ANNOTATED
GUIDE TO THE INSOLVENCY LEGISLATION

Insolvency Act 1986
Company Directors Disqualification Act 1986
Insolvency Rules 1986

ANNOTATED GUIDE TO THE INSOLVENCY LEGISLATION

Insolvency Act 1986
Company Directors Disqualification Act 1986
Insolvency Rules 1986

Fourth Edition

L S Sealy MA LLM PhD, Barrister and Solicitor (NZ)
S. J. Berwin Professor of Corporate Law,
University of Cambridge

David Milman LLB PhD
Herbert Smith Professor of Corporate and Commercial Law,
University of Manchester

CCH EDITIONS LIMITED

Published by **CCH** EDITIONS LIMITED
Telford Road, Bicester, Oxfordshire OX6 0XD
Tel. (01869) 253300, Facsimile (01869) 245814.
DX: 83750 Bicester 2.

USA CCH Incorporated, Riverwoods, Illinois.
CANADA CCH Canadian Limited, Don Mills, Ontario.
AUSTRALIA CCH Australia Limited, North Ryde, NSW.
NEW ZEALAND CCH New Zealand Limited, Auckland.
ASIA CCH Asia Limited, Singapore.
JAPAN CCH Japan Limited, Tokyo.
EUROPE CCH Europe Inc., Wiesbaden, Germany.

This publication is designed to provide accurate and authoritative information in regard to the subject-matter covered. It is sold with the understanding that the publisher is not engaged in rendering legal or other professional services. If legal advice or other expert assistance is required, the services of a competent professional person should be sought.

Ownership of Trade Mark

The trade mark is the property of

Commerce Clearing House Incorporated, Riverwoods, Illinois, USA
(**CCH** INCORPORATED)

Legislation reproduced
The publisher advises that the legislation in this publication is not the authorised official version. In its preparation, however, the greatest care has been taken to ensure exact conformity with the law as enacted.

While copyright in all the legislation resides in the Crown, copyright in indexes and annotations relating to that legislation is vested in the publisher.

British Library Cataloguing in Publication Data
A catalogue record for this book is available from the British Library.

ISBN 0 86325 365 2

First published 1987
Reprinted 1987
Second edition 1988
Reprinted 1990, 1991
Third edition 1991
Reprinted 1993
Fourth edition 1994

Typeset in Great Britain by MFK Typesetting Limited, Hitchin, Herts.
First printed in Great Britain by Hartnolls Ltd, Bodmin, Cornwall.
Reprinted in Great Britain by the Eastern Press Limited, Reading, Berkshire.

Preface to the Fourth Edition

The insolvency legislation of 1985 and 1986, based on the recommendations for reform made by the Cork Committee in 1982, established a new framework for both the law and practice in this important area. The pace of development since then can be gauged by the fact that a fourth edition of the *Annotated Guide* has become necessary less than eight years after the legislation as a whole was brought into force. Within that time, there have been many amendments both to the principal legislation and to the rules and regulations which supplement it; and the reported cases on the new law now run into several hundred. In this edition, the Insolvency Act 1986, the Company Directors Disqualification Act 1986 and the Insolvency Rules 1986 are presented in the form of an up-to-date and fully integrated text, and the commentary has been revised and enlarged in order to take account of all the cases of significance which have been reported since the legislation became operative.

It is a pleasure to acknowledge our thanks to the Insolvency Service for permission to include summaries of the information circulars known as the "Dear IP" letters, which appear as Appendix III. We are also most grateful to the various officers of the Service and those insolvency practitioners who have written to draw our attention to points in the text of the previous edition which called for correction or clarification.

The text is based on sources which were available to us up to 20 July 1994, but the publishers have kindly allowed us to incorporate some additional material which was published while the book was going to press.

The Insolvent Partnerships Order 1994 (SI 1994 No. 2421) was laid before Parliament on 16 September 1994, to come into force on 1 December 1994. It has been possible to make changes to accommodate this late development and a summary of the new order and its effect appears in the notes to s. 420 of the Insolvency Act 1986, below. Also covered are the Insolvency Regulations 1994 (SI 1994 No. 2507) and the Insolvency Fees (Amendment) Order 1994 (SI 1994 No. 2541), both operative from 24 October 1994.

Len Sealy
David Milman
September 1994

About the Publisher

CCH Editions Limited is part of a world-wide group of companies that specialises in tax, business and law publishing. The group produces a wide range of books and reporting services for the accounting, business and legal professions. The Oxfordshire premises are the centre for all UK and European operations.

All CCH publications are designed to be practical and authoritative and are written by CCH's own highly qualified and experienced editorial team and specialist outside authors.

In the UK CCH Editions currently produces a comprehensive series of reporting services on UK and international tax, business and law, and many books covering specific areas of interest for accountants, lawyers and businessmen. Irrespective of the subject matter being discussed or the depth and scope of its treatment, the material is always dealt with in the same clear and concise manner.

CCH is committed to you and your information needs, and this commitment is reflected in the constant updating and development of our reporting services and the growth and expansion of our range of publications.

If you would like to know more about our books or loose-leaf services call (01869) 253300.

Acknowledgement

The information set out in Appendix III has been kindly supplied by the Insolvency Service (now an Executive Agency within the Department of Trade and Industry).

Abbreviations

The following abbreviations are used in this work:

BA 1914	Bankruptcy Act 1914
B(A)A 1926	Bankruptcy (Amendment) Act 1926
BR 1952	Bankruptcy Rules 1952
CA	Companies Act (e.g. CA 1985 = Companies Act 1985)
CDDA 1986	Company Directors Disqualification Act 1986
CFCSA 1972	Companies (Floating Charges and Receivers) (Scotland) Act 1972
IA	Insolvency Act (e.g. IA 1985 = Insolvency Act 1985)
IR 1986	Insolvency Rules 1986
I(A)R	Insolvency (Amendment) Rules (e.g. I(A)R 1993 = Insolvency Amendment Rules 1993)
Cork Report	*Report of the Review Committee on Insolvency Law and Practice* (Cmnd 8558, 1982)
White Paper	*A Revised Framework for Insolvency Law* (Cmnd 9175, 1984)

Appendix I and Appendix II list the words and phrases which are given a special statutory definition or used in a particular sense in the legislation or the Rules, and give references to the provisions in which they and the accompanying commentary can be found.

Contents

Introduction

The insolvency legislation of 1985 and 1986

The Insolvency Act 1985 was a major piece of new legislation, implementing the most comprehensive review of the subjects of bankruptcy and corporate insolvency for over a century. It received the Royal Assent, and so became law, on 30 October 1985, but none of its provisions came into operation on that date and, indeed, only a handful of sections ever came into force – those relating to the disqualification of company directors were made operative on 28 April 1986, and those concerning the licensing of insolvency practitioners on 1 June and 1 July 1986. In regard to the bulk of the Act, the Government on 17 December 1985 announced its intention to delay implementation until a new Insolvency Act, consolidating the Act of 1985 with those parts of the Companies Act 1985 dealing with receivership and winding up, had been passed through Parliament in the course of 1986. Bills for the consolidating legislation were duly introduced into the House of Lords on 13 May 1986, and received the Royal Assent on 25 July 1986.

The consolidation took the form of two Acts: (1) the Insolvency Act 1986, dealing with winding up, receivership and other insolvency procedures affecting companies and the bankruptcy of individuals, and (2) the Company Directors Disqualification Act 1986, the title of which is self-explanatory. The Insolvency Rules 1986 (replacing the Companies (Winding up) Rules 1949 and the Bankruptcy Rules 1952) supplemented these new Acts. Detailed amendments were made to these Rules by the Insolvency (Amendment) Rules 1987. All this legislation is the subject of this Guide. The two Acts of 1986, the Insolvency Rules and various other related rules and regulations (see below) came into force on 29 December 1986, while the Insolvency (Amendment) Rules 1987 became operative on 11 January 1988.

The Cork Report

The main inspiration for the reforms made by the Insolvency Act 1985 was the *Report of the Review Committee on Insolvency Law and Practice*, the chairman of which was the late Sir Kenneth Cork (the "Cork Report", Cmnd 8558, 1982). This committee was appointed in January 1977 with a wide-ranging brief, and its Report, published in June 1982, made proposals for extensive and radical changes in the law and practice of bankruptcy and corporate insolvency, amounting virtually to the introduction of a completely new code.

The legislation of 1985

The Government's response to the Cork Report was set out in a White Paper entitled *A Revised Framework for Insolvency Law* (Cmnd 9175, February 1984). This was followed by the introduction into the House of Lords of a Bill incorporating many (but by no means all) of the Committee's recommendations on 10 December 1984.

Eventually, after considerable debate, the legislative process was completed in October 1985, when the Insolvency Act 1985 received Royal Assent.

The consolidating legislation of 1986

The Insolvency Act 1986 combines all but a very few sections of the Insolvency Act 1985 with ss. 467–650 and 659–674 of the Companies Act 1985 (together with certain minor parts of other enactments), and amounts in all to 444 sections and 14 Schedules. The major consolidating Companies Act of 1985 thus remained intact for little more than a year, and in one stroke lost some 200 sections. There is necessarily some cross-referencing between the Act of 1986 and what was left untouched of the Companies Act 1985.

The Company Directors Disqualification Act 1986, in contrast, deals with a single topic and totals only 26 sections and 4 Schedules, bringing together those parts of the Insolvency Act 1985 and the Companies Act 1985 which relate to director disqualification. Again, there are close links with those other Acts and a considerable number of cross-references.

Nature and construction of consolidating legislation

It is a fundamental principle that a consolidating Act should make no change in the substance of the law; and for this reason it is allowed an accelerated procedure in Parliament. There is a presumption in construing such a statute that no alteration of the previous law was intended, so that it is permissible to look at the superseded legislation and judicial decisions relating to it in order to determine the meaning of the new Act. This presumption applies even if the language of the two Acts is not identical. However the court will normally regard the consolidating statute as standing on its own feet, and will have recourse to the antecedent law only if the wording of the new Act is not clear.

This approach to the construction of the two new Acts will be appropriate, in the main, only to those provisions of the consolidation which were formerly contained in the Companies Act 1985 and other earlier legislation. In contrast, those sections of the 1986 Act which are derived from the Insolvency Act 1985 should be construed on the basis that that legislation was intended to make a fresh start – a view emphatically put by Millett J in *Re M C Bacon Ltd* [1990] BCC 78 at p. 87. See further the general note on Pt. IX (p. 325), preceding s. 264, below.

Later legislation

There have been only a few changes made to the Acts of 1986 since that legislation came into force. Among these may be noted the following.

Extension to building societies and friendly societies

Both the Insolvency Act 1986 and CDDA 1986 have been extended so as to apply to building societies, and the latter Act to friendly societies: see below, at pp. 124, ⁻93–594.

Disapplication of insolvency legislation to "market contracts" and "market charges"

The Companies Act 1989, Pt. VII, modifies the application of insolvency law and the enforcement of certain rights and remedies in relation to certain contracts on the financial markets. These are contracts connected with "recognised investment exchanges" and "recognised clearing houses" (CA 1989, s. 155), with certain overseas investment exchanges and clearing houses (s. 170), with certain money market institutions (s. 171) and with settlement arrangements provided by the Bank of England (s. 172). Part VII has effect in three principal ways: (1) it gives effect to contractual settlement procedures in the various financial markets, displacing the normal rules of insolvency law, where one of the contracting parties becomes insolvent (see the notes to ss. 107 and 328, below); (2) it preserves (and, in some cases, enhances) the priority of a chargee where a charge has been taken to secure obligations and liabilities arising under a market contract (see the notes to ss. 10(1), 11(2), 11(3), 15(1), 15(2), 43, 61, 127 and 284, below); and (3) it safeguards rights and remedies in relation to property provided as cover for margin in relation to market contracts and market charges (see CA 1989, ss. 177–181, and note in particular s. 180(2), which provides that an investment exchange, clearing house or chargee may authorise the commencement or continuation of enforcement proceedings by an unsecured creditor against property held as margin "notwithstanding any provision of IA 1986"). The order-making powers of Pt. VII were brought into force on 25 March 1991 and the remaining provisions (except ss. 169(4), 170–172, 176, 178 and 181) became operative on 25 April 1991. The Financial Markets and Insolvency Regulations 1991 (SI 1991 No. 880), which contain important modifications to the provisions of Pt. VII, also came into force on the latter date.

Insolvency Act 1994

The ruling of the Court of Appeal in *Powdrill & Anor* v *Watson & Anor, Re Paramount Airways Ltd (No. 3)* [1994] BCC 172 (see below, pp. 69 and 95) caused immediate concern amongst insolvency practitioners because of their possible exposure to personal liability in claims brought by former employees of companies which were, or had been, in administration or administrative receivership. The Insolvency Act 1994 was passed to clarify the question of the liability of office-holders in such circumstances, with effect from 15 March 1994 (but not retrospectively). See the notes to ss. 19 and 44, below.

Insolvency (No. 2) Act 1994

This second short Act amending IA 1986 was passed in 1994, on the initiative of the Law Society, primarily to remove doubts about the position of a person who purchases unregistered land in a transaction which is challenged as a transaction at an undervalue or a preference under IA 1986, ss. 238–241 or 339–342 (or the corresponding provisions in the Northern Ireland insolvency legislation). See the notes to ss. 241 and 342, below.

Insolvency Act 1986

The Insolvency Act 1986 brought into one composite Act the whole of the provisions of IA 1985 (except for ss. 12–14, 16, 18 and Sch. 2, which were separately consolidated into CDDA 1986) and ss. 467–650 and 659–674 of CA 1985, together with certain parts of other ancillary legislation. It deals with both corporate insolvency and the bankruptcy of individuals, but in this context "corporate insolvency" has to be understood in a much wider sense than normal, for the Act is concerned with the winding up and receivership of all companies, whether "solvent" (meaning financially viable) or not, and also with voluntary arrangements, administration orders and associated matters. Insolvent partnerships are also dealt with by subordinate legislation made under s. 420 of the Act. The Act applies to England and Wales and to Scotland in relation to corporate insolvency, but only to England and Wales in regard to the bankruptcy of individuals. The corresponding bankruptcy provisions for Scotland were revised separately by the Bankruptcy (Scotland) Act 1985. Only a few sections of the Insolvency Act 1986 apply to Northern Ireland. (See the note to s. 441.) The corresponding law for that jurisdiction is to be found in the separate legislation which is listed in the notes to s. 441, below. However, the law in Northern Ireland so closely mirrors that of Great Britain that this annotation should be of assistance to practitioners in Northern Ireland when grappling with the interpretation and application of their new insolvency legislative system.

Most Acts of Parliament, or at least the larger ones, are divided into Parts, and the Parts subdivided into Chapters, with yet further subdivisions marked by italic subheadings. The present Act has one further tier in this hierarchy: the Parts are collected into three "Groups of Parts". The "First Group of Parts" comprises "Company Insolvency" and "Companies Winding Up" – once again, we notice the ambivalence in the use of the word "insolvency" – and is broken into Parts I–VII; the Group has its own definition sections in Part VII. The Second Group deals with "Insolvency of Individuals" and "Bankruptcy", and contains four Parts, continuing in numerical sequence from VIII to XI, again with separate interpretation provisions. The Third Group, which comprises Parts XII–XIX, is concerned with the administration of the Act and miscellaneous matters affecting all types of insolvency.

Of the subordinate legislation promulgated under the new Acts, the Insolvency Rules 1986 (see page 601ff.) are by far the most significant. These Rules replace the Winding-up Rules and the Bankruptcy Rules and, like the Acts themselves, became operative on 29 December 1986. Detailed amendments to the Insolvency Rules 1986 were made by the Insolvency (Amendment) Rules 1987, which came into force on 11 January 1988, and more recently various minor amendments by the measures which are listed on p. 626–627. These amendments have been incorporated into the text of the principal Rules which is set out in this work.

The Insolvency Act 1985, apart from the few sections which had already become operative, was brought into force immediately before the consolidating legislation and was then at once repealed by the latter Acts (see SI 1986 No. 1924 (C. 71)). This brief moment of existence was sufficient to activate repeals which swept away many special features of insolvency law that had been familiar for over a century: the doctrine of relation back, acts of bankruptcy, winding up subject to the supervision of the court, and many more. Attention has been drawn to these changes at appropriate points in the discussion of the new provisions.

The Insolvency Act 1985 and the consolidating Acts introduced a good deal of new terminology: the "administration order", "administrative receivers", the "liquidation committee", and so on. It is not practicable to give a repeated explanation of these terms every time that they occur in the text, and so they have been listed in Appendix I which refers the reader to the appropriate provision of the Act, where the relevant commentary also appears. In Appendix II there is a similar list for expressions used in the Insolvency Rules.

INSOLVENCY ACT 1986

[1986 Chapter 45]

ARRANGEMENT OF SECTIONS

THE FIRST GROUP OF PARTS
COMPANY INSOLVENCY; COMPANIES WINDING UP

PART I — COMPANY VOLUNTARY ARRANGEMENTS

PART II — ADMINISTRATION ORDERS

PART III — RECEIVERSHIP

CHAPTER I — RECEIVERS AND MANAGERS (ENGLAND AND WALES)

SECTION

SECTION

CHAPTER VII — LIQUIDATORS

Preliminary

CHAPTER VIII — PROVISIONS OF GENERAL APPLICATION IN WINDING UP

Preferential debts

THE SECOND GROUP OF PARTS

INSOLVENCY OF INDIVIDUALS; BANKRUPTCY

PART VIII — INDIVIDUAL VOLUNTARY ARRANGEMENTS

PART IX — BANKRUPTCY

CHAPTER I — BANKRUPTCY PETITIONS; BANKRUPTCY ORDERS

THE THIRD GROUP OF PARTS

MISCELLANEOUS MATTERS BEARING ON BOTH COMPANY AND INDIVIDUAL INSOLVENCY; GENERAL INTERPRETATION; FINAL PROVISIONS

PART XII — PREFERENTIAL DEBTS IN COMPANY AND INDIVIDUAL INSOLVENCY

PART XIII — INSOLVENCY PRACTITIONERS AND THEIR QUALIFICATIONS

*Restrictions on unqualified persons acting as
liquidator, trustee in bankruptcy, etc.*

SCHEDULES

INSOLVENCY ACT 1986

[1986 Chapter 45]

An Act to consolidate the enactments relating to company insolvency and winding up (including the winding up of companies that are not insolvent, and of unregistered companies); enactments relating to the insolvency and bankruptcy of individuals; and other enactments bearing on those two subject matters, including the functions and qualification of insolvency practitioners, the public administration of insolvency, the penalisation and redress of malpractice and wrongdoing, and the avoidance of certain transactions at an undervalue.   [*25th July* 1986]

THE FIRST GROUP OF PARTS
COMPANY INSOLVENCY; COMPANIES WINDING UP

General comment on the First Group of Parts

The First Group of Parts deals with insolvency procedures in relation to companies (including the winding up of solvent companies), in contrast with the Second Group, which is concerned with the bankruptcy of individuals. "Company" is defined for this purpose by CA 1985, s. 735 (1) and (3), incorporated into the present Act by IA 1986, s. 251. (For the text of s. 735(1), (3), see the note to s. 73, below.) Some Parts of the Act (and, in particular, Pt. IV, dealing with winding up) are extended so as to apply to bodies and associations other than "companies", including partnerships: see the general comment preceding s. 73, below. This is true also of CDDA 1986: see the general comment to that Act and the notes to CDDA 1986, ss. 22(2) and 22A. But in the absence of any provision to this effect, the First Group of Parts and CDDA 1986 apply only to companies within the statutory definition. Accordingly, where a society incorporated under the Industrial and Provident Societies Act 1965 is in receivership, the creditors who would be entitled to preferential payment in the case of a company have no priority: *Re Devon & Somerset Farmers Ltd* [1994] Ch. 57; [1993] BCC 410.

PART I — COMPANY VOLUNTARY ARRANGEMENTS

General comment on Part I

Part I of IA 1986, which replaces IA 1985, ss. 20–26, introduced an entirely new procedure into UK company law, the "voluntary arrangement".

The Cork Committee (*Report*, paras. 400–403) considered it a weakness of the former company law that a company, unlike an individual, could not enter into a binding arrangement with its creditors for the composition of its indebtedness by some relatively simple procedure. Unless it could obtain the separate consent of every creditor, the only options previously available to a company were the formal statutory procedures of (1) a scheme of liquidation and reconstruction under CA 1985, s. 582 (formerly CA 1948, s. 287); (2) a scheme of compromise or arrangement under CA 1985, ss. 425–427 (CA 1948, ss. 206–208); and (3) the little-used "binding arrangement" under CA 1985, s. 601 (CA 1948, s. 306). Each of these methods was too slow, cumbersome and costly to be at all useful in practice.

The present sections introduce a simpler scheme, more or less along the lines recommended by the Cork Committee. The voluntary arrangement has proved to be of limited utility in practice, however, for two reasons. First, it cannot be made binding upon a secured or preferential creditor without his consent, and, secondly, there is no provision in the Act for obtaining a moratorium while the proposal for an arrangement is being drawn up and considered (contrast the "interim order" available in the case of an insolvent individual: see ss. 252–254). However, a moratorium can be achieved if a proposal for a voluntary arrangement is combined with an application to the court for the appointment of an administrator under Pt. II: this will, of course, be a more elaborate and costly procedure.

In view of these considerations, it is not surprising that the voluntary arrangement procedure has been little used. The average number has been under 100 per year – well under one per cent of recorded insolvencies – and in perhaps half of these cases the voluntary arrangement has been combined with an administration order. In the light of this experience, the Department of Trade and Industry in October 1993 published a consultative document containing proposals for radical changes in this area of the law. (It is unlikely, however, that legislation will be introduced in the immediate future.)

The initiative in setting up a voluntary arrangement is taken by the directors or, if the company is being wound up or is subject to an administration order, by the liquidator or administrator as the case may be. A "proposal" is formulated for consideration by meetings of the company's members and creditors: if the proposal is accepted at the respective meetings, the scheme becomes operative and binding upon the company and all of its creditors – even those who did not support the proposal. Thereafter, it is administered by a "supervisor" who must be qualified to act as an insolvency practitioner in relation to the company. The arrangement is conducted throughout under the aegis of the court, but the court itself is not involved in a judicial capacity unless there is some difficulty or disagreement.

It is not a prerequisite for the application of this Part of the Act that the company should be "insolvent" or "unable to pay its debts" within the statutory definitions of those terms.

Because a scheme of voluntary arrangement does not, on its own, give the company concerned any immediate protection from its creditors, the procedure is most likely to be invoked in conjunction with an administration order made under IA 1986, ss. 8ff. The purposes for which an administration order may be made specifically include "the approval of a voluntary arrangement under Part 1" (s. 8(3)(*b*)). It is also possible to give additional flexibility to an administration order which has been sought primarily for other reasons, by extending the purposes of the order to include a voluntary arrangement. For example, in *Re St. Ives Windings Ltd* (1987) 3 BCC 634, an administrator had succeeded in obtaining an advantageous realisation of the company's assets under an order which specified that purpose, but was unable to implement proposals for the distribution of the proceeds among the creditors. However, this became possible when the court, on his application, granted a variation of the order by adding as a further purpose the approval of a voluntary arrangement; the proposed distribution could then be sanctioned by the creditors in the ordinary way.

It will be the most practicable course, in any case where an administration and a voluntary scheme of arrangement are to be instituted in combination, for the administration order to be made first, and for the administrator himself to act as "nominee" and ultimately as the "supervisor" of the scheme. The administration order can be discharged as soon as the voluntary arrangement is approved.

It would probably be thought improper to present a petition for an administration order *merely* to gain a moratorium, with no intention of pursuing the application; in any case it would certainly be unwise to do so, since a petition cannot be withdrawn without the leave of the court.

A related reform effected by IA 1985 (see Sch. 10, Pt. II) was the repeal of CA 1985, s. 615(2), a provision of ancient origin which stated that any general assignment by a company of its property for the benefit of its creditors was "void to all intents".

The provision which prohibits a company from giving financial assistance in the acquisition of its own shares (CA 1985, s. 151) does not apply to anything done under a voluntary arrangement: see CA 1985, s. 153(3)(*g*) (as amended).

For the corresponding provisions relating to voluntary arrangements for insolvent individuals, see ss. 252–263.

The Act contemplates that a system will be set up by subordinate legislation for the registration of voluntary arrangements in a register open to public inspection: see Sch. 8, para. 6. The rules make provision for registration with the registrar of companies: IR 1986, rr. 1.24(5), 1.26 (2)(*b*), 1.29(3).

For the rules relating to company voluntary arrangements, see IR 1986, Pt. 1.

THE PROPOSAL

Section 1   Those who may propose an arrangement

1(1)   [Proposal by directors]   The directors of a company (other than one for which an administration order is in force, or which is being wound up) may make a proposal under this Part to the company and to its creditors for a composition in satisfaction of its debts or a scheme of arrangement of its affairs (from here on referred to, in either case, as a "voluntary arrangement").

1(2)   [Interpretation]   A proposal under this part is one which provides for some person ("the nominee") to act in relation to the voluntary arrangement either as trustee or otherwise for the purpose of supervising its implementation; and the nominee must be a person who is qualified to act as an insolvency practitioner in relation to the company.

1(3)   [Proposal by administrator or liquidator]   Such a proposal may also be made—

(a) where an administration order is in force in relation to the company, by the administrator, and

(b) where the company is being wound up, by the liquidator.

(Former provision: IA 1985, s. 20)

General note

In any case where the company is not subject to an administration order or being wound up, the initiative in proposing a voluntary arrangement is taken by the directors, and the more elaborate procedure laid down by s. 2 applies. An insolvency practitioner who is "qualified" to act in relation to the company must be brought in as "nominee" to report on the directors' proposals and to organise the meetings, etc. by which the scheme is to be implemented. (In practice, the directors will in most cases have consulted the proposed nominee in advance and invoked his help in drawing up the proposal.) Where, however, there is an administrator or liquidator already in office, he will normally himself act as the nominee and may then proceed directly to summon meetings of the company and its creditors under s. 3.

Neither creditors nor members of a company have standing to propose a voluntary arrangement.

S. 1(1)

The directors have power to act only when the company is not in liquidation or subject to an administration order.

There is no statutory definition of "creditor" for the purposes of this Part of the Act. It would be normal to give the word its dictionary meaning, "one to whom a debt is owing" – a phrase which would exclude a prospective or contingent creditor and a person whose claim was for unliquidated damages (see Goode, *Principles of Corporate Insolvency Law* (1990), pp. 31ff). This view is reinforced by the fact that the concepts of "debt" and "provable debt" are extended to include these wider categories of claim by IR 1986, rr. 13.12, 12.3; but this provision is confined to the winding up of companies. It is also noteworthy that although contingent and prospective creditors are expressly given the same rights as creditors elsewhere in the Act (see, e.g. ss. 9, 124 (standing to present petition for administration or winding-up order)), there is no similar provision here in Pt. I. It would therefore be reasonable to assume that the term "creditor" does not have the wider meaning in this section. However, r. 1.17(3) creates confusion by referring (in the context of voluntary arrangements) to "a debt for an unliquidated amount" and a "debt whose value is not ascertained". For a discussion of the terms "future", "contingent" and "prospective" liabilities, see *Burford Midland Properties Ltd* v *Marley Extensions Ltd* [1994] BCC 604.

In *Re FMS Financial Management Services Ltd* (1989) 5 BCC 191, former clients of the company who appeared to have good claims against it for damages for misrepresentation were (it is submitted, rightly) not treated as creditors for the purposes of a voluntary scheme; but an order was made by the court, after the scheme had been approved, directing that they should be admitted to prove on the same terms as the company's creditors.

S. 1(2)

The Act obviously contemplates that in most cases the "nominee" himself will in due course administer the scheme (e.g. by acting as a trustee for the benefit of the company's creditors), although it is possible in certain circumstances for someone other than the original nominee to be appointed instead (see ss. 2(4), 4(2)). When it is finally settled who it is that is to have charge of the scheme, the Act (by s. 7(2)) rather confusingly re-labels him "the supervisor". This tends to obscure the fact that in the great majority of situations "the supervisor" will be the same person as "the nominee" and, where the company is the subject of an administration order or is being wound up, also the same person as the administrator or liquidator. By whatever means he is chosen, however, the "supervisor" must be a person who is qualified to act as an insolvency practitioner in relation to the company; and in this way the legislation ensures that no voluntary scheme can be implemented without independent professional approval and supervision.

The criteria by which a person is deemed to be "qualified" to act as an insolvency practitioner "in relation to" a particular company are laid down in ss. 388–398 and 419, below.

The section provides for the nominee or supervisor to act "as trustee or otherwise". In *Re Leisure Study Group Ltd* [1994] 2 BCLC 65, Harman J held that funds in the hands of a supervisor were held on trust for the company's unsecured creditors, and had been put out of reach of the security conferred by a floating charge.

Nothing in this Part of the Act gives the supervisor, as such, power to perform any act in the name of the company or makes him an officer of the company: whatever authority he has must come from the terms of the voluntary arrangement itself, or from the fact that he is also the company's administrator or liquidator. It has been assumed by the draftsman that a decision of the company in general meeting under s. 4(1) will be competent, as a matter of company law, to give wide powers of management to a supervisor regardless of the terms of the company's articles. We must probably infer from the general tenor of the Act that the terms of a voluntary arrangement are capable of overriding the articles if necessary. The position would have been less uncertain if the supervisor had been given certain statutory powers and a more clearly defined authority. On the question of authority, cf. IR 1986, r. 1.26(1).

The nominee (and, later, the supervisor) is referred to throughout in the singular. There is nothing to prevent the appointment of joint nominees or supervisors, however: see the note to s. 7(6) below.

S. 1(3)

In the two situations referred to in this subsection, the proposal not only *may* but (by virtue of the bracketed words in s. 1(1)) *must* be made by the administrator or liquidator. In this case, the administrator or liquidator may appoint himself to be the nominee and proceed immediately to summon meetings under s. 3. If for any reason he appoints someone else, the more elaborate procedure under s. 2 must be followed.

For the rules which apply when the application is made under this subsection, see IR 1986, rr. 1.10 ff.

Section 2   Procedure where nominee is not the liquidator or administrator

2(1)   [Application]   This section applies where the nominee under section 1 is not the liquidator or administrator of the company.

2(2)   [Report to court]   The nominee shall, within 28 days (or such longer period as the court may allow) after he is given notice of the proposal for a voluntary arrangement, submit a report to the court stating—

(a) whether, in his opinion, meetings of the company and of its creditors should be summoned to consider the proposal, and

(b) if in his opinion such meetings should be summoned, the date on which, and time and place at which, he proposes the meetings should be held.

2(3)   [Information to nominee]   For the purposes of enabling the nominee to prepare his report, the person intending to make the proposal shall submit to the nominee—

(a) a document setting out the terms of the proposed voluntary arrangement, and

(b) a statement of the company's affairs containing—

(i) such particulars of its creditors and of its debts and other liabilities and of its assets as may be prescribed, and

(ii) such other information as may be prescribed.

2(4)   [Replacement of nominee by court]   The court may, on an application made by the person intending to make the proposal, in a case where the nominee has failed to submit the report required by this section, direct that the nominee be replaced as

29

such by another person qualified to act as an insolvency practitioner in relation to the company.

(Former provision: IA 1985, s. 21)

S. 2(1)

Section 2 will necessarily apply where the proposal is made by the directors under s. 1(1); and it will also apply when an administrator or liquidator designates someone other than himself as nominee.

S. 2(2)

No step towards implementing the proposal can be taken under this section until a report has first been submitted by the nominee to the court. The court's rôle is, however, primarily an administrative one, and it will not be involved judicially except when there is some dispute or difficulty. The procedure which the section envisages is as follows:

(1) The directors decide to propose an arrangement, and themselves find an insolvency practitioner who is qualified to act as nominee and who is willing, at least in principle, to do so (see IR 1986, r. 1.3(2)(*p*)). As has been mentioned above, it is likely in most cases that the directors will seek the intended nominee's professional assistance in preparing the proposal in advance. The routine contemplated by the Act will then be largely a formality.

(2) The directors give notice of the proposal for a voluntary arrangement to the nominee, and submit to him a document setting out the terms of the proposed arrangement and a statement of the company's affairs (s. 2(3)(*a*), (*b*)). (It is not clear from the section itself whether the "notice" referred to in s. 2(2) is constituted by the formal submission of the document and statement of affairs specified in s. 2(3) or is some separate and earlier notification. The former interpretation is plainly the one intended, since the 28-day period referred to in s. 2(2) only starts to run from the receipt of the document: see IR 1986, r. 1.4(3).)

(3) The nominee has 28 days (or longer, if the court allows) to prepare and submit a report to the court. This will ensure that a scheme always has the benefit of a preliminary opinion from a professional insolvency practitioner.

(4) If the nominee forms the view that the proposed scheme should go ahead, he reports to the court his opinion that meetings of the company and its creditors should be summoned, and he must himself fix their date, time and place. (On the formalities for summoning meetings, see the comment to s. 3(1) and (2), below.)

(5) Under s. 3(1), it will normally then be the nominee's rôle to summon the meetings.

(6) If the nominee considers that the proposed scheme should not be taken further, s. 2(2) appears to suggest that he should submit a negative report to the court, and this is confirmed by IR 1986, r. 1.7(2). However, nothing is made to depend on the filing of such a report, and the company is not barred from seeking a second opinion from another nominee.

(7) Where the initiative is not taken by the directors but by an administrator or liquidator who elects not to nominate himself, the responsibility for selecting the intended nominee and preparing the documentation specified in s. 2(3) falls upon that person and not on the directors.

S. 2(3)

This subsection gives details of the two documents on which the nominee is to base his report to the court.

It is made clear by the rules (IR 1986, r. 1.4(3) (as noted above (s. 2(2)) that a nominee is not to be considered as having been "given notice" of a proposal until he has received the document referred to in para. (*a*) of this subsection. The "statement of the company's affairs" may be delivered to him up to seven days later, or after a longer period if the nominee agrees: IR 1986, r. 1.5(1).

The "statement of the company's affairs" referred to is similar to the statement which must be submitted to an administrator (s. 22), an administrative receiver (ss. 47, 66) and a liquidator (ss. 99, 131). On this topic, see the note to s. 131.

S. 2(4)

If, after the expiration of the 28 days or longer period provided for by s. 2(2), the nominee has not submitted a report either in favour of or against proceeding with the proposal, this subsection allows the directors (or the administrator or liquidator, where appropriate) to invoke the court's help and have an alternative nominee appointed. However, there appears to be no reason why an intended proposal should not be aborted without the court's involvement, for at this stage no creditor will have been affected by the scheme or even have been made aware of it, and the court itself will not yet be in the picture. This course should certainly be permissible if the first intended nominee consents; if he does not, however, a professional code of conduct might possibly inhibit a colleague from replacing him against his wishes, and in that case the court's aid would be necessary.

For details of the procedure prescribed for the purpose of this section, see IR 1986, rr. 1.2–1.9.

Section 3   Summoning of meetings

3(1)   [Meetings in accordance with report]   Where the nominee under section 1 is not the liquidator or administrator, and it has been reported to the court that such meetings as are mentioned in section 2(2) should be summoned, the person making the report shall (unless the court otherwise directs) summon those meetings for the time, date and place proposed in the report.

3(2)   [Where nominee liquidator or administrator]   Where the nominee is the liquidator or administrator, he shall summon meetings of the company and of its creditors to consider the proposal for such a time, date and place as he thinks fit.

3(3)   [Persons summoned]   The persons to be summoned to a creditors' meeting under this section are every creditor of the company of whose claim and address the person summoning the meeting is aware.

(Former provision: IA 1985, s. 22)

General note

A voluntary arrangement comes into effect under s. 5 only when the proposal has been approved by both a meeting of the company and a meeting of its creditors.

Both s. 2(2)(*b*) and s. 3(2) appear to leave it to the nominee's discretion to fix such matters as the time and date of the meetings, the length of notice which is to be given and the order in which the two meetings are to be held. However such discretion as is given to the nominee by ss. 2(2)(*b*) and 3(2) is exercisable only within the constraints imposed by the rules: see IR 1986, rr. 1.9, 1.13, 1.21.

S. 3(1)

Where the nominee is not the liquidator or administrator, no step can be taken to summon meetings until he has made a favourable report to the court under s. 2(2). Once he has done so, it becomes his duty to summon the meetings (without any court order or other formality) in accordance with his own proposals.

No guidance is given by the section as to the basis on which the court might "otherwise direct", or as to who (apart from the nominee himself) might have standing to apply for such a direction.

S. 3(2)

Where the nominee is the liquidator or administrator, the procedure outlined in s. 2 is by-passed. He himself proceeds straight to the summoning of the meetings, and at this stage nothing is notified or reported to the court. There appears to be no power under this subsection for the court to "direct otherwise".

A nominee who is himself the liquidator or administrator will have received, or be entitled to receive, a "statement of affairs" under ss. 22, 99 or 131. This document, or a summary of it, must be sent, with a list of the company's creditors and the amounts of their debts, with the notices summoning the meetings: see IR 1986, r. 1.11(2).

For the appropriate rules, see IR 1986, rr. 1.10, 1.11.

S. 3(3)

A nominee who has prepared a report under s. 2(2) will have been given particulars of the company's creditors under s. 2(3)(*b*). A liquidator or administrator who has appointed himself as nominee will receive this information with the "statement of affairs".

A creditor who has not had notice of the meeting will not be bound by the arrangement: see s. 5(2)(*b*).

CONSIDERATION AND IMPLEMENTATION OF PROPOSAL

Section 4   Decisions of meetings

4(1)   **[Decision]**   The meetings summoned under section 3 shall decide whether to approve the proposed voluntary arrangement (with or without modifications).

4(2)   **[Modifications]**   The modifications may include one conferring the functions proposed to be conferred on the nominee on another person qualified to act as an insolvency practitioner in relation to the company.

But they shall not include any modification by virtue of which the proposal ceases to be a proposal such as is mentioned in section 1.

4(3)   **[Limitation on approval]**   A meeting so summoned shall not approve any proposal or modification which affects the right of a secured creditor of the company to enforce his security, except with the concurrence of the creditor concerned.

4(4)   **[Further limitation]**   Subject as follows, a meeting so summoned shall not approve any proposal or modification under which—

    (a) any preferential debt of the company is to be paid otherwise than in priority to such of its debts as are not preferential debts, or

    (b) a preferential creditor of the company is to be paid an amount in respect of a preferential debt that bears to that debt a smaller proportion than is borne to another preferential debt by the amount that is to be paid in respect of that other debt.

However, the meeting may approve such a proposal or modification with the concurrence of the preferential creditor concerned.

4(5) **[Meeting in accordance with rules]** Subject as above, each of the meetings shall be conducted in accordance with the rules.

4(6) **[Report to court, notice]** After the conclusion of either meeting in accordance with the rules, the chairman of the meeting shall report the result of the meeting to the court, and, immediately after reporting to the court, shall give notice of the result of the meeting to such persons as may be prescribed.

4(7) **[Interpretation]** References in this section to preferential debts and preferential creditors are to be read in accordance with section 386 in Part XII of this Act.

(Former provision: IA 1985, s. 23)

General note

The terms of the scheme, when approved by the meetings, bind every member and creditor (see s. 5(2)).

No provision appears to be made for any subsequent modification of the scheme unless that modification is put forward by the person who made the original proposal (see s. 6(4)). The only opportunity, therefore, for any of the company's members or creditors to seek to have the proposal modified will be at the meetings themselves.

S. 4(1)

The scheme can only go ahead in a modified form if both of the meetings approve the *same* modifications (see s. 5(1)).

S. 4(2)

The modifications may include the substitution of a different nominee to administer the scheme; but no modification may take the proceedings outside the scope of s. 1 altogether (i.e. amount to a wholly different course of action, such as putting the company into liquidation).

S. 4(3)

No voluntary arrangement can affect the rights of a secured creditor without his consent.

S. 4(4)

The rights of preferential creditors (as defined in s. 4(7)) are similarly protected, as regards both their priority *vis-à-vis* all other debts and their right to rank equally with each other. There is no provision which obliges the preferential creditors to accept a decision made by a majority of them, even if it is passed at a separate class meeting (contrast CA 1985, s. 425).

Apart from this and the preceding subsection, there is nothing in the Act which restricts the arrangements which a proposal may make, or requires creditors to be given equal treatment. It is thus permissible, e.g. for small creditors to be given more favourable treatment than larger ones.

S. 4(5)

Although this subsection refers in terms only to the *conduct* of the meetings (and not, e.g. to their summoning), it is plain that the rules apply to all aspects of such meetings: see the note to s. 3 above.

For the appropriate rules, see IR 1986, rr. 1.13ff.

S. 4(6)

The chairman of the meetings will be appointed or selected in accordance with the rules (see IR 1986, r. 1.14). The rules contemplate that the same person will be chairman of both meetings. It is perhaps odd that it is the chairman, rather than the nominee, who is saddled with this administrative chore, but the report must be filed in court very quickly (within four days: see IR 1986, r. 1.24(3)), and difficulties could arise if, e.g. the nominee was abroad. The subsection implies that separate reports of the result of each meeting are to be prepared, but the rules are less clear: see IR 1986, r. 1.24 and Form 1.1. IR 1986, r. 1.24(5) provides that if the voluntary arrangement is approved by the meetings, the *supervisor* must send a copy of the chairman's report to the registrar of companies.

The making of the chairman's report to the court and the giving of the prescribed notices have no direct legal consequences (although time is made to run for various purposes, e.g. the stay of a winding-up order, from the date that the report is made to the court). The voluntary arrangement itself takes effect as a result of the meetings alone, and the court plays no active part in the proceedings at any stage.

S. 4(7)

"Preferential debts" and "preferential creditors" are defined for the purpose of this Part of the Act by s. 386 and Sch. 6, below. The list of preferential creditors is settled by reference to a "relevant date", which determines both the existence and the amount of a preferential debt. To ascertain the "relevant date" for the purpose of the present section, see s. 387(2), (3).

The section makes no reference to the possibility that a voluntary arrangement and a receivership might co-exist – something which of course could not occur unless the charge affected a limited class of assets or the charge-holder had at some stage given his consent to the proposed arrangement. In such a case, there would also be a list of preferential creditors who were entitled to rank in priority to the charge-holder in the receivership. There would then be two lists of preferential debts defined by reference to different "relevant dates"; but those relating to the receivership would have no significance for the purposes of this Part of the Act.

Section 5 Effect of approval

5(1) [Operation]   This section has effect where each of the meetings summoned under section 3 approves the proposed voluntary arrangement either with the same modifications or without modifications.

5(2) [Effect of composition or scheme]   The approved voluntary arrangement—

(a) takes effect as if made by the company at the creditors' meeting, and

(b) binds every person who in accordance with the rules had notice of, and was entitled to vote at, that meeting (whether or not he was present or represented at the meeting) as if he were a party to the voluntary arrangement.

5(3) [Court powers]   Subject as follows, if the company is being wound up or an administration order is in force, the court may do one or both of the following, namely—

(a) by order stay or sist all proceedings in the winding up or discharge the administration order;

(b) give such directions with respect to the conduct of the winding up or the administration as it thinks appropriate for facilitating the implementation of the approved voluntary arrangement.

5(4)   [Limit on s. 5(3)(a)]   The court shall not make an order under subsection (3)(a)—

(a) at any time before the end of the period of 28 days beginning with the first day on which each of the reports required by section 4(6) has been made to the court, or

(b) at any time when an application under the next section or an appeal in respect of such an application is pending, or at any time in the period within which such an appeal may be brought.

(Former provision: IA 1985, s. 24)

General note

A scheme is not effective unless both meetings approve it, and do so in identical terms. Section 5(2), however, quite clearly makes the time of the *creditors'* meeting the critical time for the scheme to take effect, and not that of the later of the two meetings. The rules in fact require both meetings to be held on the same day and in the same place, with the creditors' meeting fixed for an earlier time: see IR 1986, rr. 1.13(3), 1.21(4). Alternatively, they may be held together (r. 1.21(1)).

It appears that the scheme takes effect at once and continues to be effective even though a challenge is mounted under s. 6; but this is subject to any directions which may be given by the court under s. 6(6).

S. 5(1)

Since the scheme cannot take effect unless any modifications are agreed to by both meetings, it may be prudent to have contingency plans for the adjournment or recall of the meeting that is held earlier, if there is any likelihood that the later meeting will wish to modify the proposals. However, there may be no adjournment of either meeting to a later date unless the other is also adjourned to the same day: IR 1986, r. 1.21(4). Alternatively, the chairman may elect to hold the two meetings together, in the hope of obtaining their simultaneous agreement to the proposal (with the same modifications, if any): see r. 1.21(1).

S. 5(2)

For the rules relating to the right to vote and the requisite majorities at the meetings of creditors and members, see IR 1986, rr. 1.17–1.20. Note that r. 1.18(2) allows voteless shareholders to vote, at least for some purposes, so that they also will be bound.

Prima facie, this subsection appears to make the scheme binding on all the company's creditors, including absentees and dissentients, or at least all those who have had notice of the meeting; and this is confirmed by IR 1986, r. 1.17(1). However, rr. 1.17(2)ff. and 1.19(3)ff. declare that in certain circumstances a creditor "shall not vote" or that his vote "shall be left out of account"; and it is arguable that such a creditor is not "entitled to vote" and so not caught by the subsection.

A voluntary arrangement does not bind a person who was not entitled to vote at the creditors' meeting, and such a person cannot take advantage of the arrangement: *R A Securities Ltd* v *Mercantile Credit Co. Ltd* [1994] BCC 598. But where a creditor who was entitled to vote assigns the benefit of his contract with the company, the assignee takes that benefit as modified by the arrangement; and where land is leased to the debtor company and the reversion is assigned, the assignee is bound by the arrangement as a matter of property law: *Burford Midland Properties Ltd* v *Marley Extrusions Ltd & Ors.* [1994] BCC 604.

On the position of creditors whose claims are for an unliquidated amount, see the note to IR 1986, r. 1.17(3).

Note that the approval of a scheme brings into operation the provisions of s. 233, which prevent the suppliers of gas, electricity, etc. from imposing certain terms as to payment as a condition of making a supply available: see s. 233(1)(*c*).

S. 5(3), (4)

If the company is being wound up or is subject to an administration order, the court is empowered to stay (or in Scotland, sist) the winding-up order or to discharge the administration order, or to give directions short of taking either of these steps which will facilitate the implementation of the scheme; but it may not make an order under s. 5(3)(*a*) until 28 days after the later of the chairman's reports has been made to the court under s. 4(6), nor while a hearing or an appeal from a ruling under s. 6 is pending.

Section 6 Challenge of decisions

6(1) [Application to court] Subject to this section, an application to the court may be made, by any of the persons specified below, on one or both of the following grounds, namely—

(a) that a voluntary arrangement approved at the meetings summoned under section 3 unfairly prejudices the interests of a creditor, member or contributory of the company;

(b) that there has been some material irregularity at or in relation to either of the meetings.

6(2) [Applicants] The persons who may apply under this section are—

(a) a person entitled, in accordance with the rules, to vote at either of the meetings;

(b) the nominee or any person who has replaced him under section 2(4) or 4(2); and

(c) if the company is being wound up or an administration order is in force, the liquidator or administrator.

6(3) [Time for application] An application under this section shall not be made after the end of the period of 28 days beginning with the first day on which each of the reports required by section 4(6) has been made to the court.

6(4) [Powers of court] Where on such an application the court is satisfied as to either of the grounds mentioned in subsection (1), it may do one or both of the following, namely—

(a) revoke or suspend the approvals given by the meetings or, in a case falling within subsection (1)(b), any approval given by the meeting in question;

(b) give a direction to any person for the summoning of further meetings to consider any revised proposal the person who made the original proposal may make or, in a case falling within subsection (1)(b), a further company or (as the case may be) creditors' meeting to reconsider the original proposal.

6(5) **[Revocation or suspension of approval]** Where at any time after giving a direction under subsection (4)(b) for the summoning of meetings to consider a revised proposal the court is satisfied that the person who made the original proposal does not intend to submit a revised proposal, the court shall revoke the direction and revoke or suspend any approval given at the previous meetings.

6(6) **[Supplemental directions]** In a case where the court, on an application under this section with respect to any meeting—

    (a) gives a direction under subsection (4)(b), or

    (b) revokes or suspends an approval under subsection (4)(a) or (5),

the court may give such supplemental directions as it thinks fit and, in particular, directions with respect to things done since the meeting under any voluntary arrangement approved by the meeting.

6(7) **[Effect of irregularity]** Except in pursuance of the preceding provisions of this section, an approval given at a meeting summoned under section 3 is not invalidated by any irregularity at or in relation to the meeting.

(Former provision: IA 1985, s. 25)

General note

Section 6 lays down a procedure whereby the various interested persons who are listed in s. 6(2) may apply to the court to challenge the fairness or regularity of a voluntary arrangement which has been approved under the preceding sections and also, it would seem (under s. 6(1)(*b*)), the regularity of a creditors' or members' meeting in the case where such approval was not forthcoming. On s. 6(2) see *Re Cranley Mansions Ltd* [1994] BCC 576. By implication, and in part by the express words of s. 6(3) and (7), a scheme of voluntary arrangement is probably not open to challenge by any other procedure or on any other grounds than are set out here.

    The section is obviously modelled on CA 1985, s. 459, a provision which allows the court to grant a remedy to a member of a company who establishes that the company's affairs are being or have been conducted in a manner which is unfairly prejudicial to the interests of some or all of the members or that some act or omission of the company is or would be so prejudicial. Similar language is used also in IA 1986, s. 27. Decisions under these related provisions may be helpful in the interpretation of s. 6.

    Section 6 is concerned only with the events leading up to the implementation of an arrangement and not with complaints about the conduct of the scheme of voluntary arrangement by the supervisor: this is dealt with by a different procedure under s. 7(3).

    For the procedure on the making of an order under s. 6, see IR 1986, r. 1.25.

    Note that it is an offence for an officer or former officer of a company to make a false representation or commit any other fraud for the purpose of obtaining the approval of the members or creditors to a proposal: IR 1986, r. 1.30. An officer would also, in principle, be civilly liable to the company or any other person who could prove damage resulting from such a fraud.

S. 6(1)

Although the word "may" appears to be permissive, it would probably be construed by a court in the sense "may and may only be" so as to make this the *only* procedure for challenging a scheme once it has been approved.

S. 6(2)

For the meaning of the phrase "a person entitled, in accordance with the rules, to vote" see the note to s. 5(2). It would appear to follow that a creditor who (perhaps by accident or oversight) has not been given notice of the meeting, or whose vote has been left out of account under IR 1986, r. 1.19(3), will have no standing to challenge the arrangement. On the other hand, a holder of shares which carry no voting rights in normal circumstances is a person entitled to vote at the meeting of the company (see IR 1986, r. 1.18(2)), and will therefore have standing under this section.

S. 6(3)

The time limit here specified is the same as that stipulated in s. 5(4). On the calculation of this time, see the note to that subsection.

S. 6(4)

The court may revoke or suspend the approvals given by the meetings, or one of the meetings, with or without giving directions as to the summoning of further meetings. If it decides to revoke but gives no such directions, it is of course always open to any of the persons mentioned in s. 1(1) or (3) to put forward a fresh scheme. However, there is probably no power to reopen the original proposal (with or without modifications) otherwise than by direction of the court under s. 6(4)(*b*).

Under s. 6(4)(*b*), the court may direct "any person" (not necessarily the nominee) to summon the further meetings. However, only the person who made the original proposal may draw up a revised one: this will be the liquidator or administrator of the company if s. 1(3) applies, and the directors if it does not. (If this person declines to co-operate, s. 6(5) applies and the arrangement falls through.)

The court seems to have no power to make any decision other than those set out in this subsection: it cannot, e.g. approve a proposal subject to modifications of its own devising, or even remit a proposal with such modifications to the meetings for reconsideration. (See, however, the note to s. 7(4), below.)

S. 6(5)

If it appears that the directors, the liquidator or the administrator, as the case may be (see s. 6(4)), do not intend to submit a revised scheme, the matter can proceed no further.

S. 6(6)

An arrangement is effective as soon as the two meetings have given their approval (s. 5). It is not suspended while an application under s. 6 is pending. This subsection empowers the court, in the event of a successful challenge, to give supplemental directions to cover acts done under an arrangement before the court gave its ruling.

S. 6(7)

An approval given at a meeting is not open to challenge as irregular otherwise than by proceeding under s. 6 itself. Once the 28 days laid down by s. 6(3) have elapsed, therefore, the approval is irrebuttably deemed valid for all purposes.

Section 7   Implementation of proposal

7(1) [Application]   This section applies where a voluntary arrangement approved by the meetings summoned under section 3 has taken effect.

7(2) [Supervisor of composition or scheme]   The person who is for the time being carrying out in relation to the voluntary arrangement the functions conferred—

(a) by virtue of the approval on the nominee, or

(b) by virtue of section 2(4) or 4(2) on a person other than the nominee,

shall be known as the supervisor of the voluntary arrangement.

7(3)   [Application to court]   If any of the company's creditors or any other person is dissatisfied by any act, omission or decision of the supervisor, he may apply to the court; and on the application the court may—

(a) confirm, reverse or modify any act or decision of the supervisor,

(b) give him directions, or

(c) make such other order as it thinks fit.

7(4)   [Application for directions by supervisor]   The supervisor—

(a) may apply to the court for directions in relation to any particular matter arising under the voluntary arrangement, and

(b) is included among the persons who may apply to the court for the winding up of the company or for an administration order to be made in relation to it.

7(5)   [Court appointment powers]   The court may, whenever—

(a) it is expedient to appoint a person to carry out the functions of the supervisor, and

(b) it is inexpedient, difficult or impracticable for an appointment to be made without the assistance of the court,

make an order appointing a person who is qualified to act as an insolvency practitioner in relation to the company, either in substitution for the existing supervisor or to fill a vacancy.

7(6)   [Limit on s. 7(5) power]   The power conferred by subsection (5) is exercisable so as to increase the number of persons exercising the functions of supervisor or, where there is more than one person exercising those functions, so as to replace one or more of those persons.

(Former provision: IA 1985, s. 26)

S. 7(1), (2)

As soon as a scheme of voluntary arrangement takes effect, the nominee (or his replacement appointed under ss. 2(4) or 4(2)) is redesignated the "supervisor". The supervisor holds funds collected by him on trust for the creditors joined to the arrangement. These funds cannot be seized by a subsequently appointed receiver: *Re Leisure Study Group Ltd* [1994] 2 BCLC 65.

For the rules relating to the implementation of the arrangement and the duties of the supervisor, see IR 1986, rr. 1.22–1.23, 1.26ff.

S. 7(3)

The court is given wide – indeed, unlimited – powers to oversee the conduct of the arrangement by the supervisor; and anyone at all (subject, no doubt, to his being able to show that he has *some* interest in the matter) may invoke the jurisdiction under this section.

S. 7(4)

The supervisor (like a liquidator, administrator, trustee, and others discharging comparable functions) may apply to the court for directions. Although the Act nowhere states explicitly that the court may give directions which modify the scheme or extend it to include persons who have not taken part in the meetings, this was in fact done in *Re FMS Financial Management Services Ltd* (1989) 5 BCC 191. Here a voluntary arrangement had been agreed to by both the members and various groups of creditors, but not by another group composed of former clients of the company who appeared to have good claims against the company for damages for misrepresentation. Hoffmann J directed that they should be treated as creditors and be given the benefit of the scheme, with the consequence that the other creditors received a substantially smaller dividend.

The supervisor may also apply for an administration order or a winding-up order (para. (*b*)), but is not listed in either s. 9 or s. 124 among the categories of persons who are entitled to petition for those orders. This difficulty has to be overcome by having the supervisor petition in the name of the company, on analogy with IR 1986, r. 4.7(7)(*a*). In the case of a petition for an administration order, this would be consistent with r. 2.1(4) (which states that the petition is to be treated as if it were the petition of the company); but it is less appropriate in relation to a winding-up petition, for r. 4.7(9) declares that this shall be treated as if it were a petition filed by contributories. On winding-up petitions presented by supervisors, see *Re Leisure Study Group Ltd* [1994] 2 BCLC 65.

S. 7(5)

This is a rather puzzling provision, for none of the preceding sections appears to give the meetings of shareholders and creditors, acting either together or independently, a power to fill a vacancy in the office of supervisor or to replace a supervisor once appointed: it seems that once the meetings have approved a proposal under s. 5, they have no further rôle. So the reference in para. (*b*) to appointing a substitute supervisor "without the assistance of the court" is strange. Since no power appears to be conferred on the meetings by the rules, it seems that the only way in which a vacancy can be filled or a replacement supervisor appointed is by invoking the jurisdiction of the court under this subsection.

S. 7(6)

This is the only reference in the Act to the possibility of appointing several persons as joint supervisors (or as joint nominees), although other "office-holders" are specifically covered by s. 231. It appears, however, that the general statutory assumption applies, so that words in the singular include the plural (Interpretation Act 1978, s. 6); and this construction may be applied throughout this Part of the Act. The rules deal with the appointment of joint supervisors in IR 1986, r. 1.22(1).

PART II — ADMINISTRATION ORDERS

General comment on Part II

The administration order procedure which is established by this Part of the Act is a novelty in English law. There is, however, a parallel with the appointment of a "judicial manager", which has been a feature of the company law of South Africa since 1926, and some similarity to the Australian "official management" which was introduced into jurisdictions in that country in 1961, but was little used in practice and has now been superseded. The reorganisation procedure prescribed under Chapter 11 of the United States Federal Bankruptcy Code is a less close equivalent. Legislation on the UK model has been introduced in Singapore and (with some significant differences) in the Republic of Ireland.

The provisions in the Act are based on the recommendations of the Cork Committee (*Report*, Ch. 9), which make no direct reference to either the South African or the Australian counterpart. The Committee thought that there was a need for a new procedure, similar to a receivership, to meet the case where a company was in difficulties but it was not possible to mount a rescue operation by having a receiver appointed because it had not given any creditor a floating charge over its undertaking.

It should be borne in mind also that both the Cork Committee and the Government in its White Paper thought it important that a board of directors which found that its company was in financial difficulties should seek outside help promptly and, if appropriate, hand over control of the company to experienced professional hands. (See the notes to s. 214 ("wrongful trading") and CDDA 1986, s. 6 (disqualification of "unfit" directors).) An administration would plainly be a proper step which a board might take in such a situation.

The timetable envisaged by the Act is leisurely (a matter of several months), and the procedure is elaborate and formal. An administrator is appointed by order of the court, which must be satisfied by evidence that the statutory grounds for an appointment exist. The administrator takes temporary charge of the company's business, calls for a "statement of the company's affairs" from the directors, and must, on the basis of this information, formulate "proposals" for consideration at a meeting of the company's creditors. If the proposals are approved at the meeting, he then proceeds to manage the company's affairs in accordance with the proposals until either the purpose is achieved or he is of opinion that it cannot be attained.

When the Act first came into force, there was considerable room for doubt whether much use would be made of the new administration regime. Its procedure was bound to be slow and expensive in comparison with the established institutions of voluntary winding up on the one hand and receivership on the other. Neither the South African nor the Australian experience gave any reason to be optimistic: over many years, only a handful of companies had been nursed back to health under the corresponding provisions in those jurisdictions. However, the new procedure has been given an encouraging start in this country. A total of 131 administration orders were made during the first year of operation of the Act and 198 in the second; since then the number has remained steadily within that range. One reason for these relatively high figures may be that the purposes for which an order can be sought under the UK legislation are wider. In South Africa, an order can be made only with a view to the financial rehabilitation of the company, and the courts there, naturally enough, have required an applicant to make out a very clear case for an order which is likely to keep the company's unpaid creditors out of their money for a very long time (see, e.g. *Tenowicz* v *Tenny Investments* 1979 (2) SA 680). In contrast, an order may be sought here to further a scheme of voluntary arrangement under Pt. I of the Act, and also to secure a more advantageous realisation of the company's assets than would be effected on a winding up. These additional purposes may well work to the advantage of creditors and the burden of satisfying a judge that such a purpose is likely to be achieved will be more easily discharged.

Where the company has given a floating charge to its bank or some other creditor, the charge-holder has a statutory right (unless the charge is invalid) to veto the appointment of an administrator and install a receiver himself instead (s. 9(3)). Since the administration procedure puts the holder of a floating charge at a considerable disadvantage (*inter alia*, subordinating his charge to all subsequently incurred debts), it might be thought inevitable that in the great majority of cases where there is a floating charge, an application for an administration order would be pointless because of the near-certainty that the charge-holder would defeat it by availing himself of his right to appoint a receiver of his own choice who could act more speedily, flexibly and cheaply. Even so, in a significant number of cases on record, the charge-holder has been prepared to give way to an administrator. In particular, where the company's objects are not purely commercial (such as a company formed to run a football club), a secured lender may avoid the unfavourable publicity which would attend a receivership and forced sale of assets by consenting to an administration order.

MAKING ETC. OF ADMINISTRATION ORDER

Section 8   Power of court to make order

8(1)   [Administration order]   Subject to this section, if the court—

(a) is satisfied that a company is or is likely to become unable to pay its debts (within the meaning given to that expression by section 123 of this Act), and

(b) considers that the making of an order under this section would be likely to achieve one or more of the purposes mentioned below,

the court may make an administration order in relation to the company.

8(2) [Definition] An administration order is an order directing that, during the period for which the order is in force, the affairs, business and property of the company shall be managed by a person ("the administrator") appointed for the purpose by the court.

8(3) [Purposes for order] The purposes for whose achievement an administration order may be made are—

(a) the survival of the company, and the whole or any part of its undertaking, as a going concern;

(b) the approval of a voluntary arrangement under Part 1;

(c) the sanctioning under section 425 of the Companies Act of a compromise or arrangement between the company and any such persons as are mentioned in that section; and

(d) a more advantageous realisation of the company's assets than would be effected on a winding up;

and the order shall specify the purpose or purposes for which it is made.

8(4) [Where order not to be made] An administration order shall not be made in relation to a company after it has gone into liquidation, nor where it is—

(a) an insurance company within the meaning of the Insurance Companies Act 1982, or

(b) an authorised institution or former authorised institution within the meaning of the Banking Act 1987.

(Former provision: IA 1985, s. 27)

S. 8(1), (2)

An administration order is defined by s. 8(2), as is the "administrator" who may be appointed to manage the affairs, etc. of a company under this section.

The term "company" is not specifically defined for the purposes of this Part, and so reference must be made to the general definition contained in CA 1985, s. 735, which applies by virtue of s. 251. Accordingly, "company" means a company formed and registered under CA 1985 or an earlier Companies Act. It follows that an administration order cannot be made in respect of a foreign company (cf. *Felixstowe Dock & Railway Co.* v *US Lines Inc.* [1989] QB 360). This will be the case also in relation to bodies other than companies, such as a building society or a society incorporated under the Industrial and Provident Societies Act 1965: see the general note to the First Group of Parts preceding s. 1. However, in the case of a foreign company, the position is different when a letter of request has been received by an English court from a court in that company's country of incorporation, for s. 426, and in particular s. 426(5), confers upon the court a jurisdiction wider than it would otherwise have: *Re Dallhold Estates (UK) Pty Ltd* [1992] BCC 394.

The prerequisites for the operation of the court's jurisdiction are set out in s. 8(1). The court must (1) be "satisfied" that the company is, or is likely to become, "unable to pay its debts" (in the statutory sense of this expression, as defined by s. 123), and (2) consider that an administration order would be likely to achieve one or more of the purposes specified in s. 8(3). The Act gives no guidance as to the nature of the evidence on which a ruling on the second of these issues is to be made; and the matter has been the subject of some judicial controversy. In *Re Consumer & Industrial Press Ltd* (1988) 4 BCC 68, Peter Gibson J was of the opinion that "likely to be achieved" meant "likely, on a balance of probabilities, to be achieved", so that the court needed to be satisfied on the evidence put before it that at least one of the purposes in s. 8(3) was likely, in the sense of "more probably than not", to be achieved. But in *Re Harris Simons Construction Ltd* [1989] 1 WLR 368, (1989) 5 BCC 11, Hoffmann J took a broader view and declined to follow this ruling. He held that the requirements of s. 8(3) would be satisfied if the court considered that there was "a real prospect" that one or more of the statutory purposes might be achieved. He thought it "not unlikely that the legislature intended to set a modest threshold of probability to found jurisdiction and to rely on the court's discretion not to make orders in cases in which, weighing all the circumstances, it seemed inappropriate to do so". Although Harman J in *Re Manlon Trading Ltd* (1988) 4 BCC 455 had accepted the earlier view of Peter Gibson J as correct, Vinelott J in *Re Primlaks (UK) Ltd* (1989) 5 BCC 710 preferred the approach of Hoffmann J; and subsequently both Peter Gibson J in *Re S C L Building Services Ltd* (1989) 5 BCC 746 and Harman J in *Re Rowbotham Baxter Ltd* [1990] BCC 113 have expressed themselves as being content to follow the "real prospect" test of Hoffmann J. The issue thus now appears to be resolved in favour of the latter view.

The order must specify the purpose or purposes for which it is made (s. 8(3)). Accordingly, the court must consider separately, in relation to each proposed purpose, whether the test of likelihood has been satisfied: see In *Re S C L Building Services Ltd* (1989) 5 BCC 746 at p. 747.

In part, the evidence on which the court bases its decision will be supplied by the affidavit filed in support of the petition under IR 1986, r. 2.3. In addition, the rules contemplate that a report by an independent person (i.e. someone not already connected with the company as a director, etc.) will be prepared for the assistance of the court (r. 2.2). This is not obligatory, but if a report has not been prepared, the court must be given an explanation (r. 2(3), (6)). (On the content of the report and the recommended practice in relation to such reports, see the discussion of the recent Practice Note in the notes to r. 2.2, below.) It is obviously appropriate to have the report prepared by the insolvency practitioner whose appointment as administrator is being proposed, and in the great majority of cases this will be the best way of providing the court with the evidence on which it can act. Where the petitioner is a creditor, however, it is unlikely that he will have access to as much evidence as the court would like to have, and this may give rise to difficulties. Another situation which may pose problems is where there are simultaneous applications by a creditor for a winding up and by the company for an administration order which seeks the rehabilitation of the company and the survival of its undertaking as a going concern. The court may well in such a case require compelling evidence before making an administration order which would keep the creditor out of his money. On the other hand, where the object of the administration is a more advantageous realisation of assets or the furtherance of a scheme of arrangement, it would be reasonable for the court to act on rather less evidence, since the order is not likely to be any less beneficial to the general creditors than a winding up.

Insolvency, for the the purposes of s. 8(1)(*a*), is at least primarily to be determined on a liquidity or "cash flow" basis (that is, on the company's ability to pay its current debts) rather than on a "balance sheet" basis (i.e. whether it is likely to have a surplus after a realisation of all its assets); but since, for this purpose, the provisions of s. 123 are relevant, the latter test is made a legitimate alternative by s. 123(2). In *Re Imperial Motors (UK) Ltd* (1989) 5 BCC 214 the court was prepared to find that the company was unable to pay its debts even though it appeared to be solvent on a balance-sheet basis. This was also the case in *Re Business Properties Ltd & Ors* (1988) 4 BCC 684. However, Harman J there expressed the view that in such a situation the court will not normally exercise its discretion to appoint an administrator, when the essential ground for seeking relief is deadlock and a breakdown of trust and confidence between the members of the company: the more appropriate remedy is winding up. An administrator, he said, has wide powers for a "short-term, intensive care" operation, but cannot achieve the realisation and distribution required to conclude the company's affairs.

If the conditions in s. 8(1)(*a*) and (*b*) are satisfied, the court then has a discretion whether to make an administration order. As Peter Gibson J observed in *Re Consumer & Industrial Press Ltd* (above), this is a complete discretion, in which account must be taken of all material circumstances, and is not limited by the wording of s. 8(1)(*a*) and (*b*). The judge's task may not be at all an easy one, for his decision may benefit some creditors at the expense of others. For example, if an administration is preferred to a winding up, preferential debts will lose their preferential status. Another factor which weighed with the judge in that case, but was not held to be decisive, was that a liquidator has wider powers to investigate the conduct of directors (e.g. in regard to fraudulent and wrongful trading) than an administrator.

Re Imperial Motors (UK) Ltd (above) is a further illustration of the exercise of the court's discretion. Here, the court took the view that the interests of the company's secured creditors should weigh lighter in the scales than those of its unsecured creditors, because they did not stand to lose so much. In *Re Arrows Ltd (No. 3)* [1992] BCC 131 a majority of the creditors opposed the making of an order. Hoffmann J. held that, while the court had a discretion to make an order in spite of such opposition, the fact that the proposals were unlikely to be approved by a creditors' meeting if an order were made would weigh strongly against making an order.

Section 8(2) refers to "the period for which the order is in force". Although it would not appear to follow necessarily from this that an order should be expressed to be made for a fixed period, the courts have so interpreted the provision, and a period of three months has become the standard. (This, of course, ties in with the obligation to report to creditors under IA 1986, s. 23, within the same period.) In *Re Newport County Association Football Club Ltd* (1987) 3 BCC 635, Harman J held that the company had standing to apply for an extension of this period, but expressed the view that such an application would be better made by the administrator.

On the making of a winding-up order, time ceases to run for the purposes of the statutes of limitation against the company's creditors (other than a petitioning creditor): *Re Cases of Taff's Well Ltd* [1992] Ch. 179; [1991] BCC 582. But in the same case (at p. 195; 589) the judge was of the view (but without expressing a concluded opinion) that the making of an administration order would not prevent time from running.

S. 8(3)

If the court makes an administration order, it must specify which of the purposes mentioned in s. 8(3) the order seeks to achieve. This requirement clearly limits the functions and powers of the administrator to acts which are consistent with the purpose or purposes stated. However, there is power under s. 18(1) to have the order varied so that it states an additional purpose.

Section 8(3) sets out under four headings the purposes which, separately or in combination, an administration order may seek to achieve. Headings (*a*) and (*d*) may not be altogether compatible with each other, although in practice they are commonly combined in the same petition or order. (In consequence, the decisive say as to the course which the administration should pursue is then left to the creditors at their meeting.) In *Re Rowbotham Baxter Ltd* [1990] BCC 113 at p. 115, Harman J stated that a proposal involving the sale of a "hived-down" company formed to take over part of the company's business could not be brought within para. (*a*) ("the survival of *the* company and part of its undertaking as a going concern"); but it is submitted that it could plainly come within para. (*d*). In *Re Maxwell Communications Corporation plc* [1992] BCC 372, Hoffmann J held that the fact that Ch. 11 proceedings, affecting a substantial proportion of the company's assets, were pending in the US was relevant to the chances of the survival of the company and all or part of its business. The remaining headings, (*b*) and (*c*), may help to make the voluntary arrangement procedure under ss. 1–7 and the scheme of arrangement provisions of CA 1985, ss. 425–427 more effective, since the appointment of an administrator in conjunction with the establishment of an arrangement or scheme will enable a moratorium or stay to be imposed, preventing individual creditors from enforcing their rights. Conversely, a company which is already subject to an administration order may, through its administrator, make a proposal for a voluntary arrangement in order to secure some modification in the rights of creditors which cannot be made under this Part of the Act alone: see *Re St Ives Windings Ltd* (1987) 3 BCC 634.

The Cork Committee (*Report*, para. 498) recommended that it should also be possible to appoint an administrator "to carry on the business where this is in the public interest"; but the Act has not implemented this proposal.

S. 8(4)

Paragraph (*b*) was substituted by the Banking Act 1987, s. 108(1) and Sch. 6, para. 25(1), as from 1 October 1987 (see SI 1987 No. 1664 (C. 50)): the former paragraph read as follows: "(b) a recognised bank or licensed institution within the meaning of the Banking Act 1979, or an institution to which sections 16 and 18 of that Act apply as if it were a licensed institution."

The administration procedure is not available where the company is an insurance company, since these companies are subject to their own special legislation. For the same reason, banks and other "authorised institutions" under the banking legislation were excluded by the Act as originally drafted – and, indeed, by the present subsection as it now appears. However, by the Banks (Administration Proceedings) Order 1989 (SI 1989 No. 1276), effective from 23 August 1989, Pt. II of the Act has been extended to apply in relation to banks and the other bodies mentioned in s. 8(3)(*b*) which are companies within the meaning of CA 1985, s. 735; and in relation to these institutions the Order provides that certain modifications to the present Act shall be made, including the "omission" of para. (*b*) of the present subsection. Other modifications give standing to the Bank of England for various purposes, such as presenting a petition for an administration order, and add as a ground of deemed insolvency a default by the institution in an obligation to pay any sum due in respect of a deposit.

The administration procedure may not be used if the company is already in liquidation. (For a general discussion of the relationship between winding up and administration orders, see the note to s. 10.)

Section 9   Application for order

9(1)   [Application to court]   An application to the court for an administration order shall be by petition presented either by the company or the directors, or by a creditor or creditors (including any contingent or prospective creditor or creditors), or by the clerk of a magistrates' court in the exercise of the power conferred by section 87A of the Magistrates' Court Act 1980 (enforcement of fines imposed on companies) or by all or any of those parties, together or separately.

9(2)   [On presentation of petition to court]   Where a petition is presented to the court—

(a) notice of the petition shall be given forthwith to any person who has appointed, or is or may be entitled to appoint, an administrative receiver of the company, and to such other persons as may be prescribed, and

(b) the petition shall not be withdrawn except with the leave of the court.

9(3)   [Duties of court]   Where the court is satisfied that there is an administrative receiver of the company, the court shall dismiss the petition unless it is also satisfied either—

45

(a) that the person by whom or on whose behalf the receiver was appointed has consented to the making of the order, or

(b) that, if an administration order were made, any security by virtue of which the receiver was appointed would—

    (i) be liable to be released or discharged under sections 238 to 240 in Part VI (transactions at an undervalue and preferences),

    (ii) be avoided under section 245 in that Part (avoidance of floating charges), or

    (iii) be challengeable under section 242 (gratuitous alienations) or 243 (unfair preferences) in that Part, or under any rule of law in Scotland.

9(4) **[Court powers on hearing petition]**   Subject to subsection (3), on hearing a petition the court may dismiss it, or adjourn the hearing conditionally or unconditionally, or make an interim order or any other order that it thinks fit.

9(5) **[Extent of interim order]**   Without prejudice to the generality of subsection (4), an interim order under that subsection may restrict the exercise of any powers of the directors or of the company (whether by reference to the consent of the court or of a person qualified to act as an insolvency practitioner in relation to the company, or otherwise).

(Former provision: IA 1985, s. 28)

General note

An administration order can be made only in consequence of an application made by petition under this section. In South Africa the court is given power to make an order for judicial management as an alternative to liquidation on the hearing of a winding-up petition. Although the Cork Committee recommended that a similar provision should apply in this country (*Report*, para. 510), the legislature has not accepted the proposal.

    For details of the procedure for making an application, see IR 1986, Pt. 2.

S. 9(1)

This list of persons who are eligible to apply for an administration order should be compared with those who may petition for a winding up under s. 124(1): see the comment to that subsection. The significant difference between the two is that the right of a member or members to seek an administration order is pointedly excluded. (This is in keeping with the rule in regard to winding up, laid down in *Re Rica Gold Washing Co.* (1879) 11 ChD 36, that a member has no standing to present a winding-up petition where the company is insolvent. Applying this principle, Harman J in *Re Chelmsford City Football Club (1980) Ltd* [1991] BCC 133 ruled that members *qua* members should not be given leave under IR 1986, r. 2.9(1)(*g*) to *oppose* an application for an administration order.) There is also no counterpart to ss. 124(4) and 124A, or to s. 124(5), which respectively empower the Secretary of State, in specified circumstances, and the official receiver to petition for a winding up. Note also that under s. 7(4)(*b*) the supervisor of a voluntary arrangement is included among the persons who may apply to the court for an administration order.

    Where the purpose of an administration order is the approval of a voluntary arrangement under Pt. I (see s. 8(3)(*a*)), it will be necessary for the directors to take steps to initiate the voluntary arrangement proceedings at the same time as the petition is presented under s. 9 (unless the voluntary arrangement is already in being), since they alone will be competent to do so.

Contingent and prospective creditors are given standing to petition under s. 9(1), as they are for a winding-up order (see s. 124 (1)). This contrasts with the position in regard to voluntary arrangements: see the note to s. 1(1).

Where a company is or has been carrying on investment business, or purporting to do so, s. 74 of the Financial Services Act 1986 empowers a "recognised self-regulating organisation", a "recognised professional body" and the Secretary of State for Trade and Industry, in certain circumstances, to apply for an administration order against it.

An application by the directors must be made by all the directors (*Re Instrumentation Electrical Services Ltd* (1988) 4 BCC 301). This could, it is submitted, be done by all the directors acting informally (even where there is not an enabling article along the lines of Table A, art. 93): see *T C B Ltd* v *Gray* [1986] Ch. 621 at p. 637; [1986] 1 All ER 587 at p. 597; *Re Tivoli Freeholds Ltd* [1972] VR 445 at pp. 459–460. An application can also be made in the name of all the directors once a proper resolution of the board of directors has been passed, for it then becomes the duty of all the directors, including those who took no part in the deliberations of the board and even those who voted against the resolution, to implement it: see *Re Equiticorp International plc* [1989] 1 WLR 1010; (1989) 5 BCC 599.

A petition presented by the supervisor of a voluntary arrangement, or by the directors, is to be treated for all purposes as the petition of the company (IR 1986, rr. 2.1(4), 2.4(3)). A supervisor should petition in the name of the company: see the note to s. 7(4).

Although s. 9(2) requires notice of the petition to be given to a charge-holder, and the rules contemplate that copies of the petition shall be served on specified persons and that they and others may appear and be represented at the hearing of the petition (IR 1986, rr. 2.6, 2.9), the court has on occasion been prepared to make an administration order *ex parte* and even, in cases of extreme urgency, to do so against an undertaking by counsel that a petition will be presented in the immediate future. Harman J in *Re Rowbotham Baxter Ltd* [1990] BCC 113 at p. 114 expressed the view that this was "an undesirable practice which should not continue". He said: "The danger is that the court hears one side only, the court has not the advantage of adversarial argument to draw its attention to points which may weigh one way or the other; and this leads . . . to a serious risk of injustice being done". However, the same judge in the later case of *Re Cavco Floors Ltd* [1990] BCC 589 qualified his earlier remarks by saying that, although it is undesirable for the court to act before presentation of the petition, it is a procedure which may need to be adopted in some cases; and in that case he did make an immediate order. See also *Re Shearing & Loader Ltd* [1991] BCC 232 and *Re Gallidoro Trawlers Ltd* [1991] BCC 691. Again, in *Re Chancery plc* [1991] BCC 171, an administration order was made *ex parte* in the case of a banking company, where the judge also took the unusual course of hearing the application in camera.

There is no provision in the Act or the rules for a petition for an administration order to be advertised.

In many applications for an administration order, and in all applications made *ex parte*, the only evidence before the court will be that submitted by the applicant company and its officers, and the proposed administrator's report under IR 1986, r. 2.2, which will be based on the same information. In *Re Sharps of Truro Ltd* [1990] BCC 94 and also in *Astor Chemical Ltd* v *Synthetic Technology Ltd* [1990] BCC 97 at pp. 107–108, the court laid stress on the importance of ensuring that all relevant information was put before the court. "All facts relevant to the exercise of the discretion to appoint an administrator must be revealed, even though to do so may be embarrassing to the applicant" (ibid.). If some material fact emerges after the making of the order, it is the duty of those who learn of it to explain it to the administrator and to put it before the court; and it is proper in such circumstances for the administrator to apply to the court for the discharge of the order, or to seek directions whether he should apply for a discharge.

The words "or by the clerk of a magistrates' court in the exercise of the power conferred by section 87A of the Magistrates' Courts Act 1980 (enforcement of fines imposed on companies) " were inserted before the words "or by all" by the Criminal Justice Act 1988, s. 62(2)(*a*) as from 5 January 1989 (see SI 1988 No. 2073 (c. 78)).

S. 9(2)

The holder of a floating charge who has power to appoint a receiver of the whole or substantially the whole of the company's property will have the power (provided that his security is not open to challenge under s. 9(3)(*b*)) to block the making of an administration order by putting the company into receivership (s. 9(3)). The notice required to be given to him by the present subsection will enable him to take this step if he wishes or, alternatively, to give his consent under s. 9(3)(*a*). In order to ensure that a debenture holder has the power to put in a receiver in these circumstances, it is necessary to make express provision in any floating charge drawn up after the Act came into force. In relation to instruments created before the commencement of the Act, there is a transitional measure in Sch. 11, para. 1, which deems such a provision to be included.

For the "other persons" prescribed by the rules as being entitled to notice of a petition, see IR 1986, r. 2.6.

The term "forthwith" has no precise meaning: "it must be done as soon as possible in the circumstances, the nature of the act to be done being taken into account" (Halsbury's *Laws of England*, 4th ed., Vol. 45, para. 1148). In the present context, it would probably be construed as "as soon as practicable" (*Sameen* v *Abeyewickrema* [1963] AC 597) or "as soon as reasonably practicable" (*Re Seagull Manufacturing Co. Ltd (in liquidation)* [1993] Ch. 345, at p. 359; [1993] BCC 241, at p. 249) rather than the peremptory "at once" (*Re Muscovitch* [1939] Ch. 694) or the lax "at any reasonable time thereafter" (*Hillingdon London Borough Council* v *Cutler* [1968] 1 QB 124).

The stipulation that a petition for an administration order shall not be withdrawn except with the leave of the court will naturally discourage irresponsible applications, and in particular the use of the procedure by a creditor for the purpose of putting pressure on a debtor company. On the other hand, it is clearly not improper for a petition to be presented under this section in order to secure a moratorium in connection with a voluntary arrangement under ss. 1–7 or a formal scheme of arrangement under CA 1985, ss. 425–427: see the note to s. 8(3).

S. 9(3)

This is the first occasion in the Act where the new term "administrative receiver" is used. In broad terms, it may be taken as meaning "a receiver or manager of the whole (or substantially the whole) of a company's property". The full statutory definition appears in ss. 29(2) and 251.

Although company law generally is able to accommodate the notion that more than one receivership can operate at the same time, or a receivership co-exist with a liquidation, the new insolvency legislation has ruled out the idea that there can be an administrator and an administrative receiver in office at the same time. To resolve the matter, the security-holder who has appointed, or has power to appoint, an administrative receiver is given the decisive say. If he has already appointed a receiver when the petition for an administration order is presented, the petition must be dismissed unless the charge-holder consents to the making of an order (s. 9(3)) and the consequent vacation of the receivership (s. 11(1)(*b*)). If he has not then appointed a receiver, he may do so before the application is heard (s. 10(2)(*b*)), and so bring about the dismissal of the petition under the present subsection. In order to enable the charge-holder to assess the position, the rules provide for him to be given five clear days' notice of the date fixed for the hearing of the application (IR 1986, rr. 2.6(2)(*a*), 2.7(1)). The court has power to abridge this period of notice in an appropriate case (*Re a Company No. 00175 of 1987* (1987) 3 BCC 124).

In the same case, the company urged the court to grant an adjournment of the application in order that the company could arrange to pay off the charge. This would have led to the termination of the receivership and so (it was argued) have enabled an administration order to be made without violation of s. 9(3). But Vinelott J held that he had no jurisdiction to take this course: the wording of s. 9(3) was mandatory and he had no alternative but to dismiss the application.

The superior claims of the charge-holder will not survive if an attack is successfully mounted upon the validity of the security on any of the grounds listed under para. (*b*) – i.e. that it is a transaction at an undervalue or preference within the scope of ss. 238–240, or a floating charge that is liable to be avoided under s. 245, or is challengeable under the equivalent Scottish provisions (ss. 242, 243). It has also been suggested that a creditor taking security might seek to clothe what is essentially a fixed charge with the appearance of a floating charge, or to combine it with a meaningless floating charge, in order to obtain the power under s. 9(3) to block an administration order by the purported appointment of an administrative receiver. An argument challenging the genuineness of a floating charge along these lines failed in *Re Croftbell Ltd* [1990] BCC 781: the court held that a charge which was expressed to extend to future assets was to be treated as a floating charge even though at the time of its creation the company had no assets of the class in question.

Paragraph (*b*) of the subsection is likely to raise procedural and evidentiary difficulties. The terms of the section make it clear that the validity or invalidity of the security may be settled in the course of the hearing of the application for an order, rather than in separate proceedings. It is plain also that the onus of satisfying the court is on the petitioner. Yet he is unlikely to have at his disposal all the evidence that an administrator or liquidator would later have when proceeding under s. 239 or s. 245. Fairly obviously, the matter cannot be determined without the security-holder as well as the company being made a party (for which, indeed, provision is made by IR 1986, r. 2.9). However, there are still difficult questions which the legislation does not address: is there any guarantee that the case will be properly put for the company (which, in the case of a creditor's petition, may well be *opposed* to the application)? There will not yet be anyone in office equivalent to the "office-holder" whose rôle it is to prosecute the proceedings under s. 239. Suppose that a decision under the present subsection is reached in favour of the security-holder: will the matter be *res judicata* if a winding-up order or an unrelated administration order is later made?

There is a further difficulty which may arise under s. 9(3)(*b*), in reckoning the statutory period during which the security must have been created if it is to be avoided. There will be no problem in the case of ss. 238–240 and 245, since the "relevant time" will be calculated from the date when the petition for an administration order was *presented* (see ss. 240(3)(*a*), 245(5)(*a*)); but the significant date for ss. 242, 243 is the date of the making of the administration *order*, and this will set the court the impossible task of ascribing a real date to a hypothetical order.

A receiver who is not an administrative receiver (e.g. a receiver of part only of the company's property, or (probably) a receiver appointed by the court) is not obliged to vacate office unless required to do so by the administrator: s. 11(2).

S. 9(4), (5)

The powers of the court, especially to make interim orders, are expressed in the widest terms, and include power to subject the decision-making powers of the corporate organs to its own supervision, or to delegate that function to a qualified insolvency practitioner. It is submitted, however, that orders made under this section can affect only the company and, presumably, such creditors as have been made parties to the application. The position as regards other creditors is dealt with in s. 10, below. One question which is not at all clear is whether an interim order under s. 9(4) and (5) could restrict the exercise of powers by a security-holder or an administrative receiver pending the determination of a question as to the validity of the security under s. 9(3)(*b*): compare s. 10(2)(*b*), (*c*).

An interim order under s. 9(4) is not an administration order for the purposes of CDDA 1986, s. 6(2)(*b*), so that time does not begin to run for the purposes of the two-year limitation prescribed CDDA 1986, s. 7(2) until an administration order under s. 8(3) is made: *Secretary of State for Trade and Industry* v *Palmer* [1993] BCC 650.

There is no power under the Act for the court to appoint an interim administrator; but in an appropriate case (e.g. where the company's property is in jeopardy) it can appoint the intended administrator or another appropriate person to take control of the property and manage the company's affairs pending the final determination of the hearing: *Re a Company No. 00175 of 1987* (1987) 3 BCC 124. Such an appointment would be analogous to the appointment of a receiver of a disputed property or of property which is in jeopardy. In *Re Gallidoro Trawlers Ltd* [1991] BCC 691 the court, instead of appointing an interim manager, made an order restricting the powers of the company's directors prior to the hearing of the petition.

Where a petition for an administration order is not proceeded with and a winding-up order is made, the court may in a proper case allow the costs of the petition to be treated as costs in the winding up: *Re Gosscott (Groundworks) Ltd* (1988) 4 BCC 372; but there have been other cases where costs have been left to be borne by the directors personally: see *Re W F Fearman Ltd (No. 2)* (1988) 4 BCC 141, *Taylor & Anor v Pace Developments Ltd* [1991] BCC 406. In *Re Land & Property Trust Co. plc; Re Andromache Properties Ltd & Ors* [1991] BCC 446, Harman J at first instance made a similar order, but his ruling was reversed on appeal (*Re Land & Property Trust Co. plc (No. 2)* [1993] BCC 462), after the Court of Appeal had ruled (*Re Land & Property Trust Co. plc* [1991] 1 WLR 601, [1991] BCC 459) that the directors' right of appeal was not barred by s. 18(1)(*f*) of the Supreme Court Act 1981.

Section 10   Effect of application

10(1)   [Limitations]   During the period beginning with the presentation of a petition for an administration order and ending with the making of such an order or the dismissal of the petition—

(a) no resolution may be passed or order made for the winding up of the company;

(b) no steps may be taken to enforce any security over the company's property, or to repossess goods in the company's possession under any hire-purchase agreement, except with the leave of the court and subject to such terms as the court may impose; and

(c) no other proceedings and no execution or other legal process may be commenced or continued, and no distress may be levied, against the company or its property except with the leave of the court and subject to such terms as aforesaid.

10(2)   [Where leave not required]   Nothing in subsection (1) requires the leave of the court—

(a) for the presentation of a petition for the winding up of the company,

(b) for the appointment of an administrative receiver of the company, or

(c) for the carrying out by such a receiver (whenever appointed) of any of his functions.

10(3)   [Period in s. 10(1)]   Where—

(a) a petition for an administration order is presented at a time when there is an administrative receiver of the company, and

(b) the person by or on whose behalf the receiver was appointed has not consented to the making of the order,

the period mentioned in subsection (1) is deemed not to begin unless and until that person so consents.

10(4) **[Hire-purchase agreements]** References in this section and the next to hire-purchase agreements include conditional sale agreements, chattel leasing agreements and retention of title agreements.

10(5) **[Scotland]** In the application of this section and the next to Scotland, references to execution being commenced or continued include references to diligence being carried out or continued, and references to distress being levied shall be omitted.

(Former provision: IA 1985, s. 29)

S. 10(1)

Unless the company is already in the hands of an administrative receiver (in which case s. 10(3) applies), the presentation of a petition for an administration order imposes an automatic moratorium, which prevents certain legal acts and processes from being performed or continued until the application is finally disposed of. The company cannot be put into voluntary liquidation, nor can a winding-up order be made (although a winding-up petition may be *presented*: s. 10(2)(*a*)); and unless the court gives leave, the enforcement of a security, the repossession of goods held under hire-purchase and similar agreements, and the commencement and prosecution of legal proceedings, etc., may not be proceeded with. (Some exceptions are listed in s. 10(2), discussed below.) The court's discretion in granting leave under paras. (*b*) and (*c*) appears to be unrestricted.

In *Re a Company No. 001448 of 1989* (1989) 5 BCC 706 Millett J held that, even though s. 10(1)(*c*) cannot be invoked until a petition for an administration order has been presented, the court has power under its *quia timet* jurisdiction to restrain the advertisement of a winding-up petition if counsel for the company has given an undertaking that a petition will be presented.

The rules have been amended to provide that notice of the presentation of a petition for an administration order be given to anyone known to be issuing execution or other legal process of distraining against the company (IR 1986, r. 2.6A), in order to avoid the risk of inadvertent contraventions of s. 10(1)(*c*).

Section 10(1)(*b*) does not apply in relation to the enforcement of "market charges" (as defined by CA 1989, s. 173): see s. 175 of that Act (as qualified by the Financial Markets and Insolvency Regulations 1991 (SI 1991 No. 880)), and the introductory note at p. 3, above.

In relation to the financial markets, nothing in s. 10(1)(*c*) affects any action taken by an exchange or clearing house for the purpose of its default proceedings: CA 1989, s. 161(4).

S. 10(2)

Although no winding-up order may be *made* while the hearing of an application for an administration order is pending, a petition for winding up may be *presented*. It may well be the case that a creditor will wish to oppose an application for an administration order and argue instead that the company should be put into liquidation. If he has not already presented a winding-up petition, s. 10(2)(*a*) confirms that he is free to do so; and in any case it is open to the court to combine the hearing of the two applications – an obviously convenient course. The leave of the court under s. 10(1)(*c*) may, however, be necessary for such a joinder of proceedings; and if liquidation is in due course to be ordered the application for an administration order must first be dismissed (s. 10(1)(*a*)), and vice versa (s. 11(1)(*a*)).

In *Re a Company No. 001992 of 1988* (1988) 4 BCC 451 the court ruled that it was proper not to proceed to advertise a winding-up petition until after determination of the application for an administration order; but in later proceedings (reported as *Re Manlon Trading Ltd* (1988) 4 BCC 455) Harman J ruled that this course should only be taken when a petition for an administration order had actually been presented or an undertaking given to the court to present one: it was not sufficient to act on affidavit evidence that administration was being contemplated.

The Act is silent on the question whether it is possible, at least without leave, to present a second administration petition specifying a different purpose (e.g. a realisation of assets rather than a voluntary arrangement, or vice versa). Gordon Stewart, *Administrative Receivers and Administrators* (CCH, 1987), p. 170, argues that the wording of s. 9(1) recognises such a right.

S. 10(3)

If an administrative receiver is already in office when a petition for an administration order is presented, the earlier "moratorium" provisions of this section do not apply, unless and until the debenture holder gives his consent to the making of an administration order (thereby signalling his willingness to vacate the receivership in favour of the proposed administratorship). There is no corresponding provision dealing with the case where the holder of the charge puts in an administrative receiver *after* the petition for an administration order is presented: the moratorium which will already be in force as regards all the company's other creditors apparently continues until the petition is disposed of in one way or another.

S. 10(4)

Of the four categories of agreement mentioned in this section, "hire-purchase agreement" and "conditional sale agreement" are defined (by reference to the Consumer Credit Act 1974) in s. 436 and "chattel leasing agreement" and "retention of title agreement" in s. 251. In each of these transactions the ownership of the goods concerned remains vested in the bailor or seller, and they do not become the company's property; but the Act for many purposes treats them as if the company has become the owner and the other party has retained only a security interest. See further the notes to ss. 15 and 43.

S. 10(5)

This provision assimilates the rules contained in the subsections above to the position under Scots law.

Section 11 Effect of order

11(1) [On making of administration order] On the making of an administration order—

    (a) any petition for the winding up of the company shall be dismissed, and

    (b) any administrative receiver of the company shall vacate office.

11(2) [Vacation of office by receiver] Where an administration order has been made, any receiver of part of the company's property shall vacate office on being required to do so by the administrator.

11(3) [Limitations] During the period for which an administration order is in force—

    (a) no resolution may be passed or order made for the winding up of the company;

    (b) no administrative receiver of the company may be appointed;

    (c) no other steps may be taken to enforce any security over the company's property, or to repossess goods in the company's possession under any hire-purchase agreement, except with the consent of the administrator or the leave of the court and subject (where the court gives leave) to such terms as the court may impose; and

(d) no other proceedings and no execution or other legal process may be commenced or continued, and no distress may be levied, against the company or its property except with the consent of the administrator or the leave of the court and subject (where the court gives leave) to such terms as aforesaid.

11(4) [Where vacation of office under s. 11(1)(b), (2)] Where at any time an administrative receiver of the company has vacated office under subsection (1)(b), or a receiver of part of the company's property has vacated office under subsection (2)—

(a) his remuneration and any expenses properly incurred by him, and

(b) any indemnity to which he is entitled out of the assets of the company,

shall be charged on and (subject to subsection (3) above) paid out of any property of the company which was in his custody or under his control at that time in priority to any security held by the person by or on whose behalf he was appointed.

11(5) [S. 40, 59] Neither an administrative receiver who vacates office under subsection (1)(b) nor a receiver who vacates office under subsection (2) is required on or after so vacating office to take any steps for the purpose of complying with any duty imposed on him by section 40 or 59 of this Act (duty to pay preferential creditors).

(Former provision: IA 1985, s. 30)

General note

On the making of an administration order, the suspension of the rights of creditors and security-holders imposed by s. 10 becomes a total ban, and the administrative receiver, if there has been one in office, must give way to the administrator.

S. 11(1)

If a petition for winding up has been presented, whether before or after the presentation of the petition for an administration order, the petitioner should take all possible steps to ensure that his case is heard before, or simultaneously with, the latter application: see the note to s. 10(2).

An administrative receiver will be required to vacate office under this provision only if his appointor has consented to the making of the administration order or if his security is found liable to be invalidated under s. 9(3)(*b*). On the effects of his vacating office, see the note to s. 11(2).

S. 11(2)

A receiver of part (i.e. not "substantially the whole") of the company's property is not an administrative receiver: see s. 29(2). He is not required automatically to vacate office – the administrator has a discretion; but any steps that he may take to enforce the security will need the consent of the administrator or the leave of the court under s. 11(3)(*c*).

The full implications of the vacation of office by a receiver under this section are not clearly spelt out in the Act. The appointment of the receiver, when it was made, will have crystallised the charge, in so far as it was a floating charge, so that the assets affected will have been subject to a fixed charge throughout the subsistence of the receivership. Section 11(4) grants the receiver a charge on the assets for his fees, etc., and in some circumstances the right to have them paid, and both this subsection and s. 15(1) confirm that the debenture holder's security continues in force during the period when the administrator is in office. Presumably it does so as a fixed charge and is not decrystallised, for otherwise s. 15(4) would make little sense. This is not now likely to be a point of great significance, however, for under the new statutory definition it will be treated for all the purposes of the Act as if it were still a floating charge: see s. 251 and the notes to ss. 175(2)(*b*) and 245. The creditors entitled to preference in the receivership will lose all claims against the discharged receiver (s. 11(5)) and will have no claim against the administrator (s. 15(1)). However, presumably it is intended that they will retain some form of priority over the debenture holder himself by virtue of s. 15(4). This is by no means a foregone conclusion, however, for (1) if the administration order is discharged without a winding up, the debenture holder will have to appoint a receiver afresh in order to enforce his security, and this will mean a new "relevant date" for the purposes of s. 387 and different "assets coming to the hands of the receiver" for the purposes of s. 40(2) or s. 59(1); while (2) if the company is put into liquidation immediately upon the discharge of the administration order, s. 175 may apply to the exclusion of s. 40 or s. 59, and under s. 387(3)(*a*) a quite different list of preferential debts would need to be drawn up.

Section 11(2) does not apply in relation to a receiver appointed to enforce a "market charge" (as defined by CA 1989, s. 173): see s. 175 of that Act (as qualified by the Financial Markets and Insolvency Regulations 1991 (SI 1991 No. 880)), and the introductory note at p. 3, above.

In relation to the financial markets, nothing in s. 11(3) affects any action taken by an exchange or clearing house for the purpose of its default proceedings: CA 1989, s. 161(4).

S. 11(3)

This subsection spells out the full details of the restrictions on the enforcement of claims and securities against the company which apply once the administration order becomes operative. In one respect, the ban is strengthened: it is no longer possible to appoint an administrative receiver. In another respect, it is slightly relaxed: the acts mentioned in paras. (*c*) and (*d*) may now be authorised by the administrator as an alternative to seeking the leave of the court.

In *Air Ecosse Ltd & Ors* v *Civil Aviation Authority & Anor* (1987) 3 BCC 492; 1987 SLT 751, the Court of Session ruled that the term "proceedings" in s. 11(3) is confined in its scope to the activities of the company's creditors in seeking to enforce their debts, and does not extend to quasi-judicial and extra-judicial proceedings such as an application made by a competitor of the company for the revocation of an aviation licence. However, a complaint or application to an industrial tribunal under the employment protection legislation, such as a complaint by a former employee of the company that he had been unfairly selected for redundancy, is within the section and requires the consent of the administrator or the leave of the court: *Carr* v *British International Helicopters Ltd* [1993] BCC 855. But in such cases it will only rarely be appropriate for consent to be refused (ibid.).

An application for an extension of time for the registration of a charge cannot be described as "proceedings against a company or its property" within s. 11(3)(*d*): *Re Barrow Borough Transport Ltd* [1990] Ch. 227; (1989) 5 BCC 646. However, once an administration order has been made and it has become clear that administration will result in the insolvent liquidation of the company, the court's discretion should be exercised against granting an extension of time for registration (ibid.).

A landlord's right of re-entry for non-payment of rent is a "security" within the meaning of para. (*c*) of this subsection: *Exchange Travel Agency Ltd* v *Triton Property Trust plc & Anor* [1991] BCC 341. In the same case Harman J also held that the exercise of such a right was the "commencement of a legal process" under para. (*d*); but this ruling was not followed by Millett J in *Re Olympia & York Canary Wharf Ltd; American Express Europe Ltd & Ors* v *Adamson & Ors* [1993] BCC 154. "Legal process", in the view of Millett J, means a process which requires the assistance of the court; and it does not include such steps as the serving by a person who is a party to a contract with the company of a notice making time of the essence of the contract, or the acceptance by such a person of a repudiatory breach of contract.

Section 11(3)(*c*) extends to goods which are the subject of a hire-purchase or similar agreement even where the agreement has been terminated before the presentation of the petition for an administration order, provided that the goods remain in the company's possession; *Re David Meek Plant Ltd; Re David Meek Access Ltd* [1993] BCC 175.

Section 11 does not affect the substantive rights of the parties: it is concerned merely with procedure. It imposes a moratorium on the enforcement of creditors' rights, but does not destroy those rights. The legal right of a security-holder to enforce his security, and that of an owner of goods to immediate possession of his goods, and the causes of action based on such rights, remain vested in that party. If he seeks and obtains the leave of the court to enforce his rights, the grant of leave does not alter the parties' legal rights, but merely grants the applicant liberty to enforce his rights: *Barclays Mercantile Business Finance Ltd & Anor* v *Sibec Developments Ltd & Ors (Re Sibec Developments Ltd)* [1992] 1 WLR 1253; [1993] BCC 148.

A proceeding (such as an application to an industrial tribunal) commenced without leave is not a nullity: it is in order for the proceeding to be adjourned while consent or leave is sought: *Carr* v *British International Helicopters Ltd* (above). This ruling means that difficulties over a possible time-bar for such applications are less likely to arise.

The judgment of Peter Gibson J in *Re Meesan Investments Ltd* (1988) 4 BCC 788 contains a discussion of the basis on which the court will exercise its discretion to allow a secured creditor to enforce his security during the currency of an administration order. The burden of making out a case lies on the creditor who is seeking leave. But it is not necessary for him to show that there is something in the conduct of the administrator deserving of criticism (e.g. that he has been guilty of undue delay). The court has to consider the interests of all concerned, including the general creditors, and not just those of the applicant. The fact that the enforcement of the security independently of the administration will increase costs is a matter that the court may take into account in refusing leave.

Section 11(3)(*c*) does not apply in relation to the enforcement of "market charges" (as defined by CA 1989, s. 173): see s. 175 of that Act (as qualified by the Financial Markets and Insolvency Regulations 1991 (SI 1991 No. 880)), and the introductory note at p. 3 above.

Section 11(3)(*d*) is similar to s. 130(2), which applies in a winding up, and decisions under that section may give guidance as to how the discretion under s. 11(3)(*d*) will be exercised.

In *Bristol Airport plc & Anor* v *Powdrill & Ors* [1990] Ch. 744 (reported as *Re Paramount Airways Ltd* [1990] BCC 130), the Court of Appeal, affirming Harman J, held that for the purposes of s. 11(3)(*c*) and (*d*): (i) aircraft held by a company under a seven-year lease was "property" of the company and (ii) the statutory right of an airport to detain aircraft pursuant to s. 88 of the Civil Aviation Act 1982 for failure to pay outstanding airport charges was a "lien or other security" which could not be exercised without the leave of the court.

Note that the reference to "any hire-purchase agreement" in para. (*c*) includes also conditional sale agreements, chattel leasing agreements and retention of title agreements: see s. 10(4).

The landmark decision of the Court of Appeal in *Re Atlantic Computer Systems plc* [1992] Ch. 505; [1990] BCC 859 contains a number of important rulings on the jurisdiction conferred by s. 11, and guidance on the principles governing the exercise of the court's discretion under the section. The company's business was leasing computers, a substantial number of which it held on hire-purchase or long lease from banks and other financial institutions (referred to in the judgment as "the funders"). Two funders applied to the court contending that the administrators, having received payments from the sub-lessees, were obliged to pay the rentals due under the head leases. Alternatively, the funders sought leave under s. 11 to repossess the computer equipment. The trial judge, applying an analogy from winding up law, held that where leased property was used for the purposes of an administration, the rent or hire charges due to the lessor should rank as an expense of the administration and as such be payable in priority to the company's other creditors; but the Court of Appeal considered that a more appropriate analogy was with administrative receivership, where such charges would not have the same priority. The court expressed the view that, in any case, the new discretionary jurisdiction conferred by s. 11 should be exercised on the broadest basis and should not be allowed to become fettered by rigid rules of automatic application. However, it went on to hold that the computers remained "goods in the company's possession", notwithstanding the sub-leases, so that the discretionary powers conferred by s. 11(3)(*c*) could be invoked; that lessors and other owners of property in the position of the funders should not be compelled to leave it in the company's hands against their will but should ordinarily be allowed to repossess it; and that this should normally be a matter where the administrator would be expected to give his consent, thus obviating the need to make application to the court for leave.

The judgment concludes with a statement giving guidance on the principles to be applied on applications for the grant of leave under s. 11. These principles, which are set out at length (see [1992] Ch. 505 at pp. 542–544; [1990] BCC 859 at pp. 879–882), may be summarised as follows:

(1) The person seeking leave has always to make out a case.

(2) If granting leave to an owner of land or goods to exercise his proprietary rights as lessor and repossess his land or goods is unlikely to impede the achievement of the purpose of the administration, leave should normally be given.

(3) In other cases where a lessor seeks possession, the court has to carry out a balancing exercise, weighing the legitimate interests of the lessor against those of the company's other creditors.

(4) In carrying out the balancing exercise, great importance is normally to be given to the lessor's proprietary interests: an administration for the benefit of unsecured creditors should not be conducted at the expense of those who have proprietary rights.

(5) It will normally be a sufficient ground for the grant of leave that significant loss would be caused to the lessor by a refusal. But if substantially greater loss would be caused to others by the grant of leave, that may outweigh the loss to the lessor caused by a refusal.

(6)–(8) These paragraphs list the various factors to which the court will have regard in assessing the respective losses under heading (5).

(9) The above considerations may be relevant not only to the decision whether or not to grant leave, but also to a decision to impose terms if leave is granted.

(10) The court may, in effect, impose conditions if leave is refused (for instance, by giving directions to the administrator), in which case the above considerations will also be applicable.

(11) A broadly similar approach will apply in many applications for leave to enforce a security.

(12) The court will not, on a leave application, seek to adjudicate upon a dispute over the existence, validity or nature of a security unless the issue raises a short point of law which it is convenient to determine without further ado.

It should perhaps be mentioned that in the original Insolvency Bill, the "freezing" of the rights of security-holders was limited to a period of 12 months (subject to extension); but this restriction has been dropped from the legislation in its final form.

S. 11(4)

An administrative receiver automatically vacates office when an order is made (s. 11(1)(*b*)), and any other receiver may be required by the administrator to do so (s. 11(2)). This subsection seeks to secure the receiver's right to remuneration, and any entitlement to an indemnity that he may have, ahead of the claims of the security-holder who appointed him. However, (like every other creditor) he cannot receive actual payment of this claim or take steps to enforce it except with the administrator's consent or the court's leave under s. 11(3).

S. 11(5)

Under the sections mentioned, it is the duty of a receiver who is appointed to enforce a floating charge to pay the company's preferential debts "out of the assets coming into his hands". This subsection makes it clear that the assets must be surrendered to the administrator by the receiver when he vacates office, without regard to this obligation, and also that he is thereafter discharged from that duty.

On "preferential debts", see the notes to ss. 386 and 387; and see also the discussion at s. 11(2) above.

Note that there is no provision in the legislation giving priority to preferential debts in a company administration, unless either a winding up follows immediately on the discharge of the administration order (s. 387(3)(*a*)) or the administration coincides with a voluntary arrangement (s. 387(2)(*a*)).

Section 12   Notification of order

12(1)   [Information in invoices etc.]   Every invoice, order for goods or business letter which, at a time when an administration order is in force in relation to a company, is issued by or on behalf of the company or the administrator, being a document on or in which the company's name appears, shall also contain the administrator's name and a statement that the affairs, business and property of the company are being managed by the administrator.

12(2)   [Penalty on default]   If default is made in complying with this section, the company and any of the following persons who without reasonable excuse authorises or permits the default, namely, the administrator and any officer of the company, is liable to a fine.

(Former provision: IA 1985, s. 31)

S. 12(1)

This is a parallel provision to those requiring notification of the appointment of a receiver (ss. 39, 64) and notification that a company is in liquidation (s. 188).

S. 12(2)

The policy reasons for making the company itself liable for this offence are not obvious. Note that the *company* is strictly liable, while any of the other persons named is liable only if he "without reasonable excuse authorises or permits the default". This language may be contrasted with that of ss. 39, 64 and 188: "who knowingly and wilfully authorises or permits the default".

On penalties, see s. 430 and Sch. 10.

ADMINISTRATORS

Section 13   Appointment of administrator

13(1)   [Appointment]   The administrator of a company shall be appointed either by the administration order or by an order under the next subsection.

13(2)   [Court may fill vacancy]   If a vacancy occurs by death, resignation or otherwise in the office of the administrator, the court may by order fill the vacancy.

13(3)   [Application for s. 13(2) order]   An application for an order under subsection (2) may be made—

(a) by any continuing administrator of the company; or

(b) where there is no such administrator, by a creditors' committee established under section 26 below; or

(c) where there is no such administrator and no such committee, by the company or the directors or by any creditor or creditors of the company.

(Former provision: IA 1985, s. 32)

General note

These provisions deal with the appointment of an administrator and with vacancies in the office of administrator.

It is apparent from s. 13(3)(*a*) and s. 231 that two or more persons may be appointed joint administrators.

There is no power under this or any other provision for the court to appoint an interim administrator: see the note to s. 9(4).

An administrator must be an insolvency practitioner and qualified to act in relation to the particular company: see s. 230(1).

S. 13(3)

On "the company" and "the directors", see the note to s. 124(1).

Section 14   General powers

14(1)   [Powers of administrator]   The administrator of a company—

(a) may do all such things as may be necessary for the management of the affairs, business and property of the company, and

(b) without prejudice to the generality of paragraph (a), has the powers specified in Schedule 1 to this Act;

and in the application of that Schedule to the administrator of a company the words "he" and "him" refer to the administrator.

14(2)   [Extra powers]   The administrator also has power—

(a) to remove any director of the company and to appoint any person to be a director of it, whether to fill a vacancy or otherwise, and

(b) to call any meeting of the members or creditors of the company.

14(3)   [Application for directions]   The administrator may apply to the court for directions in relation to any particular matter arising in connection with the carrying out of his functions.

14(4)   [Conflict with other powers]   Any power conferred on the company or its officers, whether by this Act or the Companies Act or by the memorandum or articles of association, which could be exercised in such a way as to interfere with the exercise by the administrator of his powers is not exercisable except with the consent of the administrator, which may be given either generally or in relation to particular cases.

14(5)   [Administrator agent]   In exercising his powers the administrator is deemed to act as the company's agent.

14(6) [Third party]   A person dealing with the administrator in good faith and for value is not concerned to inquire whether the administrator is acting within his powers.

(Former provision: IA 1985, s. 33)

S. 14(1)

The powers of an administrator are stated in the broadest terms in para. (*a*). In addition, some specific powers, common to both administrators and administrative receivers, are set out in more detail in Sch. 1. These powers are not restricted to the management of the company's business (as is normally the case with the board of directors). This is indicated by the use of the word "affairs" and appears also from some of the particular matters mentioned in this section and the schedule, e.g. the power to remove directors (s. 14(2)) and to petition for a winding up (Sch. 1, para. 21).

Although the powers of an administrator are similar in many respects to those of an administrative receiver, there are also important differences, and the analogy cannot be pressed too far. An administrator is appointed to manage the affairs of the company; an administrative receiver's rôle is to realise the company's assets primarily for the benefit of a particular creditor: *Astor Chemical Ltd* v *Synthetic Technology Ltd* [1990] BCC 97 at pp. 105–106. A receiver may decline to perform certain contracts which an administrator has no power to disown (ibid.). And, unlike a liquidator, an administrator has no statutory power of disclaimer (*Re P & C and R & T (Stockport) Ltd* [1991] BCC 98 at p. 104).

The powers of an administrator do not extend to acts which the company itself is not competent to perform: *Re Home Treat Ltd* [1991] BCC 165. In this case, the company's objects as stated in its memorandum did not extend to the running of a nursing home (the company's actual business which the administrators wished to continue pending a sale). The court managed to circumvent this difficulty by a somewhat indulgent ruling that there had been a *de facto* alteration of the objects clause by an informal resolution of the shareholders at an earlier stage.

For the administrator's special power to deal with charged property, see s. 15.

S. 14(2)

The power given to an administrator to appoint and remove directors has no parallel elsewhere in company law, apart of course from the powers usually conferred upon the company in general meeting. (During the currency of an administration order, these powers of the general meeting will not be exercisable without the consent of the administrator: see s. 14(4).)

If the removal of a director amounts to a breach of his service contract, the company will be liable in damages, even though the removal was in exercise of a statutory power: *Southern Foundries (1926) Ltd* v *Shirlaw* [1940] AC 701, *Shindler* v *Northern Raincoat Co. Ltd* [1960] 1 WLR 1038.

Section 14(2) does not empower the administrator to dispense with the board of directors entirely: CA 1985, s. 282 (which prescribes a minimum of two directors for every public company, and one for a private company) will still apply to a company that is subject to an administration order. See further the note to s. 14(4), below.

S. 14(3)

A similar provision applies to the supervisor of a voluntary scheme (s. 7(4)) and the liquidator in a winding up by the court (s. 168(3)).

The powers of an administrator under ss. 14(1)(*a*) and 17(2) to "manage the affairs, business and property of the company" are wide enough to make it unnecessary in many cases for an administrator to seek directions from the court, so that he may, e.g. sell a substantial asset in a proper case even before the creditors' meeting has been held: see, however, the note to s. 17(2).

For examples of applications for directions under s. 14(3), see *Re British & Commonwealth Holdings plc (No. 3)* [1992] 1 WLR 672; [1992] BCC 58 and *Re Maxwell Communications Corporation plc (No. 3)* [1993] 1 WLR 1402; [1993] BCC 369 – cases which contain important rulings on the effectiveness of debt subordination arrangements created (respectively) by trust deed and by contract.

S. 14(4)

On the appointment of an administrator, the directors remain in office, and both the board of directors and the shareholders in general meeting retain their rôles as organs of the company under the articles of association and the Companies Act – although their powers will, of course, be severely restricted by the provisions of this section. The directors' statutory and common law duties will continue to apply to them – including the duty to hold annual meetings, prepare accounts and make returns to the registrar.

S. 14(5)

This provision in part echoes the terms on which a receiver is customarily appointed to enforce a debenture holder's security – terms which are now given statutory expression in s. 44(1) of this Act. However, the subsection has only a limited effect: it does not make the administrator the company's agent in any full sense, nor even say (as does s. 44(1)) that he shall be deemed to *be* the agent of the company; only deemed to be *acting* as its agent in exercising his powers, although the difference in wording may not be material. He is not, like a normal agent, subject to control and direction by the company as his principal (see s. 14(4)); his actual authority is virtually unlimited (see s. 14(1)), and his ostensible authority completely so (see s. 14(6)).

The main object of this provision is to try to ensure that the administrator, at least in the normal case, incurs no personal liability on any contract or other obligation that he may enter into on the company's behalf. (In this, the Act departs from the original Insolvency Bill, which did make the administrator personally responsible in the absence of an express disclaimer: cf. the position of an administrative receiver (s. 44(1)).

Like an agent, the administrator will also owe the usual fiduciary duties to the company, and will be entitled to be indemnified out of its assets for obligations that he incurs.

S. 14(6)

This provision is probably inserted out of caution only, since such a third party would almost certainly be protected by the ordinary rules of agency.

Section 15   Power to deal with charged property, etc.

15(1)   [Power of disposal etc.]   The administrator of a company may dispose of or otherwise exercise his powers in relation to any property of the company which is subject to a security to which this subsection applies as if the property were not subject to the security.

15(2)   [Court orders, on application by administrator]   Where, on an application by the administrator, the court is satisfied that the disposal (with or without other assets) of—

    (a) any property of the company subject to a security to which this subsection applies, or

    (b) any goods in the possession of the company under a hire-purchase agreement, would be likely to promote the purpose or one or more of the purposes specified in the administration order, the court may by order authorise the administrator to dispose of the property as if it were not subject to the security or to dispose of the goods as if all rights of the owner under the hire-purchase agreement were vested in the company.

15(3) [Application of s. 15(1), (2)] Subsection (1) applies to any security which, as created, was a floating charge; and subsection (2) applies to any other security.

15(4) [Effect of security where property disposed of] Where property is disposed of under subsection (1), the holder of the security has the same priority in respect of any property of the company directly or indirectly representing the property disposed of as he would have had in respect of the property subject to the security.

15(5) [Conditions for s. 15(2) order] It shall be a condition of an order under subsection (2) that—

(a) the net proceeds of the disposal, and

(b) where those proceeds are less than such amount as may be determined by the court to be the net amount which would be realised on a sale of the property or goods in the open market by a willing vendor, such sums as may be required to make good the deficiency,

shall be applied towards discharging the sums secured by the security or payable under the hire-purchase agreement.

15(6) [Where s. 15(5) condition re two or more securities] Where a condition imposed in pursuance of subsection (5) relates to two or more securities, that condition requires the net proceeds of the disposal and, where paragraph (b) of that subsection applies, the sums mentioned in that paragraph to be applied towards discharging the sums secured by those securities in the order of their priorities.

15(7) [Copy of s. 15(2) order to registrar] An office copy of an order under subsection (2) shall, within 14 days after the making of the order, be sent by the administrator to the registrar of companies.

15(8) [Non-compliance with s. 15(7)] If the administrator without reasonable excuse fails to comply with subsection (7), he is liable to a fine and, for continued contravention, to a daily default fine.

15(9) [Interpretation] References in this section to hire-purchase agreements include conditional sale agreements, chattel leasing agreements and retention of title agreements.

(Former provision: IA 1985, s. 34(1)–(8), (12))

General note

This section gives to the administrator unique powers to override the rights of the holder of a security over the company's property or the owner of property held by the company under a hire-purchase or similar agreement, and to dispose of the property in question as if it were owned by the company itself unencumbered. This he may do without the consent of the chargee or owner of the property, but the authorisation of the court will be needed unless the security is (or was originally) a floating charge. The section includes provisions designed to ensure that rights roughly analogous to those previously enjoyed by the charge-holder or owner are preserved.

The power conferred by this section will be of particular value when an administrator wishes to dispose of the business of the company, or some part of it, as a going concern, and a security-holder or property-owner is not willing to co-operate. A similar power is given to an administrative receiver by s. 43.

Some guidance as to the operation of the section is given by the judgment in *Re A R V Aviation Ltd* (1988) 4 BCC 708, where the holder of a charge over land owned by the company opposed the administrators' application to be authorised to dispose of it. The charge-holder contended, *inter alia*, that the administrators were basing their application on an over-optimistic valuation of the land in question. The court ruled that a bona fide dispute as to value would clearly call into operation the discretion of the court under s. 15(2), and stated that in principle it was desirable for the court to have proper valuation evidence before being asked to exercise that jurisdiction. It also ruled (i) that "the sums secured by the security" in s. 15(5) covered interest and (subject to the court's overriding discretion) the charge-holder's costs, as well as the principal sum secured; and (ii) that it was not necessary at the time of making an order for disposal under s. 15(2) to assess the amount of the deficiency to which the secured creditor might be entitled under s. 15(5): this could be determined at a later hearing.

Note that nothing in this section or s. 16 is to be taken as prejudicing the right of a creditor or member to apply to the court for relief under s. 27: see s. 27(5).

Section 15(1) and (2) do not apply in relation to the enforcement of "market charges" (as defined by CA 1989, s. 173): see s. 175 of that Act (as qualified by the Financial Markets and Insolvency Regulations 1991 (SI 1991 No. 880)), and the introductory note at p. 3, above.

S. 15(1), (3), (4)

These subsections, taken together, deal with the case where property of the company is subject to a floating charge. The administrator is empowered to dispose of or deal with the property without the consent of the chargee and without seeking a court order. This is so even though the charge may have crystallised on or before the making of the administration order (s. 15(3), and see the note to s. 11(2)); but where the same obligation is secured by both a fixed and a floating charge, s. 15(2) will apply to such assets as are covered by the fixed charge.

The meaning of s. 15(4) is obscure. It seems to be intended to ensure that any dealing by the administrator with the property of the company will not prejudice the chargee's security rights. However, instead of providing that the *security* shall extend to the price or other property acquired by the company in substitution for the asset disposed of, it speaks merely of "priority". This could give rise to many difficult questions. For example, will the charge-holder be entitled to claim security over such substituted property if the administratorship is brought to a successful conclusion and the order discharged? Suppose that the company trades its way back into a sound financial position, though still with a modest overdraft, and control is handed back to the directors: what security will the bank have?

It is also far from clear whether the "priority" referred to means priority in the ranking of one charge *vis-à-vis* another, or priority in the order that the company's various debts are paid, or priority in some other sense. The uncertainty as to the position of those creditors whose debts would have been entitled to preferential payment in a receivership has been discussed elsewhere (see the note to s. 11(2)).

S. 15(2), (5), (6)

Property which is subject to a fixed charge (excluding a charge which was originally a floating charge but has since become fixed: see s. 15(3)) may be disposed of by the administrator under these subsections without the consent of the charge-holder, but only (1) with the authorisation of the court and (2) on terms that the whole of the net proceeds of the sale (or the open market value of the property, if it is sold for less) is applied in discharge of the amount secured – not necessarily, of course, the whole of the company's indebtedness to the particular creditor. These provisions extend also to goods in the possession of the company under a hire-purchase agreement (or a conditional sale agreement, chattel leasing agreement or retention of title agreement: see s. 15(9)): the administrator may sell the goods without the owner's consent, but must apply the realised amount (or open market value) towards discharging the sums payable to the owner under the agreement.

The phrase "payable under the agreement" (s. 15(5)) may cause some difficulty, since not all of the agreements listed in s. 15(9) will contain an express provision making the company accountable to the owner for the value of the property or the proceeds of sale in the event of a (possibly wrongful) sale to a third party. If, for instance, in regard to a chattel leasing agreement, the administrator sells the chattel unencumbered to a third party under s. 15(2) at a time when only one month's rental is outstanding, it would appear to be only the latter sum, and not the full value of the lessor's interest in the property, that must be accounted for under s. 15(5). If this is so, the lessor may have only an unsecured claim for money had and received against the company in respect of the balance of the proceeds of sale, or a right to seek relief under s. 27. No claim in tort (e.g. for wrongful interference with goods) would appear to lie against either the administrator or the company for action taken under s. 15(2); and it must be a matter of doubt whether the court can make an order subject to conditions other than that specified in s. 15(5).

If more is realised on the sale than is needed to discharge the sums in question, the balance will go into the general company funds held by the administrator. If less, the shortfall will remain due to the chargee or owner as an unsecured debt, unless the sale has been at below the market value and s. 15(5)(*b*) applies.

The administrator must satisfy the court as to the need for the sale, in the terms of s. 15(2); and the court is also charged by s. 15(5)(*b*) with the task of settling the open market value of the property, where that provision applies.

If the administrator and the chargee or owner of the property are willing to collaborate, of course, the property may be disposed of much more simply and cheaply under s. 11(3)(*c*).

In *Re Consumer & Industrial Press Ltd (No. 2)* (1988) 4 BCC 72 it was held that the court would not, except in "quite exceptional circumstances", authorise an administrator under s. 15 (2) to dispose of assets before the administrator's proposals had been considered by a creditors' meeting. However, an administrator is free to enter into an agreement with an intended purchaser conditionally upon the approval of the creditors or the leave of the court.

The administrators in *Re Newman Shopfitters (Cleveland) Ltd* [1991] BCLC 407 sought the court's authority to retain the proceeds of the sale of mortgaged property in a special bank account until they had reached a decision whether to challenge the validity of the mortgage. But the court held that it had no such power under s. 15. If, on the other hand, proceedings to challenge the mortgage had been commenced, appropriate interim relief could be sought in that action.

S. 15(6)

This deals with the application of s. 15(5) to the case where an item of property is subject to more than one charge: the normal priorities are preserved.

S. 15(7), (8)

The purpose of these provisions is, no doubt, to ensure that the register of charges kept by the registrar under CA 1985, s. 395 is kept up to date, for the benefit of people searching. However, the subsections affect all forms of security, and not merely registrable charges, and extend to hire-purchase agreements, etc., which are not charges at all.

Where charges are recorded in a register other than the Companies Registry (e.g. land, ships), it will no doubt be necessary to file a copy of the order in that register also in order to ensure that the transferee takes an unencumbered title.

S. 15(9)

See the note to s. 10(4).

Section 16   Operation of s. 15 in Scotland

16(1)   [Administrator's duty]   Where property is disposed of under section 15 in its application to Scotland, the administrator shall grant to the disponee an appropriate document of transfer or conveyance of the property, and—

(a) that document, or

(b) where any recording, intimation or registration of the document is a legal requirement for completion of title to the property, that recording, intimation or registration,

has the effect of disencumbering the property of or, as the case may be, freeing the property from the security.

16(2)   [Disposal of goods on hire-purchase etc.]   Where goods in the possession of the company under a hire-purchase agreement, conditional sale agreement, chattel leasing agreement or retention of title agreement are disposed of under section 15 in its application to Scotland, the disposal has the effect of extinguishing, as against the disponee, all rights of the owner of the goods under the agreement.

(Former provision: IA 1985, s. 34(9), (10))

General note

This section provides for the disponee who takes property under s. 15 to have such evidence as may be required under Scots law to effect or confirm the disencumbering of the property and to extinguish any claim of the previous owner of goods held under hire-purchase and similar agreements.

Section 17   General duties

17(1)   [Control of company property]   The administrator of a company shall, on his appointment, take into his custody or under his control all the property to which the company is or appears to be entitled.

17(2)   [Management of affairs, etc.]   The administrator shall manage the affairs, business and property of the company—

(a) at any time before proposals have been approved (with or without modifications) under section 24 below, in accordance with any directions given by the court, and

(b) at any time after proposals have been so approved, in accordance with those proposals as from time to time revised, whether by him or a predecessor of his.

17(3)   [Summoning of creditors' meeting]   The administrator shall summon a meeting of the company's creditors if—

(a) he is requested, in accordance with the rules, to do so by one-tenth, in value, of the company's creditors, or

(b) he is directed to do so by the court.

(Former provision: IA 1985, s. 35)

General note

The position of an administrator is in many ways broadly comparable with that of an administrative receiver, as is confirmed by the fact that by Sch. 1 they are given identical statutory powers; but there is an important difference in their rôles. A receiver, representing a single secured creditor, is entitled to give priority to the interests of that creditor. An administrator, in contrast, like a liquidator, has no particular interest to which he may give priority. In the context of a sale of company property, a receiver may effect an immediate sale whether or not that is calculated to realise the best price, though he must take reasonable care to obtain whatever is the true market value of the property at the moment he chooses to sell it. But an administrator is under a duty to take reasonable care to obtain the best price that the circumstances (as he reasonably perceives them to be) permit, and this means that he must take reasonable care in choosing the time at which to sell the property. The conduct of an administrator is to be judged by the standards of a professional insolvency practitioner of ordinary skill. (See *Re Charnley Davies Ltd* [1990] BCC 605 at p. 618).

S. 17(1)

This will include property that is encumbered and property owned by another person but in the possession of the company under a hire-purchase or similar agreement: see ss. 11 and 15. An administrative receiver will have vacated office under s. 11(1)(*b*). Exceptionally, a receiver of *part* of the company's property may be allowed by the administrator to remain in office, but he may not deal with the property in question without the consent of the administrator or the leave of the court (s. 11(2), (3)(*d*)).

S. 17(2)

The administrator's rôle is to seek to secure the financial rehabilitation of the company or one of the other purposes specified in s. 8(3); but the Act does not leave him entirely free to set about his task at once, or to do so on his own initiative. He must call for a statement of affairs (s. 22), formulate a set of proposals to define (and, by implication, to limit) the strategy he is to adopt (s. 23), and put these proposals before a specially summoned creditors' meeting for approval. This process may take a period of three months or so; hence the need to give him interim powers to act under s. 17(2)(*a*), subject to any directions that he may be given by the court.

These directions may be sought by the administrator himself or may be part of the relief granted on the application of a creditor or member under s. 27.

In an unreported hearing involving the company Charnley Davies Ltd in January 1987, Vinelott J confirmed advice given to its administrator by counsel that this section is wide enough to empower an administrator to sell the entire undertaking of the company in advance of the creditors' meeting if he considers that such a course is in the best interests of the company and its creditors, and that he does not need the sanction of the court to do so. He ruled that the words "any directions" in s. 17(2)(*a*) mean "the directions, if any". (See *Re Charnley Davies Ltd* [1990] BCC 605 at pp. 610–611.) In *Re N S Distribution Ltd* [1990] BCLC 169 Harman J took a similar view, in relation to the sale of a single asset. However, in the light of the strongly expressed opinion of Peter Gibson J in *Re Consumer & Industrial Press Ltd (No. 2)* (1988) 4 BCC 72 that a premature disposal of the company's undertaking robs the creditors of their opportunity to consider the administrator's proposals and so frustrates the purpose of the Act, it would be unwise for an administrator to proceed to sell any substantial part of the assets without taking the precaution of seeking leave.

Paragraph (*b*) makes it plain that, after the creditors' meeting, the administrator's freedom to act is limited by the terms of the "proposals" approved by the creditors under ss. 24 or 25. However, in exceptional circumstances (e.g. where the delay involved in summoning a creditors' meeting to consider a revised scheme could cause substantial loss) the court has a residual jurisdiction under s. 14(3) to authorise an administrator to depart from an approved scheme: *Re Smallman Construction Ltd* (1988) 4 BCC 784.

S. 17(3)

This provision corresponds to s. 168(2), which relates to a liquidator in a compulsory winding up. It is not necessary for the Act to provide in similar terms for the requisitioning of a shareholders' meeting, since the members' rights to do so under CA 1985, ss. 368 and 370(3) will not be affected by an administration order.

For the rules relating to this section, see IR 1986, rr. 2.21ff.

Section 18   Discharge or variation of administration order

18(1)   [Application to court by administrator]   The administrator of a company may at any time apply to the court for the administration order to be discharged, or to be varied so as to specify an additional purpose.

18(2)   [Duty to make application]   The administrator shall make an application under this section if—

(a) it appears to him that the purpose or each of the purposes specified in the order either has been achieved or is incapable of achievement, or

(b) he is required to do so by a meeting of the company's creditors summoned for the purpose in accordance with the rules.

18(3)   [Court order]   On the hearing of an application under this section, the court may by order discharge or vary the administration order and make such consequential provision as it thinks fit, or adjourn the hearing conditionally or unconditionally, or make an interim order or any other order it thinks fit.

18(4)   [Copy of order to registrar]   Where the administration order is discharged or varied the administrator shall, within 14 days after the making of the order effecting the discharge or variation, send an office copy of that order to the registrar of companies.

18(5)   [Non-compliance with s. 18(4)]   If the administrator without reasonable excuse fails to comply with subsection (4), he is liable to a fine and, for continued contravention, to a daily default fine.

(Former provision: IA 1985, s. 36)

S. 18(1), (2)

Where the purpose of an administration order is the rehabilitation of the company, an administrator will seek to have an order discharged in two contrasting situations – triumph and disaster. If the company's survival has been ensured, his discharge will enable control of the company's affairs to be restored to its directors and shareholders. If the administrator (or a meeting of the creditors) decides that the purpose is unobtainable, the administration order may be discharged and a winding-up order may then be made (very likely on the administrator's own application) if this is appropriate.

The court has no jurisdiction to make a winding-up order otherwise than on a petition lodged under s. 124. Accordingly, it is not possible for a winding-up order to be made on an application for the discharge of an administration order under the present section: *Re Brooke Marine Ltd* [1988] BCLC 546.

The Act does not seem to make provision for a company to go into voluntary liquidation following the discharge of an administration order – a choice which may commend itself on the grounds of cost – although it is no doubt within the powers of the court to sanction such a course. Particular difficulties which would have to be overcome if this method were chosen include (i) s. 11(3)(*a*), which forbids the passing of the necessary winding-up resolution (and may even prevent the passing of such a resolution conditionally upon the discharge of an administration order) and (ii) the fact that some creditors entitled to preferential payment may be disadvantaged because a different "relevant date" will apply: see s. 387(3)(*a*), (*c*).

If the purpose of an administration order is simply the approval of a voluntary arrangement under Pt. I of the Act (see s. 8(3)(*b*)), the functions of the administrator will be completed and he will be entitled to a discharge as soon as the proposal for the arrangement has been approved at the two meetings summoned under s. 3. It is the supervisor, and not the administrator, who will administer the voluntary arrangement (though these may well be the same person). Similar considerations will apply where an administration order is made in conjunction with a statutory scheme of compromise or arrangement under CA 1985, ss. 425–427 (see s. 8(3)(*c*)).

The fourth of the "purposes" specified in s. 8(3) is "a more advantageous realisation of the company's assets than would be effected on a winding up". When the administrator has achieved this object, it would seem that a liquidation is bound to follow if at the end of the exercise the company is insolvent. However, if there is a surplus, there is no reason why control should not be handed back to the company's own organs, so that they may make their own decision about its future.

An administrator who intends to apply for an administration order to be discharged before he has sent a statement of his proposals to the company's creditors under s. 23(1) must comply with IR 1986, r. 2.16(2). It appears from *Re Consumer & Industrial Press Ltd (No. 2)* (1988) 4 BCC 72 that the court will be reluctant to grant a discharge before the creditors have had an opportunity to consider the proposals. See, however, *Re Charnley Davies Business Services Ltd & Ors* (1987) 3 BCC 408, and the note to s. 23(1).

The court is also empowered under this section to vary the original order by specifying an additional purpose (but not, apparently, a *substituted* purpose), from among those listed in s. 8(3).

In *Re St. Ives Windings Ltd* (1987) 3 BCC 634 an administrator who had achieved an advantageous realisation of assets applied under this section to have the administration order varied by specifying the approval of a voluntary arrangement as an additional purpose. It was then possible for the creditors to sanction proposals for the distribution of the proceeds in a way which was binding on a dissenting minority.

An application under this section can be made only by the administrator himself: see *Re Sharps of Truro Ltd* [1990] BCC 94 at p. 95. He may do so on his own initiative, and must if so directed by a creditors' meeting.

On the discharge of an administration order, the administrator vacates office: s. 19(2)(*b*).

S. 18(3)

Consequential directions may well be needed if the affairs of the company are to be handed back to its shareholders and directors, since the Act gives no detailed guidance on this. The position of some secured creditors may need to be redefined: see the note to s. 15(4).

S. 18(4)

Notice of the making of the administration order will have been sent to the registrar under s. 21(2).

S. 18(5)

On penalties, see s. 430 and Sch. 10.

Section **19**   Vacation of office

19(1)   [Removal or resignation]   The administrator of a company may at any time be removed from office by order of the court and may, in the prescribed circumstances, resign his office by giving notice of his resignation to the court.

19(2)   [Vacation of office, etc.]   The administrator shall vacate office if—

(a) he ceases to be qualified to act as an insolvency practitioner in relation to the company, or

(b) the administration order is discharged.

19(3)   [Ceasing to be administrator]   Where at any time a person ceases to be administrator, the following subsections apply.

19(4)   [Remuneration and expenses]   His remuneration and any expenses properly incurred by him shall be charged on and paid out of any property of the company which is in his custody or under his control at that time in priority to any security to which section 15(1) then applies.

19(5)   [Debts or liabilities re contracts entered into]   Any sums payable in respect of debts or liabilities incurred, while he was administrator, under contracts entered into by him or a predecessor of his in the carrying out of his or the predecessor's functions shall be charged on and paid out of any such property as is mentioned in subsection (4) in priority to any charge arising under that subsection.

19(6)   [Debts or liabilities re contracts of employment adopted]   Any sums payable in respect of liabilities incurred, while he was administrator, under contracts of employment adopted by him or a predecessor of his in the carrying out of his or the predecessor's functions shall, to the extent that the liabilities are qualifying liabilities, be charged on and paid out of any such property as is mentioned in subsection (4) and enjoy the same priority as any sums to which subsection (5) applies.

For this purpose, the administrator is not to be taken to have adopted a contract of employment by reason of anything done or omitted to be done within 14 days after his appointment.

19(7)   [Interpretation of s. 19(6)]   For the purposes of subsection (6), a liability under a contract of employment is a qualifying liability if—

(a) it is a liability to pay a sum by way of wages or salary or contribution to an occupational pension scheme, and

(b) it is in respect of services rendered wholly or partly after the adoption of the contract.

19(8)   [Liability disregarded for s. 19(6)]   There shall be disregarded for the purposes of subsection (6) so much of any qualifying liability as represents payment in respect of services rendered before the adoption of the contract.

19(9)   [Interpretation of s. 19(7), (8)]   For the purposes of subsections (7) and (8)—

(a) wages or salary payable in respect of a period of holiday or absence from work through sickness or other good cause are deemed to be wages or (as the case may be) salary in respect of services rendered in that period, and

(b) a sum payable in lieu of holiday is deemed to be wages or (as the case may be) salary in respect of services rendered in the period by reference to which the holiday entitlement arose.

19(10)   [Interpretation of s. 19(9)(a)]   In subsection (9)(a), the reference to wages or salary payable in respect of a period of holiday includes any sums which, if they had been paid, would have been treated for the purposes of the enactments relating to social security as earnings in respect of that period.

(Former provision: IA 1985, s. 37(1)–(3))

General note

This section has been extensively amended by the Insolvency Act 1994, which received Royal Assent on 25 March 1994, (but not retrospectively so as to affect contracts of employment adopted by an administrator before 15 March 1994). The Act also affects the position of administrative receivers: see the notes to ss. 44 and 57, below.

The reform was enacted in order to allay doubts and fears following the decision of the Court of Appeal in *Powdrill & Anor* v *Watson & Anor; Re Paramount Airways Ltd (No. 3)* [1994] 2 All ER 513; [1994] BCC 172 (on which an appeal to the House of Lords is pending as this book goes to press). The effect of the *Paramount Airways* interpretation of s. 19(5), as it was formerly worded, was to subordinate the administrator's claim to remuneration and the reimbursement of his expenses to a wide range of possible claims by employees and former employees of the company, as explained below. The Act of 1994 amends s. 19(3) and (5) and (by IA 1994, s. 1(1), (4), (6), (7)) inserts new s. 19(6)–(10).

In s. 19(3), the words "next two" were substituted for the word "following" by IA 1994, s. 1(1), (2), (7).

In s. 19(5), the words "or contracts of employment adopted", formerly appearing after the words "under contracts entered into" were omitted, and what was formerly the final paragraph of s. 19(5) was moved to become the second paragraph of s. 19(6), by IA 1994, s. 1(1), (3), (7), 5 and Sch. 2.

S. 19(1)

The circumstances in which an administrator may resign his office are prescribed by IR 1986, r. 2.53. Whether a resignation is effective as soon as notice is given to the court is not made clear by the rules. The usual understanding is that it will be so effective and that, once given, it cannot be unilaterally withdrawn (see *Glossop* v *Glossop* [1907] 2 Ch. 370). The present position may be contrasted with that applicable to a liquidator (s. 171(5)), where a resignation is not effective unless it has been accepted: see IR 1986, rr. 4.108–4.110.

The death of an administrator should also be notified to the court: see s. 20(1)(*a*), and IR 1986, r. 2.54.

S. 19(2)

An administrator will cease to be "qualified to act" as an insolvency practitioner "in relation to the company" if he fails to meet any of the criteria set out in s. 390.

On the discharge of an administration order, see s. 18.

S. 19(3)–(6)

These subsections rather oddly address the question of debts and expenses incurred by an administrator only in the context of the position when he ceases to hold office. However, in the *Paramount Airways* case (above), Dillon LJ said ([1994] BCC 172, at p. 180):

"Although strictly sums payable are, under s. 19(5), only payable when the administrator vacates office, it is well understood that administrators will, in the ordinary way, pay expenses of the administration including the salaries and other payments to employees as they arise during the continuance of the administration. There is no need to wait until the end, and it would be impossible as a practical matter to do that. What is picked up at the end are those matters which fall within the phrase, but have not been paid."

The subsections provide that the administrator's remuneration and expenses and all the contractual debts and liabilities that have been incurred while he was in office are to be paid in priority to the claims of any creditor whose debt is secured by a *floating* charge (including a charge which, as created, was a floating charge but has since become fixed: see s. 15(1) and (3)). The payments under s. 19(5) and 19(6) rank in priority to those under s. 19(4). There is no mention of the preferential creditors whose claims would have ranked ahead of the holder of the floating charge in a receivership. (On the question whether these preferential claims survive the appointment of an administrator, see the comment to s. 15(4)). If a liquidation follows the administration, the administrator's costs will have priority by virtue of s. 19(4) over all claims in the winding up other than those mentioned in s. 19(5): *Re Sheridan Securities Ltd* (1988) 4 BCC 200. Where land or goods in the company's possession under a lease or hire-purchase agreement, existing at the commencement of an administration, are used for the purposes of the administration, the rent or hire charges do not rank as "expenses of the administration" within s. 19(4): *Re Atlantic Computer Systems plc* [1990] BCC 859.

Section 19(5) is confined to *contractual* debts and liabilities. This would include damages claims arising out of contracts entered into by the company while the administrator was in office, but not, e.g. any liabilities of the company in tort.

S. 19(5)–(10)

Section 19(5) gives priority over the administrator's remuneration and expenses to claims in respect of debts and liabilities under contracts entered into by him (or a predecessor) in the carrying out of his functions. Section 19(6) gives the same priority to "qualifying liabilities" (for definition, see below) under contracts of employment "adopted" by him (or a predecessor). But nothing done by the administrator within the first 14 days following his appointment is to be taken as "adopting" a contract of employment.

The making of an administration order does not terminate the company's existing contracts of employment or, for that matter, any other contract of a continuing nature; and so, strictly speaking, no affirmative act on the part of the administrator is needed to keep any such contract in being. This formerly led to much speculation and to differences of judicial opinion as to the meaning of the word "adopt", in relation to a contract of employment, as it appears in this section (and also in s. 44, in relation to an administrative receiver). In *Powdrill & Anor v Watson & Anor; Re Paramount Airways Ltd (No. 3)* [1994] BCC 172, however, it was held that where an administrator continues to use the company's existing staff, he must either "adopt" their existing contracts or negotiate new ones. "Adopted", in the view of Leggatt LJ (at p. 183) in s. 19(5) means "the continuance of which is expressly or impliedly accepted"; and (*per* Dillon at p. 180), "adoption is a matter not merely of words but of fact". These latter remarks refer to a procedure which had become virtually standard practice in all administrations and administrative receiverships following the unreported ruling of Harman J in *Re Specialised Mouldings Ltd* (13 February 1987, referred to in G Stewart, *Administrative Receivers and Administrators* (CCH Editions, 1987). Under this procedure, the office-holders wrote to the company's employees within the first 14 days after their appointment stating that they "did not and would not at any future time adopt or assume personal liability" in respect of the contracts of employment. Such a disclaimer was held by the Court of Appeal in the *Paramount Airways* case to be "mere wind with no legal effect", at least so far as concerns the question of "adoption" of the contract of employment. Earlier judicial views as to the meaning of "adopted" (e.g. that of Evans-Lombe J at first instance in *Paramount Airways* [1993] BCC 662, at p. 671, "procured the company to continue to carry out", and that of McPherson J in *Re Diesels & Components Pty Ltd* (1985) 3 ACLC 555, at p. 557, "refrained from repudiating") are accordingly no longer authoritative.

In the *Paramount Airways* case, the joint administrators were held to have impliedly "adopted" the contracts of employment of two airline pilots when they had continued, after the 14-day period, to employ them and pay them in accordance with their previous contracts. The pilots were later dismissed, and in this action successfully claimed various sums, including pay in lieu of notice, unpaid holiday pay, and pension contributions. (Certain so-called "loyalty bonuses", which had been separately agreed with the administrators, were held to be outside the contracts of employment and not recoverable.) It followed that, under s. 19(4), employees' claims were entitled to priority over the administrators' own remuneration and expenses.

The potential consequences of the Court of Appeal's ruling in *Paramount Airways* are far-reaching, for the decision may lead to the reopening of many administrations stretching back to the commencement of the Act in 1986, and the possibility that administrators will be obliged to make restitution of their fees and remuneration in order meet the claims of former employees, including perhaps claims for substantial "golden handshakes" by senior executives. Since the 1994 reforms do not have retrospective effect, the resolution of this question falls to be determined by the outcome of the appeal to the House of Lords.

In regard to contracts of employment adopted on or after 15 March 1994, however, the Act (as amended) now makes it plain that the liability of an administrator who (or whose predecessor) has adopted a contract of employment is to be limited to "qualifying liabilities". These are defined in s. 19(7)–(10), and are restricted to wages, salaries and occupational pension contributions (including holiday and sickness payments as set out in s. 19(9), (10)), but only in respect of services rendered wholly or partly *after* the adoption of the contract (s. 19(7)(*b*)) and, in the case where services are rendered partly after the adoption of the contract, so much of the qualifying liability as represents payment in respect of services rendered before the adoption are to be disregarded (s. 19(8)). An administrator can therefore now continue to retain the services of the company's employees in the knowledge that the commitment to them is only in respect of current liabilities.

The administrators in the *Paramount Airways* case in their letter to the employees also stated that they did not and would not at any future time assume personal liability in respect of the contracts of employment. There is nothing in the judgments in the Court of Appeal to suggest that such a disclaimer should not be effective – as, indeed, Evans-Lombe J had held in the court below. Moreover, the Court of Appeal expressly left open the question whether an administrator, in negotiating a fresh contract with an employee (as distinct from adopting the existing one) could contract out of the statutory rules of priority laid down by s. 19(5).

In *Paramount Airways*, interest on the sums due to the employees was also awarded.

Section 20   Release of administrator

20(1)   [Time of release]   A person who has ceased to be the administrator of a company has his release with effect from the following time, that is to say—

> (a) in the case of a person who has died, the time at which notice is given to the court in accordance with the rules that he has ceased to hold office;

> (b) in any other case, such time as the court may determine.

20(2)   [Discharge from liability, etc.]   Where a person has his release under this section, he is, with effect from the time specified above, discharged from all liability both in respect of acts or omissions of his in the administration and otherwise in relation to his conduct as administrator.

20(3)   [S. 212]   However, nothing in this section prevents the exercise, in relation to a person who has had his release as above, of the court's powers under section 212 in Chapter X of Part IV (summary remedy against delinquent directors, liquidators, etc.).

(Former provisions: IA 1985, s. 37(4), (5))

71

S. 20(1)

Except in the case of the death of an administrator, for which specific provision is made in para. (*a*), an administrator is to have his release only from such time as the court determines. The relevant rule for the purpose of para. (*a*) is IR 1986, r. 2.54.

In *Re Sibec Developments Ltd; Barclays Mercantile Finance Ltd & Anor* v *Sibec Developments Ltd & Ors* [1992] 1 WLR 1253; [1993] BCC 148, Millett J held that the administrators should not be released (and, indeed, that an administration order should not have been discharged) while there was a proper claim against them outstanding which ought to be tried. For a case where the court postponed the administrator's release because his conduct appeared to call for investigation, see *Re Sheridan Securities Ltd* (1988) 4 BCC 200. See also *Re Exchange Travel (Holdings) Ltd* [1992] BCC 954, where the order for release was made to take effect after three months, to give an opportunity for steps to be taken to have the past conduct of the administrators investigated.

S. 20(2), (3)

The release of an administrator discharges him from all liability, except for liability to account to the company under the "misfeasance" provisions of s. 212. This section applies only in a winding up, and may be invoked against an administrator in the present circumstances only with the leave of the court (s. 212(4)).

ASCERTAINMENT AND INVESTIGATION OF COMPANY'S AFFAIRS

Section 21　Information to be given by administrator

21(1)　[Duties of administrator]　Where an administration order has been made, the administrator shall—

- (a) forthwith send to the company and publish in the prescribed manner a notice of the order, and
- (b) within 28 days after the making of the order, unless the court otherwise directs, send such a notice to all creditors of the company (so far as he is aware of their addresses).

21(2)　[Copy of order to registrar]　Where an administration order has been made, the administrator shall also, within 14 days after the making of the order, send an office copy of the order to the registrar of companies and to such other persons as may be prescribed.

21(3)　[Penalty for non-compliance]　If the administrator without reasonable excuse fails to comply with this section, he is liable to a fine and, for continued contravention, to a daily default fine.

(Former provision: IA 1985, s. 38)

S. 21(1), (2)

It is the administrator's duty to see that the making of the administration order is:

- notified to the company,
- published (i.e. advertised, both in the Gazette and an appropriate newspaper (IR 1986, r. 2.10(2)),

- notified to all known creditors, and
- registered with the registrar of companies.

Notice must also be given to any person who has appointed an administrative receiver of the company, or is entitled to do so, to any administrative receiver who has been appointed, to the petitioner under any pending winding-up petition, and to any provisional liquidator (IR 1986, r. 2.10(3)). The section fixes various time limits. On the meaning of the term "forthwith", see the note to s. 9(2).

For the relevant rules and forms prescribed for the purposes of this section, see IR 1986, r. 2.10.

S. 21(3)

On penalties, see s. 430 and Sch. 10.

Section 22   Statement of affairs to be submitted to administrator

22(1)   [Duty of administrator]   Where an administration order has been made, the administrator shall forthwith require some or all of the persons mentioned below to make out and submit to him a statement in the prescribed form as to the affairs of the company.

22(2)   [Contents of statement]   The statement shall be verified by affidavit by the persons required to submit it and shall show—

- (a) particulars of the company's assets, debts and liabilities;
- (b) the names and addresses of its creditors;
- (c) the securities held by them respectively;
- (d) the dates when the securities were respectively given; and
- (e) such further or other information as may be prescribed.

22(3)   [Persons in s. 22(1)]   The persons referred to in subsection (1) are—

- (a) those who are or have been officers of the company;
- (b) those who have taken part in the company's formation at any time within one year before the date of the administration order;
- (c) those who are in the company's employment or have been in its employment within that year, and are in the administrator's opinion capable of giving the information required;
- (d) those who are or have been within that year officers of or in the employment of a company which is, or within that year was, an officer of the company.

In this subsection **"employment"** includes employment under a contract for services.

22(4)   [Time for submitting statement]   Where any persons are required under this section to submit a statement of affairs to the administrator, they shall do so (subject to the next subsection) before the end of the period of 21 days beginning with the day after that on which the prescribed notice of the requirement is given to them by the administrator.

22(5)   [Powers re release, extension of time]   The administrator, if he thinks fit, may—

(a) at any time release a person from an obligation imposed on him under sub-section (1) or (2), or

(b) either when giving notice under subsection (4) or subsequently, extend the period so mentioned;

and where the administrator has refused to exercise a power conferred by this subsection, the court, if it thinks fit, may exercise it.

22(6) [Penalty for non-compliance] If a person without reasonable excuse fails to comply with any obligation imposed under this section, he is liable to a fine and, for continued contravention, to a daily default fine.

(Former provision: IA 1985, s. 39)

General note

In this and the following sections there is set out the procedure to be followed once the administrator has been appointed. While this lengthy and formal routine may be desirable if the purpose of the administration order is to secure the rehabilitation of the company, it scarcely seems appropriate when the object of the administration is simply to smooth the path for the approval of a voluntary arrangement or the sanctioning of a statutory scheme under CA 1985, ss. 425–427 (see s. 8(3)(*b*), (*c*)). However, the Act seems to offer no alternative, unless possibly the court is empowered to dispense with the statutory requirements under the broad wording of s. 9(4).

The "statement of affairs" has long been a feature of the liquidation procedure in a compulsory winding up (see s. 131). Its use is extended by this Act to this and a number of other analogous situations. For further comment, see the notes to s. 131.

For the relevant rules and forms prescribed for the purpose of this section, see IR 1986, rr. 2.11ff and, on enforcement, r. 7.20.

S. 22(1)–(5)

On the meaning of the term "forthwith", see the note to s. 9(2).

The expression "officer", in relation to a company, includes a director, manager or secretary (CA 1985, s. 744) and at least in some contexts may extend to the holders of other offices: see the note to s. 206(3). The wide definition of "employment" used here could include professionals such as the company's auditors and bankers.

S. 22(6)

On penalties, see s. 430 and Sch. 10.

ADMINISTRATOR'S PROPOSALS

Section 23 Statement of proposals

23(1) [Duties of administrator] Where an administration order has been made, the administrator shall, within 3 months (or such longer period as the court may allow) after the making of the order—

(a) send to the registrar of companies and (so far as he is aware of their addresses) to all creditors a statement of his proposals for achieving the purpose or purposes specified in the order, and

(b) lay a copy of the statement before a meeting of the company's creditors summoned for the purpose on not less than 14 days' notice.

23(2) **[Copies of statement]** The administrator shall also, within 3 months (or such longer period as the court may allow) after the making of the order, either—

(a) send a copy of the statement (so far as he is aware of their addresses) to all members of the company, or

(b) publish in the prescribed manner a notice stating an address to which members of the company should write for copies of the statement to be sent to them free of charge.

23(3) **[Penalty for non-compliance]** If the administrator without reasonable excuse fails to comply with this section, he is liable to a fine and, for continued contravention, to a daily default fine.

(Former provision: IA 1985, s. 40)

S. 23(1)

In the light of the information given to him in the statement of affairs which he has requisitioned under s. 22, the administrator must draw up his "proposals" – his strategy for achieving the purpose or purposes specified in the administration order – and summon a meeting of the company's creditors to consider them. A copy of the proposals must be sent to the registrar of companies for registration, and also to every known creditor. (The "statement" referred to in this section is the administrator's statement of his proposals, not the statement of the company's affairs.)

A careful reading of para. *(b)* reveals that the creditors' meeting must be *held*, and not merely summoned, within the specified period of three months.

A meeting under this section cannot be held for purposes other than the consideration of the administrator's proposals, e.g. to consider whether the company should petition for its own winding up: *Re Charnley Davies Business Services Ltd & Ors* (1987) 3 BCC 408. In this case, exceptionally, Harman J discharged the administration order before a s. 23 meeting had been held because action already taken by the administrator on his own initiative had left the meeting with nothing that it could usefully do. On the question of discharge, see further the note to s. 18(1), (2).

For the procedure for summoning the creditors' meeting, see IR 1986, rr. 2.18ff.

S. 23(2)

A copy of the statement of proposals must either be sent to all members of the company individually, or advertised as being available to members free on request. This must be done *within* (and not at the end of) three months: *(Re Charnley Davies Business Services Ltd & Ors*, above), although the court may grant an extension of time. (The members have little say in, or control over, the conduct of the administration – see s. 14(4); but if a member is "unfairly prejudiced" by it, he is given a statutory remedy under s. 27, and so there is a need that members should be kept broadly in the picture.)

The relevant rules prescribed for the purpose of s. 23(2)(*b*) require the notice to be gazetted: see IR 1986, r. 2.17.

S. 23(3)

On penalties, see s. 430 and Sch. 10.

Section **24** **Consideration of proposals by creditors' meeting**

24(1) **[Creditors' meeting to decide]** A meeting of creditors summoned under section 23 shall decide whether to approve the administrator's proposals.

24(2) **[Approval, modifications]** The meeting may approve the proposals with modifications, but shall not do so unless the administrator consents to each modification.

24(3) **[Meeting in accordance with rules]** Subject as above, the meeting shall be conducted in accordance with the rules.

24(4) **[Report and notice by administrator]** After the conclusion of the meeting in accordance with the rules, the administrator shall report the result of the meeting to the court and shall give notice of that result to the registrar of companies and to such persons as may be prescribed.

24(5) **[If meeting does not approve]** If a report is given to the court under subsection (4) that the meeting has declined to approve the administrator's proposals (with or without modifications), the court may by order discharge the administration order and make such consequential provision as it thinks fit, or adjourn the hearing conditionally or unconditionally, or make an interim order or any other order that it thinks fit.

24(6) **[Where administration order discharged]** Where the administration order is discharged, the administrator shall, within 14 days after the making of the order effecting the discharge, send an office copy of that order to the registrar of companies.

24(7) **[Penalty for non-compliance]** If the administrator without reasonable excuse fails to comply with subsection (6), he is liable to a fine and, for continued contravention, to a daily default fine.

(Former provision: IA 1985, s. 41)

S. 24(1), (2)

The administrator's freedom to act in the exercise of his functions is limited by the scope of the proposals, once approved (see s. 17(2)(*b*)) – apart from "insubstantial" deviations (s. 25(1)(*b*)); and so it is important, from his point of view, that they should not be too restrictively drawn. This explains also why no modification may be made to the proposals without his consent (s. 24(2)).

S. 24(3)

For the rules governing the conduct of the meeting, see IR 1986, rr. 2.18ff. The rules, as amended, invalidate any resolution of the creditors which is opposed by a majority of the creditors who are not "connected with" the company: see IR 1986, r. 2.28(1A) and, on the meaning of "connected with", see s. 249.

S. 24(4)

The administrator is required to report the result of the meeting to the court and to notify the persons specified. If the meeting has approved the proposals, the report to the court seems to be a purely administrative matter: the administrator may, without more formality, get on with his duties under s. 17(2)(*b*).

For the persons prescribed for the purposes of this subsection, see IR 1986, r. 2.30.

S. 24(5)

If the meeting does not approve the proposals, the initiative reverts to the court, acting in its judicial capacity. The administration meantime continues provisionally under s. 17(2)(*a*).

S. 24(6), (7)

These subsections repeat the corresponding provisions in s. 18(4), (5).
   On penalties, see s. 430 and Sch. 10.

Section 25   Approval of substantial revisions

25(1)   [Application]   This section applies where—

   (a) proposals have been approved (with or without modifications) under section 24, and

   (b) the administrator proposes to make revisions of those proposals which appear to him substantial.

25(2)   [Duties of administrator]   The administrator shall—

   (a) send to all creditors of the company (so far as he is aware of their addresses) a statement in the prescribed form of his proposed revisions, and

   (b) lay a copy of the statement before a meeting of the company's creditors summoned for the purpose on not less than 14 days' notice;

and he shall not make the proposed revisions unless they are approved by the meeting.

25(3)   [Copies of statement]   The administrator shall also either—

   (a) send a copy of the statement (so far as he is aware of their addresses) to all members of the company, or

   (b) publish in the prescribed manner a notice stating an address to which members of the company should write for copies of the statement to be sent to them free of charge.

25(4)   [Approval, modifications]   The meeting of creditors may approve the proposed revisions with modifications, but shall not do so unless the administrator consents to each modification.

25(5)   [Meeting in accordance with rules]   Subject as above, the meeting shall be conducted in accordance with the rules.

25(6)   [Notification to registrar, et al.]   After the conclusion of the meeting in accordance with the rules, the administrator shall give notice of the result of the meeting to the registrar of companies and to such persons as may be prescribed.

(Former provision: IA 1985, s. 42)

S. 25(1)

Once his proposals have been approved, the administrator is bound to adhere to the course of action that they prescribe (except that he may, apparently, make "insubstantial"deviations: see para. (*b*)). If he wishes to work to a different strategy, he must go back to the creditors for approval of revised proposals. However, in exceptional circumstances (e.g. where the delay involved in summoning a creditors' meeting to consider a revised scheme could cause substantial loss) the court has a residual jurisdiction under s. 14(3) to authorise an administrator to depart from an approved scheme: *Re Smallman Construction Ltd* (1988) 4 BCC 784.

S. 25(2)–(5)

These provisions are effectively the same as ss. 23(1), (2) and 24(2), (3), except that there is no time limit prescribed and no obligation to send a copy of the statement of revised proposals to the registrar of companies.

S. 25(6)

This subsection echoes s. 24(4), except that under that provision it is necessary also to report the result of the meeting to the court.

If the meeting declines to approve the revised proposals, the administrator has the following options:

- to continue to act under the old proposals,
- to draw up a new set of revised proposals and summon a further creditors' meeting under this section,
- to apply to the court under s. 18(1) to have the purpose specified in the administration order varied, or
- to apply to the court for a discharge of the order under s. 18(2), on the ground that the purpose of the order is incapable of achievement.

For more detailed comment, see the various sections referred to.

MISCELLANEOUS

Section 26   Creditors' committee

26(1)   [Meeting may establish committee]   Where a meeting of creditors summoned under section 23 has approved the administrator's proposals (with or without modifications), the meeting may, if it thinks fit, establish a committee (**"the creditors' committee"**) to exercise the functions conferred on it by or under this Act.

26(2)   [Committee may summon administrator]   If such a committee is established, the committee may, on giving not less than 7 days' notice, require the administrator to attend before it at any reasonable time and furnish it with such information relating to the carrying out of his functions as it may reasonably require.

(Former provision: IA 1985, s. 43)

General note

Once the meeting of creditors has approved a statement of proposals, so that the administrator is empowered to act under s. 17(2)(*b*), it may delegate its functions en bloc to a committee of creditors under this section. Corresponding provisions are made in the case of an administrative receivership (see ss. 49 and 68) and in a winding up (where the committee was formerly called the "committee of inspection" and is now termed the "liquidation committee": see ss. 101, 141 and 142).

It is submitted that the phrase "conferred on it" in s. 26(1) means "conferred on the committee" and not "conferred on the meeting of creditors", as might appear on a first reading.

For the rules relating to the creditors' committee, see IR 1986, rr. 2.32ff.

Section 27 Protection of interests of creditors and members

27(1) [Application by creditor or member] At any time when an administration order is in force, a creditor or member of the company may apply to the court by petition for an order under this section on the ground—

(a) that the company's affairs, business and property are being or have been managed by the administrator in a manner which is unfairly prejudicial to the interests of its creditors or members generally, or of some part of its creditors or members (including at least himself), or

(b) that any actual or proposed act or omission of the administrator is or would be so prejudicial.

27(2) [Court order] On an application for an order under this section the court may, subject as follows, make such order as it thinks fit for giving relief in respect of the matters complained of, or adjourn the hearing conditionally or unconditionally, or make an interim order or any other order that it thinks fit.

27(3) [Limits of order] An order under this section shall not prejudice or prevent—

(a) the implementation of a voluntary arrangement approved under section 4 in Part I, or any compromise or arrangement sanctioned under section 425 of the Companies Act; or

(b) where the application for the order was made more than 28 days after the approval of any proposals or revised proposals under section 24 or 25, the implementation of those proposals or revised proposals.

27(4) [Contents of order] Subject as above, an order under this section may in particular—

(a) regulate the future management by the administrator of the company's affairs, business and property;

(b) require the administrator to refrain from doing or continuing an act complained of by the petitioner, or to do an act which the petitioner has complained he has omitted to do;

(c) require the summoning of a meeting of creditors or members for the purpose of considering such matters as the court may direct;

(d) discharge the administration order and make such consequential provision as the court thinks fit.

27(5) [Ss. 15, 16] Nothing in sections 15 or 16 is to be taken as prejudicing applications to the court under this section.

27(6) [Copy of discharge order to registrar]   Where the administration order is discharged, the administrator shall, within 14 days after the making of the order effecting the discharge, send an office copy of that order to the registrar of companies; and if without reasonable excuse he fails to comply with this subsection, he is liable to a fine and, for continued contravention, to a daily default fine.

(Former provisions: IA 1985, ss. 34(11), 44)

S. 27(1)

This section, like s. 6, is based broadly on the provisions of CA 1985, s. 459. As with s. 6, it is probable that a court would rule that a member's or creditor's *only* judicial remedy if he has any complaint is to have recourse to the procedure under this section: this would be consistent with the apparent purpose of s. 27(3)(*b*). (This would not, of course, rule out proceedings brought by the company itself, or its liquidator). The present provision differs from s. 6 in an important respect: it is concerned with the actual management of the company's affairs, etc., by the administrator, whereas s. 6 deals only with events prior to the time when the supervisor of an arrangement takes office. It may also be contrasted with CA 1985, s. 459 in that a creditor as well as a member may petition.

The scope of s. 27 is discussed in detail in the case of *Re Charnley Davies Ltd* [1990] BCC 605, where it was held that a negligent sale by an administrator of a company's assets at an under-value would be insufficient without more to establish a claim for relief under the section. The appropriate procedure in such a situation is to have the administration order discharged, the company put into compulsory liquidation, an insolvency practitioner other than the administrator appointed liquidator, and a claim brought by the liquidator against the administrator under IA 1986, s. 212. The court in *Re Charnley Davies Ltd* declined to endorse suggestions proffered by counsel as to the meaning of the words "unfairly prejudicial": "it would be wrong to substitute different language for that chosen by Parliament; if the substituted language means the same it is not helpful, and if it means something different it distorts the intention of Parliament" ([1990] BCC 605 at p. 624). "An allegation that the acts complained of are unlawful or infringe the petitioner's legal rights is not a necessary averment in a sec. 27 petition. [It] is not a sufficient averment either. The petitioner must allege and prove that they are evidence or instances of the management of the company's affairs by the administrator in a manner which is unfairly prejudicial to the petitioner's interests" (ibid., at pp. 624–625). Where the complaint may be adequately redressed by the remedy provided by law, it is unnecessary to assume the additional burden of proving unfairly prejudicial conduct. However, that burden must be assumed – but not necessarily that of proving unlawful conduct as well – if a wider remedy under s. 27 is sought.

S. 27(3)(a)

An application for an administration order may be made in conjunction with a proposed voluntary arrangement under Pt. I of this Act or a scheme of compromise or arrangement under CA 1985, ss. 425–427. A member or creditor who objects to a scheme under either of these procedures has his separate remedies under ss. 6 and 7(3) above and a right of objection under CA 1985, s. 425(2), and if he has not availed himself of these rights or has done so unsuccessfully, it is reasonable that the arrangement or scheme should stand.

S. 27(3)(b)

Under this provision, the court may upset the administration order itself only if an application is made within the 28 day period. After that, it may still grant the applicant other forms of relief, but the administration order will no longer be open to challenge.

S. 27(4)

This is modelled on CA 1985, s. 461(2); but paras. (*c*) and (*d*) have no counterpart in that section.

S. 27(5)

The two sections referred to empower the administrator to deal with charged property, in some circumstances with the authorisation of the court. The fact that an act of the administrator has the backing of a court order should not prejudice an application under the present section, since members and creditors will generally have had no standing to be heard when the order was made.

S. 27(6)

This is equivalent to s. 18(4), (5) and also to s. 24(6), (7).

PART III — RECEIVERSHIP

General comment on Part III

The Companies Acts have not previously contained many provisions dealing with receivership, at least in relation to England and Wales; matters were left to the general law and the terms of the instrument under or by which the receiver was appointed. The Cork Committee (*Report*, Ch. 8) recommended that the law should be amended so that in many respects it was placed on a statutory basis. The recommendations were broadly followed by IA 1985, Ch. IV, which is now consolidated along with a few sections of CA 1985 into the present Act.

Among the principal changes made are the introduction of the new concept of "administrative receiver" (s. 29(2)), and the requirement that an administrative receiver be a qualified insolvency practitioner. The date on which a receiver takes office and the extent to which agency rules apply have been clarified, and new provisions ensure that other creditors are kept in the picture regarding the progress of the receivership. The administrative receiver is given the statutory powers set out in Sch. 1, and other specific powers including power to dispose of encumbered property (s. 43). In many other respects an administrative receivership is placed on a similar footing to a liquidation – e.g. in regard to a statement of affairs, the appointment of a committee of creditors, and the removal of the receiver.

To all intents and purposes these days appointments of receivers to enforce security are effected out of court in pursuance of a contractual power vested in the debenture holder to make such an appointment. The advantage in this course of action is speed and lack of cost. There is however always the facility of applying to the court for such an appointment, but this is rare because of the cost and the delay – for an unusual example see *Bank of Credit and Commerce International SA* v *BRS Kumar Bros Ltd* [1994] BCLC 211.

It must be remembered that a receiver appointed to enforce a fixed charge may be subject to the old established provisions of the Law of Property Act 1925. For consideration of this statutory code see *Phoenix Properties* v *Wimpole Street Nominees Ltd* [1992] BCLC 737 and *Sargent* v *C & E Commrs* [1993] BTC 5,257. Specialised statutory regimes also exist for certain types of receivership involving (for example) companies incorporated by statute or as part of statutory insolvency regimes, but these are not our concern in this work.

The institution of receivership was unknown in Scotland until the enactment of CFCSA 1972. In the present Act the provisions of that legislation are consolidated, incorporating certain modifications made by IA 1985. Comparable provisions dealing with receivers and administrative receivers in Northern Ireland are to be found in the Insolvency (Northern Ireland) Order 1989 (SI 1989 No. 2405) (NI 19), arts. 40–59.

Although the following provisions provide some statutory framework for the mechanism of an administrative receivership there is still a substantial body of rules derived from decisions of the courts. These court-derived principles continue to be important. Many key issues are not addressed by the legislation. For example, what is the effect of the appointment of a receiver on the power of the directors to litigate on behalf of the company? Compare here *Newhart Developments* v *Cooperative Commercial Bank* [1978] QB 814 with *Tudor Grange Holdings* v *Citibank* [1992] Ch. 53, and, most recently, the Irish High Court case of *Lascomme Ltd* v *United Dominions Trust (Ireland)* [1994] ILRM 227. The question of whether a receiver owes a duty of care to the company (and those claiming through it) when managing and realising the assets has also been left for the courts to grapple with. For a generous treatment of receivers' duties by the Privy Council in this scenario see *Downsview Nominees* v *First City Corporation Ltd* [1993] AC 295; [1993] BCC 46. Here it was held that the responsibilities of receivers are essentially equitable in nature and there was no room for superimposing common law duties of care in negligence. This case is difficult to reconcile with earlier authorities such as *Standard Chartered Bank* v *Walker* [1982] 1 WLR 1410 and *Knight* v *Lawrence* [1991] BCC 411 and is best viewed as part of a general retreat on the part of the courts in the areas of economic loss and professional liability. See generally Berg [1993] JBL 213 and Fealy [1994] 45 NILQ 61. Other jurisdictions have had the foresight to address this issue through legislation – see Irish Companies Act 1963, s. 311A (introduced in 1990) and the New Zealand Receiverships Act 1993, s. 19. In both cases a statutory duty of care when selling company assets has been imposed. In Canada s. 247 of the Bankruptcy and Insolvency Act 1992 requires receivers to deal with the security in a commercially reasonable manner.

The relationship between the various corporate insolvency regimes is interesting. It has been clear from the earliest of days that the right of a secured creditor to have a receiver appointed would be protected by the law. Thus, although receivership and liquidation can run concurrently, in practice the liquidator must wait in the wings, at least so far as concerns the property covered by the charge, until the receiver has fulfilled his functions. This is so even though the agency character of the receiver's rôle changes – *Sowman* v *David Samuel Trust Ltd* [1978] 1 WLR 22 or even if liquidation precedes receivership – *Re First Express Ltd* [1991] BCC 782. The advent of the administration order regime has posed little threat to the rights of the secured creditor in that a right of veto is created by IA 1986, s. 9 in favour of a person having the power to appoint an administrative receiver (i.e. a creditor whose security includes a general floating charge). However, if this veto is not exercised, the administrator does enjoy the power to interfere with the rights of the secured creditor (see IA 1986, s. 15). A secured creditor who waits for a company voluntary arrangement to be put in place before appointing a receiver may also be in difficulties – *Re Leisure Study Group Ltd* [1994] 2 BCLC 65.

Chapter I — Receivers and Managers (England and Wales)

PRELIMINARY AND GENERAL PROVISIONS

Section 28   Extent of this Chapter

28   This Chapter does not apply to receivers appointed under Chapter II of this Part (Scotland).

(Former provisions: CA 1985, s. 488; IA 1985, s. 45(1))

General note

This emphasises that ss. 28–49 only apply to receivers and managers appointed under English law. The Scots have their own rules: see ss. 50–71.

The changes made to the law relating to receivers and managers by IA 1985 and IA 1986 are not retrospective: see Sch. 11, para. 2(2).

Section 29   Definitions

29(1) [Interpretation] It is hereby declared that, except where the context otherwise requires—

    (a) any reference in the Companies Act or this Act to a receiver or manager of the property of a company, or to a receiver of it, includes a receiver or manager, or (as the case may be) a receiver of part only of that property and a receiver only of the income arising from the property or from part of it; and

    (b) any reference in the Companies Act or this Act to the appointment of a receiver or manager under powers contained in an instrument includes an appointment made under powers which, by virtue of any enactment, are implied in and have effect as if contained in an instrument.

29(2) ["Administrative receiver"] In this Chapter **"administrative receiver"** means—

    (a) a receiver or manager of the whole (or substantially the whole) of a company's property appointed by or on behalf of the holders of any debentures of the company secured by a charge which, as created, was a floating charge, or by such a charge and one or more other securities; or

    (b) a person who would be such a receiver or manager but for the appointment of some other person as the receiver of part of the company's property.

(Former provisions: CA 1985, s. 50; IA 1985, s. 45(2))

General note

S. 29(1)

This section defines "receiver and manager" in such a way as to include partial receiverships. Receivers of income appointed under the Law of Property Act 1925 (see above) are included under the term "receiver".

S. 29(2)

This seeks to cast light upon the unhappy term "administrative receiver", a label first introduced in 1985. It is important to distinguish an administrative receiver from his untitled fellows because (inter alia) ss. 42–49, the rules on office-holders and the mitigating provisions in s. 2 of the Insolvency Act 1994 only apply to administrative receivers (though the government at present is reconsidering this strange limitation). Moreover, it is only a person having the right to appoint an administrative receiver who can veto the appointment of an administrator (see IA 1986, s. 9 and *Re Croftbell Ltd* [1990] BCC 781).

In view of the importance attached to the status of being an administrative receiver it is unfortunate that this provision was not drafted in clearer terms. A number of uncertainties exist:

1. Can there be multiple concurrent administrative receivers? The better view here would appear to be "no" – see Oditah [1991] JBL 49.
2. Can a court appointed receiver enjoy this status? The consensus here appears to deny this – see Gordon Stewart, *Administrative Receivers and Administrators* (CCH 1987), p. 13 and compare Schumacher (1993) 9 Insolvency Law and Practice 43.
3. Can an administrative receiver be appointed over the assets of a foreign company? The general rule of interpretation of companies legislation is that the word "company" does not encompass foreign companies; however, this rule can be displaced by the context. Such a displacement was accepted in the context of s. 29(2) by Mummery J in *Re International Bulk Commodities Ltd* [1993] Ch. 77; [1992] BCC 463. This ruling has not escaped criticism and the later judgment in *Re Devon and Somerset Farmers Ltd* [1994] Ch. 57; [1993] BCC 410 to the effect that an industrial and provident society cannot go into administrative receivership (because it is not a "company") sits uneasily alongside it.
4. Can an administrative receiver be appointed by a fixed chargee? The answer to this is also negative. Moreover, even if the chargee enjoys a hybrid security comprising fixed and floating charges, the appointment must be made under the floating charge element in order for an administrative receivership to result – *Meadrealm Ltd* v *Transcontinental Golf Construction* (1991, Vinelott J, unreported) noted by Marks in (1993) 6 Insolvency Intelligence 41. See also Marks and Emmett [1994] JBL 1.

Section 30 Disqualification of body corporate from acting as receiver

30 A body corporate is not qualified for appointment as receiver of the property of a company, and any body corporate which acts as such a receiver is liable to a fine.

(Former provisions: CA 1985, s. 489; CA 1948, s. 366)

General note

This provision continues the rather curious bar on corporate receivers. If a corporate receiver is appointed, a fine will be incurred and the appointment is also invalid. On penalties, see s. 430 and Sch. 10. Corporations are also barred from being qualified to act as insolvency practitioners: see s. 390(1).

Section 31 Disqualification of undischarged bankrupt

31 If a person being an undischarged bankrupt acts as receiver or manager of the property of a company on behalf of debenture holders, he is liable to imprisonment or a fine, or both.

This does not apply to a receiver or manager acting under an appointment made by the court.

(Former provisions: CA 1985, s. 490; CA 1948, s. 367)

General note

Undischarged bankrupts cannot be appointed as receivers out of court. The court is unlikely to accede to such an appointment. Undischarged bankrupts are disqualified from acting as insolvency practitioners: see s. 390(4)(*a*).

Section 32   Power for court to appoint official receiver

32   Where application is made to the court to appoint a receiver on behalf of the debenture holders or other creditors of a company which is being wound up by the court, the official receiver may be appointed.

(Former provisions: CA 1985, s. 491; CA 1948, s. 368)

General note

If a company is in liquidation, the court, in those rare cases where debenture holders apply to it to have a receiver appointed, may appoint the official receiver. For further details see ss. 399–401.

RECEIVERS AND MANAGERS APPOINTED OUT OF COURT

Section 33   Time from which appointment is effective

33(1)   [Effect of appointment]   The appointment of a person as a receiver or manager of a company's property under powers contained in an instrument—

- (a) is of no effect unless it is accepted by that person before the end of the business day next following that on which the instrument of appointment is received by him or on his behalf, and
- (b) subject to this, is deemed to be made at the time at which the instrument of appointment is so received.

33(2)   [Joint receivers or managers]   This section applies to the appointment of two or more persons as joint receivers or managers of a company's property under powers contained in an instrument, subject to such modifications as may be prescribed by the rules.

(Former provision: IA 1985, s. 46)

S.33(1)

The appointment of a receiver and manager out of court takes effect when he receives the letter of appointment, provided that he accepts the office before the end of the next business day. For administrative receivers see also IR 1986, r. 3.1.

S. 33(2)

The above rule applies to joint receivers, subject to the modifications made by the rules: see also IR 1986, r. 3.1.

Section 34   Liability for invalid appointment

34   Where the appointment of a person as the receiver or manager of a company's property under powers contained in an instrument is discovered to be invalid (whether by virtue of the invalidity of the instrument or otherwise), the court may order the person by whom or on whose behalf the appointment was made to indemnify the person appointed against any liability which arises solely by reason of the invalidity of the appointment.

(Former provision: IA 1985, s. 47)

General note

This permits the court to order that the appointor of a receiver indemnify the latter against liability in trespass, where the appointment turns out to be invalid. Invalidity may be the result of the debenture charge being unregistered or being avoided under IA 1986 s. 245. This provision will prove useful because challenges to appointments are becoming more common: see, e.g. *Shamji & Ors* v *Johnson Matthey Bankers Ltd & Ors* (1986) 2 BCC 98,910 where the challenge proved unsuccessful.

Section 35 Application to court for directions

35(1) **[Application]** A receiver or manager of the property of a company appointed under powers contained in an instrument, or the persons by whom or on whose behalf a receiver or manager has been so appointed, may apply to the court for directions in relation to any particular matter arising in connection with the performance of the functions of the receiver or manager.

35(2) **[Order, directions by court]** On such an application, the court may give such directions, or may make such order declaring the rights of persons before the court or otherwise, as it thinks just.

(Former provision: CA 1985, s. 492 (as amended by IA 1985, Sch. 6, para. 16(2)); CA 1948, s. 369)

S. 35(1)

This allows a receiver, or his appointor, to apply to the court for directions in the event of legal uncertainty arising. The latter was only given this facility by IA 1985, as a result of the recommendations of the Cork Committee (*Report*, para. 828).

S. 35(2)

The court enjoys general discretion as to any declaration it may make on such an application.

Section 36 Court's power to fix remuneration

36(1) **[Remuneration]** The court may, on an application made by the liquidator of a company, by order fix the amount to be paid by way of remuneration to a person who, under powers contained in an instrument, has been appointed receiver or manager of the company's property.

36(2) **[Extent of court's power]** The court's power under subsection (1), where no previous order has been made with respect thereto under the subsection—

(a) extends to fixing the remuneration for any period before the making of the order or the application for it,

(b) is exercisable notwithstanding that the receiver or manager has died or ceased to act before the making of the order or the application, and

(c) where the receiver or manager has been paid or has retained for his remuneration for any period before the making of the order any amount in excess of that so fixed for that period, extends to requiring him or his personal representatives to account for the excess or such part of it as may be specified in the order.

But the power conferred by paragraph (c) shall not be exercised as respects any period before the making of the application for the order under this section, unless in the court's opinion there are special circumstances making it proper for the power to be exercised.

36(3)   [Variation, amendment of order]   The court may from time to time on an application made either by the liquidator or by the receiver or manager, vary or amend an order made under subsection (1).

(Former provisions: CA 1985, s. 494; CA 1948, s. 371)

S. 36(1)

This allows the court to determine the remuneration of a receiver and manager appointed out of court where the liquidator of the company asks for this to be done. Such applications are rare, if only because of the courtesy that exists between fellow insolvency practitioners. For a recent but unsuccessful application, see *Re Potters Oils Ltd (No. 2)* [1986] 1 WLR 201; (1985) 1 BCC 99,593.

S. 36(2)

This provides further details of the powers of the court where an application has been made to it under s. 36(1).

S. 36(3)

The court can vary any order it makes fixing remuneration.

Section 37   Liability for contracts, etc.

37(1)   [Personal liability, indemnity]   A receiver or manager appointed under powers contained in an instrument (other than an administrative receiver) is, to the same extent as if he had been appointed by order of the court—

    (a) personally liable on any contract entered into by him in the performance of his functions (except in so far as the contract otherwise provides) and on any contract of employment adopted by him in the performance of those functions, and

    (b) entitled in respect of that liability to indemnity out of the assets.

37(2)   [Interpretation of s. 37(1)(a)]   For the purposes of subsection (1)(a), the receiver or manager is not to be taken to have adopted a contract of employment by reason of anything done or omitted to be done within 14 days after his appointment.

37(3)   [Extent of s. 37(1)]   Subsection (1) does not limit any right to indemnity which the receiver or manager would have apart from it, nor limit his liability on contracts entered into without authority, nor confer any right to indemnity in respect of that liability.

37(4)   [Vacation of office]   Where at any time the receiver or manager so appointed vacates office—

    (a) his remuneration and any expenses properly incurred by him, and

(b) any indemnity to which he is entitled out of the assets of the company,

shall be charged on and paid out of any property of the company which is in his custody or under his control at that time in priority to any charge or other security held by the person by or on whose behalf he was appointed.

(Former provisions: CA 1985, s. 492(3) (as amended by IA 1985, Sch. 6, paras. 16(3), (4)); CA 1948, s. 369(2))

S. 37(1), (2)

Receivers appointed out of court are personally liable on contracts entered into by them (unless they have contracted out), and existing contracts of employment adopted by them, although they have 14 days' grace to decide whether to adopt or not. This latter provision is designed to cope with the problems thrown up by *Nicoll* v *Cutts* (1985) 1 BCC 99,427. Where a receiver adopts a contract of employment under s. 37(1)(*a*) the case will be caught by the rule in *Re Paramount Airways Ltd (No. 3)* [1994] BCC 172 and this adoption will impose all accrued employment liabilities on the receiver. (See the notes to ss. 19 and 44.) The relief extended by s. 2 of the Insolvency Act 1994 to mitigate this rule has (for unconvincing reasons) deliberately not been extended to non-administrative receivers, though the government is now reconsidering this matter – see DTI Press Notice P/94/319. Such receivers may have to adopt contracts of employment if they are enforcing a fixed charge over, say, a hotel and they wish to retain staff pending a sale of the hotel as a going concern. It is implicit in s. 37(1)(*a*) that a receiver is entitled not to adopt existing contracts of the company. Where he chooses this option as a rule no injunction will lie against him to enforce observance of the contract – see *Airlines Airspares Ltd* v *Handley Page Ltd* [1970] Ch. 193. However, in some cases the contract may be enforced – see *Freevale Ltd* v *Metrostore (Holdings) Ltd & Anor* [1984] Ch. 199, *Amec Properties* v *Planning Research and Systems* [1992] 13 EG 109, and the discussion in *Astor Chemical Ltd* v *Synthetic Technology Ltd* [1990] BCC 97 and *Ash & Newman* v *Creative Devices Research Ltd* [1991] BCLC 403.

S. 37(3)

The receiver's statutory indemnity in respect of contractual liability under s. 37(1)(*b*) is not exhaustive. On the other hand, it does not apply to contracts entered into by him without authority.

S. 37(4)

This accords high priority status to the receiver's right to remuneration and indemnity. However it is important to remember that this priority only extends to the proceeds of assets caught by the security. The right to remuneration cannot be charged against assets encompassed by a prior security – *Choudri* v *Palta* [1992] BCC 787. Furthermore, in cases where the receiver has realised sufficient funds to repay the debenture holder and also (arguably) to satisfy his own claim to remuneration, etc. the court might intervene and offer interlocutory relief to prevent further sales until the quantum of remuneration has been settled – *Rottenberg* v *Monjack* [1992] BCC 688.

Section 38   Receivership accounts to be delivered to registrar

38(1)   [Where appointment under powers in instrument]   Except in the case of an administrative receiver, every receiver or manager of a company's property who has been appointed under powers contained in an instrument shall deliver to the registrar of companies for registration the requisite accounts of his receipts and payments.

38(2)   [Time for delivering accounts]   The accounts shall be delivered within one month (or such longer period as the registrar may allow) after the expiration of 12 months from the date of his appointment and of every subsequent period of 6 months, and also within one month after he ceases to act as receiver or manager.

38(3)   [Form of accounts]   The requisite accounts shall be an abstract in the prescribed form showing—

(a) receipts and payments during the relevant period of 12 or 6 months, or

(b) where the receiver or manager ceases to act, receipts and payments during the period from the end of the period of 12 or 6 months to which the last preceding abstract related (or, if no preceding abstract has been delivered under this section, from the date of his appointment) up to the date of his so ceasing, and the aggregate amount of receipts and payments during all preceding periods since his appointment.

38(4)   ["Prescribed"]   In this section **"prescribed"** means prescribed by regulations made by statutory instrument by the Secretary of State.

38(5)   [Penalty on default]   A receiver or manager who makes default in complying with this section is liable to a fine and, for continued contravention, to a daily default fine.

(Former provisions: CA 1985, s. 498 (as amended by IA 1985, Sch. 6, para. 17); CA 1948, s. 374)

S. 38(1), (2)

Receivers or managers other than administrative receivers must periodically submit accounts to Cardiff.

S. 38(3), (4)

These regulate the form of the accounts.

S. 38(5)

Criminal sanctions are imposed on the receiver in the event of default. On penalties, see s. 430 and Sch. 10. Note also the enforcement procedures laid down in s. 41.
   For administrative receivers, see IR 1986, r. 3.32.

PROVISIONS APPLICABLE TO EVERY RECEIVERSHIP

Section 39   Notification that receiver or manager appointed

39(1)   [Statement in invoices etc.]   When a receiver or manager of the property of a company has been appointed, every invoice, order for goods or business letter issued by or on behalf of the company or the receiver or manager or the liquidator of the company, being a document on or in which the company's name appears, shall contain a statement that a receiver or manager has been appointed.

39(2)   [Penalty on default]   If default is made in complying with this section, the company and any of the following persons, who knowingly and wilfully authorises or permits the default, namely, any officer of the company, any liquidator of the company and any receiver or manager, is liable to a fine.

(Former provisions: CA 1985, s. 493; CA 1948, s. 370)

S. 39(1)

Invoices, business letters, etc., must disclose the fact that a receiver and manager has been appointed. Note also that under CA 1985, s. 405(1) the fact of the appointment must be notified to Cardiff, and by virtue of IA 1986, s. 46, notice must be given to creditors.

S. 39(2)

Criminal sanctions may be imposed on various named persons in the event of a breach of s. 39(1). On penalties, see s. 430 and Sch. 10.

Section 40   Payment of debts out of assets subject to floating charge

40(1)   [Application]   The following applies, in the case of a company, where a receiver is appointed on behalf of the holders of any debentures of the company secured by a charge which, as created, was a floating charge.

40(2)   [Payment of preferential debts]   If the company is not at the time in course of being wound up, its preferential debts (within the meaning given to that expression by section 386 in Part XII) shall be paid out of the assets coming to the hands of the receiver in priority to any claims for principal or interest in respect of the debentures.

40(3)   [Recoupment of payments]   Payments made under this section shall be recouped, as far as may be, out of the assets of the company available for payment of general creditors.

(Former provisions: CA 1985, s. 196(1), (2) and (5) (as amended by IA 1985, Sch. 6, para. 15(2), (3)); CA 1948, s. 94)

S. 40(1), (2)

These subsections impose an obligation on every receiver appointed to enforce a floating charge to pay preferential claims (see s. 386 and Sch. 6). However, this obligation does not extend to receivers of industrial and provident societies – *Re Devon and Somerset Farmers Ltd* [1994] Ch. 57; [1993] BCC 410. This is a positive obligation – *IR Commrs v Goldblatt* [1972] Ch. 498. Note that the fact that the charge may have crystallised prior to the appointment of the receiver does not take the case outside the scope of s. 40. This follows from the revised definition of "floating charge" which was introduced by IA 1985 (see now IA 1986, s. 251), and which is incorporated into the wording of s. 40(1). For the significance of this change in the law see *Re Brightlife Ltd* [1987] Ch. 200; (1986) 2 BCC 99,359. The duty imposed by s. 40 is limited by s.11(5) but the fact that the company may go into liquidation during the currency of the receivership does not relieve the receiver of his obligation to pay preferential claims – *Re Eisc Teo Ltd* [1991] ILRM 760. A charge which, as created, was a fixed charge but which has since become a floating charge is not caught by s. 40: *Re New Bullas Trading Ltd* [1994] BCC 36. For a detailed analysis of the operation of s. 40 in practice, see Anderson (1994) 15 Co Law 195.

S. 40(3)

This makes it clear that the real burden of meeting the claims of preferential creditors falls on the unsecured creditors.

Section 41   Enforcement of duty to make returns

41(1)   [Court order re defaults]   If a receiver or manager of a company's property—

    (a) having made default in filing, delivering or making any return, account or other document, or in giving any notice, which a receiver or manager is by law required to file, deliver, make or give, fails to make good the default within 14 days after the service on him of a notice requiring him to do so, or

    (b) having been appointed under powers contained in an instrument, has, after being required at any time by the liquidator of the company to do so, failed to render proper accounts of his receipts and payments and to vouch them and pay over to the liquidator the amount properly payable to him,

the court may, on an application made for the purpose, make an order directing the receiver or manager (as the case may be) to make good the default within such time as may be specified in the order.

41(2)   [Application for order]   In the case of the default mentioned in subsection (1)(a), application to the court may be made by any member or creditor of the company or by the registrar of companies; and in the case of the default mentioned in subsection (1)(b), the application shall be made by the liquidator.

In either case the court's order may provide that all costs of and incidental to the application shall be borne by the receiver or manager, as the case may be.

41(3)   [Other enactments]   Nothing in this section prejudices the operation of any enactment imposing penalties on receivers in respect of any such default as is mentioned in subsection (1).

(Former provisions: CA 1985, s. 499, CA 1948, s. 375)

S. 41(1)

This subsection sets out an enforcement procedure to deal with receivers who fail to submit accounts, returns, etc.

S. 41(2)

Applicants to the court for an enforcement order are identified. Applicants may be indemnified against costs thereby arising.

S. 41(3)

Sanctions imposed by individual sections creating obligations to file returns, etc. are not prejudiced by s. 41.

ADMINISTRATIVE RECEIVERS: GENERAL

Section 42   General powers

42(1)   [Powers in Sch. 1]   The powers conferred on the administrative receiver of a company by the debentures by virtue of which he was appointed are deemed to include (except in so far as they are inconsistent with any of the provisions of those debentures) the powers specified in Schedule 1 to this Act.

42(2) **[Interpretation of Sch. 1]** In the application of Schedule 1 to the administrative receiver of a company—

    (a) the words "he" and "him" refer to the administrative receiver, and

    (b) references to the property of the company are to the property of which he is or, but for the appointment of some other person as the receiver of part of the company's property, would be the receiver or manager.

42(3) **[Deemed capacity]** A person dealing with the administrative receiver in good faith and for value is not concerned to inquire whether the receiver is acting within his powers.

(Former provision: IA 1985, s. 48)

S. 42(1)

A model list of 23 implied powers for an administrative receiver (for the definition of this term, see s. 29(2)) is set out by Sch. 1 of this Act. These are commonly found in most standard commercial debentures. These 23 implied powers would appear to cover almost every eventuality, particularly when one bears in mind the general nature of power number 23. The implied powers are the same as those accorded to an administrator by s. 14. It is clear from the extent of these powers that once a company goes into administrative receivership the control of its management passes from the directors to the receiver. For the implications of this see *Re Joshua Shaw & Sons Ltd* (1989) 5 BCC 188.

S. 42(2)

This is an interpretation provision designed to smooth out any difficulties in the application of Sch. 1.

S. 42(3)

This statutory provision is an extension of the basic company law philosophy contained in *Royal British Bank* v *Turquand* (1856) 6 E & B 327; 119 ER 886 and in CA 1985, s. 35.

Section 43   Power to dispose of charged property, etc.

43(1) **[Application to court]** Where, on an application by the administrative receiver, the court is satisfied that the disposal (with or without other assets) of any relevant property which is subject to a security would be likely to promote a more advantageous realisation of the company's assets than would otherwise be effected, the court may by order authorise the administrative receiver to dispose of the property as if it were not subject to the security.

43(2) **[Application of s. 43(1)]** Subsection (1) does not apply in the case of any security held by the person by or on whose behalf the administrative receiver was appointed, or of any security to which a security so held has priority.

43(3) **[Conditions for order]** It shall be a condition of an order under this section that—

    (a) the net proceeds of the disposal, and

    (b) where those proceeds are less than such amount as may be determined by the court to be the net amount which would be realised on the sale of the property in the open market by a willing vendor, such sums as may be required to make good the deficiency,

shall be applied towards discharging the sums secured by the security.

43(4) [Where two or more securities] Where a condition imposed in pursuance of subsection (3) relates to two or more securities, that condition shall require the net proceeds of the disposal and, where paragraph (b) of that subsection applies, the sums mentioned in that paragraph to be applied towards discharging the sums secured by those securities in the order of their priorities.

43(5) [Copy of order to registrar] An office copy of an order under this section shall, within 14 days of the making of the order, be sent by the administrative receiver to the registrar of companies.

43(6) [Penalty for non-compliance] If the administrative receiver without reasonable excuse fails to comply with subsection (5), he is liable to a fine and, for continued contravention, to a daily default fine.

43(7) ["Relevant property"] In this section **"relevant property"**, in relation to the administrative receiver, means the property of which he is or, but for the appointment of some other person as the receiver of part of the company's property, would be the receiver or manager.

(Former provision: IA 1985, s. 49)

General note

This section applies to England and Wales only (see s. 440(2)(*a*)).

Section 43 does not apply in relation to the enforcement of "market charges" (as defined by CA 1989, s. 173): see s. 175 of that Act (as qualified by the Financial Markets and Insolvency Regulations 1991 (SI 1991 No. 880)), and the introductory note at p. 3, above.

S. 43(1), (2)

These provisions create a novel facility for administrative receivers by allowing them to apply to the court for the disposal of property that is subject to a prior charge (normally a fixed charge). The court must be satisfied that such disposal would promote a more advantageous realisation of the company's assets. The word "likely" in this context would probably be construed by the courts as meaning "a reasonable prospect" – see *Re Harris Simons Construction Ltd* [1989] 1 WLR 368; (1989) 5 BCC 11. A similar power is given to an administrator by s. 15, but the power under s. 15 is wider in that it covers property subject to title retention.

"Relevant property" is defined in s. 43(7).

For further details, see IR 1986, r. 3.31.

S. 43(3), (4)

If the court orders a disposal, the net proceeds are to be paid to discharge the prior security or securities (see s.43(4)). If the court decides that the sale was at an undervalue, the deficiency must be made good.

S. 43(5), (6)

A copy of the disposal order must be registered at Cardiff within 14 days or else the administrative receiver may incur criminal sanctions.

On penalties, see s. 430 and Sch. 10.

S. 43(7)
This is an interpretation provision and is best understood in relation to s. 29(2)(*b*).

Section 44   Agency and liability for contracts

44(1)   [Position of administrative receiver]   The administrative receiver of a company—

    (a) is deemed to be the company's agent, unless and until the company goes into liquidation;

    (b) is personally liable on any contract entered into by him in the carrying out of his functions (except in so far as the contract otherwise provides) and, to the extent of any qualifying liability, on any contract of employment adopted by him in the carrying out of those functions; and

    (c) is entitled in respect of that liability to an indemnity out of the assets of the company.

44(2)   [Interpretation]   For the purposes of subsection (1)(b) the administrative receiver is not to be taken to have adopted a contract of employment by reason of anything done or omitted to be done within 14 days after his appointment.

44(2A)   [Interpretation of s. 44(1)(b)]   For the purposes of subsection (1)(b), a liability under a contract of employment is a qualifying liability if—

    (a) it is a liability to pay a sum by way of wages or salary or contribution to an occupational pension scheme,

    (b) it is incurred while the administrative receiver is in office, and

    (c) it is in respect of services rendered wholly or partly after the adoption of the contract.

44(2B)   [Further interpretation of s. 44(1)(b)]   Where a sum payable in respect of a liability which is a qualifying liability for the purposes of subsection (1)(b) is payable in respect of services rendered partly before and partly after the adoption of the contract, liability under subsection (1)(b) shall only extend to so much of the sum as is payable in respect of services rendered after the adoption of the contract.

44(2C)   [Interpretation of s. 44(2A), (2B)]   For the purposes of subsections (2A) and (2B)—

    (a) wages or salary payable in respect of a period of holiday or absence from work through sickness or other good cause are deemed to be wages or (as the case may be) salary in respect of services rendered in that period, and

    (b) a sum payable in lieu of holiday is deemed to be wages or (as the case may be) salary in respect of services rendered in the period by reference to which the holiday entitlement arose.

44(2D)   [Interpretation of s. 44(2C)(a)]   In subsection (2C)(a), the reference to wages or salary payable in respect of a period of holiday includes any sums which, if they had been paid, would have been treated for the purposes of the enactments relating to social security as earnings in respect of that period.

44(3)   [Effect on other rights]   This section does not limit any right to indemnity which the administrative receiver would have apart from it, nor limit his liability on contracts entered into or adopted without authority, nor confer any right to indemnity in respect of that liability.

(Former provision: IA 1985, s. 50)

S. 44(1), (2)

By virtue of s. 44(1)(*a*), an administrative receiver is deemed to be the company's agent, provided that the company has not gone into liquidation, whereupon the agency relationship terminates. This is merely a statutory declaration of the standard agency provision found in most commercial debentures. For the position on winding up, see *Gosling* v *Gaskell and Grocott* [1897] AC 575 and the article by Turing in (1994) 9 IL & P 163.

An agent is not normally liable personally on a contract which he makes for his principal, and in the light of this, para. (*b*) may seem somewhat surprising – especially when it is contrasted with s. 14(5), which deems an administrator to be the company's agent without a similar qualification. The explanation is that a receiver is entitled to stipulate for an indemnity from the charge-holder as a term of his accepting office, contracting out of this liability. For a case where such contracting out would have found favour with the courts see *Amec Properties* v *Planning Research and Systems* [1992] 13 EG 109.

Sections 44(1)(a) and 44(2) now need to be read in the light of amendments made by the Insolvency Act 1994. The background to these amendments can be traced back ultimately to the case of *Nicoll* v *Cutts* (1985) 1 BCC 99,427 where it was held that a receiver who continued to retain the services of company employees during the receivership did not thereby adopt their contracts of employment. This decision was immediately counteracted by an express statutory provision extending the personal contractual liability of administrative receivers to cases of adopted contracts of employment. Insolvency practitioners sought to neutralise this statutory intervention by sending all employees whose services were being retained a letter to the effect that their contracts of employment were not being adopted nor was the administrative receiver undertaking personal liability thereon. This practice drew its support from the unreported ruling of Harman J in *Re Specialised Mouldings Ltd* (13 February 1987). The ability of insolvency practitioners to avoid the effect of the statutory rules imposing liability in cases of adoption was reviewed by the Court of Appeal in *Re Paramount Airways Ltd (No. 3)* [1994] BCC 172 (see the note to s. 19 above). Here the Court of Appeal held (confirming the first instance ruling of Evans-Lombe J) that adoption could occur simply by retaining staff without changing the terms of their employment. A transparent ploy such as sending a "Specialised Mouldings" letter was of no effect. As a result of this pronouncement from the Court of Appeal administrative receivers who retained staff after the initial 14-day period for reflection did so on the basis that they became personally liable for all accrued and current rights arising under the relevant contracts of employment. Not surprisingly administrative receivers were reluctant to assume such personal risk, even though it would be covered by their indemnity. Debenture holders would be less willing to wait for their money by allowing the receiver to generate it through a corporate rescue but would instead insist on an immediate sale. The economic and political consequences of abandoning a corporate rescue strategy were so great that the government was persuaded to legislate immediately. This legislation takes the form of the Insolvency Act 1994 which applies to contracts of employment adopted on or after 15 March 1994 (this legislation is to this extent retrospective as Royal Assent was only given on 24 March). Under s. 2 of this Act where a contract of employment is adopted by an administrative receiver he will only become personally responsible for "qualifying liabilities". These are defined in the new ss. 44(2A)–(2D) (inserted by IA 1994, s. 2(1), (3), (4)) as certain liabilities accruing only after the date when the contract was adopted. In *Re Leyland Daf Ltd*; *Re Ferranti International plc* [1994] BCC 658 Lightman J confirmed that the principles laid down in *Paramount Airways (No. 3)* do indeed apply to contracts of employment adopted by administrative receivers prior to 15 March 1994. Liability thus incurred could be avoided by an express contracting out. This case is to be joined with *Paramount* when the issue is reviewed by the House of Lords later in

1994. For further comment see Mudd (1994) 10 Insolvency Law and Practice 38 and the discussion on s. 19 above. In s. 44(1)(*b*) the words ", to the extent of any qualifying liability," were inserted after " provides) and" by IA 1994, s. 2(1), (2), (4).

S. 44(3)

This, in effect, merely extends s. 37(3) to administrative receivers.

Section 45 Vacation of office

45(1) [Removal by court, resignation] An administrative receiver of a company may at any time be removed from office by order of the court (but not otherwise) and may resign his office by giving notice of his resignation in the prescribed manner to such persons as may be prescribed.

45(2) [Vacation of office] An administrative receiver shall vacate office if he ceases to be qualified to act as an insolvency practitioner in relation to the company.

45(3) [Effect of vacation of office] Where at any time an administrative receiver vacates office—

   (a) his remuneration and any expenses properly incurred by him, and

   (b) any indemnity to which he is entitled out of the assets of the company,

shall be charged on and paid out of any property of the company which is in his custody or under his control at that time in priority to any security held by the person by or on whose behalf he was appointed.

45(4) [Notice to registrar] Where an administrative receiver vacates office otherwise than by death, he shall, within 14 days after his vacation of office, send a notice to that effect to the registrar of companies.

45(5) [Penalty for non-compliance] If an administrative receiver without reasonable excuse fails to comply with subsection (4), he is liable to a fine and, for continued contravention, to a daily default fine.

(Former provision: IA 1985, s. 51)

S. 45(1), (2)

These subsections outline the situations where the tenure of an administrative receiver comes to an end. Note that (as a result of a change in the law made by IA 1985) he can only be removed by debenture holders if they successfully apply to the court. This will make it clear that he is not entirely the minion of the debenture holders who appointed him. If he loses his qualification as an insolvency practitioner (see Pt. XIII) he must also vacate office.

S. 45(3)

This subsection protects the priority status of the administrative receiver's right to remuneration and indemnity.

S. 45(4), (5)

On vacating office the administrative receiver must notify Cardiff within 14 days or incur a fine. A similar obligation is imposed by CA 1985, s. 405(2). Note prospective amendment in s. 45(5): the words " and, for continued contravention, to a daily default fine" are to be repealed by CA 1989, Sch. 16 and 24 from a day to be appointed.

On penalties, see s. 430 and Sch. 10.

For further information, see IR 1986, rr. 3.33–3.35.

ADMINISTRATIVE RECEIVERS: ASCERTAINMENT AND INVESTIGATION OF COMPANY'S AFFAIRS

Section 46   Information to be given by administrative receiver

46(1)   [Notices]   Where an administrative receiver is appointed, he shall—

- (a) forthwith send to the company and publish in the prescribed manner a notice of his appointment, and
- (b) within 28 days after his appointment, unless the court otherwise directs, send such a notice to all the creditors of the company (so far as he is aware of their addresses).

46(2)   [Non-application]   This section and the next do not apply in relation to the appointment of an administrative receiver to act—

- (a) with an existing administrative receiver, or
- (b) in place of an administrative receiver dying or ceasing to act,

except that, where they apply to an administrative receiver who dies or ceases to act before they have been fully complied with, the references in this section and the next to the administrative receiver include (subject to the next subsection) his successor and any continuing administrative receiver.

46(3)   [Where company being wound up]   If the company is being wound up, this section and the next apply notwithstanding that the administrative receiver and the liquidator are the same person, but with any necessary modifications arising from that fact.

46(4)   [Penalty for non-compliance]   If the administrative receiver without reasonable excuse fails to comply with this section, he is liable to a fine and, for continued contravention, to a daily default fine.

(Former provision: IA 1985, s. 52)

S. 46(1), (4)

These provisions impose obligations on the administrative receiver to give notice of his appointment to various named parties. Criminal sanctions are imposed in the event of default (on penalties, see s. 430 and Sch. 10). Note also s. 39, and CA 1985, s. 405(1) (entry of appointment in register of charges).

S. 46(2), (3)

Qualifications to the above obligations are imposed. Compliance with s. 46(1) is a once and for all requirement. Provision is made for the case where the company is in liquidation and the administrative receiver is also the liquidator.

For further details, see IR 1986, r. 3.2.

Section **47**   Statement of affairs to be submitted

47(1)   [Duty of administrative receiver]   Where an administrative receiver is appointed, he shall forthwith require some or all of the persons mentioned below to make out and submit to him a statement in the prescribed form as to the affairs of the company.

47(2)   [Contents of statement]   A statement submitted under this section shall be verified by affidavit by the persons required to submit it and shall show—

    (a) particulars of the company's assets, debts and liabilities;

    (b) the names and addresses of its creditors;

    (c) the securities held by them respectively;

    (d) the dates when the securities were respectively given; and

    (e) such further or other information as may be prescribed.

47(3)   [Persons in s. 47(1)]   The persons referred to in subsection (1) are—

    (a) those who are or have been officers of the company;

    (b) those who have taken part in the company's formation at any time within one year before the date of the appointment of the administrative receiver;

    (c) those who are in the company's employment, or have been in its employment within that year, and are in the administrative receiver's opinion capable of giving the information required;

    (d) those who are or have been within that year officers of or in the employment of a company which is, or within that year was, an officer of the company.

In this subsection **"employment"** includes employment under a contract for services.

47(4)   [Time for statement]   Where any persons are required under this section to submit a statement of affairs to the administrative receiver, they shall do so (subject to the next subsection) before the end of the period of 21 days beginning with the day after that on which the prescribed notice of the requirement is given to them by the administrative receiver.

47(5)   [Release, extension of time]   The administrative receiver, if he thinks fit, may—

    (a) at any time release a person from an obligation imposed on him under subsection (1) or (2), or

    (b) either when giving notice under subsection (4) or subsequently, extend the period so mentioned;

and where the administrative receiver has refused to exercise a power conferred by this subsection, the court, if it thinks fit, may exercise it.

47(6)   [Penalty for non-compliance]   If a person without reasonable excuse fails to comply with any obligation imposed under this section, he is liable to a fine and, for continued contravention, to a daily default fine.

(Former provision: IA 1985, s. 53)

S. 47(1), (2), (4)

A statement of affairs containing the information outlined in s. 47(2) and the rules must be submitted to the administrative receiver within 21 days of his requiring it (or longer, if s. 47(5) is activated).

S. 47(3), (5), (6)

The persons who may be required by the administrative receiver to participate in the submission of the statement of affairs are identified by s. 47(3), although they may be excused either by the administrative receiver or the courts. Criminal sanctions are imposed on defaulters. On penalties, see s. 430 and Sch. 10.

For further information, see IR 1986, rr. 3.3–3.7. For enforcement by the administrative receiver, see IR 1986, r. 7.20.

Section 48   Report by administrative receiver

48(1)   [Duty of administrative receiver]   Where an administrative receiver is appointed, he shall, within 3 months (or such longer period as the court may allow) after his appointment, send to the registrar of companies, to any trustees for secured creditors of the company and (so far as he is aware of their addresses) to all such creditors a report as to the following matters, namely—

    (a) the events leading up to his appointment, so far as he is aware of them;

    (b) the disposal or proposed disposal by him of any property of the company and the carrying on or proposed carrying on by him of any business of the company;

    (c) the amounts of principal and interest payable to the debenture holders by whom or on whose behalf he was appointed and the amounts payable to preferential creditors; and

    (d) the amount (if any) likely to be available for the payment of other creditors.

48(2)   [Copies of report]   The administrative receiver shall also, within 3 months (or such longer period as the court may allow) after his appointment, either—

    (a) send a copy of the report (so far as he is aware of their addresses) to all unsecured creditors of the company; or

    (b) publish in the prescribed manner a notice stating an address to which unsecured creditors of the company should write for copies of the report to be sent to them free of charge,

and (in either case), unless the court otherwise directs, lay a copy of the report before a meeting of the company's unsecured creditors summoned for the purpose on not less than 14 days' notice.

48(3)   [Conditions for s. 48(2) direction]   The court shall not give a direction under subsection (2) unless—

    (a) the report states the intention of the administrative receiver to apply for the direction, and

    (b) a copy of the report is sent to the persons mentioned in paragraph (a) of that subsection, or a notice is published as mentioned in paragraph (b) of that subsection, not less than 14 days before the hearing of the application.

48(4)   [Where company in liquidation]   Where the company has gone or goes into liquidation, the administrative receiver—

(a) shall, within 7 days after his compliance with subsection (1) or, if later, the nomination or appointment of the liquidator, send a copy of the report to the liquidator, and

(b) where he does so within the time limited for compliance with subsection (2), is not required to comply with that subsection.

48(5)   [Report to include summary of statement]   A report under this section shall include a summary of the statement of affairs made out and submitted to the administrative receiver under section 47 and of his comments (if any) upon it.

48(6)   [Limit on report only]   Nothing in this section is to be taken as requiring any such report to include any information the disclosure of which would seriously prejudice the carrying out by the administrative receiver of his functions.

48(7)   [Application of s. 46(2)]   Section 46(2) applies for the purposes of this section also.

48(8)   [Penalty for non-compliance]   If the administrative receiver without reasonable excuse fails to comply with this section, he is liable to a fine and, for continued contravention, to a daily default fine.

(Former provision: IA 1985, s. 54)

S. 48(1), (4), (7)

These subsections require an administrative receiver to submit a report (normally within 3 months of his appointment) to various named parties, including the liquidator (see s. 48(4)). The contents of the report are also detailed. It is clear from s. 48(7) that this obligation does not apply to an administrative receiver succeeding another or assisting an incumbent administrative receiver.

S. 48(2), (3)

More widespread publication of the report is required by s. 48(2). Unsecured creditors, in particular, are to be given access to this report. A meeting of unsecured creditors must also be called at which this report is presented. The court can relieve an administrative receiver from this latter obligation, provided that the conditions in s. 48(3) are satisfied.

S. 48(5), (6)

These provisions go into further detail on the administrative receiver's report. It should contain a summary of the statement of affairs submitted to him, but need not include "any information, the disclosure of which would seriously prejudice the carrying out by the administrative receiver of his functions". It is not clear whether the test to be applied here is subjective or objective. See also *Gomba Holdings UK Ltd & Ors v Homan & Bird* [1986] 1 WLR 1301; (1986) 2 BCC 99,102.

S. 48(8)

Again, criminal sanctions are imposed on a defaulting administrative receiver. On penalties, see s. 430 and Sch. 10.

Section 48 is amplified by IR 1986, rr. 3.8–3.15.

Section 49   Committee of creditors

49(1)   [Meeting may establish committee]   Where a meeting of creditors is summoned under section 48, the meeting may, if it thinks fit, establish a committee (**"the creditors' committee"**) to exercise the functions conferred on it by or under this Act.

49(2)   [Committee may summon administrative receiver]   If such a committee is established, the committee may, on giving not less than 7 days' notice, require the administrative receiver to attend before it at any reasonable time and furnish it with such information relating to the carrying out by him of his functions as it may reasonably require.

(Former provision: IA 1985, s. 55)

S. 49(1)

This empowers the unsecured creditors in their meeting called under s. 48(2) to set up a committee.

S. 49(2)

The committee of creditors can request information from the administrative receiver. The test of reasonableness is presumably designed to protect information of the type envisaged by s. 48(6).

Further details on the constitution, rôle and working of this committee are provided by IR 1986, rr. 3.16–3.30.

Chapter II — Receivers (Scotland)

Section 50   Extent of this Chapter

50   This Chapter extends to Scotland only.

(Former provisions: CA 1985, s. 487; CFCSA 1972, s. 32)

General note

Scottish debenture holders were only given the remedy of receivership in 1972 and, since that date, their law of receivership has developed separately from the English counterpart, although on similar lines. There have been problems in fitting this new remedy into the general system of Scottish corporate insolvency law, and problems of statutory interpretation have troubled the Scottish courts on a number of occasions. For the floating charge in Scotland, see CA 1985, ss. 462–466. Reference should also be made to the Receivers (Scotland) Regulations 1986 (SI 1986 No. 1917 (S. 141)).

The changes made in this area of the law by IA 1985 and IA 1986 do not operate retrospectively: see Sch. 11, para. 3(2).

Section 51   Power to appoint receiver

51(1)   [Floating charge holder may appoint receiver]   It is competent under the law of Scotland for the holder of a floating charge over all or any part of the property (including uncalled capital), which may from time to time be comprised in the property and undertaking of an incorporated company (whether a company within the meaning of the Companies Act or not) which the Court of Session has jurisdiction to wind up, to appoint a receiver of such part of the property of the company as is subject to the charge.

51(2) [Appointment by court on application] It is competent under the law of Scotland for the court, on the application of the holder of such a floating charge, to appoint a receiver of such part of the property of the company as is subject to the charge.

51(3) [Those disqualified] The following are disqualified from being appointed as receiver—

    (a) a body corporate;

    (b) an undischarged bankrupt; and

    (c) a firm according to the law of Scotland.

51(4) [Scottish firm] A body corporate or a firm according to the law of Scotland which acts as a receiver is liable to a fine.

51(5) [Undischarged bankrupt] An undischarged bankrupt who so acts is liable to imprisonment or a fine, or both.

51(6) ["Receiver"] In this section, **"receiver"** includes joint receivers.

(Former provisions: CA 1985, s. 467; CFCSA 1972, s. 11)

S. 51(1), (2)
These provisions authorise the holder of a floating charge in Scotland (for the meaning of this term, see IA 1986, s. 70) to appoint a receiver out of court or to apply to the court for such an appointment. For the meaning of "property" within subs. (1) see *Hawking* v *Hafton House Ltd* 1990 SLT 496.

S. 51(3)–(5)
These subsections deal with the question of disqualification and mirror the English provisions to a large extent. However, note that Scottish partnerships, which possess legal personality, are also disqualified. A Scottish receiver will have to be a qualified insolvency practitioner within the meaning of IA 1986, Pt. XIII, if he is an administrative receiver, as will commonly be the case (see IA 1986, s. 251). On penalties, see s. 430 and Sch. 10.

S. 51(6)
Joint receivers are permissible under Scottish law.

Section 52   Circumstances justifying appointment

52(1) [Events for s. 51(1) appointment] A receiver may be appointed under section 51(1) by the holder of the floating charge on the occurrence of any event which, by the provisions of the instrument creating the charge, entitles the holder of the charge to make that appointment and, in so far as not otherwise provided for by the instrument, on the occurrence of any of the following events, namely—

    (a) the expiry of a period of 21 days after the making of a demand for payment of the whole or any part of the principal sum secured by the charge, without payment having been made;

(b) the expiry of a period of 2 months during the whole of which interest due and payable under the charge has been in arrears;

(c) the making of an order or the passing of a resolution to wind up the company;

(d) the appointment of a receiver by virtue of any other floating charge created by the company.

52(2) **[Events for s. 51(2) appointment]** A receiver may be appointed by the court under section 51(2) on the occurrence of any event which, by the provisions of the instrument creating the floating charge, entitles the holder of the charge to make that appointment and, in so far as not otherwise provided for by the instrument, on the occurrence of any of the following events, namely—

(a) where the court, on the application of the holder of the charge, pronounces itself satisfied that the position of the holder of the charge is likely to be prejudiced if no such appointment is made;

(b) any of the events referred to in paragraphs (a) to (c) of subsection (1).

(Former provisions: CA 1985, s. 468; CFCSA 1972, s. 12)

S. 52(1)

This subsection provides a model list of grounds (which can be varied by the debenture) under which a Scots receiver can be appointed out of court by a holder of a floating charge.

S. 52(2)

A receiver can be appointed by the court on the occurrence of any of the events specified in s. 52(1) or on grounds of prejudice (a Scottish synonym for "jeopardy").

Section 53 Mode of appointment by holder of charge

53(1) **[Instrument of appointment]** The appointment of a receiver by the holder of the floating charge under section 51(1) shall be by means of a validly executed instrument in writing ("the instrument of appointment"), a copy (certified in the prescribed manner to be a correct copy) whereof shall be delivered by or on behalf of the person making the appointment to the registrar of companies for registration within 7 days of its execution and shall be accompanied by a notice in the prescribed form.

53(2) **[Penalty on default]** If any person without reasonable excuse makes default in complying with the requirements of subsection (1), he is liable to a fine and, for continued contravention, to a daily default fine.

53(3) (Repealed)

53(4) **[Execution on behalf of floating charge holder]** The instrument may be executed on behalf of the holder of the floating charge by virtue of which the receiver is to be appointed—

(a) by any person duly authorised in writing by the holder to execute the instrument, and

   (b) in the case of an appointment of a receiver by the holders of a series of secured debentures, by any person authorised by resolution of the debenture-holders to execute the instrument.

53(5) **[Entry on register]**   On receipt of the certified copy of the instrument of appointment in accordance with subsection (1), the registrar shall, on payment of the prescribed fee, enter the particulars of the appointment in the register of charges.

53(6) **[Effect of appointment]**   The appointment of a person as a receiver by an instrument of appointment in accordance with subsection (1)—

   (a) is of no effect unless it is accepted by that person before the end of the business day next following that on which the instrument of appointment is received by him or on his behalf, and

   (b) subject to paragraph (a), is deemed to be made on the day on and at the time at which the instrument of appointment is so received, as evidenced by a written docquet by that person or on his behalf;

and this subsection applies to the appointment of joint receivers subject to such modifications as may be prescribed.

53(7) **[Attachment of charge]**   On the appointment of a receiver under this section, the floating charge by virtue of which he was appointed attaches to the property then subject to the charge; and such attachment has effect as if the charge was a fixed security over the property to which it has attached.

(Former provisions: CA 1985, s. 469 (as amended by IA 1985, s. 56); CFCSA 1972, s. 13)

S. 53(1), (2), (5)

Section 53(1) specifies the exclusive method by which a receiver can be appointed out of court. Note that, as in English law (CA 1985, s. 405), a notice in proper form of the appointment must be delivered for registration to the Scottish Companies Registry in Edinburgh, whereupon the registrar must register it: see (s. 53(1)). Criminal sanctions are imposed for default. Note prospective amendment in s. 53(2): the words "and, for continued contravention, to a daily default fine" are to be repealed by CA 1989, Sch. 16 and 24 from a day to be appointed. On penalties, see s. 430 and Sch. 10. For the prescribed form under s. 53(1), see the Receivers (Scotland) Regulations 1986 (SI 1986 No. 1917 (S. 141)) Form 1 (Scot).

S. 53(3)

This subsection was repealed by the Law Reform (Miscellaneous Provisions) (Scotland) Act 1990, s. 74 and Sch. 9 – see SI 1990 No. 2328 (C. 60) (S. 197) art. 3: the former wording read as follows:

"The instrument of appointment is validly executed—

   (a) by a company, if it is executed in accordance with section 36B of the Companies Act 1985, and

   (b) by any other person, if it is executed in the manner required or permitted by the law of Scotland in the case of an attested deed."

The reference to s. 36B was substituted by CA 1989, s. 130(7) and Sch. 17, para. 10.

S. 53(4)

This subsection deals with the way in which the instrument of appointment is executed. For the meaning of "holder of the floating charge" and "series of secured debentures" in s. 53(4), see s. 70.

S. 53(6), (7)

The time of the appointment is fixed (for the English position, see IA 1986, s. 33(1)). The appointment of the receiver causes crystallisation by converting the charge into a fixed security, but this does not render it immune from attack under IA 1986, s. 245, nor from the preferential claims régime. See the Receivers (Scotland) Regulations 1986 (SI 1986 No. 1917 (S. 141)). On s. 53(7), see *Myles J. Callaghan Ltd (in receivership) & Anor* v *City of Glasgow District Council* (1987) 3 BCC 337 and *Scottish and Newcastle plc, Petitioners* [1993] BCC 634.

Section 54   Appointment by court

54(1)   [Petition to court]   Application for the appointment of a receiver by the court under section 51(2) shall be by petition to the court, which shall be served on the company.

54(2)   [Issue of interlocutor]   On such an application, the court shall, if it thinks fit, issue an interlocutor making the appointment of the receiver.

54(3)   [Copy of interlocutor to registrar, penalty on default]   A copy (certified by the clerk of the court to be a correct copy) of the court's interlocutor making the appointment shall be delivered by or on behalf of the petitioner to the registrar of companies for registration, accompanied by a notice in the prescribed form, within 7 days of the date of the interlocutor or such longer period as the court may allow.

If any person without reasonable excuse makes default in complying with the requirements of this subsection, he is liable to a fine and, for continued contravention, to a daily default fine.

54(4)   [Entry on register]   On receipt of the certified copy interlocutor in accordance with subsection (3), the registrar shall, on payment of the prescribed fee, enter the particulars of the appointment in the register of charges.

54(5)   [Date of appointment]   The receiver is to be regarded as having been appointed on the date of his being appointed by the court.

54(6)   [Attachment of charge]   On the appointment of a receiver under this section, the floating charge by virtue of which he was appointed attaches to the property then subject to the charge; and such attachment has effect as if the charge were a fixed security over the property to which it has attached.

54(7)   [Rules of court re urgent cases]   In making rules of court for the purposes of this section, the Court of Session shall have regard to the need for special provision for cases which appear to the court to require to be dealt with as a matter of urgency.

(Former provisions: CA 1985, s. 470; CFCSA 1972, s. 14(1)–(6), (8))

S. 54(1), (2)

These provisions outline the procedure by which a receiver can be appointed by the court in Scotland.

S. 54(3), (4)

The court's order (interlocutor) is to be registered at Edinburgh, normally within seven days. Criminal sanctions are imposed for failure to submit the order for registration. Note prospective amendment in s. 54(3): the words "and, for continued contravention, to a daily default fine" are to be repealed by CA 1989, Sch. 16 and 24 from a day to be appointed. On penalties, see s. 430 and Sch. 10. For the notice in prescribed form under s. 54(3), see Form 2 (Scot) in the Receivers (Scotland) Regulations 1986 (SI 1986 No. 1917 (S. 141)).

S. 54(5), (6)
These subsections regulate the timing and the effect of the appointment.

S. 54(7)
Special rules of court may be devised to expedite urgent cases.

Section 55   Powers of receiver

55(1)   [Powers in instrument]   Subject to the next subsection, a receiver has in relation to such part of the property of the company as is attached by the floating charge by virtue of which he was appointed, the powers, if any, given to him by the instrument creating that charge.

55(2)   [Powers in Sch. 2]   In addition, the receiver has under this Chapter the powers as respects that property (in so far as these are not inconsistent with any provision contained in that instrument) which are specified in Schedule 2 to this Act.

55(3)   [Restriction on powers]   Subsections (1) and (2) apply—

- (a) subject to the rights of any person who has effectually executed diligence on all or any part of the property of the company prior to the appointment of the receiver, and
- (b) subject to the rights of any person who holds over all or any part of the property of the company a fixed security or floating charge having priority over, or ranking pari passu with, the floating charge by virtue of which the receiver was appointed.

55(4)   [Enquiry as to authority not necessary]   A person dealing with a receiver in good faith and for value is not concerned to enquire whether the receiver is acting within his powers.

(Former provisions: CA 1985, s. 471 (as amended by IA 1985, s. 57); CFCSA 1972, s. 15)

S. 55(1), (2)
Scottish receivers enjoy the 23 implied powers listed in Sch. 2 of the Act. These can be added to by the debenture. For the English position, see s. 42 and Sch. 1. For a recent authority here, see *Myles J. Callaghan Ltd (in receivership) & Anor* v *City of Glasgow District Council* (1987) 3 BCC 337. The powers of the receiver do not extend to assets which cannot be regarded as the "property" of the company – see *Hawking* v *Hafton House Ltd* 1990 SLT 496.

S. 55(3), (4)
The rights of third parties, such as holders of a fixed security (for definition, see s. 70) and execution creditors, *vis-à-vis* the receiver in the exercise of his powers are regulated. Third parties need not check to see that the receiver is acting within his powers. See *Iona Hotels Ltd, Petitioners* 1991 SLT 11.

Section 56   Precedence among receivers

56(1)   [Order of precedence]   Where there are two or more floating charges subsisting over all or any part of the property of the company, a receiver may be appointed under this Chapter by virtue of each such charge; but a receiver appointed by, or on the application of, the holder of a floating charge having priority of ranking over any other floating charge by virtue of which a receiver has been appointed has the powers given to a receiver by section 55 and Schedule 2 to the exclusion of any other receiver.

56(2) **[Where floating charges rank equally]** Where two or more floating charges rank with one another equally, and two or more receivers have been appointed by virtue of such charges, the receivers so appointed are deemed to have been appointed as joint receivers.

56(3) **[Receivers to act jointly]** Receivers appointed, or deemed to have been appointed, as joint receivers shall act jointly unless the instrument of appointment or respective instruments of appointment otherwise provide.

56(4) **[Suspension of receiver's powers]** Subject to subsection (5) below, the powers of a receiver appointed by, or on the application of, the holder of a floating charge are suspended by, and as from the date of, the appointment of a receiver by, or on the application of, the holder of a floating charge having priority of ranking over that charge to such extent as may be necessary to enable the receiver second mentioned to exercise his powers under section 55 and Schedule 2; and any powers so suspended take effect again when the floating charge having priority of ranking ceases to attach to the property then subject to the charge, whether such cessation is by virtue of section 62(6) or otherwise.

56(5) **[Effect of suspension]** The suspension of the powers of a receiver under sub-section (4) does not have the effect of requiring him to release any part of the property (including any letters or documents) of the company from his control until he receives from the receiver superseding him a valid indemnity (subject to the limit of the value of such part of the property of the company as is subject to the charge by virtue of which he was appointed) in respect of any expenses, charges and liabilities he may have incurred in the performance of his functions as receiver.

56(6) **[Floating charge remains attached]** The suspension of the powers of a receiver under subsection (4) does not cause the floating charge by virtue of which he was appointed to cease to attach to the property to which it attached by virtue of section 53(7) or 54(6).

56(7) **[Same receiver by several charges]** Nothing in this section prevents the same receiver being appointed by virtue of two or more floating charges.

(Former provisions: CA 1985, s. 472; CFCSA 1972, s. 16)

S. 56(1), (2), (3)
Two competing receivers may be appointed over the same company's assets, but only the one with priority can exercise the statutory powers conferred on receivers. In the event of a "tie" they are deemed to have been appointed as joint receivers, and must act jointly.

S. 56(4), (5), (6)
These subsections deal with the situation where the receiver who was appointed first has to give way to a receiver appointed subsequently, but enjoying priority. This is a matter not dealt with by any English statutory provision. The first receiver's powers are suspended until the latter has fulfilled his rôle. However, he should not hand over property to the latter until he has received

an indemnity from him. Furthermore, the mere fact that a receiver's powers have been suspended does not cause the floating charge under which he was appointed to refloat.

S. 56(7)

To make matters easier, the same receiver can act for competing chargees, although this may produce conflicts of interest.

Section 57   Agency and liability of receiver for contracts

57(1)   **[Receiver deemed agent]**   A receiver is deemed to be the agent of the company in relation to such property of the company as is attached by the floating charge by virtue of which he was appointed.

57(1A)   **[Further qualification re receiver as agent]**   Without prejudice to subsection (1), a receiver is deemed to be the agent of the company in relation to any contract of employment adopted by him in the carrying out of his functions.

57(2)   **[Personal liability]**   A receiver (including a receiver whose powers are subsequently suspended under section 56) is personally liable on any contract entered into by him in the performance of his functions, except in so far as the contract otherwise provides, and, to the extent of any qualifying liability, on any contract of employment adopted by him in the carrying out of those functions.

57(2A)   **[Interpretation of s. 57(2)]**   For the purposes of subsection (2), a liability under a contract of employment is a qualifying liability if—

     (a) it is a liability to pay a sum by way of wages or salary or contribution to an occupational pension scheme,

     (b) it is incurred while the receiver is in office, and

     (c) it is in respect of services rendered wholly or partly after the adoption of the contract.

57(2B)   **[Further interpretation of s. 57(2)]**   Where a sum payable in respect of a liability which is a qualifying liability for the purposes of subsection (2) is payable in respect of services rendered partly before and partly after the adoption of the contract, liability under that subsection shall only extend to so much of the sum as is payable in respect of services rendered after the adoption of the contract.

57(2C)   **[Interpretation of s. 57(2A), (2B)]**   For the purposes of subsections (2A) and (2B)–

     (a) wages or salary payable in respect of a period of holiday or absence from work through sickness or other good cause are deemed to be wages or (as the case may be) salary in respect of services rendered in that period, and

     (b) a sum payable in lieu of holiday is deemed to be wages or (as the case may be) salary in respect of services rendered in the period by reference to which the holiday entitlement arose.

57(2D)   **[Interpretation of s. 57(2C)(a)]**   In subsection (2C)(a), the reference to wages or salary payable in respect of a period of holiday includes any sums which, if they had been paid, would have been treated for the purposes of the enactments relating to social security as earnings in respect of that period.

57(3)   **[Indemnity]**   A receiver who is personally liable by virtue of subsection (2) is entitled to be indemnified out of the property in respect of which he was appointed.

57(4) **[Contracts before appointment]** Any contract entered into by or on behalf of the company prior to the appointment of a receiver continues in force (subject to its terms) notwithstanding that appointment, but the receiver does not by virtue only of his appointment incur any personal liability on any such contract.

57(5) **[Interpretation of s. 57(2)]** For the purposes of subsection (2), a receiver is not to be taken to have adopted a contract of employment by reason of anything done or omitted to be done within 14 days after his appointment.

57(6) **[Effect]** This section does not limit any right to indemnity which the receiver would have apart from it, nor limit his liability on contracts entered into or adopted without authority, nor confer any right to indemnity in respect of that liability.

57(7) **[Continuation of contract]** Any contract entered into by a receiver in the performance of his functions continues in force (subject to its terms) although the powers of the receiver are subsequently suspended under section 56.

(Former provisions: CA 1985, s. 473 (as amended by IA 1985, s. 58); CFCSA 1972, s. 17)

S. 57(1)

As in English law, this subsection makes the receiver the company's agent. Indeed, it goes further, because it would appear to confer such status on court-appointed receivers. In view of this agency relationship there is no change of occupation when a receiver takes possession of the company's premises, and the receiver does not become personally liable for rates accruing on such premises – *McKillop and Watters, Petitioners* [1994] BCC 677. Having said that, it may well be in the case of certain statutory provisions that the court might find a receiver to be in joint occupation. Such a conclusion was arrived at in *Lord Advocate* v *Aero Technologies Ltd* 1991 SLT 134 in the context of s. 23 of the Explosives Act 1875.

S. 57(1A), (2A)–(2D)

These were inserted by the Insolvency Act 1994 (s. 3(1), (2), (4), (5)) to counteract the problems posed for Scottish receivers by the ruling of the Court of Appeal in *Re Paramount Airways Ltd (No. 3)* [1994] BCC 172 – see the discussion on ss. 19, 37 and 44 above.

S. 57(2), (4), (5)

These provisions reproduce the position in English law by making the receiver personally liable on contracts entered into by him and on existing contracts of employment adopted by him, although the circumstances where adoption will occur are limited by s. 57(5). Apart from contracts of employment adopted by the receiver, he is not personally liable on the company's existing contracts. For discussion of s. 57(2) see *Hill Samuel & Co. Ltd* v *Laing* 1989 SLT 760; [1991] BCC 665. In s. 57(2) the words ", to the extent of any qualifying liability," inserted after the words "provides, and" by IA 1994, s. 3(1), (3), (5) in relation to contracts of employment adopted on or after 15 March 1994.

S. 57(3), (6)

These subsections deal with the receiver's indemnity against personal liability, and make it clear that it does not extend to unauthorised contracts.

S. 57(7)

If a receiver's powers are suspended under s. 56, contracts entered into by the receiver will normally remain in force.

Section 58 Remuneration of receiver

58(1) [Remuneration by agreement] The remuneration to be paid to a receiver is to be determined by agreement between the receiver and the holder of the floating charge by virtue of which he was appointed.

58(2) [Where remuneration not specified or disputed] Where the remuneration to be paid to the receiver has not been determined under subsection (1), or where it has been so determined but is disputed by any of the persons mentioned in paragraphs (a) to (d) below, it may be fixed instead by the Auditor of the Court of Session on application made to him by—

    (a) the receiver;

    (b) the holder of any floating charge or fixed security over all or any part of the property of the company;

    (c) the company; or

    (d) the liquidator of the company.

58(3) [Accounting for excess] Where the receiver has been paid or has retained for his remuneration for any period before the remuneration has been fixed by the Auditor of the Court of Session under subsection (2) any amount in excess of the remuneration so fixed for that period, the receiver or his personal representatives shall account for the excess.

(Former provisions: CA 1985, s. 474; CFCSA 1972, s. 18)

S. 58(1)

This subsection states the general rule that the receiver's remuneration is to be fixed by agreement with the debenture holder who appointed him.

S. 58(2), (3)

This is a fall-back provision, permitting the Auditor of the Court of Session, on the application of any of various named parties, to fix remuneration in cases where there is no agreement within the meaning of s. 58(1), or where there is a dispute as to the level of remuneration. It is interesting to note that CA 1985, s. 474 fixed a time limit for such an application and also specified the correct procedure to be followed – this has been omitted in s. 58. Presumably this could be dealt with in the rules – see Sch. 8, para. 15. Section 58(3) deals with the position when a receiver has received remuneration which turns out to be excessive: surplus amounts have to be repaid.

Section 59 Priority of debts

59(1) [Certain debts to be paid in priority out of assets] Where a receiver is appointed and the company is not at the time of the appointment in course of being wound up, the debts which fall under subsection (2) of this section shall be paid out of any assets coming to the hands of the receiver in priority to any claim for principal or interest by the holder of the floating charge by virtue of which the receiver was appointed.

59(2) [Preferential debts] Debts falling under this subsection are preferential debts (within the meaning given by section 386 in Part XII) which, by the end of a period of 6 months after advertisement by the receiver for claims in the Edinburgh Gazette and in a newspaper circulating in the district where the company carries on business either—

(i) have been intimated to him, or

(ii) have become known to him.

59(3) [Recoupment of payments] Any payments made under this section shall be recouped as far as may be out of the assets of the company available for payment of ordinary creditors.

(Former provisions: CA 1985, s. 475 (as amended by IA 1985, Sch. 6, para. 20(2)); CFCSA 1972, s. 19)

S. 59(1), (2)

These subsections impose a positive obligation on the receiver to meet the preferential claims listed in Sch. 6 of the Act. The position in Scottish law differs from its English counterpart in that claims must be submitted to the receiver within six months of an advertisement being placed in the Gazette. A further difference exists between English and Scottish law with regard to preferential debts on receivership. Where the Crown wishes to exercise a set-off and has total debts owed to it which have both unsecured and preferential elements, it can exercise the set-off with respect to the unsecured debts without rateably setting off preferential debts. The effect of this is to enhance its overall priority position by preserving its preferential status – see *Turner, Petitioner* [1993] BCC 299. For the approach in English law see *Re Unit 2 Windows Ltd* (1985) 1 BCC 99,489. Note the limitation upon this duty imposed by s. 11(5).

S. 59(3)

As with s. 40(3), this makes it clear that the burden of meeting the preferential claims will ultimately fall on the unsecured creditors.

Section 60   Distribution of moneys

60(1) [Payment of moneys by receiver] Subject to the next section, and to the rights of any of the following categories of persons (which rights shall, except to the extent otherwise provided in any instrument, have the following order of priority), namely—

(a) the holder of any fixed security which is over property subject to the floating charge and which ranks prior to, or pari passu with, the floating charge;

(b) all persons who have effectually executed diligence on any part of the property of the company which is subject to the charge by virtue of which the receiver was appointed;

(c) creditors in respect of all liabilities, charges and expenses incurred by or on behalf of the receiver;

(d) the receiver in respect of his liabilities, expenses and remuneration, and any indemnity to which he is entitled out of the property of the company; and

(e) the preferential creditors entitled to payment under section 59,

the receiver shall pay moneys received by him to the holder of the floating charge by virtue of which the receiver was appointed in or towards satisfaction of the debt secured by the floating charge.

60(2) **[Balance of moneys]** Any balance of moneys remaining after the provisions of subsection (1) and section 61 below have been satisfied shall be paid in accordance with their respective rights and interests to the following persons, as the case may require—

(a) any other receiver;

(b) the holder of a fixed security which is over property subject to the floating charge;

(c) the company or its liquidator, as the case may be.

60(3) **[Doubt as to person entitled]** Where any question arises as to the person entitled to a payment under this section, or where a receipt or a discharge of a security cannot be obtained in respect of any such payment, the receiver shall consign the amount of such payment in any joint stock bank of issue in Scotland in name of the Accountant of Court for behoof of the person or persons entitled thereto.

(Former provisions: CA 1985, s. 476 (as amended by IA 1985, Sch. 6, para. 21); CFCSA 1972, s. 20)

S. 60(1)

This subsection outlines a priority ranking for claims against the assets of a company which is in receivership. There is no parallel provision in English law. When presented in this way it is not surprising that banks have become uneasy about the protection offered by the floating charge. However, IA 1986 does offer them some comfort in that it radically reduces the categories of preferential claim. For the meaning of "fixed security" in para. (*a*), see s. 70. See *Scottish and Newcastle plc, Petitioners* [1993] BCC 634.

S. 60(2)

This provision maps out the fate of any surplus moneys in the hands of the receiver, after the claims listed in s. 60(1) have been met.

S. 60(3)

In the event of a dispute over whether a claim should be met or not, the receiver should pay an appropriate sum of money into a recognised Scottish bank in the name of the Accountant of Court, pending the resolution of the dispute.

Section 61   Disposal of interest in property

61(1) **[Application to court]** Where the receiver sells or disposes, or is desirous of selling or disposing, of any property or interest in property of the company which is subject to the floating charge by virtue of which the receiver was appointed and which is—

(a) subject to any security or interest of, or burden or encumbrance in favour of, a creditor the ranking of which is prior to, or pari passu with, or post-poned to the floating charge, or

(b) property or an interest in property affected or attached by effectual diligence executed by any person,

and the receiver is unable to obtain the consent of such creditor or, as the case may be, such person to such a sale or disposal, the receiver may apply to the court for authority to sell or dispose of the property or interest in property free of such security, interest, burden, encumbrance or diligence.

61(2) **[Authorisation by court]** Subject to the next subsection, on such an application the court may, if it thinks fit, authorise the sale or disposal of the property or interest in question free of such security, interest, burden, encumbrance or diligence, and such authorisation may be on such terms or conditions as the court thinks fit.

61(3) **[Condition for authorisation]** In the case of an application where a fixed security over the property or interest in question which ranks prior to the floating charge has not been met or provided for in full, the court shall not authorise the sale or disposal of the property or interest in question unless it is satisifed that the sale or disposal would be likely to provide a more advantageous realisation of the company's assets than would otherwise be effected.

61(4) **[Condition for s. 61(3)]** It shall be a condition of an authorisation to which sub-section (3) applies that—

(a) the net proceeds of the disposal, and

(b) where those proceeds are less than such amount as may be determined by the court to be the net amount which would be realised on a sale of the property or interest in the open market by a willing seller, such sums as may be required to make good the deficiency,

shall be applied towards discharging the sums secured by the fixed security.

61(5) **[Where s. 61(4) condition re several securities]** Where a condition imposed in pursuance of subsection (4) relates to two or more such fixed securities, that condition shall require the net proceeds of the disposal and, where paragraph (b) of that subsection applies, the sums mentioned in that paragraph to be applied towards discharging the sums secured by those fixed securities in the order of their priorities.

61(6) **[Copy of authorisation to registrar]** A copy of an authorisation under subsection (2) certified by the clerk of court shall, within 14 days of the granting of the authorisation, be sent by the receiver to the registrar of companies.

61(7) **[Penalty for non-compliance]** If the receiver without reasonable excuse fails to comply with subsection (6), he is liable to a fine and, for continued contravention, to a daily default fine.

61(8) **[Receiver to give document to disponee]** Where any sale or disposal is effected in accordance with the authorisation of the court under subsection (2), the receiver shall grant to the purchaser or disponee an appropriate document of transfer or conveyance of the property or interest in question, and that document has the effect, or, where recording, intimation or registration of that document is a legal requirement for completion of title to the property or interest, then that recording, intimation or registration (as the case may be) has the effect, of—

(a) disencumbering the property or interest of the security, interest, burden or encumbrance affecting it, and

(b) freeing the property or interest from the diligence executed upon it.

61(9) **[Ranking of creditor in winding up]** Nothing in this section prejudices the right of any creditor of the company to rank for his debt in the winding up of the company.

(Former provisions: CA 1985, s. 477 (as amended by IA 1985, s. 59); CFCSA 1972, s. 21)

S. 61(1), (2)

These subsections allow a receiver to apply to the court for the sale of property subject to a fixed charge, or over which diligence has been effectually executed.

Section 61 does not apply in relation to the enforcement of "market charges" (as defined by CA 1989, s. 173): see s. 175 of that Act (as qualified by the Financial Markets and Insolvency Regulations 1991 (SI 1991 No. 880)), and the introductory note at p. 3, above.

S. 61(3), (4), (5)

If the receiver has not set aside a sufficient sum to meet the claim of the holder of the "fixed security" (for the meaning of this term, see s. 70), the court should only assent to the sale if it would promote a more effective realisation of the company's assets. Even where assent is given, the actual net proceeds (or a reasonable amount, if the sale was at an undervalue) must be set aside for the fixed chargee (or chargees).

S. 61(6), (7)

If the court permits the sale to go ahead, the receiver must register the fact at Edinburgh, or incur a default fine. On penalties, see s. 430 and Sch. 10.

S. 61(8)

This subsection provides a mechanism for assuring the purchaser under the forced sale that he can acquire an effective title from the receiver.

S. 61(9)

This is a saving provision allowing a person who has been deprived of his claim against specific property to rank instead as a creditor of the company on winding up.

Section 62   Cessation of appointment of receiver

62(1)   [Removal, resignation]   A receiver may be removed from office by the court under subsection (3) below and may resign his office by giving notice of his resignation in the prescribed manner to such persons as may be prescribed.

62(2)   [Cessation of qualification]   A receiver shall vacate office if he ceases to be qualified to act as an insolvency practitioner in relation to the company.

62(3)   [Removal on application]   Subject to the next subsection, a receiver may, on application to the court by the holder of the floating charge by virtue of which he was appointed, be removed by the court on cause shown.

62(4)   [On vacation of office]   Where at any time a receiver vacates office—

(a) his remuneration and any expenses properly incurred by him, and

(b) any indemnity to which he is entitled out of the property of the company,

shall be paid out of the property of the company which is subject to the floating charge and shall have priority as provided for in section 60(1).

62(5)   [Notice of cessation to registrar, penalty on default]   When a receiver ceases to act as such otherwise than by death he shall, and, when a receiver is removed by the court, the holder of the floating charge by virtue of which he was appointed shall, within 14 days of the cessation or removal (as the case may be) give the registrar of companies notice to that effect, and the registrar shall enter the notice in the register of charges.

If the receiver or the holder of the floating charge (as the case may require) makes default in complying with the requirements of this subsection, he is liable to a fine and, for continued contravention, to a daily default fine.

62(6) [Cessation of attachment of charge] If by the expiry of a period of one month following upon the removal of the receiver or his ceasing to act as such no other receiver has been appointed, the floating charge by virtue of which the receiver was appointed—

(a) thereupon ceases to attach to the property then subject to the charge, and

(b) again subsists as a floating charge;

and for the purposes of calculating the period of one month under this subsection no account shall be taken of any period during which an administration order under Part II of this Act is in force.

(Former provisions: CA 1985, s. 478 (as amended by IA 1985, s. 60 and Sch. 6, para. 13); CFCSA 1972, s. 22)

S. 62(1)–(3)

These subsections deal with the situations where a receiver will vacate office. Note that he can only be removed by the court on the application of the holder of the floating charge (for the meaning of this term, see s. 70), and not out of court by the holder of the floating charge who appointed him. As to the qualification as an insolvency practitioner, see Pt. XIII. For the relevant notice of resignation under s. 62(1), see the Receivers (Scotland) Regulations 1986 (SI 1986 No. 1917 (S. 141)).

S. 62(4)

This protects the priority of the receiver's right to indemity and remuneration.

S. 62(5)

Notification must be given to Edinburgh of the receiver leaving office: see Form 3 (Scot) under the Receivers (Scotland) Regulations 1986 (SI 1986 No. 1917 (S.141)). The person responsible for giving notice will incur criminal sanctions in the event of default. On penalties, see s. 430 and Sch. 10. Note prospective amendment: the words "and, for continued contravention, to a daily default fine" are to be repealed by CA 1989, Sch. 16 and 24 from a day to be appointed.

S. 62(6)

This provides for the "refloating" of the floating charge on the expiry of one month after the receiver leaves office.

Section 63 Powers of court

63(1) [Directions, on application] The court on the application of—

(a) the holder of a floating charge by virtue of which a receiver was appointed, or

(b) a receiver appointed under section 51,

may give directions to the receiver in respect of any matter arising in connection with the performance by him of his functions.

63(2) [Where receiver's appointment invalid]   Where the appointment of a person as a receiver by the holder of a floating charge is discovered to be invalid (whether by virtue of the invalidity of the instrument or otherwise), the court may order the holder of the floating charge to indemnify the person appointed against any liability which arises solely by reason of the invalidity of the appointment.

(Former provisions: CA 1985, s. 479 (as amended by IA 1985, s. 61); CFCSA 1972, s. 23)

S. 63(1)
This provision, like its English counterpart (IA 1986, s. 35), allows both the receiver or the holder of the floating charge (for definition, see s. 70) under which he was appointed to apply to the court for guidance. Such an application was the basis for the litigation in *McKillop and Watters, Petitioners* [1994] BCC 677. Prior to IA 1985, only the appointor (and not the receiver) could make such an application.

S. 63(2)
This allows the court to excuse a receiver from trespass liability arising out of an invalid appointment, and instead to impose that liability on his appointor. For the English counterpart, see s. 34.

Section 64   Notification that receiver appointed

64(1) [Statement in invoices etc.]   Where a receiver has been appointed, every invoice, order for goods or business letter issued by or on behalf of the company or the receiver or the liquidator of the company, being a document on or in which the name of the company appears, shall contain a statement that a receiver has been appointed.

64(2) [Penalty on default]   If default is made in complying with the requirements of this section, the company and any of the following persons who knowingly and wilfully authorises or permits the default, namely any officer of the company, any liquidator of the company and any receiver, is liable to a fine.

(Former provisions: CA 1985, s. 480; CFCSA 1972, s. 24)

S. 64(1)
Invoices, business letters, etc., must disclose the fact that a receiver has been appointed. The English counterpart is to be found in s. 39.

S. 64(2)
Criminal sanctions are imposed on various named parties for breach of s. 64(1). On penalties, see s. 430 and Sch. 10.

Section 65   Information to be given by receiver

65(1) [Notification of appointment]   Where a receiver is appointed, he shall—
    (a) forthwith send to the company and publish notice of his appointment, and

(b) within 28 days after his appointment, unless the court otherwise directs, send such notice to all the creditors of the company (so far as he is aware of their addresses).

65(2)   [Restriction]   This section and the next do not apply in relation to the appointment of a receiver to act—

(a) with an existing receiver, or

(b) in place of a receiver who has died or ceased to act,

except that, where they apply to a receiver who dies or ceases to act before they have been fully complied with, the references in this section and the next to the receiver include (subject to subsection (3) of this section) his successor and any continuing receiver.

65(3)   [If company being wound up]   If the company is being wound up, this section and the next apply notwithstanding that the receiver and the liquidator are the same person, but with any necessary modifications arising from that fact.

65(4)   [Penalty for non-compliance]   If a person without reasonable excuse fails to comply with this section, he is liable to a fine and, for continued contravention, to a daily default fine.

(Former provisions: CA 1985, s. 481 (as amended by IA 1985, s. 62); CFCSA 1972, s. 25)

S. 65(1), (2), (4)

These subsections provide for a receiver on taking up his appointment to give notice to the company and its creditors. See note to s. 62(5). This obligation, once complied with, does not have to be fulfilled by successor receivers, or a later appointed joint receiver. Criminal sanctions are imposed in the event of default. On penalties, see s. 430 and Sch. 10. For the notice under s. 65(1)(*a*) see Form 4 (Scot) in the Receivers (Scotland) Regulations 1986 (SI 1986 No. 1917 (S. 141)).

S. 65(3)

This caters for the situation where the receiver and liquidator are the same person. It also applies to s. 66.

Section 66   Company's statement of affairs

66(1)   [Duty of receiver]   Where a receiver of a company is appointed, the receiver shall forthwith require some or all of the persons mentioned in subsection (3) below to make out and submit to him a statement in the prescribed form as to the affairs of the company.

66(2)   [Contents of statement]   A statement submitted under this section shall be verified by affidavit by the persons required to submit it and shall show—

(a) particulars of the company's assets, debts and liabilities;

(b) the names and addresses of its creditors;

(c) the securities held by them respectively;

(d) the dates when the securities were respectively given; and

(e) such further or other information as may be prescribed.

66(3) [Persons in s. 66(1)]   The persons referred to in subsection (1) are—

    (a) those who are or have been officers of the company;

    (b) those who have taken part in the company's formation at any time within one year before the date of the appointment of the receiver;

    (c) those who are in the company's employment or have been in its employment within that year, and are in the receiver's opinion capable of giving the information required;

    (d) those who are or have been within that year officers of or in the employment of a company which is, or within that year was, an officer of the company.

In this subsection **"employment"** includes employment under a contract for services.

66(4) [Time for statement]   Where any persons are required under this section to submit a statement of affairs to the receiver they shall do so (subject to the next subsection) before the end of the period of 21 days beginning with the day after that on which the prescribed notice of the requirement is given to them by the receiver.

66(5) [Release, extension re statement]   The receiver, if he thinks fit, may—

    (a) at any time release a person from an obligation imposed on him under subsection (1) or (2), or

    (b) either when giving the notice mentioned in subsection (4) or subsequently extend the period so mentioned,

and where the receiver has refused to exercise a power conferred by this subsection, the court, if it thinks fit, may exercise it.

66(6) [Penalty for non-compliance]   If a person without reasonable excuse fails to comply with any obligation imposed under this section, he is liable to a fine and, for continued contravention, to a daily default fine.

(Former provisions: CA 1985, s. 482 (as amended by IA 1985, s. 63); CFCSA 1972, s. 26)

S. 66(1), (2)

These provisions require the receiver to ask persons listed in s. 66(3) for a statement of the company's affairs in the prescribed form (see s. 70), containing details specified in s. 66(2). For the relevant form of the statement, see Form 5 (Scot) in the Receivers (Scotland) Regulations 1986 (SI 1986 No. 1917 (S. 141)).

S. 66(3)—(6)

Section 66(3) identifies the persons who may be required to contribute towards the submission of the statement of affairs, which must normally be submitted within 21 days of a request for it. Criminal sanctions are imposed to deal with defaults. On penalties, see s. 430 and Sch. 10.

    The receiver enjoys discretion under s. 66(5) to release certain persons from their obligations in respect of the statement of affairs or to extend the deadline for submission.

Section 67   Report by receiver

67(1) [Duty of receiver]   Where a receiver is appointed under section 51, he shall within 3 months (or such longer period as the court may allow) after his appointment, send to the registrar of companies, to the holder of the floating charge by virtue of which he was appointed and to any trustees for secured creditors of the company and (so far as he is aware of their addresses) to all such creditors a report as to the following matters, namely—

(a) the events leading up to his appointment, so far as he is aware of them;

(b) the disposal or proposed disposal by him of any property of the company and the carrying on or proposed carrying on by him of any business of the company;

(c) the amounts of principal and interest payable to the holder of the floating charge by virtue of which he was appointed and the amounts payable to preferential creditors; and

(d) the amount (if any) likely to be available for the payment of other creditors.

67(2) **[Copies of report]**   The receiver shall also, within 3 months (or such longer period as the court may allow) after his appointment, either—

(a) send a copy of the report (so far as he is aware of their addresses) to all unsecured creditors of the company, or

(b) publish in the prescribed manner a notice stating an address to which unsecured creditors of the company should write for copies of the report to be sent to them free of charge,

and (in either case), unless the court otherwise directs, lay a copy of the report before a meeting of the company's unsecured creditors summoned for the purpose on not less than 14 days' notice.

67(3) **[Condition for court direction in s. 67(2)]**   The court shall not give a direction under subsection (2) unless—

(a) the report states the intention of the receiver to apply for the direction, and

(b) a copy of the report is sent to the persons mentioned in paragraph (a) of that subsection, or a notice is published as mentioned in paragraph (b) of that subsection, not less than 14 days before the hearing of the application.

67(4) . **[Where company in liquidation]**   Where the company has gone or goes into liquidation, the receiver—

(a) shall, within 7 days after his compliance with subsection (1) or, if later, the nomination or appointment of the liquidator, send a copy of the report to the liquidator, and

(b) where he does so within the time limited for compliance with subsection (2), is not required to comply with that subsection.

67(5) **[Report to involve summary of statement of affairs]**   A report under this section shall include a summary of the statement of affairs made out and submitted under section 66 and of his comments (if any) on it.

67(6) **[Information not to be disclosed]**   Nothing in this section shall be taken as requiring any such report to include any information the disclosure of which would seriously prejudice the carrying out by the receiver of his functions.

67(7) **[S. 65(2)]**   Section 65(2) applies for the purposes of this section also.

67(8) **[Penalty for non-compliance]**   If a person without reasonable excuse fails to

119

comply with this section, he is liable to a fine and, for continued contravention, to a daily default fine.

67(9) ["Secured creditor"]   In this section **"secured creditor"**, in relation to a company, means a creditor who holds in respect of his debt a security over property of the company, and **"unsecured creditor"** shall be construed accordingly.

(Former provision: CA 1985, s. 482A (as inserted by IA 1985, s. 64))

S. 67(1), (5), (6)

These subsections require the receiver to prepare a report which must be submitted to various named parties. The report should include certain specified details but need not disclose "prejudicial" information (see s. 67(6)). It should also include a summary of the statement of affairs submitted to him under s. 66, plus any comments he wishes to make.

S. 67(2)–(4)

These provisions relate to the dissemination of the receiver's report to creditors and liquidator (if applicable). The report is to be submitted to a meeting of the company's creditors, unless the court rules to the contrary. Re s. 67(2) see the Receivers (Scotland) Regulations 1986 (SI 1986 No. 1917 (S. 141)).

S. 67(7), (9)

These are merely interpretation provisions. Section 65(2) dispenses with the need for a report when an additional receiver is appointed to act with an existing receiver, or a new receiver to replace one who has ceased to act.

S. 67(8)

The receiver will incur criminal sanctions for failure to fulfil any of the stated obligations. On penalties, see s. 430 and Sch. 10.

Section 68   Committee of creditors

68(1) [Creditors' meeting may establish committee]   Where a meeting of creditors is summoned under section 67, the meeting may, if it thinks fit, establish a committee (**"the creditors' committee"**) to exercise the functions conferred on it by or under this Act.

68(2) [Powers of committee]   If such a committee is established, the committee may on giving not less than 7 days' notice require the receiver to attend before it at any reasonable time and furnish it with such information relating to the carrying out by him of his functions as it may reasonably require.

(Former provision: CA 1985, s. 482B (as introduced by IA 1985, s. 65))

S. 68(1)

A meeting of creditors summoned under s. 67(2) may set up a committee of creditors.

S. 68(2)

This committee can make reasonable requests for information from the receiver. It may be unreasonable to request information covered by s. 67(6).

Section 69   Enforcement of receiver's duty to make returns, etc.

69(1)   [Court order re receiver's default]   If any receiver—

(a) having made default in filing, delivering or making any return, account or other document, or in giving any notice, which a receiver is by law required to file, deliver, make or give, fails to make good the default within 14 days after the service on him of a notice requiring him to do so; or

(b) has, after being required at any time by the liquidator of the company so to do, failed to render proper accounts of his receipts and payments and to vouch the same and to pay over to the liquidator the amount properly payable to him,

the court may, on an application made for the purpose, make an order directing the receiver to make good the default within such time as may be specified in the order.

69(2)   [Application to court]   In the case of any such default as is mentioned in subsection 1(a), an application for the purposes of this section may be made by any member or creditor of the company or by the registrar of companies; and, in the case of any such default as is mentioned in subsection (1)(b), the application shall be made by the liquidator; and, in either case, the order may provide that all expenses of and incidental to the application shall be borne by the receiver.

69(3)   [Other enactments]   Nothing in this section prejudices the operation of any enactments imposing penalties on receivers in respect of any such default as is mentioned in subsection (1).

(Former provisions: CA 1985, s. 483; CFCSA 1972, s. 27)

S. 69(1)

The court can compel a receiver to submit returns, etc., if he fails to comply with a notice to do so. For the English counterpart, see s. 41.

S. 69(2)

This subsection identifies the applicants for an enforcement order under s. 69(1).

S. 69(3)

This enforcement mechanism is in addition to any criminal sanctions that may be imposed by individual provisions.

Section 70   Interpretation for Chapter II

70(1)   [Definitions]   In this Chapter, unless the contrary intention appears, the following expressions have the following meanings respectively assigned to them—

"**company**" means an incorporated company (whether or not a company within the meaning of the Companies Act) which the Court of Session has jurisdiction to wind up;

"**fixed security**", in relation to any property of a company, means any security, other than a floating charge or a charge having the nature of a floating charge, which on the winding up of the company in Scotland would be treated as an effective security over that property, and (without prejudice to that generality) includes a security over that property, being a heritable security within the meaning of the Conveyancing and Feudal Reform (Scotland) Act 1970;

"instrument of appointment" has the meaning given by section 53(1);

"prescribed" means prescribed by regulations made under this Chapter by the Secretary of State;

"receiver" means a receiver of such part of the property of the company as is subject to the floating charge by virtue of which he has been appointed under section 51;

"register of charges" means the register kept by the registrar of companies for the purposes of Chapter II of Part XII of the Companies Act;

"secured debenture" means a bond, debenture, debenture stock or other security which, either itself or by reference to any other instrument, creates a floating charge over all or any part of the property of the company, but does not include a security which creates no charge other than a fixed security; and

"series of secured debentures" means two or more secured debentures created as a series by the company in such a manner that the holders thereof are entitled pari passu to the benefit of the floating charge.

70(2) [Reference to holder of floating charge] Where a floating charge, secured debenture or series of secured debentures has been created by the company, then, except where the context otherwise requires, any reference in this Chapter to the holder of the floating charge shall—

    (a) where the floating charge, secured debenture or series of secured debentures provides for a receiver to be appointed by any person or body, be construed as a reference to that person or body;

    (b) where, in the case of a series of secured debentures, no such provision has been made therein but—

      (i) there are trustees acting for the debenture-holders under and in accordance with a trust deed, be construed as a reference to those trustees, and

      (ii) where no such trustees are acting, be construed as a reference to—

        (aa) a majority in nominal value of those present or represented by proxy and voting at a meeting of debenture-holders at which the holders of at least one-third in nominal value of the outstanding debentures of the series are present or so represented, or

        (bb) where no such meeting is held, the holders of at least one-half in nominal value of the outstanding debentures of the series.

70(3) [Reference to floating charge etc.] Any reference in this Chapter to a floating charge, secured debenture, series of secured debentures or instument creating a charge includes, except where the context otherwise requires, a reference to that floating charge, debenture, series of debentures or instrument as varied by any instrument.

70(4) [Reference to instrument] References in this Chapter to the instrument by which a floating charge was created are, in the case of a floating charge created by words in a bond or other written acknowledgement, references to the bond or, as the case may be, the other written acknowledgement.

(Former provisions: CA 1985, ss. 462(4), 484 and 486; CFCSA 1972, ss. 29, 31)

General note

These are general interpretation provisions for the purposes of ss. 50–71 and their main aim is to link these provisions dealing with Scottish receiverships with the sections in CA 1985 regulating the floating charge in Scotland, and also with the general rules of Scots law.

Section 71   Prescription of forms, etc.; regulations

71(1)   [Prescribed forms]   The notice referred to in section 62(5), and the notice referred to in section 65(1)(a) shall be in such form as may be prescribed.

71(2)   [Regulations]   Any power conferred by this Chapter on the Secretary of State to make regulations is exercisable by statutory instrument; and a statutory instrument made in the exercise of the power so conferred to prescribe a fee is subject to annulment in pursuance of a resolution of either House of Parliament.

(Former provisions: CA 1985, s. 485; CFCSA 1972, s. 29)

S. 71(1)

The notice of a receiver taking office or ceasing to act is in a form prescribed by the Receivers (Scotland) Regulations 1986 (SI 1986 No. 1917 (S. 141)). See note to ss. 62, 65.

S. 71(2)

The Secretary of State may make regulations, but where the power involves the prescribing of a fee it is subject to annulment by either the House of Lords or the Commons. See the regulations referred to above.

Chapter III — Receivers' Powers in Great Britain as a Whole

Section 72   Cross-border operation of receivership provisions

72(1)   [Receiver's powers]   A receiver appointed under the law of either part of Great Britain in respect of the whole or any part of any property or undertaking of a company and in consequence of the company having created a charge which, as created, was a floating charge may exercise his powers in the other part of Great Britain so far as their exercise is not inconsistent with the law applicable there.

72(2)   ["Receiver"]   In subsection (1) **"receiver"** includes a manager and a person who is appointed both receiver and manager.

(Former provisions: CA 1985, s. 724; Administration of Justice Act 1977, s. 7)

General note

This section allows a receiver appointed in England to act in Scotland, and vice versa, in so far as this is not inconsistent with local law. This provision, which can be traced back to 1970, is less important now that the Scots have a system of receivership running along similar lines to the English régime. For the utility of s. 72 see *Norfolk House* v *Repsol Petroleum* 1992 SLT 235.

PART IV — WINDING UP OF COMPANIES REGISTERED UNDER THE COMPANIES ACTS

General comment on Part IV

This Part of the Act deals with the winding up of all registered companies, whether solvent or insolvent. For this purpose, the term "company" (or "registered company") is defined by CA 1985, s. 735 (see the note to s. 73(1) below). The winding up provisions are extended to unregistered companies by Pt. V of the Act: for the definition of "unregistered company", see s. 220. Insolvent partnerships may also be wound up under Pt. V of the Act as unregistered companies by virtue of the Insolvent Partnerships Order 1994 (SI 1994 No. 2421): see the note to s. 420.

Part IV applies generally to Scotland as well as to England and Wales, apart from particular sections which are noted as they occur.

The former Companies (Winding Up) Rules 1949 have been replaced by IR 1986, Pt. 4.

The changes made to the law by IA 1985 and IA 1986 do not generally apply retrospectively, so as to affect liquidations which were already in progress when these Acts came into force: Sch. 11, para. 4. The few exceptions to this (Sch. 11, paras. 5–9) are noted at the appropriate places in the text which follows.

Where a building society is being wound up under Pt. X of the Building Societies Act 1986, Pts. IV, VI, VII, XII and XIII of the present Act (and, for Northern Ireland, Pt. XX of the Companies (Northern Ireland) Order 1986) apply, subject to the modifications made by Sch. 15 of that Act: see Building Societies Act 1986, s. 90 and Sch. 15, as amended by CA 1989, s. 211(1), (2) and Sch. 24. Note that the amendments made by CA 1989: (i) require the liquidator of a building society to be a qualified insolvency practitioner under Pt. XIII of IA 1986 (s. 211(2) (*a*)), and (ii) extend the concept of "shadow director" to building societies (s. 211(2)(*b*)). Transitional provisions contained in SI 1990 No. 1392 (C. 41), art. 7 protect the position of liquidators appointed prior to the commencement of CA 1989, s. 211(2)(*a*), i.e. 31 July 1990.

The provisions of IA 1986 are made to apply to the winding up of an industrial and provident society (such as a co-operative) by the Industrial and Provident Societies Act 1965, s. 55(*a*) (as amended by IA 1986, s. 439(2) and Sch. 14), subject to the modifications which are set out in that Act. Other bodies, such as friendly societies, which are not provided for by specific legislation, may be wound up as unregistered companies under Pt. V of IA 1986: see *Re Victoria Society, Knottingley* [1913] 1 Ch. 167.

Chapter I — Preliminary

Section 73　Alternative modes of winding up

73(1)　[Voluntary, by court]　The winding up of a company, within the meaning given to that expression by section 735 of the Companies Act, may be either voluntary (Chapters II, III, IV and V in this Part) or by the court (Chapter VI).

73(2)　[Application of Ch. I, VII–X]　This Chapter, and Chapters VII to X, relate to winding up generally, except where otherwise stated.

(Former provisions: CA 1985, s. 501; CA 1948, s. 211)

General note

Prior to the coming into force of this Act, there were three modes of winding up: (1) voluntary, (2) by the court and (3) subject to the supervision of the court. The last of these methods was little used, and was abolished by IA 1985, s. 235(3) and Sch. 10, Pt. II. A voluntary winding up is commenced by the passing of a resolution (usually a special or extraordinary resolution) by the company in general meeting (see s. 84): it may be either a "members' voluntary winding up", conducted under the control of the members, if the directors are able to make a declaration of solvency under s. 89, or a "creditors' voluntary winding up", if the directors cannot make such a declaration, in which case the creditors have control (see ss. 89–90). A winding up by the court (or "compulsory winding up"), as the name suggests, follows from the making of a court order (see ss. 122ff).

"Company", for the purposes of this section, is defined by CA 1985, s. 735(1) and (3) as follows:

"S. 735　'Company', etc.

735(1)　In this Act—

　(a)　**'company'** means a company formed and registered under this Act, or an existing company;

　(b)　**'existing company'** means a company formed and registered under the former Companies Acts, but does not include a company registered under the Joint Stock Companies Acts, the Companies Act 1862 or the Companies (Consolidation) Act 1908 in what was then Ireland;

　(c)　**'the former Companies Acts'** means the Joint Stock Companies Acts, the Companies Act 1862, the Companies (Consolidation) Act 1908, the Companies Act 1929 and the Companies Acts 1948 to 1983.

　　. . .

735(3)　**'The Joint Stock Companies Acts'** means the Joint Stock Companies Act 1856, the Joint Stock Companies Acts 1856, 1857, the Joint Stock Banking Companies Act 1857 and the Act to enable Joint Stock Banking Companies to be formed on the principle of limited liability, or any one or more of those Acts (as the case may require), but does not include the Joint Stock Companies Act 1844."

Section 74　Liability as contributories of present and past members

74(1)　[Liability to contribute]　When a company is wound up, every present and past member is liable to contribute to its assets to any amount sufficient for payment of its debts and liabilities, and the expenses of the winding up, and for the adjustment of the rights of the contributories among themselves.

74(2)   [Qualifications to liability]   This is subject as follows—

(a)   a past member is not liable to contribute if he has ceased to be a member for one year or more before the commencement of the winding up;

(b)   a past member is not liable to contribute in respect of any debt or liability of the company contracted after he ceased to be a member;

(c)   a past member is not liable to contribute, unless it appears to the court that the existing members are unable to satisfy the contributions required to be made by them in pursuance of the Companies Act and this Act;

(d)   in the case of a company limited by shares, no contribution is required from any member exceeding the amount (if any) unpaid on the shares in respect of which he is liable as a present or past member;

(e)   nothing in the Companies Act or this Act invalidates any provision contained in a policy of insurance or other contract whereby the liability of individual members on the policy or contract is restricted, or whereby the funds of the company are alone made liable in respect of the policy or contract;

(f)   a sum due to any member of the company (in his character of a member) by way of dividends, profits or otherwise is not deemed to be a debt of the company, payable to that member in a case of competition between himself and any other creditor not a member of the company, but any such sum may be taken into account for the purpose of the final adjustment of the rights of the contributories among themselves.

74(3)   [Company limited by guarantee]   In the case of a company limited by guarantee, no contribution is required from any member exceeding the amount undertaken to be contributed by him to the company's assets in the event of its being wound up; but if it is a company with a share capital, every member of it is liable (in addition to the amount so undertaken to be contributed to the assets), to contribute to the extent of any sums unpaid on shares held by him.

(Former provisions: CA 1985, s. 502; CA 1948, s. 212(1), (3))

S. 74(1)

A "contributory" is a member or past member of the company who is liable to contribute to the assets of the company in a winding up (s. 79). This includes a member whose shares are fully paid: *Re Anglesea Colliery Company* (1866) LR 1 Ch. 555, and a former member: *Re Consolidated Goldfields of New Zealand Ltd* [1953] Ch. 689. But the court has power to order the rectification of the register of members with retrospective effect, where it is satisfied that a person has never been a member: see *Barbor* v *Middleton* (1988) 4 BCC 681.

S. 74(2)

This provision defines the extent to which both present and past members are liable to contribute to the assets. The principle of limited liability will, where appropriate, apply so as to restrict the amount payable (para. (*d*)). A past member is liable only in the circumstances listed in paras. (*a*) to (*c*).

Paragraph (*f*) subordinates any sums payable by the company to any member *qua* member (e.g. a dividend declared but not paid) to the company's obligations to its general creditors. The member cannot therefore set off these sums directly against his own contribution.

S. 74(3)
This states the limit of the liability of a contributory where a company is limited by guarantee.

Section 75   Directors, etc. with unlimited liability

75(1)   [Liability in winding up]   In the winding up of a limited company, any director or manager (whether past or present) whose liability is under the Companies Act unlimited is liable, in addition to his liability (if any) to contribute as an ordinary member, to make a further contribution as if he were at the commencement of the winding up a member of an unlimited company.

75(2)   [Qualifications to liability]   However—

(a) a past director or manager is not liable to make such further contribution if he has ceased to hold office for a year or more before the commencement of the winding up;

(b) a past director or manager is not liable to make such further contribution in respect of any debt or liability of the company contracted after he ceased to hold office;

(c) subject to the company's articles, a director or manager is not liable to make such further contribution unless the court deems it necessary to require that contribution in order to satisfy the company's debts and liabilities, and the expenses of the winding up.

(Former provisions: CA 1985, s. 503; CA 1948, s. 212(2))

General note
The CA 1985, s. 306, which is virtually never used in practice, enables a limited company to provide by its memorandum for its directors and managers to have unlimited liability. This section deals with the winding up of such companies.

Section 76   Liability of past directors and shareholders

76(1)   [Application]   This section applies where a company is being wound up and—

(a) it has under Chapter VII of Part V of the Companies Act (redeemable shares; purchase by a company of its own shares) made a payment out of capital in respect of the redemption or purchase of any of its own shares (the payment being referred to below as "the relevant payment"), and

(b) the aggregate amount of the company's assets and the amounts paid by way of contribution to its assets (apart from this section) is not sufficient for payment of its debts and liabilities, and the expenses of the winding up.

76(2)   [Contribution of past shareholders, directors]   If the winding up commenced within one year of the date on which the relevant payment was made, then—

(a) the person from whom the shares were redeemed or purchased, and

(b) the directors who signed the statutory declaration made in accordance with section 173(3) of the Companies Act for purposes of the redemption or purchase (except a director who shows that he had reasonable grounds for forming the opinion set out in the declaration),

are, so as to enable that insufficiency to be met, liable to contribute to the following extent to the company's assets.

76(3)   [Amount payable]   A person from whom any of the shares were redeemed or purchased is liable to contribute an amount not exceeding so much of the relevant payment as was made by the company in respect of his shares; and the directors are jointly and severally liable with that person to contribute that amount.

76(4)   [Application to court]   A person who has contributed any amount to the assets in pursuance of this section may apply to the court for an order directing any other person jointly and severally liable in respect of that amount to pay him such amount as the court thinks just and equitable.

76(5)   [Non-application of ss. 74, 75]   Sections 74 and 75 do not apply in relation to liability accruing by virtue of this section.

76(6)   [Regulations]   This section is deemed included in Chapter VII of Part V of the Companies Act for the purposes of the Secretary of State's power to make regulations under section 179 of that Act.

(Former provisions: CA 1985, s. 504; CA 1948, ss. 58, 61)

General note

When a payment has been made out of capital by a private company in connection with a redemption or repurchase of shares under CA 1985, ss. 171ff, and the company is wound up insolvent within one year of the payment, this section applies so as to make the recipient of the payment liable to refund it in whole or part and, in some circumstances also, the directors jointly and severally liable with him.

Note that although the persons liable under this section fall within the definition of "contributory" for the purposes of this Act, they will not normally be regarded as "contributories" when construing a company's articles (see s. 79(3)).

Section 77   Limited company formerly unlimited

77(1)   [Application]   This section applies in the case of a company being wound up which was at some former time registered as unlimited but has re-registered—

(a) as a public company under section 43 of the Companies Act (or the former corresponding provision, section 5 of the Companies Act 1980), or

(b) as a limited company under section 51 of the Companies Act (or the former corresponding provision, section 44 of the Companies Act 1967).

77(2)   [Contribution by past members]   Notwithstanding section 74(2)(a) above, a past member of the company who was a member of it at the time of re-registration, if the winding up commences within the period of 3 years beginning with the day on which the company was re-registered, is liable to contribute to the assets of the company in respect of debts and liabilities contracted before that time.

77(3) **[If no past members existing members]** If no persons who were members of the company at that time are existing members of it, a person who at that time was a present or past member is liable to contribute as above notwithstanding that the existing members have satisfied the contributions required to be made by them under the Companies Act and this Act.

This applies subject to section 74(2)(a) above and to subsection (2) of this section, but notwithstanding section 74(2)(c).

77(4) **[No limitation on contribution]** Notwithstanding section 74(2)(d) and (3), there is no limit on the amount which a person who, at that time, was a past or present member of the company is liable to contribute as above.

(Former provisions: CA 1985, s. 505; CA 1948, s. 44(7) (as amended by CA 1980, s. 7(4)))

General note

The provisions of the Companies Acts mentioned in s. 77(1) enable an unlimited company to re-register as limited, but the unlimited liability of both present and past members continues if a winding up ensues within three years of the date of re-registration. The present section deals with the liability of these persons as contributories.

Section 78   Unlimited company formerly limited

78(1) **[Application]** This section applies in the case of a company being wound up which was at some former time registered as limited but has been re-registered as unlimited under section 49 of the Companies Act (or the former corresponding provision, section 43 of the Companies Act 1967).

78(2) **[Limitation on contribution]** A person who, at the time when the application for the company to be re-registered was lodged, was a past member of the company and did not after that again become a member of it is not liable to contribute to the assets of the company more than he would have been liable to contribute had the company not been re-registered.

(Former provisions: CA 1985, s. 506; CA 1948, s. 43(6))

General note

When a limited company is converted to an unlimited company under CA 1985, s. 49, the limited liability of past members is preserved by this provision.

Section 79   Meaning of "contributory"

79(1) **["Contributory"]** In this Act and the Companies Act the expression **"contributory"** means every person liable to contribute to the assets of a company in the event of its being wound up, and for the purposes of all proceedings for determining, and all proceedings prior to the final determination of, the persons who are to be deemed contributories, includes any person alleged to be a contributory.

79(2) **[Qualification]** The reference in subsection (1) to persons liable to contribute to the assets does not include a person so liable by virtue of a declaration by the court under section 213 (imputed responsibility for company's fraudulent trading) or section 214 (wrongful trading) in Chapter X of this Part.

79(3) **[Reference in articles]** A reference in a company's articles to a contributory does not (unless the context requires) include a person who is a contributory only by virtue of section 76.

This subsection is deemed included in Chapter VII of Part V of the Companies Act for the purposes of the Secretary of State's power to make regulations under section 179 of that Act.

(Former provisions: CA 1985, s. 507; CA 1948, s. 213 (as amended by CA 1981, ss. 58(6), 61); IA 1985, Sch. 6, para. 5)

General note

This section defines the term "contributory" for the purposes of both the present Act and CA 1985. It incorporates (by s. 79(2)) an amendment made by IA 1985, Sch. 6, para. 5 which makes it plain that a person is not deemed a contributory merely because he has been ordered by the court to contribute to the company's assets following a finding of fraudulent or wrongful trading under ss. 213, 214.

See also the note to s. 74(1).

Section 80　Nature of contributory's liability

80 The liability of a contributory creates a debt (in England and Wales in the nature of a specialty) accruing due from him at the time when his liability commenced, but payable at the times when calls are made for enforcing the liability.

(Former provisions: CA 1985, s. 508; CA 1948, s. 214)

General note

This section is identical with the repealed CA 1985, s. 508. The period of limitation applicable to a specialty debt is 12 years, instead of the normal six.

Section 81　Contributories in case of death of a member

81(1) **[Personal representative liable]** If a contributory dies either before or after he has been placed on the list of contributories, his personal representatives, and the heirs and legatees of heritage of his heritable estate in Scotland, are liable in a due course of administration to contribute to the assets of the company in discharge of his liability and are contributories accordingly.

81(2) **[Where personal representatives on list of contributories]** Where the personal representatives are placed on the list of contributories, the heirs or legatees of heritage need not be added, but they may be added as and when the court thinks fit.

81(3) **[Where default in payment]** If in England and Wales the personal representatives make default in paying any money ordered to be paid by them, proceedings may be taken for administering the estate of the deceased contributory and for compelling payment out of it of the money due.

(Former provisions: CA 1985, s. 509; CA 1948, s. 215)

General note

This section provides that on the death of a contributory, his personal representatives (or their Scottish counterparts) are substituted for him as contributories.

Section 82   Effect of contributory's bankruptcy

82(1)   [Application]   The following applies if a contributory becomes bankrupt, either before or after he has been placed on the list of contributories.

82(2)   [Trustee in bankruptcy a contributory]   His trustee in bankruptcy represents him for all purposes of the winding up, and is a contributory accordingly.

82(3)   [Trustee called on to admit to proof]   The trustee may be called on to admit to proof against the bankrupt's estate, or otherwise allow to be paid out of the bankrupt's assets in due course of law, any money due from the bankrupt in respect of his liability to contribute to the company's assets.

82(4)   [Estimated value of liability to future calls]   There may be proved against the bankrupt's estate the estimated value of his liability to future calls as well as calls already made.

(Former provisions: CA 1985, s. 510; CA 1948, s. 216)

S. 82(1), (2)

The trustee in bankruptcy is deemed a contributory and represents the bankrupt for all purposes of the winding up. It was held under the virtually identical wording of CA 1948, s. 216 that this section does not empower a contributory's trustee in bankruptcy to present a winding-up petition (unless the trustee has been registered as a member), since its provisions only become effective once a winding up is in place: *Re H L Bolton (Engineering) Co. Ltd* [1956] Ch. 577, at p. 582–583. In Scotland, however, the wording of the Bankruptcy (Scotland) Act 1985, s. 31 is sufficiently wide to empower a trustee to petition: *Taylor, Petitioner; Cumming's Trustee* v *Glenrinnes Farms Ltd* [1993] BCC 829.

S. 82(3), (4)

These subsections deal with the proof against the bankrupt's estate of his liability to the company as a contributory.

Section 83   Companies registered under Companies Act, Part XXII, Chapter II

83(1)   [Application]   The following applies in the event of a company being wound up which has been registered under section 680 of the Companies Act (or previous corresponding provisions in the Companies Act 1948 or earlier Acts).

83(2)   [Contributories re debts and liabilities before registration]   Every person is a contributory, in respect of the company's debts and liabilities contracted before registration, who is liable—

(a) to pay, or contribute to the payment of, any debt or liability so contracted, or

(b) to pay, or contribute to the payment of, any sum for the adjustment of the rights of the members among themselves in respect of any such debt or liability, or

(c) to pay, or contribute to the amount of, the expenses of winding up the company, so far as relates to the debts or liabilities above-mentioned.

83(3) [Amounts liable to be contributed]   Every contributory is liable to contribute to the assets of the company, in the course of the winding up, all sums due from him in respect of any such liability.

83(4) [Death, etc. of contributory]   In the event of the death, bankruptcy or insolvency of any contributory, provisions of this Act, with respect to the personal representatives, to the heirs and legatees of the heritage of the heritable estate in Scotland of deceased contributories and to the trustees of bankrupt or insolvent contributories respectively, apply.

(Former provisions: CA 1985, s. 511; CA 1948, s. 394(f), (g))

General note

The companies referred to are those not formed under the Companies Acts but authorised to register under CA 1985, s. 680 or its predecessors – e.g. a company incorporated by a private Act of Parliament.

Chapter II — Voluntary Winding Up (Introductory and General)

RESOLUTIONS FOR, AND COMMENCEMENT OF, VOLUNTARY WINDING UP

Section 84   Circumstances in which company may be wound up voluntarily

84(1) [Circumstances]   A company may be wound up voluntarily—

   (a) when the period (if any) fixed for the duration of the company by the articles expires, or the event (if any) occurs, on the occurrence of which the articles provide that the company is to be dissolved, and the company in general meeting has passed a resolution requiring it to be wound up voluntarily;

   (b) if the company resolves by special resolution that it be wound up voluntarily;

   (c) if the company resolves by extraordinary resolution to the effect that it cannot by reason of its liabilities continue its business, and that it is advisable to wind up.

84(2) [Definition]   In this Act the expression **"a resolution for voluntary winding up"** means a resolution passed under any of the paragraphs of subsection (1).

84(3) [Copy of resolution to registrar]   A resolution passed under paragraph (a) of subsection (1), as well as a special resolution under paragraph (b) and an extraordinary resolution under paragraph (c), is subject to section 380 of the Companies Act (copy of resolution to be forwarded to registrar of companies within 15 days).

(Former provisions: CA 1985, s. 572; CA 1948, ss. 278, 143(4)(e))

S. 84(1)

Paragraph (*a*) calls for a "resolution" (i.e. an *ordinary* resolution), para. (*b*) for a *special* resolution and para. (*c*) for an *extraordinary* resolution. An ordinary resolution is one passed by a simple majority of votes. The latter two terms are defined by CA 1985, s. 378: each requires a three-fourths majority vote, but a special resolution normally needs not less than 21 days' notice (unless this is waived under s. 378(3)). The intention to propose a resolution as a special or extraordinary resolution must be specifically stated in the notice.

S. 84(3)

The obligation to register these resolutions is laid down also by CA 1985, s. 380(4)(*a*), (*b*) and (*j*). The liquidator, for the purposes of these provisions, is deemed to be an officer of the company and liable accordingly to penal sanctions for non-compliance (CA 1985, s. 380(7)).

Section 85   Notice of resolution to wind up

85(1)   [Notice in Gazette]   When a company has passed a resolution for voluntary winding up, it shall, within 14 days after the passing of the resolution, give notice of the resolution by advertisement in the Gazette.

85(2)   [Penalty on default]   If default is made in complying with this section, the company and every officer of it who is in default is liable to a fine and, for continued contravention, to a daily default fine.

For purposes of this subsection the liquidator is deemed an officer of the company.

(Former provisions: CA 1985, s. 573; CA 1948, s. 279)

General note

It is the responsibility of the company and its officers (including the liquidator: s. 85(2)) to see that notice of the resolution to wind up is gazetted. The liquidator, when appointed, is under a separate obligation to publish notice of his appointment in the Gazette: see s. 109.

S. 85(2)

On penalties, see s. 430 and Sch. 10.

Section 86   Commencement of winding up

86   A voluntary winding up is deemed to commence at the time of the passing of the resolution for voluntary winding up.

(Former provisions: CA 1985, s. 574; CA 1948, s. 280)

General note

The "commencement" of a winding up is significant for many purposes under this Act and, previously, the Companies Acts. For the corresponding provision in relation to a winding up by the court, see s. 129.

It should be noted that this section refers to the "time" of commencement, as does s. 129. In contrast, s. 278, the corresponding provision in bankruptcy, states that a bankruptcy "commences *with the day* on which the order is made" – an expression which clearly relates back to the preceding midnight – while other sections of the Act and provisions in the rules refer to the "date" of an event (see, e.g. s. 183(2)(*a*): "date on which he had notice"; "date of commencement of the winding up"; s. 240(3): "date of the commencement of the winding up"; and r. 4.91 (1): "date when the company went into liquidation"). It must be inferred that the draftsmen used these different wordings deliberately, so that where the word "time" is used the normal convention that "the law takes no account of part of a day" (*Trow* v *Ind Coope (West Midlands) Ltd & Anor* [1967] 2 QB 899) is ousted, and an event is to be pinpointed to the precise time of the day when it occurred. This could be an important consideration in some areas of commerce (e.g. financial dealing rooms), where even seconds can count.

CONSEQUENCES OF RESOLUTION TO WIND UP

Section 87   Effect on business and status of company

87(1)   **[Cessation of business]**   In case of a voluntary winding up, the company shall from the commencement of the winding up cease to carry on its business, except so far as may be required for its beneficial winding up.

87(2)   **[Continuation of corporate state, etc.]**   However, the corporate state and corporate powers of the company, notwithstanding anything to the contrary in its articles, continue until the company is dissolved.

(Former provisions: CA 1985, s. 575; CA 1948, s. 281)

S. 87(1)

In the case of a compulsory winding up, the liquidator may carry on the company's business, "so far as may be necessary for its beneficial winding up" (see s. 167(1)(*a*) and Sch. IV, para. 5 and, in Scotland, s. 169), but normally only with the sanction of the court or the liquidation committee. In a voluntary winding up the question whether it is beneficial to continue the business is a matter for the liquidator's own bona fide judgment.

S. 87(2)

The corporate personality of the company in a compulsory winding up also continues until dissolution, although this is not expressly stated in the Act. It follows that acts are done by the liquidator in the name of the company, and not in his own name.

Section 88   Avoidance of share transfers, etc. after winding-up resolution

88   Any transfer of shares, not being a transfer made to or with the sanction of the liquidator, and any alteration in the status of the company's members, made after the commencement of a voluntary winding up, is void.

(Former provisions: CA 1985, s. 576; CA 1948, s. 282)

General note

In a compulsory winding up, a transfer of shares made after the commencement of the winding up is similarly void, but can be validated only by order of the court: see s. 127.

DECLARATION OF SOLVENCY

Section **89**   Statutory declaration of solvency

89(1)   [Declaration by directors]   Where it is proposed to wind up a company voluntarily, the directors (or, in the case of a company having more than two directors, the majority of them) may at a directors' meeting make a statutory declaration to the effect that they have made a full inquiry into the company's affairs and that, having done so, they have formed the opinion that the company will be able to pay its debts in full, together with interest at the official rate (as defined in section 251), within such period, not exceeding 12 months from the commencement of the winding up, as may be specified in the declaration.

89(2)   [Requirements for declaration]   Such a declaration by the directors has no effect for purposes of this Act unless—

(a) it is made within the 5 weeks immediately preceding the date of the passing of the resolution for winding up, or on that date but before the passing of the resolution, and

(b) it embodies a statement of the company's assets and liabilities as at the latest practicable date before the making of the declaration.

89(3)   [Declaration to registrar]   The declaration shall be delivered to the registrar of companies before the expiration of 15 days immediately following the date on which the resolution for winding up is passed.

89(4)   [Offence, penalty]   A director making a declaration under this section without having reasonable grounds for the opinion that the company will be able to pay its debts in full, together with interest at the official rate, within the period specified is liable to imprisonment or a fine, or both.

89(5)   [Presumption]   If the company is wound up in pursuance of a resolution passed within 5 weeks after the making of the declaration, and its debts (together with interest at the official rate) are not paid or provided for in full within the period specified, it is to be presumed (unless the contrary is shown) that the director did not have reasonable grounds for his opinion.

89(6)   [Penalty for non-compliance with s. 89(3)]   If a declaration required by subsection (3) to be delivered to the registrar is not so delivered within the time prescribed by that subsection, the company and every officer in default is liable to a fine and, for continued contravention, to a daily default fine.

(Former provisions: CA 1985, s. 577 (as amended by IA 1985, Sch. 6, para. 35); CA 1948, s. 283 (1)–(3) (as amended by CA 1981, s. 105(1)))

General note

The category of a voluntary winding up (members' or creditors': see s. 90), and the legal rules which apply to it in consequence, depend on whether a statutory declaration of solvency has been made under this section. The responsibility for assessing the likely solvency of the company is placed squarely on the directors (or a majority of them): if they make the declaration, the matter proceeds as a members' voluntary winding up under the control of the members; if they do not, the creditors take over. The severe penalties and reversed onus of proof prescribed by s. 89(4) and (5) provide directors with a strong deterrent against making a declaration of solvency irresponsibly.

There is no obligation upon the directors to make a statutory declaration when the company is insolvent or not believed to be solvent: the matter simply proceeds as a creditors' voluntary winding up.

S. 89(1)

A statutory declaration is a formal declaration made before a justice of the peace or commissioner for oaths, and is equivalent to an oath for most legal purposes, including the law of perjury. The declaration here required must be made at a directors' meeting, held before the shareholders' meeting at which the resolution for winding up is to be passed, and within the time specified in s. 89(2).

The directors must themselves fix the period, not exceeding 12 months from the commencement of the winding up, within which they predict that the company will be able to pay its debts in full. Since the directors' declaration must be made with reference to a future date, they should plainly take into account any prospective and contingent liabilities of which they are aware. On the other hand, it should be noted that they are not required to assert that the company itself is, or will be, "solvent": if the directors have a firm commitment from a third party (such as a parent company) that it will meet any liabilities that the company cannot discharge from its own resources, they may well be justified in making a declaration and allowing the liquidation to proceed as a members' voluntary winding up.

S. 89(2)

The five week period is reckoned back from the date of the winding-up resolution, and the declaration must be based on a financial statement which is as up to date as practicable.

S. 89(3)

Form 4.70 should be used.

S. 89(4)–(6)

The penalties under s. 89(4) are stringent – up to two years' imprisonment and an unlimited fine, if the proceedings are on indictment (see Sch. 10). If a director's prediction of solvency turns out in the event to be wrong, s. 89(5) reverses the normal burden of proof and requires him to show that in fact he had reasonable grounds for making it.

On penalties, see s. 430 and Sch. 10.

Section 90   Distinction between "members' " and "creditors' " voluntary winding up

90   A winding up in the case of which a directors' statutory declaration under section 89 has been made is a "members' voluntary winding up"; and a winding up in the case of which such a declaration has not been made is a "creditors' voluntary winding up".

(Former provisions: CA 1985, s. 578; CA 1948, s. 283(4))

General note

In the sections of the Act which follow, Ch. III (ss. 91–96) applies only to a members' voluntary winding up and Ch. IV (ss. 97–106) only to a creditors' voluntary winding up, while Ch. V (ss. 107–116) applies to a voluntary winding up of either kind. This was formerly made clear in the

Companies Acts by introductory sections in each case (e.g. CA 1985, ss. 579, 587, 596); in the present Act it is left (with the exception of Ch. IV) to be inferred from the title to the chapter in question. (On the relevance of chapter titles in the construction of statutes, see the comment preceding s. 230.)

Chapter III — Members' Voluntary Winding Up

Section 91   Appointment of liquidator

91(1)   [Appointment by general meeting]   In a members' voluntary winding up, the company in general meeting shall appoint one or more liquidators for the purpose of winding up the company's affairs and distributing its assets.

91(2)   [Cessation of directors' powers]   On the appointment of a liquidator all the powers of the directors cease, except so far as the company in general meeting or the liquidator sanctions their continuance.

(Former provisions: CA 1985, s. 580 (as amended by IA 1985, Sch. 10, Pt. II); CA 1948, s. 285)

S. 91(1)
For the relevant rules, see IR 1986, rr. 4.139, 4.141.

S. 91(2)
On the making of a winding-up order *by the court* the appointments of all the directors are terminated automatically: *Measures Brothers Ltd* v *Measures* [1910] 2 Ch. 248. It appears from this subsection that a resolution for voluntary winding up does not of itself operate to remove the directors from office, for if this were the case it would not be possible to sanction the continuance of their powers. This view is, perhaps, confirmed by some reported cases concerning employees, e.g. *Midland Counties District Bank Ltd* v *Attwood* [1905] 1 Ch. 357, although there are *dicta* in other cases to the contrary (e.g. *Reigate* v *Union Manufacturing Co. (Ramsbottom) Ltd & Anor* [1918] 1 KB 592, at p. 606). It is also endorsed by s. 114(2),(3).
    The equivalent section in the Companies Acts formerly empowered the company in general meeting to fix the liquidator's remuneration: see, e.g. the repealed CA 1985, s. 580(1). This matter is now provided for by the rules: see IR 1986, r. 4.148A.

Section 92   Power to fill vacancy in office of liquidator

92(1)   [Filling of vacancy]   If a vacancy occurs by death, resigation or otherwise in the office of liquidator appointed by the company, the company in general meeting may, subject to any arrangement with its creditors, fill the vacancy.

92(2)   [Convening of general meeting]   For that purpose a general meeting may be convened by any contributory or, if there were more liquidators than one, by the continuing liquidators.

92(3)   [Manner of holding meeting]   The meeting shall be held in manner provided by this Act or by the articles, or in such manner as may, on application by any contributory or by the continuing liquidators, be determined by the court.

(Former provisions: CA 1985, s. 581; CA 1948, s. 286)

S. 92(3)

The reference to "this Act" is probably a slip: fairly obviously, it should have been to CA 1985, as was the case in the pre-consolidation provision (CA 1985, s. 581(3)). The present Act contains no provisions regulating the holding of meetings in a members' voluntary winding up (apart from s. 194, which deals with resolutions passed at adjourned meetings). The subject is not dealt with in the rules apart from IR 1986, r. 4.139, concerning the appointment of the liquidator. In all other respects, the procedure will be the normal one for company meetings laid down by the company's articles and CA 1985, Pt. XI, Ch. IV.

Section 93   General company meeting at each years' end

93(1)   [If winding up for more than one year]   Subject to sections 96 and 102, in the event of the winding up continuing for more than one year, the liquidator shall summon a general meeting of the company at the end of the first year from the commencement of the winding up, and of each succeeding year, or at the first convenient date within 3 months from the end of the year or such longer period as the Secretary of State may allow.

93(2)   [Account by liquidator]   The liquidator shall lay before the meeting an account of his acts and dealings, and of the conduct of the winding up, during the preceding year.

93(3)   [Penalty for non-compliance]   If the liquidator fails to comply with this section, he is liable to a fine.

(Former provisions: CA 1985, s. 584 (as amended by IA 1985, Sch. 6, para. 36); CA 1948, s. 289)

General note

On the holding of meetings during a winding up, see the note to s. 92(3).

S. 93(3)

On penalties, see s. 430 and Sch. 10.

Section 94   Final meeting prior to dissolution

94(1)   [Account of winding up, final meeting]   As soon as the company's affairs are fully wound up, the liquidator shall make up an account of the winding up showing how it has been conducted and the company's property has been disposed of, and thereupon shall call a general meeting of the company for the purpose of laying before it the account and giving an explanation of it.

94(2)   [Advertisement in Gazette]   The meeting shall be called by advertisement in the Gazette, specifying its time, place and object and published at least one month before the meeting.

94(3)   [Copy of account, etc. to registrar]   Within one week after the meeting, the liquidator shall send to the registrar of companies a copy of the account, and shall make a return to him of the holding of the meeting and of its date.

94(4)   [Penalty on default]   If the copy is not sent or the return is not made in accordance with subsection (3), the liquidator is liable to a fine and, for continued contravention, to a daily default fine.

94(5) **[If no quorum at meeting]** If a quorum is not present at the meeting, the liquidator shall, in lieu of the return mentioned above, make a return that the meeting was duly summoned and that no quorum was present; and upon such a return being made, the provisions of subsection (3) as to the making of the return are deemed complied with.

94(6) **[Penalty if no general meeting called]** If the liquidator fails to call a general meeting of the company as required by subsection (1), he is liable to a fine.

(Former provisions: CA 1985, s. 585(1)–(4), (7); CA 1948, s. 290)

General note

When the liquidator has sent to the registrar his final account and return under this section, dissolution of the company follows automatically three months after the return is registered, unless the court makes an order deferring the date: see s. 201(2), (3).

S. 94(5)

This provision enables the liquidator to cut short the statutory formalities if the meeting, when summoned, is inquorate.

S. 94(4), (6)

On penalties, see s. 430 and Sch. 10.

Section 95   Effect of company's insolvency

95(1) **[Application]** This section applies where the liquidator is of the opinion that the company will be unable to pay its debts in full (together with interest at the official rate) within the period stated in the directors' declaration under section 89.

95(2) **[Duties of liquidator]** The liquidator shall—

(a) summon a meeting of creditors for a day not later than the 28th day after the day on which he formed that opinion;

(b) send notices of the creditors' meeting to the creditors by post not less than 7 days before the day on which that meeting is to be held;

(c) cause notice of the creditors' meeting to be advertised once in the Gazette and once at least in 2 newspapers circulating in the relevant locality (that is to say the locality in which the company's principal place of business in Great Britain was situated during the relevant period); and

(d) during the period before the day on which the creditors' meeting is to be held, furnish creditors free of charge with such information concerning the affairs of the company as they may reasonably require;

and the notice of the creditors' meeting shall state the duty imposed by paragraph (d) above.

95(3) **[Duties of liquidator re statement of affairs]** The liquidator shall also—

(a) make out a statement in the prescribed form as to the affairs of the company;

(b) lay that statement before the creditors' meeting; and

(c) attend and preside at that meeting.

95(4) **[Contents of statement of affairs]** The statement as to the affairs of the company shall be verified by affidavit by the liquidator and shall show—

    (a) particulars of the company's assets, debts and liabilities;

    (b) the names and addresses of the company's creditors;

    (c) the securities held by them respectively;

    (d) the dates when the securities were respectively given; and

    (e) such further or other information as may be prescribed.

95(5) **[Where principal place of business in different places]** Where the company's principal place of business in Great Britain was situated in different localities at different times during the relevant period, the duty imposed by subsection (2)(c) applies separately in relation to each of those localities.

95(6) **[Where no place of business in Great Britain]** Where the company had no place of business in Great Britain during the relevant period, references in subsections (2)(c) and (5) to the company's principal place of business in Great Britain are replaced by references to its registered office.

95(7) **["The relevant period"]** In this section **"the relevant period"** means the period of 6 months immediately preceding the day on which were sent the notices summoning the company meeting at which it was resolved that the company be wound up voluntarily.

95(8) **[Penalty for non-compliance]** If the liquidator without reasonable excuse fails to comply with this section, he is liable to a fine.

(Former provisions: IA 1985, s. 83(1)–(6), (9), (10), replacing CA 1985, s. 583)

General note

The earlier law had for a long time been criticised as unsatisfactory (see, e.g. the Cork Committee's *Report*, paras. 674–6). The repealed section in the Companies Act required the liquidator in a members' voluntary winding up, if he formed the opinion that the company was insolvent, to summon a meeting of the creditors and inform them of the position. However, the Act made no further provision, and so all that the creditors could then do was petition the court for a compulsory winding-up order to replace the voluntary liquidation. The new section empowers the creditors, without applying to the court, to convert the liquidation into a creditors' voluntary winding up and, if they wish, to substitute a liquidator of their own choice.

S. 95(1)

The reference is to the directors' statutory declaration of solvency by virtue of which the liquidation proceeded initially as a members' voluntary winding up: see s. 89(1).

S. 95(2)(c)

Where the company's principal place of business was situated in different localities at different times within the relevant period, s. 95(5) applies; and where the company had no place of business in Great Britain during the relevant period, s. 95(6) applies. For the meaning of "the relevant period", see s. 95(7).

S. 95(3), (4)

The "statement of affairs" provision is parallel to that which applies in a creditors' voluntary winding up (see the comments to s. 99 and s. 131), except that in the present situation the responsibilities in connection with the statement are imposed on the liquidator and not the directors.

For the rules and forms prescribed for the purposes of this section, see IR 1986, rr. 4.34ff, 4.49.

S. 95(6)

The question whether a company has established a place of business within the jurisdiction normally arises in relation to the registration requirements of CA 1985, ss. 409 and 691. The meaning of the phrase "established a place of business" has been the subject of judicial determination in a number of cases, e.g. *South India Shipping Corporation Ltd* v *The Export-Import Bank of Korea* [1985] 1 WLR 585; (1985) 1 BCC 99,350, *Re Oriel Ltd* [1986] 1 WLR 180; (1985) 1 BCC 99,444.

S. 95(8)

On penalties, see s. 430 and Sch. 10.

Section 96   Conversion to creditors' voluntary winding up

96   As from the day on which the creditors' meeting is held under section 95, this Act has effect as if—

(a) the directors' declaration under section 89 had not been made; and

(b) the creditors' meeting and the company meeting at which it was resolved that the company be wound up voluntarily were the meetings mentioned in section 98 in the next Chapter;

and accordingly the winding up becomes a creditors' voluntary winding up.

(Former provision: IA 1985, s. 83(7) (part))

General note

This section reproduces part of IA 1985, s. 83(7), omitting some final words ("and any appointment made or committee established by the creditors' meeting shall be deemed to have been made or established by the creditors' meeting so mentioned"), which were probably discarded as superfluous.

It will, of course, be competent for the creditors at their meeting to appoint a liquidator of their own choosing and to establish a liquidation committee under ss. 100 and 101, respectively, by virtue of the general provisions of the present section.

Section 97(2) makes it clear that the meeting of creditors held under s. 95(2)–(3) and the statement of affairs prepared under s. 95(4) are deemed equivalent to the meeting and statement required respectively by ss. 98 and 99, so that there is no need to duplicate either of these exercises. This is also confirmed by s. 102.

Chapter IV — Creditors' Voluntary Winding Up

Section 97   Application of this Chapter

97(1)   [Application]   Subject as follows, this Chapter applies in relation to a creditors' voluntary winding up.

97(2) **[Non-application of ss. 98, 99]** Sections 98 and 99 do not apply where, under section 96 in Chapter III, a members' voluntary winding up has become a creditors' voluntary winding up.

(Former provisions: CA 1985, s. 587; IA 1985, s. 85(1))

S. 97(1)
Chapter IV applies in every voluntary winding up where the directors do not make a statutory declaration of solvency under s. 89(1).

S. 97(2)
See the note to s. 96, above.

Section 98 Meeting of creditors

98(1) **[Duty of company]** The company shall—

    (a) cause a meeting of its creditors to be summoned for a day not later than the 14th day after the day on which there is to be held the company meeting at which the resolution for voluntary winding up is to be proposed;

    (b) cause the notices of the creditors' meeting to be sent by post to the creditors not less than 7 days before the day on which that meeting is to be held; and

    (c) cause notice of the creditors' meeting to be advertised once in the Gazette and once at least in two newspapers circulating in the relevant locality (that is to say the locality in which the company's principal place of business in Great Britain was situated during the relevant period).

98(2) **[Contents of notice of meeting]** The notice of the creditors' meeting shall state either—

    (a) the name and address of a person qualified to act as an insolvency practitioner in relation to the company who, during the period before the day on which that meeting is to be held, will furnish creditors free of charge with such information concerning the company's affairs as they may reasonably require; or

    (b) a place in the relevant locality where, on the two business days falling next before the day on which that meeting is to be held, a list of the names and addresses of the company's creditors will be available for inspection free of charge.

98(3) **[Where principal place of business in different places, etc.]** Where the company's principal place of business in Great Britain was situated in different localities at different times during the relevant period, the duties imposed by subsections (1)(c) and (2)(b) above apply separately in relation to each of those localities.

98(4) **[Where no place of business in Great Britain]** Where the company had no place of business in Great Britain during the relevant period, references in subsections (1)(c) and (3) to the company's principal place of business in Great Britain are replaced by references to its registered office.

98(5) **["The relevant period"]** In this section **"the relevant period"** means the period of 6 months immediately preceding the day on which were sent the notices summoning the company meeting at which it was resolved that the company be wound up voluntarily.

98(6) **[Penalty for non-compliance]** If the company without reasonable excuse fails to comply with subsection (1) or (2), it is guilty of an offence and liable to a fine.

(Former provisions: IA 1985, s. 85(2), (3), (6)–(8), (9)(a), (10), replacing CA 1985, s. 588)

General note

The provisions governing the convening of a creditors' meeting, after the passing by the members of the resolution for voluntary winding up, were extensively redrafted by IA 1985, s. 85, which is consolidated in this and the next section. Under the former law, the creditors' meeting was required to be held on the same day as the members' meeting or the day after, and this meant that it had to be summoned before the shareholders' meeting had been held, with little time to prepare information which would put the creditors properly in the picture. Furthermore, by the device known as "centrebinding" (see the note to s. 166), the directors were sometimes able to contrive to dispose of the company's assets, or a substantial part of them, before the creditors had a chance to consider their position at all. The new law is designed to ensure that the decisive say in a creditors' voluntary winding up really does lie with the creditors' meeting, that they have proper information on which to base their decisions, and that no action which could be adverse to their interests can be taken before their meeting is held, except to a restricted extent through the agency of a qualified insolvency practitioner (see s. 166(3), and also s. 114(3)).

For the rules relating to this section, see IR 1986, rr. 4.49, 4.53ff, 4.62.

S. 98(1)

The 14-day period replaces the former requirement that the creditors' meeting be held on the same day as the company meeting or the next day. This longer interval will enable the directors to prepare properly the information which must be laid before the creditors' meeting under s. 99. The directors have very restricted powers to act in relation to the company's property during the period between the two meetings (see s. 114) and so it will normally be necessary for the members to appoint an insolvency practitioner to act as liquidator on a provisional basis. He will be empowered to act within the limits prescribed by s. 166, and will be able also to make available to creditors the information referred to in s. 98(2)(*a*).

Where the company has had more than one "principal place of business" in Great Britain during the "relevant period", s. 98(3) will apply; and if it had no place of business in this country, s. 98(4) applies instead. The "relevant period" is defined in s. 98(5).

S. 98(2)

The directors are, in effect, given a choice. They may either hand over the task of furnishing the creditors with such information as they may require to a person qualified to act as an insolvency practitioner (for the meaning of this expression, see ss. 388ff), or they must arrange for a list of all the company's creditors to be kept available for inspection. It is not necessary that this insolvency practitioner should be the liquidator, if a liquidator has been appointed by the members on a provisional basis under s. 166; but it will obviously be convenient that he should be, and the requirements of this section will be something of an inducement to appoint a liquidator.

S. 98(3)–(5)

See the note to the corresponding s. 95(5)–(7).

S. 98(6)

On penalties, see s. 430 and Sch. 10.

Section 99   Directors to lay statement of affairs before creditors

99(1)   [Duty of directors]   The directors of the company shall—

    (a) make out a statement in the prescribed form as to the affairs of the company;

    (b) cause that statement to be laid before the creditors' meeting under section 98; and

    (c) appoint one of their number to preside at that meeting;

and it is the duty of the director so appointed to attend the meeting and preside over it.

99(2)   [Contents of statement]   The statement as to the affairs of the company shall be verified by affidavit by some or all of the directors and shall show—

    (a) particulars of the company's assets, debts and liabilities;

    (b) the names and addresses of the company's creditors;

    (c) the securities held by them respectively;

    (d) the dates when the securities were respectively given; and

    (e) such further or other information as may be prescribed.

99(3)   [Penalty for non-compliance]   If—

    (a) the directors without reasonable excuse fail to comply with subsection (1) or (2); or

    (b) any director without reasonable excuse fails to comply with subsection (1), so far as requiring him to attend and preside at the creditors' meeting,

the directors are or (as the case may be) the director is guilty of an offence and liable to a fine.

(Former provisions: IA 1985, s. 85(4), (5), 9(b), (c), (10))

General note

By this provision, introduced by the insolvency legislation of 1985, the Act imposes an obligation on those who have had control of an insolvent company to make full disclosure of its affairs in a creditors' voluntary winding up. The "statement of affairs" is called for in other situations: for detailed discussion, see the note to s. 131.

    For the rules and forms prescribed for the purposes of this section, see IR 1986, rr. 4.34ff.

    If a liquidator has been nominated by the shareholders at their meeting, he is required by s. 166(4) to attend the creditors' meeting and report to it on any exercise of his powers during the period between the two meetings.

S. 99(1)

If the designated director fails to attend the creditors' meeting, it is open to the creditors to appoint someone else to preside, and a meeting so conducted will be valid: *Re Salcombe Hotel Development Co. Ltd* (1989) 5 BCC 807.

S. 99(3)

On penalties, see s. 430 and Sch. 10.

Section 100   Appointment of liquidator

100(1)   [Nomination of liquidator at meetings]   The creditors and the company at their respective meetings mentioned in section 98 may nominate a person to be liquidator for the purpose of winding up the company's affairs and distributing its assets.

100(2)   [Person who is liquidator]   The liquidator shall be the person nominated by the creditors or, where no person has been so nominated, the person (if any) nominated by the company.

100(3)   [Where different persons nominated]   In the case of different persons being nominated, any director, member or creditor of the company may, within 7 days after the date on which the nomination was made by the creditors, apply to the court for an order either—

   (a) directing that the person nominated as liquidator by the company shall be liquidator instead of or jointly with the person nominated by the creditors, or

   (b) appointing some other person to be liquidator instead of the person nominated by the creditors.

(Former provisions: CA 1985, s. 589 (as amended by IA 1985, Sch. 6, para. 37(1), (2)); CA 1948, s. 294)

General note

This section is in substantially the same terms as the amended version of CA 1985, s. 589. The principal change made by the IA 1985 amendment was the rewording of subs. (2) so as to emphasise more positively that the decisive say in the appointment of the liquidator rests with the creditors at their meeting.

Although the section uses the word "nominate" rather than "appoint", the nomination is immediately effective in that nothing more is needed to empower the person so chosen to act. This is confirmed by s. 166, which deals with the exercise by the members' nominee of his powers as liquidator during the interval between the two meetings.

The person nominated must be qualified to act in relation to the company as an insolvency practitioner: see ss. 388, 389. A liquidator appointed under this section is not an officer of the court: *Re T H Knitwear (Wholesale) Ltd* [1988] Ch. 275; (1988) 4 BCC 102.

For the relevant rules, see IR 1986, rr. 4.101ff; and in regard to the liquidator's remuneration, rr. 4.127ff.

Section **101**   Appointment of liquidation committee

101(1)   [Creditors may appoint committee]   The creditors at the meeting to be held under section 98 or at any subsequent meeting may, if they think fit, appoint a committee ("the liquidation committee") of not more than 5 persons to exercise the functions conferred on it by or under this Act.

101(2)   [Members appointed by company]   If such a committee is appointed, the company may, either at the meeting at which the resolution for voluntary winding up is passed or at any time subsequently in general meeting, appoint such number of persons as they think fit to act as members of the committee, not exceeding 5.

101(3)   [Creditors may object to members appointed by company]   However, the creditors may, if they think fit, resolve that all or any of the persons so appointed by the company ought not to be members of the liquidation committee; and if the creditors so resolve—

   (a) the persons mentioned in the resolution are not then, unless the court otherwise directs, qualified to act as members of the committee; and

(b) on any application to the court under this provision the court may, if it thinks fit, appoint other persons to act as such members in place of the persons mentioned in the resolution.

101(4) **[Scotland]** In Scotland, the liquidation committee has, in addition to the powers and duties conferred and imposed on it by this Act, such of the powers and duties of commissioners on a bankrupt estate as may be conferred and imposed on liquidation committees by the rules.

(Former provisions: CA 1985, s. 590 (as amended by IA 1985, Sch. 6, para. 38(2)–(4)); CA 1948, s. 295)

General note

The designation of the committee as the "liquidation committee" is a novelty introduced by the draftsman of the consolidating legislation. Under CA 1948, such a committee was given the traditional name, "committee of inspection"; but this was changed to "committee established under s. 590" by IA 1985 (doubtless to reflect the fact that "inspection" of the company's affairs was no longer the primary function of such a committee). This new title is certainly more elegant than its predecessor.

Provision is made for comparable committees by ss. 26 (administration), 49 and 68 (administrative receivership) and 141, 142 (winding up by the court).

S. 101(1)

In addition to the functions conferred on the liquidation committee by the Act itself (see, e.g. s. 103), further provisions about its functions, membership and proceedings are contained in the rules: see IR 1986, rr. 4.151ff.

Section 102   Creditors' meeting where winding up converted under s. 96

102 Where, in the case of a winding up which was, under section 96 in Chapter III, converted to a creditors' voluntary winding up, a creditors' meeting is held in accordance with section 95, any appointment made or committee established by that meeting is deemed to have been made or established by a meeting held in accordance with section 98 in this Chapter.

(Former provision: IA 1985, s. 83(7) (part))

General note

This section applies when the company in a members' voluntary winding up proves to be insolvent and the liquidation has been converted into a creditors' voluntary winding up under ss. 95, 96. Its purpose is to remove any doubts that might otherwise arise about the standing and functions of a liquidator appointed or a liquidation committee established in such a case.

Section 103   Cesser of directors' powers

103 On the appointment of a liquidator, all the powers of the directors cease, except so far as the liquidation committee (or, if there is no such committee, the creditors) sanction their continuance.

(Former provisions: CA 1985, s. 591(2) (as amended by IA 1985, Sch. 6, para. 39); CA 1948, s. 296(2))

General note

It does not appear that the appointment of a liquidator operates of itself to remove the directors from office: see the note to s. 91(2).

Section 104   Vacancy in office of liquidator

104   If a vacancy occurs, by death, resignation or otherwise, in the office of a liquidator (other than a liquidator appointed by, or by the direction of, the court), the creditors may fill the vacancy.

(Former provisions: CA 1985, s. 592; CA 1948, s. 297)

General note

Where the appointment of the previous liquidator was made by or under a court order (see s. 100(3)), it appears that a further application to the court is required to fill the vacancy.

Section 105   Meetings of company and creditors at each year's end

105(1)   [Liquidator to summon meetings]   If the winding up continues for more than one year, the liquidator shall summon a general meeting of the company and a meeting of the creditors at the end of the first year from the commencement of the winding up, and of each succeeding year, or at the first convenient date within 3 months from the end of the year or such longer period as the Secretary of State may allow.

105(2)   [Liquidator to lay account]   The liquidator shall lay before each of the meetings an account of his acts and dealings and of the conduct of the winding up during the preceding year.

105(3)   [Penalty for non-compliance]   If the liquidator fails to comply with this section, he is liable to a fine.

105(4)   [Qualification to requirement]   Where under section 96 a members' voluntary winding up has become a creditors' voluntary winding up, and the creditors' meeting under section 95 is held 3 months or less before the end of the first year from the commencement of the winding up, the liquidator is not required by this section to summon a meeting of creditors at the end of that year.

(Former provisions: CA 1985, s. 594; IA 1985, s. 83(8); CA 1948, s. 299)

S. 105(1)

The corresponding provision in the case of a members' voluntary winding up is s. 93; under that section, however, the liquidator is required to report only to the members.

S. 105(3)

On penalties, see s. 430 and Sch. 10.

S. 105(4)

This subsection is linked with the new procedure prescribed by ss. 95, 96 for the situation when a company in a members' voluntary winding up proves to be insolvent. In that case, a creditors' meeting will have been held quite recently, under s. 95(2), and there would be little point in summoning a second one so soon afterwards. A general meeting of the company under s. 105 (1) must, however, still be convened.

Section 106   Final meeting prior to dissolution

106(1)   [Account of winding up, meetings]   As soon as the company's affairs are fully wound up, the liquidator shall make up an account of the winding up, showing how it has been conducted and the company's property has been disposed of, and thereupon shall call a general meeting of the company and a meeting of the creditors for the purpose of laying the account before the meetings and giving an explanation of it.

106(2)   [Advertisement in Gazette]   Each such meeting shall be called by advertisement in the Gazette specifying the time, place and object of the meeting, and published at least one month before it.

106(3)   [Copy of account, return to registrar]   Within one week after the date of the meetings (or, if they are not held on the same date, after the date of the later one) the liquidator shall send to the registrar of companies a copy of the account, and shall make a return to him of the holding of the meetings and of their dates.

106(4)   [Penalty on default re s. 106(3)]   If the copy is not sent or the return is not made in accordance with subsection (3), the liquidator is liable to a fine and, for continued contravention, to a daily default fine.

106(5)   [If quorum not present at either meeting]   However, if a quorum is not present at either such meeting, the liquidator shall, in lieu of the return required by subsection (3), make a return that the meeting was duly summoned and that no quorum was present; and upon such return being made the provisions of that subsection as to the making of the return are, in respect of that meeting, deemed complied with.

106(6)   [Penalty if no meetings called]   If the liquidator fails to call a general meeting of the company or a meeting of the creditors as required by this section, he is liable to a fine.

(Former provisions: CA 1985, ss. 595(1)–(5), (8); CA 1948, s. 300(1)–(3), (6))

General note

This section corresponds with s. 94, which deals with a members' voluntary winding up; but in that case no meeting of the creditors is required.
    See generally the notes to s. 94.
    For the relevant rules, see IR 1986, r. 4.126.
    On penalties, see s. 430 and Sch. 10.

Chapter V — Provisions Applying to both kinds of Voluntary Winding Up

Section 107   Distribution of company's property

107   Subject to the provisions of this Act as to preferential payments, the company's property in a voluntary winding up shall on the winding up be applied in satisfaction of the company's liabilities pari passu and, subject to that application, shall (unless the articles otherwise provide) be distributed among the members according to their rights and interests in the company.

(Former provisions: CA 1985, s. 597; CA 1948, s. 302)

General note

This section refers to "preferential payments", and not merely to "preferential debts", and thus includes, e.g. the expenses of the winding up (including the liquidator's remuneration) which are given priority by s. 115, as well as the preferential debts defined by ss. 386, 387.

The order of application of the assets in the hands of the liquidator will therefore be:

(1) the expenses of the winding up, including the liquidator's remuneration (s. 115);

(2) the preferential debts, as defined by ss. 386, 387 and Sch. 6 (s. 175);

(3) any preferential charge on goods distrained that arises under s. 176(3);

(4) the company's general creditors;

(5) any debts or other sums due from the company to its members *qua* members (s. 74(2)(*f*));

(6) the members generally, in accordance with their respective rights and interests (s. 107).

Secured creditors will, in principle, be entitled to be paid out of the proceeds of their security (so far as it extends) ahead of all other claims. However, where the security is by way of floating charge, the debts which are preferential debts in the liquidation must be paid first (s. 175(2)(*b*)). The expenses of the winding up will rank before both the preferential creditors and the holder of the charge in at least two situations:

(1) where the floating charge had not crystallised before the commencement of the winding up (*Re Barleycorn Enterprises Ltd* [1970] Ch 465), and

(2) where the floating charge had crystallised before the commencement of the winding up otherwise than in consequence of the appointment of a receiver (*Re Portbase Clothing Ltd, Mond* v *Taylor & Ors* [1993] Ch. 388; [1993] BCC 96).

The question whether the expenses of the winding up have a similar priority when a receivership precedes a winding up was not addressed in *Portbase Clothing*. In *Re Christonette International Ltd* [1982] 1 WLR 1245 it was held that this was not the case, but this decision was distinguished in *Portbase Clothing* in the light of the new statutory definition of "floating charge" (see s. 251) and so may now be open to reconsideration. (The position in that case would, of course, be governed by s. 40 and not by s. 175(2)(*b*): see [1993] Ch. 388 at p. 396; [1993] BCC 96 at p. 101.)

The statutory order for the application of assets may not be varied by contractual arrangements between the parties concerned, such as a pooling or clearing-house arrangement: *British Eagle International Air Lines Ltd* v *Cie Nationale Air France* [1975] 1 WLR 758. But there is a statutory exception for such arrangements in the financial markets: see the note on p. 3, and CA 1989, s. 159.

Provision is made for the proof and payment of debts in a members' voluntary winding up by IR 1986, r. 4.182A, and in a creditors' voluntary winding up by rr. 4.73ff, 4.180.

For the application of assets in a winding up by the court, see s. 148 and IR 1986, r. 4.181.

Section 108   Appointment or removal of liquidator by the court

108(1)   [If no liquidator acting]   If from any cause whatever there is no liquidator acting, the court may appoint a liquidator.

108(2)   [Removal, replacement]   The court may, on cause shown, remove a liquidator and appoint another.

(Former provisions: CA 1985, s. 599; CA 1948, s. 304)

General note

The power of the court supplements the power of the members under s. 92 (members' voluntary winding up) and that of the creditors under s. 104 (creditors' voluntary winding up) to fill any such vacancy themselves. A liquidator once appointed, however, may be removed only by the court "on cause shown" under s. 108(2). The case of *Re Keypak Homecare Ltd* (1987) 3 BCC 558 contains a useful review of the principles upon which the court will act in exercising its power to remove a liquidator under s. 108(2).

An application may be made under s. 108 by anyone whom the court considers proper, e.g. a former liquidator who has ceased to be qualified to act in relation to the company (*Re A J Adams (Builders) Ltd* [1991] BCC 62).

For the relevant rules, see IR 1986, rr. 4.103, 4.140.

Section 109   Notice by liquidator of his appointment

109(1)   [Notice in Gazette and to registrar]   The liquidator shall, within 14 days after his appointment, publish in the Gazette and deliver to the registrar of companies for registration a notice of his appointment in the form prescribed by statutory instrument made by the Secretary of State.

109(2)   [Penalty on default]   If the liquidator fails to comply with this section, he is liable to a fine and, for continued contravention, to a daily default fine.

(Former provisions: CA 1985, s. 600; CA 1948, s. 305)

S. 109(1)

The duty of the liquidator to give notice of his appointment under this section is additional to his duty to notify creditors under IR 1986, rr. 4.103, 4.139 and 4.140 and also to the obligation imposed by s. 85 on the company and its officers (including the liquidator) to notify the passing of the resolution for voluntary winding up by advertisement in the Gazette. Further advertising and registration requirements are imposed by r. 4.106.

The gazetting of the liquidator's appointment under this section constitutes an "official notification" of the event for the purposes of CA 1985, s. 42(1)(*a*): see CA 1985, s. 711(2)(*b*). If there has not been an official notification, or (in some circumstances) if the official notification is less than 15 days old, s. 42 provides that the company "is not entitled to rely against other persons on the happening" of the appointment of the liquidator. This provision has its origin in the EC First Company Law Directive; its meaning and effect (so far as English law is concerned) is obscure. What matters under the Act is the fact that the company has gone into liquidation: nothing turns on the appointment of the liquidator, as such.

S. 109(2)

On penalties, see s. 430 and Sch. 10.

Section 110 Acceptance of shares, etc., as consideration for sale of company property

110(1) [Application]   This section applies, in the case of a company proposed to be, or being, wound up voluntarily, where the whole or part of the company's business or property is proposed to be transferred or sold to another company ("the transferee company"), whether or not the latter is a company within the meaning of the Companies Act.

110(2) [Shares etc. in compensation for transfer]   With the requisite sanction, the liquidator of the company being, or proposed to be, wound up ("the transferor company") may receive, in compensation or part compensation for the transfer or sale, shares, policies or other like interests in the transferee company for distribution among the members of the transferor company.

110(3) [Sanction for s. 110(2)]   The sanction requisite under subsection (2) is—

  (a) in the case of a members' voluntary winding up, that of a special resolution of the company, conferring either a general authority on the liquidator or an authority in respect of any particular arrangement, and

  (b) in the case of a creditors' voluntary winding up, that of either the court or the liquidation committee.

110(4) [Alternative to s. 110(2)]   Alternatively to subsection (2), the liquidator may (with that sanction) enter into any other arrangement whereby the members of the transferor company may, in lieu of receiving cash, shares, policies or other like interests (or in addition thereto), participate in the profits of, or receive any other benefit from, the transferee company.

110(5) [Sale binding on transferors]   A sale or arrangement in pursuance of this section is binding on members of the transferor company.

110(6) [Special resolution]   A special resolution is not invalid for purposes of this section by reason that it is passed before or concurrently with a resolution for voluntary winding up or for appointing liquidators; but, if an order is made within a year for winding up the company by the court, the special resolution is not valid unless sanctioned by the court.

(Former provisions: CA 1985, ss. 582(1)–(4), (7), 593 (as amended by IA 1985, Sch. 6, para. 40); CA 1948, ss. 287(1), (2), (5), 298)

General note

The consolidation has brought together sections which were previously divided between what are now Ch. IV and V of Pt. IV of IA 1986; but this involves no change of substance.

The section deals with a corporate "reconstruction", under which the whole or part of the business of a company in liquidation is sold by the liquidator to another company and the members of the first company agree to accept shares or other securities in the purchasing company instead of the cash distribution to which they would normally be entitled. Provided that the sanction referred to in s. 110(3) is obtained, the scheme is binding on all the members except those who dissent in writing under s. 111(1).

S. 110(1)

For the definition of "company" referred to, see CA 1985, s. 735, and the note to s. 73 above. The word is used here in a wider sense in the phrase "the transferee company".

S. 110(2), (4)

The consideration which the members agree to accept normally consists of or includes shares in the transferee company, but it may take many other forms.

S. 110(3)

The consolidation has introduced an ambiguity into the section by running together two provisions which were formerly stated separately in CA 1985, s. 582(2) and s. 593. As it stands, para. (*b*) of the new subsection appears to read as an *alternative* to para. (*a*), but it should be an *additional* requirement; i.e. in a members' voluntary winding up, only the sanction in para. (*a*) is needed, but in a creditors' winding up, *both* para. (*a*) and para. (*b*) apply. If this were not so, the members could be obliged to accept shares without their consent, and s. 111 would not apply at all!

S. 110(5)

This should be read subject to the right of a member to dissent under s. 111. In fact, although the arrangement may be "binding" under this provision, in the sense that a dissenting member cannot prevent the deal from going ahead, nothing can oblige him to become a member of the transferee company without his consent. It is necessary in practice therefore for a scheme of reconstruction to make express provision for recalcitrant but inactive shareholders, e.g. by creating a trust to hold the new shares on their behalf.

S. 110(6)

The sanction of the court is not required before the liquidator puts a scheme of reconstruction into effect.

Section 111   Dissent from arrangement under s. 110

111(1) **[Application]**   This section applies in the case of a voluntary winding up where, for the purposes of section 110(2) or (4), there has been passed a special resolution of the transferor company providing the sanction requisite for the liquidator under that section.

111(2) **[Objections by members of transferor company]**   If a member of the transferor company who did not vote in favour of the special resolution expresses his dissent from it in writing, addressed to the liquidator and left at the company's registered office within 7 days after the passing of the resolution, he may require the liquidator either to abstain from carrying the resolution into effect or to purchase his interest at a price to be determined by agreement or by arbitration under this section.

111(3)   [Where liquidator purchases member's interest]   If the liquidator elects to purchase the member's interest, the purchase money must be paid before the company is dissolved and be raised by the liquidator in such manner as may be determined by special resolution.

111(4)   [Arbitration]   For purposes of an arbitration under this section, the provisions of the Companies Clauses Consolidation Act 1845 or, in the case of a winding up in Scotland, the Companies Clauses Consolidation (Scotland) Act 1845 with respect to the settlement of disputes by arbitration are incorporated with this Act, and—

  (a) in the construction of those provisions this Act is deemed the special Act and **"the company"** means the transferor company, and

  (b) any appointment by the incorporated provisions directed to be made under the hand of the secretary or any two of the directors may be made in writing by the liquidator (or, if there is more than one liquidator, then any two or more of them).

(Former provisions: CA 1985, s. 582(5), (6), (8); CA 1948, s. 287(3), (4), (6))

General note

This section confers on a dissenting member the right to have his shareholding in the company bought out in cash, provided that he takes the prompt action prescribed by s. 111(2).

Section 112   Reference of questions to court

112(1)   [Application to court]   The liquidator or any contributory or creditor may apply to the court to determine any question arising in the winding up of a company, or to exercise, as respects the enforcing of calls or any other matter, all or any of the powers which the court might exercise if the company were being wound up by the court.

112(2)   [Court order]   The court, if satisfied that the determination of the question or the required exercise of power will be just and beneficial, may accede wholly or partially to the application on such terms and conditions as it thinks fit, or may make such other order on the application as it thinks just.

112(3)   [Copy of order to registrar]   A copy of an order made by virtue of this section staying the proceedings in the winding up shall forthwith be forwarded by the company, or otherwise as may be prescribed, to the registrar of companies, who shall enter it in his records relating to the company.

(Former provisions: CA 1985, s. 602; CA 1948, s. 307)

S. 112(1), (2)

The powers of the court in a winding up by the court are contained in Ch. VI of the Act, and more specifically in ss. 147ff.

S. 112(2)

The court's powers are discretionary. It may refuse to permit proceedings under this provision where some other procedure is more appropriate: *Re Stetzel Thomson & Co. Ltd* (1988) 4 BCC 74. It is not a complete bar to the exercise of discretion that the applicant is using the procedure to obtain a collateral advantage: *Re Movitex Ltd* [1992] BCC 101.

S. 112(3)

No rules appear to have been prescribed for the purposes of this section.

Section 113 Court's power to control proceedings (Scotland)

113 If the court, on the application of the liquidator in the winding up of a company registered in Scotland, so directs, no action or proceeding shall be proceeded with or commenced against the company except by leave of the court and subject to such terms as the court may impose.

(Former provisions: CA 1985, s. 603; CA 1948, s. 308(1))

Section 114 No liquidator appointed or nominated by company

114(1) [Application] This section applies where, in the case of a voluntary winding up, no liquidator has been appointed or nominated by the company.

114(2) [Limit on exercise of directors' powers] The powers of the directors shall not be exercised, except with the sanction of the court or (in the case of a creditors' voluntary winding up) so far as may be necessary to secure compliance with sections 98 (creditors' meeting) and 99 (statement of affairs), during the period before the appointment or nomination of a liquidator of the company.

114(3) [Non-application of s. 114(2)] Subsection (2) does not apply in relation to the powers of the directors—

(a) to dispose of perishable goods and other goods the value of which is likely to diminish if they are not immediately disposed of, and

(b) to do all such other things as may be necessary for the protection of the company's assets.

114(4) [Penalty for non-compliance] If the directors of the company without reasonable excuse fail to comply with this section, they are liable to a fine.

(Former provision: IA 1985, s. 82)

General note

This section re-enacts with minor modifications IA 1985, s. 82, which was a new provision. It is designed as a counter to the practice of "centrebinding" which was condemned as unsatisfactory by the Cork Committee (*Report*, paras. 666ff), and should be read in conjunction with the notes to s. 166 below. The Committee drew attention to the fact that there was in every voluntary liquidation a period of time during which the directors remained in control of the company but, until the necessary meetings had been convened and a liquidator appointed, the company's assets and the interests of creditors were most inadequately protected. This period could be extended if the appointment of the liquidator was not made at the same time as the passing of the resolution for winding up but deferred until a later occasion. The Committee's recommendation was that a voluntary liquidation should commence as soon as the *directors* had decided that, because of its liabilities, the company could not carry on business, and that they should be obliged immediately to appoint a provisional liquidator who would assume effective control and safeguard the position until the appropriate meeting had made a permanent appointment.

The legislature did not accept this recommendation of the Committee, and so it remains the law that a voluntary winding up commences when the company's special resolution is passed. This section does, however, in part curb the abuse to which the report drew attention, by providing that the directors should have only very limited powers, restricted to the preservation of the company's assets, until a liquidator has been appointed. The weakness of the section is, of course, that it operates only *after* the voluntary winding up has commenced: the directors will still be in full control during the period which must elapse while the meeting of the company is being convened.

S. 114(1), (2)

In a members' voluntary winding up, the liquidator is appointed by the company in general meeting under s. 91. These new provisions should ensure that an appointment is made promptly, whereupon the powers of the directors will normally cease (see s. 91(2)). Section 114(2) should also encourage the members to nominate a liquidator promptly in the case of a creditors' voluntary winding up. In this event, it may be inferred from the wording of s. 166 that, once the company has nominated a liquidator, he automatically takes office and is vested with the powers and duties set out in that section.

S. 114(3)

The very limited powers which the directors retain are confined to the disposal of perishable goods and the protection of assets. They will not extend to continuing to manage the business in any general sense. (Note that para. (*a*) is confined in its scope to *goods*. Other property which may be likely to diminish in value (e.g. shares in a bear market) is not covered by this paragraph, although some actions of the directors in relation to such property may be justified under para. (*b*).)

S. 114(4)

On penalties, see s. 430 and Sch. 10.

Section 115   Expenses of voluntary winding up

115   All expenses properly incurred in the winding up, including the remuneration of the liquidator, are payable out of the company's assets in priority to all other claims.

(Former provisions: CA 1985, s. 604; CA 1948, s. 309)

General note

The expenses of the winding up rank ahead of the claims of the preferential creditors who are given priority by ss. 175, 176.

In the case of a creditors' voluntary winding up (including one which has commenced as a members' winding up but later proves to be insolvent), the order of priority as between the different categories of expenses is set out in IR 1986, r. 4.218, but the court has power to vary these general rules by virtue of ss. 112(1) and 156 and r. 4.220.

For the purposes of s. 115, the company's "assets" will in many, if not all, circumstances include assets covered by a floating charge: see the discussion of *Re Portbase Clothing Ltd, Mond* v *Taylor & Ors* [1993] Ch. 388, [1993] BCC 96, *Re Barleycorn Enterprises Ltd* [1970] Ch. 465 and other cases in the notes to s. 107, above.

This section does not declare that all expenses properly incurred by a liquidator are payable out of the company's assets, but only that expenses which *are* so payable should have priority to other claims. The costs of pursuing an unsuccessful claim under s. 238 (transaction at under-value), s. 239 (preference) or s. 214 (wrongful trading), however properly the claim may have been brought, are not payable out of the company's assets: *Re M C Bacon Ltd (No. 2)* [1991] Ch. 127; [1990] BCC 430.

Pre-liquidation expenses, other than those specifically incurred for the purpose of enabling the company to pass the winding-up resolution and take other steps required by statute, cannot ordinarily be claimed under this section: *Re A V Sorge & Co. Ltd* (1986) 2 BCC 99,306; *Re Sandwell Copiers Ltd* (1988) 4 BCC 227; *Re W F Fearman Ltd (No. 2)* (1988) 4 BCC 141.

Liabilities in respect of the community charge ("poll tax") arising while the company was being wound up were held not to be a "necessary disbursement" by the liquidator, and there-fore not payable as a liquidation expense, in *Re Kentish Homes Ltd* [1993] BCC 212. In this case Nicholls V-C (at p. 213) expressed the view that the position would be the same in regard to the council tax.

In *Re Berkeley Applegate (Investment Consultants) Ltd (No. 2)* (1988) 4 BCC 279, a liqui-dator had done substantial work in relation to assets in which, after investigation, the company proved to have no beneficial interest. It was held, in the circumstances, that he was entitled to be paid his proper expenses and remuneration as a charge on those assets, even though they were not "the company's assets" within s. 115. (See further *Re Berkeley Applegate (Investment Consultants)) Ltd (No. 3)* (1989) 5 BCC 803, and cf. *Re Eastern Capital Futures Ltd* (1989) 5 BCC 223.)

On the general rules regarding the distribution of assets in a voluntary winding up, see the note to s. 107.

Section 116   Saving for certain rights

116   The voluntary winding up of a company does not bar the right of any creditor or contributory to have it wound up by the court; but in the case of an application by a contributory the court must be satisfied that the rights of the contributories will be prejudiced by a voluntary winding up.

(Former provisions: CA 1985, s. 605; CA 1948, s. 310)

General note

The court has, in any case, a discretion under s. 125 to refuse a winding-up order, even where the application is made by a creditor. The wishes of a majority of the company's creditors will be taken into account, but will not be regarded as decisive: see *Re Home Remedies Ltd* [1943] Ch. 1; *Re Southard & Co. Ltd* [1979] 1 WLR 1198; *Re Medisco Equipment Ltd* (1983) 1 BCC 98,944.

Chapter VI — Winding Up by the Court

JURISDICTION (ENGLAND AND WALES)

Section 117   High Court and county court jurisdiction

117(1)   [High Court]   The High Court has jurisdiction to wind up any company registered in England and Wales.

117(2)   [County court]   Where the amount of a company's share capital paid up or credited as paid up does not exceed £120,000, then (subject to this section) the county court of the district in which the company's registered office is situated has concurrent jurisdiction with the High Court to wind up the company.

117(3)   [Increase, reduction of s. 117(2) sum]   The money sum for the time being specified in subsection (2) is subject to increase or reduction by order under section 416 in Part XV.

117(4)   [Exclusion of jurisdiction for county court]   The Lord Chancellor may by order in a statutory instrument exclude a county court from having winding-up jurisdiction, and for the purposes of that jurisdiction may attach its district, or any part thereof, to any other county court, and may by statutory instrument revoke or vary any such order.

In exercising the powers of this section, the Lord Chancellor shall provide that a county court is not to have winding-up jurisdiction unless it has for the time being jurisdiction for the purposes of Parts VIII to XI of this Act (individual insolvency).

117(5)   [Extent of winding-up jurisdiction]   Every court in England and Wales having winding-up jurisdiction has for the purposes of that jurisdiction all the powers of the High Court; and every prescribed officer of the court shall perform any duties which an officer of the High Court may discharge by order of a judge of that court or otherwise in relation to winding up.

117(6)   ["Registered office"]   For the purposes of this section, a company's **"registered office"** is the place which has longest been its registered office during the 6 months immediately preceding the presentation of the petition for winding up.

(Former provisions: CA 1985, s. 512 (as amended by IA 1985, Sch. 6, paras. 25, 26); CA 1948, s. 218 (as amended by IA 1976, Sch. 1))

General note

For the corresponding provisions relating to Scotland, see ss. 120, 121.

In CA 1985 and in the present Act, the word "court", when used in relation to a company, means the court having jurisdiction to wind up the company: see CA 1985, s. 744 and IA 1986, s. 251. This will be the appropriate court as defined by this section.

Winding-up proceedings are a form of "suit and legal process", but are not a method of "enforcing a judgment or arbitration award": *Re International Tin Council* [1989] Ch. 309; (1988) 4 BCC 653 (CA), affirming [1987] Ch. 419; (1987) 3 BCC 103.

Section 118   Proceedings taken in wrong court

118(1)   [Wrong court]   Nothing in section 117 invalidates a proceeding by reason of its being taken in the wrong court.

118(2) **[Continuation]** The winding up of a company by the court in England and Wales, or any proceedings in the winding up, may be retained in the court in which the proceedings were commenced, although it may not be the court in which they ought to have been commenced.

(Former provisions: CA 1985, s. 513; CA 1948, ss. 218(7), 219(1))

Section 119 Proceedings in county court; case stated for High Court

119(1) **[Special case]** If any question arises in any winding-up proceedings in a county court which all the parties to the proceedings, or which one of them and the judge of the court, desire to have determined in the first instance in the High Court, the judge shall state the facts in the form of a special case for the opinion of the High Court.

119(2) **[Transmission]** Thereupon the special case and the proceedings (or such of them as may be required) shall be transmitted to the High Court for the purposes of the determination.

(Former provisions: CA 1985, s. 514; CA 1948, s. 219(3))

JURISDICTION (SCOTLAND)

Section 120 Court of Session and sheriff court jurisdiction

120(1) **[Court of Session]** The Court of Session has jurisdiction to wind up any company registered in Scotland.

120(2) **[Vacation judge]** When the Court of Session is in vacation, the jurisdiction conferred on that court by this section may (subject to the provisions of this Part) be exercised by the judge acting as vacation judge.

120(3) **[Concurrent jurisdiction of sheriff court]** Where the amount of a company's share capital paid up or credited as paid up does not exceed £120,000, the sheriff court of the sheriffdom in which the company's registered office is situated has concurrent jurisdiction with the Court of Session to wind up the company; but—

  (a) the Court of Session may, if it thinks expedient having regard to the amount of the company's assets to do so—

    (i) remit to a sheriff court any petition presented to the Court of Session for winding up such a company, or

    (ii) require such a petition presented to a sheriff court to be remitted to the Court of Session; and

  (b) the Court of Session may require any such petition as above-mentioned presented to one sheriff court to be remitted to another sheriff court; and

  (c) in a winding up in the sheriff court the sheriff may submit a stated case for the opinion of the Court of Session on any question of law arising in that winding up.

120(4) **["Registered office"]** For the purposes of this section, the expression **"registered office"** means the place which has longest been the company's registered office during the 6 months immediately preceding the presentation of the petition for winding up.

120(5) **[Increase, reduction of s. 120(3) sum]** The money sum for the time being specified in subsection (3) is subject to increase or reduction by order under section 416 in Part XV.

(Former provisions: CA 1985, s. 515 (as amended by IA 1985, Sch. 6, para. 25); CA 1948, s. 220 (as amended by IA 1976, s. 1(1), (2), Sch. 1, Pt. I, II))

General note

This section lays down provisions for Scotland which correspond generally with those made for England and Wales by s. 117. There are, however, no Scottish counterparts to ss. 118 and 119.

S.120(2)

In this subsection the former words "in pursuance of section 4 of the Administration of Justice (Scotland) Act 1933" (which appeared at the end) were repealed by the Court of Session Act 1988, s. 52(2) and Sch. 2, Pt. I and III as from 29 September 1988.

Section 121 Power to remit winding up to Lord Ordinary

121(1) **[Remission to Lord Ordinary]** The Court of Session may, by Act of Sede-runt, make provision for the taking of proceedings in a winding up before one of the Lords Ordinary; and, where provision is so made, the Lord Ordinary has, for the purposes of the winding up, all the powers and jurisdiction of the court.

121(2) **[Report by Lord Ordinary]** However, the Lord Ordinary may report to the Inner House any matter which may arise in the course of a winding up.

(Former provisions: CA 1985, s. 516; CA 1948, s. 221)

GROUNDS AND EFFECT OF WINDING-UP PETITION

Section 122 Circumstances in which company may be wound up by the court

122(1) **[Circumstances]** A company may be wound up by the court if—

(a) the company has by special resolution resolved that the company be wound up by the court,

(b) being a public company which was registered as such on its original incorporation, the company has not been issued with a certificate under section 117 of the Companies Act (public company share capital requirements) and more than a year has expired since it was so registered,

(c) it is an old public company, within the meaning of the Consequential Provisions Act,

(d) the company does not commence its business within a year from its incorporation or suspends its business for a whole year,

(e) except in the case of a private company limited by shares or by guarantee, the number of members is reduced below 2,

(f) the company is unable to pay its debts,

(g) the court is of the opinion that it is just and equitable that the company should be wound up.

122(2) **[Scotland]** In Scotland, a company which the Court of Session has jurisdiction to wind up may be wound up by the Court if there is subsisting a floating charge over property comprised in the the company's property and undertaking, and the court is satisfied that the security of the creditor entitled to the benefit of the floating charge is in jeopardy.

For this purpose a creditor's security is deemed to be in jeopardy if the Court is satisfied that events have occurred or are about to occur which render it unreasonable in the creditor's interests that the company should retain power to dispose of the property which is subject to the floating charge.

(Former provisions: CA 1985, s. 517; CA 1948, s. 222 (as amended by CA 1980, Sch. 3, para. 27); Companies (Floating Charges and Receivers) (Scotland) Act 1972, s. 4)

S. 122(1)

The court has in all cases a discretion whether to make a winding-up order or not. This is implicit in the opening words of the section, and is confirmed by s. 125. Thus, it may decide that another jurisdiction is a more appropriate forum: *Re Harrods (Buenos Aires) Ltd* [1992] Ch. 72; [1991] BCC 249.

Paragraphs (*b*) and (*c*) were introduced in conjunction with the redefinition of the public company and the enactment of new statutory rules applicable to such companies by CA 1980. The remaining paragraphs of this subsection are of long standing, except that the minimum number of members for a public company was seven until 1980.

In s. 122(1)(*e*) the words "except in the case of a private company limited by shares or by guarantee" were inserted by the Companies (Single Member Private Limited Companies) Regulations 1992 (SI 1992 No. 1699), reg. 1 and Sch., para. 8, as from 15 July 1992. These regulations implemented the EC Twelfth Company Law Directive.

Paragraph (*f*) is elaborated by the presumptions set out in s. 123.

Paragraph (*g*) has been the subject of interpretation in a considerable number of cases, among the best known of which are *Re German Date Coffee Company* (1882) 20 ChD 169 (failure of object); *Re T E Brinsmead & Sons* [1897] 1 Ch. 406 (fraud); *Re Yenidje Tobacco Co. Ltd* [1916] 2 Ch. 426 (deadlock); *Loch & Anor* v *John Blackwood Ltd* [1924] AC 783 (impropriety); and *Ebrahimi* v *Westbourne Galleries Ltd & Anor* [1973] AC 360 (breakdown of confidence). The last-mentioned case established that in the exercise of its jurisdiction on the "just and equitable" ground the court is not restricted by the rights and wrongs of the position as a matter of law but may have regard to wider considerations, such as the expectation of a member of a small "quasi-partnership" company that he will have a say in matters of management. For further illustrations on this point, see *Re Zinotty Properties Ltd* [1984] 1 WLR 1249; (1984) 1 BCC 99,139, *Tay Bok Choon* v *Tahansan Snd Bhd* [1987] 1 WLR 413; (1987) 3 BCC 132. Failure on the part of the directors to pay reasonable dividends is conduct conceptually capable of supporting a winding-up petition on the "just and equitable" ground, although such a case would be extremely difficult to prove: *Re a Company No. 00370 of 1987* [1988] 1 WLR 1068; (1988) 4 BCC 506. (Note, however, that the amendment made to CA 1985, s. 459 by CA 1989,

s. 145 and Sch. 19, para. 11, from 4 February 1991 offers a minority shareholder in such a situation the possibility of alternative grounds of relief.)

The jurisdiction under s. 122(1)(*g*) may not be invoked to protect interests of the petitioner other than his interests as a member: *Re J E Cade & Son Ltd* [1991] BCC 360 (petitioner seeking to assert rights as freeholder of land in occupation of company).

Where the dispute in a petition for winding up under s. 122(1)(*g*) is essentially one which involves only rival factions of shareholders, it is a misfeasance for those in control of the company to spend its money in the proceedings, except in relation to matters in which the company, as such, is concerned, e.g. in making discovery of documents in the possession of the company, or in connection with an application under s. 127 (below) to validate a disposition of the company's property or sanction the continuance of its business pending the hearing of the petition: *Re Milgate Developments Ltd* [1991] BCC 24; *Re a Company No. 004502 of 1988, ex parte Johnson* [1991] BCC 234.

S. 122(2)

This provision can be traced back to s. 4 of the Companies (Floating Charges) (Scotland) Act 1961, the Act which first introduced the floating charge to Scotland, where it was unknown at common law. At that time, however, it was not possible in Scotland to enforce a floating charge by the appointment of a receiver, and so winding up was the only remedy which the law could provide for in a case when the security was in jeopardy. The present subsection is arguably no longer required, now that receivership is available: see s. 52(2) above.

Section 123   Definition of inability to pay debts

123(1)   [Inability to pay debts]   A company is deemed unable to pay its debts—

(a) if a creditor (by assignment or otherwise) to whom the company is indebted in a sum exceeding £750 then due has served on the company, by leaving it at the company's registered office, a written demand (in the prescribed form) requiring the company to pay the sum so due and the company has for 3 weeks thereafter neglected to pay the sum or to secure or compound for it to the reasonable satisfaction of the creditor, or

(b) if, in England and Wales, execution or other process issued on a judgment, decree or order of any court in favour of a creditor of the company is returned unsatisfied in whole or in part, or

(c) if, in Scotland, the induciae of a charge for payment on an extract decree, or an extract registered bond, or an extract registered protest, have expired without payment being made, or

(d) if, in Northern Ireland, a certificate of unenforceability has been granted in respect of a judgment against the company, or

(e) if it is proved to the satisfaction of the court that the company is unable to pay its debts as they fall due.

123(2)   [Proof that assets less than liabilities]   A company is also deemed unable to pay its debts if it is proved to the satisfaction of the court that the value of the company's assets is less than the amount of its liabilities, taking into account its contingent and prospective liabilities.

123(3)   [Increase, reduction of sum in s. 123(1)(a)]   The money sum for the time being specified in subsection (1)(a) is subject to increase or reduction by order under section 416 in Part XV.

(Former provisions: CA 1985, s. 518 (as amended by IA 1985, Sch. 6, paras. 25, 27); CA 1948, s. 223 (as amended by SI 1984 No. 1199))

General note

This section re-enacts with minor changes of wording the repealed CA 1985, s. 518, as that section was amended by IA 1985. The significant changes made by this amendment are noted below.

The question of a company's inability to pay its debts may be determined by the court as a matter of fact (s. 123(1)(*e*)) or settled by the application of a number of presumptions, four of which (s. 123(1)(*a*)–(*d*)) turn purely on the evidence, while the fifth (s. 123(2)) involves a judicial assessment of the position.

On the meaning of the term "debts", see the note to paras. 12 and 14 of Sch. 8, and the discussion of the related term "creditor" in the note to s. 1(1).

A winding-up order will not be made on the basis of a debt which is genuinely disputed: *Re LHF Wools Ltd* [1970] Ch. 27, *Re Trinity Assurance Co. Ltd* [1990] BCC 235, *Re Janeash Ltd* [1990] BCC 250, *Re a Company (No. 0010656 of 1990)* [1991] BCLC 464; contrast *Re a Company (No. 001946 of 1991), ex parte Fin Soft Holding SA* [1991] BCLC 737. In such a case, the court may strike out the petition. Where the company is solvent, it is an abuse of the process of the court to present a petition for winding up based on a disputed debt, which the court will restrain by injunction and may penalise in costs: *Re a Company (No. 0012209 of 1991)* [1992] 1 WLR 351. In the case of a prospective debt which has not yet fallen due, the court may take the view that the matter should be resolved when the petition is heard rather than on an application to strike out: *Securum Finance Ltd* v *Camswell Ltd* [1994] BCC 434. Where the company has a cross-claim against the petitioner pending in another court, the court has a discretion whether to make a winding-up order or to dismiss the petition: *Re FSA Business Software Ltd* [1990] BCC 465.

A petition may not be presented based on a statute-barred debt: *Re Karnos Property Co. Ltd* (1989) 5 BCC 14.

S. 123(1)

Paragraphs (*a*) to (*d*) correspond with events which would, in the case of an individual, have been acts of bankruptcy prior to the passing of the present Act, and survive as grounds for the making of a bankruptcy order (ss. 267, 268). Paragraph (*a*) was modified by IA 1985 by the addition of the words "in the prescribed form", so that an informal demand will now no longer be sufficient for the purpose of this provision.

Section 123(1)(*a*) specifies only one method for the service of a statutory demand, viz. by leaving it at the company's registered office. In *Re a Company* [1985] BCLC 37 Nourse J held that a demand sent by telex was not a good statutory demand; but when Morritt J in *Re a Company No. 008790 of 1990* [1992] BCC 11 was asked to follow this ruling in relation to a demand which had been sent by registered post, he held that, once it was admitted that the demand had been received at the office (albeit through the post), it had been "left at" the office and therefore properly served. Proof of posting alone, however, would not have been sufficient. It is not clear whether a similar interpretation could be applied to the case of a demand sent by telex (or fax) which had admittedly been received.

Under the previous legislation an inaccuracy in the statutory demand, such as an overstatement of the sum due, was normally regarded as fatal, but there have now been several rulings under s. 268 of the present Act which mark a departure from the earlier law, and have not treated a defective statutory demand as invalid: see the notes to that section. It is likely that a similar approach will be taken in regard to a statutory demand under s. 123.

For the form and rules relating to the statutory demand, see IR 1986, rr. 4.4ff.

Paragraph (*e*) (as CA 1985, s. 518(1)(*e*)) formerly read: "if it is proved to the satisfaction of the court that the company is unable to pay its debts (and, in determining that question, the court shall take into account the company's contingent and prospective liabilities)". This formula was unhelpful in that it ran together two issues: (1) the question whether current debts could be met as they fell due, i.e. "commercial" solvency; and (2) the question whether the company would ultimately prove solvent if its future as well as its present liabilities were brought into the reckoning. The confusion was resolved by the amendment made by IA 1985: contingent and prospective liabilities are no longer to be taken into account for the purposes of para. (*e*), while insolvency calculated on a balance-sheet basis becomes a separate test under s. 123(2).

It has been held that failure to pay a debt which is due and not disputed is of itself evidence of insolvency under s. 123(1)(*e*), even though there is other evidence showing a substantial surplus of assets over liabilities (*Cornhill Insurance plc* v *Improvement Services Ltd & Ors* [1986] 1 WLR 114; (1986) 2 BCC 98, 942), and even though a statutory demand has not been served under s. 123(1)(*e*) (*Re Taylor's Industrial Flooring Ltd* [1990] BCC 44).

S. 123(2)

It is not clear from the language of this provision whether the presumption implied by the word "deemed" may be rebutted by proof that the company is in fact able to meet all its current debts. The issue might in any case be resolved by the court deciding in its discretion (see ss. 122, 125) not to make a winding-up order.

S. 123(3)

The present figure of £750 was increased from £200 by SI 1984 No. 1199, para. 2.

Section 124 Application for winding up

124(1) [Application to court] Subject to the provisions of this section, an application to the court for the winding up of a company shall be by petition presented either by the company, or the directors, or by any creditor or creditors (including any contingent or prospective creditor or creditors), contributory or contributories or by the clerk of a magistrates' court in the exercise of the power conferred by section 87A of the Magistrates' Courts Act 1980 (enforcement of fines imposed on companies), or by all or any of those parties, together or separately.

124(2) [Conditions for contributory to present winding up petition] Except as mentioned below, a contributory is not entitled to present a winding-up petition unless either—

(a) the number of members is reduced below 2, or

(b) the shares in respect of which he is a contributory, or some of them, either were originally allotted to him, or have been held by him, and registered in his name, for at least 6 months during the 18 months before the commencement of the winding up, or have devolved on him through the death of a former holder.

124(3) [Non-application of s. 124(2)] A person who is liable under section 76 to contribute to a company's assets in the event of its being wound up may petition on either of the grounds set out in section 122(1)(f) and (g), and subsection (2) above does not then apply; but unless the person is a contributory otherwise than under section 76, he may not in his character as contributory petition on any other ground.

This subsection is deemed included in Chapter VII of Part V of the Companies

Act (redeemable shares; purchase by a company of its own shares) for the purposes of the Secretary of State's power to make regulations under section 179 of that Act.

124(4)   **[Petition by Secretary of State]**   A winding-up petition may be presented by the Secretary of State—

(a) if the ground of the petition is that in section 122(1)(b) or (c), or

(b) in a case falling within section 124A below).

124(5)   **[Petition by official receiver]**   Where a company is being wound up voluntarily in England and Wales, a winding-up petition may be presented by the official receiver attached to the court as well as by any other person authorised in that behalf under the other provisions of this section; but the court shall not make a winding-up order on the petition unless it is satisfied that the voluntary winding up cannot be continued with due regard to the interests of the creditors or contributories.

(Former provisions: CA 1985, s. 519 (as amended by IA 1985, Sch. 6, para. 28); CA 1948, s. 224 (as amended by CA 1967, s. 35(1), CA 1980, Sch. 3, para. 28, CA 1981, s. 58(7)))

General note

This section lists the persons who have standing to present a winding-up petition; but it is not exhaustive, for the Secretary of State for Trade and Industry is empowered to do so by a number of other statutes (e.g. Financial Services Act 1986, s. 72(1)), and the Attorney-General may petition in the case of a charitable company (Charities Act 1960, s. 30 (as amended by CA 1989, s. 111 and the Charities Act 1992, s. 10)). The words "or by the clerk of a magistrates' court in the exercise of the power conferred by section 87A of the Magistrates' Courts Act 1980 (enforcement of fines imposed on companies)" were inserted by the Criminal Justice Act 1988, s. 62(2)(b), with effect from 5 January 1989: see SI 1988 No. 2073 (C. 78). The reference to s. 124A in s. 124(4)(b) replaces, with effect from 21 February 1990, an earlier reference to CA 1985, s. 440, now repealed: see the note to s. 124A below.

The present Act empowers the supervisor of a voluntary scheme (s. 7(4)(b)) to apply to the court for a winding-up order and by Sch. 1, para. 21, states that an administrator and an administrative receiver may present a petition for winding up; but (no doubt as a result of a drafting slip) no mention is made of these office-holders in s. 124(1). A partial attempt has been made to overcome this difficulty without amendment of s. 124(1) by an alteration made to the rules in 1987: r. 4.7(7)(a) declares that an administrator's petition shall be expressed to be "the petition of the company by its administrator". There is no corresponding provision for an administrative receiver, but it appears that the court is prepared to accept a similar practice in this case, i.e. a petition presented by the receiver as the company's agent and in its name: see *Re Television Parlour plc & Ors* (1988) 4 BCC 95 at p. 98, and for a case before the present Act (which could well still govern the situation where the receiver is not an administrative receiver), *Re Emmadart Ltd* [1979] Ch. 540. The supervisor of a voluntary arrangement should probably also petition in the name of the company, although this is nowhere spelt out in the legislation: see the note to s. 7(4)(b).

For the procedure on an application for winding up, see IR 1986, rr. 4.7ff.

An application to restrain the presentation of a winding-up petition should be by originating motion: see the Practice Direction of 11 July 1988, [1988] PCC 404.

S. 124(1)

The directors are now empowered to present a petition for the winding up of their company, as a result of a change made by IA 1985. This has reversed the effect of the decision in *Re Emmadart Ltd* [1979] Ch. 540, in which the court ruled that the practice of allowing a company to present a petition on the strength of a resolution of the directors, which had been tolerated for many years, was irregular. The amendments make it possible in cases of urgency for a petition to be presented without the delay necessarily involved in summoning a general meeting of the company. Where the petition is presented by the directors, they petition in their own names, rather than that of the company; and – at least in the absence of a formal board resolution – they must act unanimously: *Re Instrumentation Electrical Services Ltd* (1988) 4 BCC 301. However, where a proper resolution has been passed by a majority of the directors at a board meeting, it becomes the duty of all its directors, including those who took no part in the meeting and those who voted against the resolution, to implement it; and thereafter any director has authority to present a petition on behalf of all of them: *Re Equiticorp International plc* [1989] 1 WLR 1010; (1989) 5 BCC 599 (a case decided on the similar wording of IA 1986, s. 9(1)). This ruling in effect now gives legal blessing to the practice which was declared irregular in *Re Emmadart Ltd* (above).

Under the former law, a contingent or prospective creditor could not be heard on a petition until he had given security for costs and had established that he had a prima facie case. This requirement was repealed by IA 1985, Sch. 10, Pt. II. A contingent creditor may present a petition on the "just and equitable" ground (s. 122(1)(g)): *Re a Company No. 003028 of 1987* (1987) 3 BCC 575; cf. *Re Dollar Land Holdings plc* [1993] BCC 823.

Where a person has been compelled to pay a debt owed by a company to a third party, the company is under an obligation at common law to reimburse the person who made the payment, and the latter is a prospective creditor of the company with standing to present a petition for its winding up: *Re Healing Research Trustee Co. Ltd* [1991] BCLC 716.

Where a creditor seeks to withdraw a petition, another creditor may apply to be substituted as petitioner. In *Re Wavern Engineering Co. Ltd* (1987) 3 BCC 3 leave was given by the court to a creditor to withdraw a petition in the mistaken belief that no other creditor was willing to support the petition. The court rescinded the leave to withdraw and made an order substituting another creditor as petitioner.

A person who has agreed to take a transfer of shares but whose name has not been entered on the register of members has no standing as a "contributory" to present a winding-up petition: *Re a Company No. 003160 of 1986* (1986) 2 BCC 99, 276, *Re Quickdome Ltd* (1988) 4 BCC 296. As regards the trustee in bankruptcy of a member, see the note to s. 82, above.

S. 124(2), (3)

These provisions restrict the circumstances in which winding-up proceedings may be instituted by a contributory: generally speaking, he must have been a member of at least six months' standing. Supplementing this statutory rule is the principle, long settled at common law, under which the court will dismiss a petition brought by a contributory unless he shows that he will have a financial interest in the outcome of the liquidation, so that, e.g., the holder of fully paid shares may not seek an order for the winding up of a wholly insolvent company (*Re Rica Gold Washing Company* (1879) 11 ChD 36, *Re Chesterfield Catering Co. Ltd* [1977] Ch. 373, *Re Martin-Coulter Enterprises Ltd* (1988) 4 BCC 210). Exceptionally, where the petition (on the "just and equitable" ground) is based on a failure to supply accounts, and by reason of the company's default insufficient accounts are available to tell whether there will in fact be a surplus for contributories, the petitioner is not required to prove that he has a tangible interest in the outcome: *Re Wessex Computer Stationers Ltd* [1992] BCLC 366. The persons liable under s. 76 are (1) former shareholders whose shares have been redeemed or repurchased out of capital by a company which is subsequently wound up insolvent within a year of the transaction, and (2) directors made jointly and severally liable with such former shareholders.

S. 124(5)

An example of this jurisdiction occurred in May 1988 when the Official Receiver obtained High Court Orders appointing him provisional liquidator of some 53 companies in the Manchester area, replacing three named accountants in whose hands the liquidations had been progressing. The Official Receiver was directed to take possession of papers relating to 200 companies being administered by the accountants, with a view to bringing proceedings on the ground that the voluntary liquidations could not be continued with due regard to the interests of creditors and shareholders as required by s. 124(5).

In the exercise of its discretion under this provision the court will normally have regard to the wishes of a majority in value of the company's creditors, where the company is insolvent, but will not necessarily be bound by this: *Re Southard & Co. Ltd* [1979] 1 WLR 1198, *Re Medisco Equipment Ltd* (1983) 1 BCC 98,944, *Re Falcon RJ Developments Ltd* (1987) 3 BCC 146, *Re MCH Services Ltd* (1987) 3 BCC 179, *Re Hewitt Brannan (Tools) Co. Ltd* [1990] BCC 354.

Section 124A   Petition for winding up on grounds of public interest

124A(1)   [Power of Secretary of State]   Where it appears to the Secretary of State from—

(a) any report made or information obtained under Part XIV of the Companies Act 1985 (company investigations, etc.),

(b) any report made under section 94 or 177 of the Financial Services Act 1986 or any information obtained under section 105 of that Act,

(c) any information obtained under section 2 of the Criminal Justice Act 1987 or section 52 of the Criminal Justice (Scotland) Act 1987 (fraud investigations), or

(d) any information obtained under section 83 of the Companies Act 1989 (powers exercisable for purpose of assisting overseas regulatory authorities),

that it is expedient in the public interest that a company should be wound up, he may present a petition for it to be wound up if the court thinks it just and equitable for it to be so.

124A(2)   [Non-application]   This section does not apply if the company is already being wound up by the court.

(Former provisions: CA 1985, s. 440 (as amended by Financial Services Act 1986, s. 198, Criminal Justice (Scotland) Act 1987, s. 55(a), Criminal Justice Act 1988, s. 145(a)); CA 1967, s. 35(1))

General note

When parts of CA 1985 were consolidated into IA 1986, s. 440 of CA 1985 was overlooked. This has now been remedied by CA 1989, ss. 60, 212 and Sch. 24, which repealed s. 440 and re-enacted it, with modifications, as the present s. 124A, and also made the consequential amendment to IA 1986, s. 124(4)(b), above. These changes were implemented, with effect from 21 February 1990, by SI 1990 No. 142 (C. 5), art. 4.

Section 440 of CA 1985 (as amended prior to its repeal) read as follows:

"Power of Secretary of State to present winding-up petition

If in the case of a body corporate liable to be wound up under this Act it appears to the Secretary of State from a report made by inspectors under section 437 above or section 94 of the Financial Services Act 1986, or from information or documents obtained under section 447 or 448 below or section 105 of that Act or section 52 of the Criminal Justice (Scotland) Act 1987 or section 2 of the Criminal Justice Act 1987, that it is expedient in the public interest that the body should be wound up, he may (unless the body is already being wound up by the court) present a petition for it to be so wound up if the court thinks it just and equitable for it to be so."

For an example of the exercise of this jurisdiction, see *Re Walter L. Jacob & Co. Ltd* (1989) 5 BCC 244; and of a refusal to exercise it, *Re Secure & Provide plc* [1992] BCC 405.

Where the Secretary of State decided not to pursue a petition on public interest grounds under s. 124A, Harman J declined an application by contributories of the company to be substituted as petitioners: the existing evidence, he said, would not be material to the revised petition, which would be on different grounds (*Re Xyllyx plc (No. 1)* [1992] BCLC 376).

Section 125　Powers of court on hearing of petition

125(1)　[Extent of powers]　On hearing a winding-up petition the court may dismiss it, or adjourn the hearing conditionally or unconditionally, or make an interim order, or any other order that it thinks fit; but the court shall not refuse to make a winding-up order on the ground only that the company's assets have been mortgaged to an amount equal to or in excess of those assets, or that the company has no assets.

125(2)　[Just and equitable winding up]　If the petition is presented by members of the company as contributories on the ground that it is just and equitable that the company should be wound up, the court, if it is of opinion—

(a) that the petitioners are entitled to relief either by winding up the company or by some other means, and

(b) that in the absence of any other remedy it would be just and equitable that the company should be wound up,

shall make a winding-up order; but this does not apply if the court is also of the opinion both that some other remedy is available to the petitioners and that they are acting unreasonably in seeking to have the company wound up instead of pursuing that other remedy.

(Former provisions: CA 1985, s. 520; CA 1948, s. 225)

S. 125(1)

This provision gives the court the widest discretion.

There is no established rule, comparable with that applicable in the case of a contributory petitioner (see the note to s. 124(2) above), that a creditor's petition will be dismissed unless he can show that he will have a tangible benefit from the liquidation (*Re Crigglestone Coal Co. Ltd* [1906] 2 Ch. 327), but the court's discretion is none the less unfettered, except by the concluding words of the subsection. For recent cases in which the court reviewed the authorities and discussed the basis on which the discretion will be exercised, where a petition is opposed by some creditors, see *Re Television Parlour plc & Ors* (1988) 4 BCC 95; *Re H J Tomkins & Son Ltd* [1990] BCLC 76 and *Re Leigh Estates (UK) Ltd* [1994] BCC 292.

One basis for the exercise of the court's discretion to dismiss a winding-up petition (or to grant a stay of the winding-up proceedings under s. 147) is that of *forum non conveniens*, i.e. that it is more appropriate that the matter be dealt with by a court in some other jurisdiction. In *Re Harrods (Buenos Aires) Ltd* [1992] Ch. 72; [1991] BCC 249, a petition was presented for the winding up of an English-registered company which carried on business exclusively in Argentina. The Court of Appeal ruled that the courts of Argentina were the appropriate forum, and ordered a stay of the English proceedings.

For the procedure on the making of a winding-up order, see IR 1986, rr. 4.20ff.

S. 125(2)

It is not sufficient for the purposes of this provision simply to show that the petitioner has alternative remedies open to him; he must also be acting unreasonably in not pursuing them.

In *Re a Company No. 002567 of 1982* [1983] 1 WLR 927, this subsection was relied on to refuse relief to a petitioner who had agreed to sell his shares to the majority shareholders at an independent valuation and had then reneged on this arrangement.

This was a minority shareholder's petition on the "just and equitable" ground, where it is common to seek in the alternative an order under CA 1985, s. 459, on the grounds of "unfair prejudice". In this situation the court is frequently asked to exercise its discretion under s. 125 (2) on the ground that the petitioner is unreasonably refusing to pursue some other form of relief or to accept some other remedy: see, e.g. *Re a Company No. 003028 of 1987* (1987) 3 BCC 575, *Re a Company No. 003843 of 1986* (1987) 3 BCC 624, *Re a Company No. 003096 of 1987* (1988) 4 BCC 80, *Re a Company No. 001363 of 1988* (1989) 5 BCC 18, *Vujnovich & Anor* v *Vujnovich* (1989) 5 BCC 740, *Re Abbey Leisure Ltd* [1990] BCC 60; *Re a Company No. 00330 of 1991, ex parte Holden* [1991] BCC 241.

In a Practice Direction (see *Practice Direction No. 1 of 1990* [1990] BCC 292) the attention of practitioners is drawn to the undesirability of including "as a matter of course" a prayer for winding up as an alternative to a s. 459 order. It should be included only if that is the relief which the petitioner prefers or if it is considered that it may be the only relief to which he is entitled. This may be seen as an attempt to discourage the use of an alternative prayer for winding up as a tactical device to put pressure on the company and its controllers. (See further the notes to s. 127 below.)

Section 126 Power to stay or restrain proceedings against company

126(1) [Exercise of power] At any time after the presentation of a winding-up petition, and before a winding-up order has been made, the company, or any creditor or contributory, may—

    (a) where any action or proceeding against the company is pending in the High Court or Court of Appeal in England and Wales or Northern Ireland, apply to the court in which the action or proceeding is pending for a stay of proceedings therein, and

    (b) where any other action or proceeding is pending against the company, apply to the court having jurisdiction to wind up the company to restrain further proceedings in the action or proceeding;

and the court to which application is so made may (as the case may be) stay, sist or restrain the proceedings accordingly on such terms as it thinks fit.

126(2) [Where company registered under CA, s. 680] In the case of a company registered under section 680 of the Companies Act (pre-1862 companies; companies formed under legislation other than the Companies Acts) or the previous corresponding legislation, where the application to stay, sist or restrain is by a creditor, this section extends to actions and proceedings against any contributory of the company.

(Former provisions: CA 1985, s. 521; CA 1948, ss. 226, 396)

General note

The making of a winding-up order operates automatically to stay all actions and proceedings against the company, as does also the appointment of a provisional liquidator unless the court directs otherwise (see s. 130(2)). This section empowers the court to make interim orders during the period when the hearing of a winding-up application is pending.

In relation to the financial markets, nothing in s. 126 affects any action taken by an exchange or clearing house for the purpose of its default proceedings: CA 1989, s. 161(4).

Section 127   Avoidance of property dispositions, etc.

127   In a winding up by the court, any disposition of the company's property, and any transfer of shares, or alteration in the status of the company's members, made after the commencement of the winding up is, unless the court otherwise orders, void.

(Former provisions: CA 1985, s. 522; CA 1948, s. 227)

General note

When an order is made for the winding up of a company by the court, it is deemed to have commenced from the time of the presentation of the petition or an even earlier time: see s. 129. This section accordingly operates with retrospective effect to avoid the property dispositions and other legal events mentioned, unless the court orders otherwise. It is not necessary that the company should be insolvent.

An application may be made to the court under this section for the prospective validation of a transaction before a winding-up order has been made: see, e.g. *Re A I Levy (Holdings) Ltd* [1964] Ch. 19.

Application may be made to the court by the company itself or by any interested person, such as the disponee of the property: *Re Argentum Reductions (UK) Ltd* [1975] 1 WLR 186. The principles upon which the court will act in exercising its discretion under this section are well settled. The leading case is *Re Gray's Inn Construction Co. Ltd* [1980] 1 WLR 711. Where the company is insolvent, the primary purpose of the section is to ensure that all creditors are paid *pari passu*. A transaction which has, or is likely to have, the effect of reducing the assets available to creditors will not be validated; but if there is no serious risk to creditors or if the company is likely to improve the position of its creditors by trading profitably pending the hearing of the petition, the discretion may be exercised. Payments into or out of the company's bank account were held to be "dispositions of property" for the purposes of this section: *Re Gray's Inn Construction Co. Ltd* (above); *Re McGuinness Bros. (UK) Ltd* (1987) 3 BCC 571, at p. 574; but this view was not followed, in regard to payments into an account which was in credit, in *Re Barn Crown Ltd* [1994] BCC 381. For other recent decisions under the section, see *Re a Company No. 007523 of 1986* (1987) 3 BCC 57 (order refused – company currently trading at a loss), *Re Sugar Properties (Derisley Wood) Ltd* (1987) 3 BCC 88 (order granted authorising sale of shares in racehorses), *Re French's Wine Bar Ltd* (1987) 3 BCC 173 (completion of agreement to sell leasehold property sanctioned), *Re Tramway Building & Construction Co. Ltd* [1988] Ch. 293; (1987) 3 BCC 443 (transfer of land validated: no reduction of assets), *Re Webb Electrical Ltd* (1988) 4 BCC 230 (repayment of advance made by director to company not validated: no benefit to company), *Re Fairway Graphics Ltd* [1991] BCLC 468 (order refused: benefit to creditors not shown), *Re Rafidain Bank* [1992] BCC 376 (order sought for benefit of one creditor only: refused), *Re SA & D Wright Ltd, Denney v John Hudson & Co. Ltd* [1992] BCC 503 (fuel oil supplied to company which enabled it to continue its business; seller's requirement in usual course of trading that payment for previous supplies be made as a condition for delivery of new supplies: held not a preference, and order made validating such payments).

Where the company is solvent, the same considerations do not arise. The court will be concerned to avoid paralysing the company's business, and will normally give leave for it to continue trading, the onus being on the person opposing the grant of leave to justify this course (*Re Burton & Deakin Ltd* [1977] 1 WLR 390).

"The company's property", in s. 127, means property *beneficially* owned by the company: *Re Margart Pty Ltd, Hamilton* v *Westpac Banking Corpn & Anor* (1984) 2 ACLC 709. Where a company has entered into a binding and unconditional contract for the sale of an interest in land (or, probably, any other specifically enforceable contract to alienate property) before the presentation of a winding-up petition against it, it will already have disposed of the beneficial interest in the property concerned, and so, strictly speaking, the completion of the transaction by the conveyance of the legal title after the presentation of the petition is not a "disposition" within s. 127. However, in practice it may be prudent to seek an order from the court that, in so far as the completion may involve any disposition of the property of the company, it should be treated as valid and effective: *Re French's Wine Bar Ltd* (above).

Expenditure of the company's money on litigating the disputes of an individual member will not be condoned by the court: *Re Crossmore Electrical and Civil Engineering Ltd* (1989) 5 BCC 37, *Re a Company No. 005685 of 1988* (1989) 5 BCC 79.

The section applies in the winding up of a foreign company: *Re Sugar Properties (Derisley Wood) Ltd* (above).

It has been common practice for a shareholder petitioning for relief on the grounds of unfair prejudice (CA 1985, s. 459) to add an alternative prayer for the winding up of the company. This automatically brings into operation the provisions of s. 127 so that, unless the court gives leave, the company's business will be paralysed, usually to the prejudice of all concerned. Accordingly, in a Practice Direction (*Practice Direction No. 1 of 1990* [1990] 1WLR 490; [1990] BCC 292), attention is drawn to the undesirability of including as a matter of course a prayer for winding up as an alternative to relief under s. 459; and where such a prayer is included in any petition by a contributory the petitioner is required to state in advance whether he consents or objects to a s. 127 order in the standard form which is appended to the Practice Direction. If he is prepared to consent, the registrar will normally make an order without further inquiry. The text of the standard form of order is as follows:

"ORDER that notwithstanding the presentation of the said petition,

(1) payments made into or out of the bank accounts of the company in the ordinary course of the business of the company, and
(2) dispositions of the property of the company made in the ordinary course of its business for proper value,

between the date of presentation of the petition and the date of judgment on the petition or further order in the meantime shall not be void by virtue of the provisions of s. 127 of the *Insolvency Act* 1986 in the event of an order for the winding up of the company being made on the said petition."

In *Re a Company No. 00687 of 1991* [1991] BCC 210, at p. 212 Harman J gave his approval to the addition of a proviso to the standard order in the following form which, he considered, ought to become a part of the standard order in the future:

"Provided that (the relevant bank) should be under no obligation to verify for itself whether any transaction through the company's bank accounts is in the ordinary course of business or that it represents full market value for the relevant transaction."

A similar provision is made in relation to a voluntary winding up by s. 88, except that it applies only to transfers of shares and alterations in the status of the company's members; and in this case the sanction of the liquidator and not the leave of the court is needed to validate the transaction.

In the context of the financial markets, s. 127 does not apply to a market contract or any disposition of property in pursuance of such a contract, the provision of margin in relation to market contracts, a market charge, and certain other transactions: see CA 1989, ss. 163(4), 175(3)–(5), and the note on p. 3.

Section **128**   Avoidance of attachments, etc.

128(1)   **[Attachments etc. void]**   Where a company registered in England and Wales is being wound up by the court, any attachment, sequestration, distress or execution put in force against the estate or effects of the company after the commencement of the winding up is void.

128(2)   **[Application to Scotland]**   This section, so far as relates to any estate or effects of the company situated in England and Wales, applies in the case of a company registered in Scotland as it applies in the case of a company registered in England and Wales.

(Former provisions: CA 1985, s. 523; CA 1948, s. 228)

General note

In spite of the apparently unqualified wording of s. 128, it has been held that the court may override the effect of the section by an order made under s. 126(1) or s. 130(2): see, e.g. *The Constellation* [1966] 1 WLR 272.

There is no provision in the Act which avoids attachments, etc. in a similar way in a voluntary winding up; but the liquidator may apply to the court under either s. 126(1) or s. 130(2) to have such a process stayed or set aside, by virtue of the powers conferred on the court by s. 112(1).

Further sections of the Act deal with the question of executions, etc. which have been begun but not completed at the time when the winding up of the company is deemed to commence: see ss. 183, 184.

Section 176 of the present Act is expressed to be without prejudice to this section. Section 176 imposes a charge on goods which have been distrained in the three months before a winding-up order (or their proceeds, if they have been sold) for the benefit of the company's preferential creditors.

In relation to the financial markets, nothing in s. 128 affects any action taken by an exchange or clearing house for the purpose of its default proceedings: CA 1989, s. 161(4).

COMMENCEMENT OF WINDING UP

Section **129**   Commencement of winding up by the court

129(1)   **[Time of passing of resolution]**   If, before the presentation of a petition for the winding up of a company by the court, a resolution has been passed by the company for voluntary winding up, the winding up of the company is deemed to have commenced at the time of the passing of the resolution; and unless the court, on proof of fraud or mistake, directs otherwise, all proceedings taken in the voluntary winding up are deemed to have been validly taken.

129(2)   **[Time of presentation of petition]**   In any other case, the winding up of a company by the court is deemed to commence at the time of the presentation of the petition for winding up.

(Former provisions: CA 1985, s. 524; CA 1948, s. 229)

General note

The effect of the section is to backdate the operation of the winding-up order to the time when the petition for winding up was presented (or, if the company was then already in voluntary liquidation, to the time when the resolution for voluntary winding up was passed.)

On the significance of the word "time", see the note to s. 86.

In the former bankruptcy law, the "doctrine of relation back" applied with similar retrospectivity, so that for many purposes the bankruptcy was deemed to commence from an earlier "available act of bankruptcy". Both the concept of "act of bankruptcy" and the doctrine of relation back were abolished by IA 1985, so that a bankruptcy order is no longer backdated in this way; but no corresponding change has been made in the case of corporate insolvency.

A voluntary liquidation commences at the time of the passing of the resolution for voluntary winding up: see s. 86.

The term "commencement of the winding up" is defined differently for the purposes of s. 185 (effect of diligence in Scotland): see s. 185(3).

It has been held that the periods of limitation prescribed by the Limitation Act 1980 cease to run on the making of a winding-up order, and not (except as against the petitioning creditor) at the time when the winding-up petition is presented: *Re Cases of Taff's Well Ltd* [1992] Ch. 179; [1991] BCC 582. Accordingly, in the case of a six-year period of limitation, the liquidator in a winding up by the court is at liberty to distribute the assets of the company without regard to the claims of creditors which accrued more than six years before the making of the winding-up order. In the same case the judge expressed the view, *obiter,* that an administration order would not prevent time running against a creditor of the company.

Section 130   Consequences of winding-up order

130(1)   [Copy of order to registrar]   On the making of a winding-up order, a copy of the order must forthwith be forwarded by the company (or otherwise as may be prescribed) to the registrar of companies, who shall enter it in his records relating to the company.

130(2)   [Actions stayed on winding up order]   When a winding-up order has been made or a provisional liquidator has been appointed, no action or proceeding shall be proceeded with or commenced against the company or its property, except by leave of the court and subject to such terms as the court may impose.

130(3)   [Actions stayed re companies registered under CA, s. 680]   When an order has been made for winding up a company registered under section 680 of the Companies Act, no action or proceeding shall be commenced or proceeded with against the company or its property or any contibutory of the company, in respect of any debt of the company, except by leave of the court, and subject to such terms as the court may impose.

130(4)   [Effect of order]   An order for winding up a company operates in favour of all the creditors and of all contributories of the company as if made on the joint petition of a creditor and of a contributory.

(Former provisions: CA 1985, s. 525 (as amended by IA 1985, Sch. 6, para. 29); CA 1948, ss. 230, 231, 232, 397)

General note

In relation to the financial markets, nothing in s. 130 affects any action taken by an exchange or clearing house for the purpose of its default proceedings: CA 1989, s. 161(4).

S. 130(1)

Under the rules prescribed for the purposes of this provision the court is required to send three copies of the order to the official receiver, who is then charged with the responsibility for serving the company and the registrar and for gazetting and advertising the order: see IR 1986, r. 4.21.

Neither the registration of a winding-up order in the Companies Registry nor the gazetting of the fact that a company is in liquidation or of the appointment of a liquidator operates as notice to the world that the company is in liquidation: *Ewart* v *Fryer* [1901] 1 Ch. 499, affd. *sub nom. Fryer & Ors* v *Ewart & Ors* [1902] AC 187, *Official Custodian for Charities & Ors* v *Parway Estates Developments Ltd (in liquidation)* [1985] Ch. 151 at p. 160.

The registrar is required to publish in the Gazette notice of the receipt by him of the copy of the winding-up order (CA 1985, s. 711(1)(*p*)); and this amounts to "official notification" of the making of the winding-up order for the purposes of CA 1985, s. 42. On the effect of "official notification", see the note to s. 109, above. It is not easy, however, to reconcile s. 42(1)(*a*) with the provisions contained in ss. 127–129 above which give a winding-up order retrospective effect: this is a difficult question which awaits judicial determination.

In *Re Calmex Ltd* [1989] 1 All ER 485; (1988) 4 BCC 761, a winding-up order had been made against the company in error, and the court exercised its jurisdiction under IR 1986, r. 7.47 to rescind it. The registrar of companies took the view that the winding-up order which had been recorded under s. 130(1) should remain on his files, but the court ordered it to be removed on the ground that the rescinding order had rendered it a nullity.

S. 130(2)

The power conferred on the court by this subsection complements that provided for in s. 126 (1), and has been held to qualify the apparently categorical wording of s. 128: see the note to that section.

Where the court is asked to give leave to bring an action against a company which is in liquidation, it will seek to do what is right and fair in all the circumstances. Leave will be refused if the proposed action raises issues which can with equal convenience and less delay and expense be decided in the liquidation proceedings: *Re Exchange Securities & Commodities Ltd & Ors* [1983] BCLC 186. The court will not undertake any investigation into the merits of the proposed claim or consider the background material to the s. 130 application (*Re Bank of Credit and Commerce International SA (No. 4)*) [1994] 1 BCLC 419; and accordingly in that case the court declined to make an order for specific discovery of certain documents made by the liquidators.

A criminal prosecution against a company is a "proceeding" within the meaning of this subsection. Accordingly, the leave of the court is required before any prosecution may be brought: *R* v *Dickson & Anor* [1992] BCC 719.

S. 130(3)

The companies referred to are those described in s. 126(2) as "pre-1862 companies" and "companies formed under legislation other than the Companies Acts".

INVESTIGATION PROCEDURES

Section 131   Company's statement of affairs

131(1)   [Powers of official receiver]   Where the court has made a winding-up order or appointed a provisional liquidator, the official receiver may require some or all of the persons mentioned in subsection (3) below to make out and submit to him a statement in the prescribed form as to the affairs of the company.

131(2)   [Contents of statement]   The statement shall be verified by affidavit by the persons required to submit it and shall show—

   (a) particulars of the company's assets, debts and liabilities;

   (b) the names and addresses of the company's creditors;

   (c) the securities held by them respectively;

   (d) the dates when the securities were respectively given; and

   (e) such further or other information as may be prescribed or as the official receiver may require.

131(3) **[Persons in s. 131(1)]** The persons referred to in subsection (1) are—

   (a) those who are or have been officers of the company;

   (b) those who have taken part in the formation of the company at any time within one year before the relevant date;

   (c) those who are in the company's employment, or have been in its employment within that year, and are in the official receiver's opinion capable of giving the information required;

   (d) those who are or have been within that year officers of, or in the employment of, a company which is, or within that year was, an officer of the company.

131(4) **[Time for submitting statement]** Where any persons are required under this section to submit a statement of affairs to the official receiver, they shall do so (subject to the next subsection) before the end of the period of 21 days beginning with the day after that on which the prescribed notice of the requirement is given to them by the official receiver.

131(5) **[Release, extension of time]** The official receiver, if he thinks fit, may—

   (a) at any time release a person from an obligation imposed on him under subsection (1) or (2) above; or

   (b) either when giving the notice mentioned in subsection (4) or subsequently, extend the period so mentioned;

and where the official receiver has refused to exercise a power conferred by this subsection, the court, if it thinks fit, may exercise it.

131(6) **[Definitions]** In this section—

   "employment" includes employment under a contract for services; and

   "the relevant date" means—

   (a) in a case where a provisional liquidator is appointed, the date of his appointment; and

   (b) in a case where no such appointment is made, the date of the winding-up order.

131(7) **[Penalty on default]** If a person without reasonable excuse fails to comply with any obligation imposed under this section, he is liable to a fine and, for continued contravention, to a daily default fine.

131(8)   [Scotland]   In the application of this section to Scotland references to the official receiver are to the liquidator or, in a case where a provisional liquidator is appointed, the provisional liquidator.

(Former provision: IA 1985, s. 66, replacing CA 1985, s. 528)

General note

On the making of a winding-up order, the official receiver (in England and Wales) normally becomes liquidator of the company, at least on an interim basis until a liquidator is chosen by the meetings of creditors and contributories under s. 139. (The one exception is where the company is already under the control of an administrator or of the supervisor of a voluntary arrangement: see s. 140.) In order to put the official receiver in possession of information about the company so that he may make the decisions and discharge the duties which rest upon him under the provisions of the Act which follow, the officers and employees of the company and others specified are required to complete and submit to him a "statement of affairs" under this section. This has long been a feature of a winding up by the court, and it is not simply continued in the present Act but extended to the analogous cases of a voluntary arrangement (s. 2(3)(*b*)), an administration order (s. 22), an administrative receivership (ss. 47, 66) and a creditors' voluntary winding up, whether originally so constituted (s. 99) or converted from a members' voluntary winding up when the company turns out to be insolvent (s. 95(3)(*a*)). Failure by the officers and others concerned to comply with this requirement is sanctioned by criminal penalties (s. 131(7)), and untruthfulness in the answers given is punishable as perjury, since s. 131(2) stipulates that the statement shall be verified by affidavit.

In *Re Wallace Smith Trust Co Ltd* [1992] BCC 707, the respondent director had failed to submit a statement of affairs after being required by the official receiver to do so; and the official receiver had then sought and obtained an order ex parte for his public examination in order to obtain the information which ought to have been furnished in the statement of affairs. Ferris J held that, while this course was not an abuse of the process of the court, it would have been more appropriate for a specific order or orders to have been sought under IR 1986, r. 7.20 requiring the director to complete and submit the statement of affairs, and possibly also seeking the order for public examination as an alternative in case the court refused to make the specific orders.

The information given by a person in a statement of affairs may be used in evidence in subsequent proceedings against him, and also against any other person who concurs in the making of the statement: see s. 433.

Where a provisional liquidator has been appointed by the court under s. 135 before a winding-up order has been made, the section also comes into operation and the official receiver may proceed to requisition a statement of affairs in anticipation of the making of a winding-up order which may in due course be made.

The provisions of this and the succeeding sections apply whether or not the company is insolvent.

On the office of official receiver, see ss. 399ff, below.

In Scotland, where there is no official receiver, the functions of the official receiver under this section are conferred by s. 131(8) on the liquidator, who is appointed by the court when the winding-up order is made (s. 138(1)).

For the rules and forms prescribed for the purposes of this section, see IR 1986, rr. 4.32ff. and on enforcement, r. 7.20.

S. 131(1)

Under the repealed CA 1985, s. 528(1), the official liquidator was bound to call for a statement of affairs in all cases, unless he could persuade the court to order otherwise. The present Act gives him a discretion, so that he may dispense with the procedure in any case he considers appropriate. One situation where this would be so is where the winding-up order follows the discharge of an administration order (s. 140), and the administrator is appointed liquidator by the court. (No similar discretion is given to the supervisor, administrator, etc. in the analogous cases established by ss. 2(3)(*b*), 22, etc. that are referred to in the general note to this section.)

S. 131(2)

The information listed here will be required by the official receiver in order that he may make his report to the court under s. 132, and may be relevant to the question whether an application to the court under s. 133 should be made or granted. Details of the creditors will be needed if a meeting of creditors is to be summoned under s. 136(5).

S. 131(3)

The terms "employment" and "the relevant date" are defined in s. 131(6), below. "Officer" includes a director, manager or secretary: see CA 1985, s. 744 and the note to s. 206(3).

S. 131(4)

The period for compliance has been extended from 14 days (CA 1985, s. 528) to 21 days.

S. 131(5)

The discretion here given to the official receiver supplements the general discretionary terms of s. 131(1); previously, his power of dispensation was restricted to granting an extension of time (CA 1985, s. 528(6)). The official receiver's new powers may be applied to a winding up which commenced before the present Act became operative: see Sch. 11, para. 5.

S. 131(6)

The inclusion of a person employed under a contract for services gives the section potentially a very wide scope, extending (for example) to an accountant or auditor.

S. 131(7)

On penalties, see s. 430 and Sch. 10.

S. 131(8)

As noted above, there is no official receiver in Scotland and so the liquidator or provisional liquidator is empowered to act instead. A liquidator or provisional liquidator will have the full range of discretionary powers conferred by this section on the official receiver.

Section 132   Investigation by official receiver

132(1)   [Duty of official receiver]   Where a winding-up order is made by the court in England and Wales, it is the duty of the official receiver to investigate—

  (a) if the company has failed, the causes of the failure; and

  (b) generally, the promotion, formation, business, dealings and affairs of the company,

and to make such report (if any) to the court as he thinks fit.

132(2)   [Report prima facie evidence]   The report is, in any proceedings, prima facie evidence of the facts stated in it.

(Former provision: IA 1985, s. 67, replacing CA 1985, s. 530)

S. 132(1)

Under the former law contained in CA 1985, s. 530, it was the duty of the official receiver to submit a preliminary report to the court in the case of every compulsory winding up, whether the company was solvent or insolvent, giving certain financial information about the company and, if the company had failed, explaining the causes of the failure; and stating whether in his opinion further inquiry into the company's affairs was desirable. Under this new provision, the official receiver has a discretion to decide himself whether a report to the court is called for, but he remains under a statutory duty to investigate the matters listed in paras. (*a*) and (*b*). (It is rather surprising that it has not been left to the official receiver to decide in his own judgment whether the inquiry in para. (*b*) is necessary if the company has not failed, especially since the grounds on which a winding-up order may be made under s. 122(1) include some which have no necessary connection with irregularity.)

The officers of the company (and its employees and other persons who are specified in s. 235(3)) are under a duty to co-operate with the official receiver: see s. 235, below.

S. 132(2)

The evidentiary presumption applies not only for the purpose of any immediate court hearing, but "in any proceedings".

Section 133   Public examination of officers

133(1)   [Application to court]   Where a company is being wound up by the court, the official receiver or, in Scotland, the liquidator may at any time before the dissolution of the company apply to the court for the public examination of any person who—

    (a) is or has been an officer of the company; or

    (b) has acted as liquidator or administrator of the company or as receiver or manager or, in Scotland, receiver of its property; or

    (c) not being a person falling within paragraph (a) or (b), is or has been concerned, or has taken part, in the promotion, formation or management of the company.

133(2)   [Request to make application]   Unless the court otherwise orders, the official receiver or, in Scotland, the liquidator shall make an application under subsection (1) if he is requested in accordance with the rules to do so by—

    (a) one-half, in value, of the company's creditors; or

    (b) three-quarters, in value, of the company's contributories.

133(3)   [Court's duties]   On an application under subsection (1), the court shall direct that a public examination of the person to whom the application relates shall be held on a day appointed by the court; and that person shall attend on that day and be publicly examined as to the promotion, formation or management of the company or as to the conduct of its business and affairs, or his conduct or dealings in relation to the company.

133(4)   [Persons taking part]   The following may take part in the public examination of a person under this section and may question that person concerning the matters mentioned in subsection (3), namely—

    (a) the official receiver;

(b) the liquidator of the company;

(c) any person who has been appointed as special manager of the company's property or business;

(d) any creditor of the company who has tendered a proof or, in Scotland, submitted a claim in the winding up;

(e) any contributory of the company.

(Former provisions: IA 1985, s. 68(1)–(4), replacing CA 1985, s. 564)

General note

Under CA 1985, provision was made for both a public examination (ss. 563, 564) and a private examination (s. 561) of officers and others in a compulsory winding up, but the jurisdiction under the first-mentioned sections could not be invoked unless the official receiver had made a "further report" to the court that in his opinion a fraud had been committed. For this reason, public examinations of company officers were very rarely held. The practice in this respect appeared to be very indulgent towards the officers of insolvent companies, when contrasted with that under the law governing individual bankruptcies which stipulated for a mandatory public examination of the debtor: see the Cork Committee's *Report*, paras. 653, 657. The new provisions set out in ss. 133, 134 of the present Act are designed to encourage a much wider use of the public examination procedure in corporate insolvencies: not only is the precondition of a prima facie case of fraud no longer necessary, but the creditors and the contributories are given (by s. 133(2)) an independent right to invoke the court's jurisdiction to order an examination.

The power conferred on the court by CA 1985, s. 561 to summon a somewhat wider range of persons to appear before it for private examination is preserved by ss. 236, 237, below.

Although s. 133 is by its terms expressed to apply only in a winding up by the court, it is likely that s. 112 could be invoked to make it apply also in a voluntary liquidation: see *Re Campbell Coverings Ltd (No. 2)* [1954] Ch. 225, and *Bishopsgate Investment Management Ltd (in provisional liqidation)* v *Maxwell & Anor, Mirror Group Newspapers plc & Anor* v *Maxwell & Ors* [1993] Ch. 1; [1992] BCC 222, at pp. 24, 46; 232, 249.

Under the present section, the court has power to direct the public examination of an officer of a company in compulsory liquidation who is outside the jurisdiction, and to order service of the order of the court or other relevant document to be effected on him outside the jurisdiction: *Re Seagull Manufacturing Co. Ltd (in liq.)* [1993] Ch. 345; [1993] BCC 241. (For the position in a private examination, see the notes to s. 236, below.)

For the rules regarding the procedure for obtaining an order for examination, and the conduct of the examination, see IR 1986, rr. 4.211ff. The examination is on oath: r. 4.215(1). For the sanctions for non-attendance, see s. 134, below.

S. 133(1)

The public examination provisions apply also to Scotland (unlike s. 132). They may be invoked whether the company is solvent or insolvent.

On the meaning of the term "officer", see the note to s. 206(3).

S. 133(2), (3)

The rôle of the court is curiously stated, in that it is given no discretion by s. 133(3) to refuse an order once an application has been made; but under s. 133(2) it is empowered to intervene in order to *prevent* an application from being made to it by the official receiver following a request by the creditors or contributories. The grounds on which the court may make such an order are not indicated in the present section, but IR 1986, r. 4.213(5) indicates that the official receiver may object that the creditors' request is an unreasonable one. It does, however, appear to be plain from the two subsections, read together, that any other objectors will be out of court if they do not take action before the official receiver does.

For the procedure, see IR 1986, rr. 4.213ff.

S. 133(4)

It appears that an officer or past officer of the company, though liable himself to be examined under the section, has no right to question those of his colleagues being examined with him unless he falls coincidentally within one of the categories (*a*)–(*e*). See further IR 1986, r. 4.215.

Section 134   Enforcement of s. 133

134(1)   **[Non-attendance]**   If a person without reasonable excuse fails at any time to attend his public examination under section 133, he is guilty of a contempt of court and liable to be punished accordingly.

134(2)   **[Warrant, etc. re non-attendance]**   In a case where a person without reasonable excuse fails at any time to attend his examination under section 133 or there are reasonable grounds for believing that a person has absconded, or is about to abscond, with a view to avoiding or delaying his examination under that section, the court may cause a warrant to be issued to a constable or prescribed officer of the court—

    (a) for the arrest of that person; and

    (b) for the seizure of any books, papers, records, money or goods in that person's possession.

134(3)   **[Consequences of warrant]**   In such a case the court may authorise the person arrested under the warrant to be kept in custody, and anything seized under such a warrant to be held, in accordance with the rules, until such time as the court may order.

(Former provision: IA 1985, s. 68(5), (6))

General note

This provision deals with the enforcement of s. 133. Other details relating to the conduct of the examination and summoning of those required to attend are dealt with in the rules: see IR 1986, rr. 4.211ff, 7.22.

S. 134(2)

A person who appeals unsuccessfully against an order for his arrest under s. 134(2)(*a*) is "singularly close" to being in contempt of court, and may be ordered to pay the official receiver's costs on an indemnity basis: *Re Avatar Communications Ltd* (1988) 4 BCC 473.

APPOINTMENT OF LIQUIDATOR

Section 135   Appointment and powers of provisional liquidator

135(1)   **[Time of appointment]**   Subject to the provisions of this section, the court may, at any time after the presentation of a winding-up petition, appoint a liquidator provisionally.

135(2)   [Appointment in England, Wales]   In England and Wales, the appointment of a provisional liquidator may be made at any time before the making of a winding-up order; and either the official receiver or any other fit person may be appointed.

135(3)   [Appointment in Scotland]   In Scotland, such an appointment may be made at any time before the first appointment of liquidators.

135(4)   [Provisional liquidator]   The provisional liquidator shall carry out such functions as the court may confer on him.

135(5)   [Powers of provisional liquidator]   When a liquidator is provisionally appointed by the court, his powers may be limited by the order appointing him.

(Former provisions: CA 1985, s. 532; IA 1985, s. 69(3))

General note

The primary reason for appointing a provisional liquidator is normally to ensure the preservation of the company's assets pending the hearing of the winding-up petition. Since an appointment anticipates the eventual making of a winding-up order virtually as a foregone conclusion, it is usually made only with the consent of the company itself or in a clear case of insolvency.

A provisional liquidator must be qualified to act as an insolvency practitioner in relation to the company in question: see s. 388(1)(*a*). In *Re W F Fearman Ltd (No. 2)* (1988) 4 BCC 141 it was held to be inappropriate for the court to make an order directly appointing the provisional liquidators, who were already in office, to be the liquidators of the company when the winding-up order was subsequently made, since to do so would deprive the creditors of their say in the selection of a liquidator under s. 136. However, a practical solution was found by giving leave to the official receiver to continue to use the services of the former provisional liquidators as special managers.

For the relevant rules, see IR 1986, rr. 4.25ff.

Section 136   Functions of official receiver in relation to office of liquidator

136(1)   [Application]   The following provisions of this section have effect, subject to section 140 below, on a winding-up order being made by the court in England and Wales.

136(2)   [Official receiver liquidator]   The official receiver, by virtue of his office, becomes the liquidator of the company and continues in office until another person becomes liquidator under the provisions of this Part.

136(3)   [Vacancy]   The official receiver is, by virtue of his office, the liquidator during any vacancy.

136(4)   [Powers of official receiver when liquidator]   At any time when he is the liquidator of the company, the official receiver may summon separate meetings of the company's creditors and contributories for the purpose of choosing a person to be liquidator of the company in place of the official receiver.

136(5)   [Duty of official receiver]   It is the duty of the official receiver—

(a) as soon as practicable in the period of 12 weeks beginning with the day on which the winding-up order was made, to decide whether to exercise his power under subsection (4) to summon meetings, and

(b) if in pursuance of paragraph (a) he decides not to exercise that power, to give notice of his decision, before the end of that period, to the court and to the company's creditors and contributories, and

(c) (whether or not he has decided to exercise that power) to exercise his power to summon meetings under subsection (4) if he is at any time requested, in accordance with the rules, to do so by one-quarter, in value, of the company's creditors;

and accordingly, where the duty imposed by paragraph (c) arises before the official receiver has performed a duty imposed by paragraph (a) or (b), he is not required to perform the latter duty.

136(6) [Contents of s. 136(5)(b) notice]   A notice given under subsection (5)(b) to the company's creditors shall contain an explanation of the creditors' power under subsection (5)(c) to require the official receiver to summon meetings of the company's creditors and contributories.

(Former provisions: IA 1985, s. 70(1)–(3), (4)(a), (5), (6), replacing CA 1985, s. 533)

General note

Under the former law (CA 1985, s. 533), the official receiver became provisional liquidator by virtue of his office immediately upon the making of the winding-up order, and was obliged in every case to proceed to summon the meetings of creditors and contributories now referred to in s. 136(4), for the purpose of considering whether to appoint another person as liquidator. The present provision leaves it to the official receiver himself to decide whether or not to convene the meetings. He has 12 weeks in which to reach a decision, but the creditors may in any case require him to summon the meetings.

If no meetings are convened, the official receiver continues in office as liquidator. His decision not to convene meetings is therefore, in effect, a decision to keep the liquidation in his own hands.

Section 136 should be read in conjunction with s. 137, which alternatively gives the Secretary of State power to appoint a liquidator other than the official receiver.

S. 136(1)

Section 140 applies when the company is already subject to an administration order or voluntary arrangement. The court is then empowered to make an immediate appointment of the insolvency practitioner who has been the administrator or supervisor to be the liquidator in the winding up.

S. 136(2)

Under the repealed CA 1985, s. 533(2), the official liquidator became the "provisional" liquidator. In the new Act, he is made "liquidator", and the term "provisional liquidator" is reserved for appointments made under s. 135 above *before* a winding-up order is made.

If the company is already in voluntary liquidation when a winding-up order is made, the existing liquidator is displaced: see IR 1986, rr. 4.136 and 4.147.

S. 136(4), (5)

The official receiver must make an initial decision, within the first 12 weeks after the making of the winding-up order, whether to summon meetings or not; and if he decides not to, he must give the notices specified by s. 136(5)(*b*). However, he is free to convene the meetings even after this 12-week period has expired, and the creditors' power to requisition him to call the meetings also continues. This is made clear by the use of the phrase "at any time" in s. 136(4) and 5(*c*).

For the rules dealing with the summoning of meetings under this section, see IR 1986, rr. 4.50ff; and for the official receiver's reporting obligations, see rr. 4.43ff: see also r. 4.107 (hand-over of assets).

Section 137　Appointment by Secretary of State

137(1)　[Application by official receiver]　In a winding up by the court in England and Wales the official receiver may, at any time when he is the liquidator of the company, apply to the Secretary of State for the appointment of a person as liquidator in his place.

137(2)　[Decision by official receiver]　If meetings are held in pursuance of a decision under section 136(5)(a), but no person is chosen to be liquidator as a result of those meetings, it is the duty of the official receiver to decide whether to refer the need for an appointment to the Secretary of State.

137(3)　[Duty of Secretary of State]　On an application under subsection (1), or a reference made in pursuance of a decision under subsection (2); the Secretary of State shall either make an appointment or decline to make one.

137(4)　[Notice of appointment by liquidator]　Where a liquidator has been appointed by the Secretary of State under subsection (3), the liquidator shall give notice of his appointment to the company's creditors or, if the court so allows, shall advertise his appointment in accordance with the directions of the court.

137(5)　[Contents of notice or advertisement]　In that notice or advertisement the liquidator shall—

(a) state whether he proposes to summon a general meeting of the company's creditors under section 141 below for the purpose of determining (together with any meeting of contributories) whether a liquidation committee should be established under that section, and

(b) if he does not propose to summon such a meeting, set out the power of the company's creditors under that section to require him to summon one.

(Former provision: IA 1985, s. 70(4)(b), (7)–(9))

General note

This is a new provision introduced by IA 1985. If the official receiver forms the opinion that the conduct of the winding up may be handed over to a private liquidator, he may either invite the creditors and contributories to choose an insolvency practitioner at meetings convened under s. 136, or apply under the present section to the Secretary of State to make an appointment. The Secretary of State may decline to do so (s. 137(3)), in which case the official receiver is, in effect, directed to continue in office.

There is no provision corresponding to s. 136(5)(*c*) empowering the creditors to require the official receiver to make an application to the Secretary of State under this section, or to apply to him directly themselves.

For the relevant rules, see IR 1986, rr. 4.104, 4.107.

S. 137(1)

The official receiver may make an application under this section "at any time", and may plainly do so as an alternative to summoning meetings under s. 136(4). Once he has called the meetings, however, he is probably bound to go through with that procedure, and could have recourse to his powers under the present section only if the meetings fail to choose a liquidator.

For transitional provisions affecting existing liquidations, see Sch. 11, para. 6(2).

S. 137(2)

If the meetings do not choose a liquidator, it is the "duty" of the official liquidator to make a *decision* under this subsection, but he is under no duty to make a *reference*: he may perfectly well decide to stay in office as liquidator himself.

S. 137(3)

As has already been observed, a negative decision by the Secretary of State is effectively a direction to the official receiver that he should continue in office himself.

S. 137(4), (5)

The court may allow the liquidator to advertise the fact of his appointment rather than notify creditors individually. No guidance is given as to the basis on which the court should exercise this discretion, but fairly obviously it might be used to avoid unjustified expense where there are many creditors, bearing in mind that the only purpose for which the meeting is to be summoned is to decide whether to appoint a liquidation committee.

Section 138   Appointment of liquidator in Scotland

138(1)   [Appointment]   Where a winding-up order is made by the court in Scotland, a liquidator shall be appointed by the court at the time when the order is made.

138(2)   [Period of office of interim liquidator]   The liquidator so appointed (here referred to as "the interim liquidator") continues in office until another person becomes liquidator in his place under this section or the next.

138(3)   [Meetings to be summoned]   The interim liquidator shall (subject to the next subsection) as soon as practicable in the period of 28 days beginning with the day on which the winding-up order was made or such longer period as the court may allow, summon separate meetings of the company's creditors and contributories for the purpose of choosing a person (who may be the person who is the interim liquidator) to be liquidator of the company in place of the interim liquidator.

138(4)   [Qualification to s. 138(3)]   If it appears to the interim liquidator, in any case where a company is being wound up on grounds including its inability to pay its debts, that it would be inappropriate to summon under subsection (3) a meeting of the company's contributories, he may summon only a meeting of the company's creditors for the purpose mentioned in that subsection.

138(5)   [If no person appointed at meetings]   If one or more meetings are held in pursuance of this section but no person is appointed or nominated by the meeting or meetings, the interim liquidator shall make a report to the court which shall appoint either the interim liquidator or some other person to be liquidator of the company.

138(6) **[Notification]**   A person who becomes liquidator of the company in place of the interim liquidator shall, unless he is appointed by the court, forthwith notify the court of that fact.

(Former provisions: CA 1985, s. 535 (as amended by IA 1985, Sch. 6, para. 30); IA 1985, s. 71)

General note

There is no official receiver in Scotland, or any equivalent public officer, and so the liquidator in a Scottish winding up is invariably a private insolvency practitioner. This section provides for the appointment of an "interim liquidator", whose duty it is to take custody of the company's property and to summon meetings, etc., as in a winding up in England or Wales, but he does not enjoy the discretionary powers entrusted to the official receiver under ss. 136, 137, and the court is more closely involved throughout the proceedings. The Secretary of State's powers under s. 137 do not apply in Scotland.

S. 138(5)

In contrast with the position in England and Wales (s. 137(2)), the interim liquidator's obligation is mandatory and not discretionary, and the residual power of appointment lies with the court rather than the Secretary of State.

Section 139   Choice of liquidator at meetings of creditors and contributories

139(1) **[Application]**   This section applies where a company is being wound up by the court and separate meetings of the company's creditors and contributories are summoned for the purpose of choosing a person to be liquidator of the company.

139(2) **[Nomination of liquidator]**   The creditors and the contributories at their respective meetings may nominate a person to be liquidator.

139(3) **[Liquidator]**   The liquidator shall be the person nominated by the creditors or, where no person has been so nominated, the person (if any) nominated by the contributories.

139(4) **[Where different persons nominated]**   In the case of different persons being nominated, any contributory or creditor may, within 7 days after the date on which the nomination was made by the creditors, apply to the court for an order either—

    (a) appointing the person nominated as liquidator by the contributories to be a liquidator instead of, or jointly with, the person nominated by the creditors; or

    (b) appointing some other person to be liquidator instead of the person nominated by the creditors.

(Former provision: IA 1985, s. 72)

General note

This section lays down the rules and procedure for the appointment of a liquidator when meetings of the creditors and contributories are convened for the purpose. It is very similar in terms to s. 100, which governs a creditors' voluntary winding up. Unlike ss. 136–137, it applies in Scotland as well as England and Wales.

The word "nominate" is used in a sense equivalent to "appoint": see the notes to s. 100.

For the relevant rules, see IR 1986, rr. 4.100, 4.102.

Section 140   Appointment by the court following administration or voluntary arrangement

140(1)   [Appointment of administrator]   Where a winding-up order is made immediately upon the discharge of an administration order, the court may appoint as liquidator of the company the person who has ceased on the discharge of the administration order to be the administrator of the company.

140(2)   [Appointment of supervisor]   Where a winding-up order is made at a time when there is a supervisor of a voluntary arrangement approved in relation to the company under Part I, the court may appoint as liquidator of the company the person who is the supervisor at the time when the winding-up order is made.

140(3)   [Position of official receiver]   Where the court makes an appointment under this section, the official receiver does not become the liquidator as otherwise provided by section 136(2), and he has no duty under section 136(5)(a) or (b) in respect of the summoning of creditors' or contributories' meetings.

(Former provision: IA 1985, s. 73)

General note

This section links in with the new procedures introduced by IA 1985 for the appointment of an administrator (IA 1986, ss. 8ff) and for instituting a scheme of voluntary arrangement (IA 1986, ss. 1ff). If a compulsory winding up follows immediately upon an administration or a voluntary arrangement, an insolvency practitioner who is fully aware of the company's circumstances will already be in office as the administrator or supervisor of the scheme, and it may make good sense to appoint him to the post of liquidator at the time when the winding-up order is made, so that he can get on with the conduct of the liquidation straightaway. Many of the formalities which are necessary in the case of a normal winding-up order can be by-passed in such a case. In *Re Charnley Davies Business Services Ltd & Ors* (1987) 3 BCC 408, the court (with some reluctance) appointed the former administrator as liquidator even though litigation was pending in which his conduct while administrator was to be challenged as irregular.

For the relevant rules, see IR 1986, rr. 4.49A, 4.102. The new r. 4.49A, inserted by I(A)R 1987, deals with the situation where the existence of further creditors becomes known to the insolvency practitioner who becomes liquidator.

S. 140(1), (2)

Section 140 does not empower the court to appoint as liquidator a person who has not previously occupied the position of administrator or supervisor, whether alone or as an additional liquidator (*Re Exchange Travel (Holdings) Ltd & Ors* [1992] BCC 954). If an appointment is not made under this section, the normal procedure under s. 136 and 139 must be followed.

LIQUIDATION COMMITTEES

Section 141   Liquidation committee (England and Wales)

141(1)   [Meetings may establish committee]   Where a winding-up order has been made by the court in England and Wales and separate meetings of creditors and contributories have been summoned for the purpose of choosing a person to be liquidator, those meetings may establish a committee ("the liquidation committee") to exercise the functions conferred on it by or under this Act.

141(2)   [Separate meetings may be summoned]   The liquidator (not being the official receiver) may at any time, if he thinks fit, summon separate general meetings of the company's creditors and contributories for the purpose of determining whether such a committee should be established and, if it is so determined, of establishing it.

The liquidator (not being the official receiver) shall summon such a meeting if he is requested, in accordance with the rules, to do so by one-tenth, in value, of the company's creditors.

141(3)   [Where meetings disagree]   Where meetings are summoned under this section, or for the purpose of choosing a person to be liquidator, and either the meeting of creditors or the meeting of contributories decides that a liquidation committee should be established, but the other meeting does not so decide or decides that a committee should not be established, the committee shall be established in accordance with the rules, unless the court otherwise orders.

141(4)   [Committee not to function where official receiver liquidator]   The liquidation committee is not to be able or required to carry out its functions at any time when the official receiver is liquidator; but at any such time its functions are vested in the Secretary of State except to the extent that the rules otherwise provide.

141(5)   [Where no committee etc.]   Where there is for the time being no liquidation committee, and the liquidator is a person other than the official receiver, the functions of such a committee are vested in the Secretary of State except to the extent that the rules otherwise provide.

(Former provision: IA 1985, s. 74 (replacing CA 1985, ss. 546–548)

General note

This provision is in substance the same as the repealed IA 1985, s. 74; but the committee has now been given a new name (see below), which is reflected in the side-note.

The "committee of inspection" has been a feature of the law of bankruptcy and company liquidation for over a century. The title (said to be of Scottish origin) had become a misnomer, as the Cork Committee (*Report,* para. 930) observed, for "inspection" (presumably, of the company's books) has not been part of the rôle of such a committee in recent practice. The Cork Committee recommended that the committee should be retained, to receive regular reports on the progress of the liquidation, to refer any grievances that they might have to the court, and also to discharge the traditional statutory function of giving consent on behalf of the creditors generally to certain courses of action by the liquidator. It was further recommended that similar committees should be established for other insolvency procedures, such as administration and administrative receivership; and finally that the name "committee of inspection" should be abandoned.

The legislators in IA 1985 accepted these proposals, but left the committee without any name other than "the committee established under s. 74". In the present Act, the title "liquidation committee" has been substituted, both here and in relation to a creditors' voluntary winding up (s. 101), while for the purposes of an administration (s. 26) and an administrative receivership (ss. 49, 68), where it is composed entirely of creditors, it is called the "creditors' committee" or "committee of creditors".

In marked contrast to the detailed provisions of s. 101, the present section has nothing to say about the composition of the committee, but this is clarified by the rules. It is stated in IR 1986, r. 4.152 that the committee shall consist of between three and five creditors and also (if the company is solvent) up to three contributories. Once the creditors have all been paid in full, the creditor members of the committee cease to be members: r. 4.171(4).

S. 141(1), (2)

The liquidation committee has no rôle to play while the official receiver is liquidator, as is confirmed by later subsections, and so the machinery for establishing a committee comes into operation only when there is a private liquidator, or when the appointment of a private liquidator is contemplated. The present provisions should be read in conjunction with ss. 136(4), 137(5), 139 and 140(3).

Where a liquidator has been appointed by court order under s. 140, following upon an administration or voluntary arrangement, s. 141(2) will apply, so that he or the creditors may take steps to establish a liquidation committee even though the official receiver is released from his duties in this regard by s. 140(3).

S. 141(4), (5)

A number of provisions in the Act empower the liquidator to act "with the consent of the liquidation committee" (see, e.g. s. 167(1)(*a*)), while others require him to give notice to the committee of what he has done (see, e.g. s. 167(2)). By substituting the Secretary of State for the committee in the circumstances set out, the present subsections enable the liquidator to exercise such powers when there is no committee or none competent to act.

The rules which have been made for the purposes of this section are IR 1986, rr. 4.151ff. and, for s. 141(4), (5), r. 4.172.

Section 142   Liquidation committee (Scotland)

142(1)   **[Establishing committees in Scotland]**   Where a winding-up order has been made by the court in Scotland and separate meetings of creditors and contributories have been summoned for the purpose of choosing a person to be liquidator or, under section 138(4), only a meeting of creditors has been summoned for that purpose, those meetings or (as the case may be) that meeting may establish a committee ("the liquidation committee") to exercise the functions conferred on it by or under this Act.

142(2)   **[Separate meetings may be summoned]**   The liquidator may at any time, if he thinks fit, summon separate general meetings of the company's creditors and contributories for the purpose of determining whether such a committee should be established and, if it is so determined, of establishing it.

142(3)　[Meetings to be summoned on request]　The liquidator, if appointed by the court otherwise than under section 139(4)(a), is required to summon meetings under subsection (2) if he is requested, in accordance with the rules, to do so by one-tenth, in value, of the company's creditors.

142(4)　[Where meetings disagree]　Where meetings are summoned under this section, or for the purpose of choosing a person to be liquidator, and either the meeting of creditors or the meeting of contributories decides that a liquidation committee should be established, but the other meeting does not so decide or decides that a committee should not be established, the committee shall be established in accordance with the rules, unless the court otherwise orders.

142(5)　[Where no committee etc.]　Where in the case of any winding up there is for the time being no liquidation committee, the functions of such a committee are vested in the court except to the extent that the rules otherwise provide.

142(6)　[Powers and duties of committee]　In addition to the powers and duties conferred and imposed on it by this Act, a liquidation committee has such of the powers and duties of commissioners in a sequestration as may be conferred and imposed on such committees by the rules.

(Former provision: IA 1985, s. 75)

General note

This section contains provisions for Scotland similar to those laid down for England and Wales by s. 141, and the notes to that section generally apply here also, apart from the references to the official receiver, who of course has no Scottish counterpart.

THE LIQUIDATOR'S FUNCTIONS

Section 143　General functions in winding up by the court

143(1)　[Functions]　The functions of the liquidator of a company which is being wound up by the court are to secure that the assets of the company are got in, realised and distributed to the company's creditors and, if there is a surplus, to the persons entitled to it.

143(2)　[Duty of liquidator not official receiver]　It is the duty of the liquidator of a company which is being wound up by the court in England and Wales, if he is not the official receiver—

(a)　to furnish the official receiver with such information,

(b)　to produce to the official receiver, and permit inspection by the official receiver of, such books, papers and other records, and

(c)　to give the official receiver such other assistance,

as the official receiver may reasonably require for the purposes of carrying out his functions in relation to the winding up.

(Former provision: IA 1985, s. 69(1), (2); CA 1985, s. 534(b))

S. 143(1)

The functions of a liquidator in a compulsory winding up are expressed in this subsection rather differently from those of a liquidator in a voluntary liquidation, set out in s. 107; but in substance their duties are broadly the same; and similar rules apply regarding the application of assets: see the notes to s. 107.

S. 143(2)

On enforcement of the liquidator's obligations, see IR 1986, r. 7.20.

Section 144   Custody of company's property

144(1)   [Liquidator to take property into custody]   When a winding-up order has been made, or where a provisional liquidator has been appointed, the liquidator or the provisional liquidator (as the case may be) shall take into his custody or under his control all the property and things in action to which the company is or appears to be entitled.

144(2)   [In Scotland where no liquidator]   In a winding up by the court in Scotland, if and so long as there is no liquidator, all the property of the company is deemed to be in the custody of the court.

(Former provisions: CA 1985, s. 537; CA 1948, s. 243)

S. 144(1)

The term "property" has a very comprehensive definition for the purposes of the present Act: see s. 436.

S. 144(2)

There is no equivalent to this provision for England and Wales in view of s. 136(2), (3), which ensures that the official receiver holds the office of liquidator if there is any vacancy.

Section 145   Vesting of company property in liquidator

145(1)   [Court order]   When a company is being wound up by the court, the court may on the application of the liquidator by order direct that all or any part of the property of whatsoever description belonging to the company or held by trustees on its behalf shall vest in the liquidator by his official name; and thereupon the property to which the order relates vests accordingly.

145(2)   [Action re property by liquidator]   The liquidator may, after giving such indemnity (if any) as the court may direct, bring or defend in his official name any action or other legal proceeding which relates to that property or which it is necessary to bring or defend for the purpose of effectually winding up the company and recovering its property.

(Former provisions: CA 1985, s. 538; CA 1948, s. 244)

General note

The estate of a bankrupt individual vests automatically in his trustee by operation of law: see

s. 306. In contrast, the property of a company which is in liquidation remains vested in its name unless an order is sought under the present section.

S. 145(1)

It is normally unnecessary to have a vesting order made, in view of the wide powers conferred on the liquidator to act in the company's name (see Sch. 4). However, an order may be needed in special circumstances: e.g. where the company is a foreign company which has already been wound up or dissolved in its home jurisdiction.

S. 145(2)

The liquidator would normally bring and defend actions in the name of the company: see Sch. 4, para. 4.

Section 146   Duty to summon final meeting

146(1) **[Summoning final meeting]**   Subject to the next subsection, if it appears to the liquidator of a company which is being wound up by the court that the winding up of the company is for practical purposes complete and the liquidator is not the official receiver, the liquidator shall summon a final general meeting of the company's creditors which—

     (a) shall receive the liquidator's report of the winding up, and

     (b) shall determine whether the liquidator should have his release under section 174 in Chapter VII of this Part.

146(2) **[Time for notice]**   The liquidator may, if he thinks fit, give the notice summoning the final general meeting at the same time as giving notice of any final distribution of the company's property but, if summoned for an earlier date, that meeting shall be adjourned (and, if necessary, further adjourned) until a date on which the liquidator is able to report to the meeting that the winding up of the company is for practical purposes complete.

146(3) **[Retention of sums]**   In the carrying out of his functions in the winding up it is the duty of the liquidator to retain sufficient sums from the company's property to cover the expenses of summoning and holding the meeting required by this section.

(Former provision: IA 1985, s. 78)

General note

This section applies only where a company is being wound up by the court and the liquidator is not the official receiver. It introduces a marked change from the former procedure under CA 1985, s. 545, by which the liquidator obtained his release. Previously, the liquidator had to apply for a release to the Secretary of State. He is now required instead to report to the meeting of creditors on the completion of the liquidation and it is left to that meeting to determine whether he should have his release. The creditors are thus kept in the picture throughout the winding up and the liquidator made accountable to them, and at the same time the Secretary of State is relieved from the burden of examining the liquidator's accounts, etc., in order to determine whether he is entitled to his release. The new provision complements, and in part runs parallel to, ss. 94 and 106 which apply respectively in a members' and creditors' voluntary winding up.

S. 146(1)

Where the official receiver is the liquidator, the question of his release is for the Secretary of

State to determine: see s. 174(3). The procedure governing the summoning and conduct of the meeting is in IR 1986, r. 4.125.

For transitional provisions, see Sch. 11, para. 6(3).

S. 146(2), (3)

It is clear that the winding up must in fact be completed and the company's property finally distributed (apart from what needs to be retained under s. 146(3)): the meeting cannot grant the liquidator a prospective or conditional release.

The liquidator must give notice to the court and the registrar of companies that the meeting has been held and report what decisions were made: see s. 172(8).

GENERAL POWERS OF COURT

Section 147   Power to stay or sist winding up

147(1)   [Court may order stay on application]   The court may at any time after an order for winding up, on the application either of the liquidator or the official receiver or any creditor or contributory, and on proof to the satisfaction of the court that all proceedings in the winding up ought to be stayed or sisted, make an order staying or sisting the proceedings, either altogether or for a limited time, on such terms and conditions as the court thinks fit.

147(2)   [Report by official receiver]   The court may, before making an order, require the official receiver to furnish to it a report with respect to any facts or matters which are in his opinion relevant to the application.

147(3)   [Copy of order to registrar]   A copy of every order made under this section shall forthwith be forwarded by the company, or otherwise as may be prescribed, to the registrar of companies, who shall enter it in his records relating to the company.

(Former provisions: CA 1985, s. 549; CA 1948, s. 256)

S. 147(1)

An order for the stay (or, in Scotland, sist) of the winding-up proceedings may be made either for a limited time, or "altogether". In the latter case, the order for liquidation is, in effect, terminated; the liquidator will then be entitled to a discharge and the directors reinstated in control. For the principles on which the court will grant or refuse a stay, see *Re Lowston Ltd* [1991] BCLC 570.

Prior to the 1986 legislation, it was not possible to rescind a winding-up order altogether: the nearest possible thing was the grant of a permanent stay. The consequence was that, technically, the company remained subject to the order, although its operation was suspended. In this situation, a copy of the winding-up order remains on the file at Companies House (see IA 1986, s. 130(1)), where it can be the source of misunderstanding (e.g. in relation to credit references). It is now possible, however, for the court to rescind a winding-up order under IR 1986, r. 7.47(1) (e.g. on the ground of mistake), and declare it to have been a nullity. The registrar is then bound to remove the order from his files: *Re Calmex Ltd* [1989] 1 All ER 485; (1988) 4 BCC 761.

A stay may be granted on the ground of *forum non conveniens*, i.e. that the courts of another jurisdiction are more appropriately placed to deal with the proceedings: see the note to s. 125(1).

S. 147(2)

The officers of the company and its employees and others specified are under a duty to co-operate with the official receiver: see s. 235.

S. 147(3)

No regulations appear to have been prescribed for the purposes of this section; but IR 1986, r. 4.48 empowers the court to impose requirements as to notification.

Section 148   Settlement of list of contributories and application of assets

148(1) **[Court's duties]**   As soon as may be after making a winding-up order, the court shall settle a list of contributories, with power to rectify the register of members in all cases where rectification is required in pursuance of the Companies Act or this Act, and shall cause the company's assets to be collected, and applied in discharge of its liabilities.

148(2) **[Court may dispense with list]**   If it appears to the court that it will not be necessary to make calls on or adjust the rights of contributories, the court may dispense with the settlement of a list of contributories.

148(3) **[Distinction between types of contributories]**   In settling the list, the court shall distinguish between persons who are contributories in their own right and persons who are contributories as being representatives of or liable for the debts of others.

(Former provisions: CA 1985, s. 550; CA 1948, s. 257)

S. 148(1)

On the meaning of contributories, and their liability, see the note to s. 74 above.

The powers conferred by this section have been delegated to the liquidator by rules made under s. 160, below; but the power to rectify the register of members may be exercised by the liquidator only with the special leave of the court: s. 160(2). For the relevant rules, see IR 1986, rr. 4.195ff.

The general power of the court to rectify the register of members (e.g. in the case of omission or mistake) is contained in CA 1985, s. 359.

The principles governing the application of assets in a voluntary winding up (s. 107) and in a winding up by the court under this section are substantially equivalent. See further the note to that section.

On the order of priority of the expenses of a liquidation *inter se* see IR 1986, rr. 4.218–4.220, and the note to s. 156.

S. 148(2)

This would apply, in particular, where the shares are fully paid.

S. 148(3)

The categories of contributories are known as the "A List" and "B List" contributories. The circumstances in which the latter are liable to contribute are set out in s. 74(2); see also ss. 75, 76.

Section 149   Debts due from contributory to company

149(1) **[Court may order payment from contributory]**   The court may, at any time after making a winding-up order, make an order on any contributory for the time being on the list of contributories to pay, in manner directed by the order, any money due from him (or from the estate of the person whom he represents) to the company, exclusive of any money payable by him or the estate by virtue of any call in pursuance of the Companies Act or this Act.

149(2) **[Allowances and set-offs]**   The court in making such an order may—

(a) in the case of an unlimited company, allow to the contributory by way of set-off any money due to him or the estate which he represents from the company on any independent dealing or contract with the company, but not any money due to him as a member of the company in respect of any dividend or profit, and

(b) in the case of a limited company, make to any director or manager whose liability is unlimited or to his estate the like allowance.

149(3) **[Money due to contributory may be allowed when creditors paid]**   In the case of any company, whether limited or unlimited, when all the creditors are paid in full (together with interest at the official rate), any money due on any account whatever to a contributory from the company may be allowed to him by way of set-off against any subsequent call.

(Former provisions: CA 1985, s. 552 (as amended by IA 1985, Sch. 6, para. 32); CA 1948, s. 259)

S. 149(1)

This provision allows the liquidator to recover in a summary way moneys (other than calls, which are dealt with in s. 150) due by a member to the company, thus avoiding the formality of a conventional action. However, it is confined to sums owed by the member *qua* member, e.g. dividends improperly paid to him, and may not be used to claim an ordinary debt: *Re Marlborough Club Co.* (1868) LR 5 Eq 365. One consequence of this is that the contributory loses his normal right as a debtor to set off against such a claim any sums due from the company to him (*Re Whitehouse & Co.* (1878) 9 ChD 595), apart from the special case where a contributory's liability is unlimited, which is dealt with in s. 149(2).

S. 149(2)

The right of set-off in the two situations of unlimited liability referred to is not automatic, but rests in the discretion of the court. No set-off lies in any case in regard to dividends or profits payable to the member, in keeping with the principle expressed in s. 74(2)(*f*).

On the question of set-off generally, see the general comment preceding s. 175.

S. 149(3)

The restrictions as to set-off described in the notes to s. 149(1) and (2) no longer apply once the claims of the general creditors have been fully satisfied.

On the entitlement of a creditor to interest, see the note to s. 189.

Section 150   Power to make calls

150(1) **[Court may make calls to satisfy debts]**   The court may, at any time after making a winding-up order, and either before or after it has ascertained the sufficiency of the company's assets, make calls on all or any of the contributories for the time being settled on the list of the contributories to the extent of their liability, for payment of any money which the court considers necessary to satisfy the company's debts and liabilities, and the expenses of winding up, and for the adjustment of the rights of the contributories among themselves, and make an order for payment of any calls so made.

150(2) [Matters to be considered] In making a call the court may take into consideration the probability that some of the contributories may partly or wholly fail to pay it.

(Former provisions: CA 1985, s. 553; CA 1948, s. 260)

S. 150(1)

This provision authorises the court to settle the liability of contributories to pay calls, and to enforce this liability in a summary way. The powers of the court have been delegated to the liquidator by regulations made under s. 160(1): see IR 1986, rr. 4.195, 4.202ff. In regard to the making of calls, the rules provide for the liquidator to act with the alternative sanction of the liquidation committee: r. 4.203. The liquidator may not act without authorisation unless the court gives special leave: s. 160(2).

S. 150(2)

The court may take into account the likelihood that some contributories may default, so saving the need for a further call on the remainder. If the amount thus raised is surplus to the liquidator's needs, it is of course returnable under s. 154.

Section 151   Payment into bank of money due to company

151(1) [Court may order payment into Bank of England] The court may order any contributory, purchaser or other person from whom money is due to the company to pay the amount due into the Bank of England (or any branch of it) to the account of the liquidator instead of to the liquidator, and such an order may be enforced in the same manner as if it had directed payment to the liquidator.

151(2) [Moneys in Bank subject to court orders] All money and securities paid or delivered into the Bank of England (or branch) in the event of a winding up by the court are subject in all respects to the orders of the court.

(Former provisions: CA 1985, s. 554; CA 1948, s. 261)

General note

The power to order payment to be made direct to the Bank of England is not confined to calls and other sums due from contributories, but may be invoked in relation to any debtor.

Section 152   Order on contributory to be conclusive evidence

152(1) [Order evidence that money due] An order made by the court on a contributory is conclusive evidence that the money (if any) thereby appearing to be due or ordered to be paid is due, but subject to any right of appeal.

152(2) [Other matters stated in order] All other pertinent matters stated in the order are to be taken as truly stated as against all persons and in all proceedings except proceedings in Scotland against the heritable estate of a deceased contributory; and in that case the order is only prima facie evidence for the purpose of charging his heritable estate, unless his heirs or legatees of heritage were on the list of contributories at the time of the order being made.

(Former provisions: CA 1985, s. 555; CA 1948, s. 262)

General note

This section applies only to orders against contributories, but it is not confined to orders for the payment of calls.

Section 153   Power to exclude creditors not proving in time

153   The court may fix a time or times within which creditors are to prove their debts or claims or to be excluded from the benefit of any distribution made before those debts are proved.

(Former provisions: CA 1985, s. 557; CA 1948, s. 264)

General note

A creditor who does not prove his debt within the time fixed by the court is excluded from participating in any distribution made before he proves, but his right to prove is not itself affected, and he may be paid out of such assets as remain or later become available. See further IR 1986, rr. 4.182(2) and 11.2(2).

The power of the court under this section may be delegated by rules to the liquidator: see s. 160(1). There does not appear to have been any specific exercise of this power in IR 1986, but the same result is achieved, in effect, by r. 11.2.

A creditor may, of course, be barred from claiming by the operation of the statutes of limitation. In *Re Joshua Shaw & Sons Ltd* (1989) 5 BCC 188 the debts of all the company's unsecured creditors, apart from the Crown, became statute-barred during the course of a long-running receivership. The ironic consequence was that the surplus which was found to exist at the conclusion of the receivership went to the company's shareholders.

Section 154   Adjustment of rights of contributories

154   The court shall adjust the rights of the contributories among themselves and distribute any surplus among the persons entitled to it.

(Former provisions: CA 1985, s. 558; CA 1948, s. 265)

General note

For the corresponding provision in a voluntary winding up, see s. 107.
    For the relevant rules, see IR 1986, rr. 4.221ff.

Section 155   Inspection of books by creditors, etc.

155(1)   [Court may make order for inspection]   The court may, at any time after making a winding-up order, make such order for inspection of the company's books and papers by creditors and contributories as the court thinks just; and any books and papers in the company's possession may be inspected by creditors and contributories accordingly, but not further or otherwise.

155(2)   [Statutory rights of government department]   Nothing in this section excludes or restricts any statutory rights of a government department or person acting under the authority of a government department.

(Former provisions: CA 1985, s. 559; CA 1948, s. 266)

S. 155(1)

The company's books and papers are not ordinarily accessible even to members while the company is a going concern; and although this section does confer such a right on creditors and contributories in a winding up, subject to the leave of the court, there are dicta which state that the court's leave will in practice be granted only for purposes directly connected with the liquidation: *Re North Brazilian Sugar Factories* (1887) 37 ChD 83, *Re DPR Futures Ltd* [1989] 1 WLR 778; (1989) 5 BCC 603. However, it is understood that the court will in fact grant leave in a suitable case, e.g. where a creditor needs to obtain information to defend a claim under a guarantee, or an insurance company to defend a claim made against it, even though the claim in question may not be so connected. The same cases also held that the court's jurisdiction under s. 155 extends only to books and papers in the possession of the company: it cannot, for instance, extend to documents formerly in the custody of the company which have been seized by the Serious Fraud Office.

S. 155(2)

The statutory rights most obviously referred to here are those of the Secretary of State, and inspectors appointed by him, under CA 1985, ss. 431ff.

Section 156   Payment of expenses of winding up

156   The court may, in the event of the assets being insufficient to satisfy the liabilities, make an order as to the payment out of the assets of the expenses incurred in the winding up in such order of priority as the court thinks just.

(Former provisions: CA 1985, s. 560 (as amended by IA 1985, s. 235(3) and Sch. 10); CA 1948, s. 267)

General note

The forerunner to this section used the phrase "costs, charges and expenses", but this and similar phrases were replaced throughout IA 1985 by the single word "expenses".

The rules contain provisions dealing with the payment of expenses of a winding up in the normal case, but subject to any order of the court: IR 1986, rr. 4.218, 4.220. The present section gives the court the power to make such an order where it is appropriate. The court will only in exceptional circumstances exercise its jurisdiction under this section to confer on the liquidator's remuneration, or any part of it, priority over liquidation expenses which would normally rank before it: *Re Linda Marie Ltd (in liquidation)* (1988) 4 BCC 463.

Section 157   Attendance at company meetings (Scotland)

157   In the winding up by the court of a company registered in Scotland, the court has power to require the attendance of any officer of the company at any meeting of creditors or of contributories, or of a liquidation committee, for the purpose of giving information as to the trade, dealings, affairs or property of the company.

(Former provisions: CA 1985, s. 562 (as amended by IA 1985, Sch. 6, para. 33); CA 1948, s. 269)

General note
There is no direct counterpart of this provision for England and Wales.

Section 158   Power to arrest absconding contributory

158   The court, at any time either before or after making a winding-up order, on proof of probable cause for believing that a contributory is about to quit the United Kingdom or otherwise to abscond or to remove or conceal any of his property for the purpose of evading payment of calls, may cause the contributory to be arrested and his books and papers and movable personal property to be seized and him and them to be kept safely until such time as the court may order.

(Former provisions: CA 1985, s. 565 (as amended by IA 1985, s. 235(3) and Sch. 10; CA 1948, s. 271)

General note
The former legislation, after the phrase "for the purpose of evading calls" contained the additional words "or of avoiding examination respecting the company's affairs". These words were deleted by IA 1985; the point is amply covered elsewhere in the Act: see s. 236(5).

Section 159   Powers of court to be cumulative

159   Powers conferred by this Act and the Companies Act on the court are in addition to, and not in restriction of, any existing powers of instituting proceedings against a contributory or debtor of the company, or the estate of any contributory or debtor, for the recovery of any call or other sums.

(Former provisions: CA 1985, s. 566; CA 1948, s. 272)

General note
This provision is in the same terms as the repealed CA 1985, s. 566, except that it has been necessary to add the words "and the Companies Act", reflecting the subdivision of companies legislation which has resulted from the consolidation of insolvency law.

Section 160   Delegation of powers to liquidator (England and Wales)

160(1)   **[Delegation by rules]**   Provision may be made by rules for enabling or requiring all or any of the powers and duties conferred and imposed on the court in England and Wales by the Companies Act and this Act in respect of the following matters—

   (a)   the holding and conducting of meetings to ascertain the wishes of creditors and contributories,

    (b) the settling of lists of contributories and the rectifying of the register of members where required, and the collection and application of the assets,

    (c) the payment, delivery, conveyance, surrender or transfer of money, property, books or papers to the liquidator,

    (d) the making of calls,

    (e) the fixing of a time within which debts and claims must be proved,

to be exercised or performed by the liquidator as an officer of the court, and subject to the court's control.

160(2) **[No rectification etc. without special leave]** But the liquidator shall not, without the special leave of the court, rectify the register of members, and shall not make any call without either that special leave or the sanction of the liquidation committee.

(Former provisions: CA 1985, s. 567 (as amended by IA 1985, Sch. 6, para. 34); CA 1948, s. 273)

General note

For the relevant rules, see IR 1986, rr. 4.54ff (meetings); 4.179ff (assets); 4.185 (surrender of books, etc.); 4.195ff (list of contributories); 4.196 (rectifying register); 4.202ff (calls), and see the note to s. 153 (time for proving).

ENFORCEMENT OF, AND APPEAL FROM, ORDERS

Section 161   Orders for calls on contributories (Scotland)

161(1) **[Court may order calls on contributories on receipt of list]** In Scotland, where an order, interlocutor or decree has been made for winding up a company by the court, it is competent to the court, on production by the liquidators of a list certified by them of the names of the contributories liable in payment of any calls, and of the amount due by each contributory, and of the date when that amount became due, to pronounce forthwith a decree against those contributories for payment of the sums so certified to be due, with interest from that date until payment (at 5 per cent per annum) in the same way and to the same effect as if they had severally consented to registration for execution, on a charge of 6 days, of a legal obligation to pay those calls and interest.

161(2) **[Extraction of decree]** The decree may be extracted immediately, and no suspension of it is competent, except on caution or consignation, unless with special leave of the court.

(Former provisions: CA 1985, s. 569; CA 1948, s. 275)

General note

The procedure for making calls on contributories in a winding up by the court in England and Wales is prescribed in rather different terms by s. 160(1)(*d*) and the rules made thereunder.

Section 162   Appeals from orders in Scotland

162(1) **[Appeal from order on winding up]** Subject to the provisions of this section and to rules of court, an appeal from any order or decision made or given in the winding up of a company by the court in Scotland under this Act lies in the same manner and subject to the same conditions as an appeal from an order or decision of the court in cases within its ordinary jurisdiction.

162(2)   [Orders by judge acting as vacation judge]   In regard to orders or judgments pronounced by the judge acting as vacation judge—

(a) none of the orders specified in Part I of Schedule 3 to this Act are subject to review, reduction, suspension or stay of execution, and

(b) every other order or judgment (except as mentioned below) may be submitted to review by the Inner House by reclaiming motion enrolled within 14 days from the the the date of the order or judgment.

162(3)   [Order in Sch. 3, Pt. II]   However, an order being one of those specified in Part II of that Schedule shall, from the date of the order and notwithstanding that it has been submitted to review as above, be carried out and receive effect until the Inner House have disposed of the matter.

162(4)   [Orders by Lord Ordinary]   In regard to orders or judgments pronounced in Scotland by a Lord Ordinary before whom proceedings in a winding up are being taken, any such order or judgment may be submitted to review by the Inner House by reclaiming motion enrolled within 14 days from its date; but should it not be so submitted to review during session, the provisions of this section in regard to orders or judgments pronounced by the judge acting as vacation judge apply.

162(5)   [Decrees for payment of calls in winding up]   Nothing in this section affects provisions of the Companies Act or this Act in reference to decrees in Scotland for payment of calls in the winding up of companies, whether voluntary or by the court.

(Former provisions: CA 1985, s. 571; CA 1948, s. 277)

General note

This section deals with a number of special points of Scottish procedure. It should be read in conjunction with Sch. 3, below, which makes more detailed provisions for the purposes of s. 162 (2) and (3).

S. 162(2)

In this subsection the former words "in pursuance of section 4 of the Administration of Justice (Scotland) Act 1933" (which appeared after the words "vacation judge") were repealed by the Court of Session Act 1988, s. 52(2) and Sch. 2, Pt. I and III as from 29 September 1988.

Chapter VII — Liquidators

PRELIMINARY

Section 163   Style and title of liquidators

163   The liquidator of a company shall be described—

(a) where a person other than the official receiver is liquidator, by the style of "the liquidator" of the particular company, or

(b) where the official receiver is liquidator, by the style of "the official receiver and liquidator" of the particular company;

and in neither case shall he be described by an individual name.

(Former provision: IA 1985, s. 94, replacing CA 1985, s. 533(7))

General note

This section now applies in every form of winding up. The repealed s. 533(7), which was in similar terms, was applicable only in a winding up by the court, though the practice in other types of liquidation was the same.

Section 164   Corrupt inducement affecting appointment

164   A person who gives, or agrees or offers to give, to any member or creditor of a company any valuable consideration with a view to securing his own appointment or nomination, or to securing or preventing the appointment or nomination of some person other than himself, as the company's liquidator is liable to a fine.

(Former provisions: CA 1985, s. 635; CA 1948, s. 336)

General note

It is perhaps surprising that this old provision has survived the reforms made by IA 1985, including the requirement that a liquidator must be a professional insolvency practitioner.
   On penalties, see s. 430 and Sch. 10.

LIQUIDATOR'S POWERS AND DUTIES

Section 165   Voluntary winding up

165(1)   [Application]   This section has effect where a company is being wound up voluntarily, but subject to section 166 below in the case of a creditors' voluntary winding up.

165(2)   [Powers in Sch. 4, Pt. I]   The liquidator may—

(a) in the case of a members' voluntary winding up, with the sanction of an extraordinary resolution of the company, and

(b) in the case of a creditors' voluntary winding up, with the sanction of the court or the liquidation committee (or, if there is no such committee, a meeting of the company's creditors),

exercise any of the powers specified in Part I of Schedule 4 to this Act (payment of debts, compromise of claims, etc.).

165(3)   [Powers in Sch. 4, Pt. II, III]   The liquidator may, without sanction, exercise either of the powers specified in Part II of that Schedule (institution and defence of proceedings; carrying on the business of the company) and any of the general powers specified in Part III of that Schedule.

165(4)   [Other powers]   The liquidator may—

   (a) exercise the court's power of settling a list of contributories (which list is prima facie evidence of the liability of the persons named in it to be contributories),

   (b) exercise the court's power of making calls,

   (c) summon general meetings of the company for the purpose of obtaining its sanction by special or extraordinary resolution or for any other purpose he may think fit.

165(5)   [Duty re payment of debts]   The liquidator shall pay the company's debts and adjust the rights of the contributories among themselves.

165(6)   [Notice to committee re exercise of powers]   Where the liquidator in exercise of the powers conferred on him by this Act disposes of any property of the company to a person who is connected with the company (within the meaning of section 249 in Part VII), he shall, if there is for the time being a liquidation committee, give notice to the committee of that exercise of his powers.

(Former provisions: CA 1985, ss. 539(1)(d)–(f), 598 (as amended by IA 1985, Sch. 6, para. 41); IA 1985, s. 84(1))

General note

This section deals with the powers and duties of the liquidator in a voluntary winding up. It is to be read in conjunction with Sch. 4, in which some powers are set out in detail.

S. 165(1)

The relationship between ss. 165 and 166 is a little confusing. Section 165 applies to every voluntary winding up, *including* a creditors' voluntary winding up where the liquidator has been nominated by the company; but s. 166 supplements s. 165 in the latter case (1) by imposing restrictions on the powers exercisable by the liquidator pending the holding of the creditors' meeting, and (2) by imposing on the liquidator the duty of attending the creditors' meeting (see s. 166(4)).

S. 165(2)

Schedule 4 is divided into three Parts, listing respectively:

   Pt. I: powers exercisable with sanction;

   Pt. II: powers exercisable without sanction in a voluntary winding up, but with sanction in a winding up by the court; and

   Pt. III: powers exercisable without sanction in any winding up.

The present subsection relates to Pt. I of the Schedule and specifies the appropriate sanctioning body in each case.

S. 165(3)

In the case of a voluntary winding up, no distinction is made between the powers listed in Pt. II and those in Pt. III of the Schedule. No sanction is required for the exercise of any of these powers.

S. 165(4)

These are matters for which, in the case of a winding up by the court, power is in the first instance conferred by the Act upon the court itself, but then normally delegated to the liquidator by rules made under s. 160. Note, however, that under the present section the liquidator in a voluntary winding up may make calls without any sanction (para. (*b*)), in contrast with s. 160(2) which stipulates that in a compulsory winding up he may do so only with the special leave of the court.

Reference should be made also to s. 112, which empowers the court to determine questions and exercise powers in a voluntary winding up as if the company were being wound up by the court.

S. 165(5)

There is some overlap between this provision and s. 107. On the application of assets generally, see the note to that section.

S. 165(6)

This provision, first introduced by IA 1985, is designed to ensure that, at least in any voluntary winding up where there is a liquidation committee, no property of the company shall be disposed of to someone "connected with" the company unless it is done with the modest amount of disclosure specified. (The legislators have not gone so far as to stipulate for the *sanction* of the committee.) No doubt this requirement is part of the general package of measures aimed at the abuse known as the "phoenix syndrome" (see the note to s. 216, below). If there is no liquidation committee, there is curiously no alternative obligation to notify the creditors generally, or the court.

The category of persons "connected with" a company is very widely defined, and includes a director, employee or controlling shareholder, a close relative of any of these persons, and a company in the same group. See the notes to ss. 249 and 435, below.

Section 166 Creditors' voluntary winding up

166(1) [Application] This section applies where, in the case of a creditors' voluntary winding up, a liquidator has been nominated by the company.

166(2) [Non-exercise of s. 165 powers] The powers conferred on the liquidator by section 165 shall not be exercised, except with the sanction of the court, during the period before the holding of the creditors' meeting under section 98 in Chapter IV.

166(3) [Non-application of s. 166(2)] Subsection (2) does not apply in relation to the power of the liquidator—

    (a) to take into his custody or under his control all the property to which the company is or appears to be entitled;

    (b) to dispose of perishable goods and other goods the value of which is likely to diminish if they are not immediately disposed of; and

    (c) to do all such other things as may be necessary for the protection of the company's assets.

166(4) [Liquidator to attend s. 98 meeting] The liquidator shall attend the creditors' meeting held under section 98 and shall report to the meeting on any exercise by him of his powers (whether or not under this section or under section 112 or 165).

166(5) [Where default re s. 98, 99] If default is made—

    (a) by the company in complying with subsection (1) or (2) of section 98, or

    (b) by the directors in complying with subsection (1) or (2) of section 99, the liquidator shall, within 7 days of the relevant day, apply to the court for directions as to the manner in which that default is to be remedied.

166(6) **["The relevant day"]** **"The relevant day"** means the day on which the liquidator was nominated by the company or the day on which he first became aware of the default, whichever is the later.

166(7) **[Penalty for non-compliance]** If the liquidator without reasonable excuse fails to comply with this section, he is liable to a fine.

(Former provision: IA 1985, s. 84)

General note

This section should be read in conjunction with ss. 98 and 114, above. Taken together, they should ensure (as is undoubtedly intended) that the practice which had become notorious under the name of "centrebinding" is totally stamped out. The abuse takes its name from the case of *Re Centrebind Ltd* [1967] 1 WLR 377, where the members of an insolvent company resolved to go into voluntary liquidation and appointed their own liquidator who, before any creditors' meeting had been held, took immediate steps to restrain the Inland Revenue from proceeding with a distress on the company's assets. Plowman J held that the liquidator had power to act until the creditors' meeting had been held.

Although the acts of the company and its liquidator in the *Centrebind* case itself were done entirely in good faith, it was not long before the practice developed of calling only a shareholders' meeting in the first instance to pass a winding-up resolution and, although the company was known to be insolvent, deliberately putting off for some time, or perhaps indefinitely, the holding of the creditors' meeting. This, of course, involved a technical breach of the Companies Act (CA 1985, s. 588(2)), which required the latter meeting to be held on the same day as the members' meeting or the very next day and, indeed, was a criminal offence. However, it meant that the controllers of a company, with the aid of an unscrupulous liquidator nominated by them, could effectively sell the assets off at a knock-down price to a purchaser closely connected with themselves (e.g. a new company controlled by them), and the creditors were powerless to prevent it.

The introduction by IA 1985 of a mandatory requirement that liquidators shall be of professional standing is probably in itself sufficient to ensure that "centrebinding" will no longer be part of insolvency practice; but the legislature has made doubly sure of this by provisions such as the present.

S. 166(1)

Where no liquidator has been nominated by the company the directors will remain in control of the company's property, but their powers will be limited to protecting the assets and disposing of perishable goods, unless they obtain the sanction of the court (see s. 114).

S. 166(2)

The provisions of s. 166 operate to qualify s. 165 only during the interval between the nomination of a liquidator by the company and the holding of the creditors' meeting – a period which ought not to exceed 14 days (see s. 98(1)(*a*)).

S. 166(3)

The restricted powers given to the liquidator (unless he has the sanction of the court under s. 166(2)) are, as regards paras. (*b*) and (*c*), the same as those allowed to directors by s. 114(3). In addition he has, by para. (*a*), the power to take over custody and control of the company's property from the directors. The term "property" is widely defined: see s. 436.

S. 166(4), (5)

The obligations imposed on the company by s. 98 are to convene a creditors' meeting within 14 days of the company's own meeting and to give the appropriate notices; while under s. 99 the directors are required to make out a statement of affairs to be laid before the creditors' meeting and to depute one of their number to attend the meeting. The "relevant day" is defined in s. 166(6).

The language of s. 166(5) is permissive rather than mandatory. There is no obligation on the liquidator to apply for directions where there is no need for them: *Re Salcombe Hotel Development Co. Ltd* (1989) 5 BCC 807.

S. 166(7)

On penalties, see s. 430 and Sch. 10.

Section 167 Winding up by the court

167(1) [Powers of liquidator] Where a company is being wound up by the court, the liquidator may—

(a) with the sanction of the court or the liquidation committee, exercise any of the powers specified in Parts I and II of Schedule 4 to this Act (payment of debts; compromise of ciaims, etc.; institution and defence of proceedings; carrying on of the business of the company), and

(b) with or without that sanction, exercise any of the general powers specified in Part III of that Schedule.

167(2) [Duty of liquidator] Where the liquidator (not being the official receiver), in exercise of the powers conferred on him by this Act—

(a) disposes of any property of the company to a person who is connected with the company (within the meaning of section 249 in Part VII), or

(b) employs a solicitor to assist him in the carrying out of his functions,

he shall, if there is for the time being a liquidation committee, give notice to the committee of that exercise of his powers.

167(3) [Control of court] The exercise by the liquidator in a winding up by the court of the powers conferred by this section is subject to the control of the court, and any creditor or contributory may apply to the court with respect to any exercise or proposed exercise of any of those powers.

(Former provisions: CA 1985, s. 539(1)–(3) (as amended by IA 1985, Sch. 6, para. 31); CA 1948, s. 245)

General note

The liquidator, in a winding up by the court, is given specific powers and duties by various other sections of the Act. In addition, the present provision confers on him general powers by reference to Sch. 4. Prior to the consolidation, they were set out in the body of the Act itself.

S. 167(1)

Although every liquidator has all the powers listed in Sch. 4, those of a liquidator in a winding up by the court are more restricted, in that the powers specified in Pt. II of the Schedule (instituting and defending proceedings, and carrying on the company's business) are exercisable only with the sanctions specified in para. (*a*). The rules state that any permission given under this section shall be given in the particular case, and not generally: see IR 1986, r. 4.184.

S. 167(2)

This subsection, apart from para. (*b*) relating to the employment of a solicitor, is parallel to s. 165(6) which applies in a voluntary winding up. (Note that it does not apply where the official receiver is the liquidator.)

A transitional provision extends this power to liquidations existing at the commencement of the Act: see Sch. 11, para. 6(5).

S. 167(3)

There is no provision in the Act directly corresponding to this subsection which applies in a voluntary winding up, but the supervisory powers of the court may be invoked in such a case by an application made under s. 112.

Section 168 Supplementary powers (England and Wales)

168(1) [Application] This section applies in the case of a company which is being wound up by the court in England and Wales.

168(2) [Liquidator may summon general meetings] The liquidator may summon general meetings of the creditors or contributories for the purpose of ascertaining their wishes; and it is his duty to summon meetings at such times as the creditors or contributories by resolution (either at the meeting appointing the liquidator or otherwise) may direct, or whenever requested in writing to do so by one-tenth in value of the creditors or contributories (as the case may be).

168(3) [Liquidator may apply to court for directions] The liquidator may apply to the court (in the prescribed manner) for directions in relation to any particular matter arising in the winding up.

168(4) [Liquidator to use own discretion] Subject to the provisions of this Act, the liquidator shall use his own discretion in the management of the assets and their distribution among the creditors.

168(5) [Application to court re acts of liquidator] If any person is aggrieved by an act or decision of the liquidator, that person may apply to the court; and the court may confirm, reverse or modify the act or decision complained of, and make such order in the case as it thinks just.

(Former provisions: CA 1985, s. 540(3)–(6); CA 1948, s. 246(2)–(5))

General note

This section provides in general terms for consultation between the liquidator and the meetings of creditors and contributories, either on his initiative or on requisition by one-tenth in value of those concerned, and also for the court to give directions and to supervise and control the acts and decisions of the liquidator.

For the rules relating to the summoning of meetings, see IR 1986, rr. 4.54ff, and as regards applications to the court, rr. 7.1.ff.

S. 168(5)

Notwithstanding the width of the words "may ... make such order in the case as it thinks just", the court will not normally review the exercise by the liquidator of his powers and discretions in the management and realisation of the corporate property. The words can only be construed as allowing the court to interfere with a decision of a liquidator if it was taken in bad faith or if it was so perverse as to demonstrate that no liquidator properly advised could have taken it: *Re a Debtor* [1949] Ch. 236 at p. 241, *Re Hans Place Ltd* [1992] BCC 737 at pp. 745–6.

On the meaning of "person aggrieved", see the remarks of *Warner* J (*obiter*) in *Re ACLI Metals (London) Ltd (AML Holdings Inc.* v *Auger)* (1989) 5 BCC 749 at p. 754.

S. 168(5A–5C)
The following subsections are inserted at the end of s. 168 for the purposes of the Insolvent Partnerships Order 1994 (SI 1994 No. 2421) from 1 December 1994 (by art. 14(1) of the order):

"(5A) Where at any time after a winding-up petition has been presented to the court against any person (including an insolvent partnership or other body which may be wound up under Part V of the Act as an unregistered company), whether by virtue of the provisions of the Insolvent Partnerships Order 1994 or not, the attention of the court is drawn to the fact that the person in question is a member of an insolvent partnership, the court may make an order as to the future conduct of the insolvency proceedings and any such order may apply any provisions of that Order with any necessary modifications.

(5B) Any order or directions under subsection (5A) may be made or given on the application of the official receiver, any responsible insolvency practitioner, the trustee of the partnership or any other interested person and may include provisions as to the administration of the joint estate of the partnership, and in particular how it and the separate estate of any member are to be administered.

(5C) Where the court makes an order under section 72(1)(a) of the Financial Services Act 1986 or section 92(1)(a) of the Banking Act 1987 for the winding up of an insolvent partnership, the court may make an order as to the future conduct of the winding-up proceedings, and any such order may apply any provisions of the Insolvent Partnerships Order 1994 with any necessary modifications."

Section 169 Supplementary powers (Scotland)

169(1) **[Where no liquidation committee]** In the case of a winding up in Scotland, the court may provide by order that the liquidator may, where there is no liquidation committee, exercise any of the following powers, namely—

  (a) to bring or defend any action or other legal proceeding in the name and on behalf of the company, or
  (b) to carry on the business of the company so far as may be necessary for its beneficial winding up,

without the sanction or intervention of the court.

169(2) **[Liquidator's powers]** In a winding up by the court in Scotland, the liquidator has (subject to the rules) the same powers as a trustee on a bankrupt estate.

(Former provisions: CA 1985, s. 539(4), (5) (as amended by IA 1985, Sch. 6, para. 31(4)); CA 1948, s. 245(4), (5))

S. 169(1)
This provision, brought forward from earlier Companies Acts, rather oddly allows the court to dispense with its own sanction where there is no liquidation committee. Where there is such a committee, one or other of the sanctions specified in s. 167(1)(a) must be obtained.

S. 169(2)
For the powers of the trustee on a bankrupt estate in Scotland, see the Bankruptcy (Scotland) Act 1985, especially ss. 38ff. For the relevant rules see the Insolvency (Scotland) Rules 1986 (SI 1986 No. 1915 (S. 139)), r. 4.68.

Section 170   Enforcement of liquidator's duty to make returns, etc.

170(1)   [Powers of court if liquidator fails to file returns etc.]   If a liquidator who has made any default—

    (a) in filing, delivering or making any return, account or other document, or

    (b) in giving any notice which he is by law required to file, deliver, make or give,

fails to make good the default within 14 days after the service on him of a notice requiring him to do so, the court has the following powers.

170(2)   [On application court may order to make good default]   On an application made by any creditor or contributory of the company, or by the registrar of companies, the court may make an order directing the liquidator to make good the default within such time as may be specified in the order.

170(3)   [Costs]   The court's order may provide that all costs of and incidental to the application shall be borne by the liquidator.

170(4)   [Penalties]   Nothing in this section prejudices the operation of any enactment imposing penalties on a liquidator in respect of any such default as is mentioned above.

(Former provisions: CA 1985, s. 636; CA 1948, s. 337)

General note
This section contains provisions parallel to those in CA 1985, s. 713, which deal with the enforcement of such defaults against the company itself and its officers and are, of course, not confined to a winding up. A liquidator is not normally an "officer" for the purposes of the Companies Acts: see the note to s. 206(3).

REMOVAL; VACATION OF OFFICE

Section 171   Removal, etc. (voluntary winding up)

171(1)   [Application]   This section applies with respect to the removal from office and vacation of office of the liquidator of a company which is being wound up voluntarily.

171(2)   [Removal from office]   Subject to the next subsection, the liquidator may be removed from office only by an order of the court or—

    (a) in the case of a members' voluntary winding up, by a general meeting of the company summoned specially for that purpose, or

    (b) in the case of a creditors' voluntary winding up, by a general meeting of the company's creditors summoned specially for that purpose in accordance with the rules.

171(3)   [Where liquidator appointed by court under s. 108]   Where the liquidator was appointed by the court under section 108 in Chapter V, a meeting such as is mentioned in subsection (2) above shall be summoned for the purpose of replacing him only if he thinks fit or the court so directs or the meeting is requested, in accordance with the rules—

    (a) in the case of a members' voluntary winding up, by members representing not less than one-half of the total voting rights of all the members having at the date of the request a right to vote at the meeting, or

    (b) in the case of a creditors' voluntary winding up, by not less than one-half, in value, of the company's creditors.

171(4) **[Vacation of office]** A liquidator shall vacate office if he ceases to be a person who is qualified to act as an insolvency practitioner in relation to the company.

171(5) **[Resignation]** A liquidator may, in the prescribed circumstances, resign his office by giving notice of his resignation to the registrar of companies.

171(6) **[Where final meetings held]** Where—

(a) in the case of a members' voluntary winding up, a final meeting of the company has been held under section 94 in Chapter III, or

(b) in the case of a creditors' voluntary winding up, final meetings of the company and of the creditors have been held under section 106 in Chapter IV,

the liquidator whose report was considered at the meeting or meetings shall vacate office as soon as he has complied with subsection (3) of that section and has given notice to the registrar of companies that the meeting or meetings have been held and of the decisions (if any) of the meeting or meetings.

(Former provision: IA 1985, s. 86)

General note
This section sets out in detail the manner by which a liquidator in a voluntary winding up may be removed or resign from his office, and the circumstances in which he must vacate it. It complements s. 172, which applies in a winding up by the court. Together, the two sections set out the legal position comprehensively and in some detail, in sharp contrast to the situation prior to IA 1985, where the legislation said virtually nothing about the matter (apart from CA 1985, s. 599(2), now IA 1986, s. 108(2), empowering the court to remove a liquidator "on cause shown"). An important consequence of this change is that the power of the company or of the contributories in general meeting to remove the liquidator in a creditors' voluntary winding up – even a liquidator whom they have themselves appointed – is no longer recognised.

For the liquidator's duties on vacating office, see IR 1986, rr. 4.138, 4.148.

S. 171(1), (2)
The members may remove a liquidator only in a members' voluntary winding up. The creditors alone have this power in a creditors' winding up, even where the liquidator was originally appointed by the members under s. 100(2).

For the rules prescribed for the purposes of s. 171(2)(*b*), see IR 1986, rr. 4.114, 4.120.

S. 171(3)
Section 108 empowers the court to appoint a liquidator in a voluntary winding up in the circumstances there set out. A liquidator so appointed may be removed:

(1) "on cause shown", by order of the court (s. 108(2));

(2) by the members or the creditors under s. 171(2), if the liquidator himself thinks it "fit" to summon a meeting for the purpose (s. 171(3));

(3) by the members or the creditors under s. 171(2) if the court so directs (s. 171(3)); or

(4) by the members or the creditors under s. 171(2), if the meeting is requested by members or creditors, as the case may be, having the necessary 50 per cent-plus majority stipulated for by s. 171(3)(*a*) or (*b*).

For the relevant rules, see IR 1986, r. 4.114.

S. 171(4)
The terms "act as an insolvency practitioner in relation to" a particular company, and "qualified to act as an insolvency practitioner" are defined respectively in s. 388(1) and s. 390.

When a liquidator ceases to be qualified to act as an insolvency practitioner in relation to a company, he vacates office *ipso facto* and automatically, and does not continue in office until he has complied with his obligations under the rules to notify the registrar, etc. However, the former liquidator in a voluntary liquidation who has vacated office on the ground of disqualification is a proper person to make application to the court under s. 108 to have another liquidator appointed in his place (*Re AJ Adams (Builders) Ltd* [1991] BCC 62).

For the relevant rules, see IR 1986, rr. 4.135, 4.122.

S. 171(5)

The circumstances in which a liquidator may resign are defined in IR 1986, rr. 4.108(4), 4.142 (3). Before resigning his office, the liquidator must summon a meeting of the company or the creditors (depending upon the category of winding up) for the purpose of receiving his resignation (rr. 4.108(1), 4.142(1)). The notice to the registrar must be given by the liquidator "forthwith after the meeting" (r. 4.110(2)). The meeting may decline to accept the resignation, in which event the liquidator may apply to the court for leave to resign (r. 4.111).

S. 171(6)

If the meeting in question was inquorate, so that the liquidator's report could not be considered, s. 94(5) and s. 106(5) respectively state that the liquidator shall be deemed to have complied with the requirements of the section in question. It would seem therefore that the words "whose report was considered at the meeting" in the present subsection should be taken to include such cases of deemed compliance.

Section 172   Removal, etc. (winding up by the court)

172(1)   [Application]   This section applies with respect to the removal from office and vacation of office of the liquidator of a company which is being wound up by the court, or of a provisional liquidator.

172(2)   [Removal from office]   Subject as follows, the liquidator may be removed from office only by an order of the court or by a general meeting of the company's creditors summoned specially for that purpose in accordance with the rules; and a provisional liquidator may be removed from office only by an order of the court.

172(3)   [Replacing certain types of liquidator]   Where—

   (a) the official receiver is liquidator otherwise than in succession under section 136(3) to a person who held office as a result of a nomination by a meeting of the company's creditors or contributories, or

   (b) the liquidator was appointed by the court otherwise than under section 139 (4)(a) or 140(1), or was appointed by the Secretary of State,

a general meeting of the company's creditors shall be summoned for the purpose of replacing him only if he thinks fit, or the court so directs, or the meeting is requested, in accordance with the rules, by not less that one-quarter, in value, of the creditors.

172(4)   [If liquidator appointed by Secretary of State]   If appointed by the Secretary of State, the liquidator may be removed from office by a direction of the Secretary of State.

172(5)   [Vacation of office]   A liquidator or provisional liquidator, not being the official receiver, shall vacate office if he ceases to be a person who is qualified to act as an insolvency practitioner in relation to the company.

172(6)   [Resignation]   A liquidator may, in the prescribed circumstances, resign his office by giving notice of his resignation to the court.

172(7)   [Where s. 204 order]   Where an order is made under section 204 (early dissolution in Scotland) for the dissolution of the company, the liquidator shall vacate office when the dissolution of the company takes effect in accordance with that section.

172(8)   [Where final meeting under s. 146]   Where a final meeting has been held under section 146 (liquidator's report on completion of winding up), the liquidator whose report was considered at the meeting shall vacate office as soon as he has given notice to the court and the registrar of companies that the meeting has been held and of the decisions (if any) of the meeting.

(Former provision: IA 1985, s. 79)

General note

This section contains provisions, complementary to those in s. 171, which apply in a compulsory winding up. The notes to s. 171 apply generally to the present section also, subject to the additional points below.

S. 172(1), (2)

A provisional liquidator may be removed only by court order.

There is nothing in the present section which empowers the shareholders or contributories in general meeting to remove a liquidator, even in cases where the company is demonstrably solvent, and even where the original liquidator was the members' appointee.

A contributory holding fully-paid shares in an insolvent company has no standing to apply to the court for an order removing a liquidator, on the analogy of *Re Rica Gold Washing Co.* (1879) 11 ChD 36 (see the note to s. 124(2), (3) above): *Re Corbenstoke Ltd (No. 2)* (1989) 5 BCC 767.

For the rules prescribed for the purposes of s. 172, see IR 1986, rr. 4.113ff.

S. 172(3)

The liquidator may be removed by a general meeting of the creditors without any special formality under s. 172(2) above only where:

(1) he was originally appointed by a meeting of the company's creditors or contributories (s. 172(2));

(2) the official receiver is liquidator in succession to a person who was appointed as in (1) (s. 172(3)(*a*));

(3) the liquidator was a nominee of the contributories whom the court appointed liquidator either jointly with, or instead of, a nominee of the creditors (ss. 139(4)(*a*), 172(3)(*b*)); or

(4) the liquidator was formerly the administrator of the company who was appointed by the court when the winding-up order was made immediately upon the discharge of the administration order (ss. 140(1), 172(3)(*b*)).

The special preconditions to the summoning of the creditors' general meeting will apply, however, where the official receiver is liquidator otherwise than in (2) above, where the liquidator was appointed by the Secretary of State, or where the liquidator was appointed by the court otherwise than in (3) or (4) above. (Note that this will include, first, a "neutral" liquidator who is appointed on the court's own nomination under s. 139(4)(*b*), following a disagreement between the creditors' and the contributories' meetings, and, secondly, a liquidator appointed by the court under s. 140(2), who was formerly the supervisor of a voluntary scheme.) In contrast with s. 171(3), the percentage of creditors necessary to request a meeting under s. 172(2) is one-quarter, rather than "not less than one-half".

S. 172(4)

This power is additional to that of the court under s. 172(2) and that of the creditors under s. 172(3)(*b*). For the relevant rules, see IR 1986, r. 4.123.

S. 172(5)

For the relevant rules, see IR 1986, rr. 4.134, 4.138(1).

S. 172(6)

The relevant circumstances are prescribed by IR 1986, r. 4.108(4).

S. 172(8)

When the liquidator vacates office pursuant to this provision, he must deliver up the company's books and records to the official receiver: see IR 1986, r. 4.138(3).

For transitional provisions, see Sch. 11, para. 6(3).

RELEASE OF LIQUIDATOR

Section **173** Release (voluntary winding up)

173(1) [**Application**] This section applies with respect to the release of the liquidator of a company which is being wound up voluntarily.

173(2) [**Time of release**] A person who has ceased to be a liquidator shall have his release with effect from the following time, that is to say—

(a) in the case of a person who has been removed from office by a general meeting of the company or by a general meeting of the company's creditors that has not resolved against his release or who has died, the time at which notice is given to the registrar of companies in accordance with the rules that that person has ceased to hold office;

(b) in the case of a person who has been removed from office by a general meeting of the company's creditors that has resolved against his release, or by the court, or who has vacated office under section 171(4) above, such time as the Secretary of State may, on the application of that person, determine;

(c) in the case of a person who has resigned, such time as may be prescribed;

(d) in the case of a person who has vacated office under subsection (6)(a) of section 171, the time at which he vacated office;

(e) in the case of a person who has vacated office under subsection (6)(b) of that section—

  (i) if the final meeting of the creditors referred to in that subsection has resolved against that person's release, such time as the Secretary of State may, on an application by that person, determine, and

  (ii) if that meeting has not resolved against that person's release, the time at which he vacated office.

173(3)   [Application to Scotland]   In the application of subsection (2) to the winding up of a company registered in Scotland, the references to a determination by the Secretary of State as to the time from which a person who has ceased to be liquidator shall have his release are to be read as references to such a determination by the Accountant of Court.

173(4)   [Effect of release]   Where a liquidator has his release under subsection (2), he is, with effect from the time specified in that subsection, discharged from all liability both in respect of acts or omissions of his in the winding up and otherwise in relation to his conduct as liquidator.

But nothing in this section prevents the exercise, in relation to a person who has had his release under subsection (2), of the court's powers under section 212 of this Act (summary remedy against delinquent directors, liquidators, etc.).

(Former provision: IA 1985, s. 87)

S. 173(1)

For the corresponding provisions relating to a winding up by the court, see s. 174. The effect of a release is stated in s. 173(4).

S. 173(2), (3)

The times at which the release of a liquidator becomes effective in different circumstances are set out in the various paragraphs of this subsection. For the relevant rules, see IR 1986, rr. 4.111 (2), 4.114(2), 4.122 and 4.126 (creditors' voluntary winding up) and rr. 4.144 and 4.147 (members' voluntary winding up).

It is open to the members' or creditors' meeting to resolve against the release of a liquidator in the cases mentioned in paras. (*b*) and (*e*)(i). The question of a release is then a matter for the Secretary of State (or, in Scotland, the Accountant of Court) to determine.

S. 173(4)

The terms of this subsection are in all material respects the same as those of s. 20(2), (3), relating to the release of an administrator: see, further, the notes to that section.

Section 174   Release (winding up by the court)

174(1)   [Application]   This section applies with respect to the release of the liquidator of a company which is being wound up by the court, or of a provisional liquidator.

174(2)   [Where official receiver ceases to be liquidator]   Where the official receiver has ceased to be liquidator and a person becomes liquidator in his stead, the official receiver has his release with effect from the following time, that is to say—

    (a) in a case where that person was nominated by a general meeting of creditors or contributories, or was appointed by the Secretary of State, the time at which the official receiver gives notice to the court that he has been replaced;

    (b) in a case where that person is appointed by the court, such time as the court may determine.

174(3)   [Where official receiver gives notice to Secretary of State]   If the official receiver while he is a liquidator gives notice to the Secretary of State that the winding up is for practical purposes complete, he has his release with effect from such time as the Secretary of State may determine.

174(4) **[Person other than official receiver]** A person other than the official receiver who has ceased to be a liquidator has his release with effect from the following time, that is to say—

(a) in the case of a person who has been removed from office by a general meeting of creditors that has not resolved against his release or who has died, the time at which notice is given to the court in accordance with the rules that that person has ceased to hold office;

(b) in the case of a person who has been removed from office by a general meeting of creditors that has resolved against his release, or by the court or the Secretary of State, or who has vacated office under section 172(5) or (7), such time as the Secretary of State may, on an application by that person, determine;

(c) in the case of a person who has resigned, such time as may be prescribed;

(d) in the case of a person who has vacated office under section 172(8)—

(i) if the final meeting referred to in that subsection has resolved against that person's release, such time as the Secretary of State may, on an application by that person, determine, and

(ii) if that meeting has not so resolved, the time at which that person vacated office.

174(5) **[Provisional liquidator]** A person who has ceased to hold office as a provisional liquidator has his release with effect from such time as the court may, on an application by him, determine.

174(6) **[Effect of release]** Where the official receiver or a liquidator or provisional liquidator has his release under this section, he is, with effect from the time specified in the preceding provisions of this section, discharged from all liability both in respect of acts or omissions of his in the winding up and otherwise in relation to his conduct as liquidator or provisional liquidator.

But nothing in this section prevents the exercise, in relation to a person who has had his release under this section, of the court's powers under section 212 (summary remedy against delinquent directors, liquidators, etc.).

174(7) **[Application to Scotland]** In the application of this section to a case where the order for winding up has been made by the court in Scotland, the references to a determination by the Secretary of State as to the time from which a person who has ceased to be liquidator has his release are to such a determination by the Accountant of Court.

(Former provision: IA 1985, s. 80, replacing CA 1985, s. 545)

S. 174(1)

Section 173 deals with the corresponding questions in a voluntary liquidation. The effect of a release is described in s. 174(6).

S. 174(2), (3)

These two subsections govern the release of the official receiver as liquidator. Necessarily, of course, they apply only in England and Wales.

For the relevant rules, see IR 1986, r. 4.124.

S. 174(4)

The provisions of this subsection are broadly parallel to those of s. 173(2). For the rules prescribed for the purposes of s. 174, see IR 1986, rr. 4.113, 4.121–4.125.

For transitional provisions, see Sch. 11, para. 6(3), (4).

S. 174(6)

See the corresponding provisions relating to an administrator (s. 20(2), (3)) and a liquidator in a voluntary winding up (s. 173(4)).

Chapter VIII — Provisions of General Application in Winding Up

General comment on Part IV, Ch. VIII

Those familiar with the former law relating to company liquidations, as contained in CA 1985 and its predecessors, would naturally expect to find at about this point in the present Act provisions corresponding to CA 1985, ss. 611–613. The first of these sections dealt with the question of debts provable in a liquidation, and read as follows:

"611(1) In every winding up . . . all debts payable on a contingency, and all claims against the company, present or future, certain or contingent, ascertained or sounding only in damages, are admissible to proof against the company.

(2) A just estimate is to be made (so far as possible) of the value of such debts or claims as may be subject to any contingency or sound only in damages, or for some other reason do not bear a certain value."

Section 612 provided for the application in the winding up of an insolvent company (in England and Wales) of many of the rules of the law governing the bankruptcy of individuals, and s. 613 made a corresponding, though different, provision for Scotland. It was by virtue of these sections that such rules as those relating to set-off, for instance, were imported into the law of company liquidation.

The absence of any counterpart provisions to CA 1985, ss. 611–613 in the substantive provisions of the present Act is, at first, puzzling; but the need to fill the gap left by their repeal has not been overlooked, but has been dealt with by subordinate legislation under s. 411. Schedule 8, para. 12, includes among the matters to be dealt with in this way, "provision as to the debts that may be proved in a winding up", and para. 14, "provision which, with or without modifications, applies in relation to the winding up of companies any enactment contained in Parts VIII to XI of this Act or in the Bankruptcy (Scotland) Act 1985". The debts provable in a liquidation are accordingly dealt with in IR 1986, Ch. 9 (rr. 4.73ff, and especially r. 4.86), and rr. 12.3 and 13.12, while the questions of mutual credit and set-off are provided for by r. 4.90. The corresponding provisions for bankruptcy are to be found in ss. 382 and 323, respectively.

PREFERENTIAL DEBTS

Section 175 Preferential debts (general provision)

175(1) **[Payment in priority]** In a winding up the company's preferential debts (within the meaning given by section 386 in Part XII) shall be paid in priority to all other debts.

175(2) **[Ranking and priority]** Preferential debts—

(a) rank equally among themselves after the expenses of the winding up and shall be paid in full, unless the assets are insufficient to meet them, in which case they abate in equal proportions; and

(b) so far as the assets of the company available for payment of general creditors are insufficient to meet them, have priority over the claims of holders of debentures secured by, or holders of, any floating charge created by the company, and shall be paid accordingly out of any property comprised in or subject to that charge.

(Former provision: IA 1985, s. 89(1), (2), replacing CA 1985, s. 614(1), (2))

General note

The terms of s. 175, which re-enacts IA 1985, s. 89(1), (2), are in substance the same as those of the section of the Companies Act which the latter replaced. However, the practical effect of the new provision is considerably different because the list of debts entitled to preference, set out in Sch. 6, has been radically revised. For details of these changes, see the note to s. 386.

Another important reform made by IA 1985 is of special significance for the purposes of the section. The term "floating charge" has been redefined (see now IA 1986, s. 251) so as to mean a charge which, *as created*, was a floating charge. The provisions of s. 175(2)(*b*) will therefore apply to a charge which has crystallised before the event which fixes the "relevant date" for the purposes of ss. 386, 387.

Where a company is in receivership and was not, at the time when the receiver was appointed, in course of being wound up, s. 40 applies (and not the present section), to give similar priority to preferential debts. But in that situation the list of preferential creditors is settled by reference to a different "relevant date" (see s. 387(4)). The fact that a winding up later supervenes will not, it is submitted, lead to the consequence that s. 175 displaces s. 40. The case of *Re Portbase Clothing Ltd, Mond* v *Taylor & Ors* [1993] Ch. 388; [1993] BCC 96 applied s. 175 in the situation where a floating charge had crystallised *otherwise* than by the appointment of a receiver prior to the winding up, but the judgment (at p. 396; 101) makes it plain that s. 40 will continue to apply where the receivership precedes the liquidation. See further the notes to ss. 107 and 115.

A further change made by the insolvency legislation of 1985 was to bring into line, not only the law of company insolvency and individual bankruptcy, but also that of company voluntary arrangements, receiverships and individual voluntary arrangements, so that the same rules set out in Sch. 6 apply to them all.

Note that there are no preferential debts in a company administration (IA 1986, Pt. II), except where the administration is linked with a voluntary arrangement (s. 387(2)) or where a winding-up order immediately follows upon the discharge of the administration order (s. 387(3)(*a*)).

S. 175(2)(a)

Costs incurred by a liquidator in pursuing unsuccessful claims (i) to have a transaction set aside as "at an undervalue" or a preference, and (ii) for alleged wrongful trading are not "expenses of the winding up" for the purposes of this statutory provision: *Re M C Bacon Ltd (No. 2)* [1991] Ch. 127; [1990] BCC 430.

S. 175(2)(b)

This important provision continues the rule, laid down in successive Companies Acts, which subordinates the claims of a secured creditor holding a floating charge (but not a fixed charge) to those of the preferential creditors. A similar rule applies in a receivership (ss. 40, 59).

However, the application of the rule will now be different, not only because the categories of preferential debts have been revised under the new legislation, but because the statutory definition of a floating charge has been re-worded, so that it includes any charge which, *as created*, was a floating charge (see s. 251). In consequence, any charge which was originally a floating charge but has become a fixed charge (e.g. by crystallisation, or by a notice of conversion) before the "relevant date" defined by s. 387 will now be subordinated to the preferential debts under the present section. The decisions in *Re Woodroffes (Musical Instruments) Ltd* [1986] Ch. 366, *Re Brightlife Ltd* [1987] Ch. 200; (1986) 2 BCC 99,359, *Stein v Saywell* (1969) 121 CLR 529 and *Re Griffin Hotel Co. Ltd* [1941] Ch. 129, which were previously authorities to the contrary, are accordingly no longer good law.

Section 176   Preferential charge on goods distrained

176(1)   [Application]   This section applies where a company is being wound up by the court in England and Wales, and is without prejudice to section 128 (avoidance of attachments, etc.).

176(2)   [Where distraining in previous 3 months]   Where any person (whether or not a landlord or person entitled to rent) has distrained upon the goods or effects of the company in the period of 3 months ending with the date of the winding-up order, those goods or effects, or the proceeds of their sale, shall be charged for the benefit of the company with the preferential debts of the company to the extent that the company's property is for the time being insufficient for meeting them.

176(3)   [Surrender of goods under s. 176(2)]   Where by virtue of a charge under subsection (2) any person surrenders any goods or effects to a company or makes a payment to a company, that person ranks, in respect of the amount of the proceeds of sale of those goods or effects by the liquidator or (as the case may be) the amount of the payment, as a preferential creditor of the company, except as against so much of the company's property as is available for the payment of preferential creditors by virtue of the surrender or payment.

(Former provisions: IA 1985, s. 89(3), (4); CA 1985, s. 614(3))

S. 176(1)

The present section does not apply in the case of a voluntary liquidation; and it will apply only if the distress is not void, under the provisions of s. 128, as having been put in force after the commencement of the winding up.

S. 176(2)

The effect of the subsection is to make the claims of the preferential creditors a first charge on the goods distrained or their proceeds. Note that the significant date for reckoning the three-month period is that of the winding-up *order*, and not (as in s. 128) the date of *commencement* of the winding up, which will be earlier (see s. 129).

S. 176(3)

If the person distraining pays all or part of the preferential creditors' claims out of the proceeds of sale, he is subrogated to their rights and thus has a claim to be paid in priority out of the company's assets.

SPECIAL MANAGERS

Section 177   Power to appoint special manager

177(1)   [Power of court]   Where a company has gone into liquidation or a provisional liquidator has been appointed, the court may, on an application under this section, appoint any person to be the special manager of the business or property of the company.

177(2)   [Application to court]   The application may be made by the liquidator or provisional liquidator in any case where it appears to him that the nature of the business or property of the company, or the interests of the company's creditors or contributories or members generally, require the appointment of another person to manage the company's business or property.

177(3)   [Powers of special manager]   The special manager has such powers as may be entrusted to him by the court.

177(4)   [Extent of s. 177(3) powers]   The court's power to entrust powers to the special manager includes power to direct that any provision of this Act that has effect in relation to the provisional liquidator or liquidator of a company shall have the like effect in relation to the special manager for the purposes of the carrying out by him of any of the functions of the provisional liquidator or liquidator.

177(5)   [Duties of special manager]   The special manager shall—

    (a) give such security or, in Scotland, caution as may be prescribed;

    (b) prepare and keep such accounts as may be prescribed; and

    (c) produce those accounts in accordance with the rules to the Secretary of State or to such other persons as may be prescribed.

(Former provisions: IA 1985, s. 90; CA 1985, s. 556)

General note

The former CA 1985, s. 556 provided for the appointment of a special manager when the official receiver became the liquidator or provisional liquidator of a company. The present section extends this facility to all liquidators, and now applies also to Scotland. The appointment of a special manager allows a liquidator to have assistance from someone with particular managerial or commercial expertise that he may not have himself.

    A special manager is not required to be qualified to act as an insolvency practitioner: indeed, there may be a particular need to invoke the present section when the skills in question are those which an insolvency practitioner does not normally have. (There is no longer the option of bringing in such an expert in the rôle of liquidator, or joint liquidator, unless by chance he is also qualified under this Act for appointment.)

In *Re W F Fearman Ltd (No. 2)* (1988) 4 BCC 141 the court gave leave to the official receiver to use the services of the outgoing provisional liquidators as special managers, in order to maintain continuity in the administration of the insolvency pending the choice by a creditors' meeting of liquidators on a permanent basis.

S. 177(1), (2)

The appointment must in all cases be made by the court, on the application of the liquidator or provisional liquidator himself.

S. 177(3), (4)

The powers of a special manager are determined in each case by the court, and they may be made subject to any statutory provision that applies to a liquidator – e.g., an obligation to obtain the consent of the liquidation committee on particular matters.

S. 177(5)

This provision may be contrasted with the former CA 1985, s. 556(3), which required the Secretary of State to give directions on an *ad hoc* basis in regard to security, account, etc.

The rules prescribed for the purposes of this section are to be found in IR 1986, Ch. 18 (rr. 4.206ff).

DISCLAIMER (ENGLAND AND WALES ONLY)

Section 178 Power to disclaim onerous property

178(1) [Application] This and the next two sections apply to a company that is being wound up in England and Wales.

178(2) [Disclaimer by liquidator] Subject as follows, the liquidator may, by the giving of the prescribed notice, disclaim any onerous property and may do so notwithstanding that he has taken possession of it, endeavoured to sell it, or otherwise exercised rights of ownership in relation to it.

178(3) [Onerous property] The following is onerous property for the purposes of this section—

    (a) any unprofitable contract, and

    (b) any other property of the company which is unsaleable or not readily saleable or is such that it may give rise to a liability to pay money or perform any other onerous act.

178(4) [Effect of disclaimer] A disclaimer under this section—

    (a) operates so as to determine, as from the date of the disclaimer, the rights, interests and liabilities of the company in or in respect of the property disclaimed; but

    (b) does not, except so far as is necessary for the purpose of releasing the company from any liability, affect the rights or liabilities of any other person.

178(5) [Where notice of disclaimer not to be given] A notice of disclaimer shall not be given under this section in respect of any property if—

    (a) a person interested in the property has applied in writing to the liquidator or one of his predecessors as liquidator requiring the liquidator or that predecessor to decide whether he will disclaim or not, and

    (b) the period of 28 days beginning with the day on which that application was made, or such longer period as the court may allow, has expired without a notice of disclaimer having been given under this section in respect of that property.

178(6)   **[Persons sustaining loss etc.]**   Any person sustaining loss or damage in consequence of the operation of a disclaimer under this section is deemed a creditor of the company to the extent of the loss or damage and accordingly may prove for the loss or damage in the winding up.

(Former provision: IA 1985, s. 91(1)–(4), (8))

General note

Sections 178–182 enlarge and, in some respects, modify the law regarding disclaimer which was formerly contained in CA 1985, ss. 618, 619 and 629. These provisions apply only in England and Wales. They correspond to the bankruptcy rules set out in ss. 315ff, below.

    In the context of the financial markets, s. 178 does not apply in relation to a market contract or a contract effected by an exchange or clearing house for the purpose of realising property provided as margin in relation to market contracts: see CA 1989, s. 164(1), and the note on p. 3.

S. 178(2)

Under the former law as contained in CA 1985, only the official receiver was empowered to disclaim property on his own authority; any other liquidator was required to obtain the leave of the court. Every liquidator may now exercise the power to disclaim without leave. It is left to the person affected by the proposed disclaimer to take his objection to the court, if he has one. However, the effect of the change in the law removing the requirement of leave is to make the liquidator's decision to disclaim primarily a matter for his discretion, similar to his other powers in the management and realisation of the company's property, which will normally be reviewed by the court only if it has been exercised mala fide or perversely. Cases relating to the granting of leave under the former law are now irrelevant (*Re Hans Place Ltd* [1992] BCC 737).

    A notice of disclaimer must now be "in the prescribed form": see IR 1986, r. 4.187, and Form 4.53. For the rules regulating the procedure generally, see IR 1986, Ch. 15 (rr. 4.187ff).

    The 12-month time limit which was formerly imposed by CA 1985, s. 618(3) has been abolished.

S. 178(3)

This is a new and wider definition of "onerous property". The previous specific references in CA 1985, s. 618(1) to "land (of any tenure) burdened with onerous covenants" and "shares or stock in companies" have been dropped – though such items are clearly within the wider terms of the new definition – and the former requirement that, to be "onerous", property had to be "unsaleable, or not readily saleable, *by reason of* its binding its possessor to the performance of any onerous act or to the payment of any sum of money" has now been replaced by s. 178(3)(*b*), in which these attributes are expressed as alternatives.

    The term "property" is itself widely defined for the purposes of the present Act by s. 436, below.

S. 178(4)

This provision is equivalent to the former CA 1985, s. 618(4).

The effect of a disclaimer is, apart from the operation of any vesting order made by the court under the succeeding sections, that the disclaimed property vests in the Crown as *bona vacantia* (or, in the case of land held in fee simple, by escheat).

S. 178(5)

This corresponds with the repealed CA 1985, s. 619(2), with the necessary modification that in para. (*b*) the liquidator must now give an actual notice of disclaimer within the 28-day period, instead of a notice that he intends to apply to the court for leave to disclaim. For the procedure under this subsection, see IR 1986, r. 4.191.

S. 178(6)

This is the same as the former CA 1985, s. 619(8), with the substitution of the words "sustaining loss or damage" for the less precise term "injured".

Section 179   Disclaimer of leaseholds

179(1)   **[Requirement for disclaimer to take effect]**   The disclaimer under section 178 of any property of a leasehold nature does not take effect unless a copy of the disclaimer has been served (so far as the liquidator is aware of their addresses) on every person claiming under the company as underlessee or mortgagee and either—

    (a) no application under section 181 below is made with respect to that property before the end of the period of 14 days beginning with the day on which the last notice served under this subsection was served; or

    (b) where such an application has been made, the court directs that the disclaimer shall take effect.

179(2)   **[Court's directions or orders]**   Where the court gives a direction under subsection (1)(b) it may also, instead of or in addition to any order it makes under section 181, make such orders with respect to fixtures, tenant's improvements and other matters arising out of the lease as it thinks fit.

(Former provision: IA 1985, s. 91(5), (6))

General note

Under the former law, when leave to disclaim had to be sought in every case, the court could require such notices to be given to persons interested as it thought appropriate. The present section, now that the court is no longer involved, makes express provision for notice to be given to underlessees and mortgagees of leasehold property, at least 14 days before the disclaimer can take effect.

For a case in which the effect of a disclaimer on an underlessee is discussed, see *Re A E Realisations (1985) Ltd* [1988] 1 WLR 200; (1987) 3 BCC 136.

S. 179(1)

An underlessee or mortgagee has 14 days after receiving notice of the proposed disclaimer in which to apply to the court to have a vesting order made in his favour, or such other relief as the court thinks fit.

S. 179(2)

This provision confers on the court additional powers to those prescribed by ss. 181, 182.

Section **180** Land subject to rentcharge

180(1) [Application] The following applies where, in consequence of the disclaimer under section 178 of any land subject to a rentcharge, that land vests by operation of law in the Crown or any other person (referred to in the next subsection as "the proprietor").

180(2) [Liability of proprietor et al.] The proprietor and the successors in title of the proprietor are not subject to any personal liability in repect of any sums becoming due under the rentcharge except sums becoming due after the proprietor, or some person claiming under or through the proprietor, has taken possession or control of the land or has entered into occupation of it.

(Former provision: IA 1985, s. 91(7), replacing CA 1985, s. 620)

General note

The purpose of this section is to ensure that the Crown or any other person in whom land vests as a result of a disclaimer (see the note to s. 178(4)) is not made personally liable in respect of the rentcharge unless it (or he) takes possession or control of the land.

Section **181** Powers of court (general)

181(1) [Application] This section and the next apply where the liquidator has disclaimed property under section 178.

181(2) [Application to court] An application under this section may be made to the court by—

(a) any person who claims an interest in the disclaimed property, or

(b) any person who is under any liability in respect of the disclaimed property, not being a liability discharged by the disclaimer.

181(3) [Powers of court] Subject as follows, the court may on the application make an order, on such terms as it thinks fit, for the vesting of the disclaimed property in, or for its delivery to—

(a) a person entitled to it or a trustee for such a person, or

(b) a person subject to such a liability as is mentioned in subsection (2)(b) or a trustee for such a person.

181(4) [Limit on court's powers] The court shall not make an order under subsection (3)(b) except where it appears to the court that it would be just to do so for the purpose of compensating the person subject to the liability in respect of the disclaimer.

181(5) [Relationship with s. 178(6)] The effect of any order under this section shall be taken into account in assessing for the purpose of section 178(6) the extent of any loss or damage sustained by any person in consequence of the disclaimer.

181(6) [Effect of vesting order] An order under this section vesting property in any person need not be completed by conveyance, assignment or transfer.

(Former provision: IA 1985, s. 92(1)–(4), (9), (10))

S. 181(1)–(3)

As has been explained above, the liquidator's power to disclaim no longer requires the leave of the court, and so the court becomes involved only if an application is made to it by a person who is interested in the property or otherwise affected by the disclaimer. These subsections deal with the right to make such an application, and set out the general powers of the court in such proceedings. The relevant procedure is laid down by IR 1986, r. 4.194. (In regard to vesting orders affecting leasehold property, the provisions of s. 182 apply in addition.)

The term "interest" in s. 181(2) is not confined to a proprietary interest. A subtenant of premises who is in occupation as a statutory tenant has no proprietary interest in the premises, but merely a status of irremovability; but even so, since he has a financial interest in the subsistence of the head-lease, he has a sufficient interest for the purpose of s. 181: *Re Vedmay Ltd* [1994] 1 BCLC 676.

The disclaimer of a lease brings to an end the obligations of a guarantor or surety in respect of future liabilities under the lease (*Stacey* v *Hill* [1901] 1 KB 660). It follows that a guarantor is not a "person under a liability in respect of the disclaimed property, not being a liability discharged by the disclaimer", with standing to make an application under s. 181(2)(*b*) (*Re No. 1 London Ltd* [1991] BCC 118, *Re Yarmarine (IW) Ltd* [1992] BCC 28). But the disclaimer of a lease which has been assigned does not determine a continuing liability of the original lessee and any surety for the original lessee: *Hill* v *East & West India Dock Co* (1884) 9 App Cas 448, *Hindcastle Ltd* v *Barbara Attenborough Associates Ltd & Ors* [1994] BCC 705.

Section 654 of CA 1985 provides that the property of a defunct company which has been struck off the register vests in the Crown as *bona vacantia*, subject to the Crown's right to disclaim the property under s. 656; and s. 657(2) states that, as regards property in England and Wales, ss. 178(4) and 179 to 182 of IA 1986 shall apply to such property as if it had been disclaimed by a liquidator. The case of *Allied Dunbar Assurance plc* v *Fowle & Ors* [1994] BCC 422 dealt with problems which may arise if the company concerned has been restored to the register after such a disclaimer. Garland J ruled that in such a case the obligations of a guarantor under the lease revived retroactively when the company was reinstated.

S. 181(4)

If a vesting order is made under s. 181(3)(*b*), the beneficiary will not be someone "entitled" to the property in question (cf. s. 181(3)(*a*)), but someone who is under a liability in respect of it. A vesting order allows the court to do rough justice by allowing the applicant to take over the property in exchange for the extinction of his liability, provided that the condition in this subsection is met.

S. 181(5)

The beneficiary under a vesting order proves in the winding up under s. 178(6) for any loss or damage which he may have sustained overall, after bringing into account the effect of the order, which may in itself have left him better or worse off.

S. 181(6)

The vesting order operates itself as a conveyance of the property without the need for any other legal act.

Section 182   Powers of court (leaseholds)

182(1)   [Limit on court's power]   The court shall not make an order under section 181 vesting property of a leasehold nature on any person claiming under the company as underlessee or mortgagee except on terms making that person—

(a) subject to the same liabilities and obligations as the company was subject to under the lease at the commencement of the winding up, or

(b) if the court thinks fit, subject to the same liabilities and obligations as that person would be subject to if the lease had been assigned to him at the commencement of the winding up.

182(2)   [Where order re part of property in lease]   For the purposes of an order under section 181 relating to only part of any property comprised in a lease, the requirements of subsection (1) apply as if the lease comprised only the property to which the order relates.

182(3)   [Court may vest estate in someone else]   Where subsection (1) applies and no person claiming under the company as underlessee or mortagee is willing to accept an order under section 181 on the terms required by virtue of that subsection, the court may, by order under that section, vest the company's estate or interest in the property in any person who is liable (whether personally or in a representative capacity, and whether alone or jointly with the company) to perform the lessee's covenants in the lease.

The court may vest that estate and interest in such a person freed and discharged from all estates, incumbrances and interests created by the company.

182(4)   [Where s. 182(1) applies]   Where subsection (1) applies and a person claiming under the company as underlessee or mortgagee declines to accept an order under section 181, that person is excluded from all interest in the property.

(Former provisions: IA 1985, s. 92(5)–(8))

General note

In this section, provisions which in CA 1985 had been relegated to a schedule (Sch. 20) are now restored to the body of the Act, but no changes of substance are made. They are designed to ensure that persons who have a subordinate interest in leasehold property owned by the company have an opportunity to take over the property itself on the same terms, in effect, as those upon which the company formerly held it.

S. 182(4)

This provision is limited in its application to persons who have a proprietary interest in the property. It cannot be invoked to determine a statutory tenancy: *Re Vedmay Ltd* [1994] 1 BCLC 676.

EXECUTION, ATTACHMENT AND THE SCOTTISH EQUIVALENTS

Section 183   Effect of execution or attachment (England and Wales)

183(1)   [Where creditor seeking benefit of execution or attachment]   Where a creditor has issued execution against the goods or land of a company or has attached any debt due to it, and the company is subsequently wound up, he is not entitled to retain the benefit of the execution or attachment against the liquidator unless he has completed the execution or attachment before the commencement of the winding up.

183(2) **[Qualifications]** However—

(a) if a creditor has had notice of a meeting having been called at which a resolution for voluntary winding up is to be proposed, the date on which he had notice is substituted, for the purpose of subsection (1), for the date of commencement of the winding up;

(b) a person who purchases in good faith under a sale by the sheriff any goods of a company on which execution has been levied in all cases acquires a good title to them against the liquidator; and

(c) the rights conferred by subsection (1) on the liquidator may be set aside by the court in favour of the creditor to such extent and subject to such terms as the court thinks fit.

183(3) **[Execution, attachment]** For the purposes of this Act—

(a) an execution against goods is completed by seizure and sale, or by the making of a charging order under section 1 of the Charging Orders Act 1979;

(b) an attachment of a debt is completed by receipt of the debt; and

(c) an execution against land is completed by seizure, by the appointment of a receiver, or by the making of a charging order under section 1 of the Act above mentioned.

183(4) **[Definitions]** In this section **"goods"** includes all chattels personal; and **"the sheriff"** includes any officer charged with the execution of a writ or other process.

183(5) **[Scotland]** This section does not apply in the case of a winding up in Scotland.

(Former provisions: CA 1985, s. 621; CA 1948, s. 325 (as amended by Charging Orders Act 1970, s. 4))

S. 183(1)

This section deals with the situation where a creditor has levied execution against the property of a company which then goes into liquidation. Its effect is to deprive him of the benefit of the execution unless it has been "completed" (as that term is defined in s. 183(3)) before the commencement of the winding up. Since a winding up may commence at a time earlier than the date of a winding-up order, an execution which has in fact then been completed may be avoided retrospectively.

On the "commencement" of a winding up, see ss. 86 and 129. The section may operate even earlier than this time: see s. 183(2)(*a*).

The present provisions are complementary to s. 128, which avoids all executions and attachments put in force *after* the commencement of a winding up, but whereas s. 128 is restricted to a winding up by the court, s. 183 applies to all categories of winding up.

S. 183(2)

Notice of the summoning of a meeting is here, in effect, treated as equivalent to the now discarded "notice of an act of bankruptcy" applicable in the case of an insolvent individual.

The present provision causes the execution creditor to lose the benefit of his execution, but a bona fide purchaser of goods from the sheriff is protected by para. (*b*).

On the significance of the word "date", see the note to s. 86.

The court has an overriding jurisdiction: see para. (*c*).

S. 183(3)

These provisions define with precision the point at which an execution or attachment is "completed".

S. 183(4)

The definition of "goods" is much wider than, e.g. that in the Sale of Goods Act 1979, and extends to intangible property such as choses in action.

S. 183(5)

For the position governing the winding up of a company in Scotland, see s. 185. Note, however, that where a company registered in England or Wales has assets in Scotland, the provisions of s. 185 will apply, presumably to the exclusion of the present section: see s. 185(4).

Section **184** Duties of sheriff (England and Wales)

184(1) **[Application]** The following applies where a company's goods are taken in execution and, before their sale or the completion of the execution (by the receipt or recovery of the full amount of the levy), notice is served on the sheriff that a provisional liquidator has been appointed or that a winding-up order has been made, or that a resolution for voluntary winding up has been passed.

184(2) **[Sheriff to deliver goods and money to liquidator]** The sheriff shall, on being so required, deliver the goods and any money seized or received in part satisfaction of the execution to the liquidator; but the costs of execution are a first charge on the goods or money so delivered, and the liquidator may sell the goods, or a sufficient part of them, for the purpose of satisfying the charge.

184(3) **[Costs where goods sold etc.]** If under an execution in respect of a judgment for a sum exceeding £500 a company's goods are sold or money is paid in order to avoid sale, the sheriff shall deduct the costs of the execution from the proceeds of sale or the money paid and retain the balance for 14 days.

184(4) **[If within time notice is served]** If within that time notice is served on the sheriff of a petition for the winding up of the company having been presented, or of a meeting having been called at which there is to be proposed a resolution for voluntary winding up, and an order is made or a resolution passed (as the case may be), the sheriff shall pay the balance to the liquidator who is entitled to retain it as against the execution creditor.

184(5) **[Liquidator's rights may be set aside by court]** The rights conferred by this section on the liquidator may be set aside by the court in favour of the creditor to such extent and subject to such terms as the court thinks fit.

184(6) **[Definitions]** In this section, **"goods"** includes all chattels personal; and **"the sheriff"** includes any officer charged with the execution of a writ or other process.

184(7) **[Increase, reduction of s. 184(3) sum]** The money sum for the time being specified in subsection (3) is subject to increase or reduction by order under section 416 in Part XV.

184(8) **[Scotland]** This section does not apply in the case of a winding up in Scotland.

(Former provisions: CA 1985, s. 622 (as amended by IA 1985, Sch. 6, para. 25); CA 1948, s. 326)

General note

This section defines the obligations of a sheriff where a company's goods are taken in execution, thus facilitating the operation of s. 184. For the rules relating to this section, see IR 1986, r. 12.19 and, as regards costs, r. 7.36.

S. 184(1), (2)

These subsections apply where a notice is served on the sheriff that the company in question is either actually in liquidation or in the hands of a provisional liquidator. The benefit of the execution must be surrendered to the liquidator, subject to payment of the sheriff's costs.

S. 184(3)–(5)

These provisions deal with the duties of a sheriff enforcing a judgment debt of over £500. This figure was increased from £250 by the Insolvency Proceedings (Monetary Limits) Order 1986 (SI 1986 No. 1996) as from 29 December 1986. He is required to retain in his hands the net proceeds of the sale, or any money paid to him in order to avoid sale, for 14 days; and if within that time he receives notice that a winding-up petition has been presented or a meeting called to consider a resolution for voluntary winding up, he must continue to hold the money until he learns whether a liquidation has in fact resulted and, if so, hand it to the liquidator (unless the court orders otherwise under s. 184(5)).

S. 184(6)

The definitions are identical with those in s. 183(4).

Section 185   Effect of diligence (Scotland)

185(1)   **[Application of Bankruptcy (Scotland) Act]**   In the winding up of a company registered in Scotland, the following provisions of the Bankruptcy (Scotland) Act 1985—

     (a) subsections (1) to (6) of section 37 (effect of sequestration on diligence); and

     (b) subsections (3), (4), (7) and (8) of section 39 (realisation of estate),

apply, so far as consistent with this Act, in like manner as they apply in the sequestration of a debtor's estate, with the substitutions specified below and with any other necessary modifications.

185(2)   **[Substitutions]**   The substitutions to be made in those sections of the Act of 1985 are as follows—

     (a) for references to the debtor, substitute references to the company;

     (b) for references to the sequestration, substitute references to the winding up;

     (c) for references to the date of sequestration, substitute references to the commencement of the winding up of the company; and

     (d) for references to the permanent trustee, substitute references to the liquidator.

185(3)   **[Definition]**   In this section, **"the commencement of the winding up of the company"** means, where it is being wound up by the court, the day on which the winding-up order is made.

185(4) **[English company with estate in Scotland]** This section, so far as relating to any estate or effects of the company situated in Scotland, applies in the case of a company registered in England and Wales as in the case of one registered in Scotland.

(Former provision: CA 1985, s. 623 (as amended by Bankruptcy (Scotland) Act 1985, Sch. 7, para. 21))

General note

In relation to the financial markets, nothing in s. 185 affects any action taken by an exchange or clearing house for the purpose of its default proceedings: see the note on p. 3, and CA 1989, s. 161(4).

S. 185(1)–(3)

These provisions apply to the winding up of a company in Scotland the rules relating to diligence, etc. (the Scottish equivalent of execution and attachment) in the bankruptcy of an individual. (Note, particularly, the special definition of the term "the commencement of the winding up" for this purpose.)

S. 185(4)

It is plain from ss. 183(5) and 184(8) that the converse to s. 185(4) does not apply: i.e., a company registered in Scotland which has assets in England and Wales will be governed in relation to such property by s. 185, and not by those sections.

MISCELLANEOUS MATTERS

Section 186   Rescission of contracts by the court

186(1) **[Power of court]** The court may, on the application of a person who is, as against the liquidator, entitled to the benefit or subject to the burden of a contract made with the company, make an order rescinding the contract on such terms as to payment by or to either party of damages for the non-performance of the contract, or otherwise as the court thinks just.

186(2) **[Damages]** Any damages payable under the order to such a person may be proved by him as a debt in the winding up.

(Former provisions: CA 1985, s. 619(4); CA 1948, s. 323(5))

General note

This provision was formerly included in the section of the Companies Act dealing with the disclaimer of onerous property. It is now more fittingly treated separately. The intervention of the court remains necessary in all cases.

In the context of the financial markets, s. 186 does not apply in relation to a market contract or a contract effected by an exchange or clearing house for the purpose of realising property provided as margin in relation to market contracts: see CA 1989, s. 164(1), and the note on p. 3.

Section 187   Power to make over assets to employees

187(1) **[CA, s. 719 payment on winding up]** On the winding up of a company (whether by the court or voluntarily), the liquidator may, subject to the following provisions of this section, make any payment which the company has, before the commencement of the winding up, decided to make under section 719 of the Companies Act (power to provide for employees or former employees on cessation or transfer of business).

187(2)   **[Power exercisable by liquidator]**   The power which a company may exercise by virtue only of that section may be exercised by the liquidator after the winding up has commenced if, after the company's liabilities have been fully satisfied and provision has been made for the expenses of the winding up, the exercise of that power has been sanctioned by such a resolution of the company as would be required of the company itself by section 719(3) before that commencement, if paragraph (b) of that subsection were omitted and any other requirement applicable to its exercise by the company had been met.

187(3)   **[Source of payment]**   Any payment which may be made by a company under this section (that is, a payment after the commencement of its winding up) may be made out of the company's assets which are available to the members on the winding up.

187(4)   **[Control by court]**   On a winding up by the court, the exercise by the liquidator of his powers under this section is subject to the court's control, and any creditor or contributory may apply to the court with respect to any exercise or proposed exercise of the power.

187(5)   **[Effect]**   Subsections (1) and (2) above have effect notwithstanding anything in any rule of law or in section 107 of this Act (property of company after satisfaction of liabilities to be distributed among members).

(Former provisions: CA 1985, s. 659 (as amended by IA 1985, Sch. 6, para. 48); CA 1980, s. 74(4)–(8))

General note

The provisions of this section and of CA 1985, s. 719 were first introduced (as CA 1980, s. 74) to negate the common law ruling in *Parke* v *Daily News Ltd* [1962] Ch. 927. Section 719 applies when the company is a going concern, and the present section when it is being wound up. In *Parke's* case, it was held to be ultra vires for a company which had sold its business to a third party to make substantial ex gratia payments to the employees who were thereby made redundant. Both s. 719 and the present section are framed in wide terms, so as not merely to negative any question of ultra vires (abolished by CA 1989, s. 108 from 4 February 1991), but to ensure that such payments will not be invalidated on any other grounds.

S. 187(1)

This subsection applies where the company has already resolved under CA 1985, s. 719(3), before the commencement of the winding up, to make a payment to the employees: the liquidator is authorised to implement the resolution and make that payment. This may be made only out of profits of the company which are available for dividend (s. 719(4)).

S. 187(2)

Once the winding up has commenced, it is still permissible for a company's shareholders to agree to make over assets to the employees, but the restriction to profits available for dividend no longer applies, and instead the payment must be made out of the surplus in the hands of the liquidator after all the company's debts and the costs of the winding up have been met. An ordinary resolution of the shareholders is required or, if the company's memorandum or articles so stipulate, a resolution passed by a larger majority. However, a payment cannot be made on the basis of a decision of the directors alone, even if the memorandum or articles authorise this course, since CA 1985, s. 719(3)(*b*), which permits this prior to the commencement of winding up, is nullified by the present provision.

S. 187(3)

This provision is not permissive (as it appears to be), but mandatory: the payment cannot be made out of any assets other than those available to the members.

S. 187(4), (5)

The grounds on which the court might interfere to set aside a resolution of the members are not set out. It may be assumed that a plea of ultra vires would not succeed, or an objection that the exercise of power by the majority was not in the best interests of the company (see CA 1985, s. 719(1), (2)). However, there are clearly circumstances where a minority shareholder might claim that the majority was acting oppressively or mala fide or in a discriminatory way – e.g. perhaps if the majority shareholders were themselves the employees who stood to benefit.

Section 188   Notification that company is in liquidation

188(1)   [Statement in invoices etc.]   When a company is being wound up, whether by the court or voluntarily, every invoice, order for goods or business letter issued by or on behalf of the company, or a liquidator of the company, or a receiver or manager of the company's property, being a document on or in which the name of the company appears, shall contain a statement that the company is being wound up.

188(2)   [Penalty on default]   If default is made in complying with this section, the company and any of the following persons who knowingly and wilfully authorises or permits the default, namely, any officer of the company, any liquidator of the company and any receiver or manager, is liable to a fine.

(Former provisions: CA 1985, s. 637; CA 1948, s. 338)

General note

This section is substantially the same as the provision in CA 1985 which it replaces, and has its counterpart in the provisions relating to administration (s. 12) and receivership (ss. 39, 64).

S. 188(2)

On penalties, see s. 430 and Sch. 10.

Section 189   Interest on debts

189(1)   [Payment of interest]   In a winding up interest is payable in accordance with this section on any debt proved in the winding up, including so much of any such debt as represents interest on the remainder.

189(2)   [Surplus after payment of debts]   Any surplus remaining after the payment of the debts proved in a winding up shall, before being applied for any other purpose, be applied in paying interest on those debts in respect of the periods during which they have been outstanding since the company went into liquidation.

189(3) **[Ranking of interest]** All interest under this section ranks equally, whether or not the debts on which it is payable rank equally.

189(4) **[Rate of interest]** The rate of interest payable under this section in respect of any debt (**"the official rate"** for the purposes of any provision of this Act in which that expression is used) is whichever is the greater of—

(a) the rate specified in section 17 of the Judgments Act 1838 on the day on which the company went into liquidation, and

(b) the rate applicable to that debt apart from the winding up.

189(5) **[Scotland]** In the application of this section to Scotland—

(a) references to a debt proved in a winding up have effect as references to a claim accepted in a winding up, and

(b) the reference to section 17 of the Judgments Act 1838 has effect as a reference to the rules.

(Former provision: IA 1985, s. 93)

General note

Before the reform of insolvency legislation in 1985, the legal rules governing the entitlement to interest on debts in a winding up were confused and unsatisfactory (see the Cork Committee's *Report*, Chap. 31). By virtue of BA 1914, s. 66, which was incorporated into the winding up of *insolvent* companies by CA 1985, s. 612, the rate of interest on *interest-bearing* debts was restricted to a maximum of 5 per cent per annum, and any interest payable at above that rate had to be recalculated for the purposes of proof. The Winding-up Rules 1949, r. 100, also provided for payment of interest (at the rate of 4 per cent) on *non-interest-bearing* debts in certain cases. There was no provision in a company liquidation (corresponding with BA 1914, s. 33(8)) for the payment of "statutory" interest out of any surplus remaining in the hands of the liquidator after all the creditors had been paid their debts in full. On the recommendation of the Cork Committee, all these old rules and the associated anomalies have been done away with and replaced by new provisions. Note that the new law applies in both solvent and insolvent liquidations.

For the relevant rules, see IR 1986, r. 4.93.

S. 189(1)

Interest at the "official rate" (see s. 189(4)) runs on all debts and liabilities proved in the winding up, including any debts representing interest due up to the effective date of proof, and it runs from that date until a final dividend is declared or all the proved debts have been paid in full. The date will be, in a compulsory winding up, that of the winding-up order, and in a voluntary winding up, that of the winding-up resolution: *Re Lines Bros. Ltd* [1983] Ch. 1, and cf. s. 247(2) and IR 1986, r. 4.93.

S. 189(2)

Where all the debts have been paid in full, the interest allowed for by this section is payable before any money is returned to shareholders.

In regard to debts payable at a future time, see IR 1986, r. 11.13.

S. 189(3)

The preferential and non-preferential debts rank equally as regards their right to interest. To give true effect to this provision, it is submitted that no interest should be payable on the preferential debts until the preferential and non-preferential debts have both been paid in full, without interest. Any other construction of the section (e.g. to treat the interest on a preferential debt as being itself simply a non-preferential debt – whether or not the other non-preferential debts are reckoned with interest) would be, in effect, to give the preferential creditors an additional preference in regard to interest.

S. 189(4)

The rate of interest payable under the Judgments Act 1838, s. 17, is currently 8 per cent (SI 1993 No. 564). If the debt itself carries interest at a higher rate, the latter is payable; but a creditor cannot merely by giving notice *impose* an obligation to pay interest at a rate higher than that specified in s. 189(4)(*a*): see IR 1986, rr. 4.93(5), (6) (as amended).

S. 189(5)

A rate of 15 per cent is specified in the Insolvency (Scotland) Rules 1986 (SI 1986 No. 1915 (S. 139)), r. 4.66(2)(*b*).

Section 190   Documents exempt from stamp duty

190(1)   [Application]   In the case of a winding up by the court, or of a creditors' voluntary winding up, the following has effect as regards exemption from duties chargeable under the enactments relating to stamp duties.

190(2)   [Exempt documents of company registered in England and Wales]   If the company is registered in England and Wales, the following documents are exempt from stamp duty—

> (a) every assurance relating solely to freehold or leasehold property, or to any estate, right or interest in, any real or personal property, which forms part of the company's assets and which, after the execution of the assurance, either at law or in equity, is or remains part of those assets, and
>
> (b) every writ, order, certificate, or other instrument or writing relating solely to the property of any company which is being wound up as mentioned in subsection (1), or to any proceeding under such a winding up.

"Assurance" here includes deed, conveyance, assignment and surrender.

190(3)   [Exempt document of company registered in Scotland]   If the company is registered in Scotland, the following documents are exempt from stamp duty—

> (a) every conveyance relating solely to property, which forms part of the company's assets and which, after the execution of the conveyance, is or remains the company's property for the benefit of its creditors,
>
> (b) any articles of roup or sale, submission and every other instrument and writing whatsoever relating solely to the company's property, and
>
> (c) every deed or writing forming part of the proceedings in the winding up.

"Conveyance" here includes assignation, instrument, discharge, writing and deed.

(Former provisions: CA 1985, s. 638 (as amended by Finance Act 1985, Sch. 27, Pt. IX(2); CA 1948, s. 339)

General note

This section applies only in the case of a winding up by the court or a creditors' voluntary winding up. It exempts from stamp duty all conveyances, etc. which are made to facilitate the winding up and which do not beneficially transfer assets out of the hands of the liquidator.

Section 191 Company's books to be evidence

191 Where a company is being wound up, all books and papers of the company and of the liquidators are, as between the contributories of the company, prima facie evidence of the truth of all matters purporting to be recorded in them.

(Former provision: CA 1985, s. 639; CA 1948, s. 340)

General note
The presumption which this provision creates applies only "as between the contributories of the company", and is rebuttable.

Section 192 Information as to pending liquidations

192(1) **[Statement to registrar]** If the winding up of a company is not concluded within one year after its commencement, the liquidator shall, at such intervals as may be prescribed, until the winding up is concluded, send to the registrar of companies a statement in the prescribed form and containing the prescribed particulars with respect to the proceedings in, and position of, the liquidation.

192(2) **[Penalty on default]** If a liquidator fails to comply with this section, he is liable to a fine and, for continued contravention, to a daily default fine.

(Former provisions: CA 1985, s. 641; CA 1948, s. 342)

S. 192(1)
The rules prescribed for the purposes of this provision are to be found in IR 1986, r. 4.223, which appears to apply only in a voluntary winding up; the "intervals prescribed" are every six months, after the initial year of the liquidation.

S. 192(2)
On penalties, see s. 430 and Sch. 10.
    The liquidator's obligations may also be enforced by seeking an order for compliance under s. 170. If a liquidator fails to comply with such an order, he will be in contempt of court and liable to imprisonment: *Re S & A Conversions Ltd & Ors* (1988) 4 BCC 384, *Re Allan Ellis (Transport & Packing) Services Ltd & Ors* (1989) 5 BCC 835.

Section 193 Unclaimed dividends (Scotland)

193(1) **[Application]** The following applies where a company registered in Scotland has been wound up, and is about to be dissolved.

193(2) **[Liquidator to lodge unclaimed money in bank]** The liquidator shall lodge in an appropriate bank or institution as defined in section 73(1) of the Bankruptcy (Scotland) Act 1985 (not being a bank or institution in or of which the liquidator is an acting partner, manager, agent or cashier) in the name of the Accountant of Court the whole unclaimed dividends and unapplied or undistributable balances, and the deposit receipts shall be transmitted to the Accountant of Court.

193(3)   [Application of Bankruptcy (Scotland) Act]   The provisions of section 58 of the Bankruptcy (Scotland) Act 1985 (so far as consistent with this Act and the Companies Act) apply with any necessary modifications to sums lodged in a bank or institution under this section as they apply to sums deposited under section 57 of the Act first mentioned.

(Former provisions: CA 1985, s. 643 (as amended by Bankruptcy (Scotland) Act 1985, Sch. 7, para. 22); CA 1948, s. 344)

General Note

Section 57 of the Bankruptcy (Scotland) Act 1985 provides that unclaimed dividends in an individual bankruptcy shall be held in a bank in the name of the Accountant of Court for a period of seven years, during which they may be claimed by those entitled. After the seven years, the money passes to the Secretary of State who may thereafter pay undisputed claims in his discretion.

The present section applies the same rules to a company liquidation in Scotland.

Section 194   Resolutions passed at adjourned meetings

194   Where a resolution is passed at an adjourned meeting of a company's creditors or contributories, the resolution is treated for all purposes as having been passed on the date on which it was in fact passed, and not as having been passed on any earlier date.

(Former provisions: CA 1985, s. 644; CA 1948, s. 345)

General note

This provision is confined in its application to meetings held in connection with a winding up. For other meetings, CA 1985, s. 381 lays down a similar rule, reversing the decision at common law in *Neuschild* v *British Equitorial Oil Co. Ltd* [1925] Ch. 346.

Section 195   Meetings to ascertain wishes of creditors or contributories

195(1)   [Power of court]   The court may—

(a) as to all matters relating to the winding up of a company, have regard to the wishes of the creditors or contributories (as proved to it by any sufficient evidence), and

(b) if it thinks fit, for the purpose of ascertaining those wishes, direct meetings of the creditors or contributories to be called, held and conducted in such manner as the court directs, and appoint a person to act as chairman of any such meeting and report the result of it to the court.

195(2)   [Creditors]   In the case of creditors, regard shall be had to the value of each creditor's debt.

195(3)   [Contributories]   In the case of contributories, regard shall be had to the number of votes conferred on each contributory by the Companies Act or the articles.

(Former provisions: CA 1985, s. 645; CA 1948, s. 346)

General note

The use of "may", rather than "shall", in the opening words of the section gives the court a residuary discretion to act without having regard to the wishes of the creditors (or contributories) where there are "special circumstances" – e.g. where it is not practicable to hold meetings because of the complexities of the case and the difficulty of identifying who the creditors are: *Re Bank of Credit & Commerce International SA (No. 2)* [1992] BCC 715. However, the court will not lightly disregard or overrule the views of the majority creditors whose interests are at stake: *Re Falcon R J Developments Ltd* (1987) 3 BCC 146, *Re William Thorpe & Son Ltd* (1989) 5 BCC 156. See also the note to s. 125(1), above.

The conduct of any meetings directed by the court to be called are dealt with by the rules, as well as being covered in part by the terms of the section itself. For the relevant rules, see IR 1986, rr. 4.54 ff.

Section 196   Judicial notice of court documents

196   In all proceedings under this Part, all courts, judges and persons judicially acting, and all officers, judicial or ministerial, of any court, or employed in enforcing the process of any court shall take judicial notice—

    (a)   of the signature of any officer of the High Court or of a county court in England and Wales, or of the Court of Session or a sheriff court in Scotland, or of the High Court in Northern Ireland, and also

    (b)   of the official seal or stamp of the several offices of the High Court in England and Wales or Northern Ireland, or of the Court of Session, appended to or impressed on any document made, issued or signed under the provisions of this Act or the Companies Act, or any official copy of such a document.

(Former provisions: CA 1985, s. 646; CA 1948, s. 347)

Section 197   Commission for receiving evidence

197(1)   [Courts for examination of witnesses]   When a company is wound up in England and Wales or in Scotland, the court may refer the whole or any part of the examination of witnesses—

    (a)   to a specified county court in England and Wales, or

    (b)   to the sheriff principal for a specified sheriffdom in Scotland, or

    (c)   to the High Court in Northern Ireland or a specified Northern Ireland County Court,

("specified" meaning specified in the order of the winding-up court).

197(2)   [Commissioners for taking evidence]   Any person exercising jurisdiction as a judge of the court to which the reference is made (or, in Scotland, the sheriff principal to whom it is made) shall then, by virtue of this section, be a commissioner for the purpose of taking the evidence of those witnesses.

197(3)   [Power of judge or sheriff principal]   The judge or sheriff principal has in the matter referred the same power of summoning and examining witnesses, of requiring the production and delivery of documents, of punishing defaults by witnesses, and of allowing costs and expenses to witnesses, as the court which made the winding-up order.

These powers are in addition to any which the judge or sheriff principal might lawfully exercise apart from this section.

197(4)   [Return or report re examination]   The examination so taken shall be returned or reported to the court which made the order in such manner as that court requests.

197(5)   [Northern Ireland]   This section extends to Northern Ireland.

(Former provisions: CA 1985, s. 647; CA 1948, s. 348 (as amended by SI 1984 No. 134))

Section 198   Court order for examination of persons in Scotland

198(1)   [Examination of any person on affairs of company]   The court may direct the examination in Scotland of any person for the time being in Scotland (whether a contributory of the company or not), in regard to the trade, dealings, affairs or property of any company in the course of being wound up, or of any person being a contributory of the company, so far as the company may be interested by reason of his being a contributory.

198(2)   [Directions to take examination]   The order or commission to take the examination shall be directed to the sheriff principal of the sheriffdom in which the person to be examined is residing or happens to be for the time; and the sheriff principal shall summon the person to appear before him at a time and place to be specified in the summons for examination on oath as a witness or as a haver, and to produce any books or papers called for which are in his possession or power.

198(3)   [Duties of sheriff principal re examination]   The sheriff principal may take the examination either orally or on written interrogatories, and shall report the same in writing in the usual form to the court, and shall transmit with the report the books and papers produced, if the originals are required and specified by the order or commission, or otherwise copies or extracts authenticated by the sheriff.

198(4)   [Where person fails to appear for examination]   If a person so summoned fails to appear at the time and place specified, or refuses to be examined or to make the production required, the sheriff principal shall proceed against him as a witness or haver duly cited; and failing to appear or refusing to give evidence or make production may be proceeded against by the law of Scotland.

198(5)   [Fees and allowances]   The sheriff principal is entitled to such fees, and the witness is entitled to such allowances, as sheriffs principal when acting as commissioners under appointment from the Court of Session and as witnesses and havers are entitled to in the like cases according to the law and practice of Scotland.

198(6)   [Objection by witness]   If any objection is stated to the sheriff principal by the witness, either on the ground of his incompetency as a witness, or as to the production required, or on any other ground, the sheriff principal may, if he thinks fit, report the objection to the court, and suspend the examination of the witness until it has been disposed of by the court.

(Former provisions: CA 1985, s. 648; CA 1948, s. 349)

General note

This section applies in Scotland in addition to ss. 133 and 236, which also provide for the judicial examination of persons who have been connected with a company that is in liquidation. There appears to be a considerable degree of overlap.

Section 199   Costs of application for leave to proceed (Scottish companies)

199   Where a petition or application for leave to proceed with an action or proceeding against a company which is being wound up in Scotland is unopposed and is granted by the court, the costs of the petition or application shall, unless the court otherwise directs, be added to the amount of the petitioner's or applicant's claim against the company.

(Former provisions: CA 1985, s. 649; CA 1948, s. 350)

Section 200   Affidavits etc. in United Kingdom and overseas

200(1)   **[Swearing of affidavit]**   An affidavit required to be sworn under or for the purposes of this Part may be sworn in the United Kingdom, or elsewhere in Her Majesty's dominions, before any court, judge or person lawfully authorised to take and receive affidavits, or before any of Her Majesty's consuls or vice-consuls in any place outside Her dominions.

200(2)   **[Judicial notice of signatures etc.]**   All courts, judges, justices, commissioners and persons acting judicially shall take judicial notice of the seal or stamp or signature (as the case may be) of any such court, judge, person, consul or vice-consul attached, appended or subscribed to any such affidavit, or to any other document to be used for the purposes of this Part.

(Former provisions: CA 1985, s. 650; CA 1948, s. 351)

General note

This provision is designed to simplify the normal requirements for the taking of evidence abroad, for use in winding-up proceedings.

Chapter IX — Dissolution of Companies After Winding Up

General comment on Pt. IV, Ch. IX

The dissolution of a company extinguishes its legal personality, so that it goes out of existence for all purposes. Any property and rights formerly vested in it are deemed to belong to the Crown, as *bona vacantia*.

The court is, however, given power by CA 1985, s. 651, to declare the dissolution of a company void, so that it is reinstated. An application for reinstatement under this section must normally be made within two years from the date of dissolution (s. 651(4)) but special provisions (effective from 16 November 1989: see SI 1990 No. 1392 (c. 41)) declare that this limitation shall not apply where the applicaton is made for the purpose of bringing actions for personal injuries or claims under the Fatal Accidents Act 1976 or the Damages (Scotland) Act 1976 (see s. 651(5)–(7) and, for transitional provisions, CA 1989, s. 141(4),(5)). (Note that the proposed extension from two to twelve years contemplated by IA 1985, s. 109 and Sch. 6, para. 45 was never brought into effect and has now been repealed: see CA 1989, s. 212 and Sch. 24, and SI 1990 No. 355 (C. 13), art. 5(1)(*c*).)

Under the former provisions of the Companies Acts, different rules regarding dissolution applied in a compulsory winding up and a voluntary winding up, a court order being always required in the former case. The reforms in the law of insolvency introduced by IA 1985 have dispensed with this need for a court order and so brought the various types of winding up into line. A further innovation is the provision for early dissolution now contained in s. 202 below. This enables the official receiver, in a winding up by the court, to apply to the registrar of companies to have the company dissolved at an early stage in the liquidation when the company is so hopelessly insolvent that it is pointless to proceed further. In Scotland, the liquidator is empowered to make a similar application to the court (s. 204).

In addition to these procedures, a company may be dissolved by having its name struck off the register under CA 1985, s. 652, on the ground that it has ceased to carry on business. The court has power to restore to the register the name of a company so struck off if application is made to it by the company, a member or a creditor within 20 years (CA 1985, s. 653).

Section 201   Dissolution (voluntary winding up)

201(1)   [Application]   This section applies, in the case of a company wound up voluntarily, where the liquidator has sent to the registrar of companies his final account and return under section 94 (members' voluntary) or section 106 (creditors' voluntary).

201(2)   [Duty of registrar]   The registrar on receiving the account and return shall forthwith register them; and on the expiration of 3 months from the registration of the return the company is deemed to be dissolved.

201(3)   [Power of court re deferring date]   However, the court may, on the application of the liquidator or any other person who appears to the court to be interested, make an order deferring the date at which the dissolution of the company is to take effect for such time as the court thinks fit.

201(4)   [Copy of order to registrar]   It is the duty of the person on whose application an order of the court under this section is made within 7 days after the making of the order to deliver to the registrar an office copy of the order for registration; and if that person fails to do so he is liable to a fine and, for continued contravention, to a daily default fine.

(Former provision: CA 1985, ss. 585(5), (6), 595(6), (7))

General note

This section brings together provisions relating to the dissolution of a members' and a creditors' voluntary winding up which were formerly duplicated in CA 1985, ss. 585 and 595. It makes no change of substance.

The company is automatically dissolved under this section on the expiration of three months from the filing of the liquidator's final return: no further formality is needed.

S. 201(3), (4)

The power of the court under subsection (3) is limited to extending the three-month period. On penalties, see s. 430 and Sch. 10.

Section 202   Early dissolution (England and Wales)

202(1)   **[Application]**   This section applies where an order for the winding up of a company has been made by the court in England and Wales.

202(2)   **[Official receiver may apply for dissolution]**   The official receiver, if—

    (a) he is the liquidator of the company, and

    (b) it appears to him—

        (i) that the realisable assets of the company are insufficient to cover the expenses of the winding up, and

        (ii) that the affairs of the company do not require any further investigation,

may at any time apply to the registrar of companies for the early dissolution of the company.

202(3)   **[Notice by official receiver]**   Before making that application, the official receiver shall give not less than 28 days' notice of his intention to do so to the company's creditors and contributories and, if there is an administrative receiver of the company, to that receiver.

202(4)   **[Effect of notice on official receiver]**   With the giving of that notice the official receiver ceases (subject to any directions under the next section) to be required to perform any duties imposed on him in relation to the company, its creditors or contributories by virtue of any provision of this Act, apart from a duty to make an application under subsection (2) of this section.

202(5)   **[Duty of registrar]**   On the receipt of the official receiver's application under subsection (2) the registrar shall forthwith register it and, at the end of the period of 3 months beginning with the day of the registration of the application, the company shall be dissolved.

However, the Secretary of State may, on the application of the official receiver or any other person who appears to the Secretary of State to be interested, give directions under section 203 at any time before the end of that period.

(Former provision: IA 1985, s. 76(1)–(3), (6))

General note

The Cork Committee (*Report*, paras. 649–51) recommended that a procedure should be introduced to enable the official receiver to apply to the court for the early dissolution of a company which was in compulsory liquidation and hopelessly insolvent. The legislature has gone one better and dispensed with the need for a court order: the official receiver's application is sent to the registrar of companies and takes effect automatically after three months, unless the Secretary of State intervenes in the meantime. The official receiver (and the taxpayer) is thus spared the pointless expense of completing the winding up.

S. 202(1)

For the corresponding provision for Scotland, see s. 204.

S. 202(2)

The powers under this section may be exercised only by the official receiver, and only if he is the liquidator.

Paragraph (2)(*b*)(ii) leaves it to the judgment of the official receiver to decide that the circumstances of the insolvency do not create any suspicion of impropriety, and perhaps even to consider such policy questions as whether the circumstances, though dubious, really justify the expenditure of public money which would be involved in investigating the company's affairs further.

S. 202(3), (4)

The official receiver's duties (as liquidator or otherwise) cease as soon as he gives the notice, i.e. even while the 28-day period referred to in s. 202(3) and the three-month period in s. 202(5) are running, he has no obligation to take further steps in the liquidation.

It seems that the liquidator comes under a *duty* to apply for a dissolution once he has given a notice under s. 202(3): if he starts the dissolution process, he must go through with it, and if he has second thoughts he must invoke the powers of the Secretary of State under s. 203.

S. 202(5)

The dissolution takes effect automatically on the expiry of the three-month period, unless the Secretary of State has directed that a longer period than three months be substituted.

Section 203   Consequence of notice under s. 202

203(1)   [Application for directions]   Where a notice has been given under section 202(3), the official receiver or any creditor or contributory of the company, or the administrative receiver of the company (if there is one) may apply to the Secretary of State for directions under this section.

203(2)   [Grounds for application]   The grounds on which that application may be made are—

    (a) that the realisable assets of the company are sufficient to cover the expenses of the winding up;

    (b) that the affairs of the company do require further investigation; or

    (c) that for any other reason the early dissolution of the company is inappropriate.

203(3)   [Scope of directions]   Directions under this section—

    (a) are directions making such provision as the Secretary of State thinks fit for enabling the winding up of the company to proceed as if no notice had been given under section 202(3), and

    (b) may, in the case of an application under section 202(5), include a direction deferring the date at which the dissolution of the company is to take effect for such period as the Secretary of State thinks fit.

203(4)   [Appeal to court]   An appeal to the court lies from any decision of the Secretary of State on an application for directions under this section.

203(5) **[Copy of directions etc. to registrar]** It is the duty of the person on whose application any directions are given under this section, or in whose favour an appeal with respect to an application for such directions is determined, within 7 days after the giving of the directions or the determination of the appeal, to deliver to the registrar of companies for registration such a copy of the directions or determination as is prescribed.

203(6) **[Penalty on default re s. 203(5)]** If a person without reasonable excuse fails to deliver a copy as required by subsection (5), he is liable to a fine and, for continued contravention, to a daily default fine.

(Former provisions: IA 1985, s. 76(4), (5), (7)–(10))

S. 203(1)–(3)

The Secretary of State is empowered by this section to override the official receiver's notice under s. 202(3) which initiated the dissolution process, so that the winding up proceeds as before. It also appears from s. 203(3)(*b*) that the Secretary of State may confirm the effect of the notice but delay the dissolution by substituting a longer period than three months for the operation of s. 202(5).

S. 203(4)

The use of the term "appeal" is significant, since it makes it clear that the court may substitute its own decision on the merits of the case for that of the Secretary of State. For the relevant procedure, see IR 1986, rr. 4.224, 4.225.

S. 203(5)

The seven-day period is extremely short, especially since it runs from the date of the giving of the directions or determination of the appeal, and not from the day when the applicant is notified of the outcome of his application.

It does not appear that there is any obligation to register a decision on the part of the Secretary of State to give no "directions". (However, there is equally no machinery provided to warn the registrar that an application to the Secretary of State has been made: time will continue to run for the purposes of s. 202(5) while such an application is under consideration.)

S. 203(6)

On penalties, see s. 430 and Sch. 10.

Section 204   Early dissolution (Scotland)

204(1) **[Application]** This section applies where a winding-up order has been made by the court in Scotland.

204(2) **[Application by liquidator]** If after a meeting or meetings under section 138 (appointment of liquidator in Scotland) it appears to the liquidator that the realisable assets of the company are insufficient to cover the expenses of the winding up, he may apply to the court for an order that the company be dissolved.

204(3) **[Court order]** Where the liquidator makes that application, if the court is satisfied that the realisable assets of the company are insufficient to cover the expenses of the winding up and it appears to the court appropriate to do so, the court shall make an order that the company be dissolved in accordance with this section.

204(4)   [Copy of order to registrar etc.]   A copy of the order shall within 14 days from its date be forwarded by the liquidator to the registrar of companies, who shall forthwith register it; and, at the end of the period of 3 months beginning with the day of the registration of the order, the company shall be dissolved.

204(5)   [Court may defer dissolution]   The court may, on an application by any person who appears to the court to have an interest, order that the date at which the dissolution of the company is to take effect shall be deferred for such period as the court thinks fit.

204(6)   [Copy of s. 204(5) order to registrar]   It is the duty of the person on whose application an order is made under subsection (5), within 7 days after the making of the order, to deliver to the registrar of companies such a copy of the order as is prescribed.

204(7)   [Penalty for non-compliance with s. 204(4)]   If the liquidator without reasonable excuse fails to comply with the requirements of subsection (4), he is liable to a fine and, for continued contravention, to a daily default fine.

204(8)   [Penalty for non-compliance with s. 204(6)]   If a person without reasonable excuse fails to deliver a copy as required by subsection (6), he is liable to a fine and, for continued contravention, to a daily default fine.

(Former provision: IA 1985, s. 77)

General note

There is no official receiver in Scotland, so that a private liquidator will be in office in every winding up by the court. In the absence of a public officer comparable with the official receiver, it is necessary in Scotland to refer to the court for decision the question whether an early dissolution of the company is justified. This section accordingly modifies the procedure of ss. 202, 203 to meet the different circumstances in Scotland.

S. 204(2)

There is no obligation in Scotland to give the company's creditors and contributories the 28-day notice required in England and Wales by s. 202(3). In Scotland, on the other hand, the liquidator cannot set any steps in motion to bring about an early dissolution until after the meetings of creditors and contributories have been held. It is reasonable to assume that they will have been made aware of the company's hopeless insolvency at the statutory meetings.

S. 204(3)–(8)

The whole of the proceedings in an application for early dissolution in Scotland are dealt with by the court. There is no involvement of the Secretary of State at any stage. Apart from this, the comments to ss. 202, 203 apply to the present section.
   On penalties, see s. 430 and Sch. 10.

Section 205   Dissolution otherwise than under ss. 202–204

205(1)   [Application]   This section applies where the registrar of companies receives—

   (a) a notice served for the purposes of section 172(8) (final meeting of creditors and vacation of office by liquidator), or

(b) a notice from the official receiver that the winding up of a company by the court is complete.

205(2) **[Duty of registrar etc.]** The registrar shall, on receipt of the notice, forthwith register it; and, subject as follows, at the end of the period of 3 months beginning with the day of the registration of the notice, the company shall be dissolved.

205(3) **[Deferral by Secretary of State]** The Secretary of State may, on the application of the official receiver or any other person who appears to the Secretary of State to be interested, give a direction deferring the date at which the dissolution of the company is to take effect for such period as the Secretary of State thinks fit.

205(4) **[Appeal to court]** An appeal to the court lies from any decision of the Secretary of State on an application for a direction under subsection (3).

205(5) **[Non-application of s. 205(3) in Scotland]** Subsection (3) does not apply in a case where the winding-up order was made by the court in Scotland, but in such a case the court may, on an application by any person appearing to the court to have an interest, order that the date at which the dissolution of the company is to take effect shall be deferred for such period as the court thinks fit.

205(6) **[Copy of direction etc. to registrar]** It is the duty of the person—

(a) on whose application a direction is given under subsection (3);

(b) in whose favour an appeal with respect to an application for such a direction is determined; or

(c) on whose application an order is made under subsection (5),

within 7 days after the giving of the direction, the determination of the appeal or the making of the order, to deliver to the registrar for registration such a copy of the direction, determination or order as is prescribed.

205(7) **[Penalty for non-compliance with s. 205(6)]** If a person without reasonable excuse fails to deliver a copy as required by subsection (6), he is liable to a fine and, for continued contravention, to a daily default fine.

(Former provision: IA 1985, s. 81)

S. 205(1), (2)

Under the former provisions of CA 1985, s. 568, the dissolution of a company being compulsorily wound up had to be effected by an order of the court in every case, and the company was dissolved from the date of the order. The Act now provides for the dissolution to take place automatically three months after the registrar has been given the notification by the liquidator or the official receiver required by this section.

S. 205(3)–(4)

The Secretary of State, in England and Wales, and the court are given rôles under the present section comparable with those which they discharge in relation to the early liquidation procedure under ss. 202(5), 203(3)(*b*) and 203(4): see, further, the notes to those provisions, and for the relevant procedure, see IR 1986, rr. 4.224, 4.225.

S. 205(5)

Compare s. 204(5), and see the notes to that subsection.

S. 205(6), (7)

Compare ss. 203(5), (6) and 204(6), (8), and for the relevant rule, see IR 1986, r. 4.224.

Chapter X — Malpractice before and during Liquidation; Penalisation of Companies and Company Officers; Investigations and Prosecutions

OFFENCES OF FRAUD, DECEPTION, ETC.

Section 206   Fraud, etc. in anticipation of winding up

206(1)   [Offences by officers]   When a company is ordered to be wound up by the court, or passes a resolution for voluntary winding up, any person, being a past or present officer of the company, is deemed to have committed an offence if, within the 12 months immediately preceding the commencement of the winding up, he has—

(a) concealed any part of the company's property to the value of £500 or more, or concealed any debt due to or from the company, or

(b) fraudulently removed any part of the company's property to the value of £500 or more, or

(c) concealed, destroyed, mutilated or falsified any book or paper affecting or relating to the company's property or affairs, or

(d) made any false entry in any book or paper affecting or relating to the company's property or affairs, or

(e) fraudulently parted with, altered or made any omission in any document affecting or relating to the company's property or affairs, or

(f) pawned, pledged or disposed of any property of the company which has been obtained on credit and has not been paid for (unless the pawning, pledging or disposal was in the ordinary way of the company's business).

206(2)   [Further offences]   Such a person is deemed to have committed an offence if within the period above mentioned he has been privy to the doing by others of any of the things mentioned in paragraphs (c), (d) and (e) of subsection (1); and he commits an offence if, at any time after the commencement of the winding up, he does any of the things mentioned in paragraphs (a) to (f) of that subsection, or is privy to the doing by others of any of the things mentioned in paragraphs (c) to (e) of it.

206(3)   ["Officer"]   For purposes of this section, **"officer"** includes a shadow director.

206(4)   [Defences]   It is a defence—

(a) for a person charged under paragraph (a) or (f) of subsection (1) (or under subsection (2) in respect of the things mentioned in either of those two paragraphs) to prove that he had no intent to defraud, and

(b) for a person charged under paragraph (c) or (d) of subsection (1) (or under subsection (2) in respect of the things mentioned in either of those two paragraphs) to prove that he had no intent to conceal the state of affairs of the company or to defeat the law.

243

206(5)   **[Offence re person pawning property etc. as in s. 206(1)(f)]**   Where a person pawns, pledges or disposes of any property in circumstances which amount to an offence under subsection (1)(f), every person who takes in pawn or pledge, or otherwise receives, the property knowing it to be pawned, pledged or disposed of in such circumstances, is guilty of an offence.

206(6)   **[Penalty]**   A person guilty of an offence under this section is liable to imprisonment or a fine, or both.

206(7)   **[Increase, reduction of sums in s. 206(1)(a), (b)]**   The money sums specified in paragraphs (a) and (b) of subsection (1) are subject to increase or reduction by order under section 416 in Part XV.

(Former provisions: CA 1985, s. 624 (as amended by IA 1985, Sch. 6, para. 25); CA 1948, s. 328(1)(d), (e), (i)–(k), (o), (2), (3) (as amended by SI 1984 No. 1169))

S. 206(1), (2)

This section makes it an offence for an officer of a company to conceal or remove property, falsify entries in the company's books or perpetrate other similar acts after the commencement of a winding up (s. 206(2)), and "deems" an officer or past officer to have committed an offence if he has been guilty of any of these acts and a winding up ensues within the next 12 months (s. 206(1)). The amount in s. 206(1)(*a*), (*b*) was increased from £120 by the Insolvency Proceedings (Monetary Limits) Order 1986 (SI 1986 No. 1996) as from 29 December 1986.

    The diversion of a debt due to a company into the account of the accused or a third party is equivalent to the "removal" of property for the purposes of s. 206(1)(*b*): *R v Robinson* [1990] BCC 656.

S. 206(3)

The term "officer" is not defined with precision: the definition in CA 1985, s. 744 (which is incorporated into the present Act by the concluding words of s. 251) merely states that "officer, in relation to a body corporate, *includes* a director, manager or secretary". A director "includes any person occupying the position of director, by whatever name called" (s. 251). A director (in this extended sense) and a secretary plainly will always be "officers". Shadow directors (for definition, see s. 251) are frequently declared to be officers for the purposes of a particular provision, as in the present subsection, and so it might be reasonable to infer that where there is no such statement (e.g. as in s. 207) the opposite is the case. The same argument would apply in the case of a liquidator: the fact that he is declared to be an officer for the purposes of s. 85(2), for example, suggests that he is ordinarily not to be deemed one. This is confirmed by the distinction that appears to be drawn between "officers" on the one hand and liquidators, administrators and receivers on the other (e.g. by ss. 133(1) and 212(1), and cf. also s. 219(3)).

    The word "manager", used in CA 1985, s. 744, could well be a source of difficulty. It is not clear whether a person would need to have been appointed to a post carrying managerial responsibilities to come within this concept, or whether it is sufficient that he has taken some part in the management of the company's business, even at a relatively humble level. In *Re a Company No. 00996 of 1979* [1980] Ch. 138 at p. 144, Shaw LJ said:

> "The expression 'manager' should not be too narrowly construed. It is not to be equated with a managing or other director or a general manager. ...[Any] person who in the affairs of the company exercises a supervisory control which reflects the general policy of the company for the time being or which is related to the general administration of the company is in the sphere of management. He need not be a member of the board of directors. He need not be subject to specific instructions from the board."

A number of provisions in the legislation (e.g. IA 1986, ss. 212(1)(*c*), 216(3), 217(4) and CDDA 1986, ss. 1(1)(*d*), 11, 15(4) refer to a person "taking part in the management"of a company (and cf. "involved in the management": IA 1986, s. 217(1), CDDA 1986, 2. 15(1)). It would not necessarily follow that a person coming within such a formula was a "manager" for the purposes of the present section, but cases decided under these provisions may be of some relevance. For further discussion, see the note to CDDA 1986, s. 1(1).

Both an administrator and a receiver and manager (including an administrative receiver) discharge functions which can only be described as managerial, but in the leading case of *Re B Johnson & Co. (Builders) Ltd* [1955] Ch. 634 a receiver and manager appointed by a debenture-holder was held not to be an "officer" for the purposes of what is now s. 212. (The point is now covered by s. 212(1)(*b*)). An administrator has been held to be an "officer" who may be granted relief under the court's discretionary jurisdiction conferred by CA 1985, s. 727: *Re Home Treat Ltd* [1991] BCC 165.

An auditor has been held to be an officer for the purposes of s. 212 in a number of cases, e.g. *Re London and General Bank* [1895] 2 Ch. 166, *Re Thomas Gerrard & Son Ltd* [1968] Ch. 455 at p. 473; and also under other statutory provisions similar to s. 206: *R v Shacter* [1960] 2 QB 252; but the question is not free from doubt: cf. CA 1985, s. 727 ("whether or not he is an officer of the company").

Bankers and solicitors and other professional advisers are not, as such, "officers" of the company (*Re Imperial Land Co. of Marseilles, Re National Bank* (1870) LR 10 Eq. 298), as appears to be confirmed by s. 219(3).

S. 206(4)

The onus of proof with respect to *mens rea* is, unusually, put on the defendant. In such a case, the burden of proof on the accused is less than that required at the hands of the prosecution, which must prove the case "beyond reasonable doubt": instead, the burden may be discharged by evidence which satisfies the court on a balance of probabilities: *R v Carr-Briant* [1943] KB 607, *Morton v Confer* [1963] 1 WLR 763; [1963] 2 All ER 765.

S. 206(5)

In regard to the offence created by this provision, the normal rule as to onus of proof will apply.

S. 206(6)

The sanctions fixed by Sch. 10 for these offences and the other offences involving dishonesty defined in the following sections are severe: up to seven years' imprisonment.

On penalties, see s. 430 and Sch. 10.

S. 206(7)

See the note to s. 206(1), (2) above.

Section 207   Transactions in fraud of creditors

207(1)   [Offences by officers]   When a company is ordered to be wound up by the court or passes a resolution for voluntary winding up, a person is deemed to have committed an offence if he, being at the time an officer of the company—

(a) has made or caused to be made any gift or transfer of, or charge on, or has caused or connived at the levying of any execution against, the company's property, or

   (b) has concealed or removed any part of the company's property since, or within 2 months before, the date of any unsatisfied judgment or order for the payment of money obtained against the company.

207(2) **[Exception]** A person is not guilty of an offence under this section—

   (a) by reason of conduct constituting an offence under subsection (1)(a) which occurred more than 5 years before the commencement of the winding up, or

   (b) if he proves that, at the time of the conduct constituting the offence, he had no intent to defraud the company's creditors.

207(3) **[Penalty]** A person guilty of an offence under this section is liable to imprisonment or a fine, or both.

(Former provisions: CA 1985, s. 625 (as amended by IA 1985, Sch. 6, para. 42); CA 1948, s. 330)

General note

The offences defined by this section are brought forward from earlier Companies Acts. However, a modification made by IA 1985 has had the effect of reversing the onus of proof of *mens rea*: the words "with intent to defraud creditors of the company" have been removed from the substantive definition of the crime, and s. 207(2)(*b*) (matching s. 206(4) above) has been added. Section 207(2)(*a*) is also new, fixing a time limit of five years prior to the winding up.

S. 207(1)

There is no definition of "officer", corresponding to ss. 206(3) and 208(3), extending the terms to include a shadow director for the purposes of this section.

S. 207(3)

On penalties, see s. 430 and Sch. 10.

Section 208 Misconduct in course of winding up

208(1) **[Offences by officers]** When a company is being wound up, whether by the court or voluntarily, any person, being a past or present officer of the company, commits an offence if he—

   (a) does not to the best of his knowledge and belief fully and truly discover to the liquidator all the company's property, and how and to whom and for what consideration and when the company disposed of any part of that property (except such part as has been disposed of in the ordinary way of the company's business), or

   (b) does not deliver up to the liquidator (or as he directs) all such part of the company's property as is in his custody or under his control, and which he is required by law to deliver up, or

   (c) does not deliver up to the liquidator (or as he directs) all books and papers in his custody or under his control belonging to the company and which he is required by law to deliver up, or

   (d) knowing or believing that a false debt has been proved by any person in the winding up, fails to inform the liquidator as soon as practicable, or

   (e) after the commencement of the winding up, prevents the production of any book or paper affecting or relating to the company's property or affairs.

208(2) **[Further offences]** Such a person commits an offence if after the commencement of the winding up he attempts to account for any part of the company's property by fictitious losses or expenses; and he is deemed to have committed that offence if he has so attempted at any meeting of the company's creditors within the 12 months immediately preceding the commencement of the winding up.

208(3) **["Officer"]** For purposes of this section, **"officer"** includes a shadow director.

208(4) **[Defences]** It is a defence—

(a) for a person charged under paragraph (a), (b) or (c) of subsection (1) to prove that he had no intent to defraud, and

(b) for a person charged under paragraph (e) of that subsection to prove that he had no intent to conceal the state of affairs of the company or to defeat the law.

208(5) **[Penalty]** A person guilty of an offence under this section is liable to imprisonment or a fine, or both.

(Former provisions: CA 1985, s. 626 (as amended by IA 1985, Sch. 6, para. 43); CA 1948, s. 328(1)(a)–(c), (g), (h), (l), proviso, (3))

General note

This section brings forward from the Companies Acts other offences defined by the former CA 1985, relating to wrongful conduct in the course of a winding up. The notes to s. 206 apply generally to the present section.

S. 208(1)(d)

The words "as soon as practicable" were substituted for the phrase "for the period of a month" by IA 1985, Sch. 6, para. 43.

S. 208(4)

See the note to s. 206(4).

Section 209 Falsification of company's books

209(1) **[Offence by officer or contributory]** When a company is being wound up, an officer or contributory of the company commits an offence if he destroys, mutilates, alters or falsifies any books, papers or securities, or makes or is privy to the making of any false or fraudulent entry in any register, book of account or document belonging to the company with intent to defraud or deceive any person.

209(2) **[Penalty]** A person guilty of an offence under this section is liable to imprisonment or a fine, or both.

(Former provisions: CA 1985, s. 627; CA 1948, s. 329)

General note

The offences which this section defines largely duplicate those specified in s. 206(1)(c)–(e), which apply in a winding up by virtue of s. 206(2); but those potentially liable include contributories (though not, at least in specific terms, "shadow directors"), and the element of *mens rea* is expressed differently: compare s. 206(4)(*b*).

Section 210 Material omissions from statement relating to company's affairs

210(1) **[Offence by past or present officer]** When a company is being wound up, whether by the court or voluntarily, any person, being a past or present officer of the company, commits an offence if he makes any material omission in any statement relating to the company's affairs.

210(2) **[Offence prior to winding up]** When a company has been ordered to be wound up by the court, or has passed a resolution for voluntary winding up, any such person is deemed to have committed that offence if, prior to the winding up, he has made any material omission in any such statement.

210(3) **["Officer"]** For purposes of this section, **"officer"** includes a shadow director.

210(4) **[Defence]** It is a defence for a person charged under this section to prove that he had no intent to defraud.

210(5) **[Penalty]** A person guilty of an offence under this section is liable to imprisonment or a fine, or both.

(Former provisions: CA 1985, s. 628; CA 1948, s. 328(1)(f), proviso, (3))

General note

The "statement of affairs", which under the Companies Acts was part of the standard procedure in a winding up by the court, has now become a feature of many other forms of insolvency procedure, e.g. administration and receivership (see the note to s. 131). The present section is not confined in its scope to the statutory "statement of affairs" so defined, but applies to "any statement in relation to the company's affairs". It is, however, limited to statements made when a company is being wound up, or prior to a winding up; and it is concerned only with omissions. *Positive* mis-statements relating to a company's affairs in a winding up will almost certainly amount to one or other of the offences defined in ss. 206–209; but similar wrongdoing in other insolvency proceedings may be sanctioned only by the less draconian provisions of s. 235, unless of course they are criminal offences apart from the present Act.

Liability under the section is limited to past and present officers of the company (including shadow directors: s. 210(3)). On this point and generally, see the notes to s. 206.

S. 210(4)

See the note to s. 206(4).

Section 211 False representations to creditors

211(1) **[Offences by past or present officer]** When a company is being wound up, whether by the court or voluntarily, any person, being a past or present officer of the company—

(a) commits an offence if he makes any false representation or commits any other fraud for the purpose of obtaining the consent of the company's creditors or any of them to an agreement with reference to the company's affairs or to the winding up, and

(b) is deemed to have committed that offence if, prior to the winding up, he has made any false representation, or committed any other fraud, for that purpose.

211(2) **["Officer"]** For purposes of this section, **"officer"** includes a shadow director.

211(3) **[Penalty]** A person guilty of an offence under this section is liable to imprisonment or a fine, or both.

(Former provision: CA 1985, s. 629 (as amended by IA 1985, Sch. 10, Pt. II); CA 1948, s. 328(1) (p), (3))

General note

This section applies only to past and present officers (including shadow directors). The notes to s. 206 apply generally to s. 211; but the onus of establishing fraud is here placed on the prosecution.

PENALISATION OF DIRECTORS AND OFFICERS

Section 212   Summary remedy against delinquent directors, liquidators, etc.

212(1) **[Application]** This section applies if in the course of the winding up of a company it appears that a person who—

(a) is or has been an officer of the company,

(b) has acted as liquidator, administrator or administrative receiver of the company, or

(c) not being a person falling within paragraph (a) or (b), is or has been concerned, or has taken part, in the promotion, formation or management of the company,

has misapplied or retained, or become accountable for, any money or other property of the company, or been guilty of any misfeasance or breach of any fiduciary or other duty in relation to the company.

212(2) **[Interpretation]** The reference in subsection (1) to any misfeasance or breach of any fiduciary or other duty in relation to the company includes, in the case of a person who has acted as liquidator or administrator of the company, any misfeasance or breach of any fiduciary or other duty in connection with the carrying out of his functions as liquidator or administrator of the company.

212(3) **[Examination, orders]** The court may, on the application of the official receiver or the liquidator, or of any creditor or contributory, examine into the conduct of the person falling within subsection (1) and compel him—

(a) to repay, restore or account for the money or property or any part of it, with interest at such rate as the court thinks just, or

(b) to contribute such sum to the company's assets by way of compensation in respect of the misfeasance or breach of fiduciary or other duty as the court thinks just.

212(4) [Limit on s. 212(3) application] The power to make an application under subsection (3) in relation to a person who has acted as liquidator or administrator of the company is not exercisable, except with the leave of the court, after that person has had his release.

212(5) [Exercise of s. 212(3) power] The power of a contributory to make an application under subsection (3) is not exercisable except with the leave of the court, but is exercisable notwithstanding that he will not benefit from any order the court may make on the application.

(Former provisions: IA 1985, s. 19; CA 1985, s. 631)

S. 212(1)

This re-enacts, with some amendments introduced by IA 1985, the traditional "misfeasance" section of successive Companies Acts, providing a summary remedy in the liquidation of a company for the assessment of compensation or damages for breach of duty against its former officers and others. (On the meaning of the term "officer", see the note to s. 206(3).)

The scope of the section has now been extended so as to include administrators and administrative receivers. (The supervisor of a voluntary scheme, though not specifically mentioned, would no doubt be caught by para. (*c*).) The words "breach of trust" have been replaced by "breach of any fiduciary or other duty", and this also has the effect of extending the coverage of the remedy, for although "breach of trust" and "breach of fiduciary duty" may be regarded as synonymous, it had been held that the former wording did not include claims based on negligence (*Re B Johnson & Co. (Builders) Ltd* [1955] Ch. 634). But in *Re D'Jan of London Ltd* [1993] BCC 646 Hoffmann LJ clearly accepted that the section now covers "breaches of any duty including the duty of care", and applied it in a straightforward case of negligence brought against a director.

It is well settled that the section creates no new liabilities, but only provides a simpler procedure for the recovery of property or compensation in a winding up. Even here, there are limitations on its use – e.g. it is not available to enforce a contractual debt (*Re Etic Ltd* [1928] Ch. 861).

Where directors make payments in breach of duty to one or more of their number, there may be concurrent liability under this section and under such other provisions as s. 214 (wrongful trading) and s. 239 (preference). In one such case, *Re DKG Contractors Ltd* [1990] BCC 903, it was ordered that liability under the various heads should not be cumulative but that payments made under ss. 212 and 239 should go to satisfy the liability under s. 214. However, in a later case, *Re Purpoint Ltd* [1991] BCC 121, Vinelott J made orders against the respondent for the payment of separate sums under s. 212 and 214, being satisfied that there was no injustice in the nature of overlap or "double counting" in making the orders cumulative.

The provisions of s. 212 apply to directors (including shadow directors) of building societies: see Building Societies Act 1986, s. 90 and Sch. 15, as amended by CA 1989, s. 211 and Sch. 24.

S. 212(2)

This provision is new. It is probably intended to remove any doubts on the question whether all the duties of a liquidator or administrator are owed *to* the company. It is curious, but at the same time it may well be significant, that there is no mention of an administrative receiver in this subsection, even though he is mentioned in s. 212(1)(*b*). *Johnson's* case (above) held that a receiver and manager at common law was not concerned to manage the business for the benefit of the company, but only to realise his creditor's security, and that he was under no duty to the company or its contributories to preserve the goodwill and business of the company. This view was confirmed by the Privy Council in *Downsview Nominees Ltd & Anor* v *First City Corporation Ltd & Anor* [1993] AC 295; [1993] BCC 46, where it was held that a receiver and manager owes no general duty in negligence to (inter alios) the debtor company to use reasonable care in the exercise of his powers. However, it was also stated in the latter case that equity imposes specific duties on such a receiver, including a duty to exercise his powers in good faith; and that, if a receiver decides to sell the charged property, he must take reasonable care to obtain a proper price. There is thus potentially scope (albeit of a limited nature) for s. 212 to be invoked against an administrative receiver or a receiver and manager.

S. 212(3)

This re-enacts with slight verbal changes the former CA 1985, s. 631(2). A contributory's right to make an application is qualified by s. 212(5).

S. 212(4)

This provision is new. For the release of a liquidator, see ss. 173, 174, and an administrator, s. 20.

S. 212(5)

This subsection is also new. Formerly, a contributory had standing to apply without the leave of the court, but only when he could show that he had an interest in the outcome of the proceedings.

Section 213   Fraudulent trading

213(1)   **[Application]**   If in the course of the winding up of a company it appears that any business of the company has been carried on with intent to defraud creditors of the company or creditors of any other person, or for any fraudulent purpose, the following has effect.

213(2)   **[Court may hold persons liable]**   The court, on the application of the liquidator may declare that any persons who were knowingly parties to the carrying on of the business in the manner above-mentioned are to be liable to make such contributions (if any) to the company's assets as the court thinks proper.

(Former provisions: CA 1985, s. 630(1), (2) (as amended by IA 1985, Sch. 6, para. 6(1)); CA 1948, s. 332(1))

General note

The Companies Acts have for a long time contained provisions dealing with "fraudulent trading", making it both a criminal offence (CA 1985, s. 458) and a ground for imposing personal liability upon those concerned (CA 1985, s. 630, now replaced by the present section). Originally, both the criminal and the civil sanctions could be invoked only in a winding up, but the criminal provision (s. 458) has for some years applied without this limitation.

The Cork Committee (*Report*, Chap. 44) considered that the existing law in this area was inadequate to deal with irresponsible trading, mainly because the courts have always insisted on the very strict standards of pleading and proof which are invariably applied in criminal proceedings and cases of fraud. It is not enough, for "fraudulent trading", to show that the company continued to run up debts when the directors knew that it was insolvent; there has to be "actual dishonesty, involving real moral blame" (*Re Patrick and Lyon Ltd* [1933] Ch. 786).

The Committee recommended that while this should continue to be the approach in *criminal* proceedings for fraudulent trading, *civil* liability to pay compensation could arise where loss was suffered as a result of "unreasonable" conduct, which they proposed should be termed "wrongful trading", and that for this purpose the more relaxed standard of proof appropriate to civil proceedings should apply. The former provision creating civil liability for fraudulent trading (CA 1985, s. 630) could be subsumed into the new law of wrongful trading.

In the event, the legislators have adopted the Committee's recommendations on wrongful trading in broad terms, but they have done so by creating an *additional* new provision (s. 214, below) and left the former law on fraudulent trading intact, with one or two minor amendments (the present section). There will, however, be little reason for liquidators to invoke it, since the new concept of wrongful trading, with its less onerous standard of proof, is wide enough to include all cases of fraudulent trading, and for all practical purposes the consequences will be the same.

S. 213(1)

The section, unlike the equivalent criminal provision (see above), applies only in a winding up.

The words "or for any fraudulent purpose" could not be wider, and should not be construed in any limiting way. The wording is certainly wide enough to include frauds committed against potential creditors: see *R* v *Kemp* [1988] QB 645; (1988) 4 BCC 203. See also *Re L Todd (Swanscombe) Ltd* [1990] BCC 125 (fraudulent evasion of value added tax).

S. 213(2)

Two changes are made from the former law.

First, it is only the liquidator who has standing to apply for relief under this section. Previously, an individual creditor or contributory could also apply, but this was thought undesirable because it might encourage a creditor to put improper pressure upon directors to settle his claim personally.

Secondly, the order which the court may make declares the wrongdoers "liable to make such contributions (if any) to the company's assets as the court thinks proper". This makes it clear that any sums ordered to be paid must go into the general funds in the hands of the liquidator and be held for the benefit of the whole body of creditors. Under the previous wording, the court had power to order that a defendant should directly reimburse a particular creditor (*Re Cyona Distributors Ltd* [1967] Ch. 889, *Re Gerald Cooper Chemicals Ltd (in liq.)* [1978] Ch. 262).

In other respects, the law remains the same. Thus, those who may be made liable are "any persons who were knowingly parties" to the fraudulent trading. This may be contrasted with the new wrongful trading provision (s. 214) which is limited in its scope to directors and former directors, but pointedly avoids the words "parties to" (and, indeed, "business" or "trading").

In *Re Cyona Distributors Ltd* (above), it was held appropriate to include in the order a punitive, as well as a compensatory, element. This was followed in *Re a Company No. 001418 of 1988* [1990] BCC 526, where the court ordered payment of a punitive sum of £25,000 over and above a compensatory payment of £156,420. These cases were decided under the repealed CA 1985, s. 630 (or its predecessor), where the statute empowered the court to declare "that any persons who were knowingly parties to the carrying on of the business in the manner aforesaid shall be personally responsible, without any limitation of liability, for all or any of the debts or other liabilities of the company as the court may direct". The language of s. 213 ("liable to make such contributions (if any) to the company's assets as the court thinks proper") is, if anything, less restrictive than that of s. 630, and so there is no reason why a court might not order payment of a punitive sum under the new section. This might at first sight appear to run contrary to *Re Produce Marketing Consortium Ltd* (1989) 5 BCC 569 at p. 597, where Knox J held that under the identical wording of s. 214 (below) the jurisdiction was primarily compensatory rather than penal; but (as Knox J himself observed) Parliament has chosen very wide words of discretion, which are plainly capable of supporting the continued use of a penal award by way of sanction when s. 213 is contravened, even if the same approach is not followed under s. 214.

Further provisions relating to proceedings for fraudulent trading are contained in s. 215, below.

In addition to the civil liability to pay compensation under this section and the criminal sanctions of CA 1985, s. 458, a person who is guilty of fraudulent trading may be made the subject of a disqualification order: see CDDA 1986, ss. 4, 10.

Section 214 Wrongful trading

214(1)　[Declaration by court, on application]　Subject to subsection (3) below, if in the course of the winding up of a company it appears that subsection (2) of this section applies in relation to a person who is or has been a director of the company, the court, on the application of the liquidator, may declare that that person is to be liable to make such contribution (if any) to the company's assets as the court thinks proper.

214(2)　[Application]　This subsection applies in relation to a person if—

  (a)　the company has gone into insolvent liquidation,

  (b)　at some time before the commencement of the winding up of the company, that person knew or ought to have concluded that there was no reasonable prospect that the company would avoid going into insolvent liquidation, and

  (c)　that person was a director of the company at that time;

but the court shall not make a declaration under this section in any case where the time mentioned in paragraph (b) above was before 28th April 1986.

214(3)　[Limit on declaration]　The court shall not make a declaration under this section with respect to any person if it is satisfied that after the condition specified in subsection (2)(b) was first satisfied in relation to him that person took every step with a view to minimising the potential loss to the company's creditors as (assuming him to have known that there was no reasonable prospect that the company would avoid going into insolvent liquidation) he ought to have taken.

214(4)　[Interpretation of s. 214(2),(3)]　For the purposes of subsections (2) and (3), the facts which a director of a company ought to know or ascertain, the conclusions which he ought to reach and the steps which he ought to take are those which would be known or ascertained, or reached or taken, by a reasonably diligent person having both—

  (a)　the general knowledge, skill and experience that may reasonably be expected of a person carrying out the same functions as are carried out by that director in relation to the company, and

  (b)　the general knowledge, skill and experience that that director has.

214(5)　[Interpretation of s. 214(4)]　The reference in subsection (4) to the functions carried out in relation to a company by a director of the company includes any functions which he does not carry out but which have been entrusted to him.

214(6)　[Interpretation re insolvent liquidation]　For the purposes of this section a company goes into insolvent liquidation if it goes into liquidation at a time when its assets are insufficient for the payment of its debts and other liabilities and the expenses of the winding up.

214(7) **["Director"]**   In this section **"director"** includes a shadow director.

214(8) **[S. 213]**   This section is without prejudice to section 213.

(Former provisions: IA 1985, ss. 12(9), 15(1)–(5), (7), Sch. 9, para. 4)

General note

For the background to this new provision, see the note to s. 213 above. It is framed so as to supplement the law of fraudulent trading laid down by that section, but (because of the less demanding standard of proof) it is bound in practice inevitably to supersede it.

The section, according to the marginal note, is concerned with "wrongful trading"; but it is notable that the word "trading" is not used in the text of the Act. (The marginal note may not be used as an aid for the construction of the text: *Chandler* v *Director of Public Prosecutions* [1964] AC 763.) The section itself is singularly imprecise in defining just what conduct on the part of a director will bring him within its scope.

The Cork Committee (*Report*, para. 1806) did put forward its own draft definition of "wrongful trading", the essential part of which read: ". . . at any time when the company is insolvent or unable to pay its debts as they fall due it incurs further debts or other liabilities to other persons without a reasonable prospect of meeting them in full." However, this definition was explicitly rejected by Parliament when an attempt was made to introduce it as an amendment to the Insolvency Bill 1985, and so it would be quite wrong to refer to it for guidance on the meaning of the present section. In particular, there may be wrongful trading under s. 214 even though the company does not incur further debts: one example mentioned during the parliamentary debate was the case where a company allows its assets to be depleted, e.g. by the payment of excessive directors' fees. It was, presumably, a concern to ensure that this kind of conduct was caught that led the draftsman to omit the word "trading" from his formulation.

The amount of contribution to be ordered is left entirely to the court's discretion, and is not related by the terms of the Act either to any particular period of trading or to the loss suffered by the company or creditors. However, in *Re Produce Marketing Consortium Ltd* (1989) 5 BCC 569 at p. 597, Knox J said:

"In my judgment the jurisdiction under sec. 214 is primarily compensatory rather than penal. Prime facie the appropriate amount that a director is declared to be liable to contribute is the amount by which the company's assets can be discerned to have been depleted by the director's conduct which caused the discretion under sec. 214(1) to arise. But Parliament has indeed chosen very wide words of discretion and it would be undesirable to seek to spell out limits on that discretion . . . The fact that there was no fraudulent intent is not of itself a reason for fixing the amount at a nominal or low figure, for that would amount to frustrating what I discern as Parliament's intention in adding sec. 214 to sec. 213 in the *Insolvency Act* 1986, but I am not persuaded that it is right to ignore that fact totally."

On the possibility of including a punitive element in the amount of contribution awarded, see the note to s. 213(2), above.

There will plainly be cases in which claims will be made against the former director of a company both under this section and under some other provisions of the Act, e.g. s. 212 (misfeasance) or s. 239 (preference). In such a case there may be no injustice in making orders which impose cumulative liability on the defendant: *Re Purpoint Ltd* [1991] BCC 121. However, in *Re DKG Contractors Ltd* [1990] BCC 903 the court ruled that payments made under ss. 212 and 239 should go to satisfy the liability under s. 214, and that enforcement should be limited to what was necessary to pay the company's creditors and the costs and expenses of the liquidation.

It has been ruled that, as a matter of law, CA 1985, s. 727 (which empowers the court to relieve a director from liability for breach of duty where he has acted honestly and reasonably and ought fairly to be excused) is not available to a director in s. 214 proceedings: *Re Produce Marketing Consortium Ltd (Halls v David & Anor)* [1989] 1 WLR 745; (1989) 5 BCC 399.

The proposal of the Cork Committee (*Report*, paras. 1798–1804) that it should be possible to make an application to the court, while a company was a going concern, for an anticipatory declaration that certain proposed trading would not be "wrongful" has not been implemented.

The provisions of ss. 214–217 apply to the directors of building societies: see the note to CDDA 1986, s. 7.

S. 214(1)

Four points may be noted:

(1) The section applies only to present and past directors (including shadow directors: s. 214 (7)). In *Re a Company No. 005009 of 1987* (1988) 4 BCC 424 (interlocutory proceedings in the saga of *Re M C Bacon Ltd:* see [1990] BCC 78 at p. 79G) Knox J ruled that a company's bank which, on becoming apprised of the fact that its client company is in financial difficulties, makes recommendations to its directors as to the future conduct of its business could, in principle, incur liability under the section as a "shadow director" – or, at least, that on the evidence before him the case was not so obviously unsustainable that an allegation to that effect should be struck out without proceeding to trial. A bank would not, however (it is submitted), risk liability as a shadow director if its requirements were expressed as conditions of extending loan facilities to the company rather than as instructions. In *Re Hydrodan (Corby) Ltd* [1994] BCC 161, Millett J accepted as correct a concession by counsel that s. 214 applies also to de facto directors. (See further on this point the notes to s. 251, below.)

(2) Section 214 applies only in a winding up.

(3) Only the liquidator has standing to bring proceedings.

(4) Any sum paid by a defendant goes into the general assets in the hands of the liquidator. In *Re Produce Marketing Consortium Ltd* (1989) 5 BCC 569 at p. 598, Knox J appears to have assumed that where, as in the case before him, the company had given a general floating charge to its bank, the charge would automatically attach to a sum ordered to be paid as contribution under s. 214. Such a result would be contrary to the intentions of the Cork Committee, which saw the "wrongful trading" proposals as a means of relieving a company's *unsecured* creditors: see the *Report* (Cmnd 8558, 1982), paras. 1797, 1806. The judge's view receives support from *Re Anglo-Austrian Printing and Publishing Union* [1895] 2 Ch. 891, where a similar ruling was made in relation to the proceeds of a misfeasance order made under what is now IA 1986, s. 212. The cases which hold that sums recovered as preferences are not caught by a floating charge which has crystallised prior to liquidation (e.g. *Re Yagerphone Ltd* [1935] Ch. 392, *Willmott* v *London Celluloid Co.* (1886) 31 ChD 425) might be considered as authorities to the contrary, were it not for the fact that they themselves have been the subject of some criticism. (This issue has been the subject of much academic debate: see Prentice (1990) 10 OJLS 265, Oditah (1990) LMCLQ 205, Wheeler [1993] JBL 256, Hicks (1993) 14 Co. Law. 16, 55.)

The comments to s. 213 on these points are also relevant for this subsection.

A person held liable under this section may also have a disqualification order made against him: see CDDA 1986, s. 10.

S. 214(2)

On the meaning of "has gone into insolvent liquidation" see s. 214(6); and for "the commencement of the winding up" see ss. 86 and 129.

The date 28 April 1986 was that when this provision (as IA 1985, s. 15) was first brought into force (SI 1986 No. 463).

The words "knew or ought to have concluded" are to be read in conjunction with s. 214(4). See the note to that provision, below.

S. 214(3)

The section, as has been noted, pointedly avoids giving any concrete meaning to the concept of "wrongful trading" or any positive guidance as to the types of conduct which will lead to liability. There is thus a major gap in the law, as framed, which will have to be filled by decisions of the courts in future test cases. The only objective facts that need to be established are those relating to the winding up of the company, its insolvency, and that the director held office at the material time (s. 214(2)); beyond that, liability turns on his knowledge or imputed knowledge (s. 214(2)(*b*)) and his failure to take "every step with a view to minimising the potential loss to the company's creditors as ... he ought to have taken". What a director knows, or must be taken to know, for these purposes is assessed by a mixture of subjective and objective tests (see the note to s. 214(4) below).

The phrases "took *every* step" and "*minimising* the potential loss to creditors" seem, at first sight, overstated colloquialisms. However, there is no doubt that the use of "every step" was deliberate: a proposed amendment to "every reasonable step" was expressly rejected in Parliament; and on similar reasoning, we must assume that "minimise" was fully intended, rather than, say, "reduce" or "avert".

The bracketed words in the present subsection credit a director, for the purpose of determining what he "ought" to have done, with an awareness of the company's financial position and (by virtue of s. 214(4)) with a degree of general knowledge, skill and experience which in reality he may not have had. These fictitious assumptions as to the directors' state of mind were invoked against the defendants in *Re Produce Marketing Consortium Ltd* (1989) 5 BCC 569. The company had kept inadequate accounting records, and in consequence the directors were in breach of their statutory duty to prepare accounts for the financial year ending 30 September 1985, which should have been laid before the shareholders and delivered to the registrar of companies by the end of July 1986. Knox J held that he should assume, for the purposes of s. 214, that these financial results were known to the directors at the latter date, at least to the extent of the size of the deficiency of assets over liabilities.

The Act gives no affirmative guidance as to the steps which a director "ought" to take when insolvency is threatening. It was plainly assumed in the Government's White Paper (Cmnd 9175, para. 12) that a conscientious director would seek to have the company put into receivership, administration, or voluntary liquidation as soon as possible. There is a clear risk that this may now seem the safest course for directors, faced as they are with the threat of personal liability and possible disqualification, even when in their own business judgment there is a good case for carrying on. It is clear that any decision to do so ought to be fully reasoned and documented and, where necessary, made with the benefit of outside professional advice, in order that the requirements of the present subsection can be met if a charge of wrongful trading is brought.

On principle and, it is submitted, on the language of the section, the onus of proof to show that a director has failed to take every step that he ought to have taken should be on the liquidator.

S. 214(4)

The tests to be applied under this subsection combine both subjective and objective criteria. The director is thus to be judged by the standards of the "reasonable" director, even though he himself is lacking or below average in knowledge, skill or experience, but by his own higher standards if these are above average. In *Re DKG Contractors Ltd* [1990] BCC 903 it was observed: "Patently, [the directors'] own knowledge, skill and experience were hopelessly inadequate for the task they undertook. That is not sufficient to protect them". However, it should be noted that in the *Produce Marketing* case (above), Knox J accepted a submission that the objective standards fixed by the section do require the court to have regard to the particular company and its business, so that the general knowledge, skill and experience postulated will be much less extensive in a small company in a modest way of business, with simple accounting procedures and equipment, than it will be in a large company with sophisticated procedures. This approach could also give scope for the courts to make some allowances in the case of non-executive and part-time directors.

In applying objective standards to the conduct of company directors in this way, the Act breaks new ground, for the case law has traditionally emphasised the need for honesty and conscientiousness but not demanded that directors should exercise any particular degree of competence or diligence or skill. (However, in *Re D'Jan of London Ltd* [1993] BCC 646, Hoffmann LJ expressed the view that "the duty of care owed by a director at common law is accurately stated in s. 214 of the Insolvency Act 1986".)

S. 214(5)

The remarks made in the preceding paragraph are underlined by the present subsection, which puts sins of omission into the same category as sins of commission. This, too, is a departure from the common law, which has never had effective sanctions to penalise passive defaults such as non-attendance at board meetings.

S. 214(6)

Section 214 applies only in a liquidation; but it is immaterial whether this is a compulsory or voluntary liquidation. The phrase "goes into liquidation" is defined in s. 247(2). The test of insolvency applied by s. 214(6) is on a "balance sheet" rather than a "liquidity" or "commercial" basis. (The recommendation of the Cork Committee was that *either* should be sufficient.) The definition of "inability to pay debts" in s. 123(1)(*e*) and (2) may be contrasted.

The Act gives no indication whether the company's assets are to be valued for the purpose of s. 214 on a "going concern" rather than a "break-up" basis, or whether contingent and future liabilities are to be brought into the reckoning. It is submitted that it would be wrong to judge these matters with the wisdom of hindsight, if it does happen that, e.g., the assets have had to be sold up piecemeal in the winding up which has resulted. The reference to "going into insolvent liquidation" in relation to the making of business judgments in s. 214(2)(*b*) surely indicates that the question of solvency is to be assessed on the basis of going-concern assumptions for all the purposes of the present section.

On the problems of valuation for the purposes of determining "insolvency" under the present section, see the comments of Professor R M Goode, *Principles of Corporate Insolvency Law* (Sweet & Maxwell, 1990), pp. 37–40.

S. 214(7)

For the definition of these terms, see the note to s. 206.

S. 214(8)

In view of the heavier onus of proof required by s. 213, it is unlikely that that section will be invoked in future where a liquidator has a choice of proceeding under either section. The one respect in which the two sections do not overlap, however, is that s. 213 applies to persons other than directors and shadow directors, provided that they are knowingly parties to the fraudulent trading.

Section 215   Proceedings under ss. 213, 214

215(1)   [Evidence by liquidator]   On the hearing of an application under section 213 or 214, the liquidator may himself give evidence or call witnesses.

215(2) **[Further court directions]** Where under either section the court makes a declaration, it may give such further directions as it thinks proper for giving effect to the declaration; and in particular, the court may—

(a) provide for the liability of any person under the declaration to be a charge on any debt or obligation due from the company to him, or on any mortgage or charge or any interest in a mortgage or charge on assets of the company held by or vested in him, or any person on his behalf, or any person claiming as assignee from or through the person liable or any person acting on his behalf, and

(b) from time to time make such further order as may be necessary for enforcing any charge imposed under this subsection.

215(3) **["Assignee"]** For the purposes of subsection (2), **"assignee"**—

(a) includes a person to whom or in whose favour, by the directions of the person made liable, the debt, obligation, mortgage or charge was created, issued or transferred or the interest created, but

(b) does not include an assignee for valuable consideration (not including consideration by way of marriage) given in good faith and without notice of any of the matters on the ground of which the declaration is made.

215(4) **[Directions re priority of debts]** Where the court makes a declaration under either section in relation to a person who is a creditor of the company, it may direct that the whole or any part of any debt owed by the company to that person and any interest thereon shall rank in priority after all other debts owed by the company and after any interest on those debts.

215(5) **[Ss. 213, 214]** Sections 213 and 214 have effect notwithstanding that the person concerned may be criminally liable in respect of matters on the ground of which the declaration under the section is to be made.

(Former provisions: CA 1985, s. 630(3)–(6) (as amended by IA 1985, Sch. 6, para. 6(2), (3)); IA 1985, s. 15(6))

S. 215(1)–(3), (5)

These subsections bring into the consolidation the repealed provisions of CA 1985, s. 639(3)–(5), (6), and make them applicable to proceedings for wrongful as well as fraudulent trading.

S. 215(4)

This provision was introduced as CA 1985, s. 630(5A) by IA 1985. The court is empowered to make a declaration, ancillary to an order for contribution, subordinating any debt owed by the company to a respondent so that it ranks after the company's other debts. Such a declaration was made in *Re Purpoint Ltd* [1991] BCC 121.

Section 216 Restriction on re-use of company names

216(1) **[Application]** This section applies to a person where a company **("the liquidating company")** has gone into insolvent liquidation on or after the appointed day and he was a director or shadow director of the company at any time in the period of 12 months ending with the day before it went into liquidation.

216(2)   [Prohibited name]   For the purposes of this section, a name is a prohibited name in relation to such a person if—

> (a) it is a name by which the liquidating company was known at any time in that period of 12 months, or
>
> (b) it is a name which is so similar to a name falling within paragraph (a) as to suggest an association with that company.

216(3)   [Restriction]   Except with leave of the court or in such circumstances as may be prescribed, a person to whom this section applies shall not at any time in the period of 5 years beginning with the day on which the liquidating company went into liquidation—

> (a) be a director of any other company that is known by a prohibited name, or
>
> (b) in any way, whether directly or indirectly, be concerned or take part in the promotion, formation or management of any such company, or
>
> (c) in any way, whether directly or indirectly, be concerned or take part in the carrying on of a business carried on (otherwise than by a company) under a prohibited name.

216(4)   [Penalty]   If a person acts in contravention of this section, he is liable to imprisonment or a fine, or both.

216(5)   ["The court"]   In subsection (3) **"the court"** means any court having jurisdiction to wind up companies; and on an application for leave under that subsection, the Secretary of State or the official receiver may appear and call the attention of the court to any matters which seem to him to be relevant.

216(6)   [Interpretation re name]   References in this section, in relation to any time, to a name by which a company is known are to the name of the company at that time or to any name under which the company carries on business at that time.

216(7)   [Interpretation re insolvent liquidation]   For the purposes of this section a company goes into insolvent liquidation if it goes into liquidation at a time when its assets are insufficient for the payment of its debts and other liabilities and the expenses of the winding up.

216(8)   ["Company"]   In this section **"company"** includes a company which may be wound up under Part V of this Act.

(Former provision: IA 1985, s. 17)

General note

This is one of a number of innovations made by IA 1985 which together form a package designed to strike down the "phoenix" phenomenon. This term was used to describe an abuse of the privilege of limited liability which, perhaps more than anything else, showed the inadequacies of the former insolvency law in the corporate sector. A company would be put into receivership (or voluntary liquidation) at a time when it owed large sums to its unsecured creditors. Frequently, the receiver was appointed by a controlling shareholder who had himself taken a floating charge over the whole of the company's undertaking, and there was nothing to stop him from appointing a receiver with whom he could act in collusion. The receiver would sell the entire business as a going concern at a knock-down price to a new company incorporated by the former controllers of the defunct company. As a result, what was essentially the same business would be carried on by the same people in disregard of the claims of the creditors of the first company, who in effect subsidised the launch of the new company debt-free. It was not unknown for the procedure to be repeated several times. The use of nominees or "front men" could add to the confusion and help to deceive future creditors: on the other hand, advantage could sometimes be gained from using a new company name similar to that of the old company, and cashing in on what was left of its goodwill. The present section is aimed to counter both of these latter aspects of the "phoenix syndrome". It is not based on any of the Cork Committee's recommendations, and was introduced at a late stage during the passage of the Insolvency Bill through Parliament in 1985. It makes the re-use of the name of a company which has been wound up insolvent a criminal offence in the circumstances defined; but it is rather surprisingly confined in its scope to directors and shadow directors of the extinct company. In addition, any such person and any nominee or "front man" through whom he conducts the second business may incur personal liability, without limitation, under s. 217.

S. 216(1)

Many phrases in this subsection have special meanings. "Company" and "gone into insolvent liquidation" are defined in ss. 216(8) and 216(7) respectively; the "appointed day" is the day on which the present Act came into force (29 December 1986: see ss. 436, 443); "director" and "shadow director" have the meanings ascribed to them by s. 251.

The section is not retrospective so as to apply to liquidations that were already in force when the Act took effect.

The prohibition applies to anyone who has been a director or shadow director of the old company within the 12 months prior to its liquidation, and lasts for the period of five years that follows that event (s. 216(3)).

S. 216(2)

The ban applies to the use of the same name or a similar name: see, further, the note to s. 216(6).

It should be emphasised that the present section is not directed against the re-use of an insolvent company's name in itself: there will be no ban on this practice provided that no director of the former company is associated with the second business. It is only *directors* who can contravene the section, and only directors who are liable to punishment. This explains the phrase "a prohibited name *in relation* to such a person".

S. 216(3)

The ban is not restricted to the use of a prohibited name by a newly formed company: an established company (perhaps a member of the same group as the defunct company) may well have a "similar" name already, or may change its name to a "prohibited" name, with the result that its directors may be caught by this section. (Note that IR 1986, r. 4.230, may give a director an exemption in the former of these cases.)

The court is given power to grant dispensations from the prohibition imposed by this section, which it is likely to do when the insolvency is not linked with any blameworthy conduct on the part of the director concerned. *Re Bonus Breaks Ltd* [1991] BCC 546 is an illustration of such a case. There, the applicant had been a director of a company which had gone into insolvent liquidation, but she had not behaved culpably and had lost substantial sums of her own money. A new company was set up with a capital of £50,000, including £49,000 in redeemable shares. Morritt J gave leave for her to be a director of the new company against undertakings that its capital base would be maintained and that it would not redeem any redeemable shares nor purchase its own shares out of distributable profits for a period of two years, unless such action was approved by a director independent of the company's founders.

The rules also specify three sets of circumstances where the section will not apply: see IR 1986, rr. 4.228ff. These are (1) where the whole, or substantially the whole, of the business of an insolvent company is acquired by a successor company and the liquidator (or equivalent office-holder) of the insolvent company gives notice to its creditors under r. 4.228; (2) for an interim period, where an application is made to the court within seven days of the liquidation and the court grants leave not later than six weeks from that date (r. 4.229); and (3) where the second company has been known by the name in question for at least 12 months prior to the liquidation and has not been a dormant company (r. 4.230). All other cases will have to go to the court for authorisation: the relevant rules are rr. 4.226, 4.227.

Paragraphs (*b*) and (*c*), by the use of the term "indirectly", will be effective to stop a person from controlling another company or carrying on a new business through others as "front" men. In addition, para. (*c*) makes it clear that it will be an offence to use a prohibited name even where no second company is involved, but in this case the civil consequences prescribed by s. 217 will not be applicable.

The phrase "concerned or take part in the management of a company" is not defined, but the note to s. 217 is relevant in this context.

S. 216(4)

Note that it is only a person who was a director or shadow director of the liquidating company who can be convicted of an offence under this section. In contrast, the civil liability imposed by s. 217 extends also to persons who act on the instructions of such ex-directors.

On penalties, see s. 430 and Sch. 10.

S. 216(5)

For the courts having jurisdiction to wind up companies, see ss. 117 and 120. It is clear that "the court" need not be the same court as that which may have been involved in the liquidation of the old company.

S. 216(6)

This provision should be read with s. 216(2) above. In addition to forbidding the use of an identical name, the section bans a name "so similar as to suggest an association with" the former company. It is likely that this will catch the common and, in many ways, convenient practice of calling a new company by a name such as "John Smith (1991) Ltd", after the original John Smith Ltd has gone out of business. (There will, of course, be no objection to this so long as the first company was wound up solvent.)

The offence is not confined to the use of a prohibited name by a company: an unincorporated business is caught as well (s. 216(3)(*c*)). Further, the prohibition is not confined to a company's registered name. A company may carry on business under another name. Thus, for example, John Smith Ltd, before it went into insolvent liquidation, may have used the trade name of "City Autos". It will be an offence for a former director of the company to take part in the management of any business using the name "John Smith", or "City Autos", or any name similar to either. It will also be an offence for him to be a director of any company having the registered name "John Smith Ltd" or "City Autos Ltd" and also of any other company, X Ltd, if it trades under the name "John Smith" or City Autos" – or a similar name in each case.

It is the last of these possibilities that is most likely to mislead creditors and members of the public generally, i.e. the use of the same trade name by a succession of limited companies.

S. 216(7)

This subsection defines "goes into insolvent liquidation" in terms identical to s. 214(6). See the note to that provision and, for the meaning of "goes into liquidation", s. 247(2).

S. 216(8)

The effect of this provision is to include "unregistered" as well as registered companies within the section. See the note to s. 220.

Section 217   Personal liability for debts, following contravention of s. 216

217(1) [Personal liability] A person is personally responsible for all the relevant debts of a company if at any time—

- (a) in contravention of section 216, he is involved in the management of the company, or
- (b) as a person who is involved in the management of the company, he acts or is willing to act on instructions given (without the leave of the court) by a person whom he knows at that time to be in contravention in relation to the company of section 216.

217(2) [Joint and several liability] Where a person is personally responsible under this section for the relevant debts of a company, he is jointly and severally liable in respect of those debts with the company and any other person who, whether under this section or otherwise, is so liable.

217(3) [Relevant debts of company] For the purposes of this section the relevant debts of a company are—

- (a) in relation to a person who is personally responsible under paragraph (a) of subsection (1), such debts and other liabilities of the company as are incurred at a time when that person was involved in the management of the company, and
- (b) in relation to a person who is personally responsible under paragraph (b) of that subsection, such debts and other liabilities of the company as are incurred at a time when that person was acting or was willing to act on instructions given as mentioned in that paragraph.

217(4) [Person involved in management] For the purposes of this section, a person is involved in the management of a company if he is a director of the company or if he is concerned, whether directly or indirectly, or takes part, in the management of the company.

217(5) [Interpretation] For the purposes of this section a person who, as a person involved in the management of a company, has at any time acted on instructions given (without the leave of the court) by a person whom he knew at that time to be in contravention in relation to the company of section 216 is presumed, unless the contrary is shown, to have been willing at any time thereafter to act on any instructions given by that person.

217(6) ["Company"] In this section **"company"** includes a company which may be wound up under Part V.

(Former provision: IA 1985, s. 18(1) (part), (2)–(6))

General note

This section imposes personal liability on a person who contravenes s. 216 by re-using a prohibited company name. In addition, it makes similarly liable anyone who allows himself to be used as a "front" man or nominee in breach of that section. Since the criminal liability prescribed by s. 216 affects only directors and shadow directors, the category of those who are potentially liable on a civil basis is wider than those who may be convicted of the statutory offence.

In *Thorne* v *Silverleaf* [1994] BCC 109, summary judgment was given in favour of the plaintiff against a director who had infringed s. 216. The Court of Appeal held that it was irrelevant that the plaintiff had allegedly aided and abetted the director in the commission of this offence. It was immaterial that he was aware of the facts, and even that he was aware both of the facts and that they constituted a contravention of s. 216. It was also held on the evidence that the plaintiff had not waived his right to seek recovery against the director under s. 217.

Section 217 is drafted in broadly similar terms to CDDA 1986, s. 15, which is also derived from IA 1985, s. 18.

S. 217(1)

Many of the terms used in this provision are defined or explained in the following subsections, and in particular "relevant debts", "involved in the management of a company", "is willing to act" and "company".

For a person to be made liable under para. (*b*), it will be necessary to show that he knew all the facts which are relevant to a contravention of s. 216.

Liability under the section is automatic, not requiring a special application to the court or court order of any sort and, for a case coming within para. (*a*), not requiring a prior conviction of the director concerned.

S. 217(2)

A person liable under this section is primarily liable, jointly and severally with the company and others concerned, and not in any secondary way.

S. 217(3)

Liability extends not only to debts in the narrow sense but also to all other obligations, such as claims for damages; and it applies to all debts and obligations arising during the relevant time and not merely those incurred *by* the acts of the person in question.

The phrase "willing to act" is explained in s. 217(5).

S. 217(4)

A director is irrebuttably presumed to be "involved in the management" of the company.

In regard to other persons, the best guide to the meaning of the phrase may be found in cases where the courts have construed closely similar, but not identical, provisions such as "take part in" or "be concerned in" the management of a company. For a full discussion, see the notes to CDDA 1986, s. 1(1).

S. 217(5)

This provision creates a presumption against a person who is proved at any one time to have acted on the instructions of another whom he then knew to be contravening s. 216. Once this is shown, he is rebuttably presumed to have been "willing to act" on the other's instructions at any time afterwards.

S. 217(6)

"Unregistered" companies are included by this formula. See the note to s. 220.

INVESTIGATION AND PROSECUTION OF MALPRACTICE

Section 218   Prosecution of delinquent officers and members of company

218(1)   [Court may direct matter to be referred for prosecution]   If it appears to the court in the course of a winding up by the court that any past or present officer, or any member, of the company has been guilty of any offence in relation to the company for which he is criminally liable, the court may (either on the application of a person interested in the winding up or of its own motion) direct the liquidator to refer the matter to the prosecuting authority.

218(2)   **["The prosecuting authority"]**   **"The prosecuting authority"** means—

     (a) in the case of a winding up in England and Wales, the Director of Public Prosecutions, and

     (b) in the case of a winding up in Scotland, the Lord Advocate.

218(3)   **[Report – winding up by court]**   If in the case of a winding up by the court in England and Wales it appears to the liquidator, not being the official receiver, that any past or present officer of the company, or any member of it, has been guilty of an offence in relation to the company for which he is criminally liable, the liquidator shall report the matter to the official receiver.

218(4)   **[Report – voluntary winding up]**   If it appears to the liquidator in the course of a voluntary winding up that any past or present officer of the company, or any member of it, has been guilty of an offence in relation to the company for which he is criminally liable, he shall—

     (a) forthwith report the matter to the prosecuting authority, and

     (b) furnish to that authority such information and give to him such access to and facilities for inspecting and taking copies of documents (being information or documents in the possession or under the control of the liquidator and relating to the matter in question) as the authority requires.

218(5)   **[Reference to Secretary of State]**   Where a report is made to him under subsection (4), the prosecuting authority may, if he thinks fit, refer the matter to the Secretary of State for further enquiry; and the Secretary of State—

     (a) shall thereupon investigate the matter reported to him and such other matters relating to the affairs of the company as appear to him to require investigation, and

     (b) for the purpose of his investigation may exercise any of the powers which are exercisable by inspectors appointed under section 431 or 432 of the Companies Act to investigate a company's affairs.

218(6)   **[Court may direct liquidator to make report]**   If it appears to the court in the course of a voluntary winding up that—

     (a) any past or present officer of the company, or any member of it, has been guilty as above-mentioned, and

     (b) no report with respect to the matter has been made by the liquidator to the prosecuting authority under subsection (4),

the court may (on the application of any person interested in the winding up or of its own motion) direct the liquidator to make such a report.

On a report being made accordingly, this section has effect as though the report had been made in pursuance of subsection (4).

(Former provisions: CA 1985, s. 632 (as amended by IA 1985, Sch. 6, para. 44); CA 1948, s. 334(1)–(4); CA 1981, s. 92(1))

General note

This provision establishes a reporting chain through which suspected criminal offences uncovered in the course of a winding up may be referred to the appropriate persons for investigation and, where appropriate, prosecution. The allocation of rôles to the various officers and officials does not seem wholly logical.

The words "reported to him and such other matters relating to the affairs of the company as appear to him to require investigation" were added to s. 218(5)(*a*) by CA 1989, s. 78 as from 21 February 1990: see SI 1990 No. 142 (C. 5), art. 4.

S. 218(1), (2)

In a winding up by the court, the court is empowered to take the initial step when an offence is suspected, by directing the liquidator to refer the matter to the "prosecuting authority". The latter term is explained in s. 218(2). The court may act of its own motion or on the application of "a person interested in the winding up". In England and Wales, if the liquidator (not being the official receiver) himself suspects wrongdoing, he is obliged to report the matter to the official receiver (s. 218(3)); but it is unclear whether that provision by implication debars him from making an application to the court on his own initiative under s. 218(1). In Scotland, where s. 218(3) does not apply, it would seem to be clear that the liquidator should make application to the court in all cases.

On the meaning of "officer", see the note to s. 206(3).

S. 218(3)

The section is oddly silent as to what the official receiver should do, both in the case when he is not the liquidator and receives a report of a suspected offence, and in the case where, as liquidator, he suspects an offence himself. It must be intended that he shall (either with or without conducting his own investigation into the matter) refer the case to the prosecuting authority without the need for any intervention by the court. However, the rules are silent on this point.

S. 218(4), (6)

In a voluntary winding up, the liquidator's duty is to report the matter himself directly to the prosecuting authority, and thereafter to co-operate with the authority as described, and also give the further assistance referred to in s. 219(3). However, the court has, under s. 218(6), a further power to give the liquidator directions to this effect.

S. 218(5)

The Secretary of State's powers of investigation under CA 1985, ss. 431, 432, are far-reaching, and under those sections are not restricted to pursuing inquiries in connection with suspected criminal offences. Additional provisions governing an investigation by the Secretary of State under the present subsection are laid down by s. 219 below.

The prosecuting authority may invoke the assistance of the Secretary of State under the present subsection only when a report has been made to him under s. 218(4) – which presumably includes also a report deemed to have been made under s. 218(4) by virtue of s. 218(6). There is no corresponding provision dealing with references which have been made by a liquidator to the prosecuting authority under s. 218(1), or to any information that the official receiver may have transmitted to him following a report under s. 218(3).

Section 219 Obligations arising under s. 218

219(1) [Assistance to investigation by Secretary of State] For the purpose of an investigation by the Secretary of State under section 218(5), any obligation imposed on a person by any provision of the Companies Act to produce documents or give information to, or otherwise to assist, inspectors appointed as mentioned in that subsection is to be regarded as an obligation similarly to assist the Secretary of State in his investigation.

219(2)　[Answer may be used as evidence]　An answer given by a person to a question put to him in exercise of the powers conferred by section 218(5) may be used in evidence against him.

219(3)　[Liquidator and officer to assist, where criminal proceedings instituted]　Where criminal proceedings are instituted by the prosecuting authority or the Secretary of State following any report or reference under section 218, it is the duty of the liquidator and every officer and agent of the company past and present (other than the defendant or defender) to give to that authority or the Secretary of State (as the case may be) all assistance in connection with the prosecution which he is reasonably able to give.

For this purpose **"agent"** includes any banker or solicitor of the company and any person employed by the company as auditor, whether that person is or is not an officer of the company.

219(4)　[Direction by court re assistance]　If a person fails or neglects to give assistance in the manner required by subsection (3), the court may, on the application of the prosecuting authority or the Secretary of State (as the case may be) direct the person to comply with that subsection; and if the application is made with respect to a liquidator, the court may (unless it appears that the failure or neglect to comply was due to the liquidator not having in his hands sufficient assets of the company to enable him to do so) direct that the costs shall be borne by the liquidator personally.

(Former provisions: CA 1985, s. 633; CA 1948, s. 334(5), (6); CA 1981, s. 92(2)–(4))

General note

The provisions of this section are designed to facilitate the investigations which may be made by the various officials and authorities when a suspected criminal offence is reported to them under the preceding section. The company's bankers, solicitors and auditors are specifically included among those obliged to assist (s. 219(3)).

PART V — WINDING UP OF UNREGISTERED COMPANIES

Section 220　Meaning of "unregistered company"

220(1)　["Unregistered company"]　For the purposes of this Part, the expression **"unregistered company"** includes any association and any company, with the following exceptions—

　　(a) (Repealed)

　　(b) a company registered in any part of the United Kingdom under the Joint

Stock Companies Acts or under the legislation (past or present) relating to companies in Great Britain.

(Former provision: CA 1985, s. 665 (as amended by Trustee Savings Banks Act 1981, Sch. 6, Trustee Savings Banks Act 1985, Sch. 4, IA 1985, Sch. 10, Pt. II, and Bankruptcy (Scotland) Act 1985, Sch. 8))

History note

In s. 220(1) the words "any trustee savings bank certified under the enactments relating to such banks" formerly appearing after the word "includes" ceased to have effect and were repealed by virtue of s. 220(2) from 5 July 1988: see the Trustee Savings Banks Act 1985 (Appointed Day) (No. 6) Order 1988 (SI 1988 No. 1168).

Section 220(2) reads: "On such day as the Treasury appoints by order under section 4(3) of the Trustee Savings Banks Act 1985, the words in subsection (1) from "any trustee" to "banks" cease to have effect and are hereby repealed."

Section 220(1)(*a*) ceased to have effect and was repealed by the Transport and Works Act 1992, s. 65(1)(*f*), 68(1), Sch. 4, Pt. I as from 1 January 1993 (see SI 1992 No. 2784, art. 2); s. 220(1)(*a*) formerly read as follows: "(a) a railway company incorporated by Act of Parliament,".

General note

The earliest companies legislation that enabled companies to acquire corporate status by registration was accompanied by Winding-up Acts which provided machinery for the winding up of companies which had not registered. Part V of the present Act, which consolidates CA 1985, Pt. XXI, is what survives today of that legislation. There are almost certainly, however, no "unregistered companies" in the old sense still around; and for practical purposes it is probably true to say that Pt. V will be applied to two other types of "unregistered" company – (1) statutory companies incorporated by private Act of Parliament (other than railway companies: s. 220(1)(*a*)), and (2) oversea companies which have been carrying on business in Great Britain or have some other relevant connection with this jurisdiction. Obsolete references to partnerships and limited partnerships contained in CA 1985, s. 665, were repealed by IA 1985, Sch. 10, Pt. II; but paradoxically this Part of the Act is now made to apply to the winding up of certain insolvent partnerships: see the note to s. 420.

English courts have exercised jurisdiction to wind up foreign companies under the present section or its predecessors for a very long period: s. 225, which expressly refers to companies incorporated outside Great Britain but applies in limited circumstances only, is a relative newcomer which has rarely, if ever, been invoked.

Sections 220–221 give no guidance as to the criteria which will justify an English court in assuming jurisdiction. The matter has been left to the discretion of the courts. In practice, it is normally considered a sufficient nexus for the company to have, or have had, a place of business or branch office within the jurisdiction, or to have assets here (*Banque des Marchands de Moscou (Koupetschesky)* v *Kindersley & Anor* [1951] Ch. 112; [1950] 2 All ER 549), but other factors may also be regarded as relevant, e.g. the fact that a claim may be brought by the company against an insurer in England (*Re Compania Merabello San Nicholas SA* [1973] Ch. 75; [1972] 3 All ER 448), that a winding-up order will entitle former employees of the company to claim statutory redundancy payments (*Re Eloc Electro-Optieck and Communicatie BV* [1982] Ch. 43; [1981] 2 All ER 1111), or that the debt upon which the petition is founded was incurred here (*Re a Company No. 00359 of 1987* [1988] Ch. 210; (1987) 3 BCC 160 (also known as *Re Okeanos Maritime Corp.*)). It is not necessary that the company should have assets within the jurisdiction: *Re a Company (No. 003102 of 1991), ex parte Nyckeln Finance Co. Ltd* [1991] BCLC 539. But the court must be satisfied that there is a reasonable possibility that the winding-up order will benefit those applying for it, and the court must be able to exercise jurisdiction over one or more persons interested in the distribution of the company's assets: *Re Real Estate Development Co.* [1991] BCLC 210.

The court, having exercised its discretion to hold that it has jurisdiction in respect of the particular company, has a further discretion whether or not to make an order, and if so upon what terms: see the notes to s. 221.

The object of s. 220(1)(*b*) appears fairly plainly to be to ensure that a company registered in one part of the UK may be wound up only in that jurisdiction, e.g. a company registered in England and Wales may only be wound up by the High Court or the county court (s. 117), and a company registered in Scotland only by the Court of Session or a sheriff court (s. 120). But this is not the case so far as concerns a company registered in Northern Ireland. In *Re Normandy Marketing Ltd* [1993] BCC 879 Morritt J held that by virtue of s. 220 and s. 441, read together, the court in England had jurisdiction to wind up a company registered in Northern Ireland, on the petition of the Secretary of State under s. 124A, provided that it had a principal place of business in England or Wales. In an appropriate case, s. 225 could also be invoked to give a court in Great Britain jurisdiction over a Northern Ireland company.

The allocation of jurisdiction over an oversea company as between the different parts of the United Kingdom is dealt with by s 221(2), (3).

The Civil Jurisdiction and Judgments Act 1982, which gives effect to the Brussels Convention of 1968, does not apply at all to the winding up of insolvent companies (Art. 1(2)). In regard to solvent foreign companies, Art. 16(2) has the effect of denying a British court jurisdiction where the company has its "seat" (as defined by s. 43 of the Act) in a contracting State other than the UK. But, conversely, a solvent company which is incorporated abroad in a contracting State will be subject to jurisdiction here under Pt. V of IA 1986 if it has its "seat" in this country.

An unregistered company can be wound up only by order of the court: s. 221(4).

S. 220(1)

The term "association" has been held to mean only an association formed for gain or profit: *Re St James's Club* (1852) 2 De GM & G 383; *Re The Bristol Athenaeum* (1889) 43 ChD 236. These decisions may have turned, in part, upon the special wording of the earlier legislation; but the ruling in the former case was given renewed authority when it was endorsed by the Court of Appeal in *Re International Tin Council* [1989] Ch. 309; (1988) 4 BCC 653. The Council was an organisation formed by international treaty with the legal character, status and capacities of a corporate body. In holding that it was not within CA 1985, s. 665 (the precursor of the present section), the court adopted the broad test laid down in *Re St James's Club* (above): was the association one which Parliament could reasonably have intended should be subject to the winding-up process? If any State, whether a member of the Council or not, could subject that enterprise to its own domestic law, the independence and international character of the organisation would be fragmented and destroyed. Accordingly, an English court would not assume jurisdiction under s. 665. The ruling in *Re St James's Club* was applied to a professional football club in *Re Witney Town Football and Social Club* [1993] BCC 874.

Section 221   Winding up of unregistered companies

221(1)   [Application of winding up provisions]   Subject to the provisions of this Part, any unregistered company may be wound up under this Act; and all the provisions of this Act and the Companies Act about winding up apply to an unregistered company with the exceptions and additions mentioned in the following subsections.

221(2)   [Principal place of business in Northern Ireland]   If an unregistered company has a principal place of business situated in Northern Ireland, it shall not be wound up under this Part unless it has a principal place of business situated in England and Wales or Scotland, or in both England and Wales and Scotland.

221(3) [Deemed registration, registered office] For the purpose of determining a court's winding-up jurisdiction, an unregistered company is deemed—

(a) to be registered in England and Wales or Scotland, according as its principal place of business is situated in England and Wales or Scotland, or

(b) if it has a principal place of business situated in both countries, to be registered in both countries;

and the principal place of business situated in that part of Great Britain in which proceedings are being instituted is, for all purposes of the winding up, deemed to be the registered office of the company.

221(4) [No voluntary winding up] No unregistered company shall be wound up under this Act voluntarily.

221(5) [Circumstances for winding up] The circumstances in which an unregistered company may be wound up are as follows—

(a) if the company is dissolved, or has ceased to carry on business, or is carrying on business only for the purpose of winding up its affairs;

(b) if the company is unable to pay its debts;

(c) if the court is of opinion that it is just and equitable that the company should be wound up.

221(6) (Repealed).

221(7) [Scotland] In Scotland, an unregistered company which the Court of Session has jurisdiction to wind up may be wound up by the court if there is subsisting a floating charge over property comprised in the company's property and undertaking, and the court is satisfied that the security of the creditor entitled to the benefit of the floating charge is in jeopardy.

For this purpose a creditor's security is deemed to be in jeopardy if the court is satisfied that events have occurred or are about to occur which render it unreasonable in the creditor's interest that the company should retain power to dispose of the property which is subject to the floating charge.

(Former provisions: CA 1985, s. 666 (as amended by IA 1985, Sch. 10, Pts. II, IV); CA 1948, s. 399(1)–(5), (8), (9); CFCSA 1972, s. 4)

General note

This section brings forward provisions which are in substance the same as CA 1985, s. 666, with the removal of references to winding up subject to the supervision of the court (which has been abolished: see the note to s. 73) and to partnerships and limited partnerships (see the note to s. 220).

On the question when the court will exercise jurisdiction to wind up a foreign company, see the notes to s. 220.

The court has an unrestricted discretion to make or refuse an order, or to make an order subject to conditions. Thus, in the case of an oversea company, it may decline to order a winding up, or grant a stay of proceedings here, on the ground that the courts of another country would provide a more appropriate forum (see *Re Harrods (Buenos Aires) Ltd* [1992] Ch. 72; [1991] BCC 249, *Re Wallace Smith & Co. Ltd* [1992] BCLC 970); or it may direct that the local winding up be conducted on a basis ancillary to a principal liquidation elsewhere.

S. 221(5)

The grounds for the winding up of an unregistered company which are set out in this subsection are more restricted than those for registered companies: see s. 122.

The court has jurisdiction to wind up a foreign company under this subsection even though it has no assets here, provided that a sufficiently close connection can be shown, e.g. that the debt upon which the petition is founded was incurred here: *Re a Company No. 00359 of 1987* [1988] Ch. 210; (1987) 3 BCC 160.

S.221(6)

This subsection relating to trustee savings banks was repealed with effect from 21 July 1986: see SI 1986 No. 1223 (c. 36); the former wording read as follows:

"A petition for winding up a trustee savings bank may be presented by the Trustee Savings Banks Central Board or by a commissioner appointed under section 35 of the Trustee Savings Banks Act 1981 as well as by any person authorised under Part IV of this Act to present a petition for the winding up of a company.

On such day as the Treasury appoints by order under section 4(3) of the Trustee Savings Bank Act 1985, this subsection ceases to have effect and is hereby repealed."

S. 221(7)

See the note to s. 122(2).

Section 222　　Inability to pay debts: unpaid creditor for £750 or more

222(1)　[Deemed inability to pay debts]　An unregistered company is deemed (for the purposes of section 221) unable to pay its debts if there is a creditor, by assignment or otherwise, to whom the company is indebted in a sum exceeding £750 then due and—

    (a)　the creditor has served on the company, by leaving at its principal place of business, or by delivering to the secretary or some director, manager or principal officer of the company, or by otherwise serving in such manner as the court may approve or direct, a written demand in the prescribed form requiring the company to pay the sum due, and

    (b)　the company has for 3 weeks after the service of the demand neglected to pay the sum or to secure or compound for it to the creditor's satisfaction.

222(2)　[Increase or reduction of s. 222(1) sum]　The money sum for the time being specified in subsection (1) is subject to increase or reduction by regulations under section 417 in Part XV; but no increase in the sum so specified affects any case in which the winding-up petition was presented before the coming into force of the increase.

(Former provisions: CA 1985, s. 667 (as amended by IA 1985, Sch. 6, para. 50); CA 1948, s. 399 (6)(a) (as amended by SI 1984 No. 1199))

General note

This provision modifies the definition of "inability to pay debts" contained in s. 123(1)(*a*) above to meet the case of an unregistered company. See further the notes to that section.

S. 222(1)(a)

The words "in the prescribed form" were inserted by IA 1985, Sch. 6, para. 50. For details, see IR 1986, r. 4.5ff and Form 4.1.

Section 223   Inability to pay debts: debt remaining unsatisfied after action brought

223   An unregistered company is deemed (for the purposes of section 221) unable to pay its debts if an action or other proceeding has been instituted against any member for any debt or demand due, or claimed to be due, from the company, or from him in his character of member, and—

    (a) notice in writing of the institution of the action or proceeding has been served on the company by leaving it at the company's principal place of business (or by delivering it to the secretary, or some director, manager or principal officer of the company, or by otherwise serving it in such manner as the court may approve or direct), and

    (b) the company has not within 3 weeks after service of the notice paid, secured or compounded for the debt or demand, or procured the action or proceeding to be stayed or sisted, or indemnified the defendant or defender to his reasonable satisfaction against the action or proceeding, and against all costs, damages and expenses to be incurred by him because of it.

(Former provisions: CA 1985, s. 668 (as amended by IA 1985, Sch. 6, para. 51); CA 1948, s. 399(6)(b))

General note

There is no provision corresponding directly to this section in the case of a registered company.

    The period of three weeks specified in para. (*b*) was substituted for ten days by IA 1985, Sch. 6, para. 51.

Section 224   Inability to pay debts: other cases

224(1)   [Deemed inability to pay debts]   An unregistered company is deemed (for purposes of section 221) unable to pay its debts—

    (a) if in England and Wales execution or other process issued on a judgment, decree or order obtained in any court in favour of a creditor against the company, or any member of it as such, or any person authorised to be sued as nominal defendant on behalf of the company, is returned unsatisfied;

    (b) if in Scotland the induciae of a charge for payment on an extract decree, or an extract registered bond, or an extract registered protest, have expired without payment being made;

    (c) if in Northern Ireland a certificate of unenforceability has been granted in respect of any judgment, decree or order obtained as mentioned in paragraph (a);

    (d) if it is otherwise proved to the satisfaction of the court that the company is unable to pay its debts as they fall due.

224(2)   [Deemed inability – another situation]   An unregistered company is also deemed unable to pay its debts if it is proved to the satisfaction of the court that the value of the company's assets is less than the amount of its liabilities, taking into account its contingent and prospective liabilities.

(Former provisions: CA 1985, s. 669 (as amended by IA 1985, Sch. 6, para. 52); CA 1948, s. 399(6)(c)–(e))

General note
The provisions of this section correspond with those of s. 123(1)(*b*)–(*e*), (2). Paragraph (*d*) of subs. (1) and subs. (2) have been amended by IA 1985 in the same way as the equivalent parts of s. 123: see the notes to that section.

Section 225   Oversea company may be wound up though dissolved

225   Where a company incorporated outside Great Britain which has been carrying on business in Great Britain ceases to carry on business in Great Britain, it may be wound up as an unregistered company under this Act, notwithstanding that it has been dissolved or otherwise ceased to exist as a company under or by virtue of the laws of the country under which it was incorporated.

(Former provisions: CA 1985, s. 670; CA 1948, s. 400)

General note
The jurisdiction of the court to wind up an oversea company is not, of course, limited to the circumstances set out in this section. In practice, the more widely drawn provisions of s. 221 are normally relied on: s. 225 derives originally from CA 1928, s. 91, which was enacted to remove a doubt as to the court's jurisdiction which arose in connection with the dissolution of Russian banks following the revolution of 1917; it did not confer any new power to wind up companies (per Megarry J in *Re Compania Merabello San Nicholas SA* [1973] Ch 75 at pp. 85, 87; and per Morritt J in *Re Normandy Marketing Ltd* [1993] BCC 879 at p. 883).

Section 226   Contributories in winding up of unregistered company

226(1)   [Deemed contributory]   In the event of an unregistered company being wound up, every person is deemed a contributory who is liable to pay or contribute to the payment of any debt or liability of the company, or to pay or contribute to the payment of any sum for the adjustment of the rights of members among themselves, or to pay or contribute to the payment of the expenses of winding up the company.

226(2)   [Liability for contribution]   Every contributory is liable to contribute to the company's assets all sums due from him in respect of any such liability as is mentioned above.

226(3)   [Unregistered company re mines in stannaries]   In the case of an unregistered company engaged in or formed for working mines within the stannaries, a past member is not liable to contribute to the assets if he has ceased to be a member for 2 years or more either before the mine ceased to be worked or before the date of the winding-up order.

226(4)   [Death, bankruptcy, insolvency of contributory]   In the event of the death, bankruptcy or insolvency of any contributory, the provisions of this Act with respect to the personal representatives, to the heirs and legatees of heritage of the heritable estate in Scotland of deceased contributories, and to the trustees of bankrupt or insolvent contributories, respectively apply.

(Former provisions: CA 1985, s. 671 (as amended by IA 1985, Sch. 10, Pt. II); CA 1948, s. 401)

General note
The reference in s. 226(3) to "the stannaries" is to certain Cornish tin-mining companies, which were formerly governed by separate legislation.

Section 227   Power of court to stay, sist or restrain proceedings

227 The provisions of this Part with respect to staying, sisting or restraining actions and proceedings against a company at any time after the presentation of a petition for winding up and before the making of a winding-up order extend, in the case of an unregistered company, where the application to stay, sist or restrain is presented by a creditor, to actions and proceedings against any contributory of the company.

(Former provisions: CA 1985, s. 672; CA 1948, s. 402)

Section 228   Actions stayed on winding-up order

228 Where an order has been made for winding up an unregistered company, no action or proceeding shall be proceeded with or commenced against any contributory of the company in respect of any debt of the company, except by leave of the court, and subject to such terms as the court may impose.

(Former provisions: CA 1985, s. 673; CA 1948, s. 403)

Section 229   Provisions of this Part to be cumulative

229(1) **[Pt. V in addition to Pt. IV]** The provisions of this Part with respect to unregistered companies are in addition to and not in restriction of any provisions in Part IV with respect to winding up companies by the court; and the court or liquidator may exercise any powers or do any act in the case of unregistered companies which might be exercised or done by it or him in winding up companies formed and registered under the Companies Act.

229(2) **[Unregistered company not usually company under CA]** However, an unregistered company is not, except in the event of its being wound up, deemed to be a company under the Companies Act, and then only to the extent provided by this Part of this Act.

(Former provisions: CA 1985, s. 674; CA 1948, s. 404)

PART VI — MISCELLANEOUS PROVISIONS APPLYING TO COMPANIES WHICH ARE INSOLVENT OR IN LIQUIDATION

General comment on Part VI

The heading to this Part is bound to give rise to confusion, because of the phrase "companies which are insolvent". The natural inference to be drawn from this would be that nothing in ss. 230–246 applies to a company which is solvent (in a financial sense) so that, for instance, an officer of a company is not under a duty to co-operate with an administrative receiver if the company in question is in fact solvent. The possible confusion is made worse by the absence of any statutory definition of "insolvent" company, though there is a definition of "insolvency" in

s. 247(1) (and of "onset of insolvency" in ss. 240(3) and 245(5), of "goes into insolvent liqui-dation" in ss. 214(6) and 216(7), and of "becomes insolvent" in CDDA 1986, s. 6(2)). "Insolvency" in ss. 247(1), 240(3) and 245(5) plainly refers to the various types of insolvency *proceedings* (liquidation, administration, administrative receivership, etc.), while "insolvent" in ss. 214(6), 214(7) and CDDA 1986, s. 6(2) is concerned with the company's financial state. (To add to the confusion, "insolvent" is given yet another special meaning in two chapters of the rules: see IR 1986, rr. 4.151, 4.173(2).)

In the heading to this Part, the words "which are insolvent" could be taken as meaning "which are the subject of insolvency proceedings"; and "insolvency" could then be construed in accordance with the definition in s. 247(1). This may violate to a degree the more natural con-notation of the word "insolvent"; but it would mean that the whole of Pt. VI could be applied without qualification. The alternative is to take "insolvent" as meaning "not financially viable", which raises serious problems because (1) no definition of "insolvent" is given in the body of this Part, and the word admits of many interpretations (see the note to s. 123); and (2) the whole of Pt. VI would be subject to limitations which the text of the Act does not specify.

It is probably the law that headings within a statute (in contrast to marginal notes) may be looked at to resolve an ambiguity in the sections that are grouped under them (Halsbury, *Laws of England*, 4th ed., Vol. 44, para. 818); but it would be unusual to import into the text of an Act qualifications (and ambiguities) which appear only from the words of a heading.

It is therefore submitted that Pt. VI applies to *all* companies, whether financially "solvent" or "insolvent", and that "insolvent" must be read analogously with the definition of "insolvency" in s. 247(1) – that is, as meaning "which are the subject of insolvency proceedings".

OFFICE-HOLDERS

Section 230   Holders of office to be qualified insolvency practitioners

230(1)   **[Administrator]**   Where an administration order is made in relation to a company, the administrator must be a person who is qualified to act as an insolvency practitioner in relation to the company.

230(2)   **[Administrative receiver]**   Where an administrative receiver of a company is appointed, he must be a person who is so qualified.

230(3)   **[Liquidator]**   Where a company goes into liquidation, the liquidator must be a person who is so qualified.

230(4)   **[Provisional liquidator]**   Where a provisional liquidator is appointed, he must be a person who is so qualified.

230(5)   **[Official receiver]**   Subsections (3) and (4) are without prejudice to any enactment under which the official receiver is to be, or may be, liquidator or pro-visional liquidator.

(Former provisions: IA 1985, ss. 95(1), (2), 96(1))

General note

This section requires that a person appointed to any of the various offices mentioned shall be qualified to act as an insolvency practitioner in relation to the company in question. The term "act as an insolvency practitioner" (in relation to a company) is defined by s. 388(1), and "quali-fied" and "qualified ... in relation to" by s. 390(2) and s. 390(3) respectively. It is an offence under s. 389 for a person to act as an insolvency practitioner in relation to a company at a time when he is not qualified to do so.

There is no reference in s. 230 to the nominee or the supervisor of a voluntary arrangement under Pt. I of the Act, which is a little odd since each of these is required also to be a "qualified" insolvency practitioner (see ss. 1(2), 2(4), 4(2), 7(5)).

A receiver who is not an administrative receiver is not required to be a qualified insolvency practitioner, but there are specific prohibitions in ss. 30, 31, 51(3) on the appointment of corpor-ate bodies and undischarged bankrupts as receivers.

S. 230(5)

The official receiver is an officer of the court and is responsible directly to it and to the Secretary of State (see s. 400(2)). He is not subject to the regulatory régime introduced by this Act for private insolvency practitioners.

Section 231   Appointment to office of two or more persons

231(1)   [Application]   This section applies if an appointment or nomination of any person to the office of administrator, administrative receiver, liquidator or pro-visional liquidator—

(a) relates to more than one person, or

(b) has the effect that the office is to be held by more than one person.

231(2)   [Declaration in appointment or nomination]   The appointment or nomi-nation shall declare whether any act required or authorised under any enactment to be done by the administrator, administrative receiver, liquidator or provisional liqui-dator is to be done by all or any one or more of the persons for the time being holding the office in question.

(Former provision: IA 1985, ss. 95(1), (2), 96(2))

General note

There are very few references in the present Act to joint appointments, but under the normal rules of statutory interpretation words in the singular may be taken to include the plural (Interpretation Act 1978, s. 6(c)), and (if it were needed) this section adds further confirmation.

Section 231 makes no reference to the possibility of making a joint appointment to the post of nominee or supervisor of a voluntary arrangement, but it appears from s. 7(6) that this, too, is contemplated by the Act: see the note to that provision.

Section 232   Validity of office-holder's acts

232   The acts of an individual as administrator, administrative receiver, liquidator or provisional liquidator of a company are valid notwithstanding any defect in his appointment, nomination or qualifications.

(Former provisions: IA 1985, ss. 95(1), (2), 96(3))

General note

This is a standard-form provision, similar to that applicable to directors (CA 1985, s. 285). It could not operate, however, to protect acts done where there was no power to appoint at all – e.g. where an administrative receiver is purportedly appointed under an invalid instrument. (See, on this latter point, s. 34 above, and on void appointments generally, *Morris* v *Kanssen & Ors* [1946] AC 459, *Rolled Steel Products (Holdings) Ltd* v *British Steel Corporation & Ors* [1986] Ch. 246; (1984) 1 BCC 99,158.)

The protection conferred by s. 232 is confined to acts done by an *individual*. A body corporate is not qualified to act as an insolvency practitioner (s. 390(1)), and it is extremely unlikely that in future there would ever be an attempt to appoint one to hold any of the offices listed in s. 232. It is probably correct to infer from the express limitation of s. 232 to individuals that any act done by such a corporate appointee would be wholly void. In the case of a receiver (not necessarily an administrative receiver), s. 30 adds a further statutory ban on corporate appointments, and it is established that acts done by a receiver appointed in breach of this provision are totally ineffective: see *Portman Building Society* v *Gallwey* [1955] 1 WLR 96.

There is again no reference in this section to the acts of a person as the nominee or supervisor of a voluntary arrangement. The explanation must be that such a person's rôle and functions are not statutory, but depend in each case upon the terms of the arrangement.

MANAGEMENT BY ADMINISTRATORS, LIQUIDATORS, ETC.

Section 233   Supplies of gas, water, electricity, etc.

233(1)   [Application]   This section applies in the case of a company where—

(a) an administration order is made in relation to the company, or

(b) an administrative receiver is appointed, or

(c) a voluntary arrangement under Part I, approved by meetings summoned under section 3, has taken effect, or

(d) the company goes into liquidation, or

(e) a provisional liquidator is appointed;

and **"the office-holder"** means the administrator, the administrative receiver, the supervisor of the voluntary arrangement, the liquidator or the provisional liquidator, as the case may be.

233(2)   [If request by office-holder]   If a request is made by or with the concurrence of the office-holder for the giving, after the effective date, of any of the supplies mentioned in the next subsection, the supplier—

(a) may make it a condition of the giving of the supply that the office-holder personally guarantees the payment of any charges in respect of the supply, but

(b) shall not make it a condition of the giving of the supply, or do anything which has the effect of making it a condition of the giving of the supply, that any outstanding charges in respect of a supply given to the company before the effective date are paid.

233(3)   **[Supplies in s. 233(2)]**   The supplies referred to in subsection (2) are—

(a) a public supply of gas,

(b) a public supply of electricity,

(c) a supply of water by a water undertaker or, in Scotland, a water authority,

(d) a supply of telecommunication services by a public telecommunications operator.

233(4)   **[Effective date]**   "The effective date" for the purposes of this section is whichever is applicable of the following dates—

(a) the date on which the administration order was made,

(b) the date on which the administrative receiver was appointed (or, if he was appointed in succession to another administrative receiver, the date on which the first of his predecessors was appointed),

(c) the date on which the voluntary arrangement was approved by the meetings summoned under section 3,

(d) the date on which the company went into liquidation,

(e) the date on which the provisional liquidator was appointed.

233(5)   **[Definitions]**   The following applies to expressions used in subsection (3)—

(a) **"public supply of gas"** means a supply of gas by the British Gas Corporation or a public gas supplier within the meaning of Part I of the Gas Act 1986,

(b) **"public supply of electricity"** means a supply of electricity by a public electricity supplier within the meaning of Part I of the Electricity Act 1989,

(c) **"water authority"** means the same as in the Water (Scotland) Act 1980, and

(d) **"telecommunication services"** and **"public telecommunications operator"** mean the same as in the Telecommunications Act 1984, except that the former does not include local delivery services within the meaning of Part II of the Broadcasting Act 1990.

(Former provisions: IA 1985, ss. 95, 97)

General note

This section (and its counterpart in bankruptcy, s. 372 below) implements a recommendation of the Cork Committee (*Report*, para. 1462). Prior to the present Act, a supplier of goods like gas or water or services such as the telephone was able, by virtue of its monopoly position, to compel the payment of an account incurred before the commencement of a liquidation or receivership by threatening to cut off the connection unless the arrears were paid in full or payment was personally guaranteed by the liquidator or receiver. If the supply was essential for the preservation of the company's assets (e.g. livestock or frozen food), there was little choice but to pay, and so the supplier could have its debt paid in priority even to the statutory preferential creditors. The legality of this practice was upheld in *Wellworth Cash & Carry (North Shields) Ltd v North Eastern Electricity Board* (1986) 2 BCC 99,265. This section prohibits further resort to this practice. The supplier may require the "office-holder" to undertake personal responsibility for payment for any *new* supply, but may not make the provision of a new supply conditional upon receiving payment or security for the old.

In s. 233(3)(*b*) the words "public supply of electricity" were substituted by the Electricity Act 1989, s. 112(1) and Sch. 16, para. 35(1), (2)(*a*) as from 31 March 1990: see the Electricity Act 1989, s. 113(2) and SI 1990 No. 117 (C. 4); the former words read as follows: "a supply of electricity by an Electricity Board".

In s. 233(3)(*c*) the words "a water undertaker" were substituted for the former words "statutory water undertakers" by the Water Act 1989, s. 190(1) and Sch. 25, para. 78(1), as from 1 September 1989: see the Water Act 1989, ss. 4, 194(4) and SI 1989 Nos. 1146 (C. 37) and 1530 (C. 51).

Section 233(5)(*b*) was substituted by the Electricity Act 1989, s.112(1) and Sch. 16, para. 35(1), (2) (*b*) as from 31 March 1990: see the Electricity Act 1989, s. 113(2) and SI 1990 No. 117 (C. 4), art. 3(*a*), Sch. 1; the former words read as follows: "'Electricity Board' means the same as in the Energy Act 1983".

In s. 233(5)(*d*) the words "local delivery services within the meaning of Part II of the Broadcasting Act 1990" were substituted by the Broadcasting Act 1990, s. 203(1) and Sch. 20, para. 43 as from 1 January 1991: see SI 1990 No. 2347 (C. 61), art. 3, Sch. 2; the former words read as follows: "services consisting in the conveyance of programmes included in cable programme services (within the meaning of the Cable and Broadcasting Act 1984)".

S. 233(1)

The section extends to a voluntary arrangement under Pt. I, provided that it has taken effect, as well as to the other situations listed, and "office-holder" is accordingly defined to include the supervisor of such a scheme.

S. 233(2)

The "effective date" is defined by s. 233(4).

S. 233(3)

The terms used in this subsection are explained in s. 233(5). The scope of the section is confined to statutory undertakers and similar bodies which are under a legal obligation to provide a service to the public: a private supplier of, e.g. gas or water is not affected.

S. 233(4)

The phrase "go into liquidation" is defined in s. 247(2): see the note to that subsection.

S. 233(5)

The reference to "a public supply of gas" in s. 233(3) and the definition of that term here were added during the passage of the legislation through Parliament, anticipating the privatisation of the British Gas Corporation.

Section 234   Getting in the company's property

234(1)   [Application]   This section applies in the case of a company where—

   (a) an administration order is made in relation to the company, or

   (b) an administrative receiver is appointed, or

   (c) the company goes into liquidation, or

   (d) a provisional liquidator is appointed;

and **"the office-holder"** means the administrator, the administrative receiver, the liquidator or the provisional liquidator, as the case may be.

234(2) [Court's powers]   Where any person has in his possession or control any property, books, papers or records to which the company appears to be entitled, the court may require that person forthwith (or within such period as the court may direct) to pay, deliver, convey, surrender or transfer the property, books, papers or records to the office-holder.

234(3) [Application of s. 234(4)]   Where the office-holder—

(a) seizes or disposes of any property which is not property of the company, and

(b) at the time of seizure or disposal believes, and has reasonable grounds for believing, that he is entitled (whether in pursuance of an order of the court or otherwise) to seize or dispose of that property,

the next subsection has effect.

234(4) [Liability of office-holder]   In that case the office-holder—

(a) is not liable to any person in respect of any loss or damage resulting from the seizure or disposal except in so far as that loss or damage is caused by the office-holder's own negligence, and

(b) has a lien on the property, or the proceeds of its sale, for such expenses as were incurred in connection with the seizure or disposal.

(Former provisions: IA 1985, ss. 95(1), (2), 98)

S. 234(1), (2)

The present section replaces CA 1985, s. 551, which applied only to a winding up by the court, and extends its provisions to every kind of winding up and to all other "insolvency" procedures except a voluntary arrangement. The office-holder may invoke the assistance of the court to get possession of the company's property and records.

An order under s. 234 should not be sought *ex parte*, except perhaps in very exceptional circumstances: *Re First Express Ltd* [1991] BCC 782.

Under earlier provisions corresponding to the present section, the courts had held that its procedure was not appropriate to determine questions of disputed ownership, but in *Re London Iron & Steel Co. Ltd* [1990] BCC 159 Warner J held that the words "to which the company appears to be entitled", coupled with the comprehensive rules laid down in Pt. 7 of IR 1986, are now of sufficient scope to enable the court to settle such matters. But the court has no such power where the question of ownership falls to be determined by a foreign court: *Re Leyland DAF Ltd, Talbot & Anor v Edcrest Ltd* [1994] BCC 166.

In a winding up by the court, the powers conferred on the court by this section are exercisable by the liquidator or provisional liquidator: see IR 1986, r. 4.185. The liquidator is thus empowered to impose the requirement on his own authority.

No sanction is spelt out either in the Act or in the rules for a failure to comply with a requirement imposed under this subsection. No doubt such a failure could be dealt with under the inherent powers of the court, even in the case where the requirement is imposed by a liquidator.

S. 234(3), (4)

These provisions give an immunity to the office-holder (and a lien for his expenses) where he mistakenly but bona fide seizes or disposes of property which does not belong to the company. The protection is given whether or not he has acted in pursuance of a court order granted under s. 234(2) – although such an order would go a long way towards establishing his good faith.

The immunity is "in respect of any loss or damage resulting from the seizure or sale" (negligence apart). It does not appear to extend to liability for the wrongful interference *per se*, and so the owner would not be prevented from suing to establish his right to the return of the property itself or the proceeds of its sale.

It was held in *Welsh Development Agency Ltd* v *Export Finance Co* [1992] BCC 270 that (notwithstanding the wide definition of "property" in s. 436) the protection given to office-holders by these subsections extends only to the seizure and disposal of tangible property, and that they do not apply to wrongful dealings with choses in action.

Section 235   Duty to co-operate with office-holder

235(1)   [Application]   This section applies as does section 234; and it also applies, in the case of a company in respect of which a winding-up order has been made by the court in England and Wales, as if references to the office-holder included the official receiver, whether or not he is the liquidator.

235(2)   [Duty to give information, etc.]   Each of the persons mentioned in the next subsection shall—

(a) give to the office-holder such information concerning the company and its promotion, formation, business, dealings, affairs or property as the office-holder may at any time after the effective date reasonably require, and

(b) attend on the office-holder at such times as the latter may reasonably require.

235(3)   [Persons in s. 235(2)]   The persons referred to above are—

(a) those who are or have at any time been officers of the company,

(b) those who have taken part in the formation of the company at any time within one year before the effective date,

(c) those who are in the employment of the company, or have been in its employment (including employment under a contract for services) within that year, and are in the office-holder's opinion capable of giving information which he requires,

(d) those who are, or have within that year been, officers of, or in the employment (including employment under a contract for services) of, another company which is, or within that year was, an officer of the company in question, and

(e) in the case of a company being wound up by the court, any person who has acted as administrator, administrative receiver or liquidator of the company.

235(4)   ["The effective date"]   For the purposes of subsections (2) and (3), **"the effective date"** is whichever is applicable of the following dates—

(a) the date on which the administration order was made,

(b) the date on which the administrative receiver was appointed or, if he was appointed in succession to another administrative receiver, the date on which the first of his predecessors was appointed,

(c) the date on which the provisional liquidator was appointed, and

(d) the date on which the company went into liquidation.

235(5) **[Penalty for non-compliance]** If a person without reasonable excuse fails to comply with any obligation imposed by this section, he is liable to a fine and, for continued contravention, to a daily default fine.

(Former provisions: IA 1985, ss. 95(1), (2), 99)

General note

In imposing on the former officers and employees of the company, and others, a new statutory duty to "co-operate" with the liquidator or other office-holder by giving him such information as he may reasonably require (and to attend for this purpose on the office-holder), this section supplements the traditional powers to have such persons examined either publicly (s. 133) or privately (s. 236) before the court. No court order is required under the present provisions.

Information and documents obtained by the office-holder pursuant to this section may properly be disclosed to the Secretary of State so that he may determine whether director disqualification proceedings should be brought. This is so even though the office-holder has given an assurance that the information or documents will be used only for the purposes of the administration, since such disclosure is within "the purposes of the administration" (*Re Polly Peck International plc, ex parte the joint administrators* [1994] BCC 15).

S. 235(1)

The situations to which the section applies, and the consequent definition of "office-holder", are the same as are described in s. 234(1). A voluntary arrangement is excluded. Where the liquidator in a winding up by the court in England and Wales is not the official receiver, the official receiver as well as the private liquidator has the powers conferred by the section.

S. 235(2), (3)

The "effective date" is defined in s. 235(4) below.

For the meaning of the term "officer", see the note to s. 206(3).

The extension of "employment" to include employment under a contract for services is wide enough to include accountants and others who have rendered professional services to the company.

The phrases "as the office-holder may reasonably require" and "in the office-holder's opinion" are matters left by the statute to the office-holder's discretion, but would no doubt be subject to the general powers of the court to control an office-holder if he were acting unreasonably; and in any event the question of reasonableness could be raised as a defence if a prosecution were brought.

S. 235(4)

A company "goes into liquidation" at the times described in s. 247(2): see the note to that subsection.

S. 235(5)

On penalties, see s. 430 and Sch. 10.

The duty imposed by this section may also be enforced by court order– e.g. where a director has failed to submit a statement of affairs when required by an office-holder to do so: see IR 1986, r. 7.20, and *Re Wallace Smith Trust Co. Ltd* [1992] BCC 707. For other relevant rules, see rr. 4.39ff.

Section 236   Inquiry into company's dealings, etc.

236(1) **[Application]** This section applies as does section 234; and it also applies in the case of a company in respect of which a winding-up order has been made by the court in England and Wales as if references to the office-holder included the official receiver, whether or not he is the liquidator.

236(2) **[Court's powers]**   The court may, on the application of the office-holder, summon to appear before it—

  (a) any officer of the company,

  (b) any person known or suspected to have in his possession any property of the company or supposed to be indebted to the company, or

  (c) any person whom the court thinks capable of giving information concerning the promotion, formation, business, dealings, affairs or property of the company.

236(3) **[Powers re account, production]**   The court may require any such person as is mentioned in subsection (2)(a) to (c) to submit an affidavit to the court containing an account of his dealings with the company or to produce any books, papers or other records in his possession or under his control relating to the company or the matters mentioned in paragraph (c) of the subsection.

236(4) **[Application of s. 236(5)]**   The following applies in a case where—

  (a) a person without reasonable excuse fails to appear before the court when he is summoned to do so under this section, or

  (b) there are reasonable grounds for believing that a person has absconded, or is about to abscond, with a view to avoiding his appearance before the court under this section.

236(5) **[Court's power re warrant]**   The court may, for the purpose of bringing that person and anything in his possession before the court, cause a warrant to be issued to a constable or prescribed officer of the court—

  (a) for the arrest of that person, and

  (b) for the seizure of any books, papers, records, money or goods in that person's possession.

236(6) **[Court authorisation re custody]**   The court may authorise a person arrested under such a warrant to be kept in custody, and anything seized under such a warrant to be held, in accordance with the rules, until that person is brought before the court under the warrant or until such other time as the court may order.

(Former provisions: IA 1985, ss. 95(1), (2), 100(1), (2), (6))

General note

This power of the court to summon persons to appear before it for examination was formerly provided for by CA 1985, s. 561, but that section was confined in its scope to a winding up by the court. It is now extended to other forms of corporate "insolvency" proceedings, although not to a voluntary arrangement. An examination conducted under this section is private, in contrast to the public examination of officers and others which may be ordered under s. 133.

    The court's discretion under this section is unfettered, although it is generally exercised along fairly well-settled lines. There are overriding requirements that the examination should be necessary in the interests of the winding up, and that it should not be oppressive or unfair to the respondent (*Re Embassy Art Products Ltd* (1987) 3 BCC 292, *Re Adlards Motor Group Holding Ltd* [1990] BCLC 68, and see also *British & Commonwealth Holdings plc (Joint Administrators)* v *Spicer & Oppenheim, Re British & Commonwealth Holdings plc (No. 2)*

[1993] AC 426, [1992] BCC 977). As a general (but not invariable) rule, an office-holder may not apply for examination if he has made a firm decision to commence proceedings against the respondent (*Re Castle New Homes Ltd* [1979] 1 WLR 1075; [1979] 2 All ER 775, as explained in *Cloverbay Ltd (Joint Administrators)* v *Bank of Credit and Commerce International SA (Re Cloverbay Ltd (No. 2)*) [1991] Ch. 90; [1990] BCC 414). But even the fact that criminal charges have already been brought against the respondent does not constitute an absolute bar to the making of an order (*Re Arrows Ltd (No. 2)* [1992] BCC 446). The court has to balance the importance to the office-holder of obtaining the information against the degree of oppression to the person sought to be examined, bearing in mind that the office-holder's views should be afforded great weight but are not determinative. The case for making an order against an officer or former officer of the company will usually be stronger than it would be against a third party; and an order for oral examination is much more likely to be oppressive than an order for the production of documents (*Cloverbay Ltd*, above). But (even in the case of a third party) an application is not necessarily unreasonable because it is inconvenient for the respondent or may cause him considerable work, or may make him vulnerable to future claims (*British & Commonwealth Holdings* case, above). It may be oppressive to seek an order for examination without prior notice to the respondents or without first having asked for the information by letter or some similar means, although such a course of action would be justified in some exceptional cases (*Re Embassy Art Products Ltd*, above).

Any doubts which there might have been on the question whether a respondent could be excused from complying with an order under s. 236 on the ground of self-incrimination were set at rest by a series of cases in 1992 – at least in the case where he is an officer or former officer of the insolvent company. The relevant cases are: *Re Jeffrey S Levitt Ltd* [1992] Ch. 457; [1992] BCC 137, not following *Re Barlow Clowes (Gilt Managers) Ltd (No. 2)* (Ferris J, unreported, 31 July 1990), *Re AE Farr Ltd & Ors* [1992] BCC 151 (where Ferris J decided not to follow his earlier judgment) and *Bishopsgate Investment Management Ltd (in provisional liquidation)* v *Maxwell & Anor (Re Bishopsgate Investment Management Ltd, Mirror Group Newspapers plc & Anor* v *Maxwell and Ors)* [1993] Ch. 1; [1992] BCC 222. But the fact that the privilege against self-incrimination has been impliedly abrogated by statute is a factor which can be taken into account when the court exercises its discretion whether or not to make an order ([1993] Ch. 1 at p. 63; [1992] BCC 222 at p. 262). Where the person concerned is not an officer or former officer, the plea of self-incrimination may be available (see the Australian case *O'Toole* v *Mitcham* (1978) CLC ¶40–429).

In *Re Brook Martin & Co. (Nominees) Ltd* [1993] BCLC 328, the directors of the company against whom a s. 236 order was sought were also the company's solicitors, and they raised a plea of professional privilege. Vinelott J held that no privilige could be asserted in respect of documents which belonged to the company itself. In regard to documents where the privilege arose through acts done on behalf of other clients, he left open the question whether it could, in exceptional circumstances, be overridden by an order under s. 236.

The transcripts of the examination of a person under this section attract legal professional privilege (*Dubai Bank Ltd* v *Galadari & Ors* (1989) 5 BCC 722), but this is subject to the powers of the court to allow inspection under r. 9.5(2).

The object of an order under s. 236 was said by Browne-Wilkinson V-C in the *Cloverbay Ltd* case ([1991] Ch. 90 at p. 102; [1990] BCC 415 at pp. 419–420) to be limited to enabling the office-holder "to get sufficient information to reconstitute the state of knowledge that the company should possess. In my judgment its purpose is not to put the company in a better position than it would have enjoyed if liquidation or administration had not supervened." But in *British & Commonwealth Holdings plc (Joint Administrators)* v *Spicer & Oppenheim (Re British & Commonwealth Holdings plc (No. 2)* [1993] AC 426; [1992] BCC 977, the House of Lords rejected this narrow approach, holding that an order could properly be made extending to all documents (and, it would appear, all information) which the office-holder reasonably required to have to carry out his functions.

In some early cases decided under the section, an order was made on terms that the record should not be used in subsequent criminal proceedings, or disclosed to the Serious Fraud Office (e.g. *Re Arrows Ltd (No. 2)* [1992] BCC 125 and *Re Arrows Ltd (No. 4)* (at first instance) [1992] BCC 987). But in the light of the rulings in *Rank Film Distributors Ltd* v *Video Information Centre* [1982] AC 380 and *AT & T Istel Ltd* v *Tully* [1992] QB 315 (cases decided on analogous statutory provisions) it has since been accepted that the civil courts have no jurisdiction to impose a condition on the use by prosecuting authorities in criminal proceedings of evidence given in the civil proceedings, such as a condition of the kind described: see the *Bishopsgate Investment Management Ltd* case [1992] Ch. 1 at p. 19; [1992] BCC 222 at p. 228 and *Re Arrows Ltd (No. 4); Hamilton & Anor* v *Naviede* in the House of Lords [1994] BCC 641.

In *Re Headington Investments Ltd & Ors, ex parte Maxwell* [1993] BCC 500, the Court of Appeal held that there was no public interest immunity to prevent the disclosure of s. 236 transcripts to the prosecution or regulatory authorities and that, if such disclosure is made, a person facing actual or potential prosecution was not entitled to have simultaneous disclosure made to him: the material would in due course be made available to him in the criminal proceedings, and any question of unfairness or prejudice was a matter for the judge at trial.

For the rules and procedure governing the examinations, see IR 1986, rr. 9.1ff. Application is made to the court by the office-holder. Although in many, if not most, cases it may be appropriate for the application to be made *ex parte*, Vinelott J in *Re Maxwell Communications Corporation plc, Homan & Ors* v *Vogel & Ors* [1994] BCC 741 said that some good reason must be shown to justify this course: if the person affected is given notice it may enable the scope of the order to be clarified and in this and in other ways save time and costs.

The applicant submits to the court an unsworn statement of the grounds on which the application is being made (r. 9.2(1)). The statement is confidential, and may not be inspected by anyone, without an order of the court, other than the persons mentioned in r. 9.5(2). It had been the invariable practice since *Re Gold Co.* (1879) 12 ChD 77 that this statement should not be disclosed to the person against whom the order was sought – i.e. that the court would never exercise its discretion to allow inspection by such a person. However, in *Re British & Commonwealth Holdings plc (No. 1)* [1992] Ch. 342; [1992] BCC 165, the Court of Appeal decided to depart from this practice, and ruled instead that where an application has been made to have the order set aside, inspection of the statement should prima facie be allowed if the court is of the opinion that otherwise it might be unable fairly or properly to dispose of the application. It is for the office-holder to satisfy the court that confidentiality in whole or in part would nevertheless be appropriate.

In *Re Seagull Manufacturing Co. Ltd (in liquidation)* [1993] Ch. 345; [1993] BCC 241 the Court of Appeal, affirming Mummery J [1992] Ch. 128; [1991] BCC 550, held that the public examination provisions of s. 133 have extra-territorial effect, and Mummery J in particular contrasted s. 133 with the powers under ss. 236–237 which, he said, did not extend beyond the jurisdiction. However, the Court of Session in *McIsaac & Anor, Petitioners; Joint Liquidators of First Tokyo Index Trust Ltd* [1994] BCC 410, rejected a submission that a s. 236 order could not be made against a person resident in New York. Lord Cameron of Lochbroom said (at p. 412): "The effectiveness of the court's powers to make an order, and hence the propriety of making an order, ... will then depend on whether the court can use effectively the provisions of s. 426." Since the United States was a "relevant country or territory" for the purposes of s. 426, the co-operation of the New York Court could be expected. In *Re a Company No. 003318 of 1987 (Oriental Credit Ltd)* [1988] Ch. 204; (1987) 3 BCC 564 it was held that the court has the power to grant an order restraining a person from leaving the jurisdiction pending the holding of an examination under this section.

In *Re Barlow Clowes Gilt Managers Ltd* [1992] Ch. 208; [1991] BCC 608, statements had been given voluntarily by various persons to a representative of the liquidators of a company under the threat, express or implicit, that if they did not do so voluntarily the liquidators would have recourse to their powers under ss. 236–237. Other persons, who had been charged with criminal offences in connection with the affairs of the company, sought to have access to the transcripts of these interviews; but Millett J held that the information contained in the transcripts could be used only for purposes connected with the liquidation. The liquidators had, in this instance, given the interviewees assurances of confidentiality which would not have been needed had the information been obtained under s. 236; but even so, information obtained in a private examination under the statute could also have been disclosed only to the extent that it was for the benefit of the liquidation. (On the giving of undertakings by office-holders, see further *McIsaac & Anor, Petitioners* [1994] BCC 410.)

Information or documents obtained by an office-holder pursuant to s. 236 are subject to an obligation of confidentiality, but this may in an appropriate case be waived by the court: *Re a Company No. 00534 of 1993* [1993] BCC 734. In that case administrative receivers were allowed to disclose information to the bank which had appointed them. Information may also be disclosed to the Secretary of State for the purpose of considering whether to bring disqualification proceedings: see the notes to s. 235, above.

The court has no jurisdiction to authorise anyone other than the applicant (or a solicitor or counsel instructed by him) to examine the witness, except in the rare case where there are two office-holders and IR 1986, r. 9.4(2) applies: *Re Maxwell Communications Corporation plc, Homan & Ors* v *Vogel & Ors* [1994] BCC 741.

An order under s. 236 becomes inoperative if the office-holder in whose favour it has been granted ceases to hold office: *Re Kingscroft Insurance Co. Ltd* [1994] BCC 343.

S. 236(1)

This provision is identical with s. 235(1): see the note to that subsection.

S. 236(2)

Only the office-holder has standing to make application to the court. The former legislation was not so restricted and other persons, such as contributories, were commonly allowed to apply.

The list of persons who may be summoned is shorter than that in s. 235(2), but it is potentially of wider scope in view of the discretion given to the court by para. (*c*).

S. 236(3)

The requirement as to an affidavit is new, and should significantly shorten the proceedings in most cases.

S. 236(4)–(6)

These provisions, especially when read in conjunction with s. 237, are more extensive and detailed than the former CA 1985, s. 561(4), which was confined to the apprehension of the person summoned, and also stipulated that he had to be tendered a reasonable sum for his expenses. The repealed section also stated (s. 561(3)) that if a person (e.g. a solicitor) who was ordered to produce a document relating to the company claimed a lien on it, such production should be without prejudice to the lien. The new section does not reproduce this provision. In many cases the lien will now be unenforceable by virtue of s. 246, which will allow the office-holder to demand possession of the document and so make the need for an order for its production superfluous. But even in those cases where s. 246 does not apply (e.g. where the office-holder is an administrative receiver, or where the document gives a title to property and is held as such (s. 246(3)), an order for production under s. 236 will not affect the lien: *Ex parte Bramble* (1880) 13 ChD 885, *Re Aveling Barford Ltd & Ors* [1989] 1 WLR 360; (1988) 4 BCC 548).

For relevant rules, see IR 1986, rr. 7.23, 7.24.

Section 237   Court's enforcement powers under s. 236

237(1)   [Order to deliver property]   If it appears to the court, on consideration of any evidence obtained under section 236 or this section, that any person has in his possession any property of the company, the court may, on the application of the office-holder, order that person to deliver the whole or any part of the property to the officer-holder at such time, in such manner and on such terms as the court thinks fit.

237(2) [Order to pay money due] If it appears to the court, on consideration of any evidence so obtained, that any person is indebted to the company, the court may, on the application of the office-holder, order that person to pay to the office-holder, at such time and in such manner as the court may direct, the whole or any part of the amount due, whether in full discharge of the debt or otherwise, as the court thinks fit.

237(3) [Order re examination of persons] The court may, if it thinks fit, order that any person who if within the jurisdiction of the court would be liable to be summoned to appear before it under section 236 or this section shall be examined in any part of the United Kingdom where he may for the time being be, or in a place outside the United Kingdom.

237(4) [Examination on oath etc.] Any person who appears or is brought before the court under section 236 or this section may be examined on oath, either orally or (except in Scotland) by interrogatories, concerning the company or the matters mentioned in section 236(2)(c).

(Former provisions: IA 1985, s. 100(3)–(5), (7))

General note

Most of these detailed provisions supplementing s. 236 are new. There is some overlap with s. 234.

S. 237(4)

This subsection is broadly equivalent to CA 1985, s. 561(2).

ADJUSTMENT OF PRIOR TRANSACTIONS (ADMINISTRATION AND LIQUIDATION)

Section 238 Transactions at an undervalue (England and Wales)

238(1) [Application] This section applies in the case of a company where—

(a) an administration order is made in relation to the company, or

(b) the company goes into liquidation;

and **"the office-holder"** means the administrator or the liquidator, as the case may be.

238(2) [Application to court by office-holder] Where the company has at a relevant time (defined in section 240) entered into a transaction with any person at an undervalue, the office-holder may apply to the court for an order under this section.

238(3) [Court order] Subject as follows, the court shall, on such an application, make such order as it thinks fit for restoring the position to what it would have been if the company had not entered into that transaction.

238(4) [Interpretation] For the purposes of this section and section 241, a company enters into a transaction with a person at an undervalue if—

(a) the company makes a gift to that person or otherwise enters into a transaction with that person on terms that provide for the company to receive no consideration, or

(b) the company enters into a transaction with that person for a consideration the value of which, in money or money's worth, is significantly less than the value, in money or money's worth, of the consideration provided by the company.

238(5) **[Restriction on court order]** The court shall not make an order under this section in respect of a transaction at an undervalue if it is satisfied—

(a) that the company which entered into the transaction did so in good faith and for the purpose of carrying on its business, and

(b) that at the time it did so there were reasonable grounds for believing that the transaction would benefit the company.

(Former provisions: IA 1985, ss. 95(1)(a), (b), 101(1) (part), (2), (3))

General note

To put the present section into context, it is necessary to discuss briefly the reforms made by IA 1985 in response to the recommendations made in Chapter 28 of the Cork Committee's *Report*, which appear in the present Act under the headings "transactions at an undervalue"; "preferences"; and "provisions against debt avoidance" (see respectively ss. 238 and 339; ss. 239 and 340; and ss. 423ff). The concern of the Committee was to state the existing law more logically and accurately and remove doubts as to its scope, to make the law relating to corporate insolvency and individual bankruptcy broadly the same, and to remove the former emphasis on fraud which was implicit in the traditional terms "fraudulent conveyance" and "fraudulent preference".

The new concept of "transactions at an undervalue" is based on the former BA 1914, s. 42, which declared void against the trustee in bankruptcy settlements of property made by a person who became bankrupt within a stated period thereafter. This section has now been replaced, in the case of an individual bankrupt, by the broader provisions of IA 1986, s. 339, and (in accordance with the recommendations of the Cork Committee (*Report*, para. 1237)) applied to corporate insolvency as well as bankruptcy by the present section.

The former rules relating to "fraudulent preferences" (BA 1914, s. 44; CA 1985, s. 615) are redefined (under the neutral title of "preferences") by IA 1986, s. 239 for company insolvencies and s. 340 for bankruptcies. As is indicated by the new designation, the law has been changed so that it is no longer necessary to show a *dishonest* intention to give the creditor in question an improper preference over creditors generally.

Finally, the law governing "fraudulent conveyances", which can be traced back to a statute of Elizabeth I, has been brought up to date and appears in IA 1986 as ss. 423ff, which apply to both companies and individuals. Once again, the word "fraudulent" has been pointedly dropped from the new statutory provision.

There is a considerable overlap between the three topics here discussed, and particularly, as regards transactions at an undervalue, between ss. 238 and 423ff. The distinguishing features of the latter sections are: (1) they are not confined to situations where a company is in liquidation or subject to an administration order, or an individual is bankrupt, (2) there is no time limit, and (3) application may be made to the court by any "victim" of the transaction, and not merely the "office-holder" or trustee in bankruptcy; but (4) the requisite intention to put assets out of reach of creditors or prejudice their interests must be shown.

Sections 238–241 deal with transactions at an undervalue and preferences involving companies incorporated in England and Wales: see s. 440(2)(*a*). Equivalent provision is made for

Scotland, with the distinctive labels "gratuitous alienations" and "unfair preferences", by ss. 242, 243; but these sections follow in detail the rather different bankruptcy law of Scotland.

The provisions of ss. 238–243 do not operate retrospectively so as to invalidate a transaction which occurred before the present Act came into force, unless it could have been invalidated under the corresponding provisions of the former law: see Sch. 11, para. 9.

Sections 238 and 239 (and possibly also ss. 423ff) are to be construed as having extraterritorial effect, so that an order may be made against a person who is outside the jurisdiction: *Re Paramount Airways Ltd (in administration)* [1993] Ch. 223; [1992] BCC 416. There are, however, two safeguards: first, the court has a discretion under the sections as to the order which it may make. If a foreign element is involved, it will have to be satisfied that, in respect of the relief sought against him, the respondent is a person sufficiently connected with this jurisdication for it to be just and proper to make the order. Secondly, a person who wishes to serve the proceedings has to obtain the leave of the court to do so under IR 1986, r. 12.12.

In the context of the financial markets, no order may be made under s. 238 in relation to a market contract to which a recognised investment exchange or clearing house is a party or which is entered into under its default rules, or a disposition of property in pursuance of such a market contract: see CA 1989, s. 165, and the note on p. 3.

S. 238(1)

This and the next three sections apply in a narrower range of situations than do earlier sections in this Part, i.e. only to company administrations and liquidations, and "office-holder" means the administrator or liquidator. It does not appear that the official receiver, where he is not the liquidator, is given standing also, as he is by s. 235.

For the meaning of "goes into liquidation", see s. 247(2).

S. 238(2)

Only the office-holder, as defined in s. 238(1), may make application. This may be contrasted with the wider category permitted to apply for an order under s. 423: see s. 424(1).

A "relevant time" for the purposes of this section is defined by reference not only to the calendar but also to the company's solvency: see s. 240.

S. 238(3)

This subsection (and the corresponding s. 239(3) relating to preferences) is curiously worded. On the face of it, the use of the word "shall" and the concluding phrase "for restoring the position to what it would have been if the company had not entered into that transaction" would appear to tie the court's hands, so that (subject only to s. 238(5)) it *must* make an order, and then only an order which restores the status quo. But the words "as it thinks fit" and the many and varied examples of possible orders (set out in s. 241) which it is open to the court to make clearly indicate that the applicant is not entitled to demand any particular form of order as of right, and this consideration, coupled with the fact that the court's jurisdiction in this sphere is equitable in origin, must lead to the conclusion that the court may in its discretion decline to make any order at all. In *Re Paramount Airways Ltd (in administration)* [1993] Ch. 223 at p. 239; [1992] BCC 416 at p. 425, Nicholls V-C endorsed this view.

S. 238(4)

A "transaction at an undervalue" may include an outright gift (para. (*a*)), but where consideration is given, the discrepancy in value must be "significant" (para. (*b*)).

In the leading case of *Re M C Bacon Ltd* [1990] BCC 78, Millett J held that the creation of security over a company's assets was not a transaction at an undervalue. Section 238(4)(*b*), he said, requires a comparison to be made between the value obtained by the company for the transaction and the value of the consideration provided by the company. Both values have to be measurable in money or money's worth and have to be considered from the company's point of view. The mere creation of security over the company's assets does not deplete them or diminish their value. Loss by the company of the ability to apply the proceeds of the assets otherwise than in satisfaction of the secured debt is not capable of valuation in money terms, nor is the consideration received by the company in return.

Similar reasoning would very possibly be applicable to a guarantee given by a company of another's indebtedness.

S. 238(5)

These provisions bear a distinct resemblance to the "three-fold test" of Eve J in *Re Lee, Behrens and Co. Ltd* [1932] 2 Ch. 46, which has had a chequered history in the context of the doctrine of ultra vires (and, in that context, was later declared to be largely inappropriate: see *Rolled Steel Products (Holdings) Ltd* v *British Steel Corporation & Ors* [1986] Ch. 246; (1984) 1 BCC 99,158). It may well be that s. 238(5) will prove most difficult to apply in relation to the very types of transaction illustrated by the facts of the two cases mentioned: the payment of gratuities and pensions to employees and their dependants, and the giving of guarantees (especially within corporate groups). There may be problems, too, with regard to the "genuineness" of directors' remuneration (cf. *Re Halt Garage (1964) Ltd* [1982] 3 All ER 1016), but it is very likely that the present section will make it easier to impeach such transactions.

Section 239   Preferences (England and Wales)

239(1)   [Application]   This section applies as does section 238.

239(2)   [Application to court by office-holder]   Where the company has at a relevant time (defined in the next section) given a preference to any person, the office-holder may apply to the court for an order under this section.

239(3)   [Court order]   Subject as follows, the court shall, on such an application, make such order as it thinks fit for restoring the position to what it would have been if the company had not given that preference.

239(4)   [Interpretation]   For the purposes of this section and section 241, a company gives a preference to a person if—

(a) that person is one of the company's creditors or a surety or guarantor for any of the company's debts or other liabilities, and

(b) the company does anything or suffers anything to be done which (in either case) has the effect of putting that person into a position which, in the event of the company going into insolvent liquidation, will be better than the position he would have been in if that thing had not been done.

239(5)   [Restriction on court order]   The court shall not make an order under this section in respect of a preference given to any person unless the company which gave the preference was influenced in deciding to give it by a desire to produce in relation to that person the effect mentioned in subsection (4)(b).

239(6)   [Presumption]   A company which has given a preference to a person connected with the company (otherwise than by reason only of being its employee) at the time the preference was given is presumed, unless the contrary is shown, to have been influenced in deciding to give it by such a desire as is mentioned in subsection (5).

239(7)   [Interpretation re preference]   The fact that something has been done in pursuance of the order of a court does not, without more, prevent the doing or suffering of that thing from constituting the giving of a preference.

(Former provisions: IA 1985, ss. 95(1)(a), (b), 101(1)(part), (4)–(7), (11))

General note

The former law relating to "fraudulent preferences", as contained in CA 1985 s. 615 and earlier Companies Acts, had long been thought unsatisfactory and, in particular, as the Cork Committee pointed out (*Report*, para. 1244), the word "fraudulent" was both inaccurate and misleading. The Committee recommended that the term "fraudulent preference" should be replaced by "voidable preference". The draftsman, however, has rejected this suggestion (and the expression "undue preference", which is common in Australia) in favour of simply "preference", except in Scotland, for which "unfair preference" has been chosen. These differences over terminology are unimportant. The object of the change, at least in regard to England and Wales, is to remove the implication that an improper motive must be shown (and proved to the high standard which that charge requires), and to reflect the fact that under the newly defined law it is not necessary for the liquidator even to show that the *dominant* intention of the company was to give the one creditor a preference. It need now only be established that the company was "influenced by a desire" to bring about a preference, and in some cases the burden of proof on this point is reversed (see s. 239(5), (6)).

In the first reported case under the new section, *Re M C Bacon Ltd* [1990] BCC 78, Millett J "emphatically protested" against the citation of cases decided under the old law: these, he said, could not be of any assistance in construing the language of the new statute, which had been so completely and deliberately changed.

In the context of the financial markets, no order may be made under s. 239 in relation to a market contract to which a recognised investment exchange or clearing house is a party or which is entered into under its default rules, or a disposition of property in pursuance of such a market contract: see CA 1989, s. 165, and the note on p. 3.

For the corresponding provisions in bankruptcy, see s. 340; and for the position in Scotland, see s. 243.

S. 239(1)

Section 238, which is referred to, restricts the jurisdiction to cases where a company is under administration or in liquidation, and defines "office-holder" accordingly.

S. 239(2)

"Relevant time" refers both to the period within which the preference is given and to the company's solvency: see s. 240(2). This is the time when the decision to enter into the transaction is taken, and not the time when the transaction is effected (see *Re M C Bacon Ltd* (above) at p. 88). The terms "preference" and "any person" are explained in s. 239(4).

S. 239(3)

The court's powers are similar to those conferred by s. 238(3) and include the power to decline to make any order: see the note to that subsection. In *Re Kayford Ltd* [1975] 1 WLR 279 a mail-order company in anticipation of possible insolvency had placed money sent as prepayments by its customers into a special bank account, and it was held that these sums were impressed with a trust which took them out of the insolvent estate when the company was later wound up. Under the law as it then stood, no question of fraudulent preference arose, but such an arrangement could now fall within s. 239. If this were so, the circumstances might well justify the court in refusing to make an order.

S. 239(4)

Examples of a preference given by the Cork Committee in its *Report* (para. 1208) were: paying the whole or part of a debt, providing security or further security for an existing debt, and returning goods which have been delivered but not paid for.

The phrase "going into insolvent liquidation" is not expressly defined for the purposes of the present section as it is for ss. 214 and 216. That may, however, be a more helpful definition than anything that can be inferred from ss. 240 and 247.

S. 239(5)

The phrase "was influenced . . . by a desire to produce" replaces language contained in BA 1914, s. 44(1) which had been construed as requiring the person who sought to have the payment or other transaction avoided to show that it had been made "with the dominant intention to prefer" the particular creditor. The Cork Committee (*Report*, paras. 1248–58), by a majority, took the view that the requirement of an intention (or dominant intention) to prefer should be retained, and rejected the alternative (established in Australia and the US and adopted in Scotland: see s. 243) that it should be sufficient that the conduct in question had the *effect* of giving a preference.

In *Re M C Bacon Ltd* [1990] BCC 78 at p. 87, Millett J held that it is no longer necessary to establish a *dominant* intention to prefer, nor is it sufficient to establish an *intention:* there must be a *desire* to produce the effect mentioned in the section. "Intention is objective, desire is subjective. A man can choose the lesser of two evils without desiring either . . . A man is not to be taken as *desiring* all the necessary consequences of his actions . . . It will still be possible to provide assistance to a company in financial difficulties provided that the company is actuated only by proper commercial considerations. Under the new regime a transaction will not be set aside as a voidable preference unless the company positively wished to improve the creditor's position in the event of its own insolvent liquidation." Accordingly, in that case, it was held that a decision by a company to give its bank a charge to secure existing borrowings (when the only alternative, if the bank withdrew its support, was liquidation) was not voidable as a preference under the present section.

The Cork Committee (*Report*, para. 1256) took the view that pressure for payment by the creditor should continue, as under the former law, to afford a defence to a claim for the avoidance of a preference. The decision in *Re M C Bacon Ltd* (above) suggests that the new section will be so interpreted "unless the company positively wished to improve the creditor's position in the event of its own insolvency".

S. 239(6)

This important change, introduced on the recommendation of the Cork Committee, reverses the burden of proof in regard to intention when the beneficiary of the preference is a person "connected with" the company. This phrase is defined by s. 249 and is fully discussed in the note to that section (but the special exception of employees in the present provision should be noted). The effect of s. 239(6) – not least when s. 240(2) is also taken into account – will make it very difficult indeed for directors and controlling shareholders and their relatives, and other companies in the same group (all of which are "connected persons"), to retain the benefit of a preferential payment under the new legislation. For cases where the statutory presumption against connected persons was held to have been rebutted on the evidence, see *Re Beacon Leisure Ltd* [1991] BCC 213 and *Re Fairway Magazines Ltd* [1992] BCC 924. These may be contrasted with *Re D K G Contractors Ltd* [1990] BCC 903, where the presumption was applied.

Section 240   "Relevant time" under ss. 238, 239

240(1)   **[Relevant time]**   Subject to the next subsection, the time at which a company enters into a transaction at an undervalue or gives a preference is a relevant time if the transaction is entered into, or the preference given—

(a) in the case of a transaction at an undervalue or of a preference which is given to a person who is connected with the company (otherwise than by reason only of being its employee), at a time in the period of 2 years ending with the onset of insolvency (which expression is defined below),

(b) in the case of a preference which is not such a transaction and is not so given, at a time in the period of 6 months ending with the onset of insolvency, and

(c) in either case, at a time between the presentation of a petition for the making of an administration order in relation to the company and the making of such an order on that petition.

240(2) [Where not relevant time] Where a company enters into a transaction at an undervalue or gives a preference at a time mentioned in subsection (1)(a) or (b), that time is not a relevant time for the purposes of section 238 or 239 unless the company—

(a) is at that time unable to pay its debts within the meaning of section 123 in Chapter VI of Part IV, or

(b) becomes unable to pay its debts within the meaning of that section in consequence of the transaction or preference;

but the requirements of this subsection are presumed to be satisfied, unless the contrary is shown, in relation to any transaction at an undervalue which is entered into by a company with a person who is connected with the company.

240(3) [Onset of insolvency] For the purposes of subsection (1), the onset of insolvency is—

(a) in a case where section 238 or 239 applies by reason of the making of an administration order or of a company going into liquidation immediately upon the discharge of an administration order, the date of the presentation of the petition on which the administration order was made, and

(b) in a case where the section applies by reason of a company going into liquidation at any other time, the date of the commencement of the winding up.

(Former provision: IA 1985, s. 101(8)–(11))

General note

Both ss. 238 and 239 apply only to a transaction or preference which takes place at a "relevant time". This section explains that term. Two factors may be in issue in determining the question whether a time is a "relevant time": (1) whether the transaction takes place within one of the three periods set out in s. 240(1), and (2) whether the company is, at that time, insolvent, or becomes insolvent as a result of the transaction.

Once again, as with s. 239(6), the burden of proof (this time, of "insolvency") varies with the position of the other party to the transaction: it is on the liquidator or administrator in the normal case, but on that other party if he is a person "connected with" the company (s. 240(2)). Moreover, in the case of a preference, the period by reference to which a "relevant time" is reckoned is increased from six months to two years if the other party is a "connected person" (s. 240(1)(*a*), (*b*)). In regard to a transaction at an undervalue, the period is two years in all cases (s. 240(1)(*a*).)

It is, in principle, possible, for a company's bank to come within the definition of a "connected person" for the purposes of the present group of sections, if its involvement in the company's affairs is such as to make it a "shadow director": see *Re a Company No. 005009 of 1987* (1988) 4 BCC 424 and ss. 249(*a*), 251.

S. 240(1), (3)

The periods for the purposes of ss. 238, 239 are determined by reference to a date which is defined by s. 240(3) and is very misleadingly called "the onset of insolvency". This has nothing whatever to do with the company's inability to pay its debts (although, to add to the confusion, that issue does matter for the wholly unrelated questions raised by s. 240(2)). The "onset of insolvency" means one of the following:

(1) in an administration, the date of presentation of the petition for an administration order (s. 240(3)(*a*));

(2) in a liquidation which has immediately followed an administration, the date of presentation of the petition for the administration order (s. 240(3)(*a*)); or

(3) in any other liquidation, the date of the commencement of the winding up.

(On the "commencement" of a winding up, see the notes to ss. 86 and 129, where the reference is, more precisely, to the "time" rather than the "date" of commencement. It must be assumed that this variation in language is deliberate: see the note to s. 86.)

The "relevant time" is a time within the six-month or two-year period ending with the "onset of insolvency" as defined in (1), (2) or (3) above, *plus*, in cases (1) and (2), the period between the presentation of the administration petition and the making of the administration order (s. 240(1)(*c*)). The period will be two years for all undervalue-transactions (s. 240(1)(*a*)); in the case of a preference, it will be two years if the recipient of the preference is a "connected person", and six months if he is not; but employees are again not treated as "connected persons" for this purpose (s. 240(1)(*a*), (*b*)). (For the meaning of "connected person", see the note to s. 249.)

S. 240(2)

Section 240(1) and (3) are concerned only with the calculation of time, in the ordinary sense. However, s. 240(2) introduces a further factor: a "time" will not be a "relevant" time (and therefore a transaction at an undervalue or a preference not liable to be set aside) unless the company is then unable to pay its debts, or becomes unable to pay its debts as a result of the impugned transaction. In other words, a company may enter into any transaction at an undervalue that it chooses or give any creditor a preference without violating ss. 238 or 239, so long as it is solvent or so long as the event takes place outside the period leading up to its being put under administration or into liquidation that is specified in s. 240(1): only if both these conditions are satisfied will the transaction have occurred at a "relevant time" so as to bring those sections into play. (Note, however, that s. 423 may be applicable if the necessary intent can be proved.)

The definition of "unable to pay its debts", for the purpose of s. 240(2), is the same as in s. 123, that is, either (1) deemed unable to pay because of an unpaid statutory demand for over £750 or an unsatisfied execution, or (2) proved unable in either a "commercial" or a "balance-sheet" sense. Inability may also be inferred from the fact that the company has invoices which it has not paid: *Re DKG Contractors Ltd* [1990] BCC 903. For further discussion, see the note to s. 123.

Finally, as regards inability to pay debts, there is the question of the burden of proof. This, in relation to a transaction at an undervalue, lies on the liquidator or administrator when the other party is not a "connected person", but on that other party if he is. (There is no similar provision in relation to a preference, but the question of the company's solvency will be relevant, at least indirectly, to the question of intention for which s. 239(6) places the burden of proof on the "connected person".) On the meaning of "connected person", see the note to s. 249; but note that s. 240(2) rather oddly does not repeat the exception for employees which appears in ss. 239(6) and 240(1)(*a*). (This may be a drafting error, in that the former provision corresponding to ss. 238–240, IA 1985, s. 101, applied the employee exception to all connected persons in the provision: see IA 1985, s. 101(11).)

Section **241**   Orders under ss. 238, 239

241(1)   [Extent of orders]   Without prejudice to the generality of sections 238(3) and 239(3), an order under either of those sections with respect to a transaction or preference entered into or given by a company may (subject to the next subsection)—

(a) require any property transferred as part of the transaction, or in connection with the giving of the preference, to be vested in the company,

(b) require any property to be so vested if it represents in any person's hands the application either of the proceeds of sale of property so transferred or of money so transferred,

(c) release or discharge (in whole or in part) any security given by the company,

(d) require any person to pay, in respect of benefits received by him from the company, such sums to the office-holder as the court may direct,

(e) provide for any surety or guarantor whose obligations to any person were released or discharged (in whole or in part) under the transaction, or by the giving of the preference, to be under such new or revived obligations to that person as the court thinks appropriate,

(f) provide for security to be provided for the discharge of any obligation imposed by or arising under the order, for such an obligation to be charged on any property and for the security or charge to have the same priority as a security or charge released or discharged (in whole or in part) under the transaction or by the giving of the preference, and

(g) provide for the extent to which any person whose property is vested by the order in the company, or on whom obligations are imposed by the order, is to be able to prove in the winding up of the company for debts or other liabilities which arose from, or were released or discharged (in whole or in part) under or by, the transaction or the giving of the preference.

241(2)   [Restriction on orders]   An order under section 238 or 239 may affect the property of, or impose any obligation on, any person whether or not he is the person with whom the company in question entered into the transaction or (as the case may be) the person to whom the preference was given; but such an order—

(a) shall not prejudice any interest in property which was acquired from a person other than the company and was acquired in good faith and for value, or prejudice any interest deriving from such an interest, and

(b) shall not require a person who received a benefit from the transaction or preference in good faith and for value to pay a sum to the office-holder, except where that person was a party to the transaction or the payment is to be in respect of a preference given to that person at a time when he was a creditor of the company.

241(2A)   [Presumption re good faith in s. 241(2)]   Where a person has acquired an interest in property from a person other than the company in question, or has received a benefit from the transaction or preference and at the time of that acquisition or receipt—

(a) he had notice of the relevant surrounding circumstances and of the relevant proceedings, or

(b) he was connected with, or was an associate of, either the company in question or the person with whom that company entered into the transaction or to whom that company gave the preference,

then, unless the contrary is shown, it shall be presumed for the purposes of paragraph (a) or (as the case may be) paragraph (b) of subsection (2) that the interest was acquired or the benefit was received otherwise than in good faith.

241(3)   [Relevant surrounding circumstances in s. 241(2A)(a)]   For the purposes of subsection (2A)(a), the relevant surrounding circumstances are (as the case may require)—

(a) the fact that the company in question entered into the transaction at an undervalue; or

(b) the circumstances which amounted to the giving of the preference by the company in question;

and subsections (3A) to (3C) have effect to determine whether, for those purposes, a person has notice of the relevant proceedings.

241(3A)   [Notice where administration order made]   In a case where section 238 or 239 applies by reason of the making of an administration order, a person has notice of the relevant proceedings if he has notice—

(a) of the fact that the petition on which the administration order is made has been presented, or

(b) of the fact that the administration order has been made.

241(3B)   [Notice where liquidation on discharge of administration order]   In a case where section 238 or 239 applies by reason of the company in question going into liquidation immediately upon the discharge of an administration order, a person has notice of the relevant proceedings if he has notice—

(a) of the fact that the petition on which the administration order is made has been presented;

(b) of the fact that the administration order has been made; or

(c) of the fact that the company has gone into liquidation.

241(3C)   [Notice where liquidation at other times]   In a case where section 238 or 239 applies by reason of the company in question going into liquidation at any other time, a person has notice of the relevant proceedings if he has notice—

(a) where the company goes into liquidation on the making of a winding-up order, of the fact that the petition on which the winding-up order is made has been presented or of the fact that the company has gone into liquidation;

(b) in any other case, of the fact that the company has gone into liquidation.

241(4)   [Application of s. 238–241]   The provisions of sections 238 to 241 apply without prejudice to the availability of any other remedy, even in relation to a transaction or preference which the company had no power to enter into or give.

(Former provisions: IA 1985, ss. 95(1), 102)

General note

The present section sets out in detail various orders which the court is empowered to make when avoiding a preference or a transaction at an undervalue under ss. 238, 239, although it is not intended to limit the general powers of the court. It is designed in part to meet defects in the former law which the Cork Committee (*Report*, paras. 1270–1276) identified as likely to arise when a company's obligation is backed by a surety or guarantor. For example, a payment may have been made to a creditor with a view to releasing the surety or guarantor rather than preferring the creditor, and the creditor may have released the guarantee and returned any security given before the payment is struck down as a preference. The creditor would then in all probability have had no remedy against the guarantor.

Section 241 was amended by the Insolvency (No. 2) Act 1994, ss. 1(1) and 6, with effect from 26 July 1994, as follows:

(1) in s. 241(2), in both para. (*a*) and para. (*b*), the words "in good faith and for value" were substituted for the former wording, "in good faith, for value and without notice of the relevant circumstances";

(2) new subsection (2A) was inserted, and

(3) new subsections (3), (3A), (3B) and (3C) were substituted for the former subsection (3).

The repealed s. 241(3) read as follows:

"For the purposes of this section the relevant circumstances, in relation to a transaction or preference, are—

(a) the circumstances by virtue of which an order under section 238 or (as the case may be) 239 could be made in respect of the transaction or preference if the company were to go into liquidation, or an administration order were made in relation to the company, within a particular period after the transaction is entered into or the preference given, and

(b) if that period has expired, the fact that the company has gone into liquidation or that such an order has been made."

The amendments have effect only in relation to interests acquired and benefits received after the Act came into force (s. 6(3)). For the corresponding provisions in relation to bankruptcy, see s. 342 below (as amended).

The amendment, which stems from a recommendation of the Law Society, is designed to get over a perceived difficulty in relation to unregistered land, where a bona fide purchaser might have been taken to have had notice of a transaction that was liable to be set aside under either s. 238 or 239 in the event of a later insolvency. By removing the references to notice from s. 241(2), a buyer of unregistered land is put into the same position as a buyer of registered land.

S. 241(1)

Section 241(1) is "subject to the next subsection", which protects bona fide purchasers for value.

The court's discretion extends to refusing to make any order: see the note to s. 238(3).

Paragraphs (*e*) and (*f*) will empower the court to impose revived or new obligations on a guarantor or surety if his former obligations were released or discharged by the transaction which is later impugned, and to reinstate a security with the same priority as a former security or charge.

S. 241(2)

This subsection allows third parties to be brought into the proceedings and orders to be made against them or their property instead of, or as well as, against the party with whom the company has dealt in the transaction under challenge. In particular, it will enable an order for repayment to be made directly against a surety or guarantor when the real object of a payment made by the company to a particular creditor was to release the guarantee rather than prefer the creditor. Bona fide third parties acquiring property or benefits for value will, however, be protected. Nevertheless, the concluding words of para. (*b*) indicate that the person who was the actual counterparty to a transaction at an undervalue or who himself, as a creditor, received the benefit of a preference will not be protected merely because he acted in good faith and for value. (This is in keeping with the traditional view taken in relation to fraudulent preferences, that it is the intention of the company to give an improper preference which is crucial, and that the state of mind of the creditor himself is immaterial.)

S. 241(2A)–(3C)

These subsections, which were substituted for the former s. 241(3) as described above, relate to two categories of person who have acquired an interest in property otherwise than from the company itself: (1) one who had notice of the "relevant surrounding circumstances" *and* of the "relevant proceedings" at the material time; and (2) one who was "connected with" or an "associate" of the company or the counterparty to the transaction. (For the meaning of the terms "connected with" and "associate", see ss. 249 and 435, below.) As against such a person, there is a (rebuttable) statutory presumption of a lack of good faith, thereby depriving him of the protection of s. 241(2). The requirement in s. 241(2A)(*a*) that the person (if not a "connected person" or "associate") should have notice of the insolvency proceedings as well as of the relevant surrounding circumstances is new, and is the major change effected by the 1994 reform.

Sections 241(3)–(3C) clarify the meaning of the terms "the relevant surrounding circumstances" and "notice of the relevant proceedings" used in s. 241(2A).

S. 241(4)

The phrase "a transaction which the company had no power to enter into or give" is, no doubt, a reference to the common-law doctrine of ultra vires, which has been abolished for almost all purposes by CA 1989, s. 108 (which inserted a revised s. 35(1) into CA 1985 with effect from 4 February 1991 (see SI 1991 No. 2569 (C. 68), art. 4(*a*), 7)). However, the question of corporate capacity still has some relevance in relation to charitable companies (see CA 1989, s. 111, amending Charities Act 1960 by the insertion of a new s. 30B, effective from the same date), and so the doctrine of ultra vires could apply in this restricted area. It is possible also that s. 241(1) could be construed as extending to illegal transactions, e.g. those in contravention of the "financial assistance" provisions contained in CA 1985, s. 151ff. This subsection will allow the court to override the general law by, e.g. ordering the recipient of an ultra vires loan or gift to give security for its due repayment (s. 241(1)(*f*)).

Section 242   Gratuitous alienations (Scotland)

242(1)   [Challenge to alienations]   Where this subsection applies and—

    (a) the winding up of a company has commenced, an alienation by the company is challengeable by—

        (i) any creditor who is a creditor by virtue of a debt incurred on or before the date of such commencement, or

        (ii) the liquidator;

    (b) an administration order is in force in relation to a company, an alienation by the company is challengeable by the administrator.

242(2) [Application of s. 242(1)] Subsection (1) applies where—

(a) by the alienation, whether before or after 1st April 1986 (the coming into force of section 75 of the Bankruptcy (Scotland) Act 1985), any part of the company's property is transferred or any claim or right of the company is discharged or renounced, and

(b) the alienation takes place on a relevant day.

242(3) [Interpretation of s. 242(2)(b)] For the purposes of subsection (2)(b), the day on which an alienation takes place is the day on which it becomes completely effectual; and in that subsection **"relevant day"** means, if the alienation has the effect of favouring—

(a) a person who is an associate (within the meaning of the Bankruptcy (Scotland) Act 1985) of the company, a day not earlier than 5 years before the date on which—

(i) the winding up of the company commences, or

(ii) as the case may be, the administration order is made; or

(b) any other person, a day not earlier than 2 years before that date.

242(4) [Duties of court on challenge under s. 242(1)] On a challenge being brought under subsection (1), the court shall grant decree of reduction or for such restoration of property to the company's assets or other redress as may be appropriate; but the court shall not grant such a decree if the person seeking to uphold the alienation establishes—

(a) that immediately, or at any other time, after the alienation the company's assets were greater than its liabilities, or

(b) that the alienation was made for adequate consideration, or

(c) that the alienation—

(i) was a birthday, Christmas or other conventional gift, or

(ii) was a gift made, for a charitable purpose, to a person who is not an associate of the company,

which, having regard to all the circumstances, it was reasonable for the company to make:

Provided that this subsection is without prejudice to any right or interest acquired in good faith and for value from or through the transferee in the alienation.

242(5) ["Charitable purpose" in s. 242(4)] In subsection (4) above, **"charitable purpose"** means any charitable, benevolent or philanthropic purpose, whether or not it is charitable within the meaning of any rule of law.

242(6) [Interpretation] For the purposes of the foregoing provisions of this section, an alienation in implementation of a prior obligation is deemed to be one for which there was no consideration or no adequate consideration to the extent that the prior obligation was undertaken for no consideration or no adequate consideration.

242(7) [Rights of challenge] A liquidator and an administrator have the same right as a creditor has under any rule of law to challenge an alienation of a company made for no consideration or no adequate consideration.

242(8) [Scotland only] This section applies to Scotland only.

(Former provisions: CA 1985, s. 615A; Bankruptcy (Scotland) Act 1985, Sch. 7, para. 20)

General note

This section deals with the setting aside of transactions at an undervalue (or the granting of "other redress": s. 242(4)) in Scotland. It differs on a number of points of substance from s. 238, following in these respects the Bankruptcy (Scotland) Act 1985, s. 34.

The rights of creditors under Scots common law, including the right to challenge a debtor's action as a gratuitous alienation, survive the present legislation: see *Bank of Scotland* v *Pacific Shelf (Sixty Two) Ltd & Anor* (1988) 4 BCC 457.

In the context of the financial markets, no decree may be granted under s. 242 in relation to a market contract to which a recognised investment exchange or clearing house is a party or which is entered into under its default rules, or a disposition of property in pursuance of such a market contract: see CA 1989, s. 165, and the note on p. 3.

S. 242(1)

In the case of a liquidation, a creditor is given standing to challenge under para. (*a*)(i), in contrast with s. 238(2), which restricts the right to the "office-holder". A liquidator does not require sanction under s. 167 to commence s. 242 proceedings – see *Dyer* v *Hyslop* 1994 SCLR 171. Such proceedings are not taken on behalf of or in the name of the company.

S. 242(2), (3)

The periods of five years and two years fixed by s. 242(3) are different from those prescribed for England and Wales by s. 240(1), but correspond with those that apply in the bankruptcy of an individual in Scotland: see the Bankruptcy (Scotland) Act 1985, s. 34. The meaning of "associate" under the Bankruptcy (Scotland) Act 1985, s. 74, is similar to, but not co-extensive with, that of "associate" as defined for the purposes of this Act: see s. 435 and the note to that section. For England and Wales, the term used by s. 240(1) is "connected person", which is slightly wider in scope: see s. 249.

S. 242(4)

"Gratuitous alienation" includes a transaction for consideration at an undervalue (para. (*b*)); "reasonable" gifts and charitable donations may be justified (para. (*c*)). The requirement as to solvency is here more logically placed with the substantive aspects of the statutory provision, rather than linked to the definition of "relevant day": contrast s. 240(2). See *McLuckie Bros Ltd* v *Newhouse Contracts Ltd* 1993 SLT 641.

Section 243 Unfair preferences (Scotland)

243(1) [Application of s. 243(4)] Subject to subsection (2) below, subsection (4) below applies to a transaction entered into by a company, whether before or after 1st April 1986, which has the effect of creating a preference in favour of a creditor to the prejudice of the general body of creditors, being a preference created not earlier than 6 months before the commencement of the winding up of the company or the making of an administration order in relation to the company.

243(2) [Non-application of s. 243(4)] Subsection (4) below does not apply to any of the following transactions—

(a) a transaction in the ordinary course of trade or business;

(b) a payment in cash for a debt which when it was paid had become payable, unless the transaction was collusive with the purpose of prejudicing the general body of creditors;

   (c) a transaction whereby the parties to it undertake reciprocal obligations (whether the performance by the parties of their respective obligations occurs at the same time or at different times) unless the transaction was collusive as aforesaid;

   (d) the granting of a mandate by a company authorising an arrestee to pay over the arrested funds or part thereof to the arrester where—

      (i) there has been a decree for payment or a warrant for summary diligence, and

      (ii) the decree or warrant has been preceded by an arrestment on the dependence of the action or followed by an arrestment in execution.

243(3)　[Interpretation of s. 243(1)]　For the purposes of subsection (1) above, the day on which a preference was created is the day on which the preference became completely effectual.

243(4)　[Persons who may challenge]　A transaction to which this subsection applies is challengeable by—

   (a) in the case of a winding up—

      (i) any creditor who is a creditor by virtue of a debt incurred on or before the date of commencement of the winding up, or

      (ii) the liquidator; and

   (b) in the case of an administration order, the administrator.

243(5)　[Duties of court on s. 243(4) challenge]　On a challenge being brought under subsection (4) above, the court, if satisfied that the transaction challenged is a transaction to which this section applies, shall grant decree of reduction or for such restoration of property to the company's assets or other redress as may be appropriate:

   Provided that this subsection is without prejudice to any right or interest acquired in good faith and for value from or through the creditor in whose favour the preference was created.

243(6)　[Rights of challenge]　A liquidator and an administrator have the same right as a creditor has under any rule of law to challenge a preference created by a debtor.

243(7)　[Scotland only]　This section applies to Scotland only.

(Former provisions: CA 1985, s. 615B; Bankruptcy (Scotland) Act 1985, Sch. 7, para. 20)

General note

The law relating to unfair preferences in the bankruptcy of individuals is contained in the Bankruptcy (Scotland) Act 1985, s. 36. The present section substantially follows that provision and differs in material respects from s. 239 – most notably in not requiring any proof of a desire to prefer. For the survival of the common law, see *Bank of Scotland v Pacific Shelf (Sixty Two) Ltd & Anor* (1988) 4 BCC 457.

  In the context of the financial markets, no decree may be granted under s. 243 in relation to a market contract to which a recognised investment exchange or clearing house is a party or which is entered into under its default rules, or a disposition of property in pursuance of such a market contract: see CA 1989, s. 165, and the note on p. 3.

S. 243(1), (2)

The vital factor, in contrast with the subjective requirement regarding intent in s. 239(1), (5), is whether the transaction has the *effect* of creating a preference: the intention of the parties is not relevant, unless there is collusion (s. 243(2)(*b*), (*c*)). For the purposes of s. 243(2)(*c*) there must be a *strict* equivalence of reciprocal obligations – *Nicoll* v *Steelpress (Supplies) Ltd* 1993 SLT 533.

S. 243(4)

As with s. 242, a creditor has standing to bring proceedings in the case of a winding up.

Section 244   Extortionate credit transactions

244(1)   [Application]   This section applies as does section 238, and where the company is, or has been, a party to a transaction for, or involving, the provision of credit to the company.

244(2)   [Court order re extortionate transaction]   The court may, on the application of the office-holder, make an order with respect to the transaction if the transaction is or was extortionate and was entered into in the period of 3 years ending with the day on which the administration order was made or (as the case may be) the company went into liquidation.

244(3)   [Extortionate transaction – interpretation]   For the purposes of this section a transaction is extortionate if, having regard to the risk accepted by the person providing the credit—

(a) the terms of it are or were such as to require grossly exorbitant payments to be made (whether unconditionally or in certain contingencies) in respect of the provision of the credit, or

(b) it otherwise grossly contravened ordinary principles of fair dealing;

and it shall be presumed, unless the contrary is proved, that a transaction with respect to which an application is made under this section is or, as the case may be, was extortionate.

244(4)   [Extent of court order]   An order under this section with respect to any transaction may contain such one or more of the following as the court thinks fit, that is to say—

(a) provision setting aside the whole or part of any obligation created by the transaction,

(b) provision otherwise varying the terms of the transaction or varying the terms on which any security for the purposes of the transaction is held,

(c) provision requiring any person who is or was a party to the transaction to pay to the office-holder any sums paid to that person, by virtue of the transaction, by the company,

(d) provision requiring any person to surrender to the office-holder any property held by him as security for the purposes of the transaction,

(e) provision directing accounts to be taken between any persons.

244(5)   [Exercise of powers]   The powers conferred by this section are exercisable in relation to any transaction concurrently with any powers exercisable in relation to that transaction as a transaction at an undervalue or under section 242 (gratuitous alienations in Scotland).

(Former provisions: IA 1985, ss. 95(1)(a), (b), 103)

301

General note

Section 66 of BA 1914, which was formerly applied in the winding up of insolvent companies by CA 1985, s. 612, restricted the rate of interest that could be proved for in a liquidation, in the case of a debt carrying interest, to 5 per cent p.a. In keeping with the recommendations of the Cork Committee (*Report*, para. 1380), s. 66 has now been repealed (see the note to s. 189). The removal of s. 66, without more, would allow proofs in a winding up to include sums representing exorbitant rates of interest; and accordingly the court is given power by this section to re-open credit agreements on the application of a liquidator or administrator. This is in keeping with a recommendation of the Cork Committee (*Report*, para. 1381). The section is modelled on ss. 137–140 of the Consumer Credit Act 1974.

For the corresponding provision in bankruptcy, see s. 343.

S. 244(1)

Section 238 applies to companies that are in liquidation or subject to an administration order. Although s. 238 is confined to England and Wales, it is submitted that the present section extends also to Scotland, for otherwise the reference to Scotland in s. 244(5) would be pointless. This means that the word "applies" in s. 244(1) must be construed with reference only to the different forms of insolvency proceedings and not to questions of geography or jurisdiction (even though the wording of s. 245(1) would suggest the contrary). This interpretation is supported by s. 440(2).

"Credit" is not defined.

S. 244(2)

There is a three-year time limit for the retrospective re-opening of transactions under this section. (Note, however, that the time is reckoned from the date when the company "went into liquidation", in the case of a liquidation, and not from the "commencement of the winding up".)

S. 244(3)

The onus of proof that a transaction was not extortionate is put in every case on to the person who gave the credit.

S. 244(4)

The orders which the court is empowered to make include orders affecting third parties, e.g. sureties.

S. 244(5)

On transactions at an undervalue, see ss. 238, 240, 241.

Section 245 Avoidance of certain floating charges

245(1) [Application] This section applies as does section 238, but applies to Scotland as well as to England and Wales.

245(2) [Invalidity of floating charge] Subject as follows, a floating charge on the company's undertaking or property created at a relevant time is invalid except to the extent of the aggregate of—

(a) the value of so much of the consideration for the creation of the charge as consists of money paid, or goods or services supplied, to the company at the same time as, or after, the creation of the charge,

(b) the value of so much of that consideration as consists of the discharge or reduction, at the same time as, or after, the creation of the charge, of any debt of the company, and

(c) the amount of such interest (if any) as is payable on the amount falling within paragraph (a) or (b) in pursuance of any agreement under which the money was so paid, the goods or services were so supplied or the debt was so discharged or reduced.

245(3)   [Relevant time]   Subject to the next subsection, the time at which a floating charge is created by a company is a relevant time for the purposes of this section if the charge is created—

(a) in the case of a charge which is created in favour of a person who is connected with the company, at a time in the period of 2 years ending with the onset of insolvency,

(b) in the case of a charge which is created in favour of any other person, at a time in the period of 12 months ending with the onset of insolvency, or

(c) in either case, at a time between the presentation of a petition for the making of an administration order in relation to the company and the making of such an order on that petition.

245(4)   [Qualification to s. 245(3)(b)]   Where a company creates a floating charge at a time mentioned in subsection (3)(b) and the person in favour of whom the charge is created is not connected with the company, that time is not a relevant time for the purposes of this section unless the company—

(a) is at that time unable to pay its debts within the meaning of section 123 in Chapter VI of Part IV, or

(b) becomes unable to pay its debts within the meaning of that section in consequence of the transaction under which the charge is created.

245(5)   [Onset of insolvency in s. 245(3)]   For the purposes of subsection (3), the onset of insolvency is—

(a) in a case where this section applies by reason of the making of an administration order, the date of the presentation of the petition on which the order was made, and

(b) in a case where this section applies by reason of a company going into liquidation, the date of the commencement of the winding up.

245(6)   [Value of goods, services etc. in s. 245(2)(a)]   For the purposes of subsection (2)(a) the value of any goods or services supplied by way of consideration for a floating charge is the amount in money which at the time they were supplied could reasonably have been expected to be obtained for supplying the goods or services in the ordinary course of business and on the same terms (apart from the consideration) as those on which they were supplied to the company.

(Former provisions: IA 1985, ss. 95(1)(a), (b), 104; CA 1985, s. 617)

General note

Under CA 1985, s. 617, which this section replaces, a floating charge was declared invalid if it was created within 12 months of the commencement of a winding up (unless it could be proved that the company, immediately after the creation of the charge, was solvent), except to the amount of any cash paid to the company at the time of, or subsequently to the creation of, and in consideration for, the charge. In other words, a floating charge could not be created within that time to secure past indebtedness, but only an advance of "new money".

The present Act not only formulates more elaborate provisions to apply in such circumstances, but introduces several major changes:

(1) "floating charge" is redefined so as to include any charge which was originally created as a floating charge but has since become a fixed charge (s. 251);

(2) the provisions apply in an administration as well as a liquidation;

(3) the section expressly covers some benefits conferred on the company otherwise than by the payment of "cash";

(4) the 12-month period is extended to two years if the chargee is a person "connected with" the company; and

(5) the exception where the company is proved at the material time to have been solvent will not be available to a chargee who is a person "connected with" the company.

The provisions of s. 245 do not apply to invalidate a charge created before the present Act came into force, except to the extent that it could have been invalidated under the previous law: see Sch. 11, para. 9.

S. 245(1)

The section applies where a company is in liquidation or is subject to an administration order.

S. 245(2)

A charge will not be invalidated by this section to the extent that the chargee has increased the company's assets in any of the ways described. The extended wording removes doubts about the scope of the former phrase "cash paid to the company" by stipulating that goods or services supplied to the company or the release of a debt in whole or part will be as good as "new money". Whether paras. (*a*) and (*b*) will themselves be open to a restrictive interpretation is unclear: it is hard to see why other forms of valuable consideration (e.g. the transfer of land or shares) were not included within the reform that was made.

The question whether the payment of money or the supply of goods or services is made "at the same time as" the execution of a charge is one of fact and degree: *Re Shoe Lace Ltd, Power* v *Sharp Investments Ltd & Anor* [1993] BCC 609. In that case, money was advanced in four payments on different dates in April, May, June and on 16 July, following a resolution of the company's directors to grant the debenture in March; but the debenture was not executed until 24 July. The Court of Appeal, affirming Hoffmann J [1992] BCC 367, held that the payments could not be said to have been made at the same time as the execution of the debenture. Sir Christopher Slade, giving the leading judgment, said (at p. 620):

> "In a case were no presently existing charge has been created by any agreement or company resolution preceding the execution of the formal debenture, then . . . no moneys paid before the execution of the debenture will qualify for exemption under the subsection, unless the interval between payment and execution is so short that it can be regarded as minimal and payment and execution can be regarded as contemporaneous."

However, where a promise to execute a debenture creates a present equitable right to a security, and moneys are advanced in reliance on it, any delay between the advances and the execution of the formal instrument of charge is immaterial: the charge has already been "created" and is immediately registrable, so that other creditors of the company will have had the opportunity to learn of its existence (ibid., at p. 619).

In *Re Fairway Magazines Ltd* [1992] BCC 924 it was held, following *Re Orleans Motor Co. Ltd* [1911] 2 Ch. 41, that payments made by the lender directly to the company's bank which reduced its overdraft (and consequently the lender's liability under a personal guarantee) were not payments made "to the company" within the meaning of the section: the money never became available to the company to be used as it liked.

Interest was allowable under the repealed CA 1985, s. 617, as it is under para. (*c*).

S. 245(3)–(5)

These provisions are similar to s. 240, both in their effect and in the very confusing language which is used. For more detailed comment, see the notes to that section: it is necessary to give the reminder that the phrase "the onset of insolvency" is not used with reference to the company's financial state but only with the question whether an administration or liquidation is deemed to have "commenced"; the issue of its financial well-being (or otherwise) is separately dealt with in s. 245(4) in language which avoids the words "solvent" and "insolvent".

To sum up these provisions:

- a floating charge can be retrospectively invalidated within a two-year period for a "connected" chargee, and a 12-month period in other cases; further, if there is, or has been, an administration order in force, the period is extended to include the time between the presentation of the petition and the making of the administration order;

- the "new consideration" exception applies whether the chargee is a connected person or not; and

- the "solvency" exception will now apply only where the chargee is not a connected person (using the term "solvency" in its everyday sense). The burden of establishing "solvency" under CA 1985, s. 617, was put on the person seeking to uphold the charge. This is presumably still the case, although the section does not make the point clear.

The various technical expressions which appear in the present provisions are discussed in more detail in the note to s. 240.

It is, in principle, possible for a company's bank to come within the definition of a "connected person" for the purposes of the present section, if its involvement in the company's affairs is such as to make it a "shadow director": see *Re a Company No. 005009 of 1987* (1988) 4 BCC 424 and ss. 249(*a*), 251.

All the references to time in s. 245(2) are to the time of *creation* of the charge. So it would seem that a floating charge created in favour of A will attract all the disadvantages associated with "connected" chargees if A was a "connected person" at that time, and it will be immaterial that he has since ceased to be so connected. Conversely, if A was not a connected person at the time of creation, but becomes "connected" within the two-year period, his charge will have the more favourable treatment accorded by s. 245(3)(*b*) and (4). Again, if a floating charge is created in favour of A and is later assigned to B, the only relevant question will be whether A was, at the time of creation, a "connected person": it will not matter whether B was then, or was at the time of the assignment, or has since become, a "connected person". There are clearly advantages, if one is a "connected person", of taking a charge by assignment rather than directly and, if one is not, of re-financing with a new charge rather than taking an assignment of a charge from a "connected" chargee – unless in either case the whole arrangement could be challenged as evasive.

S. 245(6)

This subsection deals with the position where goods or services, rather than "new money", is the consideration provided for a charge. It is made clear that it is the true value of the goods or services that counts, and not the price or valuation that the parties themselves have agreed on as the consideration for the supply. The chargee cannot defeat the object of the Act by having the company credit him with an unrealistic sum.

Section 246   Unenforceability of liens on books, etc.

246(1)   [Application]   This section applies in the case of a company where—

(a) an administration order is made in relation to the company, or

(b) the company goes into liquidation, or

(c) a provisional liquidator is appointed;

and **"the office-holder"** means the administrator, the liquidator or the provisional liquidator, as the case may be.

246(2)   [Lien etc. unenforceable]   Subject as follows, a lien or other right to retain possession of any of the books, papers or other records of the company is unenforceable to the extent that its enforcement would deny possession of any books, papers or other records to the office-holder.

246(3)   [Non-application]   This does not apply to a lien on documents which give a title to property and are held as such.

(Former provisions: IA 1985, ss. 95(1)(a), (b), (2), 105)

General note

This section ensures that a liquidator or administrator is not prevented from taking possession of any of the company's books, etc., because a lien is claimed over them (e.g. by a solicitor for outstanding fees). It relates only to liens on "books, papers and other records" and not to liens on other categories of goods, and operates to extinguish the lien (or, at the least, to render it unenforceable to the extent specified in s. 246(2)). Liens not caught by the section remain valid, but in the case of an administration will not be enforceable without the leave of the court under s. 11(3): *Bristol Airport plc & Anor* v *Powdrill & Ors* [1990] Ch. 744 at p. 762 (reported as *Re Paramount Airways Ltd* [1990] BCC 130 at p. 150).

  Note that s. 246 does not apply in favour of an administrative receiver or the supervisor of a voluntary arrangement.

  Section 246 does not apply to Scotland (see s. 440(2)(*a*)); but the corresponding provisions of the Bankruptcy (Scotland) Act 1985, s. 38(4), which are more limited in scope, have been extended to company liquidations by the rules: see the Insolvency (Scotland) Rules 1986 (SI 1986 No. 1915 (s. 139)), r. 4.22(1).

S. 246(3)

The exeption created by s. 246(3) is not limited to the case where the person claiming the lien does so by reason of the fact that the documents in question confer "a title to property" upon him. The words "as such" mean "in circumstances which are such as to give rise to a lien". In other words, it is sufficient that the person has a lien over the documents, and the documents are of a kind which give a title to property to somebody: *Re SEIL Trade Finance Ltd* [1992] BCC 538.

PART VII — INTERPRETATION FOR FIRST GROUP OF PARTS

Section 247   "Insolvency" and "go into liquidation"

247(1)   ["Insolvency"]   In this Group of Parts, except in so far as the context otherwise requires, **"insolvency"**, in relation to a company, includes the approval of a voluntary arrangement under Part I, the making of an administration order or the appointment of an administrative receiver.

247(2)   [Company in liquidation]   For the purposes of any provision in this Group of Parts, a company goes into liquidation if it passes a resolution for voluntary winding up or an order for its winding up is made by the court at a time when it has not already gone into liquidation by passing such a resolution.

(Former provisions: IA 1985, s. 108(3) (part), (4))

S. 247(1)

This meaning of "insolvency" is discussed in the general comment on Pt. VI, preceding s. 230, above, where attention is drawn to the fact that the Act uses the term to describe the various *proceedings*, such as winding up, administration and receivership, which are the subject of the present Act, and not to describe a company's adverse financial situation. The related word "insolvent" is not defined by this section, and at times it appears to be used in the Act in the everyday sense ("goes into insolvent liquidation": s. 214(6)) rather than analogously with the definition of "insolvency" in the present section.

S. 247(2)

The time when a company "goes into liquidation" is to be distinguished from the time when its winding up *commences*: see the notes to ss. 86 and 129. The phrase was the subject of judicial consideration (in connection with the construction of a trust deed) in *Mettoy Pension Trustees Ltd* v *Evans & Ors* [1991] 2 All ER 513, where a meaning in conformity with the definition in the present subsection was approved.

Section 248   "Secured creditor", etc.

248   In this Group of Parts, except in so far as the context otherwise requires—

(a) **"secured creditor"**, in relation to a company, means a creditor of the company who holds in respect of his debt a security over property of the company, and **"unsecured creditor"** is to be read accordingly; and

(b) **"security"** means—

    (i) in relation to England and Wales, any mortgage, charge, lien or other security, and

    (ii) in relation to Scotland, any security (whether heritable or moveable), any floating charge and any right of lien or preference and any right of retention (other than a right of compensation or set off).

(Former provision: IA 1985, s. 108(3) (part)).

General note

The term "security" as here defined does not include the owner's rights under a hire-purchase, conditional sale, chattel leasing or retention of title agreement, although for some purposes (e.g. s. 15(2)) these rights are treated analogously with security interests.

    In *Bristol Airport plc & Anor* v *Powdrill & Ors* [1990] Ch. 744 (reported as *Re Paramount Airways Ltd* [1990] BCC 130) it was held that the statutory right of an airport under the Civil Aviation Act 1982, s. 88, to detain an aircraft for failure to pay outstanding aircraft charges was a "lien or other security" within s. 248(*b*)(i). See also *Exchange Travel Agency Ltd* v *Triton Property Trust plc & Anor* [1991] BCC 341 (landlord's right of re-entry on non-payment of rent held a security).

Section 249   "Connected" with a company

249   For the purposes of any provision in this Group of Parts, a person is connected with a company if—

    (a) he is a director or shadow director of the company or an associate of such a director or shadow director, or

    (b) he is an associate of the company;

and **"associate"** has the meaning given by section 435 in Part XVIII of this Act.

(Former provision: IA 1985, s. 108(5))

General note

The meaning of "associate" (a term which the Act applies in the bankruptcy of individuals as well as in the winding up, etc. of companies) is defined at length in s. 435. The phrase "connected with" a company is used largely to put it beyond doubt that a director or shadow director is always included for the purposes of the statutory provision in question. So, also, will be the "associates" of such a director or shadow director.

    It is, in principle, possible for a company's bank to come within the definition of a "connected person", if its involvement in the company's affairs is such as to make it a "shadow director": see *Re a Company No. 005009 of 1987* (1988) 4 BCC 424.

    For the meaning of "associate", see the note to s. 435; and for "director" and "shadow director", see s. 251.

Section **250** "Member" of a company

250 For the purposes of any provision in this Group of Parts, a person who is not a member of a company but to whom shares in the company have been transferred, or transmitted by operation of law, is to be regarded as a member of the company, and references to a member or members are to be read accordingly.

(Former provision: IA 1985, s. 108(6))

General note

"Member" is defined for the purposes of the Companies Acts by CA 1985, s. 22, and under that definition the term is confined to (1) the subscribers to the memorandum, and (2) those who have agreed to become members and whose names are entered in the register of members. The present provision is designed to include the transferees of shares under unregistered transfers, and the personal representatives of deceased members and others to whom shares have been transmitted by operation of law. It is wide enough, however, to include other categories of person, e.g. holders of share warrants to bearer.

This section was no doubt inserted with the benign intention of ensuring that an unregistered transferee of shares should enjoy the same rights as a member – for instance, to petition for a winding-up order and to vote at meetings of contributories. It appears to be wide enough, however, to impose burdens upon an unregistered transferee as well – for instance, if the shares are not fully paid, to render him directly liable to the company as a contributory for calls on the shares under s. 74. Whether the legislators intended to effect such a radical change in the law by a side-wind must be open to question.

Section **251**   Expressions used generally

251   In this Group of Parts, except in so far as the context otherwise requires—

"administrative receiver" means—

(a) an administrative receiver as defined by section 29(2) in Chapter I of Part III, or

(b) a receiver appointed under section 51 in Chapter II of that Part in a case where the whole (or substantially the whole) of the company's property is attached by the floating charge;

"business day" means any day other than a Saturday, a Sunday, Christmas Day, Good Friday or a day which is a bank holiday in any part of Great Britain;

"chattel leasing agreement" means an agreement for the bailment or, in Scotland, the hiring of goods which is capable of subsisting for more than 3 months;

"contributory" has the meaning given by section 79;

"director" includes any person occupying the position of director, by whatever name called;

"floating charge" means a charge which, as created, was a floating charge and includes a floating charge within section 462 of the Companies Act (Scottish floating charges);

"office copy", in relation to Scotland, means a copy certified by the clerk of court;

"the official rate", in relation to interest, means the rate payable under section 189(4);

"prescribed" means prescribed by the rules;

"receiver", in the expression **"receiver or manager"**, does not include a receiver appointed under section 51 in Chapter II of Part III;

"retention of title agreement" means an agreement for the sale of goods to a company, being an agreement—

    (a) which does not constitute a charge on the goods, but

    (b) under which, if the seller is not paid and the company is wound up, the seller will have priority over all other creditors of the company as respects the goods or any property representing the goods;

"the rules" means rules under section 411 in Part XV; and

"shadow director", in relation to a company, means a person in accordance with whose directions or instructions the directors of the company are accustomed to act (but so that a person is not deemed a shadow director by reason only that the directors act on advice given by him in a professional capacity);

and any expression for whose interpretation provision is made by Part XXVI of the Companies Act, other than an expression defined above in this section, is to be construed in accordance with that provision.

(Former provisions: IA 1985, s. 108(3) (part); CA 1985, ss. 507, 741)

General note

Most of the definitions listed here are self-explanatory. For a discussion of terms defined by reference to other sections, see the notes to those sections.

The term "administrative receiver" may include a receiver of the property of a foreign company: see *Re International Bulk Commodities Ltd* [1993] Ch. 77; [1992] BCC 463 and the notes to s. 29(2), above.

The definition of "business day" in the Act differs from that in the rules, at least in some contexts. See the note to IR 1986, r. 13.13(1).

The definition of "floating charge" is new. The change is discussed in the notes to ss. 175(2) (*b*) and 245.

The definitions of "director" and "shadow director" have been incorporated from CA 1985, s. 741. The *concept* of a shadow director has been a feature of Companies Acts for many decades; the name itself was first introduced by CA 1980, s. 63. In *Re a Company No. 005009 of 1987* (1988) 4 BCC 424 it was recognised that the conduct of a company's bank in relation to its affairs might make it a shadow director.

A shadow director is to be distinguished from a *de facto* director: the terms do not overlap, but are alternatives, and in most if not all cases are mutually exclusive. A *de facto* director is a person who assumes to act as a director and is held out as such by the company, and who claims and purports to be a director, although never actually or validly appointed as such. A shadow director, in contrast, claims not to be a director but claims that others are the directors to the exclusion of himself. An allegation that a person has acted as a *de facto* or shadow director, without distinguishing between the two, is embarrassing: *Re Hydrodan (Corby) Ltd* [1994] BCC 161.

If a parent company is a shadow director of its subsidiary, it does not follow that the directors of the parent company are also, without more, its shadow directors. But where the director of a company is a body corporate, there must be an inference that it is accustomed to act on the directions of others, who will be shadow directors (*Re Hydrodan (Corby) Ltd*, above). There is no assumption that a director who is the nominee of a particular shareholder or creditor is the agent of his appointor or acts under his directions or instructions (*Kuwait Asia Bank EC* v *National Mutual Life Nominees Ltd* [1991] 1 AC 187; [1990] BCC 567).

In *Re Tasbian Ltd (No. 3)* [1992] BCC 358 there was held to be an arguable case that a person appointed as a consultant to a company by an outside investor was a shadow director. The dividing line between the position of a watchdog or adviser and a shadow director was difficult to draw, but there was a serious question to be tried whether the respondent might have crossed over it.

THE SECOND GROUP OF PARTS
INSOLVENCY OF INDIVIDUALS; BANKRUPTCY

Introduction to the Second Group of Parts

Bankruptcy legislation in England can be traced back to 1542, and the system with which practitioners will be familiar was contained in BA 1914 (as amended in 1926 and 1976). This system was the product of the 1883 reforms pushed through by Gladstone and Joseph Chamberlain. In view of this fact it is not surprising that both the Blagden Committee (Cmnd 221) in 1957 and the Cork Committee (Cmnd 8558) in 1982 felt that major revision was long overdue. Part III of IA 1985 did put the law on a modern footing, although its changes were less radical than the Cork Committee had hoped for. The Insolvency Act 1986, ss. 252–385 remodels the 1985 legislation mainly by fragmenting its more cumbersome provisions into several sections. Most of the provisions in the 1985 Act relating to bankruptcy never came into force. When indicating former provisions, both the provisions in the 1985 Act and those of the 1914 legislation will be cited. Indeed cases under the 1914 Act still come before the courts – see for example *Re Dent* [1994] 1 WLR 956.

What are the most obvious reforms introduced by the 1985 Act and now found in the 1986 Act? The bankruptcy procedure has been greatly simplified, with the abolition of the concept of the act of bankruptcy and the intermediate stage of the receiving order. An attempt has been made wherever possible to harmonise bankruptcy procedures with those of company liquidations, although unlike many jurisdictions there is still a distinction between corporate and personal insolvency law. Another reform which is more symbolic than significant in practice is the abolition of the concept of reputed ownership in bankruptcy law (it did not operate on corporate insolvency). Other changes worthy of mention are the rules giving increased protection to the family home (see ss. 336–338), the attempt to produce a viable alternative to bankruptcy via voluntary arrangements (ss. 252–263), plus a host of minor measures designed to streamline and improve the effectiveness of bankruptcy procedures. The liberalising trend dating back to the "Justice" Report (1975) and IA 1976 is again apparent, particularly with the new provisions on discharge (ss. 279 and 280).

Criticisms can be made of the 1986 Act. It is heavily dependent on IR 1986. On the other hand it must be conceded that the 1914 Act was considerably supplemented by BR 1952. The drafting of the provisions of Pt. III of the 1985 Act left much to be desired, and Muir Hunter QC, a leading commentator on bankruptcy law, predicted that this deficiency would lead to an increase in litigation. The drafting of the 1986 Act is much improved.

Finally, it should be noted that ss. 252–385 of the IA 1986 are not the sole source of law on personal insolvency. Parts XII and XIX of the Act also contain provisions that will be important in practice. Criminal bankruptcy (so far as concerns orders which are still in force: see the notes to ss. 264 and 277) is dealt with by the Powers of the Criminal Courts Act 1973, and the

Deeds of Arrangement Act 1914 survives largely intact. Administration orders against judgment debtors remain governed by the County Courts Act 1984 (as amended). Indeed there are still provisions of the Debtors Act 1869 which may return to haunt debtors. Thus in *Woodley* v *Woodley (No. 2)* [1994] 1 WLR 1167 a debtor (who subsequently became bankrupt on his own petition) was threatened with imprisonment by a judge under s. 5 of the 1869 Act for wilfully refusing to pay a judgment debt where he had the means to do so prior to his bankruptcy. On appeal, the committal order was quashed by the Court of Appeal because there was a sufficient degree of doubt as to whether he was deliberately defying the law or had been confused as to his obligations.

The law on personal insolvency in Scotland (or sequestration, as it is termed) is to be found in the Bankruptcy (Scotland) Act 1985 (as amended by the Bankruptcy (Scotland) Act 1993) and associated delegated legislation. Comparable provisions dealing with personal insolvency in Northern Ireland are now contained in the Insolvency (Northern Ireland) Order 1989 (SI 1989 No. 2405) (NI 19), arts. 226–345 in particular.

For a detailed guide to the law and practice of bankruptcy, relating to individuals, see Roger Gregory, *Bankruptcy of Individuals*, 2nd edn (CCH, 1992).

PART VIII — INDIVIDUAL VOLUNTARY ARRANGEMENTS

General comment on Part VIII

The provisions of Pt. VIII deal with voluntary arrangements entered into by debtors as an alternative to bankruptcy. A debtor can select a "nominee" to put his proposals into effect. Prior to 1985, a debtor who wished to make an arrangement with his creditors to avoid the consequences of bankruptcy could use the Deeds of Arrangement Act 1914, much of which will survive IA 1986. The problem with a deed of arrangement made under this 1914 legislation was that it could easily be frustrated by a dissenting creditor petitioning for bankruptcy, especially as the mere execution of a deed of arrangement was construed as an act of bankruptcy. Consequently, such deeds of arrangement came to be increasingly under-employed (there were only 51 in 1984). Deeds of arrangement have not been abolished, but rather have been left to wither on the vine. Deeds of arrangement and individual voluntary arrangements are mutually exclusive – see s. 260(3) below. There were two deeds of arrangement entered into in 1992, though this figure had leaped to eight for 1993. The annual report of the Secretary of State made under section 379 must disclose statistics concerning the Deeds of Arrangement Act 1914. Under BA 1914, ss. 16, 17, and 21 there was provision for schemes of composition or arrangement once bankruptcy proceedings had started (and even after adjudication). These provisions were little used and have now been supplanted by the more flexible system of voluntary arrangements established by the 1985 Act, and now to be found in the 1986 legislation. The Cork Committee (*Report*, para. 399) called for the introduction of a more effective system of voluntary arrangements. Although the IA 1986 has not adopted the specific Cork proposal for debts arrangement orders, the general policy of the Cork Committee has been followed.

Individual voluntary arrangements have proved popular with debtors. For background discussion see Williams (1986) 2 IL & P 11. The impact of the new system of individual voluntary arrangements is covered by Pond in (1988) 4 IL & P 66, 104 and in (1989) 5 IL & P 73. There were 4,686 IVAs entered into in 1992 (as compared to 32,106 bankruptcies). The figures for 1993 are 5,679 IVAs and 31,025 bankruptcies. This increasing popularity may be attributed to a number of factors. The moratorium initiated by the interim order does allow a period of calm during which a debtor can seek to come to a mutually beneficial arrangement with his creditors without fear of an impatient creditor throwing a spanner in the works by petitioning for bankruptcy. Statistics do show that creditors achieve a higher rate of return under an IVA because the administration costs are so much lower – rates of return double those found in bankruptcy cases are sometimes cited. An increasingly important advantage for the debtor is that in avoiding bankruptcy he also avoids the attendant restrictions and disqualifications – e.g. the bar on becoming a company director. For general discussion see Mullarkey (1993) 137 SJ 192, Oditah [1994] LMCLQ 210 and Pond (1993) 9 Insolvency Lawyer 9 continued in (1994) 10 Insolvency Lawyer 2.

Part VII of the Act is supplemented by IR 1986, rr. 5.1–5.30 and by *Practice Direction (Bankruptcy: Voluntary Arrangements)* [1992] 1 WLR 120. Note in particular that it is a crime fraudulently to procure a voluntary arrangement – IR 1986, r. 5.30.

Corresponding provisions for company voluntary arrangements are made by ss. 1–7.

MORATORIUM FOR INSOLVENT DEBTOR

Section 252 Interim order of court

252(1)   [Power of court]   In the circumstances specified below, the court may in the case of a debtor (being an individual) make an interim order under this section.

252(2)   [Effect of interim order]   An interim order has the effect that, during the period for which it is in force—

(a) no bankruptcy petition relating to the debtor may be presented or proceeded with, and

(b) no other proceedings, and no execution or other legal process, may be commenced or continued against the debtor or his property except with the leave of the court.

(Former provision: IA 1985, s. 112(1) (part), (3))

S. 252(1)

In effect, this section allows for an application for an interim order in circumstances described in s. 253.

S. 252(2)

The effect of an interim order is to impose a moratorium on proceedings against an insolvent debtor. The aim of this provision is to prevent a viable proposal being destroyed by a selfish creditor. For an early illustration of an interim order being used to prevent a sheriff acting on behalf of judgment creditors from completing the execution process, see *Re Peake* [1987] CLY 215 (Blackburn County Court). One important limitation upon the effectiveness of an interim order was revealed in *McMullen & Sons* v *Cerrone* [1994] BCC 25 where it was held not to be wide enough to debar a landlord from exercising his age-old right to levy distress for non-payment of rent. Consideration of the cases on the moratorium established when a petition for an administration order is presented in respect of an insolvent company would also be instructive in this context (see ss. 10 and 11 above) but there are differences between the two moratoria as is exemplified in the case of distress. An attempt to use an interim order to continually block bankruptcy proceedings proved unsuccessful before Scott J in *Re A Debtor (No. 83 of*

1988) [1990] 1 WLR 708 (this case is reported as *Re Cove (a debtor)* in [1990] 1 All ER 949). In *Re M,* [1991] TLR 192, Otton J held that the making of an interim order under s. 252 did not affect the right of the prosecution to make an application for a receiver of realisable property of a person against whom a restraint order had already been made under s. 8 of the Drug Trafficking Offences Act 1986. The effect of the interim order was only to protect assets not already covered by the restraint order. Assets covered by the restraint order could no longer be considered as part of the debtor's estate until the defendant was either acquitted, in which case the restraint order would be discharged, or convicted whereupon the restraint order would be converted into a confiscation order.

Section 253   Application for interim order

253(1)   [Where application made]   Application to the court for an interim order may be made where the debtor intends to make a proposal to his creditors for a composition in satisfaction of his debts or a scheme of arrangement of his affairs (from here on referred to, in either case, as a "voluntary arrangement").

253(2)   [Nominee]   The proposal must provide for some person ("the nominee") to act in relation to the voluntary arrangement either as trustee or otherwise for the purpose of supervising its implementation.

253(3)   [Applicants]   Subject as follows, the application may be made—

    (a) if the debtor is an undischarged bankrupt, by the debtor, the trustee of his estate, or the official receiver, and

    (b) in any other case, by the debtor.

253(4)   [Notice for s. 253(3)(a)]   An application shall not be made under subsection (3)(a) unless the debtor has given notice of his proposal (that is, the proposal to his creditors for a voluntary arrangement) to the official receiver and, if there is one, the trustee of his estate.

253(5)   [When application not to be made]   An application shall not be made while a bankruptcy petition presented by the debtor is pending, if the court has, under section 273 below, appointed an insolvency practitioner to inquire into the debtor's affairs and report.

(Former provisions: IA 1985, ss. 110, 111(1)–(3) (part))

S. 253(1)–(3)
These provisions define the essence of the proposal for a voluntary arrangement, to implement which the interim order is sought, and they identify who may apply for an interim order. For further details, see IR 1986, rr. 5.2–5.4.

S. 253(4)
Where the debtor is an undischarged bankrupt two days' notice is required: see IR 1986, r. 5.5(4).

S. 253(5)
This provision restricts an application for an interim order where a bankruptcy petition is pending and the affairs of the debtor are being investigated under s. 273. This is because the court can on its own initiative, in such circumstances, grant an interim order. For further details, see IR 1986, r. 5.5.

Section 254   Effect of application

254(1)   [Stay pending interim order]   At any time when an application under section 253 for an interim order is pending, the court may stay any action, execution or other legal process against the property or person of the debtor.

254(2)   [Stay or continuance]   Any court in which proceedings are pending against an individual may, on proof that an application under that section has been made in respect of that individual, either stay the proceedings or allow them to continue on such terms as it thinks fit.

(Former provisions: IA 1985, ss. 111(4), (5))

General note

Where an application for an interim order is pending, the court can take immediate steps to protect the debtor and his assets from legal action. (For the meaning of "the court", see s. 385 (1).) Indeed, any court in which proceedings are pending can also take such protective steps.

Section 255   Cases in which interim order can be made

255(1)   [Conditions for order]   The court shall not make an interim order on an application under section 253 unless it is satisfied—

  (a) that the debtor intends to make such a proposal as is mentioned in that section;
  (b) that on the day of the making of the application the debtor was an undischarged bankrupt or was able to petition for his own bankruptcy;
  (c) that no previous application has been made by the debtor for an interim order in the period of 12 months ending with that day; and
  (d) that the nominee under the debtor's proposal to his creditors is a person who is for the time being qualified to act as an insolvency practitioner in relation to the debtor, and is willing to act in relation to the proposal.

255(2)   [Order to facilitate consideration and implementation of proposal]   The court may make an order if it thinks that it would be appropriate to do so for the purpose of facilitating the consideration and implementation of the debtor's proposal.

255(3)   [Where debtor is undischarged bankrupt]   Where the debtor is an undischarged bankrupt, the interim order may contain provision as to the conduct of the bankruptcy, and the administration of the bankrupt's estate, during the period for which the order is in force.

255(4)   [Extent of s. 255(3) provision]   Subject as follows, the provision contained in an interim order by virtue of subsection (3) may include provision staying proceedings in the bankruptcy or modifying any provision in this Group of Parts, and any provision of the rules in their application to the debtor's bankruptcy.

255(5)   [Limit to interim order]   An interim order shall not, in relation to a bankrupt, make provision relaxing or removing any of the requirements of provisions in this Group of Parts, or of the rules, unless the court is satisfied that that provision is unlikely to result in any significant diminution in, or in the value of, the debtor's estate for the purposes of the bankruptcy.

255(6)   **[When order ceases to have effect]**   Subject to the following provisions of this Part, an interim order made on an application under section 253 ceases to have effect at the end of the period of 14 days beginning with the day after the making of the order.

(Former provisions: IA 1985, s. 112(1), (2), (4)–(7)(a))

S. 255(1), (2)

These subsections deal with the circumstances under which the court may make an interim order. Section 255(2) gives general discretion provided the order would facilitate the consideration and implementation of the proposals. Section 255(1) cuts down this discretion by establishing a series of pre-conditions – e.g. that the nominee whom the debtor proposes should act in relation to the scheme must be qualified to act as an insolvency practitioner (see s. 388(2)(c)). Furthermore, the debtor must not have applied for a similar order within the previous 12 months.

S. 255(3)–(5)

These provisions deal with supplementary matters that may be included in the interim order where the applicant is an undischarged bankrupt – but such a provision in an interim order must not reduce the value of the debtor's estate.

S. 255(6)

The interim order will normally expire within 14 days of the order.
   Note also IR 1986, rr. 5.6.–5.7.

Section 256   Nominee's report on debtor's proposal

256(1)   **[Report to court]**   Where an interim order has been made on an application under section 253, the nominee shall, before the order ceases to have effect, submit a report to the court stating—

    (a) whether, in his opinion, a meeting of the debtor's creditors should be summoned to consider the debtor's proposal, and

    (b) if in his opinion such a meeting should be summoned, the date on which, and time and place at which, he proposes the meeting should be held.

256(2)   **[Information to nominee]**   For the purpose of enabling a nominee to prepare his report the debtor shall submit to the nominee—

    (a) a document setting out the terms of the voluntary arrangement which the debtor is proposing, and

    (b) a statement of his affairs containing—

        (i) such particulars of his creditors and of his debts and other liabilities and of his assets as may be prescribed, and

        (ii) such other information as may be prescribed.

256(3)   **[Directions by court]**   The court may, on an application made by the debtor in a case where the nominee has failed to submit the report required by this section, do one or both of the following, namely—

    (a) direct that the nominee shall be replaced as such by another person qualified to act as an insolvency practitioner in relation to the debtor;

(b) direct that the interim order shall continue, or (if it has ceased to have effect) be renewed, for such further period as the court may specify in the direction.

256(4) **[Extension of period of interim order]** The court may, on the application of the nominee, extend the period for which the interim order has effect so as to enable the nominee to have more time to prepare his report.

256(5) **[Extension for consideration by creditors]** If the court is satisfied on receiving the nominee's report that a meeting of the debtor's creditors should be summoned to consider the debtor's proposal, the court shall direct that the period for which the interim order has effect shall be extended, for such further period as it may specify in the direction, for the purpose of enabling the debtor's proposal to be considered by his creditors in accordance with the following provisions of this Part.

256(6) **[Discharge of interim order]** The court may discharge the interim order if it is satisfied, on the application of the nominee—

(a) that the debtor has failed to comply with his obligations under subsection (2), or

(b) that for any other reason it would be inappropriate for a meeting of the debtor's creditors to be summoned to consider the debtor's proposal.

(Former provision: IA 1985, s. 113)

S. 256(1)

The nominee of the debtor must, before the interim order has expired (see s. 255(6)), report to the court whether in his opinion it is worth calling a creditors' meeting to consider the debtor's proposal.

S. 256(2)

To facilitate the nominee making his report, the debtor must submit to him details of his proposal and statement of affairs. See IR 1986, r. 5.8, 5.9.

S. 256(3)

If the nominee fails to submit a report the debtor can apply to the court to have him replaced, and the interim order may be extended in such a situation. See IR 1986, r. 5.11.

S. 256(4)

This also allows for the extension of the order where the nominee requires more time to prepare his report.

S. 256(5)

If, after receiving the nominee's report, the court is satisfied that a meeting of creditors should be summoned, the court can again extend the interim order. Note also IR 1986, rr. 5.10, 5.12. Several such extensions can be granted but the patience of the court is not limitless: *Re A Debtor (No. 83 of 1988)* [1990] 1 WLR 708.

S. 256(6)

The interim order can be discharged by the court if the debtor has failed to play his part or if it would be inappropriate to call a creditors' meeting.

Section 257   Summoning of creditors' meeting

257(1)   [Meeting to be summoned]   Where it has been reported to the court under section 256 that a meeting of the debtor's creditors should be summoned, the nominee (or his replacement under section 256(3)(a)) shall, unless the court otherwise directs, summon that meeting for the time, date and place proposed in his report.

257(2)   [Persons summoned to meeting]   The persons to be summoned to the meeting are every creditor of the debtor of whose claim and address the person summoning the meeting is aware.

257(3)   [Creditors of debtor]   For this purpose the creditors of a debtor who is an undischarged bankrupt include—

> (a)   every person who is a creditor of the bankrupt in respect of a bankruptcy debt, and
>
> (b)   every person who would be such a creditor if the bankruptcy had commenced on the day on which notice of the meeting is given.

(Former provision: IA 1985, s. 114(1) (part), (2), (3))

S. 257(1)

This provision requires the nominee to summon the meeting of creditors in accordance with his report, unless the court has directed otherwise. In *Re Debtor (No. 83 of 1988)* [1990] 1 WLR 708, Scott J held that this provision (in appropriate circumstances) enables the court to discharge any previous order directing that a creditors' meeting be convened.

S. 257(2), (3)

These subsections identify which creditors are to be summoned to the meeting – this will depend on whether the debtor is an undischarged bankrupt or not.

   For further information, reference should be made to IR 1986, rr. 5.12–5.19.

CONSIDERATION AND IMPLEMENTATION OF DEBTOR'S PROPOSAL

Section 258   Decisions of creditors' meeting

258(1)   [Decision re approval]   A creditors' meeting summoned under section 257 shall decide whether to approve the proposed voluntary arrangement.

258(2)   [Approval with modifications]   The meeting may approve the proposed voluntary arrangement with modifications, but shall not do so unless the debtor consents to each modification.

258(3)   [Extent of modifications]   The modifications subject to which the proposed voluntary arrangement may be approved may include one conferring the functions proposed to be conferred on the nominee on another person qualified to act as an insolvency practitioner in relation to the debtor.

   But they shall not include any modification by virtue of which the proposal ceases to be a proposal such as is mentioned in section 253.

258(4)   [Certain modifications not to be approved]   The meeting shall not approve any proposal or modification which affects the right of a secured creditor of the debtor to enforce his security, except with the concurrence of the creditor concerned.

258(5)   [Other modifications not to be approved]   Subject as follows, the meeting shall not approve any proposal or modification under which—

(a) any preferential debt of the debtor is to be paid otherwise than in priortity to such of his debts as are not preferential debts, or

(b) a preferential creditor of the debtor is to be paid an amount in respect of a preferential debt that bears to that debt a smaller proportion than is borne to another preferential debt by the amount that is to be paid in respect of that other debt.

However, the meeting may approve such a proposal or modification with the concurrence of the preferential creditor concerned.

258(6)   [Meeting in accordance with rules]   Subject as above, the meeting shall be conducted in accordance with the rules.

258(7)   [Definitions]   In this section **"preferential debt"** has the meaning given by section 386 in Part XII; and **"preferential creditor"** is to be construed accordingly.

(Former provisions: IA 1985, s. 115(1)–(6), (9), (10))

S. 258(1)

The meeting of creditors can either approve or reject the composition which is being put to them. No mention is made of any required majority – under BA 1914, ss. 16(2) and 21(1) it was three-fourths in value of the debtor's creditors: IR 1986, r. 5.18 retains this position.

S. 258(2)–(5)

These provisions deal with modifications to the proposed scheme. The debtor must assent to any modification and the modification may involve a change of nominee, but the basic proposal must still fall within s. 253. Changes affecting the rights of secured creditors are only permitted in so far as the secured creditors agree. Similar protection is available to consolidate the priority enjoyed by preferential creditors on bankruptcy. This confirms the position under BA 1914, s. 16(19).

S. 258(6)

The meeting must be conducted according to the rules – see IR 1986, rr. 5.14–5.19.

S. 258(7)

This defines preferential debts, etc., for the purposes of this provision.

Section 259   Report of decisions to court

259(1)   [Report to court, notice]   After the conclusion in accordance with the rules of the meeting summoned under section 257, the chairman of the meeting shall report the result of it to the court and, immediately after so reporting, shall give notice of the result of the meeting to such persons as may be prescribed.

259(2)   [Discharge of interim order]   If the report is that the meeting has declined (with or without modifications) to approve the debtor's proposal, the court may discharge any interim order which is in force in relation to the debtor.

(Former provision: IA 1985, s. 115(7), (8)

General note

The chairman of the creditors' meeting must report its decision to the court and give notice to prescribed persons. If the creditors have completely rejected the debtor's proposals, the court may discharge any interim order.

For further obligations imposed on the chairman, see IR 1986, rr. 5.22, 5.24.

Section 260 Effect of approval

260(1) [Effect] This section has effect where the meeting summoned under section 257 approves the proposed voluntary arrangement (with or without modifications).

260(2) [Effect of approved composition or scheme] The approved arrangement—

    (a) takes effect as if made by the debtor at the meeting, and

    (b) binds every person who in accordance with the rules had notice of, and was entitled to vote at, the meeting (whether or not he was present or represented at it) as if he were a party to the arrangement.

260(3) [Deeds of Arrangement Act] The Deeds of Arrangement Act 1914 does not apply to the approved voluntary arrangement.

260(4) [Certain interim orders to cease] Any interim order in force in relation to the debtor immediately before the end of the period of 28 days beginning with the day on which the report with respect to the creditors' meeting was made to the court under section 259 ceases to have effect at the end of that period.

This subsection applies except to such extent as the court may direct for the purposes of any application under section 262 below.

260(5) [Bankruptcy petition stayed by s. 260(4) interim order] Where proceedings on a bankruptcy petition have been stayed by an interim order which ceases to have effect under subsection (4), that petition is deemed, unless the court otherwise orders, to have been dismissed.

(Former provisions: IA 1985, s. 116(1)–(3), (6), (7))

S. 260(1), (2)

Where the creditors' meeting approves the debtor's proposal (whether modified or not), this will bind every creditor who had notice of, and was entitled to vote at, the meeting. (Compare BA 1914, s. 16(13).) "Notice" in the context of s. 260(2)(*b*) means actual notice. The courts will resist any attempt to introduce notions of constructive notice into this area of the law, as is attested by *Re A Debtor (No. 64 of 1992)* (*Bradford & Bingley Building Society* v *A Debtor*) [1994] BCC 55. The onus is therefore on the debtor to keep accurate records of creditors' names and addresses or else an IVA proposal might flounder through inability to contact and therefore bind certain creditors to the scheme.

Note that court approval is not required to make the scheme binding, unlike under s. 16 of the 1914 Act. Notwithstanding approval of a scheme by creditors under s. 260 an aggrieved creditor may apply to the court under s. 262 if the scheme unfairly prejudices him in his capacity as a creditor: see here *Re Naeem (A Bankrupt) (No. 18 of 1988)* [1990] 1 WLR 48.

For the effect of s. 260 in releasing old debts and creating new obligations see *Re Wisepark Ltd* [1994] BCC 221 at p. 223.

S. 260(3)

The Deeds of Arrangement Act 1914 does not apply to the approved scheme. Registration of voluntary arrangements is provided for by IR 1986, r. 5.23.

S. 260(4), (5)

Interim orders automatically lapse within 28 days of the chairman's report to the court. One effect of this is that if the interim order has "blocked" a bankruptcy petition, the petition is now to be treated as having been dismissed.

Section 261   Effect where debtor an undischarged bankrupt

261(1)   [If debtor undischarged bankrupt]   Subject as follows, where the creditors' meeting summoned under section 257 approves the proposed voluntary arrangement (with or without modifications) and the debtor is an undischarged bankrupt, the court may do one or both of the following, namely—

(a) annul the bankruptcy order by which he was adjudged bankrupt;

(b) give such directions with respect to the conduct of the bankruptcy and the administration of the bankrupt's estate as it thinks appropriate for facilitating the implementation of the approved voluntary arrangement.

261(2)   [Annulment of bankruptcy order]   The court shall not annul a bankruptcy order under subsection (1)—

(a) at any time before the end of the period of 28 days beginning with the day on which the report of the creditors' meeting was made to the court under section 259, or

(b) at any time when an application under section 262 below, or an appeal in respect of such an application, is pending or at any time in the period within which such an appeal may be brought.

(Former provisions: IA 1985, s. 116(4), (5))

General note

This section deals with the rôle of the court where the debtor was an undischarged bankrupt. The court can annul the bankruptcy order and/or modify the bankruptcy régime to facilitate the scheme. However, this is not to be done until the expiry of 28 days from the date the chairman's report or where an application under s. 262 is pending.

Section 262   Challenge of meeting's decision

262(1)   [Application to court]   Subject to this section, an application to the court may be made, by any of the persons specified below, on one or both of the following grounds, namely—

(a) that a voluntary arrangement approved by a creditor's meeting summoned under section 257 unfairly prejudices the interests of a creditor of the debtor;

   (b) that there has been some material irregularity at or in relation to such a meeting.

262(2) **[Applicants]**   The persons who may apply under this section are—

   (a) the debtor;

   (b) a person entitled, in accordance with the rules, to vote at the creditors' meeting;

   (c) the nominee (or his replacement under section 256(3)(a) or 258(3)); and

   (d) if the debtor is an undischarged bankrupt, the trustee of his estate or the official receiver.

262(3) **[Time for application]**   An application under this section shall not be made after the end of the period of 28 days beginning with the day on which the report of the creditors' meeting was made to the court under section 259.

262(4) **[Court's powers]**   Where on an application under this section the court is satisfied as to either of the grounds mentioned in subsection (1), it may do one or both of the following, namely—

   (a) revoke or suspend any approval given by the meeting;

   (b) give a direction to any person for the summoning of a further meeting of the debtor's creditors to consider any revised proposal he may make or, in a case falling within subsection (1)(b), to reconsider his original proposal.

262(5) **[Revocation of direction, approval]**   Where at any time after giving a direction under subsection (4)(b) for the summoning of a meeting to consider a revised proposal the court is satisfied that the debtor does not intend to submit such a proposal, the court shall revoke the direction and revoke or suspend any approval given at the previous meeting.

262(6) **[Further direction]**   Where the court gives a direction under subsection (4) (b), it may also give a direction continuing or, as the case may require, renewing, for such period as may be specified in the direction, the effect in relation to the debtor of any interim order.

262(7) **[Supplemental directions]**   In any case where the court, on an application made under this section with respect to a creditors' meeting, gives a direction under subsection (4)(b) or revokes or suspends an approval under subsection (4)(a) or (5), the court may give such supplemental directions as it thinks fit, and, in particular, directions with respect to—

   (a) things done since the meeting under any voluntary arrangement approved by the meeting, and

   (b) such things done since the meeting as could not have been done if an interim order had been in force in relation to the debtor when they were done.

262(8) **[Effects of irregularity at meeting]**   Except in pursuance of the preceding provisions of this section, an approval given at a creditors' meeting summoned under section 257 is not invalidated by any irregularity at or in relation to the meeting.

(Former provision: IA 1985, s. 117)

General note

Under s. 16 of BA 1914, it was the task of the court to approve the scheme, and it had to consider whether it was reasonable and for the benefit of the general creditors. Under the 1986 Act, the court's rôle is reduced and it will assume such a paternal posture only if the decision of the majority of creditors is challenged under s. 262. The court will consider whether the interests of some creditors have been unfairly prejudiced and will be less concerned with an overview of the scheme – it will assume that it is beneficial to the creditors if the majority support it. Furthermore, the court has more discretion under s. 262 to secure the revision of the scheme to meet any objections. In *Re Naeem (A Bankrupt) (No. 18 of 1988)* [1990] 1 WLR 48 a landlord successfully exploited s. 262 before a registrar to block a scheme on the ground that it unfairly prejudiced his interests, but on appeal to Hoffmann J the scheme was reinstated as no unfair prejudice to his interests *as a creditor* could be established. This case is also instructive on the question of who pays the costs of a s. 262 application. A success for s. 262 was notched up in *Re A Debtor (No. 222 of 1990) ex parte Bank of Ireland (No. 2)* [1993] BCLC 233 where Harman J found that as the nominee/chairman had conducted the IVA meeting in a materially irregular way by denying certain creditors a vote (see the earlier proceedings reported in [1992] BCLC 137) he should be personally liable for the costs of the IVA which had to be set aside. It is difficult not to feel some sympathy for the unfortunate insolvency practitioner here as the right to vote on an IVA in certain contentious cases is less than clear.

By way of comparison a s. 262 application failed in *Re A Debtor (No. 259 of 1990)* [1992] 1 WLR 226 where the court made the point that the alleged unfairness must emanate from the scheme itself.

For procedural aspects of an application under s. 262, see IR 1986, r. 5.25.

S. 262(1)–(3), (8)

Within 28 days of the chairman's report to the court a dissenter may apply to the court to challenge the scheme. Section 262(2) allows the debtor, creditors, nominee, trustee or official receiver to make such an application. The grounds for the challenge are that the scheme unfairly prejudices the interests of a creditor, or that there has been some *material* irregularity at the meeting. Unless there has been a successful challenge under this section, irregularities will not invalidate the scheme – see s. 262(8).

S. 262(4)–(7)

These provisions outline what the court may do where a scheme is challenged. It may revoke or suspend the approval or call for further meetings to be held – i.e. to reconsider the proposals or to consider revised proposals. If the debtor does not intend to put revised proposals the court can simply revoke or suspend its support for the scheme, although it can direct the interim relief to continue and also make supplementary directions. For the scope of the jurisdiction under s. 262(7) see *Re A Debtor (No. 83 of 1988)* [1990] 1 WLR 708.

Section 263 Implementation and supervision of approved voluntary arrangement

263(1) [Application] This section applies where a voluntary arrangement approved by a creditors' meeting summoned under section 257 has taken effect.

263(2) [Supervisor of voluntary arrangement] The person who is for the time being carrying out, in relation to the voluntary arrangement, the functions conferred by virtue of the approval on the nominee (or his replacement under section 256(3)(a) or 258(3)) shall be known as the supervisor of the voluntary arrangement.

263(3) [Application to court re actions of supervisor] If the debtor, any of his creditors or any other person is dissatisfied by any act, omission or decision of the supervisor, he may apply to the court; and on such an application the court may—

(a) confirm, reverse or modify any act or decision of the supervisor,

(b) give him directions, or

(c) make such other order as it thinks fit.

263(4) [Application for directions] The supervisor may apply to the court for directions in relation to any particular matter arising under the voluntary arrangement.

263(5) [Court may fill supervisor vacancy etc.] The court may, whenever—

(a) it is expedient to appoint a person to carry out the functions of the supervisor, and

(b) it is inexpedient, difficult or impracticable for an appointment to be made without the assistance of the court,

make an order appointing a person who is qualified to act as an insolvency practitioner in relation to the debtor, either in substitution for the existing supervisor or to fill a vacancy.

This is without prejudice to section 41(2) of the Trustee Act 1925 (power of court to appoint trustees of deeds of arrangement).

263(6) [Exercise of s. 263(5) power] The power conferred by subsection (5) is exercisable so as to increase the number of persons exercising the functions of the supervisor or, where there is more than one person exercising those functions, so as to replace one or more of those persons.

(Former provision: IA 1985, s. 118)

S. 263(1), (2)
Once the scheme has taken effect the "nominee" will be transformed into the "supervisor" of the composition or scheme.

S. 263(3)
This allows for the court to interfere with decisions of the supervisor which have been objected to. Compare IA 1986, s. 303(1).

S. 263(4)
The supervisor may apply to the court for directions, as can a trustee in bankruptcy under IA 1986, s. 303(2).

S. 263(5), (6)
The court can fill vacancies, appoint substitutes or increase the number of supervisors.
   For further provisions on the implementation of the voluntary arrangement and the rôle of the supervisor, see IR 1986, rr. 5.21, 5.26–5.29.

PART IX — BANKRUPTCY

General comment on Part IX

Before embarking upon the analysis of the provisions of IA 1986 with regard to bankruptcy a caveat ought to be issued. Where this is appropriate the legislative origins of particular provisions are identified in the following text. However, care must be taken in handling these former provisions (which are largely from BA 1914) for it is now clear that the courts are minded to interpret the bankruptcy sections of IA 1986 in their own light and are not necessarily going to take advantage of earlier interpretations of similar provisions in the 1914 Act. Thus in *Re a Debtor (No. 1 of 1987)* [1989] 1 WLR 271, a leading case on statutory demands, Nicholls LJ declared:

"I do not think that on this the new bankruptcy code simply incorporates and adopts the same approach as the old code. The new code has made many changes in the law of bankruptcy, and the court's task, with regard to the new code, must be to construe the new statutory provisions in accordance with the ordinary canons of construction, unfettered by previous authorities." (Ibid. at p. 276.)

More recently in the House of Lords ruling in *Smith v Braintree District Council* [1990] 2 AC 215, which was concerned with the interpretation of IA 1986, s. 285, Lord Jauncey (at pp. 237–238) reinforced this view on the *modus operandi* of interpretation:

". . . the Act of 1986, although re-enacting many provisions from earlier statutes, contains a good deal of fresh material derived from the Insolvency Act 1985. In particular, the legislation now emphasises the importance of the rehabilitation of the individual insolvent, it provides for automatic discharge from bankruptcy in many cases, and it abolishes mandatory public examinations as well as enabling a bankrupt to be discharged without public examination. Thus not only has the legislative approach to individual bankruptcy altered since the mid-19th century, but social views as to what conduct involves delinquency, as to punishment and as to the desirability of imprisonment have drastically changed . . . In these circumstances, I feel justified in construing section 285 of the Act of 1986 as a piece of new legislation without regard to 19th century authorities or similar provisions of repealed Bankruptcy Acts. . ."

These are important statements of principle that should be borne in mind when trying to attach meaning to the new statutory provisions in bankruptcy law. Having said that, there are instances where pre-1985 law has been important and therefore generalisations must be treated with caution.

It should be remembered that in addition to the Act and the Rules there are a number of relevant practice directions governing bankruptcy cases. Some of these are referred to in connection with the relevant legislative provisions. Others more general in nature are noted below – see for example *Practice Note (Bankruptcy: Consent Orders)* [1992] 1 WLR 379, *Practice Direction (Bankruptcy Hearing Dates)* [1992] 1 WLR 175, *Practice Note (Appeals from District Judges)* [1992] 3 All ER 921 and *Practice Statement (Chancery Division: Hearing Dates)* [1994] 1 WLR 776. A case of general significance in bankruptcy litigation is *Hocking v Walker*, [1993] TLR 455, where the Court of Appeal held that a bankrupt may be required to give security for costs when appealing against a bankruptcy order.

Chapter I — Bankruptcy Petitions; Bankruptcy Orders

Introductory note to Pt. IX, Ch. I

The 1985 Act implemented the recommendation of the Cork Committee (*Report*, para. 529), that the obsolete concept of acts of bankruptcy should be abolished.

PRELIMINARY

Section 264   Who may present a bankruptcy petition

264(1)   [Presentation of petition]   A petition for a bankruptcy order to be made against an individual may be presented to the court in accordance with the following provisions of this Part—

   (a) by one of the individual's creditors or jointly by more than one of them,

   (b) by the individual himself,

   (c) by the supervisor of, or any person (other than the individual) who is for the time being bound by, a voluntary arrangement proposed by the individual and approved under Part VIII, or

   (d) where a criminal bankruptcy order has been made against the individual, by the Official Petitioner or by any person specified in the order in pursuance of section 39(3)(b) of the Powers of Criminal Courts Act 1973.

264(2)   [Power of court to make order]   Subject to those provisions, the court may make a bankruptcy order on any such petition.

(Former provision: IA 1985, s. 119(1))

General note

This section describes the persons who may present a bankruptcy petition and authorises the court to make an order on such a petition. For the "Official Petitioner" in s. 264(1)(*d*) see s. 402.

   Note prospective amendment: s. 264(1)(*d*) and the word "or" immediately preceding it are to be repealed by the Criminal Justice Act 1988, s. 170(2) and Sch. 16 as from a day to be appointed. (The power to make criminal brankruptcy orders has been abolished by s. 101 of this Act, with effect from 3 April 1989 (see SI 1989 No. 264 (C. 8)), but this and other provisions of IA 1986 and IR 1986 remain in force for the time being to govern orders already existing: see further the note to s. 277.)

   The fee for a creditor's petition is now £50, with a debtor's petition costing £20: see the Supreme Court Fees (Amendment) Order 1993 (SI 1993 No. 3191). The relevant deposits for petitions presented under s. 264(1) are £330 for petitions presented under paras. (*a*), (*c*) and (*d*) and £250 for petitions presented by debtors under para. (*b*) (from 24 October 1994 – see the Insolvency Fees (Amendment) Order 1994 (SI 1994 No. 2541)).

Section 265   Conditions to be satisfied in respect of debtor

265(1)   [Conditions for presentation of petition]   A bankruptcy petition shall not be presented to the court under section 264(1)(a) or (b) unless the debtor—

   (a) is domiciled in England and Wales,

   (b) is personally present in England and Wales on the day on which the petition is presented, or

   (c) at any time in the period of 3 years ending with that day—

      (i) has been ordinarily resident, or has had a place of residence, in England and Wales, or

      (ii) has carried on business in England and Wales.

265(2) **[Interpretation]** The reference in subsection (1)(c) to an individual carrying on business includes—

    (a) the carrying on of business by a firm or partnership of which the individual is a member, and

    (b) the carrying on of business by an agent or manager for the individual or for such a firm or partnership.

(Former provisions: IA 1985, s. 119(2), (3); BA 1914, s. 1(2))

General note

This section largely repeats provisions to the same effect in BA 1914, s. 1(2). The purpose of these provisions is to establish a geographic connection between the debtor and the English bankruptcy system. For an instructive authority here, see *Re Brauch* [1978] Ch. 316. For the purposes of s. 265(1)(*c*)(ii) a person does not cease to carry on business until arrangements have been made to settle business debts – see *Re A Debtor (No. 784 of 1991)* [1992] Ch. 554 where Hoffmann J followed *Theophile* v *Solicitor General* [1950] AC 186.

Section 266   Other preliminary conditions

266(1) **[Treatment of petition]** Where a bankruptcy petition relating to an individual is presented by a person who is entitled to present a petition under two or more paragraphs of section 264(1), the petition is to be treated for the purposes of this Part as a petition under such one of those paragraphs as may be specified in the petition.

266(2) **[Limit on withdrawal of petition]** A bankruptcy petition shall not be withdrawn without the leave of the court.

266(3) **[Power of dismissal or stay]** The court has a general power, if it appears to it appropriate to do so on the grounds that there has been a contravention of rules or for any other reason, to dismiss a bankruptcy petition or to stay proceedings on such a petition; and, where it stays proceedings on a petition, it may do so on such terms and conditions as it thinks fit.

266(4) **[Where criminal bankruptcy order]** Without prejudice to subsection (3), where a petition under section 264(1)(a), (b) or (c) in respect of an individual is pending at a time when a criminal bankruptcy order is made against him, or is presented after such an order has been so made, the court may on the application of the Official Petitioner dismiss the petition if it appears to it appropriate to do so.

(Former provisions: IA 1985, s. 119(4)–(7); BA 1914, ss. 5(7), 6(2), 113)

S. 266(1)

A person may be entitled to present a petition under two or more paragraphs of s. 264(1), but he must specify which paragraph he is relying on.

S. 266(2)

The leave of the court is required before a petition can be withdrawn. This repeats BA 1914, ss. 5(7) and 6(2).

S. 266(3), (4)

The court has general discretion to stay or dismiss petitions. This was the case under BA 1914, s. 113. Section 266(4) ensures that if there is a possibility of a petition based on a criminal bankruptcy order, that should receive priority treatment. For the rôle of the Official Petitioner, see s. 402.

Note prospective amendment: s. 266(4) is to be repealed by the Criminal Justice Act 1988, s. 170(2) and Sch. 16 as from a day to be appointed: see the note to s. 264.

CREDITOR'S PETITION

Section 267   Grounds of creditor's petition

267(1)   **[Requirements]**   A creditor's petition must be in respect of one or more debts owed by the debtor, and the petitioning creditor or each of the petitioning creditors must be a person to whom the debt or (as the case may be) at least one of the debts is owed.

267(2)   **[Conditions for presentation of petition]**   Subject to the next three sections, a creditor's petition may be presented to the court in respect of a debt or debts only if, at the time the petition is presented—

- (a) the amount of the debt, or the aggregate amount of the debts, is equal to or exceeds the the bankruptcy level,
- (b) the debt, or each of the debts, is for a liquidated sum payable to the petitioning creditor, or one or more of the petitioning creditors, either immediately or at some certain, future time, and is unsecured,
- (c) the debt, or each of the debts, is a debt which the debtor appears either to be unable to pay or to have no reasonable prospect of being able to pay, and
- (d) there is no outstanding application to set aside a statutory demand served (under section 268 below) is respect of the debt or any of the debts.

267(3)   **[Interpretation]**   A debt is not to be regarded for the purposes of subsection (2) as a debt for a liquidated sum by reason only that the amount of the debt is specified in a criminal bankruptcy order.

267(4)   **["The bankruptcy level"]**   "The bankruptcy level" is £750; but the Secretary of State may by order in a statutory instrument substitute any amount specified in the order for that amount or (as the case may be) for the amount which by virtue of such an order is for the time being the amount of the bankruptcy level.

267(5)   **[Approval of order by Parliament]**   An order shall not be made under subsection (4) unless a draft of it has been laid before, and approved by a resolution of, each House of Parliament.

(Former provisions: IA 1985, s. 120(1), (2), (7)–(9); BA 1914, s. 4)

S. 267(1), (2)

These provisions explain what debts can be used as the basis of a creditor's petition. Basically, the debt must be for a liquidated sum in excess of the bankruptcy level (see s. 267(4)). The debtor must appear to be unable to pay or have no reasonable prospect of paying this debt. If an application is pending to set aside the statutory demand for payment of this debt, it falls outside the category of qualifying debts.

A sum due under an interim payments order made under RSC, O. 29, r. 10 is a "debt" for these purposes – *Maxwell* v *Bishopsgate Investment Management Ltd* [1993] TLR 67. In so deciding Chadwick J noted that the abolition of acts of bankruptcy had produced this change in the law – a final judgment was not necessary under the new bankruptcy code to justify a statutory demand. On the status of unpaid community charge see *Re Wood* [1994] 1 CL 257 (1993, Tamworth County Court). The debt can be a sum due in a foreign currency according to Morritt J in *Re A Debtor (51/SD/1991)* [1992] 1 WLR 1294.

Presumably the rule in *Re McGreavy* [1950] Ch. 269, that an unpaid rates demand is a "debt" for the purposes of a bankruptcy petition, is preserved by s. 267.

For guidance on preparing the petition see *Practice Note (Bankruptcy: Petition)* [1987] 1 WLR 81.

Section 267(2)(*d*) must, in the opinion of Mummery J, be read as being subject to s. 270 – see *Re A Debtor (No. 22 of 1993)* [1994] 1 WLR 46 (sometimes cited as *Focus Insurance* v *A Debtor*).

S. 267(3)

This narrows the definition of a liquidated sum to exclude amounts of debts specified in criminal bankruptcy orders.

Note prospective amendment: s. 267(3) is to be repealed by the Criminal Justice Act 1988, s. 170(2) and Sch. 16 as from a day to be appointed: see the note to s. 264.

S. 267(4), (5)

The current bankruptcy level is £750, although the Secretary of State can increase it. Note that this amount must still be outstanding at the date of the hearing: *Re Patel* [1986] 1 WLR 221.

Section 268   Definition of "inability to pay", etc.; the statutory demand

268(1)   [Interpretation of s. 267(2)(c)]   For the purposes of section 267(2)(c), the debtor appears to be unable to pay a debt if, but only if, the debt is payable immediately and either—

(a) the petitioning creditor to whom the debt is owed has served on the debtor a demand (known as "the statutory demand") in the prescribed form requiring him to pay the debt or to secure or compound for it to the satisfaction of the creditor, at least 3 weeks have elapsed since the demand was served and the demand has been neither complied with nor set aside in accordance with the rules, or

(b) execution or other process issued in respect of the debt on a judgment or order of any court in favour of the petitioning creditor, or one or more of the petitioning creditors to whom the debt is owed, has been returned unsatisfied in whole or in part.

268(2) **[Further interpretation]** For the purposes of section 267(2)(c) the debtor appears to have no reasonable prospect of being able to pay a debt if, but only if, the debt is not immediately payable and—

(a) the petitioning creditor to whom it is owed has served on the debtor a demand (also known as "the statutory demand") in the prescribed form requiring him to establish to the satisfaction of the creditor that there is a reasonable prospect that the debtor will be able to pay the debt when it falls due,

(b) at least 3 weeks have elapsed since the demand was served, and

(c) the demand has been neither complied with nor set aside in accordance with the rules.

(Former provisions: IA 1985, s. 120(3), (4))

General note

This section defines "inability to pay" and "statutory demand", terms featuring in s. 267. A debtor will be deemed unable to pay a debt if he fails to meet a demand in the prescribed form served on him within three weeks – under the previous law the debtor was given only ten days' grace – or an execution for a judgment debt has been returned unsatisfied. In *Re a Debtor (No. 1 of 1987)* [1989] 1 WLR 271 the Court of Appeal, confirming a ruling of Warner J, took a relaxed view of a statutory demand that contained errors as to the amount owed. The Court of Appeal refused to set aside this demand as no injustice had been done to the debtor. In so deciding the Court of Appeal departed from the position under the pre-1985 bankruptcy law and indicated that the new provisions had to be interpreted in their own context. This case is a watershed authority marking a fundamental change in attitude on the part of the courts to procedural errors in the bankruptcy process. Formerly, in the case of a defect in a bankruptcy notice the whole proceedings would be invalidated. Now that bankruptcy is viewed as a more user-friendly regime for the debtor the courts feel justified in adopting a more pragmatic stance. For a full discussion of this relaxation of judicial attitudes see Milman [1994] Conv 289–298. Thus if the debt mentioned in the demand is overstated this will not invalidate the demand (provided the undisputed element exceeds the minimum bankruptcy debt) – see here *Re A Debtor (490/SD/1991)* [1992] 1 WLR 507 where Hoffmann J disclaimed his earlier contrary view in *Re A Debtor (No. 10 of 1988)* [1989] 1 WLR 405. Similar principles would appear to apply if part of the debt is disputed but there is an undisputed balance – failure to highlight the dispute may not be critical (*Re A Debtor (657/SD/1991)* [1993] BCLC 1280 per Ferris J). Equally errors as to the degree of security enjoyed by the creditor might be overlooked – see *Re A Debtor (No. 106 of 1992)*, *The Independent*, 20 April 1992.

An important point to note is that a statutory demand is a document issued by a creditor. Unlike the old bankruptcy notice it is not issued by the court and does not form part of court proceedings. This can have implications. Thus in *Re A Debtor (No. 190 of 1987)*, *The Times*, 21 May 1988 Vinelott J held that the relieving jurisdiction in r. 7.55 was inapplicable – but in view of the more liberal attitude of the courts to procedural irregularities this hardly matters. Equally it was held in *Re A Debtor (No. 88 of 1991)* [1993] Ch. 286 that the presentation of a statutory demand is not an "action" within the meaning of s. 69 of the Solicitors Act 1974 and so the one month moratorium imposed on solicitors seeking to recover fees from debtor clients does not apply (though the moratorium would extend to the presentation of the petition). For discussion see Start (1992) 142 NLJ 1121 and Simmonds (1992) 26 Law Soc Gaz 18.

On what constitutes an unsatisfied execution within s. 268(1)(*b*) see *Re A Debtor (No. 340 of 1992)* [1993] TLR 402.

For further details on the statutory demand, see IR 1986, rr. 6.1–6.5 and *Practice Note (Bankruptcy: Statutory Demand)* [1987] 1 WLR 85. See also *Practice Note (Bankruptcy) (No. 2 of 1987)* [1987] 1 WLR 1424.

For security as to costs where s. 268(2) is relied upon see IR 1986, r. 6.17.

Section 269   Creditor with security

269(1)   [Where debt not unsecured]   A debt which is the debt, or one of the debts, in respect of which a creditor's petition is presented need not be unsecured if either—

   (a) the petition contains a statement by the person having the right to enforce the security that he is willing, in the event of a bankruptcy order being made, to give up his security for the benefit of all the bankrupt's creditors, or

   (b) the petition is expressed not to be made in respect of the secured part of the debt and contains a statement by that person of the estimated value at the date of the petition of the security for the secured part of the debt.

269(2)   [Debt in s. 269(1)(b)]   In a case falling within subsection (1)(b) the secured and unsecured parts of the debt are to be treated for the purposes of sections 267 to 270 as separate debts.

(Former provision: IA 1985, s. 120(5))

General note

Secured debts can form the basis of a creditor's petition, provided the creditor is willing to give up his security or if the petition is in respect of an unsecured part of the same debt. Note also s. 383 here (definition of "secured debt", etc.).

See also IR 1986, rr. 6.115–6.119.

Section 270   Expedited petition

270   In the case of a creditor's petition presented wholly or partly in respect of a debt which is the subject of a statutory demand under section 268, the petition may be presented before the end of the 3-week period there mentioned if there is a serious possibility that the debtor's property or the value of any of his property will be significantly diminished during that period and the petition contains a statement to that effect.

(Former provision: IA 1985, s. 120(6))

General note

The three weeks' grace given to the debtor by s. 268 can be cut short and the petition presented prematurely if the petition alleges that there is a serious possibility of a significant fall in value of the debtor's assets. This procedure can still be invoked even though there is an extant set aside application with respect to the statutory demand – see the ruling of Mummery J in *Re A Debtor (No. 22 of 1993)* [1994] 1 WLR 46 (sometimes cited as *Focus Insurance v A Debtor*). However, should the set aside application succeed at the end of the day the creditor might be exposed to some sort of personal claim by the debtor, a point considered by Mummery J.

Section 271   Proceedings on creditor's petition

271(1)   [Conditions for bankruptcy order]   The court shall not make a bankruptcy order on a creditor's petition unless it is satisfied that the debt, or one of the debts, in respect of which the petition was presented is either—

(a) a debt which, having been payable at the date of the petition or having since become payable, has been neither paid nor secured or compounded for, or

(b) a debt which the debtor has no reasonable prospect of being able to pay when it falls due.

271(2)   [Where petition contains s. 270 statement]   In a case in which the petition contains such a statement as is required by section 270, the court shall not make a bankruptcy order until at least 3 weeks have elapsed since the service of any statutory demand under section 268.

271(3)   [Dismissal of petition]   The court may dismiss the petition if it is satisfied that the debtor is able to pay all his debts or is satisfied—

(a) that the debtor has made an offer to secure or compound for a debt in respect of which the petition is presented,

(b) that the acceptance of that offer would have required the dismissal of the petition, and

(c) that the offer has been unreasonably refused;

and, in determining for the purposes of this subsection whether the debtor is able to pay all his debts, the court shall take into account his contingent and prospective liabilities.

271(4)   [Interpretation]   In determining for the purposes of this section what constitutes a reasonable prospect that a debtor will be able to pay a debt when it falls due, it is to be assumed that the prospect given by the facts and other matters known to the creditor at the time he entered into the transaction resulting in the debt was a reasonable prospect.

271(5)   [Powers of court to amend etc.]   Nothing in sections 267 to 271 prejudices the power of the court, in accordance with the rules, to authorise a creditor's petition to be amended by the omission of any creditor or debt and to be proceeded with as if things done for the purposes of those sections had been done only by or in relation to the remaining creditors or debts.

(Former provisions: IA 1985, s. 121; BA 1914, ss. 5, 110, 111)

General note

If a petition is granted under the IA 1986 it is followed by a bankruptcy order. The previous intermediate stage of a receiving order (BA 1914, s. 3) has been abolished. Note also IR 1986, rr. 6.18, 6.22 and 6.25 and 6.33.

S. 271(1), (2), (4)

The power of the court to make a bankruptcy order is qualified by these provisions. Note that in the event of a petition presented prematurely the court must wait until the three weeks have elapsed before making the order. The definition of when a debtor has a "reasonable prospect" of paying a debt certainly leaves a lot to be desired. On s. 271(1)(a) see the Practice Direction in [1986] 3 All ER 864.

S. 271(3)

This provision states that the court may dismiss the petition if the debtor is able to meet his debts, or has made a proposal to the creditor to secure or compound the debt and it has been unreasonably refused. For discussion of the operation of this provision see *Re Gilmartin (A Bankrupt)* [1989] 1 WLR 513 where Harman J concluded that the registrar had been correct in deciding that an offer had not been unreasonably refused by the petitioner and the supporting creditors. In *Re A Debtor (No. 32 of 1993)* [1994] 1 WLR 899; [1994] BCC 438 it was held by Timothy Lloyd QC (sitting as a deputy High Court judge) that a debtor can offer to secure or compound within the meaning of s. 271(3) where there is just a single creditor involved. However, in determining whether the creditor's refusal of the offer was unreasonable it must be established to the satisfaction of the court that no reasonable hypothetical creditor would have rejected the debtor's offer; the fact that some creditors might have accepted it is not conclusive. On s. 271(3) generally see *Re A Debtor (No. 415/SD/1993)* [1994] 1 WLR 917. In *Re A Debtor (No. 2389 of 1989)* [1991] Ch. 326 Vinelott J held that the proposal of a voluntary arrangement by the debtor under Pt. VIII of the Act cannot be regarded as an "offer" for the purposes of s. 271(3) in that the decision on acceptance is not solely a matter for the petitioning creditor. The consequences of acceptance or refusal of such a proposal are dealt with exclusively by Pt. VIII. For discussion, see M Griffiths (1991) 135 Sol. Jo. 598.

S. 271(5)

This protects the discretion of the court to amend petitions, etc. Presumably this would permit consolidation of petitions or changes in the carriage of proceedings (cf. the repealed BA 1914, ss. 110 and 111).

DEBTOR'S PETITION

Section 272   Grounds of debtor's petition

272(1)   [Presentation to court]   A debtor's petition may be presented to the court only on the grounds that the debtor is unable to pay his debts.

272(2)   [Statement of debtor's affairs]   The petition shall be accompanied by a statement of the debtor's affairs containing—

    (a) such particulars of the debtor's creditors and of his debts and other liabilities and of his assets as may be prescribed, and

    (b) such other information as may be prescribed.

(Former provisions: IA 1985, s. 122; BA 1914, ss. 1(1), (8), 6)

General note

This again is, in many senses, a new provision, though the break with the past is not as radical as it might appear at first sight. A debtor could file for his own bankruptcy under the old law – indeed, this was an act of bankruptcy. For further guidance on a debtor's petition see IR 1986, rr. 6.37–6.50. The fee for such a petition is £20. A debtor who petitions for his own bankruptcy does not thereby make a disposition of his property contrary to s. 37 of the Matrimonial Causes Act 1973 – *Woodley* v *Woodley (No. 2)* [1994] 1 WLR 1167.

S. 272(1)
This provision preserves a debtor's right to petition for his own bankruptcy. Note that no minimum debt is required here.

S. 272(2)
This provision details the content of the petition. The Rules are important for clarification purposes here: see IR 1986, rr. 6.38, 6.39.

Section 273   Appointment of insolvency practitioner by the court

273(1)   [Where court not to make bankruptcy order]   Subject to the next section, on the hearing of a debtor's petition the court shall not make a bankruptcy order if it appears to the court—

- (a) that if a bankruptcy order were made the aggregate amount of the bankruptcy debts, so far as unsecured, would be less than the small bankruptcies level,
- (b) that if a bankruptcy order were made, the value of the bankrupt's estate would be equal to or more than the minimum amount,
- (c) that within the period of 5 years ending with the presentation of the petition the debtor has neither been adjudged bankrupt nor made a composition with his creditors in satisfaction of his debts or a scheme of arrangement of his affairs, and
- (d) that it would be appropriate to appoint a person to prepare a report under section 274.

"The minimum amount" and **"the small bankruptcies level"** mean such amounts as may for the time being be prescribed for the purposes of this section.

273(2)   [Appointment of person to prepare report]   Where on the hearing of the petition, it appears to the court as mentioned in subsection (1), the court shall appoint a person who is qualified to act as an insolvency practitioner in relation to the debtor—

- (a) to prepare a report under the next section, and
- (b) subject to section 258(3) in Part VIII, to act in relation to any voluntary arrangement to which the report relates either as trustee or otherwise for the purpose of supervising its implementation.

(Former provisions: IA 1985, s. 123(1), (2), (8))

General note
This provision reflects the strategy of the Cork Committee, which was to use bankruptcy only as a last resort, especially where the amounts involved were small.

S. 273(1)

The power of the court to make a bankruptcy order on a debtor's petition is restricted. Where the court is satisfied that the debts do not exceed the "small bankruptcies level" (£20,000), the estate's value exceeds the "minimum amount" £2,000 (see the Insolvency Proceedings (Monetary Limits) Order 1986 (SI 1986 No. 1996)), and the debtor has not been in serious financial difficulties within the previous five years, it may feel it more appropriate to ask for a report as described below.

S. 273(2)

If the conditions in s. 273(1) are satisfied, the court can appoint a qualified insolvency practitioner to prepare a s. 274 report, and to act as supervisor of a voluntary arrangement.

See also IR 1986, rr. 6.48–6.50.

Section 274 Action on report of insolvency practitioner

274(1) **[Report to court]** A person appointed under section 273 shall inquire into the debtor's affairs and, within such period as the court may direct, shall submit a report to the court stating whether the debtor is willing, for the purposes of Part VIII, to make a proposal for a voluntary arrangement.

274(2) **[Contents of report]** A report which states that the debtor is willing as above mentioned shall also state—

    (a) whether, in the opinion of the person making the report, a meeting of the debtor's creditors should be summoned to consider the proposal, and

    (b) if in that person's opinion such a meeting should be summoned, the date on which, and time and place at which, he proposes the meetings should be held.

274(3) **[Powers of court]** On considering a report under this section the court may—

    (a) without any application, make an interim order under section 252, if it thinks that it is appropriate to do so for the purpose of facilitating the consideration and implementation of the debtor's proposal, or

    (b) if it thinks it would be inappropriate to make such an order, make a bankruptcy order.

274(4) **[Cessation of interim order]** An interim order by virtue of this section ceases to have effect at the end of such period as the court may specify for the purpose of enabling the debtor's proposal to be considered by his creditors in accordance with the applicable provisions of Part VIII.

274(5) **[Summoning of meeting]** Where it has been reported to the court under this section that a meeting of the debtor's creditors should be summoned, the person making the report shall, unless the court otherwise directs, summon that meeting for the time, date and place proposed in his report.

The meeting is then deemed to have been summoned under section 257 in Part VIII, and subsections (2) and (3) of that section, and sections 258 to 263 apply accordingly.

(Former provisions: IA 1985, ss. 111(3) (part), 112(1) (part), (7)(b), 114(1) (part), 123 (3)–(5))

S. 274(1), (2)

If the court makes a s. 273 appointment, the appointee must investigate the debtor's affairs to see whether a viable proposal for a voluntary arrangement (see ss. 252–263 above) can be constructed and, if so, whether a creditors' meeting should be held. Where the court appoints an insolvency practitioner under s. 273(2) to prepare and submit a report under s. 274 the court must, on submission of that report, pay to the practitioner a fee of £250 (which is inclusive of VAT) – see the Insolvency Fees (Amendment) Order 1994 (SI 1994 No. 2541).

S. 274(3)

This maps out the court's options on receiving the above report – these are to make either an interim order with a view to facilitating a voluntary arrangement or a bankruptcy order.

S. 274(4)

This provision describes the duration of an interim order made under s. 274(3).

S. 274(5)

This makes provision for any meeting of creditors which has to be held to consider the voluntary arrangement.

Section 275   Summary administration

275(1)   [Issue of certificate]   Where on the hearing of a debtor's petition the court makes a bankruptcy order and the case is as specified in the next subsection, the court shall, if it appears to it appropriate to do so, issue a certificate for the summary administration of the bankrupt's estate.

275(2)   [Case for issue of certificate]   That case is where it appears to the court—

   (a) that if a bankruptcy order were made the aggregate amount of the bankruptcy debts so far as unsecured would be less than the small bankruptcies level (within the meaning given by section 273), and

   (b) that within the period of 5 years ending with the presentation of the petition the debtor has neither been adjudged bankrupt nor made a composition with his creditors in satisfaction of his debts or a scheme of arrangement of his affairs,

whether the bankruptcy order is made because it does not appear to the court as mentioned in section 273(1)(b) or (d), or it is made beause the court thinks it would be inappropriate to make an interim order under section 252.

275(3)   [Revocation of certificate by court]   The court may at any time revoke a certificate issued under this section if it appears to it that, on any grounds existing at the time the certificate was issued, the certificate ought not to have been issued.

(Former provisions: IA 1985, s. 123(6), (7))

General note

These provisions relating to certificates for summary administration must be viewed in the light of ss. 289(5) and 297. The small bankruptcies level has been fixed at £20,000 – see note to s. 273. For procedural matters see IR 1986, rr. 6.48–6.50.

S. 275(1), (2)

In cases of small bankruptcy arising out of a debtor's petition, the court, if it is satisfied that the conditions in s. 275(2) are present, must issue a certificate for summary administration. This possibility was covered by BA 1914, s. 129.

S. 275(3)

Such a certificate can be revoked if it was wrongfully issued. See also IR 1986, r. 6.50 and Form 6.31 here.

OTHER CASES FOR SPECIAL CONSIDERATION

Section 276   Default in connection with voluntary arrangement

276(1)   **[Conditions for s. 264(1)(c) bankruptcy order]**   The court shall not make a bankruptcy order on a petition under section 264(1)(c) (supervisor of, or person bound by, voluntary arrangement proposed and approved) unless it is satisfied—

    (a) that the debtor has failed to comply with his obligations under the voluntary arrangement, or

    (b) that information which was false or misleading in any material particular or which contained material omissions—

       (i) was contained in any statement of affairs or other document supplied by the debtor under Part VIII to any person, or

       (ii) was otherwise made available by the debtor to his creditors at or in connection with a meeting summoned under that Part, or

    (c) that the debtor has failed to do all such things as may for the purposes of the voluntary arrangement have been reasonably required of him by the supervisor of the arrangement.

276(2)   **[Expenses]**   Where a bankruptcy order is made on a petition under section 264(1)(c), any expenses properly incurred as expenses of the administration of the voluntary arrangement in question shall be a first charge on the bankrupt's estate.

(Former provision: IA 1985, s. 124)

S. 276(1)

This allows the court to make a bankruptcy order where a debtor has failed to fulfil his obligations under a voluntary arrangement set up by virtue of ss. 252–263. This provision is similar in some respects to BA 1914, s. 16(16), although that provision also covered voluntary arrangements which, through no fault of the debtor, had become unworkable.

S. 276(2)

Where the court takes this drastic step, the expenses already incurred in connection with the scheme become a first charge on the bankrupt's estate.

Section 277 Petition based on criminal bankruptcy order

277(1) [Duty of court] Subject to section 266(3), the court shall make a bankruptcy order on a petition under section 264(1)(d) on production of a copy of the criminal bankruptcy order on which the petition is based.

This does not apply if it appears to the court that the criminal bankruptcy order has been rescinded on appeal.

277(2) [Effect of appeal pending] Subject to the provisions of this Part, the fact that an appeal is pending against any conviction by virtue of which a criminal bankruptcy order was made does not affect any proceedings on a petition under section 264(1)(d) based on that order.

277(3) [When appeal is pending] For the purposes of this section, an appeal against a conviction is pending—

(a) in any case, until the expiration of the period of 28 days beginning with the date of conviction;

(b) if notice of appeal to the Court of Appeal is given during that period and during that period the appellant notifies the official receiver of it, until the determination of the appeal and thereafter for so long as an appeal to the House of Lords is pending within the meaning of section 40(5) of the Powers of Criminal Courts Act 1973.

(Former provision: IA 1985, s. 125)

General note

This section deals with petitions arising out of criminal bankruptcy orders. Criminal bankruptcy orders were first introduced in 1972, and the legislation currently in force is the Powers of the Criminal Courts Act 1973, ss. 39, 40. However, the power to make such orders was abolished by the Criminal Justice Act 1988, s. 101, with effect from 3 April 1989 (see SI 1989 No. 264 (C.8)), and so it is most unlikely that there will be any occasion to invoke the provisions of s. 264(1)(*d*) or s. 277 in the future.

Criminal bankruptcy orders were designed to punish offenders who caused financial loss to others exceeding £15,000; but they were rarely used – there were a mere 150 in the first five years of the scheme. The Cork Committee regarded them as anomalous, and took the view that they should have no future in insolvency law (see the *Report*, ch. 41). The Committee called for the whole system of criminal bankruptcy to be re-examined (see paras. 1722–1724); and, although the ensuing review by the Hodgson Committee in 1984 recommended, with some reservations, that it should be retained, the government went ahead and abolished it in 1988.

A number of criminal bankruptcy orders remain in force, however, and will continue to do so for some time. Accordingly, although the present section, and the various other sections of IA 1986 which refer to such orders, have also been repealed by the Criminal Justice Act 1988, s. 170(2) and Sch. 16, the repeal is prospective only and will not come into effect until a day to be appointed. (See also the note to s. 264).

COMMENCEMENT AND DURATION OF BANKRUPTCY; DISCHARGE

Section 278   Commencement and continuance

278   The bankruptcy of an individual against whom a bankruptcy order has been made—

(a) commences with the day on which the order is made, and

(b) continues until the individual is discharged under the following provisions of this Chapter.

(Former provision: IA 1985, s. 126(1))

General note

Bankruptcy commences at the date of the order (and not when the petition was presented), and lasts until discharge.

See IR 1986, rr. 6.34 and 6.46.

Section 279   Duration

279(1)   [Discharge from bankruptcy]   Subject as follows, a bankrupt is discharged from bankruptcy—

(a) in the case of an individual who was adjudged bankrupt on a petition under section 264(1)(d) or who had been an undischarged bankrupt at any time in the period of 15 years ending with the commencement of the bankruptcy, by an order of the court under the section next following, and

(b) in any other case, by the expiration of the relevant period under this section.

279(2)   [Relevant period]   That period is as follows—

(a) where a certificate for the summary administration of the bankrupt's estate has been issued and is not revoked before the bankrupt's discharge, the period of 2 years beginning with the commencement of the bankruptcy, and

(b) in any other case, the period of 3 years beginning with the commencement of the bankruptcy.

279(3)   [Court order]   Where the court is satisfied on the application of the official receiver that an undischarged bankrupt in relation to whom subsection (1)(b) applies has failed or is failing to comply with any of his obligations under this Part, the court may order that the relevant period under this section shall cease to run for such period, or until the fulfilment of such conditions (including a condition requiring the court to be satisfied as to any matter), as may be specified in the order.

279(4)   [Power of annulment]   This section is without prejudice to any power of the court to annul a bankruptcy order.

(Former provisions: IA 1985, s. 126(2)–(5); BA 1914, s. 26 (as amended by B(A)A 1926, s. 1 and by IA 1976, s. 7))

General note

Automatic discharge, which was pioneered in 1976, is retained by this provision and, indeed, it becomes the norm. The Cork Committee (*Report*, para. 607) had reservations about automatic discharge, but it is hoped that s. 279(1)(*a*) and (3) will serve to prevent it being abused.

S. 279(1), (2)

Discharge will occur automatically upon the expiration of the "relevant period" from the date of commencement of bankruptcy (two years in the case of a summary administration, or three years in other cases). This period has been reduced from the five years originally prescribed by IA 1976. However, automatic discharge is not available in the case of bankruptcy based on a criminal bankruptcy order, or in the case of a second bankruptcy occurring within 15 years of the first. Application to the court under s. 280 is required in these cases. For further details on discharge see IR 1986, rr. 6.215–6.223.

S. 279(3)

The official receiver can apply to stop the running of the three-year automatic discharge period if the bankrupt is failing to comply with his obligations. Conditions may be imposed before the time begins to run again.

S. 279(4)

The court retains power to annul bankruptcy orders, see s. 282.

Section 280 Discharge by order of the court

280(1) [Application to court] An application for an order of the court discharging an individual from bankruptcy in a case falling within section 279(1)(a) may be made by the bankrupt at any time after the end of the period of 5 years beginning with the commencement of the bankruptcy.

280(2) [Powers of court] On an application under this section the court may—

(a) refuse to discharge the bankrupt from bankruptcy,

(b) make an order discharging him absolutely, or

(c) make an order discharging him subject to such conditions with respect to any income which may subsequently become due to him, or with respect to property devolving upon him, or acquired by him, after his discharge, as may be specified in the order.

280(3) [Commencement of effect of order] The court may provide for an order falling within subsection (2)(b) or (c) to have immediate effect or to have its effect suspended for such period, or until the fulfilment of such conditions (including a condition requiring the court to be satisfied as to any matter), as may be specified in the order.

(Former provisions: IA 1985, s. 127; BA 1914, s. 26 (as amended by B(A)A 1926, s. 1 and by IA 1976, s. 8))

S. 280(1)

This provision deals with the situation where an undischarged bankrupt applies to the court for his discharge. Automatic discharge is not available where a person was made bankrupt as a result of a criminal bankruptcy order or where he had experienced an earlier bankruptcy within the 15 years prior to the commencement of the present bankruptcy. In these cases he must wait for 5 years after the commencement of the bankruptcy to elapse before applying to the court for his discharge. See also IR 1986, rr. 6.215–6.223.

There is no provision in the present Act for the automatic review of cases every five years by the official receiver, as was required by IA 1976, s. 8. However, this is immaterial, as automatic discharge under s. 279 is now the general rule.

S. 280(2), (3)

On such an application the court has a variety of options open to it, including the grant of conditional or suspended discharges. The Secretary of State can appeal against a discharge order, see IR 1986, r. 7.48.

Section 281   Effect of discharge

281(1)   **[Discharge qualified release]**   Subject as follows, where a bankrupt is discharged, the discharge releases him from all the bankruptcy debts, but has no effect—

    (a)   on the functions (so far as they remain to be carried out) of the trustee of his estate, or

    (b)   on the operation, for the purposes of the carrying out of those functions, of the provisions of this Part;

and, in particular, discharge does not affect the right of any creditor of the bankrupt to prove in the bankruptcy for any debt from which the bankrupt is released.

281(2)   **[Enforcement of security]**   Discharge does not affect the right of any secured creditor of the bankrupt to enforce his security for the payment of a debt from which the bankrupt is released.

281(3)   **[Fraud etc.]**   Discharge does not release the bankrupt from any bankruptcy debt which he incurred in respect of, or forbearance in respect of which was secured by means of, any fraud or fraudulent breach of trust to which he was a party.

281(4)   **[Fines, other penalties]**   Discharge does not release the bankrupt from any liability in respect of a fine imposed for an offence or from any liability under a recognisance except, in the case of a penalty imposed for an offence under an enactment relating to the public revenue or of a recognisance, with the consent of the Treasury.

281(5)   **[Debts re damages etc.]**   Discharge does not, except to such extent and on such conditions as the court may direct, release the bankrupt from any bankruptcy debt which—

    (a)   consists in a liability to pay damages for negligence, nuisance or breach of a statutory, contractual or other duty, or to pay damages by virtue of Part I of the Consumer Protection Act 1987, being in either case damages in respect of personal injuries to any person, or

    (b)   arises under any order made in family proceedings.

281(6)   **[Other bankruptcy debts]**   Discharge does not release the bankrupt from such other bankruptcy debts, not being debts provable in his bankruptcy, as are prescribed.

281(7) [Liability as surety] Discharge does not release any person other than the bankrupt from any liability (whether as partner or co-trustee of the bankrupt or otherwise) from which the bankrupt is released by the discharge, or from any liability as surety for the bankrupt or as a person in the nature of such a surety.

281(8) [Definitions] In this section—

"**family proceedings**" means—

(a) family proceedings within the meaning of the Magistrates Courts Act 1980 and any proceedings which would be such proceedings but for section 65(1) (ii) of that Act (proceedings for variation of order for periodical payments); and

(b) family proceedings within the meaning of Part V of the Matrimonial and Family Proceedings Act 1984.

"**fine**" means the same as in the Magistrates' Courts Act 1980; and

"**personal injuries**" includes death and any disease or other impairment of a person's physical or mental condition.

(Former provisions: IA 1985, s. 128; BA 1914, s. 28)

S. 281(1)

As a general rule, discharge releases the bankrupt from liability in respect of "bankruptcy debts" (see s. 382). However, any residual functions of the trustee are not to be affected, and creditors in respect of whose debts the bankrupt has been released by the discharge may still prove in the bankruptcy. See further IR 1986, r. 6.223.

Note also the effect of discharge on disqualifications, see for example s. 427(2)(*a*).

S. 281(2)–(6), (8)

In s. 281(5)(*a*) the words "or to pay damages by virtue of Part I of the Consumer Protection Act 1987, being in either case" have been substituted for the former word "being" by the Consumer Protection Act 1987, s. 48 and Sch. 4, para. 12 as from 1 March 1988 (see SI 1988 No. 1680 (C. 51)). Subsection (5) has been amended by the Children Act 1989, Sch. 11, para. 11(1) which removed the words "or in domestic proceedings" from the original text. Subsection (8) now has a new definition of "family proceedings" provided by the Children Act 1989, Sch. 11, para. 11(2).

These provisions deal with the exceptions to the general rule of release in s. 281(1). Note especially IR 1986, r. 6.223 to explain the word "prescribed" in s. 281(6). Security enforcement rights are preserved notwithstanding the release of the debt. Debts connected with fraud or breach of trust survive, as does liability in respect of a fine (see s. 281(8)) or similar penalty (note the exception for fines, etc., in respect of public revenue offences). Liability to pay damages in respect of personal injuries (see s. 281(8)), or liability arising from family or domestic proceedings (see s. 281(8)) is not released unless the court so directs. There is also no release in respect of debts not provable in bankruptcy. Note that the list of exceptions in BA 1914, s. 28 has been widened. The Cork Committee recommended that there should be no release of fines on discharge, but by a majority voted against allowing claims for personal injury to survive – see the *Report*, paras. 1330 and 1333 respectively. Both items, however, have been added to the list of exceptions.

Section 281(4) has effect as if the reference to a fine included a reference to a confiscation order, as from 3 April 1989 (see Criminal Justice Act 1988, s. 170(1) and Sch. 15, para. 110 and Criminal Justice Act 1988 (Commencement No. 7) Order 1989 (SI 1989 No. 264) (C. 8)).

S. 281(7)

Although the bankrupt may be released from liability for a debt, any co-obligor (e.g. a partner of the bankrupt, or co-trustee, etc.) and any person liable as surety for him is not so released.

Section 282   Court's power to annul bankruptcy order

282(1)   [Power of annulment]   The court may annul a bankruptcy order if it at any time appears to the court—

   (a) that, on any grounds existing at the time the order was made, the order ought not to have been made, or

   (b) that, to the extent required by the rules, the bankruptcy debts and the expenses of the bankruptcy have all, since the making of the order, been either paid or secured for to the satisfaction of the court.

282(2)   [Where petition under s. 264(1)(a), (b), (c)]   The court may annul a bankruptcy order made against an individual on a petition under paragraph (a), (b) or (c) of section 264(1) if it at any time appears to the court, on an application by the Official Petitioner—

   (a) that the petition was pending at a time when a criminal bankruptcy order was made against the individual or was presented after such an order was so made, and

   (b) no appeal is pending (within the meaning of section 277) against the individual's conviction of any offence by virtue of which the criminal bankruptcy order was made;

and the court shall annul a bankruptcy order made on a petition under section 264(1) (d) if it at any time appears to the court that the criminal bankruptcy order on which the petition was based has been rescinded in consequence of an appeal.

282(3)   [Annulment whether or not discharged]   The court may annul a bankruptcy order whether or not the bankrupt has been discharged from the bankruptcy.

282(4)   [Effect of annulment]   Where the court annuls a bankruptcy order (whether under this section or under section 261 in Part VIII)—

   (a) any sale or other disposition of property, payment made or other thing duly done, under any provision in this Group of Parts, by or under the authority of the official receiver or a trustee of the bankrupt's estate or by the court is valid, but

   (b) if any of the bankrupt's estate is then vested, under any such provision, in such a trustee, it shall vest in such person as the court may appoint or, in default of any such appointment, revert to the bankrupt on such terms (if any) as the court may direct;

and the court may include in its order such supplemental provisions as may be authorised by the rules.

282(5)   [Undischarged bankrupt under s. 279]   In determining for the purposes of section 279 whether a person was an undischarged bankrupt at any time, any time when he was a bankrupt by virtue of an order that was subsequently annulled is to be disregarded.

(Former provisions: IA 1985, s. 129; BA 1914, s. 29)

S. 282(1), (3)

The court can annul a bankruptcy order if it should never have been made and also if the bankrupt has paid all his debts and bankruptcy expenses to the extent required by the rules – see IR 1986, s. 6.211. Annulment can be granted even though discharge has occurred. The Secretary of State can appeal against an annulment order, see IR 1986, r. 7.48. An annulment of a bankruptcy order was refused by Warner J in *Re Robertson (A Bankrupt)* [1989] 1 WLR 1139 where there had been failure to prove all debts. Harman J considered the nature of the jurisdiction to annul in *Re A Debtor (No. 68 of 1992)* [1993] TLR 69. Here the point was made that on an annulment hearing under s. 282 it was not possible for the court to consider evidence which had been unavailable to the court which had made the bankruptcy order in the first place. The answer to this problem might be for the bankrupt to utilise the s. 375 review procedure. See the discussion thereto.

There is no provision in s. 282 requiring the annulment order to be gazetted and published in a local paper, as was necessary under BA 1914, s. 29(3): now see IR 1986, r. 6.212. Formerly an application for annulment had to be supplemented with a request for rescission of the receiving order under what is now s. 375(1). With the abolition of receiving orders this is no longer necessary. For a Court of Appeal authority on rescission of receiving orders, which might have some impact on judicial practice in cases of annulment of bankruptcy orders, see *Re A Debtor (No. 707 of 1985), The Times,* 21 January 1988.

Under BA 1914, s. 29, the application for annulment had to be made by "any person interested". This requirement, which caused problems in *Re Beesley, ex parte Beesley* v *The Official Receiver & Ors* [1975] 1 All ER 385, has been dropped. See here *F* v. *F* [1994] 1 FLR 359 (application by wife of debtor). For discussion, see Miller (1994) 10 IL & P 66. A similar change has been made with regard to s. 375.

For further provisions on annulment, see IR 1986, rr. 6.206–6.214.

S. 282(2)

This provision confirms the supremacy of the system of criminal bankruptcy over ordinary bankruptcy cases. The subsection also allows the court to annul a bankruptcy order which was granted on a petition based on a criminal bankruptcy order if that latter order has been rescinded on appeal.

Note prospective amendment: s. 282(2) is to be repealed by the Criminal Justice Act 1988, s. 170(2) and Sch. 16 as from a day to be appointed; see the note to s. 264.

S. 282(4)

This deals with the practical effects of annulment – dispositions of property, etc. carried out by a trustee are valid. On annulment, the court can order the revesting of the property in the former bankrupt or some other person. For the effect of annulment on prosecutions for bankruptcy offices, see s. 350(2).

S. 282(5)

This is an explanatory provision that would be better placed in s. 279 to which it refers. It would be particularly relevant to s. 279(1)(*a*) – a person who was declared bankrupt only to have the order annulled is not to be regarded as undergoing a second bankruptcy in the event of a subsequent bankruptcy order being made against him.

Chapter II — Protection of Bankrupt's Estate and Investigation of His Affairs

Section 283 Definition of bankrupt's estate

283(1) [Bankrupt's estate] Subject as follows, a bankrupt's estate for the purposes of any of this Group of Parts comprises—

(a) all property belonging to or vested in the bankrupt at the commencement of the bankruptcy, and

(b) any property which by virtue of any of the following provisions of this Part is comprised in that estate or is treated as falling within the preceding paragraph.

283(2) [Non-application of s. 283(1)] Subsection (1) does not apply to—

(a) such tools, books, vehicles and other items of equipment as are necessary to the bankrupt for use personally by him in his employment, business or vocation;

(b) such clothing, bedding, furniture, household equipment and provisions as are necessary for satisfying the basic domestic needs of the bankrupt and his family.

This subsection is subject to section 308 in Chapter IV (certain excluded property reclaimable by trustee).

283(3) [Further non-application of s. 283(1)] Subsection (1) does not apply to—

(a) property held by the bankrupt on trust for any other person, or

(b) the right of nomination to a vacant ecclesiastical benefice.

283(3A) [Further non-application of s. 283(1)] Subject to section 308A in Chapter IV, subsection (1) does not apply to—

(a) a tenancy which is an assured tenancy or an assured agricultural occupancy, within the meaning of Part I of the Housing Act 1988, and the terms of which inhibit an assignment as mentioned in section 127(5) of the Rent Act 1977, or

(b) a protected tenancy, within the meaning of the Rent Act 1977, in respect of which, by virtue of any provision of part IX of that Act, no premium can lawfully be required as a condition of assignment, or

(c) a tenancy of a dwelling-house by virtue of which the bankrupt is, within the meaning of the Rent (Agriculture) Act 1976, a protected occupier of the dwelling-house, and the terms of which inhibit an assignment as mentioned in section 127(5) of the Rent Act 1977, or

(d) a secure tenancy, within the meaning of Part IV of the Housing Act 1985, which is not capable of being assigned, except in the cases mentioned in section 91(3) of that Act.

283(4) [References to property] References in any of this Group of Parts to property, in relation to a bankrupt, include references to any power exercisable by him over or in respect of property except in so far as the power is exercisable over or in respect of property not for the time being comprised in the bankrupt's estate and—

(a) is so exercisable at a time after either the official receiver has had his release in respect of that estate under section 299(2) in Chapter III or a meeting summoned by the trustee of that estate under section 331 in Chapter IV has been held, or

(b) cannot be so exercised for the benefit of the bankrupt;

and a power exercisable over or in respect of property is deemed for the purposes of any of this Group of Parts to vest in the person entitled to exercise it at the time of the transaction or event by virtue of which it is exercisable by that person (whether or not it becomes so exercisable at that time).

283(5)   **[Property in bankrupt's estate]**   For the purposes of any such provision in the Group of Parts, property comprised in a bankrupt's estate is so comprised subject to the rights of any person other than the bankrupt (whether as a secured creditor of the bankrupt or otherwise) in relation thereto, but disregarding—

(a) any rights in relation to which a statement such as is required by section 269(1)(a) was made in the petition on which the bankrupt was adjudged bankrupt, and

(b) any rights which have been otherwise given up in accordance with the rules.

283(6)   **[Other enactments]**   This section has effect subject to the provisions of any enactment not contained in this Act under which any property is to be excluded from a bankrupt's estate.

(Former provisions: IA 1985, s. 130; BA 1914, ss. 38, 50)

General note

The major change effected by this provision is the abolition of the doctrine of reputed ownership. This doctrine, which could trace its origins back to 1623, stated that if the debtor appeared to be in possession of property which secretly belonged to another, that would boost his creditworthiness, and therefore his creditors should be entitled to treat that property as part of the bankrupt's estate. The rationale of this doctrine, which applied only to traders who became bankrupt, was criticised by Parke B long ago in *Belcher* v *Bellamy* (1848) 2 Exch 303. It did not reflect commercial practices and it appeared particularly inappropriate with the growth of hire-purchase and consumer credit in the twentieth century. Both the courts and Parliament began to curtail the scope of the doctrine – see, e.g. Consumer Credit Act 1974, s. 192(3) and Sch. 4, para. 6. The doctrine did not apply in Ireland and many Commonwealth jurisdictions. Accordingly, calls for abolition were made by the Cork Committee (*Report*, 1093) and the White Paper, para. 116. Incidentally, the abolition of the doctrine may throw up difficulties – the problem of title retention clauses which has troubled corporate insolvency law over the past decade might now raise its ugly head. The doctrine of reputed ownership which applied only to personal and not corporate insolvency law at least served to keep that problem at bay in the law of bankruptcy. The doctrine of "relation back" of the trustee's title to the date of the act of bankruptcy has also been abandoned in the wake of the new procedures for bankruptcy. See *Re Dennis* [1993] Ch. 72 for the significance of this change. For general discussion of the new rules on the bankrupt's estate see Milman (1988) 4 IL & P 71.

S. 283(1)

This section identifies the bankrupt's estate. Note the possible impact of ss. 307–309 here and the general definition of "property" in s. 436.

    For the commencement of the bankruptcy, see s. 278(*a*).

S. 283(2), (3)

These provisions list those items that are excluded from the estate. Section 283(2) again reflects a change in the law. It was felt that a bankrupt ought to be allowed to keep a greater range of personal possessions than the BA 1914 permitted – see the Cork Report, para. 1113. Thus, the £250 limit has been dropped. It had been overtaken by inflation and discriminated against debtors with capital-intensive businesses. Vehicles are now included among the exemptions, as are general items of business equipment. Thus the old restrictive authorities on "tools" such as *Re Sherman* [1916] WN 26 have lost much of their importance. On the other hand, such property may now be "replaced" by the trustee under s. 308. Trust property is not included in the estate – see *Re Tout & Finch Ltd* [1954] 1 WLR 178 and *Re McKeown* [1974] NI 226. Section 283(3) repeats BA 1914, s. 38(*b*).

S. 283(3A)

Subsection (3A) was introduced into s. 283 by s. 117(1) of the Housing Act 1988. Its effect is to add assured tenancies, protected tenancies, protected occupancies of dwelling houses and secure tenancies to the list of exclusions from the bankrupt's estate. This provision has to be read however in the light of the newly introduced s. 308A which enables the trustee to claim such tenancies by giving notice to the bankrupt.

S. 283(4)

This deals with rights to exercise powers over the property of others.

S. 283(5)

Third party rights over the bankrupt's property are preserved, unless those rights have been surrendered.

S. 283(6)

Property may be excluded from the estate by other statutes.

Section 284   Restrictions on dispositions of property

284(1)   [Where person adjudged bankrupt]   Where a person is adjudged bankrupt, any disposition of property made by that person in the period to which this section applies is void except to the extent that it is or was made with the consent of the court, or is or was subsequently ratified by the court.

284(2)   [Application of s. 284(1) to payment]   Subsection (1) applies to a payment (whether in cash or otherwise) as it applies to a disposition of property and, accordingly, where any payment is void by virtue of that subsection, the person paid shall hold the sum paid for the bankrupt as part of his estate.

284(3)   [Relevant period]   This section applies to the period beginning with the day of the presentation of the petition for the bankruptcy order and ending with the vesting, under Chapter IV of this Part, of the bankrupt's estate in a trustee.

284(4)   [Limit to effect of s. 284(1)–(3)]   The preceding provisions of this section do not give a remedy against any person—

    (a) in respect of any property or payment which he received before the commencement of the bankruptcy in good faith, for value and without notice that the petition had been presented, or

(b) in respect of any interest in property which derives from an interest in respect of which there is, by virtue of this subsection, no remedy.

284(5) [Debt after commencement of bankruptcy]　Where after the commencement of his bankruptcy the bankrupt has incurred a debt to a banker or other person by reason of the making of a payment which is void under this section, that debt is deemed for the purposes of any of this Group of Parts to have been incurred before the commencement of the bankruptcy unless—

(a) that banker or person had notice of the bankruptcy before the debt was incurred, or

(b) it is not reasonably practicable for the amount of the payment to be recovered from the person to whom it was made.

284(6) [Property not in bankrupt's estate]　A disposition of property is void under this section notwithstanding that the property is not or, as the case may be, would not be comprised in the bankrupt's estate; but nothing in this section affects any disposition made by a person of property held by him on trust for any other person.

(Former provisions: IA 1985, s. 131; BA 1914, s. 45 and B(A)A 1926, s. 4)

General note

In the context of the financial markets, s. 284 does not apply to a market contract or any disposition of property in pursuance of such a contract, the provision of margin in relation to market contracts, a market charge, and certain other transactions: see CA 1989, ss. 163(4), 175(3)–(5), and the note on p. 3.

S. 284(1)–(3), (6)

Any disposition of property or payment of money by the debtor after the date of the petition will be void unless approved by the court, either at the time or subsequently. This is so even if the property would not have formed part of the bankrupt's estate under s. 283. Moreover it would appear that a transfer of an interest in the matrimonial home pursuant to a consent order made under s. 24 of the Matrimonial Causes Act 1973 constitutes a "disposition" for these purposes and is therefore void. This startling conclusion was arrived at by Nicholas Stewart QC (sitting as a deputy judge of the High Court) in *Re Flint* [1993] Ch. 319. This case once again illustrates that where a conflict occurs between rules of family law and principles of bankruptcy law the latter are often victorious. This critical view of the law is reinforced by *Woodley* v *Woodley (No. 2)* [1994] 1 WLR 1167 where the Court of Appeal held that the presentation of a bankruptcy petition by a debtor husband is *not* a disposition for the purposes of s. 37 of the Matrimonial Causes Act 1973 and cannot be challenged as an attempt to avoid an order for matrimonial relief.

　This provision compensates for the abolition of the doctrine of "relation back" of title and the end of the protection offered by receiving orders.

　Note that s. 284 allows the court some discretion with regard to avoidance – the provision in BA 1914 allowed no such flexibility.

S. 284(4)

This offers protection to third parties, especially bona fide purchasers for value without notice of the petition.

S. 284(5)

This provision deals with payments by the bankrupt avoided under this section, thus leaving the bankrupt indebted to the payee. If the sum of money can be recovered from the payee he will be treated as a pre-bankruptcy creditor unless he had notice of the petition at the time the debt was incurred.

Section 285   Restriction on proceedings and remedies

285(1)   [Court's power to stay]   At any time when proceedings on a bankruptcy petition are pending or an individual has been adjudged bankrupt the court may stay an action, execution or other legal process against the property or person of the debtor or, as the case may be, of the bankrupt.

285(2)   [Where proceedings pending against individual]   Any court in which proceedings are pending against any individual may, on proof that a bankruptcy petition has been presented in respect of that individual or that he is an undischarged bankrupt, either stay the proceedings or allow them to continue on such terms as it thinks fit.

285(3)   [Limit on creditors' actions]   After the making of a bankruptcy order no person who is a creditor of the bankrupt in respect of a debt provable in the bankruptcy shall—

(a) have any remedy against the property or person of the bankrupt in respect of that debt, or

(b) before the discharge of the bankrupt, commence any action or other legal proceedings against the bankrupt except with leave of the court and on such terms as the court may impose.

This is subject to sections 346 (enforcement procedures) and 347 (limited right to distress).

285(4)   [Right of secured creditor]   Subject as follows, subsection (3) does not affect the right of a secured creditor of the bankrupt to enforce his security.

285(5)   [Where goods of undischarged bankrupt held by pledge etc.]   Where any goods of an undischarged bankrupt are held by any person by way of pledge, pawn or other security, the official receiver may, after giving notice in writing of his intention to do so, inspect the goods.

Where such a notice has been given to any person, that person is not entitled, without leave of the court, to realise his security unless he has given the trustee of the bankrupt's estate a reasonable opportunity of inspecting the goods and of exercising the bankrupt's right of redemption.

285(6)   [Interpretation]   References in this section to the property or goods of the bankrupt are to any of his property or goods, whether or not comprised in his estate.

(Former provisions: IA 1985, s. 132; BA 1914, ss. 7, 9)

General note

In relation to the financial markets, nothing in s. 285 affects any action taken by an exchange or clearing house for the purpose of its default proceedings: CA 1989, s. 161(4).

S. 285(1)

This provision authorises the court (for definition, see s. 385) to stay actions, executions etc., where a bankruptcy petition is pending or, indeed, after the grant of the order. The Blagden Committee (Cmnd 221, 1957), paras. 19–20, called for the insertion of a provision *ex abundanti cautela* to the effect that High Court proceedings could be stayed under this provision. This has not been done, presumably because the existing language was deemed sufficiently wide. In *Re Smith (A Bankrupt), ex parte Braintree District Council* [1990] 2 AC 215 the House of Lords held that this provision did enable it to stay proceedings for commital for non payment of rates. There was no justification for excluding such proceedings from the scope of s. 285.

S. 285(2)

Any court may exercise such staying powers on proof that a bankruptcy petition is pending.

S. 285(3), (4)

This compels unsecured creditors of the bankrupt to look solely to bankruptcy procedures as a remedy to secure payment of their debts once the bankruptcy order has been made. This general rule is qualified by ss. 346, 347. Secured creditors do not suffer such a disability, unless s. 285(5) below applies.

S. 285(5)

This allows the official receiver to inspect any of the bankrupt's goods which have been used as security and to redeem them if necessary. The person holding the goods cannot enforce his security without the leave of the court.

S. 285(6)

This gives the words "property" and "goods" a meaning that is not restricted by s. 283.

Section 286   Power to appoint interim receiver

286(1)   [Court's power]   The court may, if it is shown to be necessary for the protection of the debtor's property, at any time after the presentation of a bankruptcy petition and before making a bankruptcy order, appoint the official receiver to be interim receiver of the debtor's property.

286(2)   [Appointment of person instead of official receiver]   Where the court has, on a debtor's petition, appointed an insolvency practitioner under section 273 and it is shown to the court as mentioned in subsection (1) of this section, the court may, without making a bankruptcy order, appoint that practitioner, instead of the official receiver, to be interim receiver of the debtor's property.

286(3)   [Rights, powers etc. of interim receiver]   The court may by an order appointing any person to be an interim receiver direct that his powers shall be limited or restricted in any respect; but, save as so directed, an interim receiver has, in relation to the debtor's property, all the rights, powers, duties and immunities of a receiver and manager under the next section.

286(4)   [Contents of court order]   An order of the court appointing any person to be an interim receiver shall require that person to take immediate possession of the debtor's property or, as the case may be, the part of it to which his powers as interim receiver are limited.

286(5) **[Duties of debtor]** Where an interim receiver has been appointed, the debtor shall give him such inventory of his property and such other information, and shall attend on the interim receiver at such times, as the latter may for the purpose of carrying out his functions under this section reasonably require.

286(6) **[Application of s. 285(3)]** Where an interim receiver is appointed, section 285(3) applies for the period between the appointment and the making of a bankruptcy order on the petition, or the dismissal of the petition, as if the appointment were the making of such an order.

286(7) **[Ceasing to be interim receiver]** A person ceases to be interim receiver of a debtor's property if the bankruptcy petition relating to the debtor is dismissed, if a bankruptcy order is made on the petition or if the court by order otherwise terminates the appointment.

286(8) **[Interpretation]** References in this section to the debtor's property are to all his property, whether or not it would be comprised in his estate if he were adjudged bankrupt.

(Former provisions: IA 1985, s. 133; BA 1914, s. 8)

S. 286(1), (2)

The court may appoint the official receiver as an interim receiver after the presentation of the bankruptcy petition if such an appointment is necessary to protect the debtor's property. The interim receiver has a company law counterpart in the provisional liquidator (IA 1986, s. 135). As an alternative to the official receiver, the person appointed on a debtor's petition under s. 273(2) to make a report on the possibility of a rescue plan can be given the rôle of interim receiver.

The law on interim receivers can be expanded by the rules – see Sch. 9, paras. 9, 30. The key provisions are IR 1986, rr. 6.51–6.57.

S. 286(3)

This describes the rôle of such an interim receiver – note the degree of control over him exercised by the court.

S. 286(4), (8)

The interim receiver should normally take immediate possession of the debtor's assets – even those assets which would not subsequently form part of the bankrupt's estate.

S. 286(5)

This requires the debtor to accede to the interim receiver's demands for assistance.

S. 286(6)

During this interim receivership the debtor's assets enjoy the same protection as if a bankruptcy order had been made.

S. 286(7)

This deals with termination of the interim receivership.

Section 287   Receivership pending appointment of trustee

287(1) **[Official receiver, receiver and manager]** Between the making of a bankruptcy order and the time at which the bankrupt's estate vests in a trustee under

Chapter IV of this Part, the official receiver is the receiver and (subject to section 370 (special manager)) the manager of the bankrupt's estate and is under a duty to act as such.

287(2) [Function and powers of official receiver] The function of the official receiver while acting as receiver or manager of the bankrupt's estate under this section is to protect the estate; and for this purpose—

    (a) he has the same powers as if he were a receiver or manager appointed by the High Court, and

    (b) he is entitled to sell or otherwise dispose of any perishable goods comprised in the estate and any other goods so comprised the value of which is likely to diminish if they are not disposed of.

287(3) [Steps re protecting property] The official receiver while acting as receiver or manager of the estate under this section—

    (a) shall take all such steps as he thinks fit for protecting any property which may be claimed for the estate by the trustee of that estate,

    (b) is not, except in pursuance of directions given by the Secretary of State, required to do anything that involves his incurring expenditure,

    (c) may, if he thinks fit (and shall, if so directed by the court) at any time summon a general meeting of the bankrupt's creditors.

287(4) [Liability of official receiver] Where—

    (a) the official receiver acting as receiver or manager of the estate under this section seizes or disposes of any property which is not comprised in the estate, and

    (b) at the time of the seizure or disposal the official receiver believes, and has reasonable grounds for believing, that he is entitled (whether in pursuance of an order of the court or otherwise) to seize or dispose of that property,

the official receiver is not liable to any person in respect of any loss or damage resulting from the seizure or disposal except in so far as that loss or damage is caused by his negligence; and he has a lien on the property, or the proceeds of its sale, for such of the expenses of the bankruptcy as were incurred in connection with the seizure or disposal.

287(5) [Non-application] This section does not apply where by virtue of section 297 (appointment of trustee; special cases) the bankrupt's estate vests in a trustee immediately on the making of the bankruptcy order.

(Former provisions: IA 1985, s. 134; BA 1914, ss. 61, 74)

S. 287(1), (2), (5)

The official receiver is to act as receiver and manager of the bankrupt's estate between the date of the bankruptcy order and when the trustee takes control. If the estate has vested immediately in the trustee by virtue of s. 297, then s. 287 does not apply. His rôle is of a caretaker nature (like a court-appointed receiver and manager), although he may sell perishables, etc.

    Under BA 1914, s. 10, the official receiver could, in the period before the receiving order and the trustee taking over, appoint a manager – under s. 287 it seems that the official receiver must fulfil this rôle himself. The court can, however, appoint a special manager under s. 370 instead of the official receiver.

Further details on the rôle of the official receiver as receiver and manager may be provided by regulations which may be made by the Secretary of State under the rules: see Sch. 9, paras. 10, 30 and IR 1986, r. 12.1(1), (2).

For the fees of the official receiver for exercising his functions under s. 287 see the Insolvency Fees Order 1986 (SI 1986 No. 2030) (as amended).

S. 287(3)

These paragraphs detail further the obligations of the official receiver while acting as receiver and manager. His duty to protect the assets is stressed, although he cannot incur expenditure unless directed to do so by the Secretary of State. He may, and, if directed by the court, must, call meetings of creditors.

S. 287(4)

This offers protection from liability for wrongful seizure of assets where the official receiver has acted reasonably and without negligence. Moreover, he has a lien over any proceeds of the wrongful sale to cover his expenses.

Section 288   Statement of affairs

288(1)   [Submission of statement to official receiver]   Where a bankruptcy order has been made otherwise than on a debtor's petition, the bankrupt shall submit a statement of his affairs to the official receiver before the end of the period of 21 days beginning with the commencement of the bankruptcy.

288(2)   [Contents of statement]   The statement of affairs shall contain—

(a) such particulars of the bankrupt's creditors and of his debts and other liabilities and of his assets as may be prescribed, and

(b) such other information as may be prescribed.

288(3)   [Powers of official receiver]   The official receiver may, if he thinks fit—

(a) release the bankrupt from his duty under subsection (1), or

(b) extend the period specified in that subsection;

and where the official receiver has refused to exercise a power conferred by this section, the court, if it thinks fit, may exercise it.

288(4)   [Penalty for non-compliance]   A bankrupt who—

(a) without reasonable excuse fails to comply with the obligation imposed by this section, or

(b) without reasonable excuse submits a statement of affairs that does not comply with the prescribed requirements,

is guilty of a contempt of court and liable to be punished accordingly (in addition to any other punishment to which he may be subject).

(Former provisions: IA 1985, s. 135; BA 1914, s. 14)

S. 288(1), (3)

Where a bankruptcy order has been made on the initiative of a creditor, the bankrupt normally has 21 days to submit a statement of affairs to the official receiver. A bankrupt may be released from this obligation by the official receiver (see IR 1986, r. 6.62 and r. 6.76), who may also extend the 21-day period. If the official receiver refuses to exercise his discretion the court may intervene. This provision differs from its predecessor in a number of respects. The time period mentioned in BA 1914, s. 14 was seven days. Furthermore, under the 1914 Act a statement of affairs was required within three days where the debtor had petitioned for his own bankruptcy: the position now is governed by s. 272(2).

S. 288(2)

This specifies the contents of the statement of affairs. The rules amplify these requirements: see IR 1986, rr. 6.58–6.66. For the evidential status of such a statement, see s. 433.

S. 288(4)

Non-compliance can result in liability for contempt of court.

Section 289   Investigatory duties of official receiver

289(1)   [Investigation and report]   Subject to subsection (5) below, it is the duty of the official receiver to investigate the conduct and affairs of every bankrupt and to make such report (if any) to the court as he thinks fit.

289(2)   [Where application under s. 280]   Where an application is made by the bankrupt under section 280 for his discharge from bankruptcy, it is the duty of the official receiver to make a report to the court with respect to the prescribed matters; and the court shall consider that report before determining what order (if any) to make under that section.

289(3)   [Report prima facie evidence]   A report by the official receiver under this section shall, in any proceedings, be prima facie evidence of the facts stated in it.

289(4)   [Interpretation of s. 289(1)]   In subsection (1) the reference to the conduct and affairs of a bankrupt includes his conduct and affairs before the making of the order by which he was adjudged bankrupt.

289(5)   [Where certificate for administration]   Where a certificate for the summary administration of the bankrupt's estate is for the time being in force, the official receiver shall carry out an investigation under subsection (1) only if he thinks fit.

(Former provisions: IA 1985, s. 136; BA 1914, s. 73)

S. 289(1), (4)

These subsections impose a duty on the official receiver to investigate the bankrupt's conduct and affairs (including his business, if any: see s. 385(2)). He can use his discretion whether to report to the court or not.

S. 289(2)

This imposes a more specific obligation – the official receiver must report to the court where a bankrupt applies for his discharge under s. 280. This report is to make reference to the "prescribed matters" – see IR 1986, r. 6.218.

S. 289(3)

Any report prepared by the official receiver under s. 289(1) or (2) is prima facie evidence of the facts stated therein.

S. 289(5)

This appears to be a new provision authorising the official receiver to omit investigations under s. 289(1) where there is a certificate for summary administration in operation (see ss. 275, 297). The policy here is to cut out expensive formalities in the case of small bankruptcies.

Section 290   Public examination of bankrupt

290(1)   [Application to court]   Where a bankruptcy order has been made, the official receiver may at any time before the discharge of the bankrupt apply to the court for the public examination of the bankrupt.

290(2)   [Duty of official receiver to make application]   Unless the court otherwise orders, the official receiver shall make an application under subsection (1) if notice requiring him to do so is given to him, in accordance with the rules, by one of the bankrupt's creditors with the concurrence of not less than one-half, in value, of those creditors (including the creditor giving notice).

290(3)   [Direction re public examination]   On an application under subsection (1), the court shall direct that a public examination of the bankrupt shall be held on a day appointed by the court; and the bankrupt shall attend on that day and be publicly examined as to his affairs, dealings and property.

290(4)   [Persons taking part in examination]   The following may take part in the public examination of the bankrupt and may question him concerning his affairs, dealings and property and the causes of his failure, namely—

   (a) the official receiver and, in the case of an individual adjudged bankrupt on a petition under section 264(1)(d), the Official Petitioner,

   (b) the trustee of the bankrupt's estate, if his appointment has taken effect,

   (c) any person who has been appointed as special manager of the bankrupt's estate or business.

   (d) any creditor of the bankrupt who has tendered a proof in the bankruptcy.

290(5)   [Penalty re non-attendance]   If a bankrupt without reasonable excuse fails at any time to attend his public examination under this section he is guilty of a contempt of court and liable to be punished accordingly (in addition to any other punishment to which he may be subject).

(Former provisions: IA 1985, s. 137; BA 1914, s. 15 (as amended by IA 1976, s. 6))

General note

Under BA 1914, s. 15, a public examination was required in every case of bankruptcy. This was unfortunate because it seemed unnecessary to ask every bankrupt to undergo such an ordeal and, in some cases, public examinations caused embarrassment to third parties not directly concerned with the bankruptcy. The most notorious example of this was provided by the public examination of John Poulson in 1972. Accordingly, IA 1976, s. 6 permitted the official receiver to ask the court to relieve certain bankrupts of this onerous procedure.

   The Bankruptcy Rules 1952, rr. 188–196 contained additional material on public examinations and the relevant provisions are now IR 1986, rr. 6.172–6.177.

S. 290(1), (2)

The position now is that a public examination will only be held where the official receiver asks for one. However, his hand can be forced by a majority of the bankrupt's creditors. It was held by the Court of Appeal in *Re Seagull Manufacturing Co. Ltd* [1993] Ch. 345; [1993] BCC 241 that the court has jurisdiction in the case of a public examination under s. 133 to order a person resident outside the jurisdiction to attend for examination. (For the position in a private examination, see the notes to s. 236, above.)

S. 290(3), (5)

The court fixes the date of the public examination and the bankrupt must attend or face liability for contempt. Self-incrimination is no excuse for refusal to answer questions (*Re Paget* [1927] 2 Ch. 85).

S. 290(4)

This determines who may attend and participate in the public examination. This means that the authority of *Re Stern (A Bankrupt)* [1982] 1 WLR 860 has been superseded.

Section 291   Duties of bankrupt in relation to official receiver

291(1)   **[Duties where bankruptcy order made]**   Where a bankruptcy order has been made, the bankrupt is under a duty—

(a) to deliver possession of his estate to the official receiver, and

(b) to deliver up to the official receiver all books, papers and other records of which he has possession or control and which relate to his estate and affairs (including any which would be privileged from disclosure in any proceedings).

291(2)   **[Property not capable of delivery to official receiver]**   In the case of any part of the bankrupt's estate which consists of things possession of which cannot be delivered to the official receiver, and in the case of any property that may be claimed for the bankrupt's estate by the trustee, it is the bankrupt's duty to do all things as may reasonably be required by the official receiver for the protection of those things or that property.

291(3)   **[Non-application of s. 291(1), (2)]**   Subsections (1) and (2) do not apply where by virtue of section 297 below the bankrupt's estate vests in a trustee immediately on the making of the bankruptcy order.

291(4)   **[Bankrupt to give information]**   The bankrupt shall give the official receiver such inventory of his estate and such other information, and shall attend on the official receiver at such times, as the official receiver may for any of the purposes of this Chapter reasonably require.

291(5)   **[Application of s. 291(4)]**   Subsection (4) applies to a bankrupt after his discharge.

291(6)   **[Penalty for non-compliance]**   If the bankrupt without reasonable excuse fails to comply with any obligation imposed by this section, he is guilty of a contempt of court and liable to be punished accordingly (in addition to any other punishment to which he may be subject).

(Former provisions: IA 1985, s. 138; BA 1914, s. 22)

S. 291(1)–(3)

This lists some of the obligations of the bankrupt towards the official receiver – this includes handing over property in his possession, assisting the recovery of other items and delivering up all relevant books and records. These obligations do not apply to the special cases covered by s. 297.

S. 291(4), (5)

This imposes an additional obligation on the bankrupt to provide information and be prepared to assist the official receiver where this is reasonably requested. The obligation continues to apply after discharge.

S. 291(6)

Failure to comply with the above obligations results in liability for contempt of court.

Chapter III — Trustees In Bankruptcy

TENURE OF OFFICE AS TRUSTEE

Section 292   Power to make appointments

292(1)   [Exercise of power]   The power to appoint a person as trustee of a bankrupt's estate (whether the first such trustee or a trustee appointed to fill any vacancy) is exercisable—

(a) except at a time when a certificate for the summary administration of the bankrupt's estate is in force, by a general meeting of the bankrupt's creditors;

(b) under section 295(2), 296(2) or 300(6) below in this Chapter, by the Secretary of State; or

(c) under section 297, by the court.

292(2)   [Qualification for trustee]   No person may be appointed as trustee of a bankrupt's estate unless he is, at the time of the appointment, qualified to act as an insolvency practitioner in relation to the bankrupt.

292(3)   [Joint trustees]   Any power to appoint a person as trustee of a bankrupt's estate includes power to appoint two or more persons as joint trustees; but such an appointment must make provision as to the circumstances in which the trustees must act together and the circumstances in which one or more of them may act for the others.

292(4)   [Requirement of acceptance of appointment]   The appointment of any person as trustee takes effect only if that person accepts the appointment in accordance with the rules. Subject to this, the appointment of any person as trustee takes effect at the time specified in his certificate of appointment.

292(5)   [Effect]   This section is without prejudice to the provisions of this Chapter under which the official receiver is, in certain circumstances, to be trustee of the estate.

(Former provisions: IA 1985, s. 139; BA 1914, ss. 19, 77)

S. 292(1)

This determines who may appoint a trustee in bankruptcy. Normally (except in cases of summary administration) it will be a decision for the creditors, although there are situations whether the Secretary of State, or the court, may assume responsibility for the appointment. See generally IR 1986, rr. 6.120–6.125.

S. 292(2)

Under BA 1914, s. 19 the trustee had to be a "fit person" – now he must be properly qualified under Pt. XIII.

S. 292(3)

This restates BA 1914, s. 77 which permitted the appointment of joint trustees.

S. 292(4)

For the appointment to take effect the trustee must accept the post in accordance with the rules (see IR 1986, r. 6.124). The date of the appointment is specified in the certificate of appointment.

S. 292(5)

The aforementioned provisions do not apply where the official receiver acts as trustee – see ss. 293(3), 295(4), 297 and 300(2).

Section 293   Summoning of meeting to appoint first trustee

293(1)   [Duty of official receiver]   Where a bankruptcy order has been made and no certificate for the summary administration of the bankrupt's estate has been issued, it is the duty of the official receiver, as soon as practicable in the period of 12 week's beginning with the day on which the order was made, to decide whether to summon a general meeting of the bankrupt's creditors for the purpose of appointing a trustee of the bankrupt's estate.

This section does not apply where the bankruptcy order was made on a petition under section 264(1)(d) (criminal bankruptcy); and it is subject to the provision made in sections 294(3) and 297(6) below.

293(2)   [Duty if no meeting summoned]   Subject to the next section, if the official receiver decides not to summon such a meeting, he shall, before the end of the period of 12 weeks above mentioned, give notice of his decision to the court and to every creditor of the bankrupt who is known to the official receiver or is identified in the bankrupt's statement of affairs.

293(3)   [Official receiver trustee from s. 293(2) notice]   As from the giving to the court of a notice under subsection (2), the official receiver is the trustee of the bankrupt's estate.

(Former provision: IA 1985, s. 140; BA 1914, ss. 13, 74 and Sch. 1)

S. 293(1)

In the normal case the official receiver must within 12 weeks of the bankruptcy order decide whether to call a general meeting of the bankrupt's creditors in order to appoint a trustee. The official receiver is entitled to a fee for summoning such a meeting: see the Insolvency Fees Order 1986 (SI 1986 No. 2030) as amended by the Insolvency Fees (Amendment) Order 1991 (SI 1991 No. 496).

Note prospective amendment: in s. 293(1) the words "does not apply where the bankruptcy order was made on a petition under section 264(1)(d) (criminal bankruptcy) and it" are to be repealed by the Criminal Justice Act 1988, s. 170(2) and Sch. 16 as from a day to be appointed. See the note to s. 264.

S. 293(2), (3)

If he decides not to summon such a meeting he must inform the court and every known creditor of his decision. He thereupon becomes trustee of the estate.

The Bankruptcy Act 1914, Sch. 1 contained details of creditors' meetings; such matters are now dealt with by the rules (Sch. 9, para. 12): see IR 1986, rr. 6.79–6.95.

Section 294   Power of creditors to requisition meeting

294(1)   [Request to official receiver]   Where in the case of any bankruptcy—

    (a)   the official receiver has not yet summoned, or has decided not to summon, a general meeting of the bankrupt's creditors for the purpose of appointing the trustee, and

    (b)   a certificate for the summary administration of the estate is not for the time being in force,

any creditor of the bankrupt may request the official receiver to summon such a meeting for that purpose.

294(2)   [Duty to summon meeting on request]   If such a request appears to the official receiver to be made with the concurrence of not less than one-quarter, in value, of the bankrupt's creditors (including the creditor making the request), it is the duty of the official receiver to summon the requested meeting.

294(3)   [Where s. 294(2) duty has arisen]   Accordingly, where the duty imposed by subsection (2) has arisen, the official receiver is required neither to reach a decision for the purposes of section 293(1) nor (if he has reached one) to serve any notice under section 293(2).

(Former provision: IA 1985, s. 141)

S. 294(1), (2)

In a normal bankruptcy case a creditor can ask the official receiver to call a creditors' meeting, with a view to appointing a trustee. Indeed, he *must* summon such a meeting if the request is backed by creditors owed 25 per cent of the bankrupt's debts. (This percentage was reduced from the original figure of 50 per cent at the Report Stage of the 1985 Bill.)

S. 294(3)

Where the creditors have forced the official receiver's hand in this way, he is excused his obligations under s. 293.

See also IR 1986, r. 6.83.

Section 295   Failure of meeting to appoint trustee

295(1)   [Duty of official receiver]   If a meeting summoned under section 293 or 294 is held but no appointment of a person as trustee is made, it is the duty of the official receiver to decide whether to refer the need for an appointment to the Secretary of State.

295(2)   [Duty of Secretary of State]   On a reference made in pursuance of that decision, the Secretary of State shall either make an appointment or decline to make one.

295(3)   [Notice to court]   If—

(a) the official receiver decides not to refer the need for an appointment to the Secretary of State, or

(b) on such a reference the Secretary of State declines to make an appointment,

the official receiver shall give notice of his decision or, as the case may be, of the Secretary of State's decision to the court.

295(4)   [As from notice official receiver trustee]   As from the giving of notice under subsection (3) in a case in which no notice has been given under section 293(2), the official receiver shall be trustee of the bankrupt's estate.

(Former provisions: IA 1985, s. 142; BA 1914, s. 19 (6))

S. 295(1), (2)

Where the creditors in meeting fail to appoint a trustee, the official receiver must decide whether to refer the matter to the Secretary of State, who has discretion whether to appoint a trustee or not. The value of the bankrupt's estate will clearly be relevant in such cases even if the small bankruptcies level (see s. 273) has been exceeded.

S. 295(3)

If the official receiver has decided not to refer the matter to the Secretary of State, or the Secretary of State has decided not to make an appointment, the official receiver must notify the court.

S. 295(4)

Where the official receiver has decided not to call on the assistance of the Secretary of State or the latter has failed to make an appointment, the official receiver will become the trustee.
    See also IR 1986, r. 6.122.

Section 296   Appointment of trustee by Secretary of State

296(1)   [Application for appointment instead of official receiver]   At any time when the official receiver is the trustee of a bankrupt's estate by virtue of any provision of this Chapter (other than section 297(1) below) he may apply to the Secretary of State for the appointment of a person as trustee instead of the official receiver.

296(2)   [Duty of Secretary of State]   On an application under subsection (1) the Secretary of State shall either make an appointment or decline to make one.

296(3)   [Making of application]   Such an application may be made notwithstanding that the Secretary of State has declined to make an appointment either on a previous application under subsection (1) or on a reference under section 295 or under section 300(4) below.

296(4) [Notice, etc., re appointment]   Where the trustee of a bankrupt's estate has been appointed by the Secretary of State (whether under this section or otherwise), the trustee shall give notice to the bankrupt's creditors of his appointment or, if the court so allows, shall advertise his appointment in accordance with the court's directions.

296(5) [Contents of notice]   In that notice or advertisement the trustee shall—

    (a) state whether he proposes to summon a general meeting of the bankrupt's creditors for the purpose of establishing a creditors' committee under section 301, and

    (b) if he does not propose to summon such a meeting, set out the power of the creditors under this Part to require him to summon one.

(Former provisions: IA 1985, s. 143; BA 1914, s. 19(6))

S. 296(1)–(3)

This permits the official receiver when acting as trustee to seek another appointment in his stead. He cannot do this where he is acting as trustee in case of summary administration or a bankruptcy initiated as the result of a criminal bankruptcy order. On the other hand, he is not precluded from making such an application by the fact that he has previously made unsuccessful applications under ss. 295, 296(1) or 300(4). On an application by the official receiver the Secretary of State has discretion whether to appoint a trustee or not. See also IR 1986, r. 6.122.

S. 296(4), (5)

Any appointment of a trustee by the Secretary of State must be notified to the creditors by the official receiver or, if the court permits, be advertised with a view to informing the creditors whether a committee should be set up under s. 301. See also IR 1986, r. 6.124 for the advertisement of the appointment.

Section 297 Special cases

297(1) [Where s. 264(1)(d) bankruptcy order]   Where a bankruptcy order is made on a petition under section 264(1)(d) (criminal bankruptcy), the official receiver shall be trustee of the bankrupt's estate.

297(2) [Where court issues certificate for summary administration]   Subject to the next subsection, where the court issues a certificate for the summary administration of a bankrupt's estate, the official receiver shall, as from the issue of that certificate, be the trustee.

297(3) [Qualification to s. 297(2)]   Where such a certificate is issued or is in force, the court may, if it thinks fit, appoint a person other than the official receiver as trustee.

297(4) [Where no certificate for summary administration]   Where a bankruptcy order is made in a case in which an insolvency practitioner's report has been submitted to the court under section 274 but no certificate for the summary administration of the estate is issued, the court, if it thinks fit, may on making the order appoint the person who made the report as trustee.

297(5) [Where there is supervisor]   Where a bankruptcy order is made (whether or not on a petition under section 264(1)(c)) at a time when there is a supervisor of a voluntary arrangement approved in relation to the bankrupt under Part VIII, the court, if it thinks fit, may on making the order appoint the supervisor of the arrangement as trustee.

297(6)   **[Exception re s. 293(1) duty]**   Where an appointment is made under subsection (4) or (5) of this section, the official receiver is not under the duty imposed by section 293(1) (to decide whether or not to summon a meeting of creditors).

297(7)   **[Notice where trustee appointed by court]**   Where the trustee of a bankrupt's estate has been appointed by the court, the trustee shall give notice to the bankrupt's creditors of his appointment or, if the court so allows, shall advertise his appointment in accordance with the directions of the court.

297(8)   **[Contents of notice]**   In that notice or advertisement he shall—

    (a) state whether he proposes to summon a general meeting of the bankrupt's creditors for the purpose of establishing a creditors' committee under section 301 below, and

    (b) if he does not propose to summon such a meeting, set out the power of the creditors under this Part to require him to summon one.

(Former provisions: IA 1985, s. 144; BA 1914, s. 129)

S. 297(1), (2)

These provisions deal with cases where the official receiver is to act as trustee – e.g. on bankruptcy initiated as the result of a criminal bankruptcy order, or in cases of summary administration (see s. 275 and IR 1986, rr. 6.48–6.50). These are not the only instances where the official receiver acts as trustee – see ss. 293(3) and 295(4).

    Note prospective amendment: s. 297(1) is to be repealed by the Criminal Justice Act 1988, s. 170(2) and Sch. 16 as from a day to be appointed; see the note to s. 264.

S. 297(3)

On a case of summary administration the court can appoint a person other than the official receiver as trustee. See IR 1986, r. 6.121 for procedural aspects.

S. 297(4)

This deals with another special case. Where in a small bankruptcy case the court has decided not to go for summary administration it can select the person who made the crucial report to it under s. 274(1) as trustee. See also IR 1986, r. 6.121.

S. 297(5)

If bankruptcy has been initiated notwithstanding the existence of a composition or scheme (see ss. 252–263) the court may appoint the supervisor as trustee. See also IR 1986, r. 6.121.

S. 297(6)

In cases covered by s. 297(4) and (5) the official receiver is not under a duty to decide whether to call a general meeting of creditors for the purpose of appointing a trustee.

S. 297(7), (8)

This mirrors s. 296(4) and (5), although the appointor here is the court and not the Secretary of State.

Section 298   Removal of trustee; vacation of office

298(1)   [Removal by court order or creditors' meeting]   Subject as follows, the trustee of a bankrupt's estate may be removed from office only by an order of the court or by a general meeting of the bankrupt's creditors summoned specially for that purpose in accordance with the rules.

298(2)   [Where official receiver trustee under s. 297(1)]   Where the official receiver is trustee by virtue of section 297(1), he shall not be removed from office under this section.

298(3)   [Where certificate for summary administration]   A general meeting of the bankrupt's creditors shall not be held for the purpose of removing the trustee at any time when a certificate for the summary administration of the estate is in force.

298(4)   [Where official receiver trustee under s. 293(3), 295(4)]   Where the official receiver is trustee by virtue of section 293(3) or 295(4) or a trustee is appointed by the Secretary of State or (otherwise than under section 297(5)) by the court, a general meeting of the bankrupt's creditors shall be summoned for the purpose of replacing the trustee only if—

(a) the trustee thinks fit, or

(b) the court so directs, or

(c) the meeting is requested by one of the bankrupt's creditors with the concurrence of not less than one-quarter, in value, of the creditors (including
the creditor making the request).

298(5)   [Where trustee appointed by Secretary of State]   If the trustee was appointed by the Secretary of State, he may be removed by a direction of the Secretary of State.

298(6)   [Vacation of office]   The trustee (not being the official receiver) shall vacate office if he ceases to be a person who is for the time being qualified to act as an insolvency practitioner in relation to the bankrupt.

298(7)   [Resignation]   The trustee may, in the prescribed circumstances, resign his office by giving notice of his resignation to the court.

298(8)   [Vacation on s. 331 notice]   The trustee shall vacate office on giving notice to the court that a final meeting has been held under section 331 in Chapter IV and of the decision (if any) of that meeting.

298(9)   [When bankruptcy order annulled]   The trustee shall vacate office if the bankruptcy order is annulled.

(Former provisions: IA 1985, s. 145; BA 1914, ss. 93–95)

S. 298(1), (2)

Trustees may as a general rule only be removed by the court or the general meeting of creditors. However, this does not apply where the official receiver is trustee.

S. 298(3)

Creditors cannot remove the trustee in the case of a summary administration.

S. 298(4)

The drafting of this provision is complex. It covers the official receiver acting as trustee by virtue of ss. 293(3) or 295(4), and trustees appointed by the Secretary of State, or by the court (but not under s. 297(5)). This allows a meeting to be called to dismiss the trustee – either the trustee himself, the court or creditors owed 25 per cent of the bankrupt's debts can call for this. This was reduced from 50 per cent in the original 1985 Bill.

S. 298(5)

The Secretary of State can remove his own appointees.

S. 298(6)

A trustee must vacate office if he ceases to be qualified to act: see Pt. XIII and r. 6.144(1).

S. 298(7)

Resignation in the circumstances prescribed is permitted.

S. 298(8)

The trustee shall vacate office after giving notice to the court of the outcome of the final meeting of creditors (see s. 331).

S. 298(9)

Annulment of the bankruptcy order will cause the trustee to vacate office.
  For further details on removal and vacation of office, see IR 1986, rr. 6.126–6.135.

Section 299   Release of trustee

299(1)   [Time of release for official receiver]   Where the official receiver has ceased to be the trustee of a bankrupt's estate and a person is appointed in his stead, the official receiver shall have his release with effect from the following time, that is to say—

  (a) where that person is appointed by a general meeting of the bankrupt's creditors or by the Secretary of State, the time at which the official receiver gives notice to the court that he has been replaced, and

  (b) where that person is appointed by the court, such time as the court may determine.

299(2)   [Time of release if notice given by official receiver]   If the official receiver while he is the trustee gives notice to the Secretary of State that the administration of the bankrupt's estate in accordance with Chapter IV of this Part is for practical purposes complete, he shall have his release with effect from such time as the Secretary of State may determine.

299(3)   [Time of release for person not official receiver]   A person other than the official receiver who has ceased to be the trustee shall have his release with effect from the following time, that is to say—

  (a) in the case of a person who has been removed from office by a general meeting of the bankrupt's creditors that has not resolved against his release or who has died, the time at which notice is given to the court in accordance with the rules that that person has ceased to hold office;

(b) in the case of a person who has been removed from office by a general meeting of the bankrupt's creditors that has resolved against his release, or by the court, or by the Secretary of State, or who has vacated office under section 298(6), such time as the Secretary of State may, on an application by that person, determine;

(c) in the case of a person who has resigned, such time as may be prescribed;

(d) in the case of a person who has vacated office under section 298(8)—

(i) if the final meeting referred to in that subsection has resolved against that person's release, such time as the Secretary of State may, on an application by that person, determine; and

(ii) if that meeting has not so resolved, the time at which the person vacated office.

299(4)   [Time of release where bankruptcy order annulled]   Where a bankruptcy order is annulled, the trustee at the time of the annulment has his release with effect from such time as the court may determine.

299(5)   [Effect of release]   Where the official receiver or the trustee has his release under this section, he shall, with effect from the time specified in the preceding provisions of this section, be discharged from all liability both in respect of acts or omissions of his in the administration of the estate and otherwise in relation to his conduct as trustee.

But nothing in this section prevents the exercise, in relation to a person who has had his release under this section, of the court's powers under section 304.

(Former provisions: IA 1985, s. 146; BA 1914, s. 93)

S. 299(1), (2)

These provisions deal with the release of an official receiver who has been acting as trustee. The procedure to be followed depends on whether he is being replaced or whether he has simply completed the administration of the estate.

For the equivalent provision for the release of liquidators, see s. 174. As to the possibility of a release being set aside, see *Re Munro, ex parte Singer* v *Trustee in Bankruptcy* [1981] 1 WLR 1358. Release is also dealt with by IR 1986, rr. 6.136, 6.137.

S. 299(3)

This fixes the date of release for trustees other than the official receiver. Again, the date will vary according to the circumstances of the case – a comprehensive list of possibilities is provided for.

S. 299(4)

Where release is the result of the annulment of the bankruptcy order the court will fix the date of release.

S. 299(5)

This is a general provision dealing with the *effect* of a release: it serves as a discharge of liabilities, unless an action is subsequently brought under s. 304.

Section 300   Vacancy in office of trustee

300(1)   [Application]   This section applies where the appointment of any person as trustee of a bankrupt's estate fails to take effect or, such an appointment having taken effect, there is otherwise a vacancy in the office of trustee.

300(2)   [Official receiver trustee]   The official receiver shall be trustee until the vacancy is filled.

300(3)   [Summoning creditors' meeting]   The official receiver may summon a general meeting of the bankrupt's creditors for the purpose of filling the vacancy and shall summon such a meeting if required to do so in pursuance of section 314(7) (creditors' requisition).

300(4)   [If no meeting summoned within 28 days]   If at the end of the period of 28 days beginning with the day on which the vacancy first came to the official receiver's attention he has not summoned, and is not proposing to summon, a general meeting of creditors for the purpose of filling the vacancy, he shall refer the need for an appointment to the Secretary of State.

300(5)   [Where certificate for summary administration]   Where a certificate for the summary administration of the estate is for the time being in force—

    (a) the official receiver may refer the need to fill any vacancy to the court or, if the vacancy arises because a person appointed by the Secretary of State has ceased to hold office, to the court or the Secretary of State, and

    (b) subsections (3) and (4) of this section do not apply.

300(6)   [Duty of Secretary of State re s. 300(4), (5)]   On a reference to the Secretary of State under subsection (4) or (5) the Secretary of State shall either make an appointment or decline to make one.

300(7)   [If no appointment on s. 300(4), (5) reference]   If on a reference under subsection (4) or (5) no appointment is made, the official receiver shall continue to be trustee of the bankrupt's estate, but without prejudice to his power to make a further reference.

300(8)   [Interpretation]   References in this section to a vacancy include a case where it is necessary, in relation to any property which is or may be comprised in a bankrupt's estate, to revive the trusteeship of that estate after holding of a final meeting summoned under section 331 or the giving by the official receiver of notice under section 299(2).

(Former provisions: IA 1985, s. 147; BA 1914, s. 78)

S. 300(1), (2)

Where the appointment of a trustee fails to take effect (e.g. because he refuses the appointment) or a casual vacancy occurs, the official receiver must act as trustee during the interregnum.

S. 300(3), (4)

The official receiver may (and, in cases under s. 314(7), must) call a general meeting to fill this vacancy. If he fails to act within 28 days he must refer the matter to the Secretary of State. See IR 1986, r. 6.122.

S. 300(5)

Where there is a summary administration, s. 300(3) and (4) do not apply, but in the event of a vacancy the official receiver must refer the matter to the court or (if it is one of his appointees who has left office) to the Secretary of State.

S. 300(6), (7)

Where a casual vacancy has been referred to the Secretary of State he has discretion whether to fill it or not. If the vacancy is not filled the official receiver must act as trustee pending the resolution of the matter.

S. 300(8)

This defines what is meant by a "vacancy" for the purposes of the present section.

CONTROL OF TRUSTEE

Section 301   Creditors' committee

301(1)   [Meeting may establish committee]   Subject as follows, a general meeting of a bankrupt's creditors (whether summoned under the preceding provisions of this Chapter or otherwise) may, in accordance with the rules, establish a committee (known as "the creditors' committee") to exercise the functions conferred on it by or under this Act.

301(2)   [Exception]   A general meeting of the bankrupt's creditors shall not establish such a committee, or confer any functions on such a committee, at any time when the official receiver is the trustee of the bankrupt's estate, except in connection with an appointment made by that meeting of a person to be trustee instead of the official receiver.

(Former provisions: IA 1985, s. 148; BA 1914, s. 20(1)–(9))

S. 301(1)

This enables the general meeting of creditors to establish a committee to supervise the trustee. Under the 1914 Act this committee was known as a "committee of inspection" but this title has now been dropped on the recommendation of the Cork Committee (*Report*, para. 932). The rôle and general position of the committee is now governed by the Rules – see now IR 1986, rr. 6.150–6.166. Under the BA 1914 many of these details were spelled out in the provisions of s. 20 itself. Under BA 1914, s. 79(1) the committee had general power to give directions to the trustee. This power was not re-enacted in the 1986 Act and therefore the rôle of the committee is more limited. Members of this committee occupy a fiduciary position vis-à-vis the bankrupt's estate – *Re Bulmer, ex parte Greaves* [1937] Ch. 499.

S. 301(2)

The committee has no rôle where the official receiver is trustee – he is supervised by the Secretary of State under s. 302. This could apply to cases of criminal bankruptcy.

Section 302   Exercise by Secretary of State of functions of creditors' committee

302(1)   [Where official receiver trustee]   The creditors' committee is not to be able or required to carry out its functions at any time when the official receiver is trustee of the bankrupt's estate; but at any such time the functions of the committee under this Act shall be vested in the Secretary of State, except to the extent that the rules otherwise provide.

302(2)   [Where no committee]   Where in the case of any bankruptcy there is for the time being no creditors' committee and the trustee of the bankrupt's estate is a person other than the official receiver, the functions of such a committee shall be vested in the Secretary of State, except to the extent that the rules otherwise provide.

(Former provisions: IA 1985, s. 149; BA 1914, s. 20(10))

S. 302(1)

This reiterates that the committee established under s. 301 cannot exercise any control functions when the official receiver is acting as trustee. Instead, control in such cases must be exercised by the Secretary of State. See IR 1986, r. 6.166. For fees payable under s. 302 see the Insolvency Fees Order 1986 (SI 1986 No. 2030) as amended by the Insolvency Fees (Amendment) Order 1991 (SI 1991 No. 496).

S. 302(2)

For the relevant rules, see IR 1986, r. 6.166.

Section 303   General control of trustee by the court

303(1)   [Application to court]   If a bankrupt or any of his creditors or any other person is dissatisfied by any act, omission or decision of a trustee of the bankrupt's estate, he may apply to the court; and on such an application the court may confirm, reverse or modify any act or decision of the trustee, may give him directions or may make such other order as it thinks fit.

303(2)   [Application by trustee for directions]   The trustee of a bankrupt's estate may apply to the court for directions in relation to any particular matter arising under the bankruptcy.

(Former provisions: IA 1985, s. 150; BA 1914, ss. 79(3), 80)

S. 303(1)

This permits any person who is dissatisfied with a decision of a trustee in bankruptcy to apply to the court for relief. On such an application the court enjoys general discretion to deal with the matter. This is a useful reserve control power, but in practice, as the Cork Committee observed (*Report*, para. 779), such applications rarely succeed – see, for an example of an unsuccessful application, *Re A Debtor, ex parte The Debtor* v *Dodwell (The Trustee)* [1949] Ch. 236. It is uncertain whether the change from "aggrieved" in the BA 1914 to "dissatisfied" will produce any practical differences. Note also IR 1986, Pt. 7.

Those lawyers looking for a more liberal use of this control facility will have been disappointed by the comments of Harman J in *Port* v *Auger* [1994] 1 WLR 862 at p. 873–4. Although Harman J appeared to accept that the change in terminology from "aggrieved" to "dissatisfied" may have indicated an intention on the part of the legislature to widen access to the court he expressed the view that the applicant must have some substantial interest that has been adversely affected and then went on to suggest that the s. 303 jurisdiction should not be invoked lightly by the court for fear of inflicting unneccessary expense on the insolvent estate.

In *Heath* v *Tang* [1993] 1 WLR 1421 it was suggested by the court that this provision might prove useful if the trustee refuses to pursue a claim of action belonging to the debtor but now vested in the estate. On this see also the notes on ss. 285(3) and 306.

S. 303(2)

This is a useful facility in that it allows a trustee in bankruptcy to apply to the court for guidance on a difficult matter. For an illustration of the court giving such directions see *Re A Debtor (No. 26A of 1975)* [1985] 1 WLR 6.

S. 303(2A)–(2C)

The following subsections are inserted at the end of s. 303 for the purposes of the Insolvent Partnerships Order 1994 (SI 1994 No. 2421) from 1 December 1994 (by art. 14(2) of the order):

"(2A) Where at any time after a bankruptcy petition has been presented to the court against any person, whether under the provisions of the Insolvent Partnerships Order 1994 or not, the attention of the court is drawn to the fact that the person in question is a member of an insolvent partnership, the court may make an order as to the future conduct of the insolvency proceedings and any such order may apply any provisions of that Order with any necessary modifications.

(2B) Where a bankruptcy petition has been presented against more than one individual in the circumstances mentioned in subsection (2A) above, the court may give such directions for consolidating the proceedings, or any of them, as it thinks just.

(2C) Any order or directions under subsection (2A) or (2B) may be made or given on the application of the official receiver, any responsible insolvency practitioner, the trustee of the partnership or any other interested person and may include provisions as to the administration of the joint estate of the partnership, and in particular how it and the separate estate of any member are to be administered."

Section 304   Liability of trustee

304(1)   [Powers of court on application]   Where on an application under this section the court is satisfied—

(a) that the trustee of a bankrupt's estate has misapplied or retained, or become accountable for, any money or other property comprised in the bankrupt's estate, or

(b) that a bankrupt's estate has suffered any loss in consequence of any misfeasance or breach of fiduciary or other duty by a trustee of the estate in the carrying out of his functions,

the court may order the trustee, for the benefit of the estate, to repay, restore or account for money or other property (together with interest at such rate as the court thinks just) or, as the case may require, to pay such sum by way of compensation in respect of the misfeasance or breach of fiduciary or other duty as the court thinks just.

This is without prejudice to any liability arising apart from this section.

304(2)   [Applicants]   An application under this section may be made by the official receiver, the Secretary of State, a creditor of the bankrupt or (whether or not there is, or is likely to be, a surplus for the purposes of section 330(5) (final distribution)) the bankrupt himself.

But the leave of the court is required for the making of an application if it is to be made by the bankrupt or if it is to be made after the trustee has had his release under section 299.

304(3)   **[Limit on liability]**   Where—

    (a) the trustee seizes or disposes of any property which is not comprised in the bankrupt's estate, and

    (b) at the time of the seizure or disposal the trustee believes, and has reasonable grounds for believing, that he is entitled (whether in pursuance of an order of the court or otherwise) to seize or dispose of that property,

the trustee is not liable to any person (whether under this section or otherwise) in respect of any loss or damage resulting from the seizure or disposal except in so far as that loss or damage is caused by the negligence of the trustee; and he has a lien on the property, or the proceeds of its sale, for such of the expenses of the bankruptcy as were incurred in connection with the seizure or disposal.

(Former provisions: IA 1985, s. 151; BA 1914, ss. 61, 93(2))

General note

The Cork Committee (*Report*, paras. 777–788) called for the introduction of a statutory duty of care imposed on trustees. This section goes some way towards this, and towards rationalising the law on the liability of trustees.

S. 304(1)

This allows the court to impose liability on the trustee for misfeasance or misapplication of money belonging to the estate, etc. The remedy is at the discretion of the court, and it is worth noting that interest can be awarded against the trustee. The comparable provision in company law is to be found in s. 212.

S. 304(2)

This determines who can apply for relief under s. 304(1). Note that if the bankrupt applies, or the application is made after the date of the trustee's release, the leave of the court must first be obtained.

S. 304(3)

This is not a new provision, but rather a reformulation of BA 1914, s. 61. It is designed to protect a trustee who innocently seizes or disposes of property belonging to a third party. Note that this protection is lost if he acts negligently. The problem of a trustee seizing property which does not belong to the bankrupt may arise more frequently in the future with the abolition of the concept of reputed ownership.

Chapter IV — Administration by Trustee

PRELIMINARY

Section 305   General functions of trustee

305(1)   **[Application of Ch. IV]**   This Chapter applies in relation to any bankruptcy where either—

    (a) the appointment of a person as trustee of a bankrupt's estate takes effect, or

    (b) the official receiver becomes trustee of a bankrupt's estate.

305(2) **[Function of trustee]** The function of the trustee is to get in, realise and distribute the bankrupt's estate in accordance with the following provisions of this Chapter; and in the carrying out of that function and in the management of the bankrupt's estate the trustee is entitled, subject to those provisions, to use his own discretion.

305(3) **[Duties of trustee]** It is the duty of the trustee, if he is not the official receiver—

(a) to furnish the official receiver with such information,

(b) to produce to the official receiver, and permit inspection by the official receiver of, such books, papers and other records, and

(c) to give the official receiver such other assistance,

as the official receiver may reasonably require for the purpose of enabling him to carry out his functions in relation to the bankruptcy.

305(4) **[Official name of trustee]** The official name of the trustee shall be "the trustee of the estate of . . . . , a bankrupt" (inserting the name of the bankrupt); but he may be referred to as "the trustee in bankruptcy" of the particular bankrupt.

(Former provisions: IA 1985, s. 152; BA 1914, ss. 76, 79(4))

S. 305(1)

Sections 305–335 apply to cases where the trustee's appointment is effective or where the official receiver is acting as trustee.

S. 305(2)

This describes the general rôle of the trustee and confers considerable residual discretion upon him.

S. 305(3)

This provision makes the trustee subordinate to the official receiver. Further details of the relationship can be seen in IR 1986, r. 6.149.

S. 305(4)

This describes the official name of the trustee and repeats BA 1914, s. 76, although his powers are not mentioned in the new provision.

ACQUISITION, CONTROL AND REALISATION OF BANKRUPT'S ESTATE

Section 306   Vesting of bankrupt's estate in trustee

306(1) **[Time of vesting]** The bankrupt's estate shall vest in the trustee immediately on his appointment taking effect or, in the case of the official receiver, on his becoming trustee.

306(2) **[Mode of vesting]** Where any property which is, or is to be, comprised in the bankrupt's estate vests in the trustee (whether under this section or under any other provision of this Part), it shall so vest without any conveyance, assignment or transfer.

(Former provisions: IA 1985, s. 153; BA 1914, ss. 18, 53)

General note

This section provides that the bankrupt's property shall vest in the trustee, on his appointment taking effect, or in the official receiver where he becomes trustee. No conveyance, etc., is required.

This automatic vesting is to be compared with the position under s. 145 where the court may direct that some or all of the company's property shall vest in the liquidator in a compulsory liquidation.

For the meaning of "property" within s. 306(2) see *London City Corp.* v *Bown, The Times*, 11 October 1989, where it was held by the Court of Appeal that a non-assignable secure periodic tenancy within the meaning of the Housing Act 1985 confers only personal rights and therefore could not be regarded as "property" for these purposes.

The rights of action possessed by the debtor at the time of his bankruptcy form part of the estate under the control of the trustee – see *Heath* v *Tang* [1993] 1 WLR 1421.

Section 307   After-acquired property

307(1)   [Power of trustee]   Subject to this section and section 309, the trustee may by notice in writing claim for the bankrupt's estate any property which has been acquired by, or has devolved upon, the bankrupt since the commencement of the bankruptcy.

307(2)   [Limit on s. 307(1) notice]   A notice under this section shall not be served in respect of—

(a) any property falling within subsection (2) or (3) of section 283 in Chapter II.

(b) any property which by virtue of any other enactment is excluded from the bankrupt's estate, or

(c) without prejudice to section 280(2)(c) (order of court on application for discharge), any property which is acquired by, or devolves upon, the bankrupt after his discharge.

307(3)   [Vesting on service of notice]   Subject to the next subsection, upon the service on the bankrupt of a notice under this section the property to which the notice relates shall vest in the trustee as part of the bankrupt's estate; and the trustee's title to that property has relation back to the time at which the property was acquired by, or devolved upon, the bankrupt.

307(4)   [Outsiders]   Where, whether before or after service of a notice under this section—

(a) a person acquires property in good faith, for value and without notice of the bankruptcy, or

(b) a banker enters into a transaction in good faith and without such notice,

the trustee is not in respect of that property or transaction entitled by virtue of this section to any remedy against that person or banker, or any person whose title to any property derives from that person or banker.

307(5)   [Interpretation]   References in this section to property do not include any property which, as part of the bankrupt's income, may be the subject of an income payments order under section 310.

(Former provisions: IA 1985, s. 154(1)–(4), (7); BA 1914, ss. 38(a), 47)

S. 307(1)

This enables the trustee to take the initiative and claim property vesting in the bankrupt after the commencement of the bankruptcy (as defined in s. 278(*a*)). Under BA 1914, s. 38(*a*) such property *automatically* vested in the trustee – see *Re Pascoe* [1944] Ch. 219. Prior to 1944 it was generally believed that positive intervention by the trustee was required. The Cork Committee (*Report*, para. 1152) felt that it would be more flexible if the trustee could be allowed to choose whether the estate wanted such property. The advantage in such a change is highlighted by the White Paper, para. 112 – it saves the trustee from wasting his time in having to disclaim onerous after-acquired property. See also IR 1986, rr. 6.200–6.202. The operation of this provision does depend on the bankrupt being honest with his trustee, as he is required to be by ss. 333(2) and 353. The bankrupt must tell the trustee within 21 days of the acquisition of the property: see IR 1986, r. 6.200(1).

S. 307(2), (5)

Certain after-acquired property cannot be claimed by the trustee: property which would not be included in the estate in any case, and property acquired after the date of discharge. Note also that income which may be caught by s. 310 cannot fall under s. 307.

S. 307(3)

On service of the trustee's notice the property in question vests in the trustee. The trustee has 42 days to claim the property after receiving notice of it from the bankrupt, see IA 1986, s. 309 (1)(*a*), or else it can be disposed of by the bankrupt.

S. 307(4)

This protects bona fide purchasers, (for value, without notice...) of after-acquired property from the bankrupt. It is based on BA 1914, s. 47 which, in turn, confirmed the rule in *Cohen* v *Mitchell* (1890) 25 QBD 262. For a comparable Australian authority see *Rimar Pty Ltd* v *Pappas* (1986) 60 ALJR 309. However, the third party loses his protection if he has notice of the bankruptcy order – thus, *Hunt* v *Fripp* [1898] 1 Ch. 675 is reversed. If the disponee is not protected the trustee can recover the property under IR 1986, r. 6.201.

Section 308   Vesting in trustee of certain items of excess value

308(1) [Claim by trustee in writing]   Subject to section 309, where—

    (a) property is excluded by virtue of section 283(2) (tools of trade, household effects, etc.) from the bankrupt's estate, and

    (b) it appears to the trustee that the realisable value of the whole or any part of that property exceeds the cost of a reasonable replacement for that property or that part of it,

the trustee may by notice in writing claim that property or, as the case may be, that part of it for the bankrupt's estate.

308(2) [Vesting on service of s. 308(1) notice]   Upon the service on the bankrupt of a notice under this section, the property to which the notice relates vests in the trustee as part of the bankrupt's estate; and, except against a purchaser in good faith, for value and without notice of the bankruptcy, the trustee's title to that property has relation back to the commencement of the bankruptcy.

308(3) [Application of funds by trustee]   The trustee shall apply funds comprised in the estate to the purchase by or on behalf of the bankrupt of a reasonable replacement for any property vested in the trustee under this section; and the duty imposed by this subsection has priority over the obligation of the trustee to distribute the estate.

308(4) **[Reasonable replacement]**   For the purposes of this section property is a reasonable replacement for other property if it is reasonably adequate for meeting the needs met by the other property.

(Former provisions: IA 1985, s. 155(1), (2), (4), (5))

General note

This is a new provision which implements the recommendations of the Cork Committee (*Report*, para. 1101). This section is supplemented by IR 1986, rr. 6.187, 6.188.

S. 308(1), (4)

The trustee is allowed to claim certain property, which would normally not be included in the bankrupt's estate by virtue of s. 283(2), if that property can be reasonably replaced (as defined in s. 308(4), producing a surplus for the estate. Note the 42 day limit in s. 309. The provision is designed to prevent bankrupts with large debts from continuing to live a life of luxury surrounded by expensive cars and consumer durables. A bankrupt who objects to replacement can complain to the court under s. 303. A third party can pay off the trustee to avert replacement: IR 1986, r. 6.188. A minor change has been made to subs. (1) to accommodate the insertion of s. 308A – see Housing Act 1988, Sch. 17, para. 73.

S. 308(2)

Once the trustee has given notice, the property in question will vest in the trustee, subject to the rights of any bona fide purchaser.

S. 308(3)

The cost of the replacement is to be met out of the estate funds and the defrayment of this cost takes priority over the trustee's obligation to distribute. The replacement may occur before or after the sale of the original item, see IR 1986, r. 6.187.

S. 308(4)

It would appear from the link with subs. (1) that the test as to what is "reasonable" is likely to be applied subjectively, i.e. does the trustee believe it is reasonable? Provided his decision is not totally erratic, the court would not intervene.

Section 308A   Vesting in trustee of certain tenancies

308A   Upon the service on the bankrupt by the trustee of a notice in writing under this section, any tenancy—

    (a) which is excluded by virtue of section 283(3A) from the bankrupt's estate, and

    (b) to which the notice relates,

vests in the trustee as part of the bankrupt's estate; and, except against a purchaser in good faith, for value and without notice of the bankruptcy, the trustee's title to that tenancy has relation back to the commencement of the bankruptcy.

General note

This provision was introduced by s. 117(2) of the Housing Act 1988. For its significance see the note to s. 283 above.

Section 309   Time-limit for notice under s. 307 or 308

309(1)   **[Timing of notice]**   Except with the leave of the court, a notice shall not be served—

(a) under section 307, after the end of the period of 42 days beginning with the day on which it first came to the knowledge of the trustee that the property in question had been acquired by, or had devolved upon, the bankrupt;

(b) under section 308 or section 308A, after the end of the period of 42 days beginning with the day on which the property or tenancy in question first came to the knowledge of the trustee.

309(2)   [Deemed knowledge]   For the purposes of this section—

(a) anything which comes to the knowledge of the trustee is deemed in relation to any successor of his as trustee to have come to the knowledge of the successor at the same time; and

(b) anything which comes (otherwise than under paragraph (a)) to the knowledge of a person before he is the trustee is deemed to come to his knowledge on his appointment taking effect or, in the case of the official receiver, on his becoming trustee.

(Former provisions: IA 1985, ss. 154(5), (6), 155(3))

General note

The trustee must claim the property or seek replacement (under ss. 307, 308 or 308A) within 42 days after it has come to his notice, as defined by s. 309(2). Note the minor changes made to subs. 1(*b*) by s. 117(3) of the Housing Act 1988.

Section 310   Income payments orders

310(1)   [Order by court]   The court may, on the application of the trustee, make an order ("an income payments order") claiming for the bankrupt's estate so much of the income of the bankrupt during the period for which the order is in force as may be specified in the order.

310(2)   [Limit on order]   The court shall not make an income payments order the effect of which would be to reduce the income of the bankrupt below what appears to the court to be necessary for meeting the reasonable domestic needs of the bankrupt and his family.

310(3)   [Extent of order]   An income payments order shall, in respect of any payment of income to which it is to apply, either—

(a) require the bankrupt to pay the trustee an amount equal to so much of that payment as is claimed by the order, or

(b) require the person making the payment to pay so much of it as is so claimed to the trustee, instead of to the bankrupt.

310(4)   [Power to discharge or vary attachment of earnings]   Where the court makes an income payments order it may, if it thinks fit, discharge or vary any attachment of earnings order that is for the time being in force to secure payments by the bankrupt.

310(5)   [Sums part of estate]   Sums received by the trustee under an income payments order form part of the bankrupt's estate.

310(6) **[After discharge of bankrupt]** An income payments order shall not be made after the discharge of the bankrupt, and if made before, shall not have effect after his discharge except—

    (a) in the case of a discharge under section 279(1)(a) (order of court), by virtue of a condition imposed by the court under section 280(2)(c) (income, etc. after discharge), or

    (b) in the case of a discharge under section 279(1)(b) (expiration of relevant period), by virtue of a provision of the order requiring it to continue in force for a period ending after the discharge but no later than 3 years after the making of the order.

310(7) **[Income of the bankrupt]** For the purposes of this section the income of the bankrupt comprises every payment in the nature of income which is from time to time made to him or to which he from time to time becomes entitled, including any payment in respect of the carrying on of any business or in respect of any office or employment.

(Former provisions: IA 1985, s. 156; BA 1914, s. 51)

General note

One of the defects in the BA 1914 was that it did not have an effective mechanism to enable the trustee to appropriate the income of the bankrupt for the benefit of the estate. BA 1914, s. 51 was largely ineffective, especially where the bankrupt was self-employed. The Cork Committee (*Report*, paras. 591–598) recommended a change in the law which would enable creditors to be paid off out of future income rather than the proceeds of a forced sale.

S. 310(1), (2)

This enables the trustee to apply to court for an income payments order, but the court cannot appropriate so great a proportion of the bankrupt's income as to reduce him and his family to penury. This restriction existed at common law – *Re Roberts* [1900] 1 QB 122. The bankrupt must be given 28 days' notice of the application, see IR 1986, r. 6.189.

S. 310(3)–(5)

These provisions deal with the effect of an income payments order. Either the bankrupt or some third party can be directed to make payments to the trustee, the sums thereby received forming part of the estate. On making such an order the court can modify any attachment of earnings order relating to the bankrupt's income. Note that s. 310(3) is amplified by the rules: see Sch. 9, para. 15 and IR 1986, rr. 6.189–6.193. The order may be reviewed on the application of either party or varied on the application of the trustee. The latter might occur where the bankrupt's income increases. Note there the obligation to notify the trustee within 21 days (s. 332(2) and r. 6.200(1)).

S. 310(6)

Income payments orders will not operate after discharge unless the discharge was conditional upon such an order surviving, or where, on automatic discharge, the order itself has specified continuance after the expiry of the "relevant period" (see s. 279); but in the latter case it cannot be allowed to continue for more than three years after the date of the order.

S. 310(7)

This defines "income" in wide terms and emphasises that it covers the income of a self-employed person. Presumably payments in the nature of capital are not covered by s. 310.

Section 311   Acquisition by trustee of control

311(1)   **[Trustee to take possession]**   The trustee shall take possession of all books, papers and other records which relate to the bankrupt's estate or affairs and which belong to him or are in his possession or under his control (including any which would be privileged from disclosure in any proceedings).

311(2)   **[Trustee like receiver]**   In relation to, and for the purpose of acquiring or retaining possession of, the bankrupt's estate, the trustee is in the same position as if he were a receiver of property appointed by the High Court; and the court may, on his application, enforce such acquisition or retention accordingly.

311(3)   **[Where estate includes transferable property]**   Where any part of the bankrupt's estate consists of stock or shares in a company, shares in a ship or any other property transferable in the books of a company, office or person, the trustee may exercise the right to transfer the property to the same extent as the bankrupt might have exercised it if he had not become bankrupt.

311(4)   **[Where estate includes things in action]**   Where any part of the estate consists of things in action, they are deemed to have been assigned to the trustee; but notice of the deemed assignment need not be given except in so far as it is necessary, in a case where the deemed assignment is from the bankrupt himself, for protecting the priority of the trustee.

311(5)   **[Where goods held by pledge]**   Where any goods comprised in the estate are held by any person by way of pledge, pawn or other security and no notice has been served in respect of those goods by the official receiver under subsection (5) of section 285 (restriction on realising security), the trustee may serve such a notice in respect of the goods; and whether or not a notice has been served under this subsection or that subsection, the trustee may, if he thinks fit, exercise the bankrupt's right of redemption in respect of any such goods.

311(6)   **[Effect of s. 311(5) notice]**   A notice served by the trustee under subsection (5) has the same effect as a notice served by the official receiver under section 285(5).

(Former provisions: IA 1985, s. 157; BA 1914, ss. 48, 59)

S. 311(1)

This describes the most basic duty of a trustee, which is to collect the bankrupt's property together. For the impact of this provision on privileged documents see *Re Konigsberg (A Bankrupt)* [1989] 1 WLR 1257.

S. 311(2)

While carrying out the above function the trustee will be treated as if he were a court-appointed receiver and will, for example, enjoy the protection of the law of contempt.

S. 311(3), (4)

These provisions deal with the trustee's rights in respect of certain intangible forms of property, such as shares or choses in action.

S. 311(5), (6)

These provisions, based on BA 1914, s. 59, deal with the situation where the bankrupt's goods have been given as security to some other person. The trustee may (if the official receiver has not already done so) serve a notice on the third party in order to redeem the goods. Such a notice has the same effect as a notice served by the official receiver under s. 285(5).

Section 312   Obligation to surrender control to trustee

312(1)   [Bankrupt to surrender property]   The bankrupt shall deliver up to the trustee possession of any property, books, papers or other records of which he has possession or control and of which the trustee is required to take possession.

This is without prejudice to the general duties of the bankrupt under section 333 in this Chapter.

312(2)   [Other persons in possession]   If any of the following is in possession of any property, books, papers or other records of which the trustee is required to take possession, namely—

(a) the official receiver,

(b) a person who has ceased to be trustee of the bankrupt's estate, or

(c) a person who has been the supervisor of a voluntary arrangement approved in relation to the bankrupt under Part VIII,

the official receiver or, as the case may be, that person shall deliver up possession of the property, books, papers or records to the trustee.

312(3)   [Bankers, agents et al. of bankrupt]   Any banker or agent of the bankrupt or any other person who holds any property to the account of, or for, the bankrupt shall pay or deliver to the trustee all property in his possession or under his control which forms part of the bankrupt's estate and which he is not by law entitled to retain as against the bankrupt or trustee.

312(4)   [Penalty for non-compliance]   If any person without reasonable excuse fails to comply with any obligation imposed by this section, he is guilty of a contempt of court and liable to be punished accordingly (in addition to any other punishment to which he may be subject).

(Former provisions: IA 1985, s. 158; BA 1914, ss. 22, 48(6))

S. 312(1)

This provision obliges the bankrupt, in addition to his general duty to assist the trustee, to hand over possession of his property, books, etc., to the trustee.

S. 312(2), (3)

This obligation extends to official receivers, former trustees, supervisors of a voluntary arrangement, bankers and agents of the bankrupt, although the latter two groups may have certain rights of retention as against the trustee.

S. 312(4)

The above obligations are reinforced by the law of contempt.

Section 313   Charge on bankrupt's home

313(1)   [Application to court by trustee]   Where any property consisting of an interest in a dwelling house which is occupied by the bankrupt or by his spouse or former spouse is comprised in the bankrupt's estate and the trustee is, for any reason, unable for the time being to realise that property, the trustee may apply to the court for an order imposing a charge on the property for the benefit of the bankrupt's estate.

313(2)   [Benefit of charge]   If on an application under this section the court imposes a charge on any property, the benefit of that charge shall be comprised in the bankrupt's estate and is enforceable, up to the value from time to time of the property secured, for the payment of any amount which is payable otherwise than to the bankrupt out of the estate and of interest on that amount at the prescribed rate.

313(3)   [Provision in order]   An order under this section made in respect of property vested in the trustee shall provide, in accordance with the rules, for the property to cease to be comprised in the bankrupt's estate and, subject to the charge (and any prior charge), to vest in the bankrupt.

313(4)   [Effect of Charging Orders Act]   Subsections (1) and (2) and (4) to (6) of section 3 of the Charging Orders Act 1979 (supplemental provisions with respect to charging orders) have effect in relation to orders under this section as in relation to charging orders under that Act.

(Former provision: IA 1985, s. 159)

General note

This is a new provision which would probably be better located next to ss. 336–338, which also deal with the matrimonial home. This new package of provisions, which was recommended by the Cork Committee (*Report*, paras. 1114–31), is designed to tilt the balance more in favour of the bankrupt and his family when it comes to selling the family home. This provision, unlike the others dealing with the matrimonial home, was included in the original Insolvency Bill of 1985. For a general view of the operation of s. 313 in practice see Hill (1990) 6 IL & P 12.

S. 313(1)

If the trustee cannot sell the bankrupt's interest in the "dwelling house" (for the definition, see s. 385) occupied by him or his family he may apply to a court for a charging order on that interest.

S. 313(2)–(4)

These provisions deal with the effect of the court granting such a charging order. It attaches to the property in question until enforced, although the property ceases to vest in the trustee and will revert to the bankrupt (subject to the charge). Certain parts of s. 3 of the Charging Orders Act 1979 will apply to such an order made by the court under s. 313(1).

The rules provide more details of the conditions which may be attached to such a charge – see IR 1986, r. 6.237.

Section 314   Powers of trustee

314(1)   [Powers in Sch. 5, Pt. I and II]   The trustee may—

   (a) with the permission of the creditors' committee or the court, exercise any of the powers specified in Part I of Schedule 5 to this Act, and

   (b) without that permission, exercise any of the general powers specified in Part II of that Schedule.

314(2)   [Powers of appointment re bankrupt]   With the permission of the creditors' committee or the court, the trustee may appoint the bankrupt—

   (a) to superintend the management of his estate or any part of it,

   (b) to carry on his business (if any) for the benefit of his creditors, or

   (c) in any other respect to assist in administering the estate in such manner and on such terms as the trustee may direct.

314(3)   [Permission in s. 314(1)(a), (2)]   A permission given for the purposes of subsection (1)(a) or (2) shall not be a general permission but shall relate to a particular proposed exercise of the power in question; and a person dealing with the trustee in good faith and for value is not to be concerned to enquire whether any permission required in either case has been given.

314(4)   [Where no permission under s. 314(1)(a), (2)]   Where the trustee has done anything without the permission required by subsection (1)(a) or (2), the court or the creditors' committee may, for the purpose of enabling him to meet his expenses out of the bankrupt's estate, ratify what the trustee has done.

But the committee shall not do so unless it is satisfied that the trustee has acted in a case of urgency and has sought its ratification without undue delay.

314(5)   [Powers in Sch. 5, Pt. III]   Part III of Schedule 5 to this Act has effect with respect to the things which the trustee is able to do for the purposes of, or in connection with, the exercise of any of his powers under any of this Group of Parts.

314(6)   [Notice to committee]   Where the trustee (not being the official receiver) in exercise of the powers conferred on him by any provision in this Group of Parts—

   (a) disposes of any property comprised in the bankrupt's estate to an associate of the bankrupt, or

   (b) employs a solicitor,

he shall, if there is for the time being a creditors' committee, give notice to the committee of that exercise of his powers.

314(7)   [Power to summon general meeting of creditors]   Without prejudice to the generality of subsection (5) and Part III of Schedule 5, the trustee may, if he thinks fit, at any time summon a general meeting of the bankrupt's creditors.

Subject to the preceding provisions in this Group of Parts, he shall summon such a meeting if he is requested to do so by a creditor of the bankrupt and the request is made with the concurrence of not less than one-tenth, in value, of the bankrupt's creditors (including the creditor making the request).

314(8)　[Capacity of trustee]　Nothing in this Act is to be construed as restricting the capacity of the trustee to exercise any of his powers outside England and Wales.

(Former provisions: IA 1985, s. 160; BA 1914, ss. 55–57, 79(2))

S. 314(1), (2), (6)

A trustee may exercise the powers listed in Pt. II of Sch. 5 without obtaining the permission of any committee of creditors (see s. 301). This list of powers is derived from BA 1914, s. 55. No major changes have been made to these basic powers. Note, however, that if property is disposed of to an "associate" of the bankrupt (for the meaning of this term see s. 435), the committee of creditors must be told. Section 314(2) refers to Pt. I of Sch. 5, which describes powers which the trustee may exercise only with the consent of the committee of creditors. These powers are based on BA 1914, ss. 56, 57. The sanction requirement is to protect the bankrupt's estate, see *Re A Debtor (No. 26A of 1975)* [1985] 1 WLR 6. The requirement that the trustee should obtain permission before employing a solicitor or agent, contained formerly in s. 56(3), has been dropped – but if he does this he must now give notice to the committee according to s. 314(6) (*b*).

S. 314(3), (4)

These provisions deal with the question of permission as required by s. 314(2) and (7) above. It must be specific. Bona fide purchasers for value dealing with the trustee need not investigate to see that it has been given: this is in line with the general policy of s. 377 validating the acts of the trustee.

S. 314(5)

This provision refers to Pt. III of Sch. 5, which gives a general account of the trustee's powers (e.g. to hold property and make contracts) that may be exercised in his "official name" (see s. 305(4)).

S. 314(7)

This deals with the calling of a general meeting of creditors by the trustee. Note that he must call such a meeting if asked to do so by creditors owed one-tenth of the bankrupt's total debts. The figure fixed by BA 1914, s. 79(2) was one-sixth in value of the total debts.

S. 314(8)

The trustee may exercise his powers outside England and Wales.

DISCLAIMER OF ONEROUS PROPERTY

Section 315　Disclaimer (general power)

315(1)　[Power of trustee to disclaim]　Subject as follows, the trustee may, by the giving of the prescribed notice, disclaim any onerous property and may do so notwithstanding that he has taken possession of it, endeavoured to sell it or otherwise exercised rights of ownership in relation to it.

315(2)　[Onerous property]　The following is onerous property for the purposes of this section, that is to say—

　　(a) any unprofitable contract, and

   (b) any other property comprised in the bankrupt's estate which is unsaleable or not readily saleable, or is such that it may give rise to a liability to pay money or perform any other onerous act.

315(3) [Effect of disclaimer] A disclaimer under this section—

   (a) operates so as to determine, as from the date of the disclaimer, the rights, interests and liabilities of the bankrupt and his estate in or in respect of the property disclaimed, and

   (b) discharges the trustee from all personal liability in respect of that property as from the commencement of his trusteeship,

but does not, except so far as is necessary for the purpose of releasing the bankrupt, the bankrupt's estate and the trustee from any liability, affect the rights or liabilities of any other person.

315(4) [Where notice of disclaimer not to be given] A notice of disclaimer shall not be given under this section in respect of any property that has been claimed for the estate under section 307 (after-acquired property) or 308 (personal property of bankrupt exceeding reasonable replacement value) or 308A, except with the leave of the court.

315(5) [Persons sustaining loss or damage] Any person sustaining loss or damage in consequence of the operation of a disclaimer under this section is deemed to be a creditor of the bankrupt to the extent of the loss or damage and accordingly may prove for the loss or damage as a bankruptcy debt.

(Former provisions: IA 1985, s. 161(1)–(4), (10); BA 1914, s. 54)

General note

This section, and the ones immediately following it, deal with the power of the trustee to disclaim onerous property, and the rôle of the court in the event of disclaimer. The Cork Committee (*Report*, paras. 1182–1199) felt that this power, which has existed since 1869, should be modified to enable the trustee to utilise it more effectively. The comparable provisions relating to disclaimers by liquidators are to be found in ss. 178–182. A disclaimer is deemed to have been validly exercised unless the contrary is established: see IR 1986, r. 6.185.

   In the context of the financial markets, s. 315 does not apply in relation to a market contract or a contract effected by an exchange or clearing house for the purpose of realising property provided as margin in relation to market contracts: see CA 1989, s. 164(1), and the note on p. 3.

S. 315(1), (2)

This authorises disclaimer of onerous property even though the trustee may have already tried to sell it. For the form of the notice see IR 1986, r. 6.178 and Form 6.61. Communication of this notice is covered by rr. 6.179–6.181. Property which may be so disclaimed is defined in s. 315(2). For the meaning of "property" here see *London City Council* v *Bown*, *The Times*, 11 October 1989 where a secure periodic tenancy was not so regarded. Note that the 12-month cut-off period for disclaimer in BA 1914, s. 54(1) has been dropped, against the wishes of the Cork Committee (*Report*, para. 1195).

S. 315(3), (5)

The effect of disclaimer is explained here. Note that third party rights are only to be prejudiced in so far as that is absolutely necessary, and anyone suffering losses as a result of disclaimer can prove in the bankruptcy in respect of it (but see s. 320(5) here). On the effect of disclaimer see

MEPC plc v *Scottish Amicable Life Assurance Association & Anor* [1993] TLR 203 which was concerned with the extent of a disclaimer initiated by a s. 315 letter. In contruing this matter the court adopted an interpretation that was most beneficial to the interests of the estate.

S. 315(4)

Notices of disclaimer are restricted by this provision. Leave of the court is required before the trustee may disclaim after-acquired property which has already been claimed for the estate (s. 307), or property claimed under s. 308 or 308A (added by the Housing Act 1988, s. 117(3)) with a view to replacement. For the leave procedure, see IR 1986, r. 6.182.

These rules on disclaimer are supplemented by IR 1986, rr. 6.178–6.186.

Section 316   Notice requiring trustee's decision

316(1)   [Where notice not to be given]   Notice of disclaimer shall not be given under section 315 in respect of any property if—

(a) a person interested in the property has applied in writing to the trustee or one of his predecessors as trustee requiring the trustee or that predecessor to decide whether he will disclaim or not, and

(b) the period of 28 days beginning with the day on which that application was made has expired without a notice of disclaimer having been given under section 315 in respect of that property.

316(2)   [Deemed adoption]   The trustee is deemed to have adopted any contract which by virtue of this section he is not entitled to disclaim.

(Former provisions: IA 1985, s. 161(5); BA 1914, s. 54)

General note

If the trustee, having been required to make a choice, decides not to disclaim, he cannot later change his mind. Failure to disclaim constitutes adoption. The 28-day period during which the trustee must make his decision has been retained from BA 1914, s. 54(4). For the form of a s. 316 application see IR 1986, r. 6.183. The trustee can force a person to declare his interest in disclaimable property by using IR 1986, r. 6.184 and Form 6.63.

Note also IR 1986, rr. 6.178–6.186.

Section 317   Disclaimer of leaseholds

317(1)   [Disclaimer of leasehold property]   The disclaimer of any property of a leasehold nature does not take effect unless a copy of the disclaimer has been served (so far as the trustee is aware of their addresses) on every person claiming under the bankrupt as underlessee or mortgagee and either—

(a) no application under section 320 below is made with respect to the property before the end of the period of 14 days beginning with the day on which the last notice served under this subsection was served, or

(b) where such an application has been made, the court directs that the disclaimer is to take effect.

317(2)   [Where court gives s. 317(1)(b) direction]   Where the court gives a direction under subsection (1)(b) it may also, instead of or in addition to any order it makes under section 320, make such orders with respect to fixtures, tenant's improvements and other matters arising out of the lease as it thinks fit.

(Former provisions: IA 1985, s. 161(6), (7); BA 1914, s. 54)

General note

These provisions deal with disclaimers in respect of onerous land. In the case of leasehold property, both underlessees and mortgagees must be served with notices of disclaimer. Note here IR 1986, rr. 6.178–6.186 (cf. the former BR 1952, r. 278).

Formerly, disclaimers of leases required the consent of the court: BA 1914, s. 54(3). Now the court will only be involved if an application is made to it within 14 days under s. 320. The trustee, after serving notice, must wait for the 14 days to elapse before the disclaimer can take effect. If application to the court has been made, obviously the trustee must wait for the outcome of the application.

The court, if it permits disclaimer, can make special provision for fixtures, etc.

Section 318 Disclaimer of dwelling house

318 Without prejudice to section 317, the disclaimer of any property in a dwelling house does not take effect unless a copy of the disclaimer has been served (so far as the trustee is aware of their addresses) on every person in occupation of or claiming a right to occupy the dwelling house and either—

    (a) no application under section 320 is made with respect to the property before the end of the period of 14 days beginning with the day on which the last notice served under this section was served, or

    (b) where such an application has been made, the court directs that the disclaimer is to take effect.

(Former provision: IA 1985, s. 161(8))

General note

In the case of dwelling houses (for definition, see s. 385), all occupiers must be notified. This is a new provision, which substantially mirrors s. 317 in many procedural respects.

Section 319 Disclaimer of land subject to rentcharge

319(1) [Application] The following applies where, in consequence of the disclaimer under section 315 of any land subject to a rentcharge, that land vests by operation of law in the Crown or any other person (referred to in the next subsection as "the proprietor").

319(2) [Limit on liability] The proprietor, and the successors in title of the proprietor, are not subject to any personal liability in respect of any sums becoming due under the rentcharge, except sums becoming due after the proprietor, or some person claiming under or through the proprietor, has taken possession or control of the land or has entered into occupation of it.

(Former provision: IA 1985, s. 161(9))

General note

These are highly specialised provisions relating to disclaimers of land subject to a rentcharge.

The person in whom the land vests subsequently is not subject to the normal rentcharge obligations.

Section 320   Court order vesting disclaimed property

320(1)   [Application]   This section and the next apply where the trustee has disclaimed property under section 315.

320(2)   [Application to court]   An application may be made to the court under this section by—

- (a) any person who claims an interest in the disclaimed property,
- (b) any person who is under any liability in respect of the disclaimed property, not being a liability discharged by the disclaimer, or
- (c) where the disclaimed property is property in a dwelling house, any person who at the time when the bankruptcy petition was presented was in occupation of or entitled to occupy the dwelling house.

320(3)   [Order by court]   Subject as follows in this section and the next, the court may, on an application under this section, make an order on such terms as it thinks fit for the vesting of the disclaimed property in, or for its delivery to—

- (a) a person entitled to it or a trustee for such a person,
- (b) a person subject to such a liability as is mentioned in subsection (2)(b) or a trustee for such a person, or
- (c) where the disclaimed property is property in a dwelling house, any person who at the time when the bankruptcy petition was presented was in occupation of or entitled to occupy the dwelling house.

320(4)   [Limit to s. 320(3)(b)]   The court shall not make an order by virtue of subsection (3)(b) except where it appears to the court that it would be just to do so for the purpose of compensating the person subject to the liability in respect of the disclaimer.

320(5)   [Effect of order in s. 315(5) assessment]   The effect of any order under this section shall be taken into account in assessing for the purposes of section 315(5) the extent of any loss or damage sustained by any person in consequence of the disclaimer.

320(6)   [Mode of vesting re order]   An order under this section vesting property in any person need not be completed by any conveyance, assignment or transfer.

(Former provisions: IA 1985, s. 162 (1)–(4), (9), (10); BA 1914, s. 54)

S. 320(1)–(4)

Where a trustee has disclaimed onerous property, certain persons have the right to apply to the court for relief. Note the three month time limit for applications, see IR 1986, r. 6.186. Note that occupiers of dwelling houses have now been given this right. The type of relief which the court may grant is described by these provisions. Vesting and delivery orders may be made according to the general discretion of the court.

S. 320(5), (6)

Where a vesting order is made, no conveyance, etc., is required to effect it. If disclaimed property is vested in a person who has suffered loss as a result of the disclaimer, that vesting is to be taken into account when assessing compensation.

Note here IR 1986, r. 6.186.

Section 321   Order under s. 320 in respect of leaseholds

321(1)   **[Terms of order re leasehold property]**   The court shall not make an order under section 320 vesting property of a leasehold nature in any person, except on terms making that person—

    (a) subject to the same liabilities and obligations as the bankrupt was subject to under the lease on the day the bankruptcy petition was presented, or

    (b) if the court thinks fit, subject to the same liabilities and obligations as that person would be subject to if the lease had been assigned to him on that day.

321(2)   **[Where order re part of property in lease]**   For the purposes of an order under section 320 relating to only part of any property comprised in a lease, the requirements of subsection (1) apply as if the lease comprised only the property to which the order relates.

321(3)   **[Where no person accepts order in s. 162(5) case]**   Where subsection (1) applies and no person is willing to accept an order under section 320 on the terms required by that subsection, the court may (by order under section 320) vest the estate or interest of the bankrupt in the property in any person who is liable (whether personally or in a representative capacity and whether alone or jointly with the bankrupt) to perform the lessee's covenants in the lease.

    The court may by virtue of this subsection vest that estate and interest in such a person freed and discharged from all estates, incumbrances and interests created by the bankrupt.

321(4)   **[Exclusion from interest in property]**   Where subsection (1) applies and a person declines to accept any order under section 320, that person shall be excluded from all interest in the property.

(Former provision: IA 1985, s. 162(5)–(8); BA 1914, s. 54)

General note

Section 321(1) deals with applications in respect of leasehold property – the person in whom the leasehold property is vested must assume the same obligations as the lessee was subject to prior to his bankruptcy. If only part of the leasehold property is so vested, the order must take this into account when determining the obligations to impose. Section 321(2) and (3) deal with cases where persons decline to accept orders made under s. 320 – the court may make adjustments to interests in the property concerned. This includes exclusion from all interest in the property in question (s. 321(4)).

DISTRIBUTION OF BANKRUPT'S ESTATE

Section 322   Proof of debts

322(1)   **[Proof in accordance with rules]**   Subject to this section and the next, the proof of any bankruptcy debt by a secured or unsecured creditor of the bankrupt and the admission or rejection of any proof shall take place in accordance with the rules.

322(2)   **[Where bankruptcy debt bears interest]**   Where a bankruptcy debt bears interest, that interest is provable as part of the debt except in so far as it is payable in respect of any period after the commencement of the bankruptcy.

322(3) [Estimation of debt] The trustee shall estimate the value of any bankruptcy debt which, by reason of its being subject to any contingency or contingencies or for any other reason, does not bear a certain value.

322(4) [Where estimate under s. 303, 322(3)] Where the value of a bankruptcy debt is estimated by the trustee under subsection (3) or, by virtue of section 303 in Chapter III, by the court, the amount provable in the bankruptcy in respect of the debt is the amount of the estimate.

(Former provisions: IA 1985, s. 163; BA 1914, ss. 30, 32 and Sch. 2)

S. 322(1)

The procedure governing proof of "bankruptcy debts" (see s. 382) is governed by the rules – see in particular IR 1986, rr. 6.96–6.114. Under BA 1914, s. 32 indicated that the details on proof of debts were to be found in Sch. 2.

For the question of proof by secured creditors see s. 383. For a case where contingent tax penalties were held provable, see *Re Hurren (A Bankrupt)* [1983] 1 WLR 183. Fines were provable debts under the old law – *Re Pascoe, ex parte Trustee of the Bankrupt* v *Lords Commissioners of His Majesty's Treasury* [1944] Ch. 310. It is not clear from the Act itself whether the recommendation of the Cork Committee (*Report*, para. 1330), that this rule should be reversed, has been implemented. However, the fact that fines are not provable is apparent from IR 1986, r. 12.3.

S. 322(2)

Under BA 1914, s. 66 there were severe restrictions on proving in respect of interest. These restrictions, which were heavily criticised by the Cork Committee (*Report*, para. 1381), have been largely removed except with regard to interest accruing after the commencement of the bankruptcy. It should also remembered that s. 343 may be relevant here.

S. 322(3), (4)

This allows the trustee to estimate the value of contingent or uncertain debts. For the costs of the trustee see IR 1986, r. 6.100(2). Under BA 1914, s. 30 there was a facility allowing a creditor to appeal against any estimate made by a trustee. This is not specifically recreated by s. 322 but possibly a disappointed creditor could make use of s. 303. This provision for estimates will be doubly useful now that the old restriction, formerly contained in BA 1914, s. 30(1), banning proof in respect of unliquidated claims, has been abolished – see s. 382(3). The Cork Committee (*Report*, para. 1318) favoured this change partly because the restriction did not apply to a corporate insolvency – *Re Berkeley Securities (Property) Ltd* [1980] 1 WLR 1589 – but this had been the subject of some uncertainty.

The change in bankruptcy law will be welcomed if it avoids such confusion.

Section 323 Mutual credit and set-off

323(1) [Application] This section applies where before the commencement of the bankruptcy there have been mutual credits, mutual debts or other mutual dealings between the bankrupt and any creditor of the bankrupt proving or claiming to prove for a bankruptcy debt.

323(2) [Account to be taken] An account shall be taken of what is due from each party to the other in respect of the mutual dealings and the sums due from one party shall be set off against the sums due from the other.

323(3) [Qualification to s. 323(2)] Sums due from the bankrupt to another party shall not be included in the account taken under subsection (2) if that other party had notice at the time they became due that a bankruptcy petition relating to the bankrupt was pending.

323(4) [Balance to trustee] Only the balance (if any) of the account taken under subsection (2) is provable as a bankruptcy debt or, as the case may be, to be paid to the trustee as part of the bankrupt's estate.

(Former provisions: IA 1985, s. 164; BA 1914, s. 31)

General note

There is little change here. The rules are those in BA 1914, s. 31, which in turn reflected common law authorities such as *Foster* v *Wilson* (1843) 12 M & W 191. The only changes in s. 323 are of a terminological or consequential nature reflecting the demise of concepts such as acts of bankruptcy and receiving orders. Notwithstanding the apparent desire of the legislature to reaffirm the old rules on set-off, in *Stein* v *Blake* [1994] Ch. 16; [1993] BCC 587 the Court of Appeal concluded that it was possible for a trustee in bankruptcy to assign a bankrupt's right of action to a third party and in so doing defeat any right of set-off which the defendant in the proposed action might have had against the bankrupt. In so deciding the Court of Appeal rejected the contrary view taken by Neill J in *Farley* v *Housing and Commercial Developments Ltd* (1984) 1 BCC 99,150 which had been decided under the old s. 31 of the Bankruptcy Act 1914. This decision of the Court of Appeal can be seen as one of a number of recent authorities favouring an "estate maximisation" policy on the part of the judiciary. Leave to appeal to the House of Lords has been granted – [1994] 1 WLR 875.

It is worth noting that s. 323 does not appear to implement the recommendation of the Cork Committee (*Report*, para. 1342) that the decision in *National Westminster Bank Ltd* v *Halesowen Presswork & Assemblies Ltd* [1972] AC 785, banning contracting out of the statutory rules, be reversed. However, there is a special exception allowing contracting out on the financial markets: see CA 1989, ss. 159, 163, and the note on p. 3, above.

For the exclusion of set-off in respect of post-insolvency VAT credits, see Finance Act 1988, s. 21 (as amended by Finance Act 1994, s. 47).

Section 324 Distribution by means of dividend

324(1) [Duty to declare and distribute] Whenever the trustee has sufficient funds in hand for the purpose he shall, subject to the retention of such sums as may be necessary for the expenses of the bankruptcy, declare and distribute dividends among the creditors in respect of the bankruptcy debts which they have respectively proved.

324(2) [Notice of intention to declare and distribute] The trustee shall give notice of his intention to declare and distribute a dividend.

324(3) [Notice of dividend etc.] Where the trustee has declared a dividend, he shall give notice of the dividend and of how it is proposed to distribute it; and a notice given under this subsection shall contain the prescribed particulars of the bankrupt's estate.

324(4) [Calculation and distribution of dividend] In the calculation and distribution of a dividend the trustee shall make provision—

(a) for any bankruptcy debts which appear to him to be due to persons who, by reason of the distance of their place of residence, may not have had sufficient time to tender and establish their proofs,

(b) for any bankruptcy debts which are the subject of claims which have not yet been determined, and

(c) for disputed proofs and claims.

(Former provisions: IA 1985, s. 165(1)–(4); BA 1914, ss. 62, 64)

S. 324(1)–(3)

These provide for the declaration of dividends to creditors when the trustee has sufficient funds at his disposal for that purpose, once expenses have been taken into account. Notice of the dividend must be given to creditors. Under BA 1914, s. 62(2) the trustee had, as a general rule, to declare the first dividend within four months of the first meeting of creditors; this specific deadline has been dropped.

For further details on declaration of dividends, see IR 1986, Pt. 11. For the mechanics of payment, see the Insolvency Regulations 1994 (SI 1994 No. 2507), reg. 23.

S. 324(4)

This is a good housekeeping provision. The trustee should set aside funds to cover disputed claims or claims by persons who have not yet lodged proofs.

If the trustee proposes to pay an interim dividend at a time when an application to the court to challenge the admission or rejection of a proof is outstanding, the leave of the court is required under IR 1986, r. 11.5(2).

Section 325 Claims by unsatisfied creditors

325(1) [Entitlements of creditors] A creditor who has not proved his debt before the declaration of any dividend is not entitled to disturb, by reason that he has not participated in it, the distribution of that dividend or any other dividend declared before his debt was proved, but—

(a) when he has proved that debt he is entitled to be paid, out of any money for the time being available for the payment of any further dividend, any dividend or dividends which he has failed to receive; and

(b) any dividend or dividends payable under paragraph (a) shall be paid before that money is applied to the payment of any such further dividend.

325(2) [Order re payment of dividend] No action lies against the trustee for a dividend, but if the trustee refuses to pay a dividend the court may, if it thinks fit, order him to pay it and also to pay, out of his own money—

(a) interest on the dividend, at the rate for the time being specified in section 17 of the Judgments Act 1838, from the time it was withheld, and

(b) the costs of the proceedings in which the order to pay is made.

(Former provisions: IA 1985, s. 165(5)(b); BA 1914, ss. 65, 68)

S. 325(1)

Late claimants cannot upset properly declared dividends, but they may make a claim on any surplus available.

S. 325(2)

This curiously worded provision is derived from BA 1914, s. 68. On the one hand, it states that no action shall lie against a trustee for a dividend, but then it permits the court to order the trustee to pay one, and, indeed, to pay interest and costs out of his own pocket.

Compare IR 1986, r. 11.8.

Section 326   Distribution of property in specie

326(1)   **[Division of unsaleable property]**   Without prejudice to sections 315 to 319 (disclaimer), the trustee may, with the permission of the creditors' committee, divide in its existing form amongst the bankrupt's creditors, according to its estimated value, any property which from its peculiar nature or other special circumstances cannot be readily or advantageously sold.

326(2)   **[Permission under s. 326(1)]**   A permission given for the purposes of subsection (1) shall not be a general permission but shall relate to a particular proposed exercise of the power in question; and a person dealing with the trustee in good faith and for value is not to be concerned to enquire whether any permission required by subsection (1) has been given.

326(3)   **[Where no permission under s. 326(1)]**   Where the trustee has done anything without the permission required by subsection (1), the court or the creditors' committee may, for the purpose of enabling him to meet his expenses out of the bankrupt's estate, ratify what the trustee has done.

But the committee shall not do so unless it is satisfied that the trustee acted in a case of urgency and has sought its ratification without undue delay.

(Former provisions: IA 1985, s. 165(7), (8))

S. 326(1)

This authorises the trustee to make distributions *in specie* of the property which is difficult to realise. This is a new facility without precedent in the 1914 Act.

S. 326(2), (3)

The trustee must obtain specific permission to exercise his power to make an *in specie* distribution under s. 326(1) above. Unauthorised distributions may, in certain circumstances, be ratified by the creditors' committee.

Section 327   Distribution in criminal bankruptcy

327   Where the bankruptcy order was made on a petition under section 264(1)(d) (criminal bankruptcy), no distribution shall be made under sections 324 to 326 so long as an appeal is pending (within the meaning of section 277) against the bankrupt's conviction of any offence by virtue of which the criminal bankruptcy order on which the petition was based was made.

(Former provision: IA 1985, s. 165(9))

General note

In cases of criminal bankruptcy no distribution is to be made until the final appeal in the criminal case is heard.

Note prospective amendment: s. 327 is to be repealed by the Criminal Justice Act 1988, s. 170(2) and Sch. 16 as from a day to be appointed; see the note to s. 264.

Section 328 Priority of debts

328(1) **[Preferential debts to be paid first]** In the distribution of the bankrupt's estate, his preferential debts (within the meaning given by section 386 in Part XII) shall be paid in priority to other debts.

328(2) **[Ranking of preferential debts]** Preferential debts rank equally between themselves after the expenses of the bankruptcy and shall be paid in full unless the bankrupt's estate is insufficient for meeting them, in which case they abate in equal proportions between themselves.

328(3) **[Debts neither preferential nor under s. 329]** Debts which are neither preferential debts nor debts to which the next section applies also rank equally between themselves and, after the preferential debts, shall be paid in full unless the bankrupt's estate is insufficient for meeting them, in which case they abate in equal proportions between themselves.

328(4) **[Surplus after payment]** Any surplus remaining after the payment of the debts that are preferential or rank equally under subsection (3) shall be applied in paying interest on those debts in respect of the periods during which they have been outstanding since the commencement of the bankruptcy; and interest on preferential debts ranks equally with interest on debts other than preferential debts.

328(5) **[Rate of interest under s. 328(4)]** The rate of interest payable under subsection (4) in respect of any debt is whichever is the greater of the following—

    (a) the rate specified in section 17 of the Judgments Act 1838 at the commencement of the bankruptcy, and

    (b) the rate applicable to that debt apart from the bankruptcy.

328(6) **[Other enactments]** This section and the next are without prejudice to any provision of this Act or any other Act under which the payment of any debt or the making of any other payment is, in the event of bankruptcy, to have a particular priority or to be postponed.

(Former provisions: IA 1985, s. 166(1)–(5), (7); BA 1914, s. 33)

General note

This section has dropped what was formerly BA 1914, s. 33(6), dealing with payment of debts in the case of partnership insolvency – see s. 420 now. The provision relating to insolvent estates of deceased persons has also not been retained – see s. 421. The text of BA 1914, s. 33(4) is now included in s. 347. See also IR 1986, rr. 6.224 and 11.2 in this context.

S. 328(1), (2)

These provisions deal with preferential debts. Those debts described as preferential by ss. 386, 387 and by Sch. 6 of this Act are to be paid in priority to other debts (but not the expenses of the bankruptcy – see Sch. 9, para. 22). In the event of a shortfall they are to abate in equal proportions. Note that the list of preferential debts has been pruned radically by Sch. 6 after considerable pressure had been exerted on the Government. This issue is considered fully in the note to s. 386 below.

S. 328(3)

Ordinary debts – i.e. those which are neither preferential nor deferred – rank equally between themselves and abate rateably in the event of a shortfall.

S. 328(4), (5)

These provisions deal with the payment of interest on debts which has accrued since the commencement of the bankruptcy (for the meaning of this phrase, see s. 278). It is to be paid only after both the preferential and ordinary creditors have been satisfied in full. Interest on preferential debts receives no special treatment. Section 328(5) specifies the maximum rate of interest allowed (currently 8 per cent (see SI 1993 No. 564)).

S. 328(6)

The general law on deferred creditors is preserved – for example, a creditor whose case falls within s. 3 of the Partnership Act 1890.

Section 329 Debts to spouse

329(1) [Application] This section applies to bankruptcy debts owed in respect of credit provided by a person who (whether or not the bankrupt's spouse at the time the credit was provided) was the bankrupt's spouse at the commencement of the bankruptcy.

329(2) [Ranking, payment] Such debts—

  (a) rank in priority after the debts and interest required to be paid in pursuance of section 328(3) and (4), and

  (b) are payable with interest at the rate specified in section 328(5) in respect of the period during which they have been outstanding since the commencement of the bankruptcy;

and the interest payable under paragraph (b) has the same priority as the debts on which it is payable.

(Former provisions: IA 1985, s. 166(6); BA 1914, s. 36)

General note

This section differs from its predecessor in the 1914 Act in a number of respects. For example, BA 1914, s. 36 related only to a loan in connection with a business or trade carried on by the bankrupt (where the lender was a husband), but not if it was lent by a wife.

Section 330 Final distribution

330(1) [Notice re dividend, etc.] When the trustee has realised all the bankrupt's estate or so much of it as can, in the trustee's opinion, be realised without needlessly protracting the trusteeship, he shall give notice in the prescribed manner either—

  (a) of his intention to declare a final dividend, or

  (b) that no dividend, or further dividend, will be declared.

330(2) [Contents of notice] The notice under subsection (1) shall contain the prescribed particulars and shall require claims against the bankrupt's estate to be established by a date ("the final date") specified in the notice.

330(3)   [Postponement of final date]   The court may, on the application of any person, postpone the final date.

330(4)   [Trustee's duties after final date]   After the final date, the trustee shall—

(a) defray any outstanding expenses of the bankruptcy out of the bankrupt's estate, and

(b) if he intends to declare a final dividend, declare and distribute that dividend without regard to the claim of any person in respect of a debt not already proved in the bankruptcy.

330(5)   [Where surplus]   If a surplus remains after payment in full and with interest of all the bankrupt's creditors and the payment of the expenses of the bankruptcy, the bankrupt is entitled to the surplus.

(Former provisions: IA 1985, s. 167; BA 1914, ss. 67, 69)

S. 330(1)–(3)

Where the trustee has realised all that can be converted into money he should notify the creditors whether he is in a position to declare a final dividend. This notice must indicate a final date for claims. This final date can be extended by the court.

S. 330(4)

Once the final date is passed the trustee should pay his final dividend, but not before the costs of the bankruptcy (which often represent a considerable figure) have been defrayed out of the proceeds of realisation.

There appears to be no provision dealing with unclaimed dividends to replace BA 1914, s. 153. Generally see IR 1986, Pt. 11.

S. 330(5)

Any surplus goes to the bankrupt.

Section 331   Final meeting

331(1)   [Application]   Subject as follows in this section and the next, this section applies where—

(a) it appears to the trustee that the administration of the bankrupt's estate in accordance with this Chapter is for practical purposes complete, and

(b) the trustee is not the official receiver.

331(2)   [Duty of trustee]   The trustee shall summon a final general meeting of the bankrupt's creditors which—

(a) shall receive the trustee's report of his administration of the bankrupt's estate, and

(b) shall determine whether the trustee should have his release under section 299 in Chapter III.

331(3)   [Time for notice]   The trustee may, if he thinks fit, give the notice summoning the final general meeting at the same time as giving notice under section 330(1); but, if summoned for an earlier date, that meeting shall be adjourned (and, if necessary, further adjourned) until a date on which the trustee is able to report to the meeting that the administration of the bankrupt's estate is for practical purposes complete.

331(4) **[Expenses]**   In the administration of the estate it is the trustee's duty to retain sufficient sums from the estate to cover the expenses of summoning and holding the meeting required by this section.

(Former provisions: IA 1985, s. 168(1), (2), (4))

S. 331(1), (2)

These provisions require a trustee (but not an official receiver) to call a final meeting of creditors to report on how things went. This appears to be an innovation.

S. 331(3)

To save money, notice of the final meeting can be sent out along with notice of the final dividend, but the meeting cannot be held until the final dividend has been paid.

S. 331(4)

This is a reminder to the trustees to set aside sufficient funds to cover the cost of this final meeting.

Section 332   Saving for bankrupt's home

332(1) **[Application]**   This section applies where—

(a) there is comprised in the bankrupt's estate property consisting of an interest in a dwelling house which is occupied by the bankrupt or by his spouse or former spouse, and

(b) the trustee has been unable for any reason to realise that property.

332(2) **[Conditions for s. 331 meeting]**   The trustee shall not summon a meeting under section 331 unless either—

(a) the court has made an order under section 313 imposing a charge on that property for the benefit of the bankrupt's estate, or

(b) the court has declined, on an application under that section, to make such an order, or

(c) the Secretary of State has issued a certificate to the trustee stating that it would be inappropriate or inexpedient for such an application to be made in the case in question.

(Former provision: IA 1985, s. 168(3))

General note

This again is a new provision. It states that as a general rule there should be no summoning of a final meeting where the bankrupt's interest in a "dwelling house" (for definition, see s. 385) has not been realised. Exceptions to this general rule are: (1) where a s. 313 charge has been imposed on the property, (2) where the court has refused to grant a s. 313 charge, or (3) where the Secretary of State has certified that it would be inappropriate for the trustee to apply for a s. 313 charge.

SUPPLEMENTAL

Section 333   Duties of bankrupt in relation to trustee

333(1)   [Duties]   The bankrupt shall—

(a) give to the trustee such information as to his affairs,

(b) attend on the trustee at such times, and

(c) do all such other things,

as the trustee may for the purposes of carrying out his functions under any of this Group of Parts reasonably require.

333(2)   [Notice re after-acquired property or income increase]   Where at any time after the commencement of the bankruptcy any property is acquired by, or devolves upon, the bankrupt or there is an increase of the bankrupt's income, the bankrupt shall, within the prescribed period, give the trustee notice of the property or, as the case may be, of the increase.

333(3)   [Application of s. 333(1)]   Subsection (1) applies to a bankrupt after his discharge.

333(4)   [Penalty for non-compliance]   If the bankrupt without reasonable excuse fails to comply with any obligation imposed by this section, he is guilty of a contempt of court and liable to be punished accordingly (in addition to any other punishment to which he may be subject).

(Former provisions: IA 1985, s. 169; BA 1914, s. 22)

S. 333(1), (3)

These provisions impose duties on a bankrupt, up to and after the date of his discharge, to provide information and assistance to enable the *trustee* to carry out his duties. The comparable provision describing the bankrupt's duties towards the *official receiver* is to be found in s. 291.

 Note also the bankrupt's more specific duties in regard to property, records, etc. under s. 312.

S. 333(2)

The obligation to provide information about the property and income is a continuing one. Such an obligation is essential for the operation of ss. 307 and 310. The prescribed period is 21 days: see IR 1986, r. 6.200(1).

S. 333(4)

A bankrupt may be held liable for contempt if he breaches any of the above obligations.

Section 334   Stay of distribution in case of second bankruptcy

334(1)   [Application, definitions]   This section and the next apply where a bankruptcy order is made against an undischarged bankrupt; and in both sections—

(a) **"the later bankruptcy"** means the bankruptcy arising from that order,

(b) **"the earlier bankruptcy"** means the bankruptcy (or, as the case may be, most recent bankruptcy) from which the bankrupt has not been discharged at the commencement of the later bankruptcy, and

395

(c) **"the existing trustee"** means the trustee (if any) of the bankrupt's estate for the purposes of the earlier bankruptcy.

334(2) **[Certain distributions void]** Where the existing trustee has been given the prescribed notice of the presentation of the petition for the later bankruptcy, any distribution or other disposition by him of anything to which the next subsection applies, if made after the giving of the notice, is void except to the extent that it was made with the consent of the court or is or was subsequently ratified by the court.

This is without prejudice to section 284 (restrictions on dispositions of property following bankruptcy order).

334(3) **[Application of s. 334(2)]** This subsection applies to—

(a) any property which is vested in the existing trustee under section 307(3) (after-acquired property);

(b) any money paid to the existing trustee in pursuance of an income payments order under section 310; and

(c) any property or money which is, or in the hands of the existing trustee represents, the proceeds of sale or application of property or money falling within paragraph (a) or (b) of this subsection.

(Former provisions: IA 1985, s. 170(1)–(3); BA 1914, s. 39 (as substituted by B(A)A 1926, s. 3))

General note

This provision is, of necessity, more sophisticated than its predecessor as a result of the advent of the new rules on after-acquired property and income payments orders.

S. 334(1)

Where a petition for bankruptcy is issued against an undischarged bankrupt who is already undergoing the bankruptcy process, his existing trustee, on receiving notice of the petition, must not make any further distributions or dispositions without the consent of the court. However, this only applies to property covered by s. 334(3).

S. 334(3)

Section 334(3) applies to after-acquired property or money from any income payments order, or the proceeds thereof. Note also IR 1986, rr. 6.225–6.228.

Section 335   Adjustment between earlier and later bankruptcy estates

335(1) **[Matters in bankrupt's estate]** With effect from the commencement of the later bankruptcy anything to which section 334(3) applies which, immediately before the commencement of that bankruptcy, is comprised in the bankrupt's estate for the purposes of the earlier bankruptcy is to be treated as comprised in the bankrupt's estate for the purposes of the later bankruptcy and, until there is a trustee of that estate, is to be dealt with by the existing trustee in accordance with the rules.

335(2) **[Sums paid under s. 310]** Any sums which in pursuance of an income payments order under section 310 are payable after the commencement of the later bankruptcy to the existing trustee shall form part of the bankrupt's estate for the purposes of the later bankruptcy; and the court may give such consequential directions for the modification of the order as it thinks fit.

335(3) [Charge re bankruptcy expenses] Anything comprised in a bankrupt's estate by virtue of subsection (1) or (2) is so comprised subject to a first charge in favour of the existing trustee for any bankruptcy expenses incurred by him in relation thereto.

335(4) [Property not in estate] Except as provided above and in section 334, property which is, or by virtue of section 308 (personal property of bankrupt exceeding reasonable replacement value) or section 308A (vesting in trustee of certain tenancies) is capable of being, comprised in the bankrupt's estate for the purposes of the earlier bankruptcy, or of any bankruptcy prior to it, shall not be comprised in his estate for the purposes of the later bankruptcy.

335(5) [Creditors of earlier bankruptcies] The creditors of the bankrupt in the earlier bankruptcy and the creditors of the bankrupt in any bankruptcy prior to the earlier one, are not to be creditors of his in the later bankruptcy in respect of the same debts; but the existing trustee may prove in the later bankruptcy for—

   (a) the unsatisfied balance of the debts (including any debt under this subsection) provable against the bankrupt's estate in the earlier bankruptcy;

   (b) any interest payable on that balance; and

   (c) any unpaid expenses of the earlier bankruptcy.

335(6) [Priority of amounts in s. 335(5)] Any amount provable under subsection (5) ranks in priority after all the other debts provable in the later bankruptcy and after interest on those debts and, accordingly, shall not be paid unless those debts and that interest have first been paid in full.

(Former provisions: IA 1985, s. 170(4)–(9); BA 1914, s. 39 (as substituted by B(A)A 1926, s. 3))

S. 335(1)–(3)

Such items, on the commencement of the second bankruptcy, must be treated as part of the estate for the purpose of that second bankruptcy. The same is true of any money paid to the first trustee under an income payments order after the date of the commencement of the second bankruptcy. Indeed, the income payments order can be modified. However, the first trustee may be entitled to a charge over such property to cover any expenses incurred in relation to it.

S. 335(4)

Other property comprised in the bankrupt's estate in the first bankruptcy does not pass to the estate on the second bankruptcy. A minor insertion has been made by the Housing Act 1988, Sch.17, para. 74.

S. 335(5), (6)

These provisions deal with the status of creditors in the first bankruptcy *vis-à-vis* the second

bankruptcy: any residual claims they may have can be proved for in the second bankruptcy, but
they only enjoy deferred status in this respect. This implements the recommendation of the
Blagden Committee (Cmnd 221, para. 114). Note also IR 1986, rr. 6.225–6.228.

S .
335

[handwritten: where the application is made after the end of the year beginning with the ... vesting of the bankrupt's estate in the T'ee, the ct. will assume, unless there are exceptional circumstances, that the interests of the bankrupt's creditors outweigh all other considerations.]

Chapter V — Effect of Bankruptcy on Certain Rights, Transactions, Etc.

RIGHTS OF OCCUPATION

Section 336   Rights of occupation etc. of bankrupt's spouse

336(1)   [Matrimonial Homes Act 1983]   Nothing occurring in the initial period of
the bankruptcy (that is to say, the period beginning with the day of the presentation of
the petition for the bankruptcy order and ending with the vesting of the bankrupt's
estate in a trustee) is to be taken as having given rise to any rights of occupation under
the Matrimonial Homes Act 1983 in relation to a dwelling house comprised in the
bankrupt's estate.

336(2)   [Where spouse's rights of occupation charge on estate]   Where a spouse's
rights of occupation under the Act of 1983 are a charge on the estate or interest of the
other spouse, or of trustees for the other spouse, and the other spouse is adjudged
bankrupt—

    (a) the charge continues to subsist notwithstanding the bankruptcy and, sub-
ject to the provisions of that Act, binds the trustee of the bankrupt's estate
and persons deriving title under that trustee, and

    (b) any application for an order under section 1 of that Act shall be made to the
court having jurisdiction in relation to the bankruptcy.

336(3)   [Where bankrupt and spouse trustees for sale of dwelling house]   Where a
person and his spouse or former spouse are trustees for sale of a dwelling house and
that person is adjudged bankrupt, any application by the trustee of the bankrupt's
estate for an order under section 30 of the Law of Property Act 1925 (powers of court
where trustees for sale refuse to act) shall be made to the court having jurisdiction in
relation to the bankruptcy.

336(4)   [Court orders]   On such an application as is mentioned in subsection (2) or
(3) the court shall make such order under section 1 of the Act of 1983 or section 30 of
the Act of 1925 as it thinks just and reasonable having regard to—

    (a) the interests of the bankrupt's creditors,

    (b) the conduct of the spouse or former spouse, so far as contributing to the
bankruptcy,

    (c) the needs and financial resources of the spouse or former spouse,

    (d) the needs of any children, and

    (e) all the circumstances of the case other than the needs of the bankrupt.

336(5) **[Assumption by court re interests of creditors]** Where such an application is made after the end of the period of one year beginning with the first vesting under Chapter IV of this Part of the bankrupt's estate in a trustee, the court shall assume, unless the circumstances of the case are exceptional, that the interests of the bankrupt's creditors outweigh all other considerations.

(Former provision: IA 1985, s. 171)

General note

This and the following two sections are part of a package to redress the balance of rights between the trustee, on the one hand, and the bankrupt and his family on the other hand, over what will probably represent the bankrupt's most valuable asset, his family home. This is a problem that has troubled the law for many years – witness the decision in *Bendall* v *McWhirter* [1952] 2 QB 466, which created a "deserted wife's equity" capable of prevailing over the trustee's rights, and its rejection by the House of Lords in *National Provincial Bank Ltd* v *Ainsworth* [1965] AC 1175. This decision, in turn, was reversed by the Matrimonial Homes Act 1967, a piece of legislation consolidated by the Matrimonial Homes Act 1983. Notwithstanding this, it was felt that the family's right to a roof over its head required greater protection in the event of the breadwinner becoming bankrupt – see the Cork Report, paras. 1114–1131. These provisions on the family home were a late insertion in the Insolvency Bill 1985. For the background to this legislation, see Miller (1986) 50 Conv. 393 and Cretney (1991) 107 LQR 177. For further discussion of this area see Creasey and Doyle (1992) 136 SJ 920.

For the definitions of "family" and "dwelling house", see s. 385.

S. 336(1)

This prevents a spouse's rights of occupation under the Matrimonial Homes Act 1983 arising during the period after the date of the petition and up to the time when the property vests in the trustee.

S. 336(2)

Where the spouse of a bankrupt has aquired statutory rights of occupation representing a charge on the house owned by the bankrupt, that charge is effective as against the trustee. Any applications made under s. 1 of the Matrimonial Homes Act 1983 (i.e. to have the spouse evicted or to enable him or her to regain possession), however, must be made to the appropriate bankruptcy court. Note that s. 336(4), commented on below, applies to such an application. This is similar to s. 1(3) of the Matrimonial Homes Act 1983.

S. 336(3)–(5)

These provisions cover the situation where the spouses or former spouses are joint owners of the property, and a trust for sale has arisen. Any application under s. 30 of the Law of Property Act 1925 to the court by the trustee in bankruptcy of one of the spouses or ex-spouses for an enforced sale is to be made to the relevant bankruptcy court. In the past, the courts have normally acceded to the trustee's request for sale, although the family interests have been considered: see *Re Solomon* [1967] Ch. 573, *Re Turner* [1974] 1 WLR 1556, *Re Densham* [1975] 1 WLR 1519, *Re Bailey* [1977] 1 WLR 278, *Re Lowrie* [1981] 3 All ER 353 and *Re Citro (A Bankrupt)* [1991] Ch. 142. A decision which went against the grain and resulted in the sale of the matrimonial home being postponed for several years until the children had finished their education was *Re Holliday* [1981] Ch. 405. A similar more "caring" approach was taken recently by Hoffmann J in *Re Mott* [1987] CLY 212 where the sick mother of the bankrupt was allowed to postpone the sale of the house until after her death. For a similar problem posed by novel facts see *Re Gorman (A Bankrupt)* [1990] 1 All ER 717. Now, if such an application is made, the court has general discretion and can consider all the circumstances (including the interests of the family and creditors and the contribution of either party towards the bankruptcy); but if it is made more than one year after the vesting of the property in the trustee in bankruptcy, it will be the interests of the creditors which will prevail unless there are exceptional counterbalancing factors. In the past, BA 1914, s. 105 has been used to protect family interests in such a case, but the Cork Committee (*Report*, para. 1118) favoured a more specific provision which would postpone the trustee's right to sell the family home for a period of a year. There is some discussion of s. 336(5) in *Re Citro (A Bankrupt)* (above) where the point is made that many of the old bankruptcy cases (which are discussed above) will be relevant to its interpretation. It is also stressed that this provision will only operate within the context of a marriage (and not to cohabitees).

Section 337 Rights of occupation of bankrupt

337(1) [Application] This section applies where—

(a) a person who is entitled to occupy a dwelling house by virtue of a beneficial estate or interest is adjudged bankrupt, and

(b) any persons under the age of 18 with whom that person had at some time occupied that dwelling house had their home with that person at the time when the bankruptcy petition was presented and at the commencment of the bankruptcy.

337(2) [Rights of occupation, etc.] Whether or not the bankrupt's spouse (if any) has rights of occupation under the Matrimonial Homes Act 1983—

(a) the bankrupt has the following rights as against the trustee of his estate—

(i) if in occupation, a right not to be evicted or excluded from the dwelling house or any part of it, except with the leave of the court,

(ii) if not in occupation, a right with the leave of the court to enter into and occupy the dwelling house, and

(b) the bankrupt's rights are a charge, having the like priority as an equitable interest created immediately before the commencement of the bankruptcy, on so much of his estate or interest in the dwelling house as vests in the trustee.

337(3) [Application of Matrimonial Homes Act] The Act of 1983 has effect, with the necessary modifications, as if—

(a) the rights conferred by paragraph (a) of subsection (2) were rights of occupation under that Act,

(b) any application for leave such as is mentioned in that paragraph were an application for an order under section 1 of that Act, and

(c) any charge under paragraph (b) of that subsection on the estate or interest of the trustee were a charge under that Act on the estate or interest of a spouse.

337(4) [Application to court] Any application for leave such as is mentioned in subsection (2)(a) or otherwise by virtue of this section for an order under section 1 of the Act of 1983 shall be made to the court having jurisdiction in relation to the bankruptcy.

337(5) [Court order under s. 337(4)]   On such an application the court shall make such order under section 1 of the Act of 1983 as it thinks just and reasonable having regard to the interests of the creditors, to the bankrupt's financial resources, to the needs of the children and to all the circumstances of the case other than the needs of the bankrupt.

337(6) [Assumption re interests of creditors]   Where such an application is made after the end of the period of one year beginning with the first vesting (under Chapter IV of this Part) of the bankrupt's estate in a trustee, the court shall assume, unless the circumstances of the case are exceptional, that the interest of the bankrupt's creditors outweigh all other considerations.

(Former provision: IA 1985, s. 172)

S. 337(1), (2)

These provisions protect the rights of occupation of the bankrupt who has dependent children living with him: he cannot be evicted from the family home without a court order and can apply to the court to regain entry if out of possession. His rights under these provisions are in the nature of an equitable interest binding on the trustee.

S. 337(3)

This extends certain provisions in the Matrimonial Homes Act 1983 to the bankrupt's right of occupation.

S. 337(4)–(6)

Applications for leave under s. 337(2)(*a*) must be made to the relevant bankruptcy court. On such an application the court should adopt a similar approach to that specified in s. 336(4) and (5) above (although the criteria are different), with the creditors' interests having priority where the application is made more than a year after the property has vested in the trustee.

Section 338   Payments in respect of premises occupied by bankrupt

338   Where any premises comprised in a bankrupt's estate are occupied by him (whether by virtue of the preceding section or otherwise) on condition that he makes payments towards satisfying any liability arising under a mortgage of the premises or otherwise towards the outgoings of the premises, the bankrupt does not, by virtue of those payments, acquire any interest in the premises.

(Former provision: IA 1985, s. 173)

General note

This provision clarifies the position where a bankrupt is allowed to remain in occupation of premises provided that he pays the mortgage, etc. Any such payment will not result in his acquiring an interest in the property.

Compare this provision with s. 1(7) of the Matrimonial Homes Act 1983.

ADJUSTMENT OF PRIOR TRANSACTIONS, ETC.

Section 339   Transactions at an undervalue

339(1) [Application to court]   Subject as follows in this section and sections 341 and 342, where an individual is adjudged bankrupt and he has at a relevant time (defined in section 341) entered into a transaction with any person at an undervalue, the trustee of the bankrupt's estate may apply to the court for an order under this section.

339(2)   [Order by court]   The court shall, on such an application, make such order as it thinks fit for restoring the position to what it would have been if that individual had not entered into that transaction.

339(3)   [Where transaction is at undervalue]   For the purposes of this section and sections 341 and 342, an individual enters into a transaction with a person at an undervalue if—

   (a) he makes a gift to that person or he otherwise enters into a transaction with that person on terms that provide for him to receive no consideration,

   (b) he enters into a transaction with that person in consideration of marriage, or

   (c) he enters into a transaction with that person for a consideration the value of which, in money or money's worth, is significantly less than the value, in money or money's worth, of the consideration provided by the individual.

(Former provisions: IA 1985, s. 174(1) (part), (2); BA 1914, ss. 42, 44)

General note

Sections 339–341 are new provisions designed to rationalise and update their outmoded predecessors in the BA 1914. They were substantially amended at the Report Stage of the 1985 Bill. For the views of the Cork Committee on the former law, see its *Report*, paras. 1226, 1285 and 1287. Unfortunately, ss. 339–341 are of Byzantine complexity. Corresponding provisions for corporate insolvency are to be found in ss. 238ff. Note also that these sections are supplemented by the more general avoidance provision in s. 423.

See further the notes to ss. 238–243.

In the context of the financial markets, no order may be made under s. 339 in relation to a market contract to which a recognised investment exchange or clearing house is a party or which is entered into under its default rules, or a disposition of property in pursuance of such a market contract: see CA 1989, s. 165, and the note on p. 3.

S. 339(1)–(3)

These provisions allow the trustee to apply to the court for relief where a person who is subsequently made bankrupt has entered into a transaction at an undervalue, at the "relevant time". Section 339(3) defines what is meant by a transaction at an undervalue, e.g. gifts, marriage settlements, etc. The meaning of the key phrase "relevant time" is supplied by s. 341. This avoidance facility was successfully invoked by the trustee in *Re Kumar* [1993] 1 WLR 224 where a transfer of an interest in a matrimonial home from debtor husband to wife was set aside by Ferris J. The interest in the equity that was given to the wife far exceeded in value the size of the mortgage commitments that she had taken over from the husband. Notwithstanding this ruling Ferris J refused to make an immediate sale order under s. 30 of the Law of Property Act 1925 – separate issues had to be tried here.

Section 340   Preferences

340(1)   [Application to court]   Subject as follows in this and the next two sections, where an individual is adjudged bankrupt and he has at a relevant time (defined in section 341) given a preference to any person, the trustee of the bankrupt's estate may apply to the court for an order under this section.

340(2)   [Order by court]   The court shall, on such an application, make such order as it thinks fit for restoring the position to what it would have been if that individual had not given that preference.

340(3)   [Where preference given]   For the purposes of this and the next two sections, an individual gives a preference to a person if—

(a) that person is one of the individual's creditors or a surety or guarantor for any of his debts or other liabilities, and

(b) the individual does anything or suffers anything to be done which (in either case) has the effect of putting that person into a position which, in the event of the individual's bankruptcy, will be better than the position he would have been in if that thing had not been done.

340(4)   [Where court not to make order]   The court shall not make an order under this section in respect of a preference given to any person unless the individual who gave the preference was influenced in deciding to give it by a desire to produce in relation to that person the effect mentioned in subsection (3)(b) above.

340(5)   [Preference to associate]   An individual who has given a preference to a person who, at the time the preference was given, was an associate of his (otherwise than by reason only of being his employee) is presumed, unless the contrary is shown, to have been influenced in deciding to give it by such a desire as is mentioned in subsection (4).

340(6)   [Things done under court order]   The fact that something has been done in pursuance of the order of a court does not, without more, prevent the doing or suffering of that thing from constituting the giving of a preference.

(Former provisions: IA 1985, s. 174(1) (part), (3)–(6), (12) (part); BA 1914, ss. 42, 44)

General note

In the context of the financial markets, no order may be made under s. 340 in relation to a market contract to which a recognised investment exchange or clearing house is a party or which is entered into under its default rules, or a disposition of property in pursuance of such a market contract: see CA 1989, s. 165, and the note on p. 3.

S. 340(1), (2)

These provisions mirror s. 339(1) and (2), although of course they relate to preferences.

S. 340(3)

This defines what is meant by the term "preference". See *Re Ledingham-Smith* [1993] BCLC 635.

S. 340(4), (5)

Preferences can only be challenged if the bankrupt was influenced by a desire to achieve the effect stated in s. 340(3)(*b*). This would appear to be a looser test than that required under the old law, which stated that the act in question must have been done "with a view" to effecting the preference. Thus under the new law an incidental or subsidiary motive to prefer could lead to the transaction being avoided. This will be presumed where the beneficiary is an "associate" (for the meaning of this term, see s. 435, as qualified here by s. 340(5)), although it is open for this presumption to be rebutted. The Cork Committee (*Report*, paras. 1256–1258) favoured this overall solution. Section 340 will be interpreted in the same light as s. 239 and therefore the comments of Millett J in *Re M C Bacon Ltd* [1990] BCC 78 must be taken cognisance of. This fact is apparent from the case of *Re Ledingham-Smith* [1993] BCLC 635. Here a payment by a debtor of arrears of fees due to a firm of accountants within the susceptible period was held not to be avoidable under s. 340. In following *Re MC Bacon Ltd* (above) Morritt J held that the debtor was not influenced by a desire to prefer but rather by a desire to retain the services of the said firm of accountants so that they would continue to advise him during his period of financial difficulties.

S. 340(6)

A preference can arise out of a court order.

Section 341 "Relevant time" under ss. 339, 340

341(1) [Where relevant time] Subject as follows, the time at which an individual enters into a transaction at an undervalue or gives a preference is a relevant time if the transaction is entered into or the preference given—

  (a) in the case of a transaction at an undervalue, at a time in the period of 5 years ending with the day of the presentation of the bankruptcy petition on which the individual is adjudged bankrupt,

  (b) in the case of a preference which is not a transaction at an undervalue and is given to a person who is an associate of the individual (otherwise than by reason only of being his employee), at a time in the period of 2 years ending with that day, and

  (c) in any other case of a preference which is not a transaction at an undervalue, at a time in the period of 6 months ending with that day.

341(2) [Conditions for relevant time] Where an individual enters into a transaction at an undervalue or gives a preference at a time mentioned in paragraph (a), (b) or (c) of subsection (1) (not being, in the case of a transaction at an undervalue, a time less than 2 years before the end of the period mentioned in paragraph (a)), that time is not a relevant time for the purposes of sections 339 and 340 unless the individual—

  (a) is insolvent at that time, or

  (b) becomes insolvent in consequence of the transaction or preference;

but the requirements of this subsection are presumed to be satisfied, unless the contrary is shown, in relation to any transaction at an undervalue which is entered into by an individual with a person who is an associate of his (otherwise than by reason only of being his employee).

341(3) [Insolvent individual under s. 341(2)] For the purposes of subsection (2), an individual is insolvent if—

  (a) he is unable to pay his debts as they fall due, or

  (b) the value of his assets is less than the amount of his liabilities, taking into account his contingent and prospective liabilities.

341(4) [Where person later bankrupt under s. 264(1)(d)] A transaction entered into or preference given by a person who is subsequently adjudged bankrupt on a petition under section 264(1)(d) (criminal bankruptcy) is to be treated as having been entered into or given at a relevant time for the purposes of sections 339 and 340 if it was entered into or given at any time on or after the date specified for the purposes of this subsection in the criminal bankruptcy order on which the petition was based.

341(5) **[Where appeal pending]** No order shall be made under section 339 or 340 by virtue of subsection (4) of this section where an appeal is pending (within the meaning of section 277) against the individual's conviction of any offence by virtue of which the criminal bankruptcy order was made.

(Former provisions: IA 1985, s. 174(7)–(11); BA 1914, ss. 42, 44)

S. 341(1)

This provides a general definition of "relevant time", for the purposes of ss. 339, 340 above. In the case of transactions at an undervalue, it covers a five-year period prior to the presentation of the petition. Formerly, a ten-year period was prescribed. For preferences, it is six months (this was favoured by the Cork Committee: *Report*, para. 1260), but this period is extended to two years prior to the petition where the beneficiary is an "associate" of the bankrupt (as defined by s. 435, although note the qualification in s. 340(5)).

S. 341(2), (3)

The time periods given in s. 341(1) are qualified by the fact that in most cases (but not a transaction at an undervalue within two years of the petition), it is necessary that the person entering the transaction should either have been insolvent at the time or reduced to insolvency by the transaction. Normally the onus of proving insolvency is on the trustee, but this is not so where the beneficiary of the transaction is an "associate" (see s. 435 as qualified by s. 340(5)). Note the special definition of insolvency in s. 341(3) which now also covers balance-sheet insolvency – this was a late amendment at the Report Stage of the 1985 Bill.

S. 341(4), (5)

These provisions modify the above rules where a person was made bankrupt as a result of a petition based on a criminal bankruptcy order. Special provision is made where an appeal is pending against the criminal conviction.

Note prospective amendment: ss. 341(4) and (5) are to be repealed by the Criminal Justice Act 1988, s. 170(2) and Sch. 16 as from a day to be appointed; see the note to s. 264.

Section 342 Orders under ss. 339, 340

342(1) **[Extent of order]** Without prejudice to the generality of section 339(2) or 340(2), an order under either of those sections with respect to a transaction or preference entered into or given by an individual who is subsequently adjudged bankrupt may (subject as follows)—

    (a) require any property transferred as part of the transaction, or in connection with the giving of the preference, to be vested in the trustee of the bankrupt's estate as part of that estate;

    (b) require any property to be so vested if it represents in any person's hands the application either of the proceeds of sale of property so transferred or of money so transferred;

(c) release or discharge (in whole or in part) any security given by the individual;

(d) require any person to pay, in respect of benefits received by him from the individual, such sums to the trustee of his estate as the court may direct;

(e) provide for any surety or guarantor whose obligations to any person were released or discharged (in whole or in part) under the transaction or by the giving of the preference to be under such new or revived obligations to that person as the court thinks appropriate;

(f) provide for security to be provided for the discharge of any obligation imposed by or arising under the order, for such an obligation to be charged on any property and for the security or charge to have the same priority as a security or charge released or discharged (in whole or in part) under the transaction or by the giving of the preference; and

(g) provide for the extent to which any person whose property is vested by the order in the trustee of the bankrupt's estate, or on whom obligations are imposed by the order, is to be able to prove in the bankruptcy for debts or other liabilities which arose from, or were released or discharged (in whole or in part) under or by, the transaction or the giving of the preference.

342(2)   **[Effect of order]**   An order under section 339 or 340 may affect the property of, or impose any obligation on, any person whether or not he is the person with whom the individual in question entered into the transaction or, as the case may be, the person to whom the preference was given; but such an order—

(a) shall not prejudice any interest in property which was acquired from a person other than that individual and was acquired in good faith and for value, or prejudice any interest deriving from such an interest, and

(b) shall not require a person who received a benefit from the transaction or preference in good faith and for value to pay a sum to the trustee of the bankrupt's estate, except where he was a party to the transaction or the payment is to be in respect of a preference given to that person at a time when he was a creditor of that individual.

342(2A)   **[Presumption re good faith in s. 342(2)]**   Where a person has acquired an interest in property from a person other than the individual in question, or has received a benefit from the transaction or preference, and at the time of that acquisition or receipt—

(a) he had notice of the relevant surrounding circumstances and of the relevant proceedings, or

(b) he was an associate of, or was connected with, either the individual in question or the person with whom that individual entered into the transaction or to whom that individual gave the preference,

then, unless the contrary is shown, it shall be presumed for the purposes of paragraph (a) or (as the case may be) paragraph (b) of subsection (2) that the interest was acquired or the benefit was received otherwise than in good faith.

342(3)   **[Sums to be paid to trustee]**   Any sums required to be paid to the trustee in accordance with an order under section 339 or 340 shall be comprised in the bankrupt's estate.

342(4) **[Relevant surrounding circumstances in s. 342(2A)(a)]**   For the purposes of subsection (2A)(a), the relevant surrounding circumstances are (as the case may require)—

(a) the fact that the individual in question entered into the transaction at an undervalue; or

(b) the circumstances which amounted to the giving of the preference by the individual in question.

342(5) **[Notice of relevant proceedings in s. 342(2A)(a)]**   For the purposes of subsection (2A)(a), a person has notice of the relevant proceedings if he has notice—

(a) of the fact that the petition on which the individual in question is adjudged bankrupt has been presented, or

(b) of the fact that the individual in question has been adjudged bankrupt.

342(6) **[Application of s. 249]**   Section 249 in Part VII of this Act shall apply for the purposes of subsection (2A)(b) as it applies for the purposes of the first Group of parts.

(Former provisions: IA 1985, s. 175; BA 1914, ss. 44(2), 45; B(A)A 1926, s. 4)

S. 342(1)

Sections 339(2) and 340(2) confer general discretion on the court where the trustee applies for relief. However, we are here given a non-exhaustive list of the possible forms of relief which the court may grant.

S. 342(2)

This subsection was amended by s. 2(1) of the Insolvency (No. 2) Act 1994 to clarify the degree of protection offered to third parties. Comparable changes have been made in the corporate context – see the annotations to s. 241. The Bill leading to this Act was sponsored by the Law Society which was concerned by the uncertainty created by the original version of s. 342 in the context of property purchases of unregistered land. Later purchasers in a chain started off by an undervalue transfer might theoretically be prejudiced and therefore be reluctant to transact with that risk in mind until the five-year limitation period had expired. This was creating further problems in the already depressed domestic property market by generating delays or additional cost caused by the necessity of taking out title insurance. For general discussion see Potterton and Cullen (1994) 138 SJ 710.

Thus the words "in good faith, for value and without notice of the relevant circumstances" have been replaced by "in good faith and for value" with the question of notice now being dealt with by a new subs. (2A). Note that these changes only apply to interests acquired and benefits received after the coming into force of the 1994 Act – i.e. 26 July 1994 (see s. 6 (ibid.)). Transactions occurring before that date will be governed by the original wording of s. 342.

S. 342(2A)

This subsection was introduced by s. 2(2) of the Insolvency (No. 2) Act 1994 and seeks to provide guidance on what is "good faith" for the purposes of the amended subs. (2) above. The burden of proving good faith switches to the person acquiring an interest in the property if he knows of the relevant surrounding circumstances *and* of the relevant proceedings. A similar reversal of the onus of proof occurs where the acquirer is an associate or connected person (see subs. (6) below). Further guidance on the relevant surrounding circumstances and notice of the relevant proceedings is provided by new subss. (4) and (5), also introduced by the 1994 Act.

S. 342(3)

This is unaffected by the 1994 changes.

S. 342(4) and (5)

See the note to subs. (2A) above.

S. 342(6)

This was inserted by s. 2(3) of the Insolvency (No. 2) Act 1994 and merely renders applicable the standard definitions of associates and connected persons as found in the Insolvency Act 1986.

Section 343 Extortionate credit transactions

343(1) [Application]   This section applies where a person is adjudged bankrupt who is or has been a party to a transaction for, or involving, the provision to him of credit.

343(2) [Order by court]   The court may, on the application of the trustee of the bankrupt's estate, make an order with respect to the transaction if the transaction is or was extortionate and was not entered into more than 3 years before the commencement of the bankruptcy.

343(3) [Extortionate transaction]   For the purposes of this section a transaction is extortionate if, having regard to the risk accepted by the person providing the credit—

  (a) the terms of it are or were such as to require grossly exorbitant payments to be made (whether unconditionally or in certain contingencies) in respect of the provision of the credit, or

  (b) it otherwise grossly contravened ordinary principles of fair dealing;

and it shall be presumed, unless the contrary is proved, that a transaction with respect to which an application is made under this section is or, as the case may be, was extortionate.

343(4) [Extent of order]   An order under this section with respect to any transaction may contain such one or more of the following as the court thinks fit, that is to say—

  (a) provision setting aside the whole or part of any obligation created by the transaction;

  (b) provision otherwise varying the terms of the transaction or varying the terms on which any security for the purposes of the transaction is held;

  (c) provision requiring any person who is or was party to the transaction to pay to the trustee any sums paid to that person, by virtue of the transaction, by the bankrupt;

  (d) provision requiring any person to surrender to the trustee any property held by him as security for the purposes of the transaction;

  (e) provision directing accounts to be taken between any persons.

343(5) [Sums to trustee]   Any sums or property required to be paid or surrendered to the trustee in accordance with an order under this section shall be comprised in the bankrupt's estate.

343(6)   **[Application under Consumer Credit Act]**   Neither the trustee of a bankrupt's estate nor an undischarged bankrupt is entitled to make an application under section 139(1)(a) of the Consumer Credit Act 1974 (re-opening of extortionate credit agreements) for any agreement by which credit is or has been provided to the bankrupt to be re-opened.

But the powers conferred by this section are exercisable in relation to any transaction concurrently with any powers exercisable under this Act in relation to that transaction as a transaction at an undervalue.

(Former provision: IA 1985, s. 176)

General note

This is a new provision enabling the trustee in bankruptcy to re-open a credit bargain made by a bankrupt, on the grounds that it was extortionate *vis-à-vis* the bankrupt. The Cork Committee (*Report*, para. 1381) called for such a provision, and its introduction in some senses can be viewed as a *quid pro quo* for the repeal of BA 1914, s. 66, which placed restrictions on a lender proving for interest – see the White Paper, para. 87.

A corresponding provision has been introduced for corporate insolvency: see s. 244.

S. 343(1), (2)

These permit the trustee to re-open extortionate credit bargains entered into by the bankrupt for the provision of credit to him within three years of the commencement of his bankruptcy (see s. 278).

S. 343(3)

The onus is on the other party to show that the bargain was not "extortionate" within the meaning of this subsection. Note that the meaning of "extortionate" is the same as that given by s. 139 of the Consumer Credit Act 1974.

S. 343(4)

This explains what the court may do if the bargain is extortionate – again this provision has been borrowed from the Consumer Credit Act 1974.

S. 343(5)

Any "proceeds" of such an action become part of the bankrupt's estate.

S. 343(6)

This makes it clear that applications under s. 139 of the Consumer Credit Act 1974 cannot be made by the trustee or the undischarged bankrupt but should be made under this section. It reminds us, however, that the transaction may also be challenged under s. 339.

Section 344   Avoidance of general assignment of book debts

344(1)   **[Application]**   The following applies where a person engaged in any business makes a general assignment to another person of his existing or future book debts, or any class of them, and is subsequently adjudged bankrupt.

344(2)   [Certain assignments void against trustee]   The assignment is void against the trustee of the bankrupt's estate as regards book debts which were not paid before the presentation of the bankruptcy petition, unless the assignment has been registered under the Bills of Sale Act 1878.

344(3)   [Definitions]   For the purposes of subsections (1) and (2)—

 (a) **"assignment"** includes an assignment by way of security or charge on book debts, and

 (b) **"general assignment"** does not include—

  (i) an assignment of book debts due at the date of the assignment from specified debtors or of debts becoming due under specified contracts, or

  (ii) an assignment of book debts included either in a transfer of a business made in good faith and for value or in an assignment of assets for the benefit of creditors generally.

344(4)   [Registration under Bills of Sale Act]   For the purposes of registration under the Act of 1878 an assignment of book debts is to be treated as if it were a bill of sale given otherwise than by way of security for the payment of a sum of money; and the provisions of that Act with respect to the registration of bills of sale apply accordingly with such necessary modifications as may be made by rules under that Act.

(Former provisions: IA 1985, s. 177; BA 1914, s. 43)

S. 344(1), (2)

This provides that a general assignment of book debts by a trader shall be void on bankruptcy unless registered under the Bills of Sale Act 1878. Note the word "general" is now used in the text of subs. (1) – in s. 43 of the 1914 Act this word merely appeared in the marginal note.

S. 344(3)

This provision clarifies s. 344(1) by stressing that assignments by way of security are covered but not specific assignments of specific book debts, nor assignments connected with a bona fide transfer of a business for value, nor a general assignment of assets for the benefit of creditors generally.

S. 344(4)

This provision describes the mechanics of registration under the 1878 Act.

Section 345   Contracts to which bankrupt is a party

345(1)   [Application]   The following applies where a contract has been made with a person who is subsequently adjudged bankrupt.

345(2)   [Court order on application]   The court may, on the application of any other party to the contract, make an order discharging obligations under the contract on such terms as to payment by the applicant or the bankrupt of damages for non-performance or otherwise as appear to the court to be equitable.

345(3)   [Damages as bankruptcy debt]   Any damages payable by the bankrupt by virtue of an order of the court under this section are provable as a bankruptcy debt.

345(4)   [Where joint contract]   Where an undischarged bankrupt is a contractor in respect of any contract jointly with any person, that person may sue or be sued in respect of the contract without the joinder of the bankrupt.

(Former provisions: IA 1985, s. 178; BA 1914, s. 118)

General note

In the context of the financial markets, s. 345 does not apply in relation to a market contract or a contract effected by an exchange or clearing house for the purpose of realising property provided as margin in relation to market contracts: see CA 1989, s. 164(1), and the note on p. 3.

S. 345(1)–(3)

This is a new provision. At common law the general rule, as laid down in *Brooke* v *Hewitt* (1796) 3 Ves 253, was that the bankruptcy of a party to a contract did not terminate that contract. Hence the need to confer on trustees a power to disclaim onerous contracts. Section 345(2) in effect redresses the balance as far as the other contracting party is concerned. He can now apply to the court to have contractual obligations discharged. The court enjoys general discretion and can order compensation payments to be paid by either party. If the bankrupt is ordered to pay compensation, that sum constitutes a provable debt.

S. 345(4)

This repeats BA 1914, s. 118 and allows a person who has entered into a contract jointly with a bankrupt to sue the other party to the contract without the joinder of the bankrupt to the proceedings.

Section 346   Enforcement procedures

346(1)   [Creditor's execution against bankrupt]   Subject to section 285 in Chapter II (restrictions on proceedings and remedies) and to the following provisions of this section, where the creditor of any person who is adjudged bankrupt has, before the commencement of the bankruptcy—

   (a) issued execution against the goods or land of that person, or

   (b) attached a debt due to that person from another person,

that creditor is not entitled, as against the official receiver or trustee of the bankrupt's estate, to retain the benefit of the execution or attachment, or any sums paid to avoid it, unless the execution or attachment was completed, or the sums were paid, before the commencement of the bankruptcy.

346(2)   [Where goods taken in execution]   Subject as follows, where any goods of a person have been taken in execution, then, if before the completion of the execution notice is given to the sheriff or other officer charged with the execution that that person has been adjudged bankrupt—

   (a) the sheriff or other officer shall on request deliver to the official receiver or trustee of the bankrupt's estate the goods and any money seized or recovered in part satisfaction of the execution, but

   (b) the costs of the execution are a first charge on the goods or money so delivered and the official receiver or trustee may sell the goods or a sufficient part of them for the purpose of satisfying the charge.

346(3)   **[Balance of sale proceeds]**   Subject to subsection (6) below, where—

  (a) under an execution in respect of a judgment for a sum exceeding such sum as may be prescribed for the purposes of this subsection, the goods of any person are sold or money is paid in order to avoid a sale, and

  (b) before the end of the period of 14 days beginning with the day of the sale or payment the sheriff or other officer charged with the execution is given notice that a bankruptcy petition has been presented in relation to that person, and

  (c) a bankruptcy order is or has been made on that petition,

the balance of the proceeds of sale or money paid, after deducting the costs of execution, shall (in priority to the claim of the execution creditor) be comprised in the bankrupt's estate.

346(4)   **[Duty of sheriff re sum in s. 346(3)]**   Accordingly, in the case of an execution in respect of a judgment for a sum exceeding the sum prescribed for the purposes of subsection (3), the sheriff or other officer charged with the execution—

  (a) shall not dispose of the balance mentioned in subsection (3) at any time within the period of 14 days so mentioned or while there is pending a bankruptcy petition of which he has been given notice under that subsection, and

  (b) shall pay that balance, where by virtue of that subsection it is comprised in the bankrupt's estate, to the official receiver or (if there is one) to the trustee of that estate.

346(5)   **[Completion of execution or attachment]**   For the purposes of this section—

  (a) an execution against goods is completed by seizure and sale or by the making of a charging order under section 1 of the Charging Orders Act 1979;

  (b) an execution against land is completed by seizure, by the appointment of a receiver or by the making of a charging order under that section;

  (c) an attachment of a debt is completed by the receipt of the debt.

346(6)   **[Setting aside of s. 346(1)–(3) rights by court]**   The rights conferred by subsections (1) to (3) on the official receiver or the trustee may, to such extent and on such terms as it thinks fit, be set aside by the court in favour of the creditor who has issued the execution or attached the debt.

346(7)   **[Acquisition in good faith]**   Nothing in this section entitles the trustee of a bankrupt's estate to claim goods from a person who has acquired them in good faith under a sale by a sheriff or other officer charged with an execution.

346(8)   **[Non-application of s. 346(2), (3)]**   Neither subsection (2) nor subsection (3) applies in relation to any execution against property which has been acquired by or has devolved upon the bankrupt since the commencement of the bankruptcy, unless, at the time the execution is issued or before it is completed—

  (a) the property has been or is claimed for the bankrupt's estate under section 307 (after-acquired property), and

  (b) a copy of the notice given under that section has been or is served on the sheriff or other officer charged with the execution.

(Former provisions: IA 1985, s. 179; BA 1914, ss. 40, 41)

S. 346(1), (5)

Where a creditor has begun an execution process before the commencement of the bankruptcy (see s. 278(*a*)), but has failed to complete before that date, he will not be allowed to proceed further and any proceeds received after the commencement of the bankruptcy must be handed over to the estate. The stages at which the various execution processes are deemed to be completed are described by s. 346(5).

Executions may also be restrained under s. 285.

S. 346(2)

This deals with the position of a sheriff who has seized goods in execution. The goods must be handed over to the estate, although the sheriff's costs are a first charge on such goods. Note also IR 1986, r. 12.19. For the sheriff's costs see r. 7.36.

S. 346(3), (4)

These provisions deal with the situation where the sheriff has received the proceeds of sale of goods seized in execution of a judgment for a "prescribed amount" (see s. 418), or has been paid not to sell them. The amount is £500 under the Insolvency Proceedings (Monetary Limits) Order 1986 (SI 1986 No. 1996) operating from 29 December 1986. If, within 14 days thereafter, the sheriff is given notice of the bankruptcy petition, the balance of the proceeds after deducting costs must be paid to the estate if the petition succeeds. The sheriff is therefore under a duty to retain proceeds for the required period, just in case this obligation is activated.

On s. 346(3)(*b*) see IR 1986, r. 12.19.

S. 346(6)

The court has discretion to set aside the rights of the estate in favour of the execution creditor.

S. 346(7)

Bona fide purchasers from the sheriff are protected.

S. 346(8)

This provision lays down special rules for execution against property acquired by the bankrupt after the commencement of the bankruptcy.

Section 347   Distress, etc.

347(1)   [Limit on distraining goods]   The right of any landlord or other person to whom rent is payable to distrain upon the goods and effects of an undischarged bankrupt for rent due to him from the bankrupt is available (subject to subsection (5) below) against goods and effects comprised in the bankrupt's estate, but only for 6 months' rent accrued due before the commencement of the bankruptcy.

347(2)   [Distraining where order later made]   Where a landlord or other person to whom rent is payable has distrained for rent upon the goods and effects of an individual to whom a bankruptcy petition relates and a bankruptcy order is subsequently made on that petition, any amount recovered by way of that distress which—

    (a) is in excess of the amount which by virtue of subsection (1) would have been recoverable after the commencement of the bankruptcy, or

    (b) is in respect of rent for a period or part of a period after the distress was levied, shall be held for the bankrupt as part of his estate.

347(3)   [Proceeds of sale re goods not held under s. 347(2)]   Where any person (whether or not a landlord or person entitled to rent) has distrained upon the goods or effects of an individual who is adjudged bankrupt before the end of the period of 3 months beginning with the distraint, so much of those goods or effects, or of the proceeds of their sale, as is not held for the bankrupt under subsection (2) shall be charged for the benefit of the bankrupt's estate with the preferential debts of the bankrupt to the extent that the bankrupt's estate is for the time being insufficient for meeting those debts.

347(4)   [Where surrender under s. 347(3)]   Where by virtue of any charge under subsection (3) any person surrenders any goods or effects to the trustee of a bankrupt's estate or makes a payment to such a trustee, that person ranks, in respect of the amount of the proceeds of the sale of those goods or effects by the trustee or, as the case may be, the amount of the payment, as a preferential creditor of the bankrupt, except as against so much of the bankrupt's estate as is available for the payment of preferential creditors by virtue of the surrender or payment.

347(5)   [Rights of landlord after discharge]   A landlord or other person to whom rent is payable is not at any time after the discharge of a bankrupt entitled to distrain upon any goods or effects comprised in the bankrupt's estate.

347(6)   [Restriction of landlord's rights]   Where in the case of any execution—

(a) a landlord is (apart from this section) entitled under section 1 of the Landlord and Tenant Act 1709 or section 102 of the County Courts Act 1984 (claims for rent where goods seized in execution) to claim for an amount not exceeding one year's rent, and

(b) the person against whom the execution is levied is adjudged bankrupt before the notice of claim is served on the sheriff or other officer charged with the execution,

the right of the landlord to claim under that section is restricted to a right to claim for an amount not exceeding 6 months' rent and does not extend to any rent payable in respect of a period after the notice of claim is so served.

347(7)   [Limit to s. 347(6)]   Nothing in subsection (6) imposes any liability on a sheriff or other officer charged with an execution to account to the official receiver or the trustee of a bankrupt's estate for any sums paid by him to a landlord at any time before the sheriff or other officer was served with notice of the bankruptcy order in question.

But this section is without prejudice to the liability of the landlord.

347(8)   [Rights to distrain other than for rent]   Nothing in this Group of Parts affects any right to distrain otherwise than for rent; and any such right is at any time exercisable without restriction against property comprised in a bankrupt's estate, even if that right is expressed by any enactment to be exercisable in like manner as a right to distrain for rent.

347(9)   [Exercise of right]   Any right to distrain against property comprised in a bankrupt's estate is exercisable notwithstanding that the property has vested in the trustee.

347(10)   [Landlord's right to prove]   The provisions of this section are without prejudice to a landlord's right in a bankruptcy to prove for any bankruptcy debt in respect of rent.

(Former provisions: IA 1985, s. 180; BA 1914, ss. 33(4), 35 (as amended by County Courts Act 1984, Sch. 2, para. 19))

S. 347(1), (2), (5), (9)

This continues the favoured treatment of landlords. A landlord may still distrain on the goods of an undischarged bankrupt (even if they have vested in the trustee – s. 347(9)), but only for a maximum of six months' rent accruing before the commencement of the bankruptcy. There is a similar rule where an administration order is in force: see County Courts Act 1984, s. 116. Where distress is levied after the petition but before the order, the landlord must hand over any proceeds in excess of the amount of rent referred to in s. 347(1). Distress cannot be levied after the discharge of the bankrupt.

S. 347(3), (4)

These make special provision out of the proceeds of a distress for the preferential creditors (see s. 328) in so far as the estate is insufficient to meet their claims. However, the landlord who loses out as a result of this provision is then subrogated to the claims of the preferential creditors against the general estate of the bankrupt.

S. 347(6), (7)

These provisions deal with special forms of distress. Although normally 12 months' rent can be claimed, this is reduced to six months' rent in the event of bankruptcy. Special protection is offered to sheriffs who inadvertently breach this provision, but the landlord himself may still incur liability.

S. 347(8)

Distress otherwise than for rent is not hampered by bankruptcy.

S. 347(10)

As an alternative to levying distress for rent, a landlord can of course prove for the unpaid amount in the bankruptcy.

Section 348   Apprenticeships, etc.

348(1)   [Application]   This section applies where—

   (a) a bankruptcy order is made in respect of an individual to whom another individual was an apprentice or articled clerk at the time when the petition on which the order was made was presented, and

   (b) the bankrupt or the apprentice or clerk gives notice to the trustee terminating the apprenticeship or articles.

348(2)   [Discharge etc.]   Subject to subsection (6) below, the indenture of apprenticeship or, as the case may be, the articles of agreement shall be discharged with effect from the commencement of the bankruptcy.

348(3)   [If money paid]   If any money has been paid by or on behalf of the apprentice or clerk to the bankrupt as a fee, the trustee may, on an application made by or on behalf of the apprentice or clerk pay such sum to the apprentice or clerk as the trustee thinks reasonable, having regard to—

    (a) the amount of the fee,

    (b) the proportion of the period in respect of which the fee was paid that has been served by the apprentice or clerk before the commencement of the bankruptcy, and

    (c) the other circumstances of the case.

348(4)   [Priority of s. 348(3) power]   The power of the trustee to make a payment under subsection (3) has priority over his obligation to distribute the bankrupt's estate.

348(5)   [Instead of s. 348(3) payment]   Instead of making a payment under subsection (3), the trustee may, if it appears to him expedient to do so on an application made by or on behalf of the apprentice or clerk, transfer the indenture or articles to a person other than the bankrupt.

348(6)   [Where s. 348(5) transfer]   Where a transfer is made under subsection (5), subsection (2) has effect only as between the apprentice or clerk and the bankrupt.

(Former provisions: IA 1985, s. 181; BA 1914, s. 34)

S. 348(1)

This section applies where a principal is declared bankrupt and notice is given to terminate a contract of apprenticeship or articled clerkship. Either party can give notice to terminate.

S. 348(2)

The effect of such notice is to discharge the contract from the date of the commencement of the bankruptcy (for the meaning of this term, see s. 278(*a*)).

S. 348(3), (4)

The trustee can repay any fee paid by the apprentice or articled clerk in whole or in part. Factors such as the duration of the apprenticeship which is unexpired and the general circumstances of the case are relevant here. The approach will be similar to that taken with regard to premiums under s. 40 of the Partnership Act 1890. The sum of money repaid under s. 348(3) ranks as a pre-preferential debt.

S. 348(5), (6)

As an alternative, the trustee can transfer the apprenticeship, etc., to another principal if the apprentice, etc., so wishes. The continuity of the apprenticeship in such a case will not be disrupted by s. 348(2). This latter provision clarifies the former law under BA 1914, s. 34.

Section 349   Unenforceability of liens on books, etc.

349(1)   [Unenforceability]   Subject as follows, a lien or other right to retain possession of any of the books, papers or other records of a bankrupt is unenforceable to the extent that its enforcement would deny possession of any books, papers or other records to the official receiver or the trustee of the bankrupt's estate.

349(2) **[Non-application of s. 349(1)]** Subsection (1) does not apply to a lien on documents which give a title to property and are held as such.

(Former provisions: IA 1985, s. 182; BR 1952, r. 386)

General note

This section renders ineffective liens, etc., on the books and records of a bankrupt in so far as they would deny possession of them to the official receiver or trustee. Liens on documents of title are not affected. Here the public interest is accorded priority over private security rights.

See also s. 333(4) for another indication of how liens on books require special treatment from the law. Regulations made by the Secretary of State pursuant to the rules may allow the trustee wide powers to deal with, and dispose of, the bankrupt's books: see IR 1986, r. 12.1(1)(c). Note also the Insolvency Regulations 1994 (SI 1994, No. 2507), reg. 30.

S. 349(2)

On the interpretation of this provision, see the note to s. 246(3).

Chapter VI — Bankruptcy Offences

PRELIMINARY

Section 350 Scheme of this Chapter

350(1) **[Application]** Subject to section 360(3) below, this Chapter applies where the court has made a bankruptcy order on a bankruptcy petition.

350(2) **[Effect of annulment of bankruptcy]** This Chapter applies whether or not the bankruptcy order is annulled, but proceedings for an offence under this Chapter shall not be instituted after the annulment.

350(3) **[Liability of bankrupt after discharge]** Without prejudice to his liability in respect of a subsequent bankruptcy, the bankrupt is not guilty of an offence under this Chapter in respect of anything done after his discharge; but nothing in this Group of Parts prevents the institution of proceedings against a discharged bankrupt for an offence committed before his discharge.

350(4) **[Where not defence]** It is not a defence in proceedings for an offence under this Chapter that anything relied on, in whole or in part, as constituting that offence was done outside England and Wales.

350(5) **[Institution of proceedings for offence]** Proceedings for an offence under this Chapter or under the rules shall not be instituted except by the Secretary of State or by or with the consent of the Director of Public Prosecutions.

350(6) **[Penalty]** A person guilty of any offence under this Chapter is liable to imprisonment or a fine, or both.

(Former provisions: IA 1985, s. 183(1)–(3), (5), (6), 192; BA 1914, s. 162)

General note

The Cork Committee (*Report*, para. 1900) called for greater use to be made of the criminal law

417

in controlling fraud in bankruptcy. In addition, it recommended a cautious tidying up of the offences (para. 1883), and this has been to some extent implemented by the following provisions in the Act. Incidentally, the Blagden Committee (Cmnd 221, 1957, paras. 206–213) also suggested that the criminal law should be applied more strictly to control fraudulent bankrupts. Note that the rules themselves create several offences, the punishments for which are prescribed by Sch. 5 of the rules. For an analysis of the new regime of bankruptcy offences see Griffiths (1986) 2 IL & P 73.

S. 350(1), (2)

These are new provisions dealing with bankruptcy offences in general. In particular, s. 350(2) makes it clear that the subsequent annulment of the bankruptcy is relevant only in so far as a prosecution cannot be instituted after this date.

S. 350(3)

This repeats the provision under the 1914 Act – the bankrupt cannot be guilty for acts done after his discharge, but he can be prosecuted after his discharge for earlier misconduct.

S. 350(4)

By way of contrast, it is not a defence to show that the conduct complained of was done outside England and Wales.

S. 350(5)

This is a new general provision replacing the fragmentary approach of the 1914 Act. Prosecutions now require the consent of the Director of Public Prosecutions or the Secretary of State. Formerly, the court's consent was needed for certain prosecutions.

S. 350(6)

For details of penalties, see s. 430 and Sch. 10.

Section 351 Definitions

351 In the following provisions of this Chapter—

(a) references to property comprised in the bankrupt's estate or to property possession of which is required to be delivered up to the official receiver or the trustee of the bankrupt's estate include any property which would be such property if a notice in respect of it were given under section 307 (after-acquired property), section 308 (personal property and effects of bankrupt having more than replacement value) or section 308A (vesting in trustee of certain tenancies);

(b) "**the initial period**" means the period between the presentation of the bankruptcy petition and the commencement of the bankruptcy; and

(c) a reference to a number of months or years before petition is to that period ending with the presentation of the bankruptcy petition.

(Former provisions: IA 1985, ss. 184(5), 187(3)(a))

General note

This section contains definitions of three concepts and phrases which recur throughout ss. 352–362:

(a) "property": see ss. 353, 354, 356, 357, 358, 359, 362;

(b) "initial period": see ss. 354, 355, 356, 358, 359, 362 (for further explanation, see s. 278 (*a*));

(c) "before petition": see ss. 354, 355, 356, 358, 359, 361, 362.

In s. 351(a) the words relating to s. 308A inserted and consequential amendment made by the Housing Act 1988, Sch. 17, para. 75.

Section 352   Defence of innocent intention

352   Where in the case of an offence under any provision of this Chapter it is stated that this section applies, a person is not guilty of the offence if he proves that, at the time of the conduct constituting the offence, he had no intent to defraud or to conceal the state of his affairs.

(Former provision: IA 1985, s. 183(4))

General note

This is an important new general defence. If the bankrupt is charged with certain offences in ss. 353–362, he has a defence if he can prove that he had not intended to defraud or conceal his affairs. The provisions creating the offences state whether s. 352 applies.

WRONGDOING BY THE BANKRUPT BEFORE AND AFTER BANKRUPTCY

Section 353   Non-disclosure

353(1)   [Offence]   The bankrupt is guilty of an offence if—

(a) he does not to the best of his knowledge and belief disclose all the property comprised in his estate to the official receiver or the trustee, or

(b) he does not inform the official receiver or the trustee of any disposal of any property which but for the disposal would be so comprised, stating how, when, to whom and for what consideration the property was disposed of.

353(2)   [Exception to s. 353(1)(b)]   Subsection (1)(b) does not apply to any disposal in the ordinary course of a business carried on by the bankrupt or to any payment of the ordinary expenses of the bankrupt or his family.

353(3)   [Application of s. 352]   Section 352 applies to this offence.

(Former provisions: IA 1985, s. 183(4), 184(1); BA 1914, s. 154(1))

S. 353(1), (2)

This makes it an offence for the bankrupt to fail to disclose items of "property" (for definition, see s. 351(*a*)) to his trustee or official receiver. Moreover, certain disposals of property which have resulted in a diminution of the estate must also be revealed. Note the positive nature of the obligations imposed here. There is a defence for bona fide business and domestic transactions.

For the appropriate penalty, see ss. 350, 430 and Sch. 10.

S. 353(3)

The general defence in s. 352 applies here.

Section 354   Concealment of property

354(1)   [Offence of concealment etc.]   The bankrupt is guilty of an offence if—

(a) he does not deliver up possession to the official receiver or trustee, or as the official receiver or trustee may direct, of such part of the property comprised in his estate as is in his possession or under his control and possession of which he is required by law so to deliver up,

(b) he conceals any debt due to or from him or conceals any property the value of which is not less than the prescribed amount and possession of which he is required to deliver up to the official receiver or trustee, or

(c) in the 12 months before petition, or in the initial period, he did anything which would have been an offence under paragraph (b) above if the bankruptcy order had been made immediately before he did it.

Section 352 applies to this offence.

354(2)   [Offence re removal of property]   The bankrupt is guilty of an offence if he removes, or in the initial period removed, any property the value of which was not less than the prescribed amount and possession of which he has or would have been required to deliver up to the official receiver or the trustee.

Section 352 applies to this offence.

354(3)   [Offence re failure to account for loss]   The bankrupt is guilty of an offence if he without reasonable excuse fails, on being required to do so by the official receiver or the court—

(a) to account for the loss of any substantial part of his property incurred in the 12 months before petition or in the initial period, or

(b) to give a satisfactory explanation of the manner in which such a loss was incurred.

(Former provisions: IA 1985, s. 183(4), 184(2)–(4); BA 1914, ss. 154, 157)

S. 354(1)

This is a related offence of failing to hand over "property" (for definition, see s.351(*a*)), or concealing debts or property which is not less than the "prescribed amount" (see s. 418). The amount is £500 under the Insolvency Proceedings (Monetary Limits) Order 1986 (SI 1986 No. 1996) (which operates from 29 December 1986). Note that, in the case of concealment, conduct in the "initial period" (i.e. between the petition and order: see s. 351(*b*)) and, indeed, in the 12 months "before petition" (see s. 351(*c*)), is covered.

The general defence in s. 352 applies.

For penalties, see ss. 350, 430 and Sch. 10.

S. 354(2)

Removal of "property" from the estate after the order or in the "initial period" is unlawful where the property exceeds the "prescribed amount" (£500 – see the note to s. 354(1)). The general defence in s. 352 applies. Settling a non-provable debt during the period in question is an offence under s. 354 – *Woodley* v *Woodley (No. 2)* [1994] 1 WLR 1167.

S. 354(3)

Failure to provide explanations for substantial losses of "property" dating back to 12 months "before petition", or in the "initial period", is unlawful, unless there is a reasonable excuse for this. The time limit referred to in s. 354(3) is the same as that in BA 1914, in spite of recommendations from the Cork Committee (*Report*, para. 1888) that it should be extended to two years.

Section 355   Concealment of books and papers; falsification

355(1)   [Offence re non-delivery of books etc.]   The bankrupt is guilty of an offence if he does not deliver up possession to the official receiver or the trustee, or as the official receiver or trustee may direct, of all books, papers and other records of which he has possession or control and which relate to his estate or his affairs.

Section 352 applies to this offence.

355(2)   [Offence re destruction, concealment etc.]   The bankrupt is guilty of an offence if—

> (a) he prevents, or in the initial period prevented, the production of any books, papers or records relating to his estate or affairs;
>
> (b) he conceals, destroys, mutilates or falsifies, or causes or permits the concealment, destruction, mutilation or falsification of, any books, papers or other records relating to his estate or affairs;
>
> (c) he makes, or causes or permits the making of, any false entries in any book, document or record relating to his estate or affairs; or
>
> (d) in the 12 months before petition, or in the initial period, he did anything which would have been an offence under paragraph (b) or (c) above if the bankruptcy order had been made before he did it.

Section 352 applies to this offence.

355(3)   [Offence re disposal, alteration etc.]   The bankrupt is guilty of an offence if—

> (a) he disposes of, or alters or makes any omission in, or causes or permits the disposal, altering or making of any omission in, any book, document or record relating to his estate or affairs, or
>
> (b) in the 12 months before petition, or in the initial period, he did anything which would have been an offence under paragraph (a) if the bankruptcy order had been made before he did it.

Section 352 applies to this offence.

(Former provisions: IA 1985, s. 183(4), 185; BA 1914, s. 154)

General note

This involved provision is somewhat tautological.

For penalties, see ss. 350, 430 and Sch. 10, and for defences, see s. 352. Note that, in the case of those basic records described by s. 361(3), the 12-month periods referred to in s. 355 are extended to two years: see s. 361(4).

S. 355(1), (2)

Failure to deliver up books and records is an offence. Moreover, if one prevents such books and records being produced, or conceals, destroys or falsifies them, this will also be unlawful. Note that for concealment and falsification, the relevant period is extended to 12 months "before petition" (see s. 351(*c*)), plus the "initial period" (see s. 351(*b*)).

S. 355(3)

It is unlawful for a bankrupt to dispose of or alter books or records – this again extends to the 12 months "before petition" and the "initial period".

Section 356   False statements

356(1) [Offence re material omission]   The bankrupt is guilty of an offence if he makes or has made any material omission in any statement made under any provision in this Group of Parts and relating to his affairs.

    Section 352 applies to this offence.

356(2) [Offence re failing to inform etc.]   The bankrupt is guilty of an offence if—

    (a) knowing or believing that a false debt has been proved by any person under the bankruptcy, he fails to inform the trustee as soon as practicable; or

    (b) he attempts to account for any part of his property by fictitious losses or expenses; or

    (c) at any meeting of his creditors in the 12 months before petition or (whether or not at such a meeting) at any time in the initial period, he did anything which would have been an offence under paragraph (b) if the bankruptcy order had been made before he did it; or

    (d) he is, or at any time has been, guilty of any false representation or other fraud for the purpose of obtaining the consent of his creditors, or any of them, to an agreement with reference to his affairs or to his bankruptcy.

(Former provisions: IA 1985, s. 183(4), 186; BA 1914, s. 154)

S. 356(1)

This is a general offence derived from BA 1914, s. 154(6), prohibiting the bankrupt from making false statements by omission. The statement must relate to his "affairs" (for definition, see s. 385(2)).

    Section 356(1) (unlike s. 356(2)) does not, on its face, require any intent to cheat or defraud, but of course the general defence under s. 352 can be utilised to offer a defence to the innocent bankrupt.

S. 356(2)

This provision specifies certain prohibited forms of conduct involving falsehoods. Such behaviour was an offence under BA 1914, s. 154(1)(7), (1)(12), and (1)(16). For definitions of "property", "before petition" and "initial period", see the note to s. 351.

    The penalties for the above offences are dealt with by ss. 350, 430 and Sch. 10.

Section 357   Fraudulent disposal of property

357(1) [Offence re transfer]   The bankrupt is guilty of an offence if he makes or causes to be made, or has in the period of 5 years ending with the commencement of the bankruptcy made or caused to be made, any gift or transfer of, or any charge on, his property.

Section 352 applies to this offence.

357(2)   [Interpretation]   The reference to making a transfer of or charge on any property includes causing or conniving at the levying of any execution against that property.

357(3)   [Offence re concealment or removal of property]   The bankrupt is guilty of an offence if he conceals or removes, or has at any time before the commencement of the bankruptcy concealed or removed, any part of his property after, or within 2 months before, the date on which a judgment or order for the payment of money has been obtained against him, being a judgment or order which was not satisfied before the commencement of the bankruptcy.

Section 352 applies to this offence.

(Former provisions: IA 1985, s. 183(4), 187(1), (3)(b); B(A)A 1926, s. 6)

S. 357(1), (3)

Based partly on BA 1914, s. 156 and partly on s. 6 of the 1926 Act, this provision prohibits fraudulent disposal by the bankrupt of any "property" (see s. 351(*a*)) within five years of his bankruptcy commencing (for the definition of "commencement," see s. 278(*a*)). It also covers attempts to defeat judgments by concealment of property.

S. 357(2)

This is a supplementary provision, based partly on s. 6 of the 1926 Act. It indicates that the bankrupt commits an offence under s. 357(1) if he causes or connives at the levying of execution on his "property".

A bankrupt charged with offences under this section can rely on the general defence in s. 352. The relevant penalties are specified by ss. 350, 430 and Sch. 10.

Section 358   Absconding

358   The bankrupt is guilty of an offence if—

(a) he leaves, or attempts or makes preparations to leave, England and Wales with any property the value of which is not less than the prescribed amount and possession of which he is required to deliver up to the official receiver or the trustee, or

(b) in the 6 months before petition, or in the initial period, he did anything which would have been an offence under paragraph (a) if the bankruptcy order had been made immediately before he did it.

Section 352 applies to this offence.

(Former provisions: IA 1985, s. 183(4), s. 187(2); BA 1914, s. 159)

General note

This largely repeats BA 1914, s. 159, although the previous arbitrary figure of £250 has been dropped – unfortunately, in favour of another arbitrary figure to be fixed under s. 418. The figure from 29 December 1986 is £500: see the Insolvency Proceedings (Monetary Limits) Order 1986 (SI 1986 No. 1996). For a critique of this, see the Cork Report, para. 1889. Note that the offence covers absconding, etc., within the six months prior to the petition.

The s. 352 defence applies here. For penalties, see ss. 350, 430 and Sch. 10. The terms "property", "before petition" and "initial period" are all defined in s. 351.

Section 359   Fraudulent dealing with property obtained on credit

359(1)   [Offence re disposal of property obtained on credit]   The bankrupt is guilty of an offence if, in the 12 months before petition, or in the initial period, he disposed of any property which he had obtained on credit and, at the time he disposed of it, had not paid for.

Section 352 applies to this offence.

359(2)   [Offence re knowingly dealing with bankrupt]   A person is guilty of an offence if, in the 12 months before petition or in the initial period, he acquired or received property from the bankrupt knowing or believing—

(a) that the bankrupt owed money in respect of the property, and

(b) that the bankrupt did not intend, or was unlikely to be able, to pay the money he so owed.

359(3)   [Disposals etc. in ordinary course of business]   A person is not guilty of an offence under subsection (1) or (2) if the disposal, acquisition or receipt of the property was in the ordinary course of a business carried on by the bankrupt at the time of the disposal, acquisition or receipt.

359(4)   [Ordinary course of business]   In determining for the purposes of this section whether any property is disposed of, acquired or received in the ordinary course of a business carried on by the bankrupt, regard may be had, in particular, to the price paid for the property.

359(5)   [Interpretation]   In this section references to disposing of property include pawning or pledging it; and references to acquiring or receiving property shall be read accordingly.

(Former provisions: IA 1985, s. 183(4), 188; BA 1914, s. 154)

S. 359(1)

Based on BA 1914, s. 154(1), (15), this provision prohibits a bankrupt from disposing of "property" (for definition, see s. 351(*a*)) obtained on credit, where the disposal occurs within 12 months "before petition" (see s. 351(*c*)), or in the "initial period" (see s. 351(*b*)).

The s. 352 defence applies here.

On penalties for the offences in this and the following subsections, see ss. 350, 430 and Sch. 10.

S. 359(2)

Derived from s. 154(3), this penalises the knowing recipient of property obtained on credit and unlawfully disposed of under s. 359(1). Note again the definitions in s. 351.

A defence for the innocent recipient is built into this subsection.

S. 359(3), (4)

These are saving provisions for disposals and receipts of "property" in the ordinary course of business. In determining whether this saving facility can operate, the price paid for the property is clearly relevant.

S. 359(5)

This provision defines disposal of "property" so as to include pawns and pledges.

Section 360 Obtaining credit; engaging in business

360(1) [Offence re credit, non-disclosure of bankruptcy]   The bankrupt is guilty of an offence if—

(a) either alone or jointly with any other person, he obtains credit to the extent of the prescribed amount or more without giving the person from whom he obtains it the relevant information about his status; or

(b) he engages (whether directly or indirectly) in any business under a name other than that in which he was adjudged bankrupt without disclosing to all persons with whom he enters into any business transaction the name in which he was so adjudged.

360(2) [Cases of bankrupt obtaining credit]   The reference to the bankrupt obtaining credit includes the following cases—

(a) where goods are bailed to him under a hire-purchase agreement, or agreed to be sold to him under a conditional sale agreement, and

(b) where he is paid in advance (whether in money or otherwise) for the supply of goods or services.

360(3) [Scotland or Northern Ireland]   A person whose estate has been sequestrated in Scotland, or who has been adjudged bankrupt in Northern Ireland, is guilty of an offence if, before his discharge, he does anything in England and Wales which would be an offence under subsection (1) if he were an undischarged bankrupt and the sequestration of his estate or the adjudication in Northern Ireland were an adjudication under this Part.

360(4) [Information for s. 360(1)(a)]   For the purposes of subsection (1)(a), the relevant information about the status of the person in question is the information that he is an undischarged bankrupt or, as the case may be, that his estate has been sequestrated in Scotland and that he has not been discharged.

(Former provisions: IA 1985, s. 189; BA 1914, s. 155 (as amended))

S. 360(1)

This prevents an undischarged bankrupt from obtaining credit to the extent of the prescribed amount, either solely or jointly, without disclosing the relevant information about his status. It also prohibits him from carrying on a business under a name which was not the name by which he was declared bankrupt. Note that a person who enters into an individual voluntary arrangement is not subject to these disabilities. Under the previous provision the credit was fixed at a minimum of £50. The figure from 29 December 1986 is £250 under the Insolvency Proceedings (Monetary Limits) Order 1986 (SI 1986 No. 1996) made under s. 418. The offence under

s. 360(1) is one of strict liability and the general defence under s. 352 does not apply, although the offence would not operate where credit is obtained for an independent third person – *R* v *Godwin* (1980) 11 Cr App Rep 97.

The sanction for breach of s. 360 is specified by ss. 350, 430 and Sch. 10.

S. 360(2)

This represents a change in the law by extending the meaning of "obtaining credit" to cover receipt of goods under a hire-purchase agreement and receiving payment in advance for goods or services. Thus, authorities such as *R* v *Miller* [1977] 3 All ER 986 and *Fisher* v *Raven* [1964] AC 210 are no longer good law on this point.

S. 360(3)

This applies the above offence to a person whose estate is sequestrated in Scotland or who is declared bankrupt in Northern Ireland and who obtains credit in England and Wales.

S. 360(4)

This provision defines the "relevant information" for the purposes of s. 360(1).

Section 361 Failure to keep proper accounts of business

361(1) [Offence re no proper accounting records] Where the bankrupt has been engaged in any business for any of the period of 2 years before petition, he is guilty of an offence if he—

(a) has not kept proper accounting records throughout that period and throughout any part of the initial period in which he was so engaged, or

(b) has not preserved all the accounting records which he has kept.

361(2) [Exception to s. 361(1)] The bankrupt is not guilty of an offence under subsection (1)—

(a) if his unsecured liabilities at the commencement of the bankruptcy did not exceed the prescribed amount, or

(b) if he proves that in the circumstances in which he carried on business the omission was honest and excusable.

361(3) [Interpretation] For the purposes of this section a person is deemed not to have kept proper accounting records if he has not kept such records as are necessary to show or explain his transactions and financial position in his business, including—

(a) records containing entries from day to day, in sufficient detail, of all cash paid and received,

(b) where the business involved dealings in goods, statements of annual stock-takings, and

(c) except in the case of goods sold by way of retail trade to the actual customer, records of all goods sold and purchased showing the buyers and sellers in sufficient detail to enable the goods and the buyers and sellers to be identified.

361(4) [Application of s. 355(2)(d), (3)(b)] In relation to any such records as are mentioned in subsection (3), subsections (2)(d) and (3)(b) of section 355 apply with the substitution of 2 years for 12 months.

(Former provisions: IA 1985, s. 190; BA 1914, s. 158 (as amended))

S. 361(1)

This creates an offence where the bankrupt has carried on business within two years "before petition" (s. 351(*c*)) without keeping proper accounting records.

  On penalties, see ss. 350, 430 and Sch. 10.

S. 361(2)

It is a defence if the bankrupt can show that his failure to keep proper records was honest and reasonable, bearing in mind the circumstances under which he carried on business. Moreover, the offence is not committed if the bankrupt's unsecured liabilities at the commencement of his bankruptcy (for the meaning of this phrase, see s. 278(*a*)) did not exceed the prescribed amount. Under the 1914 Act the limit was £6,000 for a person who had not previously been adjudged bankrupt or who had not entered into a composition or arrangement with his creditors, and £1,200 in other cases. From 29 December 1986 the amount is £20,000 under the Insolvency Proceedings (Monetary Limits) Order 1986 (SI 1986 No. 1996) made under s. 418.

S. 361(3)

Here the meaning of proper accounting records is explained by reference to certain specific sources of information about the bankrupt's finances which must be maintained.

S. 361(4)

This oddly located provision extends certain time limits in s. 355(2)(*d*) and (3)(*b*) from one year to two years in respect of the basic records mentioned in s. 361(3). This repeats the provision in the 1914 Act.

Section 362 Gambling

362(1)   [Offence re gambling, rash and hazardous speculations]   The bankrupt is guilty of an offence if he has—

  (a) in the 2 years before petition, materially contributed to, or increased the extent of, his insolvency by gambling or by rash and hazardous speculations, or

  (b) in the initial period, lost any part of his property by gambling or by rash and hazardous speculations.

362(2)   [Rash and hazardous speculations]   In determining for the purposes of this section whether any speculations were rash and hazardous, the financial position of the bankrupt at the time when he entered into them shall be taken into consideration.

(Former provisions: IA 1985, s. 191; BA 1914, s. 157)

S. 362(1)

This reproduces in part the first subsection of the relevant provision in the 1914 Act. The prohibition is on gambling or rash and hazardous speculations in the two years "before petition" (see s. 351(*c*)), which have materially contributed to the bankrupt's insolvency, or any losses caused by such activities in the "initial period" (see s. 351(*b*)). This provision formerly referred to the need for court consent to a prosecution – now, by virtue of s. 350, the consent of the Director of Public Prosecutions or Secretary of State will be required. For an explanation of this change, see the Cork Committee's *Report*, para. 1887.

  Obsolete procedural and transitional refinements have been dropped from this section. The penalty for breach of s. 362 is prescribed by ss. 350, 430 and Sch. 10.

S. 362(2)

This provision defines rash or hazardous speculations in the same terms as in the 1914 Act.

Chapter VII — Powers of Court In Bankruptcy

Section 363 General control of court

363(1) [Power of court]   Every bankruptcy is under the general control of the court and, subject to the provisions in this Group of Parts, the court has full power to decide all questions of priorities and all other questions, whether of law or fact, arising in any bankruptcy.

363(2) [Bankrupt to do as directed]   Without prejudice to any other provision in this Group of Parts, an undischarged bankrupt or a discharged bankrupt whose estate is still being administered under Chapter IV of this Part shall do all such things as he may be directed to do by the court for the purposes of his bankruptcy or, as the case may be, the administration of that estate.

363(3) [Application for directions]   The official receiver of the trustee of a bankrupt's estate may at any time apply to the court for a direction under subsection (2).

363(4) [Contempt of court]   If any person without reasonable excuse fails to comply with any obligation imposed on him by subsection (2), he is guilty of a contempt of court and liable to be punished accordingly (in addition to any other punishment to which he may be subject).

(Former provisions: IA 1985, s. 193; BA 1914, s. 105)

S. 363(1)

This confers on "the court" (see ss. 373 and 385) the power to resolve all disputes in bankruptcy matters. In *Re Colgate* [1986] Ch. 439, the court used the predecessor of this provision to fix the remuneration of a trustee where this was in dispute. The rules are also relevant here – see IR 1986, r. 6.141 and Pt. 7.

S. 363(2), (4)

This places an undischarged bankrupt squarely under the thumb of the court. If he unreasonably fails to obey its instructions he could be liable for contempt. Form 7.16 is no longer to be used for contempt proceedings, but see now Form 7.15. This change was effected by I(A)R 1987 (SI 1987 No. 1919), r. 3(1), Sch., Pt. 2, para. 159.

S. 363(3)

The trustee or official receiver may apply to the court for a direction that the undischarged bankrupt behave in a certain way. This must not be confused with the power to apply for directions under s. 303(2).

Section 364 Power of arrest

364(1) [Court's power re warrant]   In the cases specified in the next subsection the court may cause a warrant to be issued to a constable or prescribed officer of the court—

(a) for the arrest of a debtor to whom a bankruptcy petition relates or of an undischarged bankrupt, or of a discharged bankrupt whose estate is still being administered under Chapter IV of this Part, and

(b) for the seizure of any books, papers, records, money or goods in the possession of a person arrested under the warrant,

and may authorise a person arrested under such a warrant to be kept in custody, and anything seized under such a warrant to be held, in accordance with the rules, until such time as the court may order.

364(2) **[Where s. 364(1) powers exercisable]** The powers conferred by subsection (1) are exercisable in relation to a debtor or undischarged bankrupt if, at any time after the presentation of the bankruptcy petition relating to him or the making of the bankruptcy order against him, it appears to the court—

(a) that there are reasonable grounds for believing that he has absconded, or is about to abscond, with a view to avoiding or delaying the payment of any of his debts or his appearance to a bankruptcy petition or to avoiding, delaying or disrupting any proceedings in bankruptcy against him or any examination of his affairs, or

(b) that he is about to remove his goods with a view to preventing or delaying possession being taken of them by the official receiver or the trustee of his estate, or

(c) that there are reasonable grounds for believing that he has concealed or destroyed, or is about to conceal or destroy, any of his goods or any books, papers or records which might be of use to his creditors in the course of his bankruptcy or in connection with the administration of his estate, or

(d) that he has, without the leave of the official receiver or the trustee of his estate, removed any goods in his possession which exceed in value such sum as may be prescribed for the purposes of this paragraph, or

(e) that he has failed, without reasonable excuse, to attend any examination ordered by the court.

(Former provisions: IA 1985, s. 194; BA 1914, s. 23)

S. 364(1)

This provides for the issue of warrants for the arrest of debtors or undischarged bankrupts and for seizure of their books.

S. 364(2)

The court can issue such a warrant if any of the five facts listed in (*a*)–(*e*) appear to it to be present. Under BA 1914, s. 23 there were only four paragraphs ((*a*)–(*d*)), but in substance the grounds have not been added to. The grounds are aimed at debtors who are likely to abscond, avoid public examination or hide assets. What is now para. (*d*) used to include an arbitrary

has been scrapped, as the Blagden Committee recommended;
Jom figure fixed under s. 418. From 29 December 1986 under
netary Limits) Order 1986 (SI 1986 No. 1996) the figure is

..., 7.21, 7.22.

Section 365   Seizure of bankrupt's property

365(1)   [Court's power re warrant]   At any time after a bankruptcy order has been
made, the court may, on the application of the official receiver or the trustee of the
bankrupt's estate, issue a warrant authorising the person to whom it is directed to
seize any property comprised in the bankrupt's estate which is, or any books, papers
or records relating to the bankrupt's estate or affairs which are, in the possession or
under the control of the bankrupt or any other person who is required to deliver the
property, books, papers or records to the official receiver or trustee.

365(2)   [Power to break open premises etc.]   Any person executing a warrant under this section may, for the purpose of seizing any property comprised in the bankrupt's estate or any books, papers or records relating to the bankrupt's estate or
affairs, break open any premises where the bankrupt or anything that may be seized
under the warrant is or is believed to be and any receptacle of the bankrupt which
contains or is believed to contain anything that may be so seized.

365(3)   [Power of court re search]   If, after a bankruptcy order has been made, the
court is satisfied that any property comprised in the bankrupt's estate is, or any books,
papers or records relating to the bankrupt's estate or affairs are, concealed in any
premises not belonging to him, it may issue a warrant authorising any constable or
prescribed officer of the court to search those premises for the property, books, papers or records.

365(4)   [Execution of s. 365(3) warrant]   A warrant under subsection (3) shall not
be executed except in the prescribed manner and in accordance with its terms.

(Former provisions: IA 1985, s. 195; BA 1914, s. 49)

S. 365(1), (2)

These provisions allow the court to issue a warrant for the seizure of the bankrupt's property
even though it may be in the possession of a third party. Forcing entry into premises or breaking
open "receptacles" is permitted when executing such a warrant.

S. 365(3), (4)

A search warrant (in the prescribed form) for a third party's premises may also be obtained
under this section, although the court must be satisfied that the bankrupt's property, etc. is
concealed there. Fishing expeditions will not be permitted.
    Note also IR 1986, rr. 7.21, 7.25.

Section 366   Inquiry into bankrupt's dealings and property

366(1)   [Power of court to summon bankrupt to appear]   At any time after a bankruptcy order has been made the court may, on the application of the official receiver
or the trustee of the bankrupt's estate, summon to appear before it—

    (a) the bankrupt or the bankrupt's spouse or former spouse,

(b) any person known or believed to have any property comprised in the bankrupt's estate in his possession or to be indebted to the bankrupt,

(c) any person appearing to the court to be able to give information concerning the bankrupt or the bankrupt's dealings, affairs or property.

The court may require any such person as is mentioned in paragraph (b) or (c) to submit an affidavit to the court containing an account of his dealings with the bankrupt or to produce any documents in his possession or under his control relating to the bankrupt or the bankrupt's dealings, affairs or property.

366(2) [Application of s. 366(3)] Without prejudice to section 364, the following applies in a case where—

(a) a person without reasonable excuse fails to appear before the court when he is summoned to do so under this section, or

(b) there are reasonable grounds for believing that a person has absconded, or is about to abscond, with a view to avoiding his appearance before the court under this section.

366(3) [Issue of warrant re non-appearance] The court may, for the purpose of bringing that person and anything in his possession before the court, cause a warrant to be issued to a constable or prescribed officer of the court—

(a) for the arrest of that person, and

(b) for the seizure of any books, papers, records, money or goods in that person's possession.

366(4) [Power re custody etc.] The court may authorise a person arrested under such a warrant to be kept in custody, and anything seized under such a warrant to be held, in accordance with the rules, until that person is brought before the court under the warrant or until such other time as the court may order.

(Former provisions: IA 1985, s. 196(1), (2); BA 1914, s. 25)

S. 366(1)

This permits the trustee or official receiver to ask the court to examine the bankrupt privately (or his spouse, or former spouse, or third parties believed to be in possession of the bankrupt's property or of information about his affairs). On the meaning of "affairs", see s. 385(2). This changes the previous law in a number of respects. The BA 1914 provision referred to the bankrupt's "wife", which makes an assumption which can no longer be justified in an age of sex equality. The new provision also allows the court to require affidavits from the persons mentioned in paras. (*a*) and (*b*). This reform, which was recommended by the Cork Report, para. 903, reverses the rule in *Ex parte Reynolds* (1882) 21 ChD 601. It was held in *Re Tucker (A Bankrupt), ex parte Tucker* [1990] Ch. 148 that the court had no jurisdiction under s. 25(6) of BA 1914 (the precursor of the present section) over British subjects resident abroad. In *Re Seagull Manufacturing Co. Ltd* [1992] Ch. 128, at p. 137; [1991] BCC 550, at p. 555, Mummery J expressed the view that there was little doubt that, on the authority of *Re Tucker*, the court would construe ss. 366 and 367 as subject to the same territorial limitation. In the Court of Appeal in the same case, [1993] Ch. 345, [1993] BCC 241, no opinion was expressed on this point. Contrast the position in regard to a public examination under ss. 133: see the notes to that section and to s. 236. The position may be different where s. 426 can be called into aid: *McIsaac & Anor, Petitioners* [1994] BCC 410.

Further provisions on s. 366 examinations are contained in the Rules: see IR 1986, rr. 9.1–9.6.

S. 366(2)–(4)

The court can order the arrest of absconders, plus the seizure of property. Note also IR 1986, rr. 7.21, 7.23.

Section 367   Court's enforcement powers under s. 366

367(1)   [Power to order delivery]   If it appears to the court, on consideration of any evidence obtained under section 366 or this section, that any person has in his possession any property comprised in the bankrupt's estate, the court may, on the application of the official receiver or the trustee of the bankrupt's estate, order that person to deliver the whole or any part of the property to the official receiver or the trustee at such time, in such manner and on such terms as the court thinks fit.

367(2)   [Power to order payment from bankrupt debtor]   If it appears to the court, on consideration of any evidence obtained under section 366 or this section, that any person is indebted to the bankrupt, the court may, on the application of the official receiver or the trustee of the bankrupt's estate, order that person to pay to the official receiver or trustee, at such time and in such manner as the court may direct, the whole or part of the amount due, whether in full discharge of the debt or otherwise as the court thinks fit.

367(3)   [Place of examination]   The court may, if it thinks fit, order that any person who if within the jurisdiction of the court would be liable to be summoned to appear before it under section 366 shall be examined in any part of the United Kingdom where he may be for the time being, or in any place outside the United Kingdom.

367(4)   [Examination on oath]   Any person who appears or is brought before the court under section 366 or this section may be examined on oath, either orally or by interrogatories, concerning the bankrupt or the bankrupt's dealings, affairs and property.

(Former provisions: IA 1985, s. 196(3)–(6); BA 1914, s. 25)

S. 367(1), (2)

If, as a result of information gleaned from the examination, it appears that the bankrupt's property is in the possession of a third party, the court can order it to be handed over. Debts owing to the bankrupt can also be ordered to be paid.

S. 367(3)

Examinations under s. 366 do not have to be held in the UK. In *Re Tucker (A Bankrupt), ex parte Tucker* [1990] Ch. 148 (decided under BA 1914, s. 25(6)), the Court of Appeal refused to exercise its discretion to allow examination of a witness in Belgium, since it was not possible to compel him to attend such examination. On the question whether ss. 366–367 extend to the examinations of witnesses abroad, see the notes to s. 366.

S. 367(4)

This deals with the form of the examination under s. 366. Note also IR 1986, rr. 9.1–9.6.

Section 368   Provision corresponding to s. 366, where interim receiver appointed

368   Sections 366 and 367 apply where an interim receiver has been appointed under section 286 as they apply where a bankruptcy order has been made, as if—

(a) references to the official receiver or the trustee were to the interim receiver, and

(b) references to the bankrupt and to his estate were (respectively) to the debtor and his property.

(Former provision: IA 1985, s. 196(7))

General note

This extends ss. 366 and 367 to situations where the debtor has not yet been declared bankrupt, but an interim receiver has been appointed after presentation of the petition under s. 286.

Section 369   Order for production of documents by inland revenue

369(1)   [Power of court]   For the purposes of an examination under section 290 (public examination of bankrupt) or proceedings under sections 366 to 368, the court may, on the application of the official receiver or the trustee of the bankrupt's estate, order an inland revenue official to produce to the court—

(a) any return, account or accounts submitted (whether before or after the commencement of the bankruptcy) by the bankrupt to any inland revenue official,

(b) any assessment or determination made (whether before or after the commencement of the bankruptcy) in relation to the bankrupt by any inland revenue official, or

(c) any correspondence (whether before or after the commencement of the bankruptcy) between the bankrupt and any inland revenue official.

369(2)   [Order re disclosure of document]   Where the court has made an order under subsection (1) for the purposes of any examination or proceedings, the court may, at any time after the document to which the order relates is produced to it, by order authorise the disclosure of the document, or of any part of its contents, to the official receiver, the trustee of the bankrupt's estate or the bankrupt's creditors.

369(3)   [Condition for s. 369(1) order]   The court shall not address an order under subsection (1) to an inland revenue official unless it is satisfied that that official is dealing, or has dealt, with the affairs of the bankrupt.

369(4) [Where s. 369(1) document not in official's possession] Where any document to which an order under subsection (1) relates is not in the possession of the official to whom the order is addressed, it is the duty of that official to take all reasonable steps to secure possession of it and, if he fails to do so, to report the reasons for his failure to the court.

369(5) [Where document held by another official] Where any document to which an order under subsection (1) relates is in the possession of an inland revenue official other than the one to whom the order is addressed, it is the duty of the official in possession of the document, at the request of the official to whom the order is addressed, to deliver it to the official making the request.

369(6) ["Inland revenue official"] In this section **"inland revenue official"** means any inspector or collector of taxes appointed by the Commissioners of Inland Revenue or any person appointed by the Commissioners to serve in any other capacity.

369(7) [Non-application] This section does not apply for the purposes of an examination under sections 366 and 367 which takes place by virtue of section 368 (interim receiver).

(Former provision: IA 1985, s. 197)

S. 369(1), (3), (6)

The court can order inland revenue officials (as defined by s. 369(6)) to hand over tax documents relating to the bankrupt's financial affairs to assist examinations under ss. 290 or 366. Only officials dealing with the bankrupt can be so directed.

S. 369(2)

The court can order the disclosure of any document ordered to be produced under s. 369(1) to the official receiver or the trustee.

S. 369(4), (5)

Where the court makes an order under s. 369(1), an inland revenue official must use his best efforts to obtain the documents in question, and this may involve securing possession of them from another inland revenue official.

S. 369(7)

This states that s. 369 does not apply where the debtor has not been declared bankrupt and where there is merely an examination under ss. 366, 367 at the request of his interim receiver under s. 368.

For further information, see IR 1986, rr. 6.194–6.196.

Section 370 Power to appoint special manager

370(1) [Power of court] The court may, on an application under this section, appoint any person to be the special manager—

(a) of a bankrupt's estate, or

(b) of the business of an undischarged bankrupt, or

(c) of the property or business of a debtor in whose case the official receiver has been appointed interim receiver under section 286.

370(2) **[Application to court]** An application under this section may be made by the official receiver or the trustee of the bankrupt's estate in any case where it appears to the official receiver or trustee that the nature of the estate, property or business, or the interests of the creditors generally, require the appointment of another person to manage the estate, property or business.

370(3) **[Powers of special manager]** A special manager appointed under this section has such powers as may be entrusted to him by the court.

370(4) **[Powers included in s. 370(3)]** The power of the court under subsection (3) to entrust powers to a special manager include power to direct that any provision in this Group of Parts that has effect in relation to the official receiver, interim receiver or trustee shall have the like effect in relation to the special manager for the purposes of the carrying out by the special manager of any of the functions of the official receiver, interim receiver or trustee.

370(5) **[Duties of special manager]** A special manager appointed under this section shall—

(a) give such security as may be prescribed,

(b) prepare and keep such accounts as may be prescribed, and

(c) produce those accounts in accordance with the rules to the Secretary of State or to such other persons as may be prescribed.

(Former provisions: IA 1985, s. 198; BA 1914, s. 10)

S. 370(1), (2)

The court can appoint a special manager of the bankrupt's estate or business, or indeed of a debtor's estate or business where an interim receiver has been installed. The application may be made by the official receiver or trustee where it appears that it is in the interests of the creditors that such an appointment be made. Under s. 10 of the 1914 Act the official receiver made the appointment.

For the question of remuneration see Sch. 9, para. 20.

This section should be read in conjunction with s. 287 and IR 1986, rr. 6.167–6.171.

Section 371   Re-direction of bankrupt's letters, etc.

371(1) **[Power of court]** Where a bankruptcy order has been made, the court may from time to time, on the application of the official receiver or the trustee of the bankrupt's estate, order the Post Office to re-direct and send or deliver to the official receiver or trustee or otherwise any postal packet (within the meaning of the Post Office Act 1953) which would otherwise be sent or delivered by them to the bankrupt at such place or places as may be specified in the order.

371(2) **[Duration of court order]** An order under this section has effect for such period, not exceeding 3 months, as may be specified in the order.

(Former provisions: IA 1985, s. 199; BA 1914, s. 24)

S. 371(1)

This provision allows the court on an application from the official receiver or trustee to order the Post Office to redirect the bankrupt's mail after a bankruptcy order has been made. The mail can then be opened by the official receiver or trustee (see s. 365). This provision dates back to s. 85 of the Debtors Act 1869. Unfortunately there are questions as to its legality in the light of art. 8 of the European Convention on Human Rights and its relationship with the Interception of Communications Act 1985 – see Jaconelli [1994] Conv (forthcoming) on these intriguing issues.

   Note that the power to open the bankrupt's mail does not extend to outgoing mail. Moreover, a debtor who enters into an individual voluntary arrangement to settle his debts cannot have his mail opened under this provision.

S. 371(2)

The maximum period of interference permitted by the order is three months, as was the case previously.

PART X — INDIVIDUAL INSOLVENCY: GENERAL PROVISIONS

Section 372 Supplies of gas, water, electricity, etc.

372(1) [Application] This section applies where on any day **("the relevant day")**—

  (a) a bankruptcy order is made against an individual or an interim receiver of an individual's property is appointed, or

  (b) a voluntary arrangement proposed by an individual is approved under Part VIII, or

  (c) a deed of arrangement is made for the benefit of an individual's creditors;

and in this section **"the office-holder"** means the official receiver, the trustee in bankruptcy, the interim receiver, the supervisor of the voluntary arrangement or the trustee under the deed of arrangement, as the case may be.

372(2) [Where s. 372(3) request] If a request falling within the next subsection is made for the giving after the relevant day of any of the supplies mentioned in subsection (4), the supplier—

  (a) may make it a condition of the giving of the supply that the office-holder personally guarantees the payment of any charges in respect of the supply, but

  (b) shall not make it a condition of the giving of the supply, or do anything which has the effect of making it a condition of the giving of the supply, that any outstanding charges in respect of a supply given to the individual before the relevant day are paid.

372(3) [Type of request] A request falls within this subsection if it is made—

  (a) by or with the concurrence of the office-holder, and

  (b) for the purposes of any business which is or has been carried on by the individual, by a firm or partnership of which the individual is or was a member, or by an agent or manager for the individual or for such a firm or partnership.

372(4)   [Supplies in s. 372(2)]   The supplies referred to in subsection (2) are—

(a) a public supply of gas,

(b) a public supply of electricity,

(c) a supply of water by a water undertaker,

(d) a supply of telecommunication services by a public telecommunications operator.

372(5)   [Definitions]   The following applies to expressions used in subsection (4)—

(a) **"public supply of gas"** means a supply of gas by the British Gas Corporation as a public gas supplier within the meaning of Part I of the Gas Act 1986,

(b) **"a public supply of electricity"** means a supply of electricity by a public electricity supplier within the meaning of Part I of the Electricity Act 1989; and

(c) **"telecommunication services"** and **"public telecommunications operator"** mean the same as in the Telecommunications Act 1984, except that the former does not include local delivery services within the meaning of Part II of the Broadcasting Act 1990.

(Former provision: IA 1985, s. 200)

General note

This section represents a late change of mind by the Government in that it did not appear in the early forms of the 1985 Bill. It is designed to stop public utilities "blackmailing" the trustee in bankruptcy, etc. of an insolvent individual into paying arrears in respect of public utility supplies as a precondition to receiving supplies in the future. It was not clear at common law whether a public utility could behave in such a way – see *Re Flack* [1900] 2 QB 32 – but the Cork Committee (*Report*, para. 1466) favoured legislation to expressly outlaw such "priority gaining".

For the corresponding provisions in corporate insolvencies, see. s. 233.

S. 372(1)–(3)

These provisions enable an office-holder (as defined by s. 372(1)) to request a supply from a public utility. The supplier, although he may require the officer-holder to guarantee future payments personally, cannot require arrears to be paid as a precondition to the making of the supply. Section 372(3) makes special provision for supplies to partnerships where one member becomes insolvent.

S. 372(4), (5)

These provisions list the public utilities that are covered by this section – gas, electricity, water and telecommunications (but not cable services). Subsections (4) and (5) have been amended to cope with utility privatisation legislation. Thus the words "statutory water undertakers" which originally appeared in s. 372(4)(*c*) have been replaced by "a water undertaker" (see Water Act 1989, Sch. 25, para. 78(1)). The words "a supply of electricity by an Electricity Board" have been dropped from s. 374(4)(*b*) and substituted with the phrase, "a public supply of electricity", which is now defined in s. 372(5)(*b*) (see Electricity Act 1989, Sch. 16, para. 35(3)). Subsection (5)(*c*) has also been amended by the Broadcasting Act 1990, Sch. 20, para. 43.

Section **373** Jurisdiction in relation to insolvent individuals

373(1) **[High Court and county courts]** The High Court and the county courts have jurisdiction throughout England and Wales for the purposes of the Parts in this Group.

373(2) **[Powers of county court]** For the purposes of those Parts, a county court has, in addition to its ordinary jurisdiction, all the powers and jurisdiction of the High Court; and the orders of the court may be enforced accordingly in the prescribed manner.

373(3) **[Exercise of jurisdiction]** Jurisdiction for the purposes of those Parts is exercised—

(a) by the High Court in relation to the proceedings which, in accordance with the rules, are allocated to the London insolvency district, and

(b) by each county court in relation to the proceedings which are so allocated to the insolvency district of that court.

373(4) **[Operation of s. 373(3)]** Subsection (3) is without prejudice to the transfer of proceedings from one court to another in the manner prescribed by the rules; and nothing in that subsection invalidates any proceedings on the grounds that they were initiated or continued in the wrong court.

(Former provisions: IA 1985, s. 201; BA 1914, ss. 96, 100, 103)

S. 373(1)

This vests bankruptcy jurisdiction in the High Court and the county courts in the case of England and Wales. See also Pt. 7 of the rules here. For the fees in county court proceedings see the County Court Fees (Amendment No. 2) Order 1986 (SI 1986 No. 2143).

S. 373(2)

In bankruptcy matters county courts are to have all the powers of the High Court. This was the case under BA 1914, s. 103. See here *Re A Debtor (No. 2A of 1980)* [1981] Ch. 148.

S. 373(3)

This provision allocates cases between the High Court and county courts – much will depend upon the "insolvency districts" which are described in s. 374.

S. 373(4)

The transfer of proceedings from one court to another is permitted. Note IR 1986, rr. 7.11–7.15. See also IR 1986, Sch. 2, for insolvency courts.

Section **374** Insolvency districts

374(1) **[Order by Lord Chancellor]** The Lord Chancellor may by order designate the areas which are for the time being to be comprised, for the purposes of the Parts in this Group, in the London insolvency district and the insolvency district of each county court; and an order under this section may—

   (a) exclude any county court from having jurisdiction for the purposes of those Parts, or

   (b) confer jurisdiction for those purposes on any county court which has not previously had that jurisdiction.

374(2) **[Incidental provisions etc.]** An order under this section may contain such incidental, supplemental and transitional provisions as may appear to the Lord Chancellor necessary or expedient.

374(3) **[Order by statutory instrument]** An order under this section shall be made by statutory instrument and, after being made, shall be laid before each House of Parliament.

374(4) **[Relevant districts]** Subject to any order under this section—

   (a) the district which, immediately before the appointed day, is the London bankruptcy district becomes, on that day, the London insolvency district;

   (b) any district which immediately before that day is the bankruptcy district of a county court becomes, on that day, the insolvency district of that court, and

   (c) any county court which immediately before that day is excluded from having jurisdiction in bankruptcy is excluded, on and after that day, from having jurisdiction for the purposes of the Parts in this Group.

(Former provisions: IA 1985, s. 202; BA 1914, s. 96)

S. 374(1), (4)

The Lord Chancellor may by order designate the insolvency districts – certain county courts can be prevented from handling bankruptcy matters, whereas others may be given this jurisdiction for the first time. See the Civil Courts (Amendment No. 3) Order 1992 (SI 1992 No. 1810). Subject to this power, existing jurisdictional patterns are to be retained. For alternative county courts see Sch. 2 of IR 1986 (as amended).

S. 374(2), (3)

These provisions permit any order by the Lord Chancellor to deal with ancillary matters and regulate the mode by which such orders are to be made.
   See IR 1986, r. 6.40(3) and Sch. 2.

Section 375   Appeals etc. from courts exercising insolvency jurisdiction

375(1) **[Review, rescission etc.]** Every court having jurisdiction for the purposes of the Parts in this Group may review, rescind or vary any order made by it in the exercise of that jurisdiction.

375(2) **[Appeals]** An appeal from a decision made in the exercise of jurisdiction for the purposes of those Parts by a county court or by a registrar in bankruptcy of the High Court lies to a single judge of the High Court; and an appeal from a decision of that judge on such an appeal lies, with the leave of the judge or of the Court of Appeal, to the Court of Appeal.

375(3) **[No other appeals]** A county court is not, in the exercise of its jurisdiction for the purposes of those Parts, to be subject to be restrained by the order of any other court, and no appeal lies from its decision in the exercise of that jurisdiction except as provided by this section.

(Former provisions: IA 1985, s. 203; BA 1914, s. 108)

S. 375(1)

This confers a general "safety valve" power on the courts to review, rescind or vary orders on bankruptcy matters. The equivalent in corporate insolvency law is r. 7.47 and broadly speaking similar principles should be applied – *Midrome Ltd* v *Shaw* [1993] BCC 659.

S. 375(2)

This provision deals with the question of appeals, whether against a decision of the county court or High Court. Under BA 1914, s. 108(2) appeals had to be "at the instance of any person aggrieved", but the present subsection makes no mention of this. It would appear from *Re Cullinane's Applications, The Times,* 12 June 1989 (decided under s. 108 of the 1914 Act) that leave to appeal is required in the case of appeals from the High Court to the Court of Appeal involving interlocutory orders because the statutory provisions in bankruptcy law have to be read in the light of s. 18 of the Supreme Court Act 1981. A consistent interpretation of these two pieces of legislation was adopted in *Lawrence* v *European Credit Co* [1992] BCC 792, where the Court of Appeal held that the right of appeal to the Court of Appeal as conferred by s. 16 of the Supreme Court Act 1981 was not cut down by the wording of s. 375(2). Thus an appeal against the refusal of a judge to extend the time for appeals does lie to the Court of Appeal. See Fletcher [1994] JBL 279.

In *Re A Debtor (No. 32/SD/1991)* [1993] 1 WLR 314 Millett J indicated that in a s. 375 review the court can hear fresh evidence not available at the original hearing. Such a review therefore differs fundamentally from a simple appeal where this would not be permitted. Vinelott J further considered the nature of the court's jurisdiction under s. 375 in later proceedings in *Re A Debtor (No. 32/SD/1991) (No. 2)* [1994] BCC 524. According to his Lordship (at p. 528G) it was an exceptional reserve jurisdiction only to be resorted to in the most extreme of cases. It existed to prevent "miscarriages of justice" in the field of bankruptcy law where a person's reputation and freedom of action was at stake.

Note also *Practice Direction (Insolvency Appeals: Hearings Outside London) (No. 3 of 1992)* [1992] 1 WLR 791.

S. 375(3)

This complements s. 373(2) by conferring jurisdictional integrity on the county courts.
See further IR 1986, r. 7.48.

Section 376 Time-limits

376 Where by any provision in this Group of Parts or by the rules the time for doing anything is limited, the court may extend the time, either before or after it has expired, on such terms, if any, as it thinks fit.

(Former provisions: IA 1985, s. 204; BA 1914, s. 109(4))

General note

This provision once again emphasises the general control of the court over bankruptcy proceedings by allowing it to extend time-limits. Note also that under BR 1952, r. 389 the court could adjust time periods on "good cause shown" – the statutory provision makes no reference to such a precondition but see IR 1986, r. 12.9.

Section 377 Formal defects

377 The acts of a person as the trustee of a bankrupt's estate or as a special manager, and the acts of the creditors' committee established for any bankruptcy, are valid notwithstanding any defect in the appointment, election or qualifications of the trustee or manager or, as the case may be, of any member of the committee.

(Former provisions: IA 1985, s. 205; BA 1914, s. 147(2))

General note

This provision, like BR 1952, r. 388, displays a liberal attitude towards procedural defects in the appointment or qualifications of the trustee, etc. Corresponding sections in the case of company officers and office-holders are s. 232 above and CA 1985, s. 285. It is necessary to instil confidence in third parties and to preclude the need to investigate that correct procedures have been followed. Note that the predecessor of s. 377 only covered situations where the trustee, etc. acted in good faith, but this is not mentioned in s. 377. Under BA 1914, s. 147(1), which is not specifically repeated in IA 1986, other defects in bankruptcy proceedings could be excused by the court unless substantial and irreparable injustice had been caused by the irregularity. Presumably such cases could now be dealt with under ss. 363(1) and 375(1). Finally it should be remembered that the question of a trustee's qualifications must be viewed in the light of the requirements of Pt. XIII.

Schedule 9, para. 32 states that non-compliance with the rules may be made a criminal offence.

Compare also IR 1986, r. 7.55.

Section 378 Exemption from stamp duty

378 Stamp duty shall not be charged on—

    (a) any document, being a deed, conveyance, assignment, surrender, admission or other assurance relating solely to property which is comprised in a bankrupt's estate and which, after the execution of that document, is or remains at law or in equity the property of the bankrupt or of the trustee of that estate,

    (b) any writ, order, certificate or other instrument relating solely to the property of a bankrupt or to any bankruptcy proceedings.

(Former provisions: IA 1985, s. 206; BA 1914, s. 148)

General note

This section offers welcome relief from the operation of stamp duty on documents connected with bankruptcy matters.

Section 379 Annual report

379 As soon as practicable after the end of 1986 and each subsequent calendar year, the Secretary of State shall prepare and lay before each House of Parliament a report about the operation during that year of so much of this Act as is comprised in this Group of Parts, and about proceedings in the course of that year under the Deeds of Arrangement Act 1914.

(Former provisions: IA 1985, s. 210; BA 1914, s. 136)

General note

This section requires the Secretary of State to lay before Parliament an annual report on the working of IA 1986 and the Deeds of Arrangement Act 1914. This is not a new obligation. The 1984 annual report (published in November 1985) is a mine of statistical information on the working of the old bankruptcy legislation.

This provision, unlike its predecessor, makes no mention of the obligation imposed on bankruptcy officers to provide the raw statistics to the Department of Trade and Industry to facilitate the preparation of this report. However, these matters are now dealt with by the rules – see IR 1986, r. 7.29.

PART XI — INTERPRETATION FOR SECOND GROUP OF PARTS

Section 380   Introductory

380   The next five sections have effect for the interpretation of the provisions of this Act which are comprised in this Group of Parts; and where a definition is provided for a particular expression, it applies except so far as the context otherwise requires.

General note

This introduces the bankruptcy interpretation sections. Meanings attributed in ss. 381–385 can be excluded by the context. Note also Pt. XVIII of the Act and IR 1986, Pt. 13.

Section 381   "Bankrupt" and associated terminology

381(1)   **["Bankrupt"]**   **"Bankrupt"** means an individual who has been adjudged bankrupt and, in relation to a bankruptcy order, it means the individual adjudged bankrupt by that order.

381(2)   **["Bankruptcy order"]**   **"Bankruptcy order"** means an order adjudging an individual bankrupt.

381(3)   **["Bankruptcy petition"]**   **"Bankruptcy petition"** means a petition to the court for a bankruptcy order.

(Former provisions: IA 1985, s. 211(1); BA 1914, s. 167)

General note

These common phrases are hereby defined.

Section 382   "Bankruptcy debt", etc.

382(1)   **["Bankruptcy debt"]**   **"Bankruptcy debt"**, in relation to a bankrupt, means (subject to the next subsection) any of the following—

   (a) any debt or liability to which he is subject at the commencement of the bankruptcy,

   (b) any debt or liability to which he may become subject after the commencement of the bankruptcy (including after his discharge from bankruptcy) by reason of any obligation incurred before the commencement of the bankruptcy,

(c) any amount specified in pursuance of section 39(3)(c) of the Powers of Criminal Courts Act 1973 in any criminal bankruptcy order made against him before the commencement of the bankruptcy, and

(d) any interest provable as mentioned in section 322(2) in Chapter IV of Part IX.

382(2)   [Liability in tort]   In determining for the purposes of any provision in this Group of Parts whether any liability in tort is a bankruptcy debt, the bankrupt is deemed to become subject to that liability by reason of an obligation incurred at the time when the cause of action accrued.

382(3)   [References to debtor liability]   For the purposes of references in this Group of Parts to a debt or liability, it is immaterial whether the debt or liability is present or future, whether it is certain or contingent or whether its amount is fixed or liquidated, or is capable of being ascertained by fixed rules or as a matter of opinion; and references in this Group of Parts to owing a debt are to be read accordingly.

382(4)   ["Liability"]   In this Group of Parts, except in so far as the context otherwise requires, **"liability"** means (subject to subsection (3) above) a liability to pay money or money's worth, including any liability under an enactment, any liability for breach of trust, any liability in contract, tort or bailment and any liability arising out of an obligation to make restitution.

(Former provisions: IA 1985, s. 211(1)(part), (2), (3); BA 1914, s. 167)

S. 382(1), (2)

These provisions define a bankruptcy debt.

Note prospective amendment: s. 382(1)(*c*) is to be repealed by the Criminal Justice Act 1988, s. 170(2) and Sch. 16 as from a day to be appointed; see the note to s. 264.

S. 382(3), (4)

These provisions make liability in tort a bankruptcy debt and make it clear that both contingent and unliquidated liabilities are capable of forming the basis of a bankruptcy debt. On the latter point, this is a change in the law, which the Cork Committee (*Report*, para. 1318) called for. In *Re Wisepark Ltd* [1994] BCC 221 it was held that a claim for costs was not a contingent liability within s. 382 because it did not exist until the court made an order for costs. Therefore a person having such a claim could not vote on a voluntary arrangement but conversely was not bound by its terms and could pursue the debtor if the costs order was eventually made in his favour.

For the corresponding definitions in corporate insolvency, see the note to Sch. 8, paras. 12, 14.

Note that bankruptcy debts are not always provable – see the note to IR 1986, r. 12.3.

Section 383   "Creditor", "security", etc.
383(1)   ["Creditor"]   "Creditor"—

(a) in relation to a bankrupt, means a person to whom any of the bankruptcy debts is owed (being, in the case of an amount falling within paragraph (c) of the definition in section 382(1) of **"bankruptcy debt"**, the person in respect of whom that amount is specified in the criminal bankruptcy order in question), and

(b) in relation to an individual to whom a bankruptcy petition relates, means a person who would be a creditor in the bankruptcy if a bankruptcy order were made on that petition.

383(2) [Securing of debt] Subject to the next two subsections and any provision of the rules requiring a creditor to give up his security for the purposes of proving a debt, a debt is secured for the purposes of this Group of Parts to the extent that the person to whom the debt is owed holds any security for the debt (whether a mortgage, charge, lien or other security) over any property of the person by whom the debt is owed.

383(3) [Where s. 269(1)(a) statement made] Where a statement such as is mentioned in section 269(1)(a) in Chapter I of Part IX has been made by a secured creditor for the purposes of any bankruptcy petition and a bankruptcy order is subsequently made on that petition, the creditor is deemed for the purposes of the Parts in this Group to have given up the security specified in the statement.

383(4) [Qualification to s. 383(2)] In subsection (2) the reference to a security does not include a lien on books, papers or other records, except to the extent that they consist of documents which give a title to property and are held as such.

(Former provisions: IA 1985, s. 211(1)(part), (5)–(7); BA 1914, s. 167)

S. 383(1)

This defines "creditor".

Note prospective amendment: in s. 383(1)(*a*) the words from "(being," to "question)" are to be repealed by the Criminal Justice Act 1988, s. 170(2) and Sch. 16 as from a day to be appointed; see the note to s. 264.

S. 383(2)–(4)

These provisions deal with security and secured creditors. Section 383(2) defines "security", but this must be read in the light of s. 383(4), excluding liens over books, etc. See also *Re A Debtor (No. 310 of 1988)* [1989] 1 WLR 452. Section 383(3) would be better located in s. 269, to which it relates.

Section 384   "Prescribed" and "the rules"

384(1) [Definitions] Subject to the next subsection, **"prescribed"** means prescribed by the rules; and **"the rules"** means rules made under section 412 in Part XV.

384(2) [Interpretation] References in this Group of Parts to the amount prescribed for the purposes of any of the following provisions—

section 273;
section 346(3);
section 354(1) and (2);
section 358;
section 360(1);
section 361(2); and
section 364(2)(d),

and references in those provisions to the prescribed amount are to be read in accordance with section 418 in Part XV and orders made under that section.

(Former provisions: IA 1985, s. 209(1) (part), 211(1) (part))

General note

This section defines "prescribed" and "the rules" and must be read in the light of ss. 418 and 412 respectively.

Section 385   Miscellaneous definitions

385(1)   [Definitions]   The following definitions have effect—

"**the court**", in relation to any matter, means the court to which, in accordance with section 373 in Part X and the rules, proceedings with respect to that matter are allocated or transferred;

"**creditor's petition**" means a bankruptcy petition under section 264(1)(a);

"**criminal bankruptcy order**" means an order under section 39(1) of the Powers of Criminal Courts Act 1973;

"**debt**" is to be construed in accordance with section 382(3);

"**the debtor**"—

    (a) in relation to a proposal for the purposes of Part VIII, means the individual making or intending to make that proposal, and

    (b) in relation to a bankruptcy petition, means the individual to whom the petition relates;

"**debtor's petition**" means a bankruptcy petition presented by the debtor himself under section 264(1)(b);

"**dwelling house**" includes any building or part of a building which is occupied as a dwelling and any yard, garden, garage or outhouse belonging to the dwelling house and occupied with it;

"**estate**", in relation to a bankrupt is to be construed in accordance with section 283 in Chapter II of Part IX;

"**family**", in relation to a bankrupt, means the persons (if any) who are living with him and are dependent on him;

"**secured**" and related expressions are to be construed in accordance with section 383; and

"**the trustee**", in relation to a bankruptcy and the bankrupt, means the trustee of the bankrupt's estate.

385(2)   [Interpretation]   References in this Group of Parts to a person's affairs include his business, if any.

(Former provisions: IA 1985, s. 211(1)(part), (4); BA 1914, s. 167)

S. 385(1)

This provides general definitions of words commonly appearing in the Second Group of Parts. There are differences from its statutory predecessor. Thus, for example, references to resolutions passed at creditors' meetings have been omitted, as have other terms which have become obsolete. On the other hand, new terms have been included, such as "dwelling house" and "family" (note its extended meaning). Note also ss. 382 and 383, and ss. 435, 436.

Note prospective amendment: in s. 385(1) the definition of "criminal bankruptcy order" is to be repealed by the Criminal Justice Act 1988, s. 170(2) and Sch. 16 as from a day to be appointed; see the note to s. 264.

S. 385(2)

This is inserted *ex abundanti cautela* – a person's "affairs" would cover his business.

THE THIRD GROUP OF PARTS
MISCELLANEOUS MATTERS BEARING ON BOTH COMPANY AND INDIVIDUAL INSOLVENCY; GENERAL INTERPRETATION; FINAL PROVISIONS

Introduction to the Third Group of Parts

Parts XII–XIX of the IA 1986 consist of a great variety of matters. Apart from the usual "mechanical" provisions (interpretation, short title, commencement, etc.), there is a group of sections, namely ss. 386–387, which substantially reduce the significance of preferential claims in insolvency law. The provisions on the qualification of insolvency practitioners are to be found in Pt.XIII. There is also reference to official receivers (happily retained for corporate and personal insolvencies), the Official Petitioner, the Insolvency Rules Committee, insolvency service finance, insolvent estates of deceased persons and insolvent partnerships. The connection of other sections within Pt.XVII with insolvency law is more indirect – thus there are provisions dealing with Parliamentary disqualification and restrictive trade practices.

Scholars of legislative history should note ss. 423–425, which revamp s. 172 of the Law of Property Act 1925, a provision which can trace its own ancestry back to 1571! Another side of the legislative process is disclosed by s. 429, which amends provisions enacted as recently as the County Courts Act 1984.

PART XII — PREFERENTIAL DEBTS IN COMPANY AND INDIVIDUAL INSOLVENCY

General comment on Part XII

Preferential claims have been a part of insolvency law for nearly a hundred years. A preferential claim is essentially an unsecured one that is given especially favourable treatment by the legislature. Although the legislature is at liberty to create new preferential claims it seems clear that the courts will not do so on their own initiative – see here *Re Rafidain Bank* [1992]

BCC 376. It is not surprising, therefore, that the State is the main preferential claimant. In the context of corporate insolvency law, this means that preferential claims are to be satisfied out of a company's assets subject to a floating charge in priority to the debenture holder enjoying that charge. They do not rank ahead of the claims of a debenture holder secured by a fixed charge – *Re Lewis Merthyr Consolidated Collieries Ltd* [1929] 1 Ch. 498, *Re G L Saunders Ltd* [1986] 1 WLR 215. Although preferential claims enjoy no inherent priority over a fixed charge, such a priority can arise if the fixed chargee surrenders priority in respect of the charged asset to a floating chargee and fails to do so via a subrogation mechanism. A simple postponement agreement can lead to the fixed chargee inadvertently also surrendering priority to preferential claimants – see *Re Portbase (Clothing) Ltd* [1993] Ch. 388; [1993] BCC 96.

The proliferation of preferential claims since 1945 has worried banks enjoying the security of a floating charge and has led them to seek increased security in the form of the highly artificial fixed charge over future assets. The end result of these trends has been to make the position of unsecured creditors even more unhappy.

After reviewing the evidence, the Cork Committee (*Report*, para. 1450) called for a radical reduction in the number of preferential claims:

"We unhesitatingly reject the argument that debts owed to the community ought to be paid in priority to debts owed to private creditors. A bad debt owed to the State is likely to be insignificant, in terms of total Government receipts; the loss of a similar sum by a private creditor may cause substantial hardship, and bring further insolvencies in its train" (para. 1410).

In the early drafts of the Insolvency Bill 1985, the Government refused to act on this proposal because of the implications for the public exchequer. Reluctantly, however, it included provisions in IA 1985 (s. 89 and Sch. 4) which did reduce its own preferential position, and it is these provisions which have found their way into IA 1986.

The continued survival of preferential claims under English law is the subject of constant debate. It is interesting to note that the Crown's preferential rights have been entirely swept away in Australia by the 1992 amendments to the Corporations Law and in Canada have been significantly reduced by the Bankruptcy and Insolvency Act 1992.

Section 386   Categories of preferential debts

386(1)   [Debts listed in Sch. 6]   A reference in this Act to the preferential debts of a company or an individual is to the debts listed in Schedule 6 to this Act (money owed to the Inland Revenue for income tax deducted at source; VAT, insurance premium tax, car tax, betting and gaming duties, beer duty, lottery duty; social security and pension scheme contributions; remuneration etc. of employees; levies on coal and steel production); and references to preferential creditors are to be read accordingly.

386(2)   ["The debtor"]   In that Schedule **"the debtor"** means the company or the individual concerned.

386(3)   [Interpretation of Sch. 6]   Schedule 6 is to be read with Schedule 4 to the Pensions Schemes Act 1993 (occupational pension scheme contributions).

(Former provisions: CA 1985, ss. 196(2), 475(1); IA 1985, ss. 23(7), 89(1), 108(3), 115(9), 166(1), Sch. 4, para. 1(1), Sch. 6, para. 15(3))

General note

These provisions, allied to Sch. 6, reduce the number of preferential claims. Among the main preferential claims remaining there are PAYE deductions for the 12 months before the relevant date, unpaid VAT for the six months prior to the relevant date, unpaid social security contributions for the 12 months before the relevant date, contributions in respect of occupational pension schemes, "remuneration" (widely defined by Sch. 6, para. 13) due to employees for four months prior to the relevant date (subject to a maximum limit fixed by the Secretary of State), accrued holiday remuneration, sums advanced to pay employees' wages, etc. This list was added to by the Insolvency (ECSC Levy Debts) Regulations 1987 (SI 1987 No. 2093) (levies on coal and steel production), the Finance Act 1991, Sch. 2, para. 21A (beer duty), the Finance Act 1993, s. 36(1) (lottery duty), and the Finance Act 1994, Sch. 7, para. 7(2) (insurance premium tax). These additions are regrettable and run counter to the basic philosophy of the Cork Committee. The key phrase "relevant date" is explained by s. 387.

From this new list of preferential claims we can spot the "casualties" inflicted following the recommendations of the Cork Committee. These include unpaid rates and the general preference in respect of unpaid taxes owing to the Crown. The amount of unpaid VAT enjoying preferential status has been reduced by changing the period from 12 to 6 months.

Preferential creditors rank in priority not only to unsecured creditors, but also to the holder of a floating charge (s. 175(2)(*b*)). In this regard, IA 1986 has made an important change by redefining "floating charge" so as to include a charge which, though originally floating, has since become fixed. See the note to s. 175.

S. 386(3)

The reference to Sch. 4 to the Pension Scheme Act 1993 was substituted for the former reference to Sch. 3 of the Social Security Pensions Act 1975 by s. 190 of and Sch. 8, para. 18 to the 1993 Act.

Section 387 "The relevant date"

387(1) [Explanation of Sch. 6] This section explains references in Schedule 6 to the relevant date (being the date which determines the existence and amount of a preferential debt).

387(2) [Pt. I, s. 4] For the purposes of section 4 in Part I (meetings to consider company voluntary arrangement), the relevant date in relation to a company which is not being wound up is—

(a) where an administration order is in force in relation to the company, the date of the making of that order, and

(b) where no such order has been made, the date of the approval of the voluntary arrangement.

387(3) [Company being wound up] In relation to a company which is being wound up, the following applies—

(a) if the winding up is by the court, and the winding-up order was made immediately upon the discharge of an administration order, the relevant date is the date of the making of the administration order;

(b) if the case does not fall within paragraph (a) and the company—

(i) is being wound up by the court, and

    (ii) had not commenced to be wound up voluntarily before the date of the making of the winding-up order,

the relevant date is the date of the appointment (or first appointment) of a provisional liquidator or, if no such appointment has been made, the date of the winding-up order;

    (c) if the case does not fall within either paragraph (a) or (b), the relevant date is the date of the passing of the resolution for the winding up of the company.

387(4)   **[Company in receivership]**   In relation to a company in receivership (where section 40 or, as the case may be, section 59 applies), the relevant date is—

    (a) in England and Wales, the date of the appointment of the receiver by debenture-holders, and

    (b) in Scotland, the date of the appointment of the receiver under section 53(6) or (as the case may be) 54(5).

387(5)   **[Pt. VIII, s. 258]**   For the purposes of section 258 in Part VIII (individual voluntary arrangements), the relevant date is, in relation to a debtor who is not an undischarged bankrupt, the date of the interim order made under section 252 with respect to his proposal.

387(6)   **[Bankrupt]**   In relation to a bankrupt, the following applies—

    (a) where at the time the bankruptcy order was made there was an interim receiver appointed under section 286, the relevant date is the date on which the interim receiver was first appointed after the presentation of the bankruptcy petition;

    (b) otherwise, the relevant date is the date of the making of the bankruptcy order.

(Former provisions: CA 1985, ss. 196(2)–(4), 475(3), (4); IA 1985, s. 23(8), 115(10), Sch. 4, paras. 1(2), (3), Sch. 6, paras. 15(4), 20(3))

General note

The purpose of these provisions is to explain the meaning of the phrase "the relevant date", used extensively in Sch. 6. The timing for assessment of preferential claims depends on the particular insolvency regime involved, and whether corporate or individual.

    Note that there are no preferential creditors in a company administration, except (i) where the company is also the subject of a voluntary arrangement (s. 387(2)(*a*)), or (ii) where a liquidation follows immediately upon the discharge of the administration order (s. 387(3)(*a*)).

PART XIII — INSOLVENCY PRACTITIONERS AND THEIR QUALIFICATIONS

General comment on Part XIII

A major recommendation of the Cork Committee (*Report*, Ch. 15–17) was that every insolvency practitioner should be a member of a recognised professional body, or at least have some minimum professional qualification, and that all practitioners should be subject to compulsory bonding to secure the due performance of their obligations. This, it was hoped, would curb the abuses associated in the past with "cowboy" liquidators, often people with no practical experience or relevant qualifications, who engaged in dubious practices to the detriment of creditors, sometimes in league with the controllers of the defunct company whose irresponsibility (and perhaps fraud) had brought about its collapse.

These proposals were accepted by the Government in its White Paper (paras. 8–11), and the framework for the new professional régime was set up by IA 1985, ss. 1–11, now Pt. XIII of the present Act. Much of its detail, however, has been left to be prescribed in the form of rules: see the Insolvency Practitioners Regulations 1990 (SI 1990 No. 439) (as amended by SI 1993 No. 221), replacing the Insolvency Practitioners Regulations 1986 (SI 1986 No. 1995) (as amended). The law now requires every insolvency practitioner either to be a member of a recognised professional body, or to be personally authorised to act by the Secretary of State (s. 390(2)).

The Committee accepted that some concessionary arrangements would need to be made for established practitioners with substantial experience and a good record who lacked a professional qualification. However, since 1 April 1990, (the date when the 1990 Regulations referred to above came into effect), it has been necessary for persons applying to the Secretary of State for authorisation to have passed the examination set by the Joint Insolvency Examination Board or to have a similar overseas qualification, unless they already hold a current authorisation.

The introduction of professional standards for all insolvency practitioners has allowed some relaxation of the law, e.g. in such matters as the need to obtain the consent of the court before action is taken; and many of the functions which were formerly entrusted only to the official receiver have now been devolved upon private insolvency practitioners.

When the winding-up provisions of IA 1986 were extended to apply to building societies by the Building Societies Act 1986, Pt. XIII was not specifically included. This oversight has now been corrected by CA 1989, s. 211(2)(a). See the general note to Pt. IV, preceding s. 73, above.

RESTRICTIONS ON UNQUALIFIED PERSONS ACTING AS LIQUIDATOR, TRUSTEE IN BANKRUPTCY, ETC.

Section 388 Meaning of "act as insolvency practitioner"

388(1) [Acting as insolvency practitioner re company] A person acts as an insolvency practitioner in relation to a company by acting—

(a) as its liquidator, provisional liquidator, administrator or administrative receiver, or

(b) as supervisor of a voluntary arrangement approved by it under Part I.

388(2) [Acting as insolvency practitioner re individual] A person acts as an insolvency practitioner in relation to an individual by acting—

(a) as his trustee in bankruptcy or interim receiver of his property or as permanent or interim trustee in the sequestration of his estate; or

(b) as trustee under a deed which is a deed of arrangement made for the benefit of his creditors or, in Scotland, a trust deed for his creditors; or

(c) as supervisor of a voluntary arrangement proposed by him and approved under Part VIII; or

(d) in the case of a deceased individual to the administration of whose estate this section applies by virtue of an order under section 421 (application of provisions of this Act to insolvent estates of deceased persons), as administrator of that estate.

388(3) **[Interpretation]** References in this section to an individual include, except in so far as the context otherwise requires, references to a partnership and to any debtor within the meaning of the Bankruptcy (Scotland) Act 1985.

388(4) **[Definitions]** In this section—

"administrative receiver" has the meaning given by section 251 in Part VII;

"company" means a company within the meaning given by section 735(1) of the Companies Act or a company which may be wound up under Part V of this Act (unregistered companies); and

"interim trustee" and **"permanent trustee"** mean the same as in the Bankruptcy (Scotland) Act 1985.

388(5) **[Application]** Nothing in this section applies to anything done by—

(a) the official receiver; or

(b) the Accountant in Bankruptcy (within the meaning of the Bankruptcy (Scotland) Act 1985).

(Former provisions: IA 1985, s. 1(2)–(6))

General note

The first step in establishing the statutory requirement that every insolvency practitioner should be professionally qualified is taken in this section, which defines the phrase "acts as an insolvency practitioner". This is not a *general* definition describing the work or activities of such a practitioner in the abstract, but a *specific* definition of what amounts to acting as an insolvency practitioner *in relation to* a particular company or individual. The Act does not make it an offence to carry on an insolvency practitioner's business without the requisite qualification, but only to act "in relation to" a company or individual when the statutory requirements are not met (s. 389).

An important point to bear in mind is that it is possible to "act as an insolvency practitioner" in relation to a person who is not insolvent – and to do so in breach of the Act will be just as much an offence as in a case of actual insolvency. Thus, the liquidator appointed by a company in a members' voluntary winding up "acts as an insolvency practitioner" even where the company has a large cash surplus and has never been in trading difficulties.

Most of the expressions used in this section are defined or explained either in the section itself or elsewhere in the Act: for reference, see Appendix I.

S. 388(2A), (3)

The following subsection is inserted after subs. (2) and the words "to a partnership and" in subs. (3) are omitted for the purposes of the Insolvent Partnerships Order 1994 (SI 1994 No. 2421) from 1 December 1994 (by art. 15(1) and (2) of the order):

"(2A) A person acts as an insolvency practitioner in relation to an insolvent partnership by acting —

(a) as its liquidator, provisional liquidator or administrator, or

(b) as trustee of the partnership under article 11 of the Insolvent Partnerships Order 1994, or

(c) as supervisor of a voluntary arrangement approved in relation to it under Part I of this Act."

S. 388(4)

A receiver who is not an administrative receiver (i.e. a receiver of less than a "substantial" part of the company's property (ss. 29(2), 251)) is not required to be qualified to act, but certain categories of person are disqualified from acting by ss. 30, 31, 51(3).

For the meaning of "company", see further the note to s. 73(1). On "unregistered companies", see s. 220. An insolvent partnership may be treated as an unregistered company for the purposes of Pt. V: see the note to s. 420.

Part XIII of IA 1986 was extended to apply to the winding up of building societies by CA 1989, s. 211(2)(*a*) with effect from 31 July 1990, thus remedying an omission made when building societies were first made subject to the winding-up provisions by the Building Societies Act 1986.

S. 388(5)

The official receiver, as the holder of a public office, is not required to be qualified to act as an insolvency practitioner. This will include a deputy official receiver (see s. 401).

The present wording of s. 388(5) was substituted by the Bankruptcy (Scotland) Act 1993, s. 11(1) and SI 1993 No. 438 (C.9) (S.49), art. 3 as from 1 April 1993. The subsection formerly read: "Nothing in this section applies to anything done by the official receiver".

Section 389   Acting without qualification an offence

389(1)   [Penalty]   A person who acts as an insolvency practitioner in relation to a company or an individual at a time when he is not qualified to do so is liable to imprisonment or a fine, or to both.

389(2)   [Non-application to official receiver]   This section does not apply to the official receiver or the Accountant in Bankruptcy (within the meaning of the Bankruptcy (Scotland) Act 1985).

(Former provision: IA 1985, s. 1(1))

S. 389(1)

The word "qualified" refers not simply to a professional qualification (which may or may not be required: see s. 390(2)(*b*)), but to a complex set of requirements, some of them specifically related to the company or individual concerned.

On penalties, see s. 430 and Sch. 10.

S. 389(2)

The words "or the Accountant in Bankruptcy (within the meaning of the Bankruptcy (Scotland) Act 1985)" were added to s. 389(2) by the Bankruptcy (Scotland) Act 1993, s. 11(1) and SI 1993 No. 438 (C.9) (S.49), art. 3 as from 1 April 1993.

THE REQUISITE QUALIFICATION,
AND THE MEANS OF OBTAINING IT

Section 390   Persons not qualified to act as insolvency practitioners

390(1)   [Must be individual]   A person who is not an individual is not qualified to act as an insolvency practitioner.

390(2)   [Authorisation necessary]   A person is not qualified to act as an insolvency practitioner at any time unless at that time—

    (a) he is authorised so to act by virtue of membership of a professional body recognised under section 391 below, being permitted so to act by or under the rules of that body, or

452

(b) he holds an authorisation granted by a competent authority under section 393.

390(3)   [Security as condition required]   A person is not qualified to act as an insolvency practitioner in relation to another person at any time unless—

(a) there is in force at that time security or, in Scotland, caution for the proper performance of his functions, and

(b) that security or caution meets the prescribed requirements with respect to his so acting in relation to that other person.

390(4)   [Disqualification]   A person is not qualified to act as an insolvency practitioner at any time if at that time—

(a) he has been adjudged bankrupt or sequestration of his estate has been awarded and (in either case) he has not been discharged,

(b) he is subject to a disqualification order made under the Company Directors Disqualification Act 1986, or

(c) he is a patient within the meaning of Part VII of the Mental Health Act 1983 or section 125(1) of the Mental Health (Scotland) Act 1984.

(Former provisions: IA 1985, ss. 2, 3(1))

General note

As explained above, the Act uses the one term "qualified" with reference both to the general eligibility of the person to act as a practitioner and also to his specific eligibility to act *vis-à-vis* a particular company or individual. This section deals mainly with the general requirement, except for the statement in s. 390(3)(*b*) that the practitioner's bonding obligation must relate to the person or company whose affairs he is administering. However, the subject of "qualification" is further dealt with in subordinate legislation made under s. 419(2)(*b*). Reference should be made to the Insolvency Practitioners Regulations 1990 (SI 1990 No. 439) (as amended by SI 1993 No. 221), which consolidate and replace earlier regulations dating from 1986.

The Insolvency Practitioners Association publishes a *Guide to Professsional Conduct and Ethics*, which sets out guiding principles relating to the conduct of insolvency practitioners in regard to accepting appointment as a trustee or office-holder, etc.

S. 390(1)

The disqualification of corporate bodies is an extension of the prohibition that was applied in the case of a liquidator (CA 1985, s. 634) and still applies to a receiver (not necessarily an administrative receiver): see ss. 30 and 51(3)(*a*), (*c*). An act purportedly done by a corporate receiver has been held to be a nullity: see the note to s. 232.

On the question of joint appointments, see s. 231.

S. 390(2)

The Cork Committee recommended (*Report*, para. 758) that an insolvency practitioner should be required in all cases to be a member of an "approved" professional body and to have been in general practice for five years before being eligible to act. (Transitional arrangements would have allowed experienced individuals who were not professionally qualified to obtain direct authorisation to act from the Secretary of State.) The Government in its White Paper (para. 43) broadly endorsed this view, but in the Insolvency Bill as originally published in 1984 went further, and provided that every insolvency practitioner, whether a member of a profession or not, should be required to hold a certificate issued to him personally by the Secretary of State before he was eligible to act. The legislation in its final form, however, returns to a compromise position: those who are under the supervision of a recognised professional body will be permitted or authorised to act by that body, and will not be directly licensed or controlled by the Secretary of State, while others may be authorised as individuals to act, either by the Secretary of State or by a "competent authority" to which this function may be delegated (s. 392). The "direct licensing" provisions of the Act do not appear, however, to be purely a transitional arrangement as the Cork Committee envisaged.

Schedule 11, para. 21 provides that a person who was already in office (e.g. as a liquidator) when the Act came into force may continue to discharge the functions of that particular office, and so complete the liquidation, etc., without the need for acquiring a qualification under s. 390 (2) or (3).

S. 390(3)

This subsection provides for the bonding of insolvency practitioners, which is now a mandatory requirement for all office-holders. Under the former law, security had to be given only in the case of a liquidator or receiver appointed by the court. The security may be provided either generally or specially for a particular insolvency, and provides a safeguard for creditors and other interested persons who may suffer loss as a result of breach of duty by the insolvency practitioner. The maximum amount for which any bond must be given is £5 million: see the Insolvency Practitioners Regulations 1990 (SI 1990 No. 439, Sch. 2).

On the question of transitional provisions for persons holding office when the Act came into force, see the note to s. 390(2) above.

S. 390(4)

If a person comes under any of the disabilities mentioned, his disqualification is automatic, and does not depend upon the withdrawal of his authorisation under s. 393. Acts done by a disqualified person may, however, be valid by virtue of s. 232: see the note to that section.

Section 391   Recognised professional bodies

391(1)   [Order by Secretary of State]   The Secretary of State may by order declare a body which appears to him to fall within subsection (2) below to be a recognised professional body for the purposes of this section.

391(2)   [Bodies recognised]   A body may be recognised if it regulates the practice of a profession and maintains and enforces rules for securing that such of its members as are permitted by or under the rules to act as insolvency practitioners—

(a) are fit and proper persons so to act, and

(b) meet acceptable requirements as to education and practical training and experience.

391(3)   [Interpretation]   References to members of a recognised professional body are to persons who, whether members of that body or not, are subject to its rules in the practice of the profession in question.

The reference in section 390(2) above to membership of a professional body recognised under this section is to be read accordingly.

391(4)   [Revocation of order]   An order made under subsection (1) in relation to a professional body may be revoked by a further order if it appears to the Secretary of State that the body no longer falls within subsection (2).

391(5)   [Effect of order]   An order of the Secretary of State under this section has effect from such date as is specified in the order; and any such order revoking a previous order may make provision whereby members of the body in question continue to be treated as authorised to act as insolvency practitioners for a specified period after the revocation takes effect.

(Former provisions: IA 1985, s. 3(2)–(5))

General note

The Government White Paper, para. 43, stated that under the proposed new legislation a person would only be capable of acting as an insolvency practitioner if he was "a practising solicitor or member of an approved accountancy body", unless he was directly authorised by the Secretary of State. This section provides the machinery for "recognising" professional bodies (not necessarily only solicitors and accountants) whose members will be authorised to act as insolvency practitioners under s. 390(2)(*a*), and also for the withdrawal of such recognition.

S. 391(1)

The relevant order is the Insolvency Practitioners (Recognised Professional Bodies) Order 1986 (SI 1986 No. 1764) under which the following bodies are recognised:

- The Chartered Association of Certified Accountants,
- The Institute of Chartered Accountants in England and Wales,
- The Institute of Chartered Accountants of Scotland,
- The Institute of Chartered Accountants in Ireland,
- The Insolvency Practitioners Association,
- The Law Society of Scotland,
- The Law Society.

S. 391(2)

Membership of the professional body will not in itself be sufficient (nor, in some cases, even necessary: see s. 391(3)): the person must be specifically permitted by the rules of the body to act as an insolvency practitioner. This will enable the professional body to restrict eligibility to those of its members who are able to satisfy prescribed requirements as to examinations and practical experience.

S. 391(3)

Persons who are subject to the rules of a professional body without having the full status and privileges of "membership" may be authorised under this section.

S. 391(4)

The only power specifically conferred on the Secretary of State is to withdraw recognition from the body concerned. He is not given power to exercise detailed control over the activities of the professional body or to give it directions about the way it conducts its affairs. Nevertheless, the fact that the ultimate sanction of revocation is in his hands will enable him to ensure that a body is kept up to the mark in such matters as, e.g. the enforcement of its disciplinary rules. This is important, because neither the Secretary of State nor the Tribunal established under s. 396 has direct jurisdiction over an individual member of a recognised professional body, or power to revoke his authorisation.

S. 391(5)

The period of grace which the Secretary of State may allow will enable some liquidations, etc., to be completed by the existing office-holder. It will also give the individual insolvency practitioners affected by the order time to apply for direct authorisation under s. 392, or seek to become a member of another professional body.

Section 392   Authorisation by competent authority

392(1)   [Application]   Application may be made to a competent authority for authorisation to act as an insolvency practitioner.

392(2) **[Competent authorities]** The competent authorities for this purpose are—

    (a) in relation to a case of any description specified in directions given by the Secretary of State, the body or person so specified in relation to cases of that description, and

    (b) in relation to a case not falling within paragraph (a), the Secretary of State.

392(3) **[Application]** The application—

    (a) shall be made in such manner as the competent authority may direct,

    (b) shall contain or be accompanied by such information as that authority may reasonably require for the purpose of determining the application, and

    (c) shall be accompanied by the prescribed fee;

and the authority may direct that notice of the making of the application shall be published in such manner as may be specified in the direction.

392(4) **[Additional information]** At any time after receiving the application and before determining it the authority may require the applicant to furnish additional information.

392(5) **[Requirements may differ]** Directions and requirements given or imposed under subsection (3) or (4) may differ as between different applications.

392(6) **[Forms]** Any information to be furnished to the competent authority under this section shall, if it so requires, be in such form or verified in such manner as it may specify.

392(7) **[Withdrawal of application]** An application may be withdrawn before it is granted or refused.

392(8) **[Sums received]** Any sums received under this section by a competent authority other than the Secretary of State may be retained by the authority; and any sums so received by the Secretary of State shall be paid into the Consolidated Fund.

(Former provisions: IA 1985, ss. 4, 11 (part))

S. 392(1)

Most insolvency practitioners will become qualified to act by being members of a recognised professional body under s. 391. However, these professions do not have a monopoly over insolvency work. The present section allows any individual to obtain authorisation personally, either from the Secretary of State or from a "competent authority" which may be designated to discharge this function. A person who is a member of a recognised professional body is not excluded from seeking direct authorisation under this section rather than authorisation from that body.

    For the regulations relating to applications for authorisation under these provisions: see the Insolvency Practitioners Regulations 1990 (SI 1990 No. 439) (as amended) which superseded SI 1986 No. 1995 (as amended).

S. 392(2)

The Secretary of State is himself a "competent authority" and will always have a residuary power to deal with cases not specified under para. (*a*), and also during times when no alternative competent authority exists.

    No competent authority has been specified in directions given under this section, and so for the time being the only competent authority is the Secretary of State.

S. 392(3)–(7)

"Directions" relating to applications do not take the form of legislation but are made by the competent authority itself, i.e. at present, the Secretary of State.

The fee to accompany an application has been prescribed at £200, unless the applicant already holds an authorisation, in which case it is £100 (SI 1990 No. 439, reg. 9).

S. 392(8)

This provision will enable an authority other than the Secretary of State to be wholly or partly self-funded.

Section 393   Grant, refusal and withdrawal of authorisation

393(1)   [Power to grant, refuse application]   The competent authority may, on an application duly made in accordance with section 392 and after being furnished with all such information as it may require under that section, grant or refuse the application.

393(2)   [Granting application]   The authority shall grant the application if it appears to it from the information furnished by the applicant and having regard to such other information, if any, as it may have—

(a) that the applicant is a fit and proper person to act as an insolvency practitioner, and

(b) that the applicant meets the prescribed requirements with respect to education and practical training and experience.

393(3)   [Duration of authorisation]   An authorisation granted under this section, if not previously withdrawn, continues in force for such period not exceeding the prescribed maximum as may be specified in the authorisation.

393(4)   [Withdrawal of authorisation]   An authorisation so granted may be withdrawn by the competent authority if it appears to it—

(a) that the holder of the authorisation is no longer a fit and proper person to act as an insolvency practitioner, or

(b) without prejudice to paragraph (a), that the holder—

(i) has failed to comply with any provision of this Part or of any regulations made under this Part or Part XV, or

(ii) in purported compliance with any such provision, has furnished the competent authority with false, inaccurate or misleading information.

393(5)   [Withdrawal on request]   An authorisation granted under this section may be withdrawn by the competent authority at the request or with the consent of the holder of the authorisation.

(Former provision: IA 1985, s. 5)

General note

The regulations relating to the grant and refusal of authorisation in force from 1 April 1990 are the Insolvency Practitioners Regulations 1990 (SI 1990 No. 439) (as amended), replacing SI 1986 No. 1995 (as amended).

S. 393(1)

The Secretary of State is the only competent authority for the time being; see the note to s. 392(2).

S. 393(2)

The regulations referred to above set out in some detail the matters which are to be taken into account in determining whether an applicant is a fit and proper person, ranging from his personal integrity and history as a law-abiding citizen to the adequacy of the systems of control and record-keeping in his business practice: see SI 1990 No. 439, reg. 4.

The same regulations (reg. 5) give details of educational requirements, but these apply only to applicants who were born after 15 December 1951 and do not already hold an authorisation (reg. 5(2)). Practical training and experience is demanded of all applicants: this may be reckoned in a number of ways, but a minimum of five appointments to office within the past five years or 1,000 hours of "higher insolvency work experience" within the same period is stipulated (reg. 8).

S. 393(3)

The regulations referred to fix a maximum period of three years from the date on which authorisation is granted (reg. 10).

S. 393(4)

The procedure for appeal from the withdrawal, or the refusal, of an authorisation is set out in ss. 394–398.

Section 394   Notices

394(1)   **[Notice to applicant re grant]**   Where a competent authority grants an authorisation under section 393, it shall give written notice of that fact to the applicant, specifying the date on which the authorisation takes effect.

394(2)   **[Notice re proposed refusal, withdrawal]**   Where the authority proposes to refuse an application, or to withdraw an authorisation under section 393(4), it shall give the applicant or holder of the authorisation written notice of its intention to do so, setting out particulars of the grounds on which it proposes to act.

394(3)   **[Date to be stated re withdrawal]**   In the case of a proposed withdrawal the notice shall state the date on which it is proposed that the withdrawal should take effect.

394(4)   **[Notice to give details re rights]**   A notice under subsection (2) shall give particulars of the rights exercisable under the next two sections by a person on whom the notice is served.

(Former provision: IA 1985, s. 6)

General note

The Insolvency Act 1985, s. 6, from which s. 394 is derived, was brought into force on 1 July 1986 (SI 1986 No. 840, reg. 3), together with IA 1985, ss. 7–9, on which ss. 395–398 below are based.

S. 394(1)

Without authorisation, the person will not be "qualified" under s. 390(2)(*a*), and will be automatically liable to criminal prosecution under s. 389 if he acts as an insolvency practitioner; but this will not affect any appointment which he already held when the Act came into force: see Sch. 11, para. 21.

S. 394(2)–(4)

It would appear from the repeated use of the word "propose" that a decision to refuse or withdraw an authorisation does not take effect until the applicant or holder is informed of his rights to make representations under s. 395(1) and to refer the matter for consideration to the Insolvency Practitioners Tribunal under s. 396, and given an opportunity to do so. It is submitted that the word "decision" in s. 396(2)(*b*) must mean "provisional decision", to be consistent with this view. There is no indication in s. 394(3) whether the authority is free to specify any date it chooses as the effective date, but it would seem that, to make sense of the scheme of the Act as a whole, the date should be fixed at least 28 days ahead, and the notice should probably state in addition "or such later date as the authority may subsequently fix, if steps are taken by the holder to have the case reconsidered or reviewed under s. 395 or s. 396."

Section 395 Right to make representations

395(1) **[Right exercisable within 14 days]** A person on whom a notice is served under section 394(2) may within 14 days after the date of service make written representations to the competent authority.

395(2) **[Representations to be considered]** The competent authority shall have regard to any representations so made in determining whether to refuse the application or withdraw the authorisation, as the case may be.

(Former provision: IA 1985, s. 7)

General note

Section 7 of IA 1985, from which s. 395 is derived, has been in force since 1 July 1986: see the note to s. 394.

In addition to his right to have the case referred directly to the Tribunal under s. 396, the person affected by a proposed refusal or withdrawal may ask the authority itself to reconsider its decision. This will not prevent him from seeking a review by the Tribunal if he is notified that the authority's earlier decision stands; and indeed he may apparently ask for a reconsideration under the present section and then change his mind and have the matter taken to the Tribunal without waiting for the authority to complete its reconsideration.

Section 396 Reference to Tribunal

396(1) **[Application of Sch. 7]** The Insolvency Practitioners Tribunal (**"the Tribunal"**) continues in being; and the provisions of Schedule 7 apply to it.

396(2) **[Person served with notice]** Where a person is served with a notice under section 394(2), he may—

(a) at any time within 28 days after the date of service of the notice, or

(b) at any time after the making by him of representations under section 395 and before the end of the period of 28 days after the date of the service on him of a notice by the competent authority that the authority does not propose to alter its decision in consequence of the representations, give written notice to the authority requiring the case to be referred to the Tribunal.

396(3) [Reference] Where a requirement is made under subsection (2), then, unless the competent authority—

(a) has decided or decides to grant the application or, as the case may be, not to withdraw the authorisation, and

(b) within 7 days after the date of the making of the requirement, gives written notice of that decision to the person by whom the requirement was made,

it shall refer the case to the Tribunal.

(Former provisions: IA 1985, ss. 8(1), (2), (6), 11 (part))

General note

The sections of IA 1985, from which s. 396 is derived, were brought into force on 1 July 1986: see the note to s. 394.

S. 396(1)

The Insolvency Practitioners Tribunal was established by IA 1985, s. 8(6) to discharge the functions set out in ss. 396, 397 of the present Act. For further discussion, see the note to Sch. 7 and the Insolvency Practitioners Tribunal (Conduct of Investigations) Rules 1986 (SI 1986 No. 952) which continue in force.

S. 396(2)

The present section provides a procedure which is in part alternative to s. 395 and in part supplementary to it. A person who has been notified by an authority that it proposes to refuse his application or withdraw his authorisation may invoke the jurisdiction of the Tribunal *either* (1) immediately and directly, *or* (2) after the authority's own procedure for reconsideration has run its course and the decision adverse to him is confirmed; and it appears that he may also interrupt the latter procedure and have the matter referred to the Tribunal without waiting for a second decision. He must act within 28 days of being notified of the authority's provisional decision (in case (1)) or of its confirmed decision (in case (2)). The case is then referred by the authority itself to the Tribunal for review.

S. 396(3)

On receipt of a notice, the authority has seven days in which to change its mind and notify the person of its revised decision; failing this, it must refer the matter to the Tribunal (though not necessarily within that seven-day period).

Section 397   Action of Tribunal on reference

397(1) [Duties of Tribunal]   On a reference under section 396 the Tribunal shall—

(a) investigate the case, and

(b) make a report to the competent authority stating what would in their opinion be the appropriate decision in the matter and the reasons for that opinion,

and it is the duty of the competent authority to decide the matter accordingly.

397(2)   [Copy of report to applicant]   The Tribunal shall send a copy of the report to the applicant or, as the case may be, the holder of the authorisation; and the competent authority shall serve him with a written notice of the decision made by it in accordance with the report.

397(3)   [Publication of report]   The competent authority may, if he thinks fit, publish the report of the Tribunal.

(Former provision: IA 1985, s. 8(3)–(5))

General note

Section 8 of IA 1985, from which s. 397 is derived, was brought into force on 1 July 1986: see the note to s. 394.

The Tribunal makes its own investigation of the case but does not itself make a decision: instead, it gives directions to the authority (which are binding), supported by its reasons.

The requirement that the Tribunal should give a reasoned ruling plainly contemplates that it is open to a dissatisfied applicant to seek judicial review of a decision.

Section 398   Refusal or withdrawal without reference to Tribunal

398   Where in the case of any proposed refusal or withdrawal of an authorisation either—

(a) the period mentioned in section 396(2)(a) has expired without the making of any requirement under that subsection or of any representations under section 395, or

(b) the competent authority has given a notice such as is mentioned in section 396(2)(b) and the period so mentioned has expired without the making of any such requirement,

the competent authority may give written notice of the refusal or withdrawal to the person concerned in accordance with the proposal in the notice given under section 394(2).

(Former provision: IA 1985, s. 9)

General note

Section 9 of IA 1985, from which s. 398 is derived, came into force on 1 July 1986: see the note to s. 394.

If a person who has been notified under s. 394(2) of a proposal to refuse his application or withdraw his authorisation does not take the appropriate action within 28 days, he cannot prevent the refusal or withdrawal from taking effect. Whether this happens automatically, or whether a written notice must be given, depends upon whether the word "may" is to be read in a permissive or a mandatory sense. The stipulation that the notice shall be written probably indicates the latter: the point will be important only in regard to a withdrawal.

PART XIV — PUBLIC ADMINISTRATION (ENGLAND AND WALES)

OFFICIAL RECEIVERS

Section 399   Appointment, etc. of official receivers

399(1)   [Official receiver]   For the purposes of this Act the official receiver, in relation to any bankruptcy or winding up, is any person who by virtue of the following provisions of this section or section 401 below is authorised to act as the official receiver in relation to that bankruptcy or winding up.

399(2)   [Power of appointment by Secretary of State]   The Secretary of State may (subject to the approval of the Treasury as to numbers) appoint persons to the office of official receiver, and a person appointed to that office (whether under this section or section 70 of the Bankruptcy Act 1914)—

(a) shall be paid out of money provided by Parliament such salary as the Secretary of State may with the concurrence of the Treasury direct,

(b) shall hold office on such other terms and conditions as the Secretary of State may with the concurrence of the Treasury direct, and

(c) may be removed from office by a direction of the Secretary of State.

399(3)   [Attachment to particular court]   Where a person holds the office of official receiver, the Secretary of State shall from time to time attach him either to the High Court or to a county court having jurisdiction for the purposes of the second Group of Parts of this Act.

399(4)   [Person authorised to act as official receiver]   Subject to any directions under subsection (6) below, an official receiver attached to a particular court is the person authorised to act as the official receiver in relation to every bankruptcy or winding up falling within the jurisdiction of that court.

399(5)   [Each court to have official receiver]   The Secretary of State shall ensure that there is, at all times, at least one official receiver attached to the High Court and at least one attached to each county court having jurisdiction for the purposes of the second Group of Parts; but he may attach the same official receiver to two or more different courts.

399(6)   [Directions by Secretary of State]   The Secretary of State may give directions with respect to the disposal of the business of official receivers, and such directions may, in particular—

(a) authorise an official receiver attached to one court to act as the official receiver in relation to any case or description of cases falling within the jurisdiction of another court;

(b) provide, where there is more than one official receiver authorised to act as the official receiver in relation to cases falling within the jurisdiction of any court, for the distribution of their business between or among themselves.

399(7)   [Continuation of official receiver]   A person who at the coming into force of section 222 of the Insolvency Act 1985 (replaced by this section) is an official receiver attached to a court shall continue in office after the coming into force of that section as an official receiver attached to that court under this section.

(Former provisions: IA 1985, s. 222; BA 1914, s. 70)

General note

The Government in its zeal for public expenditure economies originally wanted to remove official receivers from personal insolvency law and to hive off their functions to the private sector – see its *Green Paper on Bankruptcy* (Cmnd 7967, July 1980), para. 8. The outcry that this proposal attracted, not least from the Cork Committee (*Report*, para. 723), was sufficient to force a rethink. The Insolvency Act 1986 retains the rôle of the official receivers in bankruptcy law, although their involvement is now restricted to the more serious cases. For further guidance on official receivers, see IR 1986, Pt. 10 and r. 7.52 (rights of audience).

S. 399(1)

This confirms that official receivers will continue to act both in individual and corporate insolvency cases.

S. 399(2)

The question of appointment, remuneration and tenure is to be determined by the Secretary of State. For the remuneration of the official receiver, see the Insolvency Regulations 1994 (SI 1994 No. 2507), reg. 33.

S. 399(3)–(5)

It is the responsibility of the Secretary of State to attach official receivers to the various courts having insolvency jurisdiction. Every court must have at least one official receiver attached to it, although that court may not be his sole responsibility.

S. 399(6)

This provision authorises the Secretary of State to give directions to facilitate the disposal of business by official receivers.

S. 399(7)

This is a transitional provision designed to ensure continuity.

Section 400   Functions and status of official receivers

400(1)   [Functions]   In addition to any functions conferred on him by this Act, a person holding the office of official receiver shall carry out such other functions as may from time to time be conferred on him by the Secretary of State.

400(2)   [Status]   In the exercise of the functions of his office a person holding the office of official receiver shall act under the general directions of the Secretary of State and shall also be an officer of the court in relation to which he exercises those functions.

400(3)   [Death or ceasing to hold office]   Any property vested in his official capacity in a person holding the office of official receiver shall, on his dying, ceasing to hold office or being otherwise succeeded in relation to the bankruptcy or winding up in question by another official receiver, vest in his successor without any conveyance, assignment or transfer.

(Former provisions: IA 1985, s. 223; BA 1914, ss. 70, 72)

S. 400(1)

The persons holding office as official receivers will have their functions governed either by the 1986 Act or by directions from the Secretary of State.

S. 400(2)

This provision confirms that the Secretary of State has general control over official receivers although, as was the case under BA 1914, s. 70(1), it is emphasised that they are also officers of the court. The effect of this is that any wrongful interference with them will constitute contempt of court.

S. 400(3)

The aim of this provision is to secure continuity of property ownership if an official receiver leaves office prematurely.

Section 401   Deputy official receivers and staff

401(1)   [Deputy official receiver]   The Secretary of State may, if he thinks it expedient to do so in order to facilitate the disposal of the business of the official receiver attached to any court, appoint an officer of his department to act as deputy to that official receiver.

401(2)   [Same status and functions]   Subject to any directions given by the Secretary of State under section 399 or 400, a person appointed to act as deputy to an official receiver has, on such conditions and for such period as may be specified in the terms of his appointment, the same status and functions as the official receiver to whom he is appointed deputy.

   Accordingly, references in this Act (except section 399(1) to (5)) to an official receiver include a person appointed to act as his deputy.

401(3)   [Termination of appointment]   An appointment made under subsection (1) may be terminated at any time by the Secretary of State.

401(4)   [Staff]   The Secretary of State may, subject to the approval of the Treasury as to numbers and remuneration and as to the other terms and conditions of the appointments, appoint officers of his department to assist official receivers in the carrying out of their functions.

(Former provisions: IA 1985, s. 224; BA 1914, s. 71)

S. 401(1)

To facilitate the despatch of business by official receivers, the Secretary of State may appoint deputy official receivers.

   Under BA 1914, s. 71, the deputy could be appointed on application from an official receiver but only for a two-month period at most. The present Act appears to be more flexible on this matter.

S. 401(2), (3)

A deputy enjoys the same status as an official receiver, fulfils the same functions and can be dismissed in the same way by the Secretary of State. References in IA 1986 to official receivers include references to deputies.

S. 401(4)

The Secretary of State may also appoint civil servants from his department to assist official receivers, although the consent of the Treasury must first be obtained.

THE OFFICIAL PETITIONER

Section 402   Official Petitioner

402(1)   [Continuation of officer]   There continues to be an officer known as the Official Petitioner for the purpose of discharging, in relation to cases in which a criminal bankruptcy order is made, the functions assigned to him by or under this Act; and the Director of Public Prosecutions continues, by virtue of his office, to be the Official Petitioner.

402(2)   [Functions]   The functions of the Official Petitioner include the following—

(a) to consider whether, in a case in which a criminal bankruptcy order is made, it is in the public interest that he should himself present a petition under section 264(1)(d) of this Act;

(b) to present such a petition in any case where he determines that it is in the public interest for him to do so;

(c) to make payments, in such cases as he may determine, towards expenses incurred by other persons in connection with proceedings in pursuance of such a petition; and

(d) to exercise, so far as he considers it in the public interest to do so, any of the powers conferred on him by or under this Act.

402(3)   [Discharge of functions on authority]   Any functions of the Official Petitioner may be discharged on his behalf by any person acting with his authority.

402(4)   [Inability]   Neither the Official Petitioner nor any person acting with his authority is liable to any action or proceeding in respect of anything done or omitted to be done in the discharge, or purported discharge, of the functions of the Official Petitioner.

402(5)   ["Criminal bankruptcy order"]   In this section **"criminal bankruptcy order"** means an order under section 39(1) of the Powers of Criminal Courts Act 1973.

(Former provisions: IA 1985, s. 225; Powers of the Criminal Courts Act, 1973 s. 41)

S. 402(1), (3)

This section preserves the post of Official Petitioner which will continue to be held by the Director of Public Prosecutions. The DPP can authorise junior officials to act in his stead.

S. 402(2), (5)

These provisions describe his functions, the most obvious of which is to present a petition under s. 264(1)(*d*) where a criminal bankruptcy order (as defined by s. 402(5)) has been made, although he does have discretion to present petitions in the public interest in other cases.

S. 402(4)

This confers immunity on the Official Petitioner for acts done in the discharge of his duties.
    See also IR 1986, r. 6.230.
    Note prospective amendment: s. 402 is to be repealed by the Criminal Justice Act 1988, s. 170(2) and Sch. 16 as from a day to be appointed; see the note to s. 264.

INSOLVENCY SERVICE FINANCE, ACCOUNTING AND INVESTMENT

Section 403   Insolvency Services Account

403(1)   [Payment into Account]   All money received by the Secretary of State in respect of proceedings under this Act as it applies to England and Wales shall be paid into the Insolvency Services Account kept by the Secretary of State with the Bank of England; and all payments out of money standing to the credit of the Secretary of State in that account shall be made by the Bank of England in such manner as he may direct.

403(2)   [Where excess amount]   Whenever the cash balance standing to the credit of the Insolvency Services Account is in excess of the amount which in the opinion of the Secretary of State is required for the time being to answer demands in respect of bankrupts' estates or companies' estates, the Secretary of State shall—

    (a) notify the excess to the National Debt Commissioners, and

    (b) pay into the Insolvency Services Investment Account (**"the Investment Account"**) kept by the Commissioners with the Bank of England the whole or any part of the excess as the Commissioners may require for investment in accordance with the following provisions of this Part.

403(3)   [Where invested money required]   Whenever any part of the money so invested is, in the opinion of the Secretary of State, required to answer any demand in respect of bankrupts' estates or companies' estates, he shall notify to the National Debt Commissioners the amount so required and the Commissioners—

    (a) shall thereupon repay to the Secretary of State such sum as may be required to the credit of the Insolvency Services Account, and

    (b) for that purpose may direct the sale of such part of the securities in which the money has been invested as may be necessary.

(Former provisions: Insolvency Services (Accounting and Investment Act) 1970, s. 1; IA 1976, s. 3; IA 1985, Sch. 8, para. 28)

S. 403(1)

Fees, etc. collected in England and Wales by the Secretary of State in respect of proceedings under this Act (see ss. 414, 415) are to be paid into the Insolvency Services Account at the Bank of England.

S. 403(2), (3)

These subsections regulate investment of surplus moneys from the above Account in the Investment Account at the Bank of England. See also the Insolvency Regulations 1994 (SI 1994 No. 2507).

Section 404 Investment Account

404 Any money standing to the credit of the Investment Account (including any money received by the National Debt Commissioners by way of interest on or proceeds of any investment under this section) may be invested by the Commissioners, in accordance with such directions as may be given by the Treasury, in any manner for the time being specified in Part II of Schedule 1 to the Trustee Investments Act 1961.

(Former provision: Insolvency Services (Accounting and Investment) Act 1970, s. 2)

General note
This section restricts investment of money placed in the Investment Account under s. 403(2).

Section 405 Application of income in Investment Account; adjustment of balances

405(1) **[Payment of excess into Consolidated Fund]** Where the annual account to be kept by the National Debt Commissioners under section 409 below shows that in the year for which it is made up the gross amount of the interest accrued from the securities standing to the credit of the Investment Account exceeded the aggregate of—

    (a) a sum, to be determined by the Treasury, to provide against the depreciation in the value of the securities, and

    (b) the sums paid into the Insolvency Services Account in pursuance of the next section together with the sums paid in pursuance of that section to the Commissioners of Inland Revenue,

the National Debt Commissioners shall, within 3 months after the account is laid before Parliament, cause the amount of the excess to be paid out of the Investment Account into the Consolidated Fund in such manner as may from time to time be agreed between the Treasury and the Commissioners.

405(2) **[Deficiency into Investment Account]** Where the said annual account shows that in the year for which it is made up the gross amount of interest accrued from the securities standing to the credit of the Investment Account was less than the aggregate mentioned in subsection (1), an amount equal to the deficiency shall, at such times as the Treasury direct, be paid out of the Consolidated Fund into the Investment Account.

405(3) **[If funds in Investment Account insufficient]** If the Investment Account is insufficient to meet its liabilities the Treasury may, on being informed of the insufficiency by the National Debt Commissioners, issue the amount of the deficiency out of the Consolidated Fund and the Treasury shall certify the deficiency to Parliament.

(Former provision: Insolvency Services (Accounting and Investment) Act 1970, s. 3 (as amended by IA 1976, Sch. 2, para. 5))

General note
These provisions provide for the transfer of sums to the Consolidated Fund from the Investment Account and vice versa, where it is appropriate to adjust balances.

Section 406   Interest on money received by liquidators and invested

406 Where under rules made by virtue of paragraph 16 of Schedule 8 to this Act (investment of money received by company liquidators) a company has become entitled to any sum by way of interest, the Secretary of State shall certify that sum and the amount of tax payable on it to the National Debt Commissioners; and the Commissioners shall pay, out of the Investment Account—

(a) into the Insolvency Services Account, the sum so certified less the amount of tax so certified, and

(b) to the Commissioners of Inland Revenue, the amount of tax so certified.

(Former provision: Insolvency Services (Accounting and Investment) Act 1970, s. 4 (as amended by IA 1976, Sch. 2, para. 6 and IA 1985, Sch. 8, para. 17))

General note
Where a liquidator has paid sums into the Insolvency Services Account which have been invested, and these sums have earned interest, s. 406 provides a mechanism for allocating these sums between those entitled, including the Revenue in respect of tax payable on the interest.

Section 407   Unclaimed dividends and undistributed balances

407(1)   [Duty of Secretary of State]   The Secretary of State shall from time to time pay into the Consolidated Fund out of the Insolvency Services Account so much of the sums standing to the credit of that Account as represents—

(a) dividends which were declared before such date as the Treasury may from time to time determine and have not been claimed, and

(b) balances ascertained before that date which are too small to be divided among the persons entitled to them.

407(2)   [Sums to credit of Insolvency Services Account]   For the purposes of this section the sums standing to the credit of the Insolvency Services Account are deemed to include any sums paid out of that Account and represented by any sums or securities standing to the credit of the Investment Account.

407(3)   [Power of Secretary of State]   The Secretary of State may require the National Debt Commissioners to pay out of the Investment Account into the Insolvency Services Account the whole or part of any sum which he is required to pay out of that account under subsection (1); and the Commissioners may direct the sale of such securities standing to the credit of the Investment Account as may be necessary for that purpose.

(Former provision: Insolvency Services (Accounting and Investment) Act 1970, s. 5 (as amended by IA 1976, Sch. 2, para. 7))

General note

This section states that unclaimed dividends, etc. are to be moved periodically by the Secretary of State from the Insolvency Services Account (or the Investment Account, where appropriate) to the Consolidated Fund. Investments in securities may need to be realised to achieve this end.

Section 408   Recourse to Consolidated Fund

408   If, after any repayment due to it from the Investment Account, the Insolvency Services Account is insufficient to meet its liabilities, the Treasury may, on being informed of it by the Secretary of State, issue the amount of the deficiency out of the Consolidated Fund, and the Treasury shall certify the deficiency to Parliament.

(Former provision: Insolvency Services (Accounting and Investment) Act 1970, s. 6 (as amended by IA 1976, Sch. 2, para. 8))

General note

This section provides for the Insolvency Services Account to be bailed out by the Consolidated Fund, if necessary.

Section 409   Annual financial statement and audit

409(1)   [Preparation of statement]   The National Debt Commissioners shall for each year ending on 31st March prepare a statement of the sums credited and debited to the Investment Account in such form and manner as the Treasury may direct and shall transmit it to the Comptroller and Auditor General before the end of November next following the year.

409(2)   [Duty of Secretary of State]   The Secretary of State shall for each year ending 31st March prepare a statement of the sums received or paid by him under section 403 above in such form and manner as the Treasury may direct and shall transmit each statement to the Comptroller and Auditor General before the end of November next following the year.

409(3)   [Additional information]   Every such statement shall include such additional information as the Treasury may direct.

409(4)   [Examination etc. of statement]   The Comptroller and Auditor General shall examine, certify and report on every such statement and shall lay copies of it, and of his report, before Parliament.

(Former provision: Insolvency Services (Accounting and Investment) Act 1970, s. 7 (as amended by IA 1976, Sch. 2, para. 9))

General note

This section lays down a framework for annual financial statements in respect of the Investment Account and the Insolvency Services Account, and the auditing thereof.

SUPPLEMENTARY

Section 410   Extent of this Part

410   This Part of this Act extends to England and Wales only.

(Former provision: Insolvency Services (Accounting and Investment) Act 1970, s. 9(3) (as amended by IA 1976, s. 14(6) and IA 1985, s. 236(3)(i)))

General note

Sections 399–409 do not apply in Scotland, nor in Northern Ireland. This is confirmed by ss. 440 and 441.

PART XV — SUBORDINATE LEGISLATION

GENERAL INSOLVENCY RULES

Section 411   Company insolvency rules

411(1)   **[Rules]**   Rules may be made—

     (a)   in relation to England and Wales, by the Lord Chancellor with the concurrence of the Secretary of State, or

     (b)   in relation to Scotland, by the Secretary of State,

for the purpose of giving effect to Parts I to VII of this Act.

411(2)   **[Contents of rules]**   Without prejudice to the generality of subsection (1), or to any provision of those Parts by virtue of which rules under this section may be made with respect to any matter, rules under this section may contain—

     (a)   any such provision as is specified in Schedule 8 to this Act or corresponds to provision contained immediately before the coming into force of section 106 of the Insolvency Act 1985 in rules made, or having effect as if made, under section 663(1) or (2) of the Companies Act (old winding-up rules), and

     (b)   such incidental, supplemental and transitional provisions as may appear to the Lord Chancellor or, as the case may be, the Secretary of State necessary or expedient.

411(3)   **[Interpretation of Sch. 8]**   In Schedule 8 to this Act **"liquidator"** includes a provisional liquidator; and references above in this section to Parts I to VII of this Act are to be read as including the Companies Act so far as relating to, and to matters connected with or arising out of, the insolvency or winding up of companies.

411(4)   **[Rules by statutory instrument etc.]**   Rules under this section shall be made by statutory instrument subject to annulment in pursuance of a resolution of either House of Parliament.

411(5)   **[Regulations]**   Regulations made by the Secretary of State under a power conferred by rules under this section shall be made by statutory instrument and, after being made, shall be laid before each House of Parliament.

411(6)   [Rules of court]   Nothing in this section prejudices any power to make rules of court.

(Former provision: IA 1985, s. 106)

S. 411(1), (2)

These subsections provide for the making of company insolvency rules which may include, for example, the matters specified in Sch. 8 of this Act, or former corresponding matters. The Insolvency Rules 1986 (SI 1986 No. 1925), as amended, are to be found below, commencing at p. 601 . See also the other rules, regulations and orders listed in the general note to IR 1986, r. 0.1 below, p. 626.

S. 411(3)

This is an interpretation provision, amplifying terms used in Sch. 8 and s. 411(1) and (2).

S. 411(4), (5)

These provisions explain how company insolvency rules and regulations may be made. The regulations are the Insolvency Regulations 1994 (SI 1994 No. 2507).

S. 411(6)

This is a saving provision mirrored by s. 412(5).

Section 412   Individual insolvency rules (England and Wales)

412(1)   [Rules by Lord Chancellor]   The Lord Chancellor may, with the concurrence of the Secretary of State, make rules for the purpose of giving effect to Parts VIII to XI of this Act.

412(2)   [Contents of rules]   Without prejudice to the generality of subsection (1), or to any provision of those Parts by virtue of which rules under this section may be made with respect to any matter, rules under this section may contain—

(a) any such provision as is specified in Schedule 9 to this Act or corresponds to provision contained immediately before the appointed day in rules made under section 132 of the Bankruptcy Act 1914; and

(b) such incidental, supplemental and transitional provisions as may appear to the Lord Chancellor necessary or expedient.

412(3)   [Rules to be made by statutory instrument]   Rules under this section shall be made by statutory instrument subject to annulment in pursuance of a resolution of either House of Parliament.

412(4)   [Regulations]   Regulations made by the Secretary of State under a power conferred by rules under this section shall be made by statutory instrument and, after being made, shall be laid before each House of Parliament.

412(5)   [Rules of court]   Nothing in this section prejudices any power to make rules of court.

(Former provisions: IA 1985, s. 207; BA 1914, s. 132)

S. 412(1), (2)

These subsections give authority to the Lord Chancellor, with the agreement of the Secretary of State, to make new rules which replace the 1952 rules. These are the Insolvency Rules 1986 (SI 1986 No. 1925) (see below, pp. 601 ff.) Schedule 9 of the Act provides guidelines on the matters which may be dealt with by the rules – e.g. rôle of the insolvency courts; notices; registration of voluntary arrangements; rôle of interim receivers and receivers and managers; meetings of creditors; other matters concerned with the administration of the bankrupt's estate; financial provisions; information and records; powers of the court; and miscellaneous and supplementary matters.

S. 412(3), (4)

These provisions govern how the Lord Chancellor may make rules under s. 412 and how the Secretary of State may exercise powers by regulations under the said rules (see the Insolvency Regulations 1994 (SI 1994, No. 2507), operative 24 October 1994, replacing the original Insolvency Regulations 1986 (SI 1986 No. 1994) as amended).

S. 412(5)

The power of the court to make its own rules is not to be prejudiced by this provision.

Section 413   Insolvency Rules Committee

413(1)   **[Continuation of committee]**   The committee established under section 10 of the Insolvency Act 1976 (advisory committee on bankruptcy and winding-up rules) continues to exist for the purpose of being consulted under this section.

413(2)   **[Consultation by Lord Chancellor]**   The Lord Chancellor shall consult the committee before making any rules under section 411 or 412 other than rules which contain a statement that the only provision made by the rules is provision applying rules made under section 411, with or without modifications, for the purposes of provision made by any of sections 23 to 26 of the Water Industry Act 1991 or Schedule 3 to that Act or by any of sections 59 to 65 of, or Schedule 6 or 7 to, the Railways Act 1993.

413(3)   **[Members of committee]**   Subject to the next subsection, the committee shall consist of—

    (a) a judge of the High Court attached to the Chancery Division;

    (b) a circuit judge;

    (c) a registrar in bankruptcy of the High Court;

    (d) the registrar of a county court;

    (e) a practising barrister;

    (f) a practising solicitor; and

    (g) a practising accountant;

and the appointment of any person as a member of the committee shall be made by the Lord Chancellor.

413(4)   **[Additional members]**   The Lord Chancellor may appoint as additional members of the committee any persons appearing to him to have qualifications or experience that would be of value to the committee in considering any matter with which it is concerned.

(Former provisions: IA 1985, s. 226; IA 1976, s. 10)

S. 413(1)

This provides for the continuance of the Insolvency Rules Committee established under IA 1976, s. 10. This is not to be confused with the Insolvency Court Users' Committee set up by the Vice Chancellor, Sir Nicolas Browne-Wilkinson, in April 1987 to advise on improvements to court practices: see *The Times*, 8 April 1987. In *Woodley* v *Woodley (No. 2)* [1994] 1 WLR 1167 Balcombe LJ (at p. 1179D) formally invited the Insolvency Rules Committee to consider whether lump sum payments arising out of matrimonial proceedings should be made provable debts under r. 12.3 of the Insolvency Rules and so restore the pre-1986 position.

S. 413(2)

This Committee must normally be consulted before the Lord Chancellor makes any insolvency rules under s. 411 or bankruptcy rules under s. 412.

The words from "other than rules" were inserted by the Water Act 1989, s. 190(1) and Sch. 25, para. 78(2) as from 1 September 1989 (see Water Act 1989, ss. 4, 194(4) and SI 1989 Nos. 1146 (C. 37) and 1530 (C. 51)) and this wording was in turn modified by Sch. 1 of the Water Consolidation (Consequential Provisions) Act 1991. The further words relating to the Railways Act 1993 were added by Sch. 12, para. 25 to that Act.

S. 413(3), (4)

These provisions regulate the composition of the Committee. Like s. 413(1) and (2) they represent no real change in the law.

FEES ORDERS

Section 414   Fees orders (company insolvency proceedings)

414(1)   [Fees]   There shall be paid in respect of—

    (a) proceedings under any of Parts I to VII of this Act, and

    (b) the performance by the official receiver or the Secretary of State of functions under those Parts,

such fees as the competent authority may with the sanction of the Treasury by order direct.

414(2)   [Security for fees]   That authority is—

    (a) in relation to England and Wales, the Lord Chancellor, and

    (b) in relation to Scotland, the Secretary of State.

414(3)   [Order by Treasury]   The Treasury may by order direct by whom and in what manner the fees are to be collected and accounted for.

414(4)   [Security for fees]   The Lord Chancellor may, with the sanction of the Treasury, by order provide for sums to be deposited, by such persons, in such manner and in such circumstances as may be specified in the order, by way of security for fees payable by virtue of this section.

414(5)   [Incidental matter under order]   An order under this section may contain such incidental, supplemental and transitional provisions as may appear to the Lord Chancellor, the Secretary of State or (as the case may be) the Treasury necessary or expedient.

414(6)   [Order by statutory instrument etc.]   An order under this section shall be made by statutory instrument and, after being made, shall be laid before each House of Parliament.

414(7)   [Payment into Consolidated Fund]   Fees payable by virtue of this section shall be paid into the Consolidated Fund.

414(8)   [Interpretation]   References in subsection (1) to Parts I to VII of this Act are to be read as including the Companies Act so far as relating to, and to matters connected with or arising out of, the insolvency or winding up of companies.

414(9)   [Rules of court, Scotland]   Nothing in this section prejudices any power to make rules of court; and the application of this section to Scotland is without prejudice to section 2 of the Courts of Law Fees (Scotland) Act 1895.

(Former provisions: IA 1985, s. 106(5), 107)

S. 414(1), (2)

These subsections govern the fixing of company insolvency fees in England and Wales, and in Scotland. Note the rôle of the Treasury in such matters. See the Insolvency Fees Order 1986 (SI 1986 No. 2030), as amended by the Insolvency Fees (Amendment) Order 1988 (SI 1988 No. 95), the Insolvency Fees (Amendment) Order 1990 (SI 1990 No. 560 (L. 9), the Insolvency Fees (Amendment) Order 1991 (SI 1991 No. 496), the Insolvency Fees (Amendment) Order 1992 (SI 1992 No. 34) and the Insolvency Fees (Amendment) Order 1994 (SI 1994, No. 2541). See also the County Court Fees (Amendment No. 2) Order 1986 (SI 1986 No. 2143), the Supreme Court Fees (Amendment No. 2) Order 1986 (SI 1986 No. 2144), the Department of Trade and Industry (Fees) Order 1988 (SI 1988 No. 93) and the Supreme Court Fees (Amendment) Order 1994 (SI 1994 No. 3191).

S. 414(3), (7)

These provisions deal with the manner of collection and payment into the Consolidated Fund.

S. 414(4)

Deposits by way of security may also be provided for.

S. 414(5)

This is a safety valve mechanism designed to build flexibility into the system.

S. 414(6)

This describes the parliamentary procedure to be used for orders fixing company insolvency fees.

S. 414(8), (9)

These subsections provide an interpretation facility and a saving mechanism.

Section 415   Fees orders (individual insolvency proceedings in England and Wales)

415(1)   [Payment of fees]   There shall be paid in respect of—
   (a) proceedings under Parts VIII to XI of this Act, and

(b) the performance by the official receiver or the Secretary of State of functions under those Parts,

such fees as the Lord Chancellor may with the sanction of the Treasury by order direct.

415(2) [Order by Treasury] The Treasury may by order direct by whom and in what manner the fees are to be collected and accounted for.

415(3) [Security for fees] The Lord Chancellor may, with the sanction of the Treasury, by order provide for sums to be deposited, by such persons, in such manner and in such circumstances as may be specified in the order, by way of security for—

(a) fees payable by virtue of this section, and

(b) fees payable to any person who has prepared an insolvency practitioner's report under section 274 in Chapter I of Part IX.

415(4) [Incidental provisions etc. of order] An order under this section may contain such incidental, supplemental and transitional provisions as may appear to the Lord Chancellor or, as the case may be, the Treasury, necessary or expedient.

415(5) [Order by statutory instrument etc.] An order under this section shall be made by statutory instrument and, after being made, shall be laid before each House of Parliament.

415(6) [Payment into Consolidated Fund] Fees payable by virtue of this section shall be paid into the Consolidated Fund.

415(7) [Rules of court] Nothing in this section prejudices any power to make rules of court.

(Former provisions: IA 1985, ss. 207(5), 208(1)–(3), (5); BA 1914, s. 133)

S. 415(1)–(3)

These subsections permit the Lord Chancellor, with the assent of the Treasury, to fix fees for bankruptcy proceedings and for tasks carried out by the official receiver or Secretary of State. Deposits which, e.g. represent advance payment of fees may also be similarly prescribed. See the Insolvency Fees Order 1986 (SI 1986 No. 2030), as amended by the Insolvency Fees (Amendment) Order 1988 (SI 1988 No. 95), the Insolvency Fees (Amendment) Order 1990 (SI 1990 No. 560 (L. 9)), the Insolvency Fees (Amendment) Order 1991 (SI 1991 No. 496), the Insolvency Fees (Amendment) Order 1992 (SI 1992 No. 34) and the Insolvency Fees (Amendment) Order 1994 (SI 1994, No. 2541). See also the County Court Fees (Amendment No. 2) Order 1986 (SI 1986 No. 2143), the Supreme Court Fees (Amendment No. 2) Order 1986 (SI 1986 No. 2144), the Department of Trade and Industry (Fees) Order 1988 (SI 1988 No. 93) and the Supreme Court Fees (Amendment) Order 1994 (SI 1994 No. 3191).

For the company law counterpart, see s. 414. For further details, see Sch. 9.

S. 415(4), (5)

These provisions deal with the procedural prerequisites of such an order from the Lord Chancellor and with supplementary matters which may be included therein.

S. 415(6)

Fees collected under this provision are paid into the Consolidated Fund.

S. 415(7)

This preserves the inherent power of the court to make rules of court.

SPECIFICATION, INCREASE AND REDUCTION OF MONEY SUMS
RELEVANT IN THE OPERATION OF THIS ACT

Section 416 Monetary limits (companies winding up)

416(1) [Increase or reduction of certain provisions] The Secretary of State may by order in a statutory instrument increase or reduce any of the money sums for the time being specified in the following provisions in the first Group of Parts—

> section 117(2) (amount of company's share capital determining whether county court has jurisdiction to wind it up);
>
> section 120(3) (the equivalent as respects sheriff court jurisdiction in Scotland);
>
> section 123(1)(a) (minimum debt for service of demand on company by unpaid creditor);
>
> section 184(3) (minimum value of judgment, affecting sheriff's duties on levying execution);
>
> section 206(1)(a) and (b) (minimum value of company property concealed or fraudulently removed, affecting criminal liability of company's officer).

416(2) [Transitional provisions] An order under this section may contain such transitional provisions as may appear to the Secretary of State necessary or expedient.

416(3) [Approval by Parliament] No order under this section increasing or reducing any of the money sums for the time being specified in section 117(2), 120(3) or 123(1)(a) shall be made unless a draft of the order has been laid before and approved by a resolution of each House of Parliament.

416(4) [Annulment of statutory instrument] A statutory instrument containing an order under this section, other than an order to which subsection (3) applies, is subject to annulment in pursuance of a resolution of either House of Parliament.

(Former provision: CA 1985, s. 664 (as amended by IA 1985, Sch 6, para. 49))

S. 416(1)

This provision allows the Secretary of State to use statutory instruments to increase or reduce various figures specified in the First Group of Parts without recourse to primary legislation.

S. 416(2)

The statutory instrument may provide for transitional matters.

S. 416(3), (4)

The basic parliamentary procedure to be used is mapped out by s. 416(4), although this is qualified by s. 416(3) in respect of the variation of certain figures.

Section 417 Money sum in s. 222

417 The Secretary of State may by regulations in a statutory instrument increase or reduce the money sum for the time being specified in section 222(1) (minimum debt for service of demand on unregistered company by unpaid creditor); but such regulations shall not be made unless a draft of the statutory instrument containing them has been approved by resolution of each House of Parliament.

(Former provision: CA 1985, s. 667(2) (part))

General note

This section provides a procedure for modifying the minimum debt for a statutory demand (currently £750).

Section **418**   Monetary limits (bankruptcy)

418(1)   [Powers of Secretary of State]   The Secretary of State may by order prescribe amounts for the purposes of the following provisions in the second Group of Parts—

> section 273 (minimum value of debtor's estate determining whether immediate bankruptcy order should be made; small bankruptcies level);
>
> section 346(3) (minimum amount of judgment, determining whether amount recovered on sale of debtor's goods is to be treated as part of his estate in bankruptcy);
>
> section 354(1) and (2) (minimum amount of concealed debt, or value of property concealed or removed, determining criminal liability under the section);
>
> section 358 (minimum value of property taken by a bankrupt out of England and Wales, determining his criminal liability);
>
> section 360(1) (maximum amount of credit which bankrupt may obtain without disclosure of his status);
>
> section 361(2) (exemption of bankrupt from criminal liability for failure to keep proper accounts, if unsecured debts not more than the prescribed minimum);
>
> section 364(2)(d) (minimum value of goods removed by the bankrupt, determining his liability to arrest);

and references in the second Group of Parts to the amount prescribed for the purposes of any of those provisions, and references in those provisions to the prescribed amount, are to be construed accordingly.

418(2)   [Transitional provisions]   An order under this section may contain such transitional provisions as may appear to the Secretary of State necessary or expedient.

418(3)   [Order by statutory instrument etc.]   An order under this section shall be made by statutory instrument subject to annulment in pursuance of a resolution of either House of Parliament.

(Former provision: IA 1985, s. 209(1)(part), (2), (3))

S. 418(1)

This provision authorises the Secretary of State to fix monetary amounts for a number of provisions in the Second Group of Parts. For example, he can determine the "minimum amount" and the "small bankruptcies level" for the purposes of s. 273, the minimum judgment for s. 364(3), property values for the purposes of s. 354, and so on. This represents a trend away from mentioning specific figures in the statutory provision itself to a more flexible régime suited to coping with inflation.

S. 418(2), (3)

These deal with ancillary matters and the form of any order made by the Secretary of State under s. 418(1).

INSOLVENCY PRACTICE

Section **419**   **Regulations for purposes of Part XIII**

419(1)   [Power to make regulations]   The Secretary of State may make regulations for the purpose of giving effect to Part XIII of this Act; and **"prescribed"** in that Part means prescribed by regulations made by the Secretary of State.

419(2)   [Extent of regulations]   Without prejudice to the generality of subsection (1) or to any provision of that Part by virtue of which regulations may be made with respect to any matter, regulations under this section may contain—

(a) provision as to the matters to be taken into account in determining whether a person is a fit and proper person to act as an insolvency practitioner;

(b) provision prohibiting a person from so acting in prescribed cases, being cases in which a conflict of interest will or may arise;

(c) provision imposing requirements with respect to—

   (i) the preparation and keeping by a person who acts as an insolvency practitioner of prescribed books, accounts and other records, and

   (ii) the production of those books, accounts and records to prescribed persons;

(d) provision conferring power on prescribed persons—

   (i) to require any person who acts or has acted as an insolvency practitioner to answer any inquiry in relation to a case in which he is so acting or has so acted, and

   (ii) to apply to a court to examine such a person or any other person on oath concerning such a case;

(e) provision making non-compliance with any of the regulations a criminal offence; and

(f) such incidental, supplemental and transitional provisions as may appear to the Secretary of State necessary or expedient.

419(3)   [Power exercisable by statutory instrument etc.]   Any power conferred by Part XIII or this Part to make regulations, rules or orders is exercisable by statutory instrument subject to annulment by resolution of either House of Parliament.

419(4)   [Different provisions for different cases]   Any rule or regulation under Part XIII or this Part may make different provision with respect to different cases or descriptions of cases, including different provision for different areas.

478

(Former provisions: IA 1985, ss. 10, 11 (part))

S. 419(1), (2)

This section provides for regulations to be made by the Secretary of State in order to achieve the aims of Pt. XIII (qualification of insolvency practitioners). Examples of the matters which may be provided for are listed. It would perhaps have been more sensible to include these provisions within Pt. XIII itself. For the relevant regulations see the Insolvency Practitioners Regulations 1990 (SI 1990 No. 439) which consolidate and amend earlier regulations with effect from 1 April 1990.

S. 419(3)

This lays down the parliamentary procedure to be used for creating such regulations.

S. 419(4)

This subsection, coupled with the generality of s. 419(1), gives the Secretary of State considerable freedom for manouevre.

OTHER ORDER-MAKING POWERS

Section 420   Insolvent partnerships

420(1)   [Application to insolvent partnerships]   The Lord Chancellor may, by order made with the concurrence of the Secretary of State, provide that such provisions of this Act as may be specified in the order shall apply in relation to insolvent partnerships with such modifications as may be so specified.

420(2)   [Incidental provisions etc.]   An order under this section may make different provision for different cases and may contain such incidental, supplemental and transitional provisions as may appear to the Lord Chancellor necessary or expedient.

420(3)   [Order by statutory instrument etc.]   An order under this section shall be made by statutory instrument subject to annulment in pursuance of a resolution of either House of Parliament.

(Former provision: IA 1985, s. 227)

S. 420(1)

This allows the provisions of the Act to be extended (with suitable modifications) to deal with situations where insolvent partnerships are being wound up or are subject to various other insolvency regimes. The Lord Chancellor originally exercised his power under subs. (1) to make the Insolvent Partnerships Order 1986 (SI 1986 No. 2142), which has been replaced by the Insolvent Partnerships Order 1994 (SI 1994 No. 2421). The 1994 Order provides the details of the necessary procedures with the modified primary legislation being reproduced *in extenso* in the Schedules to the Order. Appropriate forms are also appended. In the case of insolvency orders made before the coming into force of the 1994 Order (1 December 1994) the provisions of the 1986 Order will continue to apply. Transitional matters are dealt with by art. 19 of the 1994 Order.

The 1986 Order replaced the provisions in the Bankruptcy Act 1914 which dealt with insolvent partnerships – e.g., ss. 114, 116, 119 and 127, plus rr. 279–297 of the Bankruptcy Rules 1952. The 1986 Order in turn has been completely replaced by the 1994 Order. There were a number of factors which led to the introduction of the new Order. Amongst these were:

(1) a desire to promote rescue procedures for insolvent partnerships;

(2) the need to enhance the presentation of the relevant provisions to enable practitioners to interpret them more easily;

(3) the necessity of dealing with the problems of conflict between the Act and the 1986 Order as revealed by the case of *Re Marr* [1990] Ch. 773;

(4) the desirability of implementing the recommendations of the Cork Committee on distribution of assets of joint and several estates (see *Report*, paras. 1685–1690);

(5) the attractions of streamlining unnecessary procedures in order to reduce running costs.

For a fuller insight into the motivation leading to the introduction of the 1994 Order, see the Insolvency Service's Consultation Document of November 1992.

Under the 1994 Order a partnership continues to be treated as an unregistered company and therefore the provisions of Pt. V of the Insolvency Act 1986 are made applicable (with necessary modifications). The purpose of the new rules is to facilitate combined insolvency proceedings against both the firm and its members, where the business is insolvent. If the business is solvent, but an individual partner is in financial difficulties, then the general procedures relating to personal and corporate insolvency, as contained in the 1986 Act, must be used instead.

The 1994 Order (in force from 1 December 1994) deals with a number of distinct insolvency situations:

A voluntary arrangement in respect of the firm (Article 4) Full details of how Pt. I of the Act is to be modified to deal with such a case are provided by Sch. 1 to the Order.

A voluntary arrangement in respect of the members of an insolvent partnership (Article 5) This was already a possibility before 1994, but art. 5 clarifies the position (especially where both the firm and the partners are participating in voluntary arrangements).

An administration order in respect of the firm (Article 6) Details of the modus operandi here are found in Sch. 2 to the Order.

The winding up of the partnership firm (Articles 7 and 9) Here, the partnership is treated as an unregistered company with the effect that the procedures contained in Pt. V of the Act relating to the winding up of such companies are made applicable. The main ground for a winding-up petition is that the firm is unable to pay its debts. Such a petition may be presented by a creditor, or by any member of the partnership, where the firm consists of not less than eight partners. Separate provision is made for petitions presented by creditors (art. 7 and Sch. 3) and by members (art. 9 and Sch. 5).

Where the partnership is treated as an unregistered company, its members are treated as directors for the purposes of the Company Directors Disqualification Act 1986 (see art. 16).

The 1994 Order extends the availability of this winding-up procedure to the case of the winding up by creditor's petition of insolvent partnerships where the partnership has a place of business in England or Wales – it is not necessary that the principal place of business be so located. Thus certain overseas partnerships can now be brought within this regime.

Concurrent insolvency proceedings against the firm and individual partners (Articles 8 and 10) Here, it is possible to present consolidated petitions against both the partnership firm and two or more partners in that firm (whether they be individuals or companies). The petitions will be presented to and heard by the same court. The petition against the firm is treated as the principal petition. A creditor can present a petition in such a case on the ground that the partnership is unable to pay its debts. The aim of this procedure is to facilitate the concurrent insolvency regimes – thus normally a single insolvency practitioner will handle the winding up of the firm and the insolvency proceedings against the individual members. A single public examination may be used to kill two birds with one stone. The partnership assets are to be used primarily to settle partnership liabilities; the old bankruptcy rule that the separate estates of the individual partners must first be utilised towards satisfying the claims of their own individual creditors has given way to a system under which creditors of the firm who have not been able to obtain satisfaction out of the firm's assets are entitled to equal treatment in any distribution of the separate estates. Thus the rule in s. 33(6) of the Bankruptcy Act 1914 is abolished and English law is brought into line with Scottish law.

The other main changes introduced by the 1994 Order in this hybrid scenario are as follows:

- this procedure can be used where only *one* of the members (as opposed to the previous requirement of two) is facing insolvency proceedings concurrently with the partnership;
- special amendments are made to s. 271 of the Act to reduce the difficulties encountered in *Re Marr (supra)*;
- procedural changes are made to cut costs (e.g. by removing the requirement for meetings that may be deemed to be unnecessary).

A joint bankruptcy petition covering all of the partners (Article 11) It is possible for all of the partners to petition jointly for their own bankruptcy, or alternatively for some of the partners with the concurrence of the others to do this. In such a case, the trustee acting for the insolvent partners has authority to wind up the partnership firm even though no petition has been presented against it. This form of proceedings can only be initiated by the partners themselves, on the ground that the firm is unable to meet its debts, and it cannot be used if there are corporate partners or partners who dissent from this course of action. Summary administration is now available in appropriate cases.

Winding up an unregistered company where an insolvent partnership is a member (Article 12) Here the insolvent partnership is treated as if it were a corporate member of the unregistered company.

In addition to the above procedural changes the 1994 Order also makes changes, for the purposes of the Order, to ss. 168 and 303 of the Act (supplemental powers of court) and to s. 388 (meaning of "act as insolvency practitioner"): see the notes to those sections.

For a detailed analysis of the original 1986 Order, see R. Gregory, *Bankruptcy of Individuals and Partnerships* (CCH, 1988), Pt. III, and Pennington (1987) 8 Co. Law. 195. Note also *Re Hough* (1990) 6 IL & P 17.

S. 420(2), (3)

These subsections provide for flexibility of application, transitional matters and the procedure by which delegated legislation is to be made under this section.

Section 421   Insolvent estates of deceased persons

421(1) [Order by Lord Chancellor] The Lord Chancellor may, by order made with the concurrence of the Secretary of State, provide that such provisions of this Act as may be specified in the order shall apply to the administration of the insolvent estates of deceased persons with such modifications as may be so specified.

421(2) [Incidental provisions etc.] An order under this section may make different provision for different cases and may contain such incidental, supplemental and transitional provisions as may appear to the Lord Chancellor necessary or expedient.

421(3) [Order by statutory instrument] An order under this section shall be made by statutory instrument subject to annulment in pursuance of a resolution of either House of Parliament.

421(4) [Interpretation] For the purposes of this section the estate of a deceased person is insolvent if, when realised, it will be insufficient to meet in full all the debts and other liabilities to which it is subject.

(Former provisions: IA 1985, s. 228; BA 1914, s. 130)

S. 421(1), (2)

This authorises the Lord Chancellor, with the agreement of the Secretary of State, to extend the provisions of IA 1986 to the insolvent estates of deceased persons, subject to any modifications deemed necessary.

The Bankruptcy Act 1914 laid down considerable detail on the adminstration of estates of deceased insolvents, whereas the present Act clearly leaves much to the rules in delegated legislation – see Sch. 9, para. 19 and the Administration of Insolvent Estates of Deceased Persons Order 1986 (SI 1986 No. 1999).

Orders granted under s. 421 and the 1986 Order are extremely rare. The relationship between the Act, the Order and certain common law presumptions was the subject of judicial comment in *Re Palmer* [1994] 3 WLR 420. Here it was held by the Court of Appeal that the general legal presumption that a judicial act is deemed to have occurred at the earliest moment from the day on which it was done cannot be used to provide an interpretation of the Order that would make it inconsistent with the Act or make the Order ultra vires s. 421. Thus an administration order made by the court in respect of the estate of a deceased insolvent could not by using judicial fictions be deemed to have been made during the lifetime of that person. In so deciding the Court of Appeal rejected the approach adopted by Vinelott J at first instance – see [1993] 3 WLR 877.

S. 421(3)

This describes the modus operandi of such extension.

S. 421(4)

This determines when the estate of a deceased person is insolvent.

Section 422   Recognised banks, etc.

422(1)   [Order by Secretary of State]   The Secretary of State may, by order made with the concurrence of the Treasury and after consultation with the Bank of England, provide that such provisions in the first Group of Parts as may be specified in the order shall apply in relation to authorised institutions and former authorised institutions within the meaning of the Banking Act 1987, with such modifications as may be so specified.

422(2)   [Incidental provisions etc.]   An order under this section may make different provision for different cases and may contain such incidental, supplemental and transitional provisions as may appear to the Secretary of State necessary or expedient.

422(3)   [Order by statutory instrument etc.]   An order under this section shall be made by statutory instrument subject to annulment in pursuance of a resolution of either House of Parliament.

(Former provision: IA 1985, s. 229)

S. 422(1)

In this subsection the words "authorised institutions and former authorised institutions within the meaning of the Banking Act 1987" have been substituted for the former para. (*a*) and (*b*) by the Banking Act 1987, s. 108(1) and Sch. 6, para. 25(2) as from 1 October 1987 (see SI 1987 No. 1664 (C. 50)): the former paras. (*a*) and (*b*) read as follows: "(a) recognised banks and licensed institutions within the meaning of the Banking Act 1979, and (b) institutions to which sections 16 and 18 of that Act apply as if they were licensed institutions.".

This subsection enables the Secretary of State by order to make certain provisions in ss. 1–251 of this Act (which deal with corporate insolvency law) applicable to banks, licensed institutions and bodies treated as such.

See the Banks (Administration Proceedings) Order 1989 (SI 1989 No. 1276), effective 23 August 1989, which provides, *inter alia,* for the participation of the Bank of England and the Deposit Protection Board in administration proceedings involving such institutions.

S. 422(2), (3)
These provisions regulate procedural and transitional matters.

PART XVI — PROVISIONS AGAINST DEBT AVOIDANCE (ENGLAND AND WALES ONLY)

Section 423   Transactions defrauding creditors

423(1)   [Transaction at undervalue]   This section relates to transactions entered into at an undervalue; and a person enters into such a transaction with another person if—

    (a) he makes a gift to the other person or he otherwise enters into a transaction with the other on terms that provide for him to receive no consideration;

    (b) he enters into a transaction with the other in consideration of marriage; or

    (c) he enters into a transaction with the other for a consideration the value of which, in money or money's worth, is significantly less than the value, in money or money's worth, of the consideration provided by himself.

423(2)   [Order by court]   Where a person has entered into such a transaction, the court may, if satisfied under the next subsection, make such order as it thinks fit for—

    (a) restoring the position to what it would have been if the transaction had not been entered into, and

    (b) protecting the interests of persons who are victims of the transaction.

423(3)   [Conditions for court order]   In the case of a person entering into such a transaction, an order shall only be made if the court is satisfied that it was entered into by him for the purpose—

    (a) of putting assets beyond the reach of a person who is making, or may at some time make, a claim against him, or

    (b) of otherwise prejudicing the interests of such a person in relation to the claim which he is making or may make.

423(4) **["The court"]** In this section **"the court"** means the High Court or—

(a) if the person entering into the transaction is an individual, any other court which would have jurisdiction in relation to a bankruptcy petition relating to him;

(b) if that person is a body capable of being wound up under Part IV or V of this Act, any other court having jurisdiction to wind it up.

423(5) **[Interpretation]** In relation to a transaction at an undervalue, references here and below to a victim of the transation are to a person who is, or is capable of being, prejudiced by it; and in the following two sections the person entering into the transaction is referred to as **"the debtor"**.

(Former provisions: IA 1985, s. 212(1), (3), (7)(part); Law of Property Act 1925, s. 172)

General note

The purpose of this section and those immediately following it is to revamp s. 172 of the Law of Property Act 1925, which was used to avoid fraudulent conveyances. The Cork Committee wanted this provision widened, and, in particular, to cover payments of money – see the *Report*, para. 1238. This has been done. There has been a provision along these lines in English law since 1571, and ultimately it can trace its ancestry back to the Paulian action of Roman law. This provision applies to both individuals and companies alike – *Re Shilena Hosiery Co. Ltd* [1980] Ch. 219. The great utility of this provision lies in the fact that no time limit for avoidance is fixed, in contrast with the case of ss. 238, 239 and 339, 340. (For further points of comparison, see the note to s. 238.)

S. 423(1)–(3)

These provisions allow the court to set aside transactions at an undervalue designed to put assets out of reach of creditors. They explain what a transaction at an undervalue is. The definition is similar to that in ss. 238(4) and 339(3). The broad remedy which the court should have in mind is stated in s. 423(2), although the specifics are detailed in s. 425. Section 423(3) makes it clear that the transaction must have been intended to have a prejudicial effect.

Section 423 was the basis of a successful application by a creditor in *Arbuthnot Leasing International Ltd* v *Havelet Leasing Ltd & Ors (No. 2)* [1990] BCC 636. The applicant, A Ltd, had a judgment debt against L Ltd and had obtained a *Mareva* injunction against it. L Ltd had transferred the bulk of its business and assets to an associated company, F Ltd, with the effect that L Ltd exchanged its income stream from that business for an annual management fee and certain payments agreed to be made quarterly in arrears. Scott J ruled that the conditions requisite for relief under s. 423 were satisfied, and made an order reversing the transfer of assets (but without prejudice to the claims of those who had become creditors of F Ltd since the date of the transfer). He also held (i) that an intention on the part of L Ltd's managing director, M, to put assets out of the reach of A Ltd could be consistent with an honest motive on M's part; (ii) that the fact that M had acted on legal advice did not exclude M's having the purpose specified in s. 423(3)(*a*); and (iii) that on the facts the exchange of the assets and income stream for the management fee and quarterly payments in arrears was a transaction at an undervalue.

In *Chohan* v *Saggar* [1992] BCC 306 (on appeal, [1994] BCC 134) it was held that the requirements of subs (3) are satisfied provided the *dominant* purpose of the debtor was to achieve one of the prohibited aims. This analysis sits uneasily alongside the appoach the courts have taken to s. 238 (see above). The mental state of the recipient is not relevant when trying to determine the purpose of the debtor when entering into the transaction – *Moon* v *Franklin* (1990) 6 IL & P 74.

In *Agricultural Mortgage Corporation plc* v *Woodward & Anor* [1994] BCC 688 a transaction falling within s. 423(1)(c) was encountered. Here the Court of Appeal found that a grant of an agricultural tenancy by a farmer to his wife just before the mortgagee of the farm was intending to enforce the security was a transaction at an undervalue and should be set aside. Although a fair market rent had been charged by the husband that rent did not take into account the fact that the wife as tenant could effectively hold the mortgagee to ransom by denying it vacant possession and thus preventing it enforcing its security. Looking at the transaction as a whole the arrangement was designed to defeat the interests of the mortgagee and the wife received real benefits outside the formal tenancy agreement that had not been paid for. For cases falling on the other side of the line see *Menzies* v *National Bank of Kuwait* [1994] BCC 119 and *Pinewood Joinery* v. *Starelm Properties Ltd* [1994] BCC 569.

S. 423(4), (5)

These provisions define "court" and "victim" (see ss. 423(2)(*b*), 424(1)(*a*)–(*c*), 424(2)). The latter term was not used in IA 1985. In *Moon* v *Franklin (supra)* the victims were persons who were suing the debtor for professional negligence. See also *Pinewood Joinery* v *Starelm Properties (supra)*. Section 423 can be invoked by a plaintiff in any part of the High Court provided the claim does not form part of proceedings being conducted in the Bankruptcy Court or the Companies Court – *TSB Bank plc* v *Katz & Anor* [1994] TLR 231.

Section 424   Those who may apply for an order under s. 423

424(1)   [Conditions for s. 423 application]   An application for an order under section 423 shall not be made in relation to a transaction except—

(a) in a case where the debtor has been adjudged bankrupt or is a body corporate which is being wound up or in relation to which an administration order is in force, by the official receiver, by the trustee of the bankrupt's estate or the liquidator or administrator of the body corporate or (with the leave of the court) by a victim of the transaction;

(b) in a case where a victim of the transaction is bound by a voluntary arrangement approved under Part I or Part VIII of this Act, by the supervisor of the voluntary arrangement or by any person who (whether or not so bound) is such a victim; or

(c) in any other case, by a victim of the transaction.

424(2)   [Treatment of application]   An application made under any of the paragraphs of subsection (1) is to be treated as made on behalf of every victim of the transaction.

(Former provision: IA 1985, s. 212(2))

General note

These provisions explain who may make a s. 423 application. If the person entering into the transaction was a company, then it may be challenged under this provision by the liquidator or administrator. If it was an individual, then the official receiver or trustee may bring the proceedings. Supervisors of voluntary arrangements may also apply in certain cases (most avoidance provisions are not available in the cases of a company or individual voluntary arrangement), as may "victims" (for definition see s. 423(5)), who may bring an action either individually or in a representative capacity. See *Moon* v *Franklin* (1990) 6 IL&P 74 for an example of a victim making the application. A creditor of an insolvent company can be a victim – *Re Ayala Holdings Ltd* [1993] BCLC 256. See also *Pinewood Joinery* v. *Starelm Properties Ltd* [1994] BCC 569.

Section 425   Provision which may be made by order under s. 423

425(1) **[Scope of order]** Without prejudice to the generality of section 423, an order made under that section with respect to a transaction may (subject as follows)—

  (a) require any property transferred as part of the transaction to be vested in any person, either absolutely or for the benefit of all the persons on whose behalf the application for the order is treated as made;

  (b) require any property to be so vested if it represents, in any person's hands, the application either of the proceeds of sale of property so transferred or of money so transferred;

  (c) release or discharge (in whole or in part) any security given by the debtor;

  (d) require any person to pay to any other person in respect of benefits received from the debtor such sums as the court may direct;

  (e) provide for any surety or guarantor whose obligations to any person were released or discharged (in whole or in part) under the transaction to be under such new or revived obligations as the court thinks appropriate;

  (f) provide for security to be provided for the discharge of any obligation imposed by or arising under the order, for such an obligation to be charged on any property and for such security or charge to have the same priority as a security or charge released or discharged (in whole or in part) under the transaction.

425(2) **[Limit to order]** An order under section 423 may affect the property of, or impose any obligation on, any person whether or not he is the person with whom the debtor entered into the transaction; but such an order—

  (a) shall not prejudice any interest in property which was acquired from a person other than the debtor and was acquired in good faith, for value and without notice of the relevant circumstances, or prejudice any interest deriving from such an interest, and

  (b) shall not require a person who received a benefit from the transaction in good faith, for value and without notice of the relevant circumstances to pay any sum unless he was a party to the transaction.

425(3) **[Relevant circumstances]** For the purposes of this section the relevant circumstances in relation to a transaction are the circumstances by virtue of which an order under section 423 may be made in respect of the transaction.

425(4) **["Security"]** In this section **"security"** means any mortgage, charge, lien or other security.

(Former provision: IA 1985, s. 212(4)–(6), (7)(part))

S. 425(1)

This gives illustrations of the types of order the court may make under s. 423. This is similar to ss. 241(1) and 342(1), but with the omission of para. (*g*). A declaration was the basis of the relief granted in *Moon* v *Franklin* (1990) 6 IL & P 74. Interim relief may be available – *Aiglon Ltd* v *Gau Shan Co. Ltd* [1993] 1 Lloyd's Rep. 164.

S. 425(2), (3)

Although third party rights may be affected, there is protection for bona fide purchasers, for value and without notice, who have taken without notice of the relevant circumstances, as defined by s. 425(3). The relief granted in *Arbuthnot Leasing International Ltd* v *Havelet Leasing Ltd & Ors (No. 2)* [1990] BCC 636 (see the note to s. 423, above) took the form of an order that the assets improperly transferred should be held on trust for the transferor, but without prejudice to the claims of those who had become creditors of the transferee since the date of the transfer. In *Chohan* v *Saggar* [1994] BCC 134 the Court of Appeal considered the aim of an order under s. 425. Although the order should seek to restore the original pre-transaction position sometimes the need to protect third parties might prevent a complete restoration. Partial invalidation of transactions might therefore be the best answer to the problem of balancing the competing interests of creditors and bona fide third parties.

S. 425(4)

This is an interpretation provision relevant to s. 425(1)(*c*) and (*f*).

PART XVII — MISCELLANEOUS AND GENERAL

Section 426   Co-operation between courts exercising jurisdiction in relation to insolvency

426(1)   [Enforcement in other parts of UK]   An order made by a court in any part of the United Kingdom in the exercise of jurisdiction in relation to insolvency law shall be enforced in any other part of the United Kingdom as if it were made by a court exercising the corresponding jurisdiction in that other part.

426(2)   [Limit to s. 426(1)]   However, without prejudice to the following provisions of this section, nothing in subsection (1) requires a court in any part of the United Kingdom to enforce, in relation to property situated in that part, any order made by a court in any other part of the United Kingdom.

426(3)   [Order by Secretary of State]   The Secretary of State, with the concurrence in relation to property situated in England and Wales of the Lord Chancellor, may by order make provision for securing that a trustee or assignee under the insolvency law of any part of the United Kingdom has, with such modifications as may be specified in the order, the same rights in relation to any property situated in another part of the United Kingdom as he would have in the corresponding circumstances if he were a trustee or assignee under the insolvency law of that other part.

426(4)   [Assistance between courts]   The courts having jurisdiction in relation to insolvency law in any part of the United Kingdom shall assist the courts having the corresponding jurisdiction in any other part of the United Kingdom or any relevant country or territory.

426(5)   [Request under s. 426(4)]   For the purposes of subsection (4) a request made to a court in any part of the United Kingdom by a court in any other part of the United Kingdom or in a relevant country or territory is authority for the court to which the request is made to apply, in relation to any matters specified in the request, the insolvency law which is applicable by either court in relation to comparable matters falling within its jurisdiction.

In exercising its discretion under this subsection, a court shall have regard in particular to the rules of private international law.

426(6)   [Claim by trustee or assignee]   Where a person who is a trustee or assignee under the insolvency law of any part of the United Kingdom claims property situated in any other part of the United Kingdom (whether by virtue of an order under subsection (3) or otherwise), the submission of that claim to the court exercising jurisdiction in relation to insolvency law in that other part shall be treated in the same manner as a request made by a court for the purpose of subsection (4).

426(7)   [Application of Criminal Law Act]   Section 38 of the Criminal Law Act 1977 (execution of warrant of arrest throughout the United Kingdom) applies to a warrant which, in exercise of any jurisdiction in relation to insolvency law, is issued in any part of the United Kingdom for the arrest of a person as it applies to a warrant issued in that part of the United Kingdom for the arrest of a person charged with an offence.

426(8)   [Powers in subordinate legislation]   Without prejudice to any power to make rules of court, any power to make provision by subordinate legislation for the purpose of giving effect in relation to companies or individuals to the insolvency law of any part of the United Kingdom includes power to make provision for the purpose of giving effect in that part to any provision made by or under the preceding provisions of this section.

426(9)   [S. 426(3) order by statutory instrument etc.]   An order under subsection (3) shall be made by statutory instrument subject to annulment in pursuance of a resolution of either House of Parliament.

426(10)   ["Insolvency law"]   In this section **"insolvency law"** means—

   (a) in relation to England and Wales, provision made by or under this Act or sections 6 to 10, 12, 15, 19(c) and 20 (with Schedule 1) of the Company Directors Disqualification Act 1986 and extending to England and Wales;

   (b) in relation to Scotland, provision extending to Scotland and made by or under this Act, sections 6 to 10, 12, 15, 19(c) and 20 (with Schedule 1) of the Company Directors Disqualification Act 1986, Part XVIII of the Companies Act or the Bankrupty (Scotland) Act 1985;

   (c) in relation to Northern Ireland, provision made by or under the Insolvency (Northern Ireland) Order 1989 or Pt. II of the Companies (Northern Ireland) Order 1989;

   (d) in relation to any relevant country or territory, so much of the law of that country or territory as corresponds to provisions falling within any of the foregoing paragraphs;

and references in this subsection to any enactment include, in relation to any time before the coming into force of that enactment the corresponding enactment in force at that time.

426(11)   ["Relevant country or territory"]   In this section **"relevant country or territory"** means—

   (a) any of the Channel Islands or the Isle of Man, or

   (b) any country or territory designated for the purposes of this section by the Secretary of State by order made by statutory instrument.

426(12)   Application to Northern Ireland   In the application of this section to Northern Ireland—

(a) for any reference to the Secretary of State there is substituted a reference to the Department of Economic Development in Northern Ireland;

(b) in subsection (3) for the words "another part of the United Kingdom" and the words "that other part" there is substituted the words "Northern Ireland";

(c) for subsection (9) there is substituted the following subsection—

"(9)   An order made under subsection (3) by the Department of Economic Development in Northern Ireland shall be a statutory rule for the purposes of the Statutory Rules (Northern Ireland) Order 1979 and shall be subject to negative resolution within the meaning of section 41(6) of the Interpretation Act (Northern Ireland) 1954."

(Former provisions: IA 1985, s. 213; BA 1914, ss. 121–123)

General note

The Cork Report, Ch. 49, called for the rationalisation and improvement of co-operation between the insolvency courts in the UK. This section represents a step in that direction.

A number of countries and territories were designated for the purposes of s. 426 by the Co-operation of Insolvency Courts (Designation of Relevant Countries and Territories) Order 1986 (SI No. 2123), effective 29 December 1986. These were: Anguilla, Australia, the Bahamas, Bermuda, Botswana, Canada, Cayman Islands, Falkland Islands, Gibraltar, Hong Kong, the Republic of Ireland, Montserrat, New Zealand, St Helena, Turks and Caicos Islands, Tuvalu and the Virgin Islands. In consequence, the courts of these countries and territories have the right to request assistance in matters of insolvency from courts having jurisdiction in insolvency in any part of the UK.

Subsections (4), (5), (10) and (11) of s. 426 were extended to the Bailiwick of Guernsey by the Insolvency Act 1986 (Guernsey) Order 1989 (SI 1989 No. 2409), with the modifications specified in the Schedule to that Order, as from 1 February 1990. Accordingly, a co-operative insolvency régime is now established between Guernsey (including Alderney and Sark) and the UK.

In relation to the financial markets (see the note on p. 3), the provisions of s. 426 are subject to the limitations set out in CA 1989, s. 183.

S. 426(1), (2)

This allows for general enforcement of court orders throughout the UK, although there are limitations expressed with regard to enforcement of court orders against property in different parts of the UK.

S. 426(3), (9)

Assimilation of the powers of a trustee, etc. in the different UK jurisdictions is provided for here. The Secretary of State may use statutory instruments to do this.

S. 426(4), (5), (11)

The UK courts must on a matter of insolvency law co-operate with each other, and indeed with courts from the Isle of Man, Channel Isles or from any jurisdiction specified by the Secretary of State. These provisions permit the court to offer assistance to courts in other parts of the UK or in other "relevant" countries, as defined in s. 426(11). Such assistance could involve the legal principles of UK insolvency law being applied by the other court, although the rules of private international law must be taken into account in so doing. An order was made under s. 426(4) in the case of *Re Dallhold Estates (UK) Pty Ltd* [1992] BCC 394. Here the courts of Western Australia sought help from the English courts to protect the assets of an Australian company having property in this jurisdiction. Although it seems that it is not possible for the English courts to grant an administration order in respect of a foreign company on their own initiative they can in effect do this if they receive a request under s. 426. Accordingly the administration order was granted. In *Re Bank of Credit and Commerce International SA* [1993] BCC 787 Rattee J held that when faced with a request for assistance (in this case from the Grand Court of the Cayman Islands) the English courts were not restricted to rendering applicable procedural facilities of English law but could also declare principles of substantive English insolvency law applicable in the particular case.

S. 426(6)

This subsection allows trustees, etc. to claim property situated in other parts of the UK by calling on the assistance of the courts where the property is situated.

S. 426(7)

This applies s. 38 of the Criminal Law Act 1977 to warrants for arrest in connection with insolvency law matters.

S. 426(8)

Delegated legislation can be used to achieve the aim of co-operation as contained in s. 426: see the Co-operation of Insolvency Courts (Designation of Relevant Countries and Territories) Order 1986 (SI 1986 No. 2123).

S. 426(10), (11), (12)

These provisions define "insolvency law" and "relevant country or territory" for the purposes of this section and make provision for Northern Ireland. Subsection (10) was amended and subs. (12) added by Sch. 9 of the Insolvency (Northern Ireland) Order 1989 (SI 1989 No. 2045 (NI 19)).

Section 427   Parliamentary disqualification

427(1)   [Disqualification of bankrupt]   Where a court in England and Wales or Northern Ireland adjudges an individual bankrupt or a court in Scotland awards sequestration of an individual's estate, the individual is disqualified—

(a) for sitting or voting in the House of Lords,

(b) for being elected to, or sitting or voting in, the House of Commons, and

(c) for sitting or voting in a committee of either House.

427(2)   [When disqualification ceases]   Where an individual is disqualified under this section, the disqualification ceases—

(a) except where the adjudication is annulled or the award recalled or reduced without the individual having been first discharged, on the discharge of the individual, and

(b) in the excepted case, on the annulment, recall or reduction, as the case may be.

427(3) [Disqualified peer]   No writ of summons shall be issued to any lord of Parliament who is for the time being disqualified under this section for sitting and voting in the House of Lords.

427(4) [Disqualified MP]   Where a member of the House of Commons who is disqualified under this section continues to be so disqualified until the end of the period of 6 months beginning with the day of the adjudication or award, his seat shall be vacated at the end of that period.

427(5) [Certification of s. 427(1) award etc.]   A court which makes an adjudication or award such as is mentioned in subsection (1) in relation to any lord of Parliament or member of the House of Commons shall forthwith certify the adjudication or award to the Speaker of the House of Lords or, as the case may be, to the Speaker of the House of Commons.

427(6) [Further certification after s. 427(5)]   Where a court has certified an adjudication or award to the Speaker of the House of Commons under subsection (5), then immediately after it becomes apparent which of the following certificates is applicable, the court shall certify to the Speaker of the House of Commons—

(a) that the period of 6 months beginning with the day of the adjudication or award has expired without the adjudication or award having been annulled, recalled or reduced, or

(b) that the adjudication or award has been annulled, recalled or reduced before the end of that period.

427(7) [Application of relevant law to peer or MP]   Subject to the preceding provisions of this section, so much of this Act and any other enactment (whenever passed) and of any subordinate legislation (whenever made) as—

(a) makes provision for or in connection with bankruptcy in one or more parts of the United Kingdom, or

(b) makes provision conferring a power of arrest in connection with the winding up or insolvency of companies in one or more parts of the United Kingdom,

applies in relation to persons having privilege of Parliament or peerage as it applies in relation to persons not having such privilege.

(Former provisions: IA 1985, s. 214; BA 1914, ss. 106, 128)

S. 427(1), (2)

Where a person has been adjudged bankrupt in England or Wales or has experienced a similar fate in Scotland or Northern Ireland he is disqualified from both Houses of Parliament until he is discharged or the order is annulled. Similar provision is made for Scotland and Northern Ireland. Local government councillors face a similar bar – Local Government Act 1972, s. 80.

S. 427(3)

A writ of summons must not be issued in respect of any person so disqualified who is a member of the House of Lords.

S. 427(4)
A Member of Parliament who is so disqualified has six months to vacate his seat.

S. 427(5), (6)
Where a court makes a bankruptcy order, etc., the Speaker of the appropriate House of Parliament must be notified. Further, the court must notify the Speaker of the Commons of the elapse of the six-month period mentioned in s. 427(4) or of any annulment in the meantime.

S. 427(7)
This repeats BA 1914, s. 128 by providing that parliamentary privilege does not render a person immune from bankruptcy law.

Section **428**   Exemptions from Restrictive Trade Practices Act

428(1)   [No restrictions under Trade Practices Act]   No restriction in respect of any of the matters specified in the next subsection shall, on or after the appointed day, be regarded as a restriction by virtue of which the Restrictive Trade Practices Act 1976 applies to any agreement (whenever made).

428(2)   [Matters in s. 428(1)]   Those matters are—

(a) the charges to be made, quoted or paid for insolvency services supplied, offered or obtained;

(b) the terms or conditions on or subject to which insolvency services are to be supplied or obtained;

(c) the extent (if any) to which, or the scale (if any) on which, insolvency services are to be made available, supplied or obtained;

(d) the form or manner in which insolvency services are to be made available, supplied or obtained;

(e) the persons or classes of persons for whom or from whom, or the areas or places in or from which, insolvency services are to be made available or supplied or are to be obtained.

428(3)   ["Insolvency services"]   In this section **"insolvency services"** means the services of persons acting as insolvency practitioners or carrying out under the law of Northern Ireland functions corresponding to those mentioned in section 388(1) or (2) in Part XIII, in their capacity as such; and expressions which are also used in the Act of 1976 have the same meaning here as in that Act.

(Former provisions: IA 1985, s. 217(1)–(3))

General note
The effect of these provisions is to exclude agreements relating to fees charged for insolvency services, etc. being made subject to the Restrictive Trade Practices Act 1976, especially Pt. III of that Act. Schedule 14 also adds insolvency services to the list of exempt services described in

Sch. 1 of the Restrictive Trade Practices Act 1976, such as legal services, medical services, accountancy services and many other professional services. This is in accord with the general policy of the Act, and in particular Pt. XIII, which requires insolvency practitioners to be professionals.

Section 429   Disabilities on revocation of administration order against an individual

429(1)   [Application]   The following applies where a person fails to make any payment which he is required to make by virtue of an administration order under Part VI of the County Courts Act 1984.

429(2)   [Power of court]   The court which is administering that person's estate under the order may, if it thinks fit—

(a) revoke the administration order, and

(b) make an order directing that this section and section 12 of the Company Directors Disqualification Act 1986 shall apply to the person for such period, not exceeding 2 years, as may be specified in the order.

429(3)   [Restrictions]   A person to whom this section so applies shall not—

(a) either alone or jointly with another person, obtain credit to the extent of the amount prescribed for the purposes of section 360(1)(a) or more, or

(b) enter into any transaction in the course of or for the purposes of any business in which he is directly or indirectly engaged,

without disclosing to the person from whom he obtains the credit, or (as the case may be) with whom the transaction is entered into, the fact that this section applies to him.

429(4)   [Person obtaining credit]   The reference in subsection (3) to a person obtaining credit includes—

(a) a case where goods are bailed or hired to him under a hire-purchase agreement or agreed to be sold to him under a conditional sale agreement, and

(b) a case where he is paid in advance (whether in money or otherwise) for the supply of goods or services.

429(5)   [Penalty]   A person who contravenes this section is guilty of an offence and liable to imprisonment or a fine, or both.

(Former provisions: IA 1985, s. 221(1), (3)–(5); BA 1976, s. 11)

S. 429(1)

This section applies where a debtor has failed to comply with his obligations under an administration order granted under Pt. VI of the County Courts Act 1984 (as amended by s. 13 of the Courts and Legal Services Act 1990). (Note that this type of administration order, which is granted against an individual, must be distinguished from the new régime established by Pt. II of IA 1986 enabling an administration order to be made against a company which is insolvent or near-insolvent).

S. 429(2)–(4)

The court has discretion to revoke the administration order and instead apply the following restrictions for a maximum period of two years. Prior to IA 1985 there was a similar provision in IA 1976, s. 11, allowing for the revocation of administration orders and substitution of receiving orders. The new restrictions are more flexible.

The restrictions that may be imposed by the court where an administration order is revoked are then outlined. Thus, the debtor can be banned from acting as company director, liquidator or promoter, etc. (see CDDA 1986, s. 12(2)). Furthermore, he can be made subject to restrictions which are similar to the s. 360 curbs – e.g., restrictions on obtaining credit (widely defined by s. 429(4)) or, indeed, entering into business transactions without disclosing his true status. The Cork Committee (*Report*, para. 317) was in favour of such restrictions.

S. 429(5)

The sanctions for the breach of this provision are the same as for contravening s. 360 – see s. 430, and Sch. 10.

Section **430** Provision introducing Schedule of punishments

430(1) **[Sch. 10]** Schedule 10 to this Act has effect with respect to the way in which offences under this Act are punishable on conviction.

430(2) **[First, second and third columns of Schedule]** In relation to an offence under a provision of this Act specified in the first column of the Schedule (the general nature of the offence being described in the second column), the third column shows whether the offence is punishable on conviction on indictment, or on summary conviction, or either in the one way or the other.

430(3) **[Fourth column]** The fourth column of the Schedule shows, in relation to an offence, the maximum punishment by way of fine or imprisonment under this Act which may be imposed on a person convicted of the offence in the way specified in relation to it in the third column (that is to say, on indictment or summarily), a reference to a period of years or months being to a term of imprisonment of that duration.

430(4) **[Fifth column]** The fifth column shows (in relation to an offence for which there is an entry in that column) that a person convicted of the offence after continued contravention is liable to a daily default fine; that is to say, he is liable on a second or subsequent conviction of the offence to the fine specified in that column for each day on which the contravention is continued (instead of the penalty specified for the offence in the fourth column of the Schedule).

430(5) **["Officer who is in default"]** For the purpose of any enactment in this Act whereby an officer of a company who is in default is liable to a fine or penalty, the expression **"officer who is in default"** means any officer of the company who knowingly and wilfully authorises or permits the default, refusal or contravention mentioned in the enactment.

(Former provision: CA 1985, s. 730)

S. 430(1)

This directs the reader to Sch. 10 for a comprehensive list of punishments for offences created by the Act. For offences under the rules and their punishment see IR 1986, r. 12.21 and Sch. 5.

S. 430(2)–(4)

These subsections provide a guide to the use of Sch. 10. This schedule is similar in form to CA 1985, Sch. 24.

S. 430(5)

This defines the common phrase "officer who is in default" in the same terms as CA 1985, s. 730(5).

Section 431   Summary proceedings

431(1)   [Taking of summary proceedings]   Summary proceedings for any offence under any of Parts I to VII of this Act may (without prejudice to any jurisdiction exercisable apart from this subsection) be taken against a body corporate at any place at which the body has a place of business, and against any other person at any place at which he is for the time being.

431(2)   [Time for laying information]   Notwithstanding anything in section 127(1) of the Magistrates' Courts Act 1980, an information relating to such an offence which is triable by a magistrates' court in England and Wales may be so tried if it is laid at any time within 3 years after the commission of the offence and within 12 months after the date on which evidence sufficient in the opinion of the Director of Public Prosecutions or the Secretary of State (as the case may be) to justify the proceedings comes to his knowledge.

431(3)   [Time for commencement of summary proceedings in Scotland]   Summary proceedings in Scotland for such an offence shall not be commenced after the expiration of 3 years from the commission of the offence.

Subject to this (and notwithstanding anything in section 331 of the Criminal Procedure (Scotland) Act 1975), such proceedings may (in Scotland) be commenced at any time within 12 months after the date on which evidence sufficient in the Lord Advocate's opinion to justify the proceedings came to his knowledge or, where such evidence was reported to him by the Secretary of State, within 12 months after the date on which it came to the knowledge of the latter; and subsection (3) of that section applies for the purpose of this subsection as it applies for the purpose of that section.

431(4)   [Certificate by DPP et al. conclusive evidence]   For the purposes of this section, a certificate of the Director of Public Prosecutions, the Lord Advocate or the Secretary of State (as the case may be) as to the date on which such evidence as is referred to above came to his knowledge is conclusive evidence.

(Former provision: CA 1985, s. 731 (as amended by IA 1985, s. 108(1)))

S. 431(1), (2), (4)

These subsections regulate summary proceedings under this Act in England and Wales. The phrase "a place of business" is much wider than "an established place of business", which is the formula used in CA 1985, s. 409, for example.

S. 431(3), (4)

Summary proceedings in Scotland are provided for.

Section 432   Offences by bodies corporate

432(1)   [Application]   This section applies to offences under this Act other than those excepted by subsection (4).

432(2)   [Consent or connivance of various persons]   Where a body corporate is guilty of an offence to which this section applies and the offence is proved to have been committed with the consent or connivance of, or to be attributable to any neglect on the part of, any director, manager, secretary or other similar officer of the body corporate or any person who was purporting to act in any such capacity he, as well as the body corporate, is guilty of the offence and liable to be proceeded against and punished accordingly.

432(3)   [Where affairs managed by members]   Where the affairs of a body corporate are managed by its members, subsection (2) applies in relation to the acts and defaults of a member in connection with his functions of management as if he were a director of the body corporate.

432(4)   [Offences excepted]   The offences excepted from this section are those under sections 30, 39, 51, 53, 54, 62, 64, 66, 85, 89, 164, 188, 201, 206, 207, 208, 209, 210 and 211.

(Former provision: IA 1985, s. 230)

S. 432(1)–(3)

Here there is a repetition of CA 1985, s. 733. Where an offence under this Act has been committed by a body corporate, any officer who was a party to or responsible for the offence is subject to criminal liability, as well as the body corporate. *De facto* officers are similarly liable. "Body corporate" is not defined for the purposes of this Part of IA 1986; the definition contained in CA 1985, s. 740 applies only to Pts. I–VII (see s. 251). It is therefore likely that a Scottish firm and a foreign corporation would be within the scope of this provision, even though they are not within s. 740.

S. 432(3)

Some corporations, and in particular some incorporated by Royal Charter, have no body equivalent to a board of directors and are managed by their members. This is also true of a Scottish firm, if it is within the present provision. In such cases the members may incur personal liability under this section.

S. 432(4)

Offences under certain named sections of the Act are excluded from the operation of s. 432.

Section 433   Admissibility in evidence of statements of affairs, etc.

433   In any proceedings (whether or not under this Act)—

   (a) a statement of affairs prepared for the purposes of any provision of this Act which is derived from the Insolvency Act 1985, and

   (b) any other statement made in pursuance of a requirement imposed by or under any such provision or by or under rules made under this Act,

may be used in evidence against any person making or concurring in making the statement.

(Former provision: IA 1985, s. 231)

General note

This section declares that any statement of affairs prepared for the purposes of this Act (e.g. under ss. 66, 131, or 288), or other statement required by the Act, may be used in evidence against the person making it or against someone who concurred in the making of it. Thus in *R* v *Kansal* [1993] QB 244; [1992] BCC 615 the Court of Appeal held that statements made by the bankrupt in his public examination could be used against him in a prosecution for theft. The wide language used in s. 433 was not to be limited by the restrictions imposed by s. 31 of the Theft Act 1968. See also *Hamilton & Anor* v *Naviede & Anor; Re Arrows Ltd (No. 4)* [1994] BCC 641.

Section 434   Crown application

434   For the avoidance of doubt it is hereby declared that provisions of this Act which derive from the Insolvency Act 1985 bind the Crown so far as affecting or relating to the following matters, namely—

(a) remedies against, or against the property of, companies or individuals;

(b) priorities of debts;

(c) transactions at an undervalue or preferences;

(d) voluntary arrangements approved under Part I or Part VIII, and

(e) discharge from bankruptcy.

(Former provisions: IA 1985, s. 234; BA 1914, s. 151)

General note

This section makes it clear that specified provisions of the Act, whether they relate to companies or individuals, bind the Crown. Indeed, certain sections are specifically designed to take away Crown privileges – e.g., s. 386 and Sch. 6.

PART XVIII — INTERPRETATION

Section 435   Meaning of "associate"

435(1)   [Determination of whether associate]   For the purposes of this Act any question whether a person is an associate of another person is to be determined in accordance with the following provisions of this section (any provision that a person is an associate of another person being taken to mean that they are associates of each other).

435(2)   [Associate of individual]   A person is an associate of an individual if that person is the individual's husband or wife, or is a relative, or the husband or wife of a relative, of the individual or of the individual's husband or wife.

435(3)   [Associate of partner]   A person is an associate of any person with whom he is in partership, and of the husband or wife or a relative of any individual with whom he is in partnership; and a Scottish firm is an associate of any person who is a member of the firm.

435(4)   [Associate of employee, employer]   A person is an associate of any person whom he employs or by whom he is employed.

435(5)   **[Associate of trustee]**   A person in his capacity as trustee of a trust other than—

- (a) a trust arising under any of the second Group of Parts or the Bankruptcy (Scotland) Act 1985, or
- (b) a pension scheme or an employees' share scheme (within the meaning of the Companies Act),

is an associate of another person if the beneficiaries of the trust include, or the terms of the trust confer a power that may be exercised for the benefit of, that other person or an associate of that other person.

435(6)   **[Company associate of another company]**   A company is an associate of another company—

- (a) if the same person has control of both, or a person has control of one and persons who are his associates, or he and persons who are his associates, have control of the other, or
- (b) if a group of two or more persons has control of each company, and the groups either consist of the same persons or could be regarded as consisting of the same persons by treating (in one or more cases) a member of either group as replaced by a person of whom he is an associate.

435(7)   **[Company associate of another person]**   A company is an associate of another person if that person has control of it or if that person and persons who are his associates together have control of it.

435(8)   **[Person relative of individual]**   For the purposes of this section a person is a relative of an individual if he is that individual's brother, sister, uncle, aunt, nephew, niece, lineal ancestor or lineal descendant, treating—

- (a) any relationship of the half blood as a relationship of the whole blood and the stepchild or adopted child of any person as his child, and
- (b) an illegitimate child as the legitimate child of his mother and reputed father;

and references in this section to a husband or wife include a former husband or wife and a reputed husband or wife.

435(9)   **[Director employee]**   For the purposes of this section any director or other officer of a company is to be treated as employed by that company.

435(10)   **[Person with control]**   For the purposes of this section a person is to be taken as having control of a company if—

- (a) the directors of the company or of another company which has control of it (or any of them) are accustomed to act in accordance with his directions or instructions, or
- (b) he is entitled to exercise, or control the exercise of, one third or more of the voting power at any general meeting of the company or of another company which has control of it;

and where two or more persons together satisfy either of the above conditions, they are to be taken as having control of the company.

435(11)   **["Company"]**   In this section **"company"** includes any body corporate (whether incorporated in Great Britain or elsewhere); and references to directors and other officers of a company and to voting power at any general meeting of a company have effect with any necessary modifications.

(Former provision: IA 1985, s. 233)

S. 435(1)

This is a new and complex provision defining the word "associate" for the purposes of the Act. It will be particularly relevant to ss. 314(6) and 340(5), and to the definition of "connected person" (s. 249), a term extensively used in Pts. I–VII.

S. 435(2), (8)

Close family connections are sufficient to make one person an associate of another.

S. 435(3)

Partnership links with an individual, or his close family, are sufficient to give rise to an "associate" relationship.

S. 435(4)

Employers and employees are associates. However, see s. 239(6), 240(1)(*a*), 340(5).

S. 435(5)

Certain trust relationships are caught by the net, where the insolvent or his or its associates could benefit from the trust.

S. 435(6), (7), (9)–(11)

These deal with the concept of "associate" in relation to companies (including companies incorporated outside Great Britain: see s. 435(11)). A company can become an associate if it is controlled by the person in question or by his associate. Control can be determined by reference to a third of voting power at shareholders' meetings or by whether the directors normally act in accordance with his instructions. Directors and officers are to be treated as being employed by their companies – this will be relevant in connection with s. 435(4).

Section 436   Expressions used generally

436 In this Act, except in so far as the context otherwise requires (and subject to Parts VII and XI)—

> **"the appointed day"** means the day on which this Act comes into force under section 443;

> **"associate"** has the meaning given by section 435;

> **"business"** includes a trade or profession;

> **"the Companies Act"** means the Companies Act 1985;

> **"conditional sale agreement"** and **"hire-purchase agreement"** have the same meanings as in the Consumer Credit Act 1974;

> **"modifications"** includes additions, alterations and omissions and cognate expressions shall be construed accordingly;

> **"property"** includes money, goods, things in action, land and every description

of property wherever situated and also obligations and every description of interest, whether present or future or vested or contingent, arising out of, or incidental to, property;

"records" includes computer records and other non-documentary records;

"subordinate legislation" has the same meaning as in the Interpretation Act 1978; and

"transaction" includes a gift, agreement or arrangement, and references to entering into a transaction shall be construed accordingly.

(Former provision: IA 1985, s. 232(part))

General note

This is general interpretation provision for the Act. It should be read in the light of Pts. VII, XI and s. 435. Note that the general meaning given to words by s. 436 can be excluded where the context demands this.

The "appointed day" was 29 December 1986: see the note to s. 443.

A company's interest as lessee under a lease of a chattel (an aircraft) was held to be "property" within the statutory definition contained in this section in *Bristol Airport plc & Anor* v *Powdrill & Ors; Re Paramount Airways Ltd* [1990] Ch. 744; [1990] BCC 130.

PART XIX — FINAL PROVISIONS

Section 437   Transitional provisions and savings

437 The transitional provisions and savings set out in Schedule 11 to this Act shall have effect, the Schedule comprising the following Parts—

Part I: company insolvency and winding up (matters arising before appointed day, and continuance of proceedings in certain cases as before that day);

Part II: individual insolvency (matters so arising, and continuance of bankruptcy proceedings in certain cases as before that day);

Part III: transactions entered into before the appointed day and capable of being affected by orders of the court under Part XVI of this Act;

Part IV: insolvency practitioners acting as such before the appointed day; and

Part V: general transitional provisions and savings required consequentially on, and in connection with, the repeal and replacement by this Act and the Company Directors Disqualification Act 1986 of provisions of the Companies Act, the greater part of the Insolvency Act 1985 and other enactments.

(Former provision: IA 1985, s. 235 (2))

General note

This, coupled with Sch. 11, makes transitional provisions and savings.

The significant transitional provisions have been noted at the relevant places in the text.

Section 438   Repeals

438 The enactments specified in the second column of Schedule 12 to this Act are repealed to the extent specified in the third column of that Schedule.

(Former provision: none)

General note

This section refers the reader to Sch. 12, which lists the provisions repealed by IA 1986. Included amongst the repeals are a large number of provisions in CA 1985, plus virtually the entirety of IA 1985. See also Sch. 4 of CDDA 1986. Notable survivors in IA 1985 included ss. 218 and 220 discussed in turn below:

IA 1985, s. 218

This substantially amends s. 122 of the Employment Protection (Consolidation) Act 1978, which relates to claims out of the Redundancy Fund by employees of insolvent employers. Claims will only be permitted if the employment has been terminated. Statutory sick pay is now treated as arrears of pay.

IA 1985, s. 220

This amends s. 112(4)(*b*) of the County Courts Act 1984 by increasing to £1,500 the minimum debt which must be owed to a creditor before he may present a bankruptcy petition against a debtor who is the subject of an administration order. The effect of the change is understandable: it makes it more difficult for an impatient creditor to frustrate an administration order scheme. Note that this administration order regime was substantially amended by s. 13 of the Courts and Legal Services Act 1990.

This provision also amends s. 115 of the County Courts Act 1984, by increasing the minimum amount of the debtor's property from £10 to £50, or such amount as the Lord Chancellor may prescribe. Section 115 relates to execution against the property of a debtor who is subject to an administration order.

Section 220 makes fairly modest changes in the system of administration orders against insolvent judgment debtors, a system now governed by the County Courts Act 1984, ss. 112–117 (as amended by the Courts and Legal Services Act 1990). Such orders are not to be confused with administration orders against companies made under Pt. II of IA 1986. The Cork Committee (*Report*, paras. 289, 295) wanted the procedure extended to cover debts other than judgment debts, and also to allow creditors, as well as the judgment debtor, to apply to the court for such an order (instead of the position at the moment, where only the judgment debtor can apply). Neither change has been implemented.

Section 439   Amendment of enactments

439(1)   [Amendment of Companies Act]   The Companies Act is amended as shown in Parts I and II of Schedule 13 to this Act, being amendments consequential on this Act and the Company Directors Disqualification Act 1986.

439(2)   [Enactments in Sch. 14]   The enactments specified in the first column of Schedule 14 to this Act (being enactments which refer, or otherwise relate, to those which are repealed and replaced by this Act or the Company Directors Disqualification Act 1986) are amended as shown in the second column of that Schedule.

439(3)   [Consequential modifications of subordinate legislation]   The Lord Chancellor may by order make such consequential modifications of any provision contained in any subordinate legislation made before the appointed day and such transitional provisions in connection with those modifications as appear to him necessary or expedient in respect of—

    (a) any reference in that subordinate legislation to the Bankruptcy Act 1914;

    (b) any reference in that subordinate legislation to any enactment repealed by Part III or IV of Schedule 10 to the Insolvency Act 1985; or

(c) any reference in that subordinate legislation to any matter provided for under the Act of 1914 or under any enactment so repealed.

439(4)   [Order by statutory instrument etc.]   An order under this section shall be made by statutory instrument subject to annulment in pursuance of a resolution of either House of Parliament.

(Former provision: none)

General note

Apart from the consequential amendments referred to in s. 439 and Sch. 13, it should be noted that amendments and repeals in IA 1985, Sch. 6, 8 and 10 also take effect. For comments on the operation of IA 1985, see the general discussion on IA 1986 (above p. 5).

S. 439(1), (2)

These subsections refer to Sch. 13 and 14 which respectively make consequential amendments to CA 1985 and other legislation. Most of the consequential amendments of CA 1985 are purely minor textual changes. A new s. 196 of CA is enacted to apply the new preferential claims régime to the situation where the holder of a floating charge, instead of putting in a receiver, takes possession of the charged property. The consequential amendments effected by Sch. 14 are also of a minor nature.

S. 439(3), (4)

Section 439(3) allows the Lord Chancellor, by a statutory instrument created in accordance with s. 439(4), to amend existing subordinate legislation to cater for the transition to IA 1986. See the Insolvency (Amendment of Subordinate Legislation) Order 1986 (SI 1986 No. 2001), the effect of which on bankruptcy proceedings started before 21 December 1986 has been clarified by the Insolvency (Amendment of Subordinate Legislation) Order 1987 (SI 1987 No. 1398). (Note also the Insolvency (Land Registration Rules) Order 1986 (SI 1986 No. 2245).)

Section 440   Extent (Scotland)

440(1)   [Extension to Scotland except where stated]   Subject to the next subsection, provisions of this Act contained in the first Group of Parts extend to Scotland except where otherwise stated.

440(2)   [Provisions not extending to Scotland]   The following provisions of this Act do not extend to Scotland—

    (a) in the first Groups of Parts—

        section 43;
        sections 238 to 241; and
        section 246;

    (b) the second Group of Parts;

    (c) in the third Group of Parts—

        sections 399 to 402,
        sections 412, 413, 415, 418, 420 and 421,
        sections 423 to 425, and
        section 429(1) and (2); and

    (d) in the Schedules—

Parts II and III of Schedule 11; and

Schedules 12 and 14 so far as they repeal or amend enactments which extend to England and Wales only.

(Former provision: IA 1985, s. 236(3))

General note

This section identifies those provisions in IA 1986 which apply to Scotland. Most of the provisions on corporate insolvency apply equally to Scotland, except for certain receivership provisions (Scotland has its own receivership system in ss. 50–71), the rules on preferences and transactions at an undervalue (again the Scots have their own rules in ss. 242, 243 and also s. 246). The rules on personal insolvency do not apply to Scotland, which has its own system contained in the Bankruptcy (Scotland) Act 1985. Bearing in mind this point, it is not surprising that certain named miscellaneous provisions in the Third Group of Parts and the Schedules do not operate north of the border.

Section 441 Extent (Northern Ireland)

441(1) [Provisions extending to Northern Ireland] The following provisions of this Act extend to Northern Ireland—

(a) sections 197, 426, 427 and 428; and

(b) so much of section 439 and Schedule 14 as relates to enactments which extend to Northern Ireland.

441(2) [Most of provisions not extending to Northern Ireland] Subject as above, and to any provision expressly relating to companies incorporated elsewhere than in Great Britain, nothing in this Act extends to Northern Ireland or applies to or in relation to companies registered or incorporated in Northern Ireland.

(Former provision: CA 1985, s. 745 (as amended by IA 1985, s. 236(4)))

General note

The Act, generally speaking, does not apply to Northern Ireland, which has its own distinct systems of corporate and personal insolvency law. Certain exceptional provisions do apply in Northern Ireland, however – e.g. s. 426, which provides for co-operation between the various UK insolvency courts, s. 427, which deals with parliamentary disqualification, and s. 428, which amends the Restrictive Trade Practices Act 1976 (which applies in Northern Ireland).

However, legislation has since been enacted which has made the insolvency law of Northern Ireland broadly similar to that of England and Wales. New rules relating to the disqualification of company directors were introduced with effect from 24 September 1986 by the Companies (Northern Ireland) Order 1986 (SI 1986 No. 1032 (NI 6)), and these have since been re-enacted and extended by Pt. II of the Companies (Northern Ireland) Order 1989 (SI 1989 No. 2404 (NI 18)). In consequence, legislation equivalent to CDDA 1986 is now in place in Northern Ireland. The 1989 Order was brought into force with effect from 1 October 1991 by the Companies Act (1989 Order) (Commencement No. 2) Order (Northern Ireland) 1991 (SR 1991 No. 410 (C. 19)). The Insolvency (Northern Ireland) Order 1989 (SI 1989 No. 2405 (NI 19)) is the counterpart for Northern Ireland of IA 1986. The object of the order is to bring the insolvency legislation, both personal and corporate, of that jurisdiction into line with that of England and Wales. This order was made on 19 December 1989, and was brought into operation in full on 1 October 1991 by the Insolvency (1989 Order) (Commencement No. 4) Order (Northern

Ireland) 1991 (SR 1991 No. 411 (C. 20)). Previous Commencement Orders were of minimal impact. Other provisions which have been put into force as part of the new insolvency regime in Northern Ireland include the Insolvency Practitioners (Recognised Professional Bodies) Order (Northern Ireland) 1991 (SR 1991 No. 301) and the Insolvency Practitioners Regulations (Northern Ireland) 1991 (SR 1991 No. 302) (both effective 5 August 1991); the Insolvency Rules (Northern Ireland) 1991 (SR 1991 No. 364), the Insolvency (Deposits) Order (Northern Ireland) 1991 (SR 1991 No. 384), the Insolvency (Monetary Limits) Order (Northern Ireland) 1991 (SR 1991 No. 384), the Insolvency (Fees) Order (Northern Ireland) 1991 (SR 1991 No. 385), the Insolvency Regulations (Northern Ireland) 1991 (SR 1991 No. 388) and the Financial Markets and Insolvency Regulations (Northern Ireland) 1991 (SR 1991 No. 443), all effective 1 October 1991.

The Insolvency Act 1994, which amended the law relating to the "adoption" of contracts of employment by administrators and administrative receivers, also amends the law applicable in Northern Ireland: see s. 4 of and Sch. 1 to that Act. There is also an Insolvent Partnerships (Northern Ireland) Order 1991 (SR 1991 No. 366) and specific regulations dealing with proceedings and reports arising out of the disqualification of directors (see SR 1991 Nos. 367, 368 and 413). Administration of estates of deceased insolvents in Northern Ireland is covered by SR 1991 No. 365. Many of these provisions have since been the subject of amending legislation: see, e.g. SR 1992 No. 398, 1993 Nos. 302, 454, 1994 No. 26.

Section 441(2) was considered by the court in *Re Normandy Marketing Ltd* [1993] BCC 879. Here it was held that s. 221 was wide enough to cover Northern Ireland companies and therefore such a company could be wound up under English law under s. 124A of the Insolvency Act 1986 on the grounds that it was in the public interest to do so.

Section 442   Extent (other territories)

442   Her Majesty may, by Order in Council, direct that such of the provisions of this Act as are specified in the Order, being provisions formerly contained in the Insolvency Act 1985, shall extend to any of the Channel Islands or any colony with such modifications as may be so specified.

(Former provision: IA 1985, s. 236(5))

General note

This provides for the extension of the Act by Order in Council to any of the Channel Islands or any colony. The Isle of Man is not included.

The Insolvency Act 1986 (Guernsey) Order 1989 (SI 1989 No. 2409) makes provision for co-operation between the courts of the Bailiwick of Guernsey (including Alderney and Sark) and the courts of the UK: see the note to s. 426.

Section 443   Commencement

443   This Act comes into force on the day appointed under section 236(2) of the Insolvency Act 1985 for the coming into force of Part III of that Act (individual insolvency and bankruptcy), immediately after that part of that Act comes into force for England and Wales.

(Former provision: none)

General note

This odd formula ties the commencement date of the IA 1986 to the commencement date of

Pt. III of IA 1985: see SI 1986 No. 1924 (C. 71) and the general note to s. 439 above. The date was 29 December 1986. Certain other provisions in the 1985 Act, relating to corporate insolvency and the licensing of insolvency practitioners, had already been put into force (and now form part of the 1986 consolidation).

Section **444** Citation

444 This Act may be cited as the Insolvency Act 1986.

SCHEDULES

Schedule 1 — Powers of Administrator or Administrative Receiver

Sections 14, 42

1 Power to take possession of, collect and get in the property of the company and, for that purpose, to take such proceedings as may seem to him expedient.

2 Power to sell or otherwise dispose of the property of the company by public auction or private auction or private contract or, in Scotland, to sell, feu, hire out or otherwise dispose of the property of the company by public roup or private bargain.

3 Power to raise or borrow money and grant security therefor over the property of the company.

4 Power to appoint a solicitor or accountant or other professionally qualified person to assist him in the performance of his functions.

5 Power to bring or defend any action or other legal proceedings in the name and on behalf of the company.

6 Power to refer to arbitration any question affecting the company.

7 Power to effect and maintain insurances in respect of the business and property of the company.

8 Power to use the company's seal.

9 Power to do all acts and to execute in the name and on behalf of the company any deed, receipt or other document.

10 Power to draw, accept, make and endorse any bill of exchange or promissory note in the name and on behalf of the company.

11 Power to appoint any agent to do any business which he is unable to do himself or which can more conveniently be done by an agent and power to employ and dismiss employees.

12 Power to do all such things (including the carrying out of works) as may be necessary for the realisation of the property of the company.

13 Power to make any payment which is necessary or incidental to the performance of his functions.

14   Power to carry on the business of the company.

15   Power to establish subsidiaries of the company.

16   Power to transfer to subsidiaries of the company the whole or any part of the business and property of the company.

17   Power to grant or accept a surrender of a lease or tenancy of any of the property of the company, and to take a lease or tenancy of any property required or convenient for the business of the company.

18   Power to make any arrangement or compromise on behalf of the company.

19   Power to call up any uncalled capital of the company.

20   Power to rank and claim in the bankruptcy, insolvency, sequestration or liquidation of any person indebted to the company and to receive dividends, and to accede to trust deeds for the creditors of any such person.

21   Power to present or defend a petition for the winding up of the company.

22   Power to change the situation of the company's registered office.

23   Power to do all other things incidental to the exercise of the foregoing powers.

(Former provision: IA 1985, Sch. 3)

General note

Under CA 1985, the powers of a receiver (or receiver and manager) appointed out of court were left to be settled almost entirely by the provisions of the instrument under which he was appointed and the terms of the appointment itself. The Cork Committee (*Report*, para. 494) recommended that the general powers of a receiver should be set out in a statute, so that it would not be necessary for a person dealing with him to refer to the particular debenture to find out what powers he could exercise in the circumstances. (This was, in fact, already the case in Scotland under CFCSA 1972, s. 15.) The present Schedule and IA 1986, s. 42, implement those recommendations, which apply in every *administrative* receivership, and – no doubt reflecting the fact that the new administration order régime set up by ss. 8ff is closely modelled on the institution of receivership – the Schedule is made by s. 14 to apply to an administrator as well. An administrator has, in addition, the general statutory powers set out in s. 14(1)(*a*), and the specific powers given by ss. 14(2) and 15.

The powers of an administrative receiver listed in this Schedule may be overridden by the terms of the debenture under which he is appointed, but a person dealing with him in good faith and for value is not concerned to inquire whether he is acting within his powers (s. 42(3)). The Act, by s. 43, also confers special powers on an administrative receiver to dispose of charged property, etc.

A receiver who is not an administrative receiver is not affected by the changes described above, and Sch. 1 does not apply in such a case.

The Schedule applies in Scotland in the case of an administrator, but not an administrative receiver; all Scottish receivers, however, have the powers set out in s. 55 and Sch. 2.

The specific powers listed in Sch. 1 do not, on the whole, call for detailed comment, apart from para. 21 (power to present or defend a winding-up petition), which has clarified doubts regarding a receiver's ability to present such a petition at common law, and removes the limitations upon such powers as he may have had: cf. *Re Emmadart Ltd* [1979] Ch. 540. A petition by an administrator or administrative receiver is presented in the name of the company: see the note to s. 124. The power of a receiver to present a winding up petition was also the subject of comment in *Re Anvil Estates Ltd* (unreported, 1993) – discussed by Pugh and Ede in (1994) 10 Insolvency Law and Practice 48. The case was actually decided on the basis of the right of the secured creditor (as opposed to the receiver) to petition but there is some useful general discussion in the judgment. the power of an administrative receiver to oppose a winding-up petition presented by another creditor was considered in *Re Leigh Estates (UK) Ltd* [1994] BCC 292.

Schedule 2 — Powers of a Scottish Receiver (Additional to Those Conferred on him by the Instrument of Charge)

Section 55

1 Power to take possession of, collect and get in the property from the company or a liquidator thereof or any other person, and for that purpose, to take such proceedings as may seem to him expedient.

2 Power to sell, feu, hire out or otherwise dispose of the property by public roup or private bargain and with or without advertisement.

3 Power to raise or borrow money and grant security therefor over the property.

4 Power to appoint a solicitor or accountant or other professionally qualified person to assist him in the performance of his functions.

5 Power to bring or defend any action or other legal proceedings in the name and on behalf of the company.

6 Power to refer to arbitration all questions affecting the company.

7 Power to effect and maintain insurances in respect of the business and property of the company.

8 Power to use the company's seal.

9 Power to do all acts and to execute in the name and on behalf of the company any deed, receipt or other document.

10 Power to draw, accept, make and endorse any bill of exchange or promissory note in the name and on behalf of the company.

11 Power to appoint any agent to do any business which he is unable to do himself or which can more conveniently be done by an agent, and power to employ and dismiss employees.

12 Power to do all such things (including the carrying out of works), as may be necessary for the realisation of the property.

13 Power to make any payment which is necessary or incidental to the performance of his functions.

14 Power to carry on the business of the company or any part of it.

15 Power to grant or accept a surrender of a lease or tenancy of any of the property, and to take a lease or tenancy of any property required or convenient for the business of the company.

16 Power to make any arrangement or compromise on behalf of the company.

17 Power to call up any uncalled capital of the company.

18 Power to establish subsidiaries of the company.

19　Power to transfer to subsidiaries of the company the business of the company or any part of it and any of the property.

20　Power to rank and claim in the bankruptcy, insolvency, sequestrian or liquidation of any person or company indebted to the company and to receive dividends, and to accede to trust deeds for creditors of any such person.

21　Power to present or defend a petition for the winding up of the company.

22　Power to change the situation of the company's registered office.

23　Power to do all other things incidental to the exercise of the powers mentioned in section 55(1) of this Act or above in this Schedule.

(Former provision: CA 1985, s. 471(1) (as amended by IA 1985, s. 57))

General note

This Schedule provides a model list of powers for a Scottish receiver appointed by a holder of a floating charge. The list, although modified, dates back to the introduction of receivership in Scotland in 1972. The 23 implied powers mirror those of an English administrative receiver set out in Sch. 1, with only slight changes in the order. For further comment, see s. 55.

Schedule 3 — Orders in Course of Winding Up Pronounced in Vacation (Scotland)

Section 162

Part I — Orders Which are to be Final

Orders under section 153, as to the time for proving debts and claims.

Orders under section 195 as to meetings for ascertaining wishes of creditors or contributories.

Orders under section 198, as to the examination of witnesses in regard to the property or affairs of a company.

Part II — Orders Which are to take Effect until Matter Disposed of by Inner House

Orders under section 126(1), 130(2) or (3), 147, 227 or 228, restraining or permitting the commencement or the continuance of legal proceedings.

Orders under section 135(5), limiting the powers of provisional liquidators.

Orders under section 108, appointing a liquidator to fill a vacancy.

Orders under section 167 or 169, sanctioning the exercise of any powers by a liquidator, other than the powers specified in paragraphs 1, 2 and 3 of Schedule 4 to this Act.

Orders under section 158, as to the arrest and detention of an absconding contributory and his property.

(Former provision: CA 1985, Sch. 16 (as amended by IA 1985, Sch. 10, Pt. II))

General note

This Schedule re-enacts CA 1985, Sch. 16, with the deletion of one or two items consequential upon changes made in that Act.

Schedule 4 — Powers of Liquidator in a Winding Up

Sections 165, 167

Part I — Powers Exercisable with Sanction

1   Power to pay any class of creditors in full.

2   Power to make any compromise or arrangement with creditors or persons claiming to be creditors, or having or alleging themselves to have any claim (present or future, certain or contingent, ascertained or sounding only in damages) against the company, or whereby the company may be rendered liable.

3   Power to compromise, on such terms as may be agreed—

    (a)   all calls and liabilities to calls, all debts and liabilities capable of resulting in debts, and all claims (present or future, certain or contingent, ascertained or sounding only in damages) subsisting or supposed to subsist between the company and a contributory or alleged contributory or other debtor or person apprehending liability to the company, and

    (b)   all questions in any way relating to or affecting the assets or the winding up of the company,

and take any security for the discharge of any such call, debt, liability or claim and give a complete discharge in respect of it.

Part II — Powers Exercisable without Sanction in Voluntary Winding Up, with Sanction in Winding Up by the Court

4   Power to bring or defend any action or other legal proceeding in the name and on behalf of the company.

5   Power to carry on the business of the company so far as may be necessary for its beneficial winding up.

Part III — Powers Exercisable without Sanction in any Winding Up

6 Power to sell any of the company's property by public auction or private contract, with power to transfer the whole of it to any person or to sell the same in parcels.

7 Power to do all acts and execute, in the name and on behalf of the company, all deeds, receipts and other documents and for that purpose to use, when necessary, the company's seal.

8 Power to prove, rank and claim in the bankruptcy, insolvency or sequestration of any contributory for any balance against his estate, and to receive dividends in the bankruptcy, insolvency or sequestration in respect of that balance, as a separate debt due from the bankrupt or insolvent, and rateably with the other separate creditors.

9 Power to draw, accept, make and indorse any bill of exchange or promissory note in the name and on behalf of the company, with the same effect with respect to the company's liability as if the bill or note had been drawn, accepted, made or indorsed by or on behalf of the company in the course of its business.

10 Power to raise on the security of the assets of the company any money requisite.

11 Power to take out in his official name letters of administration to any deceased contributory, and to do in his official name any other act necessary for obtaining payment of any money due from a contributory or his estate which cannot conveniently be done in the name of the company.

In all such cases the money due is deemed, for the purpose of enabling the liquidator to take out the letters of administration or recover the money, to be due to the liquidator himself.

12 Power to appoint an agent to do any business which the liquidator is unable to do himself.

13 Power to do all such other things as may be necessary for winding up the company's affairs and distributing its assets.

(Former provisions: CA 1985, ss. 539(1)(a), (b), (d)–(f), (2), 598(1), (2))

General note

The powers of a liquidator in a winding up by the court were formerly set out in CA 1985, s. 539(1), (2), and those in a voluntary winding up in CA 1985, s. 598(1), (2). Many of these powers are now conveniently collected together and arranged in tabulated form in this Schedule, which applies both in England and Wales and in Scotland.

A liquidator in a winding up by the court has also the supplementary powers listed in s. 168 (England and Wales) and s. 169 (Scotland); and further powers are given to a voluntary liquidator by ss. 165, 166.

Schedule 4 makes no changes of substance from the former law.

Paras. 2, 3

It was held in *Taylor, Noter* [1992] BCC 440 that the corresponding provisions of CA 1948 empowered the liquidator of a company, with the necessary sanction, to enter into any compromise or arrangement that might have been entered into by the company itself. In that case the affairs of a number of companies controlled by the same person had been treated as one, and the liquidator had found it impossible to determine which creditors had claims against the particular companies and which had claims against the individual controller, who was now bankrupt. A scheme was agreed for a single scheme of ranking and division of all the assets and creditors. This case was followed by the Court of Appeal in England in somewhat similar circumstances in *Re Bank of Credit & Commerce International SA (No. 2)* [1992] BCC 715. The compromise powers include power to depart from the general rule that creditors are entitled to participate in the estate on a *pari passu* basis (ibid.).

Schedule 5 — Powers of Trustee in Bankruptcy

Section 314

Part I — Powers Exercisable with Sanction

1   Power to carry on any business of the bankrupt so far as may be necessary for winding it up beneficially and so far as the trustee is able to do so without contravening any requirement imposed by or under any enactment.

2   Power to bring, institute or defend any action or legal proceedings relating to the property comprised in the bankrupt's estate.

3   Power to accept as the consideration for the sale of any property comprised in the bankrupt's estate a sum of money payable at a future time subject to such stipulations as to security or otherwise as the creditors' committee or the court thinks fit.

4   Power to mortgage or pledge any part of the property comprised in the bankrupt's estate for the purpose of raising money for the payment of his debts.

5   Power, where any right, option or other power forms part of the bankrupt's estate, to make payments or incur liabilities with a view to obtaining, for the benefit of the creditors, any property which is the subject of the right, option or power.

6   Power to refer to arbitration, or compromise on such terms as may be agreed on, any debts, claims or liabilities subsisting or supposed to subsist between the bankrupt and any person who may have incurred any liability to the bankrupt.

7   Power to make such compromise or other arrangement as may be thought expedient with creditors, or persons claiming to be creditors, in respect of bankruptcy debts.

8   Power to make such compromise or other arrangement as may be thought expedient with respect to any claim arising out of or incidental to the bankrupt's estate made or capable of being made on the trustee by any person or by the trustee on any person.

Part II — General Powers

9   Power to sell any part of the property for the time being comprised in the bankrupt's estate, including the goodwill and book debts of any business.

10   Power to give receipts for any money received by him, being receipts which effectually discharge the person paying the money from all responsibility in respect of its application.

11   Power to prove, rank, claim and draw a dividend in respect of such debts due to the bankrupt as are comprised in his estate.

12   Power to exercise in relation to any property comprised in the bankrupt's estate any powers the capacity to exercise which is vested in him under Parts VIII to XI of this Act.

13 Power to deal with any property comprised in the estate to which the bankrupt is beneficially entitled as tenant in tail in the same manner as the bankrupt might have dealt with it.

Part III — Ancillary Powers

14 For the purposes of, or in connection with, the exercise of any of his powers under Parts VIII to XI of this Act, the trustee may, by his official name—

(a) hold property of every description,

(b) make contracts,

(c) sue and be sued,

(d) enter into engagements binding on himself and, in respect of the bankrupt's estate, on his successors in office,

(e) employ an agent,

(f) execute any power of attorney, deed or other instrument;

and he may do any other act which is necessary or expedient for the purposes of or in connection with the exercise of those powers.

(Former provisions: IA 1985, s. 160(1), (2), (6))

General note

This Schedule, allied to s. 314, lists the powers of a trustee in bankruptcy. Like Sch. 2, it has been hived off from the mainstream of the legislation. The crucial distinguishing factor is the need to obtain the sanction of the committee of creditors (see s. 301) before the powers listed in Pt. I can be exercised.

For a recent decision on the effect of the power now contained in Sch. 5, para. 3, see *Weddell & Anor* v *Pearce (JA) & Major & Anor* [1988] Ch. 26. This case involved the assignment of a cause of action by the trustee for future consideration without obtaining the requisite sanction. It was held by Scott J that notwithstanding this failure to obtain sanction, the assignment took effect in equity. This ruling is in line with the philosophy now expressed in ss. 314(3) and 377 of IA 1986.

For further guidance on this Schedule see the note to s. 314.

Schedule 6 — The Categories of Preferential Debts

Section 386

CATEGORY 1: DEBTS DUE TO INLAND REVENUE

1 Sums due at the relevant date from the debtor on account of deductions of income tax from emoluments paid during the period of 12 months next before that date.

The deductions here referred to are those which the debtor was liable to make under section 203 of the Income and Corporation Taxes Act 1988 (pay as you earn), less the amount of the repayments of income tax which the debtor was liable to make during that period.

2 Sums due at the relevant date from the debtor in respect of such deductions as are required to be made by the debtor for that period under section 559 of the Income and Corporation Taxes Act 1988 (sub-contractors in the construction industry).

CATEGORY 2: DEBTS DUE TO CUSTOMS AND EXCISE

3 Any value added tax which is referable to the period of 6 months next before the relevant date (which period is referred to below as **"the 6-month period"**).

For the purposes of this paragraph—

    (a) where the whole of the accounting period to which any value added tax is attributable falls within the 6-month period, the whole amount of that tax is referable to that period; and

    (b) in any other case the amount of any value added tax which is referable to the 6-month period is the proportion of the tax which is equal to such proportion (if any) of the accounting period in question as falls within the 6-month period;

and in sub-paragraph (a) **"prescribed"** means prescribed by regulations under the Value Added Tax Act 1983.

3A Any insurance premium tax which is referable to the period of 6 months next before the relevant date (which period is referred to below as **"the 6-month period"**).

For the purposes of this paragraph—

    (a) where the whole of the prescribed accounting period to which any insurance premium tax is attributable falls within the 6-month period, the whole amount of that tax is referable to that period; and

    (b) in any other case the amount of any insurance premium tax which is referable to the 6-month period is the proportion of the tax which is equal to such proportion (if any) of the accounting reference period in question as falls within the 6-month period;

and references here to accounting periods shall be construed in accordance with Part III of the Finance Act 1994.

4 The amount of any car tax which is due at the relevant date from the debtor and which became due within a period of 12 months next before that date.

5 Any amount which is due—

    (a) by way of general betting duty or bingo duty, or

    (b) under section 12(1) of the Betting and Gaming Duties Act 1981 (general betting duty and pool betting duty recoverable from agent collecting stakes), or

    (c) under section 14 of, or Schedule 2 to, that Act (gaming licence duty),

from the debtor at the relevant date and which became due within the period of 12 months next before that date.

5A The amount of any excise duty on beer which is due at the relevant date from the debtor and which became due within a period of 6 months next before that date.

5B Any amount which is due by way of lottery duty from the debtor at the relevant date and which became due within the period of 12 months next before that date.

5C Any amount which is due by way of air passenger duty from the debtor at the relevant date and which became due within the period of six months next before that date.

CATEGORY 3: SOCIAL SECURITY CONTRIBUTIONS

6 All sums which on the relevant date are due from the debtor on account of Class 1 or Class 2 contributions under the Social Security Contributions and Benefits Act 1992 or the Social Security (Northern Ireland) Act 1975 and which became due from the debtor in the 12 months next before the relevant date.

7 All sums which on the relevant date have been assessed on and are due from the debtor on account of Class 4 contributions under either of those Acts of 1975, being sums which—

(a) are due to the Commissioners of Inland Revenue (rather than to the Secretary of State or a Northern Ireland department), and

(b) are assessed on the debtor up to 5th April next before the relevant date,

but not exceeding, in the whole, any one year's assessment.

CATEGORY 4: CONTRIBUTIONS TO OCCUPATIONAL PENSION SCHEMES, ETC.

8 Any sum which is owed by the debtor and is a sum to which Schedule 4 to the Pension Schemes Act 1993 applies (contributions to occupational pension schemes and state scheme premiums).

CATEGORY 5: REMUNERATION, ETC., OF EMPLOYEES

9 So much of any amount which—

(a) is owed by the debtor to a person who is or has been an employee of the debtor, and

(b) is payable by way of remuneration in respect of the whole or any part of the period of 4 months next before the relevant date,

as does not exceed so much as may be prescribed by order made by the Secretary of State.

10 An amount owed by way of accrued holiday remuneration, in respect of any period of employment before the relevant date, to a person whose employment by the debtor has been terminated, whether before, on or after that date.

11 So much of any sum owed in respect of money advanced for the purpose as has been applied for the payment of a debt which, if it had not been paid, would have been a debt falling within paragraph 9 or 10.

12 So much of any amount which—

(a) is ordered (whether before or after the relevant date) to be paid by the debtor under the Reserve Forces (Safeguard of Employment) Act 1985, and

(b) is so ordered in respect of a default made by the debtor before that date in the discharge of his obligations under that Act.

as does not exceed such amount as may be prescribed by order made by the Secretary of State.

INTERPRETATION FOR CATEGORY 5

13(1) For the purposes of paragraphs 9 to 12, a sum is payable by the debtor to a person by way of remuneration in respect of any period if—

    (a) it is paid as wages or salary (whether payable for time or for piece work or earned wholly or partly by way of commission) in respect of services rendered to the debtor in that period, or

    (b) it is an amount falling within the following sub-paragraph and is payable by the debtor in respect of that period.

13(2)   An amount falls within this sub-paragraph if it is—

    (a) a guarantee payment under section 12(1) of the Employment Protection (Consolidation) Act 1978 (employee without work to do for a day or part of a day);

    (b) remuneration on suspension on medical grounds under section 19 of that Act or remuneration on suspension on maternity grounds under section 47 of that Act;

    (c) any payment for time off under section 31(3) or 31A(4) of that Act (looking for work, etc.; ante-natal care) or under section 169 of the Trade Union and Labour Relations (Consolidation) Act 1992 (trade union duties); or

    (d) remuneration under a protective award made by an industrial tribunal under section 189 of the latter Act (redundancy dismissal with compensation).

14(1)   This paragraph relates to a case in which a person's employment has been terminated by or in consequence of his employer going into liquidation or being adjudged bankrupt or (his employer being a company not in liquidation) by or in consequence of—

    (a) a receiver being appointed as mentioned in section 40 of this Act (debenture-holders secured by floating charge), or

    (b) the appointment of a receiver under section 53(6) or 54(5) of this Act (Scottish company with property subject to floating charge), or

    (c) the taking of possession by debenture-holders (so secured), as mentioned in section 196 of the Companies Act.

14(2)   For the purposes of paragraphs 9 to 12, holiday remuneration is deemed to have accrued to that person in respect of any period of employment if, by virtue of his contract of employment or of any enactment, that remuneration would have accrued in respect of that period if his employment had continued until he became entitled to be allowed the holiday.

14(3)   The reference in sub-paragraph (2) to any enactment includes an order or direction made under an enactment.

15   Without prejudice to paragraphs 13 and 14—

    (a) any remuneration payable by the debtor to a person in respect of a period of holiday or of absence from work through sickness or other good cause is deemed to be wages or (as the case may be) salary in respect of services rendered to the debtor in that period, and

    (b) references here and in those paragraphs to remuneration in respect of a period of holiday include any sums which, if they had been paid, would have been treated for the purposes of the enactments relating to social security as earnings in repect of that period.

CATEGORY 6: LEVIES ON COAL AND STEEL PRODUCTION

15A Any sums due at the relevant date from the debtor in respect of—

   (a) the levies on the production of coal and steel referred to in Article 49 and 50 of the E.C.S.C. Treaty, or

   (b) any surcharge for delay provided for in Article 50(3) of that Treaty and Article 6 of Decision 3/52 of the High Authority of the Coal and Steel Community.

ORDERS

16 An order under paragraph 9 or 12—

   (a) may contain such transitional provisions as may appear to the Secretary of State necessary or expedient;

   (b) shall be made by statutory instrument subject to annulment in pursuance of a resolution of either House of Parliament.

(Former provisions: IA 1985, Sch. 4, Pt. I, Pt. II, paras. 2–4)

General note

This Schedule, which is brought into play by s. 386, largely reflects the preferential claims régime as suggested by the Cork Committee (Cmnd 8558, para. 1450). Many, but not all, of this Committee's recommendations were reluctantly accepted by the economy-conscious Government. Unfortunately, the proliferation of preferential claims appears to have begun again with the addition of Category 6 by the Insolvency (ECSC Levy Debts) Regulations 1987 (SI 1987 No. 2093), which were made by the Secretary of State for Trade in exercise of the power conferred by s. 2(2) of the European Communities Act 1972. Indeed this change is retrospective to a large extent – see paras. 2(3) and 4 of these regulations.

For the meaning of the phrase "the relevant date", see s. 387. For further comment, see the general note to Pt. XII. The amount for paras. 9 and 12 is fixed at £800 — see the Insolvency Proceedings (Monetary Limits) Order 1986 (SI 1986 No. 1996), art. 4. Note also the amendments to paras. 1 and 2 by the Income and Corporation Taxes Act 1988, Sch. 29.

Para. 1

The words "203 of the Income and Corporation Taxes Act 1988" were substituted for the former words "204 of the Income and Corporation Taxes Act 1970" by the Income and Corporation Taxes Act 1988, s. 844 and Sch. 29, para. 32 for companies' accounting periods ending after 5 April 1988 (see s. 843(1)).

Para. 2

The words "559 of the Income and Corporation Taxes Act 1988" were substituted for the former words "69 of the Finance (No. 2) Act 1975" by the Income and Corporation Taxes Act 1988, s. 844 and Sch. 29, para. 32 for companies' accounting periods ending after 5 April 1988 (see s. 843(1)).

Para. 3A

This was inserted by the Finance Act 1994, Sch. 7, para. 2.

Para. 5A

This insertion was made by the Finance Act 1991, Sch. 2, para. 22.

Para. 5B

Paragraph 5B was inserted by the Finance Act 1993, s. 36(2) from 1 December 1993 (see SI 1993 No. 2842).

Para. 5C

The Finance Act 1994, Sch. 7, para. 13(1) introduces this item, with effect from 31 October 1994.

Para. 6

A minor textual amendment was made here by the Social Security (Consequential Provisions) Act 1992, Sch. 2, para. 73.

Para. 8

A minor textual amendment was made here by the Pension Schemes Act 1993, Sch. 8, para. 18.

Para. 13

Subparagraph 2(b) was added to by the Trade Union Reform and Employment Rights Act 1993, Sch. 8, para. 35. Subparagraphs 2(c) and 2(d) were amended by the Trade Union and Labour Relations (Consolidation) Act 1992, Sch. 2, para. 33.

Schedule 7 — Insolvency Practitioners Tribunal

Section 396

PANELS OF MEMBERS

1(1) The Secretary of State shall draw up and from time to time revise—

    (a) a panel of persons who

        (i) have a 7 year general qualification, within the meaning of sec. 71 of the Courts and Legal Services Act 1990;

        (ii) are advocates or solicitors in Scotland of at least 7 years' standing,

    and are nominated for the purpose by the Lord Chancellor or the Lord President of the Court of Session, and

    (b) a panel of persons who are experienced in insolvency matters;

and the members of the Tribunal shall be selected from those panels in accordance with this Schedule.

1(2) The power to revise the panels includes power to terminate a person's membership of either of them, and is accordingly to that extent subject to section 7 of the Tribunals and Inquiries Act 1992 (which makes it necessary to obtain the concurrence of the Lord Chancellor and the Lord President of the Court of Session to dismissals in certain cases).

REMUNERATION OF MEMBERS

2 The Secretary of State may out of money provided by Parliament pay to members of the Tribunal such remuneration as he may with the approval of the Treasury determine; and such expenses of the Tribunal as the Secretary of State and the Treasury may approve shall be defrayed by the Secretary of State out of money so provided.

SITTINGS OF TRIBUNAL

3(1) For the purposes of carrying out their functions in relation to any cases referred to them, the Tribunal may sit either as a single tribunal or in two or more divisions.

3(2)   The functions of the Tribunal in relation to any case referred to them shall be exercised by three members consisting of—

- (a) a chairman selected by the Secretary of State from the panel drawn up under paragraph 1(1)(a) above, and
- (b) two other members selected by the Secretary of State from the panel drawn up under paragraph 1(1)(b).

PROCEDURE OF TRIBUNAL

4(1)   Any investigation by the Tribunal shall be so conducted as to afford a reasonable opportunity for representations to be made to the Tribunal by or on behalf of the person whose case is the subject of the investigation.

4(2)   For the purposes of any such investigation, the Tribunal—

- (a) may by summons require any person to attend, at such time and place as is specified in the summons, to give evidence or to produce any books, papers and other records in his possession or under his control which the Tribunal consider it necessary for the purposes of the investigation to examine, and
- (b) may take evidence on oath, and for the purpose administer oaths, or may, instead of administering an oath, require the person examined to make and subscribe a declaration of the truth of the matter respecting which he is examined;

but no person shall be required, in obedience to such a summons, to go more than ten miles from his place of residence, unless the necessary expenses of his attendance are paid or tendered to him.

4(3)   Every person who—

- (a) without reasonable excuse fails to attend in obedience to a summons issued under this paragraph, or refuses to give evidence, or
- (b) intentionally alters, suppresses, conceals or destroys or refuses to produce any document which he may be required to produce for the purpose of an investigation by the Tribunal,

is liable to a fine.

4(4)   Subject to the provisions of this paragraph, the Secretary of State may make rules for regulating the procedure on any investigation by the Tribunal.

4(5)   In their application to Scotland, sub-paragraphs (2) and (3) above have effect as if for any reference to a summons there were substituted a reference to a notice in writing.

(Former provision: IA 1985, Sch. 1)

General note

The Insolvency Practitioners Tribunal, which was established under IA 1985, s. 8(6) and is confirmed by s. 396(1) of the present Act, is empowered to review the decisions of the Secretary of State (or other "competent authority") to refuse an application for authorisation or withdraw an authorisation to act as an insolvency practitioner: see the note to s. 396 and the Insolvency Practitioners Tribunal (Conduct of Investigations) Rules 1986 (SI 1986 No. 952). It is not concerned with decisions about authorisation made by professional bodies under ss. 390(2)(*a*) and 391, since those bodies have their own reviewing procedures.

This Schedule, which is brought forward from IA 1985, Sch. 1, contains details about the membership and procedure of the Tribunal, which consists, for the hearing of any case, of two insolvency experts and a legally qualified chairman. Although the power of selection, and also largely that of nomination, of members rests with the Secretary of State, the Tribunal is intended to function as an independent body.

Para. 1

In para. 1(1)(*a*) the words from "(i) have a 7 year general qualification" to "at least 7 years' standing," were substituted for the former words "are barristers, advocates or solicitors, in each case of at least 7 years' standing" by the Courts and Legal Services Act 1990, s. 71(2), 124(3) and Sch. 10 as from 1 January 1991 (see SI 1990 No. 2484, art. 2 and Schedule).

The reference in para. 1(2) to s. 7 of the 1992 Act replaces the former reference to s. 8 of the Tribunals and Inquiries Act 1971: see Tribunals and Inquiries Act 1992, s. 18, 19(1) and Sch. 3, para. 19, effective 1 October 1992.

Schedule 8 — Provisions Capable of Inclusion in Company Insolvency Rules

Section 411

COURTS

1   Provision for supplementing, in relation to the insolvency or winding up of companies, any provision made by or under section 117 of this Act (jurisdiction in relation to winding up).

2   Provision for regulating the practice and procedure of any court exercising jurisdiction for the purposes of Parts I to VII of this Act or the Companies Act so far as relating to, and to matters connected with or arising out of, the insolvency or winding up of companies, being any provision that could be made by rules of court.

NOTICES, ETC.

3   Provision requiring notice of any proceedings in connection with or arising out of the insolvency or winding up of a company to be given or published in the manner prescribed by the rules.

4   Provision with respect to the form, manner of serving, contents and proof of any petition, application, order, notice, statement or other document required to be presented, made, given, published or prepared under any enactment or subordinate legislation relating to, or to matters connected with or arising out of, the insolvency or winding up of companies.

5   Provision specifying the persons to whom any notice is to be given.

REGISTRATION OF VOLUNTARY ARRANGEMENTS

6   Provision for the registration of voluntary arrangements approved under Part I of this Act, including provision for the keeping and inspection of a register.

PROVISIONAL LIQUIDATOR

7   Provision as to the manner in which a provisional liquidator appointed under section 135 is to carry out his functions.

CONDUCT OF INSOLVENCY

8 Provision with respect to the certification of any person as, and as to the proof that a person is, the liquidator, administrator or administrative receiver of a company.

9 The following provision with respect to meetings of a company's creditors, contributories or members—

- (a) provision as to the manner of summoning a meeting (including provision as to how any power to require a meeting is to be exercised, provision as to the manner of determining the value of any debt or contribution for the purposes of any such power and provision making the exercise of any such power subject to the deposit of a sum sufficient to cover the expenses likely to be incurred in summoning and holding a meeting);
- (b) provision specifying the time and place at which a meeting may be held and the period of notice required for a meeting;
- (c) provision as to the procedure to be followed at a meeting (including the manner in which decisions may be reached by a meeting and the manner in which the value of any vote at a meeting is to be determined);
- (d) provision for requiring a person who is or has been an officer of the company to attend a meeting;
- (e) provision creating, in the prescribed circumstances, a presumption that a meeting has been duly summoned and held;
- (f) provision as to the manner of proving the decisions of a meeting.

10(1) Provision as to the functions, membership and proceedings of a committee established under section 26, 49, 68, 101, 141 or 142 of this Act.

10(2) The following provision with respect to the establishment of a committee under section 101, 141 or 142 of this Act, that is to say—

- (a) provision for resolving differences between a meeting of the company's creditors and a meeting of its contributories or members;
- (b) provision authorising the establishment of the committee without a meeting of contributories in a case where a company is being wound up on grounds including its inability to pay its debts; and
- (c) provision modifying the requirements of this Act with respect to the establishment of the committee in a case where a winding-up order has been made immediately upon the discharge of an administration order.

11 Provision as to the manner in which any requirement that may be imposed on a person under any Parts I to VII of this Act by the official receiver, the liquidator, administrator or administrative receiver of a company or a special manager appointed under section 177 is to be so imposed.

12 Provision as to the debts that may be proved in a winding up, as to the manner and conditions of proving a debt and as to the manner and expenses of establishing the value of any debt or security.

13 Provision with respect to the manner of the distribution of the property of a company that is being wound up, including provision with respect to unclaimed funds and dividends.

14 Provision which, with or without modifications, applies in relation to the winding up of companies any enactment contained in Parts VIII to XI of this Act or in the Bankruptcy (Scotland) Act 1985.

FINANCIAL PROVISIONS

15   Provision as to the amount, or manner of determining the amount, payable to the liquidator, administrator or administrative receiver of a company or a special manager appointed under section 177, by way of remuneration for the carrying out of functions in connection with or arising out of the insolvency or winding up of a company.

16   Provision with respect to the manner in which moneys received by the liquidator of a company in the course of carrying out his functions as such are to be invested or otherwise handled and with respect to the payment of interest on sums which, in pursuance of rules made by virtue of this paragraph, have been paid into the Insolvency Services Account.

17   Provision as to the fees, costs, charges and other expenses that may be treated as the expenses of a winding up.

18   Provisions as to the fees, costs, charges and other expenses that may be treated as properly incurred by the administrator or administrative receiver of a company.

19   Provision as to the fees, costs, charges and other expenses that may be incurred for any of the purposes of Part I of this Act or in the administration of any voluntary arrangement approved under that Part.

INFORMATION AND RECORDS

20   Provision requiring registrars and other officers of courts having jurisdiction in England and Wales in relation to, or to matters connected with or arising out of, the insolvency or winding up of companies—

   (a) to keep books and other records with respect to the exercise of that jurisdiction, and

   (b) to make returns to the Secretary of State of the business of those courts.

21   Provision requiring a creditor, member or contributory, or such a committee as is mentioned in paragraph 10 above, to be supplied (on payment in precribed cases of the prescribed fee) with such information and with copies of such documents as may be prescribed.

22   Provision as to the manner in which public examinations under sections 133 and 134 of this Act and proceedings under sections 236 and 237 are to be conducted, as to the circumstances in which records of such examinations or proceedings are to be made available to prescribed persons and as to the costs of such examinations and proceedings.

23   Provision imposing requirements with respect to—

   (a) the preparation and keeping by the liquidator, administrator or administrative receiver of a company, or by the supervisor of a voluntary arrangement approved under Part I of this Act, of prescribed books, accounts and other records;

   (b) the production of those books, accounts and records for inspection by prescribed persons;

   (c) the auditing of accounts kept by the liquidator, administrator or administrative receiver of a company, or the supervisor of such a voluntary arrangement; and

   (d) the issue by the administrator or administrative recever of a company of such a certificate as is mentioned in section 22(3)(b) of the Value Added Tax Act 1983 (refund of tax in cases of bad debts) and the supply of copies of the certificate to creditors of the company.

24 Provision requiring the person who is the supervisor of a voluntary arrangement approved under Part I, when it appears to him that the voluntary arrangement has been fully implemented and nothing remains to be done by him under the arrangement—

    (a) to give notice to that fact to persons bound by the voluntary arrangement, and

    (b) to report to those persons on the carrying out of the functions conferred on the supervisor of the arrangement.

25 Provision as to the manner in which the liquidator of a company is to act in relation to the books, papers and other records of the company, including provision authorising their disposal.

26 Provision imposing requirements in connection with the carrying out of functions under section 7(3) of the Company Directors Disqualification Act 1986 (including, in particular, requirements with respect to the making of periodic returns).

GENERAL

27 Provision conferring power on the Secretary of State to make regulations with respect to so much of any matter that may be provided for in the rules as relates to the carrying out of the functions of the liquidator, administrator or administrative receiver of a company.

28 Provision conferring a discretion on the court.

29 Provision conferring power on the court to make orders for the purpose of securing compliance with obligations imposed by or under section 22, 47, 66, 131, 143(2) or 235 of this Act or section 7(4) of the Company Directors Disqualification Act 1986.

30 Provision making non-compliance with any of the rules a criminal offence.

31 Provision making different provision for different cases or descriptions of cases, including different provisions for different areas.

(Former provision: IA 1985, Sch. 5)

General note

Much of the detail of the new insolvency régime which IA 1985 introduced and IA 1986 consolidated was left to be spelt out in subordinate legislation by regulations made under ss. 411ff. This Schedule outlines some of the matters which may be the subject of rules relating to company insolvency. The Winding-Up Rules 1949 have been superseded by IR 1986, which were brought into force contemporaneously with the commencement of the Act itself; but the Schedule is by no means confined in scope to matters which have traditionally been part of winding-up rules.

    Note that in this Schedule, "liquidator" includes a provisional liquidator (s. 411(3)). Attention should also be drawn to IR 1986, r. 12.1, which authorises the Secretary of State (pursuant to Sch. 8, para. 27 and Sch. 9, para. 30) to make regulations in regard to various matters, supplementary to the Insolvency Rules made under s. 411.

    Among the items listed which cannot be regarded as purely procedural or are not self-explanatory the following may be noted.

Para. 6

There is no mention in the body of the Act of any registration procedure for a voluntary arrangement, although certain matters must be reported to the court (see, e.g., ss. 2(2), 4(6)). The present paragraph has been implemented by IR 1986, r. 1.24(5), which provides for registration with the registrar of companies.

Paras. 12, 14

The Parts of the Act dealing with company insolvency contain no definition of "debts" and no provisions relating to proofs of debts, in marked contrast to those relating to the bankruptcy of individuals (see ss. 322, 382), and, indeed, to the repealed CA 1985, s. 611. It is only by subordinate legislation made under these paragraphs of the present Schedule that such important matters as the nature of provable debts, the quantification of such debts, allowances for mutual credit and set-off, etc., are established for company liquidations and some (but not all) analogous proceedings. This has been done by IR 1986, rr. 4.73ff, 4.86ff and 12.3.

For further discussion of the term "debts", see the note to s. 1(1).

The Companies Acts prior to the present legislation always included a substantive provision (e.g. CA 1985, s. 612) which incorporated specified aspects of bankruptcy law into the law governing the winding up of *insolvent* companies. Paragraph 14 of this Schedule is potentially of wider scope, since it applies to solvent liquidations as well.

See further the introductory note to Pt. IV, Ch. VIII, following s. 174.

Para. 26

Regulations in regard to these matters have been made by the Insolvent Companies (Reports on Conduct of Directors) No. 2 Rules 1986 (SI 1986 No. 2134, operative 29 December 1986), superseding the Insolvent Companies (Reports on Conduct of Directors) Rules 1986 (SI 1986 No. 611, operative 28 April 1986); the Insolvent Companies (Reports on Conduct of Directors) (No. 2) (Scotland) Rules 1986 (SI 1986 No. 1916 (S. 140), operative 29 December 1986), which supersedes the Insolvent Companies (Reports on Conduct of Directors) (Scotland) Rules 1986 (SI 1986 No. 626), operative 28 April 1986). See the note to CDDA 1986, s. 7.

Regulations under the same Act have also been made governing the procedure for application to the court for orders for the disqualification of directors under IA 1985, ss. 12–13 (now CDDA 1986, ss. 6–8): the Insolvent Companies (Disqualification of Unfit Directors) Proceedings Rules 1987 (SI 1987 No. 2023, operative 11 January 1988), replacing the Insolvent Companies (Disqualification of Unfit Directors) Proceedings Rules 1986 (SI 1986 No. 612, operative 28 April 1986). See the note to CDDA 1986, s. 7(1).

Para. 27

For the relevant regulations see the Insolvency Regulations 1994 (SI 1994 No. 2507), operative 24 October 1994, replacing the original Insolvency Regulations 1986 (SI 1986 No. 1994), as amended.

Schedule 9 — Provisions Capable of Inclusion in Individual Insolvency Rules

Section 412

COURTS

1 Provision with respect to the arrangement and disposition of the business under Parts VIII to XI of this Act of courts having jurisdiction for the purpose of those Parts, including provision for the allocation of proceedings under those Parts to particular courts and for the transfer of such proceedings from one court to another.

2 Provision for enabling a registrar in bankruptcy of the High Court or a registrar of a county court having jurisdiction for the purposes of those Parts to exercise such of the jurisdiction conferred for those purposes on the High Court or, as the case may be, that county court as may be prescribed.

3 Provision for regulating the practice and procedure of any court exercising jurisdiction for the purposes of those Parts, being any provision that could be made by rules of court.

4 Provision conferring rights of audience, in courts exercising jurisdiction for the purposes of those Parts, on the official receiver and on solicitors.

NOTICES ETC.

5 Provision requiring notice of any proceedings under Parts VIII to XI of this Act or of any matter relating to or arising out of a proposal under Part VIII or a bankruptcy to be given or published in the prescribed manner.

6 Provision with respect to the form, manner of serving, contents and proof of any petition, application, order, notice, statement or other document required to be presented, made, given, published or prepared under any enactment contained in Parts VIII to XI or subordinate legislation under those Parts or Part XV (including provision requiring prescribed matters to be verified by affidavit).

7 Provision specifying the persons to whom any notice under Parts VIII to XI is to be given.

REGISTRATION OF VOLUNTARY ARRANGEMENTS

8 Provision for the registration of voluntary arrangements approved under Part VIII of this Act, including provision for the keeping and inspection of a register.

INTERIM RECEIVER

9 Provision as to the manner in which an interim receiver appointed under section 286 is to carry out his functions, including any such provision as is specified in relation to the trustee of a bankrupt's estate in paragraph 21 or 27 below.

RECEIVER OR MANAGER

10 Provision as to the manner in which the official receiver is to carry out his functions as receiver or manager of a bankrupt's estate under section 287, including any such provision as is specified in relation to the trustee of a bankrupt's estate in paragraph 21 or 27 below.

ADMINISTRATION OF INDIVIDUAL INSOLVENCY

11 Provision with respect to the certification of the appointment of any person as trustee of a bankrupt's estate and as to the proof of that appointment.

12 The following provision with respect to meetings of creditors—

    (a) provision as to the manner of summoning a meeting (including provision as to how any power to require a meeting is to be exercised, provision as to the manner of determining the value of any debt for the purposes of any such power and provision making the exercise of any such power subject to the deposit of a sum sufficient to cover the expenses likely to be incurred in summoning and holding a meeting);

(b) provision specifying the time and place at which a meeting may be held and the period of notice required for a meeting;

(c) provision as to the procedure to be followed at such a meeting (including the manner in which decisions may be reached by a meeting and the manner in which the value of any vote at a meeting is to be determined);

(d) provision for requiring a bankrupt or debtor to attend a meeting;

(e) provision creating, in the prescribed circumstances, a presumption that a meeting has been duly summoned and held; and

(f) provision as to the manner of proving the decisions of a meeting.

13 Provision as to the functions, membership and proceedings of a creditors' committee established under section 301.

14 Provision as to the manner in which any requirement that may be imposed on a person under Parts VIII to XI of this Act by the official receiver, the trustee of a bankrupt's estate or a special manager appointed under section 370 is to be imposed and, in the case of any requirement imposed under section 305(3) (information etc. to be given by the trustee to the official receiver), provision conferring power on the court to make orders for the purpose of securing compliance with that requirement.

15 Provision as to the manner in which any requirement imposed by virtue of section 310(3) (compliance with income payments order) is to take effect.

16 Provision as to the terms and conditions that may be included in a charge under section 313 (dwelling house forming part of bankrupt's estate).

17 Provision as to the debts that may be proved in any bankruptcy, as to the manner and conditions of proving a debt and as to the manner and expenses of establishing the value of any debt or security.

18 Provision with respect to the manner of the distribution of a bankrupt's estate, including provision with respect to unclaimed funds and dividends.

19 Provision modifying the application of Parts VIII to XI of this Act in relation to a debtor or bankrupt who has died.

FINANCIAL PROVISIONS

20 Provision as to the amount, or manner of determining the amount, payable to an interim receiver, the trustee of a bankrupt's estate or a special manager appointed under section 370 by way of remuneration for the performance of functions in connection with or arising out of the bankruptcy of any person.

21 Provision with respect to the manner in which moneys received by the trustee of a bankrupt's estate in the course of carrying out his functions as such are to be handled.

22 Provision as to the fees, costs, charges and other expenses that may be treated as the expenses of a bankruptcy.

23 Provision as to the fees, costs, charges and other expenses that may be incurred for any of the purposes of Part VIII of this Act or in the administration of any voluntary arrangement approved under that Part.

INFORMATION AND RECORDS

24 Provision requiring registrars and other officers of courts having jurisdiction for the purposes of Parts VIII to XI—

(a) to keep books and other records with respect to the exercise of that jurisdiction and of jurisdiction under the Deeds of Arrangement Act 1914, and

(b) to make returns to the Secretary of State of the business of those courts.

25   Provision requiring a creditor or a committee established under section 301 to be supplied (on payment in prescribed cases of the prescribed fee) with such information and with copies of such documents as may be prescribed.

26   Provision as to the manner in which public examinations under section 290 and proceedings under sections 366 to 368 are to be conducted, as to the circumstances in which records of such examinations and proceedings are to be made available to prescribed persons and as to the costs of such examinations and proceedings.

27   Provision imposing requirements with respect to—

(a) the preparation and keeping by the trustee of a bankrupt's estate, or the supervisor of a voluntary arrangement approved under Part VIII, of prescribed books, accounts and other records;

(b) the production of those books, accounts and records for inspection by prescribed persons; and

(c) the auditing of accounts kept by the trustee of a bankrupt's estate or the supervisor of such a voluntary arrangement.

28   Provision requiring the person who is the supervisor of a voluntary arrangement approved under Part VIII, when it appears to him that the voluntary arrangement has been fully implemented and that nothing remains to be done by him under it—

(a) to give notice of that fact to persons bound by the voluntary arrangement, and

(b) to report to those persons on the carrying out of the functions conferred on the supervisor of it.

29   Provision as to the manner in which the trustee of a bankrupt's estate is to act in relation to the books, papers and other records of the bankrupt, including provision authorising their disposal.

GENERAL

30   Provision conferring power on the Secretary of State to make regulations with respect to so much of any matter that may be provided for in the rules as relates to the carrying out of the functions of an interim receiver appointed under section 286, of the official receiver while acting as a receiver or manager under section 287 or of a trustee of a bankrupt's estate.

31   Provision conferring a discretion on the court.

32   Provision making non-compliance with any of the rules a criminal offence.

33   Provision making different provision for different cases, including different provision for different areas.

(Former provision: IA 1985, Sch. 7)

General note

This provides a useful guide to the matters which may be provided for by the rules. Authority to make these rules is given by s. 412, and the note on that section should be referred to. The utility of para. 17 was illustrated in *Woodley* v *Woodley (No. 2)* [1994] 1 WLR 1167. For the text of the Insolvency Rules 1986 see below, at p. 626. For the regulations referred to in para. 30 see the Insolvency Regulations 1994 (SI 1994 No. 2507), operative 24 October 1994, replacing the original Insolvency Regulations 1986 (SI 1986 No. 1994), as amended.

Schedule 10 — Punishment of Offences under this Act

Note: In the fourth and fifth columns of this Schedule, "**the statutory maximum**" means—
     (a) in England and Wales, the prescribed sum under section 32 of the Magistrates' Courts Act 1980 (c. 43), and
     (b) in Scotland, the prescribed sum under section 289B of the Criminal Procedure (Scotland) Act 1975 (c. 21).

Section of Act creating offence	General nature of offence	Mode of prosecution	Punishment	Daily default fine (where applicable)
12(2) ...	Company and others failing to state in correspondence etc. that administrator appointed.	Summary.	One-fifth of the statutory maximum.	
15(8) ...	Failure of administrator to register office copy of court order permitting disposal of charged property.	Summary.	One-fifth of the statutory maximum.	One-fiftieth of the statutory maximum.
18(5) ...	Failure of administrator to register office copy of court order varying or discharging administration order.	Summary.	One-fifth of the statutory maximum.	One-fiftieth of the statutory maximum.
21(3) ...	Administrator failing to register administration order and give notice of appointment.	Summary.	One-fifth of the statutory maximum.	One-fiftieth of the statutory maximum.
22(6) ...	Failure to comply with provisions relating to statement of affairs, where administrator appointed.	1. On indictment. 2. Summary.	A fine. The statutory maximum.	One-tenth of the statutory maximum.
23(3) ...	Administrator failing to send out, register and lay before creditors statement of his proposals.	Summary.	One-fifth of the statutory maximum.	One-fiftieth of the statutory maximum.
24(7) ...	Administrator failing to file court order discharging administration order under s. 24.	Summary.	One-fifth of the statutory maximum.	One-fiftieth of the statutory maximum.
27(6) ...	Administrator failing to file court order discharging administration order under s. 27.	Summary.	One-fifth of the statutory maximum.	One-fiftieth of the statutory maximum.

Section of Act creating offence	General nature of offence	Mode of prosecution	Punishment	Daily default fine (where applicable)
30	Body corporate acting as receiver.	1. On indictment. 2. Summary.	A fine. The statutory maximum.	
31	Undischarged bankrupt acting as receiver or manager.	1. On indictment. 2. Summary.	2 years or a fine, or both. 6 months or the statutory maximum, or both.	
38(5) ...	Receiver failing to deliver accounts to registrar.	Summary.	One-fifth of the statutory maximum.	One-fiftieth of the statutory maximum.
39(2) ...	Company and others failing to state in correspondence that receiver appointed.	Summary.	One-fifth of the statutory maximum.	
43(6) ...	Administrative receiver failing to file office copy of order permitting disposal of charged property.	Summary.	One-fifth of the statutory maximum.	One-fiftieth of the statutory maximum.
45(5) ...	Administrative receiver failing to file notice of vacation of office.	Summary.	One-fifth of the statutory maximum.	One-fiftieth of the statutory maximum.
46(4) ...	Administrative receiver failing to give notice of his appointment.	Summary.	One-fifth of the statutory maximum.	One-fiftieth of the statutory maximum.
47(6) ...	Failure to comply with provisions relating to statement of affairs where administrative receiver appointed.	1. On indictment. 2. Summary.	A fine. The statutory maximum.	One-tenth of the statutory maximum.
48(8) ...	Administrative receiver failing to comply with requirements as to his report.	Summary.	One-fifth of the statutory maximum.	One-fiftieth of the statutory maximum.
51(4) ...	Body corporate or Scottish firm acting as receiver.	1. On indictment. 2. Summary.	A fine. The statutory maximum.	
51(5) ...	Undischarged bankrupt acting as receiver (Scotland).	1. On indictment. 2. Summary.	2 years or a fine, or both. 6 months or the statutory maximum, or both.	
53(2) ...	Failing to deliver to registrar copy of instrument or appointing of receiver.	Summary.	One-fifth of the statutory maximum.	One-fiftieth of the statutory maximum.

Section of Act creating offence	General nature of offence	Mode of prosecution	Punishment	Daily default fine (where applicable)
54(3) ...	Failing to deliver to registrar the court's interlocutor appointing receiver.	Summary.	One-fifth of the statutory maximum.	One-fiftieth of the statutory maximum.
61(7) ...	Receiver failing to send registrar certified copy of court order authorising disposal of charged property.	Summary.	One-fifth of the statutory maximum.	One-fiftieth of the statutory maximum.
62(5) ...	Failing to give notice to registrar of cessation or removal of receiver.	Summary.	One-fifth of the statutory maximum.	One-fiftieth of the statutory maximum.
64(2) ...	Company and others failing to state in correspondence that receiver appointed.	Summary.	One-fifth of the statutory maximum.	One-fiftieth of the statutory maximum.
65(4) ...	Receiver failing to send or publish notice of his appointment.	Summary.	One-fifth of the statutory maximum.	One-fiftieth of the statutory maximum.
66(6) ...	Failing to comply with provisions concerning statement of affairs where receiver appointed.	1. On indictment. 2. Summary.	A fine. The statutory maximum.	One-tenth of the statutory maximum.
67(8) ...	Receiver failing to comply with requirements as to his report.	Summary.	One-fifth of the statutory maximum.	One-fiftieth of the statutory maximum.
85(2) ...	Company failing to give notice in Gazette of resolution for voluntary winding up.	Summary.	One-fifth of the statutory maximum.	One-fiftieth of the statutory maximum.
89(4) ...	Director making statutory declaration of company's solvency without reasonable grounds for his opinion.	1. On indictment. 2. Summary.	2 years or a fine, or both. 6 months or the statutory maximum, or both	
89(6) ...	Declaration under section 89 not delivered to registrar within prescribed time.	Summary.	One-fifth of the statutory maximum.	One-fiftieth of the statutory maximum.
93(3) ...	Liquidator failing to summon general meeting of company at each year's end.	Summary.	One-fifth of the statutory maximum.	One-fiftieth of the statutory maximum.
94(4) ...	Liquidator failing to send to registrar a copy of account of winding up and return of final meeting.	Summary.	One-fifth of the statutory maximum.	One-fiftieth of the statutory maximum.

Section of Act creating offence	General nature of offence	Mode of prosecution	Punishment	Daily default fine (where applicable)
94(6) ...	Liquidator failing to call final meeting.	Summary.	One-fifth of the statutory maximum.	
95(8) ...	Liquidator failing to comply with s. 95, where company insolvent.	Summary.	The statutory maximum.	
98(6) ...	Company failing to comply with s. 98 in respect of summoning and giving notice of creditors' meeting.	1. On indictment. 2. Summary.	A fine. The statutory maximum.	
99(3) ...	Directors failing to attend and lay statement in prescribed form before creditors' meeting.	1. On indictment. 2. Summary.	A fine. The statutory maximum.	
105(3) ...	Liquidator failing to summon company general meeting and creditors' meeting at each year's end.	Summary.	One-fifth of the statutory maximum.	
106(4) ...	Liquidator failing to send to registrar account of winding up and return of final meetings.	Summary.	One-fifth of the statutory maximum.	One-fiftieth of the statutory maximum.
106(6) ...	Liquidator failing to call final meeting of company or creditors.	Summary.	One-fifth of the statutory maximum.	
109(2) ...	Liquidator failing to publish notice of his appointment.	Summary.	One-fifth of the statutory maximum.	One-fiftieth of the statutory maximum.
114(4) ...	Directors exercising powers in breach of s. 114, where no liquidator.	Summary.	The statutory maximum.	One-fiftieth of the statutory maximum.
131(7) ...	Failing to comply with requirements as to statement of affairs, where liquidator appointed.	1. On indictment 2. Summary.	A fine. The statutory maximum.	One-tenth of the statutory maximum.
164	Giving, offering etc. corrupt inducement affecting appointment of liquidator.	1. On indictment. 2. Summary.	A fine. The statutory maximum.	
166(7) ...	Liquidator failing to comply with requirements of s. 166 in creditors' voluntary winding up.	Summary.	The statutory maximum.	

Section of Act creating offence	General nature of offence	Mode of prosecution	Punishment	Daily default fine (where applicable)
188(2) ...	Default in compliance with s. 188 as to notification that company being wound up.	Summary.	One-fifth of the statutory maximum.	One-fiftieth of the statutory maximum.
192(2) ...	Liquidator failing to notify registrar as to progress of winding up.	Summary.	One-fifth of the statutory maximum.	One-fiftieth of the statutory maximum.
201(4) ...	Failing to deliver to registrar office copy of court order deferring dissolution.	Summary.	One-fifth of the statutory maximum.	One-fiftieth of the statutory maximum.
203(6) ...	Failing to deliver to registrar copy of directions or result of appeal under s. 203.	Summary.	One-fifth of the statutory maximum.	One-fiftieth of the statutory maximum.
204(7) ...	Liquidator failing to deliver to registrar copy of court order for early dissolution.	Summary.	One-fifth of the statutory maximum.	One-fiftieth of the statutory maximum.
204(8) ...	Failing to deliver to registrar copy of court order deferring early dissolution.	Summary.	One-fifth of the statutory maximum.	One-fiftieth of the statutory maximum.
205(7) ...	Failing to deliver to registrar copy of Secretary of State's directions or court order deferring dissolution.	Summary.	One-fifth of the statutory maximum.	One-fiftieth of the statutory maximum.
206(1) ...	Fraud etc. in anticipation of winding up.	1. On indictment. 2. Summary.	7 years or a fine, or both. 6 months or the statutory maximum, or both.	
206(2) ...	Privity to fraud in anticipation of winding up; fraud or privy to fraud. after commencement of winding up.	1. On indictment. 2. Summary.	7 years or a fine, or both. 6 months or the statutory maximum, or both.	
206(5) ...	Knowingly taking in pawn or pledge, or otherwise receiving, company property.	1. On indictment. 2. Summary.	7 years or a fine, or both. 6 months or the statutory maximum, or both.	
207 ...	Officer of company entering into transaction in fraud of company's creditors.	1. On indictment. 2. Summary.	2 years or a fine, or both. 6 months or the statutory maximum, or both.	

Section of Act creating offence	General nature of offence	Mode of prosecution	Punishment	Daily default fine (where applicable)
208	Officer of company misconducting himself in course of winding up.	1. On indictment. 2. Summary.	7 years or a fine, or both. 6 months or the statutory maximum, or both.	
209	Officer or contributory destroying, falsifying, etc. company books.	1. On indictment. 2. Summary.	7 years or a fine, or both. 6 months or the statutory maximum, or both.	
210	Officer of company making material omission from statement relating to company's affairs.	1. On indictment. 2. Summary.	7 years or a fine, or both. 6 months or the statutory maximum, or both.	
211	False representation or fraud for purpose of obtaining creditors' consent to an agreement in connection with winding up.	1. On indictment. 2. Summary.	7 years or a fine, or both. 6 months or the statutory maximum, or both.	
216(4) ...	Contravening restrictions on re-use of name of company in insolvent liquidation.	1. On indictment. 2. Summary.	2 years or a fine, or both. 6 months or the statutory maximum, or both.	
235(5) ...	Failing to co-operate with office-holder.	1. On indictment. 2. Summary.	A fine. The statutory maximum.	One-tenth of the statutory maximum.
353(1) ...	Bankrupt failing to disclose property or disposals to official receiver or trustee.	1. On indictment. 2. Summary.	7 years or a fine, or both. 6 months or the statutory maximum, or both.	
354(1) ...	Bankrupt failing to deliver property to, or concealing property from, official receiver or trustee.	1. On indictment. 2. Summary.	7 years or a fine, or both. 6 months or the statutory maximum, or both.	
354(2) ...	Bankrupt removing property which he is required to deliver to official receiver or trustee.	1. On indictment. 2. Summary.	7 years or a fine, or both. 6 months or the statutory maximum, or both.	

Section of Act creating offence	General nature of offence	Mode of prosecution	Punishment	Daily default fine (where applicable)
354(3) ...	Bankrupt failing to account for loss of substantial part of property.	1. On indictment. 2. Summary.	2 years or a fine, or both. 6 months or the statutory maximum, or both.	
355(1) ...	Bankrupt failing to deliver books, papers and records to official receiver or trustee.	1. On indictment. 2. Summary.	7 years or a fine, or both. 6 months or the statutory maximum, or both.	
355(2) ...	Bankrupt concealing, destroying etc. books, papers or records, or making false entries in them.	1. On indictment. 2. Summary.	7 years or a fine, or both. 6 months or the statutory maximum, or both.	
355(3) ...	Bankrupt disposing of, or altering, books, papers or records relating to his estate or affairs.	1. On indictment. 2. Summary.	7 years or a fine, or both. 6 months or the statutory maximum, or both.	
356(1) ...	Bankrupt making material omission in statement relating to his affairs.	1. On indictment. 2. Summary.	7 years or a fine, or both. 6 months or the statutory maximum, or both.	
356(2) ...	Bankrupt making false statement, or failing to inform trustee, where false debt proved.	1. On indictment. 2. Summary.	7 years or a fine, or both. 6 months or the statutory maximum, or both.	
357 ...	Bankrupt fraudulently disposing of property.	1. On indictment. 2. Summary.	2 years or a fine, or both. 6 months or the statutory maximum, or both.	
358 ...	Bankrupt absconding with property he is required to deliver to official receiver or trustee.	1. On indictment. 2. Summary.	2 years or a fine, or both. 6 months or the statutory maximum, or both.	
359(1) ...	Bankrupt disposing of property obtained on credit and not paid for.	1. On indictment. 2. Summary.	7 years or a fine, or both. 6 months or the statutory maximum, or both.	

Section of Act creating offence	General nature of offence	Mode of prosecution	Punishment	Daily default fine (where applicable)
359(2) ...	Obtaining property in respect of which money is owed by a bankrupt.	1. On indictment. 2. Summary.	7 years or a fine, or both. 6 months or the statutory maximum, or both.	
360(1) ...	Bankrupt obtaining credit or engaging in business without disclosing his status or name in which he was made bankrupt.	1. On indictment. 2. Summary.	2 years or a fine, or both. 6 months or the statutory maximum, or both.	
360(3) ...	Person made bankrupt in Scotland or Northern Ireland obtaining credit, etc. in England and Wales.	1. On indictment. 2. Summary.	2 years or a fine, or both. 6 months or the statutory maximum, or both.	
361(1) ...	Bankrupt failing to keep proper accounting records.	1. On indictment. 2. Summary.	2 years or a fine, or both. 6 months or the statutory maximum, or both.	
362 ...	Bankrupt increasing extent of insolvency by gambling.	1. On indictment. 2. Summary.	2 years or a fine, or both. 6 months or the statutory maximum, or both.	
389 ...	Acting as insolvency practitioner when not qualified.	1. On indictment. 2. Summary.	2 years or a fine, or both. 6 months or the statutory maximum, or both.	
429(5) ...	Contravening s. 429 in respect of disabilities imposed by county court on revocation of administrative order.	1. On indictment. 2. Summary.	2 years or a fine, or both. 6 months or the statutory maximum, or both.	
Sch. 7, para. 4(3) ...	Failure to attend and give evidence to Insolvency Practitioners Tribunal; suppressing, concealing, etc. relevant documents.	Summary.	Level 3 on the standard scale within the meaning given by section 75 of the Criminal Justice Act 1982.	

(Former provision: CA 1985, Sch. 24 and IA 1985 (passim))

General note
This technique of using a Schedule of punishments is used by CA 1985, but not by IA 1985. Guidance on the use of Sch. 10 is provided by s. 430. Sections 431 and 432 are also of assistance when applying Sch. 10.

The "statutory maximum" referred to in the introductory note to the Schedule and in columns 4 and 5 is at present £5,000 (but £2,000 in respect of offences committed before 1 October 1992): see Criminal Justice Act 1991, s. 17 and SI 1992 No. 333, 1993 No. 2118.

Schedule 11— Transitional Provisions and Savings

Section 437

Part I — Company Insolvency and Winding Up

ADMINISTRATION ORDERS

1(1)   Where any right to appoint an administrative receiver of a company is conferred by any debentures or floating charge created before the appointed day, the conditions precedent to the exercise of that right are deemed to include the presentation of a petition applying for an administration order to be made in relation to the company.

1(2)   **"Administrative receiver"** here has the meaning assigned by section 251.

RECEIVER AND MANAGERS (ENGLAND AND WALES)

2(1)   In relation to any receiver or manager of a company's property who was appointed before the appointed day, the new law does not apply; and the relevant provisions of the former law continue to have effect.

2(2)   ·**"The new law"** here means Chapter I of Part III, and Part VI, of this Act; and **"the former law"** means the Companies Act and so much of this Act as replaces provisions of that Act (without the amendments in paragraphs 15 to 17 of Schedule 6 to the Insolvency Act 1985, or the associated repeals made by that Act), and any provision of the Insolvency Act 1985 which was in force before the appointed day.

2(3)   This paragraph is without prejudice to the power conferred by the Act under which rules under section 411 may make transitional provision in connection with the coming into force of those rules; and such provision may apply those rules in relation to the receiver or manager of a company's property notwithstanding that he was appointed before the coming into force of the rules or section 411.

RECEIVERS (SCOTLAND)

3(1)   In relation to any receiver appointed under section 467 of the Companies Act before the appointed day, the new law does not apply and the relevant provisions of the former law continue to have effect.

3(2) **"The new law"** here means Chapter II of Part III, and Part VI, of this Act; and **"the former law"** means the Companies Act and so much of this Act as replaces provisions of that Act (without the amendments in paragraphs 18 to 22 of Schedule 6 to the Insolvency Act 1985 or the associated repeals made by that Act), and any provision of the Insolvency Act 1985 which was in force before the appointed day.

3(3) This paragraph is without prejudice to the power conferred by this Act under which rules under section 411 may make transitional provision in connection with the coming into force of those rules; and such provision may apply those rules in relation to a receiver appointed under section 467 notwithstanding that he was appointed before the coming into force of the rules or section 411.

WINDING UP ALREADY IN PROGRESS

4(1) In relation to any winding up which has commenced, or is treated as having commenced, before the appointed day, the new law does not apply, and the former law continues to have effect, subject to the following paragraphs.

4(2) **"The new law"** here means any provisions in the first Group of Parts of this Act which replace sections 66 to 87 and 89 to 105 of the Insolvency Act 1985; and **"the former law"** means Parts XX and XXI of the Companies Act (without the amendments in paragraphs 23 to 52 of Schedule 6 to the Insolvency Act 1985, or the associated repeals made by that Act).

Note

I(A)R 1987, r. 3(3) applies IR 1986, r. 4.223 (as amended) to those insolvency proceedings specified in para. 4(1), so that this rule applies transitionally to liquidations which commenced before 29 December 1986.

STATEMENT OF AFFAIRS

5(1) Where a winding up by the court in England and Wales has commenced, or is treated as having commenced, before the appointed day, the official receiver or (on appeal from a refusal by him) the court may, at any time on or after that day—

    (a) release a person from an obligation imposed on him by or under section 528 of the Companies Act (statement of affairs), or

    (b) extend the period specified in subsection (6) of that section.

5(2) Accordingly, on and after the appointed day, section 528(6) has effect in relation to a winding up to which this paragraph applies with the omission of the words from "or within" onwards.

PROVISIONS RELATING TO LIQUIDATOR

6(1) This paragraph applies as regards the liquidator in the case of a winding up by the court in England and Wales commenced, or treated as having commenced, before the appointed day.

6(2) The official receiver may, at any time when he is liquidator of the company, apply to the Secretary of State for the appointment of a liquidator in his (the official receiver's) place; and on any such application the Secretary of State shall either make an appointment or decline to make one.

6(3)   Where immediately before the appointed day the liquidator of the company has not made an application under section 545 of the Companies Act (release of liquidators), then—

(a) except where the Secretary of State otherwise directs, sections 146(1) and (2) and 172(8) of this Act apply, and section 545 does not apply, in relation to any liquidator of that company who holds office on or at any time after the appointed day and is not the official receiver;

(b) section 146(3) applies in relation to the carrying out at any time after that day by any liquidator of the company of any of his functions; and

(c) a liquidator in relation to whom section 172(8) has effect by virtue of this paragraph has his release with effect from the time specified in section 174 (4)(d) of this Act.

6(4)   Subsection (6) of section 174 of this Act has effect for the purposes of sub-paragraph (3)(c) above as it has for the purposes of that section, but as if the reference to section 212 were to section 631 of the Companies Act.

6(5)   The liquidator may employ a solicitor to assist him in the carrying out of his functions without the permission of the committee of inspection; but if he does so employ a solicitor he shall inform the committee of inspection that he has done so.

WINDING UP UNDER SUPERVISION OF THE COURT

7   The repeals in Part II of Schedule 10 to the Insolvency Act 1985 of references (in the Companies Act and elsewhere) to a winding up under the supervision of the court do not affect the operation of the enactments in which the references are contained in relation to any case in which an order under section 606 of the Companies Act (power to order winding up under supervision) was made before the appointed day.

SAVING FOR POWER TO MAKE RULES

8(1)   Paragraphs 4 to 7 are without prejudice to the power conferred by this Act under which rules made under section 411 may make transitional provision in connection with the coming into force of those rules.

8(2)   Such provision may apply those rules in relation to a winding up notwithstanding that the winding up commenced, or is treated as having commenced, before the coming into force of the rules or section 411.

SETTING ASIDE OF PREFERENCES AND OTHER TRANSACTIONS

9(1)   Where a provision in Part VI of this Act applies in relation to a winding up or in relation to a case in which an administration order has been made, a preference given, floating charge created or other transaction entered into before the appointed day shall not be set aside under that provision except to the extent that it could have been set aside under the law in force immediately before that day, assuming for this purpose that any relevant administration order had been a winding-up order.

9(2)   The references above to setting aside a preference, floating charge or other transaction include the making of an order which varies or reverses any effect of a preference, floating charge or other transaction.

Part II — Individual Insolvency

BANKRUPTCY (GENERAL)

10(1)   Subject to the following provisions of this Part of this Schedule, so much of this Act as replaces Part III of the Insolvency Act 1985 does not apply in relation to any case in which a petition in bankruptcy was presented, or a receiving order or adjudication in bankruptcy was made, before the appointed day.

10(2)   In relation to any such case as is mentioned above, the enactments specified in Schedule 8 to that Act, so far as they relate to bankruptcy, and those specified in Parts III and IV of Schedule 10 to that Act, so far as they so relate, have effect without the amendments and repeals specified in those Schedules.

10(3)   Where any subordinate legislation made under an enactment referred to in sub-paragraph (2) is in force immediately before the appointed day, that subordinate legislation continues to have effect on and after that day in relation to any such case as is mentioned in sub-paragraph (1).

11(1)   In relation to any such case as is mentioned in paragraph 10(1) the references in any enactment or subordinate legislation to a petition, order or other matter which is provided for under the Bankruptcy Act 1914 and corresponds to a petition, order or other matter provided for under provisions of this Act replacing Part III of the Insolvency Act 1985 continue on and after the appointed day to have effect as references to the petition, order or matter provided for by the Act of 1914; but otherwise those references have effect on and after that day as references to the petition, order or matter provided for by those provisions of this Act.

11(2)   Without prejudice to sub-paragraph (1), in determining for the purposes of section 279 of this Act (period of bankruptcy) or paragraph 13 below whether any person was an undischarged bankrupt at a time before the appointed day, an adjudication in bankruptcy and an annulment of a bankruptcy under the Act of 1914 are to be taken into account in the same way, respectively, as a bankruptcy order under the provisions of this Act replacing Part III of the Insolvency Act 1985 and the annulment under section 282 of this Act of such an order.

12   Transactions entered into before the appointed day have effect on and after that day as if references to acts of bankruptcy in the provisions for giving effect to those transactions continued to be references to acts of bankruptcy within the meaning of the Bankruptcy Act 1914, but as if such acts included failure to comply with a statutory demand served under section 268 of this Act.

DISCHARGE FROM OLD BANKRUPTCY

13(1)   Where a person—

    (a) was adjudged bankrupt before the appointed day or is adjudged on or after that day on a petition presented before that day, and

(b) that person was not an undischarged bankrupt at any time in the period of 15 years ending with the adjudication,

that person is deemed (if not previously discharged) to be discharged from his bankruptcy for the purposes of the Bankruptcy Act 1914 at the end of the discharge period.

13(2) Subject to sub-paragraph (3) below, the discharge period for the purposes of this paragraph is—

(a) in the case of a person adjudged bankrupt before the appointed day, the period of 3 years beginning with that day, and

(b) in the case of a person who is adjudged bankrupt on or after that day on a petition presented before that day, the period of 3 years beginning with the date of the adjudication.

13(3) Where the court exercising jurisdiction in relation to a bankruptcy to which this paragraph applies is satisfied, on the application of the official receiver, that the bankrupt has failed, or is failing, to comply with any of his obligations under the Bankruptcy Act 1914, any rules made under that Act or any such rules as are mentioned in paragraph 19(1) below, the court may order that the discharge period shall cease to run for such period, or until the fulfilment of such conditions (including a condition requiring the court to be satisfied as to any matter) as may be specified in the order.

PROVISIONS RELATING TO TRUSTEE

14(1) This paragraph applies as regards the trustee in the case of a person adjudged bankrupt before the appointed day, or adjudged bankrupt on or after that day on a petition presented before that day.

14(2) The official receiver may at any time when he is trustee of the bankrupt's estate apply to the Secretary of State for the appointment of a person as trustee instead of the official receiver; and on any such application the Secretary of State shall either make an appointment or decline to make one.

14(3) Where on the appointed day the trustee of a bankrupt's estate has not made an application under section 93 of the Bankruptcy Act 1914 (release of trustee), then—

(a) except where the Secretary of State otherwise directs, sections 298(8), 304 and 331(1) to (3) of this Act apply, and section 93 of the Act of 1914 does not apply, in relation to any trustee of the bankrupt's estate who holds office on or at any time after the appointed day and is not the official receiver;

(b) section 331(4) of this Act applies in relation to the carrying out at any time on or after the appointed day by the trustee of the bankrupt's estate of any of his functions; and

(c) a trustee in relation to whom section 298(8) of this Act has effect by virtue of this paragraph has his release with effect from the time specified in section 299(3)(d).

14(4) Subsection (5) of section 299 has effect for the purposes of sub-paragraph (3)(c) as it has for the purposes of that section.

14(5)   In the application of subsection (3) of section 331 in relation to a case by virtue of this paragraph, the reference in that subsection to section 330(1) has effect as a reference to section 67 of the Bankruptcy Act 1914.

14(6)   The trustee of the bankrupt's estate may employ a solicitor to assist him in the carrying out of his functions without the permission of the committee of inspection; but if he does so employ a solicitor, he shall inform the committee of inspection that he has done so.

COPYRIGHT

15   Where a person who is adjudged bankrupt on a petition presented on or after the appointed day is liable, by virtue of a transaction entered into before that day, to pay royalties or a share of the profits to any person in respect of any copyright or interest in copyright comprised in the bankrupt's estate, section 60 of the Bankruptcy Act 1914 (limitation on trustee's powers in relation to copyright) applies in relation to the trustee of that estate as it applies in relation to a trustee in bankruptcy under the Act of 1914.

SECOND BANKRUPTCY

16(1)   Sections 334 and 335 of this Act apply with the following modifications where the earlier bankruptcy (within the meaning of section 334) is a bankruptcy in relation to which the Act of 1914 applies instead of the second Group of Parts in this Act, that is to say—

    (a) references to property vested in the existing trustee under section 307(3) of this Act have effect as references to such property vested in that trustee as was acquired by or devolved on the bankrupt after the commencement (within the meaning of the Act of 1914) of the earlier bankruptcy; and

    (b) references to an order under section 310 of this Act have effect as references to an order under section 51 of the Act of 1914.

16(2)   Section 39 of the Act of 1914 (second bankruptcy) does not apply where a person who is an undischarged bankrupt under that Act is adjudged bankrupt under this Act.

SETTING ASIDE OF PREFERENCES AND OTHER TRANSACTIONS

17(1)   A preference given, assignment made or other transaction entered into before the appointed day shall not be set aside under any of sections 339 to 344 of this Act except to the extent that it could have been set aside under the law in force immediately before that day.

17(2)   References in sub-paragraph (1) to setting aside a preference assignment or other transaction include the making of any order which varies or reverses any effect of a preference, assignment or other transaction.

BANKRUPTCY OFFENCES

18(1)   Where a bankruptcy order is made under this Act on or after the appointed day, a person is not guilty of an offence under Chapter VI of Part IX in respect of anything done before that day; but, notwithstanding the repeal by the Insolvency Act 1985 of the Bankruptcy Act 1914, is guilty of an offence under the Act of 1914 in respect of anything done before the appointed day which would have been an offence under that Act if the making of the bankruptcy order had been the making of a receiving order under that Act.

18(2) Subsection (5) of section 350 of this Act applies (instead of sections 157(2), 158(2), 161 and 165 of the Act of 1914) in relation to proceedings for an offence under that Act which are instituted (whether by virtue of sub-paragraph (1) or otherwise) after the appointed day.

POWER TO MAKE RULES

19(1) The preceding provisions of this Part of this Schedule are without prejudice to the power conferred by this Act under which rules under section 412 may make transitional provision in connection with the coming into force of those rules; and such provision may apply those rules in relation to a bankruptcy notwithstanding that it arose from a petition presented before either the coming into force of the rules or the appointed day.

19(2) Rules under section 412 may provide for such notices served before the appointed day as may be prescribed to be treated for the purposes of this Act as statutory demands served under section 268.

Part III — Transitional Effect of Part XVI

20(1) A transaction entered into before the appointed day shall not be set aside under Part XVI of this Act except to the extent that it could have been set aside under the law in force immediately before that day.

20(2) References above to setting aside a transaction include the making of any order which varies or reverses any effect of a transaction.

Part IV — Insolvency Practitioners

21 Where an individual began to act as an insolvency practitioner in relation to any person before the appointed day, nothing in section 390(2) or (3) prevents that individual from being qualified to act as an insolvency practitioner in relation to that person.

Part V — General Transitional Provisions and Savings

INTERPRETATION FOR THIS PART

22 In this Part of this Schedule, **"the former enactments"** means so much of the Companies Act as is repealed and replaced by this Act, the Insolvency Act 1985 and the other enactments repealed by this Act.

GENERAL SAVING FOR PAST ACTS AND EVENTS

23　So far as anything done or treated as done under or for the purposes of any provision of the former enactments could have been done under or for the purposes of the corresponding provision of this Act, it is not invalidated by the repeal of that provision but has effect as if done under or for the purposes of the corresponding provision; and any order, regulation, rule or other instrument made or having effect under any provision of the former enactments shall, insofar as its effect is preserved by this paragraph, be treated for all purposes as made and having effect under the corresponding provision.

PERIODS OF TIME

24　Where any period of time specified in a provision of the former enactments is current immediately before the appointed day, this Act has effect as if the corresponding provision had been in force when the period began to run; and (without prejudice to the foregoing) any period of time so specified and current is deemed for the purposes of this Act—

(a) to run from the date or event from which it was running immediately before the appointed day, and

(b) to expire (subject to any provision of this Act for its extension) whenever it would have expired if this Act had not been passed;

and any rights, priorities, liabilities, reliefs, obligations, requirements, powers, duties or exemptions dependent on the beginning, duration or end of such a period as above mentioned shall be under this Act as they were or would have been under the former enactments.

INTERNAL CROSS-REFERENCES IN THIS ACT

25　Where in any provision of this Act there is a reference to another such provision, and the first-mentioned provision operates, or is capable of operating, in relation to things done or omitted, or events occurring or not occurring, in the past (including in particular past acts of compliance with any enactment, failures of compliance, contraventions, offences and convictions of offences), the reference to the other provision is to be read as including a reference to the corresponding provision of the former enactments.

PUNISHMENT OF OFFENCES

26(1)　Offences committed before the appointed day under any provision of the former enactments may, notwithstanding any repeal by this Act, be prosecuted and punished after that day as if this Act had not passed.

26(2)　A contravention of any provision of the former enactments committed before the appointed day shall not be visited with any severer punishment under or by virtue of this Act than would have been applicable under that provision at the time of the contravention; but where an offence for the continuance of which a penalty was provided has been committed under any provision of the former enactments, proceedings may be taken under this Act in respect of the continuance of the offence on and after the appointed day in the like manner as if the offence had been committed under the corresponding provision of this Act.

REFERENCES ELSEWHERE TO THE FORMER ENACTMENTS

27(1) A reference in any enactment, instrument or document (whether express or implied, and in whatever phraseology) to a provision of the former enactments (including the corresponding provision of any yet earlier enactment) is to be read, where necessary to retain for the enactment, instrument or document the same force and effect as it would have had but for the passing of this Act, as, or as including, a reference to the corresponding provision by which it is replaced in this Act.

27(2) The generality of the preceding sub-paragraph is not affected by any specific conversion of references made by this Act, nor by the inclusion in any provision of this Act of a reference (whether express or implied, and in whatever phraseology) to the provision of the former enactments corresponding to that provision, or to a provision of the former enactments which is replaced by a corresponding provision of this Act.

SAVING FOR POWER TO REPEAL PROVISIONS IN SECTION 51

28 The Secretary of State may by order in a statutory instrument repeal subsections (3) to (5) of section 51 of this Act and the entries in Schedule 10 relating to subsections (4) and (5) of that section.

SAVING FOR INTERPRETATION ACT 1978 SS. 16, 17

29 Nothing in this Schedule is to be taken as prejudicing sections 16 and 17 of the Interpretation Act 1978 (savings from, and effect of, repeals); and for the purposes of section 17(2) of that Act (construction of references to enactments repealed and replaced, etc.), so much of section 18 of the Insolvency Act 1985 as is replaced by a provision of this Act is deemed to have been repealed by this Act and not by the Company Directors Disqualification Act 1986.

(Former provision: IA 1985, Sch. 9)

General note

The greater part of IA 1985 was only brought into operation for a brief moment of time, before being repealed by the present Act as part of the consolidation exercise (see the Introduction and the general discussion on IA 1986 at pp. 1 and 5 for more details). In most respects, therefore, this Schedule has simply brought forward the transitional provisions contained in IA 1985, Sch. 9, and no adjustment was necessary because the "appointed day" contemplated by IA 1985 became the "appointed day" provided for by the present Act, i.e. 29 December 1986.

Most of the matters dealt with by this Schedule are of a routine nature, and all of them have been noted at the appropriate place in the body of the Act. However, one or two points exceptionally call for comment.

Part I

Para. 1

Under s. 9(3), the court cannot make an administration order if an administrative receiver has been appointed (unless the charge-holder consents), and under s. 9(2) notice of the presentation of a petition for an administration order must be served on any person who is or may be entitled to appoint an administrative receiver. These two provisions taken together ensure than any charge-holder who wishes to veto the making of an administration order may do so (see s. 10(2)(*b*)), but of course many currently operative instruments creating a floating charge will have been drawn up before the present Act came into force, and will not empower the charge-holder to appoint a receiver merely because an application for an administration order has been made. This transitional provision makes good the absence of such a power, but only in relation to an instrument executed *before the appointed day.* Draftsmen will need to be alert to ensure that charges created after the commencement of the Act contain an express clause to the same effect. The same is true of many other commercial documents, especially leases.

Para. 4

In *Re Hewitt Brannan (Tools) Co. Ltd* [1990] BCC 354 a petition was presented on 17 May 1989 seeking a compulsory winding-up order in respect of a company which had been in voluntary liquidation since 1983. Harman J held that the petition was properly brought under IA 1986 rather than under the former law. This ruling may not have been correct, however, for the judgment appears to overlook s. 129(1) and the words "is treated as having commenced" in para. 4(1).

Para. 7

Winding up subject to the supervision of the court (CA 1985, s. 606) was abolished by IA 1985, s. 88, with effect from 29 December 1986: see the Insolvency Act 1985 (Commencement No. 5) Order 1986 (SI 1986 No. 1924).

Para. 9

This provision ensures that the longer periods now prescribed as against "connected persons" for the invalidation of preferences and floating charges will not be applied retrospectively, nor will the more widely drawn rules relating to preferences, transactions at an undervalue, etc.

It also means, when read in conjunction with paras. 2 and 3, that the new definition of "floating charge" (see s. 251) will not operate retrospectively so as to apply to a charge created before the appointed day which has since crystallised, even if the latter event has taken place after the appointed day.

Part II

Generally speaking, the new bankruptcy régime will not apply where a bankruptcy was initiated before the appointed day (see s. 443). Note that undischarged bankrupts can take the benefit of the new liberal rules on discharge (see ss. 279, 280). Provision is made for the trustee in bankruptcy where the bankruptcy was initiated under the old régime. For example, he can claim the benefit of s. 314(6)(*b*). The rules on setting aside transactions contained in the Act are not retrospective. The same is true of the new bankruptcy offences.

Part III

Sections 423–425 are not retrospective: the old rules on avoidance apply to transactions entered into before the appointed day.

Part IV

See the note to s. 390(2)

Part V

This is a general transitional provision applying to both corporate and personal insolvency. It contains the normal transitional provisions one would expect to find, and aims to ensure that persons are not penalised by the legal metamorphosis.

Schedule 12 — Enactments Repealed

Chapter	Short title	Extent of repeal
1970 c. 8.	The Insolvency Services (Accounting and Investment) Act 1970.	The whole Act.
1976 c. 60.	The Insolvency Act 1976.	Section 3.
1985 c. 6.	The Companies Act 1985.	In Section 463(4), the words "Subject to section 617".
		Sections 467 to 485.
		In section 486, in the definition of "company" the words "other than in Chapter II of this Part"; and the definitions of "instrument of appointment", "prescribed", "receiver" and "register of charges".
		Sections 488 to 650.
		Sections 659 to 664.
		Sections 665 to 674.
		Section 709(4).
		Section 710(4).
		Section 724.
		Schedule 16.
		In Schedule 24, the entries relating to the section 467; all entries thereafter up to and including section 641(2); and the entry relating to section 710(4).
1985 c. 65.	The Insolvency Act 1985.	Sections 1 to 11.
		Section 15.
		Section 17.
		Section 19.
		Sections 20 to 107.
		Section 108(1) and (3) to (7).
		Sections 109 to 211.
		Sections 212 to 214.
		Section 216.
		Section 217(1) to (3).
		Sections 221 to 234.
		In section 235, subsections (2) to (5).

Chapter	Short title	Extent of repeal
		In section 236, subsections (3) to (5).
		In Schedule 1, paragraphs 1 to 4, and sub-paragraph (4) of paragraph 5.
		Schedules 3 to 5.
		In Schedule 6, paragraphs 5, 6, 9, 15 to 17, 20 to 22, 25 to 44 and 48 to 52.
		Schedule 7.
		In Schedule 9, paragraphs 1 and 4 to 24.
		Schedule 10.
1985 c. 66.	The Bankruptcy (Scotland) Act 1985.	In Schedule 7, paragraphs 19 to 22.
1986 c. 44.	The Gas Act 1986.	In Schedule 7, paragraph 31.

General note

This Schedule, which is introduced by s. 438, lists the repeals effected by the Act. The Companies Act 1985 suffers a large number of wounds, while IA 1985 is almost completely destroyed. For further guidance, see the note to s. 438. Also note the repeals made by IA 1985, Sch. 10; and for the relationship between IA 1985 and IA 1986, see the Introduction and the general discussion on IA 1986 at pp. 1 ff.

Schedule 13 — Consequential Amendments of Companies Act 1985

Part I — Internal and Other Section References Amended or Re-amended

Section of Act	Consequential amendment or re-amendment
Section 13(4)	After "this Act", add "and the Insolvency Act".
Section 44(7)	In paragraph (a), for "section 582" substitute "section 110 of the Insolvency Act".
Section 103(7)	In paragraph (a), the same amendment.
Section 131(7)	The same amendment.
Section 140(2)	In paragraph (b), for "section 518" substitute "section 123 of the Insolvency Act".

Section of Act	Consequential amendment or re-amendment
Section 153(3)	In paragraph (f), for "section 582" substitute "section 110 of the Insolvency Act".
	In paragraph (g), for "Chapter II of Part II of the Insolvency Act 1985" substitute "Part I of the Insolvency Act".
Section 156(3)	For "section 517" substitute "section 122 of the Insolvency Act".
Section 173(4)	The same amendment.
Section 196	For this section substitute—
	"196.—(1) The following applies in the case of a company registered in England and Wales, where debentures of the company are secured by a charge which, as created, was a floating charge.
	(2) If possession is taken, by or on behalf of the holders of any of the debentures, of any property comprised in or subject to the charge, and the company is not at that time in course of being wound up, the company's preferential debts shall be paid out of assets coming to the hands of the person taking possession in priority to any claims for principal or interest in respect of the debentures.
	(3) "Preferential debts" means the categories of debts listed in Schedule 6 to the Insolvency Act; and for the purposes of that Schedule "the relevant date" is the date of possession being taken as above mentioned.
	(4) Payments made under this section shall be recouped, as far as may be, out of the assets of the company available for payment of general creditors."
Section 380(4)	In paragraph (j), for "section 572(1)(a)" substitute "section 84(1)(a) of the Insolvency Act".
Section 441(1)	For "section 13 of the Insolvency Act 1985" substitute "section 8 of the Company Directors Disqualification Act 1986".
Section 449(1)	In paragraph (ba), for "section 12 or 13 of the Insolvency Act 1985" substitute "section 6, 7 or 8 of the Company Directors Disqualification Act 1986".
Section 461(6)	For "section 106 of the Insolvency Act 1985" substitute "section 411 of the Insolvency Act".
Section 462(5)	After "this Part" insert "and Part III of the Insolvency Act 1986".
Section 463(2)	For "Part XX (except section 623(4))" substitute "Part IV of the Insolvency Act (except section 185)".

Section of Act	Consequential amendment or re-amendment
Section 463(3)	For this subsection substitute—
	"(3) Nothing in this section derogates from the provisions of sections 53(7) and 54(6) of the Insolvency Act (attachment of floating charge on appointment of receiver), or prejudices the operation of sections 175 and 176 of that Act (payment of preferential debts in winding up)".
Section 464(6)	For "section 89 of the Insolvency Act 1985" substitute "sections 175 and 176 of the Insolvency Act".
Section 657(2)	For "subsections (3) and (5) to (7) of section 91 of the Insolvency Act 1985 and section 92 of that Act" substitute "section 178(4) and sections 179 to 182 of the Insolvency Act".
Section 658(1)	For "Subsection (7) of section 91 of the Insolvency Act 1985" substitute "Section 180 of the Insolvency Act".
Section 711(2)	In paragraph (b), for "section 600" substitute "section 109 of the Insolvency Act".
Section 733	In subsection (1), omit "295(7)".
	In subsection (3), for "216(3) or 295(7)" substitute "or 216(3)".

Part II — Amendment of Part XXVI (Interpretation)

In Part XXVI of the Companies Act, after section 735, insert the following section—

"Relationship of this Act to Insolvency Act

735A(1)   In this Act **"the Insolvency Act"** means the Insolvency Act 1986; and in the following provisions of this Act, namely, sections 375(1)(b), 425(6)(a), 440, 449(1)(a) and (d), 460(2), 675, 676, 677, 699(1), 728 and Schedule 21, paragraph 6(1), the words "this Act" are to be read as including Parts I to VII of that Act, sections 411, 413, 414, 416 and 417 in Part XV of that Act, and also the Company Directors Disqualification Act 1986.

735A(2)   In sections 704(5), 706(1), 707(1), 708(1)(a) and (4), 710(5), 713(1), 729 and 732(3) references to the Companies Acts include Parts I to VII of the Insolvency Act, sections 411, 413, 414, 416 and 417 in Part XV of that Act, and also the Company Directors Disqualification Act 1986.

735A(3)   Subsections (1) and (2) apply unless the contrary intention appears."

General note

Most of the changes made by this Schedule to CA 1985 are of a routine nature, substituting cross-references to reflect the new section numbers, etc., which follow from the consolidation. (Note also that other amendments were made to CA 1985 by IA 1985, Sch. 6 and see the Introduction and the general discussion on IA 1986 at pp. 1 and 5).

The rewording of CA 1985, s. 196 requires some comment. Previously, this section contained provision for the payment of preferential debts in priority to the holder of a floating charge, when the latter enforced his security by putting in a receiver or taking possession of the charged property. Receivership is now dealt with in the present Act (s. 40), and so s. 196 needs to cater only for taking possession. The new definition of "floating charge" (IA 1986, s. 251) applies to CA 1985, s. 196 also, in consequence of an amendment made to s. 196(1) by IA 1985, Sch. 6, para. 15(1).

The amendment of CA 1985, s. 255 allows a company to change its accounting reference date, when an administrator is in office, free of the restrictions which normally apply to making this change.

Part II of the Schedule inserts a new CA 1985, s. 735A to facilitate cross-referencing, etc. from that Act to IA 1986.

In Pt. I entries relating to s. 222(4) and 225 were repealed by CA 1989, s. 212 and Sch. 24 as from 1 April 1990 (see SI 1990 No. 355 (C. 13), art. 5(1)(d)); the entries formerly read as follows:

Section of Act	Consequential amendment or re-amendment
"Section 222(4)	For 'section 106 of the Insolvency Act 1985' substitute 'section 411 of the Insolvency Act'.
Section 225	At the end of the section add— '(8) At any time when an administration order under Part II of the Insolvency Act is in force, this section has effect as if subsections (3) and (5) to (7) were omitted'."

Schedule 14 — Consequential Amendments of other Enactments

Section 439(2)

Enactment	Amendment
Deeds of Arrangement Act 1914 (c. 47):	
Section 3(1)	For "Part III of the Insolvency Act 1985" substitute "Parts VIII to XI of the Insolvency Act 1986".
Section 3(4)	The same amendment.
Section 11(1) and (2)	In each subsection, the same amendment.
Section 15(1)	For "section 207 of the Insolvency Act 1985" substitute "section 412 of the Insolvency Act 1986".

Enactment	Amendment
Section 16	The same amendment as of section 3(1).
Section 23	The same amendment.
Section 30(1)	For the definition of "property" substitute— " 'property' has the meaning given by section 436 of the Insolvency Act 1986".
Law of Property Act 1925 (c. 20):	
Section 52(2)(b)	For "section 91 or 161 of the Insolvency Act 1985" substitute "sections 178 to 180 or sections 315 to 319 of the Insolvency Act 1986".
Land Registration Act 1925 (c. 21):	
Section 42(2)	For "section 161 of the Insolvency Act 1985" substitute "sections 315 to 319 of the Insolvency Act 1986".
Third Parties (Rights against Insurers) Act 1930 (c. 25):	
Section 1	In subsection (1)(b), for the words from "a composition" to "that Chapter" substitute "a voluntary arrangement proposed for the purposes of Part I of the Insolvency Act 1986 being approved under that Part".
	In subsection (2), for "228 of the Insolvency Act 1985" substitute "421 of the Insolvency Act 1986".
	In subsection (3), the same amendment.
Section 2	In subsection (1), the same amendment as of section 1(2).
	In subsection (1A), for the words from "composition or scheme" to the end of the subsection substitute "voluntary arrangement proposed for the purposes of, and approved under, Part I or Part VIII of the Insolvency Act 1986".
Section 4	In paragraph (b), the same amendment as of section 1(2).
Exchange Control Act 1947 (c. 14):	
Schedule 4	In paragraphs 6 and 8(4), for "section 120 of the Insolvency Act 1985" substitute "sections 267 to 270 of the Insolvency Act 1986".
Arbitration Act 1950 (c. 27):	
Section 3(2)	For "committee established under section 148 of the Insolvency Act 1985" substitute "creditors' committee established under section 301 of the Insolvency Act 1986".

Enactment	Amendment
Agricultural Marketing Act 1958 (c. 47):	
Schedule 2	For paragraph 4 substitute—
	"4.—(1) A scheme shall provide for the winding up of the board, and for that purpose may apply Part V of the Insolvency Act 1986 (winding up of unregistered companies), subject to the following modifications.
	(2) For the purposes of sections 221, 222 and 224 of the Act of 1986, the principal place of business of the board is deemed to be the office of the board the address of which is registered by the Minister under paragraph 3 above.
	(3) Section 223 does not apply.
	(4) Section 224 applies as if the words "or any member of it as such" were omitted.
	(5) A petition for winding up the board may be presented by the Minister as well as by any person authorised under Part IV of the Insolvency Act 1986 to present a petition for winding up a company".
Charities Act 1960 (c. 58):	
Section 30(1)	For "Companies Act 1985" substitute "Insolvency Act 1986".
Licensing Act 1964 (c. 26):	
Section 8(1)	In paragraph (c), for the words from "composition or scheme" to "Act 1985" substitute "voluntary arrangement proposed by the holder of the licence has been approved under Part VIII of the Insolvency Act 1986"; and for "composition or scheme" substitute "voluntary arrangement".
Section 10(5)	For the words from "composition or scheme" to "Act 1985" substitute "voluntary arrangement proposed by the holder of a justices' licence has been approved under Part VIII of the Insolvency Act 1986"; and for "composition or scheme" substitute "voluntary arrangement".
Industrial and Provident Societies Act 1965 (c. 12):	
Section 55	For "Companies Act 1985" substitute "Insolvency Act 1986".
Medicine Act 1968 (c. 67):	
Section 72(4)	For the words from "composition or scheme" to the end of the subsection substitute "voluntary arrangement proposed for the purposes of, and approved under, Part VIII of the Insolvency Act 1986".
Conveyancing and Feudal Reform (Scotland) Act 1970 (c. 35):	
Schedule 3	In Standard Condition 9(2)(b), for "228 of the Insolvency Act 1985" substitute "421 of the Insolvency Act 1986".

Enactment	Amendment
Superannuation Act 1972 (c. 11):	
Section 5(2)	For "156 of the Insolvency Act 1985" substitute "310 of the Insolvency Act 1986"; and for "the said section 156" substitute "the said section 310".
Road Traffic Act 1972 (c. 20):	
Section 150	In subsection (1)(b), for "228 of the Insolvency Act 1985" substitute "421 of the Insolvency Act 1986".
	In subsection (2), the same amendment.
Land Charges Act 1972 (c. 61):	
Section 16(2)	For "207 of the Insolvency Act 1985" substitute "412 of the Insolvency Act 1986"; and for "Part III" substitute "Parts VIII to XI".
Matrimonial Causes Act 1973 (c. 18):	
Section 39	For "section 174 of the Insolvency Act 1985" substitute "section 339 or 340 of the Insolvency Act 1986".
Powers of Criminal Courts Act 1973 (c. 62):	
Section 39(3)	In paragraph (d), for "174(10) of the Insolvency Act 1985" substitute "341(4) of the Insolvency Act 1986".
Friendly Societies Act 1974 (c. 46):	
Section 87(2)	For "Companies Act 1985" substitute "Insolvency Act 1986".
Social Security Pensions Act 1975 (c. 60):	
Section 58	The section is to have effect as originally enacted, and without the amendment made by paragraph 26(1) of Schedule 8 to the Insolvency Act 1985.
Schedule 3	At the end of paragraph 3(1) add—
	"or (in the case of a company not in liquidation)—
	(a) the appointment of a receiver as mentioned in section 40 of the Insolvency Act 1986 (debenture-holders secured by floating charge), or
	(b) the appointment of a receiver under section 53(6) or 54(5) of that Act (Scottish company with property subject to floating charge), or
	(c) the taking of possession by debenture-holders (so secured) as mentioned in section 196 of the Companies Act 1985".
	In paragraph 4, for the words from the beginning to "Act 1985" substitute "Section 196(3) of the Companies Act 1985 and section 387 of the Insolvency Act 1986 apply as regards the meaning in this Schedule of the expression 'the relevant date'.".

Enactment	Amendment
Recess Elections Act 1975 (c. 66):	
Section 1(2)	In the definition of "certificate of vacancy", for "214(6)(a) of the Insolvency Act 1985" substitute "427(6)(a) of the Insolvency Act 1986".
Policyholders Protection Act 1975 (c. 75):	
Section 5(1)(a)	For "Companies Act 1985" substitute "Insolvency Act 1986".
Section 15(1)	For "532 of the Companies Act 1985" substitute "135 of the Insolvency Act 1986".
Section 16(1)(b)	The same amendment as of section 5(1)(a).
Development Land Tax Act 1976 (c. 24):	
Section 33(1)	For "538 of the Companies Act 1985" substitute "145 of the Insolvency Act 1986".
Restrictive Trade Practices Act 1976 (c. 34):	
Schedule 1	For paragraph 9A (inserted by Insolvency Act 1985, section 217(4)) substitute— "9A. Insolvency services within the meaning of section 428 of the Insolvency Act 1986".
Employment Protection (Consolidation) Act 1978 (c. 44):	
Section 106(5)	In paragraph (b), for "228 of the Insolvency Act 1985" substitute "421 of the Insolvency Act 1986". In paragraph (c), for the words from "a composition or" to the end of the paragraph substitute "a voluntary arrangement proposed for the purposes of Part I of the Insolvency Act 1986 is approved under that Part".
Section 106(6)	The same amendment as of section 106(5)(c).
Section 122	In subsection (7), for "181 of the Insolvency Act 1985" substitute "348 of the Insolvency Act 1986"; and for "section 106" substitute "section 411". In subsection (9), for the words from "composition or scheme" to "Act 1985" substitute "voluntary arrangement proposed for the purposes of, and approved under, Part I or VIII of the Insolvency Act 1986".
Section 123(6)	For the words from "composition or scheme" to "Act 1985" substitute "voluntary arrangement proposed for the purposes of, and approved under, Part I or VIII of the Insolvency Act 1986".
Section 127(1)	In paragraph (b), for "228 of the Insolvency Act 1985" substitute "421 of the Insolvency Act 1986". In paragraph (c), for the words from "composition or" to the end of the paragraph substitute "voluntary arrangement proposed for the purposes of Part I of the Insolvency Act 1986 is approved under that Part".

Enactment	Amendment
Section 127(2)	In paragraph (c), the same amendment as of section 127(1)(c).
Credit Unions Act 1979 (c. 34):	
Section 6(1)	For "517(1)(e) of the Companies Act 1985" substitute "122(1)(e) of the Insolvency Act 1986"; and for "517(1)(e) of the Act of 1985" substitute "122(1)(e) of the Act of 1986".
Banking Act 1979 (c. 37):	
Section 6(3)	In paragraph (b), for "Part XXI of the Companies Act 1985" substitute "Part V of the Insolvency Act 1986".
Section 18	In subsection (1), for "Companies Act 1985" substitute "Insolvency Act 1986"; and in paragraph (a) of the subsection for "518" substitute "123".
	In subsection (2), for "Companies Act 1985" substitute "Insolvency Act 1986"; and for "Part XXI" substitute "Part V".
	In subsection (4)—
	in paragraph (a), for "Companies Act 1985" substitute "Insolvency Act 1986";
	in paragraph (b), for "518 of the said Act of 1985" substitute "123 of the said Act of 1986"; and
	in paragraph (c), for "Part XXI of the said Act of 1985" substitute "Part V of the said Act of 1986".
Section 19	In subsection (2), for paragraph (ba) substitute—
	"(ba) in connection with any proceedings under any provision of—
	(i) Part XVIII or XX of the Companies Act 1985, or
	(ii) Parts I to VII of the Insolvency Act 1986 (other than sections 236 and 237)".
	In subsection (8), for paragraphs (a) and (aa) substitute—
	"(a) for the references in subsection (2) to Part XVIII or XX of the Companies Act 1985 and Parts I to VII of the Insolvency Act 1986, there shall be substituted references to Parts V, VI and IX of the Companies Act (Northern Ireland) 1960 (the reference to sections 236 and 237 of the Act of 1986 being disregarded)".
Section 28	In subsection (3), in paragraph (c), for "83 of the Insolvency Act 1985" substitute "95 of the Insolvency Act 1986".
	In subsection (4), in paragraph (a), for "Part XXI of the Companies Act 1985" substitute "Part V of the Insolvency Act 1986".
	In subsection (6)(b), for sub-paragraphs (ii) to (iv) substitute—
	"(ii) to be a member of a liquidation committee established under Part IV or V of the Insolvency Act 1986;
	(iii) to be a member of a creditors committee appointed under section 301 of that Act; and
	(iv) to be a commissioner under section 30 of the Bankruptcy (Scotland) Act 1985";

554

Enactment	Amendment
	(v) to be a member of a committee of inspection appointed for the purposes of Part V or Part IX of the Companies Act (Northern Ireland) 1960;
	and (in the passage following sub-paragraph (iv)) for "such a committee as is mentioned in paragraph (b)(ii) or (iv) above" substitute "a liquidation committee, creditors' committee or committee of inspection".
	In subsection (7), in paragraph (b), for the words from "section 116(4)" to the end of the paragraph substitute "section 261(1) of the Insolvency Act 1986 to any person in whom the property of the firm is vested under section 282(4) of that Act".
Section 31(7)	For paragraph (a) substitute—
	"(a) for England and Wales, under sections 411 and 412 of the Insolvency Act 1986";
	and in paragraph (b) for "the said section 106" substitute "section 411 of that Act".
British Aerospace Act 1980 (c. 26):	
Section 9(1)	In paragraph (a), for "Companies Act 1985" substitute "Insolvency Act 1986".
Public Passenger Vehicles Act 1981 (c. 14):	
Section 19(3)	In paragraph (a), for "Chapter III of Part II of the Insolvency Act 1985" substitute "Part II of the Insolvency Act 1986".
Supreme Court Act 1981 (c. 54):	
Section 40A(2)	For "section 179 of the Insolvency Act 1985" substitute "section 346 of the Insolvency Act 1986"; and for "621 of the Companies Act 1985" substitute "183 of the Insolvency Act 1986".
Trustee Savings Banks Act 1981 (c. 65):	
Section 31	In paragraph (b), for "666 to 669 of the Companies Act 1985" substitute "221 to 224 of the Insolvency Act 1986".
Section 54(2)	For "666(6) of the Companies Act 1985" substitute "221(6) of the Insolvency Act 1986".
Iron and Steel Act 1982 (c. 25):	
Schedule 4	In paragraph 3(3) after "Companies Act 1985" insert "or the Insolvency Act 1986".
Civil Jurisdiction and Judgments Act 1982 (c. 27):	
Section 18(3)	In paragraph (ba), for "213 of the Insolvency Act 1985" substitute "426 of the Insolvency Act 1986".
Schedule 5	In paragraph (1), for "Companies Act 1985" substitute "Insolvency Act 1986".

Enactment	Amendment
Insurance Companies Act 1982 (c. 50):	
Section 53	For "Companies Act" (the first time) substitute "Insolvency Act 1986"; and for "Companies Act" (the second time) substitute "that Act of 1986".
Section 54	In subsection (1), for "the Companies Act" (the first time) substitute "Part IV or V of the Insolvency Act 1986"; and in paragraph (a), for "518 or sections 667 to 669" substitute "123 or sections 222 to 224".
	In subsection (4) for "Companies Act" (the first time) substitute "Insolvency Act 1986".
Section 55	In subsection (5), for "subsection (3) of section 540 of the Companies Act" substitute "section 168(2) of the Insolvency Act 1986".
	In subsection (6), for "631 of the Companies Act" substitute "212 of the Insolvency Act 1986".
Section 56	In subsection (4), for "Section 90(5) of the Insolvency Act 1985" substitute "Section 177(5) of the Insolvency Act 1986"; and for "section 90 of the said Act of 1985" substitute "section 177 of the said Act of 1986".
	In subsection (7), for "section 539(1) of the Companies Act" substitute "section 167 of, and Schedule 4 to, the Insolvency Act 1986".
Section 59	In subsection (1), for "106 of the Insolvency Act 1985" substitute "411 of the Insolvency Act 1986".
	In subsection (2), for "106 of the Insolvency Act 1985" substitute "411 of the Insolvency Act 1986"; and for "section 89 of, and Schedule 4 to, the Insolvency Act 1985" substitute "sections 175 and 176 of, and Schedule 6 to, the Insolvency Act 1986".
Section 96(1)	In the definition of "insolvent", for "517 and 518 or section 666 of the Companies Act" substitute "122 and 123 or section 221 of the Insolvency Act 1986".
Telecommunications Act 1984 (c. 12):	
Section 68(1)	In paragraph (a), for "Companies Act 1985" substitute "Insolvency Act 1986".
County Courts Act 1984 (c. 28):	For subsection (3) substitute—
Section 98	"(3) The provisions of this section have effect subject to those of sections 183, 184 and 346 of the Insolvency Act 1986".
Section 102	For subsection (8) substitute—
	"(8) Nothing in this section affects section 346 of the Insolvency Act 1986".
Section 109(2)	For "179 of the Insolvency Act 1985" substitute "346 of the Insolvency Act 1986".
Finance Act 1985 (c. 54):	Omit the word "altogether"; and after "Companies Act 1985"
Section 79	insert "sections 110 and 111 of the Insolvency Act 1986".

Enactment	Amendment
Housing Act 1985 (c. 68):	
Schedule 18	In paragraphs 3(4) and 5(3), for "228 of the Insolvency Act 1985" substitute "421 of the Insolvency Act 1986".

General note

Former entries relating to the Income and Corporation Taxes Act 1970, the Finance Act 1972, the Finance Act 1981 and the Finance Act 1983 were repealed by the Income and Corporation Taxes Act 1988, s. 844 and Sch. 31 for companies' accounting periods ending after 5 April 1988 (see s. 843(1)): the entries formerly read as follows:

Enactment	Amendment
Income and Corporation Taxes Act 1970 (c. 10):	
Section 247(7)	For "Companies Act 1985" substitute "Insolvency Act 1986".
Section 265(5)	For "538 of the Companies Act 1985" substitute "145 of the Insolvency Act 1986".
Finance Act 1972 (c. 41):	
Schedule 16	In paragraph 13(5), for "Companies Act 1985" substitute "Insolvency Act 1986"
Finance Act 1981 (c. 35):	
Section 55(4)	For "Companies Act 1985" substitute "Insolvency Act 1986"
Finance Act 1983 (c. 28):	
Schedule 5	In paragraph 5(4), for "Companies Act 1985" substitute "Insolvency Act 1986".

The former entry relating to s. 112AA(3)(*a*) of the Land Registration Act 1925 was repealed by s. 2 of the Land Registration Act 1988; the entry formerly read as follows:

Enactment	Amendment
Section 112AA(3)(a)	For "the Insolvency Act 1985 or the Companies Act 1985" substitute "the Insolvency Act 1986".

The former entry relating to the Employment Protection (Consolidation) Act 1978, s. 125(2) was repealed by Employment Act 1989, s.29(4) and Sch. 7 as from 16 November 1989; the entry formerly read as follows:

Enactment	Amendment
"Section 125(2)	For paragraph (a) substitute—
	"(a) the following provisions of the Insolvency Act 1986–
	(i) sections 175 and 176, 328 and 329, 348 and Schedule 6, and
	(ii) any rules under that Act applying section 348 of it to the winding up of a company; and".

The former entry relating to the Tribunals and Inquiries Act 1971 was repealed by the Tribunals and Inquiries Act 1992, s. 18(2), 19 and Sch. 4, Pt. I as from 1 October 1992; the entry formerly read as follows:

Enactment	Amendment
"Tribunals and Inquiries Act 1971 (c. 62):	
Schedule 1	For paragraph 10A substitute— '10A. The Insolvency Practitioners Tribunal referred to in section 396 of the Insolvency Act 1986'."

This Schedule lists the consequential amendments to legislation other than CA 1985. See s. 439(2). Note also that other amendments were made by IA 1985, Sch. 8. and see the Introduction and the general discussion on IA 1986 at pp. 1 and 5.

Company Directors Disqualification Act 1986

General comment to the Act

This Act brings together in consolidated form the whole of the law relating to the disqualification of company directors (and, in some circumstances, other persons) by order of the court.

There has been a power to make disqualification orders in the Companies Acts since 1947, and this power was extended in later Companies Acts, notably in CA 1976 and CA 1981; but little use was made of the sanction prior to 1985, mainly because the necessary resources were not committed to investigation and enforcement. With the enactment of the insolvency reforms of 1985, there was manifested a new resolve on the part of government to stamp out malpractice by making much greater use of the power to disqualify directors. Difficulties which had been experienced in the operation of the earlier law (e.g. as regards the heavy burden of proof required in some circumstances) were overcome by amending legislation and new grounds for disqualification introduced. These reforms were brought into force on 28 April 1986, several months ahead of the general implementation of the new insolvency legislation. The Department of Trade and Industry has set up a special unit to investigate cases of suspected breaches of the law and to institute proceedings for disqualification orders; and liquidators, receivers and other insolvency practitioners are required by law to make reports to the Department on the conduct of all the directors in every case of corporate insolvency.

Disqualification orders are now being made at a rate of over 400 per year, with several recorded cases where the maximum ban of 15 years has been imposed. Approximately half of these orders are currently being made under CDDA 1986, ss. 2–5 (fraud, criminal offences and breaches of companies legislation) and half under ss. 6 and 10 ("unfitness" and wrongful trading). (Statistics are published quarterly by the Department of Trade and Industry and annually in the Insolvency Service's *Insolvency General Annual Report.*)

The Act applies to "companies", an expression which (by s. 22(2)) "includes any company which may be wound up under the Insolvency Act 1986". This means that it applies to "unregistered companies": see the note to IA 1986, s. 220. As originally drafted, it did not apply to building societies or incorporated friendly societies, but it has since been extended so as to apply to the directors (or the members of the committee of management) and officers of both: see ss. 22A and 22B, below. However, it still does not apply to other bodies, such as industrial and provident societies: see the note to s. 22(2), below.

Where an insolvent partnership is wound up as an unregistered company under Pt. V of IA 1986 (see the note to IA 1986, s. 420), any member or former member of the partnership or any other person who has or has had control or management of the partnership business is deemed for the purposes of CDDA 1986 to be a director of the company, and ss. 6–10, 15, 19(*c*) and 20 and Sch. 1 apply: see the Insolvent Partnerships Order 1994 (SI 1994 No. 2421), art. 16.

For the purposes of the Act, "director" includes any person occupying the position of director, by whatever name called (s. 22(3)), so that it is immaterial that, in the company in question, the members of the board may be called (e.g.) "trustees" or "governors". For the purposes of ss. 6–9, the term "director" includes a "shadow director", as defined in s. 22(5). A *de facto* director has also been held to be within s. 6: see the note to s. 6(1).

All sections of CDDA 1986 apply to England and Wales and to Scotland, but not to Northern Ireland. However, equivalent legislation has been in force in that jurisdiction since 1986. Initially, this was brought about by the Companies (Northern Ireland) Order 1986 (SI 1986 No. 1032) (NI 6); but this was replaced by Pt. II of the Companies (Northern Ireland) Order 1989 (SI 1989 No. 2404 (NI 18)), equivalent to CDDA 1986, with effect from 1 October 1991.

The present Act has its own definition section (s. 22), but there is some cross-referencing between it and IA 1986, and also to CA 1985; and s. 22(8) provides that any expression not specifically defined in this Act is to be interpreted by reference to CA 1985. The terms used in all three Acts may therefore for the most part be taken to have the same meanings.

Regulations made under IA 1985 relating to director disqualification included:

the Insolvent Companies (Reports on Conduct of Directors) Rules 1986 (SI 1986 No. 611);

the Insolvent Companies (Disqualification of Unfit Directors) Proceedings Rules 1986 (SI 1986 No. 612);

the Insolvent Companies (Reports on Conduct of Directors) (Scotland) Rules 1986 (SI 1986 No. 626 (S. 59)).

All of the above rules have been revoked but have been remade in similar terms under the current legislation by:

the Insolvent Companies (Reports on Conduct of Directors) No. 2 Rules 1986 (SI 1986 No. 2134);

the Insolvent Companies (Disqualification of Unfit Directors) Proceedings Rules 1987 (SI 1987 No. 2023);

the Insolvent Companies (Reports on Conduct of Directors) (No. 2) (Scotland) Rules 1986 (SI 1986 No. 1916 (S. 140)).

Also of relevance are the Companies (Disqualification Orders) Regulations 1986 (SI 1986 No. 2067). Comparable secondary legislation has been introduced in Northern Ireland. See the note to s. 24(2).

For a more detailed account of the director disqualification legislation, see L. S. Sealy, *Disqualification and Personal Liability of Directors*, 4th edn (CCH, 1993).

COMPANY DIRECTORS DISQUALIFICATION ACT 1986

[1986 Chapter 46]

ARRANGEMENT OF SECTIONS

COMPANY DIRECTORS DISQUALIFICATION ACT 1986

[1986 Chapter 46]

An Act to consolidate certain enactments relating to the disqualification of persons from being directors of companies, and from being otherwise concerned with a company's affairs. [*25th July 1986*]

PRELIMINARY

Section 1 Disqualification orders: general

1(1) [Disqualification order] In the circumstances specified below in this Act a court may, and under section 6 shall, make against a person a disqualification order, that is to say an order that he shall not, without leave of the court—

(a) be a director of a company, or

(b) be a liquidator or administrator of a company, or

(c) be a receiver or manager of a company's property, or

(d) in any way, whether directly or indirectly, be concerned or take part in the promotion, formation or management of a company,

for a specified period beginning with the date of the order.

1(2) [Maximum, minimum periods] In each section of this Act which gives to a court power or, as the case may be, imposes on it the duty to make a disqualification order there is specified the maximum (and, in section 6, the minimum) period of disqualification which may or (as the case may be) must be imposed by means of the order.

1(3) [Where two orders] Where a disqualification order is made against a person who is already subject to such an order, the periods specified in those orders shall run concurrently.

1(4) [Criminal grounds] A disqualification order may be made on grounds which are or include matters other than criminal convictions, notwithstanding that the person in respect of whom it is to be made may be criminally liable in respect of those matters.

(Former provision: CA 1985, s. 295(1), (2), (4) (as amended by IA 1985, Sch. 6, para. 1))

General note

This section brings forward from CA 1985, s. 295, the provisions defining a disqualification order and describing its effect.

Differing views have been expressed regarding the nature and purpose of a disqualification order. On the one hand, it may be seen as a form of punishment for misconduct – a view that is reinforced by the fact that the courts have, on occasion, revised or lifted a disqualification order when a person has appealed against a criminal sentence: see, e.g. *R v Young* [1990] BCC 549, where the court said that a disqualification order was "unquestionably a punishment", and ruled that it was quite inappropriate to link such an order with a conditional discharge, and *R v Millard* (1993) 15 Cr App R (S) 445.

On the other hand, it has been stressed in many cases (and particularly those brought under ss. 6–9 and 11) that the court's primary concern is to ensure the protection of the public: see, e.g. *Re Lo-Line Electric Motors Ltd & Ors* [1988] Ch. 477 at p. 486; (1988) 4 BCC 415 at p. 419, *Re Sevenoaks Stationers (Retail) Ltd* [1991] Ch. 164 at p. 176; [1990] BCC 765 at p. 773, *Secretary of State for Trade & Industry v Langridge, Re Cedac Ltd* [1991] Ch. 402 at pp. 413–414; [1991] BCC 148 at pp. 153–155; *R v Secretary of State for Trade & Industry, ex parte Lonrho plc* [1992] BCC 325 at pp. 333, 335. But, even so, an order is clearly restrictive of the liberty of the person against whom it is made, and its contravention can have penal consequences under s. 13 (ibid.). (For a general discussion of this issue, see Dr Janet Dine, (1988) 9 Co. Law. 213.)

In *R v Holmes* [1991] BCC 394 the Court of Appeal held that it was wrong in principle to make a compensation order and at the same time to disqualify the person concerned from acting as a company director, since his ability to earn the means with which to pay the compensation order would be significantly diminished. The compensation order which had been imposed by the trial court following his conviction for fraudulent trading was accordingly quashed.

The offence of acting as a director while disqualified under this section is probably an absolute offence, on analogy with the position of an undischarged bankrupt: there is no requirement of *mens rea*. See *R v Brockley* [1994] BCC 131, and the note to s. 11 below.

A person who is subject to a disqualification order under this Act is disqualified from being a trustee of a charity, except with the leave of the court: Charities Act 1993, s. 72(1)(*f*).

S. 1(1)

A disqualification order may be made against a company or other corporate body, since the section uses the word "person" rather than "individual". This is confirmed by s. 14, below.

The word "shall" reflects the fact that s. 6 is expressed in imperative terms, but the court does in fact have a discretion: see the note to s. 6(1).

"Management" for the purposes of para. (*d*) includes both the internal and external affairs of a company: *R v Austen* (1985) 1 BCC 99,528 (a case concerning the fraudulent raising of finance). In *R v Campbell* [1984] BCLC 83, a management consultant who acted as adviser to the board of a company was held to have "been concerned in" and "taken part in" its management. It is not necessary that there should be any actual misconduct of the company's affairs: in *R v Georgiou* (1988) 4 BCC 322, a disqualification order was made against a person who had carried on an unauthorised insurance business through the medium of a limited company. In the Australian case *Re Magna Alloys & Research Pty Ltd* (1975) CLC ¶40–227: see CCH *British Company Law and Practice* Reporter, ¶37–150), a former director who acted as marketing adviser, and in that capacity attended directors' meetings, was held not to have taken part in the management of the company. In another part of the same judgment the court expressed the view that a majority shareholder might so use his position on questions of management as to infringe a prohibition on "taking part in management"; but it was thought that he would be free to vote as a shareholder, "even on a management matter".

In another Australian case, *CCA v Brecht* (1989) 7 ACLC 40, the court considered that the concept of "management" required an involvement of some kind in the decision-making process of the company, and a degree of responsibility. It may not exonerate the person concerned simply to show that some other person has the final say in decision-making or signs all the cheques. Negotiating terms of credit facilities, for instance, may be a management activity, even though those terms have to be confirmed. Advice given to management, participation in the decision-making process, and execution of management's decisions which goes beyond the mere carrying out of directions is sufficient (ibid.). In contrast, in *Re Clasper Group Services Ltd* (1988) 4 BCC 673 the respondent, who was the son of the controlling shareholder and director, was employed as a "management trainee"; he did not appear "to have risen much above the status of an office boy and messenger", but he did have authority to sign company cheques. Warner J held that his functions were too lowly to bring him within the phrase "is or has been concerned, or has taken part, in the . . . management of the company" for the purposes of IA 1986, s. 212(1)(*c*).

The requirement that the disqualification must run from the date of the order itself means that an order cannot be postdated so as, for example, to run from the end of a custodial sentence. Where an order is made pursuant to an application under CDDA 1986, ss. 7 or 8, however, it takes effect 21 days after the date of the order, unless the court orders otherwise: see SI 1987 No. 2023, r. 9. In *Re T & D Services (Timber Preservation & Damp Proofing Contractors) Ltd* [1990] BCC 592, the judge deferred the operation of the order for two weeks to allow the respondent time to try to make arrangements for the management of his company during the period of his disqualification; while in *Re Travel Mondial (UK) Ltd* [1991] BCC 224, where the director did not appear before the court and was not represented, it was ordered that the judgment should not be enforced until 21 days after personal service had been effected on him.

A disqualification order need not impose a total prohibition on the activities of the person concerned, since the court has power under this subsection to give leave. In *Re Lo-Line Electric Motors Ltd & Ors* [1988] Ch. 477; (1988) 4 BCC 415 the person disqualified was allowed to remain a director of two family companies so long as another named person remained a director with voting control. In *Re Majestic Recording Studios Ltd & Ors* (1988) 4 BCC 519 leave was given to act as a director of one specified company if a chartered accountant was willing to act as a co-director and audited accounts for the previous financial year were produced and filed. This may be compared with the condition imposed in *Re Chartmore Ltd* [1990] BCLC 673: leave was given to the respondent to act as a director of a particular company provided that monthly board meetings were held, attended by a representative of the auditors. Other cases in which leave was given include *Re Cargo Agency Ltd* [1992] BCC 388 (leave to act as a manager but not a director), *Re Godwin Warren Control Systems plc* [1992] BCC 557 and *Re Dicetrade Ltd, Secretary of State for Trade & Industry* v *Worth & Anor* [1994] BCC 371.

In *R* v *Goodman* [1992] BCC 625, it was held that there is no power under the Act to make an exception of a general kind, e.g. that the defendant be disqualified from being a director of a public company but allowed to be a director of any private company.

In *Re D J Matthews (Joinery Design) Ltd & Anor* (1988) 4 BCC 513, there was a suggestion that the court might be more willing to consider granting a disqualified person leave to act as a director of a company if it was an unlimited company and he was prepared to assume unlimited personal liability.

Leave to act under a disqualification order may be granted either at the time when the original order is made, or subsequently. The former course is desirable as "in everyone's interests" (*Re Dicetrade Ltd* (above)) [1994] BCC 371 at p. 373. In the latter case application need not be made to the same court. See further s. 17, below.

Neither the present Act nor any of the immediately relevant rules contain provisions dealing with appeals from a disqualification order. In *Re Time Utilising Business Systems Ltd* (1989) 5 BCC 851 Peter Gibson J held that an appeal from an order made by a county court registrar under CDDA, s. 6 should lie to the county court, except where some important question of law or fact was likely to arise, in which case he "inclined to the view" that the registrar might have jurisdiction to transfer the appeal to the High Court. In *Re Tasbian Ltd (No. 2)* [1990] BCC 322, the Court of Appeal ruled that an appeal from the exercise by the registrar of the High Court of jurisdiction conferred by the present Act lay to a single judge of the High Court and not to the Court of Appeal, and that such appeals should be governed by IR 1986, rr. 7.47, 7.49. This view has since been endorsed in *Re Probe Data Systems Ltd (No. 3), Secretary of State for Trade & Industry* v *Desai* [1992] BCC 110.

There is no express provision in the Act or the rules giving a court power to suspend the operation of a disqualification order pending the hearing of an appeal. It would follow on general principles that the order should run notwithstanding the fact that an appeal is pending. This would appear to be the position in relation to orders made under ss. 2, 3, 4 and 5. However, in regard to orders made under the remaining sections of the Act, RSC O. 59, rr. 13(1), 19(5) would empower both the County Court and the High Court, and also the Court of Appeal, to grant a stay pending appeal. These provisions are brought into play by reg. 2 of the Insolvent Companies (Disqualification of Unfit Directors) Rules 1987 (SI 1987 No. 2023), expressly in the case of ss. 6 and 8, and by implication in regard to s. 10.

No specific provision is made in the Act for the variation of a disqualification order; but this is something which the court may do in its inherent jurisdiction, as is indirectly confirmed by the Companies (Disqualification Orders) Regulations 1986 (SI 1986 No. 2067), reg. 4(2) and the Insolvent Companies (Disqualification of Unfit Directors) Rules 1987 (SI 1987 No. 2023), r. 8(2).

The normal rule that costs are in the discretion of the court applies to proceedings in relation to disqualification orders. For a period it had come to be accepted that certain practices favourable to the Crown should displace this rule: (1) that costs should not be awarded against the Secretary of State in situations where a *prima facie* case of unfitness had been made out against a director which was subsequently rebutted by evidence (see, e.g. *Re Douglas Construction Services Ltd* (1988) 4 BCC 553, *Re Cladrose Ltd* [1990] BCC 11), and (2) that where costs were awarded against an unsuccessful respondent in favour of the Secretary of State or Official Receiver, it should be on an indemnity and not on the standard basis (see, e.g. *Re Brooks Transport (Purfleet) Ltd* [1993] BCC 767 and the cases there cited). But the former practice was disapproved of in *Re Southbourne Sheet Metal Co. Ltd* [1993] 1 WLR 244; [1992] BCC 797, where Nourse LJ made it clear that the ruling applied also where the applicant had discontinued the proceedings, and the latter practice was rejected by Chadwick J in *Re Godwin Warren Control Systems plc* [1992] BCC 557 (a decision subsequently approved by the Court of Appeal in *Re Dicetrade Ltd, Secretary of State for Trade & Industry* v *Worth & Anor* [1994] BCC 371).

S. 1(2)

Only s. 6(4) contains provision for a minimum period of disqualification (two years). In *Re Bath Glass Ltd* (1988) 4 BCC 130 at p. 133, Peter Gibson J expressed the view that the fact that the legislature had imposed this minimum disqualification period for "unfitness" was relevant to deciding whether a person should be classed as "unfit": only conduct which was sufficiently serious to warrant such a period of disqualification would justify a conclusion that a person was unfit.

In *Re Sevenoaks Stationers (Retail) Ltd* [1991] Ch. 164; [1990] BCC 765 (the first reported director disqualification case decided by the Court of Appeal), Dillon LJ thought that it would be a helpful guide to the courts to divide the possible periods of disqualification under s. 6 into three brackets. The top period of disqualification for periods of 10–15 years should be reserved for particularly serious cases. This might include cases where a director who had already been disqualified fell to be disqualified again. The minimum bracket of two to five years' disqualification should be applied where, although disqualification was mandatory, the case was relatively not very serious. The middle bracket of disqualification, for from 6 to 10 years, should apply in serious cases which did not merit the top bracket. In *R* v *Goodman* [1992] BCC 625, at p. 628 the guidelines were not applied in criminal proceedings under s. 2; but they were referred to in *R* v *Millard* (1993) 15 Cr App R (S) 445.

S. 1(3)

This statutory prohibition on making cumulative disqualification orders was introduced as an amendment to CA 1985, s. 295(2) by IA 1985, Sch. 6, para. 1(3).

S. 1(4)

This makes it clear that disqualification proceedings may go ahead independently and without regard to the possibility that a criminal prosecution may be brought in respect of the same matter.

In *Re Rex Williams Leisure plc* [1994] BCC 551 the respondent director sought a stay of disqualification proceedings which had been brought against him by the Secretary of State until civil litigation in which he was a defendant had been disposed of. The same matters were material to both sets of proceedings. The court refused to grant a stay. The Court of Appeal, affirming Nicholls V-C [1994] Ch. 1; [1993] BCC 79, stated that the public interest in having disqualification orders made against unfit directors of insolvent companies should not be subordinated to private litigation.

DISQUALIFICATION FOR GENERAL MISCONDUCT
IN CONNECTION WITH COMPANIES

Section 2   Disqualification on conviction of indictable offence

2(1)   [Court's power]   The court may make a disqualification order against a person where he is convicted of an indictable offence (whether on indictment or summarily) in connection with the promotion, formation, management or liquidation of a company, or with the receivership or management of a company's property.

2(2)   ["The court"]   "The court" for this purpose means—

    (a) any court having jurisdiction to wind up the company in relation to which the offence was committed, or

    (b) the court by or before which the person is convicted of the offence, or

    (c) in the case of a summary conviction in England and Wales, any other magistrates' court acting for the same petty sessions area;

and for the purposes of this section the definition of **"indictable offence"** in Schedule 1 to the Interpretation Act 1978 applies for Scotland as it does for England and Wales.

2(3)   [Maximum period]   The maximum period of disqualification under this section is—

    (a) where the disqualification order is made by a court of summary jurisdiction, 5 years, and

    (b) in any other case, 15 years.

(Former provisions: CA 1985, ss. 295(2), 296)

S. 2(1)

A conviction for an indictable offence is a precondition for the operation of this section (although the proceedings need not have been on indictment). The disqualification order may be made by the court by which the offender is convicted or by the same or another court on an application made subsequently.

The scope of s. 2 is not confined to offences which arise out of the management of the internal affairs of the company: it may extend to offences in relation to third parties, e.g. defrauding finance companies (*R* v *Corbin* (1984) 6 Cr App R (S) 17) or an insurance company (*R* v *Appleyard* (1985) 81 Cr App R 319). In *R* v *Georgiou* (1988) 4 BCC 322 there was no actual misconduct of the company's affairs, internal or external: the offence of which the respondent was convicted was the carrying on of an unauthorised insurance business through the medium of a limited liability company. In *R* v *Goodman* [1992] BCC 625 the defendant had been convicted of insider dealing under the Company Securities (Insider Dealing) Act 1985, and sentenced to a term of imprisonment. The Court of Appeal held that it was competent also to impose a disqualification order: it was sufficient that the accused had been convicted of an indictable offence which had some relevant factual connection with the management of a company.

See also *R* v *Millard* (1993) 15 Cr App R (S) 445.

S. 2(2)

The court having jurisdiction to wind up a company is defined by IA 1986, ss. 117ff. (for England and Wales) and 120ff (for Scotland). Where the application is made to such a court, the procedure is governed by s. 16, below.

Section 3   Disqualification for persistent breaches of companies legislation

3(1)   [Court's power]   The court may make a disqualification order against a person where it appears to it that he has been persistently in default in relation to provisions of the companies legislation requiring any return, account or other document to be filed with, delivered or sent, or notice of any matter to be given, to the registrar of companies.

3(2)   [Conclusive proof of default]   On an application to the court for an order to be made under this section, the fact that a person has been persistently in default in relation to such provisions as are mentioned above may (without prejudice to its proof in any other manner) be conclusively proved by showing that in the 5 years ending with the date of the application he has been adjudged guilty (whether or not on the same occasion) of three or more defaults in relation to those provisions.

3(3)   [Guilty of default under s. 3(2)]   A person is to be treated under subsection (2) as being adjudged guilty of a default in relation to any provision of that legislation if—

> (a) he is convicted (whether on indictment or summarily) of an offence consisting in a contravention of or failure to comply with that provision (whether on his own part or on the part of any company), or

> (b) a default order is made against him, that is to say an order under any of the following provisions—

>> (i) section 242(4) of the Companies Act (order requiring delivery of company accounts),

>> (ia) section 245B of that Act (order requiring preparation of revised accounts),

(ii) section 713 of that Act (enforcement of company's duty to make returns),

(iii) section 41 of the Insolvency Act (enforcement of receiver's or manager's duty to make returns), or

(iv) section 170 of that Act (corresponding provision for liquidator in winding up),

in respect of any such contravention of or failure to comply with that provision (whether on his own part or on the part of any company).

3(4) **["The court"]** In this section **"the court"** means any court having jurisdiction to wind up any of the companies in relation to which the offence or other default has been or is alleged to have been committed.

3(5) **[Maximum period]** The maximum period of disqualification under this section is 5 years.

(Former provisions: CA 1985, ss. 295(2), 297)

General note

This section runs closely parallel with s. 5, which empowers the court entering a summary conviction against a person for a company law offence to make a disqualification order if he has had two or more similar convictions in the preceding five years.

S. 3(1)

"Persistent default" in complying with the filing obligations of the companies legislation is made a ground for disqualification by this section. "The companies legislation" is defined in s. 22(7), below. "Persistent default" may be established by invoking the presumptions contained in the following subsections.

In *Re Arctic Engineering Ltd* [1986] 1 WLR 686; (1985) 1 BCC 99,563 it was held that the term "persistently" requires some degree of continuance or repetition. A person may persist in the same default, or persistently commit a series of defaults. However, it is not necessary to show that he or she has been culpable, in the sense of evincing a *deliberate* disregard of the statutory requirements, although such culpability can be taken into account in considering whether to make a disqualification order and, if so, for how long.

S. 3(2)

The meaning of "adjudged guilty" is explained in s. 3(3).

S. 3(3)

The obligation to file documents with the registrar of companies is most often placed on the company itself rather than on any particular officer, but some duties (e.g. to deliver annual accounts) are specifically imposed on the directors, and others on the liquidator or some other office-holder. However, even where the duty lies with the company, it is ordinarily provided that the company and any "officer in default" shall be guilty of an offence – i.e. "any officer of the company who knowingly and wilfully authorises or permits the default... or contravention" (CA 1985, s. 730(5)). A director can thus be guilty of an offence when his company is in breach of the Act, but for para. (*a*) of the present subsection to apply, it is the director who must have been convicted, and not merely the company.

The four statutory provisions mentioned in para. (*b*) empower the court to make an order directing a company and any officer of it to make good the default in question. This may be done on the application of the registrar of companies or any member (under IA 1986, s. 170, any contributory) or creditor. Again, for para. (*b*) to apply, the default order must have been made against the director concerned and not merely his company.

In s. 3(3)(*b*) the words "section 242(4)" were substituted for the former words "section 244" by CA 1989, s. 23 and Sch. 10, para. 35(1), (2)(*a*) as from 1 April 1990, subject to transitional and saving provisions (see SI 1990 No. 355 (C. 13), art. 3, Sch. 1 and also art. 6–9); and s. 3(3)(*b*)(ia) was inserted by CA 1989, s. 232 and Sch. 10, para. 35(1), (2)(*b*) as from 7 January 1991 (see SI 1990 No. 2569 (C. 68), art. 3).

S. 3(4)

See the note to s. 2(2) and, for the procedure, s. 16.

Section 4   Disqualification for fraud, etc., in winding up

4(1)   [Court's power]   The court may make a disqualification order against a person if, in the course of the winding up of a company, it appears that he—

    (a) has been guilty of an offence for which he is liable (whether he has been convicted or not) under section 458 of the Companies Act (fraudulent trading), or

    (b) has otherwise been guilty, while an officer or liquidator of the company or receiver or manager of its property, of any fraud in relation to the company or of any breach of his duty as such officer, liquidator, receiver or manager.

4(2)   [Definitions]   In this section **"the court"** means any court having jurisdiction to wind up any of the companies in relation to which the offence or other default has been or is alleged to have been committed; and **"officer"** includes a shadow director.

4(3)   [Maximum period]   The maximum period of disqualification under this section is 15 years.

(Former provisions: CA 1985, ss. 295(2), 298)

S. 4(1)

There is some overlap between this provision and s. 2: the main points of distinction are that a conviction is a prerequisite for the operation of s. 2, but not s. 4, while a winding up is necessary for s. 4, but not s. 2.

The offence of fraudulent trading could formerly be committed only if the company ended up in liquidation, but this limitation was removed, so far as criminal proceedings are concerned, by CA 1981, s. 96. However, the same limitation continues to apply in the present section, and so if a director is convicted under CA 1985, s. 458 while his company is a going concern, any disqualification order must be sought under s. 2 and not s. 4.

There is also the possibility of an overlap between the present section and s. 10, which allows a disqualification order to be made in the case where a person has had a declaration of liability made against him for fraudulent or wrongful trading.

Paragraph (*b*) does not appear to apply to an administrator or to the supervisor of a voluntary arrangement under IA 1986, ss. 1–7.

S. 4(2)

On the meaning of "the court", see the note to s. 2(2).

The Companies Act definition of the term "officer" (CA 1985, s. 744) is incorporated into the present Act by s. 22(9). For a discussion of this definition, see the note to IA 1986, s. 206(3).

For the meaning of "shadow director", see s. 22(5).

Section 5   Disqualification on summary conviction

5(1)   [Relevant offences]   An offence counting for the purposes of this section is one of which a person is convicted (either on indictment or summarily) in consequence of a contravention of, or failure to comply with, any provision of the companies legislation requiring a return, account or other document to be filed with, delivered or sent, or notice of any matter to be given, to the registrar of companies (whether the contravention or failure is on the person's own part or on the part of any company).

5(2)   [Court's power]   Where a person is convicted of a summary offence counting for those purposes, the court by which he is convicted (or, in England and Wales, any other magistrates' court acting for the same petty sessions area) may make a disqualification order against him if the circumstances specified in the next subsection are present.

5(3)   [Circumstances in s. 5(2)]   Those circumstances are that, during the 5 years ending with the date of the conviction, the person has had made against him, or has been convicted of, in total not less than 3 default orders and offences counting for the purposes of this section; and those offences may include that of which he is convicted as mentioned in subsection (2) and any other offence of which he is convicted on the same occasion.

5(4)   [Definitions]   For the purposes of this section—

    (a) the definition of **"summary offence"** in Schedule 1 to the Interpretation Act 1978 applies for Scotland as for England and Wales, and

    (b) **"default order"** means the same as in section 3(3)(b).

5(5)   [Maximum period]   The maximum period of disqualification under this section is 5 years.

(Former provisions: CA 1985, ss. 295(2), 299)

General note

This section and s. 3 deal with very much the same situation, except that an order under s. 3 may be made only by the court having jurisdiction to wind up one of the companies concerned, i.e. the High Court or in some cases the county court, and their Scottish counterparts. Prosecutions for failure to make company law returns will, however, invariably be brought summarily, and this section enables the court exercising summary jurisdiction in such a case itself to make a disqualification order for "persistent default".

For further discussion, see the note to s. 3.

DISQUALIFICATION FOR UNFITNESS

Section 6   Duty of court to disqualify unfit directors of insolvent companies

6(1)   [Court's duty]   The court shall make a disqualification order against a person in any case where, on an application under this section, it is satisfied—

(a) that he is or has been a director of a company which has at any time become insolvent (whether while he was a director or subsequently), and

(b) that his conduct as a director of that company (either taken alone or taken together with his conduct as a director of any other company or companies) makes him unfit to be concerned in the management of a company.

6(2)   [Interpretation]   For the purposes of this section and the next, a company becomes insolvent if—

(a) the company goes into liquidation at a time when its assets are insufficient for the payment of its debts and other liabilities and the expenses of the winding up,

(b) an administration order is made in relation to the company, or

(c) an administrative receiver of the company is appointed;

and references to a person's conduct as a director of any company or companies include, where that company or any of those companies has become insolvent, that person's conduct in relation to any matter connected with or arising out of the insolvency of that company.

6(3)   [Definitions]   In this section and the next **"the court"** means—

(a) in the case of a person who is or has been a director of a company which is being wound up by the court, the court by which the company is being wound up,

(b) in the case of a person who is or has been a director of a company which is being wound up voluntarily, any court having jurisdiction to wind up the company,

(c) in the case of a person who is or has been a director of a company in relation to which an administration order is in force, the court by which that order was made, and

(d) in any other case, the High Court or, in Scotland, the Court of Session;

and in both sections **"director"** includes a shadow director.

6(4)   [Minimum, maximum periods]   Under this section the minimum period of disqualification is 2 years, and the maximum period is 15 years.

(Former provisions: CA 1985, s. 295(2); IA 1985, s. 12(1), (2), (7)–(9), 108(2))

General note

This section is in some respects more severe than CA 1985, s. 300, which was repealed by IA 1985, Sch. 10, but it falls far short of the ill-fated "automatic disqualification" provisions which the Government initially adopted as its policy in its White Paper (Cmnd 9175, para. 13) and introduced as part of the original Insolvency Bill.

Section 300 of CA 1985 provided for the disqualification, for up to 15 years, of a person who had been a director of two companies which had gone into insolvent liquidation within five years of each other, if the court considered that his conduct as a director made him "unfit to be concerned in the management of a company". The Cork Committee (*Report*, para. 1818) recommended that this provision should be tightened up in a number of respects, which have been adopted in the present section:

- an order can be made against a director who has been associated with only *one* insolvent liquidation;

- where unfitness is found, and the other requirements of the section are satisfied, disqualification is made *mandatory* rather than discretionary;

- the court must impose disqualification for a *minimum* period of two years.

Another recommendation of the Committee was not adopted: this would have allowed the application to the court for a disqualification order to be made by the liquidator, or sometimes even by an individual creditor. The Act, however, restricts the right to institute proceedings to the Secretary of State (or the official receiver acting on directions from the Secretary of State).

The "automatic disqualification" provisions in the original Insolvency Bill would have imposed a three-year automatic disqualification on every director of an insolvent company which was wound up by the court. However, the clause in question met with much criticism and opposition and was withdrawn by the Government after a defeat during the debate in the House of Lords. There is now no provision for "automatic disqualification" anywhere in the legislation, apart from the ban imposed upon an undischarged bankrupt by s. 11.

S. 6(1)

Both the word "shall" and the use of the expression "duty" in the marginal note reflect the view of the Cork Committee, referred to above, that where unfitness is found the court should be obliged to make a disqualification order. However, the court's discretion is not altogether excluded, since it is required to be "satisfied" that the director's conduct makes him "unfit to be concerned in the management of a company"; and a court which took the view that a director's conduct did not warrant the making of a disqualification order would be free to stop short of making such a finding. In *Re Bath Glass Ltd* (1988) 4 BCC 130, Peter Gibson J reached such a conclusion: though the directors' conduct had been imprudent and, in part, improper, it was not so serious as to justify a finding of unfitness. In *Re Polly Peck International plc, Secretary of State for Trade & Industry* v *Ellis & Ors (No. 2)* [1993] BCC 890, Lindsay J took this factor into account in declining to grant the Secretary of State leave to issue proceedings out of time.

Cases decided under the former legislation should be treated with caution: they may be poor guides to the likely judicial approach under the present Act. Thus, in *Re Churchill Hotel (Plymouth) Ltd & Ors* (1988) 4 BCC 112, the court found the respondent unfit to be a director but, exercising its discretion under CA 1985, s. 300 (now repealed), declined to make a disqualification order. There is no similar discretion under s. 6.

In *Re Polly Peck International plc, Secretary of State for Trade & Industry* v *Ellis & Ors (No. 2)* (above) the court declined to qualify the wording of s. 6(1)(*b*) by adding at the end the words "without the leave of the court": to do this would be to make the threshold which a complainant had to cross other than what parliament had by its language intended. In the same case it was held that "a company" in s. 6(1)(*b*) meant "companies generally".

"Director" includes a shadow director: see ss. 6(3) and 22(4) and, for the meaning of the latter term, s. 22(5). Former directors are also within the scope of the section. In *Re Lo-Line Electric Motors Ltd & Ors* [1988] Ch. 477; (1988) 4 BCC 415, a *de facto* director who had acted as such without proper appointment was also included within the ambit of the precursor to the present section (CA 1985, s. 300). In *Re Cargo Agency Ltd* [1992] BCC 388 an order was made against a person who had kept himself off the formal record as a director but had acted as one, receiving remuneration in the form of consultancy fees. In *Re Eurostem Maritime Ltd & Ors* [1987] PCC 190 the court expressed the view, *obiter*, that it had power to disqualify a director in respect of a foreign company that was being wound up in England, and it held that in proceedings against the director of an English company his conduct in relation to foreign companies of which he was also a director could be taken into consideration.

Section 6 contains no territorial restriction. It may be applied to persons, whether British subjects or foreigners, who are out of the jurisdiction at the relevant time and in respect of conduct which occurred outside the jurisdiction. However, the court has a discretion not to order that the proceedings be served out of the jurisdiction, which it will exercise where it is not satisfied that there is a good arguable case on the requirements of s. 6(1): *Re Seagull Manufacturing Co. Ltd (No. 2)* [1994] 1 WLR 453; [1993] BCC 833.

The phrase "has become insolvent" is explained in s. 6(2).

There is no anterior time limit fixed by s. 6(1)(*a*): the court may inquire right back into the defendant's history as a director of the company and any other companies, and also into his conduct after he has ceased to be a director, if it relates to a matter "connected with or arising out of the insolvency of that company" (s. 6(2)). It should be noted that an application has to be made no later than two years after the company "became insolvent": s. 7(2).

The matters to be taken into account in determining the question of "unfitness" are dealt with by s. 9 and Sch. 1: see the note to s. 9.

For a discussion of the term "management", see the note to s. 1(1).

The court may take into account a person's conduct in relation to other companies: it is not necessary that those companies should also have "become insolvent", but it is only his conduct *as a director* of those companies that is relevant. It was held, however, in *Re Bath Glass Ltd* (above), that the director's conduct in relation to other companies is to be looked at only "for the purpose of finding additional matters of complaint": in other words, it is not open to the director to adduce evidence that his conduct in relation to other companies has been impeccable in an endeavour to show that a disqualification order would be inappropriate. Despite this view, it does appear that such conduct has been taken into account as a mitigating factor in some cases (e.g. *Re D J Matthews (Joinery Design) Ltd & Anor* (1988) 4 BCC 513 and *Re Pamstock Ltd* [1994] BCC 264), at least where it relates to events subsequent to the misconduct and may be seen as evidence that the respondent has mended his ways. (On this question, see further *Re Godwin Warren Control Systems plc* [1992] BCC 557, where Chadwick J expressed the view that the words "together with" required some nexus to be shown between the conduct in relation to the other companies and that in relation to the insolvent company, and *Re Polly Peck International plc, Secretary of State for Trade & Industry* v *Ellis & Ors (No. 2)* [1993] BCC 890, especially at p. 898.)

S. 6(2)

Before the jurisdiction of s. 6 can be invoked, the company must have "become insolvent"; but this expression has an artificial meaning which will not necessarily mean that the company is insolvent in a business sense. Section 22(3) imports into the present Act the definition of "insolvency" in IA 1986, s. 247(1) – a definition which is plainly concerned with various situations in which a company may find itself (e.g., liquidation, receivership) and not with its financial viability. (See further the discussion preceding IA 1986, s. 230, and the note to s. 247(1).)

Section 6 of the present Act uses the phrase "becomes insolvent" in the same sense, and so "insolvency" at the end of the present subsection should be understood accordingly. The financial situation of the company (i.e. its solvency in an everyday sense) will be relevant only in a liquidation (para. (*a*)); in the case of an administration or an administrative receivership (paras. (*b*) and (*c*)) a company may be said to have "become insolvent" even when it would be reckoned financially solvent by at least some, and perhaps all, of the accepted tests of solvency.

Conversely, when a company *has* become insolvent in a business sense, the section will not necessarily apply – there must also have been one of the events listed in paras. (*a*)–(*c*).

The phrase "goes into liquidation" is also defined in IA 1986, s. 247(2) and extended to this Act by s. 22(3). A company "goes into liquidation" when it passes a resolution for voluntary winding up, or when an order for its winding up is made by the court (unless it is then already in voluntary liquidation, when the time of the winding-up resolution will be the relevant time): see *Re Walter L Jacob & Co. Ltd, Official Receiver* v *Jacob* [1993] BCC 512.

S. 6(3)

On "the court having jurisdiction to wind up the company", see the note to s. 2(2).

S. 6(4)

This is the only provision in the Act which fixes a minimum period of disqualification.

Section 7 Applications to court under s. 6; reporting provisions

7(1) **[Application by Secretary of State, official receiver]** If it appears to the Secretary of State that it is expedient in the public interest that a disqualification order under section 6 should be made against any person, an application for the making of such an order against that person may be made—

(a) by the Secretary of State, or

(b) if the Secretary of State so directs in the case of a person who is or has been a director of a company which is being wound up by the court in England and Wales, by the official receiver.

7(2) **[Time for application]** Except with the leave of the court, an application for the making under that section of a disqualification order against any person shall not be made after the end of the period of 2 years beginning with the day on which the company of which that person is or has been a director became insolvent.

7(3) **[Report to Secretary of State]** If it appears to the office-holder responsible under this section, that is to say—

(a) in the case of a company which is being wound up by the court in England and Wales, the official receiver,

(b) in the case of a company which is being wound up otherwise, the liquidator,

(c) in the case of a company in relation to which an administration order is in force, the administrator, or

(d) in the case of a company of which there is an administrative receiver, that receiver,

that the conditions mentioned in section 6(1) are satisfied as respects a person who is or has been a director of that company, the office-holder shall forthwith report the matter to the Secretary of State.

7(4) **[Extra information etc.]** The Secretary of State or the official receiver may require the liquidator, administrator or administrative receiver of a company, or the former liquidator, administrator or administrative receiver of a company—

(a) to furnish him with such information with respect to any person's conduct as a director of the company, and

(b) to produce and permit inspection of such books, papers and other records relevant to that person's conduct as such a director,

as the Secretary of State or the official receiver may reasonably require for the purpose of determining whether to exercise, or of exercising, any function of his under this section.

(Former provision: IA 1985, s. 12(3)–(6))

History note

A further subsection, extending the provisions of parts of this legislation as from 1 January 1987 to building societies, was inserted into IA 1985 by the Building Societies Act 1986, and survived the consolidation of IA 1985 although by oversight it was not incorporated into the present Act. The amendment has since been superseded by s. 22A, below, inserted by CA 1989, s. 211(3), as from 31 July 1990. For more details, see the note to s. 22A.

S. 7(1)

The Secretary of State, or the official receiver acting at his direction, alone has standing to make an application. The procedure is by summons in the High Court, or by originating application in the county court, and is prescribed in detail by the Insolvent Companies (Disqualification of Unfit Directors) Proceedings Rules 1987 (SI 1987 No. 2023) replacing (with effect from 11 January 1988) SI 1986 No. 612.

In *Re Carecraft Construction Co. Ltd* [1994] 1 WLR 172; [1993] BCC 336 it was held that although disqualification proceedings could not be the subject of a consent order the court could, in a proper case, adopt a summary procedure where the facts are agreed and the respondent accepts that the court will be likely to find that his conduct as a director has been such as to justify making an order. In the *Carecraft Construction* case, the respondent accepted that the court would be obliged to make an order for a minimum of two years, and the official receiver did not seek to make out a case for a longer disqualification. A similar summary procedure was adopted in *Re Aldermanbury Trust plc* [1993] BCC 598, a case brought under s. 8, where a 7-year order was made. In both cases the court gave credit to the respondent for what was, in effect, a plea of guilty in fixing the length of the disqualification.

The Secretary of State has a general power to delegate his functions to an official receiver under IA 1986, s. 400, and accordingly he may direct an official receiver to make an application under s. 7(1)(*a*) even where (because the company in question is not being wound up by the court) the case does not come within s. 7(1)(*b*). But in such a situation the proceedings must be brought in the name of the Secretary of State and not that of the official receiver; and if an error is made in this respect it cannot be cured by amendment: *Re Probe Data Systems Ltd* (1989) 5 BCC 384.

S. 7(2)

Section 6 is the only provision in CDDA 1986 which imposes a limitation period. If the two-year limit expires on a day when the court office is closed, the time is extended until the next day when it is open (*Re Philipp & Lion Ltd* [1994] BCC 261).

A company "becomes insolvent" for the purposes of s. 7(2) on the happening of any of the events mentioned in s. 6(2) (insolvent liquidation, administration, administrative receivership): see the note to that section. In the case of a compulsory winding up, the relevant date is the date of the order and not that of the petition (*Re Walter L Jacob & Co. Ltd, Official Receiver v Jacob* [1993] BCC 512).

Where, on an application for the appointment of an administrator, the court first makes an interim order under IA 1986, s. 9(4) and later makes an administration order under s. 8 of that Act, it is the date of the latter order from which time should be reckoned for the purposes of the present provision: *Secretary of State for Trade & Industry v Palmer* [1993] BCC 650.

Where more than one of the events mentioned in s. 7(2) happen in succession to the same company (e.g. the company is first put into administrative receivership and then into compulsory liquidation), the period of two years runs from the first of those events: *Re Tasbian Ltd* [1990] BCC 318. However, if the company were to return to a state of solvency between the happening of the two events, it is arguable that a fresh two-year period would start when it "became insolvent" for the second time (ibid.).

The procedure to be followed by the Secretary of State or the official receiver in making application for an extension of time under s. 7(2) has been the subject of some judicial controversy. In *Re Probe Data Systems Ltd (No. 2)* [1990] BCC 21, Millett J considered that the appropriate method was to apply *ex parte* to the registrar in the first instance, putting in the whole of the evidence; if the registrar considered that there was a prima facie case for granting leave he would then give directions to serve the respondent with the application for leave and the supporting evidence; and the respondent would then be entitled to argue that leave should not be granted. But in *Re Crestjoy Products Ltd* [1990] BCC 23 Harman J disagreed with this approach and directed that an applicant should issue an originating summons for leave, serving it on the intended respondent and then making submissions before the judge (or, possibly, the registrar) in the presence of the respondent. The latter procedure, which at least in contested cases will be considerably shorter, was adopted without comment in *Re Cedac Ltd* [1991] BCC 148.

The section does not indicate the grounds upon which the court might see fit to extend the two-year time limit. It is for the Secretary of State or Official Receiver to show a good reason for the extension of time (*Re Crestjoy Products Ltd* [1990] BCC 23 at p. 29, *Re Copecrest Ltd* [1993] BCC 844 at pp. 847, 852). The matters to be taken into account are: (1) the length of delay; (2) the reasons for the delay; (3) the strength of the case against the director; and (4) the degree of prejudice caused to the director by the delay (*Re Probe Data Systems Ltd (No. 3), Secretary of State for Trade & Industry* v *Desai* [1992] BCC 110 at p. 118). This list is not expressed to be exclusive but in most cases is likely to be so (*Re Polly Peck International plc, Secretary of State for Trade & Industry* v *Ellis & Ors (No. 2)* [1993] BCC 890 at p. 894). When each of these four matters has been looked at separately, there then needs to take place a balancing exercise; but even before this, the application for leave should be rejected if the applicant's case is so weak that it could not lead to a disqualification (ibid.).

Other cases have elaborated upon the matters listed above. In *Re Copecrest Ltd* (above) Hoffmann LJ said that the two-year period under s. 7(2) had to be treated as having built into it a contingency allowance for unexpected delays for which the applicant was not responsible, such as delays on the part of the liquidator or other office-holder; but on the other hand delays for which the respondent himself was to blame were a factor which it was proper to take into account. In *Re Crestjoy Products Ltd* (above) pressure of work and a shortage of staff in the Secretary of State's department was not considered a sufficient reason to grant leave out of time retrospectively, although the court indicated that an application made prior to the expiry of the statutory deadline would have been more favourably considered.

Rule 3(1) of the Insolvent Companies (Disqualification of Directors) Proceedings Rules 1987 (SI 1987 No. 2023) states that the evidence in support of an application for a disqualification order should be filed at the time when the summons is issued – although this provision is directory and not mandatory and failing to comply with it is an irregularity which the court may waive (*Re Jazzgold Ltd* [1992] BCC 587, *Re Copecrest Ltd* [1993] BCC 844 at p. 851). The evidence may take the form of, or include, a report by the Official Receiver (r. 3(2)). The court may take into account evidence contained in a supplementary report filed after the expiry of the two-year limitation period (*Re Jazzgold Ltd* (above)). On an application for an extension of time, it is sufficient for the evidence to show that there is an arguable case (*Re Tasbian Ltd (No. 3)* [1991] BCC 435): the court will not, even where there is a conflict of evidence, virtually try the case (*Re Packaging Direct Ltd, Jones & Anor* v *Secretary of State for Trade & Industry* [1994] BCC 213). It is not necessarily an obstacle to allowing the trial to proceed that the applicant's evidence has not been wholly accurate (*Re Tasbian Ltd (No. 3)* (above)).

An application under s. 7 may also be struck out for want of prosecution: *Re Noble Trees Ltd* [1993] BCC 318; *Official Receiver* v *B Ltd* [1994] 2 BCLC 1.

S. 7(3)

This provision makes it the duty of the liquidator or other office-holder to report any case of suspected unfitness to the Secretary of State.

Rules were made under IA 1985 to reinforce these requirements, which imposed an obligation on the insolvency practitioner concerned to complete and return prescribed forms in a number of stipulated cases. These have been reissued and are now the Insolvent Companies (Reports on Conduct of Directors) No. 2 Rules 1986 (SI 1986 No. 2134) and the Insolvent Companies (Reports on Conduct of Directors) (No. 2) (Scotland) Rules 1986 (SI 1986 No. 1916 (S. 140)). The former rules apply to (1) a voluntary winding up where the company is "insolvent" (as defined by s. 6(2)), (2) an administrative receivership, and (3) an administration. In Scotland, the rules apply in every "insolvent" winding up, administrative receivership and administration. Interim returns are also prescribed, to be made when the liquidation or receivership runs for more than six months. Fines may be imposed on a liquidator or receiver who fails to comply. The two original sets of rules became operative on 28 April 1986 (and the reissued rules on 29 December 1986).

An office-holder may disclose to the Secretary of State for the purpose of director disqualification proceedings the transcripts of interviews conducted and documents provided under IA 1986, s. 235 even when he has given assurances that the information given and documents provided will be used only for the purposes of the administration, for such disclosure is "for the purposes of the administration" (*Re Polly Peck International plc, ex parte the joint administrators* [1994] BCC 15).

S. 7(4)

The two sets of rules referred to above also provide for the enforcement of the obligations here set out by a court order, which may include a direction that the liquidator or other office-holder pay the costs personally.

Documents in the custody of an administrative receiver or other office-holder are not "in the power of" the Secretary of State by virtue of this subsection so that he can be compelled to make discovery of them under RSC, O. 24: *Re Lombard Shipping & Forwarding Ltd* [1992] BCC 700.

Section 8   Disqualification after investigation of company

8(1) [Application by Secretary of State]   If it appears to the Secretary of State from a report made by inspectors under section 437 of the Companies Act or section 94 or 177 of the Financial Services Act 1986, or from information or documents obtained under section 447 or 448 of the Companies Act or section 105 of the Financial Services Act 1986 or section 2 of the Criminal Justice Act 1987 or section 52 of the Criminal Justice (Scotland) Act 1987 or section 83 of the Companies Act 1989, that it is expedient in the public interest that a disqualification order should be made against any person who is or has been a director or shadow director of any company, he may apply to the court for such an order to be made against that person.

8(2) [Court's power]   The court may make a disqualification order against a person where, on an application under this section, it is satisfied that his conduct in relation to the company makes him unfit to be concerned in the management of a company.

8(3) ["The court"]   In this section **"the court"** means the High Court or, in Scotland, the Court of Session.

8(4) [Maximum period]   The maximum period of disqualification under this section is 15 years.

(Former provisions: CA 1985, s. 295(2); IA 1985, ss. 12(9), 13, 108(2))

S. 8(1)

The Secretary of State has powers under CA 1985, ss. 431–441 to appoint inspectors to investigate the affairs of companies in a number of situations, e.g.:

- on the application of the company itself or a section of its members (s. 431);
- if the court so orders (s. 432(1)); or
- of his own motion, if it appears to him that there are circumstances suggesting fraud or irregularity (s. 432(2)).

Under ss. 447, 448, he may also require production to him of books or papers relating to a company, and ask for an explanation of them to be given.

The references to ss. 94 or 177 of the Financial Services Act 1986 were added by s. 198(2)(*a*) of that Act from 15 November 1986 (see SI 1986 No. 1940 (C. 69)) and the reference to s. 105 by s. 198(2)(*b*) from 18 December 1986 (see SI 1986 No. 2246 (C. 88)). In addition the reference to s. 52 of the Criminal Justice (Scotland) Act 1987 was added by s. 55(*b*) of that Act from 1 January 1988 (see SI 1987 No. 2119 (C. 62) (S. 143)), that to s. 2 of the Criminal Justice Act 1987 by the Criminal Justice Act 1988, s. 145(*b*) as from 12 October 1988 (see SI 1988 No. 1676 (C. 60)), and that to s. 83 of CA 1989 by CA 1989, s. 79 as from 21 February 1990 (see SI 1990 No. 142 (C. 5), art. 4). These sections empower the Secretary of State to appoint inspectors to investigate certain matters, e.g. authorised unit trust schemes and insider dealing, and also facilitate inquiries by the Serious Fraud Office and co-operation with overseas regulatory authorities.

The present section gives the court power to make a disqualification order on the application of the Secretary of State, if it appears from a report made to him or from information or documents obtained by him under the above provisions that it is expedient in the public interest that an order should be made against a director or former director of any company.

Cases where orders have been made under s. 8 include: *Re Samuel Sherman plc* [1991] 1 WLR 1070; [1991] BCC 699 (ultra vires use of public company's assets and failure to comply with statutory obligations: five-year disqualification); *Re Looe Fish Ltd* [1993] BCC 348 (improper allotment of shares to manipulate voting: two and a half years); *Re Aldermanbury Trust plc* [1993] BCC 598 (breaches of company law, City Code and fiduciary duty, "seriously flawed" commercial judgments: seven years).

In *Re Aldermanbury Trust plc* (above) it was held that the court could properly adopt the shortened form of procedure approved in *Re Carecraft Construction Co. Ltd* (above, p. 576), and avoid a full hearing.

In *R* v *Secretary of State for Trade & Industry, ex parte Lonrho plc* [1992] BCC 325 an application for judicial review of the Secretary of State's decision not to seek a disqualification order under this section was unsuccessful.

S. 8(2)

The court must also be satisfied that the conduct of the director in relation to the company (but not, it appears, other companies) makes him unfit to be concerned in the management of a company. The notes to ss. 6(1) and 9 will be generally relevant in the present context.

The court's power here is discretionary rather than mandatory.

S. 8(3)

The procedure before the High Court takes the same form as in an application under s. 6. See the note to s. 7(1) above.

S. 8(4)

There is no minimum disqualification period under this section.

Section 9   Matters for determining unfitness of directors

9(1)   [Matters in Sch. 1]   Where it falls to a court to determine whether a person's conduct as a director or shadow director of any particular company or companies makes him unfit to be concerned in the management of a company, the court shall, as respects his conduct as a director of that company or, as the case may be, each of those companies, have regard in particular—

(a) to the matters mentioned in Part I of Schedule 1 to this Act, and

(b) where the company has become insolvent, to the matters mentioned in Part II of that Schedule;

and references in that Schedule to the director and the company are to be read accordingly.

9(2) **[Application of s. 6(2)]**   Section 6(2) applies for the purposes of this section and Schedule 1 as it applies for the purposes of sections 6 and 7.

9(3) **[Interpretation of Sch. 1]**   Subject to the next subsection, any reference in Schedule 1 to an enactment contained in the Companies Act or the Insolvency Act includes, in relation to any time before the coming into force of that enactment, the corresponding enactment in force at that time.

9(4) **[Modification of Sch. 1]**   The Secretary of State may by order modify any of the provisions of Schedule 1; and such an order may contain such transitional provisions as may appear to the Secretary of State necessary or expedient.

9(5) **[Power exercisable by statutory instrument etc.]**   The power to make orders under this section is exercisable by statutory instrument subject to annulment in pursuance of a resolution of either House of Parliament.

(Former provisions: IA 1985, ss. 12(9), 14)

S. 9(1)

Under the repealed CA 1985, s. 300 (the forerunner of the present s. 6), the question of a director's unfitness was a matter for the court to determine in its own judgment. However, IA 1985, in s. 14 and Sch. 2, prescribed a list of matters to which the court was directed to have particular regard in assessing the question of unfitness, and these provisions are re-enacted as s. 9 and Sch. 1 of the present Act.

The statutory criteria are set out in Sch. 1 in two Parts: Pt. I applies in all cases, and Pt. II applies in addition to Pt. I where the company in question has "become insolvent" (as that phrase is defined in s. 6(2)). Where the application is made under s. 6, it will always be the case that the company in respect of which the application is made has "become insolvent", so that both Parts of the Schedule will be relevant. If the director's conduct in relation to other companies is brought into the reckoning under s. 6(1)(*b*), it will be necessary for the court to determine whether any of those companies has (or had) "become insolvent" in order to see whether Pt. II applies; and this inquiry will always be necessary in an application under s. 8.

Much of what is set out in Sch. 1 is not new: it merely restates and serves to reinforce the duties of directors under the general statutory and common law rules; and there is even some overlap with the other "disqualification" provisions of this Act – e.g., in regard to persistent failure to file company returns. Read as a whole, Sch. 1 does not impose new duties on directors or demand higher standards; rather, it makes it possible to impose a salutary penalty for breaches of duty which went largely unpunished before the present Act because of inadequacies in the law enforcement process.

The matters set out in Sch. 1 are not an exhaustive list of directors' obligations, but only guidelines for the court, which may treat any other conduct as evidencing unfitness.

In *Re Bath Glass Ltd* (1988) 4 BCC 130, at p. 133, Peter Gibson J said: "To reach a finding of unfitness the court must be satisfied that the director has been guilty of a serious failure or serious failures, whether deliberately or through incompetence, to perform those duties of directors which are attendant on the privilege of trading through companies with limited liability. Any misconduct of the respondent qua director may be relevant, even if it does not fall within a specific section of the Companies Acts or the Insolvency Act."

In *Re Lo-Line Electric Motors Ltd & Ors* [1988] Ch. 447 at p. 496; (1988) 4 BCC 415 at p. 419, Browne-Wilkinson V-C said: "Ordinary commercial misjudgment is in itself not sufficient to justify disqualification. In the normal case, the conduct complained of must display a lack of commercial probity although I have no doubt that in an extreme case of gross negligence or total incompetence disqualification could be appropriate."

In *Re Polly Peck International plc, Secretary of State for Trade & Industry* v *Ellis & Ors (No. 2)* [1993] BCC 890 at p. 894, Lindsay J said that he would "pay regard to the clear thread derived from the authorities that whatever else is required of a respondent's conduct if he is to be disqualified, it must at least be 'serious' ".

However, it should be borne in mind that in *Re Sevenoaks Stationers (Retail) Ltd* [1991] Ch. 164 at p. 176; [1990] BCC 765 at p. 773 (the leading case on disqualification for "unfitness") Dillon LJ warned against treating such statements as "judicial paraphrases of the words of the statute, which fall to be construed as a matter of law in lieu of the words of the statute".

A number of reported cases have been concerned with a particular issue: the failure by a company and its directors to set aside sufficient funds to meet Crown debts for PAYE, NIC and VAT, in effect using this money as working capital as insolvency looms. The views expressed by different judges in these cases have ranged between treating such Crown debts as "quasi-trust moneys" (Harman J, *Re Wedgecraft Ltd* (unreported, 7 March 1986)), on the one hand, to a refusal to draw any distinction between these and other debts (Hoffmann J, in *Re Dawson Print Group Ltd & Anor* (1987) 3 BCC 322), on the other. Prior to the ruling of the Court of Appeal in *Re Sevenoaks Stationers (Retail) Ltd* (above), a consensus had emerged among the judges in the Chancery Division which took a middle line between these extremes, holding that the failure to pay such moneys over to the Crown was, though not a breach of trust, "more serious" and "more culpable" than the non-payment of commercial debts (*Re Stanford Services Ltd & Ors* (1987) 3 BCC 326, *Re Lo-Line Electric Motors Ltd & Ors* (1988) Ch. 477; (1988) 4 BCC 415). However, in the *Sevenoaks Stationers* case passages from the judgment of Hoffmann J in *Dawson Print* were approved, and the ruling given that non-payment of a Crown debt cannot automatically be treated as evidence of unfitness; it is necessary to look more closely in each case to see what the significance, if any, of the non-payment of the Crown debt is.

One item in Sch. 1, para. 7, perhaps deserves some comment: "the extent of the director's responsibility for any failure by the company to supply any goods or services which have been paid for (in whole or in part)." This reflects the general anxiety (especially in consumer circles) about the lack of protection given by the law to members of the public who have made payments to a company (e.g. for goods on mail-order) and find that they rank as mere unsecured creditors if it goes into liquidation, perhaps losing everything. Attempts to secure preferential treatment by law for such prepayments were defeated during the debates on the Insolvency Bill in 1985, but the present provision was inserted instead, so that the courts can use disqualification as a sanction against the irresponsible use of such prepayments to boost a company's ailing cash-flow.

Other types of conduct which have been held to be evidence of "unfitness" include:
- failure to keep proper books of account and/or to make statutory returns (*Re Rolus Properties Ltd & Anor* (1988) 4 BCC 446; *Re Western Welsh International System Buildings Ltd & Ors* (1988) 4 BCC 449; *Re T & D Services (Timber Preservation & Damp*

Proofing Contractors) Ltd [1990] BCC 592; *Re Chartmore Ltd* [1990] BCLC 673; *Re Care-craft Construction Co. Ltd* [1994] 1 WLR 172; [1993] BCC 336; *Re Synthetic Technology Ltd, Secretary of State for Trade & Industry* v *Joiner* [1993] BCC 549; *Re New Generation Engineers Ltd* [1993] BCLC 435; *Re A & C Group Services Ltd* [1993] BCLC 1297; *Re Pamstock Ltd* [1994] BCC 264));

- trading or continuing to draw remuneration while insolvent (*Re Western Welsh International System Buildings Ltd & Ors* (above); *Re Ipcon Fashions Ltd* (1989) 5 BCC 773; *Re Melcast (Wolverhampton) Ltd* [1991] BCLC 288, *Re Cargo Agency Ltd* [1992] BCC 388; *Re City Investment Centres Ltd* [1992] BCLC 956; *Re Synthetic Technology Ltd, Secretary of State for Trade & Industry* v *Joiner* (above));
- inadequate capitalisation (*Re Chartmore Ltd* (above); *Re Austinsuite Furniture Ltd* [1992] BCLC 1047; *Re Pamstock Ltd* (above));
- trading with succession of "phoenix" companies (*Re Travel Mondial Ltd* [1991] BCC 224; *Re Swift 736 Ltd* [1993] BCC 312; *Re Linvale Ltd* [1993] BCLC 654));
- misapplication of company's funds or property (*Re Keypak Homecare Ltd (No. 2)* [1990] BCC 117; *Re Tansoft Ltd* [1991] BCLC 339; *Re City Investment Centres Ltd* (above); *Re Austinsuite Furniture Ltd* (above); *Re Synthetic Technology Ltd, Secretary of State for Trade & Industry* v *Joiner* (above));
- drawing excessive remuneration (*Re Synthetic Technology Ltd, Secretary of State for Trade & Industry* v *Joiner* (above); *Re A & C Group Services Ltd* (above));
- irresponsible delegation (*Re Burnham Marketing Services Ltd & Anor, Secretary of State for Trade & Industry* v *Harper* [1993] BCC 518);
- continuing to incur liabilities after trading had ceased (*Re McNulty's Interchange Ltd* (1988) 4 BCC 533; *Re Ipcon Fashions Ltd* (above));
- deception and self-dealing (*Re Godwin Warren Control Systems plc* [1992] BCC 557);
- failure to co-operate with Official Receiver, lack of frankness with the court (*Re Tansoft Ltd* (above); *Re Godwin Warren Control Systems plc* (above)).

Of course, in many cases several of these features will have been present at the same time. Other considerations, such as the number of companies involved, their size, the extent of their losses, the position of the individual concerned in the managerial hierarchy and his experience (or lack of it), and whether there has been a lack of probity, may also go towards deciding whether unfitness has been established or determining the length of the order to be made.

Factors which have weighed with the court in deciding that a disqualification order should not be made, or that a reduced period of disqualification would be appropriate, have included the following: acting on professional advice (*Re Bath Glass Ltd* (1988) 4 BCC 130, *Re McNulty's Interchange Ltd & Anor* (1988) 4 BCC 533, *Re Douglas Construction Services Ltd & Anor* (1988) 4 BCC 553, *Re C U Fittings Ltd & Anor* (1989) 5 BCC 210, *Re Cladrose Ltd* [1990] BCC 11); employing a qualified company secretary or finance director (*Re Rolus Properties Ltd & Anor* (1988) 4 BCC 446, *Re Douglas Construction Services Ltd*); absence of dishonesty (*Re Bath Glass Ltd* (1988) 4 BCC 130, *Re Lo-Line Electric Motors Ltd & Ors* [1988] Ch. 477; (1988) 4 BCC 415, *Re D J Matthews (Joinery Design) Ltd & Anor* (1988) 4 BCC 513; *Re Burnham Marketing Services Ltd & Anor* [1993] BCC 518); readiness to make a personal financial commitment to the company or that the respondent has sustained heavy personal loss (*Re Bath Glass Ltd; Re Douglas Construction Services Ltd; Re Swift 736 Ltd* [1993] BCC 312); reliance on regular budgets and forecasts (even though subsequently shown to be inaccurate) (*Re Bath Glass Ltd*); the fact that events outside the director's control contributed to the company's misfortunes (*Re Bath Glass Ltd; Re Cladrose Ltd*); evidence that the same company or other companies have been successfully and properly run by the respondent (*Re D J Matthews (Joinery Design) Ltd; Re A & C Group Services Ltd* [1993] BCLC 1297; *Re Pamstock Ltd* [1994]

BCC 264); the fact that the business was kept going on assurances of help from others (*Re C U Fittings Ltd*); the respondent's relative youth and inexperience (*Re Chartmore Ltd* [1990] BCLC 673; *Re Austinsuite Furniture Ltd* [1992] BCLC 1047); the fact that the director was fully occupied as the company's production manager and had left board matters to others (ibid.); the fact that the proceedings have been a long time coming to a hearing and that the respondent has already been under a disqualification by reason of bankruptcy (*Re A & C Group Services Ltd* (above); the fact that the respondent has admitted his responsibility (*Re Carecraft Construction Co. Ltd* [1994] 1 WLR 172; [1993] BCC 336; *Re Aldermanbury Trust plc* [1993] BCC 598). In *Re Melcast (Wolverhampton) Ltd* [1991] BCLC 288 the court held that a ten-year disqualification was merited, but reduced the term to seven years on account of the respondent's age (68). Where other directors have also been disqualified, the court may take into account the period of disqualification imposed on them for the purpose of comparison, but should not be over-influenced by this fact (*Re Swift 736 Ltd* (above)).

A person facing disqualification proceedings under ss. 6–9 must be informed of the substance of the charges he has to meet. The standard practice of the official receiver is to include a statement of the matters allegedly going to unfitness in the affidavit which is filed in support of the application – as, indeed, is required by the Insolvent Companies (Disqualification of Unfit Directors) Proceedings Rules 1987, r. 3(3). If the applicant is the Official Receiver, he may submit a written report either instead of an affidavit, or together with affidavits of other witnesses (r. 3(2)). This report is treated as if it had been verified by affidavit and is *prima facie* evidence of any matter contained in it (ibid.). The report for this purpose may be made by a deputy official receiver (*Re Homes Assured Corpn plc* [1993] BCC 573), and the rule that it is *prima facie* evidence extends to exhibits and annexures (*Re City Investment Centres Ltd* [1992] BCLC 956). The court will, in assessing the weight to be given to statements in the report and accompanying documents, consider the source of the Official Receiver's information as well as any other evidence and all the circumstances (*Re Moonbeam Cards Ltd* [1993] BCLC 1099). In *Re Rex Williams Leisure plc* [1994] Ch. 1; [1993] BCC 79, affirmed (1994) BCC 551, the respondents objected to the inclusion as evidence (in the form of exhibits) of notes made by an examiner in the DTI's Investigations Division and his comments on those notes; but it was held that this material, although hearsay, was admissible. The court would be astute to see that a respondent was not prejudiced by the hearsay nature of the information, and would have no difficulty, should disputes arise, in identifying those parts of the notes which were comment as distinct from fact. In the same case, the respondents, in case they wished at the hearing to submit that there was no case to answer, sought a direction enabling them to file no evidence and to give evidence orally at the hearing should they wish to do so. But the court ruled that the respondents should adduce their evidence in the form of affidavits in advance of the hearing; it was open to them to make a submission of no case, but the decision on this should be taken when they had seen the applicant's evidence: it could not be postponed until after the close of the applicant's case at the hearing. Where an objection on the ground of hearsay is taken, its weight and perhaps also its final admissibility is to be argued over and ruled on at the substantive hearing (*Re Polly Peck International plc, Secretary of State for Trade & Industry* v *Ellis & Ors (No. 2)* [1993] BCC 890). Where the official receiver wishes later to rely on other allegations, the court has discretion to allow him to do so, provided that this can be done without injustice to the respondent. This may involve giving prior notice to the respondent and allowing an adjournment; see *Re Sevenoaks Stationers (Retail) Ltd* [1991] Ch. 164 at p. 177; [1990] BCC 765 at pp. 773–774). It is wrong to disqualify a director on the basis of charges which have not been made against him or for the judge to make findings on matters which have never been alleged (ibid.). It has also recently been said to be unnecessary for the Official Receiver to include in his report "every matter which could be the possible subject of a complaint". While it was right to draw the attention of the court to such matters as the failure to file returns promptly, this could be done where the failure was not serious in the form of a schedule or addendum: *Re Pamstock Ltd* [1994] BCC 264.

S. 9(2)

This incorporates the definition of "becomes insolvent" from s. 6(2).

S. 9(4), (5)

Power is given to the Secretary of State to revise the statutory criteria of unfitness by subordinate legislation.

OTHER CASES OF DISQUALIFICATION

Section 10   Participation in wrongful trading

10(1)   [Court's power]   Where the court makes a declaration under section 213 or 214 of the Insolvency Act that a person is liable to make a contribution to a company's assets, then, whether or not an application for such an order is made by any person, the court may, if it thinks fit, also make a disqualification order against the person to whom the declaration relates.

10(2)   [Maximum period]   The maximum period of disqualification under this section is 15 years.

(Former provisions: CA 1985, s. 295(2); IA 1985, ss. 16, 108(2))

General note

The sections referred to relate to fraudulent trading as well as wrongful trading. The court is empowered to make a disqualification order in addition to imposing personal liability on the person concerned (who, in the case of fraudulent trading, will not necessarily have been a director or shadow director). This it may do of its own motion, or on the application of *any* person. The section appears to assume that the disqualification order will be made in the same proceedings as the declaration of liability, but conceivably it could be the subject of a separate, later application.

   According to a note in [1990] IL & P 72, at p. 73, the respondent in *Re Purpoint Ltd* [1991] BCC 121 was disqualified under this section for two years, as well as being ordered to pay compensation under s. 214.

Section 11   Undischarged bankrupts

11(1)   [Offence]   It is an offence for a person who is an undischarged bankrupt to act as director of, or directly or indirectly to take part in or be concerned in the promotion, formation or management of, a company, except with the leave of the court.

11(2)   ["The court"]   "The court" for this purpose is the court by which the person was adjudged bankrupt or, in Scotland, sequestration of his estates was awarded.

11(3)   [Requirements for leave of court]   In England and Wales, the leave of the court shall not be given unless notice of intention to apply for it has been served on the official receiver; and it is the latter's duty, if he is of opinion that it is contrary to the public interest that the application should be granted, to attend on the hearing of the application and oppose it.

(Former provisions: CA 1985, s. 302; CA 1948, s. 187 (as amended by CA 1981, Sch. 3, para. 9; SI 1984 No. 1169, art. 2, and IA 1985, Sch. 10, Pt. I))

General note

The ban here imposed on an undischarged bankrupt is analogous in many ways to a disqualification order, except of course that it applies automatically. Some of the notes to s. 1 are relevant to this section.

The offence of acting as a director while an undischarged bankrupt under this section is an absolute offence: there is no requirement of *mens rea*. It is no defence that the defendant genuinely believes that he has been discharged from his bankruptcy: *R* v *Brockley* [1994] BCC 131.

An undischarged bankrupt is also disqualified from acting as trustee of a charity, except with the leave of the court: Charities Act 1993, s. 72(1)(*b*).

For cases where a bankrupt sought the leave of the court under this, or an equivalent, provision see *Re McQuillan* (1989) 5 BCC 137, *Re Altim Pty Ltd* [1968] 2 NSWR 762.

Section 12 Failure to pay under county court administration order

12(1) [Effect of s. 12(2)] The following has effect where a court under section 429 of the Insolvency Act revokes an administration order under Part VI of the County Courts Act 1984.

12(2) [Restriction on person] A person to whom that section applies by virtue of the order under section 429(2)(b) shall not, except with the leave of the court which made the order, act as director or liquidator of, or directly or indirectly take part or be concerned in the promotion, formation or management of, a company.

(Former provision: IA 1985, s. 221(2))

General note

The "administration order" here referred to relates to an individual debtor and has no connection with an administration order made in respect of an insolvent company under IA 1985, s. 8.

See the note to IA 1986, s. 429.

CONSEQUENCES OF CONTRAVENTION

Section 13 Criminal penalties

13 If a person acts in contravention of a disqualification order or of section 12(2), or is guilty of an offence under section 11, he is liable—

(a) on conviction on indictment, to imprisonment for not more than 2 years or a fine or both; and

(b) on summary conviction, to imprisonment for not more than 6 months or a fine not exceeding the statutory maximum, or both.

(Former provisions: CA 1985, ss. 295(7), 302(1), Sch. 24; IA 1985, s. 221(5))

General note

The breach of a disqualification order or of the analogous ban on an undischarged bankrupt is a criminal offence, as well as potentially attracting civil sanctions under s. 15.

Recent prosecutions under this section include *R* v *Theivendran* (1992) 13 Cr App R (S) 601, *R* v *Brockley* [1994] BCC 131, *R* v *Teece* (1944) 15 Cr App R 302.

On the "statutory maximum", and penalties generally, see IA 1986, s. 430 and Sch. 10.

Section 14 · Offences by body corporate

14(1) [Offence re officer]   Where a body corporate is guilty of an offence of acting in contravention of a disqualification order, and it is proved that the offence occurred with the consent or connivance of, or was attributable to any neglect on the part of any director, manager, secretary or other similar officer of the body corporate, or any person who was purporting to act in any such capacity he, as well as the body corporate, is guilty of the offence and liable to be proceeded against and punished accordingly.

14(2) [Where managers are members]   Where the affairs of a body corporate are managed by its members, subsection (1) applies in relation to the acts and defaults of a member in connection with his functions of management as if he were a director of the body corporate.

(Former provisions: CA 1985, s. 733(1)–(3); IA 1985, Sch. 6, para. 7)

General note

This is a standard provision, equivalent to IA 1986, s. 432.

"Body corporate" and "officer" are defined in CA 1985, ss. 740, 744, and these definitions are incorporated into the present Act by s. 22(6). A body corporate includes a company incorporated elsewhere than in Great Britain, but excludes a corporation sole and a Scottish firm. On the meaning of "officer", see the note to IA 1986, s. 206(3).

Section 15 Personal liability for company's debts where person acts while disqualified

15(1) [Personal liability]   A person is personally responsible for all the relevant debts of a company if at any time—

    (a) in contravention of a disqualification order or of section 11 of this Act he is involved in the management of the company, or

    (b) as a person who is involved in the management of the company, he acts or is willing to act on instructions given without the leave of the court by a person whom he knows at that time to be the subject of a disqualification order or to be an undischarged bankrupt.

15(2) [Joint and several liability]   Where a person is personally responsible under this section for the relevant debts of a company, he is jointly and severally liable in respect of those debts with the company and any other person who, whether under this section or otherwise, is so liable.

15(3) [Relevant debts of company]   For the purposes of this section the relevant debts of a company are—

    (a) in relation to a person who is personally responsible under paragraph (a) of subsection (1), such debts and other liabilities of the company as are incurred at a time when that person was involved in the management of the company, and

(b) in relation to a person who is personally responsible under paragraph (b) of that subsection, such debts and other liabilities of the company as are incurred at a time when that person was acting or was willing to act on instructions given as mentioned in that paragraph.

15(4)   [Person involved in management]   For the purposes of this section, a person is involved in the management of a company if he is a director of the company or if he is concerned, whether directly or indirectly, or takes part, in the management of the company.

15(5)   [Interpretation]   For the purposes of this section a person who, as a person involved in the management of a company, has at any time acted on instructions given without the leave of the court by a person whom he knew at that time to be the subject of a disqualification order or to be an undischarged bankrupt is presumed, unless the contrary is shown, to have been willing at any time thereafter to act on any instructions given by that person.

(Former provisions: IA 1985, s. 18(1) (part), (2)–(6))

General note

This section makes a person personally liable, without limit, for the debts of a company if he is involved in its management in breach of a disqualification order or while he is an undischarged bankrupt. It is very closely analogous to IA 1986, s. 217, which deals with the reuse of the name of a former insolvent company – indeed, the two sections are both derived from the same source.

For further comment, see the note to IA 1986, s. 217.

SUPPLEMENTARY PROVISIONS

Section 16   Application for disqualification order

16(1)   [Notice, appearance, etc.]   A person intending to apply for the making of a disqualification order by the court having jurisdiction to wind up a company shall give not less than 10 days' notice of his intention to the person against whom the order is sought; and on the hearing of the application the last-mentioned person may appear and himself give evidence or call witnesses.

16(2)   [Applicants]   An application to a court with jurisdiction to wind up companies for the making against any person of a disqualification order under any of sections 2 to 5 may be made by the Secretary of State or the official receiver, or by the liquidator or any past or present member or creditor of any company in relation to which that person has committed or is alleged to have committed an offence or other default.

16(3)   [Appearance, etc. of applicant]   On the hearing of any application under this Act made by the Secretary of State or the official receiver or the liquidator the applicant shall appear and call the attention of the court to any matters which seem to him to be relevant, and may himself give evidence or call witnesses.

(Former provisions: CA 1985, s. 295(6) (part), Sch. 12, para. 1–3; IA 1985, s. 108(2), Sch. 6, para. 1(4))

General note

The procedural provisions set out in s. 16(1) apply only where application is made to the court having jurisdiction to wind up the company. They will not apply in those cases where the court is empowered of its own motion to make an order (see, e.g. ss. 2, 10), "although doubtless the rules of natural justice will require that the person should be given some notice that the court is contemplating making a disqualification order": (*Secretary of State for Trade & Industry* v *Langridge, Re Cedac Ltd* [1991] Ch. 402 at p. 414; [1991] BCC 148 at p. 155). Again, no notice has to be served (although again the rules of natural justice will have effect) where the proceedings are before a court other than that which has winding-up jurisdiction, e.g. in a case brought under s. 5 (ibid.).

The requirement that an intended respondent should be given 10 days' notice of the intention to apply for an order is directory rather than mandatory. Failure to give proper notice is a procedural irregularity which does not nullify the application (*Secretary of State for Trade & Industry* v *Langridge, Re Cedac Ltd,* above). This decision (by a majority) of the Court of Appeal effectively overrules the earlier decision of Harman J in *Re Jaymar Management Ltd* [1990] BCC 303, but leaves undisturbed the ruling given in the latter case that "ten days' notice" means ten clear days, i.e. exclusive of both the date on which notice is given and that on which the proceedings are issued.

There is no obligation to state in the notice the grounds upon which the application will be made.

Although the second part of s. 16(1) appears to suggest that the respondent may call oral evidence at the hearing, it is clear from the rules that (exceptional cases apart) evidence must be presented in the form of affidavits and in keeping with the time limits imposed by the rules (*Re Rex Williams Leisure plc* [1994] Ch. 1; [1993] BCC 79 at p. 83, affd [1994] BCC 551). It follows that if he wishes to make a submission of no case to answer he must do so when he has seen and considered the applicant's affidavit evidence and that he cannot wait until after the close of the applicant's case at the hearing (ibid.).

Section 17   Application for leave under an order

17(1)   [Court]   As regards the court to which application must be made for leave under a disqualification order, the following applies—

   (a) where the application is for leave to promote or form a company, it is any court with jurisdiction to wind up companies, and

   (b) where the application is for leave to be a liquidator, administrator or director of, or otherwise to take part in the management of a company, or to be a receiver or manager of a company's property, it is any court having jurisdiction to wind up that company.

17(2)   [Appearance, etc. of Secretary of State et al.]   On the hearing of an application for leave made by a person against whom a disqualification order has been made on the application of the Secretary of State, the official receiver or the liquidator, the Secretary of State, official receiver or liquidator shall appear and call the attention of the court to any matters which seem to him to be relevant, and may himself give evidence or call witnesses.

(Former provisions: CA 1985, s. 295(6) (part), Sch. 12, paras. 4, 5; IA 1986, s. 108(2), Sch. 6, paras. 1(4), 14)

General note

This section deals with the procedural aspects of an application to the court, by a person who is subject to a disqualification order, for leave to act in relation to the management, etc. of a company during the currency of the order.

It is also common for an application for leave to be made at the time of the original hearing when the order is made. (In *Re Dicetrade Ltd, Secretary of State for Trade & Industry* v *Worth & Anor* [1994] BCC 371 at p. 373, Dillon LJ said that this course was "desirable" and "in everyone's interests".) In this case, the disqualification order is, in effect, made subject to a proviso which allows the respondent to act in specified ways notwithstanding the order. The normal procedure is for the respondent, after he has been served with notice of the disqualification proceedings, to issue a notice of application for the leave in question; but this pro forma request is sometimes dispensed with (e.g. in *Re Majestic Recording Studios Ltd & Ors* (1988) 4 BCC 519, in an unreported part of the judgment).

On applications for leave, see further the note to s. 1(1) above.

If an application for leave to act notwithstanding disqualification is made at the same time as the hearing for the disqualification order and does not take up a substantial part of the time of that hearing, it is convenient not to make a separate order in respect of the costs of that application. But where a separate application for leave is made some time later, it is to be regarded as free-standing for the purposes of costs. The Secretary of State may then be entitled to his costs on a standard basis; alternatively, if he simply intimates to the applicant (or to his solicitors) any particular points that are relied on so that they can be drawn to the attention of the court, but states that he does not oppose the grant of the relief sought, it may be appropriate to make no order as to costs (*Re Dicetrade Ltd* (above)).

Section 18   Register of disqualification orders

18(1)   [Regulations re furnishing information]   The Secretary of State may make regulations requiring officers of courts to furnish him with such particulars as the regulations may specify of cases in which—

(a) a disqualification order is made, or

(b) any action is taken by a court in consequence of which such an order is varied or ceases to be in force, or

(c) leave is granted by a court for a person subject to such an order to do any thing which otherwise the order prohibits him from doing;

and the regulations may specify the time within which, and the form and manner in which, such particulars are to be furnished.

18(2)   [Register of orders]   The Secretary of State shall, from the particulars so furnished, continue to maintain the register of orders, and of cases in which leave has been granted as mentioned in subsection (1)(c), which was set up by him under section 29 of the Companies Act 1976 and continued under section 301 of the Companies Act 1985.

18(3)   [Deletion of orders no longer in force]   When an order of which entry is made in the register ceases to be in force, the Secretary of State shall delete the entry from the register and all particulars relating to it which have been furnished to him under this section or any previous corresponding provision.

18(4)   [Inspection of register]   The register shall be open to inspection on payment of such fee as may be specified by the Secretary of State in regulations.

18(5)   [Regulations by statutory instrument etc.]   Regulations under this section shall be made by statutory instrument subject to annulment in pursuance of a resolution of either House of Parliament.

(Former provisions: CA 1985, s. 301; IA 1985, s. 108(2), Sch. 6, para. 2)

General note

The Secretary of State, acting through the Registrar of Companies, has kept a register of disqualification orders since first being required to do so by CA 1976, s. 29. The register is open to public inspection. This section provides for the continuation of the register, and brings forward from the pre-consolidation Acts other rules relating to the register.

S. 18(1)

The regulations currently in force are the Companies (Disqualification Orders) Regulations 1986 (SI 1986 No. 2067), which prescribe forms on which the relevant officers of the courts are to make returns.

Section **19**   Special savings from repealed enactments

19   Schedule 2 to this Act has effect—

   (a)   in connection with certain transitional cases arising under sections 93 and 94 of the Companies Act 1981, so as to limit the power to make a disqualification order, or to restrict the duration of an order, by reference to events occurring or things done before those sections came into force,

   (b)   to preserve orders made under section 28 of the Companies Act 1976 (repealed by the Act of 1981), and

   (c)   to preclude any applications for a disqualification order under section 6 or 8, where the relevant company went into liquidation before 28th April 1986.

(Former provision: CA 1985, s. 295(6))

General note

This section, read in conjunction with Sch. 2, makes transitional arrangements, preserving existing disqualification orders and making it clear that the new grounds of disqualification introduced by IA 1985 are not to apply retrospectively to events before 28 April 1986, the date when the relevant provisions of that Act become operative.

MISCELLANEOUS AND GENERAL

Section **20**   Admissibility in evidence of statements

20   In any proceedings (whether or not under this Act), any statement made in pursuance of a requirement imposed by or under sections 6 to 10, 15 or 19(c) of, or Schedule 1 to, this Act, or by or under rules made for the purposes of this Act under the Insolvency Act, may be used in evidence against any person making or concurring in making the statement.

(Former provision: IA 1985, s. 231 (part))

General note

This section is similar to IA 1986, s. 433, and is derived from the same source.

Section 21   Interaction with Insolvency Act

21(1)   [Reference to official receiver]   References in this Act to the official receiver, in relation to the winding up of a company or the bankruptcy of an individual, are to any person who, by virtue of section 399 of the Insolvency Act, is authorised to act as the official receiver in relation to that winding up or bankruptcy; and, in accordance with section 401(2) of that Act, references in this Act to an official receiver includes a person appointed as his deputy.

21(2)   [Pt. I to VII of IA]   Sections 6 to 10, 15, 19(c) and 20 of, and Schedule 1 to, this Act are deemed included in Parts I to VII of the Insolvency Act for the purposes of the following sections of that Act—

> section 411 (power to make insolvency rules);

> section 414 (fees orders);

> section 420 (orders extending provisions about insolvent companies to insolvent partnerships);

> section 422 (modification of such provisions in their application to recognised banks).

21(3)   [Application of IA, s. 434]   Section 434 of that Act (Crown application) applies to sections 6 to 10, 15, 19(c) and 20 of, and Schedule 1 to, this Act as it does to the provisions of that Act which are there mentioned.

21(4)   [Summary proceedings in Scotland]   For the purposes of summary proceedings in Scotland, section 431 of that Act applies to summary proceedings for an offence under section 11 or 13 of this Act as it applies to summary proceedings for an offence under Parts I to VII of that Act.

(Former provisions: IA 1985, ss. 106, 107, 108(1), (2), 222(1), 224(2), 227, 229, 234)

General note

This section requires a reader of this Act to make extensive cross-references to IA 1986. Most of the matters referred to are administrative or procedural in nature, but the extension of the company director disqualification régime so that it applies to the former members of insolvent partnerships is both bold and surprising. The justification for the imposition of a director disqualification order is invariably stated to be that the delinquent director has abused the privilege of limited liability (see, e.g., the Cork Committee's *Report*, para. 1807). To extend this penalty to partners, whose personal liability is necessarily unlimited, is anomalous and surely, in principle, wrong.

The Insolvency Rules 1986, and in particular the review and appeal procedures prescribed by IR 1986, rr. 7.47, 7.49, apply to orders made under this Act: *Re Tasbian Ltd (No. 2)* [1992] BCC 322, *Re Probe Data Systems Ltd (No. 3)* [1992] BCC 110.

S. 21(2)

In s. 21(2) the words "and section 431 (summary proceedings)", which formerly appeared at the end, were repealed by CA 1989, s. 212 and Sch. 24 as from 1 March 1990 (see SI 1990 No. 142

(C. 5), art. 7(*d*)). Section 21(4) was also added by this legislation with effect from the same date (art. 7(*a*)).

In regard to the entry for s. 411 see the Insolvent Companies (Reports on Conduct of Directors) No. 2 Rules 1986 (SI 1986 No. 2134) and the Insolvent Companies (Reports on Conduct of Directors) (No. 2) (Scotland) Rules 1986 (SI 1986 No. 1916 (S. 140)).

In regard to the entry for s. 420, reference should be made to the Insolvent Partnerships Order 1994 (SI 1994 No. 2421), replacing (from 1 December 1994) the Insolvent Partnerships Order 1986 (SI 1986 No. 2142).

S. 21(3)

The Crown is not bound generally, but only in relation to matters specified in paras. (*a*)–(*e*) of IA 1986, s. 434. See the note to that section.

S. 21(4)

For history, see the note to s. 21(2) above.

Section 22   Interpretation

22(1)   [Effect]   This section has effect with respect to the meaning of expressions used in this Act, and applies unless the context otherwise requires.

22(2)   ["Company"]   The expression **"company"**—

    (a)   in section 11, includes an unregistered company and a company incorporated outside Great Britain which has an established place of business in Great Britain, and

    (b)   elsewhere, includes any company which may be wound up under Part V of the Insolvency Act.

22(3)   [Application of IA, sec. 247, 251]   Section 247 in Part VII of the Insolvency Act (interpretation for the first Group of Parts of that Act) applies as regards references to a company's insolvency and to its going into liquidation; and **"administrative receiver"** has the meaning given by section 251 of that Act.

22(4)   ["Director"]   **"Director"** includes any person occupying the position of director, by whatever name called, and in sections 6 to 9 includes a shadow director.

22(5)   ["Shadow director"]   **"Shadow director"**, in relation to a company, means a person in accordance with whose directions or instructions the directors of the company are accustomed to act (but so that a person is not deemed a shadow director by reason only that the directors act on advice given by him in a professional capacity).

22(6)   [Application of CA, s. 740, 744]   Section 740 of the Companies Act applies as regards the meaning of **"body corporate"**; and **"officer"** has the meaning given by section 744 of that Act.

22(7)   [References to legislation]   In references to legislation other than this Act—

    "the Companies Act" means the Companies Act 1985;

    "the Companies Acts" has the meaning given by section 744 of that Act; and

    "the Insolvency Act" means the Insolvency Act 1986;

and in sections 3(1) and 5(1) of this Act **"the companies legislation"** means the Companies Acts (except the Insider Dealing Act), Parts I to VII of the Insolvency Act and, in Part XV of that Act, sections 411, 413, 414, 416 and 417.

22(8)   [References to former legislation]   Any reference to provisions, or a particular provision, of the Companies Acts or the Insolvency Act includes the corresponding provisions or provision of the former Companies Acts (as defined by section 735(1)(c) of the Companies Act, but including also that Act itself) or, as the case may be, the Insolvency Act 1985.

22(9)   [Application of CA, Pt. XXVI]   Any expression for whose interpretation provision is made by Part XXVI of the Companies Act (and not by subsections (3) to (8) above) is to be construed in accordance with that provision.

(Former provisions: IA 1985, s. 108(1)–(4))

General note

This section largely borrows or reproduces definitions from other Acts, notably CA 1985 and IA 1985. Further comment on the particular terms listed may be located by reference to Appendix I.

S. 22(2)

In both para. (*a*) and (*b*) of this subsection the definition of "company" was extended so as to include "a building society (within the meaning of the Building Societies Act 1986)" by the Building Societies Act 1986, s. 120 and Sch. 18, para. 16 as from 1 January 1987 (see SI 1986 No. 1560 (C. 56)). This amendment was expressed to be in regard to the former provisions, ss. 302 (4) and 295(3) of CA 1985, but would have continued to apply after the 1986 consolidation as part of s. 22(2) by virtue of Sch. 3, para. 6 of IA 1986 and s. 17(2)(*a*) of the Interpretation Act 1978. However, the amendment was itself repealed by CA 1989 simultaneously with the enactment of s. 22A, below (see CA 1989, s. 212 and Sch. 24, and SI 1990 No. 1392 (C. 41), art. 4(*b*), effective 31 July 1990), with the result that the original wording of s. 22(2) is now restored.

On the terms "company" and "unregistered company", see the note to IA 1986, s. 220.

S. 22(5)

The Act also now applies to shadow directors of building societies (see s. 22A(3)), but not to shadow directors of incorporated friendly societies (s. 22B(3)).

Section 22A   Application of Act to building societies

22A(1)   [To building societies as to companies]   This Act applies to building societies as it applies to companies.

22A(2)   [Interpretation]   References in this Act to a company, or to a director or an officer of a company include, respectively, references to a building society within the meaning of the Building Societies Act 1986 or to a director or officer, within the meaning of that Act, of a building society.

22A(3)   ["Shadow director"]   In relation to a building society the definition of "shadow director" in section 22(5) applies with the substitution of "building society" for "company".

22A(4)   [Sch. 1]   In the application of Schedule 1 to the directors of a building society, references to provisions of the Insolvency Act or the Companies Act include references to the corresponding provisions of the Building Societies Act 1986.

History note

Section 22A was inserted by CA 1989, s. 211(3) as from 31 July 1990 (see SI 1990 No. 1392 (C. 41), art. 4(*a*)).

Parts of the director disqualification legislation had already been extended to the officers and former officers of building societies from 1 January 1987 by the Building Societies Act 1986. This took the form of an amendment to IA 1985, inserting a new subs. (10) to s. 12 of that Act. (See the Building Societies Act 1986, s. 120 and Sch. 18, para. 17(3) and SI 1986 No. 1560 (C. 56).) However, by oversight it was not incorporated into the present Act in the consolidation of 1986. Its logical place would then have been as an extra subsection to s. 7. However, the amendment would have survived the legislative oversight by virtue of Sch. 3, para. 6 of CDDA 1986 and s. 17(2)(*a*) of the Interpretation Act 1978. The amendment has since been superseded by s. 22A above. Section 22A differs from the 1986 amendment in that it extends the definition of "shadow director" to include the clandestine officer of a building society.

The former provision read as follows:

"**12(10)**   In this section and in sections 14 to 19, a reference to a company or to a director (but not a shadow director) of a company includes a reference to a building society within the meaning of the Building Societies Act 1986 or to a director of a building society."

If inserted into the present Act as s. 7(5) in the course of the consolidation, and revised to take account of other relevant provisions, it would have begun: "**7(5)**   In this section and in sections 6, 9, 10 and 15 and in sections 212 and 214 to 217 of the Insolvency Act, . . .".

Section 22B   Application of Act to incorporated friendly societies

22B(1)   [Application as to companies]   This Act applies to incorporated friendly societies as it applies to companies.

22B(2)   [Interpretation]   References in this Act to a company, or to a director or an officer of a company include, respectively, references to an incorporated friendly society within the meaning of the Friendly Societies Act 1992 or to a member of the committee of management or officer, within the meaning of that Act, of an incorporated friendly society.

22B(3)   [Shadow directors]   In relation to an incorporated friendly society every reference to a shadow director shall be omitted.

22B(4)   [Sch. 1]   In the application of Schedule 1 to the members of the committee of management of an incorporated friendly society, references to provisions of the Insolvency Act or the Companies Act include references to the corresponding provisions of the Friendly Societies Act 1992.

General note

The Act in its original form did not apply to friendly societies, but it was extended so as to include incorporated friendly societies when this section was inserted by the Friendly Societies Act 1992, s. 120(1) and Sch. 21, para. 8 as from 1 February 1993 (see SI 1993 No. 16 (C. 1), art. 2 and Sch. 3).

S. 22B(3)

Shadow directors of building societies were originally also excluded, but this is no longer so: see s. 22A(3).

Section 23   Transitional provisions, savings, repeals

23(1)   [Sch. 3]   The transitional provisions and savings in Schedule 3 to this Act have effect, and are without prejudice to anything in the Interpretation Act 1978 with regard to the effect of repeals.

23(2) **[Sch. 4]** The enactments specified in the second column of Schedule 4 to this Act are repealed to the extent specified in the third column of that Schedule.

(Former provision: none)

General note

This section gives force to the repeals, transitional provisions and savings listed in the Schedules referred to.

Nothing in Sch. 4 is repealed that is not re-enacted in the consolidation, apart from the transitional provisions of IA 1985.

Section 24 Extent

24(1) **[England, Wales, Scotland]** This Act extends to England and Wales and to Scotland.

24(2) **[Northern Ireland]** Nothing in this Act extends to Northern Ireland.

General note

The disqualification regime in Northern Ireland is now contained in Pt. II of the Companies (Northern Ireland) Order 1989 as supplemented by secondary rules dealing with disqualification proceedings, reports on directors, etc. – see SR 1991 Nos. 367, 368 and 413.

Section 25 Commencement

25 This Act comes into force simultaneously with the Insolvency Act 1986.

General note

The date of commencement was 29 December 1986 – see IA 1986, s. 443 and SI 1986 No. 1924 (C.71); but most of the reforms introduced by IA 1985 which were consolidated into the present Act were brought into force on 28 April 1986: see SI 1986 No. 463 (C. 14).

Section 26 Citation

26 This Act may be cited as the Company Directors Disqualification Act 1986.

SCHEDULES

Schedule 1 — Matters for Determining Unfitness of Directors

Section 9

Part I — Matters Applicable in all Cases

1 Any misfeasance or breach of any fiduciary or other duty by the director in relation to the company.

2   Any misapplication or retention by the director of, or any conduct by the director giving rise to an obligation to account for, any money or other property of the company.

3   The extent of the director's responsibility for the company entering into any transaction liable to be set aside under Part XVI of the Insolvency Act (provisions against debt avoidance).

4   The extent of the director's responsibility for any failure by the company to comply with any of the following provisions of the Companies Act, namely—

    (a) section 221 (companies to keep accounting records);

    (b) section 222 (where and for how long records to be kept);

    (c) section 288 (register of directors and secretaries);

    (d) section 352 (obligation to keep and enter up register of members);

    (e) section 353 (location of register of members);

    (f) section 363 (duty of company to make annual returns); and

    (h) sections 399 and 415 (company's duty to register charges it creates).

5   The extent of the director's responsibility for any failure by the directors of the company to comply with—

    (a) section 226 or 227 of the Companies Act (duty to prepare annual accounts), or

    (b) section 233 of that Act (approval and signature of accounts).

General note

From 1 January 1987 to 31 July 1990 an additional para. 5A of this Schedule extended its operation to the directors of a building society; but this has now been superseded by the provisions of the new s. 22A, inserted by CA 1989. (See the notes to ss. 22(2) and 22A, above.)

    Paragraph 5A formerly read as follows:

> **"5A**   In the application of this Schedule to the directors of a building society, references to sections of the Insolvency Act or of the Companies Act other than sections which apply to building societies or their directors in any event, whether by virtue of the Insolvency Act or of the Building Societies Act 1986, shall be construed as references to the corresponding provisions (if any) of the Building Societies Act 1986".

    In para. 4, sub-para. (*f*) was substituted for the former sub-paras. (*f*) and (*g*) by CA 1989, s. 139(4) as from 1 October 1990, subject to transitional and saving provisions (see SI 1990 No. 1707 (C. 46), arts. 2(*a*), 4, 5). The former sub-paragraphs read as follows:

> "(f) sections 363 and 364 (company's duty to make annual return);
>
> (g) section 365 (time for completion of annual return);".

    Paragraph 5 was substituted by CA 1989, s. 23 and Sch. 10, para. 356(1), (3), as from 1 April 1990, subject to transitional and saving provisions (see SI 1990 No. 355 (C. 13), arts. 3, 6–9 and Sch. 1). Paragraph 5 formerly read as follows:

> "**5**   The extent of the director's responsibility for any failure by the directors of the company to comply with section 227 (directors' duty to prepare annual accounts) or section 238 (signing of balance sheet and documents to be annexed) of the Companies Act".

Part II — Matters Applicable Where Company Has Become Insolvent

6 The extent of the director's responsibility for the causes of the company becoming insolvent.

7 The extent of the director's responsibility for any failure by the company to supply any goods or services which have been paid for (in whole or in part).

8 The extent of the director's responsibility for the company entering into any transaction or giving any preference, being a transaction or preference—

    (a) liable to be set aside under section 127 or sections 238 to 240 of the Insolvency Act, or

    (b) challengeable under section 242 or 243 of that Act or under any rule of law in Scotland.

9 The extent of the director's responsibility for any failure by the directors of the company to comply with section 98 of the Insolvency Act (duty to call creditors' meeting in creditors' voluntary winding up).

10 Any failure by the director to comply with any obligation imposed on him by or under any of the following provisions of the Insolvency Act—

    (a) section 22 (company's statement of affairs in administration);

    (b) section 47 (statement of affairs to administrative receiver);

    (c) section 66 (statement of affairs in Scottish receivership);

    (d) section 99 (directors' duty to attend meeting; statement of affairs in creditors' voluntary winding up);

    (e) section 131 (statement of affairs in winding up by the court);

    (f) section 234 (duty of any one with company property to deliver it up);

    (g) section 235 (duty to co-operate with liquidator, etc.).

(For notes, see s. 9.)

Schedule 2 — Savings from Companies Act 1981 ss. 93, 94, and Insolvency Act 1985 Schedule 9

Section 19

1 Sections 2 and 4(1)(b) do not apply in relation to anything done before 15th June 1982 by a person in his capacity as liquidator of a company or as receiver or manager of a company's property.

2 Subject to paragraph 1—

    (a) section 2 applies in a case where a person is convicted on indictment of an offence which he committed (and, in the case of a continuing offence, has ceased to commit) before 15th June 1982; but in such a case a disqualification order under that section shall not be made for a period in excess of 5 years;

(b) that section does not apply in a case where a person is convicted summarily—

(i) in England and Wales, if he had consented so to be tried before that date, or

(ii) in Scotland, if the summary proceedings commenced before that date.

3 Subject to paragraph 1, section 4 applies in relation to an offence committed or other thing done before 15th June 1982; but a disqualification order made on the grounds of such an offence or other thing done shall not be made for a period in excess of 5 years.

4 The powers of a court under section 5 are not exercisable in a case where a person is convicted of an offence which he committed (and, in the case of a continuing offence, had ceased to commit) before 15th June 1982.

5 For purposes of section 3(1) and section 5, no account is to be taken of any offence which was committed, or any default order which was made, before 1st June 1977.

6 An order made under section 28 of the Companies Act 1976 has effect as if made under section 3 of this Act; and an application made before 15th June 1982 for such an order is to be treated as an application for an order under the section last mentioned.

7 Where—

(a) an application is made for a disqualification order under section 6 of this Act by virtue of paragraph (a) of subsection (2) of that section, and

(b) the company in question went into liquidation before 28th April 1986 (the coming into force of the provision replaced by section 6),

the court shall not make an order under that section unless it could have made a disqualification order under section 300 of the Companies Act as it had effect immediately before the date specified in sub-paragraph (b) above.

8 An application shall not be made under section 8 of this Act in relation to a report made or information or documents obtained before 28th April 1986.

(*For notes, see s. 19.* The Companies Act 1981, s. 93 came into force on 15 June 1982.)

Schedule 3 — Transitional Provisions and Savings

Section 23(1)

1 In this Schedule, **"the former enactments"** means so much of the Companies Act, and so much of the Insolvency Act, as is repealed and replaced by this Act; and **"the appointed day"** means the day on which this Act comes into force.

2 So far as anything done or treated as done under or for the purposes of any provision of the former enactments could have been done under or for the purposes of the corresponding provision of this Act, it is not invalidated by the repeal of that provision but has effect as if done under or for the purposes of the corresponding provision; and any order, regulation, rule or other instrument made or having effect under any provision of the former enactments shall, insofar as its effect is preserved by this paragraph, be treated for all purposes as made and having effect under the corresponding provision.

3   Where any period of time specified in a provision of the former enactments is current immediately before the appointed day, this Act has effect as if the corresponding provision had been in force when the period began to run; and (without prejudice to the foregoing) any period of time so specified and current is deemed for the purposes of this Act—

(a) to run from the date or event from which it was running immediately before the appointed day, and

(b) to expire (subject to any provision of this Act for its extension) whenever it would have expired if this Act had not been passed;

and any rights, priorities, liabilities, reliefs, obligations, requirements, powers, duties or exemptions dependent on the beginning, duration or end of such a period as above mentioned shall be under this Act as they were or would have been under the former enactments.

4   Where in any provision of this Act there is a reference to another such provision, and the first-mentioned provision operates, or is capable of operating, in relation to things done or omitted, or events occuring or not occuring, in the past (including in particular past acts of compliance with any enactment, failures of compliance, contraventions, offences and convictions of offences) the reference to the other provision is to be read as including a reference to the corresponding provision of the former enactments.

5   Offences committed before the appointed day under any provision of the former enactments may, notwithstanding any repeal by this Act, be prosecuted and punished after that day as if this Act had not passed.

6   A reference in any enactment, instrument or document (whether express or implied, and in whatever phraseology) to a provision of the former enactments (including the corresponding provision of any yet earlier enactment) is to be read, where necessary to retain for the enactment, instrument or document the same force and effect as it would have had but for the passing of this Act, as, or as including, a reference to the corresponding provision by which it is replaced in this Act.

(For notes, see s. 23.)

Schedule 4 — Repeals

Section 23(2)

Chapter	Short title	Extent of repeal
1985 c. 6.	The Companies Act 1985.	Sections 295 to 299. Section 301. Section 302. Schedule 12. In Schedule 24, the entries relating to sections 295(7) and 302(1).
1985 c. 65.	The Insolvency Act 1985.	Sections 12 to 14. Section 16. Section 18. Section 108(2). Schedule 2. In Schedule 6, paragraphs 1, 2, 7 and 14. In Schedule 9, paragraphs 2 and 3.

(For notes, see s. 23.)

THE INSOLVENCY RULES 1986

(S.I. 1986 No. 1925)

Made on 10 November 1986 by the Lord Chancellor, under ss. 411 and 412 of the Insolvency Act 1986. Operative from 29 December 1986.

[**CCH Note:** These Rules are amended by the Insolvency (Amendment) Rules 1987 (SI 1987 No. 1919) as from 11 January 1988, the Insolvency (Amendment) Rules 1989 (SI 1989, No. 397) as from 3 April 1989, the Insolvency (Amendment) Rules 1991 (SI 1991 No. 495) as from 2 April 1991 and the Insolvency (Amendment) Rules 1993 (SI 1993 No. 602) as from 5 April 1993]

ARRANGEMENT OF RULES

THE FIRST GROUP OF PARTS
COMPANY INSOLVENCY; COMPANIES WINDING UP

INTRODUCTORY PROVISIONS

RULE

PART 4 — COMPANIES WINDING UP

RULE

RULE

CHAPTER 6 — STATEMENT OF AFFAIRS AND OTHER INFORMATION

CHAPTER 7 — INFORMATION TO CREDITORS AND CONTRIBUTORIES

CHAPTER 8 — MEETINGS OF CREDITORS AND CONTRIBUTORIES

Section A: rules of general application

611

RULE

CHAPTER 17 — CALLS
(NO CVL APPLICATION)

CHAPTER 18 — SPECIAL MANAGER

CHAPTER 19 — PUBLIC EXAMINATION OF COMPANY OFFICERS AND OTHERS

CHAPTER 20 — ORDER OF PAYMENT OF COSTS, ETC., OUT OF ASSETS

CHAPTER 21 — MISCELLANEOUS RULES

Section A: return of capital
(No CVL application)

RULE

4.222. Procedure for return.

CHAPTER 22 — LEAVE TO ACT AS DIRECTOR, ETC., OF COMPANY WITH PROHIBITED NAME (SECTION 216 OF THE ACT)

THE SECOND GROUP OF PARTS

INDIVIDUAL INSOLVENCY; BANKRUPTCY

PART 5 — INDIVIDUAL VOLUNTARY ARRANGEMENTS

5.1. Introductory.

RULE

PART 6 — BANKRUPTCY

CHAPTER 1 — THE STATUTORY DEMAND

CHAPTER 2 — BANKRUPTCY PETITION (CREDITOR'S)

RULE

RULE

PART 13 — INTERPRETATION AND APPLICATION

SCHEDULES

THE INSOLVENCY RULES 1986

General

The rules in this section are prefixed with the figure 0. The remainder of the rules are grouped into Parts, numbered 1, 2, etc., and the rules in each part begin with the same figure, e.g. rr. 1.1, 1.2, etc. The sequence of Parts broadly follows the scheme of the Insolvency Act 1986.

Where a rule calls for the use of a prescribed form, the reference number of the appropriate form is shown adjacent to the rule in question.

The text incorporates amendments made to the rules by the Insolvency (Amendment) Rules 1987 (SI 1987 No. 1919), which came into force on 11 January 1988, the Insolvency (Amendment) Rules 1989 (SI 1989 No. 397), effective from 3 April 1989, the Insolvency (Amendment) Rules 1991 (SI 1991 No. 495), effective from 2 April 1991 and the Insolvency (Amendment) Rules 1993 (SI 1993 No. 602), effective from 5 April 1993. For Scotland, amendments were made by the Insolvency (Scotland) Amendment Rules 1987 (SI 1987 No. 1921 (S. 132)), effective from 11 January 1988.

INTRODUCTORY PROVISIONS

Rule 0.1 Citation and commencement

0.1 These Rules may be cited as the Insolvency Rules 1986 and shall come into force on 29th December 1986.

General Note

The day appointed for the commencement of IA 1986 and these rules was 29 December 1986. Other subordinate legislation which came into force on the same date is listed below. A number of these instruments have since been amended and/or revoked and replaced; their replacements appear in the second list below.

The Insolvency Regulations 1986 (SI 1986 No. 1994) (amended by SI 1987, No. 1959, SI 1988 No. 1739 and SI 1991 No. 380; revoked and replaced by SI 1994 No. 2507)

The Insolvency Fees Order 1986 (SI 1986 No. 2030) (since amended, see second list below)

The Insolvency Proceedings (Monetary Limits) Order 1986 (SI 1986 No. 1996)

The Insolvent Partnerships Order 1986 (SI 1986 No. 2142) (revoked and replaced by SI 1994 No. 2421)

The Administration of Insolvent Estates of Deceased Persons Order 1986 (SI 1986 No. 1999)

The Companies (Unfair Prejudice Applications) Rules 1986 (SI 1986 No. 2000)

The Insolvency Practitioners Regulations 1986 (SI 1986 No. 1995) (amended by SI 1986 No. 2247 and SI 1989 Nos. 1587 and 2170; revoked and replaced by SI 1990 No. 439)

The Insolvent Companies (Reports on Conduct of Directors) No. 2 Rules 1986 (SI 1986 No. 2134)

The Insolvency (Amendment of Subordinate Legislation) Order 1986 (SI 1986 No. 2001)

The Co-operation of Insolvency Courts (Designation of Relevant Countries and Territories) Order 1986 (SI 1986 No. 2123)

The Companies (Disqualification Orders) Regulations 1986 (SI 1986 No. 2067)

The Insurance Companies (Winding-up) (Amendment) Rules 1986 (SI 1986 No. 2002)

The Insolvency (Scotland) Rules 1986 (SI 1986 No. 1915 (S. 139))

The Receivers (Scotland) Regulations 1986 (SI 1986 No. 1917 (S. 141))

The Insolvent Companies (Reports on Conduct of Directors) (No. 2) (Scotland) Rules 1986 (SI 1986 No. 1916 (S. 140))

The Insurance Companies (Winding Up) (Scotland) Rules 1986 (SI 1986 No. 1918 (S.142))

Other secondary legislation (which came into force on 11 January 1988 unless otherwise stated) to note:

The Insolvency (Amendment of Subordinate Legislation) Order 1987 (SI 1987 No. 1398) (1 September 1987)

The Insolvency (Scotland) Amendment Rules 1987 (SI 1987 No. 1921 (S. 132))

The Insolvent Companies (Disqualification of Unfit Directors) Proceedings Rules 1987 (SI 1987 No. 2023)

The Insolvency (ECSC Levy Debts) Regulations 1987 (SI 1987 No. 2093)

The Department of Trade and Industry (Fees) Order 1988 (SI 1988 No. 93) (22 January 1988)

The Insolvency Fees (Amendment) Order 1988 (SI 1988 No. 95) (16 February 1988)

The Insolvency Act 1986 (Guernsey) Order 1989 (SI 1989 No. 2409) (1 February 1990)

The Insolvency Practitioners Regulations 1990 (SI 1990 No. 439) (1 April 1990)

The Insolvency Fees (Amendment) Order 1990 (SI 1990 No. 560) (2 April 1990)

The Bankruptcy and Companies (Department of Trade and Industry) Fees (Amendment) Order 1990 (SI 1990 No. 599) (2 April 1990)

The Insolvency Fees (Amendment) Order 1991 (SI 1991 No. 496)

The Financial Markets and Insolvency Regulations 1991 (SI 1991 No. 880) (25 April 1991)

The Insolvency Fees (Amendment) Order 1992 (SI 1992 No. 34) (14 January 1992)

The Financial Markets and Insolvency (Amendment) Regulations 1992 (SI 1992 No. 716) (1 May 1992)

The Companies (Single Member Private Limited Companies) Regulations 1992 (SI 1992 No. 1699) (15 July 1992)

The Insolvency Practitioners (Amendment) Regulations 1993 (SI 1993 No. 221) (1 April 1993)

The Insolvent Partnerships Order 1994 (SI 1994 No. 2421) (1 December 1994).

The Insolvency Regulations 1994 (SI 1994 No. 2507) (24 October 1994)

The Insolvency Fees (Amendment) Order 1994 (SI 1994 No. 2541) (24 October 1994)

Rule 0.2   Construction and interpretation

0.2(1)   [Definitions]   In these Rules—

"**the Act**" means the Insolvency Act 1986 (any reference to a numbered section being to a section of that Act);

"**the Companies Act**" means the Companies Act 1985;

"**the Rules**" means the Insolvency Rules 1986.

0.2(2)   [Pt. 13]   Subject to paragraph (1), Part 13 of the Rules has effect for their interpretation and application.

History note

Rule 0.2 was substituted by I(A)R 1987 (SI 1987 No. 1919), r. 3(1), Sch., Pt. 1, para. 1 as from 11 January 1988. The rule formerly read as follows:

"**Construction of principal references**

0.2   In these Rules—

'**the Act**' means the Insolvency Act 1986 (any reference to a numbered section being to a section of that Act);

'**the Companies Act**' means the Companies Act 1985; and

'**the Rules**' means the Insolvency Rules 1986."

Rule **0.3**   Extent

0.3(1)   **[Pt. 1, 2 and 4]**   Parts 1, 2, and 4 of the Rules, and Parts 7 to 13 as they relate to company insolvency, apply in relation to companies which the courts in England and Wales have jurisdiction to wind up.

0.3(2)   **[Pt. 3]**   Rule 3.1 applies to all receivers to whom Part III of the Act applies and the remainder of Part 3 of the Rules applies to administrative receivers appointed otherwise than under section 51 (Scottish Receivership).

0.3(3)   **[Pt. 5 and 6]**   Parts 5 and 6 of the Rules, and Parts 7 to 13 as they relate to individual insolvency, extend to England and Wales only.

History note

In r. 0.3(2) the words from the beginning to "the remainder of" were inserted by I(A)R 1987 (SI 1987 No. 1919), r. 3(1), Sch., Pt. 1, para. 2 as from 11 January 1988.

General note

The corresponding subordinate legislation for Scotland is to be found in the last four statutory instruments listed in the first part of the general note to r. 0.1 above and in the Insolvency (Scotland) Amendment Rules 1987 (SI 1987 No. 1921 (s.132)).

     For the position in Northern Ireland see the Insolvency Rules (Northern Ireland) 1991 (SR 1991 No. 364).

THE FIRST GROUP OF PARTS
COMPANY INSOLVENCY; COMPANIES WINDING UP

PART 1 — COMPANY VOLUNTARY ARRANGEMENTS

General comment on Pt. 1

The topic of company voluntary arrangements to which these rules relate is dealt with in IA 1986, ss. 1–7. On voluntary arrangements for individual debtors, see IA 1986, ss. 252ff., and IR 1986, Pt. 5.

Chapter 1 — Preliminary

Rule **1.1**   Scope of this Part; interpretation

1.1(1)   **[Application of Pt. 1 Rules]**   The Rules in this Part apply where, pursuant to Part I of the Act, it is intended to make, and there is made, a proposal to a company and its creditors for a voluntary arrangement, that is to say, a composition in satisfaction of its debts or a scheme of arrangement of its affairs.

1.1(2)   [Application of Ch. 2–6]   In this Part—

(a) Chapter 2 applies where the proposal for a voluntary arrangement is made by the directors of the company, and neither is the company in liquidation, nor is an administration order (under Part II of the Act) in force in relation to it;

(b) Chapter 3 applies where the company is in liquidation or an administration order is in force, and the proposal is made by the liquidator or (as the case may be) the administrator, he in either case being the nominee for the purposes of the proposal;

(c) Chapter 4 applies in the same case as Chapter 3, but where the nominee is an insolvency practitioner other than the liquidator or the administrator; and

(d) Chapters 5 and 6 apply in all the three cases mentioned in sub-paragraphs (a) to (c) above.

1.1(3)   ["The responsible insolvency practitioner" in Ch. 3–5]   In Chapters 3, 4 and 5, the liquidator or the administrator is referred to as "the responsible insolvency practitioner".

General note

Different procedures must be followed in the three cases listed in r. 1.1 (2)(*a*)–(*c*): see IA 1986, ss. 1, 2. The relevant rules are set out in Chs. 2, 3 and 4 respectively.

Chapter 2 — Proposal by Directors

Rule 1.2   Preparation of proposal

1.2   The directors shall prepare for the intended nominee a proposal on which (with or without amendments to be made under Rule 1.3 below) to make his report to the court under section 2.

(See general note after r. 1.6.)

Rule 1.3   Contents of proposal

1.3(1)   [Explanation why voluntary arrangement desirable]   The directors' proposal shall provide a short explanation why, in their opinion, a voluntary arrangement under Part I of the Act is desirable, and give reasons why the company's creditors may be expected to concur with such an arrangement.

1.3(2)   [Other matters]   The following matters shall be stated, or otherwise dealt with, in the directors' proposal—

(a) the following matters, so far as within the directors' immediate knowledge—

(i) the company's assets, with an estimate of their respective values,

(ii) the extent (if any) to which the assets are charged in favour of creditors,

    (iii) the extent (if any) to which particular assets are to be excluded from the voluntary arrangement;

(b) particulars of any property, other than assets of the company itself, which is proposed to be included in the arrangement, the source of such property and the terms on which it is to be made available for inclusion;

(c) the nature and amount of the company's liabilities (so far as within the directors' immediate knowledge), the manner in which they are proposed to be met, modified, postponed or otherwise dealt with by means of the arrangement, and (in particular)—

    (i) how it is proposed to deal with preferential creditors (defined in section 4(7)) and creditors who are, or claim to be, secured,

    (ii) how persons connected with the company (being creditors) are proposed to be treated under the arrangement, and

    (iii) whether there are, to the directors' knowledge, any circumstances giving rise to the possibility, in the event that the company should go into liquidation, of claims under—

section 238 (transactions at an undervalue),

section 239 (preferences),

section 244 (extortionate credit transactions), or

section 245 (floating charges invalid);

and, where any such circumstances are present, whether, and if so how, it is proposed under the voluntary arrangement to make provision for wholly or partly indemnifying the company in respect of such claims;

(d) whether any, and if so what, guarantees have been given of the company's debts by other persons, specifying which (if any) of the guarantors are persons connected with the company;

(e) the proposed duration of the voluntary arrangement;

(f) the proposed dates of distributions to creditors, with estimates of their amounts;

(g) the amount proposed to be paid to the nominee (as such) by way of remuneration and expenses;

(h) the manner in which it is proposed that the supervisor of the arrangement should be remunerated, and his expenses defrayed;

(j) whether, for the purposes of the arrangement, any guarantees are to be offered by directors, or other persons, and whether (if so) any security is to be given or sought;

(k) the manner in which funds held for the purposes of the arrangement are to be banked, invested or otherwise dealt with pending distribution to creditors;

(l) the manner in which funds held for the purpose of payment to creditors, and not so paid on the termination of the arrangement, are to be dealt with;

(m) the manner in which the business of the company is proposed to be conducted during the course of the arrangement;

(n) details of any further credit facilities which it is intended to arrange for the company, and how the debts so arising are to be paid;

(o) the functions which are to be undertaken by the supervisor of the arrangement; and

(p) the name, address and qualification of the person proposed as supervisor of the voluntary arrangement, and confirmation that he is (so far as the directors are aware) qualified to act as an insolvency practitioner in relation to the company.

1.3(3) **[Amendment of proposal]** With the agreement in writing of the nominee, the directors' proposal may be amended at any time up to delivery of the former's report to the court under section 2(2).

(See general note after r. 1.6.)

Rule **1.4** Notice to intended nominee

1.4(1) **[Written notice]** The directors shall give to the intended nominee written notice of their proposal.

1.4(2) **[Delivery of notice]** The notice, accompanied by a copy of the proposal, shall be delivered either to the nominee himself, or to a person authorised to take delivery of documents on his behalf.

1.4(3) **[Endorsement of receipt]** If the intended nominee agrees to act, he shall cause a copy of the notice to be endorsed to the effect that it has been received by him on a specified date; and the period of 28 days referred to in section 2(2) then runs from that date.

1.4(4) **[Return of endorsed notice]** The copy of the notice so endorsed shall be returned by the nominee forthwith to the directors at an address specified by them in the notice for that purpose.

(See general note after r. 1.6.)

Rule **1.5** Statement of affairs

1.5(1) **[Delivery of statement]** The directors shall, within 7 days after their proposal is delivered to the nominee, or within such longer time as he may allow, deliver to him a statement of the company's affairs.

1.5(2) **[Particulars in statement]** The statement shall comprise the following particulars (supplementing or amplifying, so far as is necessary for clarifying the state of the company's affairs, those already given in the directors' proposal)—

(a) a list of the company's assets, divided into such categories as are appropriate for easy identification, with estimated values assigned to each category;

(b) in the case of any property on which a claim against the company is wholly or partly secured, particulars of the claim and its amount, and of how and when the security was created;

  (c) the names and addresses of the company's preferential creditors (defined in section 4(7)), with the amounts of their respective claims;

  (d) the names and addresses of the company's unsecured creditors, with the amounts of their respective claims;

  (e) particulars of any debts owed by or to the company to or by persons connected with it;

  (f) the names and addresses of the company's members, with details of their respective shareholdings;

  (g) such other particulars (if any) as the nominee may in writing require to be furnished for the purposes of making his report to the court on the directors' proposal.

1.5(3) **[Relevant date]**   The statement of affairs shall be made up to a date not earlier than 2 weeks before the date of the notice to the nominee under Rule 1.4.

However, the nominee may allow an extension of that period to the nearest practicable date (not earlier than 2 months before the date of the notice under Rule 1.4); and if he does so, he shall give his reasons in his report to the court on the directors' proposal.

1.5(4) **[Certification of statement]**   The statement shall be certified as correct, to the best of their knowledge and belief, by two or more directors of the company, or by the company secretary and at least one director (other than the secretary himself).

(See general note after r. 1.6.)

Rule 1.6   Additional disclosure for assistance of nominee

1.6(1) **[Nominee may request further information]**   If it appears to the nominee that he cannot properly prepare his report on the basis of information in the directors' proposal and statement of affairs, he may call on the directors to provide him with—

  (a) further and better particulars as to the circumstances in which, and the reasons why, the company is insolvent or (as the case may be) threatened with insolvency;

  (b) particulars of any previous proposals which have been made in respect of the company under Part I of the Act;

  (c) any further information with respect to the company's affairs which the nominee thinks necessary for the purposes of his report.

1.6(2) **[Information about directors etc.]**   The nominee may call on the directors to inform him, with respect to any person who is, or at any time in the 2 years preceding the notice under Rule 1.4 had been, a director or officer of the company, whether and in what circumstances (in those 2 years or previously) that person—

  (a) has been concerned in the affairs of any other company (whether or not incorporated in England and Wales) which has become insolvent, or

  (b) has himself been adjudged bankrupt or entered into an arrangement with his creditors.

1.6(3) **[Access to accounts and records]**   For the purpose of enabling the nominee to consider their proposal and prepare his report on it, the directors must give him access to the company's accounts and records.

General note to rr. 1.2–1.6

The proposal and the statement of affairs will be relied on both by the nominee in the preparation of his report to the court under IA 1986, s. 2 and by the meetings of the company and its creditors which are summoned in due course if the proposal goes ahead. These rules seek to ensure that the decisions will be made on a basis of adequate evidence.

There is no prescribed form for the statement of affairs which is required in a voluntary arrangement, in contrast with the position in a liquidation: see rr. 4.33, 4.34.

Rule 1.7 Nominee's report on the proposal

1.7(1) [Accompanying documents] With his report to the court under section 2 the nominee shall deliver—

(a) a copy of the directors' proposal (with amendments, if any, authorised under Rule 1.3(3)); and

(b) a copy or summary of the company's statement of affairs.

1.7(2) [Nominee's opinion re meetings] If the nominee makes known his opinion that meetings of the company and its creditors should be summoned under section 3, his report shall have annexed to it his comments on the proposal.

If his opinion is otherwise, he shall give his reasons for that opinion.

1.7(3) [Endorsement of date of filing, and right to inspect] The court shall cause the nominee's report to be endorsed with the date on which it is filed in court. Any director, member or creditor of the company is entitled, at all reasonable times on any business day, to inspect the file.

1.7(4) [Copy to company] The nominee shall send a copy of his report, and of his comments (if any), to the company.

General note

The court's rôle is purely an administrative one, unless a challenge is mounted under IA 1986, s. 6.

Rule 1.8 Replacement of nominee

1.8 Where any person intends to apply to the court under section 2(4) for the nominee to be replaced, he shall give to the nominee at least 7 days' notice of his application.

Rule 1.9 Summoning of meetings under s. 3

1.9(1) [Date for meetings] If in his report the nominee states that in his opinion meetings of the company and its creditors should be summoned to consider the directors' proposal, the date on which the meetings are to be held shall be not less than 14, nor more than 28, days from that on which the nominee's report is filed in court under Rule 1.7.

1.9(2) **[Notices of meetings]**   Notices calling the meetings shall be sent by the nominee, at least 14 days before the day fixed for them to be held—

    (a) in the case of the creditors' meeting, to all the creditors specified in the statement of affairs, and any other creditors of the company of whom he is otherwise aware; and

    (b) in the case of the meeting of members of the company, to all persons who are, to the best of the nominee's belief, members of it.

1.9(3) **[Contents etc. of notice]**   Each notice sent under this Rule shall specify the court to which the nominee's report under section 2 has been delivered and shall state the effect of Rule 1.19(1), (3) and (4) (requisite majorities (creditors)); and with each notice there shall be sent—

    (a) a copy of the directors' proposal;

    (b) a copy of the statement of affairs or, if the nominee thinks fit, a summary of it (the summary to include a list of creditors and the amount of their debts); and

    (c) the nominee's comments on the proposal.

General note

The Act is largely silent about the manner of summoning meetings, but it is here made plain that a fairly strict procedure must be followed. See in addition rr. 1.13ff.

Chapter 3 — Proposal by Administrator or Liquidator (Himself the Nominee)

Rule **1.10**   Preparation of proposal

1.10(1)   **[Matters to be specified]**   The responsible insolvency practitioner's proposal shall specify—

    (a) all such matters as under Rule 1.3 in Chapter 2 the directors of the company would be required to include in a proposal by them, with the addition, where the company is subject to an administration order, of the names and addresses of the company's preferential creditors (defined in section 4(7)), with the amounts of their respective claims, and

    (b) such other matters (if any) as the insolvency practitioner considers appropriate for ensuring that members and creditors of the company are enabled to reach an informed decision on the proposal.

1.10(2)   **[Notice to official receiver]**   Where the company is being wound up by the court, the insolvency practitioner shall give notice of the proposal to the official receiver.

History note

In r. 1.10(1)(*a*) the words from ", with the addition," to "amounts of their respective claims" were inserted by I(A)R 1987 (SI 1987 No. 1919), r. 3(1), Sch., Pt. 1, para. 3 as from 11 January 1988.

(See general note after r. 1.11.)

Rule 1.11 Summoning of meetings under s. 3

1.11(1) **[Venues and notice of meetings]** The responsible insolvency practitioner shall fix a venue for the creditors' meeting and the company meeting, and give at least 14 days' notice of the meetings—

   (a) in the case of the creditors' meeting, to all the creditors specified in the company's statement of affairs, and to any other creditors of whom the insolvency practitioner is aware; and

   (b) in the case of the company meeting, to all persons who are, to the best of his belief, members of the company.

1.11(2) **[Contents etc. of notice]** Each notice sent out under this Rule shall state the effect of Rule 1.19(1), (3) and (4) (requisite majorities (creditors)); and with it there shall be sent—

   (a) a copy of the responsible insolvency practitioner's proposal, and

   (b) a copy of the statement of affairs or, if he thinks fit, a summary of it (the summary to include a list of creditors and the amounts of their debts).

General note to rr. 1.10, 1.11

Where the administrator or liquidator is himself to be the nominee, he may proceed directly to summon meetings in accordance with this chapter.

Chapter 4 — Proposal by Administrator or Liquidator (Another Insolvency Practitioner the Nominee)

Rule 1.12 Preparation of proposal and notice to nominee

1.12(1) **[Manner of giving notice etc.]** The responsible insolvency practitioner shall give notice to the intended nominee, and prepare his proposal for a voluntary arrangement, in the same manner as is required of the directors, in the case of a proposal by them, under Chapter 2.

1.12(2) **[Application of r. 1.2 and 1.4]** Rule 1.2 applies to the responsible insolvency practitioner as it applies to the directors; and Rule 1.4 applies as regards the action to be taken by the nominee.

1.12(3) **[Content of proposal]** The content of the proposal shall be as required by Rule 1.3 (and, where relevant, Rule 1.10), reading references to the directors as referring to the responsible insolvency practitioner.

1.12(4) **[Application of r. 1.6]** Rule 1.6 applies in respect of the information to be furnished to the nominee, reading references to the directors as referring to the responsible insolvency practitioner.

1.12(5) **[Copy statement of affairs]** With the proposal the responsible insolvency practitioner shall provide a copy of the company's statement of affairs.

1.12(6) **[Copy proposal to official receiver]** Where the company is being wound up by the court, the responsible insolvency practitioner shall send a copy of the proposal to the official receiver, accompanied by the name and address of the insolvency practitioner who has agreed to act as nominee.

1.12(7) **[Application of rr. 1.7–1.9]** Rules 1.7 to 1.9 apply as regards a proposal under this Chapter as they apply to a proposal under Chapter 2.

History note

In r. 1.12(3) the words "(and, where relevant, Rule 1.10)" were inserted by I(A)R 1987 (SI 1987 No. 1919), r. 3(1), Sch., Pt. 1, para. 4 as from 11 January 1988.

General note

Where the administrator or liquidator does not propose himself as nominee, the procedure is very similar to that for a directors' proposal.

Chapter 5 — Proceedings on a Proposal made by the Directors, or by the Administrator, or by the Liquidator

SECTION A: MEETINGS OF COMPANY'S CREDITORS AND MEMBERS

Rule 1.13 Summoning of meetings

1.13(1) **[Convenience of venue]** Subject as follows, in fixing the venue for the creditors' meeting and the company meeting, the person summoning the meeting ("the convener") shall have regard primarily to the convenience of the creditors.

1.13(2) **[Time of meetings]** Meetings shall in each case be summoned for commencement between 10.00 and 16.00 hours on a business day.

1.13(3) **[Creditors' meeting in advance]** The meetings shall be held on the same day and in the same place, but the creditors' meeting shall be fixed for a time in advance of the company meeting.

1.13(4) **[Forms of proxy]** With every notice summoning either meeting there shall be sent out forms of proxy.   [FORM 8.1]

(See general note after r. 1.21.)

Rule 1.14 The chairman at meetings

1.14(1) **[Convener to be chairman]** Subject as follows, at both the creditors' meeting and the company meeting, and at any combined meeting, the convener shall be chairman.

1.14(2) **[Other nominated chairman]** If for any reason he is unable to attend, he may nominate another person to act as chairman in his place; but a person so nominated must be either—

    (a) a person qualified to act as an insolvency practitioner in relation to the company, or

    (b) an employee of the convener or his firm who is experienced in insolvency matters.

(See general note after r. 1.21.)

Rule **1.15** The chairman as proxy-holder

1.15 The chairman shall not by virtue of any proxy held by him vote to increase or reduce the amount of the remuneration or expenses of the nominee or the supervisor of the proposed arrangement, unless the proxy specifically directs him to vote in that way.

(See general note after r. 1.21.)

Rule **1.16** Attendance by company officers

1.16(1) **[Notice to directors and officers]** At least 14 days' notice to attend the meetings shall be given by the convener—

    (a) to all directors of the company, and

    (b) to any persons in whose case the convener thinks that their presence is required as being officers of the company, or as having been directors or officers of it at any time in the 2 years immediately preceding the date of the notice.

1.16(2) **[Exclusion of director etc.]** The chairman may, if he thinks fit, exclude any present or former director or officer from attendance at a meeting, either completely or for any part of it; and this applies whether or not a notice under this Rule has been sent to the person excluded.

(See general note after r. 1.21.)

SECTION B: VOTING RIGHTS AND MAJORITIES

Rule **1.17** Voting rights (creditors)

1.17(1) **[Entitlement to vote]** Subject as follows, every creditor who was given notice of the creditors' meeting is entitled to vote at the meeting or any adjournment of it.

1.17(2) **[Calculation of votes]** Votes are calculated according to the amount of the creditor's debt as at the date of the meeting or, where the company is being wound up or is subject to an administration order, the date of its going into liquidation or (as the case may be) of the administration order.

1.17(3) **[Limitation on voting]** A creditor shall not vote in respect of a debt for an unliquidated amount, or any debt whose value is not ascertained, except where the chairman agrees to put upon the debt an estimated minimum value for the purpose of entitlement to vote.

1.17(4) **[Chairman's discretion]** At any creditors' meeting the chairman has power to admit or reject a creditor's claim for the purpose of his entitlement to vote, and the power is exercisable with respect to the whole or any part of the claim.

1.17(5) **[Appeal from chairman's decision]** The chairman's decision on a creditor's entitlement to vote is subject to appeal to the court by any creditor or member of the company.

1.17(6) **[Voting subject to objection]** If the chairman is in doubt whether a claim should be admitted or rejected, he shall mark it as objected to and allow the creditor to vote, subject to his vote being subsequently declared invalid if the objection to the claim is sustained.

1.17(7) **[Where chairman's decision reversed etc.]** If on an appeal the chairman's decision is reversed or varied, or a creditor's vote is declared invalid, the court may order another meeting to be summoned, or make such other order as it thinks just.

The court's power to make an order under this paragraph is exercisable only if it considers that the matter is such as gives rise to unfair prejudice or material irregularity.

1.17(8) **[Time for appeal]** An application to the court by way of appeal against the chairman's decision shall not be made after the end of the period of 28 days beginning with the first day on which each of the reports required by section 4(6) has been made to the court.

1.17(9) **[Costs of appeal]** The chairman is not personally liable for any costs incurred by any person in respect of an appeal under this Rule.

(See general note after r. 1.21.)

Rule **1.18** Voting rights (members)

1.18(1) **[Voting rights in accordance with articles]** Subject as follows, members of the company at their meeting vote according to the rights attaching to their shares respectively in accordance with the articles.

1.18(2) **[Where no voting rights]** Where no voting rights attach to a member's shares, he is nevertheless entitled to vote either for or against the proposal or any modification of it.

1.18(3) **[Interpretation]** References in this Rule to a person's shares include any other interest which he may have as a member of the company.

(See general note after r. 1.21.)

Rule **1.19** Requisite majorities (creditors)

1.19(1) **[Three-quarters majority]** Subject as follows, at the creditors' meeting for any resolution to pass approving any proposal or modification there must be a majority in excess of three-quarters in value of the creditors present in person or by proxy and voting on the resolution.

1.19(2) **[One-half majority]**   The same applies in respect of any other resolution proposed at the meeting, but substituting one-half for three-quarters.

1.19(3) **[Votes to be left out of account]**   In the following cases there is to be left out of account a creditor's vote in respect of any claim or part of a claim—

- (a) where written notice of the claim was not given, either at the meeting or before it, to the chairman or convener of the meeting;
- (b) where the claim or part is secured;
- (c) where the claim is in respect of a debt wholly or partly on, or secured by, a current bill of exchange or promissory note, unless the creditor is willing—
  - (i) to treat the liability to him on the bill or note of every person who is liable on it antecedently to the company, and against whom a bankruptcy order has not been made (or in the case of a company, which has not gone into liquidation), as a security in his hands, and
  - (ii) to estimate the value of the security and (for the purpose of entitlement to vote, but not of any distribution under the arrangement) to deduct it from his claim.

1.19(4) **[Voting rendering resolution invalid]**   Any resolution is invalid if those voting against it include more than half in value of the creditors, counting in these latter only those—

- (a) to whom notice of the meeting was sent;
- (b) whose votes are not to be left out of account under paragraph (3); and
- (c) who are not, to the best of the chairman's belief, persons connected with the company.

1.19(5) **[Chairman's powers]**   It is for the chairman of the meeting to decide whether under this Rule—

- (a) a vote is to be left out of account in accordance with paragraph (3), or
- (b) a person is a connected person for the purposes of paragraph (4)(c);

and in relation to the second of these two cases the chairman is entitled to rely on the information provided by the company's statement of affairs or otherwise in accordance with this Part of the Rules.

1.19(6) **[Use of proxy contrary to r. 1.15]**   If the chairman uses a proxy contrary to Rule 1.15, his vote with that proxy does not count towards any majority under this Rule.

1.19(7) **[Application of r. 1.17]**   Paragraphs (5) to (9) of Rule 1.17 apply as regards an appeal against the decision of the chairman under this Rule.

(See general note after r. 1.21.)

Rule 1.20   Requisite majorities (members)

1.20(1) **[One-half majority]**   Subject as follows, and to any express provision made in the articles, at a company meeting any resolution is to be regarded as passed if voted for by more than one-half in value of the members present in person or by proxy and voting on the resolution.

The value of members is determined by reference to the number of votes conferred on each member by the company's articles.

1.20(2)   **[Rule 1.18(2) votes to be left out]**   In determining whether a majority for any resolution has been obtained, there is to be left out of account any vote cast in accordance with Rule 1.18(2).

1.20(3)   **[Use of proxy contrary to r. 1.15]**   If the chairman uses a proxy contrary to Rule 1.15, his vote with that proxy does not count towards any majority under this Rule.

History note

In r. 1.20(1) the words "in value" after the words "one-half" were inserted and the second subparagraph was added by I(A)R 1987 (SI 1987 No. 1919), r. 3(1), Sch., Pt. 1, para. 5 as from 11 January 1988.

(See general note after r. 1.21.)

Rule **1.21**   Proceedings to obtain agreement on the proposal

1.21(1)   **[Meetings may be adjourned, and held together]**   On the day on which the meetings are held, they may from time to time be adjourned; and, if the chairman thinks fit for the purpose of obtaining the simultaneous agreement of the meetings to the proposal (with the same modifications, if any), the meetings may be held together.

1.21(2)   **[Adjournment]**   If on that day the requisite majority for the approval of the voluntary arrangement (with the same modifications, if any) has not been obtained from both creditors and members of the company, the chairman may, and shall if it is so resolved, adjourn the meetings for not more than 14 days.

1.21(3)   **[Final adjournment]**   If there are subsequently further adjournments, the final adjournment shall not be to a day later than 14 days after the date on which the meetings were originally held.

1.21(4)   **[Meetings must be adjourned to same day]**   There shall be no adjournment of either meeting unless the other is also adjourned to the same business day.

1.21(5)   **[Notice of adjournment]**   In the case of a proposal by the directors, if the meetings are adjourned under paragraph (2), notice of the fact shall be given by the nominee forthwith to the court.

1.21(6)   **[Deemed rejection of proposal]**   If following any final adjournment of the meetings the proposal (with the same modifications, if any) is not agreed by both meetings, it is deemed rejected.

General note to rr. 1.13–1.21

The detailed procedure for the summoning and conduct of meetings is here set out, and a number of points which the Insolvency Act appears to leave in doubt are settled.

Although the creditors' meeting must be *fixed* for a time in advance of the company meeting (r. 1.13(3)), it need not conclude its business before the company meeting begins (r. 1.22(2)); and the meetings may be held together (r. 1.21(1)).

Rules 1.16(1)(*b*) and 1.16(2) allow the chairman a wide discretion, on the one hand to insist on the attendance of a director whose presence he may consider helpful and, on the other, to exclude any director who may be thought likely to hinder the proceedings.

Rule 1.17(2) makes no provision for the case where a creditor in a liquidation or administration has had the amount of his debt reduced since the making of the order. In equity, his vote should be proportionately diminished.

A claim for an unliquidated amount or for a sum whose value is not ascertained is not, strictly speaking, a "debt", and the claimant is not a "creditor": see the note to s. 1(1). Of course, it is open to the legislature to extend these definitions for the purpose of specific statutory provisions, but this has not been done for Pt. I of IA 1986 or this Part of the rules, and so the supervisor of a voluntary scheme would be right not to treat such a claimant as a "creditor" (compare *Re FMS Financial Management Services Ltd* (1989) 5 BCC 191). The legitimacy of r. 1.17(3) is accordingly open to question. A problem arose in connection with this provision in *Re Cranley Mansions Ltd* [1994] BCC 576 (noted by R Gregory in CCH *Company Law News* No. 158, p. 10). A creditor who alleged that she had an unliquidated claim for £900,000 had this claim valued at a nominal £1 by the chairman (which entitled her to vote at the creditors' meeting, but not in respect of a realistic valuation of her claim if it was in due course substantiated). Ferris J rejected this approach. He drew attention to the word "agrees", in r. 1.17(3), and ruled that there was no agreement unless the creditor accepted the chairman's figure. It followed that the creditor was not entitled to vote at all, and accordingly she was not bound by the arrangement. This ruling has led to some disquiet among practitioners and commentators, for the utility of a voluntary arrangement is lessened if substantial creditors are not bound by it.

The majority required by r. 1.19 is, unusually, not simply three-quarters of those present and voting, but a majority *in excess of* three-quarters. Note in addition, however, that both this majority and the ordinary majority required by r. 1.19(2) are qualified by r. 1.19(4), which in effect nullifies the votes of any creditors "connected with" the company (and certain others) who support the proposal. (For the meaning of a "connected" person, see IA 1986, s. 249.)

Rule 1.18(2) enfranchises voteless shareholders for the purpose of considering a proposal, but not for the purpose of determining whether a majority on any resolution has been obtained. It is therefore not necessary for the rules to ascribe a "value" to the vote given by a voteless shareholder. However, these votes could be a useful indication to the nominee of the degree of general support for the proposal, and could be taken into account by the court if an application is made under s. 6 of the Act. (Note that a voteless shareholder has standing to make such an application: see s. 6(2).)

The rules assume that the same person will be chairman of both meetings: see r. 1.24(1).

SECTION C: IMPLEMENTATION OF THE ARRANGEMENT

Rule 1.22   Resolutions to follow approval

1.22(1)   [Joint supervisors]   If the voluntary arrangement is approved (with or without modifications) by the two meetings, a resolution may be taken by the creditors, where two or more insolvency practitioners are appointed to act as supervisor, on the question whether acts to be done in connection with the arrangement may be done by any one of them, or must be done by both or all.

1.22(2)   [Resolution in anticipation of approval]   A resolution under paragraph (1) may be passed in anticipation of the approval of the voluntary arrangement by the company meeting if that meeting has not then been concluded.

1.22(3)   [Other than nominee to be supervisor]   If at either meeting a resolution is moved for the appointment of some person other than the nominee to be supervisor of the arrangement, there must be produced to the chairman, at or before the meeting—

(a) that person's written consent to act (unless he is present and then and there signifies his consent), and

(b) his written confirmation that he is qualified to act as an insolvency practitioner in relation to the company.

(See general note after r. 1.29.)

Rule **1.23**   **Hand-over of property etc. to supervisor**

1.23(1)   [Putting supervisor into possession of assets]   After the approval of the voluntary arrangement—

(a) the directors, or

(b) where the company is in liquidation or is subject to an administration order, and a person other than the responsible insolvency practitioner is appointed as supervisor of the voluntary arrangement, the insolvency practitioner,

shall forthwith do all that is required for putting the supervisor into possession of the assets included in the arrangement.

1.23(2)   [Discharge of insolvency practitioner's remuneration etc.]   Where the company is in liquidation or is subject to an administration order, the supervisor shall on taking possession of the assets discharge any balance due to the insolvency practitioner by way of remuneration or on account of—

(a) fees, costs, charges and expenses properly incurred and payable under the Act or the Rules, and

(b) any advances made in respect of the company, together with interest on such advances at the rate specified in section 17 of the Judgments Act 1838 at the date on which the company went into liquidation or (as the case may be) became subject to the administration order.

1.23(3)   [Undertaking to discharge]   Alternatively, the supervisor must, before taking possession, give the responsible insolvency practitioner a written undertaking to discharge any such balance out of the first realisation of assets.

1.23(4)   [Charge on assets]   The insolvency practitioner has a charge on the assets included in the voluntary arrangement in respect of any sums due as above until they have been discharged, subject only to the deduction from realisations by the supervisor of the proper costs and expenses of such realisations.

1.23(5)   [Discharge of guarantees etc.]   The supervisor shall from time to time out of the realisation of assets discharge all guarantees properly given by the responsible insolvency practitioner for the benefit of the company, and shall pay all the insolvency practitioner's expenses.

1.23(6)   [Interpretation]   References in this Rule to the responsible insolvency practitioner include, where a company is being wound up by the court, the official receiver, whether or not in his capacity as liquidator; and any sums due to the official receiver take priority over those due to a liquidator.

(See general note after r. 1.29.)

Rule **1.24** Report of meetings

1.24(1) **[Chairman to prepare report]** A report of the meetings shall be prepared by the person who was chairman of them.

1.24(2) **[Contents of report]** The report shall—

    (a) state whether the proposal for a voluntary arrangement was approved or rejected and, if approved, with what (if any) modifications;

    (b) set out the resolutions which were taken at each meeting, and the decision on each one;

    (c) list the creditors and members of the company (with their respective values) who were present or represented at the meetings, and how they voted on each resolution; and

    (d) include such further information (if any) as the chairman thinks it appropriate to make known to the court.

1.24(3) **[Copy report to be filed in court]** A copy of the chairman's report shall, within 4 days of the meetings being held, be filed in court; and the court shall cause that copy to be endorsed with the date of filing.

1.24(4) **[Notice of result]** In respect of each of the meetings, the persons to whom notice of its result is to be sent by the chairman under section 4(6) are all those who were sent notice of the meeting under this Part of the Rules.

    The notice shall be sent immediately after a copy of the chairman's report is filed in court under paragraph (3).

1.24(5) **[Copy report to registrar of companies]** If the voluntary arrangement has been approved by the meetings (whether or not in the form proposed), the supervisor shall forthwith send a copy of the chairman's report to the registrar of companies.

[FORM 1.1]

(See general note after r. 1.29.)

Rule **1.25** Revocation or suspension of the arrangement

1.25(1) **[Application of Rule]** This Rule applies where the court makes an order of revocation or suspension under section 6.

1.25(2) **[Service of copy orders]** The person who applied for the order shall serve sealed copies of it—

    (a) on the supervisor of the voluntary arrangement, and

    (b) on the directors of the company or the administrator or liquidator (according to who made the proposal for the arrangement).

    Service on the directors may be effected by service of a single copy of the order on the company at its registered office.

1.25(3) **[Notice re further meetings]** If the order includes a direction by the court under section 6(4)(b) for any further meetings to be summoned, notice shall also be given (by the person who applied for the order) to whoever is, in accordance with the direction, required to summon the meetings.

1.25(4) **[Notice of order, and of intention re proposal]** The directors or (as the case may be) the administrator or liquidator shall—

(a) forthwith after receiving a copy of the court's order, give notice of it to all persons who were sent notice of the creditors' and company meetings or who, not having been sent that notice, appear to be affected by the order;

(b) within 7 days of their receiving a copy of the order (or within such longer period as the court may allow), give notice to the court whether it is intended to make a revised proposal to the company and its creditors, or to invite re-consideration of the original proposal.

1.25(5) **[Copy order to registrar of companies]** The person on whose application the order of revocation or suspension was made shall, within 7 days after the making of the order, deliver a copy of the order to the registrar of companies. [FORM 1.2]

(See general note after r. 1.29.)

Rule **1.26** Supervisor's accounts and reports

1.26(1) **[Obligation to keep accounts etc.]** Where the voluntary arrangement authorises or requires the supervisor—

(a) to carry on the business of the company or trade on its behalf or in its name, or

(b) to realise assets of the company, or

(c) otherwise to administer or dispose of any of its funds,

he shall keep accounts and records of his acts and dealings in and in connection with the arrangement, including in particular records of all receipts and payments of money.

1.26(2) **[Abstract of receipts and payments]** The supervisor shall, not less often than once in every 12 months beginning with the date of his appointment, prepare an abstract of such receipts and payments, and send copies of it, accompanied by his comments on the progress and efficacy of the arrangement, to—

(a) the court,

(b) the registrar of companies,

(c) the company, [FORM 1.3]

(d) all those of the company's creditors who are bound by the arrangement,

(e) subject to paragraph (5) below, the members of the company who are so bound, and

(f) if the company is not in liquidation, the company's auditors for the time being.

If in any period of 12 months he has made no payments and had no receipts, he shall at the end of that period send a statement to that effect to all those specified in sub-paragraphs (a) to (f) above.

1.26(3) **[Abstract under r. 1.26(2)]** An abstract provided under paragraph (2) shall relate to a period beginning with the date of the supervisor's appointment or (as the case may be) the day following the end of the last period for which an abstract was prepared under this Rule; and copies of the abstract shall be sent out, as required by paragraph (2), within the 2 months following the end of the period to which the abstract relates.

1.26(4)   [If supervisor not authorised as in r. 1.26(1)]   If the supervisor is not authorised as mentioned in paragraph (1), he shall, not less often than once in every 12 months beginning with the date of his appointment, send to all those specified in paragraph (2)(a) to (f) a report on the progress and efficacy of the voluntary arrangement.

1.26(5)   [Powers of court]   The court may, on application by the supervisor—

    (a) dispense with the sending under this Rule of abstracts or reports to members of the company, either altogether or on the basis that the availability of the abstract or report to members is to be advertised by the supervisor in a specified manner;

    (b) vary the dates on which the obligation to send abstracts or reports arises.

(See general note after r. 1.29.)

Rule 1.27   Production of accounts and records to Secretary of State

1.27(1)   [Powers of Secretary of State]   The Secretary of State may at any time during the course of the voluntary arrangement or after its completion require the supervisor to produce for inspection—

    (a) his records and accounts in respect of the arrangement, and

    (b) copies of abstracts and reports prepared in compliance with Rule 1.26.

1.27(2)   [Production and duty to comply]   The Secretary of State may require production either at the premises of the supervisor or elsewhere; and it is the duty of the supervisor to comply with any requirement imposed on him under this Rule.

1.27(3)   [Audit of accounts and records]   The Secretary of State may cause any accounts and records produced to him under this Rule to be audited; and the supervisor shall give to the Secretary of State such further information and assistance as he needs for the purposes of his audit.

(See general note after r. 1.29.)

Rule 1.28   Fees, costs, charges and expenses

1.28   The fees, costs, charges and expenses that may be incurred for any of the purposes of the voluntary arrangement are —

    (a) any disbursements made by the nominee prior to the approval of the arrangement, and any remuneration for his services as such agreed between himself and the company (or, as the case may be, the administrator or liquidator);

    (b) any fees, costs, charges or expenses which—

    (i) are sanctioned by the terms of the arrangement, or

    (ii) would be payable, or correspond to those which would be payable, in an administration or winding up.

(See general note after r. 1.29.)

Rule 1.29   Completion of the arrangement

1.29(1)   [Supervisor to send notice]   Not more than 28 days after the final completion of the voluntary arrangement, the supervisor shall send to all the creditors and members of the company who are bound by it a notice that the voluntary arrangement has been fully implemented.

1.29(2)   [Supervisor's report]   With the notice there shall be sent to each creditor and member a copy of a report by the supervisor summarising all receipts and payments made by him in pursuance of the arrangement, and explaining any difference in the actual implementation of it as compared with the proposal as approved by the creditors' and company meetings.

1.29(3)   [Copy notice and report to registrar]   The supervisor shall, within the 28 days mentioned above, send to the registrar of companies and to the court a copy of the notice to creditors and members under paragraph (1), together with a copy of the report under paragraph (2).   [FORM 1.4]

1.29(4)   [Extension of time]   The court may, on application by the supervisor, extend the period of 28 days under paragraphs (1) and (3).

General note to rr. 1.22–1.29

The detailed procedure for the implementation of the proposals, if approved, is set out here. The scheme takes effect without further formality from the time of the creditors' meeting, even though under the rules the members' meeting must be fixed for a later time on the same day: see IA 1986, s. 5(2)(*a*).

Chapter 6 — General

Rule 1.30   False representations, etc.

1.30(1)   [Offence]   A person being a past or present officer of a company commits an offence if he makes any false representation or commits any other fraud for the purpose of obtaining the approval of the company's members or creditors to a proposal for a voluntary arrangement under Part I of the Act.

1.30(2)   ["Officer"]   For this purpose "officer" includes a shadow director.

1.30(3)   [Penalties]   A person guilty of an offence under this Rule is liable to imprisonment or a fine, or both.

General note

The scope of this provision is, somewhat surprisingly, confined to "officers", including "shadow directors". For the meaning of these terms, see CA 1986, s. 744 and IA 1986, s. 251, and the note to IA 1986, s. 206(3).

PART 2 — ADMINISTRATION PROCEDURE

Chapter 1 — Application for, and Making of, the Order

Rule 2.1 Affidavit to support petition

2.1(1) [Affidavit required] Where it is proposed to apply to the court by petition for an administration order to be made in relation to a company, an affidavit complying with Rule 2.3 below must be prepared and sworn, with a view to its being filed in court in support of the petition.   [FORM 2.1]

2.1(2) [Petition presented by company or directors] If the petition is to be presented by the company or by the directors, the affidavit must be made by one of the directors, or the secretary of the company, stating himself to make it on behalf of the company or, as the case may be, on behalf of the directors.

2.1(3) [Creditor's petition] If the petition is to be presented by creditors, the affidavit must be made by a person acting under the authority of them all, whether or not himself one of their number. In any case there must be stated in the affidavit the nature of his authority and the means of his knowledge of the matters to which the affidavit relates.

2.1(4) [Supervisor's petition] If the petition is to be presented by the supervisor of a voluntary arrangement under Part I of the Act, it is to be treated as if it were a petition by the company.

(See general note after r. 2.3.)

Rule 2.2 Independent report on company's affairs

2.2(1) [Report that administrator's appointment expedient] There may be prepared, with a view to its being exhibited to the affidavit in support of the petition, a report by an independent person to the effect that the appointment of an administrator for the company is expedient.

2.2(2) [Who may report] The report may be by the person proposed as administrator, or by any other person having adequate knowledge of the company's affairs, not being a director, secretary, manager, member, or employee of the company.

2.2(3) **[Report to specify purpose of order]** The report shall specify the purposes which, in the opinion of the person preparing it, may be achieved for the company by the making of an administration order, being purposes particularly specified in section 8(3).

(See general note after r. 2.3.)

Rule **2.3** Contents of affidavit

2.3(1) **[Statements in affidavit]** The affidavit shall state—

  (a) the deponent's belief that the company is, or is likely to become, unable to pay its debts and the grounds of that belief; and

  (b) which of the purposes specified in section 8(3) is expected to be achieved by the making of an administration order.

2.3(2) **[Company's financial position]** There shall in the affidavit be provided a statement of the company's financial position, specifying (to the best of the deponent's knowledge and belief) assets and liabilities, including contingent and prospective liabilities.

2.3(3) **[Details of creditors' security]** Details shall be given of any security known or believed to be held by creditors of the company, and whether in any case the security is such as to confer power on the holder to appoint an administrative receiver. If an administrative receiver has been appointed, that fact shall be stated.

2.3(4) **[Details of winding-up petition]** If any petition has been presented for the winding up of the company, details of it shall be given in the affidavit, so far as within the immediate knowledge of the deponent.

2.3(5) **[Other matters]** If there are other matters which, in the opinion of those intending to present the petition for an administration order, will assist the court in deciding whether to make such an order, those matters (so far as lying within the knowledge or belief of the deponent) shall also be stated.

2.3(6) **[Rule 2.2 report]** If a report has been prepared for the company under Rule 2.2, that fact shall be stated. If not, an explanation shall be provided why not.

General note to rr. 2.1–2.3

These rules give guidance as to the evidence required in support of a petition for an administration order.

It is not obligatory to obtain the report of an independent person under r. 2.2, but the absence of such a report must be explained (r. 2. 3(6)). It is customary for the report to cover such matters as: the qualifications of the independent person and the fact of his independence; how far he is relying on his own work and judgment and how far on the work and opinions of others; the company's insolvency; the factors influencing his opinion in favour of recommending the making of an order and the factors against it; which of the statutory purposes are likely to be achieved; and proposals for the provision of working capital during the administration.

The Vice-Chancellor in a Practice Note dated 17 January 1994 (*Practice Note (Administration order applications: content of independent reports)* [1994] 1 WLR 160; [1994] BCC 35) has stressed the importance of ensuring that the primary aim of administration orders (namely, to facilitate the rescue and rehabilitation of insolvent companies) is not frustrated by expense, and urged that the costs of obtaining an administration order should not operate as a disincentive or put the process out of the reach of smaller companies.

Accordingly, the Note states that the contents of a r. 2(2) report should not be unnecessarily elaborate and detailed. While the extent of the necessary investigation and the amount of material to be provided must be a matter of judgment for the person concerned and will vary from case to case, what is ordinarily required is a concise assessment of the company's situation and of the prospects of an order achieving one or more of the statutory purposes, normally including an explanation of the availability of any finance required during administration. Where the court finds that it has insufficient material on which to base a decision, the proposed administrator, if he is in court, may offer to supplement the material by giving oral evidence, and later filing a supplemental report covering this extra information.

In suitable cases the court may appoint an administrator but require him to report back to the court within a short time so that the court can consider whether to allow the administration to continue or to discharge the order. In some cases the court may require the administrator to hold a meeting of creditors before reporting back to the court, both within a relatively short period.

The Note concludes by reminding practitioners that there may be straightforward cases in which a report is not necessary.

The significance of the report was stressed by Harman J in *Re Newport County Association Football Club Ltd* [1987] BCC 635 at p. 635 in the following passage: "Such a report, which is of course an objective assessment by persons with no axe to grind (using that phrase non-pejoratively), that is to say by persons not having any reason to wish a particular result or to be optimistic about a particular outcome, is one which very much influences the court, because it is prepared by experienced people who are detached from the emotions raised by failure . . . , and can make a serious and objective assessment of the chances." This may be contrasted with *Re W F Fearman Ltd* (1988) 4 BCC 139, where the absence of a report in the making of an order was regarded as fatal to the application.

The reference to "all" the creditors in r. 2.1(3) is to all the *petitioning* creditors (if there are more than one), and not to all the creditors of the company: cf. r. 2.4(4).

Rule 2.4   Form of petition

2.4(1)   **[Petition presented by company or directors]**   If presented by the company or by the directors, the petition shall state the name of the company and its address for service, which (in the absence of special reasons to the contrary) is that of the company's registered office.

2.4(2)   **[Single creditor's petition]**   If presented by a single creditor, the petition shall state his name and address for service.

2.4(3)   **[Director's petition]**   If the petition is presented by the directors, it shall state that it is so presented under section 9; but from and after presentation it is to be treated for all purposes as the petition of the company.

2.4(4)   **[Creditor's petition]**   If the petition is presented by two or more creditors, it shall state that it is so presented (naming them); but from and after presentation it is to be treated for all purposes as the petition of one only of them, named in the petition as petitioning on behalf of himself and other creditors. An address for service for that one shall be specified.

2.4(5)   **[Specification of proposed administrator]**   The petition shall specify the name and address of the person proposed to be appointed as administrator; and it shall be stated that, to the best of the petitioner's knowledge and belief, the person is qualified to act as an insolvency practitioner in relation to the company.

2.4(6) [Documents to be exhibited] There shall be exhibited to the affidavit in support of the petition—

    (a) a copy of the petition;

    (b) a written consent by the proposed administrator to accept appointment, if an administration order is made; and   [FORM 2.2]

    (c) if a report has been prepared under Rule 2.2, a copy of it.

(See general note after r. 2.8.)

Rule 2.5 Filing of petition

2.5(1) [Filing in court] The petition and affidavit shall be filed in court, with a sufficient number of copies for service and use as provided by Rule 2.6.

2.5(2) [Sealed copies] Each of the copies delivered shall have applied to it the seal of the court and be issued to the petitioner; and on each copy there shall be endorsed the date and time of filing.

2.5(3) [Venue for hearing] The court shall fix a venue for the hearing of the petition and this also shall be endorsed on each copy of the petition issued under paragraph (2).

2.5(4) [After petition filed] After the petition is filed, it is the duty of the petitioner to notify the court in writing of any winding-up petition presented against the company, as soon as he becomes aware of it.

(See general note after r. 2.8.)

Rule 2.6 Service of petition

2.6(1) [Interpretation] In the following paragraphs of this Rule, references to the petition are to a copy of the petition issued by the court under Rule 2.5(2) together with the affidavit in support of it and the documents (other than the copy petition) exhibited to the affidavit.

2.6(2) [Persons to be served] The petition shall be served—

    (a) on any person who has appointed, or is or may be entitled to appoint, an administrative receiver for the company;

    (b) if an administrative receiver has been appointed, on him;

    (c) if there is pending a petition for the winding up of the company, on the petitioner (and also on the provisional liquidator, if any); and

    (d) on the person proposed as administrator.

2.6(3) **[Creditors' petition]** If the petition for the making of an administration order is presented by creditors of the company, the petition shall be served on the company.

History note

In r. 2.6(2) para. (a) was substituted by I(A)R 1987 (SI 1987 No. 1919), r. 3(1), Sch., Pt. 1, para. 6 as from 11 January 1988. The paragraph formerly read as follows:

"(a) on any person who has appointed an administrative receiver for the company, or has the power to do so;".

(See general note after r. 2.8.)

Rule 2.6A   Notice to sheriff, etc.

2.6A   The petitioner shall forthwith after filing the petition give notice of its presentation to—

    (a) any sheriff or other officer who to his knowledge is charged with an execution or other legal process against the company or its property, and

    (b) any person who to his knowledge has distrained against the company or its property.

History note

Rule 2.6A was inserted by I(A)R 1987 (SI 1987 No. 1919), r. 3(1), Sch., Pt. 1, para. 7 as from 11 January 1988.

(See general note after r. 2.8.)

Rule 2.7   Manner in which service to be effected

2.7(1) **[Person to effect service]** Service of the petition in accordance with Rule 2.6 shall be effected by the petitioner, or his solicitor, or by a person instructed by him or his solicitor, not less than 5 days before the date fixed for the hearing.

2.7(2) **[How effected]** Service shall be effected as follows—

    (a) on the company (subject to paragraph (3) below), by delivering the documents to its registered office;

    (b) on any other person (subject to paragraph (4)), by delivering the documents to his proper address;

    (c) in either case, in such other manner as the court may direct.

2.7(3) **[Service to registered office not practicable]** If delivery to the company's registered office is not practicable, service may be effected by delivery to its last known principal place of business in England and Wales.

2.7(4) **[Proper address under r. 2.7(2)(b)]** Subject to paragraph (4A), for the purposes of paragraph (2)(b), a person's proper address is any which he has previously notified as his address for service; but if he has not notified any such address, service may be effected by delivery to his usual or last known address.

2.7(4A) **[Other person re rr. 2.7(2)(b), 2.7(4)]** In the case of a person who—

(a) is an authorised institution or former authorised institution within the meaning of the Banking Act 1987,

(b) has appointed, or is or may be entitled to appoint, an administrative receiver of the company, and

(c) has not notified an address for service,

the proper address is the address of an office of that person where, to the knowledge of the petitioner, the company maintains a bank account or, where no such office is known to the petitioner, the registered office of that person, or, if there is no such office, his usual or last known address.

2.7(5) **[What constitutes delivery]** Delivery of documents to any place or address may be made by leaving them there, or sending them by first class post.

History note

In r. 2.7(4) the words "Subject to paragraph (4A)," were inserted by I(A)R 1987 (SI 1987 No. 1919), r. 3(1), Sch., Pt. 1, para. 8(1) as from 11 January 1988.

Rule 2.7(4A) was inserted by I(A)R 1987 (SI 1987 No. 1919), r. 3(1), Sch., Pt. 1, para. 8(2) as from 11 January 1988.

(See general note after r. 2.8.)

Rule **2.8** Proof of service

2.8(1) **[Verifying affidavit]** Service of the petition shall be verified by affidavit, specifying the date on which, and the manner in which, service was effected.

[FORM 2.3]

2.8(2) **[Filing in court]** The affidavit, with a sealed copy of the petition exhibited to it, shall be filed in court forthwith after service, and in any event not less than one day before the hearing of the petition.

General note to rr. 2.4–2.8

Here are set out the requirements regarding the form, filing and service of the petition. A petition by the directors (rr. 2.4(1), (3)) must be presented by all the directors: see the note to IA 1986, s. 9(1).

The court has power to abridge the period of five days specified by r. 2.7(1): *Re a Company No. 00175 of 1987* (1987) 3 BCC 124.

Although the rules plainly contemplate that the proceedings for an administration order shall be by way of hearing on notice to interested parties, the courts are willing in a case of urgency to make an order *ex parte* (and indeed, before the presentation of the petition), against suitable undertakings by counsel: see the note to s. 9(1) and the cases there cited.

The amendment of r. 2.6(2)(*a*) is purely textual, and designed to bring the wording of the rule into line with that of the Act.

The new r. 2.6A seeks to prevent executions, etc. from being proceeded with in innocent contravention of IA 1986, s. 11(3)(*d*).

Rule 2.7(4A) is intended to ensure that notice to the company's bank is given at a place where its account can most easily be traced.

Rule 2.9   The hearing

2.9(1) **[Appearances]**   At the hearing of the petition, any of the following may appear or be represented—

(a) the petitioner;

(b) the company;

(c) any person who has appointed, or is or may be entitled to appoint, an administrative receiver of the company;

(d) if an administrative receiver has been appointed, he;

(e) any person who has presented a petition for the winding up of the company;

(f) the person proposed for appointment as administrator; and

(g) with the leave of the court, any other person who appears to have an interest justifying his appearance.

2.9(2) **[Costs]**   If the court makes an administration order, the costs of the petitioner, and of any person appearing whose costs are allowed by the court, are payable as an expense of the administration.

History note

Rule 2.9(1)(*c*) was substituted by I(A)R 1987 (SI 1987 No. 1919), r. 3(1), Sch., Pt. 1, para. 9 as from 11 January 1988: it formerly read as follows:

"(c) any person who has appointed an administrative receiver, or has the power to do so;".

General note

This rule ensures that all those likely to have an interest in the outcome of the proceedings may be heard, but those not particularly specified in para. (*a*)–(*f*) of r. 2.9(1) need the leave of the court. This would include a member, a director or an unsecured creditor.

On the willingness of the courts in special cases to hear applications *ex parte*, see the note to rr. 2.4–2.8.

The court will not normally give members of the company, *qua* members, leave to be heard under this rule, at least where the company is plainly insolvent, notwithstanding the possibility that if the administration achieves its purpose they may have some interest in the outcome: *Re Chelmsford City Football Club (1980) Ltd* [1991] BCC 133.

On the amendment to r. 2.9(1)(*c*), see the preceding note.

Rule 2.10   Notice and advertisement of administration order

2.10(1) **[Court to give notice]**   If the court makes an administration order, it shall forthwith give notice to the person appointed as administrator.   [FORM 2.4A]

2.10(2) **[Advertisement]** Forthwith after the order is made, the administrator shall advertise its making once in the Gazette, and once in such newspaper as he thinks most appropriate for ensuring that the order comes to the notice of the company's creditors. [FORM 2.5]

2.10(3) **[Administrator to give notice]** The administrator shall also forthwith give notice of the making of the order—

    (a) to any person who has appointed, or is or may be entitled to appoint, an administrative receiver of the company;

    (b) if an administrative receiver has been appointed, to him;

    (c) if there is pending a petition for the winding up of the company, to the petitioner (and also to the provisional liquidator, if any); and

    (d) to the registrar of companies. [FORM 2.6]

2.10(4) **[Sealed copies]** Two sealed copies of the order shall be sent by the court to the administrator, one of which shall be sent by him to the registrar of companies in accordance with section 21(2). [FORM 2.7]

2.10(5) **[Directions under s. 9(4)]** If under section 9(4) the court makes any other order, it shall give directions as to the persons to whom, and how, notice of it is to be given.

History note

Against r. 2.10(1) the words "[FORM 2.4A]" were inserted by I(A)R 1987 (SI 1987 No. 1919), r. 3(1), Sch., Pt. 2, para. 156(1) as from 11 January 1988.

    Rule 2.10(3)(*a*) was substituted by I(A)R 1987 (SI 1987 No. 1919), r. 3(1), Sch., Pt. 1, para. 10 as from 11 January 1988: it formerly read as follows:

    "(a) to any person who has appointed an administrative receiver, or has power to do so;".

General note

This rule dealing with the notification and publicity of the administration order is supplemented by IA 1986, s. 12, which requires notification on the company's business letters, etc.

    On the amendment to r. 2.10(3)(*a*), see the general note to rr. 2.4–2.8.

    There is no power under the Act or the rules for the court to appoint an interim administrator, although if the court is satisfied that the assets or business of a company are in jeopardy and that there exists a prima facie case for the making of an administration order, it can under its inherent jurisdiction appoint a person to take control of the property of the company and manage its affairs pending the hearing of the application. Such an appointment is analogous to the appointment of a receiver of a disputed property which is in jeopardy (*Re a Company No. 00175 of 1987* (1987) 3 BCC 124). An alternative course, where a petition for winding up has also been presented, is for the court to appoint a provisional liquidator.

Chapter 2 — Statement of Affairs and Proposals to Creditors

Rule 2.11 Notice requiring statement of affairs

2.11(1) **[Notice]** Where the administrator determines to require a statement of the company's affairs to be made out and submitted to him in accordance with section

22, he shall send notice to each of the persons whom he considers should be made responsible under that section, requiring them to prepare and submit the statement.

[FORM 2.8]

2.11(2) **["The deponents"]** The persons to whom the notice is sent are referred to in this Chapter as "the deponents".

2.11(3) **[Contents of notice]** The notice shall inform each of the deponents—

(a) of the names and addresses of all others (if any) to whom the same notice has been sent;

(b) of the time within which the statement must be delivered;

(c) of the effect of section 22(6) (penalty for non-compliance); and

(d) of the application to him, and to each of the other deponents, of section 235 (duty to provide information, and to attend on the administrator if required).

2.11(4) **[Instructions for preparation of statement]** The administrator shall, on request, furnish each deponent with the forms required for the preparation of the statement of affairs.

History note

In r. 2.11(1) the first word "Where" was substituted for the former word "If " by I(A)R 1987 (SI 1987 No. 1919), r. 3(1), Sch., Pt. 1, para. 11 as from 11 January 1988.

In r. 2.11(4) the words "the forms required" to the end were substituted by I(A)R 1987 (SI 1987 No. 1919), r. 3(1), Sch., Pt. 1, para. 12 as from 11 January 1988: the former words were "instructions for the preparation of the statement and with the forms required for that purpose".

(See general note after r. 2.15.)

Rule 2.12 Verification and filing

2.12(1) **[Form and verification]** The statement of affairs shall be in Form 2.9, shall contain all the particulars required by that form and shall be verified by affidavit by the deponents (using the same form). [FORM 2.9]

2.12(2) **[Affidavits of concurrence]** The administrator may require any of the persons mentioned in section 22(3) to submit an affidavit of concurrence, stating that he concurs in the statement of affairs.

2.12(3) **[Affidavit may be qualified]** An affidavit of concurrence may be qualified in respect of matters dealt with in the statement of affairs, where the maker of the affidavit is not in agreement with the deponents, or he considers the statement to be erroneous or misleading, or he is without the direct knowledge necessary for concurring with it.

2.12(4) **[Delivery of statement to administrator]** The statement of affairs shall be delivered to the administrator by the deponent making the affidavit of verification (or by one of them, if more than one), together with a copy of the verified statement.

2.12(5) **[Delivery of affidavit of concurrence]** Every affidavit of concurrence shall be delivered by the person who makes it, together with a copy.

2.12(6)   [Filing in court]   The administrator shall file the verified copy of the state-ment, and the affidavits of concurrence (if any) in court.

(See general note after r. 2.15.)

Rule 2.13   Limited disclosure

2.13(1)   [Administrator may apply to court]   Where the administrator thinks that it would prejudice the conduct of the administration for the whole or part of the state-ment of affairs to be disclosed, he may apply to the court for an order of limited disclosure in respect of the statement, or any specified part of it.

2.13(2)   [Powers of court]   The court may on the application order that the state-ment or, as the case may be, the specified part of it, be not filed in court, or that it is to be filed separately and not be open to inspection otherwise than with leave of the court.

2.13(3)   [Directions]   The court's order may include directions as to the delivery of documents to the registrar of companies and the disclosure of relevant information to other persons.

(See general note after r. 2.15.)

Rule 2.14   Release from duty to submit statement of affairs; extension of time

2.14(1)   [Exercise of s. 22(5) power]   The power of the administrator under section 22(5) to give a release from the obligation imposed by that section, or to grant an extension of time, may be exercised at the administrator's own discretion, or at the request of any deponent.

2.14(2)   [Deponent may apply to court]   A deponent may, if he requests a release or extension of time and it is refused by the administrator, apply to the court for it.

2.14(3)   [Court may dismiss application etc.]   The court may, if it thinks that no sufficient cause is shown for the application, dismiss it; but it shall not do so unless the applicant has had an opportunity to attend the court for an *ex parte* hearing, of which he has been given at least 7 days' notice.

　　If the application is not dismissed under this paragraph, the court shall fix a venue for it to be heard, and give notice to the deponent accordingly.

2.14(4)   [Deponent to send notice to administrator]   The deponent shall, at least 14 days before the hearing, send to the administrator a notice stating the venue and accompanied by a copy of the application, and of any evidence which he (the deponent) intends to adduce in support of it.

2.14(5)   [Appearance etc. by administrator]   The administrator may appear and be heard on the application; and, whether or not he appears, he may file a written report of any matters which he considers ought to be drawn to the court's attention.

　　If such a report is filed, a copy of it shall be sent by the administrator to the deponent, not later than 5 days before the hearing.

2.14(6) **[Sealed copies of order]** Sealed copies of any order made on the application shall be sent by the court to the deponent and the administrator.

2.14(7) **[Applicant's costs]** On any application under this Rule the applicant's costs shall be paid in any event by him and, unless the court otherwise orders, no allowance towards them shall be made out of the assets.

(See general note after r. 2.15.)

Rule 2.15 Expenses of statement of affairs

2.15(1) **[Payment of expenses]** A deponent making the statement of affairs and affidavit shall be allowed, and paid by the administrator out of his receipts, any expenses incurred by the deponent in so doing which the administrator considers reasonable.

2.15(2) **[Appeal to court]** Any decision by the administrator under this Rule is subject to appeal to the court.

2.15(3) **[Effect of Rule]** Nothing in this Rule relieves a deponent from any obligation with respect to the preparation, verification and submission of the statement of affairs, or to the provision of information to the administrator.

General note to rr. 2.11–2.15
These rules give details regarding the statement of affairs, which must in this case follow a prescribed form (r. 2.12).

Rule 2.16 Statement to be annexed to proposals

2.16(1) **[Contents of statement]** There shall be annexed to the administrator's proposals, when sent to the registrar of companies under section 23 and laid before the creditors' meeting to be summoned under that section, a statement by him showing—

- (a) details relating to his appointment as administrator, the purposes for which an administration order was applied for and made, and any subsequent variation of those purposes;
- (b) the names of the directors and secretary of the company;
- (c) an account of the circumstances giving rise to the application for an administration order;
- (d) if a statement of affairs has been submitted, a copy or summary of it, with the administrator's comments, if any;
- (e) if no statement of affairs has been submitted, details of the financial position of the company at the latest practicable date (which must, unless the court otherwise orders, be a date not earlier than that of the administration order);
- (f) the manner in which the affairs and business of the company—
  - (i) have, since the date of the administrator's appointment, been managed and financed, and

      (ii) will, if the administrator's proposals are approved, continue to be managed and financed; and

    (g) such other information (if any) as the administrator thinks necessary to enable creditors to decide whether or not to vote for the adoption of the proposals.

2.16(2) **[Where s. 18 application]** Where the administrator intends to apply to the court under section 18 for the administration order to be discharged at a time before he has sent a statement of his proposals to creditors in accordance with section 23(1), he shall, at least 10 days before he makes such an application, send to all creditors of the company (so far as he is aware of their addresses) a report containing the information required by paragraph (1)(a)–(f)(i) of this Rule.

History note

Rule 2.16(1) was renumbered as such and para. (*f*) was substituted by I(A)R 1987 (SI 1987 No. 1919), r. 3(1), Sch., Pt. 1, para. 12(1) as from 11 January 1988; para. (*f*) formerly read as follows:

   "(f) the manner in which the affairs of the company will be managed and its business financed, if the administrator's proposals are approved; and".

Rule 2.16(2) was added by I(A)R 1987 (SI 1987 No. 1919), r. 3(1), Sch., Pt. 1, para. 12(2) as from 11 January 1988.

Rule 2.17   Notice to members of proposals to creditors

2.17 The manner of publishing—

    (a) under section 23(2)(b), notice to members of the administrator's proposals to creditors, and

    (b) under section 25(3)(b), notice to members of substantial revisions of the proposals,

shall be by gazetting; and the notice shall also in either case be advertised once in the newspaper in which the administration order was advertised.

General note

The administrator's proposals must be sent to the registrar of companies and to every known creditor individually (IA 1986, s. 23(2)). The administrator must also send copies of the statement directly to members; or alternatively, by virtue of s. 23(2)(*b*) and r. 2.17, he may publish in the Gazette an address to which members should write for copies.

Chapter 3 — Creditors' and Company Meetings

SECTION A: CREDITORS' MEETINGS

Rule 2.18   Meeting to consider administrator's proposals

2.18(1) **[Notice of s. 23(1) meeting]** Notice of the creditors' meeting to be summoned under section 23(1) shall be given to all the creditors of the company who are identified in the statement of affairs, or are known to the administrator and had claims against the company at the date of the administration order.

2.18(2) **[Newspaper advertisement]**   Notice of the meeting shall also (unless the court otherwise directs) be given by advertisement in the newspaper in which the administration order was advertised.

2.18(3) **[Notice to directors etc.]**   Notice to attend the meeting shall be sent out at the same time to any directors or officers of the company (including persons who have been directors or officers in the past) whose presence at the meeting is, in the administrator's opinion, required.   [FORM 2.10]

2.18(4) **[Adjournment of meeting]**   If at the meeting there is not the requisite majority for approval of the administrator's proposals (with modifications, if any), the chairman may, and shall if a resolution is passed to that effect, adjourn the meeting for not more than 14 days.

(See general note after r. 2.29.)

Rule 2.19   Creditors' meetings generally

2.19(1) **[Application of Rule]**   This Rule applies to creditors' meetings summoned by the administrator under—

(a) section 14(2)(b) (general power to summon meetings of creditors);

(b) section 17(3) (requisition by creditors; direction by the court);

(c) section 23(1) (to consider administrator's proposals); or

(d) section 25(2)(b) (to consider substantial revisions).

2.19(2) **[Convenience of venue]**   In fixing the venue for the meeting, the administrator shall have regard to the convenience of creditors.

2.19(3) **[Time of meeting]**   The meeting shall be summoned for commencement between 10.00 and 16.00 hours on a business day, unless the court otherwise directs.

2.19(4) **[Notice]**   Notice of the meeting shall be given to all creditors who are known to the administrator and had claims against the company at the date of the administration order; and the notice shall specify the purpose of the meeting and contain a statement of the effect of Rule 2.22(1) (entitlement to vote). [FORM 2.11]
                                                                                      [FORM 2.22]

2.19(4A) **[Period of notice]**   Except in relation to a meeting summoned under section 23(1) or 25(2), at least 21 days' notice of the meeting shall be given.

2.19(5) **[Forms of proxy]**   With the notice summoning the meeting there shall be sent out forms of proxy.   [FORM 8.2]

2.19(6) **[Adjournment if no chairman]**   If within 30 minutes from the time fixed for commencement of the meeting there is no person present to act as chairman, the meeting stands adjourned to the same time and place in the following week or, if that is not a business day, to the business day immediately following.

2.19(7) **[Further adjournments]**   The meeting may from time to time be adjourned, if the chairman thinks fit, but not for more than 14 days from the date on which it was fixed to commence.

History note

In r. 2.19(4) the words "At least 21 days' " formerly appearing at the beginning were omitted by I(A)R 1987 (SI 1987 No. 1919), r. 3(1), Sch., Pt. 1, para. 13(1) as from 11 January 1988. Also against r. 2.19(4) the words "[FORM 2.22]" were inserted by I(A)R 1987 (SI 1987 No. 1919), r. 3(1), Sch., Pt. 2, para. 156(1) as from the same date.

Rule 2.19(4A) was inserted by I(A)R 1987 (SI 1987 No. 1919), r. 3(1), Sch., Pt. 1, para. 13(2) as from 11 January 1988.

(See general note after r. 2.29.)

Rule 2.20   The chairman at meetings

2.20(1)   [Administrator or his nominee to be chairman]   At any meeting of creditors summoned by the administrator, either he shall be chairman, or a person nominated by him in writing to act in his place.

2.20(2)   [Nominee chairman]   A person so nominated must be either—

(a) one who is qualified to act as an insolvency practitioner in relation to the company, or

(b) an employee of the administrator or his firm who is experienced in insolvency matters.

(See general note after r. 2.29.)

Rule 2.21   Meeting requisitioned by creditors

2.21(1)   [Documents to accompany request]   Any request by creditors to the administrator for a meeting of creditors to be summoned shall be accompanied by—

(a) a list of the creditors concurring with the request, showing the amounts of their respective claims in the administration;

(b) from each creditor concurring, written confirmation of his concurrence; and

(c) a statement of the purpose of the proposed meeting.

This paragraph does not apply if the requisitioning creditor's debt is alone sufficient, without the concurrence of other creditors.

2.21(2)   [Fixing of venue]   The administrator shall, if he considers the request to be properly made in accordance with section 17(3), fix a venue for the meeting, not more than 35 days from his receipt of the request, and give at least 21 days' notice of the meeting to creditors.

2.21(3)   [Expenses]   The expenses of summoning and holding a meeting at the instance of any person other than the administrator shall be paid by that person, who shall deposit with the administrator security for their payment.

2.21(4)   [Deposit under r. 2.21(3)]   The sum to be deposited shall be such as the administrator may determine, and he shall not act without the deposit having been made.

2.21(5)   [Resolution of meeting re expenses]   The meeting may resolve that the expenses of summoning and holding it are to be payable out of the assets of the company, as an expense of the administration.

2.21(6) [Repayment of deposit] To the extent that any deposit made under this Rule is not required for the payment of expenses of summoning and holding the meeting, it shall be repaid to the person who made it.

(See general note after r. 2.29.)

Rule **2.22** Entitlement to vote

2.22(1) [Conditions for voting] Subject as follows, at a meeting of creditors in administration proceedings a person is entitled to vote only if—

- (a) he has given to the administrator, not later than 12.00 hours on the business day before the day fixed for the meeting, details in writing of the debt which he claims to be due to him from the company, and the claim has been duly admitted under the following provisions of this Rule, and
- (b) there has been lodged with the administrator any proxy which he intends to be used on his behalf.

Details of the debt must include any calculation for the purposes of Rules 2.24 to 2.27.

2.22(2) [Failure to comply with r. 2.22(1)(a)] The chairman of the meeting may allow a creditor to vote, notwithstanding that he has failed to comply with paragraph (1)(a), if satisfied that the failure was due to circumstances beyond the creditor's control.

2.22(3) [Production of documents] The administrator or, if other, the chairman of the meeting may call for any document or other evidence to be produced to him, where he thinks it necessary for the purpose of substantiating the whole or any part of the claim.

2.22(4) [Calculation of votes] Votes are calculated according to the amount of a creditor's debt as at the date of the administration order, deducting any amounts paid in respect of the debt after that date.

2.22(5) [Limitation on voting] A creditor shall not vote in respect of a debt for an unliquidated amount, or any debt whose value is not ascertained, except where the chairman agrees to put upon the debt an estimated minimum value for the purpose of entitlement to vote and admits the claim for that purpose.

(See general note after r. 2.29.)

Rule **2.23** Admission and rejection of claims

2.23(1) [Power of chairman] At any creditors' meeting the chairman has power to admit or reject a creditor's claim for the purpose of his entitlement to vote; and the power is exercisable with respect to the whole or any part of the claim.

2.23(2) [Appeal from chairman's decision] The chairman's decision under this Rule, or in respect of any matter arising under Rule 2.22, is subject to appeal to the court by any creditor.

2.23(3)   [Voting subject to objection]   If the chairman is in doubt whether a claim should be admitted or rejected, he shall mark it as objected to and allow the creditor to vote, subject to his vote being subsequently declared invalid if the objection to the claim is sustained.

2.23(4)   [If chairman's decision reversed etc.]   If on an appeal the chairman's decision is reversed or varied, or a creditor's vote is declared invalid, the court may order that another meeting be summoned, or make such other order as it thinks just.

2.23(5)   [In case of s. 23 meeting]   In the case of the meeting summoned under section 23 to consider the administrator's proposals, an application to the court by way of appeal under this Rule against a decision of the chairman shall not be made later than 28 days after the delivery of the administrator's report in accordance with section 24(4).

2.23(6)   [Costs of appeal]   Neither the administrator nor any person nominated by him to be chairman is personally liable for costs incurred by any person in respect of an appeal to the court under this Rule, unless the court makes an order to that effect.

(See general note after r. 2.29.)

Rule 2.24   Secured creditors

2.24   At a meeting of creditors a secured creditor is entitled to vote only in respect of the balance (if any) of his debt after deducting the value of his security as estimated by him.

(See general note after r. 2.29.)

Rule 2.25   Holders of negotiable instruments

2.25   A creditor shall not vote in respect of a debt on, or secured by, a current bill of exchange or promissory note, unless he is willing—

  (a) to treat the liability to him on the bill or note of every person who is liable on it antecedently to the company, and against whom a bankruptcy order has not been made (or, in the case of a company, which has not gone into liqui-dation), as a security in his hands, and

  (b) to estimate the value of the security and, for the purpose of his entitlement to vote, to deduct it from his claim.

(See general note after r. 2.29.)

Rule 2.26   Retention of title creditors

2.26   For the purpose of entitlement to vote at a creditors' meeting in administration proceedings, a seller of goods to the company under a retention of title agreement shall deduct from his claim the value, as estimated by him, of any rights arising under that agreement in respect of goods in possession of the company.

(See general note after r. 2.29.)

Rule 2.27   Hire-purchase, conditional sale and chattel leasing agreements

2.27(1)   [Entitlement to vote]   Subject as follows, an owner of goods under a hire-purchase or chattel leasing agreement, or a seller of goods under a conditional sale agreement, is entitled to vote in respect of the amount of the debt due and payable to him by the company as at the date of the administration order.

2.27(2)   [Calculating amount of debt]   In calculating the amount of any debt for this purpose, no account shall be taken of any amount attributable to the exercise of any right under the relevant agreement, so far as the right has become exercisable solely by virtue of the presentation of the petition for an administration order or any matter arising in consequence of that, or of the making of the order.

(See general note after r. 2.29.)

Rule 2.28   Resolutions and minutes

2.28(1)   [Resolution passed by majority in value]   Subject to paragraph (1A), at a creditors' meeting in administration proceedings, a resolution is passed when a majority (in value) of those present and voting, in person or by proxy, have voted in favour of it.

2.28(1A)   [Resolution invalid]   Any resolution is invalid if those voting against it include more than half in value of the creditors to whom notice of the meeting was sent and who are not, to the best of the chairman's belief, persons connected with the company.

2.28(2)   [Minute book]   The chairman of the meeting shall cause minutes of its proceedings to be entered in the company's minute book.

2.28(3)   [Contents of minutes]   The minutes shall include a list of the creditors who attended (personally or by proxy) and, if a creditors' committee has been established, the names and addresses of those elected to be members of the committee.

History note

In r. 2.28(1) the words "Subject to paragraph (1A)," at the beginning were inserted by I(A)R 1987 (SI 1987 No. 1919), r. 3(1), Sch., Pt. 1, para. 14(1) as from 11 January 1988.

Rule 2.28(1A) was inserted by I(A)R 1987 (SI 1987 No. 1919), r. 3(1), Sch., Pt. 1, para. 14(2) as from 11 January 1988.

(See general note after r. 2.29.)

Rule 2.29   Reports and notices under s. 23 and 25

2.29   Any report or notice by the administrator of the result of a creditors' meeting held under section 23 or 25 shall have annexed to it details of the proposals which were considered by the meeting and of the revisions and modifications to the proposals which were so considered.

History note

Rule 2.29 was substituted by I(A)R 1987 (SI 1987 No. 1919), r. 3(1), Sch., Pt. 1, para. 15 as from 11 January 1988: it formerly read as follows:

"Rule 2.29   Administrator's report

2.29 Any report by the administrator of the result of creditors' meetings held under section 23 or 25 shall have annexed to it details of the proposals which were considered by the meeting in question and of the modifications which were so considered."

General note to rr. 2.18–2.29

These are the rules governing the summoning and conduct of creditors' meetings. A meeting may be summoned either by the administrator himself or on the requisition of one-tenth in value of the creditors (IA 1986, s. 17(3)(*b*)). A creditor is required to prove his debt prior to the meeting (r. 2.22), although the chairman has a limited discretion to make exceptions (r. 2.22 (2)). Voting is prima facie by a simple majority in value of those creditors present and voting (including proxy votes): r. 2.28(1); but the new r. 2.28(1A) prevents a resolution from being carried against the wish of a majority of the "outside" creditors. On the meaning of "connected with", see IA 1986, s. 249, and cf. IR 1986, r. 1.19(4).

Rule 2.22(5), like r. 1.17(3), appears to assume that a claimant for an unliquidated amount or for a sum whose value is not ascertained may be regarded as a "creditor" for the purposes of an administration. There is, perhaps, more support for this in the case of an administration than in a voluntary arrangement, since s. 9(1) gives contingent and prospective creditors the right to present a petition, but the assumption lacks explicit statutory justification. See the notes to s. 1(1) and rr. 1.13–1.21; and contrast the position in a winding up (rr. 12.3(1), 13.12).

A creditor may, if he wishes, split the vote to which he is entitled so as to cast his vote as to £x in value in one way and as to £y in value in the other, provided that £x + £y does not exceed the total debt in respect of which he is qualified to vote under r. 2.22: *Re Polly Peck International plc* [1991] BCC 503. Accordingly, a trustee for debenture holders can give effect to the wishes of the debenture holders where they differ *inter se*, or are at variance with those of the trustee as a creditor in its own right.

Rule 2.30   Notices to creditors

2.30(1)   [Notice of result of meeting]   Within 14 days of the conclusion of a meeting of creditors to consider the administrator's proposals or revised proposals, the administrator shall send notice of the result of the meeting (including, where appropriate, details of the proposals as approved) to every creditor who received notice of the meeting under the Rules, and to any other creditor of whom the administrator has since become aware.   [FORM 2.12]

2.30(2)   [Administrator's report]   Within 14 days of the end of every period of 6 months beginning with the date of approval of the administrator's proposals or revised proposals, the administrator shall send to all creditors of the company a report on the progress of the administration.

2.30(3)   [Administrator vacating office]   On vacating office the administrator shall send to creditors a report on the administration up to that time.

This does not apply where the administration is immediately followed by the company going into liquidation, nor when the administrator is removed from office by the court or ceases to be qualified as an insolvency practitioner.

General note

The result of the meeting must be notified to all known creditors.

SECTION B: COMPANY MEETINGS

Rule 2.31 Venue and conduct of company meeting

2.31(1) **[Fixing of venue]** Where the administrator summons a meeting of members of the company, he shall fix a venue for it having regard to their convenience.

2.31(2) **[Chairman]** The chairman of the meeting shall be the administrator or a person nominated by him in writing to act in his place.

2.31(3) **[Nominee chairman]** A person so nominated must be either—

(a) one who is qualified to act as an insolvency practitioner in relation to the company, or

(b) an employee of the administrator or his firm who is experienced in insolvency matters.

2.31(4) **[Adjournment if no chairman]** If within 30 minutes from the time fixed for commencement of the meeting there is no person present to act as chairman, the meeting stands adjourned to the same time and place in the following week or, if that is not a business day, to the business day immediately following.

2.31(5) **[Summoning and conduct of meeting]** Subject as above, the meeting shall be summoned and conducted as if it were a general meeting of the company summoned under the company's articles of association, and in accordance with the applicable provisions of the Companies Act.

2.31(6) **[Minutes]** The chairman of the meeting shall cause minutes of its proceedings to be entered in the company's minute book.

General note

Any meeting of the shareholders held during the currency of an administration order is summoned and conducted in accordance with the articles of association, but where it is summoned by the administrator, it is he or his nominee who takes the chair.

Chapter 4 — The Creditors' Committee

Rule 2.32 Constitution of committee

2.32(1) **[Three–five creditors]** Where it is resolved by a creditors' meeting to establish a creditors' committee for the purposes of the administration, the committee shall consist of at least 3 and not more than 5 creditors of the company elected at the meeting.

2.32(2) **[Eligibility of creditors]** Any creditor of the company is eligible to be a member of the committee, so long as his claim has not been rejected for the purpose of his entitlement to vote.

2.32(3) **[Body corporate as member]** A body corporate may be a member of the committee, but it cannot act as such otherwise than by a representative appointed under Rule 2.37 below.

(See general note after r. 2.46A.)

Rule 2.33   Formalities of establishment

2.33(1)   [Certificate of due constitution]   The creditors' committee does not come into being, and accordingly cannot act, until the administrator has issued a certificate of its due constitution.

2.33(2)   [Agreement to act]   No person may act as a member of the committee unless and until he has agreed to do so and, unless the relevant proxy or authorisation contains a statement to the contrary, such agreement may be given by his proxy-holder or representative under section 375 of the Companies Act present at the meeting establishing the committee.

2.33(2A)   [Issue of administrator's certificate]   The administrator's certificate of the committee's due constitution shall not issue unless and until at least 3 of the persons who are to be members of the committee have agreed to act.

2.33(3)   [Amended certificate]   As and when the others (if any) agree to act, the administrator shall issue an amended certificate.

2.33(4)   [Filing of certificates]   The certificate, and any amended certificate, shall be filed in court by the administrator.   [FORM 2.13]

2.33(5)   [Change in membership]   If after the first establishment of the committee there is any change in its membership, the administrator shall report the change to the court.   [FORM 2.14]

History note

Rule 2.33(2) and (2A) were substituted for the former r. 2.33(2) by I(A)R 1987 (SI 1987 No. 1919), r. 3(1), Sch., Pt. 1, para. 16 as from 11 January 1988: the former r. 2.33(2) read as follows:

"**2.33(2)** No person may act as a member of the committee unless and until he has agreed to do so; and the administrator's certificate of the committee's due constitution shall not issue unless and until at least 3 of the persons who are to be members of it have agreed to act."

(See general note after r. 2.46A.)

Rule 2.34   Functions and meetings of the committee

2.34(1)   [Functions]   The creditors' committee shall assist the administrator in discharging his functions, and act in relation to him in such manner as may be agreed from time to time.

2.34(2)   [Holding of meetings]   Subject as follows, meetings of the committee shall be held when and where determined by the administrator.

2.34(3)   [First and subsequent meetings]   The administrator shall call a first meeting of the committee not later than 3 months after its first establishment; and thereafter he shall call a meeting—

  (a) if so requested by a member of the committee or his representative (the meeting then to be held within 21 days of the request being received by the administrator), and

  (b) for a specified date, if the committee has previously resolved that a meeting be held on that date.

2.34(4)   [Notice of venue]   The administrator shall give 7 days' written notice of the venue of any meeting to every member of the committee (or his representative designated for that purpose), unless in any case the requirement of notice has been waived by or on behalf of any member.

Waiver may be signified either at or or before the meeting.

(See general note after r. 2.46A.)

Rule 2.35 The chairman at meetings

2.35(1) **[Administrator to be chairman]** Subject to Rule 2.44(3), the chairman at any meeting of the creditors' committee shall be the administrator or a person nominated by him in writing to act.

2.35(2) **[Other nominated chairman]** A person so nominated must be either—

 (a) one who is qualified to act as an insolvency practitioner in relation to the company, or

 (b) an employee of the administrator or his firm who is experienced in insolvency matters.

(See general note after r. 2.46A.)

Rule 2.36 Quorum

2.36 A meeting of the committee is duly constituted if due notice of it has been given to all the members, and at least 2 members are present or represented.

(See general note after r. 2.46A.)

Rule 2.37 Committee-members' representatives

2.37(1) **[Representation]** A member of the committee may, in relation to the business of the committee, be represented by another person duly authorised by him for that purpose.

2.37(2) **[Letter of authority]** A person acting as a committee-member's representative must hold a letter of authority entitling him so to act (either generally or specially) and signed by or on behalf of the committee-member, and for this purpose any proxy or any authorisation under section 375 of the Companies Act in relation to any meeting of creditors of the company shall, unless it contains a statement to the contrary, be treated as a letter of authority to act generally signed by or on behalf of the committee-member.

2.37(3) **[Production of letter of authority]** The chairman at any meeting of the committee may call on a person claiming to act as a committee-member's representative to produce his letter of authority, and may exclude him if it appears that his authority is deficient.

2.37(4) **[Who may not be a representative]** No member may be represented by a body corporate, or by a person who is an undischarged bankrupt, or is subject to a composition or arrangement with his creditors.

2.37(5)   [No dual representation]   No person shall—
- (a) on the same committee, act at one and the same time as representative of more than one committee-member, or
- (b) act both as a member of the committee and as representative of another member.

2.37(6)   [Signing as representative]   Where a member's representative signs any document on the member's behalf, the fact that he so signs must be stated below his signature.

History note

In r. 2.37(2) the words ", and for this purpose" to the end were added by I(A)R 1987 (SI 1987 No. 1919), r. 3(1), Sch., Pt. 1, para. 17 as from 11 January 1988.

(See general note after r. 2.46A.)

Rule 2.38   Resignation

2.38   A member of the committee may resign by notice in writing delivered to the administrator.

(See general note after r. 2.46A.)

Rule 2.39   Termination of membership

2.39(1)   [Automatic termination]   Membership of the creditors' committee is automatically terminated if the member—
- (a) becomes bankrupt, or compounds or arranges with his creditors, or
- (b) at 3 consecutive meetings of the committee is neither present nor represented (unless at the third of those meetings it is resolved that this Rule is not to apply in his case), or
- (c) ceases to be, or is found never to have been, a creditor.

2.39(2)   [Termination on bankruptcy]   However, if the cause of termination is the member's bankruptcy, his trustee in bankruptcy replaces him as a member of the committee.

(See general note after r. 2.46A.)

Rule 2.40   Removal

2.40   A member of the committee may be removed by resolution at a meeting of creditors, at least 14 days' notice having been given of the intention to move that resolution.

(See general note after r. 2.46A.)

Rule 2.41   Vacancies

2.41(1)   [Application of Rule]   The following applies if there is a vacancy in the membership of the creditors' committee.

2.41(2) **[Agreement not to fill vacancy]** The vacancy need not be filled if the administrator and a majority of the remaining members of the committee so agree, provided that the total number of members does not fall below the minimum required under Rule 2.32.

2.41(3) **[Filling vacancy]** The administrator may appoint any creditor (being qualified under the Rules to be a member of the committee) to fill the vacancy, if a majority of the other members of the committee agree to the appointment, and the creditor concerned consents to act.

(See general note after r. 2.46A.)

Rule 2.42   Procedure at meetings

2.42(1) **[Votes and passing of resolutions]** At any meeting of the creditors' committee, each member of it (whether present himself, or by his representative) has one vote; and a resolution is passed when a majority of the members present or represented have voted in favour of it.

2.42(2) **[Record of resolutions]** Every resolution passed shall be recorded in writing, either separately or as part of the minutes of the meeting.

2.42(3) **[Signing of records etc.]** A record of each resolution shall be signed by the chairman and placed in the company's minute book.

(See general note after r. 2.46A.)

Rule 2.43   Resolutions by post

2.43(1) **[Proposed resolution sent to members]** In accordance with this Rule, the administrator may seek to obtain the agreement of members of the creditors' committee to a resolution by sending to every member (or his representative designated for the purpose) a copy of the proposed resolution.

2.43(2) **[Copy of proposed resolution]** Where the administrator makes use of the procedure allowed by this Rule, he shall send out to members of the committee or their representatives (as the case may be) a copy of any proposed resolution on which a decision is sought, which shall be set out in such a way that agreement with or dissent from each separate resolution may be indicated by the recipient on the copy so sent.

2.43(3) **[Member may require meeting]** Any member of the committee may, within 7 business days from the date of the administrator sending out a resolution, require him to summon a meeting of the committee to consider the matters raised by the resolution.

2.43(4) **[Deemed passing of resolution]** In the absence of such a request, the resolution is deemed to have been passed by the committee if and when the administrator is notified in writing by a majority of the members that they concur with it.

2.43(5) **[Copy resolution etc. in minute book]** A copy of every resolution passed under this Rule, and a note that the committee's concurrence was obtained, shall be placed in the company's minute book.

History note

In r. 2.43(2) the words "a copy of any proposed resolution" to the end were substituted by

I(A)R 1987 (SI 1987 No. 1919), r. 3(1), Sch. Pt. 1, para. 18 as from 11 January 1988: the former words were as follows:

> "a statement incorporating the resolution to which their agreement is sought, each resolution (if more than one) being sent out in a separate document."

(See general note after r. 2.46A.)

Rule 2.44   Information from administrator

2.44(1)   [Notice to administrator]   Where the committee resolves to require the attendance of the administrator under section 26(2), the notice to him shall be in writing signed by the majority of the members of the committee for the time being. A member's representative may sign for him.

2.44(2)   [Time and place of meeting]   The meeting at which the administrator's attendance is required shall be fixed by the committee for a business day, and shall be held at such time and place as he determines.

2.44(3)   [Chairman]   Where the administrator so attends, the members of the committee may elect any one of their number to be chairman of the meeting, in place of the administrator or a nominee of his.

(See general note after r. 2.46A.)

Rule 2.45   Expenses of members

2.45(1)   [Expenses defrayed out of assets]   Subject as follows, the administrator shall out of the assets of the company defray any reasonable travelling expenses directly incurred by members of the creditors' committee or their representatives in relation to their attendance at the committee's meetings, or otherwise on the committee's business, as an expense of the administration.

2.45(2)   [Non-application of r. 2.45(1)]   Paragraph (1) does not apply to any meeting of the committee held within 3 months of a previous meeting, unless the meeting in question is summoned at the instance of the administrator.

(See general note after r. 2.46A.)

Rule 2.46   Members' dealings with the company

2.46(1)   [Effect of membership]   Membership of the committee does not prevent a person from dealing with the company while the administration order is in force, provided that any transactions in the course of such dealings are in good faith and for value.

2.46(2)   [Court may set aside transaction]   The court may, on the application of any person interested, set aside any transaction which appears to it to be contrary to the requirements of this Rule, and may give such consequential directions as it thinks fit for compensating the company for any loss which it may have incurred in consequence of the transaction.

(See general note after r. 2.46A.)

Rule 2.46A   Formal defects

2.46A   The acts of the creditors' committee established for any administration are valid notwithstanding any defect in the appointment, election or qualifications of any member of the committee or any committee-member's representative or in the formalities of its establishment.

History note

Rule 2.46A was inserted by I(A)R 1987 (SI 1987 No. 1919), r. 3(1), Sch., Pt. 1, para. 19 as from 11 January 1988.

General note to rr. 2.32–2.46A

The IA 1986, s. 26 provides for the establishment of a creditors' committee, corresponding to the liquidation committee in a liquidation. These rules deal with its constitution and functioning. The amendments to rr. 2.33 and 2.37 are intended to make it easier for insolvency practitioners to convene committee meetings immediately after the creditor's meeting. The new r. 2.43(2) will save a good deal of unnecessary work, as well as paper! Rule 2.46A (and rr. 3.30A, 4.172A and 6.156(7)) is in standard form, although one would normally expect to find such a provision in the substantive legislation rather than the rules.

Rule 2.32 envisages that the election to membership of the creditors' committee will be conducted by a single ballot, with the five creditors who attract the greatest number of votes by value being chosen to form the committee: *Re Polly Peck International plc* [1991] BCC 503.

Chapter 5 — The Administrator

Rule 2.47   Fixing of remuneration

2.47(1)   **[Entitlement to remuneration]**   The administrator is entitled to receive remuneration for his services as such.

2.47(2)   **[How fixed]**   The remuneration shall be fixed either—

     (a)   as a percentage of the value of the property with which he has to deal, or

     (b)   by reference to the time properly given by the insolvency practitioner (as administrator) and his staff in attending to matters arising in the administration.

2.47(3)   **[Determination under r. 2.47(2)]**   It is for the creditors' committee (if there is one) to determine whether the remuneration is to be fixed under paragraph (2)(a) or (b) and, if under paragraph (2)(a), to determine any percentage to be applied as there mentioned.

2.47(4)   **[Matters relevant to r. 2.47(3) determination]**   In arriving at that determination, the committee shall have regard to the following matters—

    (a) the complexity (or otherwise) of the case,

    (b) any respects in which, in connection with the company's affairs, there falls on the administrator any responsibility of an exceptional kind or degree,

    (c) the effectiveness with which the administrator appears to be carrying out, or to have carried out, his duties as such, and

    (d) the value and nature of the property with which he has to deal.

2.47(5) **[If no committee or determination]** If there is no creditors' committee, or the committee does not make the requisite determination, the administrator's remuneration may be fixed (in accordance with paragraph (2)) by a resolution of a meeting of creditors; and paragraph (4) applies to them as it does to the creditors' committee.

2.47(6) **[Fixed by court]** If not fixed as above, the administrator's remuneration shall, on his application, be fixed by the court.

2.47(7) **[Where joint administrators]** Where there are joint administrators, it is for them to agree between themselves as to how the remuneration payable should be apportioned. Any dispute arising between them may be referred—

    (a) to the court, for settlement by order, or

    (b) to the creditors' committee or a meeting of creditors, for settlement by resolution.

2.47(8) **[Where administrator solicitor]** If the administrator is a solicitor and employs his own firm, or any partner in it, to act on behalf of the company, profit costs shall not be paid unless this is authorised by the creditors' committee, the creditors or the court.

History note

Rules 2.47(7) and (8) were substituted for the former r. 2.47(7) by I(A)R 1987 (SI 1987 No. 1919), r. 3(1), Sch., Pt. 1, para. 20 as from 11 January 1988: the former r. 2.47(7) read as follows:

> "**2.47(7)** Rule 4.128 (2) and (3) in Part 4 of the Rules (remuneration of joint liquidators; solicitors' profit costs) applies to an administrator as it applies to a liquidator, with any necessary modifications."

(See general note after r. 2.55.)

Rule 2.48   Recourse to meeting of creditors

2.48 If the administrator's remuneration has been fixed by the creditors' committee, and he considers the rate or amount to be insufficient, he may request that it be increased by resolution of the creditors.

(See general note after r. 2.55.)

Rule 2.49   Recourse to the court

2.49(1) **[Administrator may apply to court]** If the administrator considers that the remuneration fixed for him by the creditors' committee, or by resolution of the creditors, is insufficient, he may apply to the court for an order increasing its amount or rate.

2.49(2) **[Notice to committee members etc.]** The administrator shall give at least 14 days' notice of his application to the members of the creditors' committee; and the committee may nominate one or more members to appear or be represented, and to be heard, on the application.

2.49(3) **[Where no committee]** If there is no creditors' committee, the administrator's notice of his application shall be sent to such one or more of the company's creditors as the court may direct, which creditors may nominate one or more of their number to appear or be represented.

2.49(4) **[Costs of application]** The court may, if it appears to be a proper case, order the costs of the administrator's application, including the costs of any member of the creditors' committee appearing or being represented on it, or any creditor so appearing or being represented, to be paid as an expense of the administration.

History note

In r. 2.49(4) the words "or being represented" in both places where they occur were inserted by I(A)R 1987 (SI 1987 No. 1919), r. 3(1), Sch., Pt. 1, para. 21 as from 11 January 1988.

(See general note after r. 2.55.)

Rule 2.50   Creditors' claim that remuneration is excessive

2.50(1) **[Creditor may apply to court]** Any creditor of the company may, with the concurrence of at least 25 per cent. in value of the creditors (including himself), apply to the court for an order that the administrator's remuneration be reduced, on the grounds that it is, in all the circumstances, excessive.

2.50(2) **[Power of court to dismiss etc.]** The court may, if it thinks that no sufficient cause is shown for a reduction, dismiss the application; but it shall not do so unless the applicant has had an opportunity to attend the court for an *ex parte* hearing, of which he has been given at least 7 days' notice.

If the application is not dismissed under this paragraph, the court shall fix a venue for it to be heard, and given notice to the applicant accordingly.

2.50(3) **[Notice to administrator]** The applicant shall, at least 14 days before the hearing, send to the administrator a notice stating the venue and accompanied by a copy of the application, and of any evidence which the applicant intends to adduce in support of it.

2.50(4) **[Court order]** If the court considers the application to be well-founded, it shall make an order fixing the remuneration at a reduced amount or rate.

2.50(5) **[Costs of application]** Unless the court orders otherwise, the costs of the application shall be paid by the applicant, and are not payable as an expense of the administration.

(See general note after r. 2.55.)

Rule 2.51   Disposal of charged property, etc.

2.51(1) **[Application of Rule]** The following applies where the administrator applies to the court under section 15(2) for authority to dispose of property of the company which is subject to a security, or goods in the possession of the company under an agreement, to which that subsection relates.

2.51(2)   [Venue and notice]   The court shall fix a venue for the hearing of the application, and the administrator shall forthwith give notice of the venue to the person who is the holder of the security or, as the case may be, the owner under the agreement.

2.51(3)   [Notice of s. 15(2) order]   If an order is made under section 15(2), the administrator shall forthwith give notice of it to that person or owner.

2.51(4)   [Sealed copies of order]   The court shall send 2 sealed copies of the order to the administrator, who shall send one of them to that person or owner.

(See general note after r. 2.55.)

Rule 2.52   Abstract of receipts and payments

2.52(1)   [Adminstrator to send accounts etc.]   The administrator shall—

    (a) within 2 months after the end of 6 months from the date of his appointment, and of every subsequent period of 6 months, and

    (b) within 2 months after he ceases to act as administrator,

send to the court, and to registrar of companies, and to each member of the creditors' committee, the requisite accounts of the receipts and payments of the company. [FORM 2.15]

2.52(2)   [Extension of time]   The court may, on the administrator's application, extend the period of 2 months mentioned above.

2.52(3)   [Form of abstract]   The accounts are to be in the form of an abstract showing—

    (a) receipts and payments during the relevant period of 6 months, or

    (b) where the administrator has ceased to act, receipts and payments during the period from the end of the last 6-month period to the time when he so ceased (alternatively, if there has been no previous abstract, receipts and payments in the period since his appointment as administrator).

2.52(4)   [Penalty on default]   If the administrator makes default in complying with this Rule, he is liable to a fine and, for continued contravention, to a daily default fine.

(See general note after r. 2.55.)

Rule 2.53   Resignation

2.53(1)   [Grounds for resignation]   The administrator may give notice of his resignation on grounds of ill health or because— [FORM 2.16]

    (a) he intends ceasing to be in practice as an insolvency practitioner, or

    (b) there is some conflict of interest, or change of personal circumstances, which precludes or makes impracticable the further discharge by him of the duties of administrator.

2.53(2)   [Other grounds]   The administrator may, with the leave of the court, give notice of his resignation on grounds other than those specified in paragraph (1).

[FORM 2.17]

2.53(3)   [Notice to specified persons]   The administrator must give to the persons specified below at least 7 days' notice of his intention to resign, or to apply for the court's leave to do so—

    (a) if there is a continuing administrator of the company, to him;

    (b) if there is no such administrator, to the creditors' committee; and

    (c) if there is no such administrator and no creditors' committee, to the company and its creditors.

(See general note after r. 2.55.)

Rule 2.54   Administrator deceased

2.54(1)   [Notice to court]   Subject as follows, where the administrator has died, it is the duty of his personal representatives to give notice of the fact to the court, specifying the date of the death.

This does not apply if notice has been given under any of the following paragraphs of this Rule.

2.54(2)   [Notice by partner etc.]   If the deceased administrator was a partner in a firm, notice may be given by a partner in the firm who is qualified to act as an insolvency practitioner, or is a member of any body recognised by the Secretary of State for the authorisation of insolvency practitioners.

2.54(3)   [Notice by others]   Notice of the death may be given by any person producing to the court the relevant death certificate or a copy of it.

(See general note after r. 2.55.)

Rule 2.55   Order filling vacancy

2.55   Where the court makes an order filling a vacancy in the office of administrator, the same provisions apply in respect of giving notice of, and advertising, the order as the case of the administration order.

History note

In r. 2.55 the words "administration order" were substituted for the former words "original appointment of an administrator" by I(A)R 1987 (SI 1987 No. 1919), r. 3(1), Sch., Pt. 1, para. 22 as from 11 January 1988.

General note to rr. 2.47–2.55

Here are found miscellaneous rules in regard to the administrator's remuneration, his power to deal with charged property, his duties as regards accounting, and vacancies in the office resulting from his resignation, death, etc.

Chapter 6 — VAT Bad Debt Relief

Rule 2.56   Issue of certificate of insolvency

2.56(1) **[Duty of administrator]** In accordance with this Rule, it is the duty of the administrator to issue a certificate in the terms of paragraph (b) of section 22(3) of the Value Added Tax Act 1983 (which specifies the circumstances in which a company is deemed insolvent for the purposes of that section) forthwith upon his forming the opinion described in that paragraph.

2.56(2) **[Contents of certificate]** There shall in the certificate be specified—

  (a) the name of the company and its registered number;

  (b) the name of the administrator and the date of his appointment;

  (c) the date on which the certificate is issued.

2.56(3) **[Title of certificate]** The certificate shall be intituled "CERTIFICATE OF INSOLVENCY FOR THE PURPOSES OF SECTION 22(3)(b) OF THE VALUE ADDED TAX ACT 1983".

General note

Bad debt relief was available under the Value Added Tax Act 1983 only where the debtor had become insolvent. The Finance Act 1985, s. 32 amended that section so as to include the case where an administrator or administrative receiver is appointed. This rule and r. 3.36 provide the necessary machinery for these cases.

    See also Finance Act 1994, s. 47 (effective 10 May 1994), excluding the obligation to set off post-insolvency VAT credits against pre-insolvency debts.

Rule 2.57   Notice to creditors

2.57(1) **[Time for giving notice]** Notice of the issue of the certificate shall be given by the administrator within 3 months of his appointment or within 2 months of issuing the certificate, whichever is the later, to all of the company's unsecured creditors of whose address he is then aware and who have, to his knowledge, made supplies to the company, with a charge to value added tax, at any time before his appointment.

2.57(2) **[Later notice]** Thereafter, he shall give the notice to any such creditor of whose address and supplies to the company he becomes aware.

2.57(3) **[No obligation re certificate]** He is not under obligation to provide any creditor with a copy of the certificate.

Rule 2.58   Preservation of certificate with company's records

2.58(1)   [Retention of certificate]   The certificate shall be retained with the company's accounting records, and section 222 of the Companies Act (where and for how long records are to be kept) shall apply to the certificate as it applies to those records.

2.58(2)   [Duty of administrator]   It is the duty of the administrator, on vacating office, to bring this Rule to the attention of the directors or (as the case may be) any successor of his as administrator.

PART 3—ADMINISTRATIVE RECEIVERSHIP

General comment on Pt. 3

These rules are new and they have no counterpart in the previous legislation. The bulk of the rules deal with the creditors' committee which was an innovation introduced by IA 1986. It should be noted that the following rules do not apply to Scottish receiverships or receivers in Northern Ireland.

Chapter 1 — Appointment of Administrative Receiver

Rule 3.1   Acceptance and confirmation of acceptance of appointment

3.1(1)   [Two or more persons appointed jointly]   Where two or more persons are appointed as joint receivers or managers of a company's property under powers contained in an instrument, the acceptance of such an appointment shall be made by each of them in accordance with section 33 as if that person were a sole appointee, but the joint appointment takes effect only when all such persons have so accepted and is then deemed to have been made at the time at which the instrument of appointment was received by or on behalf of all such persons.

3.1(2)   [Sole or joint receiver]   Subject to the next paragraph, where a person is appointed as the sole or joint receiver of a company's property under powers contained in an instrument, the appointee shall, if he accepts the appointment, within 7 days confirm his acceptance in writing to the person appointing him.

3.1(3)   [Non-application of r. 3.1(2)]   Paragraph (2) does not apply where an appointment is accepted in writing.   [FORM 3.1]

3.1(4)   [Who may accept or confirm]   Any acceptance or confirmation of acceptance of appointment as a receiver or manager of a company's property, whether under the Act or the Rules, may be given by any person (including, in the case of a joint appointment, any joint appointee) duly authorised for that purpose on behalf of the receiver or manager.

3.1(5) [Statements in confirmation] In confirming acceptance the appointee or person authorised for that purpose shall state—

(a) the time and date of receipt of the instrument of appointment, and

(b) the time and date of acceptance.

History note

Rule 3.1 was substituted by I(A)R 1987 (SI 1987 No. 1919), r. 3(1), Sch., Pt. 1, para. 23 as from 11 January 1988: r. 3.1 formerly read as follows:

"Rule 3.1 Acceptance of appointment

3.1(1) Where a person is appointed as the sole or joint administrative receiver of a company's property under powers contained in an instrument, the appointee, if he accepts the appointment, shall within 7 days confirm his acceptance in writing to the appointer.

3.1(2) If two or more persons are appointed jointly as administrative receivers, each of them shall confirm acceptance on his own behalf; but the appointment is effective only when all those jointly appointed have complied with this Rule.

3.1(3) Confirmation under this Rule may be given on the appointee's behalf by a person whom he has duly authorised to give it.

3.1(4) In confirming his acceptance, the appointee shall state—

(a) the time and date of his receipt of notice of the appointment, and

(b) the time and date of his acceptance."

Also against r. 3.1(3) the words "[FORM 3.1]" were inserted by I(A)R 1987 (SI 1987 No. 1919), r. 3(1), Sch., Pt. 2, para. 156(1) as from 11 January 1988.

General note

This rule should be viewed in the light of s. 33. It deals with acceptance and confirmation of appointment as receiver or manager (not just an administrative receiver) despite the title of this Part and Chapter of the rules – see r. 03(2) as amended.

Rule 3.2 Notice and advertisement of appointment

3.2(1) [Notice required by s. 46(1)] This Rule relates to the notice which a person is required by section 46(1) to send and publish, when appointed as administrative receiver.

3.2(2) [Matters to be stated in notice] The following matters shall be stated in the notices sent to the company and the creditors—

(a) the registered name of the company, as at the date of the appointment, and its registered number;

(b) any other name with which the company has been registered in the 12 months preceding that date;

(c) any name under which the company has traded at any time in those 12 months, if substantially different from its then registered name;

(d) the name and address of the administrative receiver, and the date of his appointment;

(e) the name of the person by whom the appointment was made;

(f) the date of the instrument conferring the power under which the appointment was made, and a brief description of the instrument;

(g) a brief description of the assets of the company (if any) in respect of which the person appointed is not made the receiver.

3.2(3) **[Advertisement]** The administrative receiver shall cause notice of his appointment to be advertised once in the Gazette, and once in such newspaper as he thinks most appropriate for ensuring that it comes to the notice of the company's creditors.   [FORM 3.1A]

3.2(4) **[Contents of advertisement]** The advertisement shall state all the matters specified in sub-paragraphs (a) to (e) of paragraph (2) above.

History note

In r. 3.2(2) the words "notices sent to the company and the creditors" were substituted for the former word "notice" by I(A)R 1987 (SI 1987 No. 1919), r. 3(1), Sch., Pt. 1, para. 24 as from 11 January 1988.

Against r. 3.2(3) the words "[FORM 3.1A]" were inserted by I(A)R 1987 (SI 1987 No. 1919), r. 3(1), Sch., Pt. 2, para. 156(1) as from 11 January 1988.

General note

Details of the notices required to be given by an administrative receiver under IA 1986, s. 46 to the company and the public at large are here provided.

Chapter 2 — Statement of Affairs and Report to Creditors

Rule 3.3   Notice requiring statement of affairs

3.3(1) **[Notice re s. 47 statement]** Where the administrative receiver determines to require a statement of the company's affairs to be made out and submitted to him in accordance with section 47, he shall send notice to each of the persons whom he considers should be made responsible under that section, requiring them to prepare and submit the statement.   [FORM 3.1B]

3.3(2) **["The deponents"]** The persons to whom the notice is sent are referred to in this Chapter as "the deponents".

3.3(3) **[Contents of notice]** The notice shall inform each of the deponents—

(a) of the names and addresses of all others (if any) to whom the same notice has been sent;

(b) of the time within which the statement must be delivered;

(c) of the effect of section 47(6) (penalty for non-compliance); and

(d) of the application to him, and to each of the other deponents, of section 235 (duty to provide information, and to attend on the administrative receiver if required).

3.3(4) **[Instructions for preparation of statement]** The administrative receiver shall, on request, furnish each deponent with the forms required for the preparation of the statement of affairs.

History note
In r. 3.3(1) the word "Where" was substituted for the former word "If" by I(A)R 1987 (SI 1987 No. 1919), r. 3(1), Sch., Pt. 1, para. 25(1) as from 11 January 1988. Also against r. 3.3(1) the words "[FORM 3.1B]" were substituted for the former words "[FORM 3.1]" by I(A)R 1987 (SI 1987 No. 1919), r. 3(1), Sch., Pt. 2, para. 156(2) as from the same date.

In r. 3.3(4) the words "the forms required for the preparation of the statement of affairs" were substituted by I(A)R 1987 (SI 1987 No. 1919), r. 3(1), Sch., Pt. 1, para. 25(2) as from 11 January 1988: the former words were as follows:

"instructions for the preparation of the statement and with the forms required for that purpose."

General note

This rule fills out the contents of any notice given by an administrative receiver under IA 1986, s. 47 to "deponents" who must submit a statement of the company's affairs to him.

The receiver *must* demand a statement from someone: his only discretion is in determining who to "require" it from (see s. 47 itself).

Rule 3.4 Verification and filing

3.4(1) [**Form of statement and verification**]   The statement of affairs shall be in Form 3.2, shall contain all the particulars required by that form and shall be verified by affidavit by the deponents (using the same form).   [FORM 3.2]

3.4(2) [**Affidavits of concurrence**]   The administrative receiver may require any of the persons mentioned in section 47(3) to submit an affidavit of concurrence, stating that he concurs in the statement of affairs.

3.4(3) [**Affidavit may be qualified**]   An affidavit of concurrence may be qualified in respect of matters dealt with in the statement of affairs, where the maker of the affidavit is not in agreement with the deponents, or he considers the statement to be erroneous or misleading, or he is without the direct knowledge necessary for concurring with it.

3.4(4) [**Delivery of statement to receiver**]   The statement of affairs shall be delivered to the receiver by the deponent making the affidavit of verification (or by one of them, if more than one), together with a copy of the verified statement.

3.4(5) [**Delivery of affidavit of concurrence**]   Every affidavit of concurrence shall be delivered by the person who makes it, together with a copy.

3.4(6) [**Retention of copy statement etc.**]   The administrative receiver shall retain the verified copy of the statement and the affidavits of concurrence (if any) as part of the records of the receivership.

General note

This relates to the form of the statement of affairs submitted under IA 1986, s. 47.

Rule 3.5 Limited disclosure

3.5(1) [**Application to court**]   Where the administrative receiver thinks that it would prejudice the conduct of the receivership for the whole or part of the statement of affairs to be disclosed, he may apply to the court for an order of limited disclosure in respect of the statement or a specified part of it.

3.5(2)   [Powers of court]   The court may on the application order that the statement, or, as the case may be, the specified part of it, be not open to inspection otherwise than with leave of the court.

3.5(3)   [Directions]   The court's order may include directions as to the delivery of documents to the registrar of companies and the disclosure of relevant information to other persons.

General note

This allows the administrative receiver to apply to the court to censor the statement of affairs if publication would prejudice his task. Compare IA 1986, s. 48(6).

Rule 3.6   Release from duty to submit statement of affairs; extension of time

3.6(1)   [Exercise of s. 47(5) power]   The power of the administrative receiver under section 47(5) to give a release from the obligation imposed by that section, or to grant an extension of time, may be exercised at the receiver's own discretion, or at the request of any deponent.

3.6(2)   [Application to court]   A deponent may, if he requests a release or extension of time and it is refused by the receiver, apply to the court for it.

3.6(3)   [Court may dismiss application etc.]   The court may, if it thinks that no sufficient cause is shown for the application, dismiss it; but it shall not do so unless the applicant has had an opportunity to attend the court for an *ex parte* hearing, of which he has been given at least 7 days' notice.

If the application is not dismissed under this paragraph, the court shall fix a venue for it to be heard, and give notice to the deponent accordingly.

3.6(4)   [Deponent to send notice to receiver]   The deponent shall, at least 14 days before the hearing, send to the receiver a notice stating the venue and accompanied by a copy of the application, and of any evidence which he (the deponent) intends to adduce in support of it.

3.6(5)   [Appearance etc. by receiver]   The receiver may appear and be heard on the application; and, whether or not he appears, he may file a written report of any matters which he considers ought to be drawn to the court's attention.

If such a report is filed, a copy of it shall be sent by the receiver to the deponent, not later than 5 days before the hearing.

3.6(6)   [Sealed copies of order]   Sealed copies of any order made on the application shall be sent by the court to the deponent and the receiver.

3.6(7)   [Costs]   On any application under this Rule the applicant's costs shall be paid in any event by him and, unless the court otherwise orders, no allowance towards them shall be made out of the assets under the administrative receiver's control.

General note

Further details of any release given by an administrative receiver under IA 1986, s. 47(5) are provided by this rule.

Rule 3.7   Expenses of statement of affairs

3.7(1)   [Payment of expenses]   A deponent making the statement of affairs and affidavit shall be allowed, and paid by the administrative receiver out of his receipts, any expenses incurred by the deponent in so doing which the receiver thinks reasonable.

3.7(2)   [Appeal to court]   Any decision by the receiver under this Rule is subject to appeal to the court.

3.7(3)   [Effect of Rule]   Nothing in this Rule relieves a deponent from any obligation with respect to the preparation, verification and submission of the statement of affairs, or to the provision of information to the receiver.

General note

This allows a "deponent" (see r. 3.3(2)) to recover from the company's assets his expenses incurred in producing the statement of affairs.

Rule 3.8   Report to creditors

3.8(1)   [Notice under s. 48(2)]   If under section 48(2) the administrative receiver determines not to send a copy of his report to creditors, but to publish notice under paragraph (b) of that subsection, the notice shall be published in the newspaper in which the receiver's appointment was advertised.

3.8(2)   [No s. 48(2) meeting proposed]   If he proposes to apply to the court to dispense with the holding of the meeting of unsecured creditors (otherwise required by section 48(2)), he shall in his report to creditors or (as the case may be) in the notice published as above, state the venue fixed by the court for the hearing of the application.

3.8(3)   [Documents to be attached to report]   Subject to any order of the court under Rule 3.5, the copy of the receiver's report which under section 48(1) is to be sent to the registrar of companies shall have attached to it a copy of any statement of affairs under section 47, and copies of any affidavits of concurrence.

3.8(4)   [Late submission of documents]   If the statement of affairs or affidavits of concurrence, if any, have not been submitted to the receiver by the time he sends a copy of his report to the registrar of companies, he shall send a copy of the statement and any affidavits of concurrence as soon thereafter as he receives them.[FORM 3.3]

General note

If the administrative receiver opts to inform creditors under IA 1986, s. 48(2) by a notice, then this rule will apply. This rule also deals with other actions of the administrative receiver under IA 1986, s. 48.

Chapter 3 — Creditors' Meeting

Rule 3.9   Procedure for summoning meeting under s. 48(2)

3.9(1)   [Convenience of venue]   In fixing the venue for a meeting of creditors summoned under section 48(2), the administrative receiver shall have regard to the convenience of the persons who are invited to attend.

3.9(2)   [Time of meeting]   The meeting shall be summoned for commencement between 10.00 and 16.00 hours on a business day, unless the court otherwise directs.

3.9(3)   [Notice of venue]   At least 14 days' notice of the venue shall be given to all creditors of the company who are identified in the statement of affairs, or are known to the receiver and had claims against the company at the date of his appointment.

3.9(4)   [Forms of proxy]   With the notice summoning the meeting there shall be sent out forms of proxy.   [FORM 8.3]

3.9(5)   [Statement in notice]   The notice shall include a statement to the effect that creditors whose claims are wholly secured are not entitled to attend or be represented at the meeting.

3.9(6)   [Publication of notice]   Notice of the venue shall also be published in the newspaper in which the receiver's appointment was advertised.

3.9(7)   [Rule 3.11(1) statement]   The notice to creditors and the newspaper advertisement shall contain a statement of the effect of Rule 3.11(1) below (voting rights).

General note

This outlines the procedure to be followed if the administrative receiver calls a meeting of creditors under IA 1986, s. 48(2). For the definition of "venue" and "business day" see rr. 13.6 and 13.3(1).

Rule 3.10   The chairman at the meeting

3.10(1)   [Receiver or his nominee to be chairman]   The chairman at the creditors' meeting shall be the receiver, or a person nominated by him in writing to act in his place.

3.10(2)   [Nominee chairman]   A person so nominated must be either—

    (a) one who is qualified to act as an insolvency practitioner in relation to the company, or

    (b) an employee of the receiver or his firm who is experienced in insolvency matters.

General note

Where the chairman of the meeting is not the administrative receiver, then he must also be qualified as an insolvency practitioner or have experience to satisfy r. 3.10(2)(b) – see Pt. XIII of the Act.

Rule **3.11** Voting rights

3.11(1) **[Entitlement to vote]** Subject as follows, at the creditors' meeting a person is entitled to vote only if—

(a) he has given to the receiver, not later than 12.00 hours on the business day before the day fixed for the meeting, details in writing of the debt that he claims to be due to him from the company, and the claim has been duly admitted under the following provisions of this Rule, and

(b) there has been lodged with the administrative receiver any proxy which the creditor intends to be used on his behalf.

3.11(2) **[Failure to comply with r. 3.11(1)(a)]** The chairman of the meeting may allow a creditor to vote, notwithstanding that he has failed to comply with paragraph (1)(a), if satisfied that the failure was due to circumstances beyond the creditor's control.

3.11(3) **[Production of documents]** The receiver or (if other) the chairman of the meeting may call for any document or other evidence to be produced to him where he thinks it necessary for the purpose of substantiating the whole or any part of the claim.

3.11(4) **[Calculation of votes]** Votes are calculated according to the amount of a creditor's debt as at the date of the appointment of the receiver, after deducting any amounts paid in respect of that debt after that date.

3.11(5) **[Limitation on voting]** A creditor shall not vote in respect of a debt for an unliquidated amount, or any debt whose value is not ascertained, except where the chairman agrees to put upon the debt an estimated minimum value for the purpose of entitlement to vote and admits the claim for that purpose.

3.11(6) **[Secured creditors]** A secured creditor is entitled to vote only in respect of the balance (if any) of his debt after deducting the value of his security as estimated by him.

3.11(7) **[Further limitation on voting]** A creditor shall not vote in respect of a debt on, or secured by, a current bill of exchange or promissory note, unless he is willing—

(a) to treat the liability to him on the bill or note of every person who is liable on it antecedently to the company, and against whom a bankruptcy order has not been made (or, in the case of a company, which has not gone into liquidation), as a security in his hands, and

(b) to estimate the value of the security and, for the purpose of his entitlement to vote, to deduct it from his claim.

General note

This regulates the exercise of voting rights at the creditors' meeting. The voting is likely to favour larger creditors. Note the special rules for persons having unliquidated claims in damages, etc., against the company.

Rule **3.12**   Admission and rejection of claim

3.12(1)   [Power of chairman]   At the creditors' meeting the chairman has power to admit or reject a creditor's claim for the purpose of his entitlement to vote; and the power is exercisable with respect to the whole or any part of the claim.

3.12(2)   [Appeal from chairman's decision]   The chairman's decision under this Rule, or in respect of any matter arising under Rule. 3.11, is subject to appeal to the court by any creditor.

3.12(3)   [Voting subject to objection]   If the chairman is in doubt whether a claim should be admitted or rejected, he shall mark it as objected to and allow the creditor to vote, subject to his vote being subsequently declared invalid if the objection to the claim is sustained.

3.12(4)   [If chairman's decision reversed etc.]   If on an appeal the chairman's decision is reversed or varied, or a creditor's vote is declared invalid, the court may order that another meeting be summoned, or make such other order as it thinks just.

3.12(5)   [Costs of appeal]   Neither the receiver nor any person nominated by him to be chairman is personally liable for costs incurred by any person in respect of an appeal to the court under this Rule, unless the court makes an order to that effect.

General note

The chairman can regulate the acceptance of claims and therefore voting rights. Appeal to the court is possible.

Rule **3.13**   Quorum

(Omitted by the Insolvency (Amendment) Rules 1987 (S.I. 1987 No. 1919), r. 3(1), Sch., Pt. 1, para. 26 as from 11 January 1988.)

History note

Rule 3.13 formerly read as follows:

> "**3.13(1)**   The creditors' meeting is not competent to act unless there are present in person or by proxy at least 3 creditors (or all of the creditors, if their number does not exceed 3), being in either case entitled to vote.
>
> **3.13(2)**   One person constitutes a quorum if—
>
> (a) he is himself a creditor or representative under section 375 of the Companies Act, with entitlement to vote, and he holds a number of proxies sufficient to ensure that, with his own vote, paragraph (1) is complied with, or
>
> (b) being the chairman or any other person, he holds that number of proxies."

General note

See now the general provision in r. 12.4A.

Rule **3.14**   Adjournment

3.14(1)   [Chairman's decision]   The creditors' meeting shall not be adjourned, even if no quorum is present, unless the chairman decides that it is desirable; and in that case he shall adjourn it to such date, time and place as he thinks fit.

3.14(2) **[Application of r. 3.9]**　Rule 3.9(1) and (2) applies, with necessary modifications, to any adjourned meeting.

3.14(3) **[If no quorum or adjournment]**　If there is no quorum, and the meeting is not adjourned, it is deemed to have been duly summoned and held.

Rule 3.15　Resolutions and minutes

3.15(1) **[Resolution passed by majority in value]**　At the creditors' meeting, a resolution is passed when a majority (in value) of those present and voting in person or by proxy have voted in favour of it.

3.15(2) **[Record of proceedings]**　The chairman of the meeting shall cause a record to be made of the proceedings and kept as part of the records of the receivership.

3.15(3) **[Contents of record]**　The record shall include a list of the creditors who attended (personally or by proxy) and, if a creditors' committee has been established, the names and addresses of those elected to be members of the committee.

General note

Resolutions are to be passed by simple majority.

Chapter 4 — The Creditors' Committee

Rule 3.16　Constitution of committee

3.16(1) **[Three–five creditors]**　Where it is resolved by the creditors' meeting to establish a creditors' committee, the committee shall consist of at least 3 and not more than 5 creditors of the company elected at the meeting.

3.16(2) **[Eligibility]**　Any creditor of the company is eligible to be a member of the committee, so long as his claim has not been rejected for the purpose of his entitlement to vote.

3.16(3) **[Body corporate as member]**　A body corporate may be a member of the committee, but it cannot act as such otherwise than by a representative appointed under Rule 3.21 below.

General note

This details the constitution and size of any committee set up under IA 1986, s. 49.

Rule 3.17　Formalities of establishment

3.17(1) **[Certificate of due constitution]**　The creditors' committee does not come into being, and accordingly cannot act, until the administrative receiver has issued a certificate of its due constitution.

3.17(2) **[Agreement to act]** No person may act as a member of the committee unless and until he has agreed to do so and, unless the relevant proxy or authorisation contains a statement to the contrary, such agreement may be given by his proxy-holder or representative under section 375 of the Companies Act present at the meeting establishing the committee.

3.17(2A) **[Issue of certificate]** The receiver's certificate of the committee's due constitution shall not issue unless and until at least 3 of the persons who are to be members of the committee have agreed to act.

3.17(3) **[Amended certificate]** As and when the others (if any) agree to act, the receiver shall issue an amended certificate.

3.17(4) **[Certificates to be sent to registrar]** The certificate, and any amended certificate, shall be sent by the receiver to the registrar of companies.   [FORM 3.4]

3.17(5) **[Change in membership]** If, after the first establishment of the committee, there is any change in its membership, the receiver shall report the change to the registrar of companies.   [FORM 3.5]

History note

Rules 3.17(2) and (2A) were substituted for the former r. 3.17(2) by I(A)R 1987 (SI 1987 No. 1919), r. 3(1), Sch., Pt. 1, para. 27 as from 11 January 1988: the former r. 3.17(2) read as follows:

> "**3.17(2)** No person may act as a member of the committee unless and until he has agreed to do so; and the receiver's certificate of the committee's due constitution shall not issue unless and until at least 3 of the persons who are to be members of it have agreed to act."

General note

It is for the administrative receiver to certify this committee.

Rules 3.17(2) and 3.17(2A) aim to facilitate the immediate establishment of a committee after the creditors' meeting.

Rule 3.18   Functions and meetings of the committee

3.18(1) **[Functions]** The creditors' committee shall assist the administrative receiver in discharging his functions, and act in relation to him in such manner as may be agreed from time to time.

3.18(2) **[Holding of meetings]** Subject as follows, meetings of the committee shall be held when and where determined by the receiver.

3.18(3) **[First and subsequent meetings]** The receiver shall call a first meeting of the committee not later than 3 months after its establishment; and thereafter he shall call a meeting—

(a) if requested by a member of the committee or his representative (the meeting then to be held within 21 days of the request being received by the receiver), and

(b) for a specified date, if the committee has previously resolved that a meeting be held on that date.

3.18(4) **[Notice of venue]** The receiver shall give 7 days' written notice of the venue of any meeting to every member (or his representative designated for that purpose), unless in any case the requirement of notice has been waived by or on behalf of any member.

Waiver may be signified either at or before the meeting.

General note

This outlines the rôle of the committee. The committee's functions are left vague by IA 1986, s. 49. For "venue" in r. 3.18(4) see r. 13.6.

Rule 3.19   The chairman at meetings

3.19(1)   [Chairman]   Subject to Rule 3.28(3), the chairman at any meeting of the creditors' committee shall be the administrative receiver, or a person nominated by him in writing to act.

3.19(2)   [Nominated chairman]   A person so nominated must be either—

(a) one who is qualified to act as an insolvency practitioner in relation to the company, or

(b) an employee of the receiver or his firm who is experienced in insolvency matters.

General note

This is similar to r. 3.10.

Rule 3.20   Quorum

3.20   A meeting of the committee is duly constituted if due notice has been given to all the members, and at least 2 members are present or represented.

General note

The committee's quorum is two.

Rule 3.21   Committee-members' representatives

3.21(1)   [Representation]   A member of the committee may, in relation to the business of the committee, be represented by another person duly authorised by him for that purpose.

3.21(2)   [Letter of authority]   A person acting as a committee-member's representative must hold a letter of authority entitling him so to act (either generally or specially) and signed by or on behalf of the committee-member, and for this purpose any proxy or any authorisation under section 375 of the Companies Act in relation to any meeting of creditors of the company shall, unless it contains a statement to the contrary, be treated as a letter of authority to act generally signed by or on behalf of the committee-member.

3.21(3)   [Production of letter of authority]   The chairman at any meeting of the committee may call on a person claiming to act as a committee-member's representative to produce his letter of authority, and may exclude him if it appears that his authority is deficient.

3.21(4) **[Who may not be a representative]** No member may be represented by a body corporate, or by a person who is an undischarged bankrupt, or is subject to a composition or arrangement with his creditors.

3.21(5) **[No dual representation]** No person shall—

(a) on the same committee, act at one and the same time as representative of more than one committee-member, or

(b) act both as a member of the committee and as representative of another member.

3.21(6) **[Signing as representative]** Where a member's representative signs any document on the member's behalf, the fact that he so signs must be stated below his signature.

History note

In r. 3.21(2) the words from ", and for this purpose any proxy" to the end were added by I(A)R 1987 (SI 1987 No. 1919), r. 3(1), Sch., Pt. 1, para. 27 as from 11 January 1988.

General note

Committee members may appoint representatives to act for them.

Rule 3.22 Resignation

3.22 A member of the committee may resign by notice in writing delivered to the administrative receiver.

Rule 3.23 Termination of membership

3.23(1) **[Automatic termination]** Membership of the creditors' committee is automatically terminated if the member—

(a) becomes bankrupt, or compounds or arranges with his creditors, or

(b) at 3 consecutive meetings of the committee is neither present nor represented (unless at the third of those meetings it is resolved that this Rule is not to apply in his case), or

(c) ceases to be, or is found never to have been, a creditor.

3.23(2) **[Termination on bankruptcy]** However, if the cause of termination is the member's bankruptcy, his trustee in bankruptcy replaces him as a member of the committee.

General note

Note the sanction against absentees.

Rule 3.24 Removal

3.24 A member of the committee may be removed by resolution at a meeting of creditors, at least 14 days' notice having been given of the intention to move that resolution.

General note
The committee is thus controlled by the creditors' meeting.

Rule 3.25　Vacancies

3.25(1)　[Application of Rule]　The following applies if there is a vacancy in the membership of the creditors' committee.

3.25(2)　[Agreement not to fill vacancy]　The vacancy need not be filled if the administrative receiver and a majority of the remaining members of the committee so agree, provided that the total number of members does not fall below the minimum required under Rule 3.16.

3.25(3)　[Filling vacancy]　The receiver may appoint any creditor (being qualified under the Rules to be a member of the committee) to fill the vacancy, if a majority of the other members of the committee agree to the appointment and the creditor concerned consents to act.

Rule 3.26　Procedure at meetings

3.26(1)　[Votes and passing of resolutions]　At any meeting of the committee, each member of it (whether present himself or by his representative) has one vote; and a resolution is passed when a majority of the members present or represented have voted in favour of it.

3.26(2)　[Record of resolutions]　Every resolution passed shall be recorded in writing, either separately or as part of the minutes of the meeting.

3.26(3)　[Signing of records etc.]　A record of each resolution shall be signed by the chairman and kept as part of the records of the receivership.

General note
Votes at the committee are passed by a simple majority. There is no weighting of votes here.

Rule 3.27　Resolutions by post

3.27(1)　[Proposed resolution sent to members]　In accordance with this Rule, the administrative receiver may seek to obtain the agreement of members of the creditors' committee to a resolution by sending to every member (or his representative designated for the purpose) a copy of the proposed resolution.

3.27(2)　[Copies of proposed resolution]　Where the receiver makes use of the procedure allowed by this Rule, he shall send out to members of the committee or their representatives (as the case may be) a copy of any proposed resolution on which a decision is sought, which shall be set out in such a way that agreement with or dissent from each separate resolution may be indicated by the recipient on the copy so sent.

3.27(3)　[Member may require meeting]　Any member of the committee may, within 7 business days from the date of the receiver sending out a resolution, require him to summon a meeting of the committee to consider the matters raised by the resolution.

3.27(4) **[Deemed passing of resolution]** In the absence of such a request, the resolution is deemed to have been passed by the committee if and when the receiver is notified in writing by a majority of the members that they concur with it.

3.27(5) **[Copy resolution etc. with records]** A copy of every resolution passed under this Rule, and a note that the committee's concurrence was obtained, shall be kept with the records of the receivership.

History note

In r. 3.27(2) the words from "a copy of any proposed resolution" to the end were substituted by I(A)R 1987 (SI 1987 No. 1919), r. 3(1), Sch., Pt. 1, para. 29 as from 11 January 1988: the former words were as follows:·

"a statement incorporating the resolution to which their agreement is sought, each resolution (if more than one) being sent out in a separate document."

General note

Postal voting is acceptable if no member objects.

Rule 3.27(2) was amended to prevent duplication of papers and so to save money. For "business days" in r. 3.27(3), see r. 13.13(1).

Rule 3.28 Information from receiver

3.28(1) **[Notice to administrative receiver]** Where the committee resolves to require the attendance of the administrative receiver under section 49(2), the notice to him shall be in writing signed by the majority of the members of the committee for the time being. A member's representative may sign for him.

3.28(2) **[Time and place of meeting]** The meeting at which the receiver's attendance is required shall be fixed by the committee for a business day, and shall be held at such time and place as he determines.

3.28(3) **[Chairman]** Where the receiver so attends, the members of the committee may elect any one of their number to be chairman of the meeting, in place of the receiver or any nominee of his.

General note

This provides essential procedural guidance on the operation of IA 1986, s. 49(2). "Business day" (r. 3.28(2)) is defined in r. 13.13(1).

Rule 3.29 Expenses of members

3.29(1) **[Expenses defrayed out of assets]** Subject as follows, the administrative receiver shall out of the assets of the company defray any reasonable travelling expenses directly incurred by members of the creditors' committee or their representatives in relation to their attendance at the committee's meetings, or otherwise on the committee's business, as an expense of the receivership.

3.29(2) **[Non-application of r. 3.29(1)]** Paragraph (1) does not apply to any meeting of the committee held within 3 months of a previous meeting, unless the meeting in question is summoned at the instance of the administrative receiver.

Rule 3.30   Members' dealings with the company

3.30(1) **[Effect of membership]** Membership of the committee does not prevent a person from dealing with the company while the receiver is acting, provided that any transactions in the course of such dealings are entered into in good faith and for value.

3.30(2) **[Court may set aside transaction]** The court may, on the application of any person interested, set aside a transaction which appears to it to be contrary to the requirements of this Rule, and may give such consequential directions as it thinks fit for compensating the company for any loss which it may have incurred in consequence of the transaction.

General note

This allows committee members to deal with the company in good faith and for value. The court can invalidate transactions entered into in breach of this provision. Surely this power of invalidation would have been better located within the Insolvency Act itself.

Rules 3.30A   Formal defects

3.30A The acts of the creditors' committee established for any administrative receivership are valid notwithstanding any defect in the appointment, election or qualifications of any member of the committee or any committee-member's representative or in the formalities of its establishment.

History note

Rule 3.30A was inserted by I(A)R 1987 (SI 1987 No. 1919), r. 3(1), Sch., Pt. 1, para. 30 as from 11 January 1988.

General note

Rule 3.30A reflects a common philosophy in the new insolvency legislation: see, for example, s. 377 of the Act and rr. 6.156(7) and 7.55. The insertion of rr. 2.46A and 4.172A has a similar rationale.

Chapter 5 — The Administrative Receiver (Miscellaneous)

Rule 3.31   Disposal of charged property

3.31(1) **[Application of Rule]** The following applies where the administrative receiver applies to the court under section 43(1) for authority to dispose of property of the company which is subject to a security.

3.31(2) **[Venue for hearing]** The court shall fix a venue for the hearing of the application, and the receiver shall forthwith give notice of the venue to the person who is the holder of the security.

3.31(3) **[Notice of s. 43(1) order]** If an order is made under section 43(1), the receiver shall forthwith give notice of it to that person.

3.31(4) **[Sealed copies of order]** The court shall send 2 sealed copies of the order to the receiver, who shall send one of them to that person.

General note

This clarifies the position where applications are made by the administrative receiver to the court under IA 1986, s. 43(1). For "venue" in r. 3.31(2) see r. 13.6.

Rule 3.32 Abstract of receipts and payments

3.32(1) **[Administrative receiver to send accounts etc.]** The administrative receiver shall—

    (a) within 2 months after the end of 12 months from the date of his appointment, and of every subsequent period of 12 months, and

    (b) within 2 months after he ceases to act as administrative receiver,

send to the registrar of companies, to the company and to the person by whom he was appointed, and to each member of the creditors' committee (if there is one), the requisite accounts of his receipts and payments as receiver. [FORM 3.6]

3.32(2) **[Extension of time]** The court may, on the receiver's application, extend the period of 2 months referred to in paragraph (1).

3.32(3) **[Form of abstract]** The accounts are to be in the form of an abstract showing—

    (a) receipts and payments during the relevant period of 12 months, or

    (b) where the receiver has ceased to act, receipts and payments during the period from the end of the last 12-month period to the time when he so ceased (alternatively, if there has been no previous abstract, receipts and payments in the period since his appointment as administrative receiver).

3.32(4) **[Effect of Rule]** This Rule is without prejudice to the receiver's duty to render proper accounts required otherwise than as above.

3.32(5) **[Penalty on default]** If the administrative receiver makes default in complying with this Rule, he is liable to a fine and, for continued contravention, to a daily default fine.

General note

This imposes accounting requirements on the administrative receiver. Compare these with the requirements of IA 1986, s. 38. Rule 3.32(4) preserves the common law duty to account — see *Smiths Ltd* v *Middleton* [1979] 3 All ER 842. For the sanction in r. 3.32(5), see IR 1986, Sch. 5.

Rule 3.33 Resignation

3.33(1) **[Notice of intention]** Subject as follows, before resigning his office the administrative receiver shall give at least 7 days' notice of his intention to do so to—

    (a) the person by whom he was appointed,

    (b) the company or, if it is then in liquidation, its liquidator, and

    (c) in any case, to the members of the creditors' committee (if any).

3.33(2) **[Contents of notice]** A notice given under this Rule shall specify the date on which the receiver intends his resignation to take effect.

3.33(3) **[Where no notice necessary]** No notice is necessary if the receiver resigns in consequence of the making of an administration order.

History note

In r. 3.33(1) the word "and" formerly appearing at the end of subpara. (a) has been omitted and the word ", and" and subpara. (c) added at the end of subpara. (b) by I(A)R 1987 (SI 1987 No. 1919), r. 3(1), Sch., Pt. 1, para. 31 as from 11 January 1988.

General note

This expands upon the provisions of IA 1986, s. 45.

Rule 3.34 Receiver deceased

3.34 If the administrative receiver dies, the person by whom he was appointed shall, forthwith on his becoming aware of the death, give notice of it to—

    (a) the registrar of companies,   [FORM 3.7]

    (b) the company or, if it is in liquidation, the liquidator, and

    (c) in any case, to the members of the creditors' committee (if any).

History note

In r. 3.34 the word "and" formerly appearing at the end of subpara. (a) has been omitted and the word ", and" and subpara. (c) added at the end of subpara. (b) by I(A)R 1987 (SI 1987 No. 1919), r. 3(1), Sch., Pt. 1, para. 32 as from 11 January 1988.

Rule 3.35 Vacation of office

3.35(1) **[Notice]** The administrative receiver, on vacating office on completion of the receivership, or in consequence of his ceasing to be qualified as an insolvency practitioner, shall forthwith give notice of his doing so—

    (a) to the company or, if it is in liquidation, the liquidator, and

    (b) to the members of the creditors' committee (if any).

3.35(2) **[Indorsement on notice]** Where the receiver's office is vacated, the notice to the registrar of companies which is required by section 45(4) may be given by means of an indorsement on the notice required by section 405(2) of the Companies Act (notice for the purposes of the register of charges).

History note

In r. 3.35(1), subpara. (a) was substituted and in subpara. (b) the words "in any case," formerly appearing at the beginning, were omitted by I(A)R 1987 (SI 1987 No. 1919), r. 3(1), Sch., Pt. 1, para. 33 as from 11 January 1988: subpara. (a) formerly read as follows:

    "(a) if the company is in liquidation, to the liquidator, and".

General note

This rule should be viewed in the light of IA 1986, s. 45. As a result of CA 1989, at some unspecified time in the future CA 1985, s. 405(2) will be renumbered as s. 409(2).

Chapter 6 — VAT Bad Debt Relief

Rule 3.36   Issue of certificate of insolvency

3.36(1)   [Duty of administrative receiver]   In accordance with this Rule, it is the duty of the administrative receiver to issue a certificate in the terms of paragraph (b) of section 22(3) of the Value Added Tax Act 1983 (which specifies the circumstances in which a company is deemed insolvent for the purposes of that section) forthwith upon his forming the opinion described in that paragraph.

3.36(2)   [Contents of certificate]   There shall in the certificate be specified—

- (a) the name of the company and its registered number;
- (b) the name of the administrative receiver and the date of his appointment; and
- (c) the date on which the certificate is issued.

3.36(3)   [Title of certificate]   The certificate shall be intituled "CERTIFICATE OF INSOLVENCY FOR THE PURPOSES OF SECTION 22(3)(B) OF THE VALUE ADDED TAX ACT 1983".

General note

This obliges the administrative receiver to issue a certificate of insolvency for the purposes of VAT bad debt relief. See the note to r. 2.56.

Rule 3.37   Notice to creditors

3.37(1)   [Time for giving notice]   Notice of the issue of the certificate shall be given by the administrative receiver within 3 months of his appointment or within 2 months of issuing the certificate, whichever is the later, to all of the company's unsecured creditors of whose address he is then aware and who have, to his knowledge, made supplies to the company, with a charge to value added tax, at any time before his appointment.

3.37(2)   [Later notice]   Thereafter, he shall give the notice to any such creditor of whose address and supplies to the company he becomes aware.

3.37(3)   [No obligation re certificate]   He is not under obligation to provide any creditor with a copy of the certificate.

General note

This provides for dissemination of the fact of the issue of the certificate under r. 3.36 to creditors and suppliers.

Rule 3.38   Preservation of certificate with company's records

3.38(1)   [Retention of certificate]   The certificate shall be retained with the company's accounting records, and section 222 of the Companies Act (where and for how long records are to be kept) shall apply to the certificate as it applies to those records.

3.38(2) **[Duty of administrative receiver]** It is the duty of the administrative receiver, on vacating office, to bring this Rule to the attention of the directors or (as the case may be) any successor of his as receiver.

PART 4 — COMPANIES WINDING UP

Chapter 1 — The Scheme of this Part of the Rules

Rule 4.1 Voluntary winding up; winding up by the court

4.1(1) **[Members' voluntary winding up]** In a members' voluntary winding up, the Rules in this Part do not apply, except as follows—

   (a) Rule 4.3 applies in the same way as it applies in a creditors' voluntary winding up;

   (b) Rule 4.72 (additional provisions concerning meetings in relation to Bank of England and Deposit Protection Board) applies in the winding up of authorised institutions or former authorised institutions within the meaning of the Banking Act 1987, whether members' or creditors' voluntary or by the court;

   (c) Chapters 9 (proof of debts in a liquidation), 10 (secured creditors), 15 (disclaimer) and 18 (special manager) apply wherever, and in the same way as, they apply in a creditors' voluntary winding up;

   (d) Section F of Chapter 11 (the liquidator) applies only in a members' voluntary winding up, and not otherwise;

   (e) Section G of that Chapter (court's power to set aside certain transactions; rule against solicitation) applies in any winding up, whether members' or creditors' voluntary or by the court;

   (f) Rule 4.182A applies only in a members' voluntary winding up, and not otherwise; and

   (g) Rule 4.223-CVL (liquidator's statements) applies in the same way as it applies in a creditors' voluntary winding up.

4.1(2) **[Creditors' voluntary winding up and winding up by court]** Subject as follows, the Rules in this Part apply both in a creditors' voluntary winding up and in a winding up by the court; and for this purpose a winding up is treated as a creditors' voluntary winding up if, and from the time when, the liquidator forms the opinion that the company will be unable to pay its debts in full, and determines accordingly to summon a creditors' meeting under section 95.

4.1(3) **[Creditors' voluntary winding up]** The following Chapters, or Sections of Chapters, of this Part do not apply in a creditors' voluntary winding up—

Chapter 2 — The statutory demand;

Chapter 3 — Petition to winding-up order;

Chapter 4 — Petition by contributories;

Chapter 5 — Provisional liquidator;

Chapter 11 (Section F) — The liquidator in a members' voluntary winding up;

Chapter 13 — The liquidation committee where winding up follows immediately on administration;

Chapter 16 — Settlement of list of contributories;

Chapter 17 — Calls;

Chapter 19 — Public examination of company officers and others; and

Chapter 21 (Section A) — Return of capital;

Chapter 21 (Section C) — Dissolution after winding up.

4.1(4) ["(NO CVL APPLICATION)"] Where at the head of any Rule, or at the end of any paragraph of a Rule, there appear the words "(NO CVL APPLICATION)", this signifies that the Rule or, as the case may be, the paragraph does not apply in a creditors' voluntary winding up.

However, this does not affect the court's power to make orders under section 112 (exercise in relation to voluntary winding up of powers available in winding up by the court).

4.1(5) ["CVL"] Where to any Rule or paragraph there is given a number incorporating the letters "CVL", that signifies that the Rule or (as the case may be) the paragraph applies in a creditors' voluntary winding up, and not in a winding up by the court.

History note

Rule 4.1(1) was substituted by I(A)R 1987 (SI 1987 No. 1919), r. 3(1), Sch., Pt. 1, para. 34(1) as from 11 January 1988: r. 4.1(1) formerly read as follows:

"**4.1(1)** In a members' voluntary winding up, the Rules in this Part do not apply, except as follows—

(a) Chapters 9 (proof of debts in a liquidation), 10 (secured creditors) and 18 (special manager) apply wherever, and in the same way as, they apply in a creditors' voluntary winding up;

(b) Section B of Chapter 8 (additional provisions concerning meetings in relation to Bank of England and Deposit Protection Board) applies in the winding up of recognised banks, etc., whether members' or creditors' voluntary or by the court;

(c) Section F of Chapter 11 (the liquidator) applies only in a members' voluntary winding up, and not otherwise;

(d) Section G of that Chapter (court's power to set aside certain transactions; rule against solicitation) applies in any winding up, whether members' or creditors' voluntary or by the court; and

(e) Section B of Chapter 21 (liquidator's statements) applies in the same way as it applies in a creditors' voluntary winding up."

In r. 4.1(2) the words "winding up" were inserted after the words "creditors' voluntary" and before the words "if, and from the time" by I(A)R 1987 (SI 1987 No. 1919), r. 3(1), Sch., Pt. 1, para. 34(2) as from 11 January 1988.

In r. 4.1(3) the line beginning "Chapter 11 (Section F)" was inserted and the line beginning "Chapter 21 (Section C)" was added by I(A)R 1987 (SI 1987 No. 1919), r. 3(1), Sch., Pt. 1, para. 34(3) as from 11 January 1988.

General note

The rules in this Part do not apply to a members' voluntary winding up, except as stated in r. 4.1(1).

Section F of Ch. 11 (rr. 4.139–4.148) applies *only* in a members' voluntary winding up.

The remaining rules apply generally to *both* a winding up by the court *and* a creditors' voluntary winding up (including a creditors' voluntary winding up that begins as a members' winding up but later proves insolvent); but some rules or parts of rules apply only in a winding up by the court, and these are marked NO CVL APPLICATION; while others apply only in a creditors' voluntary winding up, and are marked CVL.

The amendments made by I(A)R 1987 have corrected drafting deficiencies in the original rules.

Rule **4.2**   Winding up by the court: the various forms of petition (NO CVL APPLICATION)

4.2(1)   [S. 122(1)]   Insofar as the Rules in this Part apply to winding up by the court, they apply (subject as follows) whether the petition for winding up is presented under any of the several paragraphs of section 122(1), namely—

> paragraph (a) — company special resolution for winding up by the court;

> paragraph (b) — public company without certificate under section 117 of the Companies Act;

> paragraph (c) — old public company;

> paragraph (d) — company not commencing business after formation, or suspending business;

> paragraph (e) — number of company's members reduced below 2;

> paragraph (f) — company unable to pay its debts;

> paragraph (g) — court's power under the "just and equitable" rule,

or under any enactment enabling the presentation of a winding-up petition.

4.2(2)   [Petitioners]   Except as provided by the following two paragraphs or by any particular Rule, the Rules apply whether the petition for winding up is presented by the company, the directors, one or more creditors, one or more contributories, the Secretary of State, the official receiver, or any person entitled under any enactment to present such a petition.

4.2(3)   [Application of Ch. 2]   Chapter 2 (statutory demand) has no application except in relation to an unpaid creditor of the company satisfying section 123(1)(a) (the first of the two cases specified, in relation to England and Wales, of the company being deemed unable to pay its debts within section 122(1)(f)) or section 222(1) (the equivalent provision in relation to unregistered companies).

4.2(4)   [Application of Ch. 3 and 4]   Chapter 3 (petition to winding-up order) has no application to a petition for winding up presented by one or more contributories; and in relation to a petition so presented Chapter 4 has effect.

In r. 4.2 the words "(NO CVL APPLICATION)" in the heading were inserted by I(A)R 1987 (SI 1987 No. 1919), r. 3(1), Sch., Pt. 1, para. 35 as from 11 January 1988.

General note

Rule 4.2(1) lists all the circumstances in which a company may be wound up by the court, and r. 4.2(2) all the possible petitioners: see IA 1986, ss. 122, 124. Where a receiver or administrator or the supervisor of a voluntary arrangement petitions, he does so in the name of the company: see the note to s. 124.

Rule 4.3   Time-limits

4.3   Where by any provision of the Act or the Rules about winding up, the time for doing anything is limited, the court may extend the time, either before or after it has expired, on such terms, if any, as it thinks fit.

General note

See Practice Direction from the Companies Court in [1987] 1 All ER 107 (reproduced in Appendix IV of this Guide).

Chapter 2 — The Statutory Demand (NO CVL APPLICATION)

Rule 4.4   Preliminary

4.4(1)   **[Non-application of Ch. 2]**   This Chapter does not apply where a petition for the winding up of a company is presented under section 124 on or after the date on which the Rules come into force and the petition is based on failure to comply with a written demand served on the company before that date.

4.4(2)   **["The statutory demand"]**   A written demand served by a creditor on a company under section 123(1)(a) (registered companies) or 222(1)(a) (unregistered companies) is known in winding-up proceedings as "the statutory demand".

4.4(3)   **[Must be dated and signed]**   The statutory demand must be dated, and be signed either by the creditor himself or by a person stating himself to be authorised to make the demand on the creditor's behalf.

(See general note after r. 4.6.)

Rule 4.5   Form and content of statutory demand

4.5(1)   **[Form of demand]**   The statutory demand must state the amount of the debt and the consideration for it (or, if there is no consideration, the way in which it arises)
                                                                [FORM 4.1]

4.5(2)   **[Interest and accruing charges]**   If the amount claimed in the demand includes—

(a) any charge by way of interest not previously notified to the company as included in its liability, or

(b) any other charge accruing from time to time,

the amount or rate of the charge must be separately identified, and the grounds on which payment of it is claimed must be stated.

In either case the amount claimed must be limited to that which has accrued due at the date of the demand.

(See general note after r. 4.6.)

Rule 4.6 Information to be given in statutory demand

4.6(1) [Explanation of demand generally] The statutory demand must include an explanation to the company of the following matters—

(a) the purpose of the demand, and the fact that, if the demand is not complied with, proceedings may be instituted for the winding up of the company;

(b) the time within which it must be complied with, if that consequence is to be avoided; and

(c) the methods of compliance which are open to the company.

4.6(2) [Information re named individuals] Information must be provided for the company as to how an officer or representative of it may enter into communication with one or more named individuals, with a view to securing or compounding for the debt to the creditor's satisfaction.

In the case of any individual so named in the demand, his address and telephone number (if any) must be given.

General note to rr. 4.4–4.6

This chapter has no application except in relation to an unpaid creditor of the company satisfying CA 1986, s. 123(1)(*a*) or s. 222(1): see r. 4.2(3).

Under IA 1986, s. 123, a written demand for the payment of a debt must be "in the prescribed form". These rules deal with the form and content of the statutory demand.

A statutory demand may be effective despite some inaccuracy, e.g. in relation to the sum stated to be due: see the note to s. 123.

Chapter 3 — Petition to Winding-up Order
(NO CVL APPLICATION)
(No Application to Petition by Contributories)

Rule 4.7 Presentation and filing of petition

4.7(1) [Filing with verifying affidavit] The petition, verified by affidavit in accordance with Rule 4.12 below, shall be filed in court.   [FORM 4.2]
[FORM 4.3]

4.7(2)   [Receipt for deposit payable on presentation]   No petition shall be filed unless there is produced with it the receipt for the deposit payable on presentation.

4.7(3)   [Petitioner other than company]   If the petitioner is other than the company itself, there shall be delivered with the petition—

(a) one copy for service on the company, and

(b) one copy to be exhibited to the affidavit verifying service.

4.7(4)   [Accompanying documents]   There shall in any case be delivered with the petition—

(a) if the company is in course of being wound up voluntarily, and a liquidator has been appointed, one copy of the petition to be sent to him;

(b) if an administration order is in force in relation to the company, one copy to be sent to the administrator;

(c) if an administrative receiver has been appointed in relation to the company, one copy to be sent to him;

(d) if there is in force for the company a voluntary arrangement under Part I of the Act, one copy for the supervisor of the arrangement; and

(e) if the company is an authorised institution or former authorised institution within the meaning of the Banking Act 1987 and the petitioner is not the Bank of England, one copy to be sent to the Bank.

4.7(5)   [Sealed copies issued to petitioner]   Each of the copies delivered shall have applied to it the seal of the court, and shall be issued to the petitioner.

4.7(6)   [Venue for hearing]   The court shall fix a venue for the hearing of the petition; and this shall be endorsed on any copy issued to the petitioner under paragraph (5).

4.7(7)   [Petition by administrator]   Where a petition is filed at the instance of a company's administrator the petition shall—

(a) be expressed to be the petition of the company by its administrator,

(b) state the name of the administrator, the number of the petition on which the administration order was made and the date of that order, and

(c) contain an application under section 18 requesting that the administration order be discharged and that the court make any such order consequential upon that discharge as it thinks fit.

4.7(8)   [Filing if in administration or voluntary arrangement]   Any petition filed in relation to a company in respect of which there is in force an administration order or a voluntary arrangement under Part I of the Act shall be presented to the court which made the administration order or, as the case may be, to which the nominee's report under section 2 was submitted.

4.7(9)   [Treatment of petition of administrator or supervisor]   Any petition such as is mentioned in paragraph (7) above or presented by the supervisor of a voluntary arrangement under Part I of the Act in force for the company shall be treated as if it were a petition filed by contributories, and Chapter 4 in this Part of the Rules shall apply accordingly.

4.7(10) [Request for appointment under s. 140] Where a petition contains a request for the appointment of a person as liquidator in accordance with section 140 (appointment of former administrator or supervisor as liquidator) the person whose appointment is sought shall, not less than 2 days before the return day for the petition, file in court a report including particulars of—

    (a) a date on which he notified creditors of the company, either in writing or at a meeting of creditors, of the intention to seek his appointment as liquidator, such date to be at least 10 days before the day on which the report under this paragraph is filed, and

    (b) details of any response from creditors to that notification, including any objections to his appointment.

History note

In r. 4.7(4)(*e*) the words from "an authorised institution" to "Banking Act 1987" were substituted by I(A)R 1987 (SI 1987 No. 1919), r. 3(1), Sch., Pt. 1, para. 36(1) as from 11 January 1988: the former words were as follows:

    "(i) a recognised bank or licensed institution within the meaning of the Banking Act 1979, or

    (ii) an institution to which sections 16 and 18 of that Act apply as if it were licensed."

Rules 4.7(7) to (10) were added by I(A)R 1987 (SI 1987 No. 1919), r. 3(1), Sch., Pt. 1, para. 36(2) as from 11 January 1988.

(See general note after r. 4.14.)

Rule **4.8** Service of petition

4.8(1) [Application of Rule] The following paragraphs apply as regards service of the petition on the company (where the petitioner is other than the company itself); and references to the petition are to a copy of the petition bearing the seal of the court in which it is presented.

4.8(2) [Service] Subject as follows, the petition shall be served at the company's registered office, that is to say—

    (a) the place which is specified, in the company's statement delivered under section 10 of the Companies Act as the intended situation of its registered office on incorporation, or

    (b) if notice has been given by the company to the registrar of companies under section 287 of that Act (change of registered office), the place specified in that notice or, as the case may be, in the last such notice.

4.8(3) [Means of service] Service of the petition at the registered office may be effected in any of the following ways—

    (a) it may be handed to a person who there and then acknowledges himself to be, or to the best of the server's knowledge, information and belief is, a director or other officer, or employee, of the company; or

    (b) it may be handed to a person who there and then acknowledges himself to be authorised to accept service of documents on the company's behalf; or

    (c) in the absence of any such person as is mentioned in sub-paragraph (a) or (b), it may be deposited at or about the registered office in such a way that it is likely to come to the notice of a person attending at the office.

4.8(4)   [Service at registered office not practicable etc.]   If for any reason service at the registered office is not practicable, or the company has no registered office or is an unregistered company, the petition may be served on the company by leaving it at the company's last known principal place of business in such a way that it is likely to come to the attention of a person attending there, or by delivering it to the secretary or some director, manager or principal officer of the company, wherever that person may be found.

4.8(5)   [Oversea company]   In the case of an oversea company, service may be effected in any manner provided for by section 695 of the Companies Act.

4.8(6)   [Service in another manner]   If for any reason it is impracticable to effect service as provided by paragraphs (2) to (5), the petition may be served in such other manner as the court may approve or direct.

4.8(7)   [Application under r. 4.8(6)]   Application for leave of the court under paragraph (6) may be made *ex parte*, on affidavit stating what steps have been taken to comply with paragraphs (2) to (5), and the reasons why it is impracticable to effect service as there provided.

History note

Rule 4.8(4) was substituted by I(A)R 1987 (SI 1987 No. 1919), r. 3(1), Sch., Pt. 1, para. 37(1) as from 11 January 1988: r. 4.8(4) formerly read as follows:

> **"4.8(4)**   If for any reason service at the registered office is not practicable, or the company has no registered office, or it is an unregistered company, the petition may be served at the company's last known principal place of business in England and Wales, or at some place in England and Wales at which it has carried on business, by handing it to such a person as is mentioned in paragraph (3)(a) or (b) above."

In r. 4.8(6) the words "approve or" after the words "the court may" were inserted by I(A)R 1987 (SI 1987 No. 1919), r. 3(1), Sch., Pt. 1, para. 37(2) as from 11 January 1988.

Rule 4.8(6)

See Practice Direction by Companies Court in [1987] 1 All ER 107 (reproduced in Appendix IV of this Guide).

(See general note after r. 4.14.)

Rule 4.9   Proof of service

4.9(1)   [Affidavit of service]   Service of the petition shall be proved by affidavit, specifying the manner of service.   [FORM 4.4]
                                                                          [FORM 4.5]

4.9(2)   [Exhibits]   The affidavit shall have exhibited to it—

(a) a sealed copy of the petition, and

(b) if substituted service has been ordered, a sealed copy of the order;

and it shall be filed in court immediately after service.

(See general note after r. 4.14.)

Rule **4.10**   Other persons to receive copies of petition

4.10(1)   [Company being wound up voluntarily]   If to the petitioner's knowledge the company is in course of being wound up voluntarily, a copy of the petition shall be sent by him to the liquidator.

4.10(2)   [Administrative receiver appointed etc.]   If to the petitioner's knowledge an administrative receiver has been appointed in relation to the company, or an administration order is in force in relation to it, a copy of the petition shall be sent by him to the receiver or, as the case may be, the administrator.

4.10(3)   [Voluntary arrangement in force]   If to the petitioner's knowledge there is in force for the company a voluntary arrangement under Part I of the Act, a copy of the petition shall be sent by him to the supervisor of the voluntary arrangement.

4.10(4)   [If company is authorised institution under Banking Act]   If the company is an authorised institution or former authorised institution within the meaning of the Banking Act 1987, a copy of the petition shall be sent by the petitioner to the Bank of England.

This does not apply if the petitioner is the Bank of England itself.

4.10(5)   [Time for sending copy of petition]   A copy of the petition which is required by this Rule to be sent shall be despatched on the next business day after the day on which the petition is served on the company.

History note

In r. 4.10(4) the words from "an authorised institution" to "Banking Act 1987" were substituted by I(A)R 1987 (SI 1987 No. 1919), r. 3(1), Sch., Pt. 1, para. 38 as from 11 January 1988: the former words read as follows:

"a recognised bank or a licensed institution within the meaning of the Banking Act 1979, or an institution to which sections 16 and 18 of that Act apply as if it were a licensed institution".

(See general note after r. 4.14.)

Rule **4.11**   Advertisement of petition

4.11(1)   [Advertisement in Gazette]   Unless the court otherwise directs, the petition shall be advertised once in the Gazette.   [FORM 4.6]

4.11(2)   [Time for advertisement]   The advertisement must be made to appear—

(a) if the petitioner is the company itself, not less than 7 business days before the day appointed for the hearing, and

(b) otherwise, not less than 7 business days after service of the petition on the company, nor less than 7 business days before the day so appointed.

4.11(3)   [Newspaper instead of Gazette]   The court may, if compliance with paragraph (2) is not reasonably practicable, direct that advertisement of the petition be made to appear in a specified newspaper, instead of in the Gazette.

4.11(4) **[Contents of advertisement]** The advertisement of the petition must state—

   (a) the name of the company and the address of its registered office, or—

      (i) in the case of an unregistered company, the address of its principal place of business;

      (ii) in the case of an oversea company, the address at which service of the petition was effected;

   (b) the name and address of the petitioner;

   (c) where the petitioner is the company itself, the address of its registered office or, in the case of an unregistered company, of its principal place of business;

   (d) the date on which the petition was presented;

   (e) the venue fixed for the hearing of the petition;

   (f) the name and address of the petitioner's solicitor (if any); and

   (g) that any person intending to appear at the hearing (whether to support or oppose the petition) must give notice of his intention in accordance with Rule 4.16.

4.11(5) **[Court may dismiss petition]** If the petition is not duly advertised in accordance with this Rule, the court may dismiss it.

(See general note after r. 4.14.)

Rule **4.12**   Verification of petition

4.12(1) **[Verifying affidavit]** The petition shall be verified by an affidavit that the statements in the petition are true, or are true to the best of the deponent's knowledge, information and belief.   [FORM 4.2]
[FORM 4.3]

4.12(2) **[Debts due to different creditors]** If the petition is in respect of debts due to different creditors, the debts to each creditor must be separately verified.

4.12(3) **[Petition to be exhibited]** The petition shall be exhibited to the affidavit verifying it.

4.12(4) **[Who shall make affidavit]** The affidavit shall be made—

   (a) by the petitioner (or if there are two or more petitioners, any one of them), or

   (b) by some person such as a director, company secretary or similar company officer, or a solicitor, who has been concerned in the matters giving rise to the presentation of the petition, or

   (c) by some responsible person who is duly authorised to make the affidavit and has the requisite knowledge of those matters.

4.12(5) **[Where deponent not petitioner]** Where the deponent is not the petitioner himself, or one of the petitioners, he must in the affidavit identify himself and state—

(a) the capacity in which, and the authority by which, he makes it, and

(b) the means of his knowledge of the matters sworn to in the affidavit.

4.12(6) **[Affidavit as prima facie evidence]** The affidavit is prima facie evidence of the statements in the petition to which it relates.

4.12(7) **[Affidavit verifying more than one petition]** An affidavit verifying more than one petition shall include in its title the names of the companies to which it relates and shall set out, in respect of each company, the statements relied on by the petitioner; and a clear and legible photocopy of the affidavit shall be filed with each petition which it verifies.

(See general note after r. 4.14.)

Rule 4.13 Persons entitled to copy of petition

4.13 Every director, contributory or creditor of the company is entitled to be furnished by the solicitor for the petitioner (or by the petitioner himself, if acting in person) with a copy of the petition within 2 days after requiring it, on payment of the appropriate fee.

(See general note after r. 4.14.)

Rule 4.14 Certificate of compliance

4.14(1) **[Filing in court]** The petitioner or his solicitor shall, at least 5 days before the hearing of the petition, file in court a certificate of compliance with the Rules relating to service and advertisement.   [FORM 4.7]

4.14(2) **[Contents of certificate]** The certificate shall show—

(a) the date of presentation of the petition,

(b) the date fixed for the hearing, and

(c) the date or dates on which the petition was served and advertised in compliance with the Rules.

A copy of the advertisement of the petition shall be filed in court with the certificate.

4.14(3) **[Effect of non-compliance]** Non-compliance with this Rule is a ground on which the court may, if it thinks fit, dismiss the petition.

General note to rr. 4.7–4.14

These rules deal with the filing, service, advertisement and verification of the petition. Any director, contributory or creditor of the company is entitled to a copy of the petition on payment of the appropriate fee (r. 4.13).

The court is given a discretion by r. 4.11(5) to dismiss the petition if it has not been duly advertised. It has been the practice of the court since the ruling in *Re Signland Ltd* [1982] 2 All ER 609 to strike out any petition where the petitioning creditor has not observed the provisions as to time set out in r. 4.11(2)(*b*), and in particular where the petition has been advertised without giving the company the prescribed seven days' notice. However, in two more recent cases Hoffmann J has exercised his discretion to allow a petition to stand where the company had changed its registered office and the petition had been served at the address of the company's former office. In *Re Corbenstoke Ltd* (1989) 5 BCC 197 the mistake was due to an error made in the companies registry, and the petitioning creditor was in no way to blame; it also appeared that the company had suffered no prejudice. In the second case, *Re Garton (Western) Ltd* (1989) 5 BCC 198, the solicitors acting for the petitioner had relied on a stale search, but there was evidence that even a petitioner who had searched diligently might have found the register somewhat out of date. The petition was not struck out but adjourned on terms as to costs.

The word "advertised" has two meanings: (1) a paid announcement in a general publication, and (2) notifying the existence of the matter in question. Where the court has made an order restraining the advertisement of a winding-up petition, the word is to be construed in a wide sense, and any communication to an unauthorised party (e.g. informing the company's bank) of the fact that the petition has been presented will be a breach of the order: see the note to r. 4.23(1)(*c*). But in r. 4.11 and 4.14 the word refers to publication in the Gazette – i.e. is used in the former sense (*SN Group plc* v *Barclays Bank plc* [1993] BCC 506), and a notification to a third party of the existence of the petition will not in itself be a breach or r. 4.11 or 4.14. Such a communication may, however be open to condemnation as an abuse of the process of the court, if made for an improper purpose such as putting pressure on the company: if so, the petition may be struck out for this reason (*Re Bill Hennessy Associates Ltd* [1992] BCC 386).

The amendment made by the new r. 4.7(7) goes some way to meet drafting deficiencies in the Act, but it does not deal with the case of a petition instituted by an administrative receiver (as might have been expected) or meet all the problems that may arise with a supervisor's petition under IA 1986, s. 7(4)(*b*). See the note to s. 124(1).

The procedure on a petition presented by contributories is set out in Ch. 4 (rr. 4.22ff).

The new r. 4.8(4) enables service to be effected more easily on a company which has ceased trading.

An application to restrain the presentation of a winding-up petition should be by originating motion: see the Practice Direction of 11 July 1988, [1988] PCC 404.

History note

In r. 4.11(3) the words "London morning newspaper, or other" formerly appearing before the word "newspaper" were omitted by I(A)R 1991 (SI 1991 No. 495), r. 3, Sch., para. 1 as from 2 April 1991.

Rule 4.15   Leave for petitioner to withdraw

4.15   If at least 5 days before the hearing the petitioner, on an *ex parte* application, satisfies the court that—

(a) the petition has not been advertised, and

(b) no notices (whether in support or in opposition) have been received by him with reference to the petition, and

(c) the company consents to an order being made under this Rule,

the court may order that the petitioner has leave to withdraw the petition on such terms as to costs as the parties may agree.   [FORM 4.8]

General note

The circumstances in which a petition may be withdrawn are limited to those prescribed. See Practice Direction by Companies Court in [1987] 1 All ER 107 (reproduced in Appendix IV of this Guide).

Rule 4.16 Notice of appearance

4.16(1) [Notice of intention] Every person who intends to appear on the hearing of the petition shall give to the petitioner notice of his intention in accordance with this Rule. [FORM 4.9]

4.16(2) [Contents of notice] The notice shall specify—

    (a) the name and address of the person giving it, and any telephone number and reference which may be required for communication with him or with any other person (to be also specified in the notice) authorised to speak or act on his behalf;

    (b) whether his intention is to support or oppose the petition; and

    (c) the amount and nature of his debt.

4.16(3) [Address for sending notice] The notice shall be sent to the petitioner at the address shown for him in the court records, or in the advertisement of the petition required by Rule 4.11; or it may be sent to his solicitor.

4.16(4) [Time for sending notice] The notice shall be sent so as to reach the addressee not later than 16.00 hours on the business day before that which is appointed for the hearing (or, where the hearing has been adjourned, for the adjourned hearing).

4.16(5) [Effect of non-compliance] A person failing to comply with this Rule may appear on the hearing of the petition only with the leave of the court.

(See general note after r. 4.21A.)

Rule 4.17 List of appearances

4.17(1) [Petitioner to prepare list] The petitioner shall prepare for the court a list of the persons (if any) who have given notice under Rule 4.16, specifying their names and addresses and (if known to him) their respective solicitors. [FORM 4.10]

4.17(2) [Whether creditors support or oppose] Against the name of each creditor in the list it shall be stated whether his intention is to support the petition, or to oppose it.

4.17(3) [Copy of list handed to court] On the day appointed for the hearing of the petition, a copy of the list shall be handed to the court before the commencement of the hearing.

4.17(4) [Leave under r. 4.16(5)] If any leave is given under Rule 4.16(5), the petitioner shall add to the list the same particulars in respect of the person to whom leave has been given.

(See general note after r. 4.21A.)

Rule 4.18 Affidavit in opposition

4.18(1) [Filing in court] If the company intends to oppose the petition, its affidavit in opposition shall be filed in court not less than 7 days before the date fixed for the hearing.

4.18(2) **[Copy to petitioner]** A copy of the affidavit shall be sent by the company to the petitioner, forthwith after filing.

(See general note after r. 4.21A.)

Rule **4.19** Substitution of creditor or contributory for petitioner

4.19(1) **[Application of Rule]** This Rule applies where a person petitions and is subsequently found not entitled to do so, or where the petitioner—

- (a) fails to advertise his petition within the time prescribed by the Rules or such extended time as the court may allow, or
- (b) consents to withdraw his petition, or to allow it to be dismissed, consents to an adjournment, or fails to appear in support of his petition when it is called on in court on the day originally fixed for the hearing, or on a day to which it is adjourned, or
- (c) appears, but does not apply for an order in the terms of the prayer of his petition.

4.19(2) **[Power of court]** The court may, on such terms as it thinks just, substitute as petitioner any creditor or contributory who in its opinion would have a right to present a petition, and who is desirous of prosecuting it.

4.19(3) **[Making of order]** An order of the court under this Rule may, where a petitioner fails to advertise his petition within the time prescribed by these Rules, or consents to withdraw his petition, be made at any time.

General note
See Practice Direction by Companies Court in [1987] 1 All ER 107 (reproduced in Appendix IV of this Guide) and *Re Goldthorpe & Lacey Ltd* (1987) 3 BCC 595. See also general note after r. 4.21A.

Rule **4.20** Notice and settling of winding-up order

4.20(1) **[Notice to official receiver]** When a winding-up order has been made, the court shall forthwith give notice of the fact to the official receiver.   [FORM 4.11]
[FORM 4.12]
[FORM 4.13]

4.20(2) **[Documents to be left at court]** The petitioner and every other person who has appeared on the hearing of the petition shall, not later than the business day following that on which the order is made, leave at the court all the documents required for enabling the order to be completed forthwith.

4.20(3) **[Appointment of venue]** It is not necessary for the court to appoint a venue for any person to attend to settle the order, unless in any particular case the special circumstances make an appointment necessary.

(See general note after r. 4.21A.)

Rule **4.21** Transmission and advertisement of order

4.21(1) **[Copy of orders to official receiver]** When the winding-up order has been made, 3 copies of it, sealed with the seal of the court, shall be sent forthwith by the court to the official receiver.

4.21(2)   [Service on company etc.]   The official receiver shall cause a sealed copy of the order to be served on the company by prepaid letter addressed to it at its registered office (if any) or, if there is no registered office, at its principal or last known principal place of business.

Alternatively, the order may be served on such other person or persons, or in such other manner, as the court directs.

4.21(3)   [Copy of order to registrar]   The official receiver shall forward to the registrar of companies the copy of the order which by section 130(1) is directed to be so forwarded by the company.

4.21(4)   [Advertisement]   The official receiver shall forthwith—

    (a) cause the order to be gazetted, and

    (b) advertise the order in such newspaper as the official receiver may select.

(See general note after r. 4.21A)

Rule **4.21A**   Expenses of voluntary arrangement

4.21A   Where a winding-up order is made and there is at the time of the presentation of the petition in force for the company a voluntary arrangement under Part I of the Act, any expenses properly incurred as expenses of the administration of the arrangement in question shall be a first charge on the company's assets.

History note

In r. 4.21(4) the word "local" formerly appearing before the word "newspaper" was omitted by I(A)R 1991 (SI 1991 No. 495), r. 3, Sch., para. 2 as from 2 April 1991.

    Rule 4.21A was inserted by I(A)R 1987 (SI 1987 No. 1919), r. 3(1), Sch., Pt. 1, para. 39 as from 11 January 1988.

General note to rr. 4.16–4.21A

These rules deal with the conduct of the hearing, and the steps which are to be taken once a winding-up order has been made. This includes the registration of a copy of the winding-up order in the Companies Registry.

    Where the court orders the rescission of a winding-up order under r. 7.47, the registrar of companies may be directed to remove the order from his files; but he may, if he thinks it desirable, record the fact that it has been removed in a note: *Re Calmex Ltd* (1988) 4 BCC 761.

Chapter 4 — Petition by Contributories
(NO CVL APPLICATION)

Rule **4.22**   Presentation and service of petition

4.22(1)   [Form of petition and filing in court]   The petition shall specify the grounds on which it is presented and shall be filed in court with one copy for service under this Rule.   [FORM 4.14]

4.22(1A) **[Deposit receipt to be produced]** No petition shall be filed unless there is produced with it the receipt for the deposit payable on presentation.

4.22(2) **[Fixing return day]** The court shall fix a hearing for a day ("the return day") on which, unless the court otherwise directs, the petitioner and the company shall attend before the registrar in chambers for directions to be given in relation to the procedure on the petition.

4.22(3) **[Copy of petition for service]** On fixing the return day, the court shall return to the petitioner a sealed copy of the petition for service, endorsed with the return day and time of hearing.

4.22(4) **[Service on company]** The petitioner shall, at least 14 days before the return day, serve a sealed copy of the petition on the company.

History note

In r. 4.22(1) the words "and the nature of the relief which is sought by the petitioner," formerly appearing after the words "on which it is presented" were omitted by I(A)R 1987 (SI 1987 No. 1919), r. 3(1), Sch., Pt. 1, para. 40(1) as from 11 January 1988.

Rule 4.22(1A) was inserted by I(A)R 1987 (SI 1987 No. 1919), r. 3(1), Sch., Pt. 1, para. 40(2) as from 11 January 1988.

Rule 4.22(2)

See Practice Direction by Companies Court in [1987] 1 All ER 107 (reproduced in Appendix IV of this Guide).

(See general note after r. 4.24.)

Rule 4.23   Return of petition

4.23(1) **[Directions]** On the return day, or at any time after it, the court shall give such directions as it thinks appropriate with respect to the following matters—

- (a) service of the petition, whether in connection with the venue for a further hearing, or for any other purpose;
- (b) whether particulars of claim and defence are to be delivered, and generally as to the procedure on the petition;
- (c) whether, and if so by what means, the petition is to be advertised;
- (d) the manner in which any evidence is to be adduced at any hearing before the judge and in particular (but without prejudice to the generality of the above) as to—
  - (i) the taking of evidence wholly or in part by affidavit or orally;
  - (ii) the cross-examination of any deponents to affidavits;
  - (iii) the matters to be dealt with in evidence;
- (e) any other matter affecting the procedure on the petition or in connection with the hearing and disposal of the petition.

4.23(2) **[Directions under r. 4.23(1)(a)]** In giving directions under paragraph (1) (a), the court shall have regard to whether any of the persons specified in Rule 4.10 should be served with a copy of the petition.

(See general note after r. 4. 24.)

Rule **4.24** Application of Rules in Chapter 3

4.24 The following Rules in Chapter 3 apply, with the necessary modifications—

Rule 4.16 (notice of appearance);

Rule 4.17 (list of appearances);

Rule 4.20 (notice and settling of winding-up order);

Rule 4.21 (transmission and advertisement of order); and

Rule 4.21A (expenses of voluntary arrangement)

History note

In r. 4.24 the word "and" at the end of the line beginning "Rule 4.20" was omitted and the words "; and" and the line beginning "Rule 4.21A" were added by I(A)R 1987 (SI 1987 No. 1919), r. 3(1), Sch., Pt. 1, para. 41 as from 11 January 1988.

General note to rr. 4.22–4.24

The procedure to be followed on a contributory's petition is generally the same as that for other petitions, with the modifications set out here. Directions from the court regarding the service, advertisement and hearing of the petition must be sought in every case.

    The word "advertised" has two meanings: primarily, a paid announcement in a general publication, but also notifying the existence of the matter in question in any way. Where the court has made an order restraining the advertisement of a winding-up petition under r. 4.23(1)(*c*), the word may be construed in the latter sense, and any communication to an unauthorised party (e.g. informing the company's bank) of the fact that the petition has been presented will be a breach of the order (*Re a Company No. 00687 of 1991* [1991] BCC 210). (See also the note to r. 4.11, above.)

Chapter 5 — Provisional Liquidator (NO CVL APPLICATION)

Rule **4.25** Appointment of provisional liquidator

4.25(1) **[Who may apply to court]** An application to the court for the appointment of a provisional liquidator under section 135 may be made by the petitioner, or by a creditor of the company, or by a contributory, or by the company itself, or by the Secretary of State, or by any person who under any enactment would be entitled to present a petition for the winding up of the company.

4.25(2) **[Supporting affidavit]** The application must be supported by an affidavit stating—

    (a) the grounds on which it is proposed that a provisional liquidator should be appointed;

    (b) if some person other than the official receiver is proposed to be appointed, that the person has consented to act and, to the best of the applicant's belief, is qualified to act as an insolvency practitioner in relation to the company;

   (c) whether or not the official receiver has been informed of the application and, if so, has been furnished with a copy of it;

   (d) whether to the applicant's knowledge—

      (i) there has been proposed or is in force for the company a voluntary arrangement under Part I of the Act, or

      (ii) an administrator or administrative receiver is acting in relation to the company, or

      (iii) a liquidator has been appointed for its voluntary winding up; and

   (e) the applicant's estimate of the value of the assets in respect of which the provisional liquidator is to be appointed.

4.25(3) **[Copies to official receiver etc.]** The applicant shall send copies of the application and of the affidavit in support to the official receiver, who may attend the hearing and make any representations which he thinks appropriate.

If for any reason it is not practicable to comply with this paragraph, the official receiver must be informed of the application in sufficient time for him to be able to attend.

4.25(4) **[Powers of court]** The court may on the application, if satisfied that sufficient grounds are shown for the appointment, make it on such terms as it thinks fit.

(See general note after r. 4.31.)

Rule 4.25A   Notice of appointment

4.25A(1) **[Notice to official receiver]** Where a provisional liquidator has been appointed the court shall forthwith give notice of the fact to the official receiver.

4.25A(2) **[Copy to provisional liquidator]** A copy of that notice shall at the same time be sent by the court to the provisional liquidator where he is not the official receiver.   [FORM 4.14A]

History note

Rule 4.25A was inserted by I(A)R 1987 (SI 1987 No. 1919), r. 3(1), Sch., Pt. 1, para. 42 as from 11 January 1988. Also against r. 4.25A the words "[FORM 4.14A]" were inserted by I(A)R 1987 (SI 1987 No. 1919), r. 3(1), Sch., Pt. 2, para. 156(1) as from the same date.

(See general note after r. 4.31.)

Rule 4.26   Order of appointment

4.26(1) **[Form of order]** The order appointing the provisional liquidator shall specify the functions to be carried out by him in relation to the company's affairs.   [FORM 4.15]

4.26(2) **[Sealed copies]** The court shall, forthwith after the order is made, send sealed copies of the order as follows—

   (a) if the official receiver is appointed, two copies to him;

   (b) if a person other than the official receiver is appointed—

      (i) two copies to that person, and

  (ii) one copy to the official receiver;
 (c) if there is an administrative receiver acting in relation to the company, one
     copy to him.

4.26(3) **[One r. 4.26(2) copy sent to company or liquidator]** Of the two copies of
the order sent to the official receiver under paragraph (2)(a), or to another person
under paragraph (2)(b)(i), one shall in each case be sent by the recipient to the company or, if a liquidator has been appointed for the company's voluntary winding up, to
him.

(See general note after r. 4.31.)

Rule 4.27 Deposit

4.27(1) **[Security for official receiver's remuneration etc.]** Before an order
appointing the official receiver as provisional liquidator is issued, the applicant for it
shall deposit with him, or otherwise secure to his satisfaction, such sum as the court
directs to cover the official receiver's remuneration and expenses.

4.27(2) **[Insufficiency of deposit etc.]** If the sum deposited or secured subsequently proves to be insufficient, the court may, on application by the official
receiver, order that an additional sum be deposited or secured. If the order is not
complied with within 2 days after service of it on the person to whom it is directed, the
court may discharge the order appointing the provisional liquidator.

4.27(3) **[Repayment of deposit etc.]** If a winding-up order is made after a provisional liquidator has been appointed, any money deposited under this Rule shall
(unless it is required by reason of insufficiency of assets for payment of remuneration
and expenses of the provisional liquidator) be repaid to the person depositing it (or as
that person may direct) out of the assets, in the prescribed order of priority.

(See general note after r. 4.31.)

Rule 4.28 Security

4.28(1) **[Application of Rule]** The following applies where an insolvency practitioner is appointed to be provisional liquidator under section 135.

4.28(2) **[Cost of providing security]** The cost of providing the security required
under the Act shall be paid in the first instance by the provisional liquidator; but—
 (a) if a winding-up order is not made, the person so appointed is entitled to be
     reimbursed out of the property of the company, and the court may make an
     order on the company accordingly, and
 (b) if a winding-up order is made, he is entitled to be reimbursed out of the
     assets in the prescribed order of priority.

(See general note after r. 4.31.)

Rule 4.29 Failure to give or keep up security

4.29(1) **[Powers of court]** If the provisional liquidator fails to give or keep up his
security, the court may remove him, and make such order as it thinks fit as to costs.

4.29(2)　[Directions for replacement]　If an order is made under this Rule removing the provisional liquidator, or discharging the order appointing him, the court shall give directions as to whether any, and if so what, steps should be taken for the appointment of another person in his place.

(See general note after r. 4.31.)

Rule **4.30**　Remuneration

4.30(1)　[To be fixed by court]　The remuneration of the provisional liquidator (other than the official receiver) shall be fixed by the court from time to time on his application.

4.30(2)　[Matters to be taken into account]　In fixing his remuneration, the court shall take into account—

- (a) the time properly given by him (as provisional liquidator) and his staff in attending to the company's affairs;
- (b) the complexity (or otherwise) of the case;
- (c) any respects in which, in connection with the company's affairs, there falls on the provisional liquidator any responsibility of an exceptional kind or degree;
- (d) the effectiveness with which the provisional liquidator appears to be carrying out, or to have carried out, his duties; and
- (e) the value and nature of the property with which he has to deal.

4.30(3)　[Source of payment of remuneration etc.]　Without prejudice to any order the court may make as to costs, the provisional liquidator's remuneration (whether the official receiver or another) shall be paid to him, and the amount of any expenses incurred by him (including the remuneration and expenses of any special manager appointed under section 177) reimbursed—

- (a) if a winding-up order is not made, out of the property of the company; and
- (b) if a winding-up order is made, out of the assets, in the prescribed order of priority,

or, in either case (the relevant funds being insufficient), out of the deposit under Rule 4.27.

4.30(3A)　[Power of retention]　Unless the court otherwise directs, in a case falling within paragraph (3)(a) above the provisional liquidator may retain out of the company's property such sums or property as are or may be required for meeting his remuneration and expenses.

4.30(4)　[Provisional liquidator other than official receiver]　Where a person other than the official receiver has been appointed provisional liquidator, and the official receiver has taken any steps for the purpose of obtaining a statement of affairs or has performed any other duty under the Rules, he shall pay the official receiver such sum (if any) as the court may direct.

History note

In r. 4.30(3) the words from the beginning to "out of the property of the company" in para. (*a*) were substituted by I(A)R 1987 (SI 1987 No. 1919), r. 3(1), Sch., Pt. 1, para. 43(1) as from 11 January 1988: the former words read as follows:

"**4.30(3)**   The provisional liquidator's remuneration (whether the official receiver or another) shall be paid to him, and the amount of any expenses incurred by him reimbursed—

    (a)   if a winding-up order is not made, out of the property of the company (and the court may make an order on the company accordingly)".

Rule 4.30(3A) was inserted by I(A)R 1987 (SI 1987 No. 1919), r. 3(1), Sch., Pt. 1, para. 43(2) as from 11 January 1988.

(See general note after r. 4.31.)

Rule **4.31**   Termination of appointment

4.31(1)   **[Termination by court]**   The appointment of the provisional liquidator may be terminated by the court on his application, or on that of any of the persons specified in Rule 4.25(1).

4.31(2)   **[Directions on termination]**   If the provisional liquidator's appointment terminates, in consequence of the dismissal of the winding-up petition or otherwise, the court may give such directions as it thinks fit with respect to the accounts of his administration or any other matters which it thinks appropriate.

4.31(3)   (Omitted by the Insolvency (Amendment) Rules 1987 (S.I. 1987 No. 1919), r. 3(1), Sch. , Pt. 1, para. 44 as from 11 January 1988.)

History note

Rule 4.31(3) formerly read as follows:

"**4.31(3)**   The court may under paragraph (2)—

    (a)   direct that any expenses properly incurred by the provisional liquidator during the period of his appointment, including any remuneration to which he is entitled, be paid out of the property of the company, and

    (b)   authorise him to retain out of that property such sums as are required for meeting those expenses.

Alternatively, the court may make such order as it thinks fit with respect to those matters."

General note to rr. 4.25–4.31

These rules set out the procedure governing an application to the court for the appointment of a provisional liquidator under IA 1986, s. 135, and the associated questions of furnishing a deposit (where the official receiver is appointed) or security (where the provisional liquidator is an insolvency practitioner), and the liquidator's remuneration.

The new r. 4.25A gives formal sanction to the procedure which had been operating in practice since the rules came into force.

The provisions in rr. 4.28 and 4.30 are directory, although subject to the overall discretion conferred by r. 4.31(2) (and formerly also by r. 4.31(3)); and so a court will not normally make an order that an unsuccessful petitioner should pay the remuneration of a provisional liquidator: *Re Walter L Jacob & Co. Ltd* (1987) 3 BCC 532. (See, however, *Re Secure & Provide plc* [1992] BCC 405, where such an order was made against the Secretary of State following the failure of a petition under s. 124A, and cf. *Re Xyllyx plc (No. 2)* [1992] BCLC 378.)

Chapter 6 — Statement of Affairs and Other Information

Rule 4.32 Notice requiring statement of affairs

(NO CVL APPLICATION)

4.32(1) [Application of Rule] The following applies where the official receiver determines to require a statement of the company's affairs to be made out and submitted to him in accordance with section 131.   [FORM 4.16]

4.32(2) [Notice] He shall send notice to each of the persons whom he considers should be made responsible under that section, requiring them to prepare and submit the statement.

4.32(3) ["The deponents"] The persons to whom that notice is sent are referred to in this Chapter as "the deponents".

4.32(4) [Contents of notice] The notice shall inform each of the deponents—

   (a) of the names and addresses of all others (if any) to whom the same notice has been sent;

   (b) of the time within which the statement must be delivered;

   (c) of the effect of section 131(7) (penalty for non-compliance); and

   (d) of the application to him, and to each of the other deponents, of section 235 (duty to provide information, and to attend on the official receiver if required).

4.32(5) [Instructions for preparation of statement] The official receiver shall, on request, furnish a deponent with instructions for the preparation of the statement and with the forms required for that purpose.

(See general note after r. 4. 33.)

Rule 4.33 Verification and filing

(NO CVL APPLICATION)

4.33(1) [Form and verification] The statement of affairs shall be in Form 4.17, shall contain all the particulars required by that form and shall be verified by affidavit by the deponents (using the same form).   [FORM 4.17]

4.33(2) [Affidavits of concurrence] The official receiver may require any of the persons mentioned in section 131(3) to submit an affidavit of concurrence, stating that he concurs in the statement of affairs.

4.33(3) [Affidavit may be qualified] An affidavit of concurrence made under paragraph (2) may be qualified in respect of matters dealt with in the statement of affairs, where the maker of the affidavit is not in agreement with the deponents, or he considers the statement to be erroneous or misleading, or he is without the direct knowledge necessary for concurring in the statement.

4.33(4)   **[Delivery of statement to official receiver]**   The statement of affairs shall be delivered to the official receiver by the deponent making the affidavit of verification (or by one of them, if more than one), together with a copy of the verified statement.

4.33(5)   **[Delivery of affidavit of concurrence]**   Every affidavit of concurrence shall be delivered to the official receiver by the person who makes it, together with a copy.

4.33(6)   **[Filing in court]**   The official receiver shall file the verified copy of the statement and the affidavits of concurrence (if any) in court.

4.33(7)   **[Swearing of affidavit]**   The affidavit may be sworn before an official receiver or a deputy official receiver, or before an officer of the Department or the court duly authorised in that behalf.

General note to rr. 4.32, 4.33

The statement of affairs referred to in these rules is that which the official receiver may require when an order for winding up or for the appointment of a provisional liquidator has been made.

Rule 4.34   Statement of affairs

4.34–CVL(1)   **[Application of Rule]**   This Rule applies with respect to the statement of affairs made out by the liquidator under section 95(3) or (as the case may be) by the directors under section 99(1).   [FORM 4.18]
                                                       [FORM 4.19]

4.34(2)   **[Made out by liquidator]**   Where it is made out by the liquidator, the statement of affairs shall be delivered by him to the registrar of companies within 7 days after the creditors' meeting summoned under section 95(2).   [FORM 4.20]

4.34(3)   **[Made out by directors]**   Where it is made out by the directors under section 99(1) the statement of affairs shall be delivered by them to the liquidator in office following the creditors' meeting summoned under section 98 forthwith after that meeting has been held; and he shall, within 7 days, deliver it to the registrar of companies.   [FORM 4.20]

4.34(4)   **[Date where made out by directors]**   A statement of affairs under section 99(1) may be made up to a date not more than 14 days before that on which the resolution for voluntary winding up is passed by the company.

History note

Rules 4.34(3) and (4) were substituted for the former r. 4.34(3) by I(A)R 1987 (SI 1987 No. 1919), r. 3(1), Sch., Pt. 1, para. 45 as from 11 January 1988: the former r. 4.34(3) read as follows:

"**4.34(3)** Where it is made out by the directors under section 99(1), the statement of affairs shall be delivered by them to the liquidator, when appointed; and he shall, within 7 days, deliver it to the registrar of companies."

(See general note after r. 4.34A)

Rule 4.34A   Copy statement of affairs

4.34A–CVL   Where a liquidator is nominated by the company at a general meeting held on a day prior to that on which the creditors' meeting summoned under section 98 is held, the directors shall forthwith after his nomination or the making of the statement of affairs, whichever is the later, deliver to him a copy of the statement of affairs.

History note

Rule 4.34A–CVL was inserted by I(A)R 1987 (SI 1987 No. 1919), r. 3(1), Sch., Pt. 1, para. 46 as from 11 January 1988.

General note to rr. 4.34, 4.34A

These rules deal with the registration of the statement of affairs made out in a creditors' voluntary winding up.

The amendments made by I(A)R 1987 are designed to eliminate some time-tabling difficulties experienced in practice under the original rules.

Rule 4.35   Limited disclosure

(NO CVL APPLICATION)

4.35(1)   [Official receiver may apply to court]   Where the official receiver thinks that it would prejudice the conduct of the liquidation for the whole or part of the statement of affairs to be disclosed, he may apply to the court for an order of limited disclosure in respect of the statement, or any specified part of it.

4.35(2)   [Powers of court]   The court may on the application order that the statement or, as the case may be, the specified part of it be not filed, or that it is to be filed separately and not be open to inspection otherwise than with leave of the court.

General note

See Practice Direction by Companies Court in [1987] 1 All ER 107 (reproduced in Appendix IV of this Guide). See also general note after r. 4.37.

Rule 4.36   Release from duty to submit statement of affairs; extension of time

(NO CVL APPLICATION)

4.36(1)   [Exercise of s. 131(5) power]   The power of the official receiver under section 131(5) to give a release from the obligation imposed by that section, or to grant an extension of time, may be exercised at the official receiver's own discretion, or at the request of any deponent.

4.36(2)   [Deponent may apply to court]   A deponent may, if he requests a release or extension of time and it is refused by the official receiver, apply to the court for it.

4.36(3)   [Court may dismiss application etc.]   The court may, if it thinks that no sufficient cause is shown for the application, dismiss it; but it shall not do so unless the applicant has had an opportunity to attend the court for an *ex parte* hearing, of which he has been given at least 7 days' notice.

If the application is not dismissed under this paragraph, the court shall fix a venue for it to be heard, and give notice to the deponent accordingly.

4.36(4)   [Deponent to send notice to official receiver]   The deponent shall, at least 14 days before the hearing, send to the official receiver a notice stating the venue and accompanied by a copy of the application, and of any evidence which he (the deponent) intends to adduce in support of it.

4.36(5)   [Appearance etc. by official receiver]   The official receiver may appear and be heard on the application; and, whether or not he appears, he may file a written report of any matters which he considers ought to be drawn to the court's attention.

If such a report is filed, a copy of it shall be sent by the official receiver to the deponent, not later than 5 days before the hearing.

4.36(6)   [Sealed copies of order]   Sealed copies of any order made on the application shall be sent by the court to the deponent and the official receiver.

4.36(7)   [Applicant's costs]   On any application under this Rule the applicant's cost shall be paid in any event by him and, unless the court otherwise orders, no allowance towards them shall be made out of the assets.

(See general note after r. 4.37.)

Rule 4.37   Expenses of statement of affairs

(NO CVL APPLICATION)

4.37(1)   [Persons assisting in preparation of statement]   If any deponent cannot himself prepare a proper statement of affairs, the official receiver may, at the expense of the assets, employ some person or persons to assist in the preparation of the statement.

4.37(2)   [Allowance towards expenses]   At the request of any deponent, made on the grounds that he cannot himself prepare a proper statement, the official receiver may authorise an allowance, payable out of the assets, towards expenses to be incurred by the deponent in employing some person or persons to assist him in preparing it.

4.37(3)   [Estimate of expenses]   Any such request by the deponent shall be accompanied by an estimate of the expenses involved; and the official receiver shall only authorise the employment of a named person or a named firm, being in either case approved by him.

4.37(4)   [Authorisation subject to conditions]   An authorisation given by the official receiver under this Rule shall be subject to such conditions (if any) as he thinks fit to impose with respect to the manner in which any person may obtain access to relevant books and papers.

4.37(5) [Effect of Rule] Nothing in this Rule relieves a deponent from any obligation with respect to the preparation, verification and submission of the statement of affairs, or to the provision of information to the official receiver or the liquidator.

4.37(6) [Priority of payment out of assets] Any payment out of the assets under this Rule shall be made in the prescribed order of priority.

4.37(7) [Application of rr. 4.37(2)–(6)] Paragraphs (2) to (6) of this Rule may be applied, on application to the official receiver by any deponent, in relation to the making of an affidavit of concurrence.

General note to rr. 4.35–4.37

These rules are concerned with various discretionary powers conferred on the official receiver in regard to the statement of affairs: to apply to the court for an order authorising limited disclosure in the statement of affairs, to grant a release or an extension of time, and to provide a deponent with professional help.

Rule 4.38 Expenses of statement of affairs

4.38–CVL(1) [Payment out of assets] Payment may be made out of the company's assets, either before or after the commencement of the winding up, of any reasonable and necessary expenses of preparing the statement of affairs under section 99.

Any such payment is an expense of the liquidation.

4.38(2) [Payment before commencement of winding up] Where such a payment is made before the commencement of the winding up, the director presiding at the creditors' meeting held under section 98 shall inform the meeting of the amount of the payment and the identity of the person to whom it was made.

4.38(3) [Payment by liquidator] The liquidator appointed under section 100 may make such a payment (subject to the next paragraph); but if there is a liquidation committee, he must give the committee at least 7 days' notice of his intention to make it.

4.38(4) [No payment by liquidator to himself] Such a payment shall not be made by the liquidator to himself, or to any associate of his, otherwise than with the approval of the liquidation committee, the creditors, or the court.

4.38(5) [Powers of court under r. 4.219] This Rule is without prejudice to the powers of the court under Rule 4.219 (voluntary winding up superseded by winding up by the court).

General note

In a creditors' voluntary liquidation, the expenses of preparing the statement may be met from the assets, on the authority of the various persons or bodies mentioned.

Rule **4.39**   Submission of accounts

(NO CVL APPLICATION)

4.39(1)   [Request to persons specified in s. 235(3)]   Any of the persons specified in section 235(3) shall, at the request of the official receiver, furnish him with accounts of the company of such nature, as at such date, and for such period, as he may specify.

4.39(2)   [Beginning of specified period]   The period specified may begin from a date up to 3 years preceding the date of the presentation of the winding-up petition, or from an earlier date to which audited accounts of the company were last prepared.

4.39(3)   [Accounts for earlier period]   The court may, on the official receiver's application, require accounts for any earlier period.

4.39(4)   [Application of r. 4.37]   Rule 4.37 applies (with the necessary modification) in relation to accounts to be furnished under this Rule as it applies in relation to the statement of affairs.

4.39(5)   [Verification and delivery]   The accounts shall, if the official receiver so requires, be verified by affidavit and (whether or not so verified) delivered to him within 21 days of the request under paragraph (1), or such longer period as he may allow.

4.39(6)   [Copies to official receiver etc.]   Two copies of the accounts and (where required) the affidavit shall be delivered to the official receiver by whoever is required to furnish them; and the official receiver shall file one copy in court (with the affidavit, if any).

General note

The official receiver may call for accounts for up to three years past or up to the date of the last audited accounts, or for a longer period on an order of the court.

Professional assistance may be authorised under r. 4.37. The official receiver may call for further disclosure under r. 4.42.

Rule **4.40**   Submission of accounts

4.40–CVL(1)   [Request to persons specified in s. 235(3)]   Any of the persons specified in section 235(3) shall, at the request of the liquidator, furnish him with accounts of the company of such nature, as at such date, and for such period, as he may specify.

4.40(2)   [Beginning of specified period]   The specified period for the accounts may begin from a date up to 3 years preceding the date of the resolution for winding up, or from an earlier date to which audited accounts of the company were last prepared.

4.40(3)   [Verification and delivery]   The accounts shall, if the liquidator so requires, be verified by affidavit and (whether or not so verified) delivered to him, with the affidavit if required, within 21 days from the request under paragraph (1), or such longer period as he may allow.

(See general note after r. 4.41.)

Rule **4.41**   Expenses of preparing accounts

4.41–CVL(1)   [Persons assisting in preparation of accounts]   Where a person is required under Rule 4.40–CVL to furnish accounts, the liquidator may, with the sanction of the liquidation committee (if there is one) and at the expense of the assets, employ some person or persons to assist in the preparation of the accounts.

4.41(2) **[Allowance towards expenses]** At the request of the person subject to the requirement, the liquidator may, with that sanction, authorise an allowance, payable out of the assets, towards expenses to be incurred by that person in employing others to assist him in preparing the accounts.

4.41(3) **[Estimate of expenses]** Any such request shall be accompanied by an estimate of the expenses involved; and the liquidator shall only authorise the employment of a named person or a named firm, being in either case approved by him.

General note to rr. 4.40, 4.41

These rules make provision corresponding to r. 4.39, to apply in a creditors' voluntary liquidation. If accounts are required for a period more than three years back, the court's jurisdiction under IA 1986, s. 112 may be invoked.

Rule **4.42** Further disclosure

(NO CVL APPLICATION)

4.42(1) **[Official receiver may require further information]** The official receiver may at any time require the deponents, or any one or more of them, to submit (in writing) further information amplifying, modifying or explaining any matter contained in the statement of affairs, or in accounts submitted in pursuance of the Act or the Rules.

4.42(2) **[Verification and delivery]** The information shall, if the official receiver so directs, be verified by affidavit, and (whether or not so verified) delivered to him within 21 days of the requirement under paragraph (1), or such longer period as he may allow.

4.42(3) **[Copies to official receiver etc.]** Two copies of the documents containing the information and (where verification is directed) the affidavit shall be delivered by the deponent to the official receiver, who shall file one copy in court (with the affidavit, if any).

General note

This rule should be read in conjunction with rr. 4.32ff. (statement of affairs) and r. 4.39 (submission of accounts).

Chapter 7 — Information to Creditors and Contributories

Rule **4.43** Reports by official receiver

(NO CVL APPLICATION)

4.43(1) **[Winding-up proceedings and state of affairs]** The official receiver shall, at least once after the making of the winding-up order, send a report to creditors and contributories with respect to the proceedings in the winding up, and the state of the company's affairs.

4.43(2)   [Copy to court]   The official receiver shall file in court a copy of any report sent under this Chapter.

History note

Rule 4.43(1) was renumbered as such and r. 4.43(2) added by I(A)R 1987 (SI 1987 No. 1919), r. 3(1), Sch., Pt. 1, para. 47 as from 11 January 1988.

(See general note after r. 4.49A.)

Rule **4.44**   Meaning of "creditors"

4.44   Any reference in this Chapter to creditors is to creditors of the company who are known to the official receiver or (as the case may be) the liquidator or, where a statement of the company's affairs has been submitted, are identified in the statement.

(See general note after r. 4.49A.)

Rule **4.45**   Report where statement of affairs lodged

(NO CVL APPLICATION)

4.45(1)   [Report to creditors and contributories]   Where a statement of affairs has been submitted and filed in court, the official receiver shall send out to creditors and contributories a report containing a summary of the statement (if he thinks fit, as amplified, modified or explained by virtue of Rule 4.42) and such observations (if any) as he thinks fit to make with respect to it, or to the affairs of the company in general.

4.45(2)   [Where no need to comply with r. 4.45(1)]   The official receiver need not comply with paragraph (1) if he has previously reported to creditors and contributories with respect to the company's affairs (so far as known to him) and he is of opinion that there are no additional matters which ought to be brought to their attention.

History note

In r. 4.45(1) the words from "(if he thinks fit" to "of Rule 4.42)" were inserted by I(A)R 1987 (SI 1987 No. 1919), r. 3(1), Sch., Pt. 1, para. 48 as from 11 January 1988.

(See general note after r. 4.49A.)

Rule **4.46**   Statement of affairs dispensed with

(NO CVL APPLICATION)

4.46(1)   [Application of Rule]   This Rule applies where, in the company's case, release from the obligation to submit a statement of affairs has been granted by the official receiver or the court.

4.46(2) **[Report to creditors and contributories]** As soon as may be after the release has been granted, the official receiver shall send to creditors and contributories a report containing a summary of the company's affairs (so far as within his knowledge), and his observations (if any) with respect to it, or to the affairs of the company in general.

4.46(3) **[Where no need to comply with r. 4.46(2)]** The official receiver need not comply with paragraph (2) if he has previously reported to creditors and contributories with respect to the company's affairs (so far as known to him) and he is of opinion that there are no additional matters which ought to be brought to their attention.

(See general note after r. 4.49A.)

Rule **4.47**   General rule as to reporting

(NO CVL APPLICATION)

4.47(1) **[Powers of court]** The court may, on the official receiver's application, relieve him of any duty imposed on him by this Chapter, or authorise him to carry out the duty in a way other than there required.

4.47(2) **[Matters for court to consider]** In considering whether to act under this Rule, the court shall have regard to the cost of carrying out the duty, to the amount of the assets available, and to the extent of the interest of creditors or contributories, or any particular class of them.

General note

See Practice Direction by Companies Court in [1987] 1 All ER 107 (reproduced in Appendix IV of this Guide). See also general note after r. 4.49A.

Rule **4.48**   Winding up stayed

(NO CVL APPLICATION)

4.48(1) **[Cessation of official receiver's duty]** If proceedings in the winding up are stayed by order of the court, any duty of the official receiver to send reports under the preceding Rules in this Chapter ceases.

4.48(2) **[Notice of stay]** Where the court grants a stay, it may include in its order such requirements on the company as it thinks fit with a view to bringing the stay to the notice of creditors and contributories.

(See general note after r. 4.49A.)

Rule **4.49**   Information to creditors and contributories

4.49–CVL The liquidator shall, within 28 days of a meeting held under section 95 or 98, send to creditors and contributories of the company—

(a) a copy or summary of the statement of affairs, and

(b) a report of the proceedings at the meeting.

(See general note after r. 4.49A)

725

Rule **4.49A** Further information where liquidation follows administration

4.49A Where under section 140 the court appoints as the company's liquidator a person who was formerly its administrator and that person becomes aware of creditors not formerly known to him in his capacity as administrator, he shall send to those creditors a copy of any statement or report sent by him to creditors under Rule 2.16, so noted as to indicate that it is being sent under this Rule.

History note

Rule 4.49A was inserted by I(A)R 1987 (SI 1987 No. 1919), r. 3(1), Sch., Pt. 1, para. 49 as from 11 January 1988.

General note to rr. 4.43–4.49A

These rules are designed to ensure that creditors and contributories are kept informed of the state of the company's affairs in the various situations referred to.

Chapter 8 — Meetings of Creditors and Contributories

SECTION A: RULES OF GENERAL APPLICATION

Rule **4.50** First meetings

(NO CVL APPLICATION)

4.50(1) **[Venue for meetings etc.]** If under section 136(5) the official receiver decides to summon meetings of the company's creditors and contributories for the purpose of nominating a person to be liquidator in place of himself, he shall fix a venue for each meeting, in neither case more than 4 months from the date of the winding-up order.

4.50(2) **[Notice of meetings]** When for each meeting a venue has been fixed, notice of the meetings shall be given to the court and—

(a) in the case of the creditors' meeting, to every creditor who is known to the official receiver or is identified in the company's statement of affairs; and

(b) in the case of the contributories' meeting, to every person appearing (by the company's books or otherwise) to be a contributory of the company.

4.50(3) **[Time for giving notice]** Notice to the court shall be given forthwith, and the other notices shall be given at least 21 days before the date fixed for each meeting respectively.

4.50(4) **[Contents of notice]** The notice to creditors shall specify a time and date, not more than 4 days before the date fixed for the meeting, by which they must lodge proofs and (if applicable) proxies, in order to be entitled to vote at the meeting; and the same applies in respect of contributories and their proxies.

4.50(5) **[Public advertisement]** Notice of the meetings shall also be given by public advertisement.

4.50(6) **[Request by creditors under s. 136(5)(c)]** Where the official receiver receives a request by creditors under section 136(5)(c) for meetings of creditors and contributories to be summoned, and it appears to him that the request is properly made in accordance with the Act, he shall—

    (a) withdraw any notices previously given by him under section 136(5)(b) (that he has decided not to summon such meetings),

    (b) fix the venue of each meeting for not more than 3 months from his receipt of the creditors' request, and

    (c) act in accordance with paragraphs (2) to (5) above, as if he had decided under section 136 to summon the meetings. [FORM 4.21]

4.50(7) **[Names of meetings]** Meetings summoned by the official receiver under this Rule are known respectively as "the first meeting of creditors" and "the first meeting of contributories", and jointly as "the first meetings in the liquidation".

4.50(8) **[Where company is authorised institution under Banking Act]** Where the company is an authorised institution or former authorised institution within the meaning of the Banking Act 1987, additional notices are required by Rule 4.72.

History note

In r. 4.50(8) the words from "an authorised institution" to "Banking Act 1987" were substituted by I(A)R 1987 (SI 1987 No. 1919), r. 3(1), Sch., Pt. 1, para. 50 as from 11 January 1988: the former words were:

    "a recognised bank or licensed institution under the Banking Act 1979, or an institution to which sections 16 and 18 of that Act apply as if it were a licensed institution".

(See general note after r. 4.71.)

Rule 4.51 First meeting of creditors

4.51–CVL(1) **[Application of Rule]** This Rule applies in the case of a meeting of creditors summoned by the liquidator under section 95 (where, in what starts as a members' voluntary winding up, he forms the opinion that the company will be unable to pay its debts) or a meeting under section 98 (first meeting of creditors in a creditors' voluntary winding up).

4.51(2) **[Contents of notice]** The notice summoning the meeting shall specify a venue for the meeting and the time (not earlier than 12.00 hours on the business day before the day fixed for the meeting) by which, and the place at which, creditors must lodge any proxies necessary to entitle them to vote at the meeting.

4.51(3) **[Where company is authorised institution under Banking Act]** Where the company is an authorised institution or former authorised institution within the meaning of the Banking Act 1987, additional notices are required by Rule 4.72.

History note
In r. 4.51(2) the words from "any proxies necessary" to the end were substituted for the former words "proofs and (if applicable) proxies" by I(A)R 1987 (SI 1987 No. 1919), r. 3(1), Sch., Pt. 1, para. 51(1) as from 11 January 1988.
In r. 4.51(3) the words from "an authorised institution" to "Banking Act 1987" were substituted by I(A)R 1987 (SI 1987 No. 1919), r. 3(1), Sch., Pt. 1, para. 51(2) as from 11 January 1988: the former words read as follows:
"a recognised bank or licensed institution under the Banking Act 1979, or an institution to which sections 16 and 18 of that Act apply as if it were a licensed institution".

(See general note after r. 4.71.)

Rule 4.52   Business at first meetings in the liquidation

(NO CVL APPLICATION)

4.52(1)   [Limitation on resolutions at first meeting of creditors]   At the first meeting of creditors, no resolutions shall be taken other than the following—

(a) a resolution to appoint a named insolvency practitioner to be liquidator, or two or more insolvency practitioners as joint liquidators;

(b) a resolution to establish a liquidation committee;

(c) (unless it has been resolved to establish a liquidation committee) a resolution specifying the terms on which the liquidator is to be remunerated, or to defer consideration of that matter;

(d) (if, and only if, two or more persons are appointed to act jointly as liquidator) a resolution specifying whether acts are to be done by both or all of them, or by only one;

(e) (where the meeting has been requisitioned under section 136), a resolution authorising payment out of the assets, as an expense of the liquidation, of the cost of summoning and holding the meeting and any meeting of contributories so requisitioned and held;

(f) a resolution to adjourn the meeting for not more than 3 weeks;

(g) any other resolution which the chairman thinks it right to allow for special reasons.

4.52(2)   [At first meeting of contributories]   The same applies as regards the first meeting of contributories, but that meeting shall not pass any resolution to the effect of paragraph (1)(c) or (e).

4.52(3)   [Limitation at either meeting]   At neither meeting shall any resolution be proposed which has for its object the appointment of the official receiver as liquidator.

(See general note after r. 4.71.)

Rule 4.53   Business at meeting under s. 95 or 98

4.53–CVL   Rule 4.52(1), except sub-paragraph (e), applies to a creditors' meeting under section 95 or 98.

(See general note after r. 4.71.)

Rule **4.53A** Effect of adjournment of company meeting

4.53A–CVL Where a company meeting at which a resolution for voluntary winding up is to be proposed is adjourned, any resolution passed at a meeting under section 98 held before the holding of the adjourned company meeting only has effect on and from the passing by the company of a resolution for winding up.

History note

See note after r. 4.53B.

(See general note after r. 4.71.)

Rule **4.53B** Report by director, etc.

4.53B–CVL(1) **[State of company's affairs]** At any meeting held under section 98 where the statement of affairs laid before the meeting does not state the company's affairs as at the date of the meeting, the directors of the company shall cause to be made to the meeting, either by the director presiding at the meeting or by another person with knowledge of the relevant matters, a report (written or oral) on any material transactions relating to the company occurring between the date of the making of the statement of affairs and that of the meeting.

4.53B(2) **[Recorded in minutes]** Any such report shall be recorded in the minutes of the meeting kept under Rule 4.71.

History note

Rules 4.53A and 4.53B were inserted by I(A)R 1987 (SI 1987 No. 1919), r. 3(1), Sch., Pt. 1, para. 52 as from 11 January 1988.

(See general note after r. 4.71.)

Rule **4.54** General power to call meetings

4.54(1) **[General power, "the convener"]** The official receiver or the liquidator may at any time summon and conduct meetings of creditors or of contributories for the purpose of ascertaining their wishes in all matters relating to the liquidation; and in relation to any meeting summoned under the Act or the Rules, the person summoning it is referred to as "the convener".

4.54(2) **[Notice of venue]** When (in either case) a venue for the meeting has been fixed, notice of it shall be given by the convener—

    (a) in the case of a creditors' meeting, to every creditor who is known to him or is identified in the company's statement of affairs; and   [FORM 4.22]

    (b) in the case of a meeting of contributories, to every person appearing (by the company's books or otherwise) to be a contributory of the company.   [FORM 4.23]

4.54(3) [Time for giving notice etc.] Notice of the meeting shall be given at least 21 days before the date fixed for it, and shall specify the purpose of the meeting.

4.54(4) [Contents of notice] The notice shall specify a time and date, not more than 4 days before the date fixed for the meeting, by which, and the place at which, creditors must lodge proofs and proxies, in order to be entitled to vote at the meeting; and the same applies in respect of contributories and their proxies.

(NO CVL APPLICATION)

4.54(5–CVL) [Contents of notice] The notice shall specify a time and date, not more than 4 days before that fixed for the meeting, by which, and the place at which, creditors (if not individuals attending in person) must lodge proxies, in order to be entitled to vote at the meeting.

4.54(6) [Additional notice by public advertisement] Additional notice of the meeting may be given by public advertisement if the convener thinks fit, and shall be so given if the court orders.

(See general note after r. 4.71.)

Rule 4.55   The chairman at meetings

(NO CVL APPLICATION)

4.55(1) [Application of Rule] This Rule applies both to a meeting of creditors and to a meeting of contributories.

4.55(2) [Where convener official receiver] Where the convener of the meeting is the official receiver, he, or a person nominated by him, shall be chairman.

A nomination under this paragraph shall be in writing, unless the nominee is another official receiver or a deputy official receiver.

4.55(3) [Where convener not official receiver] Where the convener is other than the official receiver, the chairman shall be he, or a person nominated in writing by him.

A person nominated under this paragraph must be either—

   (a) one who is qualified to act as an insolvency practitioner in relation to the company, or

   (b) an employee of the liquidator or his firm who is experienced in insolvency matters.

(See general note after r. 4.71.)

Rule 4.56   The chairman at meetings

4.56–CVL(1) [Application of Rule] This Rule applies both to a meeting of creditors (except a meeting under section 95 or 98) and to a meeting of contributories.

4.56(2) [Liquidator or his nominee to be chairman] The liquidator, or a person nominated by him in writing to act, shall be chairman of the meeting.

A person nominated under this paragraph must be either—

    (a) one who is qualified to act as an insolvency practitioner in relation to the company, or

    (b) an employee of the liquidator or his firm who is experienced in insolvency matters.

History note

In r. 4.56–CVL(1) the words "section 95 or 98" were substituted for the former words "section 98" by I(A)R 1987 (SI 1987 No. 1919), r. 3(1), Sch., Pt. 1, para. 53 as from 11 January 1988.

(See general note after r. 4.71.)

Rule 4.57 Requisitioned meetings

4.57(1) **[Documents to accompany creditors' request]** Any request by creditors to the liquidator (whether or not the official receiver) for a meeting of creditors or contributories, or meetings of both, to be summoned shall be accompanied by—

    (a) a list of the creditors concurring with the request and the amount of their respective claims in the winding up;

    (b) from each creditor concurring, written confirmation of his concurrence; and

    (c) a statement of the purpose of the proposed meeting.

Sub-paragraphs (a) and (b) do not apply if the requisitioning creditor's debt is alone sufficient, without the concurrence of other creditors. [FORM 4.21]

4.57(2) **[Liquidator to fix venue]** The liquidator shall, if he considers the request to be properly made in accordance with the Act, fix a venue for the meeting, not more than 35 days from his receipt of the request.

4.57(3) **[Notice of meeting]** The liquidator shall give 21 days' notice of the meeting, and the venue for it, to creditors.

4.57(4) **[Application of rr. 4.57(1)–(3) to contributories' meetings]** Paragraphs (1) to (3) above apply to the requisitioning by contributories of contributories' meetings, with the following modifications—

    (a) for the reference in paragraph (1)(a) to the creditors' respective claims substitute the contributories' respective values (being the amounts for which they may vote at any meeting); and

    (b) the persons to be given notice under paragraph (3) are those appearing (by the company's books or otherwise) to be contributories of the company. [FORM 4.24]

(NO CVL APPLICATION)

(See general note after r. 4.71.)

Rule 4.58 Attendance at meetings of company's personnel

4.58(1) **[Application of Rule]** This Rule applies to meetings of creditors and to meetings of contributories.

4.58(2) **[Notice to company's personnel]**   Whenever a meeting is summoned, the convener shall give at least 21 days' notice to such of the company's personnel as he thinks should be told of, or be present at, the meeting.

"The company's personnel" means the persons referred to in paragraphs (a) to (d) of section 235(3) (present and past officers, employees, etc.).

4.58(3) **[Notice of adjournment]**   If the meeting is adjourned, the chairman of the meeting shall, unless for any reason he thinks it unnecessary or impracticable, give notice of the adjournment to such (if any) of the company's personnel as he considers appropriate, being persons who were not themselves present at the meeting.

4.58(4) **[Notice that presence required]**   The convener may, if he thinks fit, give notice to any one or more of the company's personnel that he is, or they are, required to be present at the meeting, or to be in attendance.

4.58(5) **[Admission to meetings]**   In the case of any meeting, any one or more of the company's personnel, and any other persons, may be admitted, but—

(a) they must have given reasonable notice of their wish to be present, and

(b) it is a matter for the chairman's discretion whether they are to be admitted or not, and his decision is final as to what (if any) intervention may be made by any of them.

4.58(6) **[Adjournment for obtaining attendance]**   If it is desired to put questions to any one of the company's personnel who is not present, the chairman may adjourn the meeting with a view to obtaining his attendance.

4.58(7) **[Chairman's discretion re questions]**   Where one of the company's personnel is present at a meeting, only such questions may be put to him as the chairman may in his discretion allow.

(See general note after r. 4.71.)

Rule 4.59   Notice of meetings by advertisement only

4.59(1) **[Power of court]**   In the case of any meeting of creditors or contributories to be held under the Act or the Rules, the court may order that notice of the meeting be given by public advertisement, and not by individual notice to the persons concerned.

4.59(2) **[Matters for court to consider]**   In considering whether to act under this Rule, the court shall have regard to the cost of public advertisement, to the amount of the assets available, and to the extent of the interest of creditors or of contributories, or any particular class of either of them.

General note

See Practice Direction in [1987] 1 All ER 107 (reproduced in Appendix IV of this Guide). See also general note after r. 4.71.

Rule 4.60   Venue

4.60(1) **[Convenience of venue]**   In fixing the venue for a meeting of creditors or contributories, the convener shall have regard to the convenience of the persons (other than whoever is to be chairman) who are invited to attend.

4.60(2) **[Time of meetings]** Meetings shall in all cases be summoned for commencement between the hours of 10.00 and 16.00 hours on a business day, unless the court otherwise directs.

4.60(3) **[Forms of proxy]** With every notice summoning a meeting of creditors or contributories there shall be sent out forms of proxy. [FORM 8.4]
or [FORM 8.5]

(See general note after r. 4.71.)

Rule **4.61** Expenses of summoning meetings

4.61(1) **[Deposit for payment of expenses]** Subject as follows, the expenses of summoning and holding a meeting of creditors or contributories at the instance of any person other than the official receiver or the liquidator shall be paid by that person, who shall deposit with the liquidator security for their payment.

4.61(2) **[Appropriate security]** The sum to be deposited shall be such as the official receiver or liquidator (as the case may be) determines to be appropriate; and neither shall act without the deposit having been made.

4.61(3) **[Vote for expenses to be paid out of assets]** Where a meeting of creditors is so summoned, it may vote that the expenses of summoning and holding it, and of summoning and holding any meeting of contributories requisitioned at the same time, shall be payable out of the assets, as an expense of the liquidation.

4.61(4) **[Contributories' meeting]** Where a meeting of contributories is summoned on the requisition of contributories, it may vote that the expenses of summoning and holding it shall be payable out of the assets, but subject to the right of creditors to be paid in full, with interest.

4.61(5) **[Repayment of deposit]** To the extent that any deposit made under this Rule is not required for the payment of expenses of summoning and holding a meeting, it shall be repaid to the person who made it.

(See general note after r. 4.71.)

Rule **4.62** Expenses of meeting under s. 98

4.62–CVL(1) **[Payment out of assets]** Payment may be made out of the company's assets, either before or after the commencement of the winding up, of any reasonable and necessary expenses incurred in connection with the summoning, advertisement and holding of a creditors' meeting under section 98.

Any such payment is an expense of the liquidation.

4.62(2) **[Payment before commencement of winding up]** Where such payments are made before the commencement of the winding up, the director presiding at the creditors' meeting shall inform the meeting of their amount and the identity of the persons to whom they were made.

4.62(3) **[Payment by s. 100 liquidator]** The liquidator appointed under section 100 may make such a payment (subject to the next paragraph); but if there is a liquidation committee, he must give the committee at least 7 days' notice of his intention to make the payment.

4.62(4) **[No payment by liquidator to himself]**   Such a payment shall not be made by the liquidator to himself, or to any associate of his, otherwise than with the approval of the liquidation committee, the creditors, or the court.

4.62(5) **[Powers of court under r. 4.219]**   This Rule is without prejudice to the powers of the court under Rule 4.219 (voluntary winding up superseded by winding up by the court).

(See general note after r. 4.71.)

Rule 4.63   Resolutions

4.63(1) **[Resolution passed by majority in value]**   Subject as follows, at a meeting of creditors or contributories, a resolution is passed when a majority (in value) of those present and voting, in person or by proxy, have voted in favour of the resolution.

The value of contributories is determined by reference to the number of votes conferred on each contributory by the company's articles.

4.63(2) **[Resolution for appointment of liquidator]**   In the case of a resolution for the appointment of a liquidator—

- (a) subject to paragraph (2A), if on any vote there are two nominees for appointment, the person who obtains the most support is appointed;
- (b) if there are three or more nominees, and one of them has a clear majority over both or all the others together, that one is appointed; and
- (c) in any other case, the chairman of the meeting shall continue to take votes (disregarding at each vote any nominee who has withdrawn and, if no nominee has withdrawn, the nominee who obtained the least support last time), until a clear majority is obtained for any one nominee.

4.63(2A) **[Majority in value]**   In a winding up by the court the support referred to in paragraph (2)(a) must represent a majority in value of all those present (in person or by proxy) at the meeting and entitled to vote. (NO CVL APPLICATION).

4.63(3) **[Resolution for joint appointment]**   The chairman may at any time put to the meeting a resolution for the joint appointment of any two or more nominees.

4.63(4) **[Resolution affecting liquidator etc.]**   Where a resolution is proposed which affects a person in respect of his remuneration or conduct as liquidator, or as proposed or former liquidator, the vote of that person, and of any partner or employee of his, shall not be reckoned in the majority required for passing the resolution.

This paragraph applies with respect to a vote given by a person (whether personally or on his behalf by a proxy-holder) either as creditor or contributory or as proxy-holder for a creditor or a contributory (but subject to Rule 8.6 in Part 8 of the Rules).

History note

In r. 4.63(1) the words "Subject as follows," at the beginning were inserted by I(A)R 1987 (SI 1987 No. 1919), r. 3(1), Sch., Pt. 1, para. 54(1) as from 11 January 1988.

In r. 4.63(2)(*a*) the words "Subject to paragraph (2A), "at the beginning were inserted by I(A)R 1987 (SI 1987 No. 1919), r. 3(1), Sch., Pt. 1, para. 54(2) as from 11 January 1988.

Rule 4.63(2A) was inserted by I(A)R 1987 (SI 1987 No. 1919), r. 3(1), Sch., Pt. 1, para. 54(3) as from 11 January 1988.

In the second paragraph of r. 4.63(4) the words "whether personally or on his behalf by a proxy-holder)" were inserted and the word "proxy-holder" was substituted for the former word "proxy" by I(A)R 1987 (SI 1987 No. 1919), r. 3(1), Sch., Pt. 1, para. 54(4) as from 11 January 1988.

(See general note after r. 4.71.)

Rule 4.64   Chairman of meeting as proxy-holder

4.64   Where the chairman at a meeting of creditors or contributories holds a proxy which requires him to vote for a particular resolution, and no other person proposes that resolution—

    (a) he shall himself propose it, unless he considers that there is good reason for not doing so, and

    (b) if he does not propose it, he shall forthwith after the meeting notify his principal of the reason why not.

(See general note after r. 4.71.)

Rule 4.65   Suspension and adjournment

4.65(1)   [Application of Rule]   This Rule applies to meetings of creditors and to meetings of contributories.

4.65(2)   [Suspension at chairman's discretion]   Once only in the course of any meeting, the chairman may, in his discretion and without an adjournment, declare the meeting suspended for any period up to one hour.

4.65(3)   [Adjournment]   The chairman at any meeting may in his discretion, and shall if the meeting so resolves, adjourn it to such time and place as seems to him to be appropriate in the circumstances.

This is subject to Rule 4.113(3) or, as the case may be, 4.114–CVL(3), in a case where the liquidator or his nominee is chairman, and a resolution has been proposed for the liquidator's removal.

4.65(4)   [Adjourned if inquorate]   If within a period of 30 minutes from the time appointed for the commencement of a meeting a quorum is not present, then the chairman may, at his discretion, adjourn the meeting to such time and place as he may appoint.

4.65(5)   [Period of adjournment]   An adjournment under this Rule shall not be for a period of more than 21 days; and Rule 4.60(1) and (2) applies.

4.65(6)   [If no chairman]   If there is no person present to act as chairman, some other person present (being entitled to vote) may make the appointment under paragraph (4), with the agreement of others present (being persons so entitled).

Failing agreement, the adjournment shall be to the same time and place in the next following week or, if that is not a business day, to the business day immediately following.

4.65(7) **[Use of proofs and proxies at adjourned meeting]** Where a meeting is adjourned under this Rule, proofs and proxies may be used if lodged at any time up to midday on the business day immediately before the adjourned meeting.

History note

In r. 4.65(3) the words "or, as the case may be, 4.114–CVL(3)," were inserted by I(A)R 1987 (SI 1987 No. 1919), r. 3(1), Sch., Pt. 1, para. 55(1) as from 11 January 1988.

   In r. 4.65(4) the words from "the chairman may, at his discretion," to the end were substituted by I(A)R 1987 (SI 1987 No. 1919), r. 3(1), Sch., Pt. 1, para. 55(2) as from 11 January 1988: the former words read as follows:

> "by virtue of this Rule the meeting stands adjourned to such time and place as may be appointed by the chairman."

(See general note after r. 4.71.)

Rule 4.66   Quorum

4.66 (Omitted by the Insolvency (Amendment) Rules 1987 (S.I. 1987 No. 1919), r. 3(1), Sch., Pt. 1, para. 56 as from 11 January 1988).

History note

Rule 4.66 formerly read as follows:

> **"4.66(1)** A meeting is not competent to act, in the absence of a quorum, for any purpose except—
>
> >   (a) the election of a chairman,
> >
> >   (b) in the case of a creditors' meeting, the admission by the chairman of proofs for the purpose of entitlement of creditors to vote, and
> >
> >   (c) (c) the adjournment of the meeting.
>
> (NO CVL APPLICATION)
>
> **4.66(2–CVL)** A meeting is not competent to act, in the absence of a quorum, for any purpose except the election of a chairman, or the adjournment of the meeting.
>
> **4.66(3)** Subject to paragraph (4), a quorum is—
>
> >   (a) in the case of a creditors' meeting, at least 3 creditors entitled to vote, or all the creditors so entitled, if their number does not exceed 3;
> >
> >   (b) in the case of a meeting of contributories, at least 2 contributories so entitled, or all the contributories, if their number does not exceed 2.
>
> The references to creditors and contributories are to those present in person or by proxy, or duly represented under section 375 of the Companies Act.
>
> **4.66(4)** One person present constitutes a quorum if—
>
> >   (a) he is himself a creditor or representative under section 375 of the Companies Act or (as the case may be) a contributory with entitlement to vote and he holds a number of proxies sufficient to ensure that, with his own vote, paragraph (3) is complied with, or
> >
> >   (a) being the chairman or any other person, he holds that number of proxies."

Rule 4.67   Entitlement to vote (creditors)

4.67(1) **[Conditions for voting]** Subject as follows in this Rule and the next, at a meeting of creditors a person is entitled to vote as a creditor only if—

(a) there has been duly lodged (in a winding up by the court by the time and date stated in the notice of the meeting) a proof of the debt claimed to be due to him from the company, and the claim has been admitted under Rule 4.70 for the purpose of entitlement to vote, and

(b) there has been lodged, by the time and date stated in the notice of the meeting, any proxy requisite for that entitlement.

4.67(2) **[Powers of court]** The court may, in exceptional circumstances, by order declare the creditors, or any class of them, entitled to vote at creditors' meetings, without being required to prove their debts.

Where a creditor is so entitled, the court may, on the application of the liquidator, make such consequential orders as it thinks fit (as for example an order treating a creditor as having proved his debt for the purpose of permitting payment of dividend).

4.67(3) **[Limitation on voting]** A creditor shall not vote in respect of a debt for an unliquidated amount, or any debt whose value is not ascertained, except where the chairman agrees to put upon the debt an estimated minimum value for the purpose of entitlement to vote and admits his proof for that purpose.

4.67(4) **[Secured creditor]** A secured creditor is entitled to vote only in respect of the balance (if any) of his debt after deducting the value of his security as estimated by him.

4.67(5) **[Further limitation on voting]** A creditor shall not vote in respect of a debt on, or secured by, a current bill of exchange or promissory note, unless he is willing—

(a) to treat the liability to him on the bill or note of every person who is liable on it antecedently to the company, and against whom a bankruptcy order has not been made (or, in the case of a company, which has not gone into liquidation), as a security in his hands, and

(b) to estimate the value of the security and (for the purpose of entitlement to vote, but not for dividend) to deduct it from his proof.

(See general note after r. 4.71.)

Rule 4.68 Chairman's discretion to allow vote

4.68–CVL At a creditors' meeting, the chairman may allow a creditor to vote, notwithstanding that he has failed to comply with Rule 4.67(1)(a), if satisfied that the failure was due to circumstances beyond the creditor's control.

(See general note after r. 4.71.)

Rule 4.69 Entitlement to vote (contributories)

4.69 At a meeting of contributories, voting rights are as at a general meeting of the company, subject to any provision in the articles affecting entitlement to vote, either generally or at a time when the company is in liquidation.

(See general note after r. 4.71.)

Rule 4.70 Admission and rejection of proof (creditors' meeting)

4.70(1) **[Power of chairman]** At any creditors' meeting the chairman has power to admit or reject a creditor's proof for the purpose of his entitlement to vote; and the power is exercisable with respect to the whole or any part of the proof.

4.70(2) **[Appeal from chairman's decision]** The chairman's decision under this Rule, or in respect of any matter arising under Rule 4.67, is subject to appeal to the court by any creditor or contributory.

4.70(3) **[Voting subject to objection]** If the chairman is in doubt whether a proof should be admitted or rejected, he shall mark it as objected to and allow the creditor to vote, subject to his vote being subsequently declared invalid if the objection to the proof is sustained.

4.70(4) **[If chairman's decision reversed etc.]** If on an appeal the chairman's decision is reversed or varied, or a creditor's vote is declared invalid, the court may order that another meeting be summoned, or make such other order as it thinks just.

4.70(5) **[Costs re application]** Neither the official receiver, nor any person nominated by him to be chairman, is personally liable for costs incurred by any person in respect of an application under this Rule; and the chairman (if other than the official receiver or a person so nominated) is not so liable unless the court makes an order to that effect.

(NO CVL APPLICATION)

4.70(6–CVL) **[Costs re application]** The liquidator or his nominee as chairman is not personally liable for costs incurred by any person in respect of an application under this Rule, unless the court makes an order to that effect.

(See general note after r. 4.71.)

Rule 4.71 Record of proceedings

4.71(1) **[Minutes of proceedings]** At any meeting, the chairman shall cause minutes of the proceedings to be kept. The minutes shall be signed by him, and retained as part of the records of the liquidation.

4.71(2) **[List of creditors or contributories attending]** The chairman shall also cause to be made up and kept a list of all the creditors or, as the case may be, contributories who attended the meeting.

4.71(3) **[Record of resolutions]** The minutes of the meeting shall include a record of every resolution passed.

4.71(4) **[Chairman's duty to deliver particulars]** It is the chairman's duty to see to it that particulars of all such resolutions, certified by him, are filed in court not more than 21 days after the date of the meeting.

(NO CVL APPLICATION)

General note to rr. 4.50–4.71

The official receiver has a discretion under IA 1986 whether to summon first meetings. If he decides to do so, the procedure to be followed in a winding up by the court is set out in rr. 4.50 and 4.52; rr. 4.51 and 4.53 deal with the first meeting of creditors in a creditors' voluntary winding up.

The remaining rules in this chapter provide for the summoning of other meetings and the conduct of creditors' and contributories' meetings generally. Voting at creditors' meetings is by a majority in *value* only, instead of the majority in *number and value* required under r. 134 of the former winding-up rules.

Note in regard to r. 4.57(1),(2) that the statutory power of the creditors and contributories to requisition meetings is contained in IA 1986, s. 168(2), which requires the support of at least one-tenth in value of the creditors or contributories, as the case may be.

The amendment to r. 4.51(2) removes an apparent restriction upon the time within which a creditor may lodge a proof. (Under r. 4.67(1), in a creditors' voluntary winding up, a proof may be delivered or produced at any time up to the taking of the vote.)

The new r. 4.53A brings back into operation a provision equivalent to the repealed CA 1985, s. 588(4), and allows the creditors to pass a resolution in anticipation of and conditionally upon the passing in due course of a resolution for winding up at an adjourned shareholders' meeting.

Rule 4.53B reflects a change in the form relating to the statement of affairs (Form 4.19). Previously, this had to be made up to the date of the creditors' meeting – a requirement which could not be met in practice. The date may now be anything up to 14 days before the meeting; and r. 4.53B imposes an obligation to make a report (which may be oral) to the meeting, bringing the statement up to date.

The new r. 4.63(2A) prevents the election of a liquidator on a minority vote in the case where there are several nominees. The exclusion of its application to a creditors' voluntary winding up ensures that a liquidator who has the greatest support among the creditors (even if only a minority of them overall) is preferred to the company's nominee.

The repealed r. 4.66 has been replaced by the new r. 12.4A.

The language of r. 4.67(3) is similar to that used in other rules, e.g. r. 1.17(3) and r. 5.17(3), and accordingly decisions on those provisions (such as *Re a Debtor (No. 222 of 1990), ex parte Bank of Ireland & Ors* [1992] BCLC 137) are relevant to its interpretation. In *Re Bank of Credit & Commerce International SA (No. 5), Sheik Khalid v Bank of Credit & Commerce International SA* [1994] 1 BCLC 429 the court considered an application by a person claiming to be a creditor before any ruling had been given by the chairman (who had not yet been appointed).

SECTION B: WINDING UP OF RECOGNISED BANKS, ETC.

Rule 4.72   Additional provisions as regards certain meetings

4.72(1)   [Application of Rule]   This Rule applies where a company goes, or proposes to go, into liquidation and it is an authorised institution or former authorised institution within the meaning of the Banking Act 1987.

4.72(2)   [Notice re proposed winding up]   Notice of any meeting of the company at which it is intended to propose a resolution for its winding up shall be given by the directors to the Bank of England and to the Deposit Protection Board.

4.72(3)   [Form of notice]   Notice to the Bank and the Board shall be the same as given to members of the company.

4.72(4)   [Where creditors' meeting summoned under s. 95 or 98]   Where a creditors' meeting is summoned by the liquidator under section 95 or, in a creditors' voluntary winding up, is summoned under section 98, the same notice of the meeting must be given to the Bank and the Board as is given to creditors under Rule 4.51–CVL.

4.72(5)   [Where company being wound up by court]   Where the company is being wound up by the court, notice of the first meetings of creditors and contributories shall be given to the Bank and the Board by the official receiver.

4.72(6) [Where meeting to receive liquidator's resignation etc.]   Where in the winding up (whether voluntary or by the court) a meeting of creditors or contributories or of the company is summoned for the purpose of—

(a) receiving the liquidator's resignation, or

(b) removing the liquidator, or

(c) appointing a new liquidator,

the person summoning the meeting and giving notice of it shall also give notice to the Bank and the Board.

4.72(7) [Representation of Deposit Protection Board]   The Board is entitled to be represented at any meeting of which it is required by this Rule to be given notice; and Schedule 1 to the Rules has effect with respect to the voting rights of the Board at such a meeting.

History note

In r. 4.72(1) the words from "an authorised institution" to the end were substituted by I(A)R 1987 (SI 1987 No. 1919), r. 3(1), Sch., Pt. 1, para. 57 as from 11 January 1988: the former words were as follows:

"(a) a recognised bank or licensed institution within the meaning of the Banking Act 1979, or

(b) an institution to which sections 16 and 18 of that Act apply as if it were a licensed institution."

General note

This rule ensures that the Bank of England and the Deposit Protection Board are notified of meetings summoned in connection with the winding up of a recognised bank or an authorised institution under the Banking Act 1987.

Chapter 9 — Proof of Debts in a Liquidation

SECTION A: PROCEDURE FOR PROVING

Rule 4.73   Meaning of "prove"

4.73(1) [Winding up by court]   Where a company is being wound up by the court, a person claiming to be a creditor of the company and wishing to recover his debt in whole or in part must (subject to any order of the court under Rule 4.67(2)) submit his claim in writing to the liquidator. (NO CVL APPLICATION)

4.73(2–CVL) [Voluntary winding up]   In a voluntary winding up (whether members' or creditors') the liquidator may require a person claiming to be a creditor of the company and wishing to recover his debt in whole or in part, to submit the claim in writing to him.

4.73(3) ["Proving" and "proof"]   A creditor who claims (whether or not in writing) is referred to as "proving" for his debt; and a document by which he seeks to establish his claim is his "proof".

4.73(4) **["Proof of debt"]** Subject to the next paragraph, a proof must be in the form known as "proof of debt" (whether the form prescribed by the Rules, or a substantially similar form), which shall be made out by or under the directions of the creditor, and signed by him or a person authorised in that behalf. (NO CVL APPLICATION) [FORM 4.25]

4.73(5) **[Debt due to Crown etc.]** Where a debt is due to a Minister of the Crown or a Government Department, the proof need not be in that form, provided that there are shown all such particulars of the debt as are required in the form used by other creditors, and as are relevant in the circumstances. (NO CVL APPLICATION)

4.73(6–CVL) **[Creditor's proof]** The creditor's proof may be in any form.

4.73(7) **[Proof in form of affidavit]** In certain circumstances, specified below in this Chapter, the proof must be in the form of an affidavit.

(See general note after r. 4.85.)

Rule **4.74** Supply of forms

(NO CVL APPLICATION)

4.74(1) **[Forms to be sent to every creditor]** Forms of proof shall be sent out by the liquidator to every creditor of the company who is known to him, or is identified in the company's statement of affairs.

4.74(2) **[Forms to accompany first notice]** The forms shall accompany (whichever is first)—

(a) the notice to creditors under section 136(5)(b) (official receiver's decision not to call meetings of creditors and contributories), or

(b) the first notice calling a meeting of creditors, or

(c) where a liquidator is appointed by the court, the notice of his appointment sent by him to creditors.

4.74(3) **[Where liquidator advertises his appointment]** Where, with the leave of the court under Rule 4.102(5), the liquidator advertises his appointment, he shall send proofs to the creditors within 4 months after the date of the winding-up order.

4.74(4) **[Rule subject to order of court]** The above paragraphs of this Rule are subject to any order of the court dispensing with the requirement to send out forms of proof, or altering the time at which the forms are to be sent.

Rule 4.74(4)

See Practice Direction in [1987] 1 All ER 107 (reproduced in Appendix IV of this Guide).

(See general note after r. 4.85.)

Rule **4.75**   Contents of proof

(NO CVL APPLICATION)

4.75(1)   [Matters to be stated in creditor's proof]   Subject to Rule 4.73(5), the following matters shall be stated in a creditor's proof of debt—

   (a) the creditor's name and address;

   (b) the total amount of his claim as at the date on which the company went into liquidation;

   (c) whether or not that amount includes outstanding uncapitalised interest;

   (d) whether or not the claim includes value added tax;

   (e) whether the whole or any part of the debt falls within any (and if so which) of the categories of preferential debts under section 386 of, and Schedule 6 to, the Act (as read with Schedule 3 to the Social Security Pensions Act 1975);

   (f) particulars of how and when the debt was incurred by the company;

   (g) particulars of any security held, the date when it was given and the value which the creditor puts upon it; and

   (h) the name, address and authority of the person signing the proof (if other than the creditor himself).

4.75(2)   [Specified documents]   There shall be specified in the proof any documents by reference to which the debts can be substantiated; but (subject as follows) it is not essential that such documents be attached to the proof or submitted with it.

4.75(3)   [Production of documents etc.]   The liquidator, or the chairman or convener of any meeting, may call for any document or other evidence to be produced to him, where he thinks it necessary for the purpose of substantiating the whole or any part of the claim made in the proof.

History note

In r. 4.75(1) the words "Subject to Rule 4.73(5)," at the beginning were inserted by I(A)R 1987 (SI 1987 No. 1919), r. 3(1), Sch., Pt. 1, para. 58 as from 11 January 1988.

(See general note after r. 4.85.)

Rule **4.76**   Particulars of creditor's claim

4.76 CVL   The liquidator, or the convenor or chairman of any meeting, may, if he thinks it necessary for the purpose of clarifying or substantiating the whole or any part of a creditor's claim made in his proof, call for details of any matter specified in paragraphs (a) to (h) of Rule 4.75(1), or for the production to him of such documentary or other evidence as he may require.

(See general note after r. 4.85.)

Rule **4.77**　Claim established by affidavit

4.77(1)　**[Liquidator may require "affidavit of debt"]**　The liquidator may, if he thinks it necessary, require a claim of debt to be verified by means of an affidavit, for which purpose there shall be used the form known as "affidavit of debt", or a substantially similar form.　　　　　　　　　　　　　　　　　　[FORM 4.26]

4.77(2)　**[In addition to proof]**　An affidavit may be required notwithstanding that a proof of debt has already been lodged.

4.77(3)　**[Swearing of affidavit]**　The affidavit may be sworn before an official receiver or deputy official receiver, or before an officer of the Department or of the court duly authorised in that behalf. (NO CVL APPLICATION)

(See general note after r. 4.85.)

Rule **4.78**　Cost of proving

4.78(1)　**[Creditor bears cost of proving own debt]**　Subject as follows, every creditor bears the cost of proving his own debt, including such as may be incurred in providing documents or evidence under Rule 4.75(3) or 4.76–CVL.

4.78(2)　**[Liquidator's costs]**　Costs incurred by the liquidator in estimating the quantum of a debt under Rule 4.86 (debts not bearing a certain value) are payable out of the assets, as an expense of the liquidation.

4.78(3)　**[Application of rr. 4.78(1), (2)]**　Paragraphs (1) and (2) apply unless the court otherwise orders.

(See general note after r. 4.85.)

Rule **4.79**　Liquidator to allow inspection of proofs

4.79　The liquidator shall, so long as proofs lodged with him are in his hands, allow them to be inspected, at all reasonable times on any business day, by any of the following persons—

> (a)　any creditor who has submitted his proof of debt (unless his proof has been wholly rejected for purposes of dividend or otherwise);
>
> (b)　any contributory of the company;
>
> (c)　any person acting on behalf of either of the above.

(See general note after r. 4.85.)

Rule **4.80**　Transmission of proofs to liquidator

(NO CVL APPLICATION)

4.80(1)　**[On liquidator's appintment]**　Where a liquidator is appointed, the official receiver shall forthwith transmit to him all the proofs which he has so far received, together with an itemised list of them.

4.80(2) **[Receipt for proofs]**   The liquidator shall sign the list by way of receipt for the proofs, and return it to the official receiver.

4.80(3) **[All later proofs to liquidator]**   From then on, all proofs of debt shall be sent to the liquidator, and retained by him.

(See general note after r. 4.85.)

Rule **4.81**   New liquidator appointed

4.81(1) **[On appointment]**   If a new liquidator is appointed in place of another, the former liquidator shall transmit to him all proofs which he has received, together with an itemised list of them.

4.81(2) **[Receipt for proofs]**   The new liquidator shall sign the list by way of receipt for the proofs, and return it to his predecessor.

(See general note after r. 4.85.)

Rule **4.82**   Admission and rejection of proofs for dividend

4.82(1) **[Admission]**   A proof may be admitted for dividend either for the whole amount claimed by the creditor, or for part of that amount.

4.82(2) **[Rejection]**   If the liquidator rejects a proof in whole or in part, he shall prepare a written statement of his reasons for doing so, and send it forthwith to the creditor.

(See general note after r. 4.85.)

Rule **4.83**   Appeal against decision on proof

4.83(1) **[Application by creditor]**   If a creditor is dissatisifed with the liquidator's decision with respect to his proof (including any decision on the question of preference), he may apply to the court for the decision to be reversed or varied.

    The application must be made within 21 days of his receiving the statement sent under Rule 4.82(2).

4.83(2) **[Application by contributory etc.]**   A contributory or any other creditor may, if dissatisfied with the liquidator's decision admitting or rejecting the whole or any part of a proof, make such an application within 21 days of becoming aware of the liquidator's decision.

4.83(3) **[Venue and notice]**   Where application is made to the court under this Rule, the court shall fix a venue for the application to be heard, notice of which shall be sent by the applicant to the creditor who lodged the proof in question (if it is not himself) and to the liquidator.

4.83(4) **[Relevant proof etc. to be filed in court]**   The liquidator shall, on receipt of the notice, file in court the relevant proof, together (if appropriate) with a copy of the statement sent under Rule 4.82(2).

4.83(5) **[Return of proof]**   After the application has been heard and determined, the proof shall, unless it has been wholly disallowed, be returned by the court to the liquidator.

4.83(6) **[Costs re application]**   The official receiver is not personally liable for costs incurred by any person in respect of an application under this Rule; and the liquidator (if other than the official receiver) is not so liable unless the court makes an order to that effect.

(See general note after r. 4.85.)

Rule 4.84   Withdrawal or variation of proof

4.84   A creditor's proof may at any time, by agreement between himself and the liquidator, be withdrawn or varied as to the amount claimed.

(See general note after r. 4.85.)

Rule 4.85   Expunging of proof by the court

4.85(1) **[Expunging or reduction of amount]**   The court may expunge a proof or reduce the amount claimed—

    (a) on the liquidator's application, where he thinks that the proof has been improperly admitted, or ought to be reduced; or

    (b) on the application of a creditor, if the liquidator declines to interfere in the matter.

4.85(2) **[Venue and notice]**   Where application is made to the court under this Rule, the court shall fix a venue for the application to be heard, notice of which shall be sent by the applicant—

    (a) in the case of an application by the liquidator, to the creditor who made the proof, and

    (b) in the case of an application by a creditor, to the liquidator and to the creditor who made the proof (if not himself).

General note to rr. 4.73–4.85

Here are set out the rules governing the proof of debts, the rights of inspection of proofs, appeals against a liquidator's decision with respect to a proof, etc. See generally the comment preceding s. 175.

On the meaning of "went into liquidation", in r. 4.75, see IA 1986, s. 247.

See Practice Direction in [1987] 1 All ER 107 (reproduced in Appendix IV of this Guide).

SECTION B: QUANTIFICATION OF CLAIM

Rule 4.86   Estimate of quantum

4.86(1) **[Estimating value of debts etc.]**   The liquidator shall estimate the value of any debt which, by reason of its being subject to any contingency or for any other reason, does not bear a certain value; and he may revise any estimate previously made, if he thinks fit by reference to any change of circumstances or to information becoming available to him.

He shall inform the creditor as to his estimate and any revision of it.

4.86(2)   [Amount provable in winding up]   Where the value of a debt is estimated under this Rule, or by the court under section 168(3) or (5), the amount provable in the winding up in the case of that debt is that of the estimate for the time being.

(See general note after r. 4.89.)

Rule **4.87**   Negotiable instruments, etc.

4.87   Unless the liquidator allows, a proof in respect of money owed on a bill of exchange, promissory note, cheque or other negotiable instrument or security cannot be admitted unless there is produced the instrument or security itself or a copy of it, certified by the creditor or his authorised representative to be a true copy.

(See general note after r. 4.89.)

Rule **4.88**   Secured creditors

4.88(1)   [Proving for balance of debt]   If a secured creditor realises his security, he may prove for the balance of his debt, after deducting the amount realised.

4.88(2)   [Proving for whole debt]   If a secured creditor voluntarily surrenders his security for the general benefit of creditors, he may prove for his whole debt, as if it were unsecured.

(See general note after r. 4.89.)

Rule **4.89**   Discounts

4.89   There shall in every case be deducted from the claim all trade and other discounts which would have been available to the company but for its liquidation, except any discount for immediate, early or cash settlement.

General note to rr. 4.86–4.89

These are the rules for assessing a debt for the purposes of proof in the special cases of contingent and secured debts, etc.

Rule **4.90**   Mutual credit and set-off

4.90(1)   [Application of Rule]   This Rule applies where, before the company goes into liquidation there have been mutual credits, mutual debts or other mutual dealings between the company and any creditor of the company proving or claiming to prove for a debt in the liquidation.

4.90(2)   [Account of mutual dealings and set-off]   An account shall be taken of what is due from each party to the other in respect of the mutual dealings, and the sums due from one party shall be set off against the sums due from the other.

4.90(3) **[Sums not to be included in account]** Sums due from the company to another party shall not be included in the account taken under paragraph (2) if that other party had notice at the time they became due that a meeting of creditors had been summoned under section 98 or (as the case may be) a petition for the winding up of the company was pending.

4.90(4) **[Only balance (if any) provable etc.]** Only the balance (if any) of the account is provable in the liquidation. Alternatively (as the case may be) the amount shall be paid to the liquidator as part of the assets.

General note

There is no provision in the Insolvency Act itself for the case of mutual credit and set-off in company insolvency corresponding to IA 1986, s. 323, which deals with individual bankruptcy. The present rule makes good this shortcoming. See the general comment on Pt. IV, Ch. VIII preceding IA 1986, s. 175.

The new law removes some uncertainties that were not fully resolved previously. First, it is now clear that the rules as to mutual credit and set-off apply to all liquidations, irrespective of the solvency or otherwise of the company and whether the liquidation is voluntary or compulsory. Secondly, it is also clear that the relevant date (or time: see the note to s. 86) for all purposes of proof and set-off is that when the company goes into liquidation. (For the meaning of this expression, see s. 247(2).) On the other hand, some difficult questions remain to be resolved, e.g. the rules give no guidance as to the set-off of contingent liabilities, and in particular how such liabilities of the company should be quantified. (On this point see Wood (1987) 8 Co. Law. 262 and *MS Fashions Ltd & Ors v Bank of Credit & Commerce International SA (No. 2)* [1993] Ch. 425, at p. 435; [1993] BCC 70, at p. 75; and note that the court will take into account for this purpose events which have happened since the date of the winding up (ibid., at p. 432, 73).)

The rules as to set-off in insolvency are different from those which apply between solvent parties. The object of the latter is to avoid cross-actions, and their scope is restricted. The former, in contrast, are intended to do substantial justice between the parties, and their application is not limited to particular categories of claim, but apply to all cross-claims provided that they are mutual and measurable in money terms (*Stein v Blake* [1993] BCC 587, at p. 590, per Balcombe LJ). The rules as to set-off are mandatory and cannot be excluded by agreement between the parties (*National Westminster Bank Ltd v Halesowen Presswork & Assemblies Ltd* [1972] AC 785). In the *MS Fashions* case (above, affirmed [1993] Ch. 425, at p. 439; *sub nom. High Street Services Ltd & Ors v Bank of Credit & Commerce International SA* [1993] BCC 360), it was held that where several persons were each liable to the company as principal debtors in respect of the same debt, a set-off available against one of them operated automatically to reduce the debt for the benefit of them all. It was not open to a liquidator to seek to avoid this consequence by electing to claim the full amount in the first instance from the other debtors. (For earlier proceedings in the same case, see *MS Fashions Ltd & Ors v Bank of Credit & Commerce International SA & Anor* [1992] BCC 571.) In contrast, in a later case, *Re Bank of Credit & Commerce International SA (No. 3)* [1994] BCC 462, the court held that the bank's liquidators could proceed first against the principal debtors concerned, without bringing into account the amounts of certain deposits made with the bank by other persons and allegedly charged to secure the debts. In this case the depositors had no personal liability for the principal debts, and accordingly there was no sum "due" from them on which a set-off could operate.

The holder of a secured debt is not required by r. 4.90 to set off money owed by the company to him against that debt, unless he elects to give up his security and prove his debt in the liquidation: *Re Norman Holding Co. Ltd (in liquidation)* [1991] 1 WLR 10; [1991] BCC 11.

For the exclusion of set-off in respect of post-insolvency VAT credits, see Finance Act 1988, s. 21 (as amended by Finance Act 1994, s. 47).

In *Myles J Callaghan Ltd (in receivership) & Anor* v *City of Glasgow District Council* (1987) 3 BCC 337 it was held competent in Scots law for a creditor in a liquidation to set off a claim for damages for breach of a building contract against a claim by the company for the return of its plant and equipment or payment of its value, and to do so notwithstanding the appointment of a receiver.

See also the notes to s. 323, above.

Rule **4.91**   Debt in foreign currency

4.91(1)   [Conversion into sterling]   For the purpose of proving a debt incurred or payable in a currency other than sterling, the amount of the debt shall be converted into sterling at the official exchange rate prevailing on the date when the company went into liquidation.

4.91(2)   ["The official exchange rate"]   "The official exchange rate" is the middle market rate at the Bank of England, as published for the date in question. In the absence of any such published rate, it is such rate as the court determines.

General note

This confirms the ruling in *Re Lines Bros Ltd* [1983] Ch. 1 in which comments made (*obiter*) in the earlier decision of the House of Lords in *Miliangos* v *George Frank (Textiles) Ltd* [1976] AC 443 were not followed. For the meaning of "went into liquidation", see s. 247(2). Note that the rule refers to the *date*, rather than the *time*. (On this point, see the note to s. 86.)

Rule **4.92**   Payments of a periodical nature

4.92(1)   [Rent etc.]   In the case of rent and other payments of a periodical nature, the creditor may prove for any amounts due and unpaid up to the date when the company went into liquidation.

4.92(2)   [If accruing from day to day]   Where at that date any payment was accruing due, the creditor may prove for so much as would have fallen due at that date, if accruing from day to day.

Rule **4.93**   Interest

4.93(1)   [Where debt bears interest]   Where a debt proved in the liquidation bears interest, that interest is provable as part of the debt except in so far as it is payable in respect of any period after the company went into liquidation.

4.93(2)   [Where claim may include interest]   In the following circumstances the creditor's claim may include interest on the debt for periods before the company went into liquidation, although not previously reserved or agreed.

4.93(3)   [Debt due by written instrument]   If the debt is due by virtue of a written instrument, and payable at a certain time, interest may be claimed for the period from that time to the date when the company went into liquidation.

4.93(4)   [Debt due otherwise]   If the debt is due otherwise, interest may only be claimed if, before that date, a demand for payment of the debt was made in writing by or on behalf of the creditor, and notice given that interest would be payable from the date of the demand to the date of payment.

4.93(5) **[Claiming r. 4.93(4) interest]** Interest under paragraph (4) may only be claimed for the period from the date of the demand to that of the company's going into liquidation and for all the purposes of the Act and the Rules shall be chargeable at a rate not exceeding that mentioned in paragraph (6).

4.93(6) **[Rate of interest under r. 4.93(3) and (4)]** The rate of interest to be claimed under paragraphs (3) and (4) is the rate specified in section 17 of the Judgments Act 1838 on the date when the company went into liquidation.

History note

In r. 4.93(5) the words from "and for all purposes" to the end were added by I(A)R 1987 (SI 1987 No. 1919), r. 3(1), Sch., Pt. 1, para. 59(1) as from 11 January 1988; and by para. 59(2) of the same schedule r. 4.93(6) was substituted. Rule 4.93(6) formerly read as follows:

"**4.93(6)** The rate of interest to be claimed under paragraph (3) or (4) of this Rule is the rate specified in section 17 of the Judgments Act 1838 on the date when the company went into liquidation, except that, where the case falls within paragraph (4), the rate is that specified in the notice there referred to, not exceeding the rate under the Judgments Act mentioned above."

General note

See the notes to IA 1986, s. 189.

Rule 4.94   Debt payable at future time

4.94 A creditor may prove for a debt of which payment was not yet due on the date when the company went into liquidation, but subject to Rule 11.13 in Part 11 of the Rules (adjustment of dividend where payment made before time).

Chapter 10 — Secured Creditors

Rule 4.95   Value of security

4.95(1) **[Altering value]** A secured creditor may, with the agreement of the liquidator or the leave of the court, at any time alter the value which he has, in his proof of debt, put upon his security.

4.95(2) **[Limitation on re-valuation]** However, if a secured creditor—

(a) being the petitioner, has in the petition put a value on his security, or

(b) has voted in respect of the unsecured balance of his debt,

he may re-value his security only with leave of the court. (NO CVL APPLICATION)

(See general note after r. 4.99.)

Rule 4.96 Surrender for non-disclosure

4.96(1) [Omission to disclose security] If a secured creditor omits to disclose his security in his proof of debt, he shall surrender his security for the general benefit of creditors, unless the court, on application by him, relieves him for the effect of this Rule on the ground that the omission was inadvertent or the result of honest mistake.

4.96(2) [Relief from effect of r. 4.96(1)] If the court grants that relief, it may require or allow the creditor's proof of debt to be amended, on such terms as may be just.

(See general note after r. 4.99.)

Rule 4.97 Redemption by liquidator

4.97(1) [Notice of proposed redemption] The liquidator may at any time give notice to a creditor whose debt is secured that he proposes, at the expiration of 28 days from the date of the notice, to redeem the security at the value put upon it in the creditor's proof.

4.97(2) [Time for re-valuation etc.] The creditor then has 21 days (or such longer period as the liquidator may allow) in which, if he so wishes, to exercise his right to re-value his security (with the leave of the court, where Rule 4.95(2) applies).

If the creditor re-values his security, the liquidator may only redeem at the new value.

4.97(3) [If liquidator redeems] If the liquidator redeems the security, the cost of transferring it is payable out of the assets.

4.97(4) [Notice to liquidator to elect etc.] A secured creditor may at any time, by a notice in writing, call on the liquidator to elect whether he will or will not exercise his power to redeem the security at the value then placed on it; and the liquidator then has 6 months in which to exercise the power or determine not to exercise it.

(See general note after r. 4.99.)

Rule 4.98 Test of security's value

4.98(1) [Offer for sale] Subject as follows, the liquidator, if he is dissatisfied with the value which a secured creditor puts on his security (whether in his proof or by way of re-valuation under Rule 4.97), may require any property comprised in the security to be offered for sale.

4.98(2) [Terms of sale] The terms of sale shall be such as may be agreed, or as the court may direct; and if the sale is by auction, the liquidator on behalf of the company, and the creditor on his own behalf, may appear and bid.

(See general note after r. 4.99.)

Rule 4.99 Realisation of security by creditor

4.99 If a creditor who has valued his security subsequently realises it (whether or not at the instance of the liquidator)—

(a) the net amount realised shall be substituted for the value previously put by the creditor on the security, and

(b) that amount shall be treated in all respects as an amended valuation made by him.

General note to rr. 4.95–4.99

These rules deal with the valuation of his security by a secured creditor, the liquidator's right to redeem the security, the consequences of the realisation of a security, and various related matters.

Chapter 11 — The Liquidator

SECTION A: APPOINTMENT AND ASSOCIATED FORMALITIES

Rule 4.100   Appointment by creditors or contributories
(NO CVL APPLICATION)

4.100(1)   [Application of Rule]   This Rule applies where a person is appointed as liquidator either by a meeting of creditors or by a meeting of contributories.

4.100(2)   [Certification of appointment]   The chairman of the meeting shall certify the appointment, but not unless and until the person appointed has provided him with a written statement to the effect that he is an insolvency practitioner, duly qualified under the Act to be the liquidator, and that he consents so to act.   [FORM 4.27]
[FORM 4.28]

4.100(3)   [Effective date of appointment]   The liquidator's appointment is effective from the date on which the appointment is certified, that date to be endorsed on the certificate.

4.100(4)   [Where chairman not official receiver]   The chairman of the meeting (if not himself the official receiver) shall send the certificate to the official receiver.

4.100(5)   [Certificate to liquidator; filing]   The official receiver shall in any case send the certificate to the liquidator and file a copy of it in court.

History note

Rules 4.100(3), (4) and (5) were substituted by I(A)R 1987 (SI 1987 No. 1919), r. 3(1), Sch., Pt. 1, para. 60 as from 11 January 1988: they formerly read as follows:

"**4.100(3)**   Where the chairman of the meeting is not the official receiver, he shall send the certificate to him.

4.100(4)   The official receiver shall in any case file a copy of the certificate in court; and the liquidator's appointment is effective as from the date on which the official receiver files the copy certificate in court, that date to be endorsed on the copy certificate.

4.100(5)   The certificate, so endorsed, shall be sent by the official receiver to the liquidator."

(See general note after r. 4.106.)

Rule **4.101**   Appointment by creditors or by the company

4.101–CVL(1)   [Application of Rule]   This Rule applies where a person is appointed as liquidator either by a meeting of creditors or by a meeting of the company.

4.101(2)   [Certification and effective date of appointment]   Subject as follows, the chairman of the meeting shall certify the appointment, but not unless and until the person appointed has provided him with a written statement to the effect that he is an insolvency practitioner, duly qualified under the Act to be the liquidator, and that he consents so to act; the liquidator's appointment takes effect upon the passing of the resolution for that appointment.   [FORM 4.27]
[FORM 4.28]

4.101(3)   [Certificate to liquidator]   The chairman shall send the certificate forthwith to the liquidator, who shall keep it as part of the records of the liquidation.

4.101(4)   [Where no need to comply with rr. 4.101(2), (3)]   Paragraphs (2) and (3) need not be complied with in case of a liquidator appointed by a company meeting and replaced by another liquidator appointed on the same day by a creditors' meeting.

History note

In r. 4.101(2) the words from "takes effect upon the passing" to the end were substituted for the former words "is effective from the date of the certificate" by I(A)R 1987 (SI 1987 No. 1919), r. 3(1), Sch., Pt. 1, para. 61 as from 11 January 1988.

(See general note after r. 4.106.)

Rule **4.101A**   Power to fill vacancy in office of liquidator

4.101A–CVL   Where a vacancy in the office of liquidator occurs in the manner mentioned in section 104 a meeting of creditors to fill the vacancy may be convened by any creditor or, if there were more liquidators than one, by the continuing liquidators.

History note

Rule 4.101A was inserted by I(A)R 1987 (SI 1987 No. 1919), r. 3(1), Sch., Pt. 1, para. 62, as from 11 January 1988.

(See general note after r. 4.106.)

Rule **4.102**   Appointment by the court

(NO CVL APPLICATION)

4.102(1)   [Application of Rule]   This Rule applies where the liquidator is appointed by the court under section 139(4) (different persons nominated by creditors and contributories) or section 140 (liquidation following administration or voluntary arrangement).   [FORM 4.29]
[FORM 4.30]

4.102(2)   [Issue of court order]   The court's order shall not issue unless and until the person appointed has filed in court a statement to the effect that he is an insolvency practitioner, duly qualified under the Act to be the liquidator, and that he consents so to act.

4.102(3)   [Copy of orders to official receiver etc.]   Thereafter, the court shall send 2 copies of the order to the official receiver. One of the copies shall be sealed, and this shall be sent to the person appointed as liquidator.

4.102(4)   [Commencement of appointment]   The liquidator's appointment takes effect from the date of the order.

4.102(5)   [Notice of appointment etc.]   The liquidator shall, within 28 days of his appointment, give notice of it to all creditors and contributories of the company of whom he is aware in that period. Alternatively, if the court allows, he may advertise his appointment in accordance with the court's directions.

4.102(6)   [Contents of notice etc.]   In his notice or advertisement under this Rule the liquidator shall—

> (a) state whether he proposes to summon meetings of creditors and contributories for the purpose of establishing a liquidation committee, or proposes to summon only a meeting of creditors for that purpose, and
>
> (b) if he does not propose to summon any such meeting, set out the powers of the creditors under the Act to require him to summon one.

General note

See Practice Direction in [1987] 1 All ER 107 (reproduced in Appendix IV of this Guide). See also general note after r. 4.106.

Rule **4.103**   Appointment by the court

4.103–CVL(1)   [Application of Rule]   This Rule applies where the liquidator is appointed by the court under section 100(3) or 108.   [FORM 4.29]
                                                                                   [FORM 4.30]

4.103(2)   [Issue of court order]   The court's order shall not issue unless and until the person appointed has filed in court a statement to the effect that he is an insolvency practitioner, duly qualified under the Act to be the liquidator, and that he consents so to act.

4.103(3)   [Sealed copy to liquidator]   Thereafter, the court shall send a sealed copy of the order to the liquidator, whose appointment takes effect from the date of the order.

4.103(4)   [Notice etc. of appointment]   Not later than 28 days from his appointment, the liquidator shall give notice of it to all creditors of the company of whom he is aware in that period. Alternatively, if the court allows, he may advertise his appointment in accordance with the court's directions.

General note

See Practice Direction in [1987] 1 All ER 107 (reproduced in Appendix IV of this Guide). See also general note after r. 4.106.

Rule **4.104**   Appointment by Secretary of State

(NO CVL APPLICATION)

4.104(1)   [Application of Rule]   This Rule applies where the official receiver applies to the Secretary of State to appoint a liquidator in place of himself, or refers to the Secretary of State the need for an appointment.

4.104(2)   **[Copy of certificates to official receiver etc.]**   If the Secretary of State makes an appointment, he shall send two copies of the certificate of appointment to the official receiver, who shall transmit one such copy to the person appointed, and file the other in court.

4.104(3)   **[Content of certificate]**   The certificate shall specify the date from which the liquidator's appointment is to be effective.

(See general note after r. 4.106.)

Rule 4.105   Authentication of liquidator's appointment

4.105   A copy of the certificate of the liquidator's appointment or (as the case may be) a sealed copy of the court's order, may in any proceedings be adduced as proof that the person appointed is duly authorised to exercise the powers and perform the duties of liquidator in the company's winding up.

(See general note after r. 4.106.)

Rule 4.106   Appointment to be advertised and registered

4.106(1)   **[Where liquidator appointed by meeting]**   Subject as follows, where the liquidator is appointed by a creditors' or contributories' meeting, or by a meeting of the company, he shall, on receiving his certificate of appointment, give notice of his appointment in such newspaper as he thinks most appropriate for ensuring that it comes to the notice of the company's creditors and contributories.

4.106(2–CVL)   **[Where no need to comply with r. 4.106(1)]**   Paragraph (1) need not be complied with in the case of a liquidator appointed by a company meeting and replaced by another liquidator appointed on the same day by a creditors' meeting.

4.106(3)   **[Expense of giving notice]**   The expense of giving notice under this Rule shall be borne in the first instance by the liquidator; but he is entitled to be reimbursed out of the assets, as an expense of the liquidation.

    The same applies also in the case of the notice or advertisement required where the appointment is made by the court or the Secretary of State.

4.106(4)   **[Notice to registrar]**   In the case of a winding up by the court, the liquidator shall also forthwith notify his appointment to the registrar of companies.

    This applies however the liquidator is appointed.   [FORM 4.31]

(NO CVL APPLICATION)

History note

The words "(NO CVL APPLICATION)" at the end of r. 4.106 were inserted by I(A)R 1987 (SI 1987 No. 1919), r. 3(1), Sch., Pt. 1, para. 63 as from 11 January 1988.

General note to rr. 4.100–4.106
These rules are concerned with the formalities relating to the appointment of a liquidator by the creditors or contributories (rr. 4.100, 4.101), by the court (rr. 4.102, 4.103), and by the Secretary of State (r. 4.104), and the certification, registration and notification of the appointment. The amendments to rr. 4.100, 4.101 and the new r. 4.101A are designed to resolve practical difficulties experienced in the operation of the rules as originally drafted.

Rule **4.107**   Hand-over of assets to liquidator

(NO CVL APPLICATION)

4.107(1)   **[Application of Rule]**   This Rule applies only where the liquidator is appointed in succession to the official receiver acting as liquidator.

4.107(2)   **[On liquidator's appointment]**   When the liquidator's appointment takes effect, the official receiver shall forthwith do all that is required for putting him into possession of the assets.

4.107(3)   **[Discharge of balance due to official receiver]**   On taking possession of the assets, the liquidator shall discharge any balance due to the official receiver on account of—

    (a) expenses properly incurred by him and payable under the Act or the Rules, and

    (b) any advances made by him in respect of the assets, together with interest on such advances at the rate specified in section 17 of the Judgments Act 1838 at the date of the winding-up order.

4.107(4)   **[Undertaking to discharge]**   Alternatively, the liquidator may (before taking office) give to the official receiver a written undertaking to discharge any such balance out of the first realisation of assets.

4.107(5)   **[Official receiver's charge]**   The official receiver has a charge on the assets in respect of any sums due to him under paragraph (3). But, where the liquidator has realised assets with a view to making those payments, the official receiver's charge does not extend in respect of sums deductible by the liquidator from the proceeds of realisation, as being expenses properly incurred therein.

4.107(6)   **[Discharge of guarantees etc.]**   The liquidator shall from time to time out of the realisation of assets discharge all guarantees properly given by the official receiver for the benefit of the estate, and shall pay all the official receiver's expenses.

4.107(7)   **[Official receiver to give liquidator information]**   The official receiver shall give to the liquidator all such information relating to the affairs of the company and the course of the winding up as he (the official receiver) considers to be reasonably required for the effective discharge by the liquidator of his duties as such.

4.107(8)   **[Copy of Ch. 7 report]**   The liquidator shall also be furnished with a copy of any report made by the official receiver under Chapter 7 of this Part of the Rules.

General note

This rule applies following the appointment of a private liquidator under IA 1986, ss. 136 and 139, or s. 137.

SECTION B: RESIGNATION AND REMOVAL; VACATION OF OFFICE

Rule **4.108**   Creditors' meeting to receive liquidator's resignation

4.108(1)   [Liquidator must call meeting etc.]   Before resigning his office, the liquidator must call a meeting of creditors for the purpose of receiving his resignation. The notice summoning the meeting shall indicate that this is the purpose, or one of the purposes, of it, and shall draw the attention of creditors to Rule 4.121 or, as the case may be, Rule 4.122–CVL with respect to the liquidator's release.   [FORM 4.22]

4.108(2)   [Copy of notice to official receiver]   A copy of the notice shall at the same time also be sent to the official receiver. (NO CVL APPLICATION)

4.108(3)   [Account of liquidator's administration]   The notice to creditors under paragraph (1) must be accompanied by an account of the liquidator's administration of the winding up, including—

(a) a summary of his receipts and payments, and

(b) a statement by him that he has reconciled his account with that which is held by the Secretary of State in respect of the winding up.

4.108(4)   [Grounds for proceeding under Rule]   Subject as follows, the liquidator may only proceed under this Rule on grounds of ill health or because—

(a) he intends ceasing to be in practice as an insolvency practitioner, or

(b) there is some conflict of interest or change of personal circumstances which precludes or makes impracticable the further discharge by him of the duties of liquidator.

4.108(5)   [Where joint liquidators]   Where two or more persons are acting as liquidator jointly, any one of them may proceed under this Rule (without prejudice to the continuation in office of the other or others) on the ground that, in his opinion and that of the other or others, it is no longer expedient that there should continue to be the present number of joint liquidators.

4.108(6)   [If no quorum]   If there is no quorum present at the meeting summoned to receive the liquidator's resignation, the meeting is deemed to have been held, a resolution is deemed to have been passed that the liquidator's resignation be accepted and the creditors are deemed not to have resolved against the liquidator having his release.

4.108(7)   [Application of r. 4.108(6)]   Where paragraph (6) applies any reference in the Rules to a resolution that the liquidator's resignation be accepted is replaced by a reference to the making of a written statement, signed by the person who, had there been a quorum present, would have been chairman of the meeting, that no quorum was present and that the liquidator may resign.

History note

Rules 4.108(6) and (7) were added by I(A)R 1987 (SI 1987 No. 1919), r. 3(1), Sch., Pt. 1, para. 64 as from 11 January 1988.

(See general note after r. 4.112.)

Rule **4.109** Action following acceptance of resignation

(NO CVL APPLICATION)

4.109(1) [Application of Rule] This Rule applies where a meeting is summoned to receive the liquidator's resignation.

4.109(2) [Copy of resolutions to official receiver etc.] If the chairman of the meeting is other than the official receiver, and there is passed at the meeting any of the following resolutions—

(a) that the liquidator's resignation be accepted,

(b) that a new liquidator be appointed,

(c) that the resigning liquidator be not given his release,

the chairman shall, within 3 days, send to the official receiver a copy of the resolution.

   If it has been resolved to accept the liquidator's resignation, the chairman shall send to the official receiver a certificate to that effect.

4.109(3) [If creditors resolve to appoint new liquidator] If the creditors have resolved to appoint a new liquidator, the certificate of his appointment shall also be sent to the official receiver within that time; and Rule 4.100 shall be complied with in respect of it.

4.109(4) [If liquidator's resignation accepted] If the liquidator's resignation is accepted, the notice of it required by section 172(6) shall be given by him forthwith after the meeting; and he shall send a copy of the notice to the official receiver.

   The notice shall be accompanied by a copy of the account sent to creditors under Rule 4.108(3).   [FORM 4.32]

4.109(5) [Copy notice] The official receiver shall file a copy of the notice in court.

4.109(6) [Effective date of resignation] The liquidator's resignation is effective as from the date on which the official receiver files the copy notice in court, that date to be endorsed on the copy notice.

(See general note after r. 4.112.)

Rule **4.110** Action following acceptance of resignation

4.110–CVL(1) [Application of Rule] This Rule applies where a meeting is summoned to receive the liquidator's resignation.

4.110(2) [S. 171(5) notice] If his resignation is accepted, the notice of it required by section 171(5) shall be given by him forthwith after the meeting.

[FORM 4.33]

4.110(3) [Certificate of new liquidator's appointment] Where a new liquidator is appointed in place of the one who has resigned, the certificate of his appointment shall be delivered forthwith by the chairman of the meeting to the new liquidator.

(See general note after r. 4.112.)

Rule **4.111** Leave to resign granted by the court

4.111(1) [If liquidator's resignation not accepted] If at a creditors' meeting summoned to accept the liquidator's resignation it is resolved that it be not accepted, the court may, on the liquidator's application, make an order giving him leave to resign.   [FORM 4.34]

4.111(2)   [Extent of order under r. 4.111(1)]   The court's order may include such provision as it thinks fit with respect to matters arising in connection with the resignation, and shall determine the date from which the liquidator's release is effective.

4.111(3)   [Sealed copies of order]   The court shall send two sealed copies of the order to the liquidator, who shall send one of the copies forthwith to the official receiver. (NO CVL APPLICATION)

4.111(4–CVL)   [Sealed copies]   The court shall send two sealed copies of the order to the liquidator, who shall forthwith send one of them to the registrar of companies.   [FORM 4.35]

4.111(5)   [Copy notice to court and official receiver]   On sending notice of his resignation to the court, the liquidator shall send a copy of it to the official receiver. (NO CVL APPLICATION)   [FORM 4.36]

General note

See Practice Direction in [1987] 1 All ER 107 (reproduced in Appendix IV of this Guide). See also general note after r. 4.112.

Rule 4.112   Advertisement of resignation

4.112   Where a new liquidator is appointed in place of one who has resigned, the former shall, in giving notice of his appointment, state that his predecessor has resigned and (if it be the case) that he has been given his release.

General note to rr. 4.108–4.112

The circumstances in which a liquidator may resign are set out in r. 108(4), (5). These rules detail the procedure to be followed, and the date when the resignation takes effect. The question of the release of the liquidator is covered by rr. 4.121, 4.122.

Rule 4.113   Meeting of creditors to remove liquidator

(NO CVL APPLICATION)

4.113(1)   [Notice]   Where a meeting of creditors is summoned for the purpose of removing the liquidator, the notice summoning it shall indicate that this is the purpose, or one of the purposes, of the meeting; and the notice shall draw the attention of creditors to section 174(4) with respect to the liquidator's release.

[FORM 4.22]

4.113(2)   [Copy notice to official receiver]   A copy of the notice shall at the same time also be sent to the official receiver.

4.113(3)   [Chairman; if liquidator chairman etc.]   At the meeting, a person other than the liquidator or his nominee may be elected to act as chairman; but if the liquidator or his nominee is chairman and a resolution has been proposed for the liquidator's removal, the chairman shall not adjourn the meeting without the consent of at least one-half (in value) of the creditors present (in person or by proxy) and entitled to vote.

4.113(4) [Copy resolutions to official receiver]   Where the chairman of the meeting is other than the official receiver, and there is passed at the meeting any of the following resolutions—

(a) that the liquidator be removed,

(b) that a new liquidator be appointed,

(c) that the removed liquidator be not given his release,

the chairman shall, within 3 days, send to the official receiver a copy of the resolution.

If it has been resolved to remove the liquidator, the chairman shall send to the official receiver a certificate to that effect.   [FORM 4.37]

4.113(5) [If creditors resolve to appoint new liquidator]   If the creditors have resolved to appoint a new liquidator, the certificate of his appointment shall also be sent to the official receiver within that time; and Rule 4.100 above shall be complied with in respect of it.

(See general note after r. 4.120.)

Rule 4.114   Meeting of creditors to remove liquidator

4.114–CVL(1) [S. 171(2)(b) meeting requested]   A meeting held under section 171(2)(b) for the removal of the liquidator shall be summoned by him if requested by 25 per cent in value of the company's creditors, excluding those who are connected with it.

4.114(2) [Notice]   The notice summoning the meeting shall indicate that the removal of the liquidator is the purpose, or one of the purposes, of the meeting; and the notice shall draw the attention of creditors to section 173(2) with respect to the liquidator's release.   [FORM 4.22]

4.114(3) [Chairman; if liquidator chairman etc.]   At the meeting, a person other than the liquidator or his nominee may be elected to act as chairman, but if the liquidator or his nominee is chairman and a resolution has been proposed for the liquidator's removal, the chairman shall not adjourn the meeting without the consent of at least one-half (in value) of the creditors present (in person or by proxy) and entitled to vote.

(See general note after r. 4.120.)

Rule 4.115   Court's power to regulate meetings under Rules 4.113, 4.114–CVL

4.115   Where a meeting under Rule 4.113 or 4.114–CVL is to be held, or is proposed to be summoned, the court may, on the application of any creditor, give directions as to the mode of summoning it, the sending out and return of forms of proxy, the conduct of the meeting, and any other matter which appears to the court to require regulation or control under this Rule.

(See general note after r. 4.120.)

Rule **4.116**　Procedure on removal

(NO CVL APPLICATION)

4.116(1)　**[Certificate of removal to be filed]**　Where the creditors have resolved that the liquidator be removed, the official receiver shall file in court the certificate of removal.

4.116(2)　**[Effective date of removal resolution]**　The resolution is effective as from the date on which the official receiver files the certificate of removal in court, and that date shall be endorsed on the certificate.

4.116(3)　**[Copy of certificate]**　A copy of the certificate, so endorsed, shall be sent by the official receiver to the liquidator who has been removed and, if a new liquidator has been appointed, to him.

4.116(4)　**[Reconciliation of accounts]**　The official receiver shall not file the certificate in court unless and until the Secretary of State has certified to him that the removed liquidator has reconciled his account with that held by the Secretary of State in respect of the winding up.

(See general note after r. 4. 120.)

Rule **4.117**　Procedure on removal

4.117–CVL　Where the creditors have resolved that the liquidator be removed, the chairman of the creditors' meeting shall forthwith—

(a) if at the meeting another liquidator was not appointed, send the certificate of the liquidator's removal to the registrar of companies, and

(b) otherwise, deliver the certificate to the new liquidator, who shall send it to the registrar.　　　　　　　　　　　　　　[FORM 4.38]

(See general note after r. 4.120.)

Rule **4.118**　Advertisement of removal

4.118　Where a new liquidator is appointed in place of one removed, the former shall, in giving notice of his appointment, state that his predecessor has been removed and (if it be the case) that he has been given his release.

(See general note after r. 4.120.)

Rule **4.119**　Removal of liquidator by the court

(NO CVL APPLICATION)

4.119(1)　**[Application of Rule]**　This Rule applies where application is made to the court for the removal of the liquidator, or for an order directing the liquidator to summon a meeting of creditors for the purpose of removing him.　　　[FORM 4.39]

4.119(2)　**[Court may dismiss application etc.]**　The court may, if it thinks that no sufficient cause is shown for the application, dismiss it; but it shall not do so unless the applicant has had an opportunity to attend the court for an *ex parte* hearing, of which he has been given at least 7 days' notice.

If the application is not dismissed under this paragraph, the court shall fix a venue for it to be heard.

4.119(3)   [Deposit or security for costs]   The court may require the applicant to make a deposit or give security for the costs to be incurred by the liquidator on the application.

4.119(4)   [Notice etc.]   The applicant shall, at least 14 days before the hearing, send to the liquidator and the official receiver a notice stating the venue and accompanied by a copy of the application, and of any evidence which he intends to adduce in support of it.

4.119(5)   [Costs]   Subject to any contrary order of the court, the costs of the application are not payable out of the assets.

4.119(6)   [Where court removes liquidator]   Where the court removes the liquidator—

- (a) it shall send copies of the order of removal to him and to the official receiver;
- (b) the order may include such provision as the court thinks fit with respect to matters arising in connection with the removal; and
- (c) if the court appoints a new liquidator, Rule 4.102 applies.

(See general note after r. 4.120.)

Rule **4.120**   Removal of liquidator by the court

4.120–CVL(1)   [Application of Rule]   This Rule applies where application is made to the court for the removal of the liquidator, or for an order directing the liquidator to summon a creditors' meeting for the purpose of removing him.   [FORM 4.39]

4.120(2)   [Court may dismiss application etc.]   The court may, if it thinks that no sufficient cause is shown for the application, dismiss it; but it shall not do so unless the applicant has had an opportunity to attend the court for an *ex parte* hearing, of which he has been given at least 7 days' notice.

If the application is not dismissed under this paragraph, the court shall fix a venue for it to be heard.

4.120(3)   [Deposit or security for costs]   The court may require the applicant to make a deposit or give security for the costs to be incurred by the liquidator on the application.

4.120(4)   [Notice etc.]   The applicant shall, at least 14 days before the hearing, send to the liquidator a notice stating the venue and accompanied by a copy of the application, and of any evidence which he intends to adduce in support of it.

4.120(5)   [Costs]   Subject to any contrary order of the court, the costs of the application are not payable out of the assets.

4.120(6)   [Where court removes liquidator]   Where the court removes the liquidator—

(a) it shall send 2 copies of the order of removal to him, one to be sent by him forthwith to the registrar of companies, with notice of his ceasing to act;

(b) the order may include such provision as the court thinks fit with respect to matters arising in connection with the removal; and

(c) if the court appoints a new liquidator, Rule 4.103–CVL applies.

[FORM 4.40]

General note to rr. 4.113–4.120

The removal of a liquidator is dealt with in IA 1986, ss. 171, 172, which these rules supplement. On the liquidator's release, see rr. 4.121, 4.122.

Rule 4.121   Release of resigning or removed liquidator

(NO CVL APPLICATION)

4.121(1) **[Where liquidator's resignation accepted]** Where the liquidator's resignation is accepted by a meeting of creditors which has not resolved against his release, he has his release from when his resignation is effective under Rule 4.109.

4.121(2) **[Where liquidator removed by meeting]** Where the liquidator is removed by a meeting of creditors which has not resolved against his release, the fact of his release shall be stated in the certificate of removal.

4.121(3) **[Application to Secretary of State]** Where—

(a) the liquidator resigns, and the creditors' meeting called to receive his resignation has resolved against his release, or

(b) he is removed by a creditors' meeting which has so resolved, or is removed by the court,

he must apply to the Secretary of State for his release.   [FORM 4.41]

4.121(4) **[Certificate of release]** When the Secretary of State gives the release, he shall certify it accordingly, and send the certificate to the official receiver, to be filed in court.

4.121(5) **[Copy of certificate]** A copy of the certificate shall be sent by the Secretary of State to the former liquidator, whose release is effective from the date of the certificate.

(See general note after r. 4.122.)

Rule 4.122   Release of resigning or removed liquidator

4.122–CVL(1) **[Where liquidator's resignation accepted]** Where the liquidator's resignation is accepted by a meeting of creditors which has not resolved against his release, he has his release from when he gives notice of his resignation to the registrar of companies.   [FORM 4.40]

4.122(2) **[Where liquidator removed by meeting]** Where the liquidator is removed by a creditors' meeting which has not resolved against his release, the fact of his release shall be stated in the certificate of removal.

4.122(3)   [Application to Secretary of State]   Where—

(a) the liquidator resigns, and the creditors' meeting called to receive his resignation has resolved against his release, or

(b) he is removed by a creditors' meeting which has so resolved, or is removed by the court,

he must apply to the Secretary of State for his release.   [FORM 4.41]

4.122(4)   [Certificate of release]   When the Secretary of State gives the release, he shall certify it accordingly, and send the certificate to the registrar of companies.

4.122(5)   [Copy of certificate]   A copy of the certificate shall be sent by the Secretary of State to the former liquidator, whose release is effective from the date of the certificate.

General note to rr. 4.121, 4.122

These rules deal with the liquidator's release following his resignation or removal. On the question of release following completion of the administration of the winding up, see rr. 4.124ff.

Rule 4.123   Removal of liquidator by Secretary of State

(NO CVL APPLICATION)

4.123(1)   [Notice to liquidator etc.]   If the Secretary of State decides to remove the liquidator, he shall before doing so notify the liquidator and the official receiver of his decision and the grounds of it, and specify a period within which the liquidator may make representations against implementation of the decision.

4.123(2)   [On removal]   If the Secretary of State directs the removal of the liquidator, he shall forthwith—

(a) file notice of his decision in court, and

(b) send notice to the liquidator and the official receiver.

4.123(3)   [If liquidator removed]   If the liquidator is removed by direction of the Secretary of State—

(a) Rule 4.121 applies as regards the liquidator obtaining his release, as if he had been removed by the court, and

(b) the court may make any such order in his case as it would have power to make if he had been so removed.

General note

The removal of a liquidator by the Secretary of State is provided for by IA 1986, s. 172(4).

SECTION C: RELEASE ON COMPLETION OF ADMINISTRATION

Rule 4.124   Release of official receiver

(NO CVL APPLICATION)

4.124(1)   [Notice of intention]   The official receiver shall, before giving notice to the Secretary of State under section 174(3) (that the winding up is for practical purposes complete), send out notice of his intention to do so to all creditors who have proved their debts.

4.124(2)   [Accompanying summary]   The notice shall in each case be accompanied by a summary of the official receiver's receipts and payments as liquidator.

4.124(3)   [Notice to court of date of release]   The Secretary of State, when he has determined the date from which the official receiver is to have his release, shall give notice to the court that he has done so. The notice shall be accompanied by the summary referred to in paragraph (2).

(See general note after r. 4.126.)

Rule 4.125   Final meeting

(NO CVL APPLICATION)

4.125(1)   [Notice to creditors etc.]   Where the liquidator is other than the official receiver, he shall give at least 28 days' notice of the final meeting of creditors to be held under section 146. The notice shall be sent to all creditors who have proved their debts; and the liquidator shall cause it to be gazetted at least one month before the meeting is to be held.   [FORM 4.22]

4.125(2)   [Liquidator's report]   The liquidator's report laid before the meeting under that section shall contain an account of the liquidator's administration of the winding up, including—

    (a) a summary of his receipts and payments, and

    (b) a statement by him that he has reconciled his account with that which is held by the Secretary of State in respect of the winding up.

4.125(3)   [Questioning of liquidator]   At the final meeting, the creditors may question the liquidator with respect to any matter contained in his report, and may resolve against him having his release.

4.125(4)   [Notice to court]   The liquidator shall give notice to the court that the final meeting has been held; and the notice shall state whether or not he has been given his release, and be accompanied by a copy of the report laid before the final meeting. A copy of the notice shall be sent by the liquidator to the official receiver.   [FORM 4.42]

4.125(5)   [No quorum at final meeting]   If there is no quorum present at the final meeting, the liquidator shall report to the court that a final meeting was summoned in accordance with the Rules, but there was no quorum present; and the final meeting is then deemed to have been held, and the creditors not to have resolved against the liquidator having his release.

4.125(6) **[Release of liquidator]** If the creditors at the final meeting have not so resolved, the liquidator is released when the notice under paragraph (4) is filed in court. If they have so resolved, the liquidator must obtain his release from the Secretary of State and Rule 4.121 applies accordingly.

(See general note after r. 4.126.)

Rule **4.126**   Final meeting

4.126–CVL(1) **[Notice to creditors]** The liquidator shall give at least 28 days' notice of the final meeting of creditors to be held under section 106. The notice shall be sent to all creditors who have proved their debts.   [FORM 4.22]

4.126(2) **[Questioning of liquidator]** At the final meeting, the creditors may question the liquidator with respect to any matter contained in the account required under the section, and may resolve against the liquidator having his release.

4.126(3) **[Release of liquidator]** Where the creditors have so resolved, he must obtain his release from the Secretary of State; and Rule 4.122–CVL applies accordingly.

General note to rr. 4.124–4.126

These rules deal with the liquidator's release following the completion of his administration of the estate. On the question of his release upon his resignation or removal, see rr. 4.121, 4.122.

SECTION D: REMUNERATION

Rule **4.127**   Fixing of remuneration

4.127(1) **[Entitlement to remuneration]** The liquidator is entitled to receive remuneration for his services as such.

4.127(2) **[How fixed]** The remuneration shall be fixed either—

  (a) as a percentage of the value of the assets which are realised or distributed, or of the one value and the other in combination, or

  (b) by reference to the time properly given by the insolvency practitioner (as liquidator) and his staff in attending to matters arising in the winding up.

4.127(3) **[Determination under r. 4.127(2)]** Where the liquidator is other than the official receiver, it is for the liquidation committee (if there is one) to determine whether the remuneration is to be fixed under paragraph (2)(a) or (b) and, if under paragraph (2)(a), to determine any percentage to be applied as there mentioned.

4.127(4) **[Matters relevant r. 4.127(3) determination]** In arriving at that determination, the committee shall have regard to the following matters—

  (a) the complexity (or otherwise) of the case,

  (b) any respects in which, in connection with the winding up, there falls on the insolvency practitioner (as liquidator) any responsibility of an exceptional kind or degree,

(c) the effectiveness with which the insolvency practitioner appears to be carrying out, or to have carried out, his duties as liquidator, and

(d) the value and nature of the assets with which the liquidator has to deal.

4.127(5) **[If no committee or no determination]** If there is no liquidation committee, or the committee does not make the requisite determination, the liquidator's remuneration may be fixed (in accordance with paragraph (2)) by a resolution of a meeting of creditors; and paragraph (4) applies to them as it does to the liquidation committee.

4.127(6) **[Otherwise fixed]** If not fixed as above, the liquidator's remuneration shall be in accordance with the scale laid down for the official receiver by general regulations.

(See general note after r. 4.131.)

Rule **4.128** Other matters affecting remuneration

4.128(1) **[Where liquidator sells for secured creditor]** Where the liquidator sells assets on behalf of a secured creditor, he is entitled to take for himself, out of the proceeds of sale, a sum by way of remuneration equivalent to that which is chargeable in corresponding circumstances by the official receiver under general regulations.

4.128(2) **[Where joint liquidators]** Where there are joint liquidators, it is for them to agree between themselves as to how the remuneration payable should be apportioned. Any dispute arising between them may be referred—

(a) to the court, for settlement by order, or

(b) to the liquidation committee or a meeting of creditors, for settlement by resolution.

4.128(3) **[If liquidator is a solicitor]** If the liquidator is a solicitor and employs his own firm, or any partner in it, to act on behalf of the company, profit costs shall not be paid unless this is authorised by the liquidation committee, the creditors or the court.

(See general note after r. 4.131.)

Rule **4.129** Recourse of liquidator to meeting of creditors

4.129 If the liquidator's remuneration has been fixed by the liquidation committee, and he considers the rate or amount to be insufficient, he may request that it be increased by resolution of the creditors.

(See general note after r. 4.131.)

Rule **4.130** Recourse to the court

4.130(1) **[Liquidator may apply to court]** If the liquidator considers that the remuneration fixed for him by the liquidation committee, or by resolution of the creditors, or as under Rule 4.127(6), is insufficient, he may apply to the court for an order increasing its amount or rate.

4.130(2)   **[Notice to committee etc.]**   The liquidator shall give at least 14 days' notice of his application to the members of the liquidation committee; and the committee may nominate one or more members to appear or be represented, and to be heard, on the application.

4.130(3)   **[Where no committee]**   If there is no liquidation committee, the liquidator's notice of his application shall be sent to such one or more of the company's creditors as the court may direct, which creditors may nominate one or more of their number to appear or be represented.

4.130(4)   **[Costs of application]**   The court may, if it appears to be a proper case, order the costs of the liquidator's application, including the costs of any member of the liquidation committee appearing or being represented on it, or any creditor so appearing or being represented, to be paid out of the assets.

History note

In r. 4.130(4) the words "or being represented" in both places where they occur were inserted by I(A)R 1987 (SI 1987 No. 1919), r. 3(1), Sch., Pt. 1, para. 65 as from 11 January 1988.

(See general note after r. 4.131.)

Rule **4.131**   Creditors' claim that remuneration is excessive

4.131(1)   **[Creditor may apply to court]**   Any creditor of the company may, with the concurrence of at least 25 per cent. in value of the creditors (including himself), apply to the court for an order that the liquidator's remuneration be reduced, on the grounds that it is, in all the circumstances, excessive.

4.131(2)   **[Power of court to dismiss etc.]**   The court may, if it thinks that no sufficient cause is shown for a reduction, dismiss the application; but it shall not do so unless the applicant has had an opportunity to attend the court for an *ex parte* hearing, of which he has been given at least 7 days' notice.

    If the application is not dismissed under this paragraph, the court shall fix a venue for it to be heard, and give notice to the applicant accordingly.

4.131(3)   **[Notice to liquidator]**   The applicant shall, at least 14 days before the hearing, send to the liquidator a notice stating the venue and accompanied by a copy of the application, and of any evidence which the applicant intends to adduce in support of it.

4.131(4)   **[Court order]**   If the court considers the application to be well-founded, it shall make an order fixing the remuneration at a reduced amount or rate.

4.131(5)   **[Costs of application]**   Unless the court orders otherwise, the costs of the application shall be paid by the applicant, and are not payable out of the assets.

General note to rr. 4.127–4.131

Here are set out the provisions relating to fixing the liquidator's remuneration and the various ways in which a decision on this question may be reviewed or challenged. On the remuneration of a liquidator in a members' voluntary winding up, see r. 4.148A.

A liquidator may, in an appropriate case, also be paid remuneration and allowed expenses for work done in relation to property which does not form part of the assets in the liquidation, for instance property held by the company on trust. In *Re Berkeley Applegate (Investment Consultants) Ltd (No. 2)* (1988) 4 BCC 279 the liquidator in a creditors' voluntary winding up discovered, after extensive investigations, that certain assets standing in the name of the company were held by it on trust for people who had paid money to the company for investment. Although there was no statutory authority for payment, the court held that fair compensation could be awarded to the liquidator on general equitable principles. In later proceedings (*Re Berkeley Applegate (Investment Consultants) Ltd (No. 3)* (1989) 5 BCC 803, it was held that this remuneration could not properly be charged on the company's assets in the liquidation but only on the trust funds themselves.

SECTION E: SUPPLEMENTARY PROVISIONS

Rule 4.132   Liquidator deceased
(NO CVL APPLICATION)

4.132(1)   [Notice to official receiver]   Subject as follows, where the liquidator (other than the official receiver) has died, it is the duty of his personal representatives to give notice of the fact to the official receiver, specifying the date of the death.

This does not apply if notice has been given under any of the following paragraphs of this Rule.

4.132(2)   [Notice by partner etc.]   If the deceased liquidator was a partner in a firm, notice may be given to the official receiver by a partner in the firm who is qualified to act as an insolvency practitioner, or is a member of any body recognised by the Secretary of State for the authorisation of insolvency practitioners.

4.132(3)   [Notice by others]   Notice of the death may be given by any person producing to the official receiver the relevant death certificate or a copy of it.

4.132(4)   [Notice by official receiver]   The official receiver shall give notice to the court, for the purpose of fixing the date of the deceased liquidator's release.

(See general note after r. 4.138.)

Rule 4.133   Liquidator deceased

4.133–CVL(1)   [Notice to registrar and committee]   Subject as follows, where the liquidator has died, it is the duty of his personal representatives to give notice of the fact, and of the date of death, to the registrar of companies and to the liquidation committee (if any) or a member of that committee.   [FORM 4.44]

4.133(2)   [Notice by others]   In the alternative, notice of the death may be given—

   (a) if the deceased liquidator was a partner in a firm, by a partner qualified to act as an insolvency practitioner or who is a member of any body approved by the Secretary of State for the authorisation of insolvency practitioners, or

(b) by any person, if he delivers with the notice a copy of the relevant death certificate.

(See general note after r. 4.138.)

Rule 4.134 Loss of qualification as insolvency practitioner

(NO CVL APPLICATION)

4.134(1) [Application of Rule] This Rule applies where the liquidator vacates office on ceasing to be qualified to act as an insolvency practitioner in relation to the company.

4.134(2) [Notice to official receiver etc.] He shall forthwith give notice of his doing so to the official receiver, who shall give notice to the Secretary of State.

The official receiver shall file in court a copy of his notice under this paragraph. [FORM 4.45]

4.134(3) [Application of r. 4.121] Rule 4.121 applies as regards the liquidator obtaining his release, as if he had been removed by the court.

(See general note after r. 4.138.)

Rule 4.135 Loss of qualification as insolvency practitioner

4.135–CVL(1) [Application of Rule] This Rule applies where the liquidator vacates office on ceasing to be qualified to act as an insolvency practitioner in relation to the company.

4.135(2) [Notice] He shall forthwith give notice of his doing so to the registrar of companies and the Secretary of State. [FORM 4.46]
[FORM 4.45]

4.135(3) [Application of r. 4.122–CVL] Rule 4.122–CVL applies as regards the liquidator obtaining his release, as if he had been removed by the court.

(See general note after r. 4.138.)

Rule 4.136 Vacation of office on making of winding-up order

4.136–CVL Where the liquidator vacates office in consequence of the court making a winding-up order against the company, Rule 4.122–CVL applies as regards his obtaining his release, as if he had been removed by the court.

(See general note after r. 4.138.)

Rule 4.137 Notice to official receiver of intention to vacate office

(NO CVL APPLICATION)

4.137(1) [Notice to official receiver] Where the liquidator intends to vacate office, whether by resignation or otherwise, he shall give notice of his intention to the official receiver together with notice of any creditors' meeting to be held in respect of his vacation of office, including any meeting to receive his resignation.

4.137(2)   [Time limit for notice]   The notice to the official receiver must be given at least 21 days before any such creditors' meeting.

4.137(3)   [Details of property]   Where there remains any property of the company which has not been realised, applied, distributed or otherwise fully dealt with in the winding up, the liquidator shall include in his notice to the official receiver details of the nature of that property, its value (or the fact that it has no value), its location, any action taken by the liquidator to deal with that property or any reason for his not dealing with it, and the current position in relation to it.

History note

Rule 4.137 was substituted by I(A)R 1987 (SI 1987 No. 1919), r. 3(1), Sch., Pt. 1, para. 66 as from 11 January 1988: r. 4.137 formerly read as follows:

"**4.137(1)**   Where the liquidator intends to vacate office, whether by resignation or otherwise, and there remain any unrealised assets, he shall give notice of his intention to the official receiver, informing him of the nature, value and whereabouts of the assets in question.

4.137(2)   Where there is to be a creditors' meeting to receive the liquidator's resignation, or otherwise in respect of his vacation of office, the notice to the official receiver must be given at least 21 days before the meeting."

(See general note after r. 4.138.)

Rule **4.138**   Liquidator's duties on vacating office

4.138(1)   [Obligation to deliver up assets etc.]   Where the liquidator ceases to be in office as such, in consequence of removal, resignation or cesser of qualification as an insolvency practitioner, he is under obligation forthwith to deliver up to the person succeeding him as liquidator the assets (after deduction of any expenses properly incurred, and distributions made, by him) and further to deliver up to that person—

   (a)   the records of the liquidation, including correspondence, proofs and other related papers appertaining to the administration while it was within his responsibility, and

   (b)   the company's books, papers and other records.

4.138(2)   [When winding up complete]   When the winding up is for practical purposes complete, the liquidator shall forthwith file in court all proofs remaining with him in the proceedings. (NO CVL APPLICATION)

4.138(3)   [Vacation following creditors' final meeting]   Where the liquidator vacates office under section 172(8) (final meeting of creditors), he shall deliver up to the official receiver the company's books, papers and other records which have not already been disposed of in accordance with general regulations in the course of the liquidation. (NO CVL APPLICATION).

History note
Rule 4.138(3) was added by I(A)R 1987 (SI 1987 No. 1919), r. 3(1), Sch., Pt. 1, para. 67 as from 11 January 1988.

General note to rr. 4.132–4.138

Apart from resignation and removal, which are dealt with in rr. 4.108 ff., the office of liquidator may be vacated by death or disqualification or in consequence of a court order. The present rules are concerned with these situations and with various other matters incidental to vacating office.

The amendment to r. 4.137 makes it plain that the official receiver must be informed about all property, whether or not it is considered to be of value (thus resolving doubts as to the meaning of the term "assets" in the former rule). The new r. 4.138(3) fills a gap in the rule as previously framed.

SECTION F: THE LIQUIDATOR IN A MEMBERS' VOLUNTARY WINDING UP

Rule 4.139 Appointment by the company

4.139(1) [Application of Rule] This Rule applies where the liquidator is appointed by a meeting of the company.

4.139(2) [Certifying appointment etc.] Subject as follows, the chairman of the meeting shall certify the appointment, but not unless and until the person appointed has provided him with a written statement to the effect that he is an insolvency practitioner, duly qualified under the Act to be the liquidator, and that he consents so to act.   [FORM 4.27]
[FORM 4.28]

4.139(3) [Certificate to liquidator] The chairman shall send the certificate forthwith to the liquidator, who shall keep it as part of the records of the liquidation.

4.139(4) [Notice to creditors] Not later than 28 days from his appointment, the liquidator shall give notice of it to all creditors of the company of whom he is aware in that period.

(See general note after r. 4.148A.)

Rule 4.140 Appointment by the court

4.140(1) [Application of Rule] This Rule applies where the liquidator is appointed by the court under section 108.

4.140(2) [Issue of court order] The court's order shall not issue unless and until the person appointed has filed in court a statement to the effect that he is an insolvency practitioner, duly qualified under the Act to be the liquidator, and that he consents so to act.   [FORM 4.29]
[FORM 4.30]

4.140(3) [Copy of order to liquidator] Thereafter, the court shall send a sealed copy of the order to the liquidator, whose appointment takes effect from the date of the order.

4.140(4) **[Notice to creditors]** Not later than 28 days from his appointment, the liquidator shall give notice of it all to creditors of the company of whom he is aware in that period.

(See general note after r. 4.148A.)

Rule **4.141** Authentication of liquidator's appointment

4.141 A copy of the certificate of the liquidator's appointment or (as the case may be) a sealed copy of the court's order appointing him may in any proceedings be adduced as proof that the person appointed is duly authorised to exercise the powers and perform the duties of liquidator in the company's winding up.

(See general note after r. 4.148A.)

Rule **4.142** Company meeting to receive liquidator's resignation

4.142(1) **[Liquidator must call meeting etc.]** Before resigning his office, the liquidator must call a meeting of the company for the purpose of receiving his resignation. The notice summoning the meeting shall indicate that this is the purpose, or one of the purposes, of it.

4.142(2) **[Account of liquidator's administration]** The notice under paragraph (1) must be accompanied by an account of the liquidator's administration of the winding up, including—

(a) a summary of his receipts and payments, and

(b) a statement by him that he has reconciled his account with that which is held by the Secretary of State in respect of the winding up.

4.142(3) **[Grounds for proceeding under Rule]** Subject as follows, the liquidator may only proceed under this Rule on grounds of ill health or because—

(a) he intends ceasing to be in practice as an insolvency practitioner, or

(b) there is some conflict of interest or change of personal circumstances which precludes or makes impracticable the further discharge by him of the duties of liquidator.

4.142(4) **[Where joint liquidators]** Where two or more persons are acting as liquidator jointly, any one of them may proceed under this Rule (without prejudice to the continuation in office of the other or others) on the ground that, in his opinion or that of the other or others, it is no longer expedient that there should continue to be the present number of joint liquidators.

4.142(4A) **[If no quorum]** If there is no quorum present at the meeting summoned to receive the liquidator's resignation, the meeting is deemed to have been held.

4.142(5) **[S. 171(5) notice]** The notice of the liquidator's resignation required by section 171(5) shall be given by him forthwith after the meeting. [FORM 4.33]

4.142(6) **[Where new liquidator appointed]** Where a new liquidator is appointed in place of one who has resigned, the former shall, in giving notice of his appointment, state that his predecessor has resigned.

History note

Rule 4.142(4A) was inserted by I(A)R 1987 (SI 1987 No. 1919), r. 3(1), Sch., Pt. 1, para. 68 as from 11 January 1988.

(See general note after r. 4.148A.)

Rule **4.143** Removal of liquidator by the court

4.143(1) **[Application of Rule]** This Rule applies where application is made to the court for the removal of the liquidator, or for an order directing the liquidator to summon a company meeting for the purpose of removing him.

4.143(2) **[Court may dismiss application etc.]** The court may, if it thinks that no sufficient cause is shown for the application, dismiss it; but it shall not do so unless the applicant has had an opportunity to attend the court for an *ex parte* hearing, of which he has been given at least 7 days' notice.

If the application is not dismissed under this paragraph, the court shall fix a venue for it to be heard.

4.143(3) **[Deposit or security for costs]** The court may require the applicant to make a deposit or give security for the costs to be incurred by the liquidator on the application.

4.143(4) **[Notice etc.]** The applicant shall, at least 14 days before the hearing, send to the liquidator a notice stating the venue and accompanied by a copy of the application, and of any evidence which he intends to adduce in support of it.

Subject to any contrary order of the court, the costs of the application are not payable out of the assets.

4.143(5) **[Where court removes liquidator]** Where the court removes the liquidator—

    (a) it shall send 2 copies of the order of removal to him, one to be sent by him forthwith to the registrar of companies, with notice of his ceasing to act;

    (b) the order may include such provision as the court thinks fit with respect to matters arising in connection with the removal; and

    (c) if the court appoints a new liquidator, Rule 4.140 applies.   [FORM 4.39]
                                                               [FORM 4.40]

(See general note after r. 4.148A.)

Rule **4.144** Release of resigning or removed liquidator

4.144(1) **[Where liquidator resigns]** Where the liquidator resigns, he has his release from the date on which he gives notice of his resignation to the registrar of companies.   [FORM 4.40]

4.144(2) **[Where removed by meeting]** Where the liquidator is removed by a meeting of the company, he shall forthwith give notice to the registrar of companies of his ceasing to act.   [FORM 4.40]

4.144(3) **[Where removed by court]** Where the liquidator is removed by the court, he must apply to the Secretary of State for his release.   [FORM 4.41]

4.144(4) **[Certifying release etc.]** When the Secretary of State gives the release, he shall certify it accordingly, and send the certificate to the registrar of companies.

4.144(5) **[Copy of certificate]** A copy of the certificate shall be sent by the Secretary of State to the former liquidator, whose release is effective from the date of the certificate.

(See general note after r. 4.148A.)

Rule **4.145** Liquidator deceased

4.145(1) **[Duty to give notice]** Subject as follows, where the liquidator has died, it is the duty of his personal representatives to give notice of the fact, and of the date of death, to the company's directors, or any one of them, and to the registrar of companies. [FORM 4.44]

4.145(2) **[Notice by partner or others]** In the alternative, notice of the death may be given—

    (a) if the deceased liquidator was a partner in a firm, by a partner qualified to act as an insolvency practitioner or who is a member of any body approved by the Secretary of State for the authorisation of insolvency practitioners, or

    (b) by any person, if he delivers with the notice a copy of the relevant death certificate.

(See general note after r. 4.148A.)

Rule **4.146** Loss of qualification as insolvency practitioner

4.146(1) **[Application of Rule]** This Rule applies where the liquidator vacates office on ceasing to be qualified to act as an insolvency practitioner in relation to the company.

4.146(2) **[Notice]** He shall forthwith give notice of his doing so to the registrar of companies and the Secretary of State. [FORM 4.46]
[FORM 4.45]

4.146(3) **[Application of r. 4.144]** Rule 4.144 applies as regards the liquidator obtaining his release, as if he had been removed by the court.

(See general note after r. 4.148A.)

Rule **4.147** Vacation of office on making of winding-up order

4.147 Where the liquidator vacates office in consequence of the court making a winding-up order against the company. Rule 4.144 applies as regards his obtaining his release, as if he had been removed by the court.

(See general note after r. 4.148A.)

Rule **4.148** Liquidator's duties on vacating office

4.148 Where the liquidator ceases to be in office as such, in consequence of removal, resignation or cesser of qualification as an insolvency practitioner, he is under obligation forthwith to deliver up to the person succeeding him as liquidator the assets (after deduction of any expenses properly incurred, and distributions made, by him) and further to deliver up to that person—

(a) the records of the liquidation, including correspondence, proofs and other related papers appertaining to the administration while it was within his responsibility, and

(b) the company's books, papers and other records.

(See general note after r. 4.148A.)

Rule 4.148A   Remuneration of liquidator in members' voluntary winding up

4.148A(1)   [Entitlement]   The liquidator is entitled to receive remuneration for his services as such.

4.148A(2)   [How fixed]   The remuneration shall be fixed either —

(a) as a percentage of the value of the assets which are realised or distributed, or of the one value and the other in combination, or

(b) by reference to the time properly given by the insolvency practitioner (as liquidator) and his staff in attending to matters arising in the winding up;

and the company in general meeting shall determine whether the remuneration is to be fixed under subparagraph (a) or (b) and, if under subparagraph (a), the percentage to be applied as there mentioned.

4.148A(3)   [Matters in determination]   In arriving at that determination the company in general meeting shall have regard to the matters set out in paragraph (4) of Rule 4.127.

4.148A(4)   [Otherwise fixed]   If not fixed as above, the liquidator's remuneration shall be in accordance with the scale laid down for the official receiver by general regulations.

4.148A(5)   [Application of r. 4.128]   Rule 4.128 shall apply in relation to the remuneration of the liquidator in respect of the matters there mentioned and for this purpose references in that Rule to "the liquidation committee" and "a meeting of creditors" shall be read as references to the company in general meeting.

4.148A(6)   [Liquidator may apply to court]   If the liquidator considers that the remuneration fixed for him by the company in general meeting, or as under paragraph (4), is insufficient, he may apply to the court for an order increasing its amount or rate.

4.148A(7)   [Notice to contributories]   The liquidator shall give at least 14 days' notice of an application under paragraph (6) to the company's contributories, or such one or more of them as the court may direct, and the contributories may nominate any one or more of their number to appear or be represented.

4.148A(8)   [Costs of application]   The court may, if it appears to be a proper case, order the costs of the liquidator's application, including the costs of any contributory appearing or being represented on it, to be paid out of the assets.

History note

Rule 4.148A was inserted by I(A)R 1987 (SI 1987 No. 1919), r. 3(1), Sch., Pt. 1, para. 69 as from 11 January 1988.

This is the only part of the rules which deals exclusively with a members' voluntary winding up. The rules set out here relate to the questions of the appointment of the liquidator and the vacation of his office, corresponding to earlier sections of this chapter which govern compulsory and insolvent liquidations. On the liquidator's remuneration, the rules were formerly silent, but a specific provision has now been included in order to remove uncertainty (r. 4.148A).

SECTION G: RULES APPLYING IN EVERY WINDING UP, WHETHER VOLUNTARY OR BY THE COURT

Rule 4.149   Power of court to set aside certain transactions

4.149(1)   [Liquidator's transaction with associate]   If in the administration of the estate the liquidator enters into any transaction with a person who is an associate of his, the court may, on the application of any person interested, set the transaction aside and order the liquidator to compensate the company for any loss suffered in consequence of it.

4.149(2)   [Where r. 4.149(1) does not apply]   This does not apply if either—

(a) the transaction was entered into with the prior consent of the court, or

(b) it is shown to the court's satisfaction that the transaction was for value, and that it was entered into by the liquidator without knowing, or having any reason to suppose, that the person concerned was an associate.

4.149(3)   [Effect of Rule]   Nothing in this Rule is to be taken as prejudicing the operation of any rule of law or equity with respect to a liquidator's dealings with trust property, or the fiduciary obligations of any person.

General note
This rule imposes statutory duties of a quasi-fiduciary character on a liquidator, supplementing the rules of equity and the common law. For the meaning of "associate", see IA 1986, s. 435.

Rule 4.150   Rule against solicitation

4.150(1)   [Power of court]   Where the court is satisfied that any improper solicitation has been used by or on behalf of the liquidator in obtaining proxies or procuring his appointment, it may order that no remuneration out of the assets be allowed to any person by whom, or on whose behalf, the solicitation was exercised.

4.150(2)   [Effect of court order]   An order of the court under this Rule overrides any resolution of the liquidation committee or the creditors, or any other provision of the Rules relating to the liquidator's remuneration.

General note

This rule similarly supplements principles of equity and the common law; and see also IA 1986, s. 164 (corrupt inducement affecting liquidator's appointment).

Chapter 12 — The Liquidation Committee

Rule **4.151** Preliminary

(NO CVL APPLICATION)

4.151 For the purposes of this Chapter—

    (a) an "insolvent winding up" is where the company is being wound up on grounds which include inability to pay its debts, and

    (b) a "solvent winding up" is where the company is being wound up on grounds which do not include that one.

General note

Note that this is a special use of the word "solvent": a company which is ordered to be wound up on grounds other than inability to pay debts may well be "insolvent" in any of the normal senses of that word, but the liquidation will be "solvent" within this definition, and conversely. See the general comment to IA 1986, Pt. VI, preceding s. 230, and the note to IA 1986, s. 247.

    For the meaning of "inability to pay its debts", see IA 1986, see s. 123.

    For the rules which apply where a winding up follows immediately upon an administration, see rr. 4.173 ff.

Rule **4.152** Membership of committee

4.152(1) **[Numbers to be elected]** Subject to Rule 4.154 below, the liquidation committee shall consist as follows—

    (a) in any case of at least 3, and not more than 5, creditors of the company, elected by the meeting of creditors held under section 141 of the Act, and

    (b) also, in the case of a solvent winding up, where the contributories' meeting held under that section so decides, of up to 3 contributories, elected by that meeting.

(NO CVL APPLICATION)

4.152 (2–CVL) **[At least three members]** The committee must have at least 3 members before it can be established.

4.152(3) **[Eligibility]** Any creditor of the company (other than one whose debt is fully secured) is eligible to be a member of the committee, so long as—

    (a) he has lodged a proof of his debt, and

    (b) his proof has neither been wholly disallowed for voting purposes, nor wholly rejected for purposes of distribution or dividend.

4.152(4) **[No dual membership]** No person can be a member as both a creditor and a contributory.

4.152(5) [Representation of body corporate] A body corporate may be a member of the committee, but it cannot act as such otherwise than by a representative appointed under Rule 4.159.

4.152(6) ["Creditor members", "contributory members"] Members of the committee elected or appointed to represent the creditors are called "creditor members"; and those elected or appointed to represent the contributories are called "contributory members".

4.152(7) [Deposit Protection Board as creditor member] Where a representative of the Deposit Protection Board exercises the right (under section 58 of the Banking Act 1987) to be a member of the committee, he is to be regarded as an additional creditor member.

History note

In r. 4.152(7) the words "58 of the Banking Act 1987" were substituted for the former words "28 of the Banking Act 1979" by I(A)R 1987 (SI 1987 No. 1919), r. 3(1), Sch., Pt. 1, para. 70 as from 11 January 1988.

(See general note after r. 4.155.)

Rule 4.153   Formalities of establishment

4.153(1) [Liquidator's certificate] The liquidation committee does not come into being, and accordingly cannot act, until the liquidator has issued a certificate of its due constitution.   [FORM 4.47]

4.153(2) [If chairman of meeting not liquidator] If the chairman of the meeting which resolves to establish the committee is not the liquidator, he shall forthwith give notice of the resolution to the liquidator (or, as the case may be, the person appointed as liquidator by that same meeting), and inform him of the names and addresses of the persons elected to be members of the committee.

4.153(3) [Agreement to act] No person may act as a member of the committee unless and until he has agreed to do so and, unless the relevant proxy or authorisation contains a statement to the contrary, such agreement may be given by his proxyholder or representative under section 375 of the Companies Act present at the meeting establishing the committee.

4.153(3A) [No certificate without agreement] The liquidator's certificate of the committee's due constitution shall not issue before the minimum number of persons (in accordance with Rule 4.152) who are to be members of the committee have agreed to act.

4.153(4) [Amended certificate] As and when the others (if any) agree to act, the liquidator shall issue an amended certificate.

4.153(5) [Certificate to be filed in court] The certificate, and any amended certificate, shall be filed in court by the liquidator.

(NO CVL APPLICATION)

4.153(6–CVL) [Certificate to registrar] The certificate, and any amended certificate, shall be sent by the liquidator to the registrar of companies.   [FORM 4.47]
                                                                              [FORM 4.48]

4.153(7) [Change in membership] If after the first establishment of the committee there is any change in its membership, the liquidator shall report the change to the court. (NO CVL APPLICATION)   [FORM 4.49]

4.153(8–CVL) **[Change in membership]** If after the first establishment of the committee there is any change in its membership, the liquidator shall report the change to the registrar of companies.　　　　　　　　　　[FORM 4.49]
[FORM 4.48]

History note

Rules 4.153(3) and (3A) were substituted for the former r. 4.153(3) by I(A)R 1987 (SI 1987 No. 1919), r. 3(1), Sch., Pt. 1, para. 71 as from 11 January 1988: the former r. 4.153(3) read as follows:

"**4.153(3)** No person may act as a member of the committee unless and until he has agreed to do so; and the liquidator's certificate of the committee's due constitution shall not issue before the minimum number of persons (in accordance with Rule 4.152) who are to be members of it have agreed to act."

(See general note after r. 4.155.)

Rule **4.154** Committee established by contributories

(NO CVL APPLICATION)

4.154(1) **[Application of Rule]** The following applies where the creditors' meeting under section 141 does not decide that a liquidation committee should be established, or decides that a committee should not be established.

4.154(2) **[Further creditors' meeting]** The meeting of contributories under that section may appoint one of their number to make application to the court for an order to the liquidator that a further creditors' meeting be summoned for the purpose of establishing a liquidation committee; and—

(a) the court may, if it thinks that there are special circumstances to justify it, make that order, and

(b) the creditors' meeting summoned by the liquidator in compliance with the order is deemed to have been summoned under section 141.

4.154(3) **[Meeting of contributories]** If the creditors' meeting so summoned does not establish a liquidation committee, a meeting of contributories may do so.

4.154(4) **[Constitution of committee]** The committee shall then consist of at least 3, and not more than 5, contributories elected by that meeting; and Rule 4.153 applies, substituting for the reference in paragraph (3A) of that Rule to Rule 4.152 a reference to this paragraph.

History note

In r. 4.154(4) the words from "substituting" to the end were substituted for the former words "substituting references to contributories for references to creditors" by I(A)R 1987 (SI 1987 No. 1919), r. 3(1), Sch., Pt. 1, para. 72 as from 11 January 1988.

(See general note after r. 4.155.)

Rule **4.155** Obligations of liquidator to committee

4.155(1) **[Liquidator's duty to report]** Subject as follows, it is the duty of the liquidator to report to the members of the liquidation committee all such matters as appear to him to be, or as they have indicated to him as being, of concern to them with respect to the winding up.

4.155(2)   **[Non-compliance with request for information]**   In the case of matters so indicated to him by the committee, the liquidator need not comply with any request for information where it appears to him that—

(a) the request is frivolous or unreasonable, or

(b) the cost of complying would be excessive, having regard to the relative importance of the information, or

(c) there are not sufficient assets to enable him to comply.

4.155(3)   **[Report in summary form]**   Where the committee has come into being more than 28 days after the appointment of the liquidator, he shall report to them, in summary form, what actions he has taken since his appointment, and shall answer all such questions as they may put to him regarding his conduct of the winding up hitherto.

4.155(4)   **[Summary report for subsequent member]**   A person who becomes a member of the committee at any time after its first establishment is not entitled to require a report to him by the liquidator, otherwise than in summary form, of any matters previously arising.

4.155(5)   **[Access to liquidator's records]**   Nothing in this Rule disentitles the committee, or any member of it from having access to the liquidator's records of the liquidation, or from seeking an explanation of any matter within the committee's responsibility.

General note to rr. 4.152–4.155

These rules deal with the membership of the liquidation committee in different circumstances (rr. 4.152, 4.154), and with the liquidator's reporting obligations (r. 4.155). Note that the contributories may be represented on the committee only in the case of a "solvent" winding up (as that term is defined by r. 4.151(*b*)). On the termination of membership, see rr. 4.160–4.164 and 4.171; and for further reporting obligations, see r. 4.168.

    The amendment to r. 4.153(3) is intended to enable a meeting of the liquidation committee to be held immediately after the meeting at which the liquidator is appointed.

    Documents passing between the liquidator and the Department of Trade and Industry concerning possible disqualification of directors are not documents which are within any of the statutory rights of the liquidation committee to inspect, or in respect of which the committee can properly put questions to the liquidator and ask him to report to them: *Re W & A Glaser Ltd* [1994] BCC 199.

Rule **4.156** Meetings of the committee

4.156(1)   **[Holding of meetings]**   Subject as follows, meetings of the liquidation committee shall be held when and where determined by the liquidator.

4.156(2)   **[First and subsequent meetings]**   The liquidator shall call a first meeting of the committee to take place within 3 months of his appointment or of the committee's establishment (whichever is the later); and thereafter he shall call a meeting—

(a) if so requested by a creditor member of the committee or his representative (the meeting then to be held within 21 days of the request being received by the liquidator), and

(b) for a specified date, if the committee has previously resolved that a meeting be held on that date.

4.156(3) **[Notice of venue]** The liquidator shall give 7 days' written notice of the venue of a meeting to every member of the committee (or his representative, if designated for that purpose), unless in any case the requirement of the notice has been waived by or on behalf of any member.

Waiver may be signified either at or before the meeting.

(See general note after r. 4.159.)

Rule **4.157** The chairman at meetings

4.157(1) **[Liquidator or his nominee]** The chairman at any meeting of the liquidation committee shall be the liquidator, or a person nominated by him to act.

4.157(2) **[Nominated chairman]** A person so nominated must be either—

(a) one who is qualified to act as an insolvency practitioner in relation to the company, or

(b) an employee of the liquidator or his firm who is experienced in insolvency matters.

(See general note after r. 4.159.)

Rule **4.158** Quorum

4.158(1) **[Two creditor members]** A meeting of the committee is duly constituted if due notice of it has been given to all the members, and at least 2 creditor members are present or represented.

(NO CVL APPLICATION)

4.158(2–CVL) **[Two members]** A meeting of the committee is duly constituted if due notice of it has been given to all the members, and at least 2 members are present or represented.

(See general note after r. 4.159.)

Rule **4.159** Committee-members' representatives

4.159(1) **[Representation]** A member of the liquidation committee may, in relation to the business of the committee, be represented by another person duly authorised by him for that purpose.

4.159(2) **[Letter of authority]** A person acting as a committee-member's representative must hold a letter of authority entitling him so to act (either generally or specially) and signed by or on behalf of the committee-member, and for this purpose any proxy or any authorisation under section 375 of the Companies Act in relation to any meeting of creditors (or, as the case may be, members or contributories) of the company shall, unless it contains a statement to the contrary, be treated as such a letter of authority to act generally signed by or on behalf of the committee-member.

4.159(3) **[Production of letter of authority]**   The chairman at any meeting of the committee may call on a person claiming to act as a committee-member's representative to produce his letter of authority, and may exclude him if it appears that his authority is deficient.

4.159(4) **[Who may not be a representative]**   No member may be represented by a body corporate, or by a person who is an undischarged bankrupt or is subject to a composition or arrangement with his creditors.

4.159(5) **[No dual representation]**   No person shall—

    (a) on the same committee, act at one and the same time as representative of more than one committee-member, or

    (b) act both as a member of the committee and as representative of another member.

4.159(6) **[Signing as representative]**   Where a member's representative signs any document on the member's behalf, the fact that he so signs must be stated below his signature.

History note

In r. 4.159(2) the words ", and for this purpose" to the end were added by I(A)R 1987 (SI 1987 No. 1919), r. 3(1), Sch., Pt. 1, para. 73 as from 11 January 1988.

General note to rr. 4.156–4.159

Some of the rules regarding the holding and conduct of meetings of the liquidation committee are set out here. The remainder are at rr. 4.165–4.168. On the members' expenses, see r. 4.169, and on the amendment to r. 4.159(2), see the general note to rr. 4.152–4.155. On the rôle of representatives, see *Re W & A Glaser Ltd* [1994] BCC 199, at p. 208.

Rule 4.160   Resignation

4.160   A member of the liquidation committee may resign by notice in writing delivered to the liquidator.

(See general note after r. 4.164.)

Rule 4.161   Termination of membership

4.161(1) **[Automatic termination]**   A person's membership of the liquidation committee is automatically terminated if—

    (a) he becomes bankrupt or compounds or arranges with his creditors, or

    (b) at 3 consecutive meetings of the committee he is neither present nor represented (unless at the third of those meetings it is resolved that this Rule is not to apply in his case).

4.161(2) **[Termination on bankruptcy]** However, if the cause of termination is the member's bankruptcy, his trustee in bankruptcy replaces him as a member of the committee.

4.161(3) **[Not a creditor]** The membership of a creditor member is also automatically terminated if he ceases to be, or is found never to have been, a creditor.

(See general note after r. 4.164.)

Rule **4.162** Removal

4.162(1) **[Removal by resolution]** A creditor member of the committee may be removed by resolution at a meeting of creditors; and a contributory member may be removed by a resolution of a meeting of contributories.

4.162(2) **[Notice of intention]** In either case, 14 days' notice must be given of the intention to move the resolution.

(See general note after r. 4.164.)

Rule **4.163** Vacancy (creditor members)

4.163(1) **[Application of Rule]** The following applies if there is a vacancy among the creditor members of the committee.

4.163(2) **[Agreement not to fill vacancy]** The vacancy need not be filled if the liquidator and a majority of the remaining creditor members so agree, provided that the total number of members does not fall below the minimum required by Rule 4.152.

4.163(3) **[Appointment by liquidator]** The liquidator may appoint any creditor (being qualified under the Rules to be a member of the committee) to fill the vacancy, if a majority of the other creditor members agree to the appointment, and the creditor concerned consents to act.

4.163(4) **[Appointment by resolution]** Alternatively, a meeting of creditors may resolve that a creditor be appointed (with his consent) to fill the vacancy. In this case, at least 14 days' notice must have been given of the resolution to make such an appointment (whether or not of a person named in the notice).

4.163(5) **[Report to liquidator]** Where the vacancy is filled by an appointment made by a creditors' meeting at which the liquidator is not present, the chairman of the meeting shall report to the liquidator the appointment which has been made.

(See general note after r. 4.164.)

Rule **4.164** Vacancy (contributory members)

4.164(1) **[Application of Rule]** The following applies if there is a vacancy among the contributory members of the committee.

4.164(2) **[Agreement not to fill vacancy]** The vacancy need not be filled if the liquidator and a majority of the remaining contributory members so agree, provided that, in the case of a committee of contributory members only, the total number of members does not fall below the minimum required by r. 4.154(4) or, as the case may be, 4.171(5).

4.164(3)   [Appointment by liquidator]   The liquidator may appoint any contributory member (being qualified under the Rules to be a member of the committee) to fill the vacancy, if a majority of the other contributory members agree to the appointment, and the contributory concerned consents to act.

4.164(4)   [Appointment by resolution]   Alternatively, a meeting of contributories may resolve that a contributory be appointed (with his consent) to fill the vacancy. In this case, at least 14 days' notice must have been given of the resolution to make such an appointment (whether or not of a person named in the notice).

4.164(5–CVL)   [Where contributories make r. 4.164(4) appointment]   Where the contributories make an appointment under paragraph (4), the creditor members of the committee may, if they think fit, resolve that the person appointed ought not to be a member of the committee; and—

  (a) that person is not then, unless the court otherwise directs, qualified to act as a member of the committee, and

  (b) on any application to the court for a direction under this paragraph the court may, if it thinks fit, appoint another person (being a contributory) to fill the vacancy on the committee.

4.164(6)   [Report to liquidator]   Where the vacancy is filled by an appointment made by a contributories' meeting at which the liquidator is not present, the chairman of the meeting shall report to the liquidator the appointment which has been made.

General note to rr. 4.160–4.164

Note also that the membership of the creditor members of the committee automatically ceases when it is certified that the creditors have been paid in full (r. 4.171).

Rule 4.165   Voting rights and resolutions

(NO CVL APPLICATION)

4.165(1)   [Creditor members' votes]   At any meeting of the committee, each member of it (whether present himself, or by his representative) has one vote; and a resolution is passed when a majority of the creditor members present or represented have voted in favour of it.

4.165(2)   [Contributory members' votes]   Subject to the next paragraph, the votes of contributory members do not count towards the number required for passing a resolution, but the way in which they vote on any resolution shall be recorded.

4.165(3)   [Only contributory members]   Paragraph (2) does not apply where, by virtue of Rule 4.154 or 4.171, the only members of the committee are contributories. In that case the committee is to be treated for voting purposes as if all its members were creditors.

4.165(4)   **[Record of resolutions]**   Every resolution passed shall be recorded in writing, either separately or as part of the minutes of the meeting. The record shall be signed by the chairman and kept with the records of the liquidation.

(See general note after r. 4.169.)

Rule **4.166**   Voting rights and resolutions

4.166–CVL(1)   **[Votes etc.]**   At any meeting of the committee, each member of it (whether present himself, or by his representative) has one vote; and a resolution is passed when a majority of the members present or represented have voted in favour of it.   ·

4.166(2)   **[Record of resolutions]**   Every resolution passed shall be recorded in writing, either separately or as part of the minutes of the meeting. The record shall be signed by the chairman and kept with the records of the liquidation.

(See general note after r. 4.169.)

Rule **4.167**   Resolutions by post

4.167(1)   **[Sending proposed resolution]**   In accordance with this Rule, the liquidator may seek to obtain the agreement of members of the liquidation committee to a resolution by sending to every member (or his representative designated for the purpose) a copy of the proposed resolution.

4.167(2)   **[Copy of proposed resolution]**   Where the liquidator makes use of the procedure allowed by this Rule, he shall send out to members of the committee or their representatives (as the case may be) a copy of any proposed resolution on which a decision is sought, which shall be set out in such a way that agreement with or dissent from each separate resolution may be indicated by the recipient on the copy so sent.

4.167(3)   **[Creditor requiring meeting]**   Any creditor member of the committee may, within 7 business days from the date of the liquidator sending out a resolution, require him to summon a meeting of the committee to consider the matters raised by the resolution. (NO CVL APPLICATION)

4.167(4–CVL)   **[Member requiring meeting]**   Any member of the committee may, within 7 business days from the date of the liquidator sending out a resolution, require him to summon a meeting of the committee to consider the matters raised by the resolution.

4.167(5)   **[Deemed passing of resolution]**   In the absence of such a request, the resolution is deemed to have been passed by the committee if and when the liquidator is notified in writing by a majority of the creditor members that they concur with it. (NO CVL APPLICATION)

4.167(6–CVL)   **[Deemed passing of resolution where no request]**   In the absence of such a request, the resolution is deemed to have been passed by the committee if and when the liquidator is notified in writing by a majority of the members that they concur with it.

4.167(7)   **[Copy of resolutions]**   A copy of every resolution passed under this Rule, and a note that the committee's concurrence was obtained, shall be kept with the records of the liquidation.

History note

In r. 4.167(2) the words "a copy of any proposed resolution" to the end were substituted by I(A)R 1987 (SI 1987 No. 1919), r. 3(1), Sch., Pt. 1, para. 74 as from 11 January 1988: the former words read as follows:

> "a statement incorporating the resolution to which their agreement is sought, each resolution (if more than one) being set out in a separate document."

(See general note after r. 4.169.)

Rule **4.168** Liquidator's reports

4.168(1) **[Liquidator directed to report]** The liquidator shall, as and when directed by the liquidation committee (but not more often than once in any period of 2 months), send a written report to every member of the committee setting out the position generally as regards the progress of the winding up and matters arising in connection with it, to which he (the liquidator) considers the committee's attention should be drawn.

4.168(2) **[If no directions to report]** In the absence of such directions by the committee, the liquidator shall send such a report not less often than once in every period of 6 months.

4.168(3) **[Effect of Rule]** The obligations of the liquidator under this Rule are without prejudice to those imposed by Rule 4.155.

(See general note after r. 4.169.)

Rule **4.169** Expenses of members, etc.

4.169 The liquidator shall defray out of the assets, in the prescribed order of priority, any reasonable travelling expenses directly incurred by members of the liquidation committee or their representatives in respect of their attendance at the committee's meetings, or otherwise on the committee's business.

General note to rr. 4.165–4.167, 4.169

See also rr. 4.155–4.159 and, on the question of priority, r. 4.218(1)(*m*).

The amendment to r. 4.167(2) removes the former requirement that each resolution be set out on a separate piece of paper.

Rule **4.170** Dealings by committee-members and others

4.170(1) **[Application of Rule]** This Rule applies to—

(a) any member of the liquidation committee,

(b) any committee-member's representative,

(c) any person who is an associate of a member of the committee or a committee-member's representative, and

(d) any person who has been a member of the committee at any time in the last 12 months.

4.170(2) [Prohibited transactions]   Subject as follows, a person to whom this Rule applies shall not enter into any transaction whereby he—

(a) receives out of the company's assets any payment for services given or goods supplied in connection with the administration, or

(b) obtains any profit from the administration, or

(c) acquires any asset forming part of the estate.

4.170(3) [Leave or sanction for r. 4.170(2) transaction]   Such a transaction may be entered into by a person to whom this Rule applies—

(a) with the prior leave of the court, or

(b) if he does so as a matter of urgency, or by way of performance of a contract in force before the date on which the company went into liquidation, and obtains the court's leave for the transaction, having applied for it without undue delay, or

(c) with the prior sanction of the liquidation committee, where it is satisfied (after full disclosure of the circumstances) that the person will be giving full value in the transaction.

4.170(4) [Resolution to sanction transaction]   Where in the committee a resolution is proposed that sanction be accorded for a transaction to be entered into which, without that sanction or the leave of the court, would be in contravention of this Rule, no member of the committee, and no representative of a member, shall vote if he is to participate directly or indirectly in the transaction.

4.170(5) [Powers of court]   The court may, on the application of any person interested—

(a) set aside a transaction on the ground that it has been entered into in contravention of this Rule, and

(b) make with respect to it such other order as it thinks fit, including (subject to the following paragraph) an order requiring a person to whom this Rule applies to account for any profit obtained from the transaction and compensate the estate for any resultant loss.

4.170(6) [Member's or representative's associate]   In the case of a person to whom this Rule applies as an associate of a member of the committee or of a committee-member's representative, the court shall not make any order under paragraph (5), if satisfied that he entered into the relevant transaction without having any reason to suppose that in doing so he would contravene this Rule.

4.170(7) [Costs of application]   The costs of an application to the court for leave under this Rule are not payable out of the assets, unless the court so orders.

General note

This rule makes provision to guard against the risks of conflicts of interest on the part of committee members and their associates. (For the meaning of "associate", see IA 1986, s. 435.)

Rule 4.171 Composition of committee when creditors paid in full

4.171(1) [Application of Rule]   This Rule applies if the liquidator issues a certificate that the creditors have been paid in full, with interest in accordance with section 189.

4.171(2)   [Liquidator to file certificate in court]   The liquidator shall forthwith file the certificate in court. (NO CVL APPLICATION)   [FORM 4.50]

4.171(3–CVL)   [Copy of certificate to registrar]   The liquidator shall forthwith send a copy of the certificate to the registrar of companies.   [FORM 4.51]
                                                                                                              [FORM 4.50]

4.171(4)   [Creditor members]   The creditor members of the liquidation committee cease to be members of the committee.

4.171(5)   [Contributory members]   The committee continues in being unless and until abolished by decision of a meeting of contributories, and (subject to the next paragraph) so long as it consists of at least 3 contributory members.

4.171(6)   [Cessation or suspension]   The committee does not cease to exist on account of the number of contributory members falling below 3, unless and until 28 days have elapsed since the issue of the liquidator's certificate under paragraph (1).

But at any time when the committee consists of less than 3 contributory members, it is suspended and cannot act.

4.171(7)   [Co-opting etc. of contributories]   Contributories may be co-opted by the liquidator, or appointed by a contributories' meeting, to be members of the committee; but the maximum number of members is 5.

4.171(8)   [Application of Rules]   The foregoing Rules in this Chapter continue to apply to the liquidation committee (with any necessary modifications) as if all the members of the committee were creditor members.

History note

Against r. 4.171(3–CVL) the words "[FORM 4.50]" were inserted by I(A)R 1987 (SI 1987 No. 1919), r. 3(1), Sch., Pt. 2, para. 156(1) as from 11 January 1988.

General note

The liquidation committee continues in being without creditor members after the creditors have been paid in full, subject to rr. 4.171(5), (6).

Rule **4.172**   Committee's functions vested in Secretary of State

(NO CVL APPLICATION)

4.172(1)   [Liquidator's notices and reports]   At any time when the functions of the liquidation committee are vested in the Secretary of State under section 141(4) or (5), requirements of the Act or the Rules about notices to be given, or reports to be made, to the committee by the liquidator do not apply, otherwise than as enabling the committee to require a report as to any matter.

4.172(2)   [Exercise by official receiver]   Where the committee's functions are so vested under section 141(5), they may be exercised by the official receiver.

General note

The IA 1986, s. 141(4) applies when the official receiver is liquidator, and s. 141(5) where there is for the time being no liquidation committee.

Rule **4.172A**   Formal defects

4.172A   The acts of the liquidation committee established for any winding up are valid notwithstanding any defect in the appointment, election or qualifications of any member of the committee or any committee-member's representative or in the formalities of its establishment.

History note

Rule 4.172A was inserted by I(A)R 1987 (SI 1987 No. 1919), r. 3(1), Sch., Pt. 1, para. 75 as from 11 January 1988.

General note

This is a standard-form provision designed to prevent technical objections to the constitution of the committee. (See, however, *Re W & A Glaser Ltd* [1994] BCC 199, which makes it clear that the court itself is free to go into this question.)

Chapter 13 — The Liquidation Committee Where Winding Up Follows Immediately on Administration (NO CVL APPLICATION)

Rule **4.173**   Preliminary

4.173(1)   **[Application of Rules]**   The Rules in this Chapter apply where—

    (a) the winding-up order has been made immediately upon the discharge of an administration order under Part II of the Act, and

    (b) the court makes an order under section 140(1) of the Act appointing as liquidator the person who was previously the administrator.

4.173(2)   **[Definitions]**   In this Chapter, **"insolvent winding up"**, **"solvent winding up"**, **"creditor member"** and **"contributory member"** mean the same as in Chapter 12.

(See general note after r. 4.178.)

Rule **4.174**   Continuation of creditors' committee

4.174(1)   **[Creditors' committee as liquidation committee]**   If under section 26 a creditors' committee has been established for the purposes of the administration, then (subject as follows in this Chapter) that committee continues in being as the liquidation committee for the purposes of the winding up, and—

    (a) it is deemed to be a committee established as such under section 141, and

    (b) no action shall be taken under subsections (1) to (3) of that section to establish any other.

4.174(2) **[Non-application of Rule]** This Rule does not apply if, at the time when the court's order under section 140(1) is made, the committee under section 26 consists of less than 3 members; and a creditor who was, immediately before that date, a member of it, ceases to be a member on the making of the order if his debt is fully secured.

(See general note after r. 4.178.)

Rule **4.175** Membership of committee

4.175(1) **[Three–five creditors]** Subject as follows, the liquidation committee shall consist of at least 3, and not more than 5, creditors of the company, elected by the creditors' meeting held under section 26 or (in order to make up numbers or fill vacancies) by a creditors' meeting summoned by the liquidator after the company goes into liquidation.

4.175(2) **[In a solvent winding up]** In the case of a solvent winding up, the liquidator shall, on not less than 21 days' notice, summon a meeting of contributories, in order to elect (if it so wishes) contributory members of the liquidation committee, up to 3 in number.

(See general note after r. 4.178.)

Rule **4.176** Liquidator's certificate

4.176(1) **[Certificate of continuance]** The liquidator shall issue a certificate of the liquidation committee's continuance, specifying the persons who are, or are to be, members of it. [FORM 4.52]

4.176(2) **[Contents of certificate]** It shall be stated in the certificate whether or not the liquidator has summoned a meeting of contributories under Rule 4.175(2), and whether (if so) the meeting has elected contributories to be members of the committee.

4.176(3) **[Effect of certificate]** Pending the issue of the liquidator's certificate, the committee is suspended and cannot act.

4.176(4) **[Agreement to act]** No person may act, or continue to act, as a member of the committee unless and until he has agreed to do so; and the liquidator's certificate shall not issue until at least the minimum number of persons required under Rule 4.175 to form a committee have signified their agreement.

4.176(5) **[Amended certificate]** As and when the others signify their agreement, the liquidator shall issue an amended certificate. [FORM 4.52]

4.176(6) **[Certificate to be filed in court]** The liquidator's certificate (or, as the case may be, the amended certificate) shall be filed by him in court.

4.176(7) **[Change in membership]** If subsequently there is any change in the committee's membership, the liquidator shall report the change to the court.

[FORM 4.49]

(See general note after r. 4.178.)

Rule 4.177 Obligations of liquidator to committee

4.177(1) **[Liquidator's report]** As soon as may be after the issue of the liquidator's certificate under Rule 4.176, the liquidator shall report to the liquidation committee what actions he has taken since the date on which the company went into liquidation.

4.177(2) **[Summary report]** A person who becomes a member of the committee after that date is not entitled to require a report to him by the liquidator, otherwise than in a summary form, of any matters previously arising.

4.177(3) **[Access to records etc.]** Nothing in this Rule disentitles the committee, or any member of it, from having access to the records of the liquidation (whether relating to the period when he was administrator, or to any subsequent period), or from seeking an explanation of any matter within the committee's responsibility.

(See general note after r. 4.178.)

Rule 4.178 Application of Chapter 12

4.178 Except as provided above in this Chapter, Rules 4.155 to 4.172A in Chapter 12 apply to the liquidation committee following the issue of the liquidator's certificate under Rule 4.176, as if it had been established under section 141.

History note

In r. 4.178 "4.172A" was substituted for the former "4.172" by I(A)R 1987 (SI 1987 No. 1919), r. 3(1), Sch., Pt. 1, para. 76 as from 11 January 1988.

General note to rr. 4.173–4.178

These rules adapt those generally applicable to the liquidation committee (rr. 4.151–4.172A) for the special case where a winding up follows immediately on an administration. The creditors' committee appointed for the purpose of the administration continues in being as the liquidation committee, subject to the right of the contributories (where it is a "solvent" liquidation – see r. 4.151) to appoint their own members.

Chapter 14 — Collection and Distribution of Company's Assets by Liquidator

Rule 4.179 General duties of liquidator

(NO CVL APPLICATION)

4.179(1) **[Officer of the court]** The duties imposed on the court by the Act with regard to the collection of the company's assets and their application in discharge of its liabilities are discharged by the liquidator as an officer of the court subject to its control.

4.179(2) **[Same powers as a receiver]** In the discharge of his duties the liquidator, for the purposes of acquiring and retaining possession of the company's property, has the same powers as a receiver appointed by the High Court, and the court may on his application enforce such acquisition or retention accordingly.

General note

For the statutory source of this rule, see IA 1986, ss. 148(1), 160(1)(*b*).

Rule 4.180   Manner of distributing assets

4.180(1)   [Dividends]   Whenever the liquidator has sufficient funds in hand for the purpose he shall, subject to the retention of such sums as may be necessary for the expenses of the winding up, declare and distribute dividends among the creditors in respect of the debts which they have respectively proved.

4.180(2)   [Notice of intention]   The liquidator shall give notice of his intention to declare and distribute a dividend.

4.180(3)   [Notice of dividend]   Where the liquidator has declared a dividend, he shall give notice of it to the creditors, stating how the dividend is proposed to be distributed. The notice shall contain such particulars with respect to the company, and to its assets and affairs, as will enable the creditors to comprehend the calculation of the amount of the dividend and the manner of its distribution.

(See general note after r. 4.183.)

Rule 4.181   Debts of insolvent company to rank equally

(NO CVL APPLICATION)

4.181(1)   [Ranking and priority]   Debts other than preferential debts rank equally between themselves in the winding up and, after the preferential debts, shall be paid in full unless the assets are insufficient for meeting them, in which case they abate in equal proportions between themselves.

4.181(2)   [Application of r. 4.181(1)]   Paragraph (1) applies whether or not the company is unable to pay its debts.

History note

Rule 4.181(1) was renumbered as such and r. 4.181(2) was added by I(A)R 1987 (SI 1987 No. 1919), r. 3(1), Sch., Pt. 1, para. 77 as from 11 January 1988.

(See general note after r. 4.183.)

Rule 4.182   Supplementary provisions as to dividend

4.182(1)   [Calculation and distribution]   In the calculation and distribution of a dividend the liquidator shall make provision—

   (a) for any debts which appear to him to be due to persons who, by reason of the distance of their place of residence, may not have had sufficient time to tender and establish their proofs,
   (b) for any debts which are the subject of claims which have not yet been determined, and
   (c) for disputed proofs and claims.

4.182(2)   [Proof after dividend declared]   A creditor who has not proved his debt before the declaration of any dividend is not entitled to disturb, by reason that he has not participated in it, the distribution of that dividend or any other dividend declared before his debt was proved, but—

(a) when he has proved that debt he is entitled to be paid, out of any money for the time being available for the payment of any further dividend, any dividend or dividends which he has failed to receive, and

(b) any dividend or dividends payable under sub-paragraph (a) shall be paid before that money is applied to the payment of any such further dividend.

4.182(3)   [Order for payment etc.]   No action lies against the liquidator for a dividend; but if he refuses to pay a dividend the court may, if it thinks fit, order him to pay it and also to pay, out of his own money—

(a) interest on the dividend, at the rate for the time being specified in section 17 of the Judgments Act 1838, from the time when it was withheld, and

(b) the costs of the proceedings in which the order to pay is made.

(See general note after r. 4.183.)

Rule **4.182A**   Distribution in members' voluntary winding up

(NO CVL APPLICATION)

4.182A(1)   [Notice of intention]   In a members' voluntary winding up the liquidator may give notice in such newspaper as he considers most appropriate for the purpose of drawing the matter to the attention of the company's creditors that he intends to make a distribution to creditors.

4.182A(2)   ["The last date for proving"]   The notice shall specify a date ("the last date for proving") up to which proofs may be lodged. The date shall be the same for all creditors and not less than 21 days from that of the notice.

4.182A(3)   [Proofs lodged out of time]   The liquidator is not obliged to deal with proofs lodged after the last date for proving; but he may do so, if he thinks fit.

4.182A(4)   [Distribution not to be disturbed]   A creditor who has not proved his debt before the last date for proving or after that date increases the claim in his proof is not entitled to disturb, by reason that he has not participated in it, either at all or, as the case may be, to the extent that his increased claim would allow, that distribution or any other distribution made before his debt was proved or his claim increased; but when he has proved his debt or, as the case may be, increased his claim, he is entitled to be paid, out of any money for the time being available for the payment of any further distribution, any distribution or distributions which he has failed to receive.

4.182A(5)   [Only or final distribution]   Where the distribution proposed to be made is to be the only or the final distribution in that winding up, the liquidator may, subject to paragraph (6), make that distribution without regard to the claim of any person in respect of a debt not already proved.

4.182A(6)   [Notice in r. 4.182A(5)]   Where the distribution proposed to be made is one specified in paragraph (5), the notice given under paragraph (1) shall state the effect of paragraph (5).

History note

Rule 4.182A was inserted by I(A)R 1987 (SI 1987 No. 1919), r. 3(1), Sch., Pt. 1, para. 78 as from 11 January 1988.

(See general note after r. 4.183.)

Rule **4.183**   Division of unsold assets

4.183 Without prejudice to provisions of the Act about disclaimer, the liquidator may, with the permission of the liquidation committee, divide in its existing form amongst the company's creditors, according to its estimated value, any property which from its peculiar nature or other special circumstances cannot be readily or advantageously sold.

General note to rr. 4.180–4.183

These rules deal with the distribution of dividends and the ranking of debts *inter se*. For further provisions regarding dividends, see rr. 4.186 and 11.1ff; and on preferential debts see IA 1986, s. 386 and Sch. 6.

If the liquidator proposes to pay an interim dividend at a time when an application to the court to challenge the admission or rejection of a proof is outstanding, the leave of the court is required under IR 1986, r. 11.5(2).

The amendment to r. 4.181 seems to have added more confusion than it has dispelled. If the new para. (2) was necessary at all, it ought to have been accompanied by the removal of the reference to insolvency in the heading to the rule. It appears that para. (2) was introduced to refer to the words "shall be paid in full" in para. (1); but there can hardly be any question of the "ranking" of debts that are all to be paid in full.

Note that a sum due to a member *qua* member is not deemed to be a debt, and ranks after the claims of the company's creditors: s. 74(2)(*f*).

Provision equivalent to r. 4.181 is made for a voluntary winding up by s. 107.

Rule **4.184**   General powers of liquidator

4.184(1)   **[Particular permission]**   Any permission given by the liquidation committee or the court under section 167(1)(a), or under the Rules, shall not be a general permission but shall relate to a particular proposed exercise of the liquidator's power in question; and a person dealing with the liquidator in good faith and for value is not concerned to enquire whether any such permission has been given.

4.184(2)   **[Ratification]**   Where the liquidator has done anything without that permission, the court or the liquidation committee may, for the purpose of enabling him to meet his expenses out of the assets, ratify what he has done; but neither shall do so unless it is satisfied that the liquidator has acted in a case of urgency and has sought ratification without undue delay.

General note

The powers referred to in IA 1986, s. 167(1)(*a*) are the payment of debts, the compromise of claims, the institution and defence of proceedings, and the carrying on of the business of the company.

Rule **4.185**   Enforced delivery up of company's property

(NO CVL APPLICATION)

4.185(1)   **[Powers under s. 234]**   The powers conferred on the court by section 234 (enforced delivery of company property) are exercisable by the liquidator or, where a provisional liquidator has been appointed, by him.

4.185(2) **[Duty to comply]** Any person on whom a requirement under section 234 (2) is imposed by the liquidator or provisional liquidator shall, without avoidable delay, comply with it.

General note

For the statutory source of this rule, see IA 1986, ss. 160(1)(*c*), 234.

Rule **4.186** Final distribution

4.186(1) **[Notice under Pt. 11]** When the liquidator has realised all the company's assets or so much of them as can, in his opinion, be realised without needlessly protracting the liquidation, he shall give notice, under Part 11 of the Rules, either—

(a) of his intention to declare a final dividend, or

(b) that no dividend, or further dividend, will be declared.

4.186(2) **[Contents of notice]** The notice shall contain all such particulars as are required by Part 11 of the Rules and shall require claims against the assets to be established by a date specified in the notice.

4.186(3) **[Final dividend]** After that date, the liquidator shall—

(a) defray any outstanding expenses of the winding up out of the assets, and

(b) if he intends to declare a final dividend, declare and distribute that dividend without regard to the claim of any person in respect of a debt not already proved.

4.186(4) **[Postponement]** The court may, on the application of any person, postpone the date specified in the notice.

General note

On dividends generally, see rr. 4.180–4.183 and 11.1ff.

Chapter 15 — Disclaimer

Rule **4.187** Liquidator's notice of disclaimer

4.187(1) **[Contents of notice]** Where the liquidator disclaims property under section 178, the notice of disclaimer shall contain such particulars of the property disclaimed as enable it to be easily identified.   [FORM 4.53]

4.187(2) **[Notice to be signed etc.]** The notice shall be signed by the liquidator and filed in court, with a copy. The court shall secure that both the notice and the copy are sealed and endorsed with the date of filing.

4.187(3) **[Copy of notice returned to liquidator]** The copy notice, so sealed and endorsed, shall be returned by the court to the liquidator as follows—

(a) if the notice has been delivered at the offices of the court by the liquidator in person, it shall be handed to him,

  (b) if it has been delivered by some person acting on the liquidator's behalf, it shall be handed to that person, for immediate transmission to the liquidator, and

  (c) otherwise, it shall be sent to the liquidator by first class post.

The court shall cause to be endorsed on the original notice, or otherwise recorded on the file, the manner in which the copy notice was returned to the liquidator.

4.187(4)   **[Date of notice]**   For the purposes of section 178, the date of the prescribed notice is that which is endorsed on it, and on the copy, in accordance with this Rule.

(See general note after r. 4.194.)

Rule **4.188**   Communication of disclaimer to persons interested

4.188(1)   **[Copy of notices]**   Within 7 days after the day on which the copy of the notice of disclaimer is returned to him under Rule 4.187, the liquidator shall send or give copies of the notice (showing the date endorsed as required by that Rule) to the persons mentioned in paragraphs (2) to (4) below.   [FORM 4.53]

4.188(2)   **[Leasehold property]**   Where the property disclaimed is of a leasehold nature, he shall send or give a copy to every person who (to his knowledge) claims under the company as underlessee or mortgagee.

4.188(3)   **[Giving notice]**   He shall in any case send or give a copy of the notice to every person who (to his knowledge)—

  (a) claims an interest in respect of the property, or

  (b) is under any liability in respect of the property, not being a liability discharged by the disclaimer.

4.188(4)   **[Unprofitable contract]**   If the disclaimer is of an unprofitable contract, he shall send or give copies of the notice to all such persons as, to his knowledge, are parties to the contract or have interests under it.

4.188(5)   **[Late communication]**   If subsequently it comes to the liquidator's knowledge, in the case of any person, that he has such an interest in the disclaimed property as would have entitled him to receive a copy of the notice of disclaimer in pursuance of paragraphs (2) to (4), the liquidator shall then forthwith send or give to that person a copy of the notice.

  But compliance with this paragraph is not required if—

  (a) the liquidator is satisfied that the person has already been made aware of the disclaimer and its date, or

  (b) the court, on the liquidator's application, orders that compliance is not required in that particular case.

(See general note after r. 4.194.)

Rule **4.189**   Additional notices

4.189   The liquidator disclaiming property may, without prejudice to his obligations under sections 178 to 180 and Rules 4.187 and 4.188, at any time give notice of the disclaimer to any persons who in his opinion ought, in the public interest or otherwise, to be informed of it.   [FORM 4.53]

(See general note after r. 4.194.)

Rule **4.190**   Duty to keep court informed

4.190   The liquidator shall notify the court from time to time as to the persons to whom he has sent or given copies of the notice of disclaimer under the two preceding Rules, giving their names and addresses, and the nature of their respective interests.

(See general note after r. 4.194.)

Rule **4.191**   Application by interested party under s. 178(5)

4.191   Where, in the case of any property, application is made to the liquidator by an interested party under section 178(5) (request for decision whether the property is to be disclaimed or not), the application—

(a) shall be delivered to the liquidator personally or by registered post, and

(b) shall be made in the form known as "notice to elect", or a substantially similar form.   [FORM 4.54]

(See general note after r. 4.194.)

Rule **4.192**   Interest in property to be declared on request

4.192(1)   [Notice to declare interest]   If, in the case of property which the liquidator has the right to disclaim, it appears to him that there is some person who claims, or may claim, to have an interest in the property, he may give notice to that person calling on him to declare within 14 days whether he claims any such interest and, if so, the nature and extent of it.   [FORM 4.55]

4.192(2)   [Failing compliance with notice]   Failing compliance with the notice, the liquidator is entitled to assume that the person concerned has no such interest in the property as will prevent or impede its disclaimer.

(See general note after r. 4.194.)

Rule **4.193**   Disclaimer presumed valid and effective

4.193   Any disclaimer of property by the liquidator is presumed valid and effective, unless it is proved that he has been in breach of his duty with respect to the giving of notice of disclaimer, or otherwise under sections 178 to 180, or under this Chapter of the Rules.

(See general note after r. 4.194.)

Rule **4.194**   **Application for exercise of court's powers under s. 181**

4.194(1)   [Application of Rule]   This Rule applies with respect to an application by any person under section 181 for an order of the court to vest or deliver disclaimed property.

4.194(2)   [Time for application]   The application must be made within 3 months of the applicant becoming aware of the disclaimer, or of his receiving a copy of the liquidator's notice of disclaimer sent under Rule 4.188, whichever is the earlier.

4.194(3)   [Contents of affidavit]   The applicant shall with his application file in court an affidavit—

(a) stating whether he applies under paragraph (a) of section 181(2) (claim of interest in the property) or under paragraph (b) (liability not discharged);

(b) specifying the date on which he received a copy of the liquidator's notice of disclaimer, or otherwise became aware of the disclaimer; and

(c) specifying the grounds of his application and the order which he desires the court to make under section 181.

4.194(4)   [Venue for hearing]   The court shall fix a venue for the hearing of the application; and the applicant shall, not later than 7 days before the date fixed, give to the liquidator notice of the venue, accompanied by copies of the application and the affidavit under paragraph (3).

4.194(5)   [Directions for notice etc.]   On the hearing of the application, the court may give directions as to other persons (if any) who should be sent or given notice of the application and the grounds on which it is made.

4.194(6)   [Sealed copies of order]   Sealed copies of any order made on the application shall be sent by the court to the applicant and the liquidator.

4.194(7)   [Leasehold property]   In a case where the property disclaimed is of a leasehold nature, and section 179 applies to suspend the effect of the disclaimer, there shall be included in the court's order a direction giving effect to the disclaimer.

This paragraph does not apply if, at the time when the order is issued, other applications under section 181 are pending in respect of the same property.

General note to rr. 4.187–4.194

The statutory powers of disclaimer are contained in IA 1986, ss. 178–182. These rules supplement those provisions. On property "of a leasehold nature", see IA 1986, ss. 179, 182.

Chapter 16 — Settlement of List of Contributories

(NO CVL APPLICATION)

Rule **4.195**   **Preliminary**

4.195   The duties of the court with regard to the settling of the list of contributories are, by virtue of the Rules, delegated to the liquidator.

(See general note after r. 4.196.)

Rule **4.196**   Duty of liquidator to settle list

4.196(1)   **[Settling list of contributories]**   Subject as follows, the liquidator shall, as soon as may be after his appointment, exercise the court's power to settle a list of the company's contributories for the purposes of section 148 and, with the court's approval, rectify the register of members.

4.196(2)   **[Officer of the court]**   The liquidator's duties under this Rule are performed by him as an officer of the court subject to the court's control.

General note to rr. 4.195, 4. 196

For the statutory source of these rules, see IA 1986, ss. 148, 160(1)(*b*).

Rule **4.197**   Form of list

4.197(1)   **[Contents of list]**   The list shall identify—

(a) the several classes of the company's shares (if more than one), and

(b) the several classes of contributories, distinguishing between those who are contributories in their own right and those who are so as representatives of, or liable for the debts of, others.

4.197(2)   **[Further contents]**   In the case of each contributory there shall in the list be stated—

(a) his address,

(b) the number and class of shares, or the extent of any other interest to be attributed to him, and

(c) if the shares are not fully paid up, the amounts which have been called up and paid in respect of them (and the equivalent, if any, where his interest is other than shares).

(See general note after r. 4.201.)

Rule **4.198**   Procedure for settling list

4.198(1)   **[Notice]**   Having settled the list, the liquidator shall forthwith give notice, to every person included in the list, that he has done so.

4.198(2)   **[Contents of notice]**   The notice given to each person shall state—

(a) in what character, and for what number of shares or what interest, he is included in the list,

(b) what amounts have been called up and paid up in respect of the shares or interest, and

(c) that in relation to any shares or interest not fully paid up, his inclusion in the list may result in the unpaid capital being called.

4.198(3)   **[Objection to list]**   The notice shall inform any person to whom it is given that, if he objects to any entry in, or omission from, the list, he should so inform the liquidator in writing within 21 days from the date of the notice.

4.198(4) **[Amendment of list]** On receipt of any such objection, the liquidator shall within 14 days give notice to the objector either—
(a) that he has amended the list (specifying the amendment), or
(b) that he considers the objection to be not well-founded and declines to amend the list.
The notice shall in either case inform the objector of the effect of Rule 4.199.

(See general note after r. 4.201.)

Rule 4.199 Application to court for variation of the list

4.199(1) **[Application to court]** If a person objects to any entry in, or exclusion from, the list of contributories as settled by the liquidator and, notwithstanding notice by the liquidator declining to amend the list, maintains his objection, he may apply to the court for an order removing the entry to which he objects or (as the case may be) otherwise amending the list.

4.199(2) **[Time for application]** The application must be made within 21 days of the service on the applicant of the liquidator's notice under Rule 4.198(4).

(See general note after r. 4.201.)

Rule 4.200 Variation of, or addition to, the list

4.200 The liquidator may from time to time vary or add to the list of contributories as previously settled by him, but subject in all respects to the preceding Rules in this Chapter.

(See general note after r. 4.201.)

Rule 4.201 Costs not to fall on official receiver

4.201 The official receiver is not personally liable for any costs incurred by a person in respect of an application to set aside or vary his act or decision in settling the list of contributories, or varying or adding to the list; and the liquidator (if other than the official receiver) is not so liable unless the court makes an order to that effect.

General note to rr. 4.197–4.201
Here are set out the rules prescribing the form of the list of contributories and the procedure for settling it. Note that the power to rectify the register of members may be exercised only with the special leave of the court: IA 1986, s. 160(2), r. 4.196(1).

Chapter 17 — Calls (NO CVL APPLICATION)

Rule 4.202 Calls by liquidator

4.202 Subject as follows, the powers conferred by the Act with respect to the making of calls on contributories are exercisable by the liquidator as an officer of the court subject to the court's control.

(See general note after r. 4.205.)

Rule 4.203   Control by liquidation committee

4.203(1)   [Meeting to sanction call]   Where the liquidator proposes to make a call, and there is a liquidation committee, he may summon a meeting of the committee for the purpose of obtaining its sanction.

4.203(2)   [Notice]   At least 7 days' notice of the meeting shall be given by the liquidator to each member of the committee.

4.203(3)   [Contents of notice]   The notice shall contain a statement of the proposed amount of the call, and the purpose for which it is intended to be made.

(See general note after r. 4.205.)

Rule 4.204   Application to court for leave to make a call

4.204(1)   [Form of application]   For the purpose of obtaining the leave of the court for the making of a call on any contributories of the company, the liquidator shall apply *ex parte*, supporting his application by affidavit.   [FORM 4.56]

4.204(2)   [Contents of application]   There shall in the application be stated the amount of the proposed call, and the contributories on whom it is to be made.

4.204(3)   [Powers of court]   The court may direct that notice of the order be given to the contributories concerned, or to other contributories, or may direct that the notice be publicly advertised.   [FORM 4.57]

(See general note after r. 4.205.)

Rule 4.205   Making and enforcement of the call

4.205(1)   [Notice of call]   Notice of the call shall be given to each of the contributories concerned, and shall specify—

(a) the amount or balance due from him in respect of it, and

(b) whether the call is made with the sanction of the court or the liquidation committee.   [FORM 4.58]

4.205(2)   [Enforcement by order]   Payment of the amount due from any contributory may be enforced by order of the court.   [FORM 4.59]

General note to rr. 4.202–4.205

For the statutory source of these rules, see IA 1986, ss. 150, 160(1)(*d*). The exercise of the power of the liquidator to make a call requires the special leave of the court or the sanction of the liquidation committee (s. 160(2), rr. 4.203, 4.204).

Chapter 18 — Special Manager

Rule 4.206   Appointment and remuneration

4.206(1)   [Liquidator's report]   An application made by the liquidator under section 177 for the appointment of a person to be special manager shall be supported by a report setting out the reasons for the application.

The report shall include the applicant's estimate of the value of the assets in respect of which the special manager is to be appointed.

4.206(2)   **[Application of Chapter]**   This Chapter applies also with respect to an application by the provisional liquidator, where one has been appointed, and references to the liquidator are to be read accordingly as including the provisional liquidator. (NO CVL APPLICATION).

4.206(3)   **[Duration of appointment]**   The court's order appointing the special manager shall specify the duration of his appointment, which may be for a period of time, or until the occurrence of a specified event. Alternatively, the order may specify that the duration of the appointment is to be subject to a further order of the court.   [FORM 4.60]

4.206(4)   **[Renewal]**   The appointment of a special manager may be renewed by order of the court.

4.206(5)   **[Remuneration]**   The special manager's remuneration shall be fixed from time to time by the court.

4.206(6)   **[Validation of acts]**   The acts of the special manager are valid notwithstanding any defect in his appointment or qualifications.

(See general note after r. 4.210.)

Rule 4.207   Security

4.207(1)   **[Effect of giving security]**   The appointment of the special manager does not take effect until the person appointed has given (or being allowed by the court to do so, undertaken to give) security to the person who applies for him to be appointed.

4.207(2)   **[Special or general security]**   It is not necessary that security shall be given for each separate company liquidation; but it may be given specially for a particular liquidation, or generally for any liquidation in relation to which the special manager may be employed as such.

4.207(3)   **[Amount of security]**   The amount of the security shall not be less than the value of the assets in respect of which he is appointed, as estimated by the applicant in his report under Rule 4.206.

4.207(4)   **[Certificate of adequacy]**   When the special manager has given security to the person applying for his appointment, that person shall file in court a certificate as to the adequacy of the security.

4.207(5)   **[Cost of security]**   The cost of providing the security shall be paid in the first instance by the special manager; but—

     (a) where a winding-up order is not made, he is entitled to be reimbursed out of the property of the company, and the court may make an order on the company accordingly, and

     (b) where a winding-up order is made, he is entitled to be reimbursed out of the assets in the prescribed order of priority.

(NO CVL APPLICATION)

4.207(6–CVL) **[Cost of providing security]** The cost of providing the security shall be paid in the first instance by the special manager; but he is entitled to be reimbursed out of the assets, in the prescribed order of priority.

(See general note after r. 4.210.)

Rule 4.208 Failure to give or keep up security

4.208(1) **[Failure to give security]** If the special manager fails to give the required security within the time stated for that purpose by the order appointing him, or any extension of that time that may be allowed, the liquidator shall report the failure to the court, which may thereupon discharge the order appointing the special manager.

4.208(2) **[Failure to keep up security]** If the special manager fails to keep up his security, the liquidator shall report his failure to the court, which may thereupon remove the special manager, and make such order as it thinks fit as to costs.

4.208(3) **[Directions on removal]** If an order is made under this Rule removing the special manager, or discharging the order appointing him, the court shall give directions as to whether any, and if so what, steps should be taken for the appointment of another special manager in his place.

(See general note after r. 4.210.)

Rule 4.209 Accounting

4.209(1) **[Contents of accounts]** The special manager shall produce accounts, containing details of his receipts and payments, for the approval of the liquidator.

4.209(2) **[Period of accounts]** The accounts shall be in respect of 3-month periods for the duration of the special manager's appointment (or for a lesser period, if his appointment terminates less than 3 months from its date, or from the date to which the last accounts were made up).

4.209(3) **[When accounts approved]** When the accounts have been approved, the special manager's receipts and payments shall be added to those of the liquidator.

(See general note after r. 4.210.)

Rule 4.210 Termination of appointment

4.210(1) **[Automatic termination]** The special manager's appointment terminates if the winding-up petition is dismissed or if, a provisional liquidator having been appointed, the latter is discharged without a winding-up order having been made. (NO CVL APPLICATION).

4.210(2) **[Application to court]** If the liquidator is of opinion that the employment of the special manager is no longer necessary or profitable for the company, he shall apply to the court for directions, and the court may order the special manager's appointment to be terminated.

4.210(3) **[Resolution of creditors]**   The liquidator shall make the same application if a resolution of the creditors is passed, requesting that the appointment be terminated.

General note to rr. 4.206–4.210

On the appointment of a special manager, see IA 1986, s. 177 and the notes thereto. A special manager need not be qualified to act as an insolvency practitioner. These rules deal with his appointment and remuneration, the furnishing of security, his obligation to keep accounts and the termination of his appointment.

Chapter 19 — Public Examination of Company Officers and Others

Rule **4.211**   Order for public examination

4.211(1) **[Service of copy order]**   If the official receiver applies to the court under section 133 for the public examination of any person, a copy of the court's order shall, forthwith after its making, be served on that person.   [FORM 4.61]

4.211(2) **[Official receivers' report]**   Where the application relates to a person falling within section 133(1)(c) (promoters, past managers, etc.), it shall be accompanied by a report by the official receiver indicating—

   (a) the grounds on which the person is supposed to fall within that paragraph, and

   (b) whether, in the official receiver's opinion, it is likely that service of the order on the person can be effected by post at a known address.

4.211(3) **[Means of service]**   If in his report the official receiver gives it as his opinion that, in a case to which paragraph (2) applies, there is no reasonable certainty that service by post will be effective, the court may direct that the order be served by some means other than, or in addition to, post.

4.211(4) **[Rescission of order]**   In a case to which paragraphs (2) and (3) apply, the court shall rescind the order if satisfied by the person to whom it is directed that he does not fall within section 133(1)(c).

(See general note after r. 4.217.)

Rule **4.212**   Notice of hearing

4.212(1) **[Venue and direction to attend]**   The court's order shall appoint a venue for the examination of the person to whom it is directed ("the examinee"), and direct his attendance thereat.

4.212(2) **[Notice of hearing]**   The official receiver shall give at least 14 days' notice of the hearing—

   (a) if a liquidator has been nominated or appointed, to him;

   (b) if a special manager has been appointed, to him; and

(c) subject to any contrary direction of the court, to every creditor and contributory of the company who is known to the official receiver or is identified in the company's statement of affairs.

4.212(3) **[Advertisement]** The official receiver may, if he thinks fit, cause notice of the order to be given, by advertisement in one or more newspapers, at least 14 days before the date fixed for the hearing; but, unless the court otherwise directs, there shall be no such advertisement before at least 7 days have elapsed since the examinee was served with the order.

(See general note after r. 4.217.)

Rule **4.213** Order on request by creditors or contributories

4.213(1) **[Form of request etc.]** A request to the official receiver by creditors or contributories under section 133(2) shall be made in writing and be accompanied by—

(a) a list of the creditors concurring with the request and the amounts of their respective claims in the liquidation or (as the case may be) of the contributories so concurring, with their respective values, and

(b) from each creditor or contributory concurring, written confirmation of his concurrence.

This paragraph does not apply if the requisitioning creditor's debt or, as the case may be, requisitioning contributory's shareholding is alone sufficient, without the concurrence of others. [FORM 4.62]
[FORM 4.63]

4.213(2) **[Further contents]** The request must specify the name of the proposed examinee, the relationship which he has, or has had, to the company and the reasons why his examination is requested.

4.213(3) **[Security for expenses of hearing]** Before an application to the court is made on the request, the requisitionists shall deposit with the official receiver such sum as the latter may determine to be appropriate by way of security for the expenses of the hearing of a public examination, if ordered.

4.213(4) **[Time for application]** Subject as follows, the official receiver shall, within 28 days of receiving the request, make the application to the court required by section 133(2).

4.213(5) **[Relief from unreasonable request]** If the official receiver is of opinion that the request is an unreasonable one in the circumstances, he may apply to the court for an order relieving him from the obligation to make the application otherwise required by that subsection.

4.213(6) **[Notice of relief order etc.]** If the court so orders, and the application for the order was made *ex parte*, notice of the order shall be given forthwith by the official receiver to the requisitionists. If the application for an order is dismissed, the official receiver's application under section 133(2) shall be made forthwith on conclusion of the hearing of the application first mentioned.

(See general note after r. 4.217.)

Rule **4.214**   Witness unfit for examination

4.214(1)   [Application for stay etc.]   Where the examinee is suffering from any mental disorder or physical affliction or disability rendering him unfit to undergo or attend for public examination, the court may, on application in that behalf, either stay the order for his public examination or direct that it shall be conducted in such manner and at such place as it thinks fit.   [FORM 4.64]

4.214(2)   [Who may apply]   Application under this Rule shall be made—

  (a) by a person who has been appointed by a court in the United Kingdom or elsewhere to manage the affairs of, or to represent, the examinee, or

  (b) by a relative or friend of the examinee whom the court considers to be a proper person to make the application, or

  (c) by the official receiver.

4.214(3)   [Application not by official receiver]   Where the application is made by a person other than the official receiver, then—

  (a) it shall, unless the examinee is a patient within the meaning of the Mental Health Act 1983, be supported by the affidavit of a registered medical practitioner as to the examinee's mental and physical condition;

  (b) at least 7 days' notice of the application shall be given to the official receiver and the liquidator (if other than the official receiver); and

  (c) before any order is made on the application, the applicant shall deposit with the official receiver such sum as the latter certifies to be necessary for the additional expenses of any examination that may be ordered on the application.

An order made on the application may provide that the expenses of the examination are to be payable, as to a specified proportion, out of the deposit under subparagraph (c), instead of out of the assets.

4.214(4)   [Application by official receiver]   Where the application is made by the official receiver it may be made *ex parte*, and may be supported by evidence in the form of a report by the official receiver to the court.

(See general note after r. 4.217.)

Rule **4.215**   Procedure at hearing

4.215(1)   [Examination on oath]   The examinee shall at the hearing be examined on oath; and he shall answer all such questions as the court may put, or allow to be put, to him.

4.215(2)   [Appearances etc.]   Any of the persons allowed by section 133(4) to question the examinee may, with the approval of the court (made known either at the hearing or in advance of it), appear by solicitor or counsel; or he may in writing authorise another person to question the examinee on his behalf.

4.215(3)   [Representation of examinee]   The examinee may at his own expense employ a solicitor with or without counsel, who may put to him such questions as the court may allow for the purpose of enabling him to explain or qualify any answers given by him, and may make representations on his behalf.

4.215(4)   [Record of examination]   There shall be made in writing such record of the examination as the court thinks proper. The record shall be read over either to or by the examinee, signed by him, and verified by affidavit at a venue fixed by the court.   [FORM 4.65]

4.215(5)   [Record as evidence]   The written record may, in any proceedings (whether under the Act or otherwise) be used as evidence against the examinee of any statement made by him in the course of his public examination.

4.215(6)   [Criminal proceedings etc.]   If criminal proceedings have been instituted against the examinee, and the court is of opinion that the continuance of the hearing would be calculated to prejudice a fair trial of those proceedings, the hearing may be adjourned.

(See general note after r. 4.217.)

Rule **4.216**   Adjournment

4.216(1)   [Adjourned by court]   The public examination may be adjourned by the court from time to time, either to a fixed date or generally.   [FORM 4.66]

4.216(2)   [Resumption]   Where the examination has been adjourned generally, the court may at any time on the application of the official receiver or of the examinee—

(a) fix a venue for the resumption of the examination, and

(b) give directions as to the manner in which, and the time within which, notice of the resumed public examination is to be given to persons entitled to take part in it.   [FORM 4.67]

4.216(3)   [Deposit for expenses re application]   Where application under paragraph (2) is made by the examinee, the court may grant it on terms that the expenses of giving the notices required by that paragraph shall be paid by him and that, before a venue for the resumed public examination is fixed, he shall deposit with the official receiver such sum as the latter considers necessary to cover those expenses.

(See general note after r. 4.217.)

Rule **4.217**   Expenses of examination

4.217(1)   [Expenses paid out of r. 4.213 deposit]   Where a public examination of the examinee has been ordered by the court on a creditors' or contributories' requisition under Rule 4.213, the court may order that the expenses of the examination are to be paid, as to a specified proportion, out of the deposit under Rule 4.213(3), instead of out of the assets.

4.217(2)   [Official receiver not liable for costs]   In no case do the costs and expenses of a public examination fall on the official receiver personally.

General note to rr. 4.211–4.217

It is expected that the official receiver will make more frequent use of the power to have company officers and others attend for public examination under the more broadly drawn terms of the new insolvency legislation: see the note to IA 1986, s. 133.

On the *private* examination of persons connected with an insolvent company, see IA 1986, ss. 236, 237 and rr. 9.1ff., and the notes thereto.

Subject to r. 4.211(2)(*a*) and (4), the official receiver is entitled to an order *ipso facto*, i.e. he need not make out any case to the court.

In r. 4.211(1) the word "forthwith" means "as soon as is reasonably practicable": *Re Seagull Manufacturing Co. Ltd. (in liquidation)* [1993] Ch. 345, at p. 359; [1993] BCC 241, at p. 248.

Chapter 20 — Order of Payment of Costs, etc., out of Assets

Rule 4.218   General rule as to priority

4.218(1)   [Priority of expenses]   The expenses of the liquidation are payable out of the assets in the following order of priority—

- (a) expenses properly chargeable or incurred by the official receiver or the liquidator in preserving, realising or getting in any of the assets of the company;
- (b) any other expenses incurred or disbursements made by the official receiver or under his authority, including those incurred or made in carrying on the business of the company;
- (c) (i) the fee payable under any order made under section 414 for the performance by the official receiver of his general duties as official receiver;
  - (ii) any repayable deposit lodged by the petitioner under any such order as security for the fee mentioned in sub-paragraph (i);
- (d) any other fees payable under any order made under section 414, including those payable to the official receiver, and any remuneration payable to him under general regulations;
- (e) the cost of any security provided by a provisional liquidator, liquidator or special manager in accordance with the Act or the Rules;
- (f) the remuneration of the provisional liquidator (if any);
- (g) any deposit lodged on an application for the appointment of a provisional liquidator;
- (h) the costs of the petitioner, and of any person appearing on the petition whose costs are allowed by the court;
- (j) the remuneration of the special manager (if any);
- (k) any amount payable to a person employed or authorised, under Chapter 6 of this Part of the Rules, to assist in the preparation of a statement of affairs or of accounts;
- (l) any allowance made, by order of the court, towards costs on an application

for release from the obligation to submit a statement of affairs, or for an extension of time for submitting such a statement;

(m) any necessary disbursements by the liquidator in the course of his administration (including any expenses incurred by members of the liquidation committee or their representatives and allowed by the liquidator under Rule 4.169, but not including any payment of corporation tax in circumstances referred to in sub-paragraph (p) below);

(n) the remuneration or emoluments of any person who has been employed by the liquidator to perform any services for the company, as required or authorised by or under the Act or the Rules;

(o) the remuneration of the liquidator, up to any amount not exceeding that which is payable to the official receiver under general regulations;

(p) the amount of any corporation tax on chargeable gains accruing on the realisation of any asset of the company (without regard to whether the realisation is effected by the liquidator, a secured creditor, or a receiver or manager appointed to deal with a security);

(q) the balance, after payment of any sums due under sub-paragraph (o) above, of any remuneration due to the liquidator.

4.218(2) **[Costs of shorthand writer]** The costs of employing a shorthand writer, if appointed by an order of the court made at the instance of the official receiver in connection with an examination, rank in priority with those specified in paragraph (1)(a). The costs of employing a shorthand writer so appointed in any other case rank after the allowance mentioned in paragraph (1)(l) and before the disbursements mentioned in paragraph (1)(m).

4.218(3) **[Expenses of r. 4.214 examination]** Any expenses incurred in holding an examination under Rule 4.214 (examinee unfit), where the application for it is made by the official receiver, rank in priority with those specified in paragraph (1)(a).

History note

In r. 4.218(1)(*m*) and (*p*) the word "corporation" was substituted for the former words "capital gains" by I(A)R 1987 (SI 1987 No. 1919), r. 3(1), Sch., Pt. 1, para. 79 as from 11 January 1988.

(See general note after r. 4.220.)

Rule 4.219 Winding up commencing as voluntary

4.219 In a winding up by the court which follows immediately on a voluntary winding up (whether members' voluntary or creditors' voluntary), such remuneration of the voluntary liquidator and costs and expenses of the voluntary liquidation as the court may allow are to rank in priority with the expenses specified in Rule 4.218(1)(a).

(See general note after r. 4.220.)

Rule 4.220 Saving for powers of the court

4.220(1) **[Powers of court under s. 156]** In a winding up by the court, the priorities laid down by Rules 4.218 and 4.219 are subject to the power of the court to make orders under section 156, where the assets are insufficient to satisfy the liabilities.

4.220(2)   [Powers of court re costs etc.]   Nothing in those Rules applies to or affects the power of any court, in proceedings by or against the company, to order costs to be paid by the company, or the liquidator; nor do they affect the rights of any person to whom such costs are ordered to be paid.

General note to rr. 4.218–4.220
The new list giving the order of priority for payment of the expenses of the liquidation is longer and more detailed than under the old winding-up rules.

Rule 4.218, unlike the former r. 195 of the 1949 Rules, applies to a creditors' voluntary winding up (including one that was originally a members' winding up): see r. 4.1(2).

The word "assets" in the opening sentence of r. 4.218(1) includes assets covered by the security of a floating charge which has crystallised (in other words, the claims for expenses under r. 4.218(1) rank ahead of those of the preferential creditors and the floating charge-holder): see the discussion of *Re Barleycorn Enterprises Ltd* [1970] Ch. 465 and *Re Portbase (Clothing) Ltd* [1993] Ch. 388; [1993] BCC 96 in the note to s. 107.

In *Re W F Fearman Ltd (No. 2)* (1988) 4 BCC 141 it was held that the costs of an administration petition (although bona fide presented and proving in the event to have been in the interests of the creditors) could not be allowed as a liquidation expense when the administration proceedings were terminated and a winding-up order was made. However, in the later case of *Re Gosscott (Groundworks) Ltd* (1988) 4 BCC 372, an order was made in such circumstances.

In *Re M C Bacon Ltd (No. 2)* [1990] BCC 430; [1991] Ch. 127, a liquidator had unsuccessfully brought proceedings to have a floating charge set aside as a transaction at an undervalue or a preference under ss. 238, 239, or to have the company's bank (as a "shadow director") ordered to pay compensation to the company for wrongful trading under s. 214. The court ruled that costs which had been awarded against the liquidator in those proceedings could not be recouped out of the company's assets (either as "expenses of the winding up" or as "expenses … incurred in realising or getting in any of the assets").

In the later case of *Re Movitex Ltd* [1990] BCC 491 the liquidators had continued an action, which had been commenced by the company before the winding up, to have certain property transactions set aside on the ground that they had been entered into without authority or in breach of directors' duty. Judgment had been given for the defendants with costs against the company, but the company's assets were insufficient to pay the costs order. It was held that the litigation costs were payable in full to the extent of the company's assets, but only after allowing the liquidators a deduction in respect of their costs in realising those assets.

Where rent is paid by a liquidator who has retained a lease in the hope of realising the company's assets to better advantage (as distinct from preserving the lease as an asset of the company) the rent does not rank as an expense of the liquidation under para. (*a*) of r. 4.218(1) but as a necessary disbursement under para. (*m*): *Re Linda Marie Ltd (in liq.)* (1988) 4 BCC 463. In the same case, the court declined to exercise its discretion to confer priority on the liquidator's remuneration over the landlord's claim for rent.

Chapter 21 — Miscellaneous Rules

SECTION A: RETURN OF CAPITAL
(NO CVL APPLICATION)

Rule 4.221   Application to court for order authorising return
4.221(1)   [Application of Rule]   This Rule applies where the liquidator intends to apply to the court for an order authorising a return of capital.

4.221(2) **[Accompanying list]** The application shall be accompanied by a list of the persons to whom the return is to be made.

4.221(3) **[Contents of list]** The list shall include the same details of those persons as appears in the settled list of contributories, with any necessary alterations to take account of matters after settlement of the list, and the amount to be paid to each person.

4.221(4) **[Copy order]** Where the court makes an order authorising the return, it shall send a sealed copy of the order to the liquidator.

General note

See Practice Direction in [1987] 1 All ER 107 (reproduced in Appendix IV of this Guide). See also general note after r. 4.222.

Rule 4.222 Procedure for return

4.222(1) **[Rate of return etc.]** The liquidator shall inform each person to whom a return is made of the rate of return per share, and whether it is expected that any further return will be made.

4.222(2) **[Method of payment]** Any payments made by the liquidator by way of the return may be sent by post, unless for any reason another method of making the payment has been agreed with the payee.

General note to rr. 4.221, 4.222

In a winding up by the court, the court must "adjust the rights of the contributories among themselves and distribute any surplus among the persons entitled to it" (IA 1986, s. 154). Although it might have been thought from the language of IA 1986, ss. 143(1) and 160(1)(*b*), (2) that capital could be returned to contributories on the liquidator's own authority, these rules confirm that he must have the sanction of the court.

SECTION B: CONCLUSION OF WINDING UP

Rule 4.223 Statements to registrar of companies under s. 192

4.223–CVL(1) **[Time limit for s. 192 statement]** Subject to paragraphs (3) and (3A), the statement which section 192 requires the liquidator to send to the registrar of companies, if the winding up is not concluded within one year from its commencement, shall be sent not more than 30 days after the expiration of that year, and thereafter 6-monthly until the winding up is concluded. [FORM 4.68]

4.223(2) **[Conclusion of winding up etc.]** For this purpose the winding up is concluded at the date of the dissolution of the company, except that if at that date any assets or funds of the company remain unclaimed or undistributed in the hands or under the control of the liquidator, or any former liquidator, the winding up is not concluded until those assets or funds have either been distributed or paid into the Insolvency Services Account.

4.223(3) **[Final statement]** Subject as above, the liquidator's final statement shall be sent forthwith after the conclusion of the winding up.

4.223(3A) **[No statement required]** No statement shall be required to be delivered under this Rule where the return of the final meeting in respect of the company under sections 94 or 106 is delivered before the date at which the statement is to be delivered and that return shows that no assets or funds of the company remain unclaimed or undistributed in the hands or under the control of the liquidator or any former liquidator; but where this paragraph applies, the liquidator shall deliver a copy of that return to the Secretary of State.

4.223(4) **[Duplicate statements]** Every statement sent to the registrar of companies under section 192 shall be in duplicate.

History note

Rule 4.223(1) was substituted by I(A)R 1987 (SI 1987 No. 1919), r. 3(1), Sch., Pt. 1, para. 80(1) as from 11 January 1988: the former r. 4.223(1) read as follows:

"**4.223–CVL(1)** The statement which section 192 requires the liquidator to send to the registrar of companies, if the winding up is not concluded within one year from its commencement, shall be sent not more than 30 days after the expiration of that year, and thereafter not less often than 6-monthly until the winding up is concluded."

Rule 4.223(3A) was inserted by I(A)R 1987 (SI 1987 No. 1919), r. 3(1), Sch., Pt. 1, para. 80(2) as from 11 January 1988.

General note

The detailed reporting requirements imposed on the liquidator by IA 1986, s. 192 are spelt out in this rule, and in particular the statutory "intervals" are prescribed at six months. (The amendment of r. 4.223(1) makes it clear that shorter periods may not be substituted.) This rule applies to both a creditors' and a members' voluntary winding up; see r. 4.1(1)(*g*).

The new r. 4.223(3A) avoids a duplication of returns where no assets remain at the end of the administration.

The amended version of r. 4.223 applies retrospectively to liquidations started before 29 December 1986: see I(A)R 1987, r. 3(3).

SECTION C: DISSOLUTION AFTER WINDING UP

Rule 4.224   Secretary of State's directions under s. 203, 205

4.224(1) **[Copy of directions]** Where the Secretary of State gives a direction under—

(a) section 203 (where official receiver applies to registrar of companies for a company's early dissolution), or

(b) section 205 (application by interested person for postponement of dissolution),

he shall send two copies of the direction to the applicant for it.

4.224(2) **[Copy to registrar]** Of those copies one shall be sent by the applicant to the registrar of companies, to comply with section 203(5) or, as the case may be, 205(6).

(See general note after r. 4.225.)

Rule **4.225**   Procedure following appeal under ss. 203(4) or 205(4)

4.225   Following an appeal under section 203(4) or 205(4) (against a decision of the Secretary of State under the applicable section) the court shall send two sealed copies of its order to the person in whose favour the appeal was determined; and that party shall send one of the copies to the registrar of companies to comply with section 203 (5) or, as the case may be, 205(6).   [FORM 4.69]

General note to rr. 4.224, 4.225

These rules provide machinery for the exercise of the official receiver's new power under IA 1986, ss. 202ff., to apply to the registrar of companies for the early dissolution of the company where the assets are not worth the expense of administration.

Chapter 22 — Leave to Act as Director, etc., of Company with Prohibited Name (Section 216 of the Act)

Rule **4.226**   Preliminary

4.226   The Rules in this Chapter—

- (a) relate to the leave required under section 216 (restriction on re-use of name of company in insolvent liquidation) for a person to act as mentioned in section 216(3) in relation to a company with a prohibited name,
- (b) prescribe the cases excepted from that provision, that is to say, those in which a person to whom the section applies may so act without that leave, and
- (c) apply to all windings up to which section 216 applies, whether or not the winding up commenced before the coming into force of the Rules.

History note

In r. 4.226 the word "and" formerly appearing at the end of subpara. (*a*) was omitted and the word ", and" and subpara. (*c*) were added at the end of subpara. (*b*) by I(A)R 1987 (SI 1987 No. 1919), r. 3(1), Sch., Pt. 1, para. 81 as from 11 January 1988.

(See general note after r. 4.227.)

Rule **4.227**   Application for leave under s. 216(3)

4.227   When considering an application for leave under section 216, the court may call on the liquidator, or any former liquidator, of the liquidating company for a report of the circumstances in which that company became insolvent, and the extent (if any) of the applicant's apparent responsibility for its doing so.

General note to rr. 4.226, 4.227

A former director or shadow director may not re-use a prohibited company name "except with the leave of the court or in such circumstances as may be prescribed" (IA 1986, s. 216(3)). Rule 4.227 deals with an application for such leave, while rr. 4.228–4.230 specify three sets of circumstances which are to be treated as excepted cases. The new r. 4.226(*c*) makes the rules in this chapter coextensive with s. 216, so that the rules apply (for example) to a winding up where the petition was presented before 29 December 1986 (the commencement date for IR 1986) but the winding-up order was not made until after that date.

Rule 4.228   First excepted case

4.228(1)   [Notice to creditors]   Where a company ("the successor company") acquires the whole, or substantially the whole, of the business of an insolvent company, under arrangements made by an insolvency practitioner acting as its liquidator, administrator or administrative receiver, or as supervisor of a voluntary arrangement under Part I of the Act, the successor company may for the purposes of section 216 give notice under this Rule to the insolvent company's creditors.

4.228(2)   [Time for notice and contents]   To be effective, the notice must be given within 28 days from the completion of the arrangements, to all creditors of the insolvent company of whose addresses the successor company is aware in that period; and it must specify—

(a) the name and registered number of the insolvent company and the circumstances in which its business has been acquired by the successor company,

(b) the name which the successor company has assumed, or proposes to assume for the purpose of carrying on the business, if that name is or will be a prohibited name under section 216, and

(c) any change of name which it has made, or proposes to make, for that purpose under section 28 of the Companies Act.

4.228(3)   [Notice may name director etc.]   The notice may name a person to whom section 216 may apply as having been a director or shadow director of the insolvent company, and give particulars as to the nature and duration of that directorship, with a view to his being a director of the successor company or being otherwise associated with its management.

4.228(4)   [Effect of notice]   If the successor company has effectively given notice under this Rule to the insolvent company's creditors, a person who is so named in the notice may act in relation to the successor company in any of the ways mentioned in section 216(3), notwithstanding that he has not the leave of the court under that section.

General note

The essential elements of this exception are:

● there must have been a transfer of the defunct company's business by its liquidator, etc., to a successor company;

● notice must be given to all known creditors of the insolvent company within 28 days of the completion of the arrangements, specifying the names used and proposed to be used by the two companies;

● the former director or shadow director must be named and the details in r. 4.228(3) also given.

Rule 4.229   Second excepted case

4.229(1)   [Where director applies for leave]   Where a person to whom section 216 applies as having been a director or shadow director of the liquidating company applies for leave of the court under that section not later than 7 days from the date on which the company went into liquidation, he may, during the period specified in paragraph (2) below, act in any of the ways mentioned in section 216(3), notwithstanding that he has not the leave of the court under that section.

4.229(2) [Period in r. 4.229(1)] The period referred to in paragraph (1) begins with the day on which the company goes into liquidation and ends either on the day falling six weeks after that date or on the day on which the court disposes of the application for leave under section 216, whichever of those days occurs first.

History note

Rule 4.229 was substituted by I(A)R 1987 (SI 1987 No. 1919), r. 3(1), Sch., Pt. 1, para. 82 as from 11 January 1988: the former r. 4.229 read as follows:

"**4.229(1)** In the circumstances specified below, a person to whom section 216 applies as having been a director or shadow director of the liquidating company may act in any of the ways mentioned in section 216(3), notwithstanding that he has not the leave of the court under that section.

4.229(2) Those circumstances are that—

(a) he applies to the court for leave, not later than 7 days from the date on which the company went into liquidation, and

(b) leave is granted by the court not later than 6 weeks from that date."

General note

This exception enables a person who is seeking the leave of the court to act as a director, etc. of a company with a prohibited name for a brief period while his application is awaiting a hearing. Note the strict time limits. The revised wording avoids the risk that an applicant who was unsuccessful would have unwittingly committed an offence while the hearing of his case was pending.

Rule 4.230 Third excepted case

4.230 The court's leave under section 216(3) is not required where the company there referred to, though known by a prohibited name within the meaning of the section—

(a) has been known by that name for the whole of the period of 12 months ending with the day before the liquidating company went into liquidation, and

(b) has not at any time in those 12 months been dormant within the meaning of section 252(5) of the Companies Act.

General note

This exception allows a former director to continue to act in the affairs of an established company even though it is known by a prohibited name, provided that it has been using that name for at least a year before his other company went into liquidation.

THE SECOND GROUP OF PARTS
INDIVIDUAL INSOLVENCY; BANKRUPTCY

PART 5 — INDIVIDUAL VOLUNTARY ARRANGEMENTS

Rule 5.1 Introductory

5.1(1) **[Application of Pt. 5 Rules]** The Rules in this Part apply where a debtor, with a view to an application for an interim order under Part VIII of the Act, makes a proposal to his creditors for a voluntary arrangement, that is to say, a composition in satisfaction of his debts or a scheme of arrangement of his affairs.

5.1(2) **["Case 1", "Case 2"]** The Rules apply whether the debtor is an undischarged bankrupt ("Case 1"), or he is not ("Case 2").

General note

These rules supplement IA 1986, ss. 252-263, which introduced new procedures enabling a debtor to make voluntary arrangements with his creditors instead of being declared bankrupt. This facility is also available to undischarged bankrupts in certain cases. The following rules distinguish between these two possibilities by using the label "Case 1" to cover situations where the debtor is an undischarged bankrupt and "Case 2" to relate to the scenario where he is not an undischarged bankrupt.

SECTION A: THE DEBTOR'S PROPOSAL

Rule 5.2 Preparation of proposal

5.2 The debtor shall prepare for the intended nominee a proposal on which (with or without amendments to be made under Rule 5.3(3) below) to make his report to the court under section 256.

Rule 5.3 Contents of proposal

5.3(1) **[Explanation why voluntary arrangement desirable]** The debtor's proposal shall provide a short explanation why, in his opinion, a voluntary arrangement under Part VIII is desirable, and give reasons why his creditors may be expected to concur with such an arrangement.

5.3(2) **[Other matters]** The following matters shall be stated, or otherwise dealt with, in the proposal—

(a) the following matters, so far as within the debtor's immediate knowledge—

    (i) his assets, with an estimate of their respective values,

    (ii) the extent (if any) to which the assets are charged in favour of creditors,

    (iii) the extent (if any) to which particular assets are to be excluded from the voluntary arrangement;

(b) particulars of any property, other than assets of the debtor himself, which is proposed to be included in the arrangement, the source of such property and the terms on which it is to be made available for inclusion;

(c) the nature· and amount of the debtor's liabilities (so far as within his immediate knowledge), the manner in which they are proposed to be met, modified, postponed or otherwise dealt with by means of the arrangement and (in particular)—

    (i) how it is proposed to deal with preferential creditors (defined in section 258(7)) and creditors who are, or claim to be, secured,

    (ii) how associates of the debtor (being creditors of his) are proposed to be treated under the arrangement, and

    (iii) in Case 1 whether, to the debtor's knowledge, claims have been made under section 339 (transactions at an undervalue), section 340 (preferences) or section 343 (extortionate credit transactions), or there are circumstances giving rise to the possibility of such claims, and in Case 2 whether there are circumstances which would give rise to the possibility of such claims in the event that he should be adjudged bankrupt,

and, where any such circumstances are present, whether, and if so how, it is proposed under the voluntary arrangement to make provision for wholly or partly indemnifying the insolvent estate in respect of such claims;

(d) whether any, and if so what, guarantees have been given of the debtor's debts by other persons, specifying which (if any) of the guarantors are associates of his;

(e) the proposed duration of the voluntary arrangement;

(f) the proposed dates of distributions to creditors, with estimates of their amounts;

(g) the amount proposed to be paid to the nominee (as such) by way of remuneration and expenses;

(h) the manner in which it is proposed that the supervisor of the arrangement should be remunerated, and his expenses defrayed;

(j) whether, for the purposes of the arrangement, any guarantees are to be offered by any persons other than the debtor, and whether (if so) any security is to be given or sought;

(k) the manner in which funds held for the purposes of the arrangement are to be banked, invested or otherwise dealt with pending distribution to creditors;

(l) the manner in which funds held for the purpose of payment to creditors, and not so paid on the termination of the arrangement, are to be dealt with;

(m) if the debtor has any business, the manner in which it is proposed to be conducted during the course of the arrangement;

(n) details of any further credit facilities which it is intended to arrange for the debtor, and how the debts so arising are to be paid;

(o) the functions which are to be undertaken by the supervisor of the arrangement;

(p) the name, address and qualification of the person proposed as supervisor of the voluntary arrangement, and confirmation that he is (so far as the debtor is aware) qualified to act as an insolvency practitioner in relation to him.

5.3(3)   [Amendment of proposal]   With the agreement in writing of the nominee, the debtor's proposal may be amended at any time up to the delivery of the former's report to the court under section 256.

History note

In r. 5.3(2)(*c*)(iii) the words from the beginning to "should be adjudged bankrupt" were substituted by I(A)R 1987 (SI 1987 No. 1919), r. 3(1), Sch., Pt. 1, para. 83 as from 11 January 1988: the former words read as follows:

"(iii) (Case 2 only) whether there are, to the debtor's knowledge, any circumstances giving rise to the possibility, in the event that he should be adjudged bankrupt, of claims under—
section 339 (transactions at an undervalue),
section 340 (preferences), or
section 343 (extortionate credit transactions),".

General note

This explains in great detail what the debtor's proposal to his nominee should contain. It also requires the debtor to justify a voluntary arrangement.

Rule 5.3(2)(*c*)(iii) was replaced to make the bankrupt disclose any claims against him in respect of preferences, etc.

Rule 5.4   Notice to intended nominee

5.4(1)   [Written notice]   The debtor shall give to the intended nominee written notice of his proposal.

5.4(2)   [Delivery of notice]   The notice, accompanied by a copy of the proposal, shall be delivered either to the nominee himself, or to a person authorised to take delivery of documents on his behalf.

5.4(3)   [Endorsement of receipt]   If the intended nominee agrees to act, he shall cause a copy of the notice to be endorsed to the effect that it has been received by him on a specified date.

5.4(4)   [Return of endorsed notice]   The copy of the notice so endorsed shall be returned by the nominee forthwith to the debtor at an address specified by him in the notice for that purpose.

5.4(5)   [Notice in Case 1]   Where (in Case 1) the debtor gives notice of his proposal to the official receiver and (if any) the trustee, the notice must contain the name and address of the insolvency practitioner who has agreed to act as nominee.

General note

The intended nominee must receive written notice of the debtor's proposal. If the debtor is an undischarged bankrupt, the official receiver or trustee may have to be notified.

Rule 5.5   Application for interim order

5.5(1)   [Accompanying affidavit]   An application to the court for an interim order under Part VIII of the Act shall be accompanied by an affidavit of the following matters—

- (a) the reasons for making the application;
- (b) particulars of any execution or other legal process which, to the debtor's knowledge, has been commenced against him;
- (c) that he is an undischarged bankrupt or (as the case may be) that he is able to petition for his own bankruptcy;
- (d) that no previous application for an interim order has been made by or in respect of the debtor in the period of 12 months ending with the date of the affidavit; and
- (e) that the nominee under the proposal (naming him) is a person who is qualified to act as an insolvency practitioner in relation to the debtor, and is willing to act in relation to the proposal.

5.5(2)   [Rule 5.4 notice to be exhibited]   A copy of the notice to the intended nominee under Rule 5.4, endorsed to the effect that he agrees so to act, and a copy of the debtor's proposal given to the nominee under that Rule shall be exhibited to the affidavit.

5.5(3)   [Court to fix venue]   On receiving the application and affidavit, the court shall fix a venue for the hearing of the application.

5.5(4)   [Notice of hearing]   The applicant shall give at least 2 days' notice of the hearing—

- (a) in Case 1, to the bankrupt, the official receiver and the trustee (whichever of those three is not himself the applicant),
- (b) in Case 2, to any creditor who (to the debtor's knowledge) has presented a bankruptcy petition against him, and
- (c) in either case, to the nominee who has agreed to act in relation to the debtor's proposal.

History note

In r. 5.5(2) the words "and a copy of the debtor's proposal given to the nominee under that Rule" were inserted by I(A)R 1987 (SI 1987 No. 1919), r. 3(1), Sch., Pt. 1, para. 84 as from 11 January 1988.

General note

This supplements IA 1986, s. 253 by outlining what the debtor's affidavit to the court should contain. At least two days' notice of the hearing should be given to the intended nominee, official receiver or trustee (where the debtor is an undischarged bankrupt) or to any petitioning creditor.

The amendment to r. 5.5(2) provides additional information for the court, i.e. a copy of the debtor's proposal is to be attached to the affidavit.

Rule 5.5A   Court in which application to be made

5.5A(1)   [Debtor not bankrupt]   Except in the case of a bankrupt, an application to the court under Part VIII of the Act shall be made to a court in which the debtor would be entitled to present his own petition in bankruptcy under Rule 6.40.

5.5A(2)   [Information in application]   The application shall contain sufficient information to establish that it is brought in the appropriate court.

5.5A(3)   [Debtor bankrupt]   In the case of a bankrupt such an application shall be made to the court having the conduct of his bankruptcy and shall be filed with those bankruptcy proceedings.

History note

Rule 5.5A was inserted by I(A)R 1987 (SI 1987 No. 1919), r. 3(1), Sch., Pt. 1, para. 85 as from 11 January 1988.

General note

The new r. 5.5A was inserted to identify the court to which the application is to be made. This would be the appropriate bankruptcy court, see r. 6.40.

Rule 5.6   Hearing of the application

5.6(1)   [Appearances etc.]   Any of the persons who have been given notice under Rule 5.5(4) may appear or be represented at the hearing of the application.

5.6(2)   [Representations re order]   The court, in deciding whether to make an interim order on the application, shall take into account any representations made by or on behalf of any of those persons (in particular, whether an order should be made containing such provision as is referred to in section 255(3) and (4)).

5.6(3)   [Consideration of nominee's report]   If the court makes an interim order, it shall fix a venue for consideration of the nominee's report. Subject to the following paragraph, the date for that consideration shall be not later than that on which the interim order ceases to have effect under section 255(6).

5.6(4)   [Extension of time under s. 256(4)]   If under section 256(4) an extension of time is granted for filing the nominee's report, the court shall, unless there appear to be good reasons against it, correspondingly extend the period for which the interim order has effect.

General note

This outlines the hearing procedure on any application for an interim order under IA 1986, s. 253. The provision further adds to IA 1986, ss. 255, 256.

Rule 5.7 Action to follow making of order

5.7(1) [Sealed copies] Where an interim order is made, at least 2 sealed copies of the order shall be sent by the court forthwith to the person who applied for it; and that person shall serve one of the copies on the nominee under the debtor's proposal.

[FORM 5.2]

5.7(2) [Notice of order] The applicant shall also forthwith give notice of the making of the order to any person who was given notice of the hearing pursuant to Rule 5.5(4) and was not present or represented at it.

History note

Against r. 5.7(1) the words "[FORM 5.2]" were inserted by I(A)R 1987 (SI 1987 No. 1919), r. 3(1), Sch., Pt. 2, para. 156(1) as from 11 January 1988.

General note

This provides for dissemination of the interim order.

Rule 5.8 Statement of affairs

5.8(1) [In Case 1] In Case 1, if the debtor has already delivered a statement of affairs under section 272 (debtor's petition) or 288 (creditor's petition), he need not deliver a further statement unless so required by the nominee, with a view to supplementing or amplifying the former one.

5.8(2) [In Case 2] In Case 2, the debtor shall, within 7 days after his proposal is delivered to the nominee, or within such longer time as the latter may allow, deliver to the nominee a statement of his (the debtor's) affairs.

5.8(3) [Particulars in statement] The statement shall comprise the following particulars (supplementing or amplifying, so far as is necessary for clarifying the state of the debtor's affairs, those already given in his proposal)—

> (a) a list of his assets, divided into such categories as are appropriate for easy indentification, with estimated values assigned to each category;
>
> (b) in the case of any property on which a claim against the debtor is wholly or partly secured, particulars of the claim and its amount, and of how and when the security was created;
>
> (c) the names and addresses of the debtor's preferential creditors (defined in section 258(7)), with the amounts of their respective claims;
>
> (d) the names and addresses of the debtor's unsecured creditors, with the amounts of their respective claims;
>
> (e) particulars of any debts owed by or to the debtor to or by persons who are associates of his;
>
> (f) such other particulars (if any) as the nominee may in writing require to be furnished for the purposes of making his report to the court on the debtor's proposal.

5.8(4) [Relevant date] The statement of affairs shall be made up to a date not earlier than 2 weeks before the date of the notice to the nominee under Rule. 5.4.

However, the nominee may allow an extension of that period to the nearest practicable date (not earlier than 2 months before the date of the notice under Rule 5.4); and if he does so, he shall give his reasons in his report to the court on the debtor's proposal.

5.8(5) [Certification of statement] The statement shall be certified by the debtor as correct, to the best of his knowledge and belief.

General note

This relates to the statement of affairs which the debtor must submit to his nominee under IA 1986, s. 256(2). For undischarged bankrupts, any previous statements of affairs submitted under IA 1986, ss. 278 or 288 will suffice. The contents and topicality of the statement are regulated by this provision.

Rule 5.9   Additional disclosure for assistance of nominee

5.9(1)   [Nominee may request further information] If it appears to the nominee that he cannot properly prepare his report on the basis of information in the debtor's proposal and statement of affairs, he may call on the debtor to provide him with—

  (a) further and better particulars as to the circumstances in which, and the reasons why, he is insolvent or (as the case may be) threatened with insolvency;

  (b) particulars of any previous proposals which have been made by him under Part VIII of the Act;

  (c) any further information with respect to his affairs which the nominee thinks necessary for the purposes of his report.

5.9(2)   [Whether debtor concerned with insolvent company, bankrupt etc.] The nominee may call on the debtor to inform him whether and in what circumstances he has at any time—

  (a) been concerned in the affairs of any company (whether or not incorporated in England and Wales) which has become insolvent, or

  (b) been adjudged bankrupt, or entered into an arrangement with his creditors.

5.9(3)   [Access to accounts and records] For the purpose of enabling the nominee to consider the debtor's proposal and prepare his report on it, the latter must give him access to his accounts and records.

General note

This allows the nominee to call for additional information to supplement the proposal and the statement of affairs already submitted by the debtor.

Rule 5.10   Nominee's report on the proposal

5.10(1)   [Time for delivery] The nominee's report shall be delivered by him to the court not less than 2 days before the interim order ceases to have effect.

5.10(2)   [Accompanying documents] With his report the nominee shall deliver—

  (a) a copy of the debtor's proposal (with amendments, if any, authorised under Rule 5.3(3)); and

  (b) a copy or summary of any statement of affairs provided by the debtor.

5.10(3)   [Nominee's opinion re meeting]   If the nominee makes known his opinion that a meeting of the debtor's creditors should be summoned under section 257, his report shall have annexed to it his comments on the debtor's proposal.

If his opinion is otherwise, he shall give his reasons for that opinion.

5.10(4)   [Endorsement of date of filing and right to inspect]   The court shall cause the nominee's report to be endorsed with the date on which it is filed in court. Any creditor of the debtor is entitled, at all reasonable times on any business day, to inspect the file.

5.10(5)   [Directions in Cases 1 and 2]   In Case 1, the nominee shall send to the official receiver and (if any) the trustee—

    (a) a copy of the debtor's proposal,

    (b) a copy of his (the nominee's) report and his comments accompanying it (if any), and

    (c) a copy or summary of the debtor's statement of affairs.

In Case 2, the nominee shall send a copy of each of those documents to any person who has presented a bankruptcy petition against the debtor.

History note

In r. 5.10(5) the words "and (if any) the trustee" were inserted by I(A)R 1987 (SI 1987 No. 1919), r. 3(1), Sch., Pt. 1, para. 86 as from 11 January 1988.

General note

This provides further information on the content and mode of presentation of the nominee's report under IA 1986, s. 256. The procedure for dissemination will vary depending on whether the debtor is an undischarged bankrupt or not.

For "business day" in r. 5.10(4), see r. 13.13(1).

Rule 5.11   Replacement of nominee

5.11   Where the debtor intends to apply to the court under section 256(3) for the nominee to be replaced, he shall give to the nominee at least 7 days' notice of his application.

SECTION B: ACTION ON THE PROPOSAL; CREDITORS' MEETING

Rule 5.12   Consideration of nominee's report

5.12(1)   [Appearances etc.]   At the hearing by the court to consider the nominee's report, any of the persons who have been given notice under Rule 5.5(4) may appear or be represented.

5.12(2)   [Application of r. 5.7]   Rule 5.7 applies to any order made by the court at the hearing.

General note

This rule supplements IA 1986, s. 256(5).

Rule **5.13** Summoning of creditors' meeting

5.13(1) **[Date for meeting]** If in his report the nominee states that in his opinion a meeting of creditors should be summoned to consider the debtor's proposal, the date on which the meeting is to be held shall be not less than 14 days from that on which the nominee's report is filed in court under Rule 5.10, nor more than 28 days from that on which that report is considered by the court under Rule 5.12.

5.13(2) **[Notices of meeting]** Notices calling the meeting shall be sent by the nominee, at least 14 days before the day fixed for it to be held, to all the creditors specified in the debtor's statement of affairs, and any other creditors of whom the nominee is otherwise aware.

5.13(3) **[Contents etc. of notice]** Each notice sent under this Rule shall specify the court to which the nominee's report on the debtor's proposal has been delivered and shall state the effect of Rule 5.18(1), (3) and (4) (requisite majorities); and with it there shall be sent—

    (a) a copy of the proposal,

    (b) a copy of the statement of affairs or, if the nominee thinks fit, a summary of it (the summary to include a list of the creditors and the amounts of their debts), and

    (c) the nominee's comments on the proposal.

History note

In r. 5.13(1) the words ", nor more than 28," formerly appearing after "14" were omitted and the words ", nor more than 28 days from that" to the end were added by I(A)R 1987 (SI 1987 No. 1919), r. 3(1), Sch., Pt. 1, para. 87 as from 11 January 1988.

General note

This provision should be viewed in the light of IA 1986, s. 257. The creditors' meeting must take place within the period of not less than 14 days and not more than 28 days after the filing of the report.

Rule 5.13(1) was amended to allow the nominee a little more time. The court has discretion to extend the 28-day deadline imposed by r. 5.13(1) – see the case of *Re Young* [1993] CLY 2367.

Rule **5.14** Creditors' meeting: supplementary

5.14(1) **[Convenience of venue]** Subject as follows, in fixing the venue for the creditors' meeting, the nominee shall have regard to the convenience of creditors.

5.14(2) **[Time of meeting]** The meeting shall be summoned for commencement between 10.00 and 16.00 hours on a business day.

5.14(3) **[Forms of proxy]** With every notice summoning the meeting there shall be sent out forms of proxy. [FORM 8.1]

General note

For "venue" and "business day", see rr. 13.6 and 13.13(1) respectively. For proxies, see Pt. 8.

Rule **5.15** The chairman at the meeting

5.15(1) **[Nominee to be chairman]** Subject as follows, the nominee shall be chairman of the creditors' meeting.

5.15(2) **[Other nominated chairman]** If for any reason the nominee is unable to attend, he may nominate another person to act as chairman in his place; but a person so nominated must be either—

(a) a person qualified to act as an insolvency practitioner in relation to the debtor, or

(b) an employee of the nominee or his firm who is experienced in insolvency matters.

General note

This rule ensures that the chairman will have professional insolvency experience. In the conduct of a creditors' meeting at which an IVA proposal is being considered the chairman is assumed to act as an independent professional person and not as the agent of the debtor. Accordingly, the chairman is personally responsible for procedural lapses – *Re A Debtor (No. 222 of 1990), ex parte Bank of Ireland (No. 2)* [1993] BCLC 233 (per Harman J).

Rule **5.16** The chairman as proxy-holder

5.16 The chairman shall not by virtue of any proxy held by him vote to increase or reduce the amount of the remuneration or expenses of the nominee or the supervisor of the proposed arrangement, unless the proxy specifically directs him to vote in that way.

Rule **5.17** Voting rights

5.17(1) **[Entitlement to vote]** Subject as follows, every creditor who was given notice of the creditors' meeting is entitled to vote at the meeting or any adjournment of it.

5.17(2) **[Calculation of votes]** In Case 1, votes are calculated according to the amount of the creditor's debt as at the date of the bankruptcy order, and in Case 2 according to the amount of the debt as at the date of the meeting.

5.17(3) **[Limitation on voting]** A creditor shall not vote in respect of a debt for an unliquidated amount, or any debt whose value is not ascertained, except where the chairman agrees to put upon the debt an estimated minimum value for the purpose of entitlement to vote.

5.17(4) **[Chairman's discretion]** The chairman has power to admit or reject a creditor's claim for the purpose of his entitlement to vote, and the power is exercisable with respect to the whole or any part of the claim.

5.17(5) **[Appeal from chairman's decision]** The chairman's decision on entitlement to vote is subject to appeal to the court by any creditor, or by the debtor.

5.17(6) **[Voting subject to objection]** If the chairman is in doubt whether a claim should be admitted or rejected, he shall mark it as objected to and allow the creditor to vote, subject to his vote being subsequently declared invalid if the objection to the claim is sustained.

5.17(7) **[Where chairman's decision reversed etc.]** If on an appeal the chairman's decision is reversed or varied, or a creditor's vote is declared invalid, the court may order another meeting to be summoned, or make such other order as it thinks just.

The court's power to make an order under this paragraph is exercisable only if it considers that the matter is such as to give rise to unfair prejudice or a material irregularity.

5.17(8)　[Time for appeal]　An application to the court by way of appeal under this Rule against the chairman's decision shall not be made after the end of the period of 28 days beginning with the day on which the chairman's report to the court is made under section 259.

5.17(9)　[Costs of appeal]　The chairman is not personally liable for any costs incurred by any person in respect of an appeal under this Rule.

General note

Voting rights are weighted according to value, the method of computation varying depending on whether the debtor is an undischarged bankrupt or not. Note the special rules for persons claiming unliquidated amounts, etc. Appeals to the court against a determination by the chairman on an entitlement to vote are permissible. If the court decides that a person should have been allowed to vote, it can reconvene the meeting but will only do so where the wrongful disqualification of the vote led to unfair prejudice or material irregularity (see IA 1986, s. 262): see *Re A Debtor (No. 83 of 1988)* [1990] 1 WLR 708 and *Re Cove (A Debtor)* [1990] 1 All ER 949.

The question of who is entitled to vote at a meeting to consider an IVA is a vexed issue and the statutory provisions here are less than helpful. In *Re A Debtor (No. 222 of 1990)* [1992] BCLC 137 the chairman was found to have made an error of interpretation as to entitlement to vote and Harman J suggested a procedure to be adopted in future to deal with contested voting rights on disputed debts. As a result of the material irregularity occurring in this case the IVA was cancelled by Harman J where one of the excluded creditors brought a s. 262 action. For discussion of this case and the difficult issues raised by it see Glithero, *Insolvency Lawyer* (February 1993) 7–9 and the response by Twemlow, *Insolvency Lawyer* (October 1993), 6–9. See also *Calor Gas* v *Piercy* [1994] BCC 69 (partly secured creditor can vote on unsecured balance) and *Re Cranley Mansions Ltd* [1994] BCC 576 (a ruling on r. 1.17(3)).

Rule 5.18　Requisite majorities

5.18(1)　[Three-quarters majority]　Subject as follows, at the creditors' meeting for any resolution to pass approving any proposal or modification there must be a majority in excess of three-quarters in value of the creditors present in person or by proxy and voting on the resolution.

5.18(2)　[One-half majority]　The same applies in respect of any other resolution proposed at the meeting, but substituting one-half for three-quarters.

5.18(3)　[Votes to be left out of account]　In the following cases there is to be left out of account a creditor's vote in respect of any claim or part of a claim—

(a)　where written notice of the claim was not given, either at the meeting or before it, to the chairman or the nominee;

(b)　where the claim or part is secured;

(c)　where the claim is in respect of a debt wholly or partly on, or secured by, a current bill of exchange or promissory note, unless the creditor is willing—

(i)　to treat the liability to him on the bill or note of every person who is liable on it antecendently to the debtor, and against whom a bankruptcy order has not been made (or, in the case of a company, which has not gone into liquidation), as a security in his hands, and

    (ii) to estimate the value of the security and (for the purpose of entitlement to vote, but not of any distribution under the arrangement) to deduct it from his claim.

5.18(4) [Votes rendering resolution invalid]   Any resolution is invalid if those voting against it include more than half in value of the creditors, counting in these latter only those—

    (a) to whom notice of the meeting was sent;

    (b) whose votes are not to be left out of account under paragraph (3); and

    (c) who are not, to the best of the chairman's belief, associates of the debtor.

5.18(5) [Chairman's powers]   It is for the chairman of the meeting to decide whether under this Rule—

    (a) a vote is to be left out of account in accordance with paragraph (3), or

    (b) a person is an associate of the debtor for the purposes of paragraph (4)(c);

and in relation to the second of these two cases the chairman is entitled to rely on the information provided by the debtor's statement of affairs or otherwise in accordance with this Part of the Rules.

5.18(6) [Chairman's use of proxy]   If the chairman uses a proxy contrary to Rule 5.16, his vote with that proxy does not count towards any majority under this Rule.

5.18(7) [Application of r. 5.17]   Paragraphs (5) to (9) of Rule 5.17 apply as regards an appeal against the decision of the chairman under this Rule.

General note

A majority in excess of three-quarters is required for the approval or modification of proposals. This matter was left unclear by IA 1986, s. 258: see *Re A Debtor (No. 2389) of 1989, ex parte Travel and General Insurance Co. plc* v *The Debtor* [1990] 3 All ER 984. Other votes can be passed by a majority in excess of one-half. The votes of certain persons (e.g., associates of the debtor – see IA 1986, s. 435) may in effect be disqualified. Rule 5.18(3) was considered in *Calor Gas* v *Piercy* [1994] BCC 69 where it was held that a partly secured creditor could vote in respect of the unsecured balance of his debt.

Rule 5.19   Proceedings to obtain agreement on the proposal

5.19(1) [Adjournments]   On the day on which the creditors' meeting is held, it may from time to time be adjourned.

5.19(2) [Failure to obtain requisite majority]   If on that day the requisite majority for the approval of the voluntary arrangement (with or without modifications) has not been obtained, the chairman may, and shall if it is so resolved, adjourn the meeting for not more than 14 days.

5.19(3) [Final adjournment]   If there are subsequently further adjournments, the final adjournment shall not be to a day later than 14 days after that on which the meeting was originally held.

5.19(4) [Notice of adjournment]   If the meeting is adjourned under paragraph (2), notice of the fact shall be given by the chairman forthwith to the court.

5.19(5) **[Deemed rejection of proposal]** If following any final adjournment of the meeting the proposal (with or without modifications) is not agreed to, it is deemed rejected.

General note
The meeting may be adjourned to improve the prospects of approval of the proposals.

SECTION C: IMPLEMENTATION OF THE ARRANGEMENT

Rule 5.20 Resolutions to follow approval

5.20(1) **[Resolution re supervisory acts]** If the voluntary arrangement is approved (with or without modifications), a resolution may be taken by the creditors, where two or more insolvency practitioners are appointed to act as supervisor, on the question whether acts to be done in connection with the arrangement may be done by any one of them, or must be done by both or all.

5.20(2) **[Other than nominee to be supervisor]** If at the creditors' meeting a resolution is moved for the appointment of some person other than the nominee to be supervisor of the arrangement, there must be produced to the chairman, at or before the meeting—

(a) that person's written consent to act (unless he is present and then and there signifies his consent), and

(b) his written confirmation that he is qualified to act as an insolvency practitioner in relation to the debtor.

General note
This amplifies the provisions of IA 1986, s. 263, particularly with regard to the possibility of joint supervisors.

Rule 5.21 Hand-over of property, etc. to supervisor

5.21(1) **[Putting supervisor into possession of assets]** Forthwith after the approval of the voluntary arrangement, the debtor in Case 2, and the official receiver or trustee in Case 1, shall do all that is required for putting the supervisor into possession of the assets included in the arrangement.

5.21(2) **[Discharge of official receiver's remuneration etc.]** On taking possession of the assets in Case 1, the supervisor shall discharge any balance due to the official receiver and (if other) the trustee by way of remuneration or on account of—

(a) fees, costs, charges and expenses properly incurred and payable under the Act or the Rules, and

(b) any advances made in respect of the insolvent estate, together with interest on such advances at the rate specified in section 17 of the Judgments Act 1838 at the date of the bankruptcy order.

5.21(3)   [Undertaking to discharge etc.]   Alternatively in Case 1, the supervisor must, before taking possession, give the official receiver or the trustee a written undertaking to discharge any such balance out of the first realisation of assets.

5.21(4)   [Charge on assets]   The official receiver and (if other) the trustee has in Case 1 a charge on the assets included in the voluntary arrangement in respect of any sums due as above until they have been discharged, subject only to the deduction from realisations by the supervisor of the proper costs and expenses of realisation.

Any sums due to the official receiver take priority over those due to a trustee.

5.21(5)   [Discharge of guarantees etc.]   The supervisor shall from time to time out of the realisation of assets discharge all guarantees properly given by the official receiver or the trustee for the benefit of the estate, and shall pay all their expenses.

General note

This is a mechanical provision relating to the hand-over of property to the supervisor. The procedure varies depending on whether the debtor is an undischarged bankrupt or not.

Rule 5.22   Report of creditors' meeting

5.22(1)   [Chairman to prepare report]   A report of the creditors' meeting shall be prepared by the chairman of the meeting.

5.22(2)   [Contents of report]   The report shall—

   (a) state whether the proposal for a voluntary arrangement was approved or rejected and, if approved, with what (if any) modifications;

   (b) set out the resolutions which were taken at the meeting, and the decision on each one;

   (c) list the creditors (with their respective values) who were present or represented at the meeting, and how they voted on each resolution; and

   (d) include such further information (if any) as the chairman thinks it appropriate to make known to the court.

5.22(3)   [Copy of report to be filed in court]   A copy of the chairman's report shall, within 4 days of the meeting being held, be filed in court; and the court shall cause that copy to be endorsed with the date of filing.

5.22(4)   [Notice of result]   The persons to whom notice of the result is to be given, under section 259(1), are all those who were sent notice of the meeting under this Part of the Rules and, in Case 1, the official receiver and (if any) the trustee.

The notice shall be sent immediately after a copy of the chairman's report is filed in court under paragraph (3).

History note

In r. 5.22(4) the words "and, in Case 1, the official receiver and (if any) the trustee" were inserted by I(A)R 1987 (SI 1987 No. 1919), r. 3(1), Sch., Pt. 1, para. 88 as from 11 January 1988.

This oddly located provision supplements IA 1986, s. 259.

Rule 5.22(4) was amended to clarify who is to receive a notice of the result.

Rule 5.23 Register of voluntary arrangements

5.23(1) [Register maintained by Secretary of State] The Secretary of State shall maintain a register of individual voluntary arrangements, and shall enter in it all such matters as are reported to him in pursuance of Rules 5.24, 5.25 and 5.29.

5.23(2) [Open to public inspection] The register shall be open to public inspection.

History note

In r. 5.23(1) the words "Rules 5.24, 5.25 and 5.29" were substituted for the former words "this Part of the Rules" by I(A)R 1987 (SI 1987 No. 1919), r. 3(1), Sch., Pt. 1, para. 89 as from 11 January 1988.

General note

A public register of voluntary arrangements is hereby provided for. This provision would have been more appropriately located in the text of the Insolvency Act itself.

The scope of r. 5.23(1) has been clarified by specific reference to numbered rules.

Rule 5.24 Reports to Secretary of State

5.24(1) [Details of arrangement] Immediately after the chairman of the creditors' meeting has filed in court a report that the meeting has approved the voluntary arrangement, he shall report to the Secretary of State the following details of the arrangement—

(a) the name and address of the debtor;

(b) the date on which the arrangement was approved by the creditors;

(c) the name and address of the supervisor; and

(d) the court in which the chairman's report has been filed.

5.24(2) [Notice of appointment as supervisor etc.] A person who is appointed to act as supervisor of an individual voluntary arrangement (whether in the first instance or by way of replacement of another person previously appointed) shall forthwith give written notice to the Secretary of State of his appointment.

If he vacates office as supervisor, he shall forthwith give written notice of that fact also to the Secretary of State.

General note

This adds to IA 1986, s. 259 by requiring the chairman to notify the result of the meeting to the Secretary of State.

Rule 5.25 Revocation or suspension of the arrangement

5.25(1) [Application of Rule] This Rule applies where the court makes an order of revocation or suspension under section 262.

(a) any disbursements made by the nominee prior to the approval of the arrangement, and any remuneration for his services as such agreed between himself and the debtor, the official receiver or the trustee;

(b) any fees, costs, charges or expenses which—

   (i) are sanctioned by the terms of the arrangement, or

  (ii) would be payable, or correspond to those which would be payable, in the debtor's bankruptcy.

Rule 5.29   Completion of the arrangement

5.29(1) [Supervisor to send notice] Not more than 28 days after the final completion of the voluntary arrangement, the supervisor shall send to all creditors of the debtor who are bound by the arrangement, and to the debtor, a notice that the arrangement has been fully implemented.

5.29(2) [Supervisor's report] With the notice there shall be sent to each of those persons a copy of a report by the supervisor summarising all receipts and payments made by him in pursuance of the arrangement, and explaining any difference in the actual implementation of it as compared with the proposal as approved by the creditors' meeting.

5.29(3) [Copies of notices and reports] The supervisor shall, within the 28 days mentioned above, send to the Secretary of State and to the court a copy of the notice under paragraph (1), together with a copy of the report under paragraph (2).

5.29(4) [Extension of time] The court may, on application by the supervisor, extend the period of 28 days under paragraphs (1) and (3).

General note

This rule governs the completion of the voluntary arrangement.

SECTION D: GENERAL

Rule 5.30   False representations, etc.

5.30(1) [Offence] The debtor commits an offence if he makes any false representation or commits any other fraud for the purpose of obtaining the approval of his creditors to a proposal for a voluntary arrangement under Part VIII of the Act.

5.30(2) [Penalties] A person guilty of an offence under this Rule is liable to imprisonment or a fine, or both.

General note

This rule creates an offence of fraudulently procuring a voluntary arrangement. It is surely inappropriate to include such a provision in the Insolvency Rules and it would be better located in Pt. VIII of the Act (or possibly in Pt. IX, Ch. VI). For the appropriate penalty, see Sch. 5.

PART 6 — BANKRUPTCY

Chapter 1 — The Statutory Demand

General comment on Pt. 6

The following rules supplement IA 1986, Pt. IV.

Rule 6.1   Form and content of statutory demand

6.1(1)   **[Must be dated and signed]**   A statutory demand under section 268 must be dated, and be signed either by the creditor himself or by a person stating himself to be authorised to make the demand on the creditor's behalf.   [FORM 6.1]
or [FORM 6.2]
or [FORM 6.3]

6.1(2)   **[Whether s. 268(1) or (2)]**   The statutory demand must specify whether it is made under section 268(1) (debt payable immediately) or section 268(2) (debt not so payable).

6.1(3)   **[Further contents]**   The demand must state the amount of the debt, and the consideration for it (or, if there is no consideration, the way in which it arises) and—

    (a) if made under section 268(1) and founded on a judgment or order of a court, it must give details of the judgment or order, and

    (b) if made under section 268(2), it must state the grounds on which it is alleged that the debtor appears to have no reasonable prospect of paying the debt.

6.1(4)   **[Interest and accruing charges]**   If the amount claimed in the demand includes—

    (a) any charge by way of interest not previously notified to the debtor as a liability of his, or

    (b) any other charge accruing from time to time,

the amount or rate of the charge must be separately identified, and the grounds on which payment of it is claimed must be stated.

    In either case the amount claimed must be limited to that which has accrued due at the date of the demand.

6.1(5)   **[If creditor holds security]**   If the creditor holds any security in respect of the debt, the full amount of the debt shall be specified, but—

    (a) there shall in the demand be specified the nature of the security, and the value which the creditor puts upon it as at the date of the demand, and

    (b) the amount of which payment is claimed by the demand shall be the full amount of the debt, less the amount specified as the value of the security.

General note

    See also *Practice Note (Bankruptcy: Prescribed Forms) (No. 2/88)* [1988] 1 WLR 557.

    For judicial consideration of this provision see *Re A Debtor (No. 310 of 1988)* [1989] 1 WLR 452. Here Knox J held that the phrase "any security in respect of the debt" when used in

r. 6.1(5) must have the same meaning as when used in IA 1986, ss. 383 and 385(1). Therefore the security that had to be referred to in the statutory demand was security over any property of the alleged debtor and not security in connection with a third party. Failure to specify the security held as required under r. 6.1(5) may not always be fatal for the creditor, as the court now tends to consider whether the debtor has suffered any real injustice – see *Re A Debtor (No. 106 of 1992), The Independent,* 20 April, 1992 and the comments on s. 268.

(See general note after r. 6.2.)

Rule 6.2   Information to be given in statutory demand

6.2(1)   [Explanation of demand generally]   The statutory demand must include an explanation to the debtor of the following matters—

    (a) the purpose of the demand, and the fact that, if the debtor does not comply with the demand, bankruptcy proceedings may be commenced against him;

    (b) the time within which the demand must be complied with, if that consequence is to be avoided;

    (c) the methods of compliance which are open to the debtor; and

    (d) his right to apply to the court for the statutory demand to be set aside.

6.2(2)   [Information re named individuals]   The demand must specify one or more named individuals with whom the debtor may, if he wishes, enter into communication with a view to securing or compounding for the debt to the satisfaction of the creditor or (as the case may be) establishing to the creditor's satisfaction that there is a reasonable prospect that the debt will be paid when it falls due.

In the case of any individual so named in the demand, his address and telephone number (if any) must be given.

General note to rr. 6.1, 6.2

These rules describe the statutory demand mentioned in IA 1986, s. 268(1)(*a*), (2)(*a*). The form and contents are detailed.

Rule 6.3   Requirements as to service

6.3(1)   [Effect of r. 6.11]   Rule 6.11 in Chapter 2 below has effect as regards service of the statutory demand, and proof of that service by affidavit to be filed with a bankruptcy petition.

6.3(2)   [Creditor's obligation to effect personal service etc.]   The creditor is, by virtue of the Rules, under an obligation to do all that is reasonable for the purpose of bringing the statutory demand to the debtor's attention and, if practicable in the particular circumstances, to cause personal service of the demand to be effected.

6.3(3)   [Advertisement of demand for sum due under judgment etc.]   Where the statutory demand is for payment of a sum due under a judgment or order of any court and the creditor knows, or believes with reasonable cause—

(a) that the debtor has absconded or is keeping out of the way with a view to avoiding service, and

(b) there is no real prospect of the sum due being recovered by execution or other process,

the demand may be advertised in one or more newspapers; and the time limited for compliance with the demand runs from the date of the advertisement's appearance or (as the case may be) its first appearance.

General note

The rules as to service of the statutory demand are hereby prescribed. Personal service is normally required, subject to r. 6.3(3). See also *Practice Note (Bankruptcy: Substituted Service)* [1987] 1 WLR 82. For service out of the jurisdiction see *Practice Note (Bankruptcy: Service Abroad) (No. 1/88)* [1988] 1 WLR 461.

In *Re A Debtor (Nos. 234 and 236 of 1991)*, *The Independent*, 29 June 1992 it was confirmed by Blackett-Ord QC (sitting as a judge of the High Court) that in some cases it may be appropriate to serve the statutory demand upon the solicitors of the debtor.

Rule 6.4   Application to set aside statutory demand

6.4(1)   [Time for application]   The debtor may, within the period allowed by this Rule, apply to the appropriate court for an order setting the statutory demand aside.   [FORM 6.4]

That period is 18 days from the date of the service on him of the statutory demand or, where the demand is advertised in a newspaper pursuant to Rule 6.3, from the date of the advertisement's appearance or (as the case may be) its first appearance.

6.4(2)   [Appropriate court where creditor is Minister etc.]   Where the creditor issuing the statutory demand is a Minister of the Crown or a Government Department, and—

(a) the debt in respect of which the demand is made, or a part of it equal to or exceeding the bankruptcy level (within the meaning of section 267), is the subject of a judgment or order of any court, and

(b) the statutory demand specifies the date of the judgment or order and the court in which it was obtained, but indicates the creditor's intention to present a bankruptcy petition against the debtor in the High Court,

the appropriate court under this Rule is the High Court; and in any other case it is that to which the debtor would, in accordance with paragraphs (1) and (2) of Rule 6.40 in Chapter 3 below, present his own bankruptcy petition.

6.4(3)   [Effect of filing application in court]   As from (inclusive) the date on which the application is filed in court, the time limited for compliance with the statutory demand ceases to run, subject to any order of the court under Rule 6.5(6).

6.4(4)   [Supporting affidavit]   The debtor's application shall be supported by an affidavit—

(a) specifying the date on which the statutory demand came into his hands, and

(b) stating the grounds on which he claims that is should be set aside.

The affidavit shall have exhibited to it a copy of the statutory demand.

[FORM 6.5]

General note

The debtor can, by using Forms 6.4 and 6.5, apply to the court to have the statutory demand set aside. He has 18 days after service to make such an application. If an application is made, the three weeks' deadline for compliance with the demand ceases to run.

See also *Practice Note (Bankruptcy: Statutory Demand: Setting Aside)* [1987] 1 WLR 119.

Rule **6.5**   Hearing of application to set aside

6.5(1)   **[Court may dismiss application etc.]** On receipt of an application under Rule 6.4, the court may, if satisfied that no sufficient cause is shown for it, dismiss it without giving notice to the creditor. As from (inclusive) the date on which the application is dismissed, the time limited for compliance with the statutory demand runs again.

6.5(2)   **[Application not dismissed under r. 6.5(1)]** If the application is not dismissed under paragraph (1), the court shall fix a venue for it to be heard, and shall give at least 7 days' notice of it to—

(a) the debtor or, if the debtor's application was made by a solicitor acting for him, to the solicitor,

(b) the creditor, and

(c) whoever is named in the statutory demand as the person with whom the debtor may enter into communication with reference to the demand (or, if more than one person is so named, the first of them).

6.5(3)   **[Summary determination or adjournment]** On the hearing of the application, the court shall consider the evidence then available to it, and may either summarily determine the application or adjourn it, giving such directions as it thinks appropriate.

6.5(4)   **[Setting aside demand]** The court may grant the application if—

(a) the debtor appears to have a counterclaim, set-off or cross demand which equals or exceeds the amount of the debt or debts specified in the statutory demand; or

(b) the debt is disputed on grounds which appear to the court to be substantial; or

(c) it appears that the creditor holds some security in respect of the debt claimed by the demand, and either Rule 6.1(5) is not complied with in respect of it, or the court is satisfied that the value of the security equals or exceeds the full amount of the debt; or

(d) the court is satisfied, on other grounds, that the demand ought to be set aside.   [FORM 6.6]

6.5(5)   **[Under-valued security]** Where the creditor holds some security in respect of his debt, and Rule 6.1(5) is complied with in respect of it but the court is satisfied that the security is under-valued in the statutory demand, the creditor may be required to amend the demand accordingly (but without prejudice to his right to present a bankruptcy petition by reference to the original demand).

6.5(6) [On dismissal of application] If the court dismisses the application, it shall make an order authorising the creditor to present a bankruptcy petition either forthwith, or on or after a date specified in the order.

A copy of the order shall be sent by the court forthwith to the creditor.

General note

This rule outlines the hearing procedure for an application made under r. 6.4. If the application succeeds, the court's order should be in the style of Form 6.6. If the application fails the court can permit the immediate presentation of the bankruptcy petition. The leading case on r. 6.5(4) is *Re A Debtor (No. 1 of 1987)* [1989] 1 WLR 271 where the Court of Appeal held that a document purporting to be a statutory demand was to be treated as such until set aside. In cases of setting aside under r. 6.5(4)(*d*) the debtor must not merely convince the court that the demand was perplexing but also prove what the true position was between himself and the creditor. See the general note after s. 268.

The jurisdiction to set aside statutory demands is permissive; the court is under no obligation to act, as was stressed in *Re A Debtor (No. 106 of 1992) The Independent*, 20 April 1992.

The court cannot make a conditional order on a set-aside application. Either the demand must be set aside or the application rejected – *Re A Debtor (No. 90 of 1992)* [1993] TLR 387 and *Re Debtor No. 32 of 1991 (No. 2)* [1994] BCC 524.

In *Re A Debtor (No. 960/SD/1992)* [1993] STC 218 Mummery J refused to set aside a statutory demand under r. 6.5(4) in a case where a tax assessment was being challenged by the taxpayer; the case did not appear to be covered by this provision.

A set-aside application also proved unsuccessful in *Re A Debtor (No. 415/SD/1993)* [1994] 1 WLR 917. Here the debtor was seeking to set aside the demand by arguing that he had made a reasonable offer of security to the creditor. In discussing the meaning of "other grounds" in r. 6.5(4)(*d*) Jacob J made it clear that set-aside applications were designed to deal with procedural flaws in the demand and were not meant to raise substantive issues of reasonableness – these issues could be considered when the petition was heard. Equally in *Platts* v *Western Trust and Savings Ltd* [1993] TLR 210 the court indicated that it would not investigate such questions as whether the creditor was secured or not as these were issues best dealt with when the petition was heard.

If the creditor bases his petition upon a judgment debt the court will not on a set-aside application look behind the earlier judgment – see Ferris J in *Re A Debtor (657/SD/1991)* [1993] BCLC 1280 applying *Practice Direction* [1987] 1 WLR 119.

For the position where the debt is disputed within the context of r. 6.5(4)(*b*), see *Re A Debtor (No. 11 of 1987), The Independent*, 28 March 1988 and *Re A Debtor (No. 10 of 1988)* [1989] 1 WLR 405. Another interesting case involving a disputed debt was *Re A Debtor (Nos. 49 and 50 of 1992)* [1994] 3 WLR 847. Here part of the debt upon which the statutory demand was based was disputed by the debtor. The undisputed element was for an amount less than the statutory minimum upon which a creditor could petition for bankruptcy. In those circumstances the Court of Appeal held that although the demand could not be set aside in its entirety under r. 6.5(4)(*b*) the court could set aside the whole demand using its residual descretion under r. 6.5(4)(*d*).

Rule 7.55 cannot apply in the context of the statutory demand – *Re A Debtor (No. 190 of 1987), The Times*, 21 May 1988.

Chapter 2 — Bankruptcy Petition (Creditor's)

Rule 6.6 Preliminary

6.6   The Rules in this Chapter relate to a creditor's petition, and the making of a bankruptcy order thereon; and in those Rules **"the debt"** means, except where the context otherwise requires, the debt (or debts) in respect of which the petition is presented.

Those Rules also apply to a petition under section 264(1)(c) (supervisor of, or person bound by, voluntary arrangement), with any necessary modifications.

[FORM 6.7]
or [FORM 6.8]
or [FORM 6.9]
or [FORM 6.10]

General note

See the guidance in *Practice Note (Bankruptcy: Petition)* [1987] 1 WLR 81 and the *Practice Direction 3/86* noted in (1987) 3 *Insolvency Law & Practice* 101.

Rule 6.7 Identification of debtor

6.7(1)   **[Contents of petition]**   The petition shall state the following matters with respect to the debtor, so far as they are within the petitioner's knowledge—

(a) his name, place of residence and occupation (if any);

(b) the name or names in which he carries on business, if other than his true name, and whether, in the case of any business of a specified nature, he carries it on alone or with others;

(c) the nature of his business, and the address or addresses at which he carries it on;

(d) any name or names, other than his true name, in which he has carried on business at or after the time when the debt was incurred, and whether he has done so alone or with others;

(e) any address or addresses at which he has resided or carried on business at or after that time, and the nature of that business.

6.7(2)   **[Title of proceedings]**   The particulars of the debtor given under this Rule determine the full title of the proceedings.

6.7(3)   **[Debtor's other names]**   If to the petitioner's personal knowledge the debtor has used any name other than the one specified under paragraph (1)(a), that fact shall be stated in the petition.

(See general note after r. 6.8.)

Rule 6.8 Identification of debt

6.8(1)   **[Contents of petition]**   There shall be stated in the petition, with reference to every debt in respect of which it is presented—

(a) the amount of the debt, the consideration for it (or, if there is no consideration, the way in which it arises) and the fact that it is owed to the petitioner;

(b) when the debt was incurred or became due;

(c) if the amount of the debt includes—

   (i) any charge by way of interest not previously notified to the debtor as a liability of his, or

   (ii) any other charge accruing from time to time,

the amount or rate of the charge (separately identified) and the grounds on which it is claimed to form part of the debt, provided that such amount or rate must, in the case of a petition based on a statutory demand, be limited to that claimed in that demand;

  (d) either—

   (i) that the debt is for a liquidated sum payable immediately, and the debt-or appears to be unable to pay it, or

   (ii) that the debt is for a liquidated sum payable at some certain, future time (that time to be specified), and the debtor appears to have no reasonable prospect of being able to pay it,

and, in either case (subject to section 269) that the debt is unsecured.

6.8(2)   **[Where statutory demand served]**   Where the debt is one for which, under section 268, a statutory demand must have been served on the debtor—

  (a) there shall be specified the date and manner of service of the statutory demand, and

  (b) it shall be stated that, to the best of the creditor's knowledge and belief—

   (i) the demand has been neither complied with nor set aside in accordance with the Rules, and

   (ii) no application to set it aside is outstanding.

6.8(3)   **[If case within sec. 268(1)(b)]**   If the case is within section 268(1)(b) (debt arising under judgment or order of court; execution returned unsatisfied), the court from which the execution or other process issued shall be specified, and particulars shall be given relating to the return.

History note

In r. 6.8(1)(*c*) the words from ", provided that such amount" to the end were added by I(A)R 1987 (SI 1987 No 1919), r.3(1), Sch., Pt. 1, para. 91 as from 11 January 1988.

General note to rr. 6.7, 6.8

These rules outline the contents of a creditor's petition.

  See also *Practice Note (Bankruptcy) (No. 2/87)* dated 30 September 1987, [1987] 1 WLR 1424 which amended the *Practice Note* in [1987] 1 WLR 81.

Rule 6.9   Court in which petition to be presented

6.9(1)   **[Presentation to High Court]**   In the following cases, the petition shall be presented to the High Court—

  (a) if the petition is presented by a Minister of the Crown or a Government Department, and either in any statutory demand on which the petition is based the creditor has indicated the intention to present a bankruptcy pet-ition to that Court, or the petition is presented under section 268(1)(b), or

  (b) if the debtor has resided or carried on business within the London insol-vency district for the greater part of the 6 months immediately preceding the presentation of the petition, or for a longer period in those 6 months than in any other insolvency district, or

(c) if the debtor is not resident in England and Wales, or

(d) if the petitioner is unable to ascertain the residence of the debtor, or his place of business.

6.9(2) [County court] In any other case the petition shall be presented to the county court for the insolvency district in which the debtor has resided or carried on business for the longest period during those 6 months.

6.9(3) [Insolvency districts] If the debtor has for the greater part of those 6 months carried on business in one insolvency district and resided in another, the petition shall be presented to the court for the insolvency district in which he has carried on business.

6.9(4) [Principal place of business] If the debtor has during those 6 months carried on business in more than one insolvency district, the petition shall be presented to the court for the insolvency district in which is, or has been for the longest period in those 6 months, his principal place of business.

6.9(4A) [Voluntary arrangement] Notwithstanding any other provision of this Rule, where there is in force for the debtor a voluntary arrangement under Part VIII of the Act, the petition shall be presented to the court to which the nominee's report under section 256 was submitted.

6.9(5) [Establishing appropriate court] The petition shall contain sufficient information to establish that it is brought in the appropriate court.

History note

R. 6.9(4A) was inserted by I(A)R 1987 (SI 1987 No. 1919), r. 3(1), Sch., Pt. 1, para. 92 as from 11 January 1988.

General note

The court to which the creditor's petition must be presented is hereby identified.

Rule 6.10 Procedure for presentation and filing

6.10(1) [Filing with verifying affidavit] The petition, verified by affidavit in accordance with Rule 6.12(1) below, shall be filed in court.

6.10(2) [Receipt for deposit payable on presentation] No petition shall be filed unless there is produced with it the receipt for the deposit payable on presentation.

6.10(3) [Copies of petition] The following copies of the petition shall also be delivered to the court with the petition—

(a) one for service on the debtor,

(b) one to be exhibited to the affidavit verifying that service, and

(c) if there is in force for the debtor a voluntary arrangement under Part VIII of the Act, and the petitioner is not the supervisor of the arrangement, one copy for him.

Each of these copies shall have applied to it the seal of the court, and shall be issued to the petitioner.

6.10(4)   [Endorsing of r. 6.10(3) copies]   The date and time of filing the petition shall be endorsed on the petition and on any copy issued under paragraph (3).

6.10(5)   [Venue for hearing]   The court shall fix a venue for hearing the petition, and this also shall be endorsed on the petition and on any copy so issued.

6.10(6)   [Former supervisor requested as trustee]   Where a petition contains a request for the appointment of a person as trustee in accordance with section 297(5) (appointment of former supervisor as trustee) the person whose appointment is sought shall, not less than 2 days before the day appointed for hearing the petition, file in court a report including particulars of—

    (a) a date on which he gave written notification to creditors bound by the arrangement of the intention to seek his appointment as trustee, such date to be at least 10 days before the day on which the report under this paragraph is filed, and

    (b) details of any response from creditors to that notice, including any objections to his appointment.

History note

In r. 6.10(3) the word "and" formerly at the end of subpara. (*a*) was omitted and the word ", and" and subpara. (*c*) were added at the end of subpara. (*b*) by I(A)R 1987 (SI 1987 No. 1919), r. 3(1), Sch., Pt. 1, para. 93(1) as from 11 January 1988.

    Rule 6.10(6) was added by I(A)R 1987 (SI 1987 No. 1919), r. 3(1), Sch., Pt. 1, para. 93(2) as from 11 January 1988.

(See general note after r. 6.12.)

Rule **6.11**   Proof of service of statutory demand

6.11(1)   [Affidavit of service]   Where under section 268 the petition must have been preceded by a statutory demand, there must be filed in court, with the petition, an affidavit or affidavits proving service of the demand.

6.11(2)   [Copy of demand to be exhibited]   Every affidavit must have exhibited to it a copy of the demand as served.

6.11(3)   [Affidavit of personal service]   Subject to the next paragraph, if the demand has been served personally on the debtor, the affidavit must be made by the person who effected that service.   [FORM 6.11]

6.11(4)   [If service of demand acknowledged]   If service of the demand (however effected) has been acknowleged in writing either by the debtor himself, or by some person stating himself in the acknowledgment to be authorised to accept service on the debtor's behalf, the affidavit must be made either by the creditor or by a person acting on his behalf, and the acknowledgement of service must be exhibited to the affidavit.

6.11(5) **[If neither r. 6.11(3) or (4) applies]** If neither paragraph (3) nor paragraph (4) applies, the affidavit or affidavits must be made by a person or persons having direct personal knowledge of the means adopted for serving the statutory demand, and must—

(a) give particulars of the steps which have been taken with a view to serving the demand personally, and

(b) state the means whereby (those steps having been ineffective) it was sought to bring the demand to the debtor's attention, and

(c) specify a date by which, to the best of the knowledge, information and belief of the person making the affidavit, the demand will have come to the debtor's attention. [FORM 6.12]

6.11(6) **[Sufficiency of r. 6.11(5)(a) particulars]** The steps of which particulars are given for the purposes of paragraph (5)(a) must be such as would have sufficed to justify an order for substituted service of a petition.

6.11(7) **[Deemed date of service]** If the affidavit specifies a date for the purposes of compliance with paragraph (5)(c), then unless the court otherwise orders, that date is deemed for the purposes of the Rules to have been the date on which the statutory demand was served on the debtor.

6.11(8) **[Newspaper advertisement]** Where the creditor has taken advantage of Rule 6.3(3) (newspaper advertisement), the affidavit must be made either by the creditor himself or by a person having direct personal knowledge of the circumstances; and there must be specified in the affidavit—

(a) the means of the creditor's knowledge or (as the case may be) belief required for the purposes of that Rule, and

(b) the date or dates on which, and the newspaper in which, the statutory demand was advertised under that Rule;

and there shall be exhibited to the affidavit a copy of any advertisement of the statutory demand.

6.11(9) **[Discharge of r. 6.3(2) obligation]** The court may decline to file the petition if not satisfied that the creditor has discharged the obligation imposed on him by Rule 6.3(2).

History note

In r. 6.11(1) the words "or affidavits" were inserted by I(A)R 1987 (SI 1987 No. 1919), r. 3(1), Sch., Pt. 1, para. 94(1) as from 11 January 1988.

In r. 6.11(2) the words "Every affidavit" were substituted for the former words "The affidavit" by I(A)R 1987 (SI 1987 No. 1919), r. 3(1), Sch., Pt. 1, para. 94(2) as from 11 January 1988.

In r. 6.11(5) the words "or affidavits", "or persons" and "personally" (in subpara. (*a*)) were inserted by I(A)R 1987 (SI 1987 No. 1919), r. 3(1), Sch., Pt. 1, para. 94(3) as from 11 January 1988.

General note

See *Practice Note (Bankruptcy: Statutory Demand)* [1987] 1 WLR 85. See also general note after r. 6.12.

Rule 6.12   Verification of petition

6.12(1)   **[Verifying affidavit]**   The petition shall be verified by an affidavit that the statements in the petition are true, or are true to the best of the deponent's knowledge, information and belief.   [FORM 6.13]

6.12(2)   **[Debts due to different creditors]**   If the petition is in respect of debts to different creditors, the debts to each creditor must be separately verified.

6.12(3)   **[Petition to be exhibited]**   The petition shall be exhibited to the affidavit verifying it.

6.12(4)   **[Who shall make the affidavit]**   The affidavit shall be made—

    (a)   by the petitioner (or if there are two or more petitioners, any one of them), or

    (b)   by some person such as a director, company secretary or similar company officer, or a solicitor, who has been concerned in the matters giving rise to the presentation of the petition, or

    (c)   by some responsible person who is duly authorised to make the affidavit and has the requisite knowledge of those matters.

6.12(5)   **[Where deponent not petitioner]**   Where the maker of the affidavit is not the petitioner himself, or one of the petitioners, he must in the affidavit identify himself and state—

    (a)   the capacity in which, and the authority by which, he makes it, and

    (b)   the means of his knowledge of the matters sworn to in the affidavit.

6.12(6)   **[Affidavit as prima facie evidence]**   The affidavit is prima facie evidence of the truth of the statements in the petition to which it relates.

6.12(7)   **[Delay between demand and petition]**   If the petition is based upon a statutory demand, and more than 4 months have elapsed between the service of the demand and the presentation of the petition, the affidavit must also state the reasons for the delay.

General note to rr. 6.10–6.12

The procedure for filing a creditor's petition is described in these rules. The petition should be accompanied by proof of service of the statutory demand, and by an affidavit of verification. Compare BR 1952, r. 150.

Rule 6.13   Notice to Chief Land Registrar

6.13   When the petition is filed, the court shall forthwith send to the Chief Land Registrar notice of the petition together with a request that it may be registered in the register of pending actions.   [FORM 6.14]

General note

Compare BR 1952, r. 147.

    Form 6.14 is now contained in modified form in I(A)R 1987 (SI 1987 No. 1919), r. 3(1), Sch., Pt. 5, s. 1.

Rule 6.14   Service of petition

6.14(1)   **[Personal service]**   Subject as follows, the petition shall be served personally on the debtor by an officer of the court, or by the petitioning creditor or his solicitor, or by a person instructed by the creditor or his solicitor for that purpose; and service shall be effected by delivering to him a sealed copy of the petition.

6.14(2) **[Substituted service]** If the court is satisfied by affidavit or other evidence on oath that prompt personal service cannot be effected because the debtor is keeping out of the way to avoid service of the petition or other legal process, or for any other cause, it may order substituted service to be effected in such manner as it thinks fit.

6.14(3) **[Deemed service]** Where an order for substituted service has been carried out, the petition is deemed duly served on the debtor. [FORM 6.15]
[FORM 6.16]

6.14(4) **[If voluntary arrangement in force]** If to the petitioner's knowledge there is in force for the debtor a voluntary arrangement under Part VIII of the Act, and the petitioner is not himself the supervisor of the arrangement, a copy of the petition shall be sent by him to the supervisor.

History note

Rule 6.14(4) was added by I(A)R 1987 (SI 1987 No. 1919), r. 3(1), Sch., Pt. 1, para. 95 as from 11 January 1988.

General note

Personal service of a creditor's petition is required unless it is a case where substituted service may be appropriate – see *Re A Debtor (Nos. 234 and 236 of 1991)*, *The Independent*, 29 June 1992 (Blackett-Ord QC sitting as a judge of the High Court).

See *Practice Note (Bankruptcy: Substituted Service)* [1987] 1 WLR 82.

For service outside the jurisdiction see r. 12.12(2).

Rule 6.15   Proof of service

6.15(1) **[Affidavit of service]** Service of the petition shall be proved by affidavit.

6.15(2) **[Exhibits]** The affidavit shall have exhibited to it—

(a) a sealed copy of the petition, and

(b) if substituted service has been ordered, a sealed copy of the order;

and it shall be filed in court immediately after service. [FORM 6.17]
or [FORM 6.18]

General note to rr. 6.14, 6.15

These map out the rules as to service of the creditor's petition. Note the use of substituted service (Forms 6.15, 6.16), and the requirement of proof of service by affidavit (Forms 6.17, 6.18). Compare BR 1952, rr. 153, 154.

Rule 6.16   Death of debtor before service

6.16 If the debtor dies before service of the petition, the court may order service to be effected on his personal representatives or on such other persons as it thinks fit.

Rule 6.17   Security for costs (s. 268(2) only)

6.17(1) **[Application of Rule]** This Rule applies where the debt in respect of which the petition is presented is for a liquidated sum payable at some future time, it being claimed in the petition that the debtor appears to have no reasonable prospect of being able to pay it.

6.17(2)   [Debtor's application for security]   The petitioning creditor may, on the debtor's application, be ordered to give security for the debtor's costs.

6.17(3)   [Court's discretion]   The nature and amount of the security to be ordered is in the court's discretion.

6.17(4)   [If order made]   If an order is made under this Rule, there shall be no hearing of the petition until the whole amount of the security has been given.

General note

This imposes additional financial requirements for petitions based on IA 1986, s. 268(2).

Rule **6.18**   Hearing of petition

6.18(1)   [Time for hearing]   Subject as follows, the petition shall not be heard until at least 14 days have elapsed since it was served on the debtor.

6.18(2)   [Expedited hearing]   The court may, on such terms as it thinks fit, hear the petition at an earlier date, if it appears that the debtor has absconded, or the court is satisfied that is is a proper case for an expedited hearing, or the debtor consents to a hearing within the 14 days.

6.18(3)   [Appearances]   Any of the following may appear and be heard, that is to say, the petitioning creditor, the debtor, the supervisor of any voluntary arrangement under Part VIII of the Act in force for the debtor and any creditor who has given notice under Rule 6.23 below.

History note

In r. 6.18(3) the words from ", the supervisor" to "in force for the debtor" were inserted by I(A)R 1987 (SI 1987 No. 1919), r. 3(1), Sch., Pt. 1, para. 96 as from 11 January 1988.

General note

Normally, 14 days must elapse between the petition being served and the hearing.

Rule **6.19**   Petition against two or more debtors

(Omitted by the Insolvency (Amendment) Rules 1987 (S.I. 1987 No. 1919), r. 3(1), Sch., Pt. 1, para. 97 as from 11 January 1988).

History note

Rule 6.19 formerly read as follows:

> "**6.19**   Where two or more debtors are named in the petition, and the petition has not been served on both or all of them, the petition may be heard separately or collectively as regards any of those who have been served, and may subsequently be heard (separately or collectively) as regards the others, as and when service on them is effected."

General note

This rule was omitted because it was felt that a joint petition against multiple debtors would create problems. The general rule of one petition for each debtor should prevail.

Rule 6.20 Petition by moneylender

6.20 A petition in respect of a moneylending transaction made before 27th January 1980 of a creditor who at the time of the transaction was a licensed moneylender shall at the hearing of the petition be supported by an affidavit incorporating a statement setting out in detail the particulars mentioned in section 9(2) of the Moneylenders Act 1927.

General note

Compare BR 1952, r. 165.

Rule 6.21 Petition opposed by debtor

6.21 Where the debtor intends to oppose the petition, he shall not later than 7 days before the day fixed for the hearing—

(a) file in court a notice specifying the grounds on which he will object to the making of a bankruptcy order, and

(b) send a copy of the notice to the petitioning creditor or his solicitor.

[FORM 6.19]

Rule 6.22 Amendment of petition

6.22 With the leave of the court (given on such terms, if any, as the court thinks fit to impose), the petition may be amended at any time after presentation by the omission of any creditor or any debt.

Rule 6.23 Notice by persons intending to appear

6.23(1) **[Notice of intention]** Every creditor who intends to appear on the hearing of the petition shall give to the petitioning creditor notice of his intention in accordance with this Rule. [FORM 6.20]

6.23(2) **[Contents of notice]** The notice shall specify—

(a) the name and address of the person giving it, and any telephone number and reference which may be required for communication with him or with any other person (to be also specified in the notice) authorised to speak or act on his behalf;

(b) whether his intention is to support or oppose the petition; and

(c) the amount and nature of his debt.

6.23(3) **[Time for sending notice]** The notice shall be sent so as to reach the addressee not later than 16.00 hours on the business day before that which is appointed for the hearing (or, where the hearing has been adjourned, for the adjourned hearing).

6.23(4)   [Effect of non-compliance]   A person failing to comply with this Rule may appear on the hearing of the petition only with the leave of the court.

(See general note after r. 6.24.)

Rule 6.24   List of appearances

6.24(1)   [Petitioning creditor to prepare list]   The petitioning creditor shall pre-pare for the court a list of the creditors (if any) who have given notice under Rule 6.23, specifying their names and addresses and (if known to him) their respective solici-tors.   [FORM 6.21]

6.24(2)   [Whether creditors support or oppose]   Against the name of each creditor in the list it shall be stated whether his intention is to support the petition, or to oppose it.

6.24(3)   [Copy list handed to court]   On the day appointed for the hearing of the petition, a copy of the list shall be handed to the court before the commencement of the hearing.

6.24(4)   [Leave under r. 6.23(4)]   If any leave is given under Rule 6.23(4), the pet-itioner shall add to the list the same particulars in respect of the person to whom leave has been given.

General note to rr. 6.23, 6.24

Creditors who wish to attend the hearing must notify the petitioning creditor, informing him of their attitude to the petition. The petitioning creditor must draw up a list of such persons (Form 6.21), and hand it to the court before the start of the hearing.

Rule 6.25   Decision on the hearing

6.25(1)   [Bankruptcy order]   On the hearing of the petition, the court may make a bankruptcy order if satisfied that the statements in the petition are true, and that the debt on which it is founded has not been paid, or secured or compounded for.

6.25(2)   [Stay or dismissal]   If the petition is brought in respect of a judgment debt, or a sum ordered by any court to be paid, the court may stay or dismiss the petition on the ground that an appeal is pending from the judgment or order, or that execution of the judgment has been stayed.   [FORM 6.22]

6.25(3)   [Debt over-stated in demand]   A petition preceded by a statutory demand shall not be dismissed on the ground only that the amount of the debt was over-stated in the demand, unless the debtor, within the time allowed for complying with the demand, gave notice to the creditor disputing the validity of the demand on that ground; but, in the absence of such notice, the debtor is deemed to have complied with the demand if he has, within the time allowed, paid the correct amount.

General note

See *Practice Note (Bankruptcy: Certificate of Debt)* [1987] 1 WLR 120. See also general note after r. 6.26.

Rule 6.26   Non-appearance of creditor

6.26   If the petitioning creditor fails to appear on the hearing of the petition, no subsequent petition against the same debtor, either alone or jointly with any other person, shall be presented by the same creditor in respect of the same debt, without the leave of the court to which the previous petition was presented.

General note to rr. 6.25, 6.26

These supplement IA 1986, s. 271. Note the sanction against non-appearance by a petitioning creditor – this largely repeats BR 1952, r. 168.

Rule 6.27   Vacating registration on dismissal of petition

6.27   If the petition is dismissed or withdrawn by leave of the court, an order shall be made at the same time permitting vacation of the registration of the petition as a pending action; and the court shall send to the debtor two sealed copies of the order.   [FORM 6.22]

General note

This should be viewed in the light of r. 6.13.

Rule 6.28   Extension of time for hearing

6.28(1)   [If petition not served]   The petitioning creditor may, if the petition has not been served, apply to the court to appoint another venue for the hearing.

6.28(2)   [Why petition not served]   The application shall state the reasons why the petition has not been served.

6.28(3)   [Costs]   No costs occasioned by the application shall be allowed in the proceedings except by order of the court.

6.28(4)   [Notification of creditors]   If the court appoints another day for the hearing, the petitioning creditor shall forthwith notify any creditor who has given notice under Rule 6.23.

General note

"Venue" in r. 6.28(1) is defined in r. 13.6. See *Practice Direction (Bankruptcy 1/92)* [1992] 1 All ER 704.

Rule 6.29   Adjournment

6.29(1)   [Application of Rule]   If the court adjourns the hearing of the petition, the following applies.   [FORM 6.23]

6.29(2)   [Notice of adjournment]   Unless the court otherwise directs, the petitioning creditor shall forthwith send—

(a) to the debtor, and

(b) where any creditor has given notice under Rule 6.23 but was not present at the hearing, to him,

notice of the making of the order of adjournment. The notice shall state the venue for the adjourned hearing.   [FORM 6.24]

General note

The order for adjournment is to take the style of Form 6.23, whereas Form 6.24 is to be used when giving notice of the adjournment to the debtor.

Rule 6.30   Substitution of petitioner

6.30(1) **[Application of Rule]**   This Rule applies where a creditor petitions and is subsequently found not entitled to do so, or where the petitioner—

    (a) consents to withdraw his petition or to allow it to be dismissed, or consents to an adjournment, or fails to appear in support of his petition when it is called on in court on the day originally fixed for the hearing, or on a day to which it is adjourned, or

    (b) appears, but does not apply for an order in terms of the prayer of his petition.

6.30(2) **[Substitution]**   The court may, on such terms as it thinks just, order that there be substituted as petitioner any creditor who—

    (a) has under Rule 6.23 given notice of his intention to appear at the hearing,

    (b) is desirous of prosecuting the petition, and

    (c) was, at the date on which the petition was presented, in such a position in relation to the debtor as would have enabled him (the creditor) on that date to present a bankruptcy petition in respect of a debt or debts owed to him by the debtor, paragraphs (a) to (d) of section 267(2) being satisfied in respect of that debt or those debts.   **[FORM 6.24A]**

History note

Against r. 6.30(2) the words "[FORM 6.24A]" were inserted by I(A)R 1987 (SI 1987 No. 1919), r. 3(1), Sch., Pt. 2, para. 156(1) as from 11 January 1988.

General note

This allows the court to substitute petitioners in appropriate circumstances.

Rule 6.31   Change of carriage of petition

6.31(1) **[Application by creditor]**   On the hearing of the petition, any person who claims to be a creditor of the debtor, and who has given notice under Rule 6.23 of his intention to appear at the hearing, may apply to the court for an order giving him carriage of the petition in place of the petitioning creditor, but without requiring any amendment of the petition.

6.31(2) **[Powers of court]**   The court may, on such terms as it thinks just, make a change of carriage order if satisfied that—

    (a) the applicant is an unpaid and unsecured creditor of the debtor, and

    (b) the petitioning creditor either—

        (i) intends by any means to secure the postponement, adjournment or withdrawal of the petition, or

        (ii) does not intend to prosecute the petition, either diligently or at all.   **[FORM 6.24B]**

6.31(3) [Where court not to make order]   The court shall not make the order if satisfied that the petitioning creditor's debt has been paid, secured or compounded for by means of—

    (a) a disposition of property made by some person other than the debtor, or

    (b) a disposition of the debtor's own property made with the approval of, or ratified by, the court.

6.31(4) [Appearance by petitioning creditor]   A change of carriage order may be made whether or not the petitioning creditor appears at the hearing.

6.31(5) [If order made]   If the order is made, the person given the carriage of the petition is entitled to rely on all evidence previously adduced in the proceedings (whether by affidavit or otherwise).

History note

Against r. 6.31(2) the words "[FORM 6.24B]" were inserted by I(A)R 1987 (SI 1987 No. 1919), r. 3(1), Sch., Pt. 2, para. 156(1) as from 11 January 1988.

General note

Other creditors can apply to the court for carriage of the petition. A formal amendment of the petition is not required.

Rule 6.32   Petitioner seeking dismissal or leave to withdraw

6.32(1) [Affidavit specifying grounds of application etc.]   Where the petitioner applies to the court for the petition to be dismissed, or for leave to withdraw it, he must, unless the court otherwise orders, file in court an affidavit specifying the grounds of the application and the circumstances in which it is made.

6.32(2) [If payment made since petition filed]   If, since the petition was filed, any payment has been made to the petitioner by way of settlement (in whole or in part) of the debt or debts in respect of which the petition was brought, or any arrangement has been entered into for securing or compounding it or them, the affidavit must state—

    (a) what dispositions of property have been made for the purposes of the settlement or arrangement, and

    (b) whether, in the case of any disposition, it was property of the debtor himself, or of some other person, and

    (c) whether, if it was property of the debtor, the disposition was made with the approval of, or has been ratified by, the court (if so, specifying the relevant court order).

6.32(3) [No order before hearing]   No order giving leave to withdraw a petition shall be given before the petition is heard.   [FORM 6.22]

General note

This restricts the right of a petitioner to change his mind, so to speak. Bankruptcy proceedings are essentially a class remedy for the benefit of all creditors.

Rule 6.33   Settlement and content of bankruptcy order

6.33(1)   [Order to be settled by court]   The bankruptcy order shall be settled by the court.   [FORM 6.25]

6.33(2)   [Contents of order]   The order shall—

(a) state the date of the presentation of the petition on which the order is made, and the date and time of the making of the order, and

(b) contain a notice requiring the bankrupt, forthwith after service of the order on him, to attend on the official receiver at the place stated in the order.

6.33(3)   [Order staying proceedings]   Subject to section 346 (effect of bankruptcy on enforcement procedures), the order may include provision staying any action or proceeding against the bankrupt.

6.33(4)   [Where petitioning creditor represented by solicitor]   Where the petitioning creditor is represented by a solicitor, the order shall be endorsed with the latter's name, address, telephone number and reference (if any).

General note

This regulates the form of any bankruptcy order made under IA 1986, s. 271.

Rule 6.34   Action to follow making of order

6.34(1)   [Copies of order to official receiver etc.]   At least two sealed copies of the bankruptcy order shall be sent forthwith by the court to the official receiver, who shall forthwith send one of them to the bankrupt.

6.34(2)   [Official receiver to send notice etc.]   Subject to the next paragraph, the official receiver shall—

(a) send notice of the making of the order to the Chief Land Registrar, for registration in the register of writs and orders affecting land,

(b) cause the order to be advertised in such newspaper as the official receiver thinks fit, and

(c) cause the order to be gazetted.   [FORM 6.26]

6.34(3)   [Suspension of action under r. 6.34(2)]   The court may, on the application of the bankrupt or a creditor, order the official receiver to suspend action under paragraph (2), pending a further order of the court.

An application under this paragraph shall be supported by an affidavit stating the grounds on which it is made.

6.34(4)   [Where order made under r.6.34(3)]   Where an order is made under paragraph (3), the applicant for the order shall forthwith deliver a copy of it to the official receiver.

General note

This provides for the dissemination, advertisement and gazetting of the bankruptcy order.

Rule 6.34(2)

Formerly it was required that the notice be placed in a "local paper" but this restriction was removed by I(A)R 1991 (SI 1991 No. 495), r. 3, Sch., para. 3 as from 2 April 1991. Any newspaper will now suffice.

Rule 6.35 Amendment of title of proceedings

6.35(1) [Application for amendment] At any time after the making of a bankruptcy order, the official receiver or the trustee may apply to the court for an order amending the full title of the proceedings.

6.35(2) [Where amendment order made] Where such an order is made, the official receiver shall forthwith send notice of it to the Chief Land Registrar, for corresponding amendment of the register; and, if the court so directs he shall also cause notice of the order to be gazetted, and to be advertised in such newspaper as the official receiver thinks fit.

Rule 6.35(2)

The restriction that the newspaper had to be "local" was removed by I(A)R 1991 (SI 1991 No. 495), r. 3, Sch., para 3 as from 2 April 1991.

Rule 6.36 Old bankruptcy notices

6.36(1) [Proceeding on old notice] Subject as follows, a person who has before the appointed day for the purposes of the Act served a bankruptcy notice under the Bankruptcy Act 1914 may, on or after that day, proceed on the notice as if it were a statutory demand duly served under Chapter 1 of this Part of the Rules.

6.36(2) [Conditions of application of Rule] The conditions of the application of this Rule are that—

(a) the debt in respect of which the bankruptcy notice was served has not been paid, secured or compounded for in the terms of the notice and the Act of 1914;

(b) the date by which compliance with the notice was required was not more than 3 months before the date of presentation of the petition; and

(c) there has not, before the appointed day, been presented any bankruptcy petition with reference to an act of bankruptcy arising from non-compliance with the bankruptcy notice.

6.36(3) [Application to set old notice aside] If before, on or after the appointed day, application is made (under the Act of 1914) to set the bankruptcy notice aside, that application is to be treated, on and after that day, as an application duly made (on the date on which it was in fact made) to set aside a statutory demand duly served on the date on which the bankruptcy notice was in fact served.

General note

This is a necessary transitional provision. See IA 1986, s. 443 for further guidance on "the appointed day". Note also r. 13.14(2).

Chapter 3 — Bankruptcy Petition (Debtor's)

Rule 6.37 Preliminary

6.37 The Rules in this Chapter relate to a debtor's petition, and the making of a bankruptcy order thereon.   [FORM 6.27]

(See general note after r. 6.39.)

Rule 6.38 Identification of debtor

6.38(1) [Contents of petition] The petition shall state the following matters with respect to the debtor—

(a) his name, place of residence and occupation (if any);

(b) the name or names in which he carries on business, if other than his true name, and whether, in the case of any business of a specified nature, he carries it on alone or with others;

(c) the nature of his business, and the address or addresses at which he carries it on;

(d) any name or names, other than his true name, in which he has carried on business in the period in which any of his bankruptcy debts were incurred and, in the case of any such business, whether he had carried it on alone or with others; and

(e) any address or addresses at which he has resided or carried on business during that period, and the nature of that business.

6.38(2) [Title of proceedings] The particulars of the debtor given under this Rule determine the full title of the proceedings.

6.38(3) [Debtor's other names] If the debtor has at any time used a name other than the one given under paragraph (1)(a), that fact shall be stated in the petition.

(See general note after r. 6.39.)

Rule 6.39 Admission of insolvency

6.39(1) [Contents of petition] The petition shall contain the statement that the petitioner is unable to pay his debts, and a request that a bankruptcy order be made against him.

6.39(2) [Particulars in preceding five-year period] If within the period of 5 years

854

ending with the date of the petition the petitioner has been adjudged bankrupt, or has made a composition with his creditors in satisfaction of his debts or a scheme of arrangement of his affairs, or he has entered into any voluntary arrangement or been subject to an administration order under Part VI of the County Courts Act 1984, particulars of these matters shall be given in the petition.

6.39(3) **[If voluntary arrangement in force]** If there is at the date of the petition in force for the debtor a voluntary arrangement under Part VIII of the Act, the particulars required by paragraph (2) above shall contain a statement to that effect and the name and address of the supervisor of the arrangement.

History note

Rule 6.39(3) was added by I(A)R 1987 (SI 1987 No. 1919), r. 3(1), Sch., Pt. 1, para. 98 as from 11 January 1988.

General note to rr. 6.37–6.39

These rules map out the form and the contents of a debtor's petition (see IA 1986, s. 272). Form 6.27 should be employed for such a bankruptcy petition.

Rule 6.40 Court in which petition to be filed

6.40(1) **[Presentation to High Court]** In the following cases, the petition shall be presented to the High Court—

    (a) if the debtor has resided or carried on business in the London insolvency district for the greater part of the 6 months immediately preceding the presentation of the petition, or for a longer period in those 6 months than in any other insolvency district, or

    (b) if the debtor is not resident in England and Wales.

6.40(2) **[County court]** In any other case, the petition shall (subject to paragraph (3) below), be presented to the debtor's own county court, which is—

    (a) the county court for the insolvency district in which he has resided or carried on business for the longest period in those 6 months, or

    (b) if he has for the greater part of those 6 months carried on business in one insolvency district and resided in another, the county court for that in which he has carried on business, or

    (c) if he has during those 6 months carried on business in more than one insolvency district, the county court for that in which is, or has been for the longest period in those 6 months, his principal place of business.

6.40(3) **[Case not falling within r. 6.40(1)]** If, in a case not falling within paragraph (1), it is more expedient for the debtor with a view to expediting his petition—

    (a) it may in any case be presented to whichever court is specified by Schedule 2 to the Rules as being, in relation to the debtor's own court, the nearest full-time court, and

    (b) it may alternatively, in a case falling within paragraph (2)(b), be presented to the court for the insolvency district in which he has resided for the greater part of the 6 months there referred to.

6.40(3A) **[Where voluntary arrangement in force]** Notwithstanding any other provision of this Rule, where there is in force for the debtor a voluntary arrangement under Part VIII of the Act the petition shall be presented to the court to which the nominee's report under section 256 was submitted.

6.40(4) **[Establishing appropriateness of court]** The petition shall contain sufficient information to establish that it is brought in the appropriate court.

History note

Rules 6.40(3) and (3A) were substituted for the former r. 6.40(3) by I(A)R 1987 (SI 1987 No. 1919), r. 3(1), Sch., Pt. 1, para. 99 as from 11 January 1988: the former r. 6.40(3) read as follows:

"**6.40(3)** If, in a case not falling within paragraph (1), it is more expedient for the debtor with a view to expediting his petition, it may be presented to whichever county court is specified by Schedule 2 to the Rules as being, in relation to the debtor's own county court, the nearest full-time court."

General note

Compare r. 6.9.

Rule 6.40(3) was amended to facilitate the presentation of bankruptcy petitions by debtor traders. The possibility of using the court where one resides (as opposed to where one trades) is in addition to the alternatives in Sch. 2. Rule 6.40(3A) is equally sensible in its approach, in that it ensures that the court which dealt with the voluntary arrangement should be the one to hear the bankruptcy petition.

Rule 6.41 Statement of affairs

6.41(1) **[Accompanying statement etc.]** The petition shall be accompanied by a statement of the debtor's affairs, verified by affidavit. [FORM 6.28]

6.41(2) **[Application of Section B of Ch. 5]** Section B of Chapter 5 below applies with respect to the statement of affairs.

General note

This supplements IA 1986, s. 272(2). Note also rr. 6.67, 6.68.

Rule 6.42 Procedure for presentation and filing

6.42(1) **[Filing in court]** The petition and the statement of affairs shall be filed in court, together with three copies of the petition, and two copies of the statement. No petition shall be filed unless there is produced with it the receipt for the deposit payable on presentation.

6.42(2) **[Powers of court]** Subject to paragraph (2A), the court may hear the petition forthwith. If it does not do so, it shall fix a venue for the hearing.

6.42(2A) **[If petition refers to voluntary arrangement]** If the petition contains particulars of a voluntary arrangement under Part VIII of the Act in force for the debtor, the court shall fix a venue for the hearing and give at least 14 days' notice of it to the supervisor of the arrangement; the supervisor may appear and be heard on the petition.

6.42(3) **[Copies of petition]** Of the three copies of the petition delivered—

(a) one shall be returned to the petitioner, endorsed with any venue fixed;

(b) another, so endorsed, shall be sent by the court to the official receiver; and

(c) the remaining copy shall be retained by the court, to be sent to an insolvency practitioner (if appointed under section 273(2)).

6.42(4) **[Copies of statement of affairs]** Of the two copies of the statement of affairs—

(a) one shall be sent by the court to the official receiver; and

(b) the other shall be retained by the court to be sent to the insolvency practitioner (if appointed).

6.42(5) **[Swearing verifying affidavit]** The affidavit verifying the debtor's statement of affairs may be sworn before an officer of the court duly authorised in that behalf.

6.42(6) **[Documents to official receiver]** Where the court hears a petition forthwith, or it will in the opinion of the court otherwise expedite the delivery of any document to the official receiver, the court may, instead of sending that document to the official receiver, direct the bankrupt forthwith to deliver it to him.

6.42(7) **[Former supervisor requested as trustee]** Where a petition contains a request for the appointment of a person as trustee in accordance with section 297(5) (appointment of former supervisor as trustee) the person whose appointment is sought shall, not less than 2 days before the day appointed for hearing the petition, file in court a report including particulars of—

(a) a date on which he gave written notification to creditors bound by the arrangement of the intention to seek his appointment as trustee, such date to be at least 10 days before the day on which the report under this paragraph is filed, and

(b) details of any response from creditors to that notice, including any objections to his appointment.

History note

In r. 6.42(2) the words "Subject to paragraph (2A)," were inserted by I(A)R 1987 (SI 1987 No. 1919), r. 3(1), Sch., Pt. 1, para. 100(1) as from 11 January 1988.

Rule 6.42(2A) was inserted by I(A)R 1987 (SI 1987 No. 1919), r. 3(1), Sch., Pt. 1, para. 100(2) as from 11 January 1988.

In r. 6.42(3)(*b*) the words "sent by the court to the official receiver; and" were substituted by I(A)R 1987 (SI 1987 No. 1919), r. 3(1), Sch., Pt. 1, para. 100(3) as from 11 January 1988: the former words read as follows:

"retained by the court, to be sent to the official receiver if he is appointed interim receiver or a bankruptcy order is made; and".

Rule 6.42(4)(*a*) was substituted by I(A)R 1987 (SI 1987 No. 1919), r. 3(1), Sch., Pt. 1, para. 100(4) as from 11 January 1988: the former words read as follows:

"(a) one shall be retained by the court, to be sent to the official receiver if he is appointed interim receiver or a bankruptcy order is made; and".

Rules 6.42(6) and (7) were added by I(A)R 1987 (SI 1987 No. 1919), r. 3(1), Sch., Pt. 1, para. 100(5) as from 11 January 1988.

General note

Rule 6.42 was substantially modified by I(A)R 1987. The change to r. 6.42(4) was to give the official receiver early access to the statement of affairs to facilitate his examination of the debtor. Note the addition of rr. 6.42(2A), 6.42(6) and 6.42(7).

Rule 6.43   Notice to Chief Land Registrar

6.43   When the petition is filed, the court shall forthwith send to the Chief Land Registrar notice of the petition, for registration in the register of pending actions. [FORM 6.14]

Rule 6.44   Report of insolvency practitioner

6.44(1)   [If court appoints insolvency practitioner]   If the court under section 273 (2) appoints an insolvency practitioner to act in the debtor's case, it shall forthwith—

(a) send to the person appointed—

(i) a sealed copy of the order of appointment, and

(ii) copies of the petition and statement of affairs,

(b) fix a venue for the insolvency practitioner's report to be considered, and

(c) send notice of the venue to the insolvency practitioner and the debtor.

[FORM 6.29]

6.44(2)   [Insolvency practitioner's report]   The insolvency practitioner shall file his report in court and send one copy of it to the debtor, so as to be in his hands not less than 3 days before the date fixed for consideration of the report, and a further copy to the official receiver.

6.44(3)   [Debtor's attendance etc.]   The debtor is entitled to attend when the report is considered, and shall attend if so directed by the court. If he attends, the court shall hear any representations which he makes with respect to any of the matters dealt with in the report.

6.44(4)   (Omitted by the Insolvency (Amendment) Rules 1987 (S.I. 1987 No. 1919), r. 3(1), Sch., Pt. 1, para. 101(2) as from 11 January 1988).

History note

In r. 6.44(2) the words "with one copy," formerly appearing after the words "report in court" were omitted and the words ", and a further copy to the official receiver" added by I(A)R 1987 (SI 1987 No. 1919), r. 3(1), Sch., Pt. 1, para. 101(1) as from 11 January 1988.

Rule 6.44(4) formerly read as follows:

"**6.44(4)**   If the official receiver is appointed interim receiver or a bankruptcy order is made, a copy of the insolvency practitioner's report, the debtor's petition and his statement of affairs shall be sent by the court to the official receiver."

General note

This adds to IA 1986, s. 273(2) (appointment of insolvency practitioner in small bankruptcies). It deals with the form of the court's order (see Form 6.29), and the production of the report under IA 1986, s. 274.

Rule 6.44(2) was amended to give the official receiver early access to the report.

Rule 6.45   Settlement and content of bankruptcy order

6.45(1)   [Order to be settled by court]   The bankruptcy order shall be settled by the court.   [FORM 6.30]

6.45(2)   [Contents of order]   The order shall—

   (a) state the date of the presentation of the petition on which the order is made, and the date and time of the making of the order, and

   (b) contain a notice requiring the bankrupt, forthwith after the service of the order on him, to attend on the official receiver at the place stated in the order.

6.45(3)   [Order staying proceedings]   Subject to section 346 (effect of bankruptcy on enforcement procedures), the order may include provision staying any action or proceeding against the bankrupt.

6.45(4)   [Where bankrupt represented by solicitor]   Where the bankrupt is represented by a solicitor, the order shall be endorsed with the latter's name, address, telephone number and reference.

Rule 6.46   Action to follow making of order

6.46(1)   [Copy orders to official receiver etc.]   At least two sealed copies of the bankruptcy order shall be sent forthwith by the court to the official receiver, who shall forthwith send one of them to the bankrupt.

6.46(2)   [Official receiver to send notice etc.]   Subject to the next paragraph, the official receiver shall—

   (a) send notice of the making of the order to the Chief Land Registrar, for registration in the register of writs and orders affecting land,

   (b) cause the order to be advertised in such newspaper as the official receiver thinks fit, and

   (c) cause notice of the order to be gazetted.   [FORM 6.26]

6.46(3)   [Suspension of action under r. 6.46(2)]   The court may, on the application of the bankrupt or a creditor, order the official receiver to suspend action under paragraph (2), pending a further order of the court.

   An application under this paragraph shall be supported by an affidavit stating the grounds on which it is made.

6.46(4)   [Where order made under r. 6.46(3)]   Where an order is made under paragraph (3), the applicant shall forthwith deliver a copy of it to the official receiver.

General note

This regulates the dissemination, advertisement and gazetting of the order. Note the use of Form 6.26 and the connection with r. 6.43.

   Formerly under r. 6.46(2)(*b*) the notice had to be placed in a "local paper" as such and not a national newspaper circulating in a local area: *Re A Bankrupt (No. 1273 of 1990), The Independent,* 26 February 1990. This restriction was removed by I(A)R 1991 (SI 1991 No. 495), r. 3, Sch., para 3 as from 2 April 1991.

Rule 6.46A Expenses of voluntary arrangement

6.46A Where a bankruptcy order is made on a debtor's petition and there is at the time of the petition in force for the debtor a voluntary arrangement under Part VIII of the Act, any expenses properly incurred as expenses of the administration of the arrangement in question shall be a first charge on the bankrupt's estate.

History note

Rule 6.46A was inserted by I(A)R 1987 (SI 1987 No. 1919), r. 3(1), Sch., Pt. 1, para. 102 as from 11 January 1988.

Rule 6.47 Amendment of title of proceedings

6.47(1) [Application for amendment] At any time after the making of the bankruptcy order, the official receiver or the trustee may apply to the court for an order amending the full title of the proceedings.

6.47(2) [Where amendment order made] Where such an order is made, the official receiver shall forthwith send notice of it to the Chief Land Registrar, for corresponding amendment of the register; and, if the court so directs, he shall also—

(a) cause notice of the order to be gazetted, and

(b) cause notice of the order to be advertised in such newspaper as the official receiver thinks appropriate.

Rule 6.47(2)

The category of newspapers that can be used for placing notices has been extended by I(A)R 1991 (SI 1991 No. 495), r. 3, Sch., para 3 as from 2 April 1991). See the comment on r. 6.46(2)(*b*) above.

Rule 6.48 Certificate of summary administration

6.48(1) [S. 275 certificate] If the court under section 275 issues a certificate for the summary administration of the bankrupt's estate, the certificate may be included in the bankruptcy order. [FORM 6.30]

6.48(2) [Copy of certificate] If the certificate is not so included, the court shall forthwith send copies of it to the official receiver and the bankrupt.

(See general note after r. 6.50.)

Rule 6.49 Duty of official receiver in summary administration

6.49(1) [Where trustee appointed] Where a trustee has been appointed, the official receiver shall send a copy of the certificate of summary administration (whether or not included in the bankruptcy order) to him.

6.49(2) [Notice to creditors] Within 12 weeks after the issue of the certificate the official receiver shall (in so far as he has not already done so) give notice to creditors of the making of the bankruptcy order.

(See general note after r. 6.50.)

Rule 6.50 Revocation of certificate of summary administration

6.50(1) **[Powers of court]** The court may under section 275(3) revoke a certificate for summary administration, either of its own motion or on the application of the official receiver. [FORM 6.31]

6.50(2) **[Notice to bankrupt]** If the official receiver applies for the certificate to be revoked, he shall give at least 14 days' notice of the application to the bankrupt.

6.50(3) **[Notice of revocation]** If the court revokes the certificate, it shall forthwith give notice to the official receiver and the bankrupt.

6.50(4) **[Copy of notice to trustee]** If at the time of revocation there is a trustee other than the official receiver, the official receiver shall send a copy of the court's notice to him.

General note to rr. 6.48–6.50

These rules provide much needed guidance on the operation of summary administrations (see IA 1986, s. 275). Rule 6.50 is to be viewed in the light of s. 275(3).

Chapter 4 — The Interim Receiver

Rule 6.51 Application for appointment of interim receiver

6.51(1) **[Who may apply]** An application to the court for the appointment of an interim receiver under section 286 may be made by a creditor or by the debtor, or by an insolvency practitioner appointed under section 273(2).

6.51(2) **[Supporting affidavit]** The application must be supported by an affidavit stating—

(a) the grounds on which it is proposed that the interim receiver should be appointed,

(b) whether or not the official receiver has been informed of the application and, if so, has been furnished with a copy of it,

(c) whether to the applicant's knowledge there has been proposed or is in force a voluntary arrangement under Part VIII of the Act, and

(d) the applicant's estimate of the value of the property or business in respect of which the interim receiver is to be appointed.

6.51(3) **[If insolvency practitioner to be interim receiver]** If an insolvency practitioner has been appointed under section 273, and it is proposed that he (and not the official receiver) should be appointed interim receiver, and it is not the insolvency practitioner himself who is the applicant under this Rule, the affidavit under paragraph (2) must state that he has consented to act.

6.51(4) **[Copies of application and affidavit]** The applicant shall send copies of the application and the affidavit to the person proposed to be appointed interim receiver. If that person is the official receiver and an insolvency practitioner has been appointed under section 273 (and he is not himself the applicant), copies of the application and affidavit shall be sent by the applicant to the insolvency practitioner.

If, in any case where a copy of the application is to be sent to a person under this paragraph, it is for any reason not practicable to send a copy, that person must be informed of the application in sufficient time to enable him to be present at the hearing.

6.51(5)   [Appearances]   The official receiver and (if appointed) the insolvency practitioner may attend the hearing of the application and make representations.

6.51(6)   [Powers of court]   The court may on the application, if satisfied that sufficient grounds are shown for the appointment, make it on such terms as it thinks fit.

(See general note after r. 6.57.)

Rule 6.52   Order of appointment

6.52(1)   [Contents of order]   The order appointing the interim receiver shall state the nature and a short description of the property of which the person appointed is to take possession, and the duties to be performed by him in relation to the debtor's affairs.   [FORM 6.32]

6.52(2)   [Sealed copies]   The court shall, forthwith after the order is made, send 2 sealed copies of it to the person appointed interim receiver (one of which shall be sent by him forthwith to the debtor).

(See general note after r. 6.57.)

Rule 6.53   Deposit

6.53(1)   [Security for official receiver's remuneration etc.]   Before an order appointing the official receiver as interim receiver is issued, the applicant for it shall deposit with him, or otherwise secure to his satisfaction, such sum as the court directs to cover his remuneration and expenses.

6.53(2)   [Sufficiency of deposit etc.]   If the sum deposited or secured subsequently proves to be insufficient, the court may, on application by the official receiver, order that an additional sum be deposited or secured. If the order is not complied with within 2 days after service on the person to whom the order is directed, the court may discharge the order appointing the interim receiver.

6.53(3)   [Repayment etc. of deposit]   If a bankruptcy order is made after an interim receiver has been appointed, any money deposited under this Rule shall (unless it is required by reason of insufficiency of assets for payment of remuneration and expenses of the interim receiver, or the deposit was made by the debtor out of his own property) be repaid to the person depositing it (or as that person may direct) out of the bankrupt's estate, in the prescribed order of priority.

(See general note after r. 6.57.)

Rule 6.54   Security

6.54(1)   [Application of Rule]   The following applies where an insolvency practitioner is appointed to be interim receiver under section 286(2).

6.54(2)   [Cost of providing security]   The cost of providing the security required
under the Act shall be paid in the first instance by the interim receiver; but—

- (a) if a bankruptcy order is not made, the person so appointed is entitled to be
  reimbursed out of the property of the debtor, and the court may make an
  order on the debtor accordingly, and
- (b) if a bankruptcy order is made, he is entitled to be reimbursed out of the
  estate in the prescribed order of priority.

(See general note after r. 6.57.)

Rule 6.55   Failure to give or keep up security

6.55(1)   [Powers of court]   If the interim receiver fails to give or keep up his security, the court may remove him, and make such order as it thinks fit as to costs.

6.55(2)   [Directions on removal etc.]   If an order is made under this Rule removing
the interim receiver, or discharging the order appointing him, the court shall give
directions as to whether any, and if so what, steps should be taken for the appointment
of another person in his place.

(See general note after r. 6.57.)

Rule 6.56   Remuneration

6.56(1)   [To be fixed by court]   The remuneration of the interim receiver (other
than the official receiver) shall be fixed by the court from time to time on his
application.

6.56(2)   [Matters to be taken into account]   In fixing the interim receiver's
remuneration, the court shall take into account—

- (a) the time properly given by him (as interim receiver) and his staff in attending to the debtor's affairs,
- (b) the complexity (or otherwise) of the case,
- (c) any respects in which, in connection with the debtor's affairs, there falls on
  the interim receiver any responsibility of an exceptional kind or degree,
- (d) the effectiveness with which the interim receiver appears to be carrying out,
  or to have carried out, his duties as such, and
- (e) the value and nature of the property with which he has to deal.

6.56(3)   [Source of payment of remuneration etc.]   Without prejudice to any order the court may make as to costs, the interim receiver's remuneration (whether the official receiver or another) shall be paid to him, and the amount of any expenses incurred by him (including the remuneration and expenses of any special manager appointed under section 370) reimbursed—

(a) if a bankruptcy order is not made, out of the property of the debtor, and

(b) if a bankruptcy order is made, out of the estate in the prescribed order of priority,

or, in either case (the relevant funds being insufficient), out of the deposit under Rule 6.53.

6.56(4)   [Power of retention]   Unless the court otherwise directs, in a case falling within paragraph (3)(a) above the interim receiver may retain out of the debtor's property such sums or property as are or may be required for meeting his remuneration and expenses.

History note

In r. 6.56(3) the words from the beginning to "out of the property of the debtor" were substituted by I(A)R 1987 (SI 1987 No. 1919), r. 3(1), Sch., Pt. 1, para. 103(1) as from 11 January 1988: the former words read as follows:

"The interim receiver's remuneration (whether the official receiver or another) shall be paid to him, and the amount of any expenses incurred by him reimbursed—

(a) if a bankruptcy order is not made, out of the property of the debtor (and the court may make an order on the debtor accordingly)".

Rule 6.56(4) was added by I(A)R 1987 (SI 1987 No. 1919), r. 3(1), Sch., Pt. 1, para. 103(2) as from 11 January 1988.

(See general note after r. 6.57.)

Rule 6.57   Termination of appointment

6.57(1)   [Termination by court]   The appointment of the interim receiver may be terminated by the court on his application, or on that of the official receiver, the debtor or any creditor.

6.57(2)   [Directions on termination]   If the interim receiver's appointment terminates, in consequence of the dismissal of the bankruptcy petition or otherwise, the court may give such directions as it thinks fit with respect to the accounts of his administration and any other matters which it thinks appropriate.

6.57(3)   (Omitted by the Insolvency (Amendment) Rules 1987 (S.I. 1987 No. 1919), r. 3(1), Sch., Pt. 1, para. 104 as from 11 January 1988).

History note

Rule 6.57(3) formerly read as follows:

"**6.57(3)**   The court may under paragraph (2)—

(a) direct that any expenses properly incurred by the interim receiver during the period of his appointment, and any remuneration to which he is entitled, be paid out of property of the debtor, and

(b) authorise him to retain out of that property such sums as are required for meeting his expenses and remuneration.

Alternatively, the court may make such order as it thinks fit with respect to those matters."

General note to rr. 6.51–6.57

These rules all deal with the appointment of an interim receiver to protect the debtor's assets under IA 1986, s. 286. The application procedure is detailed. The order of appointment takes the style of Form 6.32. A deposit may be required from the applicant. The interim receiver may be required to give security; failure to do so could result in his removal by the court. The court is to determine the remuneration of an interim receiver. The question of the termination of his appointment is governed by r. 6.57, which should be cross-referenced to IA 1986, s. 286(7). For the former position, see BR 1952, rr. 157–161.

Chapter 5 — Disclosure by Bankrupt with Respect to the State of his Affairs

SECTION A: CREDITOR'S PETITION

Rule 6.58   Preliminary

6.58 The Rules in this Section apply with respect to the statement of affairs required by section 288(1) to be submitted by the bankrupt, following a bankruptcy order made on a creditor's petition, and the further and other disclosure which is required of him in that case.

(See general note after r. 6.59.)

Rule 6.59   The statement of affairs

6.59 The bankrupt's statement of affairs shall be in Form 6.33, and contain all the particulars required by that form.   [FORM 6.33]

General note to rr. 6.58, 6.59

These rules expand upon the provisions of IA 1986, s. 288.

Rule 6.60   Verification and filing

6.60(1) **[Instructions for preparation of statement]** The bankrupt shall be furnished by the official receiver with instructions for the preparation of his statement of affairs, and the forms required for that purpose.

6.60(2) **[Verification and delivery]**   The statement of affairs shall be verified by affidavit and delivered to the official receiver, together with one copy.

6.60(3) **[Filing in court]**   The official receiver shall file the verified statement in court.

6.60(4) **[Swearing verifying affidavit]**   The affidavit may be sworn before an official receiver or a deputy official receiver, or before an officer of the Department or the court duly authorised in that behalf.

Rule 6.61   Limited disclosure

6.61(1) **[Official receiver may apply to court]**   Where the official receiver thinks that it would prejudice the conduct of the bankruptcy for the whole or part of the statement of affairs to be disclosed, he may apply to the court for an order of limited disclosure in respect of the statement, or any specified part of it.

6.61(2) **[Powers of court]**   The court may on the application order that the statement or, as the case may be, the specified part of it be not filed in court, or that it is to be filed separately and not be open to inspection otherwise than with leave of the court.

General note

This is the standard provision in the rules enabling the court to censor sensitive information.

Rule 6.62   Release from duty to submit statement of affairs; extension of time

6.62(1) **[Exercise of s. 288(3) power]**   The power of the official receiver under section 288(3) to release the bankrupt from his duty to submit a statement of affairs, or to grant an extension of time, may be exercised at the official receiver's own discretion, or at the bankrupt's request.

6.62(2) **[Bankrupt may apply to court]**   The bankrupt may, if he requests a release or extension of time and it is refused by the official receiver, apply to the court for it.

6.62(3) **[Court may dismiss application etc.]**   The court may, if it thinks that no sufficient cause is shown for the application, dismiss it; but it shall not do so unless the bankrupt has had an opportunity to attend the court for an *ex parte* hearing, of which he has been given at least 7 days' notice.

If the application is not dismissed under this paragraph, the court shall fix a venue for it to be heard, and give notice to the bankrupt accordingly.

6.62(4) **[Bankrupt to send notice to official receiver]**   The bankrupt shall, at least 14 days before the hearing, send to the official receiver a notice stating the venue and accompanied by a copy of the application, and of any evidence which he (the bankrupt) intends to adduce in support of it.

6.62(5) **[Appearance etc. by official receiver]**   The official receiver may appear and be heard on the application; and, whether or not he appears, he may file a written report of any matters which he considers ought to be drawn to the court's attention.

If such a report is filed, a copy of it shall be sent by the official receiver to the bankrupt, not later than 5 days before the hearing.

6.62(6) **[Sealed copies of order]** Sealed copies of any order made on the application shall be sent by the court to the bankrupt and the official receiver.

6.62(7) **[Bankrupt's costs]** On any application under this Rule the bankrupt's costs shall be paid in any event by him and, unless the court otherwise orders, no allowance towards them shall be made out of the estate.

General note
This builds upon IA 1986, s. 288(3).

Rule 6.63   Expenses of statement of affairs

6.63(1) **[Persons assisting in preparation of statement]** If the bankrupt cannot himself prepare a proper statement of affairs, the official receiver may, at the expense of the estate, employ some person or persons to assist in the preparation of the statement.

6.63(2) **[Allowance towards expenses]** At the request of the bankrupt, made on the grounds that he cannot himself prepare a proper statement, the official receiver may authorise an allowance payable out of the estate (in accordance with the prescribed order of priority) towards expenses to be incurred by the bankrupt in employing some person or persons to assist him in preparing it.

6.63(3) **[Estimate of expenses]** Any such request by the bankrupt shall be accompanied by an estimate of the expenses involved; and the official receiver shall only authorise the employment of a named person or a named firm, being in either case approved by him.

6.63(4) **[Authorisation subject to conditions]** An authorisation given by the official receiver under this Rule shall be subject to such conditions (if any) as he thinks fit to impose with respect to the manner in which any person may obtain access to relevant books and papers.

6.63(5) **[Effect of Rule]** Nothing in this Rule relieves the bankrupt from any obligation with respect to the preparation, verification and submission of his statement of affairs, or to the provision of information to the official receiver or the trustee.

General note
This deals with the funding of the statement of affairs where the bankrupt is unable to prepare it himself.

Rule 6.64   Requirement to submit accounts

6.64(1) **[At request of official receiver]** The bankrupt shall, at the request of the official receiver, furnish him with accounts relating to his affairs of such nature, as at such date and for such period as he may specify.

6.64(2) **[Beginning of specified period]** The period specified may begin from a date up to 3 years preceding the date of the presentation of the bankruptcy petition.

6.64(3) **[Accounts for earlier period]**   The court may, on the official receiver's application, require accounts in respect of any earlier period.

6.64(4) **[Application of r. 6.63]**   Rule 6.63 applies (with the necessary modifications) in relation to accounts to be furnished under this Rule as it applies in relation to the statement of affairs.

(See general note after r. 6.66.)

Rule 6.65   Submission and filing of accounts

6.65(1) **[Verification and delivery]**   The accounts to be furnished under Rule 6.64 shall, if the official receiver so requires, be verified by affidavit, and (whether or not so verified) delivered to him within 21 days of the request under Rule 6.64(1), or such longer period as he may allow.

6.65(2) **[Copies of accounts etc. to official receiver]**   Two copies of the accounts and (where required) the affidavit shall be delivered by the bankrupt to the official receiver, who shall file one copy in court (with the affidavit, if any).

(See general note after r. 6.66.)

Rule 6.66   Further disclosure

6.66(1) **[Official receiver may require further information]**   The official receiver may at any time require the bankrupt to submit (in writing) further information amplifying, modifying or explaining any matter contained in his statement of affairs, or in accounts submitted in pursuance of the Act or the Rules.

6.66(2) **[Verification and delivery]**   The information shall, if the official receiver so directs, be verified by affidavit, and (whether or not so verified) delivered to him within 21 days of the requirement under this Rule, or such longer period as he may allow.

6.66(3) **[Copies to official receiver etc.]**   Two copies of the documents containing the information and (where verification is directed) the affidavit shall be delivered by the bankrupt to the official receiver, who shall file one copy in court (with the affidavit, if any).

General note to rr. 6.64–6.66

These provisions clarify IA 1986, s. 288(2)(*b*). Note how far back the official receiver can request accounts for.

SECTION B: DEBTOR'S PETITION

Rule 6.67   Preliminary

6.67   The Rules in this Section apply with respect to the statement of affairs required in the case of a person petitioning for a bankruptcy order to be made against him, and the further disclosure which is required of him in that case.

General note
This provision and r. 6.68 are to be linked with r. 6.41.

Rule 6.68   Contents of statement

6.68   The statement of affairs required by Rule 6.41 to accompany the debtor's petition shall be in Form 6.28, and contain all the particulars required by that form.   [FORM 6.28]

Rule 6.69   Requirement to submit accounts

6.69(1)   [At request of official receiver]   The bankrupt shall, at the request of the official receiver, furnish him with accounts relating to his affairs of such nature, as at such date and for such period as he may specify.

6.69(2)   [Beginning of specified period]   The period specified may begin from a date up to 3 years preceding the date of the presentation of the bankruptcy petition.

6.69(3)   [Accounts for earlier period]   The court may, on the official receiver's application, require accounts in respect of any earlier period.

(See general note after r. 6.72.)

Rule 6.70   Submission and filing of accounts

6.70(1)   [Verification and delivery]   The accounts to be furnished under Rule 6.69 shall, if the official receiver so requires, be verified by affidavit, and (whether or not so verified) delivered to him within 21 days of the request under Rule 6.69, or such longer period as he may allow.

6.70(2)   [Copies of accounts etc. to official receiver]   Two copies of the accounts and (where required) the affidavit shall be delivered by the bankrupt to the official receiver, who shall file one copy in court (with the affidavit, if any).

(See general note after r. 6.72.)

Rule 6.71   Expenses of preparing accounts

6.71(1)   [Persons assisting in preparation of accounts]   If the bankrupt cannot himself prepare proper accounts under Rule 6.69, the official receiver may, at the expense of the estate, employ some person or persons to assist in their preparation.

6.71(2) [Allowance towards expenses]   At the request of the bankrupt, made on the grounds that he cannot himself prepare the accounts, the official receiver may authorise an allowance payable out of the estate (in accordance with the prescribed order of priority) towards expenses to be incurred by the bankrupt in employing some person or persons to assist him in their preparation.

6.71(3) [Estimate of expenses]   Any such request by the bankrupt shall be accompanied by an estimate of the expenses involved; and the official receiver shall only authorise the employment of a named person or a named firm, being in either case approved by him.

6.71(4) [Authorisation subject to conditions]   An authorisation given by the official receiver under this Rule shall be subject to such conditions (if any) as he thinks fit to impose with respect to the manner in which any person may obtain access to relevant books and papers.

6.71(5) [Effect of Rule]   Nothing in this Rule relieves the bankrupt from any obligation with respect to the preparation and submission of accounts, or to the provision of information to the official receiver or the trustee.

(See general note after r. 6.72.)

Rule 6.72 Further disclosure

6.72(1) [Official receiver may require further information]   The official receiver may at any time require the bankrupt to submit (in writing) further information amplifying, modifying or explaining any matter contained in his statement of affairs, or in accounts submitted in pursuance of the Act or the Rules.

6.72(2) [Verification and delivery]   The information shall, if the official receiver so directs, be verified by affidavit, and (whether or not so verified) delivered to him within 21 days from the date of the requirement under paragraph (1), or such longer period as he may allow.

6.72(3) [Copies to official receiver etc.]   Two copies of the documents containing the information and (where verification is directed) the affidavit shall be delivered by the bankrupt to the official receiver, who shall file one copy in court, with the affidavit (if any).

General note to rr. 6.69–6.72
These provisions largely mirror rr. 6.63–6.66.

Chapter 6 — Information to Creditors

Rule 6.73   General duty of official receiver

6.73(1)   [Report to creditors]   In accordance with this Chapter, the official receiver shall, at least once after the making of the bankruptcy order, send a report to creditors with respect to the bankruptcy proceedings, and the state of the bankrupt's affairs.

6.73(2)   [Copy of report]   The official receiver shall file in court a copy of any report sent under this Chapter.

History note

Rule 6.73(1) was renumbered as such and r. 6.73(2) added by I(A)R 1987 (SI 1987 No. 1919), r. 3(1), Sch., Pt. 1, para. 105 as from 11 January 1988.

General note

The rules in Ch. 6 impose additional duties upon the official receiver to keep creditors informed.

Rule 6.74   Those entitled to be informed

6.74   Any reference in this Chapter to creditors is to creditors of the bankrupt who are known to the official receiver or, where the bankrupt has submitted a statement of affairs, are identified in the statement.

General note

This narrows the definition of "creditors".

Rule 6.75   Report where statement of affairs lodged

6.75(1)   [Report to creditors]   Where the bankrupt has submitted a statement of affairs, and it has been filed in court, the official receiver shall send out to creditors a report containing a summary of the statement (if he thinks fit, as amplified, modified or explained by virtue of Rule 6.66 or 6.72) and such observations (if any) as he thinks fit to make with respect to it or to the bankrupt's affairs generally.

6.75(2)   [Where no need to comply with r. 6.75(1)]   The official receiver need not comply with paragraph (1) if he has previously reported to creditors with respect to the bankrupt's affairs (so far as known to him) and he is of opinion that there are no additional matters which ought to be brought to their attention.

History note

In r. 6.75(1) the words from "(if he thinks fit" to "or 6.72)" were inserted by I(A)R 1987 (SI 1987 No. 1919), r. 3(1), Sch., Pt. 1, para. 106 as from 11 January 1988.

General note

This develops IA 1986, s. 288 and relates to the dissemination of the statement of affairs.

Rule 6.76 Statement of affairs dispensed with

6.76(1) [Application of Rule] This Rule applies where the bankrupt has been released from the obligation to submit a statement of affairs.

6.76(2) [Report to creditors] As soon as may be after the release has been granted, the official receiver shall send to creditors a report containing a summary of the bankrupt's affairs (so far as within his knowledge), and his observations (if any) with respect to it or the bankrupt's affairs generally.

6.76(3) [Where no need to comply with r. 6.76(2)] The official receiver need not comply with paragraph (2) if he has previously reported to creditors with respect to the bankrupt's affairs (so far as known to him) and he is of opinion that there are no additional matters which ought to be brought to their attention.

General note

If IA 1986, s. 288(3)(*a*) has been activated, the official receiver must supply a report to the creditors dealing with the financial position of the bankrupt.

Rule 6.77 General rule as to reporting

6.77(1) [Powers of court] The court may, on the official receiver's application, relieve him of any duty imposed on him by this Chapter of the Rules, or authorise him to carry out the duty in a way other than there required.

6.77(2) [Matters for court to consider] In considering whether to act as above, the court shall have regard to the cost of carrying out the duty, to the amount of the funds available in the estate, and to the extent of the interest of creditors or any particular class of them.

(See general note after r. 6.78.)

Rule 6.78 Bankruptcy order annulled

6.78 If the bankruptcy order is annulled, the duty of the official receiver to send reports under the preceding Rules in this Chapter ceases.

General note to rr. 6.77, 6.78

These rules modify the above obligations which have been imposed on the official receiver. Note the court's power of waiver under r. 6.77.

Chapter 7 — Creditors' Meetings

Rule 6.79 First meeting of creditors

6.79(1) [Venue for meeting etc.] If under section 293(1) the official receiver decides to summon a meeting of creditors, he shall fix a venue for the meeting, not more than 4 months from the date of the bankruptcy order.

6.79(2)   [Notice of meeting]   When a venue has been fixed, notice of the meeting shall be given—

(a) to the court, and

(b) to every creditor of the bankrupt who is known to the official receiver or is identified in the bankrupt's statement of affairs.

6.79(3)   [Time for giving notice]   Notice to the court shall be given forthwith; and the notice to creditors shall be given at least 21 days before the date fixed for the meeting.

6.79(4)   [Contents of notice]   The notice to creditors shall specify a time and date, not more than 4 days before the date fixed for the meeting, by which they must lodge proofs and (if applicable) proxies, in order to be entitled to vote at the meeting.

6.79(5)   [Public advertisement]   Notice of the meeting shall also be given by public advertisement.

6.79(6)   [Request by creditor under s. 294]   Where the official receiver receives a request by a creditor under section 294 for a meeting of creditors to be summoned, and it appears to him that the request is properly made in accordance with the Act, he shall—

(a) withdraw any notice already given by him under section 293(2) (that he has decided not to summon such a meeting), and

(b) fix the venue of the meeting for not more than 3 months from his receipt of the creditor's request, and

(c) act in accordance with paragraphs (2) to (5) above, as if he had decided under section 293(1) to summon the meeting.   [FORM 6.34]

6.79(7)   [Name of meeting]   A meeting summoned by the official receiver under section 293 or 294 is known as "the first meeting of creditors".

General note

If the official receiver decides to call a first meeting of creditors under IA 1986, s. 293, it must take place within four months of the date of the bankruptcy order. The meeting must be properly notified to the court (immediately), and to creditors (who should have 21 days' notice). It should also be advertised. Creditors should be given an opportunity to lodge proofs. Rule 6.79(6) develops the provisions of IA 1986, s. 294. Note the use of Form 6.34 for the purposes of s. 294. For the meaning of "venue" see r. 13.6.

Rule 6.80   Business at first meeting

6.80(1)   [Limitation on resolutions]   At the first meeting of creditors, no resolutions shall be taken other than the following—

(a) a resolution to appoint a named insolvency practitioner to be trustee in bankruptcy or two or more named insolvency practitioners as joint trustees;

(b) a resolution to establish a creditors' committee;

(c) (unless it has been resolved to establish a creditors' committee) a resolution specifying the terms on which the trustee is to be remunerated, or to defer consideration of that matter;

(d) (if, and only if, two or more persons are appointed to act jointly as trustee) a resolution specifying whether acts are to be done by both or all of them, or by only one;

(e) (where the meeting has been requisitioned under section 294) a resolution authorising payment out of the estate, as an expense of the bankruptcy, of the cost of summoning and holding the meeting;

(f) a resolution to adjourn the meeting for not more than 3 weeks;

(g) any other resolution which the chairman thinks it right to allow for special reasons.

6.80(2)   [Further limitation]   No resolution shall be proposed which has for its object the appointment of the official receiver as trustee.

General note

This restricts the agenda of the first meeting of creditors. Note the importance of securing the appointment of a trustee.

Rule 6.81   General power to call meetings

6.81(1)   [General power, "the convener"]   The official receiver or the trustee may at any time summon and conduct meetings of creditors for the purpose of ascertaining their wishes in all matters relating to the bankruptcy.

In relation to any meeting of creditors, the person summoning it is referred to as "the convener".

6.81(2)   [Notice of meeting]   When a venue for the meeting has been fixed, notice of the meeting shall be given by the convener to every creditor who is known to him or is identified in the bankrupt's statement of affairs.

The notice shall be given at least 21 days before the date fixed for the meeting.   [FORM 6.35]

6.81(3)   [Contents of notice]   The notice to creditors shall specify the purpose for which the meeting is summoned, and a time and date (not more than 4 days before the meeting) by which creditors must lodge proxies and those who have not already lodged proofs must do so, in order to be entitled to vote at the meeting.

6.81(4)   [Public advertisement]   Additional notice of the meeting may be given by public advertisement if the convener thinks fit, and shall be so given if the court so orders.

General note

Subsequent meetings of creditors are held normally at the discretion of the official receiver, or trustee (subject to requisitions under r. 6.83).

Rule 6.82   The chairman at a meeting

6.82(1)   [Where convener official receiver]   Where the convener of a meeting is the official receiver, he, or a person nominated by him, shall be chairman.

A nomination under this paragraph shall be in writing, unless the nominee is another official receiver or a deputy official receiver.

6.82(2) **[Where convener other than official receiver]** Where the convener is other than the official receiver, the chairman shall be he, or a person nominated by him in writing to act.

A person nominated under this paragraph must be either—

(a) one who is qualified to act as an insolvency practitioner in relation to the bankrupt, or

(b) an employee of the trustee or his firm who is experienced in insolvency matters.

General note

For the qualification of insolvency practitioners, see IA 1986, Pt. XIII.

Rule 6.83 Requisitioned meetings

6.83(1) **[Documents to accompany creditors' request]** A request by creditors to the official receiver for a meeting of creditors to be summoned shall be accompanied by—

(a) a list of the creditors concurring with the request and the amount of their respective claims in the bankruptcy,

(b) from each creditor concurring, written confirmation of his concurrence, and

(c) a statement of the purpose of the proposed meeting.

Sub-paragraphs (a) and (b) do not apply if the requisitioning creditor's debt is alone sufficient, without the concurrence of other creditors.   [FORM 6.34]

6.83(2) **[Official receiver to fix venue etc.]** The official receiver, if he considers the request to be properly made in accordance with the Act, shall—

(a) fix a venue for the meeting, to take place not more than 35 days from the receipt of the request, and

(b) give 21 days' notice of the meeting, and of the venue for it, to creditors.

6.83(3) **[Application of Rule]** Where a request for a creditors' meeting is made to the trustee, this Rule applies to him as it does to the official receiver.

General note

This qualifies r. 6.81. No minimum level of support is specified here — but see IA 1986, s. 294. For the meaning of "venue" see r. 13.6.

Rule 6.84 Attendance at meetings of bankrupt, etc.

6.84(1) **[Notice to bankrupt]** Whenever a meeting of creditors is summoned, the convener shall give at least 21 days' notice of the meeting to the bankrupt.
[FORM 6.36]

6.84(2) **[Notice of adjournment]** If the meeting is adjourned, the chairman of the meeting shall (unless for any reason it appears to him to be unnecessary or impracticable) give notice of the fact to the bankrupt, if the latter was not himself present at the meeting.

6.84(3) **[Notice that presence required]** The convener may, if he thinks fit, give notice to the bankrupt that he is required to be present, or in attendance.

6.84(4) **[Admission to meetings]** In the case of any meeting, the bankrupt or any other person may, if he has given reasonable notice of his wish to be present, be admitted; but this is at the discretion of the chairman.

The chairman's decision is final as to what (if any) intervention may be made by the bankrupt, or by any other person admitted to the meeting under this paragraph.

6.84(5) **[Adjournment for obtaining attendance]** If the bankrupt is not present, and it is desired to put questions to him, the chairman may adjourn the meeting with a view to obtaining his attendance.

6.84(6) **[Chairman's discretion re questions]** Where the bankrupt is present at a creditors' meeting, only such questions may be put to him as the chairman may in his discretion allow.

General note

This is largely self-explanatory. Form 6.36 is used to notify the bankrupt. Bankrupts may be forced to attend. Note the wide powers of the chairman of the meeting.

Rule 6.85   Notice of meetings by advertisement only

6.85(1) **[Power of court]** In the case of any meeting to be held under the Act or the Rules, the court may order that notice of it be given by public advertisement, and not by individual notice to the persons concerned.

6.85(2) **[Matters for court to consider]** In considering whether to act under this Rule, the court shall have regard to the cost of public advertisement, to the amount of the funds available in the estate, and to the extent of the interest of creditors or any particular class of them.

General note

This is an economy measure that the court may adopt in appropriate circumstances.

Rule 6.86   Venue of meetings

6.86(1) **[Convenience of venue]** In fixing the venue for a meeting of creditors, the person summoning the meeting shall have regard to the convenience of the creditors.

6.86(2) **[Time of meetings]** Meetings shall in all cases be summoned for commencement between the hours of 10.00 and 16.00 hours on a business day, unless the court otherwise directs.

6.86(3) **[Forms of proxy]** With every notice summoning a creditors' meeting there shall be sent out forms of proxy.   [FORM 8.5]

General note

For the meaning of "venue" and "business day" see rr. 13.6 and 13.13(1).

Rule 6.87   Expenses of summoning meetings

6.87(1) **[Security for payment of expenses]** Subject to paragraph (3) below, the expenses of summoning and holding a meeting of creditors at the instance of any person other than the official receiver or the trustee shall be paid by that person, who shall deposit security for their payment with the trustee or, if no trustee has been appointed, with the official receiver.

6.87(2)   [Appropriate security]   The sum to be deposited shall be such as the trustee or (as the case may be) the official receiver determines to be appropriate; and neither shall act without the deposit having been made.

6.87(3)   [Vote for expenses to be paid out of estate]   Where a meeting is so summoned, it may vote that the expenses of summoning and holding it shall be payable out of the estate, as an expense of the bankruptcy.

6.87(4)   [Repayment of deposit]   To the extent that any deposit made under this Rule is not required for the payment of expenses of summoning and holding the meeting, it shall be repaid to the person who made it.

General note

This serves as a deterrent to persons wishing to requisition meetings under r. 6.83.

Rule 6.88   Resolutions

6.88(1)   [Resolution passed by majority in value]   Subject as follows, at a meeting of creditors, a resolution is passed when a majority (in value) of those present and voting, in person or by proxy, have voted in favour of the resolution.

6.88(2)   [Resolution for appointment of trustee]   In the case of a resolution for the appointment of a trustee—

    (a) if on any vote there are two nominees for appointment, the person who obtains the most support is appointed, provided that such support represents a majority in value of all those present (in person or by proxy) at the meeting and entitled to vote;

    (b) if there are three or more nominees, and one of them has a clear majority over both or all the others together, that one is appointed; and

    (c) in any other case the chairman shall continue to take votes (disregarding at each vote any nominee who has withdrawn and, if no nominee has withdrawn, the nominee who obtained the least support last time), until a clear majority is obtained for any one nominee.

6.88(3)   [Resolution for joint appointment]   The chairman may at any time put to the meeting a resolution for the joint appointment of any two or more nominees.

6.88(4)   [Resolution affecting trustee etc.]   Where a resolution is proposed which affects a person in respect of his remuneration or conduct as trustee, or as proposed or former trustee, the vote of that person, and of any partner or employee of his, shall not be reckoned in the majority required for passing the resolution.

This paragraph applies with respect to a vote given by a person (whether personally or on his behalf by a proxy-holder) either as creditor or as proxy-holder for a creditor (but subject to Rule 8.6 in Part 8 of the Rules).

History note

In r. 6.88(1) the words "Subject as follows," were inserted by I(A)R 1987 (SI 1987 No. 1919), r. 3(1), Sch., Pt. 1, para. 107(1) as from 11 January 1988.

In r. 6.88(2)(*a*) the words from "provided that" to the end were added by I(A)R 1987 (SI 1987 No. 1919), r. 3(1), Sch., Pt. 1, para. 107(2) as from 11 January 1988.

In the second paragraph of r. 6.88(4) the words "(whether personally or on his behalf by a proxy-holder)" were inserted and the word "proxy-holder" was substituted for the former word "proxy" by I(A)R 1987 (SI 1987 No. 1919), r. 3(1), Sch., Pt. 1, para. 107(3) as from 11 January 1988.

General note

Simple majorities are required to pass resolutions.

Rule 6.89   Chairman of meeting as proxy-holder

6.89   Where the chairman at a meeting holds a proxy for a creditor, which requires him to vote for a particular resolution, and no other person proposes that resolution—

(a) he shall himself propose it, unless he considers that there is good reason for not doing so, and

(b) if he does not propose it, he shall forthwith after the meeting notify his principal of the reason why not.

Rule 6.90   Suspension of meeting

6.90   Once only in the course of any meeting, the chairman may, in his discretion and without an adjournment, declare the meeting suspended for any period up to one hour.

Rule 6.91   Adjournment

6.91(1)   [At chairman's discretion]   The chairman at any meeting may, in his discretion, and shall if the meeting so resolves, adjourn it to such time and place as seems to him to be appropriate in the circumstances.

This is subject to Rule 6.129(3) in a case where the trustee or his nominee is chairman and a resolution has been proposed for the trustee's removal.

6.91(2)   [Adjournment if inquorate]   If within a period of 30 minutes from the time appointed for the commencement of a meeting a quorum is not present, then the chairman may, at his discretion, adjourn the meeting to such time and place as he may appoint.

6.91(3)   [Period of adjournment]   An adjournment under this Rule shall not be for a period of more than 21 days; and Rule 6.86(1) and (2) applies with regard to the venue of the adjourned meeting.

6.91(4)   [If no chairman]   If there is no person present to act as chairman, some other person present (being entitled to vote) may make the appointment under paragraph (2), with the agreement of others present (being persons so entitled).

Failing agreement, the adjournment shall be to the same time and place in the next following week or, if that is not a business day, to the business day immediately following.

6.91(5) [Use of proof and proxies at adjourned meeting] Where a meeting is adjourned under this Rule, proofs and proxies may be used if lodged at any time up to midday on the business day immediately before the adjourned meeting.

History note

In r. 6.91(2) the words from "the chairman may" to the end were substituted by I(A)R 1987 (SI 1987 No. 1919), r. 3(1), Sch., Pt. 1, para. 108 as from 11 January 1988: the former words read as follows:

> "by virtue of this Rule the meeting stands adjourned to such time and place as may be appointed by the chairman."

General note

For the meaning of "venue" and "business day" see rr. 13.6 and 13.13(1).
  Rule 6.91(2) was amended to allow the chairman discretion to adjourn.

Rule 6.92 Quorum

6.92 (Omitted by the Insolvency (Amendment) Rules 1987 (S.I. 1987 No. 1919), r. 3(1), Sch., Pt. 1, para. 109 as from 11 January 1988).

History note

Rule 6.92 formerly read as follows:

> "**6.92(1)** A creditors' meeting is not competent to act for any purpose, except—
>
>   (a) the election of a chairman,
>   (b) the admission by the chairman of creditors' proofs, for the purpose of their entitlement to vote, and
>   (c) the adjournment of the meeting,
>
> unless there are present in person or by proxy at least 3 creditors, or all the creditors, if their number does not exceed 3, being in either case persons entitled to vote.
>
> **6.92(2)** One person present constitutes a quorum if—
>
>   (a) he is himself a creditor with entitlement to vote and he holds a number of proxies sufficient to ensure that, with his own vote, paragraph (1) of this Rule is complied with, or
>   (b) being the chairman or any other person, he holds that number of proxies."

General note

See now r. 12.4A.

Rule 6.93 Entitlement to vote

6.93(1) [Conditions for voting] Subject as follows, at a meeting of creditors a person is entitled to vote as a creditor only if—

  (a) there has been duly lodged, by the time and date stated in the notice of the meeting, a proof of the debt claimed to be due to him from the bankrupt, and the claim has been admitted under Rule 6.94 for the purpose of entitlement to vote, and
  (b) there has been lodged, by that time and date, any proxy requisite for that entitlement.

6.93(2) **[Powers of court]**   The court may, in exceptional circumstances, by order declare the creditors, or any class of them, entitled to vote at creditors' meetings, without being required to prove their debts.

Where a creditor is so entitled, the court may, on the application of the trustee, make such consequential orders as it thinks fit (as for example an order treating a creditor as having proved his debt for the purpose of permitting payment of dividend).

6.93(3) **[Limitation on voting]**   A creditor shall not vote in respect of a debt for an unliquidated amount, or any debt whose value is not ascertained, expect where the chairman agrees to put upon the debt an estimated minimum value for the purpose of entitlement to vote and admits his proof for that purpose.

6.93(4) **[Secured creditor]**   A secured creditor is entitled to vote only in respect of the balance (if any) of his debt after deducting the value of his security as estimated by him.

6.93(5) **[Further limitation on voting]**   A creditor shall not vote in respect of a debt on, or secured by, a current bill of exchange or promissory note, unless he is willing—

    (a) to treat the liability to him on the bill or note of every person who is liable on it antecedently to the bankrupt, and against whom a bankruptcy order has not been made (or, in the case of a company, which has not gone into liquidation), as a security in his hands, and

    (b) to estimate the value of the security and (for the purpose of entitlement to vote, but not for dividend) to deduct it from his proof.

General note

As a general rule, only creditors who have lodged proofs which have been admitted can vote. Note the special rules for persons claiming unliquidated amounts, etc.

Rule 6.94   Admission and rejection of proof

6.94(1) **[Power of chairman]**   At any creditors' meeting the chairman has power to admit or reject a creditor's proof for the purpose of his entitlement to vote; and the power is exercisable with respect to the whole or any part of the proof.

6.94(2) **[Appeal from chairman's decision]**   The chairman's decision under this Rule, or in respect of any matter arising under Rule 6.93, is subject to appeal to the court by any creditor, or by the bankrupt.

6.94(3) **[Voting subject to objection]**   If the chairman is in doubt whether a proof should be admitted or rejected, he shall mark it as objected to and allow the creditor to vote, subject to his vote being subsequently declared invalid if the objection to the proof is sustained.

6.94(4) **[If chairman's decision reversed etc.]**   If on an appeal the chairman's decision is reversed or varied, or a creditor's vote is declared invalid, the court may order that another meeting be summoned, or make such other order as it thinks just.

6.94(5) **[Costs re application]**   Neither the official receiver nor any person nominated by him to be chairman is personally liable for costs incurred by any person in respect of an application to the court under this Rule; and the chairman (if other than the official receiver or a person so nominated) is not so liable unless the court makes an order to that effect.

General note

Admission of proofs is a matter for the chairman (subject to an appeal to the court).

Rule 6.95   Record of proceedings

6.95(1)   [Minutes of proceedings]   The chairman at any creditors' meeting shall cause minutes of the proceedings at the meeting, signed by him, to be retained by him as part of the records of the bankruptcy.

6.95(2)   [List of creditors attending]   He shall also cause to be made up and kept a list of all the creditors who attended the meeting.

6.95(3)   [Record of resolutions]   The minutes of the meeting shall include a record of every resolution passed; and it is the chairman's duty to see to it that particulars of all such resolutions, certified by him, are filed in court not more than 21 days after the date of the meeting.

Chapter 8 — Proof of Bankruptcy Debts

SECTION A: PROCEDURE FOR PROVING

Rule 6.96   Meaning of "prove"

6.96(1)   [Claim to be submitted in writing etc.]   A person claiming to be a creditor of the bankrupt and wishing to recover his debt in whole or in part must (subject to any order of the court under Rule 6.93(2)) submit his claim in writing to the official receiver, where acting as receiver and manager, or to the trustee.

6.96(2)   ["Proving" and "proof"]   The creditor is referred to as **"proving"** for his debt; and the document by which he seeks to establish his claim is his **"proof"**.

6.96(3)   ["Proof of debt"]   Subject to the next two paragraphs, the proof must be in the form known as **"proof of debt"** (whether the form prescribed by the Rules, or a substantially similar form), which shall be made out by or under the directions of the creditor, and signed by him or a person authorised in that behalf.   [FORM 6.37]

6.96(4)   [Debt due to Crown etc.]   Where a debt is due to a Minister of the Crown or a Government Department, the proof need not be in that form, provided that there are shown all such particulars of the debt as are required in the form used by other creditors, and as are relevant in the circumstances.

6.96(5)   [Proof under s. 335(5)]   Where an existing trustee proves in a later bankruptcy under section 335(5), the proof must be in Form 6.38.   [FORM 6.38]

6.96(6)   [Proof in form of affidavit]   In certain circumstances, specified below in this Chapter, the proof must be in the form of an affidavit.   [FORM 6.39]

General note
This supplements IA 1986, s. 322.

Rule 6.97   Supply of forms

6.97(1)   [Forms to be sent to every creditor]   Forms of proof shall be sent out by the official receiver or the trustee to every creditor of the bankrupt who is known to the sender, or is identified in the bankrupt's statement of affairs.

6.97(2)   [Forms to accompany first notice]   The forms shall accompany (whichever is first)—

(a) the notice to creditors under section 293(2) (official receiver's decision not to call meeting of creditors), or

(b) the first notice calling a meeting of creditors, or

(c) where a certificate of summary administration has been issued by the court, the notice sent by the official receiver under Rule 6.49(2), or

(d) where a trustee is appointed by the court, the notice of his appointment sent by him to creditors.

6.97(3)   [Where trustee advertises his appointment]   Where, with leave of the court under section 297(7), the trustee advertises his appointment, he shall send proofs to the creditors within 4 months after the date of the bankruptcy order.

6.97(4)   [Rule subject to order of court]   The above paragraphs of this Rule are subject to any order of the court dispensing with the requirement to send out forms of proof, or altering the time at which the forms are to be sent.

History note
In r. 6.97(1) the words "of proof" were substituted for the former words "to be used for the purpose of proving bankruptcy debts" by I(A)R 1987 (SI 1987 No. 1919), r. 3(1), Sch., Pt. 1, para. 110 as from 11 January 1988.

General note
Rule 6.97(1) was amended to make it clear that forms of proof can be in a mode other than that prescribed.

Rule 6.98   Contents of proof

6.98(1)   [Matters to be stated]   Subject to Rule 6.96(4), the following matters shall be stated in a creditor's proof of debt—

(a) the creditor's name and address;

(b) the total amount of his claim as at the date of the bankruptcy order;

(c) whether or not that amount includes outstanding uncapitalised interest;

(d) whether or not the claim includes value added tax;

(e) whether the whole or any part of the debt falls within any (and if so which) of the categories of preferential debts under section 386 of, and Schedule 6 to, the Act (as read with Schedule 3 to the Social Security Pensions Act 1975);

(f) particulars of how and when the debt was incurred by the debtor;

(g) particulars of any security held, the date when it was given and the value which the creditor puts upon it; and

(h) the name, address and authority of the person signing the proof (if other than the creditor himself).

6.98(2) **[Specified documents]** There shall be specified in the proof any documents by reference to which the debt can be substantiated; but (subject as follows) it is not essential that such documents be attached to the proof or submitted with it.

6.98(3) **[Production of documents etc.]** The trustee, or the convener or chairman of any meeting, may call for any document or other evidence to be produced to him, where he thinks it necessary for the purpose of substantiating the whole or any part of the claim made in the proof.

History note

In r. 6.98(1) the words "Subject to Rule 6.96(4)," were inserted by I(A)R 1987 (SI 1987 No. 1919), r. 3(1), Sch., Pt. 1, para. 111 as from 11 January 1988.

General note

Rule 6.98(1) was qualified by I(A)R 1987 to deal with forms of proof submitted by Government Departments by specifically referring to r. 6.96(4).

Rule 6.99 Claim established by affidavit

6.99(1) **[Trustee may require "affidavit of debt"]** The trustee may, if he thinks it necessary, require a claim of debt to be verified by affidavit, for which purpose there shall be used the form known as **"affidavit of debt"**. [FORM 6.39]

6.99(2) **[In addition to proof]** An affidavit may be required notwithstanding that a proof of debt has already been lodged.

6.99(3) **[Swearing of affidavit]** The affidavit may be sworn before an official receiver or a deputy official receiver, or before an officer of the Department or of the court duly authorised in that behalf.

General note

Affidavits of debt (see Form 6.39) may be required to support proofs. "Department" is defined in r. 13.13(2).

Rule 6.100 Cost of proving

6.100(1) **[Creditor bears cost of proving own debt]** Subject as follows, every creditor bears the cost of proving his own debt, including such as may be incurred in providing documents or evidence under Rule 6.98(3).

6.100(2)   [Trustee's costs]   Costs incurred by the trustee in estimating the value of a bankruptcy debt under section 322(3) (debts not bearing a certain value) fall on the estate, as an expense of the bankruptcy.

6.100(3)   [Application of rr. 6.100(1), (2)]   Paragraphs (1) and (2) apply unless the court otherwise orders.

Rule 6.101   Trustee to allow inspection of proofs

6.101   The trustee shall, so long as proofs lodged with him are in his hands, allow them to be inspected, at all reasonable times on any business day, by any of the following persons—

    (a) any creditor who has submitted his proof of debt (unless his proof has been wholly rejected for purposes of dividend or otherwise),

    (b) the bankrupt, and

    (c) any person acting on behalf of either of the above.

General note

Proofs are available for inspection by the creditors and the bankrupt and their representatives.

Rule 6.102   Proof of licensed moneylender

6.102   A proof of debt in respect of a moneylending transaction made before 27th January 1980, where the creditor was at the time of the transaction a licensed moneylender, shall have endorsed on or annexed to it a statement setting out in detail the particulars mentioned in section 9(2) of the Moneylenders Act 1927.

General note

Compare BR 1952, r. 251.

Rule 6.103   Transmissions of proofs to trustee

6.103(1)   [On trustee's appointment]   Where a trustee is appointed, the official receiver shall forthwith transmit to him all the proofs which he has so far received, together with an itemised list of them.

6.103(2)   [Receipt for proofs]   The trustee shall sign the list by way of receipt for the proofs, and return it to the official receiver.

6.103(3)   [All later proofs to trustee]   From then on, all proofs of debt shall be sent to the trustee and retained by him.

General note

This deals with the transfer of responsibilities from the official receiver to the trustee.

Rule 6.104   Admission and rejection of proofs for dividend

6.104(1)   [Admission]   A proof may be admitted for dividend either for the whole amount claimed by the creditor, or for part of that amount.

6.104(2)   [Rejection]   If the trustee rejects a proof in whole or in part, he shall prepare a written statement of his reasons for doing so, and send it forthwith to the creditor.

General note
For dividend distributions see IA 1986, s. 324. Note also Pt. 11 of the rules.

Rule **6.105**   Appeal against decision on proof

6.105(1)   [Application by creditor]   If a creditor is dissatisfied with the trustee's decision with respect to his proof (including any decision on the question of preference), he may apply to the court for the decision to be reversed or varied.

The application must be made within 21 days of his receiving the statement sent under Rule 6.104(2).

6.105(2)   [Application by bankrupt etc.]   The bankrupt or any other creditor may, if dissatisfied with the trustee's decision admitting or rejecting the whole or any part of a proof, make such an application within 21 days of becoming aware of the trustee's decision.

6.105(3)   [Venue and notice]   Where application is made to the court under this Rule, the court shall fix a venue for the application to be heard, notice of which shall be sent by the applicant to the creditor who lodged the proof in question (if it is not himself) and to the trustee.

6.105(4)   [Relevant proof etc. to be filed in court]   The trustee shall, on receipt of the notice, file in court the relevant proof, together (if appropriate) with a copy of the statement sent under Rule 6.104(2).

6.105(5)   [Return of proof]   After the application has been heard and determined, the proof shall, unless it has been wholly disallowed, be returned by the court to the trustee.

6.105(6)   [Costs re application]   The official receiver is not personally liable for costs incurred by any person in respect of an application under this Rule; and the trustee (if other than the official receiver) is not so liable unless the court makes an order to that effect.

General note
Rejection of proof under r. 6.104 may be appealed against to the court. For the meaning of "venue" in r. 6.105(3) see r. 13.6.

Rule **6.106**   Withdrawal or variation of proof

6.106   A creditor's proof may at any time, by agreement between himself and the trustee, be withdrawn or varied as to the amount claimed.

Rule **6.107**   Expunging of proof by the court

6.107(1)   [Expunging or reduction of amount]   The court may expunge a proof or reduce the amount claimed—

(a) on the trustee's application, where he thinks that the proof has been improperly admitted, or ought to be reduced; or

(b) on the application of a creditor, if the trustee declines to interfere in the matter.

6.107(2) **[Venue and notice]** Where application is made to the court under this Rule, the court shall fix a venue for the application to be heard, notice of which shall be sent by the applicant—

(a) in the case of an application by the trustee, to the creditor who made the proof, and

(b) in the case of an application by a creditor, to the trustee and to the creditor who made the proof (if not himself).

General note

For the meaning of "venue" in r. 6.107(2) see r. 13.6.

SECTION B: QUANTIFICATION OF CLAIM

Rule **6.108**　Negotiable instruments, etc.

6.108 Unless the trustee allows, a proof in respect of money owed on a bill of exchange, promissory note, cheque or other negotiable instrument or security cannot be admitted unless there is produced the instrument or security itself or a copy of it, certified by the creditor or his authorised representative to be a true copy.

Rule **6.109**　Secured creditors

6.109(1) **[Proving for balance of debt]** If a secured creditor realises his security, he may prove for the balance of his debt, after deducting the amount realised.

6.109(2) **[Proving for whole debt]** If a secured creditor voluntarily surrenders his security for the general benefit of creditors, he may prove for his whole debt, as if it were unsecured.

General note

This should be viewed in the light of IA 1986, ss. 269 and 383(2), and also rr. 6.15–6.19. For a useful discussion of the operation of this rule see Anderson (1989) 5 I L & P 180.

Rule **6.110**　Discounts

6.110 There shall in every case be deducted from the claim all trade and other discounts which would have been available to the bankrupt but for his bankruptcy, except any discount for immediate, early or cash settlement.

Rule **6.111**　Debt in foreign currency

6.111(1) **[Conversion into sterling]** For the purpose of proving a debt incurred or payable in a currency other than sterling, the amount of the debt shall be converted into sterling at the official exchange rate prevailing on the date of the bankruptcy order.

6.111(2)   ["The official exchange rate"]   **"The official exchange rate"**   is the middle market rate at the Bank of England, as published for the date in question. In the absence of any such published rate, it is such rate as the court determines.

General note

A similar rule applies in company law – *Re Dynamics Corporation of America (No. 2)* [1976] 1 WLR 757. Note that conversion into sterling under r. 6.111(1) is not required at the stage when a statutory demand is presented – see the ruling of Morritt J in *Re A Debtor (51/SD/1991)* [1992] 1 WLR 1294.

Rule 6.112   Payments of a periodical nature

6.112(1)   [Rent etc.]   In the case of rent and other payments of a periodical nature, the creditor may prove for any amounts due and unpaid up to the date of the bankruptcy order.

6.112(2)   [If accruing from day to day]   Where at that date any payment was accruing due, the creditor may prove for so much as would have fallen due at that date, if accruing from day to day.

Rule 6.113   Interest

6.113(1)   [Where claim may include interest]   In the following circumstances the creditor's claim may include interest on the debt for periods before the bankruptcy order, although not previously reserved or agreed.

6.113(2)   [Debt due by written instrument]   If the debt is due by virtue of a written instrument and payable at a certain time, interest may be claimed for the period from that time to the date of the bankruptcy order.

6.113(3)   [Debt due otherwise]   If the debt is due otherwise, interest may only be claimed if, before the presentation of the bankruptcy petition, a demand for payment was made in writing by or on behalf of the creditor, and notice given that interest would be payable from the date of the demand to the date of payment and for all the purposes of the Act and the Rules shall be chargeable at a rate not exceeding that mentioned in paragraph (5).

6.113(4)   [Period of claim]   Interest under paragraph (3) may only be claimed for the period from the date of the demand to that of the bankruptcy order.

6.113(5)   [Rate of interest]   The rate of interest to be claimed under paragraphs (2) and (3) is the rate specified in section 17 of the Judgments Act 1838 on the date of the bankruptcy order.

History note

In r. 6.113(3) the words from "and for all the purposes" to the end were added by I(A)R 1987 (SI 1987 No. 1919), r. 3(1), Sch., Pt. 1, para. 112(1) as from 11 January 1988.
   Rules 6.113(4) and (5) were substituted for the former second paragraph of r. 6.113(3) and

the former r. 6.113(4) by I(A)R (SI 1987 No. 1919), r. 3(1), Sch., Pt. 1, para. 112(2) as from 11 January 1988: the former second paragraph of r. 6.113(3) and r. 6.113(4) read as follows:

> "In that case interest may be claimed under this Rule for the period from the date of the demand to that of the bankruptcy order.
>
> **6.113(4)** The rate of interest to be claimed under this Rule is the rate specified in section 17 of the Judgments Act 1838 on the date of the bankruptcy order; except that, where the case falls within paragraph (3), the rate is that specified in the notice there referred to, not exceeding the rate under the Judgments Act as mentioned above."

General note

For further guidance on claims in respect of interest, see IA 1986, s. 328(4), (5).

     Rule 6.113 was amended to limit the rate of interest that may be claimed. See also r. 4.93. This is achieved by qualifying r. 6.113(3) and replacing r. 6.113(4).

Rule **6.114**   Debt payable at future time

6.114   A creditor may prove for a debt of which payment was not yet due at the date of the bankruptcy order, but subject to Rule 11.13 in Part 11 of the Rules (adjustment of dividend where payment made before time).

Chapter 9 — Secured Creditors

Rule **6.115**   Value of security

6.115(1)   **[Altering value]**   A secured creditor may, with the agreement of the trustee or the leave of the court, at any time alter the value which he has, in his proof of debt, put upon his security.

6.115(2)   **[Limitation on re-valuation]**   However, if a secured creditor—

    (a) being the petitioner, has in the petition put a value on his security, or

    (b) has voted in respect of the unsecured balance of his debt,

he may re-value his security only with leave of the court.

(See general note after r. 6.119.)

Rule **6.116**   Surrender for non-disclosure

6.116(1)   **[Omission to disclose security]**   If a secured creditor omits to disclose his security in his proof of debt, he shall surrender his security for the general benefit of creditors, unless the court, on application by him, relieves him from the effect of this Rule on the ground that the omission was inadvertent or the result of honest mistake.

6.116(2)   **[Relief from effect of r. 6.116(1)]**   If the court grants that relief, it may require or allow the creditor's proof of debt to be amended, on such terms as may be just.

(See general note after r. 6.119.)

Rule 6.117   Redemption by trustee

6.117(1)   [Notice of proposed redemption]   The trustee may at any time give notice to a creditor whose debt is secured that he proposes, at the expiration of 28 days from the date of the notice, to redeem the security at the value put upon it in the creditor's proof.

6.117(2)   [Time for re-valuation]   The creditor then has 21 days (or such longer period as the trustee may allow) in which, if he so wishes, to exercise his right to re-value his security (with the leave of the court, where Rule 6.115(2) applies).

If the creditor re-values his security, the trustee may only redeem at the new value.

6.117(3)   [If trustee redeems]   If the trustee redeems the security, the cost of transferring it is borne by the estate.

6.117(4)   [Notice to trustee to elect etc.]   A secured creditor may at any time, by a notice in writing, call on the trustee to elect whether he will or will not exercise his power to redeem the security at the value then placed on it; and the trustee then has 6 months in which to exercise the power or determine not to exercise it.

(See general note after r. 6.119.)

Rule 6.118   Test of security's value

6.118(1)   [Offer for sale]   Subject as follows, the trustee, if he is dissatisfied with the value which a secured creditor puts on his security (whether in his proof or by way of re-valuation under Rule 6.117), may require any property comprised in the security to be offered for sale.

6.118(2)   [Terms of sale]   The terms of sale shall be such as may be agreed, or as the court may direct; and if the sale is by auction, the trustee on behalf of the estate, and the creditor on his own behalf, may appear and bid.

6.118(3)   [Non-application of Rule]   This Rule does not apply if the security has been re-valued and the re-valuation has been approved by the court.

(See general note after r. 6.119.)

Rule 6.119   Realisation of security by creditor

6.119   If a creditor who has valued his security subsequently realises it (whether or not at the instance of the trustee)—

(a) the net amount realised shall be substituted for the value previously put by the creditor on the security, and

(b) that amount shall be treated in all respects as an amended valuation made by him.

General note to rr. 6.115–6.119

These rules relate to secured creditors. Revaluation of security is permitted, subject to certain restrictions. Non-disclosure of security can lead to it being forfeited. Security may be redeemed by the trustee. If the secured creditor realises his security, the original valuation is replaced by the amount of the net proceeds of realisation.

Chapter 10 — The Trustee in Bankruptcy

SECTION A: APPOINTMENT AND ASSOCIATED FORMALITIES

Rule 6.120　Appointment by creditors' meeting

6.120(1)　[Application of Rule]　This Rule applies where a person has been appointed trustee by resolution of a creditors' meeting.

6.120(2)　[Certification of appointment]　The chairman of the meeting shall certify the appointment, but not unless and until the person to be appointed has provided him with a written statement to the effect that he is an insolvency practitioner, duly qualified under the Act to act as trustee in relation to the bankrupt, and that he consents so to act.　　　　　　　　　　　　　　　　　　　　[FORM 6.40]
or [FORM 6.41]

6.120(3)　[Date when appointment effective]　The trustee's appointment is effective from the date on which the appointment is certified, that date to be endorsed on the certificate.

6.120(4)　[Certificate to official receiver]　The chairman of the meeting (if not himself the official receiver) shall send the certificate to the official receiver.

6.120(5)　[Certificate to trustee, copy to be filed]　The official receiver shall in any case send the certificate to the trustee and file a copy of it in court.

History note

Rules 6.120(3), (4) and (5) were substituted for the former rr. 6.120(3) and (4) by I(A)R 1987 (SI 1987 No 1919), r. 3(1), Sch., Pt. 1, para. 113 as from 11 January 1988: the former rr. 6.120(3) and (4) read as follows:

"**6.120(3)**　The chairman (if not himself the official receiver) shall send the certificate to the official receiver.
6.120(4)　The official receiver shall in any case file a copy of the certificate in court; and the trustee's appointment is effective as from the date on which the official receiver files the copy certificate in court, that date to be endorsed on the copy certificate.
The certificate, so endorsed, shall be sent by the official receiver to the trustee."

General note

This supplements IA 1986, s. 293.
Rules 6.120(3)–(5) were substituted to facilitate handovers to insolvency practitioners.

Rule 6.121　Appointment by the court

6.121(1)　[Application of Rule]　This Rule applies where the court under section 297(3), (4) or (5) appoints the trustee.　　　　　　　　　　　　[FORM 6.42]
or [FORM 6.43]

6.121(2) **[Issue of court order]** The court's order shall not issue unless and until the person appointed has filed in court a statement to the effect that he is an insolvency practitioner, duly qualified under the Act to be the trustee, and that he consents so to act.

6.121(3) **[Copies of orders to official receiver etc.]** Thereafter, the court shall send 2 copies of the order to the official receiver. One of the copies shall be sealed, and this shall be sent by him to the person appointed as trustee.

6.121(4) **[Commencement of appointment]** The trustee's appointment takes effect from the date of the order.

General note

This rule should be viewed in the light of IA 1986, s. 297(3), (4), (5). If the court appoints a trustee under these provisions, Forms 6.42 and 6.43 are to be adopted.

Rule 6.122 Appointment by Secretary of State

6.122(1) **[Application of Rule]** This Rule applies where the official receiver—

(a) under section 295 or 300, refers to the Secretary of State the need for an appointment of a trustee, or

(b) under section 296, applies to the Secretary of State to make the appointment.

6.122(2) **[Copies of certificate to official receiver etc.]** If the Secretary of State makes an appointment he shall send two copies of the certificate of appointment to the official receiver, who shall transmit one such copy to the person appointed, and file the other copy in court.

The certificate shall specify the date which the trustee's appointment is to be effective.

General note

This rule clarifies the provisions of IA 1986, ss. 295, 296 and 300.

Rule 6.123 Authentication of trustee's appointment

6.123 Where a trustee is appointed under any of the 3 preceding Rules, a sealed copy of the order of appointment or (as the case may be) a copy of the certificate of his appointment may in any proceedings be adduced as proof that he is duly authorised to exercise the powers and perform the duties of trustee of the bankrupt's estate.

General note

This relates to rr. 6.120–6.122 by providing for the authentication of the trustee's appointment.

Rule 6.124 Advertisement of appointment

6.124(1) **[Where trustee appointed by meeting]** Where the trustee is appointed by a creditors' meeting, he shall, forthwith after receiving his certificate of appointment, give notice of his appointment in such newspaper as he thinks most appropriate for ensuring that it comes to the notice of the bankrupt's creditors.

6.124(2) [Expense of giving notice] The expense of giving the notice shall be borne in the first instance by the trustee; but he is entitled to be reimbursed by the estate, as an expense of the bankruptcy.

The same applies also in the case of the notice or advertisement under section 296(4) (appointment of trustee by Secretary of State), and of the notice or advertisement under section 297(7) (appointment by the court).

General note

The onus is on the trustee to ensure that his appointment is advertised in the newspapers.

Rule **6.125** Hand-over of estate to trustee

6.125(1) [Application of Rule] This Rule applies only where—

- (a) the bankrupt's estate vests in the trustee under Chapter IV of Part IX of the Act, following a period in which the official receiver is the receiver and manager of the estate according to section 287, or
- (b) the trustee is appointed in succession to the official. receiver acting as trustee.

6.125(2) [On trustee's appointment] When the trustee's appointment takes effect, the official receiver shall forthwith do all that is required for putting him into possession of the estate.

6.125(3) [Discharge of balance due to official receiver] On taking possession of the estate, the trustee shall discharge any balance due to the official receiver on account of—

- (a) expenses properly incurred by him and payable under the Act or the Rules, and
- (b) any advances made by him in respect of the estate, together with interest on such advances at the rate specified in section 17 of the Judgments Act 1838 on the date of the bankruptcy order.

6.125(4) [Undertaking to discharge] Alternatively, the trustee may (before taking office) give to the official receiver a written undertaking to discharge any such balance out of the first realisation of assets.

6.125(5) [Official receiver's charge] The official receiver has a charge on the estate in respect of any sums due to him under paragraph (3). But, where the trustee has realised assets with a view to making those payments, the official receiver's charge does not extend in respect of sums deductible by the trustee from the proceeds of realisation, as being expenses properly incurred therein.

6.125(6) [Discharge of guarantees etc.] The trustee shall from time to time out of the realisation of assets discharge all guarantees properly given by the official receiver for the benefit of the estate, and shall pay all the official receiver's expenses.

6.125(7) [Official receiver to give trustee information] The official receiver shall give to the trustee all such information, relating to the affairs of the bankrupt and the course of the bankruptcy, as he (the official receiver) considers to be reasonably required for the effective discharge by the trustee of his duties in relation to the estate.

6.125(8) [Ch. 6 report] The trustee shall also be furnished with any report of the official receiver under Chapter 6 of this Part of the Rules.

General note
See IA 1986, ss. 287 and 306 for the relevant statutory provisions here.

SECTION B: RESIGNATION AND REMOVAL; VACATION OF OFFICE

Rule **6.126** Creditors' meeting to receive trustee's resignation

6.126(1) [Trustee must call meeting etc.] Before resigning his office, the trustee must call a meeting of creditors for the purpose of receiving his resignation. Notice of the meeting shall be sent to the official receiver at the same time as it is sent to creditors.

6.126(2) [Account of trustee's administration] The notice to creditors must be accompanied by an account of the trustee's administration of the bankrupt's estate, including—

(a) a summary of his receipts and payments and

(b) a statement by him that he has reconciled his accounts with that which is held by the Secretary of State in respect of the bankruptcy.

6.126(3) [Grounds for proceedings under Rule] Subject as follows, the trustee may only proceed under this Rule on grounds of ill health or because—

(a) he intends ceasing to be in practice as an insolvency practitioner, or

(b) there is some conflict of interest or change of personal circumstances which precludes or makes impracticable the further discharge by him of the duties of trustee.

6.126(4) [Where joint trustees] Where two or more persons are acting as trustee jointly, any one of them may proceed under this Rule (without prejudice to the continuation in office of the other or others) on the ground that, in his opinion and that of the other or others, it is no longer expedient that there should continue to be the present number of joint trustees.

6.126(5) [If no quorum] If there is no quorum present at the meeting summoned to receive the trustee's resignation, the meeting is deemed to have been held, a resolution is deemed to have been passed that the trustee's resignation be accepted and the creditors are deemed not to have resolved against the trustee having his release.

6.126(6) [Application of r. 6.126(5)] Where paragraph (5) applies any reference in the Rules to a resolution that the trustee's resignation be accepted is replaced by a reference to the making of a written statement, signed by the person who, had there been a quorum present, would have been chairman of the meeting, that no quorum was present and that the trustee may resign.

History note
Rules 6.126(5) and (6) were added by I(A)R 1987 (SI 1987 No. 1919), r. 3(1), Sch., Pt. 1, para. 114 as from 11 January 1988.

General note
The relevant statutory provision here is IA 1986, s. 298(7). Note the restriction in r. 6.126(3) on the grounds for resignation.

Rule 6.127　Action following acceptance of resignation

6.127(1)　[Notice of meeting to indicate purpose etc.]　Where a meeting of creditors is summoned for the purpose of receiving the trustee's resignation, the notice summoning it shall indicate that this is the purpose, or one of the purposes, of the meeting; and the notice shall draw the attention of creditors to Rule 6.135 with respect to the trustee's release.　　　　　　　　　　　　　　　　[FORM 6.35]

6.127(2)　[Copy of notice to official receiver]　A copy of the notice shall at the same time also be sent to the official receiver.

6.127(3)　[Where chairman other than official receiver]　Where the chairman of the meeting is other than the official receiver, and there is passed at the meeting any of the following resolutions—

(a) that the trustee's resignation be accepted,

(b) that a new trustee be appointed,

(c) that the resigning trustee be not given his release,

the chairman shall, within 3 days, send to the official receiver a copy of the resolution.

　　If it has been resolved to accept the trustee's resignation, the chairman shall send to the official receiver a certificate to that effect.　　　　　　　　[FORM 6.44]

6.127(4)　[If creditors resolve to appoint new trustee]　If the creditors have resolved to appoint a new trustee, the certificate of his appointment shall also be sent to the official receiver within that time; and Rule 6.120 above shall be complied with in respect of it.

6.127(5)　[If trustee's resignation accepted]　If the trustee's resignation is accepted, the notice of it required by section 298(7) shall be given by him forthwith after the meeting; and he shall send a copy of the notice to the official receiver.

　　The notice shall be accompanied by a copy of the account sent to creditors under Rule 6.126(2).

6.127(6)　[Copy of notice]　The official receiver shall file a copy of the notice in court.

6.127(7)　[Effective date of resignation]　The trustee's resignation is effective as from the date on which the official receiver files the copy notice in court, that date to be endorsed on the copy notice.

General note
Form 6.44 is to be used by the chairman of the creditors' committee to notify the official receiver of the resignation. The trustee must also notify the court.

Rule 6.128　Leave to resign granted by the court

6.128(1)　[If creditors resolve not to accept resignation]　If at a creditors' meeting summoned to accept the trustee's resignation it is resolved that it be not accepted, the court may, on the trustee's application, make an order giving him leave to resign.   [FORM 6.45]

6.128(2)   [Extent of order under r. 6.128(1)]   The court's order under this Rule may include such provision as it thinks fit with respect to matters arising in connection with the resignation, and shall determine the date from which the trustee's release is effective.

6.128(3)   [Sealed copies of order]   The court shall send two sealed copies of the order to the trustee, who shall send one of the copies forthwith to the official receiver.

6.128(4)   [Copy notice to court and official receiver]   On sending notice of his resignation to the court, as required by section 298(7), the trustee shall send a copy of it to the official receiver.   [FORM 6.46]

General note

This allows the court to accept a trustee's resignation notwithstanding opposition from the creditors.

Rule 6.129   Meeting of creditors to remove trustee

6.129(1)   [Notice]   Where a meeting of creditors is summoned for the purpose of removing the trustee, the notice summoning it shall indicate that this is the purpose, or one of the purposes, of the meeting; and the notice shall draw the attention of creditors to section 299(3) with respect to the trustee's release.   [FORM 6.35]

6.129(2)   [Copy of notice to official receiver]   A copy of the notice shall at the same time also be sent to the official receiver.

6.129(3)   [Chairman, if trustee chairman etc.]   At the meeting, a person other than the trustee or his nominee may be elected to act as chairman; but if the trustee or his nominee is chairman and a resolution has been proposed for the trustee's removal, the chairman shall not adjourn the meeting without the consent of at least one-half (in value) of the creditors present (in person or by proxy) and entitled to vote.

6.129(4)   [Where chairman other than official receiver]   Where the chairman of the meeting is other than the official receiver, and there is passed at the meeting any of the following resolutions—

    (a) that the trustee be removed,

    (b) that a new trustee be appointed,

    (c) that the removed trustee be not given his release,

the chairman shall, within 3 days, send to the official receiver a copy of the resolution.

    If it has been resolved to remove the trustee, the chairman shall send to the official receiver a certificate to that effect.   [FORM 6.47]

6.129(5)   [If creditors resolve to appoint new trustee]   If the creditors have resolved to appoint a new trustee, the certificate of his appointment shall also be sent to the official receiver within that time; and Rule 6.120 shall be complied with in respect of it.

General note

This develops IA 1986, s. 298(1).

Rule 6.130   Court's power to regulate meeting under r. 6.129

6.130   Where a meeting under Rule 6.129 is to be held, or is proposed to be summoned, the court may on the application of any creditor give directions as to the mode of summoning it, the sending out and return of forms of proxy, the conduct of the meeting, and any other matter which appears to the court to require regulation or control.

Rule 6.131   Procedure on removal

6.131(1)   [Certificate of removal to be filed]   Where the creditors have resolved that the trustee be removed, the official receiver shall file the certificate of removal in court.

6.131(2)   [Effective date]   The resolution is effective as from the date on which the official receiver files the certificate of removal in court, and that date shall be endorsed on the certificate.

6.131(3)   [Copy of certificate]   A copy of the certificate, so endorsed, shall be sent by the official receiver to the trustee who has been removed and, if a new trustee has been appointed, to him.

6.131(4)   [Reconciliation of accounts]   The official receiver shall not file the certificate in court until the Secretary of State has certified to him that the removed trustee has reconciled his account with that held by the Secretary of State in respect of the bankruptcy.

Rule 6.132   Removal of trustee by the court

6.132(1)   [Application of Rule]   This Rule applies where application is made to the court for the removal of the trustee, or for an order directing the trustee to summon a meeting of creditors for the purpose of removing him.   [FORM 6.48]

6.132(2)   [Court may dismiss application etc.]   The court may, if it thinks that no sufficient cause is shown for the application, dismiss it; but it shall not do so unless the applicant has had an opportunity to attend the court for an *ex parte* hearing, of which he has been given at least 7 days' notice.

If the application is not dismissed under this paragraph, the court shall fix a venue for it to be heard.

6.132(3)   [Notice etc.]   The applicant shall, at least 14 days before the hearing, send to the trustee and the official receiver notice stating the venue so fixed; and the notice shall be accompanied by a copy of the application, and of any evidence which the applicant intends to adduce in support of it.

6.132(4)   [Costs]   Subject to any contrary order of the court, the costs of the application do not fall on the estate.

6.132(5)   [Where court removes trustee]   Where the court removes the trustee—

   (a) it shall send copies of the order of removal to him and to the official
       receiver;

(b) the order may include such provision as the court thinks fit with respect to matters arising in connection with the removal; and

(c) if the court appoints a new trustee, Rule 6.121 applies.

General note

The court enjoys power to remove trustees under IA 1986, s. 298(1). For the meaning of "venue" in rr. 6.132(2) and (3), see r. 13.6.

Rule 6.133   Removal of trustee by Secretary of State

6.133(1)   [Notice to trustee etc.]   If the Secretary of State decides to remove the trustee, he shall before doing so notify the trustee and the official receiver of his decision and the grounds of it, and specify a period within which the trustee may make representations against implementation of the decision.

6.133(2)   [On removal]   If the Secretary of State directs the removal of the trustee, he shall forthwith—

(a) file notice of his decision in court, and

(b) send notice to the trustee and the official receiver.

6.133(3)   [If trustee removed]   If the trustee is removed by direction of the Secretary of State, the court may make any such order in his case as it would have power to make if he had been removed by itself.

General note

See IA 1986, s. 298(5).

Rule 6.134   Advertisement of resignation or removal

6.134   Where a new trustee is appointed in place of one who has resigned or been removed, the new trustee shall, in the advertisement of his appointment, state that his predecessor has resigned or, as the case may be, been removed and (if it be the case) that he has been given his release.

Rule 6.135   Release of resigning or removed trustee

6.135(1)   [Where trustee's resignation accepted]   Where the trustee's resignation is accepted by a meeting of creditors which has not resolved against his release, he has his release from when his resignation is effective under Rule 6.127.

6.135(2)   [Where trustee removed by meeting]   Where the trustee is removed by a meeting of creditors which has not resolved against his release, the fact of his release shall be stated in the certificate of removal.

6.135(3)   [Application to Secretary of State]   Where—

(a) the trustee resigns, and the creditor's meeting called to receive his resignation has resolved against his release, or

(b) he is removed by a creditors' meeting which has so resolved, or is removed by the court, he must apply to the Secretary of State for his release. [FORM 6.49]

6.135(4) **[Certificate of release]** When the Secretary of State gives the release, he shall certify it accordingly, and send the certificate to the official receiver, to be filed in court.

6.135(5) **[Copy of certificate]** A copy of the certificate shall be sent by the Secretary of State to the former trustee, whose release is effective from the date of the certificate.

(See general note after r. 6.136.)

SECTION C: RELEASE ON COMPLETION OF ADMINISTRATION

Rule 6.136   Release of official receiver

6.136(1) **[Notice of intention]** The official receiver shall, before giving notice to the Secretary of State under section 299(2) (that the administration of the estate is for practical purposes complete), send out notice of his intention to do so to all creditors who have proved their debts, and to the bankrupt.

6.136(2) **[Accompanying summary]** The notice shall in each case be accompanied by a summary of the official receiver's receipts and payments as trustee.

6.136(3) **[Notice to court of date of release]** The Secretary of State, when he has under section 299(2) determined the date from which the official receiver is to have his release, shall give notice to the court that he has done so. The notice shall be accompanied by the summary referred to in paragraph (2).

General note to rr. 6.135, 6.136
These supplement IA 1986, s. 299 (release of trustees).

Rule 6.137   Final meeting of creditors

6.137(1) **[Notice to creditors etc.]** Where the trustee is other than the official receiver, he shall give at least 28 days' notice of the final meeting of creditors to be held under section 331. The notice shall be sent to all creditors who have proved their debts, and to the bankrupt. [FORM 6.35]

6.137(2) **[Trustee's report]** The trustee's report laid before the meeting under that section shall include—

    (a) a summary of his receipts and payments, and

    (b) a statement by him that he has reconciled his account with that which is held by the Secretary of State in respect of the bankruptcy.

6.137(3) **[Questioning of trustee]** At the final meeting, the creditors may question the trustee with respect to any matter contained in his report, and may resolve against him having his release.

6.137(4) **[Notice to court]** The trustee shall give notice to the court that the final meeting has been held; and the notice shall state whether or not he has given his release, and be accompanied by a copy of the report laid before the final meeting. A copy of the notice shall be sent by the trustee to the official receiver.   [FORM 6.50]

6.137(5)   [No quorum at final meeting]   If there is no quorum present at the final meeting, the trustee shall report to the court that a final meeting was summoned in accordance with the Rules, but there was no quorum present; and the final meeting is then deemed to have been held, and the creditors not to have resolved against the trustee having his release.

6.137(6)   [Release of trustee]   If the creditors at the final meeting have not so resolved, the trustee is released when the notice under paragraph (4) is filed in court. If they have so resolved, the trustee must obtain his release from the Secretary of State, as provided by Rule 6.135.

General note

See IA 1986, s. 331. 28 days' notice of the final meeting must be given.

SECTION D: REMUNERATION

Rule 6.138   Fixing of remuneration

6.138(1)   [Entitlement to remuneration]   The trustee is entitled to receive remuneration for his services as such.

6.138(2)   [How fixed]   The remuneration shall be fixed either—

    (a) as a percentage of the value of the assets in the bankrupt's estate which are realised or distributed, or of the one value and the other in combination, or

    (b) by reference to the time properly given by the insolvency practitioner (as trustee) and his staff in attending to matters arising in the bankruptcy.

6.138(3)   [Determination under r. 6.138(2)]   Where the trustee is other than the official receiver, it is for the creditors' committee (if there is one) to determine whether his remuneration is to be fixed under paragraph (2)(a) or (b) and, if under paragraph (2)(a), to determine any percentage to be applied as there mentioned.

6.138(4)   [Matters relevant to r. 6.138(3) determination]   In arriving at that determination, the committee shall have regard to the following matters—

    (a) the complexity (or otherwise) of the case,

    (b) any respects in which, in connection with the administration of the estate, there falls on the insolvency practitioner (as trustee) any responsibility of an exceptional kind or degree,

    (c) the effectiveness with which the insolvency practitioner appears to be carrying out, or to have carried out, his duties as trustee, and

    (d) the value and nature of the assets in the estate with which the trustee has to deal.

6.138(5)   [If no committee or no determination]   If there is no creditors' committee, or the committee does not make the requisite determination, the trustee's remuneration may be fixed (in accordance with paragraph (2)) by a resolution of a meeting of creditors; and paragraph (4) applies to them as it does to the creditors' committee.

6.138(6) **[Otherwise fixed]**   If not fixed as above, the trustee's remuneration shall be on the scale laid down for the official receiver by general regulations.

General note

The IA 1986 is silent on the question of the trustee's remuneration. This provision lays down the general rules for determining the rate of remuneration by the creditors' committee. Compare BR 1952, rr. 335–337. For the meaning of "general regulations" in r. 6.138(6), see r. 13.13(5).

Rule 6.139   Other matters affecting remuneration

6.139(1) **[Where trustee sells for secured creditor]**   Where the trustee sells assets on behalf of a secured creditor, he is entitled to take for himself, out of the proceeds of sale, a sum by way of remuneration equivalent to the remuneration chargeable in corresponding circumstances by the official receiver under general regulations.

6.139(2) **[Where joint trustees]**   Where there are joint trustees, it is for them to agree between themselves as to how the remuneration payable should be apportioned. Any dispute arising between them may be referred—

    (a) to the court, for settlement by order, or

    (b) to the creditors' committee or a meeting of creditors, for settlement by resolution.

6.139(3) **[If trustee is a solicitor]**   If the trustee is a solicitor and employs his own firm, or any partner in it, to act on behalf of the estate, profit costs shall not be paid unless this is authorised by the creditors' committee, the creditors or the court.

Rule 6.139(1)

This relates to remuneration where the trustee is really acting for the benefit of a secured creditor.

Rule 6.140   Recourse of trustee to meeting of creditors

6.140   If the trustee's remuneration has been fixed by the creditors' committee, and he considers the rate or amount to be insufficient, he may request that it be increased by resolution of the creditors.

General note

The creditors can override any decision of their committee on remuneration.

Rule 6.141   Recourse to the court

6.141(1) **[Trustee may apply to court]**   If the trustee considers that the remuneration fixed for him by the creditors' committee, or by resolution of the creditors, or as under Rule 6.138(6), is insufficient, he may apply to the court for an order increasing its amount or rate.

6.141(2) **[Notice to committee etc.]** The trustee shall give at least 14 days' notice of his application to the members of the creditors' committee; and the committee may nominate one or more members to appear or be represented, and to be heard, on the application.

6.141(3) **[If no committee]** If there is no creditors' committee, the trustee's notice of his application shall be sent to such one or more of the bankrupt's creditors as the court may direct, which creditors may nominate one or more of their number to appear or be represented.

6.141(4) **[Costs of application]** The court may, if it appears to be a proper case, order the costs of the trustee's application, including the costs of any member of the creditors' committee appearing or being represented on it, or any creditor so appearing or being represented, to be paid out of the estate.

History note

In r. 6.141(4) the words "or being represented" in both places where they occur were inserted by I(A)R 1987 (SI 1987 No. 1919), r. 3(1), Sch., Pt. 1, para. 115 as from 11 January 1988.

(See general note after r. 6.142.)

Rule 6.142 Creditor's claim that remuneration is excessive

6.142(1) **[Creditor may apply to court]** Any creditor of the bankrupt may, with the concurrence of at least 25 per cent. in value of the creditors (including himself), apply to the court for an order that the trustee's remuneration be reduced, on the grounds that it is, in all the circumstances, excessive.

6.142(2) **[Court may dismiss application etc.]** The court may, if it thinks that no sufficient cause is shown for the application, dismiss it; but it shall not do so unless the applicant has had an opportunity to attend the court for an *ex parte* hearing, of which he has been given at least 7 days' notice.

If the application is not dismissed under this paragraph, the court shall fix a venue for it to be heard.

6.142(3) **[Notice to trustee]** The applicant shall, at least 14 days before the hearing, send to the trustee a notice stating the venue so fixed; and the notice shall be accompanied by a copy of the application, and of any evidence which the applicant intends to adduce in support of it.

6.142(4) **[Court order]** If the court considers the application to be well-founded, it shall make an order fixing the remuneration at a reduced amount or rate.

6.142(5) **[Costs of application]** Unless the court orders otherwise, the costs of the application shall be paid by the applicant, and do not fall on the estate.

General note to rr. 6.141, 6.142

The court will always have the final say on issues of remuneration. If a creditor wishes to challenge the trustee's remuneration he must have the support of 25% in value of the creditors.

SECTION E: SUPPLEMENTARY PROVISIONS

Rule 6.143 Trustee deceased

6.143(1) **[Notice to official receiver]** Subject as follows, where the trustee (other than the official receiver) has died, it is the duty of his personal representatives to give notice of the fact to the official receiver, specifying the date of the death.

This does not apply if notice has been given under any of the following paragraphs of this Rule.

6.143(2) **[Notice by partner etc.]** If the deceased trustee was a partner in a firm, which may be given to the official receiver by a partner in the firm who is qualified to act as an insolvency practitioner, or is a member of any body recognised by the Secretary of State for the authorisation of insolvency practitioners.

6.143(3) **[Notice by others]** Notice of the death may be given by any person producing to the official receiver the relevant death certificate or a copy of it.

6.143(4) **[Notice to court by official receiver]** The official receiver shall give notice to the court, for the purpose of fixing the date of the deceased trustee's release in accordance with section 299(3)(a).

Rule 6.144 Loss of qualification as insolvency practitioner

6.144(1) **[Application of Rule]** This Rule applies where the trustee vacates office, under section 298(6), on his ceasing to be qualified to act as an insolvency practitioner in relation to the bankrupt.

6.144(2) **[Notice to official receiver etc.]** The trustee vacating office shall forthwith give notice of his doing so to the official receiver, who shall give notice to the Secretary of State.

The official receiver shall file in court a copy of his notice under this paragraph. [FORM 6.51]

6.144(3) **[Application of r. 6.135]** Rule 6.135 applies as regards the trustee obtaining his release, as if he had been removed by the court.

General note

This expands IA 1986, s. 298(6). On qualification, see IA 1986, Pt. XIII.

Rule 6.145 Notice to official receiver of intention to vacate office

6.145(1) **[Notice of official receiver]** Where the trustee intends to vacate office, whether by resignation or otherwise, he shall give notice of his intention to the official receiver together with notice of any creditors' meeting to be held in respect of his vacation of office, including any meeting to receive his resignation.

6.145(2)   [Time limit for notice]   The notice to the official receiver must be given at least 21 days before any such creditors' meeting.

6.145(3)   [Details of property]   Where there remains in the bankrupt's estate any property which has not been realised, applied, distributed or otherwise fully dealt with in the bankruptcy, the trustee shall include in his notice to the official receiver details of the nature of that property, its value (or the fact that it has no value), its location, any action taken by the trustee to deal with that property or any reason for his not dealing with it, and the current position in relation to it.

History note

Rule 6.145 was substituted by I(A)R 1987 (SI 1987 No. 1919), r. 3(1), Sch., Pt. 1, para. 116 as from 11 January 1988: r. 6.145 formerly read as follows:

"**6.145(1)**   Where the trustee intends to vacate office, whether by resignation or otherwise, and there remain in the estate any unrealised assets, he shall give notice of his intention to the official receiver, informing him of the nature, value and whereabouts of the assets in question.

6.145(2)   Where there is to be a creditors' meeting to receive the trustee's resignation, or otherwise in respect of his vacation of office, the notice to the official receiver must be given at least 21 days before the meeting."

General note

Rule 6.145(3) makes it clear that valueless property must now be detailed in the report to the official receiver. The word "assets" used in the previous version of r. 6.145 has now been dropped to clarify matters.

Rule 6.146   Trustee's duties on vacating office

6.146(1)   [Obligation to deliver any assets etc.]   Where the trustee ceases to be in office as such, in consequence of removal, resignation or cesser of qualification as an insolvency practitioner, he is under obligation forthwith to deliver up to the person succeeding him as trustee the assets of the estate (after deduction of any expenses properly incurred, and distributions made, by him) and further to deliver up to that person—

(a) the records of the bankruptcy, including correspondence, proofs and other related papers appertaining to the bankruptcy while it was within his responsibility, and

(b) the bankrupt's books, papers and other records.

6.146(2)   [When administration complete]   When the administration of the bankrupt's estate is for practical purposes complete, the trustee shall forthwith file in court all proofs remaining with him in the proceedings.

General note

This ties up matters left unresolved by IA 1986, s. 298.

Rule 6.147   Power of court to set aside certain transactions

6.147(1)   [Trustee's transaction with associate]   If in the administration of the estate the trustee enters into any transaction with a person who is an associate of his,

903

the court may, on the application of any person interested, set the transaction aside and order the trustee to compensate the estate for any loss suffered in consequence of it.

6.147(2)   [Where r. 6.147(1) does not apply]   This does not apply if either—

(a) the transaction was entered into with the prior consent of the court, or

(b) it is shown to the court's satisfaction that the transaction was for value, and that it was entered into by the trustee without knowing, or having any reason to suppose, that the person concerned was an associate.

6.147(3)   [Effect of Rule]   Nothing in this Rule is to be taken as prejudicing the operation of any rule of law or equity with respect to a trustee's dealings with trust property, or the fiduciary obligations of any person.

General note

This power is sufficiently important to have been located within the text of IA 1986. For "associate" – see IA 1986, s. 435.

Rule 6.148   Rule against solicitation

6.148(1)   [Power of court]   Where the court is satisfied that any improper solicitation has been used by or on behalf of the trustee in obtaining proxies or procuring his appointment, it may order that no remuneration out of the estate be allowed to any person by whom, or on whose behalf, the solicitation was exercised.

6.148(2)   [Effect of court order]   An order of the court under this Rule overrides any resolution of the creditors' committee or the creditors, or any other provision of the Rules relating to the trustee's remuneration.

Rule 6.149   Enforcement of trustee's obligations to official receiver

6.149(1)   [Powers of court]   The court may, on the application of the official receiver, make such orders as it thinks necessary for enforcement of the duties of the trustee under section 305(3) (information and assistance to be given; production and inspection of books and records relating to the bankruptcy).

6.149(2)   [Extent of order]   An order of the court under this Rule may provide that all costs of and incidental to the official receiver's application shall be borne by the trustee.

General note

See IA 1986, s. 305(3).

Chapter 11 — The Creditors' Committee

Rule 6.150   Membership of creditors' committee

6.150(1)   [Three–five members]   The creditors' committee shall consist of at least 3, and not more than 5, members.

6.150(2) **[Eligibility]** All the members of the committee must be creditors of the bankrupt; and any creditor (other than one who is fully secured) may be a member, so long as—

(a) he has lodged a proof of his debt, and

(b) his proof has neither been wholly disallowed for voting purposes, nor wholly rejected for the purposes of distribution or dividend.

6.150(3) **[Representation of body corporate]** A body corporate may be a member of the committee, but it cannot act as such otherwise than by a representative appointed under Rule 6.156.

General note

This develops IA 1986, s. 301.

Rule **6.151** Formalities of establishment

6.151(1) **[Trustee's certificate of due constitution]** The creditors' committee does not come into being, and accordingly cannot act, until the trustee has issued a certificate of its due constitution.   [FORM 6.52]

6.151(2) **[If chairman of meeting not trustee]** If the chairman of the creditors' meeting which resolves to establish the committee is not the trustee, he shall forthwith give notice of the resolution to the trustee (or, as the case may be, the person appointed as trustee by that same meeting), and inform him of the names and addresses of the persons elected to be members of the committee.

6.151(3) **[Agreement to act]** No person may act as a member of the committee unless and until he has agreed to do so and, unless the relevant proxy contains a statement to the contrary, such agreement may be given by his proxy-holder present at the meeting establishing the committee.

6.151(3A) **[No certificate without agreement]** The trustee's certificate of the committee's due constitution shall not issue before at least 3 persons elected to be members of the committee have agreed to act.

6.151(4) **[Amended certificate]** As and when the others (if any) agree to act, the trustee shall issue an amended certificate.   [FORM 6.52]

6.151(5) **[Certificate to be filed]** The certificate, and any amended certificate, shall be filed in court by the trustee.

6.151(6) **[Change in membership]** If after the first establishment of the committee there is any change in its membership, the trustee shall report the change to the court.   [FORM 6.53]

History note

Rules 6.151(3) and (3A) were substituted for the former r. 6.151(3) by I(A)R 1987 (SI 1987 No. 1919), r. 3(1), Sch., Pt. 1, para. 117 as from 11 January 1988: the former r. 6.151(3) read as follows:

"**6.151(3)** No person may act as a member of the committee unless and until he has agreed to do so; and the trustee's certificate of the committee's due constitution shall not issue before at least 3 persons elected to be members of it have agreed to act."

This rule was amended to facilitate immediate committee meetings after the creditors' meeting. The original r. 6.151(3) has been broken down into (3) and (3A).

Rule 6.152 Obligations of trustee to committee

6.152(1) [Trustee's duty to report]   Subject as follows, it is the duty of the trustee to report to the members of the creditors' committee all such matters as appear to him to be, or as they have indicated to him as being, of concern to them with respect to the bankruptcy.

6.152(2) [Non-compliance with request for information]   In the case of matters so indicated to him by the committee, the trustee need not comply with any request for information where it appears to him that—

(a) the request is frivolous or unreasonable, or

(b) the cost of complying would be excessive, having regard to the relative importance of the information, or

(c) the estate is without funds sufficient for enabling him to comply.

6.152(3) [Report in summary form]   Where the committee has come into being more than 28 days after the appointment of the trustee, the latter shall report to them, in summary form, what actions he has taken since his appointment, and shall answer such questions as they may put to him regarding his conduct of the bankruptcy hitherto.

6.152(4) [Summary report for subsequent member]   A person who becomes a member of the committee at any time after its first establishment is not entitled to require a report to him by the trustee, otherwise than in summary form, of any matters previously arising.

6.152(5) [Access to trustee's records]   Nothing in this Rule disentitles the committee, or any member of it, from having access to the trustee's records of the bankruptcy, or from seeking an explanation of any matter within the committee's responsibility.

General note

This imposes a duty on the trustee to keep the committee informed (subject to r. 6.152(2)). Note also r. 6.163.

Rule 6.153 Meetings of the committee

6.153(1) [Holding of meetings]   Subject as follows, meetings of the creditors' committee shall be held when and where determined by the trustee.

6.153(2) [First and subsequent meetings]   The trustee shall call a first meeting of the committee to take place within 3 months of his appointment or of the committee's establishment (whichever is the later); and thereafter he shall call a meeting—

(a) if so requested by a member of the committee or his representative (the meeting then to be held within 21 days of the request being received by the trustee), and

(b) for a specified date, if the committee has previously resolved that a meeting be held on that date.

6.153(3) [Notice of venue] The trustee shall give 7 days' notice in writing of the venue of any meeting to every member of the committee (or his representative, if designated for that purpose), unless in any case the requirement of the notice has been waived by or on behalf of any member.

Waiver may be signified either at or before the meeting.

(See general note after r. 6.156.)

Rule 6.154 The chairman at meetings

6.154(1) [Trustee or his nominee] The chairman at any meeting of the creditors' committee shall be the trustee, or a person appointed by him in writing to act.

6.154(2) [Nominated chairman] A person so nominated must be either—

(a) one who is qualified to act as an insolvency practitioner in relation to the bankrupt, or

(b) an employee of the trustee or his firm who is experienced in insolvency matters.

(See general note after r. 6.156.)

Rule 6.155 Quorum

6.155 A meeting of the committee is duly constituted if due notice of it has been given to all the members and at least 2 of the members are present or represented.

(See general note after r. 6.156.)

Rule 6.156 Committee-members' representatives

6.156(1) [Representation] A member of the creditors' committee may, in relation to the business of the committee, be represented by another person duly authorised by him for that purpose.

6.156(2) [Letter of authority] A person acting as a committee-member's representative must hold a letter of authority entitling him so to act (either generally or specially) and signed by or on behalf of the committee-member, and for this purpose any proxy in relation to any meeting of creditors of the bankrupt shall, unless it contains a statement to the contrary, be treated as such a letter of authority to act generally signed by or on behalf of the committee-member.

6.156(3) [Production of letter of authority] The chairman at any meeting of the committee may call on a person claiming to act as a committee-member's representative to produce his letter of authority, and may exclude him if it appears that his authority is deficient.

6.156(4) [Who may not be a representative] No member may be represented by a body corporate, or by a person who is an undischarged bankrupt or is subject to a composition or arrangement with his creditors.

6.156(5) [No dual representation]   No person shall—

(a) on the same committee, act at one and the same time as representative of more than one committee-member, or

(b) act both as a member of the committee and as representative of another member.

6.156(6) [Signing as representative]   Where the representative of a committee-member signs any document on the latter's behalf, the fact that he so signs must be stated below his signature.

6.156(7) [Validity of acts]   The acts of the committee are valid notwithstanding any defect in the appointment or qualifications of any committee-member's representative.

History note

In r. 6.156(2) the words from "specially)" to the end were substituted by I(A)R 1987 (SI 1987 No. 1919), r. 3(1), Sch., Pt. 1, para. 118(1) as from 11 January 1988: the former words read as follows:

"specially). The letter must be signed by or on behalf of the committee-member."

Rule 6.156(7) was added by I(A)R 1987 (SI 1987 No. 1919), r. 3(1), Sch., Pt. 1, para. 118(2) as from 11 January 1988.

General note to rr. 6.153–6.156

These rules regulate meetings of the committee. Note that the quorum is fixed at two members. Committee members may appoint representatives to act on their behalf.

Rule 6.157   Resignation

6.157   A member of the creditors' committee may resign by notice in writing delivered to the trustee.

Rule 6.158   Termination of membership

6.158(1) [Automatic termination]   A person's membership of the creditors' committee is automatically terminated if—

(a) he becomes bankrupt or compounds or arranges with his creditors, or

(b) at 3 consecutive meetings of the committee he is neither present nor represented (unless at the third of those meetings it is resolved that this Rule is not to apply in his case), or

(c) he ceases to be, or is found never to have been, a creditor.

6.158(2) [Termination on bankruptcy]   However, if the cause of termination is the member's bankruptcy, his trustee in bankruptcy replaces him as a member of the committee.

Rule 6.159 Removal

6.159 A member of the creditors' committee may be removed by resolution at a meeting of creditors, at least 14 days' notice having been given of the intention to move that resolution.

Rule 6.160 Vacancies

6.160(1) [Application of Rule] The following applies if there is a vacancy in the membership of the creditors' committee.

6.160(2) [Agreement not to fill vacancy] The vacancy need not be filled if the trustee and a majority of the remaining committee-members so agree, provided that the number of members does not fall below the minimum required by Rule 6.150(1).

6.160(3) [Appointment by trustee] The trustee may appoint any creditor (being qualified under the Rules to be a member of the committee) to fill the vacancy, if a majority of the other members of the committee agree to the appointment and the creditor concerned consents to act.

6.160(4) [Appointment by resolution] Alternatively, a meeting of creditors may resolve that a creditor be appointed (with his consent) to fill the vacancy. In this case at least 14 days' notice must have been given of a resolution to make such an appointment (whether or not of a person named in the notice).

6.160(5) [Report to trustee] Where the vacancy is filled by an appointment made by a creditors' meeting at which the trustee is not present, the chairman of the meeting shall report to the trustee the appointment which has been made.

Rule 6.161 Voting rights and resolutions

6.161(1) [Votes etc.] At any meeting of the committee, each member (whether present himself, or by his representative) has one vote; and a resolution is passed when a majority of the members present or represented have voted in favour of it.

6.161(2) [Record of resolutions] Every resolution passed shall be recorded in writing, either separately or as part of the minutes of the meeting. The record shall be signed by the chairman and kept with the records of the bankruptcy.

General note

Committee resolutions are to be passed by simple majority and there is to be no weighting of votes.

Rule 6.162 Resolutions by post

6.162(1) [Sending proposed resolution] In accordance with this Rule, the trustee may seek to obtain the agreement of members of the creditors' committee to a resolution by sending to every member (or his representative designated for the purpose) a copy of the proposed resolution.

6.162(2) **[Copy of proposed resolution]** Where the trustee makes use of the procedure allowed by this Rule, he shall send out to members of the committee or their representatives (as the case may be) a copy of any proposed resolution on which a decision is sought, which shall be set out in such a way that agreement with or dissent from each separate resolution may be indicated by the recipient on the copy so sent.

6.162(3) **[Member requiring meeting]** Any member of the committee may, within 7 business days from the date of the trustee sending out a resolution, require the trustee to summon a meeting of the committee to consider the matters raised by the resolution.

6.162(4) **[Deemed passing of resolution]** In the absence of such a request, the resolution is deemed to have been carried in the committee if and when the trustee is notified in writing by a majority of the members that they concur with it.

6.162(5) **[Copy resolutions]** A copy of every resolution passed under this Rule, and a note that the concurrence of the committee was obtained, shall be kept with the records of the bankruptcy.

History note

In r. 6.162(2) the words from "a copy of any proposed resolution" to the end were substituted by I(A)R 1987 (SI 1987 No. 1919), r. 3(1), Sch., Pt. 1, para. 119(1) as from 11 January 1988: the former words read as follows:

"a statement incorporating the resolution to which their agreement is sought, each resolution (if more than one) being set out in a separate document."

In r. 6.162(3) the word "business" was inserted by I(A)R 1987 (SI 1987 No. 1919), r. 3(1), Sch., Pt. 1, para. 119(2) as from 11 January 1988.

General note

This is to make life easy for committee members (and for the trustee).

The change to r. 6.162(2) is intended to prevent proliferation of documents. Rule 6.162(3) now refers to "business days".

Rule **6.163** Trustee's reports

6.163(1) **[Trustee directed to report]** The trustee shall, as and when directed by the creditors' committee (but not more often than once in any period of 2 months), send a written report to every member of the committee setting out the position generally as regards the progress of the bankruptcy and matters arising in connection with it, to which he (the trustee) considers the committee's attention should be drawn.

6.163(2) **[If no directions to report]** In the absence of any such directions by the committee, the trustee shall send such a report not less often than once in every period of 6 months.

6.163(3) **[Effect of Rule]** The obligations of the trustee under this Rule are without prejudice to those imposed by Rule 6.152.

General note

The trustee can be required to submit two-monthly reports to the committee.

Rule **6.164**   Expenses of members etc.

6.164   The trustee shall defray out of the estate, in the prescribed order of priority, any reasonable travelling expenses directly incurred by members of the creditors' committee or their representatives in respect of their attendance at the committee's meetings, or otherwise on the committee's business.

Rule **6.165**   Dealings by committee-members and others

6.165(1)   [Application of Rule]   This Rule applies to—

(a) any member of the creditors' committee,

(b) any committee-member's representative,

(c) any person who is an associate of a member of the committee or a committee-member's representative, and

(d) any person who has been a member of the committee at any time in the last 12 months.

6.165(2)   [Prohibited transactions]   Subject as follows, a person to whom this Rule applies shall not enter into any transaction whereby he—

(a) receives out of the estate any payment for services given or goods supplied in connection with the estate's administration, or

(b) obtains any profit from the administration, or

(c) acquires any asset forming part of the estate.

6.165(3)   [Leave or sanction for r. 6.165(2) transaction]   Such a transaction may be entered into by a person to whom this Rule applies—

(a) with the prior leave of the court, or

(b) if he does so as a matter of urgency, or by way of performance of a contract in force before the commencement of the bankruptcy, and obtains the court's leave for the transaction, having applied for it without undue delay, or

(c) with the prior sanction of the creditors' committee, where it is satisfied (after full disclosure of the circumstances) that the person will be giving full value in the transaction.

6.165(4)   [Resolution to sanction transaction]   Where in the committee a resolution is proposed that sanction be accorded for a transaction to be entered into which, without the sanction or the leave of the court, would be in contravention of this Rule, no member of the committee, and no representative of a member, shall vote if he is to participate directly or indirectly in the transaction.

6.165(5)   [Powers of court]   The court may, on application of any person interested—

(a) set aside a transaction on the ground that it has been entered into in contravention of this Rule, and

(b) make with respect to it such other order as it thinks fit, including (subject to the following paragraph) an order requiring a person to whom this Rule applies to account for any profit obtained from the transaction and compensate the estate for any resultant loss.

6.165(6)   [Member's or representative's associate]   In the case of a person to whom this Rule applies as an associate of a member of the committee or of a committee-member's representative the court shall not make any order under paragraph (5), if satisfied that he entered into the relevant transaction without having any reason to suppose that in doing so he would contravene this Rule.

6.165(7)   [Costs of application]   The costs of an application to the court for leave under this Rule do not fall on the estate, unless the court so orders.

General note

This imposes strict controls on dealings between committee members, et al. and the estate. Full disclosure is required and the permission of the court or of the creditors must first be obtained. The court can set aside transactions contravening these rules. Once again, an important substantive provision like this would have been more appropriately placed in IA 1986 itself. Compare BR 1952, r. 350. See also *Re Gallard* [1896] 1 QB 68 and *Re Bulmer, ex parte Greaves* [1937] Ch. 499.

Rule 6.166   Committee's functions vested in Secretary of State

6.166(1)   [Trustee's notices and reports]   At any time when the functions of the creditors' committee are vested in the Secretary of State under section 302(1) or (2), requirements of the Act or the Rules about notices to be given, or reports to be made, to the committee by the trustee do not apply, otherwise than as enabling the committee to require a report as to any matter.

6.166(2)   [Exercise by official receiver]   Where the committee's functions are so vested under section 302(2), they may be exercised by the official receiver.

General note

See IA 1986, s. 302.

Chapter 12 — Special Manager

Rule 6.167   Appointment and remuneration

6.167(1)   [Application under sec. 370 to be supported by report]   An application made by the official receiver or trustee under section 370 for the appointment of a person to be special manager shall be supported by a report setting out the reasons for the application.

The report shall include the applicant's estimate of the value of the estate, property or business in respect of which the special manager is to be appointed.

6.167(2)   [Duration of appointment]   The court's order appointing the special manager shall specify the duration of his appointment, which may be for a period of time, or until the occurrence of a specified event. Alternatively, the order may specify that the duration of the appointment is to be subject to a further order of the court.   [FORM 6.54]

6.167(3) [Renewal] The appointment of a special manager may be renewed by order of the court.

6.167(4) [Remuneration] The special manager's remuneration shall be fixed from time to time by the court.

(See general note after r. 6.171.)

Rule 6.168 Security

6.168(1) [Effect of giving security] The appointment of the special manager does not take effect until the person appointed has given (or, being allowed by the court to do so, undertaken to give) security to the person who applies for him to be appointed.

6.168(2) [Special or general security] It is not necessary that security shall be given for each separate bankruptcy; but it may be given either specially for a particular bankruptcy, or generally for any bankruptcy in relation to which the special manager may be employed as such.

6.168(3) [Amount of security] The amount of the security shall be not less than the value of the estate, property or business in respect of which he is appointed, as estimated by the applicant in his report under Rule 6.167(1).

6.168(4) [Certificate of adequacy] When the special manager has given security to the person applying for his appointment, that person's certificate as to the adequacy of the security shall be filed in court.

6.168(5) [Cost of providing security] The cost of providing the security shall be paid in the first instance by the special manager; but—

    (a) where a bankruptcy order is not made, he is entitled to be reimbursed out of the property of the debtor, and the court may make an order on the debtor accordingly, and

    (b) where a bankruptcy order is made, he is entitled to be reimbursed out of the estate in the prescribed order of priority.

(See general note after r. 6.171.)

Rule 6.169 Failure to give or keep up security

6.169(1) [Failure to give security] If the special manager fails to give the required security within the time stated for that purpose by the order appointing him, or any extension of that time may be allowed, the official receiver or trustee (as the case may be) shall report the failure to the court, which may thereupon discharge the order appointing the special manager.

6.169(2) [Failure to keep up security] If the special manager fails to keep up his security, the official receiver or trustee shall report his failure to the court, which may thereupon remove the special manager, and make such order as it thinks fit as to costs.

6.169(3) [Directions on removal] If an order is made under this Rule removing the special manager, or discharging the order appointing him, the court shall give directions as to whether any, and if so what, steps should be taken for the appointment of another special manager in his place.

(See general note after r. 6.171.)

Rule **6.170**   Accounting

6.170(1)   [Contents of accounts]   The special manager shall produce accounts, containing details of his receipts and payments, for the approval of the trustee.

6.170(2)   [Period of accounts]   The accounts shall be in respect of 3-month periods for the duration of the special manager's appointment (or for a lesser period, if his appointment terminates less than 3 months from its date, or from the date to which the last accounts were made up).

6.170(3)   [When accounts approved]   When the accounts have been approved, the special manager's receipts and payments shall be added to those of the trustee.

(See general note after r. 6.171.)

Rule **6.171**   Termination of appointment

6.171(1)   [Automatic termination]   The special manager's appointment terminates if the bankruptcy petition is dismissed or if, an interim receiver having been appointed, the latter is discharged without a bankruptcy order having been made.

6.171(2)   [Application to court]   If the official receiver or the trustee is of opinion that the employment of the special manager is no longer necessary or profitable for the estate, he shall apply to the court for directions, and the court may order the special manager's appointment to be terminated.

6.171(3)   [Resolution of creditors]   The official receiver or the trustee shall make the same application if a resolution of the creditors is passed, requesting that the appointment be terminated.

General note to rr. 6.167–6.171

These rules develop the provisions of IA 1986, s. 370. If the court appoints a special manager, Form 6.54 is to be used. The court fixes his remuneration. Security is required. The special manager must provide three-monthly accounts for the trustee. The circumstances leading to the termination of the appointment of the special manager are mapped out. Compare BR 1952, rr. 353, 354.

Chapter 13 — Public Examination of Bankrupt

Rule **6.172**   Order for public examination

6.172(1)   [Copy of order to bankrupt]   If the official receiver applies to the court, under section 290, for the public examination of the bankrupt, a copy of the court's order shall, forthwith after its making, be sent by the official receiver to the bankrupt.   [FORM 6.55]

6.172(2)   [Venue and bankrupt's attendance]   The order shall appoint a venue for the hearing, and direct the bankrupt's attendance thereat.

6.172(3) **[Notice of hearing]** The official receiver shall give at least 14 days' notice of the hearing—

- (a) if a trustee has been nominated or appointed, to him;
- (b) if a special manager has been appointed, to him; and
- (c) subject to any contrary direction of the court, to every creditor of the bankrupt who is known to the official receiver or is identified in the bankrupt's statement of affairs.

6.172(4) **[Advertisement]** The official receiver may, if he thinks fit, cause notice of the order to be given, by public advertisement in one or more newspapers, at least 14 days before the day fixed for the hearing.

(See general note after r. 6.177.)

Rule 6.173   Order on request by creditors

6.173(1) **[Form of request etc.]** A request by a creditor to the official receiver, under section 290(2), for the bankrupt to be publicly examined shall be made in writing and be accompanied by—

- (a) a list of the creditors concurring with the request and the amount of their respective claims in the bankruptcy,
- (b) from each creditor concurring, written confirmation of his concurrence, and
- (c) a statement of the reasons why the examination is requested.

Sub-paragraphs (a) and (b) do not apply if the requisitioning creditor's debt is alone sufficient, without the concurrence of others.   [FORM 6.56]

6.173(2) **[Security for expenses of hearing]** Before an application to the court is made on the request, the requisitionist shall deposit with the official receiver such sum as the latter may determine to be appropriate by way of security for the expenses of the hearing of a public examination, if ordered.

6.173(3) **[Time for application]** Subject as follows, the official receiver shall, within 28 days of receiving the request, make the application to the court required by section 290(2).

6.173(4) **[Relief from unreasonable request]** If the official receiver is of opinion that the request is an unreasonable one in the circumstances, he may apply to the court for an order relieving him from the obligation to make the application otherwise required by that subsection.

6.173(5) **[Notice of relief order etc.]** If the court so orders, and the application for the order was made *ex parte*, notice of the order shall be given forthwith by the official receiver to the requisitionist. If the application for an order is dismissed, the official receiver's application under section 290(2) shall be made forthwith on conclusion of the hearing of the application first mentioned.

(See general note after r. 6.177.)

Rule 6.174   Bankrupt unfit for examination

6.174(1) **[Application for stay etc.]** Where the bankrupt is suffering from any mental disorder or physical affliction or disability rendering him unfit to undergo or attend for public examination, the court may, on application in that behalf, either stay the order for his public examination or direct that it shall be conducted in such manner and at such place as it thinks fit.   [FORM 6.57]

6.174(2) **[Who may apply]** Application under this Rule shall be made—

 (a) by a person who has been appointed by a court in the United Kingdom or elsewhere to manage the affairs of, or to represent, the bankrupt, or

 (b) by a relative or friend of the bankrupt whom the court considers to be a proper person to make the application, or

 (c) by the official receiver.

6.174(3) **[Application not by official receiver]** Where the application is made by a person other than the official receiver, then—

 (a) it shall, unless the bankrupt is a patient within the meaning of the Mental Health Act 1983, be supported by the affidavit of a registered medical practitioner as to the bankrupt's mental and physical condition;

 (b) at least 7 days' notice of the application shall be given to the official receiver and the trustee (if any); and

 (c) before any order is made on the application, the applicant shall deposit with the official receiver such sum as the latter certifies to be necessary for the additional expenses of any examination that may be ordered on the application.

An order made on the application may provide that the expenses of the examination are to be payable, as to a specified proportion, out of the deposit under subparagraph (c), instead of out of the estate.

6.174(4) **[Application by official receiver]** Where the application is made by the official receiver, it may be made *ex parte*, and may be supported by evidence in the form of a report by the official receiver to the court.

(See general note after r. 6.177.)

Rule **6.175** Procedure at hearing

6.175(1) **[Examination on oath]** The bankrupt shall at the hearing be examined on oath; and he shall answer all such questions as the court may put, or allow to be put, to him.

6.175(2) **[Appearances etc.]** Any of the persons allowed by section 290(4) to question the bankrupt may, with the approval of the court (made known either at the hearing or in advance of it), appear by solicitor or counsel; or he may in writing authorise another person to question the bankrupt on his behalf.

6.175(3) **[Representation of bankrupt]** The bankrupt may at his own expense employ a solicitor with or without counsel, who may put to him such questions as the court may allow for the purpose of enabling him to explain or qualify any answers given by him, and may make representations on his behalf.

6.175(4) **[Record of examination]** There shall be made in writing such record of the examination as the court thinks proper. The record shall be read over either to or by the bankrupt, signed by him, and verified by affidavit at a venue fixed by the court.   [FORM 6.58]

6.175(5)   [Record as evidence]   The written record may, in any proceedings (whether under the Act or otherwise) be used as evidence against the bankrupt of any statement made by him in the course of his public examination.

6.175(6)   [Criminal proceedings etc.]   If criminal proceedings have been instituted against the bankrupt, and the court is of opinion that the continuance of the hearing would be calculated to prejudice a fair trial of those proceedings, the hearing may be adjourned.

(See general note after r. 6.177.)

Rule 6.176   Adjournment

6.176(1)   [Adjourned by court]   The public examination may be adjourned by the court from time to time, either to a fixed date or generally.   [FORM 6.59]

6.176(2)   [Resumption]   Where the examination has been adjourned generally, the court may at any time on the application of the official receiver or of the bankrupt—

   (a) fix a venue for the resumption of the examination, and

   (b) give directions as to the manner in which, and the time within which, notice of the resumed public examination is to be given to persons entitled to take part in it.   [FORM 6.60]

6.176(3)   [Deposit for expenses re application]   Where application under paragraph (2) is made by the bankrupt, the court may grant it on terms that the expenses of giving the notices required by that paragraph shall be paid by him and that, before a venue for the resumed public examination is fixed, he shall deposit with the official receiver such sum as the latter considers necessary to cover those expenses.

6.176(4)   [Official receiver's application under s. 279(3)]   Where the examination is adjourned generally, the official receiver may, there and then, make application under section 279(3) (suspension of automatic discharge).

(See general note after r. 6.177.)

Rule 6.177   Expenses of examination

6.177(1)   [Expenses paid out of r. 6.173(2) deposit]   Where a public examination of the bankrupt has been ordered by the court on a creditors' requisition under Rule 6.173, the court may order that the expenses of the examination are to be paid, as to a specified proportion, out of the deposit under Rule 6.173(2), instead of out of the estate.

6.177(2)   [Official receiver not liable for costs]   In no case do the costs and expenses of a public examination fall on the official receiver personally.

These rules provide detailed guidance on the conduct of a public examination of a bankrupt under IA 1986, s. 290. If the official receiver applies to the court, Form 6.55 is to be used, whereas if a creditor applies to the official receiver for a public examination, Form 6.56 is the appropriate document. A creditor seeking a public examination must provide security. If the bankrupt is not fit to be publicly examined, the court can excuse him. Note the use of Form 6.57 in this context. The hearing procedure is mapped out by rr. 6.175 and 6.176. The public examination is normally to be funded out of the estate, unless the deposit furnished by a requisitioning creditor is made use of. Compare BR 1952, rr. 188–196A.

Chapter 14 — Disclaimer

Rule **6.178**   Trustee's notice of disclaimer

6.178(1)   **[Contents of notice]**   Where the trustee disclaims property under section 315, the notice of disclaimer shall contain such particulars of the property disclaimed as enable it to be easily identified.   [FORM 6.61]

6.178(2)   **[Notice to be signed etc.]**   The notice shall be signed by the trustee and filed in court, with a copy. The court shall secure that both the notice and the copy are sealed and endorsed with the date of filing.

6.178(3)   **[Copy notice returned to trustee]**   The copy notice, so sealed and endorsed, shall be returned by the court to the trustee as follows—

  (a) if the notice has been delivered at the offices of the court by the trustee in person, it shall be handed to him,

  (b) if it has been delivered by some person acting on the trustee's behalf, it shall be handed to that person, for immediate transmission to the trustee, and

  (c) otherwise, it shall be sent to the trustee by first class post.

The court shall cause to be endorsed on the original notice, or otherwise recorded on the file, the manner in which the copy notice was returned to the trustee.

6.178(4)   **[Date of notice]**   For the purposes of section 315 the date of the prescribed notice is that which is endorsed on it, and on the copy, in accordance with this Rule.

(See general note after r. 6.186.)

Rule **6.179**   Communication of disclaimer to persons interested

6.179(1)   **[Copy notices]**   Within 7 days after the day on which a copy of the notice of disclaimer is returned to him, the trustee shall send or give copies of the notice (showing the date endorsed as required by Rule 6.178) to the persons mentioned in paragraphs (2) to (5) below.

6.179(2)   **[Leasehold property]**   Where the property disclaimed is of a leasehold nature, he shall send or give a copy to every person who (to his knowledge) claims under the bankrupt as underlessee or mortgagee.

6.179(3)   **[Property in a dwelling-house]**   Where the disclaimer is of property in a dwelling-house, he shall send or give a copy to every person who (to his knowledge) is in occupation of, or claims a right to occupy, the house.

6.179(4)   **[Giving notice]**   He shall in any case send or give a copy of the notice to every person who (to his knowledge)—

(a) claims an interest in the disclaimed property, or

(b) is under any liability in respect of the property, not being a liability discharged by the disclaimer.

6.179(5)   **[Unprofitable contract]**   If the disclaimer is of an unprofitable contract, he shall send or give copies of the notice to all such persons as, to his knowledge, are parties to the contract or have interests under it.

6.179(6)   **[Late communication]**   If subsequently it comes to the trustee's knowledge, in the case of any person, that he has such an interest in the disclaimed property as would have entitled him to receive a copy of the notice of disclaimer in pursuance of paragraphs (2) to (5), the trustee shall then forthwith send or give to that person a copy of the notice.

But compliance with this paragraph is not required if—

(a) the trustee is satisfied that the person has already been made aware of the disclaimer and its date, or

(b) the court, on the trustee's application, orders that compliance is not required in that particular case.

6.179(7)   **[Notice to minor re dwelling-house]**   A notice or copy notice to be served on any person under the age of 18 in relation to the disclaimer of property in a dwelling-house is sufficiently served if sent or given to the parent or guardian of that person.

History note

Rule 6.179(7) was added by I(A)R 1987 (SI 1987 No. 1919), r. 3(1), Sch., Pt. 1, para. 120 as from 11 January 1988.

General note

Note the use of Pt. 3 of Form 6.61 here.

(See also general note after r. 6.186.)

Rule 6.180   Additional notices

6.180   The trustee disclaiming property may, without prejudice to his obligations under sections 315 to 319 and Rules 6.178 and 6.179, at any time give notice of the disclaimer to any persons who in his opinion ought, in the public interest or otherwise, to be informed of it.

General note

Note the use of Pt. 3 of Form 6.61 here.

(See also general note after r. 6.186.)

Rule 6.181   Duty to keep court informed

6.181 The trustee shall notify the court from time to time as to the persons to whom he has sent or given copies of the notice of disclaimer under the two preceding Rules, giving their names and addresses, and the nature of their respective interests.

(See general note after r. 6.186.)

Rule 6.182   Application for leave to disclaim

6.182(1) **[Applying ex parte]** Where under section 315(4) the trustee requires the leave of the court to disclaim property claimed for the bankrupt's estate under section 307 or 308, he may apply for that leave *ex parte*.

6.182(2) **[Accompanying report]** The application must be accompanied by a report—

    (a) giving such particulars of the property proposed to be disclaimed as enable it to be easily identified,

    (b) setting out the reasons why, the property having been claimed for the estate, the court's leave to disclaim is now applied for, and

    (c) specifying the persons (if any) who have been informed of the trustee's intention to make the application.

6.182(3) **[Copy of consent to disclaimer]** If it is stated in the report that any person's consent to the disclaimer has been signified, a copy of that consent must be annexed to the report.

6.182(4) **[Court may grant leave etc.]** The court may, on consideration of the application, grant the leave applied for; and it may, before granting leave—

    (a) order that notice of the application be given to all such persons who, if the property is disclaimed, will be entitled to apply for a vesting or other order under section 320, and

    (b) fix a venue for the hearing of the application under section 315(4).

(See general note after r. 6.186.)

Rule 6.183   Application by interested party under s. 316

6.183(1) **[Application of Rule]** The following applies where, in the case of any property, application is made to the trustee by an interested party under section 316 (request for decision whether the property is to be disclaimed or not).

6.183(2) **[Delivery and form of application]** The application—

    (a) shall be delivered to the trustee personally or by registered post, and

    (b) shall be made in the form known as "notice to elect", or a substantially similar form.   [FORM 6.62]

6.183(3) **[Where property cannot be disclaimed without leave of court]** This paragraph applies in a case where the property concerned cannot be disclaimed by the trustee without the leave of the court.

If within the period of 28 days mentioned in section 316(1) the trustee applies to the court for leave to disclaim, the court shall extend the time allowed by that section for giving notice of disclaimer to a date not earlier than the date fixed for the hearing of the application.

(See general note after r. 6.186.)

Rule **6.184**   Interest in property to be declared on request

6.184(1)   **[Notice to declare interest]**   If, in the case of property which the trustee has the right to disclaim, it appears to him that there is some person who claims, or may claim, to have an interest in the property, he may give notice to that person calling on him to declare within 14 days whether he claims any such interest and, if so, the nature and extent of it.   [FORM 6.63]

6.184(2)   **[Failing compliance with notice]**   Failing compliance with the notice, the trustee is entitled to assume that the person concerned has no such interest in the property as will prevent or impede its disclaimer.

(See general note after r. 6.186.)

Rule **6.185**   Disclaimer presumed valid and effective

6.185   Any disclaimer of property by the trustee is presumed valid and effective, unless it is proved that he has been in breach of his duty with respect to the giving of notice of disclaimer, or otherwise under sections 315 to 319, or under this Chapter of the Rules.

(See general note after r. 6.186.)

Rule **6.186**   Application for exercise of court's powers under s. 320

6.186(1)   **[Application of Rule]**   This Rule applies with respect to an application by any person under section 320 for an order of the court to vest or deliver disclaimed property.

6.186(2)   **[Time for application]**   The application must be made within 3 months of the applicant becoming aware of the disclaimer, or of his receiving a copy of the trustee's notice of disclaimer sent under Rule 6.179, whichever is the earlier.

6.186(3)   **[Contents of affidavit]**   The applicant shall with his application file an affidavit—

  (a) stating whether he applies under paragraph (a) of section 320(2) (claim of interest in the property), under paragraph (b) (liability not discharged) or under paragraph (c) (occupation of dwelling-house);

  (b) specifying the date on which he received a copy of the trustee's notice of disclaimer, or otherwise became aware of the disclaimer; and

  (c) specifying the grounds of his application and the order which he desires the court to make under section 320.

6.186(4) [Venue for hearing] The court shall fix a venue for the hearing of the application; and the applicant shall, not later than 7 days before the date fixed, give to the trustee notice of the venue, accompanied by copies of the application and the affidavit under paragraph (3).

6.186(5) [Directions for notice etc.] On the hearing of the application, the court may give directions as to other persons (if any) who should be sent or given notice of the application and the grounds on which it is made.

6.186(6) [Sealed copies of order] Sealed copies of any order made on the application shall be sent by the court to the applicant and the trustee.

6.186(7) [Leasehold property or property in a dwelling-house] In a case where the property disclaimed is of a leasehold nature, or is property in a dwelling-house, and section 317 or (as the case may be) section 318 applies to suspend the effect of the disclaimer, there shall be included in the court's order a direction giving effect to the disclaimer.

This paragraph does not apply if, at the time when the order is issued, other applications under section 320 are pending in respect of the same property.

General note to rr. 6.178–6.186

These rules complement IA 1986, ss. 315–321 (disclaimer of property, etc. by the trustee). This disclaimer is to take the style of Form 6.61 and must be filed with the court. Rules 6.179 and 6.180 relate to the dissemination of the notice of disclaimer. The court must always be kept informed of the dissemination process. Rule 6.182 develops IA 1986, s. 315(4) (leave of court for certain notices of disclaimer). Section 316 must be read in the light of r. 6.183 and Form 6.62. The trustee can, under r. 6.184 and by using Form 6.63, compel persons to declare their interest in any property which he is considering disclaiming. The onus of proving that a disclaimer has been exercised improperly is naturally cast upon the person challenging it (r. 6.185). Section 320 is to be viewed in the light of r. 6.186. Note especially the time limitation upon applications under s. 320. Compare BR 1952, r. 278.

Chapter 15 — Replacement of Exempt Property

Rule 6.187 Purchase of replacement property

6.187(1) [Time for purchase] A purchase of replacement property under section 308(3) may be made either before or after the realisation by the trustee of the value of the property vesting in him under the section.

6.187(2) [Sufficiency of funds in estate] The trustee is under no obligation, by virtue of the section, to apply funds to the purchase of a replacement for property vested in him, unless and until he has sufficient funds in the estate for that purpose.

(See general note after r. 6.188.)

Rule 6.188 Money provided in lieu of sale

6.188(1) [Application of Rule] The following applies where a third party proposes to the trustee that he (the former) should provide the estate with a sum of money enabling the bankrupt to be left in possession of property which other-wise be made to vest in the trustee under section 308.

6.188(2)   [Reasonableness of proposal]   The trustee may accept that proposal, if satisfied that it is a reasonable one, and that the estate will benefit to the extent of the value of the property in question less the cost of a reasonable replacement.

General note to rr. 6.187, 6.188

These rules provide further guidance on the operation of IA 1986, s. 308, which is a novel provision in the Act. A third party can provide funds for the estate to prevent a sale and replacement of assets.

Chapter 16 — Income Payments Orders

Rule 6.189   Application for order

6.189(1)   [Court to fix venue]   Where the trustee applies for an income payments order under section 310, the court shall fix a venue for the hearing of the application.

6.189(2)   [Notice etc. to bankrupt]   Notice of the application, and of the venue, shall be sent by the trustee to the bankrupt at least 28 days before the day fixed for the hearing, together with a copy of the trustee's application and a short statement of the grounds on which it is made.   [FORM 6.64]

6.189(3)   [Contents of notice]   The notice shall inform the bankrupt that—

   (a) unless at least 7 days before the date fixed for the hearing he sends to the court and to the trustee written consent to an order being made in the terms of the application, he is required to attend the hearing, and

   (b) if he attends, he will be given an opportunity to show cause why the order should not be made, or an order should be made otherwise than as applied for by the trustee.

General note

For the meaning of "venue" see r. 13.6.

(See general note after r. 6.193.)

Rule 6.190   Action to follow making of order

6.190(1)   [Copy of order to bankrupt]   Where the court makes an income pay-ments order, a sealed copy of the order shall, forthwith after it is made, be sent by the trustee to the bankrupt.   [FORM 6.65]
or [FORM 6.66]

6.190(2)   [Copy of order under s. 310(3)(b)]   If the order is made under section 310(3)(b), a sealed copy of the order shall also be sent by the trustee to the person to whom the order is directed.

(See general note after r. 6.193.)

Rule 6.191   Variation of order

6.191(1)   [Non-compliance with s. 310(3)(a) order]   If an income payments order is made under section 310(3)(a), and the bankrupt does not comply with it, the trustee may apply to the court for the order to be varied, so as to take effect under section 310(3)(b) as an order to the payor of the relevant income.   [FORM 6.67]

6.191(2)   [Ex parte application]   The trustee's application under this Rule may be made *ex parte*.

6.191(3)   [Copy of order to trustee and bankrupt]   Sealed copies of any order made on the application shall, forthwith after it is made, be sent by the court to the trustee and the bankrupt.

6.191(4)   [Variation etc. of s. 310(3)(b) order]   In the case of an order varying or discharging an income payments order made under section 310(3)(b), an additional sealed copy shall be sent to the trustee, for transmission forthwith to the payor of the relevant income.

(See general note after r. 6.193.)

Rule 6.192   Order to payor of income: administration

6.192(1)   [Compliance by payer]   Where a person receives notice of an income payments order under section 310(3)(b), with reference to income otherwise payable by him to the bankrupt, he shall make the arrangements requisite for immediate compliance with the order.

6.192(2)   [Costs of compliance]   When making any payment to the trustee, he may deduct the appropriate fee towards the clerical and administrative costs of compliance with the income payments order.

He shall give to the bankrupt a written statement of any amount deducted by him under this paragraph.

6.192(3)   [Where payer no longer liable etc.]   Where a person receives notice of an income payments order imposing on him a requirement under section 310(3)(b), and either—

(a) he is then no longer liable to make to the bankrupt any payment of income, or

(b) having made payments in compliance with the order, he ceases to be so liable,

he shall forthwith give notice of that fact to the trustee.

(See general note after r. 6.193.)

Rule 6.193   Review of order

6.193(1)   [Application to court]   Where an income payments order is in force, either the trustee or the bankrupt may apply to the court for the order to be varied or discharged.

6.193(2) **[Application by trustee]**   If the application is made by the trustee, Rule 6.189 applies (with any necessary modification) as in the case of an application for an income payments order.

6.193(3) **[Application by bankrupt]**   If the application is made by the bankrupt, it shall be accompanied by a short statement of the grounds on which it is made.

6.193(4) **[Court may dismiss application etc.]**   The court may, if it thinks that no sufficient cause is shown for the application, dismiss it; but it shall not do so unless the applicant has had an opportunity to attend the court for an *ex parte* hearing, of which he has been given at least 7 days' notice.

If the application is not dismissed under this paragraph, the court shall fix a venue for it to be heard.

6.193(5) **[Notice of venue etc.]**   At least 28 days before the date fixed for the hearing, the applicant shall send to the trustee or the bankrupt (whichever of them is not himself the applicant) notice of the venue, accompanied by a copy of the application.

Where the applicant is the bankrupt, the notice shall be accompanied by a copy of the statement of grounds under paragraph (3).

6.193(6) **[Appearance etc. by trustee]**   The trustee may, if he thinks fit, appear and be heard on the application; and, whether or not he intends to appear, he may, not less than 7 days before the date fixed for the hearing, file a written report of any matters which he considers ought to be drawn to the court's attention.

If such a report is filed, a copy of it shall be sent by the trustee to the bankrupt.

6.193(7) **[Sealed copies of order]**   Sealed copies of any order made on the application shall, forthwith after the order is made, be sent by the court to the trustee, the bankrupt and the payor (if other than the bankrupt).   [FORM 6.66]

General note to rr. 6.189–6.193

Once again these rules develop an innovation introduced by IA 1986, s. 310, the income payments order. The trustee's application should adopt Form 6.64, whereas the court order should follow Forms 6.65 and 6.66. Variation of orders is provided for (see Form 6.67). Provision is made for third parties whose payments to the bankrupt may be diverted under IA 1986, s. 310(3)(*b*). Note the special fee, which is 50p, under r. 6.192(2)—see r. 13.11(*a*).

Chapter 17 — Action by Court Under Section 369
Order to Inland Revenue Official

Rule **6.194**   Application for order

6.194(1) **[Application to specify documents etc.]**   An application by the official receiver or the trustee for an order under section 369 (order to inland revenue official to produce documents) shall specify (with such particularity as will enable the order, if made, to be most easily complied with) the documents whose production to the court is desired, naming the official to whom the order is to be addressed.

6.194(2) **[Court to fix venue]** The court shall fix a venue for the hearing of the application.

6.194(3) **[Notice of venue etc. to Commissioners]** Notice of the venue, accompanied by a copy of the application, shall be sent by the applicant to the Commissioners of Inland Revenue ("the Commissioners") at least 28 days before the hearing.

6.194(4) **[Whether Commissioners consent or object]** The notice shall require the Commissioners, not later than 7 days before the date fixed for the hearing of the application, to inform the court whether they consent or object to the making of an order under the section.

6.194(5) **[If Commissioners consent]** If the Commissioners consent to the making of an order, they shall inform the court of the name of the official to whom it should be addressed, if other than the one named in the application.

6.194(6) **[If Commissioners object]** If the Commissioners object to the making of an order, they shall secure that an officer of theirs attends the hearing of the application and, not less than 7 days before it, deliver to the court a statement in writing of their grounds of objection.

A copy of the statement shall be sent forthwith to the applicant.

General note

For the meaning of "venue" see r. 13.6.

(See also general note after r. 6.196.)

Rule 6.195 Making and service of the order

6.195(1) **[Powers of court]** If on the hearing of the application it appears to the court to be a proper case, the court may make the order applied for, with such modifications (if any) as appear appropriate having regard to any representations made on behalf of the Commissioners. [FORM 6.69]

6.195(2) **[Form and contents of order]** The order—

    (a) may be addressed to an inland revenue official other than the one named in the application,

    (b) shall specify a time, not less than 28 days after service on the official to whom the order is addressed, within which compliance is required, and

    (c) may include requirements as to the manner in which documents to which the order relates are to be produced.

6.195(3) **[Service of copy of order]** A sealed copy of the order shall be served by the applicant on the official to whom it is addressed.

6.195(4) **[If official unable to comply]** If the official is unable to comply with the order because he has not the relevant documents in his possession, and has been unable to obtain possession of them, he shall deliver to the court a statement in writing as to the reasons for his non-compliance.

A copy of the statement shall be sent forthwith by the official to the applicant.

(See general note after r. 6.196.)

Rule **6.196**   **Custody of documents**

6.196   Where in compliance with an order under section 369 original documents are produced, and not copies, any person who, by order of the court under section 369(2) (authorised disclosure to persons with right of inspection), has them in his possession or custody is responsible to the court for their safe keeping and return as and when directed.

General note to rr. 6.194–6.196

These rules provide further details on orders made under IA 1986, s. 369. Form 6.69 is to be used for orders against the Inland Revenue under s. 369. A maximum of 28 days after service is fixed for compliance with a s. 369 order.

Chapter 18 — Mortgaged Property

Rule **6.197**   **Claim by mortgagee of land**

6.197(1)   [Application for order for sale, "land"]   Any person claiming to be the legal or equitable mortgagee of land belonging to the bankrupt may apply to the court for an order directing that the land be sold.

"Land" includes any interest in, or right over, land.

6.197(2)   [Court may direct accounts to be taken etc.]   The court, if satisfied as to the applicant's title, may direct accounts to be taken and enquiries made to ascertain—

> (a) the principal, interest and costs due under the mortgage, and
>
> (b) where the mortgagee has been in possession of the land or any part of it, the rents and profits, dividends, interest, or other proceeds received by him or on his behalf.

Directions may be given by the court under this paragraph with respect to any mortgage (whether prior or subsequent) on the same property, other than that of the applicant.

6.197(3)   [Powers of court]   For the purpose of those accounts and enquiries, and of making title to the purchaser, any of the parties may be examined by the court, and shall produce on oath before the court all such documents in their custody or under their control relating to the estate of the bankrupt as the court may direct.

The court may under this paragraph authorise the service of interrogatories on any party.

6.197(4)   [In like manner as in High Court]   In any proceedings between a mortgagor and mortgagee, or the trustee of either of them, the court may order accounts to be taken and enquiries made in like manner as in the Chancery Division of the High Court.

(See general note after r. 6.199.)

Rule **6.198**   Power of court to order sale

6.198(1)   [Order for sale etc.]   The court may order that the land, or any specified part of it, be sold; and any party bound by the order and in possession of the land or part, or in receipt of the rents and profits from it, may be ordered to deliver up possession or receipt to the purchaser or to such other person as the court may direct.

6.198(2)   [Directions re sale]   The court may permit the person having the conduct of the sale to sell the land in such manner as he thinks fit. Alternatively, the court may direct that the land be sold as directed by the order.

6.198(3)   [Contents of order]   The court's order may contain directions—

    (a) appointing the persons to have the conduct of the sale;

    (b) fixing the manner of sale (whether by contract conditional on the court's approval, private treaty, public auction, or otherwise);

    (c) settling the particulars and conditions of sale;

    (d) obtaining evidence of the value of the property, and fixing a reserve or minimum price;

    (e) requiring particular persons to join in the sale and conveyance;

    (f) requiring the payment of the purchase money into court, or to trustees or others;

    (g) if the sale is to be by public auction, fixing the security (if any) to be given by the auctioneer, and his remuneration.

6.198(4)   [Sale by auction]   The court may direct that, if the sale is to be by public auction, the mortgagee may appear and bid on his own behalf.

(See general note after r. 6.199.)

Rule **6.199**   Proceeds of sale

6.199(1)   [Application of proceeds]   The proceeds of sale shall be applied—

    (a) first, in payment of the expenses of the trustee, of and occasioned by the application to the court, of the sale and attendance thereat, and of any costs arising from the taking of accounts, and making of enquiries, as directed by the court under Rule 6.197; and

    (b) secondly, in payment of the amount found due to any mortgagee, for principal, interest and costs;

and the balance (if any) shall be retained by or paid to the trustee.

6.199(2)   [Where proceeds insufficient]   Where the proceeds of the sale are insufficient to pay in full the amount found due to any mortgagee, he is entitled to prove as a creditor for any deficiency, and to receive dividends rateably with other creditors, but not so as to disturb any dividend already declared.

These provisions regulate the rights of mortgagees of the bankrupt's land. The court can order the sale of the mortgage property. Note the priority of claims against the proceeds of sale (r. 6.199). Compare BR 1952, rr. 73 and 74.

Chapter 19 — After-Acquired Property

Rule 6.200   Duties of bankrupt in respect of after-acquired property

6.200(1)   [Time for bankrupt to give notice]   The notice to be given by the bankrupt to the trustee, under section 333(2), of property acquired by, or devolving upon, him, or of any increase of his income, shall be given within 21 days of his becoming aware of the relevant facts.

6.200(2)   [Not to dispose of property]   Having served notice in respect of property acquired by or devolving upon him, the bankrupt shall not, without the trustee's consent in writing, dispose of it within the period of 42 days beginning with the date of the notice.

6.200(3)   [To identify etc. disponee]   If the bankrupt disposes of property before giving the notice required by this Rule or in contravention of paragraph (2), it is his duty forthwith to disclose to the trustee the name and address of the disponee, and to provide any other information which may be necessary to enable the trustee to trace the property and recover it for the estate.

6.200(4)   [Property to which rr. 6.200 (1)–(3) do not apply]   Subject as follows, paragraphs (1) to (3) do not apply to property acquired by the bankrupt in the ordinary course of a business carried on by him.

6.200(5)   [If bankrupt carries on business]   If the bankrupt carries on a business, he shall, not less often than 6-monthly, furnish to the trustee information with respect to it, showing the total of goods bought and sold (or, as the case may be, services supplied) and the profit or loss arising from the business.

The trustee may require the bankrupt to furnish fuller details (including accounts) of the business carried on by him.

(See general note after r. 6.202.)

Rule 6.201   Trustee's recourse to disponee of property

6.201(1)   [Trustee may serve notice on disponee]   Where property has been disposed of by the bankrupt before giving the notice required by Rule 6.200 or otherwise in contravention of that Rule, the trustee may serve notice on the disponee, claiming the property as part of the estate by virtue of section 307(3).

6.201(2) **[Time for serving notice]** The trustee's notice under this rule must be served within 28 days of his becoming aware of the disponee's identity and an address at which he can be served.

(See general note after r. 6.202.)

Rule 6.202 Expenses of getting in property for the estate

6.202 Any expenses incurred by the trustee in acquiring title to after-acquired property shall be paid out of the estate, in the prescribed order of priority.

General note to rr. 6.200–6.202

The key provision on after-acquired property is IA 1986, s. 307, which represents a new departure in bankruptcy law. Section 333(2) is also relevant. The bankrupt has 21 days after becoming aware that after-acquired property has become vested in him to notify the trustee. The bankrupt must then wait 42 days before disposing of that property. If property is wrongfully disposed of, it may be traced by the trustee at the expense of the estate.

Chapter 20 — Leave to Act as Director, Etc.

Rule 6.203 Application for leave

6.203(1) **[Application supported by affidavit]** An application by the bankrupt for leave, under section 11 of the Company Directors Disqualification Act 1986, to act as director of, or to take part or be concerned in the promotion, formation or management of a company, shall be supported by an affidavit complying with this Rule.

6.203(2) **[Contents of affidavit]** The affidavit must identify the company and specify—

- (a) the nature of its business or intended business, and the place or places where that business is, or is to be, carried on,
- (b) whether it is, or is to be, a private or a public company,
- (c) the persons who are, or are to be, principally responsible for the conduct of its affairs (whether as directors, shadow directors, managers or otherwise),
- (d) the manner and capacity in which the applicant proposes to take part or be concerned in the promotion or formation of the company or, as the case may be, its management, and
- (e) the emoluments and other benefits to be obtained from the directorship.

6.203(3) **[If company in existence]** If the company is already in existence, the affidavit must specify the date of its incorporation and the amount of its nominal and issued share capital; and if not, it must specify the amount, or approximate amount, of its proposed commencing share capital, and the sources from which that capital is to be obtained.

6.203(4)   [Taking part in promotion etc.]   Where the bankrupt intends to take part or be concerned in the promotion or formation of a company, the affidavit must contain an undertaking by him that he will, within not less than 7 days of the company being incorporated, file in court a copy of its memorandum of association and certificate of incorporation under section 13 of the Companies Act.

6.203(5)   [Venue and notice]   The court shall fix a venue for the hearing of the bankrupt's application, and give notice to him accordingly.

(See general note after r. 6.205.)

Rule 6.204   Report of official receiver

6.204(1)   [Notice of venue etc.]   The bankrupt shall, not less than 28 days before the date fixed for the hearing, give to the official receiver and the trustee notice of the venue, accompanied by copies of the application and the affidavit under Rule 6.203.

6.204(2)   [Official receiver's report]   The official receiver may, not less than 14 days before the date fixed for the hearing, file in court a report of any matters which he considers ought to be drawn to the court's attention. A copy of the report shall be sent by him, forthwith after it is filed, to the bankrupt and to the trustee.

6.204(3)   [Where bankrupt disputes report]   The bankrupt may, not later than 7 days before the date of the hearing, file in court a notice specifying any statements in the official receiver's report which he intends to deny or dispute.

If he gives notice under this paragraph, he shall send copies of it, not less than 4 days before the date of the hearing, to the official receiver and the trustee.

6.204(4)   [Appearances]   The official receiver and the trustee may appear on the hearing of the application, and may make representations and put to the bankrupt such questions as the court may allow.

(See general note after r. 6.205.)

Rule 6.205   Court's order on application

6.205(1)   [If court grants application]   If the court grants the bankrupt's application for leave under section 11 of the Company Directors Disqualification Act 1986, its order shall specify that which by virtue of the order the bankrupt has leave to do.

6.205(2)   [Powers of court]   The court may at the same time, having regard to any representations made by the trustee on the hearing of the application—

    (a) include in the order provision varying an income payments order already in force in respect of the bankrupt, or

    (b) if no income payments order is in force, make one.

6.205(3)   [Copies of order]   Whether or not the application is granted, copies of the order shall be sent by the court to the bankrupt, the trustee and the official receiver.

General note to rr. 6.203–6.205

The placement of these provisions within the Insolvency Rules is puzzling (but a similar provision was contained in BR 1952, r. 238). These rules relate to applications by a bankrupt for leave to participate in company management under CDDA 1986, s. 11. The official receiver is to be notified to give him a chance to put his views to the court.

Chapter 21 — Annulment of Bankruptcy Order

Rule 6.206 Application for annulment

6.206(1) [Form of application]   An application to the court under section 282(1) for the annulment of a bankruptcy order shall specify whether it is made—

    (a) under subsection (1)(a) of the section (claim that the order ought not to have been made), or

    (b) under subsection (1)(b) (debts and expenses of the bankruptcy all paid or secured).

6.206(2) [Supporting affidavit]   The application shall, in either case, be supported by an affidavit stating the grounds on which it is made; and, where it is made under section 282(1)(b), there shall be set out in the affidavit all the facts by reference to which the court is, under the Act and the Rules, required to be satisfied before annulling the bankruptcy order.

6.206(3) [Copy of application etc.]   A copy of the application and supporting affidavit shall be filed in court; and the court shall give to the applicant notice of the venue fixed for the hearing.

6.206(4) [Notice of venue]   The applicant shall give to the official receiver and (if other) the trustee notice of the venue, accompanied by copies of the application and the affidavit under paragraph (2)—

    (a) where the application is made under section 282(1)(a), in sufficient time to enable them to be present at the hearing, and

    (b) where the application is made under section 282(1)(b), not less than 28 days before the hearing.

6.206(5) [Where application under s. 282(1)(a)]   Where the application is made under section 282(1)(a), paragraph (4) shall additionally be complied with in relation to the person on whose petition the bankruptcy order was made.

History note

In r. 6.206(4) the words ", not less than 28 days before the hearing," formerly appearing after the words "The applicant shall" were omitted and paras. (*a*) and (*b*) were added by I(A)R 1987 (SI 1987 No. 1919), r. 3(1), Sch., Pt. 1, para. 121(1) as from 11 January 1988.

    Rule 6.206(5) was added by I(A)R 1987 (SI 1987 No. 1919), r. 3(1), Sch., Pt. 1, para. 121(2) as from 11 January 1988.

General note

The general 28-day limit originally fixed by r. 6.206(4) was modified to deal with applications under s. 282(1)(*a*).

(See also general note after r. 6.215.)

Rule 6.207   Report by trustee

6.207(1)   [Application of Rule]   The following applies where the application is made under section 282(1)(b) (debts and expenses of the bankruptcy all paid or secured).

6.207(2)   [Contents of report]   Not less than 21 days before the date fixed for the hearing, the trustee or, if no trustee has been appointed, the official receiver shall file in court a report with respect to the following matters—

(a) the circumstances leading to the bankruptcy;

(b) (in summarised form) the extent of the bankrupt's assets and liabilities at the date of the bankruptcy order and at the date of the present application;

(c) details of creditors (if any) who are known to him to have claims, but have not proved; and

(d) such other matters as the person making the report considers to be, in the circumstances, necessary for the information of the court.

6.207(3)   [Particulars of debts etc.]   The report shall include particulars of the extent (if any) to which, and the manner in which, the debts and expenses of the bankruptcy have been paid or secured.

In so far as debts and expenses are unpaid but secured, the person making the report shall state in it whether and to what extent he considers the security to be satisfactory.

6.207(4)   [Copy of report to applicant]   A copy of the report shall be sent to the applicant at least 14 days before the date fixed for the hearing; and he may, if he wishes, file further affidavits in answer to statements made in the report.

Copies of any such affidavits shall be sent by the applicant to the official receiver and (if other) the trustee.

6.207(5)   [If trustee not official receiver]   If the trustee is other than the official receiver, a copy of his report shall be sent to the official receiver at least 21 days before the hearing. The official receiver may then file an additional report, a copy of which shall be sent to the applicant at least 7 days before the hearing.

(See also general note after r. 6.215.)

Rule 6.208   Power of court to stay proceedings

6.208(1)   [Interim order]   The court may, in advance of the hearing, make an interim order staying any proceedings which it thinks ought, in the circumstances of the application, to be stayed.

6.208(2)   [Ex parte application]   Except in relation to an application for an order staying all or any part of the proceedings in the bankruptcy, application for an order under this Rule may be made *ex parte*.

6.208(3)   [Copies of application]   Where application is made under this Rule for an order staying all or any part of the proceedings in the bankruptcy, the applicant shall send copies of the application to the official receiver and (if other) the trustee in sufficient time to enable them to be present at the hearing and (if they wish to do so) make representations.

6.208(4)   **[Effect of staying order on annulment]**   Where the court makes an order under this Rule staying all or any part of the proceedings in the bankruptcy, the rules in this Chapter nevertheless continue to apply to any application for, or other matters in connection with, the annulment of the bankruptcy order.

6.208(5)   **[Copies of staying order]**   If the court makes an order under this Rule, it shall send copies of the order to the applicant, the official receiver and (if other) the trustee.

History note

Rules 6.208(2) to (5) were substituted for the former r. 6.208(2) by I(A)R 1987 (SI 1987 No. 1919), r. 3(1), Sch., Pt. 1, para. 122 as from 11 January 1988: the former r. 6.208(2) read as follows:

   "**6.208(2)** Application for an interim order under this Rule may be made *ex parte*".

General note

Rule 6.208 was substantially expanded to enable the official receiver to have an early warning of an application to stay. There is also provision for annulment proceedings.

(See also general note after r. 6.215.)

Rule 6.209   Notice to creditors who have not proved

6.209   Where the application for annulment is made under section 282(1)(b) and it has been reported to the court Rule 6.207 that there are known creditors of the bankrupt who have not proved, the court may—

    (a)   direct the trustee or, if no trustee has been appointed, the official receiver to send notice of the application to such of those creditors as the court thinks ought to be informed of it, with a view to their proving their debts (if they so wish) within 21 days, and

    (b)   direct the trustee or, if no trustee has been appointed, the official receiver to advertise the fact that the application has been made, so that creditors who have not proved may do so within a specified time, and

    (c)   adjourn the application meanwhile, for any period not less than 35 days.

History note

In r. 6.209(*a*) and (*b*) the words "or, if no trustee has been appointed, the official receiver" in both places where they occur were inserted by I(A)R 1987 (SI 1987 No. 1919), r. 3(1), Sch., Pt. 1, para. 123 as from 11 January 1988.

General note

For the significance of r. 6.209 see the comments of Warner J in *Re Robertson (A Bankrupt)* [1989] 1 WLR 1139.

(See general note after r. 6.215.)

Rule 6.210   The hearing

6.210(1)   **[Trustee to attend]**   The trustee shall attend the hearing of the application.

6.210(2)   [Attendance of official receiver]   The official receiver, if he is not the trustee, may attend, but is not required to do so unless he has filed a report under Rule 6.207.

6.210(3)   [Copies of order]   If the court makes an order on the application, it shall send copies of the order to the applicant, the official receiver and (if other) the trustee.   [FORM 6.71]

(See general note after r. 6.215.)

Rule 6.211   Matters to be proved under s. 282(1)(b)

6.211(1)   [Application of Rule]   This rule applies with regard to the matters which must, in an application under section 282(1)(b), be proved to the satisfaction of the court.

6.211(2)   [Debts paid in full]   Subject to the following paragraph, all bankruptcy debts which have been proved must have been paid in full.

6.211(3)   [If debt disputed etc.]   If a debt is disputed, or a creditor who has proved can no longer be traced, the bankrupt must have given such security (in the form of money paid into court, or a bond entered into with approved sureties) as the court considers adequate to satisfy any sum that may subsequently be proved to be due to the creditor concerned and (if the court thinks fit) costs.

6.211(4)   [Advertisement in case of untraced creditor]   Where under paragraph (3) security has been given in the case of an untraced creditor, the court may direct that particulars of the alleged debt, and the security, be advertised in such manner as it thinks fit.

If advertisement is ordered under this paragraph, and no claim on the security is made within 12 months from the date of the advertisement (or the first advertisement, if more than one), the court shall, on application in that behalf, order the security to be released.

General note

For the significance of r. 6.211 see *Re Robertson (A Bankrupt)* [1989] 1 WLR 1139.

(See general note after r. 6.215.)

Rule 6.212   Notice to creditors

6.212(1)   [Notice of annulment]   Where the official receiver has notified creditors of the debtor's bankruptcy, and the bankruptcy order is annulled, he shall forthwith notify them of the annulment.

6.212(2)   [Expenses of giving notice]   Expenses incurred by the official receiver in giving notice under this Rule are a charge in his favour on the property of the former bankrupt, whether or not actually in his hands.

6.212(3)   [Property in hands of trustee etc.]   Where any property is in the hands of a trustee or any person other than the former bankrupt himself, the official receiver's charge is valid subject only to any costs that may be incurred by the trustee or that other person in effecting realisation of the property for the purpose of satisfying the charge.

(See general note after r. 6.215.)

Rule 6.212A   Annulment under s. 261

6.212A   Rules 6.206 to 6.212 apply to an application for annulment under section 261 as they apply to such an application under section 282(1)(a).

History note

Rule 6.212A was inserted by I(A)R 1987 (SI 1987 No. 1919), r. 3(1), Sch., Pt. 1, para. 124 as from 11 January 1988.

General note

Rule 6.212A was intended to fill a lacuna in the case of annulments following acceptance of a proposal for an individual voluntary arrangement.

Rule 6.213   Other matters arising on annulment

6.213(1)   **[Contents of ss. 261 or 282 order]**   In an order under section 261 or 282 the court shall include provision permitting vacation of the registration of the bankruptcy petition as a pending action, and of the bankruptcy order, in the register of writs and orders affecting land.

6.213(2)   **[Notice of order]**   The court shall forthwith give notice of the making of the order to the Secretary of State.

6.213(3)   **[Requiring advertisement of order]**   The former bankrupt may require the Secretary of State to give notice of the making of the order—

     (a) in the Gazette, or

     (b) in any newspaper in which the bankruptcy order was advertised, or

     (c) in both.

6.213(4)   **[Requirement under r. 6.213(3), cost of advertisement]**   Any requirement by the former bankrupt under paragraph (3) shall be addressed to the Secretary of State in writing. The Secretary of State shall notify him forthwith as to the cost of the advertisement, and is under no obligation to advertise until that sum has been paid.

6.213(5)   **[Former bankrupt deceased etc.]**   Where the former bankrupt has died, or is a person incapable of managing his affairs (within the meaning of Chapter 7 in Part 7 of the Rules), the references to him in paragraphs (3) and (4) are to be read as referring to his personal representative or, as the case may be, a person appointed by the court to represent or act for him.

History note

In r. 6.213(1) the words "261 or" were inserted by I(A)R 1987 (SI 1987 No. 1919), r. 3(1), Sch., Pt. 1, para. 125 as from 11 January 1988.

(See general note after r. 6.215.)

Rule 6.214   Trustee's final account

6.214(1)   [Duty to account for all transactions]   Where a bankruptcy order is annulled under section 261 or 282, this does not of itself release the trustee from any duty or obligation, imposed on him by or under the Act or the Rules, to account for all his transactions in connection with the former bankrupt's estate.

6.214(2)   [Final account to Secretary of State etc.]   The trustee shall submit a copy of his final account to the Secretary of State, as soon as practicable after the court's order annulling the bankruptcy order; and he shall file a copy of the final account in court.

6.214(3)   [Contents of final account]   The final account must include a summary of the trustee's receipts and payments in the administration, and contain a statement to the effect that he has reconciled his account with that which is held by the Secretary of State in respect of the bankruptcy.

6.214(4)   [Release of trustee]   The trustee is released from such time as the court may determine, having regard to whether—

    (a) paragraph (2) of this Rule has been complied with, and

    (b) any security given under Rule 6.211(3) has been, or will be, released.

History note

In r. 6.214(1) the words "261 or" were inserted by I(A)R 1987 (SI 1987 No. 1919), r. 3(1), Sch., Pt. 1, para. 126 as from 11 January 1988.

(See general note after r. 6.215.)

Chapter 22 — Discharge

Rule 6.215   Application for suspension of discharge

6.215(1)   [Application of Rule]   The following applies where the official receiver applies to the court for an order under section 279(3) (suspension of automatic discharge), but not where he makes that application, pursuant to Rule 6.176(4), on the adjournment of the bankrupt's public examination.

6.215(2)   [Official receiver's report]   The official receiver shall with his application file a report setting out the reasons why it appears to him that such an order should be made.

6.215(3)   [Venue and notice]   The court shall fix a venue for the hearing of the application, and give notice of it to the official receiver, the trustee and the bankrupt.

6.215(4)   [Copies of report to trustee and bankrupt]   Copies of the official receiver's report under this Rule shall be sent by him to the trustee and the bankrupt, so as to reach them at least 21 days before the date fixed for the hearing.

6.215(5)   [Where bankrupt disputes report]   The bankrupt may, not later than 7 days before the date of the hearing, file in court a notice specifying any statements in the official receiver's report which he intends to deny or dispute.

If he gives notice under this paragraph, he shall send copies of it, not less than 4 days before the date of the hearing, to the official receiver and the trustee.

6.215(6)   [Copies of order]   If on the hearing the court makes an order suspending the bankrupt's discharge, copies of the order shall be sent by the court to the official receiver, the trustee and the bankrupt.   [FORM 6.72]

General note to rr. 6.206–6.215

The key provisions on annulment of bankruptcy orders, IA 1986, ss. 261 and 282, leave many questions unanswered. These rules provide the necessary answers. The form of the application to the court is prescribed and if the application is under s. 282(1)(*b*), a full report from the trustee is required. Proceedings can be stayed where an annulment application is pending. Notice of the application may have to be sent to known creditors who have not proved. Public advertisements may also be required. The court order for the annulment should be in the style of Form 6.71, which has been amended by I(A)R 1991 (SI 1991 No. 495), r. 3, Sch., para. 5 from 2 April 1991, to remove the word "local" before "newspaper". Rule 6.211 explains further s. 282(1)(*b*). Creditors must be notified of the annulment, entries in the Land Register, etc. will have to be vacated, the Secretary of State must be told and the former bankrupt can demand that the annulment be publicly advertised. Rule 6.214 is a necessary saving provision relating to the trustee's accounts. Note the amendments of rr. 6.213 and 6.214 to include annulments under s. 261.

Rule 6.216   Lifting of suspension of discharge

6.216(1)   [Bankrupt may apply to court]   Where the court has made an order under section 279(3) that the relevant period (that is to say, the period after which the bankrupt may under that section have his discharge) shall cease to run, the bankrupt may apply to it for the order to be discharged.

6.216(2)   [Venue and notice]   The court shall fix a venue for the hearing of the application; and the bankrupt shall, not less than 28 days before the date fixed for hearing, give notice of the venue to the official receiver and the trustee, accompanied in each case by a copy of the application.

6.216(3)   [Appearances etc.]   The official receiver and the trustee may appear and be heard on the bankrupt's application; and, whether or not he appears, the official receiver may file in court a report of any matters which he considers ought to be drawn to the court's attention.

6.216(4)   [If conditions specified in order]   If the court's order under section 279(3) was for the relevant period to cease to run until the fulfilment of specified conditions, the court may request a report from the official receiver as to whether those conditions have or have not been fulfilled.

6.216(5)   [Copies of rr. 6.216(3), (4) report]   If a report is filed under paragraph (3) or (4), copies of it shall be sent by the official receiver to the bankrupt and the trustee, not later than 14 days before the hearing.

6.216(6)   [Where bankrupt disputes report]   The bankrupt may, not later than 7 days before the date of the hearing, file in court a notice specifying any statements in the official receiver's report which he intends to deny or dispute.

If he gives notice under this paragraph, he shall send copies of it, not less than 4 days before the date of the hearing, to the official receiver and the trustee.

6.216(7) **[If court discharges s. 279(3) order]** If on the bankrupt's application the court discharges the order under section 279(3) (being satisfied that the relevant period should begin to run again), it shall issue to the bankrupt a certificate that it has done so, with effect from a specified date. [FORM 6.73]
[FORM 6.74]

General note

For the meaning of "venue" in r. 6.216(2) see r. 13.6.

(See also general note after r. 6.223.)

Rule 6.217 Application by bankrupt for discharge

6.217(1) **[If bankrupt makes s. 280 application]** If the bankrupt applies under section 280 for an order discharging him from bankruptcy, he shall give to the official receiver notice of the application, and deposit with him such sum as the latter may require to cover his costs of the application.

6.217(2) **[Venue and notice]** The court, if satisfied that paragraph (1) has been complied with, shall fix a venue for the hearing of the application, and give at least 42 days' notice of it to the official receiver and the bankrupt.

6.127(3) **[Notice by official receiver]** The official receiver shall give notice accordingly—

(a) to the trustee, and

(b) to every creditor who, to the official receiver's knowledge, has a claim outstanding against the estate which has not been satisfied.

6.127(4) **[Time for r. 6.127(3) notice]** Notices under paragraph (3) shall be given not later than 14 days before the date fixed for the hearing of the bankrupt's application.

(See also general note after r. 6.223.)

Rule 6.218 Report of official receiver

6.218(1) **[Contents etc. of report]** Where the bankrupt makes an application under section 280, the official receiver shall, at least 21 days before the date fixed for the hearing of the application, file in court a report containing the following information with respect to the bankrupt—

(a) any failure by him to comply with his obligations under Parts VIII to XI of the Act;

(b) the circumstances surrounding the present bankruptcy, and those surrounding any previous bankruptcy of his;

(c) the extent to which, in the present and in any previous bankruptcy, his liabilities have exceeded his assets; and

(d) particulars of any distribution which has been, or is expected to be, made to creditors in the present bankruptcy or, if such is the case, that there has been and is to be no distribution;

and the official receiver shall include in his report any other matters which in his opinion ought to be brought to the court's attention.

6.218(2) **[Copies of reports]** The official receiver shall send a copy of the report to the bankrupt and the trustee, so as to reach them at least 14 days before the date of the hearing of the application under section 280.

6.218(3) **[Where bankrupt disputes report]** The bankrupt may, not later than 7 days before the date of the hearing, file in court a notice specifying any statements in the official receiver's report which he intends to deny or dispute.

If he gives notice under this paragraph, he shall send copies of it, not less than 4 days before the date of the hearing, to the official receiver and the trustee.

[FORM 6.75]

6.218(4) **[Appearances]** The official receiver, the trustee and any creditor may appear on the hearing of the bankrupt's application, and may make representations and put to the bankrupt such questions as the court may allow.

(See general note after r. 6.223.)

Rule 6.219   Order of discharge on application

6.219(1) **[Order to take effect when drawn up by court]** An order of the court under section 280(2)(b) (discharge absolutely) or (c) (discharge subject to conditions with respect to income or property) shall bear the date on which it is made, but does not take effect until such time as it is drawn up by the court.   [FORM 6.76]

6.219(2) **[Retrospective effect]** The order then has effect retrospectively to the date on which it was made.

6.219(3) **[Copies of order]** Copies of any order made by the court on an application by the bankrupt for discharge under section 280 shall be sent by the court to the bankrupt, the trustee and the official receiver.

(See general note after r. 6.223.)

Rule 6.220   Certificate of discharge

6.220(1) **[Where bankrupt is discharged]** Where it appears to the court that a bankrupt is discharged, whether by expiration of time or otherwise, the court shall, on his application, issue to him a certificate of his discharge, and the date from which it is effective.   [FORM 6.77]

6.220(2) **[Requiring advertisement of discharge]** The discharged bankrupt may require the Secretary of State to give notice of the discharge—

(a) in the Gazette, or

(b) in any newspaper in which the bankruptcy was advertised, or

(c) in both.

6.220(3)   **[Requirement in r. 6.220(2), cost of advertisement]**   Any requirement by the former bankrupt under paragraph (2) shall be addressed to the Secretary of State in writing. The Secretary of State shall notify him forthwith as to the cost of the advertisement, and is under no obligation to advertise until that sum has been paid.

6.220(4)   **[Former bankrupt deceased etc.]**   Where the former bankrupt has died, or is a person incapable of managing his affairs (within the meaning of Chapter 7 in Part 7 of the Rules), the references to him in paragraphs (2) and (3) are to be read as referring to his personal representative or, as the case may be, a person appointed by the court to represent or act for him.

(See general note after r. 6.223.)

Rule 6.221   Deferment of issue of order pending appeal

6.221   An order made by the court on an application by the bankrupt for discharge under section 280 shall not be issued or gazetted until the time allowed for appealing has expired or, if an appeal is entered, until the appeal has been determined.

(See general note after r. 6.223.)

Rule 6.222   Costs under this Chapter

6.222   In no case do any costs or expenses arising under this Chapter fall on the official receiver personally.

(See general note after r. 6.223.)

Rule 6.223   Bankrupt's debts surviving discharge

6.223   Discharge does not release the bankrupt from any obligation arising under a confiscation order made under section 1 of the Drug Trafficking Offences Act 1986 or section 1 of the Criminal Justice (Scotland) Act 1987 or section 71 of the Criminal Justice Act 1988.

History note

In r. 6.223 the words "or section 1 of the Criminal Justice (Scotland) Act 1987" were added by I(A)R 1987 (SI 1987 No. 1919), r. 3(1), Sch., Pt. 1, para. 127 as from 11 January 1988, and the words "or section 71 of the Criminal Justice Act 1988" by I(A)R 1989 (SI 1989 No. 397), r. 3(1), Sch., as from 3 April 1989.

General note to rr. 6.216–6.223

These rules provide additional information on the effect of IA 1986, ss. 279–281. Compare BR 1952, rr. 225–237G. Applications for suspension of automatic discharge under s. 279(3) are explained. If the court orders suspension, Form 6.72 is to be used. Suspension orders can be varied by the court. Note the use of Forms 6.73 and 6.74 here. Rules 6.217 and 6.218 are specially referable to applications by the bankrupt to the court for discharge under IA 1986, s. 280. The official receiver must be notified and he must file a report on the bankrupt's conduct. Form 6.76 is to be used for any court order under s. 280. Certificates of discharge must normally adopt the style of Form 6.77. Rule 6.223 is a specialised provision dealing with the enforcement of sanctions against drug dealers – compare s. 281(4).

Chapter 23 — Order of Payment of Costs, Etc., out of Estate

Rule 6.224 General rule as to priority

6.224(1) **[Priority of expenses]** The expenses of the bankruptcy are payable out of the estate in the following order of priority—

- (a) expenses properly chargeable or incurred by the official receiver or the trustee in preserving, realising or getting in any of the assets of the bankrupt, including those incurred in acquiring title to after-acquired property;
- (b) any other expenses incurred or disbursements made by the official receiver or under his authority, including those incurred or made in carrying on the business of a debtor or bankrupt;
- (c) (i) the fee payable under any order made under section 415 for the performance by the official receiver of his general duties as official receiver;
- (ii) any repayable deposit lodged by the petitioner under any such order as security for the fee mentioned in subparagraph (i) (except where the deposit is applied to the payment of the remuneration of an insolvency practitioner appointed under section 273 (debtor's petition));
- (d) any other fees payable under any order made under section 415, including those payable to the official receiver, and any remuneration payable to him under general regulations;
- (e) the cost of any security provided by an interim receiver, trustee or special manager in accordance with the Act or the Rules;
- (f) the remuneration of the interim receiver (if any);
- (g) any deposit lodged on an application for the appointment of an interim receiver;
- (h) the costs of the petitioner, and of any person appearing on the petition whose costs are allowed by the court;
- (j) the remuneration of the special manager (if any);
- (k) any amount payable to a person employed or authorised, under Chapter 5 of this Part of the Rules, to assist in the preparation of a statement of affairs or of accounts;

(l) any allowance made, by order of the court, towards costs on an application for release from the obligation to submit a statement of affairs, or for an extension of time for submitting such a statement;

(m) any necessary disbursements by the trustee in the course of his administration (including any expenses incurred by members of the creditors' committee or their representatives and allowed by the trustee under Rule 6.164, but not including any payment of capital gains tax in circumstances referred to in sub-paragraph (p) below);

(n) the remuneration or emoluments of any person (including the bankrupt) who has been employed by the trustee to perform any services for the estate, as required or authorised by or under the Act or the Rules;

(o) the remuneration of the trustee, up to any amount not exceeding that which is payable to the official receiver under general regulations;

(p) the amount of any capital gains tax on chargeable gains accruing on the realisation of any asset of the bankrupt (without regard to whether the realisation is effected by the trustee, a secured creditor, or a receiver or manager appointed to deal with a security);

(q) the balance, after payment of any sums due under sub-paragraph (o) above, of any remuneration due to the trustee.

6.224(2)   [Costs of shorthand writer]   The costs of employing a shorthand writer, if appointed by an order of the court made at the instance of the official receiver in connection with an examination, rank in priority with those specified in paragraph (1)(a). The costs of employing a shorthand writer so appointed in any other case rank after the allowance mentioned in paragraph (1)(l) and before the disbursements mentioned in paragraph (1)(m).

6.224(3)   [Expenses of r. 6.174 examination]   Any expenses incurred in holding an examination under Rule 6.174 (examinee unfit), where the application for it is made by the official receiver, rank in priority with those specified in paragraph (1)(a).

General note

This is the normal priority régime though it is described in great detail here. Link this list with IA 1986, s. 328. Compare BR 1952, r. 115. For "general regulations" see r. 13.13(5).

Chapter 24 — Second Bankruptcy

Rule 6.225   Scope of this Chapter

6.225(1)   [Application of Ch. 24 Rules]   The Rules in this Chapter relate to the manner in which, in the case of a second bankruptcy, the trustee in the earlier bankruptcy is to deal with property and money to which section 334(3) applies, until there is a trustee of the estate in the later bankruptcy.

6.225(2)   [Definitions]   "The earlier bankruptcy", "the later bankruptcy" and **"the existing trustee"** have the meanings given by section 334(1).

(See general note after r. 6.228.)

Rule 6.226   General duty of existing trustee

6.226(1)   **[Duty to get in property etc.]**   Subject as follows, the existing trustee shall take into his custody or under his control all such property and money, in so far as he has not already done so as part of his duties as trustee in the earlier bankruptcy.

6.226(2)   **[Power to sell perishable goods etc.]**   Where any of that property consists of perishable goods, or goods the value of which is likely to diminish if they are not disposed of, the existing trustee has power to sell or otherwise dispose of those goods.

6.226(3)   **[Proceeds of sale]**   The proceeds of any such sale or disposal shall be held, under the existing trustee's control, with the other property and money comprised in the bankrupt's estate.

(See general note after r. 6.228.)

Rule 6.227   Delivery up to later trustee

6.227   The existing trustee shall, as and when requested by the trustee for the purposes of the later bankruptcy, deliver up to the latter all such property and money as is in his custody or under his control in pursuance of Rule 6.226.

(See general note after r. 6.228.)

Rule 6.228   Existing trustee's expenses

6.228   Any expenses incurred by the existing trustee in compliance with section 335 (1) and this Chapter of the Rules shall be defrayed out of, and are a charge on, all such property and money as is referred to in section 334(3), whether in the hands of the existing trustee or of the trustee for the purposes of the later bankruptcy.

General note to rr. 6.225–6.228

These rules supplement IA 1986, s. 334 and deal with the complex relationship between the two successive bankruptcy régimes.

Chapter 25 — Criminal Bankruptcy

Rule 6.229   Presentation of petition

6.229(1)   **[Presentation to High Court]**   In criminal bankruptcy, the petition under section 264(1)(d) shall be presented to the High Court, and accordingly Rule 6.9 in Chapter 2 (court in which other petitions to be presented) does not apply.

[FORM 6.79]

6.229(2)   **[Effect of Rule]**   This does not affect the High Court's power to order that the proceedings be transferred.

(See general note after r. 6.234.)

Rule **6.230** Status and functions of Official Petitioner

6.230(1) **[Official Petitioner as a creditor]** Subject as follows, the Official Petitioner is to be regarded for all purposes of the Act and the Rules as a creditor of the bankrupt.

6.230(2) **[Attendance, representation etc.]** He may attend or be represented at any meeting of creditors, and is to be given any notice under the Act or the Rules which is required or authorised to be given to creditors; and the requirements of the Rules as to the lodging or use of proxies do not apply.

(See general note after r. 6.234.)

Rule **6.231** Interim receivership

6.231 Chapter 4 of this Part of the Rules applies in criminal bankruptcy only in so far as it provides for the appointment of the official receiver as interim receiver.

(See general note after r. 6.234.)

Rule **6.232** Proof of bankruptcy debts and notice of order

6.232(1) **[Effect of order]** The making of a bankruptcy order on a criminal bankruptcy petition does not affect the right of creditors to prove for their debts arising otherwise than in consequence of the criminal proceedings.

6.232(2) **[Person suffering loss etc.]** A person specified in a criminal bankruptcy order as having suffered loss or damage shall be treated as a creditor of the bankrupt; and a copy of the order is sufficient evidence of his claim, subject to its being shown by any party to the bankruptcy proceedings that the loss or damage actually suffered was more or (as the case may be) less than the amount specified in the order.

6.232(3) **[Non-application of Rules]** The requirements of the Rules with respect to the proof of debts do not apply to the Official Petitioner.

6.232(4) **[Forms of proof]** In criminal bankruptcy, forms of proof shall be sent out by the official receiver within 12 weeks from the making of the bankruptcy order, to every creditor who is known to him, or is identified in the bankrupt's statements of affairs.

6.232(5) **[Notice to creditors]** The official receiver shall, within those 12 weeks, send to every such creditor notice of the making of the bankruptcy order.

History note

Rule 6.232(4) was substituted by I(A)R 1987 (SI 1987 No. 1919), r. 3(1), Sch., Pt. 1, para. 128 as from 11 January 1988: the former r. 6.232(4) read as follows:

"**6.232(4)** In criminal bankruptcy, the forms to be used by any person for the purpose of proving bankruptcy debts shall be sent out by the official receiver, not less than 12 weeks from the making of the bankruptcy order, to every creditor who is known to him, or is identified in the bankrupt's statement of affairs."

General note

The new r. 6.232(4) makes it clear that forms of proof do not have to be in a prescribed format. The deadline has been changed to within 12 weeks, which was what was originally intended but not conveyed by the language of the previous provision.

(See also general note after r. 6.234.)

Rule 6.233 Meetings under the Rules

6.233(1) **[Non-application of Ch. 6 Rules]** The following Rules in Chapter 6 of this Part do not apply in criminal bankruptcy—

Rules 6.79 and 6.80 (first meeting of creditors, and business thereat);

Rule 6.82(2) (the chairman, if other than the official receiver);

Rule 6.88(2) and (3) (resolution for appointment of trustee).

6.233(2) **[Non-application of r. 6.97]** Rule 6.97 (supply of forms for proof of debts) does not apply.

(See general note after r. 6.234.)

Rule 6.234 Trustee in bankruptcy; creditors' committee; annulment of bankruptcy order

6.234(1) **[Non-application of Ch. 10 Rules]** Chapter 10 of this Part of the Rules does not apply in criminal bankruptcy, except Rules 6.136 (release of official receiver) and 6.147 (power of court to set aside transactions).

6.234(2) **[Non-application of Ch. 11 Rules]** Chapter 11 (creditors' committee) does not apply.

6.234(3) **[Application of Ch. 21 Rules]** Chapter 21 (annulment of bankruptcy order) applies to an application to the court under section 282(2) as it applies to an application under section 282(1), with any necessary modifications.

History note

In r. 6.234(1) the words "Chapter 10" were substituted for the former words "Chapter 11" by I(A)R 1987 (SI 1987 No. 1919), r. 3(1), Sch., Pt. 1, para. 129(1) as from 11 January 1988.

In r. 6.234(2) the words "Chapter 11" were substituted for the former words "Chapter 12" by I(A)R 1987 (SI 1987 No. 1919), r. 3(1), Sch., Pt. 1, para. 129(2) as from 11 January 1988.

General note to rr. 6.229–6.234

The criminal bankruptcy régime (see IA 1986, s. 277) sits uneasily alongside the other facets of bankruptcy law. Further details of its operation are hereby provided. The form of the petition (Form 6.79) and the rôle of the Official Petitioner (see IA 1986, s. 402) are described. Proof of debts, meetings of creditors, etc., are also regulated by these rules.

The amendment to r. 6.232(4) by I(A)R 1987 is discussed above. Typographical errors in r. 6.234 have also been amended.

The criminal bankruptcy régime is to be abolished by the Criminal Justice Act 1988 — see the note to IA 1986, s. 277.

Chapter 26 — Miscellaneous Rules in Bankruptcy

Rule 6.235   Bankruptcy of solicitors

6.235   Where a bankruptcy order is made against a solicitor, or such an order made against a solicitor is rescinded or annulled, the court shall forthwith give notice to the Secretary of the Law Society of the order that it has made.

Rule 6.236   Consolidation of petitions

6.236   Where two or more bankruptcy petitions are presented against the same debtor, the court may order the consolidation of the proceedings, on such terms as it thinks fit.

General note

This provision would have been better located perhaps towards the beginning of this Part of the rules.

Rule 6.237   Bankrupt's dwelling-house and home

6.237(1)   **[Application of Rule]**   This Rule applies where the trustee applies to the court under section 313 for an order imposing a charge on property consisting of an interest in a dwelling-house.   [FORM 6.79A]

6.237(2)   **[Respondents to application]**   The bankrupt's spouse or former spouse shall be made respondent to the application; and the court may, if it thinks fit, direct other persons to be made respondents also, in respect of any interest which they may have in the property.

6.237(3)   **[Contents of trustee's report]**   The trustee shall make a report to the court, containing the following particulars—

- (a) the extent of the bankrupt's interest in the property which is the subject of the application; and
- (b) the amount which, at the date of the application, remains owing to unsecured creditors of the bankrupt.

6.237(4)   **[Terms of charge]**   The terms of the charge to be imposed shall be agreed between the trustee and the bankrupt or, failing agreement, shall be settled by the court.

6.237(5) **[Rate of interest]** The rate of interest applicable under section 313(2) is the rate specified in section 17 of the Judgments Act 1838 on the day on which the charge is imposed, and the rate so applicable shall be stated in the court's order imposing the charge.

6.237(6) **[Contents of order]** The court's order shall also—

   (a) describe the property to be charged;

   (b) state whether the title to the property is registered and, if it is, specify the title number;

   (c) set out the extent of the bankrupt's interest in the property which has vested in the trustee;

   (d) indicate, by reference to any, or the total, amount which is payable otherwise than to the bankrupt out of the estate and of interest on that amount, how the amount of the charge to be imposed is to be ascertained;

   (e) set out the conditions (if any) imposed by the court under section 3(1) of the Charging Orders Act 1979;

   (f) identify when any property charged under section 313 shall cease to be comprised in the bankrupt's estate and, subject to the charge (and any prior charge), to vest in the bankrupt.

6.237(7) **[Date under r. 6.237(6)(f)]** Unless the court is of the opinion that a different date is appropriate, the date under paragraph (6)(f) shall be that of the registration of the charge in accordance with section 3(2) of the Charging Orders Act 1979.

6.237(8) **[Notice to Chief Land Registrar]** The trustee shall, forthwith after the making of the court's order, send notice of it and its effect to the Chief Land Registrar.

History note

Against r. 6.237(1) the words "[FORM 6.79A]" were inserted by I(A)R 1987 (SI 1987 No. 1919), r. 3(1), Sch., Pt. 2, para. 156(1) as from 11 January 1988.

   In r. 6.237(6) paras. (*d*) and (*f*) were substituted by I(A)R 1987 (SI 1987 No. 1919), r. 3(1), Sch., Pt. 1, para. 130 as from 11 January 1988: the former paras. (*d*) and (*f*) read as follows:

"(d) indicate, by reference to the amount which remains owing to unsecured creditors of the bankrupt, the amount of the charge to be imposed;

   (f) provide for any property comprised in the charge to vest again in the bankrupt as from a specified date."

General note

See IA 1986, s. 313 for the substantive law. Note the detailed information on the trustee's report and any court order made under s. 313.

   Form 6.79A is to be used for application under r. 6.237(1).

   The changes to r. 6.237(6) are designed to get the language of the rules in line with that used in s. 313 itself.

THE THIRD GROUP OF PARTS

PART 7 — COURT PROCEDURE AND PRACTICE

General comment on Pt. 7

Part 7 deals with the practice and procedure on all applications to the court, whether in corporate insolvency or individual bankruptcy, except for the three categories of petition listed in r. 7.1

Chapter 1 — Applications

Rule 7.1   Preliminary

7.1 This Chapter applies to any application made to the court under the Act or Rules except a petition for—

    (a) an administration order under Part II,

    (b) a winding-up order under Part IV, or

    (c) a bankruptcy order under Part IX

of the Act.

(See general note after r. 7.18.)

Rule 7.2   Interpretation

7.2(1)   **[Definitions]**   In this Chapter, except in so far as the context otherwise requires—

    "originating application" means an application to the court which is not an application in pending proceedings before the court; and   [FORM 7.1]

    "ordinary application" means any other application to the court.   [FORM 7.2]

7.2(2)   **[Form of application]**   Every application shall be in the form appropriate to the application concerned.

(See general note after r. 7.18.)

Rule 7.3   Form and contents of application

7.3(1)   **[Contents etc. of application]**   Each application shall be in writing and shall state—

    (a) the names of the parties;

    (b) the nature of the relief or order applied for or the directions sought from the court;

(c) the names and addresses of the persons (if any) on whom it is intended to serve the application or that no person is intended to be served;

(d) where the Act or Rules require that notice of the application is to be given to specified persons, the names and addresses of all those persons (so far as known to the applicant); and

(e) the applicant's address for service.

7.3(2) **[Grounds for application]**   An originating application shall set out the grounds on which the applicant claims to be entitled to the relief or order sought.

7.3(3) **[Application must be signed etc.]**   The application must be signed by the applicant if he is acting in person or, when he is not so acting, by or on behalf of his solicitor.

(See general note after r. 7.18.)

Rule 7.4   Filing and service of application

7.4(1) **[Filing etc.]**   The application shall be filed in court, accompanied by one copy and a number of additional copies equal to the number of persons who are to be served with the application.

7.4(2) **[Venue]**   Subject as follows in this Rule and the next, or unless the Rule under which the application is brought provides otherwise, or the court otherwise orders, upon the presentation of the documents mentioned in paragraph (1) above, the court shall fix a venue for the application to be heard.

7.4(3) **[Service]**   Unless the court otherwise directs, the applicant shall serve a sealed copy of the application, endorsed with the venue for the hearing, on the respondent named in the application (or on each respondent if more than one).

7.4(4) **[Directions]**   The court may give any of the following directions—

(a) that the application be served upon persons other than those specified by the relevant provision of the Act or Rules;

(b) that the giving of notice to any person may be dispensed with;

(c) that notice be given in some way other than that specified in paragraph (3).

7.4(5) **[Time for service]**   Unless the provision of the Act or Rules under which the application is made provides otherwise, and subject to the next paragraph, the application must be served at least 14 days before the date fixed for the hearing.

7.4(6) **[In case of urgency]**   Where the case is one of urgency, the court may (without prejudice to its general power to extend or abridge time limits)—

(a) hear the application immediately, either with or without notice to, or the attendance of, other parties, or

(b) authorise a shorter period of service than that provided for by paragraph (5);

and any such application may be heard on terms providing for the filing or service of documents, or the carrying out of other formalities, as the court thinks fit.

(See general note after r. 7.18.)

Rule 7.5   Other hearings ex parte

7.5(1)   [Ex parte applications]   Where the relevant provisions of the Act or Rules do not require service of the application on, or notice of it to be given to, any person, the court may hear the application *ex parte.*

7.5(2)   [Power of court]   Where the application is properly made *ex parte*, the court may hear it forthwith, without fixing a venue as required by Rule 7.4(2).

7.5(3)   [Alternative power]   Alternatively, the court may fix a venue for the application to be heard, in which case Rule 7.4 applies (so far as relevant).

(See general note after r. 7.18.)

Rule 7.6   Hearing of application

7.6(1)   [Hearing in chambers]   Unless allowed or authorised to be made otherwise, every application before the registrar shall, and every application before the judge may, be heard in chambers.

7.6(2)   [Registrar's jurisdiction]   Unless either—

(a) the judge has given a general or special direction to the contrary, or

(b) it is not within the registrar's power to make the order required,

the jurisdiction of the court to hear and determine the application may be exercised by the registrar, and the application shall be made to the registrar in the first instance.

7.6(3)   [Reference to judge]   Where the application is made to the registrar he may refer to the judge any matter which he thinks should properly be decided by the judge, and the judge may either dispose of the matter or refer it back to the registrar with such directions as he thinks fit.

7.6(4)   [Effect of Rule]   Nothing in this Rule precludes an application being made directly to the judge in a proper case.

(See general note after r. 7.18.)

Rule 7.7   Use of affidavit evidence

7.7(1)   [Affidavit evidence, attendance for cross-examination]   In any proceedings evidence may be given by affidavit unless by any provision of the Rules it is otherwise provided or the court otherwise directs; but the court may, on the application of any party, order the attendance for cross-examination of the person making the affidavit.

7.7(2)   [Where attendance for cross-examination ordered]   Where, after such an order has been made, the person in question does not attend, his affidavit shall not be used in evidence without the leave of the court.

(See general note after r. 7.18.)

951

Rule **7.8** Filing and service of affidavits

7.8(1) **[Filing in court etc.]** Unless the provision of the Act or Rules under which
the application is made provides otherwise, or the court otherwise allows—

(a) if the applicant intends to rely at the first hearing on affidavit evidence, he
shall file the affidavit or affidavits (if more than one) in court and serve a
copy or copies on the respondent, not less than 14 days before the date fixed
for the hearing, and

(b) where a respondent to an application intends to oppose it and to rely for
that purpose on affidavit evidence, he shall file the affidavit or affidavits (if
more than one) in court and serve a copy or copies on the applicant, not less
than 7 days before the date fixed for the hearing.

7.8(2) **[Swearing of affidavits]** Any affidavit may be sworn by the applicant or by
the respondent or by some other person possessing direct knowledge of the subject
matter of the application.

(See general note after r. 7.18.)

Rule **7.9** Use of reports

7.9(1) **[Filing report instead of affidavit]** A report may be filed in court instead of
an affidavit—

(a) in any case, by the official receiver (whether or not he is acting in any capacity mentioned in sub-paragraph (b)), or a deputy official receiver, or

(b) unless the application involves other parties or the court otherwise orders,
by—

(i) an administrator, a liquidator or a trustee in bankruptcy,

(ii) a provisional liquidator or an interim receiver,

(iii) a special manager, or

(iv) an insolvency practitioner appointed under section 273(2).

7.9(2) **[Report to be treated as affidavit]** In any case where a report is filed instead
of an affidavit, the report shall be treated for the purposes of Rule 7.8(1) and any
hearing before the court as if it were an affidavit.

7.9(3) **[Official receiver's report as prima facie evidence]** Any report filed by the
official receiver in accordance with the Act or the Rules is prima facie evidence of any
matter contained in it.

(See general note after r. 7.18.)

Rule **7.10** Adjournment of hearing; directions

7.10(1) **[Powers of court]** The court may adjourn the hearing of an application on
such terms (if any) as it thinks fit.

7.10(2) **[Directions]** The court may at any time give such directions as it thinks fit as to—

    (a) service or notice of the application on or to any person, whether in connection with the venue of a resumed hearing or for any other purpose;

    (b) whether particulars of claim and defence are to be delivered and generally as to the procedure on the applications;

    (c) the manner in which any evidence is to be adduced at a resumed hearing and in particular (but without prejudice to the generality of this sub-paragraph) as to—

        (i) the taking of evidence wholly or in part by affidavit or orally;

        (ii) the cross-examination either before the judge or registrar on the hearing in court or in chambers, of any deponents to affidavits;

        (iii) any report to be given by the official receiver or any person mentioned in Rule 7.9(1)(b);

    (d) the matters to be dealt with in evidence.

(See general note after r. 7.18.)

Chapter 2 — Transfer of Proceedings Between Courts

Rule 7.11   General power of transfer

7.11(1) **[Transfer to county court]** Where winding-up or bankruptcy proceedings are pending in the High Court, the court may order them to be transferred to a specified county court.

7.11(2) **[Transfer to High Court etc.]** Where winding-up or bankruptcy proceedings are pending in a county court, the court may order them to be transferred either to the High Court or to another county court.

7.11(3) **[Transfer to county court with jurisdiction]** In any case where proceedings are transferred to a county court, the transfer must be to a court which has jurisdiction to wind up companies or, as the case may be, jurisdiction in bankruptcy.

7.11(4) **[Power of High Court judge]** Where winding-up or bankruptcy proceedings are pending in a county court, a judge of the High Court may order them to be transferred to that Court.

7.11(5) **[Order for transfer]** A transfer of proceedings under this Rule may be ordered—

    (a) by the court of its own motion, or

    (b) on the application of the official receiver, or

    (c) on the application of a person appearing to the court to have an interest in the proceedings.

7.11(6) **[Proceedings commenced before coming into force of Rules]** A transfer of proceedings under this Rule may be ordered notwithstanding that the proceedings commenced before the coming into force of the Rules.

General note

See Practice Direction in [1987] 1 All ER 107 (reproduced in Appendix IV of this Guide). See also general note after r. 7.18. For a case under the old law (BA 1914, s. 100) where proceedings were transferred to the High Court see *Re A Debtor (No. 26A of 1975)* [1985] 1 WLR 6.

Rule 7.12   Proceedings commenced in wrong court

7.12   Where winding-up or bankruptcy proceedings are commenced in a court which is, in relation to those proceedings, the wrong court, that court may—

    (a) order the transfer of the proceedings to the court in which they ought to have been commenced;

    (b) order that the proceedings be continued in the court in which they have been commenced; or

    (c) order the proceedings to be struck out.

(See general note after r. 7.18.)

Rule 7.13   Applications for transfer

7.13(1)   **[Official receiver's report]**   An application by the official receiver for proceedings to be transferred shall be made with a report by him—

    (a) setting out the reasons for the transfer, and

    (b) including a statement either that the petitioner consents to the transfer, or that he has been given at least 14 days' notice of the official receiver's application.

7.13(2)   **[More convenient conduct of proceedings]**   If the court is satisfied from the official receiver's report that the proceedings can be conducted more conveniently in another court, the proceedings shall be transferred to that court.

7.13(3)   **[Application not made by official receiver]**   Where an application for the transfer of proceedings is made otherwise than by the official receiver, at least 14 days' notice of the application shall be given by the applicant—

    (a) to the official receiver attached to the court in which the proceedings are pending, and

    (b) to the official receiver attached to the court to which it is proposed that they should be transferred.

(See general note after r. 7.18.)

Rule 7.14   Procedure following order for transfer

7.14(1)   **[Copy of order etc. to transferee court]**   Subject as follows, the court making an order under Rule 7.11 shall forthwith send to the transferee court a sealed copy of the order, and the file of the proceedings.

7.14(2) **[On receipt]** On receipt of these, the transferee court shall forthwith send notice of the transfer to the official receivers attached to that court and the transferor court respectively.

7.14(3) **[Non-application of r. 7.14(1)]** Paragraph (1) does not apply where the order is made by the High Court under Rule 7.11(4). In that case—

(a) the High Court shall send sealed copies of the order to the county court from which the proceedings are to be transferred, and to the official receivers attached to that court and the High Court respectively, and

(b) that county court shall send the file of the proceedings to the High Court.

7.14(4) **[Following compliance with Rule]** Following compliance with this Rule, if the official receiver attached to the court to which the proceedings are ordered to be transferred is not already, by virtue of directions given by the Secretary of State under section 399(6)(a), the official receiver in relation to those proceedings, he becomes, in relation to those proceedings, the official receiver in place of the official receiver attached to the other court concerned.

(See general note after r. 7.18.)

Rule 7.15   Consequential transfer of other proceedings

7.15(1) **[Application of Rule]** This Rule applies where—

(a) an order for the winding up of a company, or a bankruptcy order in the case of an individual, has been made by the High Court, or

(b) in either such case, a provisional liquidator or (as the case may be) an interim receiver has been appointed, or

(c) winding-up or bankruptcy proceedings have been transferred to that Court from a county court.

7.15(2) **[Power of High Court judge]** A judge of any Division of the High Court may, of his own motion, order the transfer to that Division of any such proceedings as are mentioned below and are pending against the company or individual concerned ("the insolvent") either in another Division of the High Court or in a court in England and Wales other than the High Court.

7.15(3) **[Proceedings which may be transferred]** Proceedings which may be so transferred are those brought by or against the insolvent for the purpose of enforcing a claim against the insolvent estate, or brought by a person other than the insolvent for the purpose of enforcing any such claim (including in either case proceedings of any description by a debenture-holder or mortgagee).

7.15(4) **[Where proceedings are transferred]** Where proceedings are transferred under this Rule, the registrar may (subject to general or special directions of the judge) dispose of any matter arising in the proceedings which would, but for the transfer, have been disposed of in chambers or, in the case of proceedings transferred from a county court, by the registrar of that court.

(See general note after r. 7.18.)

Chapter 3 — Shorthand Writers

Rule 7.16   Nomination and appointment of shorthand writers

7.16(1)   [Nomination]   In the High Court the judge and, in a county court, the registrar may in writing nominate one or more persons to be official shorthand writers to the court.   [FORM 7.3]

7.16(2)   [Appointment]   The court may, at any time in the course of insolvency proceedings, appoint a shorthand writer to take down the evidence of a person examined under section 133, 236, 290 or 366.   [FORM 7.4]

7.16(3)   [Application by official receiver etc.]   Where the official receiver applies to the court for an order appointing a shorthand writer, he shall name the person he proposes for appointment; and that appointment shall be made, unless the court otherwise orders.

(See general note after r. 7.18.).

Rule 7.17   Remuneration

7.17(1)   [Payment]   The remuneration of a shorthand writer appointed in insolvency proceedings shall be paid by the party at whose instance the appointment was made, or out of the insolvent estate, or otherwise, as the court may direct.

7.17(2)   [Court's discretion]   Any question arising as to the rates of remuneration payable under this Rule shall be determined by the court in its discretion.

History note

Rule 7.17(2) was substituted by the Insolvency (Amendment) Rules 1993 (SI 1993 No. 602), r. 3 and Sch., para. 1, as from 5 April 1993. Rule 7.17(2) formerly read: "The remuneration payable shall be calculated in accordance with Schedule 3 to the Rules". Schedule 3 has consequentially been deleted.

(See also general note after r. 7.18.)

Rule 7.18   Cost of shorthand note

7.18   Where in insolvency proceedings the court appoints a shorthand writer on the application of the official receiver, in order that a written record may be taken of the evidence of a person to be examined, the cost of the written record is deemed an expense of the official receiver in the proceedings.

General note to rr. 7.1–7.18

There are only two forms of application: originating and ordinary. The distinction is relevant primarily in relation to the forms to be used (r. 7.2). In the case of an originating application, r. 7.3(2) also applies.

The procedure here laid down is largely similar to that prescribed by the rules of court. The following provisions perhaps call for special note:

r. 7.4(6) – hearings in case of urgency;

r. 7.5 – other hearings *ex parte*;

r. 7.9 – use of reports of the official receiver or of an insolvency practitioner instead of affidavits;

r. 7.15 – transfer to the insolvency court of other proceedings pending against the insolvent.

The meaning and nature of an "ordinary application" under r. 7.2 was discussed by Harman J in *Port* v *Auger* [1994] 1 WLR 862. An ordinary application as defined in r. 7.2(1) cannot be struck out under RSC O.18, r. 19, since it is not within the definition of "pleadings" under the latter rule; but the court may strike out such an application under its inherent jurisdiction to stay proceedings which are frivolous, vexatious or an abuse of its process (ibid.).

R. 7.17

The rates of remuneration for shorthand writers were formerly fixed by Sch. 3. The court is now given a discretion to settle any disputed charge.

Chapter 4 — Enforcement Procedures

Rule 7.19 Enforcement of court orders

7.19(1) [Orders enforced as judgments]   In any insolvency proceedings, orders of the court may be enforced in the same manner as a judgment to the same effect.

7.19(2) [Enforcement etc. by any county court]   Where an order in insolvency proceedings is made, or any process is issued, by a county court ("the primary court"), the order or process may be enforced, executed and dealt with by any other county court ("the secondary court"), as if it had been made or issued for the enforcement of a judgment or order to the same effect made by the secondary court.

This applies whether or not the secondary court has jurisdiction to take insolvency proceedings.

(See general note after r. 7.25.)

Rule 7.20 Orders enforcing compliance with the Rules

7.20(1) [Application by competent person]   The court may, on application by the competent person, make such orders as it thinks necessary for the enforcement of obligations falling on any person in accordance with—

(a) section 22, 47 or 131 (duty to submit statement of affairs in administration, administrative receivership or winding up),

(b) section 143(2) (liquidator to furnish information, books, papers, etc.), or

(c) section 235 (duty of various persons to co-operate with office-holder).

7.20(2) [Who is competent person] The competent person for this purpose is—

(a) under section 22, the administrator,

(b) under section 47, the administrative receiver,

(c) under section 131 or 143(2), the official receiver, and

(d) under section 235, the official receiver, the administrator, the administrative receiver, the liquidator or the provisional liquidator, as the case may be.

7.20(3) [Costs] An order of the court under this Rule may provide that all costs of and incidental to the application for it shall be borne by the person against whom the order is made.

(See general note after r. 7.25.)

Rule 7.21 Warrants (general provisions)

7.21(1) [Address for warrant] A warrant issued by the court under any provision of the Act shall be addressed to such officer of the High Court or of a county court (whether or not having jurisdiction in insolvency proceedings) as the warrant specifies, or to any constable.

7.21(2) [Prescribed officer of the court] The persons referred to in sections 134 (2), 236(5), 364(1), 365(3) and 366(3) (court's powers of enforcement) as the prescribed officer of the court are—

(a) in the case of the High Court, the tipstaff and his assistants of the court, and

(b) in the case of a county court, the registrar and the bailiffs.

7.21(3) [Definition] In this Chapter references to property include books, papers and records.

(See general note after r. 7.25.)

Rule 7.22 Warrants under ss. 134, 364

7.22 When a person is arrested under a warrant issued by the court under section 134 (officer of company failing to attend for public examination), or section 364 (arrest of debtor or bankrupt)—

(a) the officer apprehending him shall give him into the custody of the governor of the prison named in the warrant, who shall keep him in custody until such time as the court otherwise orders and shall produce him before the court as it may from time to time direct; and   [FORM 7.9]

(b) any property in the arrested person's possession which may be seized shall be—

  (i) lodged with, or otherwise dealt with as instructed by, whoever is specified in the warrant as authorised to receive it, or

  (ii) kept by the officer seizing it pending the receipt of written orders from the court as to its disposal,

as may be directed by the court in the warrant.   [FORM 7.6]
                                                                     [FORM 7.7]

History note

Against r. 7.22(*a*) the words "[FORM 7.9]" were inserted by 1987 (SI 1987 No. 1919), r. 3(1), Sch., Pt. 2, para. 156(1) as from 11 January 1988.

(See general note after r. 7.25.)

Rule 7.23   Warrants under ss. 236, 366

7.23(1)   [When person arrrested]   When a person is arrested under a warrant issued under section 236 (inquiry into insolvent company's dealings) or 366 (the equivalent in bankruptcy), the officer arresting him shall forthwith bring him before the court issuing the warrant in order that he may be examined.   [FORM 7.8]

7.23(2)   [If not brought before court immediately]   If he cannot immediately be brought up for examination, the officer shall deliver him into the custody of the governor of the prison named in the warrant, who shall keep him in custody and produce him before the court as it may from time to time direct.   [FORM 7.9]

7.23(3)   [Report of arrest etc.]   After arresting the person named in the warrant, the officer shall forthwith report to the court the arrest or delivery into custody (as the case may be) and apply to the court to fix a venue for the person's examination.

7.23(4)   [Time for examination etc.]   The court shall appoint the earliest practicable time for the examination, and shall—

    (a)   direct the governor of the prison to produce the person for examination at the time and place appointed, and

    (b)   forthwith give notice of the venue to the person who applied for the warrant.   [FORM 7.9]

7.23(5)   [Property in arrested person's possession]   Any property in the arrested person's possession which may be seized shall be—

    (a)   lodged with, or otherwise dealt with as instructed by, whoever is specified in the warrant as authorised to receive it, or

    (b)   kept by the officer seizing it pending the receipt of written orders from the court as to its disposal,

as may be directed by the court.

(See general note after r. 7.25.)

Rule 7.24   Execution of warrants outside court's district

7.24(1)   [Application of Rule]   This Rule applies where a warrant for a person's arrest has been issued in insolvency proceedings by a county court ("the primary court") and is addressed to another county court ("the secondary court") for execution in its district.   [FORM 7.10]

7.24(2)   [Power of secondary court]   The secondary court may send the warrant to the registrar of any other county court (whether or not having jurisdiction to take insolvency proceedings) in whose district the person to be arrested is or is believed to be, with a notice to the effect that the warrant is transmitted to that court under this Rule for execution in its district at the request of the primary court.

7.24(3) [Court receiving warrant] The court receiving a warrant transmitted by the secondary court under this Rule shall apply its seal to the warrant, and secure that all such steps are taken for its execution as would be appropriate in the case of a warrant issued by itself.

(See general note after r. 7.25.)

Rule 7.25   Warrants under s. 365

7.25(1) [Seizure] A warrant issued under section 365(3) (search of premises not belonging to the bankrupt) shall authorise any person executing it to seize any property of the bankrupt found as a result of the execution of the warrant.

7.25(2) [Seized property] Any property seized under a warrant issued under section 365(2) or (3) shall be—

(a) lodged with, or otherwise dealt with as instructed by, whoever is specified in the warrant as authorised to receive it, or

(b) kept by the officer seizing it pending the receipt of written orders from the court as to its disposal,

as may be directed by the warrant.   [FORM 7.12]
                                                                [FORM 7.13]

General note to rr. 7.19–7.25

Chapter 4, as the title indicates, deals with the procedures for the enforcement of court orders, of statutory duties and of warrants issued under IA 1986. In particular, r. 7.20 sanctions with the backing of the court the general duty of corporate officers and others to co-operate with the official receiver and with insolvency practitioners holding office as liquidator, etc.

Chapter 5 — Court Records and Returns

Rule 7.26   Title of proceedings

7.26(1) [Proceedings under Pt. I–VII] Every proceeding under Parts I to VII of the Act shall, with any necessary additions, be intituled "IN THE MATTER OF …(naming the company to which the proceedings relate) AND IN THE MATTER OF THE INSOLVENCY ACT 1986".

7.26(2) [Proceedings under Pt. IX–XI] Every proceeding under Parts IX to XI of the Act shall be intituled "IN BANKRUPTCY".

(See general note after r. 7.32.)

Rule 7.27   Court records

7.27   The court shall keep records of all insolvency proceedings, and shall cause to be entered in the records the taking of any step in the proceedings, and such decisions of the court in relation thereto, as the court thinks fit.

(See general note after r. 7.32.)

Rule 7.28   Inspection of records

7.28(1)   [Open to inspection by any person]   Subject as follows, the court's records of insolvency proceedings shall be open to inspection by any person.

7.28(2)   [Application to inspect etc.]   If in the case of a person applying to inspect the records the registrar is not satisfied as to the propriety of the purpose for which inspection is required, he may refuse to allow it. The person may then apply forthwith and *ex parte* to the judge, who may refuse the inspection, or allow it on such terms as he thinks fit.

7.28(3)   [Judge's decision final]   The judge's decision under paragraph (2) is final.

(See general note after r. 7.32.)

Rule 7.29   Returns to Secretary of State

7.29(1)   [Particulars of proceedings]   The court shall from time to time send to the Secretary of State the following particulars relating to winding-up and bankruptcy proceedings—

(a) the full title of the proceedings, including the number assigned to each case;

(b) where a winding-up or bankruptcy order has been made, the date of the order.

7.29(2)   [Request for particulars etc.]   The Secretary of State may, on the request of any person, furnish him with particulars sent by the court under this Rule.

(See general note after r. 7.32.)

Rule 7.30   File of court proceedings

7.30(1)   [Court file]   In respect of all insolvency proceedings, the court shall open and maintain a file for each case; and (subject to directions of the registrar) all documents relating to such proceedings shall be placed on the relevant file.

7.30(2)   [No filing in Central Office]   No proceedings shall be filed in the Central Office of the High Court.

(See general note after r. 7.32.)

Rule 7.31   Right to inspect the file

7.31(1)   [Who has right to inspect]   In the case of any insolvency proceedings, the following have the right, at all reasonable times, to inspect the court's file of the proceedings—

(a) the person who, in relation to those proceedings, is the responsible insolvency practitioner;

(b) any duly authorised officer of the Department; and

(c) any person stating himself in writing to be a creditor of the company to which, or the individual to whom, the proceedings relate.

7.31(2) [Exercise of right] The same right of inspection is exercisable—

(a) in proceedings under Parts I to VII of the Act, by every person who is, or at any time has been, a director or officer of the company to which the proceedings relate, or who is a member of the company or a contributory in its winding up;

(b) in proceedings with respect to a voluntary arrangement proposed by a debtor under Part VIII of the Act, by the debtor;

(c) in bankruptcy proceedings, by—

   (i) the bankrupt,

   (ii) any person against whom, or by whom, a bankruptcy petition has been presented, and

   (iii) any person who has been served, in accordance with Chapter 1 of Part 6 of the Rules, with a statutory demand.

7.31(3) [Authority to inspect] The right of inspection conferred as above on any person may be exercised on his behalf by a person properly authorised by him.

7.31(4) [Leave to inspect] Any person may, by special leave of the court, inspect the file.

7.31(5) [When right not exercisable etc.] The right of inspection conferred by this Rule is not exercisable in the case of documents, or parts of documents, as to which the court directs (either generally or specially) that they are not to be made open to inspection without the court's leave.

An application for a direction of the court under this paragraph may be made by the official receiver, by the person who in relation to any proceedings is the responsible insolvency practitioner, or by any party appearing to the court to have an interest.

7.31(6) [If Secretary of State etc. requires to inspect] If, for the purpose of powers conferred by the Act or the Rules, the Secretary of State, the Department or the official receiver requires to inspect the file of any insolvency proceedings, and requests the transmission of the file, the court shall comply with the request (unless the file is for the time being in use for the court's own purposes).

7.31(7) [Application of r. 7.28] Paragraphs (2) and (3) of Rule 7.28 apply in respect of the court's file of any proceedings as they apply in respect of court records.

(See general note after r. 7.32.)

Rule 7.32 Filing of Gazette notices and advertisements

7.32(1) [Filing by officer of the court] In any court in which insolvency proceedings are pending, an officer of the court shall file a copy of every issue of the Gazette which contains an advertisement relating to those proceedings.

7.32(2) **[Filing by advertiser]** Where there appears in a newspaper an advertisement relating to insolvency proceedings pending in any court, the person inserting the advertisement shall file a copy of it in that court.

The copy of the advertisement shall be accompanied by, or have endorsed on it, such particulars as are necessary to identify the proceedings and the date of the advertisement's appearance.

7.32(3) **[Court officer's memorandum]** An officer of any court in which insolvency proceedings are pending shall from time to time file a memorandum giving the dates of, and other particulars relating to, any notice published in the Gazette, and any newspaper advertisements, which relate to proceedings so pending.

The officer's memorandum is prima facie evidence that any notice or advertisement mentioned in it was duly inserted in the issue of the newspaper or the Gazette which is specified in the memorandum.

General note to rr. 7.26–7.32

These rules give instructions about court records and files and the respective rights to inspect them; and also about the returns to be made by the court to the Secretary of State and the filing of Gazette notices.

For an analysis of the relationship between the various sub-rules in r. 7.31 see the judgment of Vinelott J in *Astor Chemical Ltd* v *Synthetic Technology Ltd* [1990] BCC 97.

An "insolvency consultant" who sought to search the records of insolvency proceedings for the names and addresses of potential customers for his services was not inspecting the records for a proper purpose, within r. 7.28(2), and was rightly refused inspection: *Re an Application pursuant to r. 7.28 of the Insolvency Rules 1986* [1994] BCC 369.

Chapter 6 — Costs and Taxation

Rule 7.33   Application of Rules of Supreme Court and County Court Rules

7.33 Subject to provision to inconsistent effect made as follows in this Chapter—

   (a) Order 62 of the Rules of the Supreme Court applies to insolvency proceedings in the High Court, and

   (b) Order 38 of the County Court Rules applies to such proceedings in a county court,

in either case, with any necessary modifications.

General note

The relationship between r. 7.33 and s. 51 of the Supreme Court Act 1981 was considered by Mervyn Davies J in *Re Gosscott (Groundworks) Ltd* (1988) 4 BCC 372 where it was held that the discretion conferred by s. 51 authorised the court to treat costs of an unsuccessful administration order petition as costs of the subsequent winding up.

(See general note after r. 7.42.)

Rule 7.34   Requirement to tax costs

7.34(1)   [Costs etc. payable out of estate]   Subject as follows, where the costs, charges or expenses of any person are payable out of the insolvent estate, those costs, charges or expenses shall be taxed unless agreed between the responsible insolvency practitioner and the person entitled to payment, and in the absence of such agreement the responsible insolvency practitioner may require taxation by notice in writing requiring that person to deliver his bill of costs to the appropriate taxing officer for taxation; the appropriate taxing officer is that in relation to the court to which the insolvency proceedings are allocated or, where in relation to a company there is no such court, that in relation to any court having jurisdiction to wind up the company.

7.34(2)   [Resolution that costs etc. be taxed]   If a liquidation or creditors' committee established in insolvency proceedings (except administrative receivership) resolves that any such costs, charges or expenses be taxed, the insolvency practitioner shall require taxation.

7.34(3)   [Where costs etc. are required to be taxed]   Where the costs, charges or expenses of any person employed by an insolvency practitioner in insolvency proceedings are required to be taxed or fixed by order of the court this does not preclude the insolvency practitioner from making payments on account to such person on the basis of an undertaking by that person to repay immediately any money which may, on taxation, prove to have been overpaid, with interest at the rate specified in section 17 of the Judgments Act 1838 on the date payment was made and for the period from the date of payment to that of repayment.

7.34(4)   [Power of court]   In any proceedings before the court, including proceedings on a petition, the court may order costs to be taxed.

7.34(5)   [Costs of trustee or liquidator]   Unless otherwise directed or authorised, the costs of a trustee in bankruptcy or a liquidator are to be allowed on the standard basis specified in Rule 12 of Order 62 of the Rules of the Supreme Court.

7.34(6)   [Application of Rule]   This Rule applies additionally (with any necessary modifications) to winding-up and bankruptcy proceedings commenced before the coming into force of the Rules.

History note

Rule 7.34(1) was substituted by I(A)R 1987 (SI 1987 No. 1919), r. 3(1), Sch., Pt. 1, para. 131(1) as from 11 January 1988: r. 7.34(1) formerly read as follows:

"**7.34(1)**   Subject as follows, where any costs, charges or expenses of any person are payable out of the insolvent estate, the responsible insolvency practitioner may agree them with the person entitled to payment or may require them to be taxed by the court to which the insolvency proceedings are allocated or, where in relation to a company there is no such court, by a court having jurisdiction to wind up the company."

In r. 7.34(3) the words "fixed by order of the court" were inserted by I(A)R 1987 (SI 1987 No. 1919), r. 3(1), Sch., Pt. 1, para. 131(2) as from 11 January 1988.

In r. 7.34(5) the words from "specified in Rule 12" to the end were inserted by I(A)R 1987 (SI 1987 No. 1919), r. 3(1), Sch., Pt. 1, para. 131(3) as from 11 January 1988.

(See general note after r. 7.42.)

Rule 7.35   Procedure where taxation required

7.35(1)   [Before taxing costs]   Before taxing the costs of any person employed in insolvency proceedings by a responsible insolvency practitioner, the taxing officer shall require a certificate of employment, which shall be endorsed on the bill and signed by the insolvency practitioner.

7.35(2)   [Contents of certificate of employment]   The certificate shall include—

(a) the name and address of the person employed,

(b) details of the functions to be carried out under the employment, and

(c) a note of any special terms of remuneration which have been agreed.

7.35(3)   [Delivery of bill of costs]   Every person whose costs are required to be taxed in insolvency proceedings shall, on being required in writing to do so by the insolvency practitioner, deliver his bill of costs to the taxing officer for taxation.

7.35(4)   [If bill delivered out of time]   If that person does not so deliver his bill within 3 months of the requirement under paragraph (3), or within such further time as the court, on application, may grant, the insolvency practitioner may deal with the insolvent estate without regard to any claim by that person, whose claim is forfeited.

7.35(5)   [Additional claim forfeited]   Where in any such case such a claim lies additionally against an insolvency practitioner in his personal capacity, that claim is also forfeited.

7.35(6)   [Where proceedings transferred]   Where costs have been incurred in insolvency proceedings in the High Court and those proceedings are subsequently transferred to a county court, all costs of those proceedings directed by the court or otherwise required to be taxed may nevertheless, on the application of the person who incurred the costs, be ordered to be taxed in the High Court.

History note

Rule 7.35(6) was added by I(A)R 1987 (SI 1987 No. 1919), r. 3(1), Sch., Pt. 1, para. 132 as from 11 January 1988.

(See general note after r. 7.42.)

Rule 7.36   Costs of sheriff

7.36(1)   [Taxing sheriff's bill]   Where a sheriff—

(a) is required under section 184(2) or 346(2) to deliver up goods or money, or

(b) has under section 184(3) or 346(3) deducted costs from the proceeds of an execution or money paid to him,

the responsible insolvency practitioner may require in writing that the sheriff's bill of costs be taxed.

7.36(2)   [Application of r. 7.35(4)]   Where such a requirement is made, Rule 7.35 (4) applies.

7.36(3)   [In case of r. 7.36(1)(b) deduction]   Where, in the case of a deduction under paragraph (1)(b), any amount is disallowed on taxation, the sheriff shall forthwith pay a sum equal to that amount to the insolvency practitioner for the benefit of the insolvent estate.

(See general note after r. 7.42.)

Rule 7.37   Petitions presented by insolvents

7.37(1)   [Credit for security etc.]   In any case where a petition is presented by a company or individual ("the insolvent") against himself, any solicitor acting for the insolvent shall in his bill of costs give credit for any sum or security received from the insolvent as a deposit on account of the costs and expenses to be incurred in respect of the filing and prosecution of the petition; and the deposit shall be noted by the taxing officer on the taxing certificate.

7.37(2)   [Application of r. 7.37(3)]   Paragraph (3) applies where a petition is presented by a person other than the insolvent to whom the petition relates and before it is heard the insolvent presents a petition for the same order, and that order is made.

7.37(3)   [No costs allowed to insolvent etc.]   Unless the court considers that the insolvent estate has benefitted by the insolvent's conduct, or that there are otherwise special circumstances justifying the allowance of costs, no costs shall be allowed to the insolvent or his solicitor out of the insolvent estate.

(See general note after r. 7.42.)

Rule 7.38   Costs paid otherwise than out of the insolvent estate

7.38   Where a bill of costs is taxed under an order of the court directing that the costs are to be paid otherwise than out of the insolvent estate, the taxing officer shall note on the certificate of taxation by whom, or the manner in which, the costs are to be paid.

(See general note after r. 7.42.)

Rule 7.39   Award of costs against official receiver or responsible insolvency practitioner

7.39   Without prejudice to any provision of the Act or Rules by virtue of which the official receiver is not in any event to be liable for costs and expenses, where the official receiver or a responsible insolvency practitioner is made a party to any proceedings on the application of another party to the proceedings, he shall not be personally liable for costs unless the court otherwise directs.

(See general note after r. 7.42.)

Rule 7.40   Applications for costs

7.40(1)   [Application of Rule]   This Rule applies where a party to, or person affected by, any proceedings in an insolvency—

  (a) applies to the court for an order allowing his costs, or part of them, incidental to the proceedings, and

  (b) that application is not made at the time of the proceedings.

7.40(2) **[Copies of application]** The person concerned shall serve a sealed copy of his application on the responsible insolvency practitioner, and, in winding up by the court or bankruptcy, on the official receiver.

7.40(3) **[Appearances]** The insolvency practitioner and, where appropriate, the official receiver may appear on the application.

7.40(4) **[Costs]** No costs of or incidental to the application shall be allowed to the applicant unless the court is satisfied that the application could not have been made at the time of the proceedings.

(See general note after r. 7.42.)

Rule 7.41   Costs and expenses of witnesses

7.41(1) **[No allowance to bankrupt etc.]** Except as directed by the court, no allowance as a witness in any examination or other proceedings before the court shall be made to the bankrupt or an officer of the insolvent company to which the proceedings relate.

7.41(2) **[Petitioner's expenses]** A person presenting any petition in insolvency proceedings shall not be regarded as a witness on the hearing of the petition, but the taxing officer may allow his expenses of travelling and subsistence.

(See general note after r. 7.42.)

Rule 7.42   Certificate of taxation

7.42(1) **[Certificate is final etc.]** A certificate of taxation of the taxing officer is final and conclusive as to all matters which have not been objected to in the manner provided for under the rules of the court.

7.42(2) **[Duplicate certificate]** Where it is proved to the satisfaction of a taxing officer that a certificate of taxation has been lost or destroyed, he may issue a duplicate.

7.42(3) **[Definition]** "Certificate of taxation" includes, for the purposes of the Rules, an order of the registrar in a county court.

General note to rr. 7.33–7.42

Chapter 6 applies to insolvency proceedings the Rules of the Supreme Court and the County Court Rules relating to the taxation of costs, and deals with other aspects of costs in insolvency matters.

Chapter 7 — Persons Incapable of Managing Their Affairs

Rule 7.43   Introductory

7.43(1) **[Application of Ch. 7 Rules]** The Rules in this Chapter apply where in insolvency proceedings it appears to the court that a person affected by the proceedings is one who is incapable of managing and administering his property and affairs either—

(a) by reason of mental disorder within the meaning of the Mental Health Act 1983, or

(b) due to physical affliction or disability.

7.43(2)   ["The incapacitated person"]   The person concerned is referred to as "the incapacitated person".

(See general note after r. 7.46.)

Rule 7.44   Appointment of another person to act

7.44(1)   [Power of court]   The court may appoint such person as it thinks fit to appear for, represent or act for the incapacitated person.   [FORM 7.19]

7.44(2)   [General or particular appointment]   The appointment may be made either generally or for the purpose of any particular application or proceeding, or for the exercise of particular rights or powers which the incapacitated person might have exercised but for his incapacity.

7.44(3)   [Appointment by court or on application]   The court may make the appointment either of its own motion or on application by—

(a) a person who has been appointed by a court in the United Kingdom or elsewhere to manage the affairs of, or to represent, the incapacitated person, or

(b) any relative or friend of the incapacitated person who appears to the court to be a proper person to make the application, or

(c) the official receiver, or

(d) the person who, in relation to the proceedings, is the responsible insolvency practitioner.

7.44(4)   [Ex parte application, powers of court]   Application under paragraph (3) may be made *ex parte*; but the court may require such notice of the application as it thinks necessary to be given to the person alleged to be incapacitated, or any other person, and may adjourn the hearing of the application to enable the notice to be given.

(See general note after r. 7.46.)

Rule 7.45   Affidavit in support of application

7.45(1)   [Affidavit of registered medical practitioner]   Except where made by the official receiver, an application under Rule 7.44(3) shall be supported by an affidavit of a registered medical practitioner as to the mental or physical condition of the incapacitated person.

7.45(2) **[Official receiver's report]** In the excepted case, a report made by the official receiver is sufficient.

(See general note after r. 7.46.)

Rule **7.46** Service of notices following appointment

7.46 Any notice served on, or sent to, a person appointed under Rule 7.44 has the same effect as if it had been served on, or given to, the incapacitated person.

General note to rr. 7.43–7.46

The court is empowered by these rules to make special provision for any person subject to a disability who is affected by insolvency proceedings.

Chapter 8 — Appeals in Insolvency Proceedings

Rule **7.47** Appeals and reviews of court orders (winding up)

7.47(1) **[Powers of courts]** Every court having jurisdiction under the Act to wind up companies may review, rescind or vary any order made by it in the exercise of that jurisdiction.

7.47(2) **[Appeal to High Court etc.]** An appeal from a decision made in the exercise of that jurisdiction by a county court or by a registrar of the High Court lies to a single judge of the High Court; and an appeal from a decision of that judge on such an appeal lies, with the leave of that judge or the Court of Appeal, to the Court of Appeal.

7.47(3) **[County court not to be restrained etc.]** A county court is not, in the exercise of its jurisdiction to wind up companies, subject to be restrained by the order of any other court, and no appeal lies from its decision in the exercise of that jurisdiction except as provided by this Rule.

7.47(4) **[Application for rescission of winding-up order]** Any application for the rescission of a winding-up order shall be made within 7 days after the date on which the order was made.

General note

Appeals from a registrar's winding up order go to the High Court, not the Court of Appeal – *Re Calahurst Ltd* (1989) 5 BCC 318. This point was confirmed by the Court of Appeal in *Re Tasbian Ltd (No. 2)* [1990] BCC 322. This is also true in relation to an order made by a district judge in the county court: *Re Langley Marketing Services Ltd* [1992] BCC 585; and the rule applies to an order made under CDDA 1986 (ibid.). It applies also to administration orders: *Cornhill Insurance plc* v *Cornhill Financial Services Ltd & Ors* [1992] BCC 818. The appeal may take the form either of an appeal against the original decision of the registrar, or of an appeal from the registrar's refusal to review his original decision (*Re SN Group plc* [1993] BCC 808). The jurisdiction under r. 7.47 is very wide, and extends even to the review, rescission or variation by a

High Court judge of a decision of any judge of that court: *Re W & A Glaser Ltd* [1994] BCC 199, at p. 208, per Harman J. Leave is not required for an appeal to the High Court (*Re Busytoday Ltd* [1992] BCC 480), but is necessary for a further appeal to the Court of Appeal (*Midrome Ltd* v *Shaw* [1993] BCC 659).

Practice Direction No. 3 of 1992 [1992] 1 WLR 791; [1992] BCC 998 states that appeals from decisions of district judges exercising insolvency jurisdiction over companies or over individuals may be heard either in London or by a circuit judge who exercises the powers of a judge of the Chancery Division at Birmingham, Bristol, Cardiff, Leeds, Liverpool, Manchester, Newcastle upon Tyne or Preston. In such cases, notices of appeal may be lodged in the appropriate High Court district registry in company insolvency proceedings and with the Registrar in Bankruptcy of the High Court in London in individual insolvency proceedings. However (notwithstanding r. 13.2(3)), if the parties agree, notice of appeal from a district judge in individual insolvency proceedings may be lodged with the appropriate High Court district registry.

Appeals under r. 747(2) are true appeals and do not require a hearing *de novo*. Thus a decision of the registrar will only be overturned if it was based on an error of law or wrongful exercise of discretion: *Re Probe Data Systems Ltd (No. 3)* [1991] BCC 428 and *Re Tasbian Ltd (No. 3)* [1991] BCC 435. See also *Re Industrial & Commercial Securities plc* (1989) 5 BCC 320.

(See also general note after r. 7.50.)

Rule 7.48   Appeals in bankruptcy

7.48(1)   [Appeal at instance of Secretary of State]   In bankruptcy proceedings, an appeal lies at the instance of the Secretary of State from any order of the court made on an application for the rescission or annulment of a bankruptcy order, or for a bankrupt's discharge.

7.48(2)   [Appeal to High Court etc.]   In the case of an order made by a county court or by a registrar of the High Court, the appeal lies to a single judge of the High Court; and an appeal from a decision of that judge on such an appeal lies, with the leave of that judge or the Court of Appeal, to the Court of Appeal.

General note
An appeal under r. 7.48(2) from either a county court judge or a registrar of the High Court to a single judge of the High Court was a true appeal and not a re-hearing *de novo: Re Gilmartin (A Bankrupt)* [1989] 1 WLR 513.

(See general note after r. 7.50)

Rule 7.49   Procedure on appeal

7.49(1)   [Application of Supreme Court procedure etc.]   Subject as follows, the procedure and practice of the Supreme Court relating to appeals to the Court of Appeal apply to appeals in insolvency proceedings.

7.49(2)   [Re appeal to single judge]   In relation to any appeal to a single judge of the High Court under section 375(2) (individual insolvency) or Rule 7.47(2) above (company insolvency), any reference in the Rules of the Supreme Court to the Court of Appeal is replaced by a reference to that judge and any reference to the registrar of civil appeals is replaced by a reference to the registrar of the High Court who deals with insolvency proceedings of the kind involved.

7.49(3) **[Appeal by application]** In insolvency proceedings, the procedure under Order 59 of the Rules of the Supreme Court (appeal to the Court of Appeal) is by application, and not by summons.

History note

In r. 7.49(2) the words from "and any reference to the registrar" to the end were added by I(A)R 1987 (SI 1987 No. 1919), r. 3(1), Sch., Pt. 1, para. 133 as from 11 January 1988.

(See general note after r. 7.50.)

Rule 7.50   Appeal against decision of Secretary of State or official receiver

7.50 An appeal under the Act or the Rules against a decision of the Secretary of State or the official receiver shall be brought within 28 days of the notification of the decision.

General note to rr. 7.47 – 7.50

The various procedures and time limits listed here govern reviews and appeals from decisions of the courts, the Secretary of State and the official receiver. For further details, see the general note after r. 7.47.

Chapter 9 — General

Rule 7.51   Principal court rules and practice to apply

7.51 Except so far as inconsistent with the Insolvency Rules, the Rules of the Supreme Court and the practice of the High Court apply to insolvency proceedings in the High Court, and the County Court Rules and the practice of the county court apply to insolvency proceedings in a county court, in either case with any necessary modifications.

General note

This rule provides for the application generally of the Rules of the Supreme Court and the County Court Rules in insolvency proceedings. In regard to costs, see rr. 7.33–7.42.

Rule **7.52**   Right of audience

7.52(1)   [Official receivers and their deputies]   Official receivers and deputy official receivers have right of audience in insolvency proceedings, whether in the High Court or a county court.

7.52(2)   [Rights as obtained before Rules]   Subject as above, rights of audience in insolvency proceedings are the same as obtained before the coming into force of the Rules.

General note
There appears to have been no express provision governing rights of audience in the former rules: the matter was presumably left to be settled by the ordinary rules of court and the common law.

Rule **7.53**   Right of attendance (company insolvency)

7.53(1)   [Creditor or member or contributory]   Subject as follows, in company insolvency proceedings any person stating himself in writing, in records kept by the court for that purpose, to be a creditor or member of the company or, where the company is being wound up, a contributory, is entitled, at his own cost, to attend in court or in chambers at any stage of the proceedings.

7.53(2)   [Attendance in person etc.]   Attendance may be by the person himself, or his solicitor.

7.53(3)   [Notice of proceedings]   A person so entitled may request the court in writing to give him notice of any step in the proceedings; and, subject to his paying the costs involved and keeping the court informed as to his address, the court shall comply with the request.

7.53(4)   [Costs]   If the court is satisfied that the exercise by a person of his rights under this Rule has given rise to costs for the insolvent estate which would not otherwise have been incurred and ought not, in the circumstances, to fall on that estate, it may direct that the costs be paid by the person concerned, to an amount specified.

The person's rights under this Rule are in abeyance so long as those costs are not paid.

7.53(5)   [Power of court to appoint representatives etc.]   The court may appoint one or more persons to represent the creditors, the members or the contributories of an insolvent company, or any class of them, to have the rights conferred by this Rule, instead of the rights being exercisable by any or all of them individually.

If two or more persons are appointed under this paragraph to represent the same interest, they must (if at all) instruct the same solicitor.

The right of individual creditors, members and contributories to participate in company insolvency proceedings is here confirmed, subject to the power of the court to direct that such persons should be represented as a class under r. 7.53(5).

Rule 7.54   Insolvency practitioner's solicitor

7.54   Where in any proceedings the attendance of the responsible insolvency practitioner's solicitor is required, whether in court or in chambers, the insolvency practitioner himself need not attend, unless directed by the court.

Rule 7.55   Formal defects

7.55   No insolvency proceedings shall be invalidated by any formal defect or by any irregularity, unless the court before which objection is made considers that substantial injustice has been caused by the defect or irregularity, and that the injustice cannot be remedied by any order of the court.

General note

This rule appears to be based on BA 1914, s. 147(1). For its relevance in the context of setting aside a statutory demand, see *Re A Debtor (No. 1 of 1987)* [1988] 1 WLR 419. In the later case of *Re A Debtor (No. 190 of 1987), The Times,* 21 May 1988, Vinelott J held that r. 7.55 did not apply to cure defects in the statutory demand. He thereby followed *Re Cartwright* [1975] 1 WLR 573, which was decided under the old law.

In *Re A Debtor (No. 340 of 1992)* [1993] TLR 402 it was held that r. 7.55 did not validate an improperly executed writ of fieri facias as in the circumstances of the case the irregularity was so serious as to mean that the writ could not be said to have been served at all. Here apart from knocking on a debtor's door the bailiff had left the premises without any serious attempt to gain access.

Rule 7.55 did however come into play in *Re A Debtor (No. 22 of 1993)* [1994] 1 WLR 46 (sometimes cited as *Focus Insurance* v *A Debtor*) where an omission by a creditor to state in his petition that there was an extant set-aside application by the debtor was waved through by Mummery J.

Rule 7.56   Restriction on concurrent proceedings and remedies

7.56   Where, in insolvency proceedings the court makes an order staying any action, execution or other legal process against the property of a company, or against the property or person of an individual debtor or bankrupt, service of the order may be effected by sending a sealed copy of the order to whatever is the address for service of the plaintiff or other party having the carriage of the proceedings to be stayed.

Rule 7.57   Affidavits

7.57(1)   [Applicability of High Court rules etc.]   Subject as follows, the rules and practice obtaining in the High Court with regard to affidavits, their form and contents, and the procedure governing their use, are to be taken as applicable in all insolvency proceedings in any court.

7.57(2)   [Application of RSC, O. 41]   In applying RSC Order 41 (which relates to affidavits generally), there are to be disregarded provisions which are inconsistent with, or necessarily excluded by, the following paragraphs of this Rule.

7.57(3)   [Affidavit by official receiver or responsible insolvency practitioner]   Where in insolvency proceedings an affidavit is made by the official receiver or the responsible insolvency practitioner, the deponent shall state the capacity in which he makes it, the position which he holds, and the address at which he works.

7.57(4)   [Swearing creditor's affidavit of debt]   Notwithstanding RSC Order 41 Rule 8 (affidavit not to be sworn before party's own solicitor), a creditor's affidavit of debt may be sworn before his own solicitor.

7.57(5)   [Power of official receiver etc.]   The official receiver, any deputy official receiver, or any officer of the court duly authorised in that behalf, may take affidavits and declarations.

Rule 7.58   Security in court

7.58(1)   [Form of security]   Where security has to be given to the court (otherwise than in relation to costs), it may be given by guarantee, bond or the payment of money into court.

7.58(2)   [Notice re bond]   A person proposing to give a bond as security shall give notice to the party in whose favour the security is required, and to the court, naming those who are to be sureties to the bond.

7.58(3)   [Court to give notice]   The court shall forthwith give notice to both the parties concerned of a venue for the execution of the bond and the making of any objection to the sureties.

7.58(4)   [Sureties' affidavits etc.]   The sureties shall make an affidavit of their sufficiency (unless dispensed with by the party in whose favour the security is required) and shall, if required by the court, attend the court to be cross-examined.

Rule 7.59   Payment into court

7.59   The Rules of the Supreme Court and the County Court Rules relating to payment into and out of court of money lodged in court as security for costs apply, in the High Court and a county court respectively, to money lodged in court under the Rules.

Rule 7.60 Discovery

7.60(1) [Interrogatories or discovery] Any party to insolvency proceedings may, with the leave of the court, administer interrogatories to, or obtain discovery from, any other party to those proceedings.

7.60(2) [Ex parte application] Application under this Rule may be made *ex parte*.

General note

The operation of this particular rule was considered in detail by Harman J in *Re Primlaks (UK) Ltd (No. 2)* [1990] BCLC 234. Here it was held that in an unfair prejudice application under s. 6 of the Act arising out of a corporate voluntary arrangement, discovery should be ordered if it was in the interests of justice to do so; and clearly if a particular creditor was making an application under s. 6 it was necessary for him to know the full facts of the transactions which he alleged were unfair.

Rule 7.61 Office copies of documents

7.61(1) [Right to require office copy] Any person who has under the Rules the right to inspect the court file of insolvency proceedings may require the court to provide him with an office copy of any document from the file.

7.61(2) [Exercise of right] A person's rights under this Rule may be exercised on his behalf by his solicitor.

7.61(3) [Form of copy] An office copy provided by the court under this Rule shall be in such form as the registrar thinks appropriate, and shall bear the court's seal.

PART 8 — PROXIES AND COMPANY REPRESENTATION

Rule 8.1 Definition of "proxy"

8.1(1) [Definition] For the purposes of the Rules, a proxy is an authority given by a person (**"the principal"**) to another person (**"the proxy-holder"**) to attend a meeting and speak and vote as his representative.   [FORMS 8.1 to 8.5]

8.1(2) [Use of proxies] Proxies are for use at creditors', company or contributories' meetings summoned or called under the Act or the Rules.

8.1(3) [Giving proxies] Only one proxy may be given by a person for any one meeting at which he desires to be represented; and it may only be given to one person, being an individual aged 18 or over. But the principal may specify one or more other such individuals to be proxy-holder in the alternative, in the order in which they are named in the proxy.

8.1(4) [Chairman etc. as proxy-holder] Without prejudice to the generality of paragraph (3), a proxy for a particular meeting may be given to whoever is to be the chairman of the meeting; and for a meeting held as part of the proceedings in a winding up by the court, or in a bankruptcy, it may be given to the official receiver.

8.1(5) **[Chairman etc. cannot decline]** A person given a proxy under paragraph (4) cannot decline to be the proxy-holder in relation to that proxy.

8.1(6) **[Conduct of proxy-holder]** A proxy requires the holder to give the principal's vote on matters arising for determination at the meeting, or to abstain, or to propose, in the principal's name, a resolution to be voted on by the meeting, either as directed or in accordance with the holder's own discretion.

History note

In r. 8.1(2) the words "summoned or called" were inserted by I(A)R 1987 (SI 1987 No. 1919), r. 3(1), Sch., Pt. 1, para. 134(1) as from 11 January 1988.

   Rules 8.1(5) and (6) were substituted for the former r. 8.1(5) by I(A)R 1987 (SI 1987 No. 1919), r. 3(1), Sch., Pt. 1, para. 134(2) as from 11 January 1988: the former r. 8.1(5) read as follows:

   "**8.1(5)** A proxy requires the holder to give the principal's vote on matters arising for determination at the meeting, or to abstain, either as directed or in accordance with the holder's own discretion; and it may authorise or require the holder to propose, in the principal's name, a resolution to be voted on by the meeting."

(See general note after r. 8.6.)

Rule 8.2   Issue and use of forms

8.2(1) **[When forms are sent with notice]** When notice is given of a meeting to be held in insolvency proceedings, and forms of proxy are sent out with the notice, no form so sent out shall have inserted in it the name or description of any person.

8.2(2) **[Forms of proxy]** No form of proxy shall be used at any meeting except that which is sent out with the notice summoning the meeting, or a substantially similar form.

8.2(3) **[Proxy to be signed etc.]** A form of proxy shall be signed by the principal, or by some person authorised by him (either generally or with reference to a particular meeting). If the form is signed by a person other than the principal, the nature of the person's authority shall be stated.

(See general note after r. 8.6.)

Rule 8.3   Use of proxies at meetings

8.3(1) **[Use at adjournment]** A proxy given for a particular meeting may be used at any adjournment of that meeting.

8.3(2) **[Official receiver etc. as proxy-holder]** Where the official receiver holds proxies for use at any meeting, his deputy, or any other official receiver, may act as proxy-holder in his place.

   Alternatively, the official receiver may in writing authorise another officer of the Department to act for him at the meeting and use the proxies as if that other officer were himself proxy-holder.

8.3(3) **[Chairman etc. as proxy-holder]** Where the responsible insolvency practitioner holds proxies to be used by him as chairman of a meeting, and some other person acts as chairman, the other person may use the insolvency practitioner's proxies as if he were himself proxy-holder.

8.3(4) **[Appointment of responsible insolvency practitioner]** Where a proxy directs a proxy-holder to vote for or against a resolution for the nomination or appointment of a person as the responsible insolvency practitioner, the proxy-holder may, unless the proxy states otherwise, vote for or against (as he thinks fit) any resolution for the nomination or appointment of that person jointly with another or others.

8.3(5) **[Proposal by proxy-holder]** A proxy-holder may propose any resolution which, if proposed by another, would be a resolution in favour of which by virtue of the proxy he would be entitled to vote.

8.3(6) **[Specific directions to proxy-holder]** Where a proxy gives specific directions as to voting, this does not, unless the proxy states otherwise, preclude the proxy-holder from voting at his discretion on resolutions put to the meeting which are not dealt with in the proxy.

History note

Rules 8.3(4), (5) and (6) were added by I(A)R 1987 (SI 1987 No. 1919), r. 3(1), Sch., Pt. 1, para. 135 as from 11 January 1988.

General note

Rules 8.3(4), (5) and (6) were inserted to improve the effectiveness of the proxy system allowing a proxy more discretion (if his principal desires).

(See general note after r. 8.6.)

Rule 8.4 Retention of proxies

8.4(1) **[Chairman to retain proxies]** Subject as follows, proxies used for voting at any meeting shall be retained by the chairman of the meeting.

8.4(2) **[Delivery]** The chairman shall deliver the proxies, forthwith after the meeting, to the responsible insolvency practitioner (where that is someone other than himself).

(See general note after r. 8.6.)

Rule 8.5 Right of inspection

8.5(1) **[Who may inspect]** The responsible insolvency practitioner shall, so long as proxies lodged with him are in his hands, allow them to be inspected, at all reasonable times on any business day, by—

    (a) the creditors, in the case of proxies used at a meeting of creditors, and

    (b) a company's members or contributories, in the case of proxies used at a meeting of the company or of its contributories.

8.5(2) [Who are r. 8.5(1) creditors]   The reference in paragraph (1) to creditors is—

(a) in the case of a company in liquidation or of an individual's bankruptcy, those creditors who have proved their debts, and

(b) in any other case, persons who have submitted in writing a claim to be creditors of the company or individual concerned;

but in neither case does it include a person whose proof or claim has been wholly rejected for purposes of voting, dividend or otherwise.

8.5(3) [Who may also inspect]   The right of inspection given by this Rule is also exercisable—

(a) in the case of an insolvent company, by its directors, and

(b) in the case of an insolvent individual, by him.

8.5(4) [Person attending meeting]   Any person attending a meeting in insolvency proceedings is entitled, immediately before or in the course of the meeting, to inspect proxies and associated documents (including proofs) sent or given, in accordance with directions contained in any notice convening the meeting, to the chairman of that meeting or to any other person by a creditor, member or contributory for the purpose of that meeting.

History note

In r. 8.5(4) the words from "(including proofs)" to the end were substituted for the former words "to be used in connection with that meeting" by I(A)R 1987 (SI 1987 No. 1919), r. 3(1), Sch., Pt. 1, para. 136 as from 11 January 1988.

(See general note after r. 8.6.)

Rule 8.6   Proxy-holder with financial interest

8.6(1) [Limitation on voting by proxy-holder]   A proxy-holder shall not vote in favour of any resolution which would directly or indirectly place him, or any associate of his, in a position to receive any remuneration out of the insolvent estate, unless the proxy specifically directs him to vote in that way.

8.6(1A) [Written authorisation]   Where a proxy-holder has signed the proxy as being authorised to do so by his principal and the proxy specifically directs him to vote in the way mentioned in paragraph (1), he shall nevertheless not vote in that way unless he produces to the chairman of the meeting written authorisation from his principal sufficient to show that the proxy-holder was entitled so to sign the proxy.

8.6(2) [Application of Rule]   This Rule applies also to any person acting as chairman of a meeting and using proxies in that capacity under Rule 8.3; and in its application to him, the proxy-holder is deemed an associate of his.

History note

Rule 8.6(1A) was inserted by I(A)R 1987 (SI 1987 No. 1919), r. 3(1), Sch., Pt. 1, para. 137(1) as from 11 January 1988.

   In r. 8.6(2) the words "under Rule 8.3" were inserted by I(A)R 1987 (SI 1987 No. 1919), r. 3(1), Sch., Pt. 1, para. 137(2) as from 11 January 1988.

The use of proxies in insolvency proceedings is fairly strictly controlled by these rules.

For the meaning of "associate" in r. 8.6, see IA 1986, s. 435.

Rule 8.6(1A) was added to r. 8.6 to restrict the possibility of a proxy profiting from his position unless expressly authorised to do so by his principal. Specific reference to r. 8.3 was also included in r. 8.6(2).

Rule 8.7   Company representation

8.7(1)   [Production of copy of resolution]   Where a person is authorised under section 375 of the Companies Act to represent a corporation at a meeting of creditors or of the company or its contributories, he shall produce to the chairman of the meeting a copy of the resolution from which he derives his authority.

8.7(2)   [Copy of resolution to be sealed or certified]   The copy resolution must be under the seal of the corporation, or certified by the secretary or a director of the corporation to be a true copy.

8.7(3)   [Authority to sign proxy]   Nothing in this Rule requires the authority of a person to sign a proxy on behalf of a principal which is a corporation to be in the form of a resolution of that corporation.

History note

Rule 8.7(3) was added by I(A)R 1987 (SI 1987 No. 1919), r. 3(1), Sch., Pt. 1, para. 138 as from 11 January 1988.

PART 9 — EXAMINATION OF PERSONS CONCERNED IN COMPANY AND INDIVIDUAL INSOLVENCY

Rule 9.1   Preliminary

9.1(1)   [Application of Pt. 9 Rules]   The Rules in this Part relate to applications to the court for an order under—

    (a) section 236 (inquiry into company's dealings when it is, or is alleged to be, insolvent), or   [FORM 9.1]

    (b) section 366 (inquiry in bankruptcy, with respect to the bankrupt's dealings)   [FORM 9.1]

9.1(2)   [Definitions]   The following definitions apply—

    (a) the person in respect of whom an order is applied for is "the respondent";

    (b) "the applicable section" is section 236 or section 366, according to whether the affairs of a company or those of a bankrupt or (where the application under section 366 is made by virtue of section 368) a debtor are in question;

(c) the company or, as the case may be, the bankrupt or debtor concerned is "the insolvent".

(See general note after r. 9.6.)

Rule 9.2   Form and contents of application

9.2(1)   [In writing, statement of grounds]   The application shall be in writing, and be accompanied by a brief statement of the grounds on which it is made.

9.2(2)   [Respondent sufficiently identified]   The respondent must be sufficiently identified in the application.

9.2(3)   [Purpose to be stated]   It shall be stated whether the application is for the respondent—

(a) to be ordered to appear before the court, or
(b) to answer interrogatories (if so, particulars to be given of the matters in respect of which answers are required), or
(c) to submit affidavits (if so, particulars to be given of the matters to which he is required to swear), or
(d) to produce books, papers or other records (if so, the items in question to be specified),

or for any two or more of those purposes.

9.2(4)   [Ex parte application]   The application may be made *ex parte*.

(See general note after r. 9.6.)

Rule 9.3   Order for examination, etc.

9.3(1)   [Powers of court]   The court may, whatever the purpose of the application, make any order which it has power to make under the applicable section.

9.3(2)   [Venue]   The court, if it orders the respondent to appear before it, shall specify a venue for his appearance, which shall be not less than 14 days from the date of the order.

9.3(3)   [Order to submit affidavits]   If he is ordered to submit affidavits, the order shall specify—

(a) the matters which are to be dealt with in his affidavits, and
(b) the time within which they are to be submitted to the court.

9.3(4)   [Order to produce books etc.]   If the order is to produce books, papers or other records, the time and manner of compliance shall be specified.

9.3(5)   [Service]   The order must be served forthwith on the respondent; and it must be served personally, unless the court otherwise orders.

General note
For the meaning of "venue" see r. 13.6.

(See also general note after r. 9.6.)

Rule **9.4** Procedure for examination

9.4(1) [Applicant may attend etc.] At any examination of the respondent, the applicant may attend in person, or be represented by a solicitor with or without counsel, and may put such questions to the respondent as the court may allow.

9.4(2) [Other attendances etc.] Any other person who could have applied for an order under the applicable section in respect of the insolvent's affairs may, with the leave of the court and if the applicant does not object, attend the examination and put questions to the respondent (but only through the applicant).

9.4(3) [Interrogatories] If the respondent is ordered to answer interrogatories, the court shall direct him as to the questions which he is required to answer, and as to whether his answers (if any) are to be made on affidavit.

9.4(4) [Attendance etc. of creditor] Where application has been made under the applicable section on information provided by a creditor of the insolvent, that creditor may, with the leave of the court and if the applicant does not object, attend the examination and put questions to the respondent (but only through the applicant).

9.4(5) [Representation of respondent] The respondent may at his own expense employ a solicitor with or without counsel, who may put to him such questions as the court may allow for the purpose of enabling him to explain or qualify any answers given by him, and may make representations on his behalf.

9.4(6) [Record of examination] There shall be made in writing such record of the examination as the court thinks proper. The record shall be read over either to or by the respondent and signed by him at a venue fixed by the court.

9.4(7) [Record as evidence] The written record may, in any proceedings (whether under the Act or otherwise) be used as evidence against the respondent of any statement made by him in the course of his examination.

(See general note after r. 9.6.)

Rule **9.5** Record of examination

9.5(1) [Record etc. not to be filed] Unless the court otherwise directs, the written record of the respondent's examination, and any answer given by him to interrogatories, and any affidavits submitted by him in compliance with an order to the court under the applicable section, shall not be filed in court.

9.5(2) [Inspection] The written record, answers and affidavits shall not be open to inspection, without an order of the court, by any person other than—

(a) the applicant for an order under the applicable section, or

(b) any person who could have applied for such an order in respect of the affairs of the same insolvent.

9.5(3) [Application of r. 9.5(2)] Paragraph (2) applies also to so much of the court file as shows the grounds of the application for an order under the applicable section and to any copy of proposed interrogatories.

9.5(4)   **[Powers of court]**   The court may from time to time give directions as to the custody and inspection of any documents to which this Rule applies, and as to the furnishing of copies of, or extracts from, such documents.

(See general note after r. 9.6.)

Rule 9.6   Costs of proceedings under ss. 236, 366

9.6(1)   **[Power of court]**   Where the court has ordered an examination of any person under the applicable section, and it appears to it that the examination was made necessary because information had been unjustifiably refused by the respondent, it may order that the costs of the examination be paid by him.

9.6(2)   **[Further power]**   Where the court makes an order against a person under—

    (a)   section 237(1) or 367(1) (to deliver up property in his possession which belongs to the insolvent), or

    (b)   section 237(2) or 367(2) (to pay any amount in discharge of a debt due to the insolvent),

the costs of the application for the order may be ordered by the court to be paid by the respondent.

9.6(3)   **[Applicant's costs]**   Subject to paragraphs (1) and (2) above, the applicant's costs shall, unless the court otherwise orders, be paid out of the insolvent estate.

9.6(4)   **[Travelling expenses etc.]**   A person summoned to attend for examination under this Chapter shall be tendered a reasonable sum in respect of travelling expenses incurred in connection with his attendance. Other costs falling on him are at the court's discretion.

9.6(5)   **[No order against official receiver]**   Where the examination is on the application of the official receiver otherwise than in the capacity of liquidator or trustee, no order shall be made for the payment of costs by him.

General note to rr. 9.1–9.6

The examinations authorised by IA 1986, ss. 236, 366, to which this Part refers, are private examinations, in contrast to the public examinations which may be ordered under IA 1986, ss. 133, 134 and 290. For further discussion, see notes to those sections, and for the rules applicable in the latter case, see rr. 4.211ff. In addition, ss. 237 and 367, referred to in r. 9.6, empower the court to order a person to deliver up property to the liquidator or other office holder, or to pay money in discharge of a debt.

The explanatory words "when it is, or is alleged to be, insolvent" in r. 9.1(1)(*a*) are misleading. For the circumstances in which s. 236 applies, reference should be made to s. 236(1) and 234(1).

Under the former winding-up rules, it was the practice for an applicant seeking an order to support his application by a memorandum which was required to be verified by affidavit in every case except where the applicant, as a liquidator, was an officer of the court. Rule 9.2(1) appears to have abolished this distinction, so that an unsworn statement is now sufficient in all cases. The statement is confidential: *Re Aveling Barford Ltd & Ors* [1989] 1 WLR 360; (1988) 4 BCC 548; but (in a departure from the previous practice) the court may order that it be disclosed in whole or in part to the person against whom the order is sought in a proper case: see the note to s. 236.

An order requiring a person to give "an account of full particulars of all dealings" by him with the company may be open to objection on the grounds that it lacks the particularity called for by rr. 9.2(3)(*c*) and 9.3(*a*): *Re Aveling Barford Ltd* (above). It was held in the same case that the phrase "a person summoned to attend for examination under this Chapter" in r. 9.6(4) includes a person required to give information by the alternative methods permitted under s. 236. On the question of the examinee's costs, Hoffmann J declined to make an order in advance or to say that there should be a presumption in favour of allowing costs, over and above the travelling expenses mentioned in r. 9.6(4)

PART 10 — OFFICIAL RECEIVERS

General comment on Pt. 10
The rules in this Part supplement IA 1986, ss. 399–401.

Rule 10.1 Appointment of official receivers
10.1 Judicial notice shall be taken of the appointment under sections 399 to 401 of official receivers and deputy official receivers.

Rule 10.2 Persons entitled to act on official receiver's behalf
10.2(1) **[In absence of official receiver]** In the absence of the official receiver authorised to act in a particular case, an officer authorised in writing for the purpose by the Secretary of State, or by the official receiver himself, may, with the leave of the court, act on the official receiver's behalf and in his place—

    (a) in any examination under section 133, 236, 290 or 366, and

    (b) in respect of any application to the court.

10.2(2) **[In case of emergency]** In case of emergency, where there is no official receiver capable of acting, anything to be done by, to or before the official receiver may be done by, to or before the registrar of the court.

General note
The possibility of a person acting on behalf of the official receiver would appear to be in addition to the appointment of a deputy under IA 1986, s. 401.

Rule 10.3 Application for directions
10.3 The official receiver may apply to the court for directions in relation to any matter arising in insolvency proceedings.

General note
This is a standard facility for all insolvency practitioners. Compare BR 1952, r. 323.

Rule 10.4 Official receiver's expenses
10.4(1) **["Expenses"]** Any expenses incurred by the official receiver (in whatever capacity he may be acting) in connection with proceedings taken against him in insolvency proceedings are to be treated as expenses of the insolvency proceedings.

    "Expenses" includes damages.

10.4(2) **[Official receiver's charge]** In respect of any sums due to him under paragraph (1), the official receiver has a charge on the insolvent estate.

General note

Note the wide definition of "expenses".

PART 11 — DECLARATION AND PAYMENT OF DIVIDEND (WINDING UP AND BANKRUPTCY)

General comment on Pt. 11

The rules in this Part are to be viewed in light of the provisions of IA 1986 – e.g. see ss. 324 and 330.

Rule 11.1 Preliminary

11.1(1) **[Application of Pt. 11 Rules]** The Rules in this Part relate to the declaration and payment of dividends in companies winding up and in bankruptcy.

11.1(2) **[Definitions]** The following definitions apply—

(a) **"the insolvent"** means the company in liquidation or, as the case may be, the bankrupt; and

(b) **"creditors"** means those creditors of the insolvent of whom the responsible practitioner is aware, or who are identified in the insolvent's statement of affairs.

Rule 11.2 Notice of intended dividend

11.2(1) **[Before declaring dividend]** Before declaring a dividend, the responsible insolvency practitioner shall give notice of his intention to do so to all creditors whose addresses are known to him and who have not proved their debts.

11.2(1A) **[Public advertisement]** Before declaring a first dividend, the responsible insolvency practitioner shall, unless he has previously by public advertisement invited creditors to prove their debts, give notice of the intended dividend by public advertisement.

11.2(2) **["The last date for proving"]** Any notice under paragraph (1) and any notice of a first dividend under paragraph (1A) shall specify a date ("the last date for proving") up to which proofs may be lodged. The date shall be the same for all creditors, and not less than 21 days from that of the notice.

11.2(3) **[Contents of notice]** The insolvency practitioner shall in the notice state his intention to declare a dividend (specified as interim or final, as the case may be) within the period of 4 months from the last date for proving.

History note

In r. 11.2(1) the words "whose addresses are known to him and" were inserted by I(A)R 1987 (SI 1987 No. 1919), r. 3(1), Sch., Pt. 1, para. 139(1) as from 11 January 1988.

Rule 11.2(1A) was inserted by I(A)R 1987 (SI 1987 No. 1919), r. 3(1), Sch., Pt. 1, para. 139(2) as from 11 January 1988.

In r. 11.2(2) the words from "Any notice" to "paragraph (1A)" were substituted for the former words "The notice" by I(A)R 1987 (SI 1987 No. 1919), r. 3(1), Sch., Pt. 1, para. 139(3) as from 11 January 1988.

General note

This is to give tardy creditors a last chance to lodge their proofs.

Notice need only be given under r. 11.2(1) to known creditors. Rule 11.2(1A) confers a discretion on the trustee to advertise for claims, in the case of a first dividend, where he has not previously advertised inviting creditors to prove.

Rule 11.3   Final admission/rejection of proofs

11.3(1)   [Dealing with every proof]   The responsible insolvency practitioner shall, within 7 days from the last date for proving, deal with every creditor's proof (in so far as not already dealt with) by admitting or rejecting it in whole or in part, or by making such provision as he thinks fit in respect of it.

11.3(2)   [Proofs lodged out of time]   The insolvency practitioner is not obliged to deal with proofs lodged after the date for proving; but he may do so, if he thinks fit.

General note

Late proofs may be accepted at the discretion of the insolvency practitioner.

Rule 11.4   Postponement or cancellation of dividend

11.4   If in the period of 4 months referred to in Rule 11.2(3)—

   (a)   the responsible insolvency practitioner has rejected a proof in whole or in part and application is made to the court for his decision to be reversed or varied, or

   (b)   application is made to the court for the insolvency practitioner's decision on a proof to be reversed or varied, or for a proof to be expunged, or for a reduction of the amount claimed,

the insolvency practitioner may postpone or cancel the dividend.

General note

An application to the court to have the decision of the insolvency practitioner on the admission or rejection of proofs varied is made, in the case of a winding up, under r. 4.83(1) or (2) and in a bankruptcy, under r. 6.105(1) or (2). There is a time-limit of 21 days in each case. If such an application has been made, the insolvency practitioner may postpone or cancel the dividend under this rule; but, if he proposes to pay a dividend, r. 11.5(2) applies.

Rule 11.5   Decision to declare dividend

11.5(1)   [Proceeding to declare dividend]   If the responsible insolvency practitioner has not, in the 4-month period referred to in Rule 11.2(3), had cause to postpone or cancel the dividend, he shall within that period proceed to declare the dividend of which he gave notice under that Rule.

11.5(2) [Pending application re proof etc.]   Except with the leave of the court, the insolvency practitioner shall not declare the dividend so long as there is pending any application to the court to reverse or vary a decision of his on a proof, or to expunge a proof or to reduce the amount claimed.

If the court gives leave under this paragraph, the insolvency practitioner shall make such provision in respect of the proof in question as the court directs.

General note

If no application has been made to the court to challenge a decision on the admission or rejection of a proof, the dividend must be declared within the four-month period. If the insolvency practitioner wishes to declare an interim dividend pending the outcome of such an application, the leave of the court is required under r. 11.5(2). Where this rule applies, the normal rules as to the payment of interim dividends (IA 1986, s. 324, IR 1986, rr. 4.180, 4.182) are displaced.

Rule 11.6   Notice of declaration

11.6(1) [Notice to all creditors who have proved]   The responsible insolvency practitioner shall give notice of the dividend to all creditors who have proved their debts.

11.6(2) [Particulars in notice]   The notice shall include the following particulars relating to the insolvency and the administration of the insolvent estate—

    (a) amounts realised from the sale of assets, indicating (so far as practicable) amounts raised by the sale of particular assets;

    (b) payments made by the insolvency practitioner in the administration of the insolvent estate;

    (c) provision (if any) made for unsettled claims, and funds (if any) retained for particular purposes;

    (d) the total amount to be distributed, and the rate of dividend;

    (e) whether, and if so when, any further dividend is expected to be declared.

11.6(3) [Simultaneous distribution]   The dividend may be distributed simultaneously with the notice declaring it.

11.6(4) [Method of payment]   Payment of dividend may be made by post, or arrangements may be made with any creditor for it to be paid to him in another way, or held for his collection.

11.6(5) [Endorsement in negotiable instrument]   Where a dividend is paid on a bill of exchange or other negotiable instrument, the amount of the dividend shall be endorsed on the instrument, or on a certified copy of it, if required to be produced by the holder for that purpose.

General note
Creditors are to receive full information relating to the payment of dividends, etc.

Rule 11.7 Notice of no, or no further, dividend

11.7 If the responsible insolvency practitioner gives notice to creditors that he is unable to declare any dividend or (as the case may be) any further dividend, the notice shall contain a statement to the effect either—

> (a) that no funds have been realised, or
> (b) that the funds realised have already been distributed or used or allocated for defraying the expenses of administration.

Rule 11.8 Proof altered after payment of dividend

11.8(1) **[If amount claimed in proof increased]** If after payment of dividend the amount claimed by a creditor in his proof is increased, the creditor is not entitled to disturb the distribution of the dividend; but he is entitled to be paid, out of any money for the time being available for the payment of any further dividend, any dividend or dividends which he has failed to receive.

11.8(2) **[Payments under r. 11.8(1)]** Any dividend or dividends payable under paragraph (1) shall be paid before the money there referred to is applied to the payment of any such further dividend.

11.8(3) **[Proof withdrawn etc.]** If, after a creditor's proof has been admitted, the proof is withdrawn or expunged, or the amount of it is reduced, the creditor is liable to repay to the responsible insolvency practitioner, for the credit of the insolvent estate, any amount overpaid by way of dividend.

General note
Here we have a "heads I win, tails you lose" situation.

Rule 11.9 Secured creditors

11.9(1) **[Application of Rule]** The following applies where a creditor re-values his security at a time when a dividend has been declared.

11.9(2) **[Reduction of unsecured claim]** If the revaluation results in a reduction of his unsecured claim ranking for dividend, the creditor shall forthwith repay to the responsible insolvency practitioner, for the credit of the insolvent estate, any amount received by him as dividend in excess of that to which he would be entitled having regard to the revaluation of the security.

11.9(3) **[Increase of unsecured claim]** If the revaluation results in an increase of his unsecured claim, the creditor is entitled to receive from the insolvency practitioner, out of any money for the time being available for the payment of a further dividend, before any such further dividend is paid, any dividend or dividends which he has failed to receive, having regard to the revaluation of the security.

However, the creditor is not entitled to disturb any dividend declared (whether or not distributed) before the date of the revaluation.

General note

This again shows that the law will not disturb dividends that have already been declared.

Rule **11.10**　Disqualification from dividend

11.10　If a creditor contravenes any provision of the Act or the Rules relating to the valuation of securities, the court may, on the application of the responsible insolvency practitioner, order that the creditor be wholly or partly disqualified from participation in any dividend.

General note

This is a useful sanction.

Rule **11.11**　Assignment of right to dividend

11.11(1)　**[Notice of assignment etc.]**　If a person entitled to a dividend gives notice to the responsible insolvency practitioner that he wishes the dividend to be paid to another person, or that he has assigned his entitlement to another person, the insolvency practitioner shall pay the dividend to that other accordingly.

11.11(2)　**[Contents of notice]**　A notice given under this Rule must specify the name and address of the person to whom payment is to be made.

General note

The right to receive a dividend can be assigned.

Rule **11.12**　Preferential creditors

11.12(1)　**[Application of Pt. 11 Rules]**　Subject as follows, the Rules in this Part apply with respect to any distribution made in the insolvency to preferential creditors, with such adaptions as are appropriate considering that such creditors are of a limited class.

11.12(2)　**[Rule 11.2 notice]**　The notice by the responsible insolvency practitioner under Rule 11.2, where a dividend is to be declared for preferential creditors, need only be given to those creditors in whose case he has reason to believe that their debts are preferential and public advertisement of the intended dividend need only be given if the insolvency practitioner thinks fit.

History note

In r. 11.12(2) the words from "and public advertisement" to the end were added by I(A)R 1987 (SI 1987 No. 1919), r. 3(1), Sch., Pt. 1, para. 140 as from 11 January 1988.

General note
This makes necessary modifications to the above rules where the declaration is for the benefit of preferential creditors – see IA 1986, Pt. XII.

Rule 11.13   Debt payable at future time

11.13(1)   [Entitlement to dividend]   Where a creditor has proved for a debt of which payment is not due at the date of the declaration of dividend, he is entitled to dividend equally with other creditors, but subject as follows.

11.13(2)   [Calculation of amount of reduction]   For the purpose of dividend (and for no other purpose), the amount of the creditor's admitted proof (or, if a distribution has previously been made to him, the amount remaining outstanding in respect of his admitted proof) shall be reduced by a percentage calculated as follows—

$$\frac{I \times M}{12}$$

where I is 5 per cent. and M is the number of months (expressed, if need be, as, or as including, fractions of months) between the declaration of dividend and the date when payment of the creditor's debt would otherwise be due.

11.13(3)   [Other creditors' entitlement to interest]   Other creditors are not entitled to interest out of surplus funds under section 189(2) or (as the case may be) 328(4) until any creditor to whom paragraphs (1) and (2) apply has been paid the full amount of his debt.

History note

In r. 11.13(2) the words "a percentage" were substituted for the former words "an amount" by I(A)R 1987 (SI 1987 No. 1919), r. 3(1), Sch., Pt. 1, para. 141 as from 11 January 1988.

General note

This deals with interest payable on future debts.
    Rule 11.13(2) was amended on a point of mathematical semantics.

PART 12 — MISCELLANEOUS AND GENERAL

Rule 12.1   Power of Secretary of State to regulate certain matters

12.1(1)   [Power to make regulations]   Pursuant to paragraph 27 of Schedule 8 to the Act, and paragraph 30 of Schedule 9 to the Act, the Secretary of State may, subject to the Act and the Rules, make regulations with respect to any matter provided for in the Rules as relates to the carrying out of the functions of a liquidator, provisional liquidator, administrator or administrative receiver of a company, an interim receiver appointed under section 286, of the official receiver while acting as receiver or manager under section 287 or of a trustee of a bankrupt's estate, including, without prejudice to the generality of the foregoing, provision with respect to the following matters arising in companies winding up and individual bankruptcy—

(a) the preparation and keeping by liquidators, trustees, provisional liquidators, interim receivers and the official receiver, of books, accounts and other records, and their production to such persons as may be authorised or required to inspect them.

(b) the auditing of liquidators' and trustees' accounts;

(c) the manner in which liquidators and trustees are to act in relation to the insolvent company's or bankrupt's books, papers and other records, and the manner of their disposal by the responsible insolvency practitioner or others;

(d) the supply—

(i) in company insolvency, by the liquidator to creditors and members of the company, contributories in its winding up and the liquidation committee, and

(ii) in individual insolvency, by the trustee to creditors and the creditors' committee,

of copies of documents relating to the insolvency and the affairs of the insolvent company or individual (on payment, in such cases as may be specified by the regulations, of the specified fee);

(e) the manner in which insolvent estates are to be distributed by liquidators and trustees, including provision with respect to unclaimed funds and dividends;

(f) the manner in which moneys coming into the hands of a liquidator or trustee in the course of his administration are to be handled and, in the case of a liquidator, invested, and the payment of interest on sums which, in pursuance of regulations made by virtue of this sub-paragraph, have been paid into the Insolvency Services Account;

(g) the amount (or the manner of determining the amount) to be paid to the official receiver by way of remuneration when acting as provisional liquidator, liquidator, interim receiver or trustee.

12.1(2)   [Reference to trustee in r. 12.1(1)]   Any reference in paragraph (1) to a trustee includes a reference to the official receiver when acting as receiver and manager under section 287.

12.1(3)   [Contents of regulations]   Regulations made pursuant to paragraph (1) may—

(a) confer a discretion on the court;

(b) make non-compliance with any of the regulations a criminal offence;

(c) make different provision for different cases, including different provision for different areas; and

(d) contain such incidental, supplemental and transitional provisions as may appear to the Secretary of State necessary or expedient.

History note

In r. 12.1(1) the words from ", subject to the Act and the Rules" to "generality of the foregoing, provision" were substituted for the former words "make regulations" by I(A)R 1987 (SI 1987 No. 1919), r. 3(1), Sch., Pt. 1, para. 142(1) as from 11 January 1988.

In r. 12.1(3) the word ", and" and para. (*d*) were added by I(A)R 1987 (SI 1987 No. 1919), r. 3(1), Sch., Pt. 1, para. 142(2) as from 11 January 1988.

General note

This clarifies the power of the Secretary of State to make regulations to supplement the existing framework: see the Insolvency Regulations 1994 (SI 1994 No. 2507), operative from 24 October 1994, replacing the original Insolvency Regulations 1986 (SI 1986 No. 1994) as amended which like the Rules and the two 1986 statutes operated from 29 December 1986.

Rule **12.2** Costs, expenses, etc.

12.2 All fees, costs, charges and other expenses incurred in the course of winding up or bankruptcy proceedings are to be regarded as expenses of the winding up or, as the case may be, of the bankruptcy.

Rule **12.3** Provable debts

12.3(1) [What is provable] Subject as follows, in both winding up and bankruptcy, all claims by creditors are provable as debts against the company or, as the case may be, the bankrupt, whether they are present or future, certain or contingent, ascertained or sounding only in damages.

12.3(2) [What is not provable] The following are not provable—

(a) in bankruptcy, any fine imposed for an offence, and any obligation arising under an order made in family proceedings or under a maintenance assessment made under the Child Support Act 1991;

(b) in winding up or bankruptcy, any obligation arising under a confiscation order made under section 1 of the Drug Trafficking Offences Act 1986 or section 1 of the Criminal Justice (Scotland) Act 1987 or section 71 of the Criminal Justice Act 1988.

"Fine" and **"family proceedings"** have the meanings given by section 281(8) of the Act (which applies the Magistrates' Courts Act 1980 and the Matrimonial and Family Proceedings Act 1984).

12.3(2A) [Postponed debts] The following are not provable except at a time when all other claims of creditors in the insolvency proceedings (other than any of a kind mentioned in this paragraph) have been paid in full with interest under section 189(2) or, as the case may be, section 328(4)—

  (a) in a winding up or a bankruptcy, any claim arising by virtue of—

     (i) section 6(3)(a) of the Financial Services Act 1986, not being a claim also arising by virtue of section 6(3)(b) of that Act, or

    (ii) section 61(3)(a) of that Act, not being a claim also arising by virtue of section 61(3)(b) of that Act;

  (b) in a winding up or a bankruptcy, any claim arising by virtue of section 49 of the Banking Act 1987;

  (c) in a winding up, any claim which by virtue of the Act or any other enactment is a claim the payment of which in a bankruptcy or a winding up is to be postponed.

12.3(3)   **[Effect of Rule]**   Nothing in this Rule prejudices any enactment or rule of law under which a particular kind of debt is not provable, whether on grounds of public policy or otherwise.

History note

In r. 12.3(2)(*b*) the words "or section 1 of the Criminal Justice (Scotland) Act 1987" were added by I(A)R 1987 (SI 1987 No. 1919), r. 3(1), Sch., Pt. 1, para. 143(1) as from 11 January 1988, and the words "or section 71 of the Criminal Justice Act 1988" by I(A)R 1989 (SI 1989 No. 397), r. 3(1), Sch., as from 3 April 1989. Minor textual amendments to r. 12.3(2) were made by the Insolvency (Amendment) Rules 1993 (SI 1993 No. 602).

    Rule 12.3(2A) was inserted by I(A)R 1987 (SI 1987 No. 1919), r. 3(1), Sch., Pt. 1, para. 143(2) as from 11 January 1988.

General note

This provision complements IA 1986, ss. 322 and 382. It must be read in the light of r. 13.12. Not all bankruptcy debts are provable debts – see the discussion in *Woodley* v *Woodley (No. 2)* [1994] 1 WLR 1167 at p. 1175. Note that fines are now regarded as not provable. The opposite conclusion was arrived at in *Re Pascoe* [1944] Ch. 310. The Cork Committee (Cmnd 8558, para. 1330) suggested this change in the law.

    Rule 12.3(2A) further restricts the categories of provable debt.

    The legal status of r. 12.3 came under consideration in the Court of Appeal in *Woodley* v *Woodley (No. 2)* [1994] 1 WLR 1167. Here the suggestion that r. 12.3 might be ultra vires the 1986 Act was considered and then dismissed. Authority for it was based upon para. 17 of Sch. 9 to the Insolvency Act 1986 and ultimately upon s. 412(2)(*a*). In spite of this reassuring finding the Court of Appeal suggested that the Insolvency Rules Committee should look at the question of whether lump sum orders made in family proceedings should be restored as provable debts, which was the position before the 1986 rules came into effect.

    Foreign tax debts provide an example of a debt which is regarded as non-provable on policy grounds – see *Government of India, Ministry of Finance (Revenue Division)* v *Taylor & Anor* [1955] AC 491 which is discussed by Miller in [1991] JBL 144.

Rule **12.4**   Notices

12.4(1)   **[Notices in writing etc.]**   All notices required or authorised by or under the Act or the Rules to be given must be in writing, unless it is otherwise provided, or the court allows the notice to be given in some other way.

12.4(2)   **[Certificates of posting]**   Where in any proceedings a notice is required to be sent or given by the official receiver or by the responsible insolvency practitioner, the sending or giving of it may be proved by means of a certificate—

(a) in the case of the official receiver, by him or a member of his staff, and

(b) in the case of the insolvency practitioner, by him, or his solicitor, or a partner or an employee of either of them,

that the notice was duly posted.

12.4(3) [Certificates of posting] In the case of a notice to be sent or given by a person other than the official receiver or insolvency practitioner, the sending or giving of it may be proved by means of a certificate by that person that he posted the notice, or instructed another person (naming him) to do so.

12.4(4) [Certificate endorsed on copy of notice] A certificate under this Rule may be endorsed on a copy or specimen of the notice to which it relates.

Rule 12.4A   Quorum at meeting of creditors or contributories

12.4A(1) [Meeting competent] Any meeting of creditors or contributories in insolvency proceedings is competent to act if a quorum is present.

12.4A(2) [Quorum] Subject to the next paragraph, a quorum is—

(a) in the case of a creditors' meeting, at least one creditor entitled to vote;

(b) in the case of a meeting of contributories, at least 2 contributories so entitled, or all the contributories, if their number does not exceed 2.

12.4A(3) [Persons present or represented] For the purposes of this Rule, the reference to the creditor or contributories necessary to constitute a quorum is to those persons present or represented by proxy by any person (including the chairman) and in the case of any proceedings under Parts I–VII of the Act includes persons duly represented under section 375 of the Companies Act.

12.4A(4) [Meeting to be delayed] Where at any meeting of creditors or contributories—

(a) the provisions of this Rule as to a quorum being present are satisfied by the attendance of—

(i) the chairman alone, or

(ii) one other person in addition to the chairman, and

(b) the chairman is aware, by virtue of proofs and proxies received or otherwise, that one or more additional persons would, if attending, be entitled to vote,

the meeting shall not commence until at least the expiry of 15 minutes after the time appointed for its commencement.

History note

Rule 12.4A was inserted by I(A)R 1987 (SI 1987 No. 1919), r. 3(1), Sch., Pt. 1, para. 144 as from 11 January 1988.

General note

In part r. 12.4A fills the void created by the deletion of rr. 3.13, 4.66 and 6.92. The quorum for creditors' meetings has now been reduced from three creditors to one.

Rule **12.5**   Evidence of proceedings at meetings

12.5(1)   [Minute of proceedings admissible]   A minute of proceedings at a meeting (held under the Act or the Rules) of a person's creditors, or of the members of a company, or of the contributories in a company's liquidation, signed by a person describing himself as, or appearing to be, the chairman of that meeting is admissible in insolvency proceedings without further proof.

12.5(2)   [Minute as prima facie evidence]   The minute is prima facie evidence that—

   (a) the meeting was duly convened and held,

   (b) all resolutions passed at the meeting were duly passed, and

   (c) all proceedings at the meeting duly took place.

Rule **12.6**   Documents issuing from Secretary of State

12.6(1)   [Presumption re documents]   Any document purporting to be, or to contain, any order, directions or certificate issued by the Secretary of State shall be received in evidence and deemed to be or (as the case may be) contain that order or certificate, or those directions, without further proof, unless the contrary is shown.

12.6(2)   [Application of r. 12.6(1)]   Paragraph (1) applies whether the document is signed by the Secretary of State himself or an officer on his behalf.

12.6(3)   [Certificate as conclusive evidence]   Without prejudice to the foregoing, a certificate signed by the Secretary of State or an officer on his behalf and confirming—

   (a) the making of any order,

   (b) the issuing of any document, or

   (c) the exercise of any discretion, power or obligation arising or imposed under the Act or the Rules,

is conclusive evidence of the matters dealt with in the certificate.

Rule **12.7**   Forms for use in insolvency proceedings

12.7(1)   [Sch. 4 forms]   The forms contained in Schedule 4 to the Rules shall be used in and in connection with, insolvency proceedings, whether in the High Court or a county court.

12.7(2)   [Variations]   The forms shall be used with such variations, if any, as the circumstances may require.

12.7(3)   [Use of old forms]   Where any form contained in Schedule 4 is substantially the same as one used for a corresponding purpose under either—

   (a) the law and practice obtaining before the coming into force of the Rules; or

   (b) if the form was first required to be used after the coming into force of the Rules, the law and practice obtaining before the making of the requirement,

whichever shall be appropriate in any case, the latter may continue to be used (with the necessary modifications) until 1 March 1988.

History note

Rule 12.7(3) was substituted by I(A)R 1987 (SI 1987 No. 1919), r. 3(1), Sch., Pt. 1, para. 145 as from 11 January 1988: the former r. 12.7(3) read as follows:

"**12.7(3)** Where any form contained in Schedule 4 is substantially the same as one used for a corresponding purpose under the law and practice obtaining before the coming into force of the Rules, the latter may continue to be used (with the necessary modifications) until the Lord Chancellor otherwise directs."

General note

The appropriate insolvency forms are in Sch. 4 – but are not reproduced in this Guide, although a full list of the relevant names and numbers is included. Note the transitional concession made by r. 12.7(3). This was substituted and provided with a specific deadline by I(A)R 1987 (see history note above) to cover old forms in an amended form; they ceased to be acceptable on 1 March 1988.

Rule 12.8 Insolvency practitioner's security

12.8(1) [Duty re appointee's security] Wherever under the Rules any person has to appoint, or certify the appointment of, an insolvency practitioner to any office, he is under a duty to satisfy himself that the person appointed or to be appointed has security for the proper performance of his functions.

12.8(2) [Duty to review adequacy of security] It is the duty—

   (a) of the creditors' committee in companies administration, administrative receivership and bankruptcy,

   (b) of the liquidation committee in companies winding up, and

   (c) of any committe of creditors established for the purposes of a voluntary arrangement under Part I or VIII of the Act,

to review from time to time the adequacy of the responsible insolvency practitioner's security.

12.8(3) [Cost of security] In any insolvency proceedings the cost of the responsible insolvency practitioner's security shall be defrayed as an expense of the proceedings.

General note

For the requirement of security, see IA 1986, s. 390(3) in general. The provision of security is not a once and for all requirement, as r. 12.8(2) makes clear.

Rule 12.9 Time-limits

12.9 The provisions of Order 3 of the Rules of the Supreme Court, except Rules 3 and 6, apply as regards computation of time in respect of anything required or authorised by the Rules to be done.

General note

Under this rule, the court has power to abridge the period of five days' notice of a petition for an administration order that is normally required to be given to a floating chargeholder by r. 2.7(1): *Re a Company No. 00175 of 1987* (1987) 3 BCC 124.

Rule **12.10**   Service by post

12.10(1)   [Proper service by post]   For a document to be properly served by post, it must be contained in an envelope addressed to the person on whom service is to be effected, and pre-paid for either first or second class post.

12.10(1A)   [Where to be served]   A document to be served by post may be sent to the last known address of the person to be served.

12.10(2)   [First class post]   Where first class post is used, the document is treated as served on the second business day after the date of posting, unless the contrary is shown.

12.10(3)   [Second class post]   Where second class post is used, the document is treated as served on the fourth business day after the date of posting, unless the contrary is shown.

12.10(4)   [Presumed date of posting]   The date of posting is presumed, unless the contrary is shown, to be the date shown in the post-mark on the envelope in which the document is contained.

History note

Rule 12.10(1A) was inserted by I(A)R 1987 (SI 1987 No. 1919) r. 3(1), Sch., Pt. 1, para. 146 as from 11 January 1988.

Rule **12.11**   General provisions as to service

12.11(1)   [Application of RSC, O.65]   Subject to Rule 12.10 and as follows, Order 65 of the Rules of the Supreme Court applies as regards any matter relating to the service of documents and the giving of notice in insolvency proceedings.

12.11(2)   [Application of O.65, r. 7]   In Order 65 Rule 7, the expression "other originating process" does not include any application in insolvency proceedings.

12.11(3)   [Non-application of O.65, r. 9]   Order 65 Rule 9 does not apply.

12.11(4)   [Application of O.65, r. 10]   In Order 65 Rule 10, the expression "process" includes any application in insolvency proceedings.

History note

In r. 12.11(1) the words "to Rule 12.10 and" were inserted by I(A)R 1987 (SI 1987 No. 1919), r.3(1), Sch., Pt. 1, para. 147 as from 11 January 1988.

Rule **12.12**   Service outside the jurisdiction

12.12(1)   [Non-application of RSC, O.11 etc.]   Order 11 of the Rules of the Supreme Court, and the corresponding County Court Rules, do not apply in insolvency proceedings.

12.12(2) **[Service of bankruptcy petition outside England and Wales]** A bankruptcy petition may, with the leave of the court, be served outside England and Wales in such manner as the court may direct.

12.12(3) **[Service on a person not in England and Wales]** Where for the purposes of insolvency proceedings any process or order of the court, or other document, is required to be served on a person who is not in England and Wales, the court may order service to be effected within such time, on such person, at such place and in such manner as it thinks fit, and may also require such proof of service as it thinks fit.

12.12(4) **[Supporting affidavit]** An application under this Rule shall be supported by an affidavit stating—

(a) the grounds on which the application is made, and

(b) in what place or country the person to be served is, or probably may be found.

General note

The position under the old law (BR 1952, r. 86) was considered in *Re Jogia (A Bankrupt)* [1988] 1 WLR 484, *Re Tucker (A Bankrupt)* [1988] 1 WLR 497 and *Re Tucker (A Bankrupt), ex parte Tucker* [1990] Ch. 148 at p. 162. For a case where a winding-up petition was served outside the jurisdiction, see *Re Baby Moon (UK) Ltd* (1985) 1 BCC 99,298. Rule 12.12 is of growing importance as the UK courts strive to give extraterritorial effect to more and more provisions of the Insolvency Act 1986 and the Company Directors Disqualification Act 1986. Recently the following judicial decisions have leaned in favour of extraterritoriality – *Re Paramount Airways Ltd (in Administration)* [1993] Ch. 223 (reported as *Re Paramount Airways Ltd (No. 2)* [1992] BCC 416) (use of s. 238 of IA 1986), *Re Seagull Manufacturing Co. Ltd* [1993] Ch. 345; [1993] BCC 241 (examinations of officers conducted under s. 133 of IA 1986), *Re Seagull Manufacturing Co. Ltd (No. 2)* [1994] 2 WLR 453; [1993] BCC 833 (disqualification proceedings under CDDA 1986) and *McIsaac & Anor, Petitioners* [1994] BCC 410 (orders under ss. 236, 237 and 426 of IA 1986). This drive towards extending the territorial scope of UK insolvency law is in response to the increasingly transnational nature of commercial activity and in particular the fact that with modern technology UK companies can be effectively managed from abroad.

RSC O.11 continues to apply to applications for relief on the ground of unfairly prejudicial conduct under CA 1985, s. 459. Accordingly, where a petitioner for a winding-up order contains an alternative prayer for relief under s. 459, leave to serve the proceedings on a respondent who is outside the jurisdiction must be sought under O.11: *Re Harrods (Buenos Aires) Ltd* [1992] Ch. 72; [1991] BCC 249.

Rule 12.13   Confidentiality of documents

12.13(1) **[Power of responsible insolvency practitioner]** Where in insolvency proceedings the responsible insolvency practitioner considers, in the case of a document forming part of the records of the insolvency, that—

(a) it should be treated as confidential, or

(b) it is of such a nature that its disclosure would be calculated to be injurious to the interests of the insolvent's creditors or, in the case of a company's insolvency, its members or the contributories in its winding up,

he may decline to allow it to be inspected by a person who would otherwise be entitled to inspect it.

12.13(2) **[Who may be refused inspection]**　The persons to whom the insolvency practitioner may under this Rule refuse inspection include the members of a liquidation committee or a creditors' committee.

12.13(3) **[Application to court etc.]**　Where under this Rule the insolvency practitioner determines to refuse inspection of a document, the person wishing to inspect it may apply to the court for that determination to be overruled; and the court may either overrule it altogether, or sustain it subject to such conditions (if any) as it thinks fit to impose.

12.13(4) **[Inspection of proof or proxy]**　Nothing in this Rule entitles the insolvency practitioner to decline to allow the inspection of any proof or proxy.

History note

Rule 12.13(4) was added by I(A)R 1987 (SI 1987 No. 1919), r. 3(1), Sch., Pt. 1, para. 148 as from 11 January 1988.

General note

This reinforces a theme reflected in several IA 1986 provisions (e.g., s. 48(6)), and also in many of the rules themselves (e.g., rr. 3.5 and 6.61).

　　Rule 12.13(4) was inserted to curb refusal of inspection of proofs or proxy on grounds of confidentiality.

Rule **12.14**　Notices sent simultaneously to the same person

12.14　Where under the Act or the Rules a document of any description is to be sent to a person (whether or not as a member of a class of persons to whom that same document is to be sent), it may be sent as an accompaniment to any other document or information which the person is to receive, with or without modification or adaption of the form applicable to that document.

Rule **12.15**　Right to copy documents

12.15　Where the Act or the Rules confer a right for any person to inspect documents, the right includes that of taking copies of those documents, on payment—

(a) in the case of documents on the court's file of proceedings, of the fee chargeable under any order made under section 130 of the Supreme Court Act 1981 or under section 128 of the County Courts Act 1984, and

(b) otherwise, of the appropriate fee.

History note

In r. 12.15 the words "Act or the" were inserted by I(A)R 1987 (SI 1987 No. 1919), r. 3(1), Sch., Pt. 1, para. 149 as from 11 January 1988.

General note

This is a standard facility where inspection is permitted. The scope of r. 12.15 was extended to cover documents which may be inspected under the Act. See also r. 12.17. For the meaning of "appropriate fee", see r. 13.11.

Rule **12.15A** Charge for copy documents

12.15A Where the responsible insolvency practitioner or the official receiver is requested by a creditor, member, contributory or member of a liquidation or creditors' committee to supply copies of any documents he is entitled to require the payment of the appropriate fee in respect of the supply of the documents.

History note

Rule 12.15A was inserted by I(A)R 1987 (SI 1987 No. 1919), r. 3(1), Sch., Pt. 1, para. 150 as from 11 January 1988.

General note

For details of "the appropriate fee", see r. 13.11. Apparently insolvency practitioners called for the insertion of r. 12.15A to enable them to charge for copies in cases where there is no right to inspect and so the case is not covered by r. 12.15.

Rule **12.16** Non-receipt of notice of meeting

12.16 Where in accordance with the Act or the Rules a meeting of creditors or other persons is summoned by notice, the meeting is presumed to have been duly summoned and held, notwithstanding that not all those to whom the notice is to be given have received it.

General note

This is somewhat similar to art. 39 in Table A of the Companies (Tables A to F) Regulations 1985 (SI 1985 No. 805). Compare BR 1952, r. 242. See *Re A Debtor No. 64 of 1992* [1994] 1 WLR 264; [1994] BCC 55 for a limitation on the utility of rule 12.16.

Rule **12.17** Right to have list of creditors

12.17(1) **[Application of Rule]** This Rule applies in any of the following proceedings—

    (a) proceedings under Part II of the Act (company administration),

    (b) a creditors' voluntary winding up, or a winding up by the court, and

    (c) proceedings in bankruptcy.

12.17(2) **[Creditor's right to list etc.]** In any such proceedings a creditor who under the Rules has the right to inspect documents on the court file also has the right to require the responsible insolvency practitioner to furnish him with a list of the insolvent's creditors and the amounts of their respective debts.

    This does not apply if a statement of the insolvent's affairs has been filed in court or, in the case of a creditors' voluntary winding up, been delivered to the registrar of companies.

12.17(3) **[Fee for sending list]** The insolvency practitioner, on being required by any person to furnish the list, shall send it to him, but is entitled to charge the appropriate fee for doing so.

General note

This complements r. 12.15.

For the meaning of "appropriate fee" in r. 12.17(3), see r. 13.11.

Rule 12.18   False claim of status as creditor, etc.

12.18(1)   [Offence]   Where the Rules provide for creditors, members of a company or contributories in a company's winding up a right to inspect any documents, whether on the court's file or in the hands of a responsible insolvency practitioner or other person, it is an offence for a person, with the intention of obtaining a sight of documents which he has not under the Rules any right to inspect, falsely to claim a status which would entitle him to inspect them.

12.18(2)   [Penalties]   A person guilty of an offence under this Rule is liable to imprisonment or a fine, or both.

General note

This is a useful deterrent to restrict bogus claims to inspect. For the appropriate penalty, see r. 12.21 and Sch. 5.

Rule 12.19   Execution overtaken by judgment debtor's insolvency

12.19(1)   [Application of Rule]   This Rule applies where execution has been taken out against property of a judgment debtor, and notice is given to the sheriff or other officer charged with the execution—

(a) under section 184(1) (that a winding-up order has been made against the debtor, or that a provisional liquidator has been appointed, or that a resolution for voluntary winding up has been passed); or

(b) under section 184(4) (that a winding-up petition has been presented or a winding-up order made, or that a meeting has been called at which there is to be proposed a resolution for voluntary winding up, or that such a resolution has been passed); or

(c) under section 346(2) (that the judgment debtor has been adjudged bankrupt); or

(d) under section 346(3)(b) (that a bankruptcy petition has been presented in respect of him).

12.19(2)   [Notice]   Subject as follows, the notice shall be in writing and be delivered by hand at, or sent by recorded delivery to, the office of the under-sheriff or (as the case may be) of the officer charged with the execution.

12.19(3)   [Execution in county court etc.]   Where the execution is in a county court, and the officer in charge of it is the registrar of that court, then if—

(a) there is filed in that court in respect of the judgment debtor a winding-up or bankruptcy petition, or

(b) there is made by that court in respect of him a winding-up order or an order appointing a provisional liquidator, or a bankruptcy order or an order appointing an interim receiver,

section 184 or (as the case may be) 346 is deemed satisfied as regards the requirement of a notice to be served on, or given to, the officer in charge of the execution.

General note
General note

This provision supplements IA 1986, ss. 184 and 346 on procedural matters.

Rule **12.20**   The Gazette

12.20(1)   [Gazetted notice as evidence]   A copy of the Gazette containing any notice required by the Act or the Rules to be gazetted is evidence of any facts stated in the notice.

12.20(2)   [Gazetted notice of court order as conclusive evidence]   In the case of an order of the court notice of which is required by the Act or the Rules to be gazetted, a copy of the Gazette containing the notice may in any proceedings be produced as conclusive evidence that the order was made on the date specified in the notice.

12.20(3)   [Where gazetted order varied etc.]   Where an order of the court which is gazetted has been varied, and where any matter has been erroneously or inaccurately gazetted, the person whose responsibility it was to procure the requisite entry in the Gazette shall forthwith cause the variation of the order to be gazetted or, as the case may be, a further entry to be made in the Gazette for the purpose of correcting the error or inaccuracy.

Rule **12.21**   Punishment of offences

12.21(1)   [Effect of Sch. 5]   Schedule 5 to the Rules has effect with respect to the way in which contraventions of the Rules are punishable on conviction.

12.21(2)   [First, second and third columns of Schedule]   In relation to an offence under a provision of the Rules specified in the first column of the Schedule (the general nature of the offence being described in the second column), the third column shows whether the offence is punishable on conviction on indictment, or on summary conviction, or either in the one way or the other.

12.21(3)   [Fourth column]   The fourth column shows, in relation to an offence, the maximum punishment by way of fine or imprisonment which may be imposed on a person convicted of the offence in the way specified in relation to it in the third column (that is to say, on indictment or summarily), a reference to a period of years or months being to a term of imprisonment of that duration.

12.21(4)   [Fifth column]   The fifth column shows (in relation to an offence for which there is an entry in that column) that a person convicted of the offence after continued contravention is liable to a daily default fine; that is to say, he is liable on a second or subsequent conviction of the offence to the fine specified in that column for each day on which the contravention is continued (instead of the penalty specified for the offence in the fourth column of the Schedule).

12.21(5)   [Application of s. 431]   Section 431 (summary proceedings), as it applies to England and Wales, has effect in relation to offences under the Rules as to offences under the Act.

General note

This explains the mechanics of Sch. 5. Note the connection with IA 1986, s. 431 for summary proceedings.

PART 13 — INTERPRETATION AND APPLICATION

General comment on Pt. 13

This interpretation Part should be viewed in the light of the IA 1986 interpretation provisions, especially ss. 247–251, 380–385, and 435–436.

Rule 13.1 Introductory

13.1 This Part of the Rules has effect for their interpretation and application; and any definition given in this Part applies except, and in so far as, the context otherwise requires.

Rule 13.2 "The court"; "the registrar"

13.2(1) ["The court"]   Anything to be done under or by virtue of the Act or the Rules by, to or before the court may be done by, to or before a judge or the registrar.

13.2(2) ["The registrar"]   The registrar may authorise any act of a formal or administrative character which is not by statute his responsibility to be carried out by the chief clerk or any other officer of the court acting on his behalf, in accordance with directions given by the Lord Chancellor.

13.2(3) ["The registrar" in individual insolvency proceedings]   In individual insolvency proceedings, **"the registrar"** means a Registrar in Bankruptcy of the High Court, or the registrar or deputy registrar of a county court.

13.2(4) [In company insolvency proceedings in High Court]   In company insolvency proceedings in the High Court, **"the registrar"** means—

  (a) subject to the following paragraph, a Registrar in Bankruptcy of the High Court;

  (b) where the proceedings are in the District Registry of Birmingham, Bristol, Cardiff, Leeds, Liverpool, Manchester, Newcastle-upon-Tyne or Preston, the District Registrar.

13.2(5) [In a county court]   In company insolvency proceedings in a county court, **"the registrar"** means the officer of the court whose duty it is to exercise the functions which in the High Court are exercised by a registrar.

General note

The registrar handles much of the day-to-day business of insolvency work. Compare BR 1952, r. 9.

Rule 13.2(2)

See *Practice Direction* in [1987] 1 All ER 107 (reproduced in Appendix IV of this Guide).

Rule 13.2(3)

See *Practice Direction (Insolvency Appeals: Hearings Outside London) (No. 3 of 1992)* [1992] 1 WLR 791; [1992] BCC 998.

Rule 13.3 "Give notice", etc.

13.3(1) [Sending by post] A reference in the Rules to giving notice, or to delivering, sending or serving any document, means that the notice or document may be sent by post, unless under a particular Rule personal service is expressly required.

13.3(2) [Form of post] Any form of post may be used, unless under a particular Rule a specified form is expressly required.

13.3(3) [Personal service] Personal service of a document is permissible in all cases.

13.3(4) [Notice of venue] Notice of the venue fixed for an application may be given by service of the sealed copy of the application under Rule 7.4(3).

Rule 13.4 Notice, etc. to solicitors

13.4 Where under the Act or the Rules a notice or other document is required or authorised to be given to a person, it may, if he has indicated that his solicitor is authorised to accept service on his behalf, be given instead to the solicitor.

General note

Solicitors have no implied authority to receive notices — *Re Munro* [1981] 1 WLR 1358.

Rule 13.5 Notice to joint liquidators, joint trustees, etc.

13.5 Where two or more persons are acting jointly as the responsible insolvency practitioner in any proceedings, delivery of a document to one of them is to be treated as delivery to them all.

Rule 13.6 "Venue"

13.6 References to the **"venue"** for any proceeding or attendance before the court, or for a meeting, are to the time, date and place for the proceeding, attendance or meeting.

Rule 13.7 "Insolvency proceedings"

13.7 **"Insolvency proceedings'** means any proceedings under the Act or the Rules.

Rule 13.8 "Insolvent estate"

13.8 References to **"the insolvent estate"** are—

(a) in relation to a company insolvency, the company's assets, and

(b) in relation to an individual insolvency, the bankrupt's estate or (as the case may be) the debtor's property.

Rule 13.9 "Responsible insolvency practitioner", etc.

13.9(1) [Definition] In relation to any insolvency proceedings, **"the responsible insolvency practitioner"** means—

(a) the person acting in a company insolvency, as supervisor of a voluntary arrangement under Part I of the Act, or as administrator, administrative receiver, liquidator or provisional liquidator;

(b) the person acting in an individual insolvency, as the supervisor of a voluntary arrangement under Part VIII of the Act, or as trustee or interim receiver;

(c) the official receiver acting as receiver and manager of a bankrupt's estate.

13.9(2) **[Official receiver acting in relevant capacity]** Any reference to the liquidator, provisional liquidator, trustee or interim receiver includes the official receiver when acting in the relevant capacity.

General note
See IA 1986, Pt. XIII.

Rule 13.10 "Petitioner"

13.10 In winding up and bankruptcy, references to **"the petitioner"** or **"the petitioning creditor"** include any person who has been substituted as such, or been given carriage of the petition.

General note
See rr. 4.19, 6.30 and 6.31.

Rule 13.11 "The appropriate fee"

13.11 **"The appropriate fee"** means—

(a) in Rule 6.192(2) (payor under income payments order entitled to clerical etc. costs), 50 pence; and

(b) in other cases, 15 pence per A4 or A5 page, and 30 pence per A3 page.

General note
Note the special higher fee for cases under r. 6.192(2).

Rule 13.12 "Debt", "liability" (winding up)

13.12(1) **[Definition]** **"Debt"**, in relation to the winding up of a company, means (subject to the next paragraph) any of the following—

(a) any debt or liability to which the company is subject at the date on which it goes into liquidation;

(b) any debt or liability to which the company may become subject after that date by reason of any obligation incurred before that date; and

(c) any interest provable as mentioned in Rule 4.93(1).

13.12(2) **[Liability in tort]** In determining for the purposes of any provision of the

Act or the Rules about winding up, whether any liability in tort is a debt provable in the winding up, the company is deemed to become subject to that liability by reason of an obligation incurred at the time when the cause of action accrued.

13.12(3) **[Debt or liability]** For the purposes of references in any provision of the Act or the Rules about winding up to a debt or liability, it is immaterial whether the debt or liability is present or future, whether it is certain or contingent, or whether its amount is fixed or liquidated, or is capable of being ascertained by fixed rules or as a matter of opinion; and references in any such provision to owing a debt are to be read accordingly.

13.12(4) **["Liability"]** In any provision of the Act or the Rules about winding up, except in so far as the context otherwise requires, **"liability"** means (subject to paragraph (3) above) a liability to pay money or money's worth, including any liability under an enactment, any liability for breach of trust, any liability in contract, tort or bailment, and any liability arising out of an obligation to make restitution.

General note

This would have been better located in IA 1986, Pt. VII. Compare IA 1986, s. 382 ("debt" in bankruptcy cases), and see also r. 12.3 (provable debts), and note that there are no corresponding definitions for other corporate insolvency proceedings, such as voluntary arrangements and administrations – a somewhat surprising omission in view of the references to "contingent and prospective creditors" in s. 9(1) and to "debts for an unliquidated amount . . . or whose value is not ascertained" in rr. 1.17(3) and 2.22(5). For a general discussion of the terms "debt" and "creditor", see the note to s.1(1).

In *Re Kentish Homes Ltd* [1993] BCC 212 a rare example of non-provable debt arose. In this case a Law of Property Act receiver had incurred community charges in respect of premises which had been constructed by the receiver in order to fulfil contractual obligations of the insolvent company, but which had remained unoccupied until they were sold. This property development company had gone into liquidation after the commencement of a Law of Property Act receivership but the liquidator had not been allowed into possession. On the subsequent liquidation of the company it was held by Nicholls VC that the conditions laid down in r. 13.12 (1) had not been satisfied in respect of this sum and the local authority could not prove in respect of it. The liability to pay the community charge did not exist at the date of entry into liquidation nor did it arise in respect of a pre-liquidation obligation. The receiver was empowered to settle this debt but he had no legal obligation under s. 109(8)(*i*) of the Law of Property Act 1925 to do so nor would the court require him to do so. His Lordship made the point that the position would be the same in respect of the new council tax.

By way of contrast it was held in *Tottenham Hotspur plc* v *Edennote plc* [1994] BCC 681 that an order for costs was debt for the purposes of r. 13.12(1)(*b*) and (3) and so could form the basis of a winding-up petition.

Rule 13.12(2)

This rule would appear to settle the inconsistency between *Re Berkeley Securities (Property) Ltd* [1980] 1 WLR 1589 and *Re Islington Metal and Plating Works Ltd* [1984] 1 WLR 14; (1983) 1 BCC 98,933. The Cork Committee (*Report*, para. 1310) favoured the former decision. This new rule is not ultra vires but is authorised by IA 1986, Sch. 8, para. 12.

Rule 13.13 Expressions used generally

13.13(1) **["Business day"]** **"Business day"** has the same meaning as in section 251 of the Act except in Rules 1.7, 4.10, 4.11, 4.16, 4.20, 5.10 and 6.23, where, if the court is the High Court, it has the same meaning as is given in Order 65, Rule 5(4) of the Rules of the Supreme Court, and, in relation to a county court, it means any day on which the court office is open in accordance with Order 2, Rule 2 of the County Court Rules.

13.13(2) ["The Department"] "The Department" means the Department of Trade and Industry.

13.13(3) ["File in court"] "File in court" means deliver to the court for filing.

13.13(4) ["The Gazette"] "The Gazette" means the London Gazette.

13.13(5) ["General regulations"] "General regulations" means regulations made by the Secretary of State under Rule 12.1.

13.13(6) ["Prescribed order of priority"] "Prescribed order of priority" means the order of priority of payments laid down by Chapter 20 of Part 4 of the Rules, or Chapter 23 of Part 6.

History note

Rule 13.13(1) was substituted by I(A)R 1987 (SI 1987 No. 1919), r. 3(1), Sch., Pt. 1, para. 151 as from 11 January 1988: the former Rule 13.13(1) read as follows:

"**13.13(1) 'Business day'**—

   (a) in relation to the High Court has the same meaning as in Order 65, Rule 5(4) of the Rules of the Supreme Court, and

   (b) in relation to a county court means any day on which the court office is open in accordance with Order 2, Rule 2 of the County Court Rules."

General note

The definition of "business day" for the purposes of the rules is not always the same as that contained in IA 1986, s. 251.

   The reference to RSC, O. 65, r.5(4) appears to be a slip for r. 5(3).

   The relevant provisions of the Rules of the Supreme Court and the County Court Rules are as follows:

RSC, O. 65, r. 5(3)

   "In this rule 'business day' means any day other than a Saturday, a Sunday, Christmas Day, Good Friday or a bank holiday under the Banking and Financial Dealings Act 1971."

County Court Rules 1981, O. 2, r. 2

   "**2. (1)** Every court office or, if a court has two or more offices, at least one of those offices, shall be open on every day of the year except—

   (a) Saturdays and Sundays.

   (b) the day before Good Friday from noon onwards and Good Friday,

   (c) the Tuesday after the spring holiday,

   (d) Christmas Eve or—

      (i) if that day is a Saturday, then 23rd December,

      (ii) if that day is a Sunday or a Tuesday, then 27th December,

   (e) Christmas Day and, if that day is a Friday or Saturday, then 28th December,

   (f) bank holidays, and

   (g) such other days as the Lord Chancellor may by general or special order direct.

(2) in the foregoing paragraph 'bank holiday' means a bank holiday in England and Wales under the Banking and Financial Dealings Act 1971 and 'spring holiday' means the bank holiday on the last Monday in May or any day appointed instead of that day under section 1(2) of that Act."

Rule **13.14** Application

13.14(1) [Application of Rules] Subject to paragraph (2) of this Rule, and save where otherwise expressly provided, the Rules apply—

- (a) to receivers appointed on or after the day on which the Rules come into force,
- (b) to bankruptcy proceedings where the bankruptcy petition is presented on or after the day on which the Rules come into force, and
- (c) to all other insolvency proceedings commenced on or after that day.

13.14(2) [Further application] The Rules also apply to winding-up and bankruptcy proceedings commenced before that day to which provisions of the Act are applied by Schedule 11 to the Act, to the extent necessary to give effect to those provisions.

History note

In r. 13.14(1)(*a*) the word "administrative" formerly appearing before the word "receiver" was omitted by I(A)R 1987 (SI 1987 No. 1919), r. 3(1), Sch., Pt. 1, para. 152 as from 11 January 1988.

General note

Rule 13.14(1)(*a*) was amended to extend the scope of the rules, where appropriate, to non-administrative receivers.

Schedule 1 — Deposit Protection Board's Voting Rights

Rule 4.72(7)

1 This Schedule applies as does Rule 4.72.

2 In relation to any meeting at which the Deposit Protection Board is under Rule 4.72 entitled to be represented, the Board may submit in the liquidation, instead of a proof, a written statement of voting rights ("the statement").

3 The statement shall contain details of—

- (a) the names of creditors of the company in respect of whom an obligation of the Board has arisen or may reasonably be expected to arise as a result of the liquidation or proposed liquidation;
- (b) the amount of the obligation so arising; and
- (c) the total amount of all such obligations specified in the statement.

4 The Board's statement shall, for the purpose of voting at a meeting (but for no other purpose), be treated in all respects as if it were a proof.

5 Any voting rights which a creditor might otherwise exercise at a meeting in respect of a claim against the company are reduced by a sum equal to the amount of that claim in relation to which the Board, by virtue of its having submitted a statement, is entitled to exercise voting rights at that meeting.

6   The Board may from time to time submit a further statement, and, if it does so, that statement supersedes any statement previously submitted.

Schedule 2 — Alternative Courts for Debtors' Petitions in Bankruptcy

Rule 6.40(3)

Debtor's own county court	*Nearest full-time court*
ABERDARE	CARDIFF
ABERYSTWYTH	CARDIFF
AYLESBURY	LUTON
BANBURY	LUTON or GLOUCESTER or READING
BANGOR	BIRKENHEAD or CHESTER
BARNSLEY	SHEFFIELD
BARNSTAPLE	EXETER
BARROW IN FURNESS	BLACKPOOL or PRESTON
BATH	BRISTOL
BEDFORD	LUTON
BLACKBURN	PRESTON
BLACKWOOD	CARDIFF
BOSTON	NOTTINGHAM
BRIDGEND	CARDIFF
BRIDGWATER	BRISTOL
BURNLEY	BOLTON or PRESTON
BURTON ON TRENT	LEICESTER or DERBY or NOTTINGHAM
BURY ST. EDMUNDS	CAMBRIDGE
CANTERBURY	CROYDON or THE HIGH COURT (LONDON)
CARLISLE	PRESTON or BLACKPOOL
CARMARTHEN	CARDIFF
CHELMSFORD	SOUTHEND or THE HIGH COURT (LONDON)
CHELTENHAM	GLOUCESTER
CHESTERFIELD	SHEFFIELD
COLCHESTER	SOUTHEND or THE HIGH COURT (LONDON)
COVENTRY	BIRMINGHAM
CREWE	STOKE or CHESTER
DARLINGTON	MIDDLESBROUGH
DEWSBURY	LEEDS
DONCASTER	SHEFFIELD
DUDLEY	BIRMINGHAM
DURHAM	NEWCASTLE
EASTBOURNE	BRIGHTON
GREAT GRIMSBY	HULL

GREAT YARMOUTH	NORWICH
GUILDFORD	CROYDON
HALIFAX	LEEDS
HARROGATE	LEEDS
HASTINGS	BRIGHTON
HAVERFORDWEST	CARDIFF
HEREFORD	GLOUCESTER
HERTFORD	LUTON
HUDDERSFIELD	LEEDS
IPSWICH	NORWICH or SOUTHEND
KENDAL	BLACKPOOL or PRESTON
KIDDERMINSTER	BIRMINGHAM
KING'S LYNN	NORWICH or CAMBRIDGE
LANCASTER	BLACKPOOL or PRESTON
LINCOLN	NOTTINGHAM
MACCLESFIELD	STOKE or MANCHESTER
MAIDSTONE	CROYDON or THE HIGH COURT (LONDON)
MEDWAY	CROYDON or THE HIGH COURT (LONDON)
MERTHYR TYDFIL	CARDIFF
MILTON KEYNES	LUTON
NEATH	CARDIFF
NEWBURY	READING
NEWPORT (GWENT)	CARDIFF
NEWPORT (I.O.W.)	SOUTHAMPTON or PORTSMOUTH
NORTHAMPTON	LUTON
OXFORD	READING
PETERBOROUGH	CAMBRIDGE
PONTYPRIDD	CARDIFF
PORTMADOC	BIRKENHEAD or STOKE or CHESTER
RHYL	BIRKENHEAD or CHESTER
ROCHDALE	OLDHAM or MANCHESTER
SALISBURY	BOURNEMOUTH or SOUTHAMPTON
SCARBOROUGH	YORK or HULL or MIDDLESBROUGH
SCUNTHORPE	HULL or SHEFFIELD
SHREWSBURY	STOKE
ST. ALBANS	LUTON
STAFFORD	STOKE
STOCKTON ON TEES	MIDDLESBROUGH
STOCKPORT	MANCHESTER
STOURBRIDGE	BIRMINGHAM
SUNDERLAND	NEWCASTLE
SWANSEA	CARDIFF
SWINDON	GLOUCESTER or READING
TAMESIDE	MANCHESTER
TAUNTON	EXETER or BRISTOL
TORQUAY	EXETER
TRURO	PLYMOUTH
TUNBRIDGE WELLS	CROYDON
WAKEFIELD	LEEDS

WARRINGTON	CHESTER or LIVERPOOL or MANCHESTER
WARWICK	BIRMINGHAM
WELSHPOOL	STOKE or CHESTER
WEST BROMWICH	BIRMINGHAM
WEYMOUTH	BOURNEMOUTH
WIGAN	BOLTON or MANCHESTER or PRESTON
WINCHESTER	SOUTHAMPTON
WORCESTER	GLOUCESTER
WORKINGTON	PRESTON or BLACKPOOL
WREXHAM	BIRKENHEAD or STOKE or CHESTER
YEOVIL	EXETER or BRISTOL

History note

Schedule 2 was replaced by I(A)R 1987 (SI 1987 No. 1919), r. 3(1), Sch., Pt. 2, para. 153 and Pt. 3 as from 11 January 1988.

Schedule 3 — Shorthand Writers' Remuneration

[Deleted]

History note

Schedule 3 was deleted by the Insolvency (Amendment) Rules 1993 (SI 1993 No. 602), r. 3 and Sch., para. 4, as from 5 April 1993, following the amendment to r. 7.17(2). The Schedule formerly read as follows:

Rule 7.17

1 For attendance   £66.20

2 Per folio of written record   92.4p plus 5p per folio for all copies.

3 Travelling time   £7.00 per hour after first hour of each journey.

4 In addition to the items in paragraphs 1 to 3, the following London weighting allowances (see note below) are payable in relation to the location of the court or other place concerned—

Inner	Intermediate	Outer
£8.74 per day	£5.00 per day	£2.63 per day

5 The amounts shown in paragraph 4 are subject to a maximum annual allowance of—

Inner	Intermediate	Outer
£1,750	£1,000	£725

Note:

The rate at which London weighting allowances are payable is determined as follows:

(a) Inner

The area within a radius of 5 miles from Charing Cross (statue of King Charles I).

(b) Intermediate

The area outside that specified in paragraph (a) but within a radius of 10 miles from Charing Cross.

(c) Outer

    (i) The area outside those specified in paragraphs (a) and (b) but within a radius of 18 miles from Charing Cross; or

(ii) the former Borough of St Albans, Herts; or

(iii) the former Urban District of Slough, Bucks; or

(iv) the following towns whose boundary is intersected by the 18 miles radius from Charing Cross:—

>   Abbots Langley
>   Chertsey
>   Egham
>   Fetcham
>   Godstone
>   Hatfield
>   Redhill .
>   Rickmansworth
>   South Ockenden
>   Stone
>   Swanscombe
>   Weybridge"

Schedule 4 — Forms

Rule 12.7

Index
Part 1: Company Voluntary Arrangements

Part 2: Administration Procedure

Part 3: Administrative Receivership

Part 4: Companies Winding Up

Part 5: Individual Voluntary Arrangements

Part 6: Bankruptcy

Part 7: Court Procedure and Practice

Part 8: Proxies and Company Representation

FORM NO.	TITLE
8.4	Proxy—winding up by the court or bankruptcy
8.5	Proxy—members' or creditors' voluntary winding up

Part 9: Examination of Persons Concerned in Company and Individual Insolvency

9.1   Order under section 236 or 366 of the Insolvency Act 1986

History note

A number of changes to the forms were made by I(A)R 1987 (SI 1987 No. 1919), r. 3(1), Sch., Pt. 2, paras. 157 to 159 as from 11 January 1988:

   Forms 2.4A, 3.1, 3.1A, 4.14A, 5.1, 5.2, 5.3, 5.4, 6.24A, 6.24B and 6.79A were added;

   Forms 1.1, 2.1, 2.5, 2.8, 2.11, 2.12, 2.16, 2.17, 4.1, 4.12, 4.13, 4.14, 4.16, 4.53, 4.61, 4.64, 4.66, 4.67, 4.68, 4.70, 6.1, 6.2, 6.3, 6.11, 6.14, 6.26, 6.30, 6.55, 6.57, 6.59, 6.60, 6.61, 6.78, 7.9 and 7.15 were substituted for the former forms with identical numbers;

   Form 3.1B was substituted for the former Form 3.1;

   Form 7.16 was omitted.

Further changes were made by I(A)R 1991 (SI 1991 No. 495), r. 3, Sch., para. 5, 6: the forms affected are Forms 4.71, 4.72, 6.71, 6.76 and 6.77.

Note

This Schedule sets out the prescribed forms referred to in the above list. The use of the new prescribed forms of statutory demand and creditors' petition was made mandatory after 31 March 1988: see *Practice Note (Bankruptcy: Prescribed Forms)* [1988] 1 WLR 557. The forms are not reproduced here.

Schedule 5 — Punishment of Offences under the Rules

Rule 12.21

Note: In the fourth and fifth columns of this Schedule, **"the statutory maximum"** means the prescribed sum under section 32 of the Magistrates' Courts Act 1980 (c. 43).

Rule creating offence	General nature of offence	Mode of prosecution	Punishment	Daily default fine (where applicable)
In Part 1, Rule 1.30.	False representation or fraud for purpose of obtaining members' or creditors' consent to proposal for voluntary arrangement.	1. On indictment. 2. Summary.	7 years or a fine, or both. 6 months or the statutory maximum, or both.	
In Part 2, Rule 2.52(4).	Administrator failing to send notification as to progress of administration.	Summary.	One-fifth of the statutory maximum.	One-fiftieth of the statutory maximum.
In Part 3, Rule 3.32(5).	Administrative receiver failing to send notification as to progress of receivership.	Summary.	One-fifth of the statutory maximum.	One-fiftieth of the statutory maximum.
In Part 5, Rule 5.30.	False representation or fraud for purpose of obtaining creditors' consent to proposal for voluntary arrangement.	1. On indictment. 2. Summary.	7 years or a fine, or both. 6 months or the statutory maximum, or both.	
In Part 12, Rule 12.18.	False representation of status for purpose of inspecting documents.	1. On indictment. 2. Summary.	2 years or a fine, or both. 6 months or the statutory maximum, or both.	

General note

For an explanation of **"the statutory maximum"** see IA 1986, Sch. 10 notes.

EXPLANATORY NOTE

(This Note does not form part of the Rules.)

These Rules set out the detailed procedure for the conduct of all company and individual insolvency proceedings in England and Wales under the Insolvency Act 1986 and otherwise give effect to that Act. The insolvency proceedings concerned are—

company voluntary arrangements (Part 1 of the Rules),
administration (Part 2),
administrative receivership (Part 3),
companies winding up (Part 4),
individual voluntary arrangements (Part 5),and
bankruptcy (Part 6).

Parts 7 to 13 of the Rules apply to both company and individual insolvency proceedings and are concerned with the following matters—

court procedure and practice (Part 7),
proxies and company representation (Part 8),
examination of persons concerned in company and individual insolvency (Part 9),
official receivers (Part 10),
declaration and payment of dividend (winding up and bankruptcy) (Part 11),
miscellaneous and general (Part 12), and interpretation and application (Part 13).

The Arrangement of Rules at the beginning of the statutory instrument lists the number and contents of all the Rules and Schedules. The Rules come into force on 29 December 1986 and generally apply to all insolvency proceedings commenced on or after that date. The Rules also apply to such proceedings commenced before that date to which provisions of the Insolvency Act 1986 are applied by Schedule 11 of the Act to the extent necessary to give effect to those provisions. In addition, Rules 6.36, 7.11 and 7.34 expressly provide for their application to insolvency proceedings, whenever commenced.

Appendix I

Index to Statutory Definitions

The words and phrases listed below are given special meanings for the purpose of all or part of the insolvency legislation of 1986 which is the subject of this *Guide*. The numbers shown refer to the section of IA 1986 (or where indicated, CDDA 1986) in which the statutory definition appears and, in most cases, is discussed in the note adjoining that section.

An asterisk (*) means that the term has a special meaning for only a limited part of the Act, as will be indicated in the section referred to. Some words or phrases have been used by the draftsman with more than one meaning and where this is the case, each reference has been separately asterisked.

Where a definition applies to all the *bankruptcy* Parts of the Act, this is shown by *^b; if it applies to all the *company* insolvency Parts, by *^c; if to the whole of CDDA 1986, by *^d.

(An index to definitions in the Insolvency Rules 1986 is given in Appendix II.)

Appendix I: Index to Statutory Definitions

Statutory definition	*Provision*
associate	ss. 435, 436
assurance	s. 190(1)*
attachment completed	s. 179(5)
bankrupt	s. 381(1)*ᵇ
bankruptcy debt	s. 382*ᵇ
bankruptcy level	s. 267(4)*
bankruptcy order	s. 381(2)*
bankruptcy petition	s. 381(3)*ᵇ
bankrupt's estate	ss. 283*ᵇ, 385(1)*ᵇ
become insolvent	CDDA, ss. 6(2),* 7,* 9(2),* Sch. 1*
body corporate	CDDA, s. 22(6)*ᵈ
business	s. 436
business day	s. 251*ᶜ
cable programme services	ss. 233(5)(*d*),* 372(5)(*c*)*
carrying on business	s. 265(2)*
charitable purpose	s. 242(5)*
chattel leasing agreement	s. 251*ᶜ
commencement of bankruptcy	s. 278
commencement of winding up	ss. 86, 129, 185(3)*
Companies Act	s. 436; CDDA, s. 22(7)*ᵈ
Companies Acts	Sch. 13, Pt. II;* CDDA s. 22(8)*ᵈ
companies legislation	CDDA, s. 22(6)*
company	ss. 70(1),* 111(4)(*a*),* 216(8),* 217(6)* 388(4),* 435(11);*CDDA s. 22(2)*
competent authority	s. 392(2)*
conditional sale agreement	s. 436
conduct and affairs of a bankrupt	s. 289(4)*
conduct as a director of a company	CDDA, ss. 6(2),* 9(2), * Sch. 1*
connected with a company	s. 249*ᶜ
contributory	ss. 79, 83(2), 226(1),* 251*ᶜ
control of a company	s. 435(10)*
conveyance	s. 190(3)*
court	ss. 216(5),* 385(1),*ᵇ 423(4);* CDDA, ss. 2(2),* 3(4),* 4(2),* 6(2),* 7,* 8(3),* 11(2), 17*

[Note that for the purposes of Pts. I–VII of IA 1986, "the court" means, in relation to a company, the court having jurisdiction to wind up the company: CA 1985, s. 744, as incorporated by IA 1986, s. 251.]

Appendix II

Index to Definitions in the Rules

The words and phrases listed below have special definitions for all or part of the Insolvency Rules 1986. The numbers shown refer to the rule in which the definition appears. An asterisk (*) means that the term has a special meaning for only a limited part of the Rules, as will be indicated in the rule referred to.

Appendix III

Insolvency Service Information

Since the coming into force of the 1985–86 legislation, the Insolvency Service (now an Executive Agency within the Department of Trade and Industry) has regularly published information for insolvency practitioners in the form of a series of letters entitled "Dear IP". The following table gives a list of the letters issued to date, with a brief note of their principal contents. Further details may be obtained from: The Insolvency Service, P.O. Box 203, 21 Bloomsbury Street, London WC1B 3QW, tel. 0171–637 1110.

Issue no. 1 (12 December 1986):
Referrals by courts under IA 1986, ss. 273, 297; appointments by Secretary of State in compulsory liquidations and bankruptcies under IA 1986, ss. 137, 296.

Issue no. 2 (16 December 1986):
Security and bonding requirements under IA 1986.

Issue no. 3 (16 June 1987):
Referrals and appointments: further information. Guidance notes in respect of the director-disqualification reporting provisions under CDDA 1986.

Issue no. 4 (June 1987):
Structure of the new Fees Order. Practice regarding payments into the Insolvency Services Account.

Issue no. 5 (3 July 1987):
Disqualification: revised guidance notes relating to conduct reports. New insolvency fees and regulations. Operation of the Insolvency Practitioner appointments schedules. Schedule of trade classifications. Use of Form 600a (*Gazette* notices of appointments). Notices of meetings to HM Customs and Excise.

Issue no. 6 (23 February 1988):
Insolvency (Fees) Amendment Order 1988. Disclosure of information in disqualification reports. Taxation of costs in "old Act" cases. Vacation of office and release of voluntary liquidator. Inspection of the Land Register. The receipts and payments accounts in voluntary liquidation. Voluntary arrangement notice to Inland Revenue. ECSC levy preferential debt. Review of statement of affairs forms. Voluntary liquidations – payments into Insolvency Services Account. Priority of payment of costs. Global bonds.

Issue no. 7 (7 June 1988):

The move of Insolvency Headquarters to Bridge Place. Insolvency Services Account – voluntary liquidation cases. Insolvency practitioner court appointment schedules. Disqualification reports – desirability of early reporting, on an interim basis if necessary. Notice to Official Liquidator of intention to vacate office and of final meeting in compulsory liquidations and bankruptcies.

Issue no. 8 (7 November 1988):

Contracts at Bridge Place. The Insolvency (Amendment) Regulations 1988. The proposed move of certain functions of Insolvency Headquarters to Birmingham. Information and guidance notes for members of the creditors' committee or liquidation committee.

Issue no. 9 (22 December 1988):

Companies Bill: financial markets and insolvency law.

Issue no. 10 (12 April 1989):

Move of some HQ staff to Birmingham. Insolvency Services Account (Birmingham branch, Bank of England). Insolvency (Amendment) Rules 1989. Information and guidance notes for members of the creditors' committee or the liquidation committee. Examination of lists of creditors. Proposals by administrators under IA 1986 – no power to make distributions to creditors without additional procedure such as a voluntary arrangement.

Issue no. 11 (3 August 1989):

Applications to the Secretary of State for authorisation to act as an insolvency practitioner – introduction of JIEB examinations. Disqualification "D" forms – respective roles of Birmingham and London. Disqualification – Scottish sub-unit. Faxed proxies and proofs of debt.

Issue no. 12 (24 October 1989):

Move of the Disqualification Unit to Bridge Place. Bank giro slips and unclaimed dividends. Delegation of powers to act as committee of inspection from Secretary of State to official receivers. Annual meetings of creditors and members in voluntary liquidations – need for explanation of delay.

Issue no. 13 (12 December 1989):

Disqualification "D" forms: reminder letter discontinued. Further authorisation of practitioners by the Secretary of State. The Banks (Administration Proceedings) Order 1989. Payments into the Insolvency Account – endorsement.

Issue no. 14 (July 1990):

Relocation of official receiver, London. Payments into the Insolvency Services Account: form of endorsement, and when endorsement is not needed. Form of application for payments out of the Account. Remuneration – how it is fixed where there is no committee. Annual returns of statutory interest no longer required.

Notification of individual voluntary arrangements to government departments. Joint Insolvency Examination Board – examinations. Directory of insolvency practitioners.

Issue no. 15 (15 November 1990):

Recent developments concerning administration of CDDA 1986 (internal administration; statistics; need for timely reporting; the "ten-day letter"; reports on progress of cases; case results; criteria for case selection; what the Unit is looking for in reports; completion of conduct reports and supplementary documentation required; insolvency practitioner's costs in disqualification cases.

Issue no. 16 (February 1991):

Guidelines on the operation of the Secretary of State's discretion on extension of time for holding meetings of creditors. Fees on VAT element of realisations. Payments into the Insolvency Services Account – criteria for retention of funds. Notification of voluntary arrangements and voluntary liquidations to government departments. Directory of Insolvency Practitioners, 1991.

Issue no. 17 (April 1991):

Sanction of legal proceedings by the official receiver or Secretary of State – contingency fee arrangements. Disqualification returns. Central Accounting Unit account numbers. Four new statutory instruments. Disqualification Unit (Edinburgh office). Directory of Authorised Insolvency Practitioners.

Issue no. 18 (July 1991):

Fees for preparation of statement of affairs and for holding meeting of creditors. Suspension of discharge period in bankruptcy. User's guide to the Central Accounting Unit. Insolvency Services Account: (a) charging of fee 10 (Secretary of State fee) where compulsory liquidation follows a voluntary liquidation; (b) payments into the account; (c) withdrawals from the account; (d) credit balances outstanding in respect of closed cases; (e) debit balances in bankruptcy and compulsory cases. Preservation of company records for investigation purposes.

Issue no. 19 (November 1991):

Destruction of records held by Official Receivers, London. Central Accounting Unit matters: (a) fees on VAT element of realisations; (b) amendment of cheques drawn on the Insolvency Services Account; (c) unclaimed dividends in bankruptcy and compulsory liquidation; (d) account numbers; (e) completion of requisitions. Section 98 notice to the Inland Revenue. Dealing with Employment Protection Act claims. Preparation for the 1992 edition of the Directory of Authorised Insolvency Practitioners. Addressing correspondence to Insolvency Service Headquarters. Land Registration Fees Order 1991.

Issue no. 20 (January 1992):

The Insolvency Fees (Amendment) Order 1992. Discharge of administration: administrator becoming liquidator. Insolvent Partnerships Order 1986 – forms. Addressing correspondence to Insolvency Service Headquarters. Voluntary administration – gazetting appointment as liquidator.

Issue no. 21 (May 1992):

Central Accounting Unit matters: (a) CAU fax number; (b) endorsement of payments into the Insolvency Services Account consequent upon new Cheques Act coming into force on 16 June; (c) investments in Treasury bills; (d) CAU account numbers – changes being introduced from July; (e) practitioners' specimen signatures; (f) CAU cheque requisition forms. Monitoring visits by Insolvency Practitioner Section, Control Unit.

Issue no. 22 (August 1992):

Central Accounting Unit matters: (a) reissues of cheques drawn from the ISA; (b) The Cheques Act 1992. Registration of individual voluntary arrangements and deeds of arrangement. Destruction of files held by the High Court. Acceptance of assessed debts by chairman at a meeting of creditors. Bankruptcy (Scotland) Act 1985. Transfer of Post Release Section, Official Receiver, London. Duty of practitioners to report offences in voluntary liquidations. Settlement of Official Receiver's costs. Directory of Authorised Insolvency Practitioners 1992.

Issue no. 23 (September 1992):

The Cheques Act 1992.

Issue no. 24 (October 1992):

CDDA 1986: payment of practitioner's costs for further investigation, etc. Land Registration Fees Order 1992. Shorthand writer's charges. Individual and company voluntary arrangements – position of preferential creditors. Interest earned on Employment Protection Act funds. Move of Disqualification Unit, Edinburgh.

Issue no. 25 (January 1993):

New arrangements for insolvency bond. Central Accounting Unit customer survey. Disposal of company records after dissolution. Notifications to HM Customs & Excise. Revision of County Court fees.

Issue no. 26 (March 1993):

HM Customs & Excise matters. London Support Unit, accounts section. Interest paid on Employment Protection Act funds. New arrangements for insolvency bond: the Insolvency Practitioners (Amendment) Regulations 1993. The Insolvency (Amendment) Rules 1993. Notifications to London Electricity plc. Revised guidance notes to IPs reporting under the CDDA 1986.

Issue no. 27 (August 1993):

CAU matters: (a) fixed charge realisations and the Insolvency Services Account; (b) CAU computer developments; (c) Insolvency Services Account – unpaid receipts. Disqualification matters: (a) costs of disqualification work; (b) CDDA Act 1986 – guidance notes on reporting. Customs & Excise matters: (a) s. 98 creditors' meetings – use of Customs & Excise proxy; (b) split period VAT returns in individual voluntary arrangements; (c) VAT 100 returns for insolvent firms; (d) relocation of VAT Insolvency Branch DMD4. Applications to Official Receiver acting as liquidation or creditors' committee for sanction to employ solicitors. Interest paid on Employment Protection Act funds. Distress for Council Tax. Insolvency bond. Guidance notes for trustees and liquidators in dealing with the Inland Revenue. CAU market survey.

Issue no. 28 (December 1993):

Standards agreed between the Insolvency Service and the recognised professional bodies for monitoring visits to insolvency practitioners.

Issue no. 29 (January 1994):

CAU matters: (a) market testing; (b) new postal address for CAU; (c) control systems over banking. Relationship between Official Receivers London and the London Support Unit. Insolvency bond. Directory of Authorised Insolvency Practitioners.

Issue no. 30 (March 1994):

Relocation of Insolvency Headquarters (London). Destruction of bankruptcy files by the High Court. Insolvency bond. IVAs – notices to the Official Receiver and the Secretary of State. Completion of preliminary questionnaire by advisers. Land Registration Fees Order 1993.

Appendix IV

Practice Direction No. 3 of 1986

Chancery Division (Companies Court)

10 December 1986

COMPANIES COURT: INSOLVENCY

(1) As from 29 December 1986 the following applications shall be made direct to the judge and, unless otherwise ordered, shall be heard in open court:

   (i)   applications to commit any person to prison for contempt;

   (ii) applications for urgent interlocutory relief (e.g. applications pursuant to s. 127 of the Insolvency Act 1986 prior to any winding-up order being made);

   (iii) applications to restrain the presentation or advertisement of a petition to wind up;

   (iv) petitions for administration orders or an interim order upon such a petition;

   (v)   applications after an administration order has been made pursuant to s. 14(3) of the 1986 Act (for directions) or s. 18(3) of the Act (to vary or discharge the order);

   (vi) applications pursuant to s. 5(3) of the 1986 Act (to stay a winding up or discharge an administration order or for directions) where a voluntary arrangement has been approved;

   (vii) appeals from a decision made by a county court or by a registrar of the High Court.

(2) Subject to para. 4 below all other applications shall be made to the registrar in the first instance, who may give any necessary directions and may, in the exercise of his discretion, either hear and determine it himself or refer it to the judge.

(3) The following matters will also be heard in open court:

   (i)   petitions to wind up (whether opposed or unopposed);

   (ii) public examinations;

   (iii) all matters and applications heard by the judge except those referred by the registrar to be heard in chambers or so directed by the judge to be heard.

(4) In accordance with directions given by the Lord Chancellor the registrar has authorised certain applications to be dealt with by the Chief Clerk of the Companies Court pursuant to r. 13.2(2) of the Insolvency Rules 1986 (SI 1986, No. 1925). The applications are:

   (a)   to extend or abridge time prescribed by the rules in connection with winding up (r. 4.3);

   (b)   for substituted service of winding-up petitions (r. 4.8(6));

   (c)   to withdraw petitions (r. 4.15);

(d)   for the substitution of a petitioner (r. 4.19);

(e)   for directors on a petition presented by a contributory (r. 4.22(2));

(f)   by the official receiver for limited disclosure of a statement of affairs (r. 4.35);

(g)   by the official receiver for relief from duties imposed on him by the rules (r. 4.47);

(h)   by the official receiver for leave to give notice of a meeting by advertisement only (r. 4.59);

(i)   by a liquidator for relief from the requirement to send out forms or proof of debt (r. 4.74(4));

(j)   to expunge or reduce a proof of debt (r. 4.85);

(k)   to appoint a liquidator in either a compulsory or a voluntary winding up (rr. 4.102 and 4.103));

(l)   for leave to a liquidator to resign (r. 4.111);

(m)   by a liquidator for leave to make a return of capital (r. 4.221);

(n)   to transfer proceedings from the High Court to the county courts (r. 7.11);

(o)   for leave to amend any originating application.

(5) The Practice Directions dated 5 October 1979, *Practice Direction (Companies Court: Chief Clerk)* [1979] 3 All ER 613; [1979] 1 WLR 1416 and 3 March 1982, *Practice Direction (Companies Court: Chief Clerk) (No. 2)* [1982] 1 All ER 846; [1982] 1 WLR 389 are hereby revoked.

By direction of the Vice-Chancellor.

Case Table

This is a list of all cases cited, practice notes and directions in the notes to the Insolvency Act 1986, the Company Directors Disqualification Act 1986 and the Insolvency Rules 1986.

Abbreviations in the provision column are to the Insolvency Act 1986 (IA) or the Company Directors Disqualification Act 1986 (CDDA) or to the Insolvency Rules 1986 (IR).

	Provision
A	
A & C Group Services Ltd, Re [1993] BCLC 1297	CDDA 9(1)
Abbey Leisure Ltd, Re [1990] BCC 60	IA 125(2)
ACLI Metals (London) Ltd, Re (1989) 5 BCC 749	IA 168(5)
Adams (AJ) (Builders) Ltd, Re [1991] BCC 62	IA 108, 171(4)
Adlards Motor Group Holding Ltd, Re [1990] BCLC 68	IA 236
AE Realisations (1985) Ltd, Re (1987) 3 BCC 136	IA 179
Agricultural Mortgage Corp plc v Woodward [1994] BCC 688	IA 423(1)–(3)
Aiglon Ltd v Gau Shan Co [1993] 1 Lloyd's Rep 164	IA 425(1)
Air Ecosse Ltd v Civil Aviation Authority (1987) 3 BCC 492	IA 11(3)
Airlines Airspares Ltd v Handley Page Ltd [1970] Ch 193	IA 37(1), (2)
Aldermanbury Trust plc, Re [1993] BCC 598	CDDA 7(1), 8(1)
Allan Ellis (Transport & Packing) Services Ltd, Re (1989) 5 BCC 835	IA 192(2)
Allied Dunbar Assurance plc v Fowle [1994] BCC 422	IA 181(1)–(3)
Altim Pty Ltd, Re [1968] 2 NSWR 762	CDDA 11
Amec Properties v Planning Research and Systems [1992] 13 EG 109; [1992] 1 EGLR 70	IA 37(1), (2), 44(1), (2)
American Express Europe Ltd v Adamson [1993] BCC 154	IA 11(3)
AML Holdings Inc v Auger (1989) 5 BCC 749	IA 168(5)

	Provision
Andromache Properties Ltd, Re [1991] BCC 446	IA 9(4), (5)
Anglesea Colliery Co, Re (1866) LR 1 Ch 555	IA 74(1)
Anglo-Austrian Printing and Publishing Union, Re [1895] 2 Ch 891	IA 214(1)
Anvil Estates Ltd, Re (unreported, 1993)	IA Sch. 1
Application pursuant to r. 7.28 of the Insolvency Rules 1986, Re an [1994] BCC 369	IR 7.26–7.32
Arbuthnot Leasing International Ltd v Havelet Leasing Ltd (No. 2) [1990] BCC 636	IA 423, 425(2), (3)
Arctic Engineering Ltd, Re [1986] 1 WLR 686; (1985) 1 BCC 99,563	CDDA 3(1)
Argentum Reductions (UK) Ltd, Re [1975] 1 WLR 186	IA 127
Arrows Ltd, Re (No. 2) [1992] BCC 446	IA 236
Arrows Ltd, Re (No. 3) [1992] BCC 131	IA 8(1), (2)
Arrows Ltd, Re (No. 4) [1994] BCC 641	IA 236, 433
Ash & Newman v Creative Devices Research Ltd [1991] BCLC 403 .	IA 37(1), (2)
Astor Chemical Ltd v Synthetic Technology Ltd [1990] BCC 97 ..	IA 9(1), 14(1), 37(1), (2); IR 7.26–7.32
Atlantic Computer Systems plc, Re [1992] Ch 505; [1990] BCC 859 ..	IA 11(3), 19(3)–(6)
Austinsuite Furniture Ltd, Re [1992] BCLC 1047	CDDA 9(1)
Avatar Communications Ltd, Re (1988) 4 BCC 473	IA 134

Legislation Finding List

This Legislation Finding List enables the user to locate references to legislative provisions other than the Insolvency Act 1986, the Company Directors Disqualification Act 1986 and the Insolvency Rules 1986 in the provisions of those Acts and Rules or their notes.

Abbreviations in the provision column are to the Insolvency Act 1986 (IA) or the Company Directors Disqualification Act 1986 (CDDA) or to the Insolvency Rules 1986 (IR).

	Provision
Administration of Insolvent Estates of Deceased	
Persons Order 1986 (SI 1986/1999)	...IA 421; IR 0.1
Administration of Justice (Scotland) Act 1933	
See generally	IA 120
4	IA 162(2)
Banking Act 1979	
See generally	IA 8(4), 422(1); IR 4.51(3), 4.72
16	IR 4.50, 4.51, 4.72
18	IR 4.50, 4.51, 4.72
18(1), (2), (4)	IA 438
19(2), (8)	IA 438
Banking Act 1987	
See generally	IR 4.50
28	IR 4.152
58	IR 4.152
92(1)(a)	IA 168(5A)–(5C)
108(1)	IA 8(4)
Sch. 6, para. 25(1)	IA 8(4)
Banking and Financial Dealings Act 1971	
See generally	IR 13.13
1(2)	IR 13.13
Bankruptcy Act 1914	
See generally	IA Pt. VIII–XI, IX, 326(1), 420(1), 439(3), Sch. 11, para. 11(1), 12, 13
1(2)	IA 265(1), (2)
5(7)	IA 266(2)
10	IA 287(1), (2), (5), 370(1), (2)
14	IA 288(1), (3)
15	IA 290
16	IA Pt. VIII, 260(1), (2), 262
16(2)	IA 258(1)
16(13)	IA 260(1), (2)
16(16)	IA 276(1)
16(19)	IA 258(2)–(5)
17	IA Pt. VIII

	Provision
19	IA 292(2)
21	IA Pt. VIII
21(1)	IA 258(1)
23	IA 364(2)
25(6)	IA 366(1)
28	IA 281(2)–(6), (8)
29(3)	IA 282(1), (3)
30, 30(1)	IA 322(3), (4)
31	IA 323, 323(1)–(4)
32	IA 322(1)
33(4)	IA 328
33(6)	IA 328, 420(1)
33(8)	IA 189
34	IA 348(5), (6)
36	IA 329(1), (2)
38(a)	IA 307(1)
38(b)	IA 283(2)–(3)
39	IA Sch. 11, para. 16(2)
42	IA 238
44	IA 238
44(1)	IA 239(5)
47	IA 307(4)
51	IA 310, Sch. 11, para. 16(1)
54(1)	IA 315(1), (2)
54(3)	IA 317(1), (2)
54(4)	IA 316(1), (2)
55–57	IA 314(1), (2), (6)
59	IA 311(5), (6)
60	IA Sch. 11, para. 15
61	IA 304(3)
62(2)	IA 324(1)–(3)
66	IA 189, 244, 322(2), 343
67	IA Sch. 11, para. 14(5)
68	IA 325(2)
70(1)	IA 400(2)
71	IA 401(1)
76	IA 305(4)
77	IA 292(3)

1053

Index

Abbreviations in the provision column are to the Insolvency Act 1986 (IA) or the Company Directors Disqualification Act 1986 (CDDA) or the Insolvency Rules 1986 (IR).

1077